SOCIOLOGY

ACADEMIC REVIEWERS

We would like to express our thanks to the following people, who have reviewed all or various portions of the manuscript.

Richard T. Schaefer
Robert P. Lamm

Patrick Ashwood
Indian Hills Community College
Laura A. Dowd
University of Georgia
Jan Fiola
University of Minnesota
Karen E. Gilbert
University of Georgia
Michael Goslin
Tallahassee Community College
Stanford W. Gregory
Kent State University

Harlowe Hatle
University of South Dakota
John R. Henderson
Scottsdale Community College
Sean-Shong Hwang
University of Alabama–
Birmingham
Mark Kassop
Bergen County Community College
Martha Loustaunau
New Mexico State University
Patrick McNamara
University of New Mexico
David H. Malone
University of North Texas
William Michelson
University of Toronto
Laura L. Miller
Northwestern University
Mari Molseed
Drake University
Karen Nardone-Lemons
Massachusetts Bay Community
College

Brian Powell
Indiana University
Kathryn Strother Ratcliff
University of Connecticut
Beth Rubin
Tulane University
Jon A. Schlenker
University of Maine–Augusta
Robert L. Seufert
Miami University–Middletown
Dale R. Spady
Northern Michigan University
Steven Stack
Wayne State University
Randy Stoecker
University of Toledo
Leann M. Tigges
University of Georgia
Wen-Hui Tsai
Indiana University
J. Sherwood Williams
Virginia Commonwealth University
William C. Yoels
University of Alabama

FIFTH EDITION

SOCIOLOGY

RICHARD T. SCHAEFER

Western Illinois University

ROBERT P. LAMM

McGRAW-HILL, INC.

*New York   St. Louis   San Francisco   Auckland   Bogotá   Caracas   Lisbon
London   Madrid   Mexico City   Milan   Montreal   New Delhi   San Juan
Singapore   Sydney   Tokyo   Toronto*

SOCIOLOGY

Copyright ©1995, 1992, 1989, 1986, 1983 by McGraw-Hill, Inc. All rights reserved. Printed in the United States of America. Except as permitted under the United States Copyright Act of 1976, no part of this publication may be reproduced or distributed in any form or by any means, or stored in a data base or retrieval system, without the prior written permission of the publisher.

Acknowledgments appear on pages 658–662, and on this page by reference.

This book is printed on acid-free paper.

1 2 3 4 5 6 7 8 9 0 VNH VNH 9 0 9 8 7 6 5 4

ISBN 0-07-056959-2

Library of Congress Cataloging-in-Publication Data

Schaefer, Richard T.
    Sociology / Richard T. Schaefer, Robert P. Lamm.
        —5th ed.
        p.   cm.
    Includes bibliographical references and index.
    ISBN 0-07-056959-2
    1. Sociology.   2. Social problems.   3. United
States—Social policy.   I. Lamm, Robert P.   II. Title.
HM51.S345   1995
301—dc20   94-13650

This book was set in New Baskerville by York Graphic Services, Inc.
The editors were Rhona Robbin, Jill S. Gordon, and Curt Berkowitz; the designer was Joan E. O'Connor; the production supervisor was Elizabeth J. Strange.
The photo editor was Elyse Rieder; the permissions editor was Elsa Peterson.
New drawings were done by Fine Line Illustrations, Inc.
Von Hoffmann Press, Inc., was printer and binder.

Cover Painting

West Church, Boston, 1900–1901
Prendergast, Maurice Brazil.
American, 1858–1924
Watercolor over graphite
18 15/16 × 15 3/8 in. (276 × 392 mm.)
Hayden Collection. Charles Henry Hayden Fund
Courtesy, Museum of Fine Arts, Boston.

ABOUT THE
AUTHORS

Richard T. Schaefer, born and raised in Chicago, is Professor of Sociology and Dean of the College of Arts and Sciences at Western Illinois University. He received his B.A. in sociology from Northwestern University and his M.A. and Ph.D. from the University of Chicago. He has taught introductory sociology for 26 years to students in colleges, adult education programs, nursing programs, and a maximum-security prison. He is the author of the well-received *Racial and Ethnic Groups* (HarperCollins, 1993), now in its fifth edition. His articles and book reviews have appeared in many journals, including *American Journal of Sociology, Phylon: Review of Race and Culture, Contemporary Sociology, Sociology and Social Research,* and *Teaching Sociology.* He is currently the president of the Midwest Sociological Society.

Robert P. Lamm is a New York-based free-lance writer with extensive experience on social science textbooks and supplements. His essays, profiles, reviews, and fiction have appeared in two anthologies and in more than 30 periodicals in the United States, Canada, and Great Britain. He received his B.A. in political science from Yale University, also studied at Sarah Lawrence College, and has taught at Yale, Queens College, and the New School for Social Research. He is a long-time activist in the National Writers Union.

Schaefer and Lamm have collaborated on all five editions of Sociology *(McGraw-Hill, 1995) and its supplements. They served as co-authors of* Sociology: A Brief Introduction *(McGraw-Hill, 1994) and as editors of the reader* Introducing Sociology *(McGraw-Hill, 1987).*

To my wife, Sandra L. Schaefer

R.T.S.

To Mary Wollstonecraft (1759–1797) and
all the other women and men—some
famous, some not—who have joined in
the struggle for justice, equality,
and liberation for women

R.P.L.

CONTENTS
IN BRIEF

List of Boxes   xv
Preface   xvii

PART ONE
THE SOCIOLOGICAL PERSPECTIVE   1
 1 THE NATURE OF SOCIOLOGY   3
 2 METHODS OF SOCIOLOGICAL
   RESEARCH   31

PART TWO
ORGANIZING SOCIAL LIFE   59
 3 CULTURE   61
 4 SOCIALIZATION   91
 5 SOCIAL INTERACTION AND SOCIAL
   STRUCTURE   119
 6 GROUPS AND ORGANIZATIONS   143
 7 DEVIANCE AND SOCIAL CONTROL   173

PART THREE
SOCIAL INEQUALITY   205
 8 STRATIFICATION AND SOCIAL
   MOBILITY   207
 9 SOCIAL INEQUALITY WORLDWIDE   241
10 RACIAL AND ETHNIC INEQUALITY   271
11 STRATIFICATION BY GENDER   305
12 STRATIFICATION BY AGE   333

PART FOUR
SOCIAL INSTITUTIONS   357
13 THE FAMILY   359
14 RELIGION   391
15 GOVERNMENT AND THE
   ECONOMY   419
16 EDUCATION   449
17 HEALTH AND MEDICINE   477

PART FIVE
CHANGING SOCIETY   507
18 COMMUNITIES   509
19 POPULATION AND THE
   ENVIRONMENT   539
20 COLLECTIVE BEHAVIOR AND
   SOCIAL CHANGE   567
**EPILOGUE: SOCIOLOGY,
   TECHNOLOGY, AND THE
   FUTURE**   595

Glossary   601
References   613
Acknowledgments   658
Indexes   663

CONTENTS

List of Boxes   xv
Preface   xvii

PART ONE
THE SOCIOLOGICAL
PERSPECTIVE   1

1 THE NATURE OF SOCIOLOGY   3
WHAT IS SOCIOLOGY?   5
*The Sociological Imagination / Sociology and
the Social Sciences / Sociology and Common
Sense*
WHAT IS SOCIOLOGICAL THEORY?   9
ORIGINS OF SOCIOLOGY   10
*Early Thinkers: Comte, Martineau, and
Spencer / Émile Durkheim / Max Weber /
Karl Marx / Twentieth-Century Sociology*
MAJOR THEORETICAL PERSPECTIVES   18
*Functionalist Perspective / Conflict
Perspective / Interactionist Perspective /
The Sociological Approach*

APPLIED AND CLINICAL SOCIOLOGY   25
SOCIOLOGY AND SOCIAL POLICY   25
APPENDIX: CAREERS IN SOCIOLOGY   26

2 METHODS OF SOCIOLOGICAL
RESEARCH   31
WHAT IS THE SCIENTIFIC METHOD?   33
*Defining the Problem / Reviewing the
Literature / Formulating the
Hypothesis / Collecting and Analyzing
Data / Developing the Conclusion /
In Summary: The Scientific Method*
RESEARCH DESIGNS FOR
   COLLECTING DATA   39
*Surveys / Observation / Experiments /
Use of Existing Sources*
ETHICS OF RESEARCH   46
*Case Studies of Ethical Controversies /
Neutrality and Politics in Research*
APPENDIX I: WRITING A LIBRARY
   RESEARCH REPORT   52

APPENDIX II: UNDERSTANDING TABLES
AND GRAPHS 54

PART TWO
ORGANIZING SOCIAL LIFE 59

3 CULTURE 61
CULTURE AND SOCIETY 62
DEVELOPMENT OF CULTURE 63
Cultural Universals / Innovation / Diffusion
ELEMENTS OF CULTURE 67
Language / Norms / Sanctions / Values
CULTURAL INTEGRATION 76
CULTURAL VARIATION 77
*Aspects of Cultural Variation / Attitudes toward
Cultural Variation*
CULTURE AND THE DOMINANT
IDEOLOGY 83
SOCIAL POLICY AND CULTURE:
MULTICULTURALISM 84

4 SOCIALIZATION 91
THE ROLE OF SOCIALIZATION 93
*Environment: The Impact of Isolation /
The Influence of Heredity / Sociobiology*
THE SELF AND SOCIALIZATION 98
*Sociological Approaches to the Self /
Psychological Approaches to the Self*
SOCIALIZATION AND THE LIFE CYCLE 102
*Stages of Socialization / Anticipatory
Socialization and Resocialization*
AGENTS OF SOCIALIZATION 105
*Family / School / Peer Group / Mass
Media / Workplace / The State*
SOCIAL POLICY AND SOCIALIZATION:
THE NEED FOR CHILD CARE 113

**5 SOCIAL INTERACTION AND
SOCIAL STRUCTURE** 119
SOCIAL INTERACTION AND REALITY 121
*Defining and Reconstructing Reality /
Negotiated Order*
ELEMENTS OF SOCIAL STRUCTURE 124
*Statuses / Social Roles / Groups /
Social Institutions*
SOCIAL STRUCTURE AND MODERN
SOCIETY 133
*Durkheim's Mechanical and Organic
Solidarity / Tönnies's Gemeinschaft and
Gesellschaft*
SOCIAL POLICY AND SOCIAL JUSTICE:
THE AIDS CRISIS 136

6 GROUPS AND ORGANIZATIONS 143
UNDERSTANDING GROUPS 145
Types of Groups / Studying Small Groups
UNDERSTANDING ORGANIZATIONS 151
*Formal Organizations and Bureaucracies /
Voluntary Associations / Organizational
Change*
SOCIAL POLICY AND ORGANIZATIONS:
SEXUAL HARASSMENT 167

7 DEVIANCE AND SOCIAL CONTROL 173
SOCIAL CONTROL 176
*Conformity and Obedience / Informal and
Formal Social Control / Law and Society*
DEVIANCE 179
What Is Deviance? / Explaining Deviance
CRIME 190
Types of Crime / Crime Statistics
SOCIAL POLICY AND CRIMINAL JUSTICE:
GUN CONTROL 198

PART THREE
SOCIAL INEQUALITY 205

**8 STRATIFICATION AND SOCIAL
MOBILITY** 207
UNDERSTANDING STRATIFICATION 210
*Systems of Stratification / Perspectives on
Stratification / Is Stratification Universal?*
STRATIFICATION BY SOCIAL CLASS 219
*Measuring Social Class / Consequences
of Social Class in the United States*
SOCIAL MOBILITY 230
*Open versus Closed Class Systems / Types
of Social Mobility / Social Mobility in the
United States*
SOCIAL POLICY AND STRATIFICATION:
RETHINKING WELFARE 234

9 SOCIAL INEQUALITY WORLDWIDE 241
STRATIFICATION IN THE WORLD SYSTEM:
A GLOBAL PERSPECTIVE 243
*Colonialism, Neocolonialism, and World Systems
Theory / Modernization / Multinational
Corporations / Consequences of Stratification
for Developing Nations*
STRATIFICATION WITHIN NATIONS:
A COMPARATIVE PERSPECTIVE 253
*Distribution of Wealth and Income /
Prestige / Social Mobility*
STRATIFICATION IN BRAZIL:
A CASE STUDY 259

Race Relations in Brazil: The Legacy of Slavery / The Status of Brazilian Women / Brazil's Economy and Environment
SOCIAL POLICY AND WORLDWIDE INEQUALITY: UNIVERSAL HUMAN RIGHTS 264

10 RACIAL AND ETHNIC INEQUALITY 271
MINORITY, RACIAL, AND ETHNIC GROUPS 273
Minority Groups / Race / Ethnicity
STUDYING RACE AND ETHNICITY 279
Functionalist Perspective / Conflict Perspective / Interactionist Perspective
PREJUDICE AND DISCRIMINATION 280
The Structural Component / Discriminatory Behavior / Institutional Discrimination
PATTERNS OF INTERGROUP RELATIONS 283
Amalgamation / Assimilation / Segregation / Pluralism
RACE AND ETHNICITY IN THE UNITED STATES 286
Racial Groups / Ethnic Groups
SOCIAL POLICY AND RACE AND ETHNICITY: REGULATING IMMIGRATION 297

11 STRATIFICATION BY GENDER 305
GENDER IDENTITY AND GENDER ROLES 307
Gender Roles in the United States / Cross-Cultural Perspective
EXPLAINING STRATIFICATION BY GENDER 311
The Functionalist View / The Conflict Response / The Interactionist Approach
WOMEN: THE OPPRESSED MAJORITY 313
The Global Perspective / Women in the Work Force of the United States / Women: Emergence of a Collective Consciousness / Minority Women: Double Jeopardy
SOCIAL POLICY AND GENDER STRATIFICATION: THE BATTLE OVER ABORTION 327

12 STRATIFICATION BY AGE 333
AGING AND SOCIETY 335
AGING WORLDWIDE 336
EXPLAINING THE AGING PROCESS 337
Functionalist Approach: Disengagement Theory / Interactionist Approach: Activity Theory / The Conflict Response

AGE STRATIFICATION IN THE UNITED STATES 341
The "Graying of America" / Ageism / Competition in the Labor Force / The Elderly: Emergence of a Collective Consciousness
ROLE TRANSITIONS IN LATER LIFE 347
Adjusting to Retirement / Death and Dying
SOCIAL POLICY AND AGE STRATIFICATION: THE RIGHT TO DIE 350

PART FOUR
SOCIAL INSTITUTIONS 357
13 THE FAMILY 359
THE FAMILY: UNIVERSAL BUT VARIED 361
Composition: What Is the Family? / Descent Patterns: To Whom Are We Related? / Family Residence: Where Do We Live? / Authority Patterns: Who Rules?
FUNCTIONS OF THE FAMILY 365
MARRIAGE AND FAMILY IN THE UNITED STATES 367
Courtship and Mate Selection / Parenthood and Grandparenthood / Adoption / Dual-Career Families / Variations in Family Life
DIVORCE IN THE UNITED STATES 376
Statistical Trends in Divorce / Factors Associated with Divorce
ALTERNATIVE LIFESTYLES 379
Cohabitation / Remaining Single / Gay Relationships / Marriage without Children / Single-Parent Families
SOCIAL POLICY AND THE FAMILY: DOMESTIC VIOLENCE 384

14 RELIGION 391
DURKHEIM AND THE SOCIOLOGICAL APPROACH TO RELIGION 395
FUNCTIONS OF RELIGION 396
The Integrative Function of Religion / Religion and Social Control: The Marxist Critique / Religion and Social Support / Religion and Social Change: The Weberian Thesis
DIMENSIONS OF RELIGION 401
Belief / Ritual / Experience
ORGANIZATION OF RELIGIOUS BEHAVIOR 403
Ecclesiae / Denominations / Sects / Cults / Comparing Forms of Religious Organization
RELIGION IN THE UNITED STATES 407

Beliefs and Practices / Resurgent
Fundamentalism / Jews in the United
States / Sects and Cults in the United States
SOCIAL POLICY AND RELIGION:
   RELIGION IN THE SCHOOLS   414

**15 GOVERNMENT AND THE
ECONOMY**   419
ECONOMIC SYSTEMS   421
Preindustrial Societies / Industrial Societies /
Postindustrial and Postmodern Societies
POLITICS AND GOVERNMENT   426
Power / Types of Authority
POLITICAL BEHAVIOR IN THE
   UNITED STATES   428
Political Socialization / Participation and
Apathy / Women in Politics / Interest Groups
MODELS OF POWER STRUCTURE
   IN THE UNITED STATES   435
Elite Model / Pluralist Model
ASPECTS OF THE ECONOMY   439
Occupations and Professions / Work and
Alienation: Marx's View
SOCIAL POLICY, GOVERNMENT, AND
   THE ECONOMY: AFFIRMATIVE ACTION   442

16 EDUCATION   449
SOCIOLOGICAL PERSPECTIVES ON
   EDUCATION   452
Functionalist View / Conflict View /
Interactionist View
SCHOOLS AS FORMAL ORGANIZATIONS   461
Bureaucratization of Schools / Teachers:
Employees and Instructors / The Student
Subculture
EDUCATION IN THE UNITED STATES:
   CURRENT TRENDS   466
Minimum-Competency Testing / Mainstreaming
and Inclusion / Women in Education /
Adult Education
SOCIAL POLICY AND EDUCATION:
   SCHOOL CHOICE PROGRAMS   471

17 HEALTH AND MEDICINE   477
SOCIOLOGICAL PERSPECTIVES ON
   HEALTH AND ILLNESS   480
Functionalist Approach / Conflict Approach /
Interactionist Approach / Labeling Approach /
An Overview
SOCIAL EPIDEMIOLOGY AND HEALTH   486
Gender / Social Class / Race and Ethnicity
HEALTH CARE IN THE UNITED STATES   491

A Historical View / Physicians, Nurses,
and Patients / The Role of Government /
Alternatives to Traditional Health Care
MENTAL ILLNESS IN THE
   UNITED STATES   497
Theoretical Models of Mental Disorders /
Patterns of Care
SOCIAL POLICY AND HEALTH:
   NATIONAL HEALTH INSURANCE   500

PART FIVE
CHANGING SOCIETY   507
18 COMMUNITIES   509
HOW DID COMMUNITIES ORIGINATE?   511
Early Communities / Preindustrial Cities /
Industrial Cities
SOCIOLOGICAL APPROACHES
   TO COMMUNITIES   513
Ecological Views of Urban Growth / Conflict
View of Urban Growth / Models of Community
Attachment
TYPES OF COMMUNITIES   521
Central Cities / Suburbs / Rural Communities
SOCIAL POLICY AND COMMUNITIES:
   HOMELESSNESS   532

**19 POPULATION AND THE
ENVIRONMENT**   539
DEMOGRAPHY: THE STUDY OF
   POPULATION   541
Malthus's Thesis and Marx's Response /
Studying Population Today / Elements
of Demography
WORLD POPULATION HISTORY   544
Demographic Transition / The Population
Explosion
FERTILITY PATTERNS IN THE UNITED
   STATES   551
The Baby Boom / Stable Population Growth
POPULATION AND MIGRATION   553
International Migration / Internal Migration
THE ENVIRONMENT   554
Environmental Problems: An Overview /
Functionalism and Human Ecology / Conflict
View of Environmental Issues
SOCIAL POLICY AND THE ENVIRONMENT:
   OPPOSITION TO LANDFILLS   560

**20 COLLECTIVE BEHAVIOR AND
SOCIAL CHANGE**   567

THEORIES OF COLLECTIVE BEHAVIOR 569
Emergent-Norm Perspective / Value-Added Perspective / Assembling Perspective
FORMS OF COLLECTIVE BEHAVIOR 573
Crowds / Disaster Behavior / Fads and Fashions / Panics and Crazes / Rumors / Publics and Public Opinion / Social Movements
THEORIES OF SOCIAL CHANGE 582
Evolutionary Theory / Functionalist Theory / Conflict Theory
RESISTANCE TO SOCIAL CHANGE 586
SOCIAL POLICY AND SOCIAL MOVEMENTS: DISABILITY RIGHTS 588

EPILOGUE: SOCIOLOGY, TECHNOLOGY, AND THE FUTURE 595

Glossary 601
References 613
Acknowledgments 658
Indexes
  Name Index 663
  Subject Index 673

LIST
OF BOXES

BOX

1-1 Everyday Behavior: Functionalist, Conflict, and Interactionist Views of Sports   20

1-2 Everyday Behavior: A Feminist View of Public Places   24

2-1 Current Research: Racial "Eye Work" on the Street   43

2-2 Speaking Out: Preserving Confidentiality—One Sociologist's View   47

3-1 Around the World: Sexism in Languages—English and Japanese   70

3-2 Around the World: The Skinhead Counterculture   79

4-1 Everyday Behavior: Impression Management by Students after Exams   101

4-2 Everyday Behavior: Socialization in Mexican American Families   107

5-1 Current Research: The Process of Role Exit   126

5-2 Speaking Out: Savage Inequalities in Public Education   132

6-1 Current Research: Multicultural Small Groups   148

6-2 Everyday Behavior: Self-Help Groups   163

7-1 Current Research: Neutralization of Deviance and Female Bodybuilders   186

7-2 Around the World: Police Power in Japan   195

8-1 Around the World: Slavery in the 1990s   211

8-2 Speaking Out: Blaming the Victim   227

9-1 Around the World: The Informal Economy   251

9-2 Around the World: Inequality in Japan   256

10-1 Speaking Out: Hispanics as an Invisible Minority   277

10-2 Current Research: Asian Americans and the "Model Minority" Stereotype   291

11-1 Current Research: Gendered Spaces   314

11-2 Current Research: Male Nurses in a Traditional "Women's Job"   321

12-1 Around the World: The Elderly in !Kung Society   338

12-2 Speaking Out: An Older Person Speaks to Younger Generations   348

13-1 Everyday Behavior: Marital Power   366

13-2 Current Research: The Effects of Divorce on Female and Male Children   378

14-1 Around the World: Liberation Theology   399

14-2 Everyday Behavior: Women in the Clergy   410

15-1 Speaking Out: Martin Luther King on War and Peace   429

15-2 Everyday Behavior: Farm Workers and the Abolition of the Short-Handled Hoe   441

16-1 Around the World: Inequality in Education   459

16-2 Everyday Behavior: Violence in the Schools   464

17-1 Around the World: Bitter Pills—Prescription Drugs in the Third World   484

17-2 Current Research: Sexism in Medical Research   488

18-1 Current Research: Urban Apartheid in the United States   525

18-2 Speaking Out: The Death of a Family Farm   531

19-1 Around the World: Japan's Declining Fertility   545

19-2 Current Research: The Demography of Islamic Nations   548

20-1 Around the World: Exit Polling in the Former Soviet Union   579

20-2 Everyday Behavior: The Social Movement for Prostitutes' Rights   583

xvi

PREFACE

Sociology seeks to unravel the social factors that have created the crisis in health care in the United States. It assesses the differential impact of divorce on a couple's sons and daughters. Sociology investigates the social forces that promote prejudice, the persistence of slavery in the 1990s, the process of growing old in different cultures, and the educational prospects for people in Third World countries. These issues, along with many others, are of great interest to me, but it is the sociological explanations for them which I find especially compelling. It is little surprise, then, that I have found the introductory sociology class to be the ideal laboratory in which to confront our society and our global neighbors.

After 26 years of teaching sociology to students in colleges, adult education programs, nursing programs, an overseas program based in London, and even a maximum-security prison, I am firmly convinced that the discipline can play a valuable role in teaching critical thinking skills. Sociology can help students to better understand the workings of their own society and of other cultures. Through the distinctive emphasis on social policy found in this text, students will be shown how the sociological imagination can be useful in examining such public policy issues as multiculturalism, the AIDS crisis, sexual harassment, the "right to die," affirmative action, and homelessness.

The first four editions of *Sociology* were aimed at instructors seeking a textbook which would be thorough, challenging, and comprehensive—and, at the same time, clear, readable, and lively. In view of the adoption of the text in more than 400 colleges and universities and the enthusiastic response of both instructors and students, I feel that *Sociology* has succeeded in this important goal. Nevertheless, revising the text provides an opportunity to draw on my own experiences with using it in class, as well as on the suggestions of instructors who have used it and of expert reviewers.

As in the earlier editions, I have taken great care to present the basic concepts and research methods of sociology through the use of understandable definitions and carefully chosen examples. Thus, in Chapter 2, a study of the employment patterns of African American corporate executives is described as a means of introducing the five steps of the scientific method. In Chapter 3, studies of Skinhead groups in the United States, Great Britain, and western Europe are used to illustrate the meaning of a counterculture. In Chapter 4, I draw on a study of college students' interactions after exams to explain the concept of impression management.

Through their reading of *Sociology*, students will become familiar with the theoretical approaches of functionalism, the conflict perspective, and interactionism. Ideally, they will begin to think like sociologists and will be able to use sociological theories and concepts in evaluating human interactions and institutions. From the first pages of Chapter 1—which draw on a study that a colleague and I conducted of the food bank system of the United States—the text stresses the distinctive way sociologists examine and question even the most familiar patterns of social behavior.

ORGANIZATION

Sociology is divided into five parts which provide a systematic introduction to the study of human behavior. Part One focuses on sociological theories and research methods. The origins of sociology as a social science are described; and the functionalist, conflict, and interactionist approaches are clearly defined. The challenges and difficulties of sociological research are thoroughly presented; particular attention is given to ethical issues faced by sociologists in conducting research.

In Part Two, students learn how social life is organized. The basic sociological concepts of culture, society, socialization, social interaction, and social structure are defined and explored. The impact of groups and organizations on social behavior is discussed, as are conformity to and deviance from accepted social norms.

Part Three addresses the persistence of social inequality in the United States and other societies. The key sociological concepts of stratification and social mobility are introduced. Separate chapters focus on inequality based on social class, race and ethnicity, gender, and age; and a distinctive chapter (Chapter 9) examines social inequality worldwide.

In Part Four, the critical social institutions of human societies—the family, religion, government, the economy, education, and health care—are analyzed. The discussion of each institution highlights its functions, patterns of organization, and differential treatment of individuals and groups.

Part Five emphasizes change as a characteristic aspect of human societies. Students learn about changes in human communities, the social consequences of population growth, the deterioration of our physical environment, attempts to achieve change through involvement in social movements, and theories of social change.

Finally, a new Epilogue presents a sociological view of technological changes and the impact these changes may have on human societies in the twenty-first century.

SPECIAL FEATURES

"Looking Ahead" Questions

Each chapter of *Sociology* begins with "Looking Ahead"—a set of questions designed to interest students in the most significant subjects and issues that will be raised.

Chapter Introduction

Following "Looking Ahead," a lively chapter introduction conveys the importance of sociological inquiry. For example, students begin their work on worldwide inequality (Chapter 9) by learning about the life of a 42-year-old woman in rural Brazil who has seen 13 of her 18 children die. Students begin their work on religion (Chapter 14) by reading about Islamic day schools in the United States and about the resurgence of religion in Russia since the overthrow of communist rule.

Chapter Overview

Reflecting the positive responses to the format of the first four editions, the introduction is again followed by a chapter overview that describes the content of the chapter in narrative form.

Key Terms

Careful attention has been given to presenting understandable and accurate definitions of each key term. These terms are highlighted in **bold italics** when they are introduced. A list of key terms and definitions in each chapter—with page references—is found at the end of the chapter. In addition, the *glossary* at the end of the book includes the definitions of the textbook's 398 key terms and the page references for each term.

Boxes

The boxes which appeared in earlier editions were praised by both adopters and students because they supplemented the text discussions so closely. The boxed material in the fifth edition is again carefully tied to the basic themes of each chapter. Certain boxes illustrate the application of sociological theories, such as the analysis of functionalist, conflict, and interactionist views of sports in Chapter 1. Others provide detailed analysis of sociological research, such as the box on male nurses in a traditional "women's job" (Chapter 11). Still other boxes focus on contemporary issues, such as inequality in public education (Chapter 5) or the pervasive stereotype of Asian Americans as a "model minority" (Chapter 10).

Illustrations and Tables

Like the boxes, the *photographs, cartoons, figures,* and *tables* are closely linked to the themes of the text, and their captions make the links explicit.

Social Policy Sections

The social policy sections which close virtually all 20 chapters play a critical role in helping students to think like sociologists. These sections focus on current and often controversial issues of public policy such as child care (Chapter 4), gun control (Chapter 7), U.S. immigration and refugee policy (Chapter 10), domestic violence (Chapter 13), national health insurance (Chapter 17), and disability rights (Chapter 20). In all cases, students are shown the utility of sociological theory and research in understanding and resolving major political issues confronting policymakers and the general public. To help students appreciate the relevance of sociology in studying policy issues, each section begins with a set of questions designed to underscore the connection.

Chapter Summaries

Each chapter includes a brief and numbered summary to aid students in reviewing the important themes.

Critical Thinking Questions

After the summary, each chapter includes critical thinking questions that will help students analyze the social world in which they participate. Such critical thinking is an essential element in the sociological imagination.

Additional Readings

An annotated list of additional readings concludes each chapter. These works have been selected because of their sociological soundness and their accessibility for introductory students. For the fifth edition, as before, I have included a list of sociological journals and periodicals which focus on the issues discussed in the chapter.

References

Some 2050 books, articles, government documents, scholarly presentations, dissertations, and pamphlets are included in the list of references at the end of the book. These materials have been listed with complete bibliographic information so that they can be retrieved easily by instructors or students. More than 40 percent of the references have been added especially for the fifth edition.

CHANGES IN THE FIFTH EDITION

Among the most important changes in the fifth edition of *Sociology* are the following:

New Focus on the Environment

In the 1990s, people around the planet are worried about the continuing deterioration of the environment. In 1992, some 106 heads of government—the largest gathering of the world's political leaders in history—met in Rio de Janeiro to attend the United Nations Conference on Environment and Development (commonly known as the "Earth Summit"). The Earth Summit occurred within a climate of grave concern about serious environmental disasters and about the day-to-day environmental damage caused by present population levels and production and consumption patterns. Consequently, it seems important to teach introductory students about environmental issues and about the complex relationship between population and the environment.

The environment is being threatened not only be physical forces, but also by social action and inaction. With this in mind, sociologists conduct observation research, surveys, and secondary analysis to investigate people's role in environmental protection and deterioration. Sociological theories are helpful in guiding and interpreting such research, and in examining the controversy over the relationship between population and the environment.

Chapter 19 has therefore been substantially revised as a chapter on Population and the Environment. Among the major topics added to the chapter are:

- An overview of environmental problems, including air pollution, water pollution, and contamination of land
- Functionalism and human ecology
- Conflict view of environmental issues
- Opposition to landfills (social policy section)

New Material in Age Chapter

In response to requests from adopters, we have revised the chapter on "Stratification by Age" (Chapter 12) by adding a major concluding section on Role Transitions in Later Life. This section includes material on "Adjusting to Retirement" and "Death and Dying" and leads into a new social policy section on physician-assisted suicide and the "right to die."

Epilogue on Sociology, Technology, and the Future

When viewed from a sociological perspective, individuals, institutions, and societies will face unprecedented adaptive challenges in adjusting to the technological advances soon to come. In an epilogue written specifically for the fifth edition, we examine the sociological implications of such advances as sex selection, biotechnology, telecommuting, and virtual reality. The epilogue concludes with an examination of how technological advances may intensify inequality based on gender, race, and class, as well as the inequality between industrial core nations and the developing world.

Renewed Emphasis on Issues of Gender, Race, Ethnicity, and Class

Earlier editions of *Sociology* have been praised by reviewers and adopters for including material on gender, race, ethnicity, and class in *all* chapters—not only in the chapters on "Stratification and Social Mobility" (Chapter 8), "Racial and Ethnic Inequality" (Chapter 10), and "Stratification by Gender" (Chapter 11). The fifth edition has even more material on gender, race, ethnicity, and class throughout the text. We also examine the interplay among these variables, such as how poverty is linked to race and gender and the manner in which poverty sometimes fosters conflict between members of different subordinate racial and ethnic groups.

Important additions to the fifth edition include the following topics:

- Sexual stereotyping in magazine advertisements (Chapter 2)
- Racial "eye work" on the street (Chapter 2)
- Multiculturalism (Chapter 3)
- Socialization in Mexican American families (Chapter 4)

- Conformity to racial prejudice (Chapter 7)
- Rethinking welfare (Chapter 8)
- Hispanics as an invisible minority (Chapter 10)
- Korean Americans (Chapter 10)
- Male nurses in a traditional "women's job" (Chapter 11)
- Domestic violence (Chapter 13)
- Farm workers and the abolition of the short-handled hoe (Chapter 15)
- Urban apartheid in the United States (Chapter 18)

A Stronger Global Perspective

The fifth edition includes not only an entire chapter on "Social Inequality Worldwide" (Chapter 9) but also new cross-cultural material throughout the text.

Special attention has been given to Japan. It is important that students gain a balanced understanding of this Pacific Rim nation and go beyond the simplistic images presented in the mass media and the hand-wringing about the U.S. balance of payments. Consequently, Japanese examples are used in many text discussions and social policy sections, while four boxes (three of which are new to this edition) present sociological analysis of various aspects of Japanese society. Among the topics covered are Christmas in Japan (Chapter 3), sexism in the Japanese language (Chapter 3), socialization of children in schools (Chapter 4), sexual harassment in Japan (Chapter 6), the nation's relative lack of crime (Chapter 7), sexual and racial inequality in Japan (Chapter 9), respect for the elderly (Chapter 12), the relationship between Japanese religious faiths and capitalism (Chapter 14), the high salaries paid to teachers (Chapter 16), and Japan's declining fertility (Chapter 19).

Among the other important new cross-cultural topics in the fifth edition are:

- Slavery in the 1990s (Chapter 8)
- Universal human rights (Chapter 9)
- Schooling in Vietnam (Chapter 16)
- Prescription drugs in the Third World (Chapter 17)
- Exit polling in the former Soviet Union (Chapter 20)

New Boxes

More than half the boxed inserts in the fifth edition are new. As in the fourth edition, the boxes are divided into four broad categories: "Around the World," "Speaking Out," "Current Research," and "Everyday Behavior." Among the new boxes are:

- Around the World: The Skinhead Counterculture (Chapter 3)
- Speaking Out: Savage Inequalities in Public Education (Chapter 5)
- Current Research: Gendered Spaces (Chapter 11)
- Around the World: The Elderly in !Kung Society (Chapter 12)
- Current Research: The Effects of Divorce on Female and Male Children (Chapter 13)
- Everyday Behavior: Violence in the Schools (Chapter 16)
- Speaking Out: The Death of a Family Farm (Chapter 18)
- Everyday Behavior: The Social Movement for Prostitutes' Rights (Chapter 20)

In response to feedback from adopters, we have limited the number of boxes in our new edition of *Sociology* to two per chapter.

New Social Policy Sections

The fifth edition includes 10 new social policy sections:

- Multiculturalism (Chapter 3)
- Gun Control (Chapter 7)
- Rethinking Welfare (Chapter 8)
- Universal Human Rights (Chapter 9)
- The Right to Die (Chapter 12)
- Domestic Violence (Chapter 13)
- Religion in the Schools (Chapter 14)
- School Choice Programs (Chapter 16)
- National Health Insurance (Chapter 17)
- Opposition to Landfills (Chapter 19)

Critical Thinking Questions

As noted earlier, critical thinking questions have been added at the end of each chapter, just after the chapter summary. These questions may be useful in sparking class discussion.

Updating

The fifth edition includes the most recent data and research findings. It draws on 845 new sources, of which almost 550 were published in 1992, 1993, or 1994. The results of the 1990 Census are fully integrated into figures, tables, and text discussions. Recent data from *Current Population Reports,* the Centers for Disease Control, the World Bank, and the Population Reference Bureau have been incorporated as well.

SUPPLEMENTS

Annotated Instructor's Edition

An *Annotated Instructor's Edition (AIE)* of the text, prepared by Richard T. Schaefer and Robert P. Lamm, offers page-by-page annotations to assist instructors in using textbook material. These include several categories: *Classroom Tips* (suggested teaching techniques); *Let's Discuss* (ideas for classroom discussion); *Student Alert* (which anticipate common student misconceptions; *Policy Pointers* (which show tie-ins between important concepts and social policy applications); *Theory* (examples of the application of the functionalist, conflict, interactionist, and labeling perspectives); *Methods* (examples of the use of surveys, observation, experiments, and existing sources); *Global View* (examples of cross-cultural material); *Race/Ethnicity* (material on racial and ethnic minorities in the United States); and *Transparencies* (cross-references to overhead transparencies available from McGraw-Hill).

The *Annotated Instructor's Edition* begins with a 160-page *Instructor's Resource Manual.* This manual provides sociology instructors with detailed *key points, additional lecture ideas* (among them alternative social policy issues), *class discussion topics, essay questions, topics for student research* (along with suggested research materials for each topic), and suggested *additional readings* (unlike those in the text itself, these are meant for instructors rather than students). Finally, *media materials* will be suggested for each chapter, including audiotapes, videotapes, and films. I have updated this media list in order to include the latest available sources.

The *Classroom Tips* annotations provided in each chapter of the *Annotated Instructor's Edition* will alert instructors to material in the *Instructor's Resource Manual* (front matter) which is relevant to a particular text discussion, box, or social policy section.

Instructor's Resource Manual

As noted above, an *Instructor's Resource Manual* is provided as the front matter for the *Annotated Instructor's Edition.* This *Manual* is also available to instructors as a separate supplement. It includes chapter contents, the material in the front matter of the *Annotated Instructor's Edition,* and a list (with page references) of the annotations in the AIE.

Students' Guide

The *Students' Guide,* written by Richard T. Schaefer and Robert P. Lamm, includes standard features such as detailed *key points,* definitions of *key terms, multiple-choice questions, fill-in questions,* and *true-false questions.* Many chapters include a *"name that sociologist"* section. Perhaps the most distinctive feature is the *social policy exercise,* which is closely tied to the social policy section in the text. All study guide questions are keyed to specific pages in the textbook, and page references are provided for *key points* and definitions of *key terms.*

Test Banks

The two *Test Banks* which accompany *Sociology,* written by sociologist Mark Kassop of Bergen Community College in New Jersey and Robert P. Lamm, can be used with computerized test-generating systems. Each contains over 1900 short-answer questions. Both *multiple-choice questions* and *true-false questions* are included for each chapter; they will be useful in testing students on basic sociological concepts, application of theoretical perspectives, and recall of important factual information. (Multiple-choice questions in the *Test Banks* are labeled "definition," "application," or "information" questions.) Correct answers and page references are provided for all questions.

In addition to the printed format, the *Test Banks* are available in computerized form for use on IBM PCs and compatibles and the Apple Macintosh. Tests can also be prepared by our customized test service. The telephone number for Customized

Tests is 800-888-EXAM. McGraw-Hill's local representative can assist professors in obtaining these supplements.

Guide to Critical Thinking

A Guide to Critical Thinking, written by sociologist Mark Kassop of Bergen Community College, provides a general introduction to critical thinking and contains critical thinking exercises for each of the text's 20 chapters. These exercises will be useful for the instructor's lectures, small group discussions, class debates, homework assignments, or essay examination questions.

Guide for Non-Native Speakers

This booklet was written by Sylvia Bloch, who is a specialist on English for non-native speakers. It is designed as an additional aid for students for whom English is not their native language. It explains idiomatic expressions, provides assistance in determining the meaning of unfamiliar words, and offers other aids to help students who are non-native speakers understand and review text material.

Overhead Transparencies

Adopters of *Sociology* can also receive a set of 75 color *overhead transparencies* especially developed for this edition by Richard T. Schaefer. These transparencies include figures, tables, and maps drawn from the textbook and from other academic and governmental sources. Cross-references to these transparencies are included in the *Annotated Instructor's Edition* and in the separate *Instructor's Manual*.

Sociology Update

Users of the first four editions of *Sociology* responded enthusiastically to a unique supplementary feature: the newsletter *Sociology Update*, written by Richard T. Schaefer and Robert P. Lamm. This newsletter will be continued for the fifth edition and is projected to come out in early January and early September each year. It is intended primarily for instructors but may be photocopied or reproduced for students. It will update tables and figures with the latest data, offer sketches of newly developing policy issues, discuss contemporary research findings in the social sciences, and summarize legislative and judicial decisions that have sociological relevance. All material will be keyed to text pages, thereby aiding instructors in integrating *Update* material into lecture and class discussions.

Other Materials and Services

Finally, McGraw-Hill also makes available to adopters videos, interactive software, classroom management software, and other materials and services. For more details, contact McGraw-Hill's main office or your local McGraw-Hill representative.

ACKNOWLEDGMENTS

Robert P. Lamm serves as coauthor of this book and has been an integral part of my writing with McGraw-Hill since the first edition of *Sociology*.

Both of us are deeply appreciative of the contributions to this project made by our editors. Rhona Robbin, a senior editor at McGraw-Hill, has worked tirelessly as our development editor since this project began more than 14 years ago. Rhona has continually challenged us to make each edition *better* than its predecessor; her talent, commitment, and sensitivity have helped us to achieve that goal. Phillip Butcher has worked with us since the second edition, either as our sociology editor or (once again) as our publisher. Phil has consistently supported our work with his confidence and enthusiasm, with constructive criticisms, and with a commitment to ensure that we have the best possible team of people working with us.

The fifth edition of *Sociology* benefited as well from the expertise and dedication of two new members of our team: Jill Gordon, our sponsoring editor; and Curt Berkowitz, senior editing supervisor. Additional guidance and support were provided by Sally Constable, marketing manager; Elyse Rieder, photo editor; Elsa Peterson, permissions editor; William O'Neal, copy editor; Joan O'Connor, designer; and Elizabeth Strange, production supervisor. Special thanks go to Matt Zimbelmann and Linda Gal, whose work as editorial assistants made our lives easier. Finally, we'd like to acknowledge Eric Munson, the signing editor for *Sociology,* whose encouragement and advice helped us get off to a good start (despite formidable competitors) in the early 1980s.

I have had the good fortune to be able to introduce students to sociology for many years. These students have been enormously helpful in spurring on my own sociological imagination. In ways I can fully appreciate but cannot fully acknowledge, their questions in class and queries in the hallway have found their way into this textbook.

This edition of *Sociology* continues to reflect many insightful suggestions made by reviewers of the first four editions. The current edition has benefited from constructive and thorough evaluations provided by 29 sociologists from both two-year and four-year institutions. These academic reviewers are listed on page ii. In addition, my colleagues at Western Illinois University have been most supportive.

As is evident from these acknowledgments, the preparation of a textbook is truly a team effort. The most valuable members of this effort continue to be my wife, Sandy; and my son, Peter. They provide the support so necessary in my creative and scholarly activities.

Richard T. Schaefer

SOCIOLOGY

PART ONE

THE

SOCIOLOGICAL

PERSPECTIVE

Part One will introduce the fundamental theories and research methods used by sociologists and other social scientists to understand social behavior. Chapter 1 defines the sociological imagination; compares sociology with other social sciences; discusses the origins and founders of sociology; and presents the functionalist, conflict, and interactionist approaches that will be utilized throughout the book. Chapter 2 outlines the basic principles and steps of the scientific method, examines the methods through which sociologists generate data for their research, and explores the ethical issues that sociologists face as they study human behavior. These discussions of sociological theory and research serve as the foundation for our study of the organization of social life (Part Two), social inequality (Part Three), social institutions (Part Four), and social change (Part Five).

1

THE NATURE
OF SOCIOLOGY

WHAT IS SOCIOLOGY?
The Sociological Imagination
Sociology and the Social Sciences
Sociology and Common Sense

WHAT IS SOCIOLOGICAL THEORY?

ORIGINS OF SOCIOLOGY
Early Thinkers: Comte, Martineau,
    and Spencer
Émile Durkheim
Max Weber
Karl Marx
Twentieth-Century Sociology

**MAJOR THEORETICAL
PERSPECTIVES**
Functionalist Perspective

Manifest and Latent Functions
    Dysfunctions
Conflict Perspective
Interactionist Perspective
The Sociological Approach

APPLIED AND CLINICAL SOCIOLOGY

SOCIOLOGY AND SOCIAL POLICY

APPENDIX: CAREERS IN SOCIOLOGY

BOXES
1-1 Everyday Behavior: Functionalist,
    Conflict, and Interactionist Views
    of Sports
1-2 Everyday Behavior: A Feminist View
    of Public Places

LOOKING AHEAD

- How does the sociological imagination, as a unique feature of sociology, distinguish sociology from the other social sciences?
- Why is sociology more than a collection of commonsense observations?
- Why do sociologists regard suicide as a social as well as an individual act?
- How did Émile Durkheim, Max Weber, and Karl Marx contribute to the development of sociological thought?
- How can the sociological perspectives of functionalism, conflict theory, and interactionism be used to better understand the world of sports?
- What career options are available to sociologists?

In 1992, sociologist David Miller spent a cold and wet Saturday afternoon transporting donated food items from the parking lot of a local supermarket in Macomb, Illinois, to the basement food pantry of his local church. Miller was impressed by the substantial amount of food that had been donated, and soon learned that the church's pantry was an important source of food for some of his neighbors. This church regularly distributes canned and boxed food products to any needy person in the community. Miller was curious as to what the source of these food products was and how widespread such pantries were.

Since that day, Miller and Richard Schaefer (this textbook's senior author) have joined forces to study the food bank system of the United States, which distributes food to hungry individuals and families. As part of their research, they have examined government documents and other reference materials in libraries; they have conducted phone interviews with food bank directors in Illinois, Iowa, Oregon, and California; and they have observed the distribution of food at various churches and Salvation Army facilities.

Miller and Schaefer learned that more than one out of four children in the United States are hungry. One-third of the nation's homeless people report eating one meal per day or less. With these disturbing realities in mind, charities are redistributing food to pantries and shelters that just a decade ago was destined for landfills. In fact, the fourth-largest charity in the United States, Second Harvest, is a food distribution organization with an annual revenue of more than half a billion dollars. In 1991, Second Harvest distributed 500 million pounds of food from hundreds of individual and corporate donors to more than 43,000 food pantries, soup kitchens, and social service agencies.

In writing about hunger in the United States, a newspaper reporter might look for exposés or unusual human interest stories. However, as sociologists, Miller and Schaefer (1993) focus on broad social meanings evident in the nation's food distribution system. For example, they note the value judgments made in determining which food items are "proper" to distribute to hungry people. Alco-

The United States has an extensive food bank system which distributes food to hungry individuals and families.

hol and tobacco products are banned from the "food pipeline," but it is literally crammed full of "junk food" such as candy and ice cream.

Many observers would uncritically applaud the distribution of tons of food to the needy. While supportive of and personally involved in such efforts, Miller and Schaefer nevertheless draw on the insights of sociology to offer a more probing view of these activities. They note that powerful forces in our society—such as the federal government, major food retailers, and other large corporations—have joined in charitable food distribution arrangements. Perhaps as a result, the focus of such relief programs is specific and limited. The homeless are to be fed, not housed; the unemployed are to be given meals, not jobs. Relief efforts assist hungry individuals and families without challenging the existing social order (for example, by demanding a redistribution of wealth). Miller and Schaefer add that without these limited successes in distributing food, hoards of starving people might assault patrons of restaurants, loot grocery stores, or literally die of starvation on the steps of city halls and across from the White House. Such critical thinking is typical of the theoretical and research efforts of sociologists in studying a social issue such as hunger (see also Cohn et al., 1993).

WHAT IS SOCIOLOGY?

As we have seen, the sociologist has a distinctive way of examining human interactions. *Sociology* is the systematic study of social behavior and human groups. It focuses primarily on the influence of social relationships upon people's attitudes and behavior and on how societies are established and change. As a field of study, sociology has an extremely broad scope. Therefore, this textbook deals with families, gangs, business firms, political parties, schools, religions, and labor unions. It is concerned with love, poverty, conformity, discrimination, illness, alienation, overpopulation, and community.

In the United States, newspapers, television, and radio are the usual sources of information about such groups and problems. However, while the basic function of journalists is to report the news, sociologists bring a different type of understanding to such issues. The vision of sociology involves seeing through the outside appearances of people's actions and organizations (Berger, 1963:31–37).

One major goal of sociology is to identify underlying, recurring patterns of and influences on social behavior. For example, sociologists study the passionate desire of movie or rock music fans to see in person, to talk with, even to grab the clothing of a star. Why do people feel this need so powerfully? To what extent does participation in a crowd of fans allow individuals to act more boldly than they otherwise might? Will people gain greater respect from family members or friends if they have shaken hands with Madonna and exchanged three sentences of conversation?

Sociology goes beyond identifying patterns of social behavior; it also attempts to provide explanations for such patterns. Here the impact of broad societal forces becomes a central consideration of sociology. Sociologists are not content to look at the individual fan's personality or "unique" reasons for wanting to meet Tom Cruise, Julia Roberts, or Denzel Washington. Rather, they recognize that millions of people want to meet celebrities, and they examine the *shared* feelings and behavior of fans within the larger social context of the culture of the United States.

The Sociological Imagination

In attempting to understand social behavior, sociologists rely on an unusual type of creative thinking. C. Wright Mills (1959) described such thinking as the *sociological imagination*—an awareness of the relationship between an individual and the wider society. This awareness allows people (not simply sociologists) to comprehend the links between their immediate, personal social settings and the remote, impersonal social world that surrounds them and helps to shape them.

A key element in the sociological imagination is the ability to view one's own society as an outsider would, rather than from the limited perspective of personal experiences and cultural biases. Thus, instead of simply accepting the fact that movie stars and rock stars are the "royalty" of our society, we could ask, in a more critical sense, why this is the case. Conceivably, an outsider unfamiliar with the United States might wonder why we are not as interested in meeting outstanding scientists, elementary school teachers, or architects.

As was true of the study of hunger and food distribution by Miller and Schaefer, the sociological imagination allows us to go beyond personal experiences and observations to understand broader public issues. Unemployment, for example, is unquestionably a personal hardship for a man or woman without a job. However, C. Wright Mills pointed out that when unemployment is a social problem shared by *millions* of people, it is appropriate to question the way that a society is structured. Similarly, Mills advocated use of the sociological imagination to view divorce not simply as the personal problem of a particular man and woman, but rather as a structural problem, since it was the outcome of so many marriages. And he was writing this in the 1950s, when the divorce rate was but a fraction of what it is today (I. Horowitz, 1983:87–108).

Sociological imagination can bring new understanding to daily life around us. Sociologist Murray Melbin (1978, 1987) has likened the social life in cities of the United States during late nighttime hours to social life on frontiers of the old west. In his view, there are many similarities in the social and behavioral patterns of people in cities at night and on the frontier, among them the following: (1) the population tends to be sparse and homogeneous, (2) there is a welcome solitude with fewer social constraints, (3) there is more lawlessness and violence, and (4) interest groups emerge which have concerns specific to the night or the frontier.

One of Melbin's most surprising assertions is that both in the city at night and on the frontier, there is *more* helpfulness and friendliness than in other times and places. He attempted to substantiate this view by conducting four tests of Boston residents' helpfulness and friendliness at various times during the 24-hour cycle. Melbin found that between midnight and 7 A.M.—as compared with other times during the day—people were more likely to give directions, to consent to an interview, and to be sociable with a stranger. Apparently, when aware that they are out in a dangerous environment (the night or the frontier), people identify with the vulnerability of others and become more outgoing. By drawing on the sociological imagination, Melbin's intriguing study helps us to view nighttime social activity as different from—and not necessarily more threatening than—activity during "normal hours."

Sociologists put their imagination to work in a variety of areas. Table 1-1 presents a partial list of the specializations within contemporary sociology. Throughout this textbook, the sociological imagination will be used to examine the United States (and other societies) from the viewpoint of respectful but questioning outsiders.

In this chapter, the nature of sociology as a science and its relationship to other social sciences will be explored. The contributions of three pioneering thinkers—Émile Durkheim, Max Weber, and Karl Marx—to the development of sociology will be evaluated. A number of important theoretical perspectives used by sociologists will be discussed. Finally, practical applications of the discipline of sociology for human behavior and organizations will be described.

Sociology and the Social Sciences

In a general sense, sociology can be considered a science. The term *science* refers to the body of knowledge obtained by methods based upon systematic observation. Like other scientific disciplines, sociology engages in organized, systematic study of phenomena (in this case, human behavior) in order to enhance understanding. All scientists, whether studying mushrooms or murderers, attempt to collect precise information through methods of study which are as objective as possible. They rely on careful recording of observations and accumulation of data.

Of course, there is a great difference between sociology and physics, between psychology and astronomy. For this reason, the sciences are commonly divided into natural and social sciences. *Natural science* is the study of the physical features of nature and the ways in which they interact and change. Astronomy, biology, chemistry, geology, and physics are all natural sciences. *Social science* is the study of various aspects of human society. The social sciences include sociology, anthropology, economics, history, psychology, and political science.

These academic disciplines have a common focus on the social behavior of people, yet each has a particular orientation in studying such behavior. Anthropologists usually study cultures of the past and preindustrial societies that remain in existence today, as well as the origins of men and women; this knowledge is used to examine contemporary societies, including even industrial societies. Econo-

TABLE 1-1	Specializations within Sociology

A PARTIAL LISTING

Methodology and research technology
Sociology: history and theory
Social psychology
Group interactions
Culture and social structure
Complex organization
Social change and economic development
Mass phenomena
Political sociology and interactions
Social stratification and mobility
Sociology of occupations and professions
Rural sociology and agriculture
Urban sociology
Sociology of language and the arts
Sociology of education
Sociology of religion
Social control
Sociology of law
Police, penology, and correctional problems
Sociology of science
Demography and human behavior
The family and socialization
Sociology of sexual behavior
Sociology of health and medicine
Sociology of knowledge
Community and regional development
Policy planning and forecasting
Radical sociology
Studies in poverty
Studies in violence
Feminist and gender studies
Marxist sociology
Sociological practice (clinical and applied)
Sociology of business and entrepreneurism

SOURCE: Adapted from *Sociological Abstracts*, 1994.

As reflected in this excerpt from the table of contents of Sociological Abstracts*—an online and hardcover database of articles, papers, and books on topics of sociology—the discipline of sociology can be divided into a diverse variety of subfields.*

In their examination of gambling, sociologists focus on the social networks that develop among many participants.

mists explore the ways in which people produce and exchange goods and services, along with money and other resources. Historians are concerned with the peoples and events of the past and their significance for us today. Political scientists study international relations, the workings of government, and the exercise of power and authority. Psychologists investigate personality and individual behavior. In contrast to other social sciences, sociology emphasizes the influence that society has on people's attitudes and behavior and the ways in which people shape society. Humans are social animals; therefore, sociologists scientifically examine our social relationships with people.

To better illustrate the distinctive perspectives of the social sciences, let us examine sociological and psychological approaches to the issue of gambling. The growing legalization of gambling in the United States has, in effect, increased the number of participants and contributed to a rise in the number of "problem gamblers"—that is, people who consistently lose more money than they can afford to lose. Gamblers' professed goal is economic gain; yet, because the vast majority end up losing money, their perspective is commonly viewed as "irrational" or even "pathological." Viewed from the perspective of psychology, gambling represents an escape into a fantasy world where great fortune can be attained easily. Eventually, people become so dependent on gambling that the activity fills an emotional need. As a result, they cannot give up gambling without feeling nervous and upset.

By contrast, in their examination of gambling, sociologists focus on the social networks that develop among many participants. Whether they be offtrack bettors, sports bettors, or poker players, gamblers establish friendship groups and work hard to create feelings of conviviality even among casual acquaintances whom they meet through gambling. Consequently, for such people, gambling is a form of recreation and may even be their primary social activity. This sociological perspective on gambling casts a shadow on recurring efforts to discourage particular individuals from gambling and to discourage the practice in general. Giving up gambling may, in fact, mean forgoing all social interaction that a person has previously found to be meaningful. Alternatively, participation in Gamblers Anonymous—a self-help group for "problem gamblers" modeled on Alcoholics Anonymous—provides a new forum to which ex-gamblers can turn for interaction, understanding, and encouragement. The individual can find social support to replace the friendship groups developed in his or her betting days (Rosecrance, 1986, 1987).

Sociologist Ronald Pavalko has initiated many studies of gambling and has founded the Center for Gambling Studies at the University of Wisconsin-

Parkside. In teaching undergraduate classes on "The Sociology of Gambling," Pavalko approaches gambling as a booming industry (which accounted for $330 billion in legal wages in the United States in 1992), as a public policy issue, and as an interpersonal and family problem. Pavalko and his colleagues have examined such issues as the role of gambling in the workplace, gambling as a leisure time activity for older people, and compulsive gambling within Native American tribes that operate casinos (Howery, 1993).

Sociology and Common Sense

As we have seen, sociology and the other social sciences focus on the study of certain aspects of human behavior. Yet human behavior is something with which we all have experience and about which we have at least a bit of knowledge. Many of us, even without Ph.D. degrees in the social sciences, might have suggestions about how society could ease the difficulties faced by dual-career couples with young children. All of us might well have theories about why movie stars and rock music stars are the subjects of so much attention and adulation. Our theories and suggestions come from our experiences and from a cherished source of wisdom: common sense.

In our daily lives, we rely on common sense to get us through many unfamiliar situations. However, this knowledge is not always accurate, because it rests on commonly held beliefs rather than systematic analysis of facts. It was once considered "common sense" to accept that the earth was flat—a view rightly questioned by Pythagoras and Aristotle. Incorrect commonsense notions are not just a part of the distant past; they remain with us today.

In the United States, common sense tells us that when a racial minority group moves into a previously all-White neighborhood, property values decline. Common sense tells us that people panic when faced with natural disasters, such as floods and earthquakes, with the result that all social organization disintegrates. However, these particular commonsense notions—like the notion that the earth is flat—are *untrue;* neither of them is supported by sociological research. Race has been found to have little relationship to property values; such factors as zoning changes, overcrowding, and age of housing

are more significant. Disasters do not generally produce panic. In the aftermath of natural disasters, greater social organization and structure emerge to deal with a community's problems.

Like other social scientists, sociologists do not accept something as a fact because "everyone knows it." Instead, each piece of information must be tested and recorded, then analyzed in relationship to other data. Sociology relies on scientific studies in order to describe and understand a social environment. At times, the findings of sociologists may seem like common sense because they deal with facets of everyday life. Yet it is important to stress that such findings have been *tested* by researchers. Common sense now tells us that the earth is round. But this particular commonsense notion is based on centuries of scientific work upholding the breakthrough made by Pythagoras and Aristotle.

WHAT IS SOCIOLOGICAL THEORY?

Why do people commit suicide? One traditional commonsense answer is that people inherit the desire to kill themselves. Another view is that sunspots drive people to take their own lives. These explanations may not seem especially convincing to contemporary researchers, but they represent beliefs widely held as recently as 1900.

Sociologists are not particularly interested in why any one individual commits suicide; they are more concerned with why *people in general* take their own lives. This leads sociologists to examine the social forces that influence people in deciding whether or not to attempt suicide. In order to undertake such research, sociologists develop theories that offer a general explanation of some type of behavior.

Theories can be regarded as attempts to explain events, forces, materials, ideas, or behavior in a comprehensive manner. Within sociology, a **theory** is a set of statements that seeks to explain problems, actions, or behavior. An effective theory may have both explanatory and predictive power. That is, it can help us to develop a broad and integrated view of the relationships among seemingly isolated phenomena as well as to understand how one type of change in an environment leads to others.

An essential task in building a sociological theory is to examine the relationship between bits of

9

data, gathered through research, that may seem completely unrelated. For example, suppose that you are given data about the number of reported suicides in various European nations in 1869. You are told that there were 5144 reported suicides in France in that year, 1588 in England, and only 462 in Denmark. If you restricted yourself to those data, you might attempt to develop a theory about why there were so many suicides in France and so few in Denmark. However, in researching this very problem, Émile Durkheim (1951, original edition 1897) looked into suicide data in much greater detail and developed a highly original theory about the relationship between suicide and social factors.

Durkheim was primarily concerned not with the personalities of individual suicide victims, but rather with suicide *rates* and how they varied from country to country. As a result, when he looked at the number of reported suicides in France, England, and Denmark in 1869, he also examined the populations of these nations to determine their rates of suicide. In doing so, he found that whereas England had only 67 reported suicides per million inhabitants, France had 135 per million and Denmark had 277 per million. Thus, in terms of national comparisons, the question then became: "Why did Denmark (rather than France) have a comparatively high rate of reported suicides?"

Durkheim went much deeper into his investigation of suicide rates, and the result was his landmark work *Suicide,* published in 1897. Durkheim refused to automatically accept unproven explanations regarding suicide, including the beliefs that such deaths were caused by cosmic forces or by inherited tendencies. Instead, he focused on such problems as the cohesiveness or lack of cohesiveness of religious and occupational groups.

Durkheim's research suggested that suicide, while a solitary act, is related to group life. Protestants had much higher suicide rates than Catholics did; the unmarried had much higher rates than married people did; soldiers were more likely to take their lives than civilians were. In addition, it appeared that there were higher rates of suicide in times of peace than in times of war and revolution, and in times of economic instability and recession rather than in times of prosperity. Durkheim concluded that the suicide rates of a society reflected the extent to which people were or were not integrated into the group life of the society.

Émile Durkheim, like many other social scientists, developed a theory to explain how individual behavior can be understood within a social context. He pointed out the influence of groups and societal forces on what had always been viewed as a highly personal act. Clearly, Durkheim offered a more *scientific* explanation for the causes of suicide than that of sunspots or inherited tendencies. His theory has predictive power, since it suggests that suicide rates will rise or fall in conjunction with certain social and economic changes.

It is important to understand that a theory—even the best of theories—is not a final statement about human behavior. Durkheim's theory of suicide is no exception; sociologists continue to examine factors which contribute to a society's rate of suicide. For example, people across the United States were shocked by the national news reports in 1987 concerning four New Jersey teenagers who together drove into a garage, closed the door, and let carbon monoxide fumes take their lives, thereby engaging in a collective act of suicide. Within little more than a week, 10 more teenagers in four different states killed themselves in garages using carbon monoxide. These suicides were more than a coincidence; sociological research from 1973 through the present documents that the incidence of suicide increases following nationally televised stories about suicide and that teenagers are especially vulnerable to such "copycat" behavior. Studies show that the impact is greatest after the publicized suicide of an entertainer or politician and is somewhat less after the suicide of an artist, criminal, or member of the economic elite (Israel and Stack, 1987; Phillips and Carstensen, 1986; Stack, 1987; Wasserman, 1984).

ORIGINS OF SOCIOLOGY

People have always been curious about how we get along, what we do, and whom we select as our leaders. Philosophers and religious authorities of ancient and medieval societies made countless observations about human behavior. These observations were not tested or verified scientifically; nevertheless, they often became the foundation for moral codes. Several of the early social philosophers predicted that a systematic study of human behavior would one day emerge. Beginning in the nineteenth century, European theorists made pioneering contributions to the development of a science of human behavior.

Early Thinkers: Comte, Martineau, and Spencer

In France, the nineteenth century was an unsettling time for that nation's intellectuals. The French monarchy had been deposed earlier in the revolution of 1789, and Napoleon had subsequently been defeated in his effort to conquer Europe. Amidst this chaos, philosophers considered how society might be improved. Auguste Comte (1798–1857), credited with being the most influential of these philosophers of the early 1800s, believed that a theoretical science of society and systematic investigation of behavior were needed to improve society. Comte coined the term *sociology* to apply to the science of human behavior and insisted that sociology could make a critical contribution to a new and improved human community. Writing in the 1800s, Comte feared that France's stability had been permanently impaired by the excesses of the French Revolution. Yet he hoped that the study of social behavior in a systematic way would eventually lead to more rational human interactions. In Comte's hierarchy of sciences, sociology was at the top. He called it the "queen" and its practitioners "scientist-priests." This French theorist did not simply give sociology its name; he also presented a rather ambitious challenge to the fledgling discipline.

Scholars were able to learn of Comte's works largely through translations by the English sociologist Harriet Martineau (1802–1876). But Martineau was a path breaker in her own right as a sociologist; she offered insightful observations of the customs and social practices of both her native Britain and the United States. Martineau's book *Society in America* (1962, original edition 1837) examines religion, politics, child rearing, and immigration in the young nation. Martineau gives special attention to status distinctions and to such factors as gender and race.

Martineau's writings emphasized the impact that the economy, law, trade, and population could have on the social problems of contemporary society. She spoke out in favor of the rights of women, the emancipation of slaves, and religious tolerance. In

Betmann

Harriet Martineau (1802–1876), an English scholar, was an early pioneer of sociology who studied social behavior both in her native country and in the United States.

Martineau's (1896) view, intellectuals and scholars should not simply offer observations of social conditions; they should act upon their convictions in a manner that will benefit society. In line with this view, Martineau conducted research on the nature of female employment and pointed to the need for much more research on this important issue (Hoecker-Drysdale, 1992).

Another important contributor to the discipline of sociology was Herbert Spencer (1820–1903). Writing from the viewpoint of relatively prosperous Victorian England, Spencer (unlike Martineau) did not feel compelled to correct or improve society; instead, he merely hoped to understand it better. Drawing on Charles Darwin's study *On the Origin of Species,* Spencer used the concept of evolution of animals to explain how societies change over time. Similarly, he adapted Darwin's evolutionary view of the "survival of the fittest" by arguing that it is "natural" that some people are rich while others are poor.

Spencer's approach to societal change was extremely popular in his own lifetime. Unlike Comte, Spencer suggested that societies are bound to change; therefore, one need not be highly critical of present social arrangements or work actively for social change. This position appealed to many influential people in England and the United States who had a vested interest in the status quo and were suspicious of social thinkers who endorsed change. We will consider Spencer's views on society and social change in more detail in Chapter 20.

Émile Durkheim

Émile Durkheim's important theoretical work on suicide was but one of his many pioneering contributions to sociology. The son of a rabbi, Durkheim (1858–1917) was educated in both France and Germany. He established an impressive academic reputation and was appointed as one of the first professors of sociology in France.

Above all, Durkheim will be remembered for his insistence that behavior cannot be fully understood in individualistic terms, that it must be understood within a larger social context. As one example of this emphasis, Durkheim (1947, original edition 1912) developed a fundamental thesis to help understand all forms of society through intensive study of the Arunta, an Australian tribe. He focused on the functions that religion performed for the Arunta and underscored the role that group life plays in defining that which we consider religious. Durkheim concluded that, like other forms of group behavior, religion reinforces a group's solidarity.

Another of Durkheim's main interests was the consequences of work in modern societies. In his view, the growing division of labor found in industrial societies as workers became much more specialized in their tasks led to what he called *anomie*. *Anomie* refers to a loss of direction that is felt in a society when social control of individual behavior has become ineffective. The state of anomie occurs when people have lost their sense of purpose or direction, often during a time of profound social change. In a period of anomie, people are so confused and unable to cope with the new social environment that they may resort to taking their own lives.

As will be seen in the examination of work and the economy in Chapter 15, Durkheim was concerned about the dangers that such alienation, loneliness, and isolation might pose for modern industrial societies. He shared Comte's belief that sociology should provide direction for social change. As a result, he advocated the creation of new social groups—between the individual's family and the state—which would ideally provide a sense of belonging for members of huge, impersonal societies.

Like many other sociologists, Durkheim's interests were not limited to one aspect of social behavior. Later in this book, we will give further attention to his thinking on crime and punishment, religion, and the workplace. Few sociologists have had such a dramatic impact on so many different areas within the discipline.

Max Weber

Another important theorist who contributed to the scientific study of society was Max Weber (pronounced "VAY-ber"). Born in Germany in 1864, Weber took his early academic training in legal and economic history, but he gradually developed an interest in sociology. Eventually, he became a professor at various German universities. Weber told his students that they should employ *Verstehen,* the German word for "understanding" or "insight," in their intellectual work. He pointed out that much of our social behavior cannot be analyzed by the kinds of objective criteria we use to measure weight or temperature. To fully comprehend behavior, we must learn the subjective meanings people attach to their actions—how they themselves view and explain their behavior.

For example, suppose that sociologists were studying the social ranking of individuals within an electricians' union. Weber would expect researchers to employ *Verstehen* in order to determine the significance of the union's social hierarchy for its members. Sociologists would seek to learn how these electricians relate to union members of higher or lower status; they might examine the effects of seniority on standing within the union. While investigating these questions, researchers would take into account people's emotions, thoughts, beliefs, and attitudes (L. Coser, 1977:130).

We also owe credit to Weber for a key conceptual tool: the ideal type. An *ideal type* is a construct,

FIGURE 1-1 *The Early Social Thinkers*

Émile Durkheim
1858–1917

Max Weber
1864–1920

Karl Marx
1818–1883

Left, Bibliothèque Nationale, Paris; middle, Culver; right, Culver.

Academic training	Philosophy	Law, economics, history, philosophy	Philosophy, law

| Key works | 1893 – *The Division of Labor in Society*
 1897 – *Suicide: A Study in Sociology*
 1912 – *Elementary Forms of Religious Life* | 1904-1905 – *The Protestant Ethic and the Spirit of Capitalism*
 1922 — *Wirtshaft und Gesellschaft* | 1848 — *The Communist Manifesto*
 1867 — *Das Kapital* |

Most of today's sociological studies draw on the work of these three nineteenth-century thinkers.

a model that serves as a measuring rod against which actual cases can be evaluated. In his own works, Weber identified various characteristics of bureaucracy as an ideal type (these will be discussed in detail in Chapter 6). In presenting this model of bureaucracy, Weber was not describing any particular business, nor was he using the term *ideal* in a way that suggested a positive evaluation. Instead, his purpose was to provide a useful standard for measuring how bureaucratic an actual organization is (Gerth and Mills, 1958:219). Later in this textbook, the concept of ideal type will be used to study the family, religion, authority, and economic systems and to analyze bureaucracy.

Although their professional careers came at the same time, Émile Durkheim and Max Weber never met and probably were unaware of each other's existence, let alone ideas. This was certainly not true of the work of Karl Marx. Durkheim's thinking about anomie was related to Marx's writings, while Weber's concern for a value-free, objective sociology (which will be explored in Chapter 2) was a direct response to Marx's deeply held convictions.

Thus, it is no surprise that Karl Marx is viewed as a major figure in the development of several social sciences, among them sociology. (See Figure 1-1.)

Karl Marx

Karl Marx (1818–1883) shared with Durkheim and Weber a dual interest in abstract philosophical issues and in the concrete reality of everyday life. Unlike the others, Marx was so critical of existing institutions that a conventional academic career was impossible, and although he was born and educated in Germany, most of his life was spent in exile.

Marx's personal life was a difficult struggle. When a paper that he had written was suppressed, he fled his native land and went to France. In Paris, he met Friedrich Engels (1820–1895), with whom he formed a lifelong friendship. They lived during a time in which European and North American economic life was increasingly being dominated by the factory rather than the farm.

In 1847, Marx and Engels attended secret meetings in London of an illegal coalition of labor unions, the Communist League. The following year, they finished preparing a platform called *The Communist Manifesto,* in which they argued that the masses of people who have no resources other than their labor (whom they referred to as the *proletariat*) should unite to fight for the overthrow of capitalist societies. In the words of Marx and Engels:

> The history of all hitherto existing society is the history of class struggles. . . . The proletarians have nothing to lose but their chains. They have a world to win. WORKING MEN OF ALL COUNTRIES UNITE! (Feuer, 1959:7, 41).

After completing *The Communist Manifesto,* Marx returned to Germany, only to be expelled. He then moved to England, where he continued to write books and essays. Marx's life there was one of extreme poverty. He pawned most of his possessions, and several of his children died of malnutrition and disease. Marx clearly was an outsider in British society, a fact which may well have affected his view of western cultures (R. Collins and Makowsky, 1978:40).

Marx's thinking was strongly influenced by the work of a German philosopher, Georg Hegel. Hegel saw history as a *dialectical process*—a series of clashes between conflicting ideas and forces. At the end of each clash, a new and improved set of ideas was expected to emerge. In Hegel's view, conflict was an essential element in progress. Conflict led to progress; progress came only through conflict.

In applying Hegel's theories, Marx focused on conflict between social classes, as represented by industrial workers and the owners of factories and businesses. Under Marx's analysis, society was fundamentally divided between classes who clash in pursuit of their own class interests. He argued that history could be understood in dialectical terms as a record of the inevitable conflicts between economic groups. This view forms the basis for the contemporary sociological perspective of conflict theory, which will be examined later in the chapter.

When Marx examined the industrial societies of his time, such as Germany, England, and the United States, he saw the factory as the center of conflict between the exploiters (the owners of the means of production) and the exploited (the workers). Marx viewed these relationships in systematic terms; that is, he believed that an entire system of economic, social, and political relationships had been established to maintain the power and dominance of the owners over the workers. Consequently, Marx and Engels argued that the working class needed to overthrow the existing class system. Marx's writings inspired those who were subsequently to lead communist revolutions in Russia, China, Cuba, Vietnam, and elsewhere.

Even apart from the political revolutions that his work helped to foster, Marx's influence on contemporary thinking has been dramatic. Although he certainly did not view himself as a sociologist, Marx nevertheless made a critical contribution to the development of sociology and other social sciences. Partly, this reflected Marx's emphasis on carefully researching the actual, measurable conditions of people's lives, a practice which foreshadowed the scientific nature of today's social sciences.

In addition, Marx placed great value on the *group* identifications and associations that influenced an individual's place in society. As we have seen, this area of study is the major focus of contemporary sociology. Throughout this textbook, we will consider how membership in a particular gender classification, age group, racial group, or economic class affects a person's attitudes and behavior. In an important sense, this way of understanding society can be traced back to the pioneering work of Karl Marx. (See Figure 1-2.)

Twentieth-Century Sociology

Sociology, as we know it in the 1990s, draws upon the firm foundation developed by Émile Durkheim, Max Weber, and Karl Marx. However, the discipline has certainly not remained stagnant over the last century. Sociologists have gained new insights which have helped them to better understand the workings of society.

Charles Horton Cooley (1864−1929) was typical of the sociologists who became prominent in the early 1900s. Born in Ann Arbor, Michigan, Cooley received his graduate training in economics but later became a sociology professor at the University

FIGURE 1-2 *Prominent Contributors to Sociological Thought*

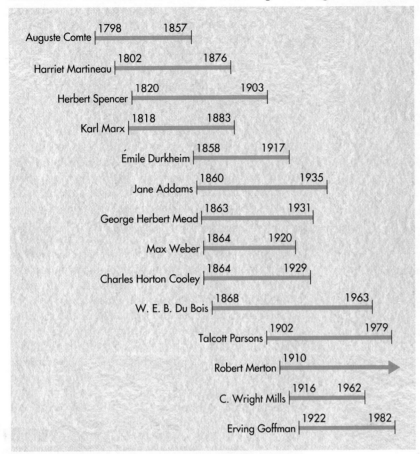

The "time lines" shown here give an idea of relative chronology.

of Michigan. Like other early sociologists, he became interested in this "new" discipline while pursuing a related area of study.

Cooley shared the desire of Durkheim, Weber, and Marx to learn more about society. But to do so effectively, Cooley preferred to use the sociological perspective to look first at smaller units—intimate, face-to-face groups such as families, gangs, and friendship networks. He saw these groups as the seedbeds of society in the sense that they shape people's ideals, beliefs, values, and social nature. Cooley's work brought new understanding to groups of relatively small size.

In the early 1900s, many of the leading sociologists of the United States saw themselves as social reformers dedicated to systematically studying and then improving a corrupt society. They were genuinely concerned about the lives of immigrants in the nation's growing cities, whether these immigrants came from Europe or from the American south. Early female sociologists, in particular, were often active in poor urban areas as leaders of community centers known as *settlement houses*. For example, Jane Addams (1860–1935), a member of and speaker before the American Sociological Society, cofounded the famous Chicago settlement, Hull House.

Addams and other pioneering female sociologists commonly combined intellectual inquiry, social service work, and political activism—all with the goal

Early female sociologists were often active in poor urban areas as leaders of community centers known as settlement houses. *For example, Jane Addams (1860–1935) was a cofounder of the famous Chicago settlement, Hull House.*

of assisting the underprivileged and creating a more egalitarian society. For example, working with the Black journalist and educator Ida B. Wells, Addams successfully prevented the implementation of a racial segregation policy in the Chicago public schools. The practical focus of her work was also evident in Addams' efforts to establish a juvenile court system and a women's trade union (Addams, 1910, 1930; Deegan, 1991; Wells, 1970).

By the middle of the twentieth century, however, the focus of the discipline had shifted. Sociologists restricted themselves to theorizing and gathering information, while the aim of transforming society was left to social workers and others. This shift away from social reform was accompanied by a growing commitment to scientific methods of research and to value-free interpretation of data.

Sociologist Robert Merton (1968:39–72) made an important contribution to the discipline by successfully combining theory and research. Born in 1910 of Slavic immigrant parents in Philadelphia, Merton subsequently won a scholarship to Temple University. He continued his studies at Harvard, where he acquired his lifelong interest in sociology. Merton's teaching career has been based at Columbia University.

Merton has produced a theory that is one of the most frequently cited explanations of deviant behavior. He noted different ways in which people attempt to achieve success in life. In his view, some may not share the socially agreed-upon goal of accumulating material goods or the accepted means of achieving this goal. For example, in Merton's classification scheme, "innovators" are people who accept the goal of pursuing material wealth but use illegal means to do so, including robbery, burglary, and extortion. Merton's explanation of crime is based on individual behavior—influenced by society's approved goals and means—yet it has wider applications. It helps to account for the high crime rates among the nation's poor, who may see no hope of advancing themselves through traditional roads to success. Merton's theory will be discussed in greater detail in Chapter 7.

Merton also emphasized that sociology should strive to bring together the "macro-level" and "micro-level" approaches to the study of society. **Macrosociology** concentrates on large-scale phenomena or entire civilizations. Thus, Émile Durkheim's cross-cultural study of suicide is an example of macro-level research. More recently, macrosociologists have examined international crime rates (see Chapter 7), the stereotype of Asian Americans as a "model minority" (see Chapter 10), and the population patterns of Islamic countries (see Chapter 19). By contrast, *microsociology* stresses study of small groups and often uses experimental study in laboratories. Sociological research on the micro level has included studies of how divorced men and women, ex-convicts, and others disengage from significant social roles (see Chapter 5); of how conformity can influence the expression of prejudiced attitudes (see Chapter 7); and of how a teacher's expectations can affect a student's academic performance (see Chapter 16).

Sociologists find it useful to employ both these approaches. In fact, we can learn a great deal by us-

A macrosociological examination of marriage ceremonies would seek to identify cross-cultural differences in religious customs and traditions, types of dress and music, wording of wedding vows, and so forth; and it would assess the sociological significance of these differences. Pictured are observant Jews at a wedding in Jerusalem, a bride and groom throwing rice on a "sacred fire" at a Hindu wedding in New Delhi, India, and a Shinto wedding at a shrine in Japan.

ing macrosociological and microsociological analysis to study the same problem. For example, we might try to understand criminal behavior at the macro level by analyzing crime rates in various countries and at the micro level by examining the social interactions that influence individuals to become criminals or delinquents.

Contemporary sociology reflects the diverse contributions of earlier theorists. As sociologists approach such topics as divorce, drug addiction, and religious cults, they can draw upon the theoretical insights of the discipline's pioneers. A careful reader can hear Comte, Durkheim, Weber, Marx, Cooley, Addams, and many others speaking through the pages of current research. In describing the work of today's sociologists, it is helpful to examine a number of influential theoretical approaches (also known as *perspectives*).

MAJOR THEORETICAL PERSPECTIVES

Sociologists view society in different ways. Some see the world basically as a stable and ongoing entity. They are impressed with the endurance of the family, organized religion, and other social institutions. Some sociologists see society as composed of many groups in conflict, competing for scarce resources. To other sociologists, the most fascinating aspects of the social world are the everyday, routine interactions among individuals that we sometimes take for granted.

These differing perspectives of society are all ways of examining the same phenomena. Sociological imagination may employ any of a number of theoretical approaches in order to study human behavior. From these approaches, sociologists develop theories to explain specific types of behavior. The three perspectives that are most widely used by sociologists will provide an introductory look at the discipline. These are the functionalist, conflict, and interactionist perspectives.

Functionalist Perspective

In the view of functionalists, each part of a society contributes to its survival. The *functionalist perspective* emphasizes the way that parts of a society are structured to maintain its stability. Émile Durkheim's analysis of religion represented a critical contribution to the development of functionalism. As noted earlier, Durkheim focused on the role of religion in reinforcing feelings of solidarity and unity within group life.

Talcott Parsons (1902–1979), a Harvard University sociologist, was a key figure in the development of functionalist theory. Parsons had been greatly influenced by the work of Émile Durkheim, Max Weber, and other European sociologists. For more than four decades, Parsons dominated sociology in the United States with his advocacy of functionalism. He saw any society as a vast network of connected parts, each of which contributes to the maintenance of the system as a whole. Under the functionalist approach, if an aspect of social life does not contribute to a society's stability or survival—if it does not serve some identifiably useful function or promote value consensus among members of a society—it will not be passed on from one generation to the next.

As an example of the functionalist perspective, let us examine prostitution. Why is it that a practice so widely condemned continues to display such persistence and vitality? Functionalists suggest that prostitution satisfies needs of patrons that may not be readily met through more socially acceptable forms such as courtship or marriage. The "buyer" receives sex without any responsibility for procreation or sentimental attachment; at the same time, the "seller" gains a livelihood through this exchange.

Through such an examination, we can conclude that prostitution does perform certain functions that society seems to need. However, this is not to suggest that prostitution is a desirable or legitimate form of social behavior. Functionalists do not make such judgments and do not wish to condone the abuses or crimes that prostitutes and their clients may commit. Rather, advocates of the functionalist perspective hope to explain how an aspect of society that is so frequently attacked can nevertheless manage to survive (K. Davis, 1937).

Manifest and Latent Functions A university catalog typically presents various stated functions of the institution. It may inform us, for example, that the university intends to "offer each student a broad education in classical and contemporary thought, in the humanities, in the sciences, and in the arts." However, it would be quite a surprise if we came across a catalog which declared: "This university was founded in 1895 to keep people between the ages of 18 and 22 out of the job market, thus reducing unemployment." No college catalog will declare that this is the purpose of the university. Yet societal institutions serve many functions, some of them quite subtle. The university, in fact, *does* delay people's entry into the job market.

To better examine the functions of institutions, Robert Merton (1968:115–120) made an important distinction between manifest and latent functions. *Manifest functions* of institutions are open, stated, conscious functions. They involve the intended, recognized consequences of an aspect of society, such as the university's role in certifying academic competence and excellence. By contrast, *latent functions* are unconscious or unintended functions and may reflect hidden purposes of an institution.

One latent function of universities is to serve as a meeting ground for people seeking marital partners.

Dysfunctions Functionalists acknowledge that not all parts of a society contribute to its stability all the time. A *dysfunction* refers to an element or a process of society that may actually disrupt a social system or lead to a decrease in stability.

Many dysfunctional behavior patterns, such as homicide, are widely regarded as undesirable. Yet dysfunctions should not automatically be interpreted as negative. The evaluation of a dysfunction depends on one's own values, or, as the saying goes, on "where you sit." For example, the official view in prisons in the United States is that inmates' gangs should be eradicated because they are dysfunctional to smooth operations. Yet some guards have actually come to view the presence of prison gangs as functional for their jobs. The danger posed by gangs creates a "threat to security" and thereby requires increased surveillance and more overtime work for guards (Hunt et al., 1993:400).

Conflict Perspective

In contrast to functionalists' emphasis on stability and consensus, conflict sociologists see the social world in continual struggle. The *conflict perspective* assumes that social behavior is best understood in terms of conflict or tension between competing groups. Such conflict need not be violent; it can take the form of labor negotiations, party politics, competition among religious groups for members, or disputes over cuts in the federal budget.

As we saw earlier, Karl Marx viewed struggle between social classes as inevitable, given the exploitation of workers under capitalism. Expanding on Marx's work, sociologists and other social scientists have come to see conflict not merely as a class phenomenon but as a part of everyday life in all societies. Thus, in studying any culture, organization, or social group, sociologists want to know who benefits, who suffers, and who dominates at the expense of others. They are concerned with the conflicts between women and men, parents and children, cities and suburbs, and Whites and Blacks, to name only a few. In studying such questions, conflict theorists are interested in how society's insti-

tutions—including the family, government, religion, education, and the media—may help to maintain the privileges of some groups and keep others in a subservient position.

Although contemporary conflict theory was clearly inspired by Karl Marx's analysis, there are important differences between Marxist theories and the conflict perspective. Whereas Marx foretold an end to conflict through the emergence of a classless communist society, current conflict theorists view conflict as unavoidable. They are less likely to anticipate, much less predict, that the social tensions arising from inequality will be entirely resolved. Moreover, while Marx viewed a total restructuring of society as fundamentally necessary to resolve social problems, contemporary conflict theorists believe that poverty, racism, sexism, inadequate housing, and other problems can be understood and attacked somewhat independently (Agger, 1989).

Like functionalists, conflict sociologists tend to use the macro-level approach. Obviously, though, there is a striking difference between these two sociological perspectives (see Box 1-1 on page 20 on the functionalist, conflict, and interactionist views of sports). Conflict theorists are primarily concerned with the kinds of changes that conflict can bring about, whereas functionalists look for stability and consensus. The conflict model is viewed as more "radical" and "activist" because of its emphasis on social change and redistribution of resources. On the other hand, the functionalist perspective, because of its focus on stability, is generally seen as more "conservative" (Dahrendorf, 1958).

Throughout most of the 1900s, sociology in the United States was more influenced by the functionalist perspective. However, the conflict approach has become increasingly persuasive since the late 1960s. The widespread social unrest resulting from battles over civil rights, bitter divisions over the war in Vietnam, the rise of the feminist and gay liberation movements, the Watergate scandal, urban riots, and confrontations at abortion clinics offered support for the conflict approach—the view that our social world is characterized by continual struggle between competing groups. Currently, conflict theory is accepted within the discipline of sociology as one valid way to gain insight into a society.

BOX 1-1 • EVERYDAY BEHAVIOR

FUNCTIONALIST, CONFLICT, AND INTERACTIONIST VIEWS OF SPORTS

We generally think of the functionalist, conflict, and interactionist perspectives of sociology as being applied to "serious" subjects such as the family, health care, and criminal behavior. Yet even sports can be analyzed using these theoretical perspectives.

FUNCTIONALIST VIEW

In examining any aspect of society, including sports, functionalists emphasize the contribution it makes to overall social stability. Functionalists regard sports as an almost religious institution which uses ritual and ceremony to reinforce the common values of a society:

- Sports provide learning experiences that socialize young people into such values as competition and patriotism. Athletes became role models and are treated with awe and respect.
- Sports contribute to the adaptive needs of the social system by helping to maintain people's physical well-being.
- Sports serve as a safety valve for both participants and spectators, who are allowed to shed tension and aggressive energy in a socially acceptable way.
- Sports "bring together" members of a community or even a nation and promote an overall feeling of unity and social solidarity.

CONFLICT VIEW

Conflict theorists argue that the social order is based on coercion and exploitation. They emphasize that sports reflect and even exacerbate many of the divisions of society, including those based on gender, race, ethnicity, and social class:

- Sports are a form of big business in which profits are more important than the health and safety of the workers (athletes).
- Sports perpetuate the false idea that success can be achieved simply through hard work, while failure should be blamed on the individual alone (rather than on injustices in the larger social system). Sports serve as an "opiate" which encourages people to seek a "fix" or temporary "high" rather than focus on personal problems and social issues.
- Sports maintain the subordinate role of Blacks and Hispanics, who toil as athletes but are largely barred from supervisory positions as coaches, managers, and general managers. In 1993, for example, African Americans accounted for only 7 percent of all executives and department heads in professional basketball and football and less than 4 percent in baseball.
- Sports relegate women to a secondary role as spectators and sexual "prizes" and tend to equate masculinity with brute strength, insensitivity, and domination.

INTERACTIONIST VIEW

In studying the social order, interactionists are especially interested in shared understandings of everyday behavior. Consequently, interactionists examine sports on the micro level by focusing on how day-to-day social behavior is shaped by the distinctive norms, values, and demands of the world of sports:

- Sports often heighten parent-child involvement; they may lead to parental expectations for participation and (sometimes unrealistically) for success.
- Participation in sports contributes to the emergence of friendship networks that can permeate everyday life.
- Despite class, racial, and religious differences, teammates may work together harmoniously and may even abandon previous stereotypes and prejudices.
- Relationships in the sports world are defined by people's social positions as players, coaches, and referees—as well as by the high or low status that individuals hold as a result of their performances and reputations.

Clearly, there is more to sports than exercise or recreation. From a functionalist perspective, sports reinforce societal traditions, consensus on values, and stability. By contrast, conflict theorists view sports as merely another reflection of the political and social struggles within a society. Interactionists focus on social relationships in sports, as people work together as teammates or compete in athletic contests.

SOURCES: Commission on Civil Rights, 1993; Edwards, 1973:84–130; Eitzen, 1984a, 1984b; G. Fine, 1987; Hasbrook, 1986; Lapchick and Jackson, 1993; Messner, 1989; Theberge, 1993.

One important contribution of conflict theory is that it has encouraged sociologists to view society through the eyes of those segments of the population that rarely influence decision making. Early Black sociologists such as W. E. B. Du Bois (1868–1963) provided research that they hoped would assist the struggle for a racially egalitarian society. Du Bois believed that knowledge was essential in combating prejudice and achieving tolerance and justice. Sociology, Du Bois contended, had to draw on scientific principles to study social problems such as those experienced by Blacks in the United States.

Du Bois had little patience for theorists such as Herbert Spencer who seemed content with the status quo. He advocated basic research on the lives of Blacks that would separate opinion from fact, and he documented their relatively low status in Philadelphia and Atlanta. Du Bois believed that the granting of full political rights to Blacks was essential to their social and economic progress in the United States. Many of his ideas challenging the status quo did not find a receptive audience within either the government or the academic world. As a result, Du Bois became increasingly involved with organizations questioning the established social order and helped to found the National Association for the Advancement of Colored People, better known as the NAACP (Green and Driver, 1978).

As is true of the work of African American sociologists, feminist scholarship in sociology has helped to enhance our understanding of social behavior. For example, a family's social standing is no longer viewed as defined solely by the husband's position and income. Feminist scholars have not only challenged stereotyping of women; they have argued for a gender-balanced study of society in which women's experiences and contributions are as visible as those of men (Brewer, 1989; Komarovsky, 1991).

Feminist theory builds in important ways on the conflict perspective. Like other conflict theorists, feminist scholars see gender differences as a reflection of the subjugation of one group (women) by another group (men). Drawing on the work of Marx and Engels, contemporary feminist theorists often view women's subordination as inherent in capitalist societies. Some radical feminist theorists, however, view the oppression of women as inevitable in *all* male-dominated societies, including

Sociologist W. E. B. Du Bois (1868–1963), the first Black person to receive a doctorate from Harvard University, later helped organize the National Association for the Advancement of Colored People (NAACP).

those labeled as *capitalist, socialist,* and *communist* (Tuchman, 1992).

Interactionist Perspective

The functionalist and conflict perspectives both analyze behavior in terms of societywide patterns. However, many contemporary sociologists are more interested in understanding society as a whole through an examination of social interactions such as small groups conducting meetings, two friends talking casually with each other, a family celebrating a birthday, and so forth. The *interactionist perspective* generalizes about fundamental or everyday forms of social interaction. Interactionism is a sociological framework for viewing human beings as living in a world of meaningful objects. These "objects" may include material things, actions, other people, relationships, and even symbols (Henslin, 1972:95).

21

Interactionists recognize that symbols, as in these photographs, can carry very different meanings in different social contexts.

Focusing on everyday behavior permits interactionists to better understand the larger society.

In a classic example of interactionist research, sociologist Howard S. Becker (1963) studied the process through which people become successful marijuana users. Becker found that novices are typically introduced to marijuana by their friends, but rarely "get high" the first time they experiment with this drug. Instead, people must *learn* (through the assistance of more experienced users) how to detect and enjoy the effects of marijuana. Consequently, Becker views marijuana smoking as a social act and learning to enjoy marijuana as a social process. More generally, interactionists emphasize that most forms of criminal or norm-defying behavior are learned, often from close acquaintances (Ritzer, 1992a).

George Herbert Mead (1863–1931) is widely regarded as the founder of the interactionist perspective. Mead taught at the University of Chicago from 1893 until his death in 1931. Mead's sociological analysis, like that of Charles Horton Cooley, often focused on human interactions within one-to-one situations and small groups. Mead was interested in observing the most minute forms of communication—smiles, frowns, nods of the head—and in understanding how such individual behavior was influenced by the larger context of a group or society. However, despite his innovative views, Mead only occasionally wrote articles, and never a book. Most of his insights have been passed along to us through edited volumes of his lectures which his students published after his death.

Interactionists see symbols as an especially important part of human communication. In fact, the interactionist perspective is sometimes referred to as the *symbolic interactionist perspective*. Such researchers note that both a clenched fist and a salute have social meanings which are shared and understood by members of a society. In the United States, a salute symbolizes respect, while a clenched fist signifies defiance. However, in another culture different gestures might be used to convey a feeling of respect or defiance.

Let us examine how various societies portray suicide without the use of words. People in the United States point a finger at the head (shooting); urban

TABLE 1-2	Comparing Major Theoretical Perspectives		
	FUNCTIONALIST	CONFLICT	INTERACTIONIST
View of Society	Stable, well-integrated	Characterized by tension and struggle between groups	Active in influencing and affecting everyday social interaction
Level of Analysis Emphasized	Macro	Macro	Micro analysis as a way of understanding the larger macro phenomena
View of the Individual	People are socialized to perform societal functions	People are shaped by power, coercion, and authority	People manipulate symbols and create their social worlds through interaction
View of the Social Order	Maintained through cooperation and consensus	Maintained through force and coercion	Maintained by shared understanding of everyday behavior
View of Social Change	Predictable, reinforcing	Change takes place all the time and may have positive consequences	Reflected in people's social positions and their communications with others
Proponents	Émile Durkheim Talcott Parsons Robert Merton	Karl Marx W. E. B. Du Bois C. Wright Mills	George Herbert Mead Charles Horton Cooley Erving Goffman

This table shows how the three theoretical perspectives can be compared along several important dimensions.

Japanese bring a fist against the stomach (stabbing); and the South Fore of Papua, New Guinea, clench a hand at the throat (hanging). These types of symbolic interaction are classified as forms of **nonverbal communication,** which can include many other gestures, facial expressions, and postures.

Interactionists realize the importance of nonverbal communication as a form of human behavior. George Muedeking (1992:232–233) observed interactions in visiting rooms at three state prisons for men in California. He found that guards typically use a form of nonverbal communication which he called "gazing" to control the behavior of inmates and their wives or girlfriends. A guard will slowly shift his gaze back and forth across the visiting room. If a couple's interactions are becoming overly intimate, the guard will stare directly into the inmate's eyes. This is a warning that a more direct confrontation will follow if the intimate behavior continues. Interestingly, the inmate will attempt to *avoid* eye contact with the guard, rather than acknowledge that he has received the guard's warning.

Since Mead's teachings have become well known, sociologists have expressed greater interest in the interactionist perspective. Many have moved away from what may have been an excessive preoccupa-

tion with the macro level of social behavior and have redirected their attention toward behavior which occurs in small groups. Erving Goffman (1922–1982) made a distinctive contribution by popularizing a particular type of interactionist method known as the **dramaturgical approach.** The dramaturgist compares everyday life to the setting of the theater and stage. Just as actors present certain images, all of us seek to present particular features of our personalities while we hide other qualities. Thus, in a class, we may feel the need to project a serious image; at a party, it may seem important to look like a relaxed and entertaining person. In Box 1-2 on page 24, Goffman's work on public places is reviewed to see how accurately it speaks to the experiences of women.

The Sociological Approach

Which perspective should a sociologist use in studying human behavior? The functionalist? The conflict? The interactionist? Sociology makes use of all three perspectives (see Table 1-2), since each offers

BOX 1-2 • EVERYDAY BEHAVIOR

A FEMINIST VIEW OF PUBLIC PLACES

Feminist sociology is often associated with the conflict perspective because that perspective emphasizes the struggle among competing groups in a society. However, sociologist Carol Brooks Gardner (1989), a symbolic interactionist interested in gender issues, has offered a feminist critique of the influential work on the sociology of public places developed by her dissertation adviser, Erving Goffman (1963b, 1971).

In Gardner's view, the classical sociological examinations of public places present public streets, parks, and roadways as innocuous settings in which strangers either leave each other alone or interact politely. Consequently, Goffman's studies of routine interactions in public places (such as "helping" encounters when a person is lost and asks for directions) underestimate the difficulties commonly experienced by subordinate groups. In Gardner's view (1989:45): "Rarely does Goffman emphasize the habitual disproportionate fear that women can come to feel in public toward

men, much less the routine trepidation that ethnic and racial minorities and the disabled can experience." For example, women are well-aware that the ostensibly innocuous helping encounter with a man in a public place can too easily lead to undesired sexual queries or advances. If a man asks for directions or for a match, a woman may have reason to fear that he has a hidden agenda that has sparked the conversation.

As part of her dissertation research, Gardner observed gender behavior in public places in Santa Fe, New Mexico, over an 18-month period; she also conducted 35 in-depth interviews with women and men from Santa Fe about their experiences in public places. In comparing her findings with those of Goffman, she places particular emphasis on the impact of street remarks on women.

Whereas Goffman suggests that street remarks occur rarely—and that they generally hold no unpleasant or threatening implications—Gardner counters (1989:49) that

"for young women especially, . . . appearing in public places carries with it the constant possibility of evaluation, compliments that are not really so complimentary after all, and harsh or vulgar insults if the woman is found wanting." She adds that street remarks are occasionally followed by tweaks, pinches, or even blows, which unmask the latent hostility of many male-to-female street remarks.

Gardner acknowledges the pioneering contribution of Erving Goffman to the study of public places, calling his work "original" and "conceptually rich." But she suggests that Goffman's view of interactions in public places gives insufficient attention to the impact of gender. For Gardner, many women have a well-founded fear of the sexual harassment, assault, and rape that can occur in public places. She therefore concludes that "public places are arenas for the enactment of inequality in everyday life for women and for many others" (Gardner, 1989:56; see also Gardner, 1990).

---

unique insights into the same problem. Thus, in studying the continued high levels of unemployment in the United States, the functionalist might wish to study how unemployment reduces the demand for goods but simultaneously increases the need for public services, thereby leading to new jobs in the government sector. The interactionist might encourage us to focus on the overall impact of unemployment on family life, as manifested in divorce, domestic violence, and dependence on drugs and alcohol. Researchers with a conflict perspective might draw our attention to the uneven distribution of unemployment within the labor

force and how it is particularly likely to affect women and racial and ethnic minorities—those groups least likely to influence decision making about economic and social policy.

No one of these approaches to the issues related to unemployment is "correct." Within this textbook, it is assumed that we can gain the broadest understanding of our society by drawing upon all three perspectives in the study of human behavior and institutions. These perspectives overlap as their interests coincide but can diverge according to the dictates of each approach and of the issue being studied.

APPLIED AND CLINICAL SOCIOLOGY

As noted before in this chapter, many early sociologists—notably Jane Addams—were quite concerned with social reform. They wanted their theories and findings to be relevant to policymakers and to people's lives in general. Today, *applied sociology* is the use of the discipline of sociology with the specific intent of yielding practical applications for human behavior and organizations.

Often, the goal of such work is to assist in resolving a social problem. For example, in the last 25 years, six presidents of the United States have established commissions to delve into major societal concerns facing our nation. Sociologists have been called upon to apply their expertise to studying such issues as violence, pornography, crime, immigration, and population. In Europe, both academic and governmental research departments are offering increasing financial support for applied studies.

Another example of applied sociology is the growing local community research movement. One institution which has pioneered in this effort is the Center for the Study of Local Issues, a research unit of Anne Arundel Community College, located in Arnold, Maryland. The center encourages students and faculty to apply social scientific research methods in studying community issues such as employment opportunities for people with disabilities and patterns of armed robberies. Similarly, in an effort to improve services, the Social Science Center for Community Education, Research, and Service of the University of Wisconsin–Stout has studied the effectiveness of state-funded programs designed to prevent child abuse and the attitudes of college students toward local retail stores and other community resources (Pamperin et al., 1985; see also P. Rossi, 1987).

The growing popularity of applied sociology has led to the rise of the specialty of clinical sociology. Louis Wirth (1931) wrote about clinical sociology more than 60 years ago, but the term itself has become popular only in recent years. *Clinical sociology* employs a variety of techniques to facilitate change and is similar in certain respects to applied sociology. However, while applied sociology may be evaluative, clinical sociology is dedicated to altering social relationships (as in family therapy)

or to restructuring social institutions (as in the reorganization of a medical center).

The Sociological Practice Association was founded in 1978 to promote the application of sociological knowledge to intervention for individual and social change. This professional group has developed a procedure for certifying clinical sociologists—much as physical therapists or psychologists are certified. As another indication of the rise of clinical sociology, as of 1989 the American Sociological Association began publishing a new journal of clinical sociology, *Sociological Practice Review.*

Applied sociologists generally leave it to others to act on their evaluations. By contrast, clinical sociologists bear direct responsibility for implementation and view those with whom they work as their clients. This specialty has become increasingly attractive to sociology graduate students because it offers an opportunity to apply intellectual learning in a practical way. Moreover, shrinking prospects for academic employment have made such alternative career routes appealing (H. Freeman et al., 1983; H. Freeman and Rossi, 1984; R. Straus, 1985:18).

Applied and clinical sociology can be contrasted with *basic* (or *pure*) *sociology,* which has the objective of gaining a more profound knowledge of the fundamental aspects of social phenomena. This type of research does not necessarily hope to generate specific applications, although such ideas may result once findings are analyzed. When Durkheim studied suicide rates, he was not primarily interested in discovering a way to eliminate suicide. In this sense, his research was an example of basic rather than applied sociology.

SOCIOLOGY AND SOCIAL POLICY

One important way in which the sociological imagination can be usefully applied is to enhance our understanding of current social issues. Beginning with Chapter 3 of this textbook, which focuses on culture, each chapter will conclude with a discussion of a contemporary social policy issue. In some cases, a specific issue facing Congress will be examined; in others, there will be a more decentralized issue facing city councils or school boards. For example, government funding of child care centers will be discussed in Chapter 4, Socialization; the

AIDS crisis in Chapter 5, Social Interaction and Social Structure; domestic violence in Chapter 13, The Family; and national health insurance in Chapter 17, Health and Medicine. These social policy sections will demonstrate how fundamental sociological concepts can enhance our critical thinking skills and help us to better understand current public policy debates.

In addition, sociology has been used to evaluate the success of programs or the impact of changes brought about by policymakers and political activists. Chapter 2, Methods of Sociological Research, will focus on a study of how the corporate response to Blacks' demands for civil rights affected top-ranking African American executives. Chapter 8, Stratification and Social Mobility, includes discussion of research on the effectiveness of welfare programs. Chapter 18, Communities, examines a study of how activism by homeless people improved their individual situations and led to broader changes in public policy. These discussions, along with the social policy sections of the text, will underscore the many practical applications of sociological theory and research.

Sociologists expect the next quarter of a century to be perhaps the most exciting and critical period in the history of the discipline. This is because of a growing recognition—both in the United States and around the world—that current social problems *must* be addressed before their magnitude overwhelms human societies. If such predictions prove to be accurate, we can expect sociologists to play an increasing role in the government sector by researching and developing public policy alternatives. Therefore, it seems appropriate for this textbook to include a unique focus on the connection between the work of sociologists and the difficult questions confronting the policymakers and people of the United States.

APPENDIX

CAREERS IN SOCIOLOGY

The primary source of employment for sociologists is higher education. About 75 percent of recent Ph.D. recipients in sociology sought employment in two-year community colleges, liberal arts colleges, and universities. These sociologists will teach not only majors committed to the discipline but also students hoping to become doctors, nurses, lawyers, police officers, and so forth (B. Huber, 1985).

For sociology students interested in academic careers, the road to a Ph.D. degree (or doctorate) can be long and difficult. This degree symbolizes competence in original research; each candidate must prepare a book-length study known as a *dissertation*. Typically, a graduate student in sociology will engage in four to six years of intensive work, including the time required to complete the dissertation. Yet this effort is no guarantee of a job as a sociology professor. Over the next decade, the demand for instructors is expected to decline, since there will be fewer students of college age. Consequently, anyone who launches an academic career must be prepared for considerable uncertainty and competition in the college job market (American Sociological Association, 1977:10–11; B. Huber, 1985).

Of course, not all people working as sociologists teach or hold doctoral degrees. Government is the second-largest source of employment for people in this discipline. The Census Bureau relies on people with sociological training to interpret data in a way that is useful for other government agencies and the general public. Virtually every agency depends on survey research—a field in which sociology students can specialize—in order to assess everything from community needs to the morale of the agency's own workers. In addition, people with sociological training can put their academic knowledge to effective use in probation and parole, health sciences, community development, and recreational services. Some people working in government or private industry have a master's degree (an M.A. or M.S.) in sociology; others have a bachelor's degree (a B.A. or B.S.).

The accompanying figure summarizes sources of employment for those with B.A. or B.S. degrees in

Where Sociology Graduates Find Employment

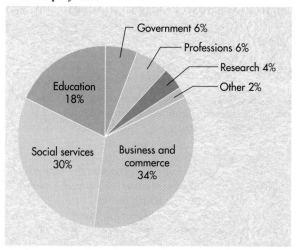

SOURCE: Watts and Ellis, 1989:301.

Graduates with baccalaureate degrees in sociology find employment in a number of areas, but particularly in business and commerce, social services, and education.

sociology. Like other liberal arts graduates, sociology majors can generally offer their employers essential job-related skills. Job applicants with sociology degrees find that their refinement in such areas as oral and written communication, interpersonal skills, problem solving, and critical thinking gives them an advantage over graduates who have pursued more technical degrees (Benner and Hitchcock, 1986; Billson and Huber, 1993).

Reflecting the utility of applied and clinical sociology, the figure shows that the areas of human services, business, and government offer important career opportunities for sociology graduates. Un-

dergraduates are commonly advised to enroll in sociology courses and specialties (refer back to Table 1-1) best-suited for their career interests. For example, students hoping to become health planners would take a class in medical sociology; students seeking employment as social science research assistants would refine their skills in statistics and methods. Internships, such as placements at city planning agencies and survey research organizations, offer sociology undergraduates an important opportunity to prepare for careers. Studies show that students who choose an internship placement have less trouble finding jobs, obtain better jobs, and enjoy greater job satisfaction than students without internship placements (Salem and Grabarek, 1986).

Many college students view social work as the field most closely associated with sociology. Traditionally, social workers received their undergraduate training in sociology and allied fields such as psychology and counseling. After some practical experience, social workers would generally seek a master's degree in social work (M.S.W.) to be considered for supervisory or administrative positions. Today, however, some students choose (where it is available) to pursue an undergraduate degree in social work (B.S.W.). This degree prepares graduates for direct service positions such as caseworker or group worker, rather than for the broader occupational areas served by the sociology baccalaureate.

Finally, underscoring the renewed interest in applied sociology, it is clear that an increasing number of sociologists with graduate degrees are being hired by business firms, industry, hospitals, and nonprofit organizations. Indeed, studies show that many sociology graduates are making career changes from social services areas to business and commerce. As an undergraduate major, sociology is excellent preparation for employment in many parts of the business world (B. Huber, 1985, 1987; W. Watts and Ellis, 1989; Wilkinson, 1980).

SUMMARY

Sociology is the systematic study of social behavior and human groups. In this chapter, we examine the nature of sociological theory, the founders of the discipline, theoretical perspectives of contemporary sociology, and the application of sociology to current issues of public policy.

1 An important element in the **sociological imagination** is the ability to view our own society as an outsider might, rather than from the perspective of our limited experiences and cultural biases.

2 In contrast to other **social sciences,** sociology emphasizes the influence that groups can have on people's behavior and attitudes and the ways in which people shape society.

3 Sociologists employ **theories** to examine the relationships between observations or between data that may seem completely unrelated.

4 In his pioneering work *Suicide,* published in 1897, Émile Durkheim focused on social factors that contributed to the rates of suicide found among various groups and nations.

5 Max Weber told his students that they should employ **Verstehen,** the German word for "understanding" or "insight," in their intellectual work. In employing *Verstehen,* sociologists consider the thoughts and feelings of those people under study.

6 Karl Marx argued that history could be understood in dialectical terms as a record of the inevitable conflict between the owners of the means of production and the masses of people who have no resources other than their labor (the proletariat).

7 *Macrosociology* concentrates on large-scale phenomena or entire civilizations, whereas *microsociology* stresses study of small groups.

8 In contrast to the emphasis on stability which characterizes the **functionalist perspective** of sociology, the **conflict perspective** assumes that social behavior is best understood in terms of conflict or tension between competing groups.

9 Within the discipline of sociology, the **interactionist perspective** is primarily concerned with fundamental or everyday forms of interaction, including symbols and other types of **nonverbal communication.**

10 *Applied sociology*—the use of the discipline with the specific intent of yielding practical applications for human behavior and organizations—can be contrasted with **basic sociology,** the objective of which is to gain a more profound knowledge of the fundamental aspects of social phenomena.

11 Sociologists expect the next quarter of a century to be perhaps the most exciting and critical period in the history of the discipline because of a growing recognition that social problems *must* be addressed in the near future.

CRITICAL THINKING QUESTIONS

1 If a sociologist was present in a college cafeteria, what aspects of the social and work environment would be of particular interest because of his or her "sociological imagination"?

2 Some sociologists see themselves as social reformers dedicated to systematically studying and then improving society, while others counter that sociologists should restrict themselves to theorizing and gathering information. In your view, which of these positions represents a more appropriate goal for the discipline of sociology?

3 How might functionalist, conflict, and interactionist theorists view popular music?

KEY TERMS

Anomie Durkheim's term for the loss of direction felt in a society when social control of individual behavior has become ineffective. (page 12)

Applied sociology The use of the discipline of sociology with the specific intent of yielding practical applications for human behavior and organizations. (25)

Basic sociology Sociological inquiry conducted with the objective of gaining a more profound knowledge of the fundamental aspects of social phenomena. Also known as *pure sociology.* (25)

Clinical sociology The use of the discipline of sociology with the specific intent of altering social relationships and facilitating change. (25)

Conflict perspective A sociological approach which assumes that social behavior is best understood in terms of conflict or tension between competing groups. (19)

Dialectical process A series of clashes between conflicting ideas and forces. (14)

Dramaturgical approach A view of social interaction, popularized by Erving Goffman, under which people are examined as if they were theatrical performers. (23)

Dysfunction An element or a process of society that may disrupt a social system or lead to a decrease in stability. (19)

Functionalist perspective A sociological approach which emphasizes the way that parts of a society are structured to maintain its stability. (18)

Ideal type A construct or model that serves as a measuring rod against which actual cases can be evaluated. (12)

Interactionist perspective A sociological approach which generalizes about fundamental or everyday forms of social interaction. (21)

Latent functions Unconscious or unintended functions; hidden purposes. (18)

Macrosociology Sociological investigation which concentrates on large-scale phenomena or entire civilizations. (16)

Manifest functions Open, stated, and conscious functions. (18)

Microsociology Sociological investigation which stresses study of small groups and often uses laboratory experimental studies. (16)

Natural science The study of the physical features of nature and the ways in which they interact and change. (7)

Nonverbal communication The sending of messages through the use of posture, facial expressions, and gestures. (23)

Science The body of knowledge obtained by methods based upon systematic observation. (7)

Social science The study of various aspects of human society. (7)

Sociological imagination An awareness of the relationship between an individual and the wider society. (6)

Sociology The systematic study of social behavior and human groups. (5)

Theory In sociology, a set of statements that seeks to explain problems, actions, or behavior. (9)

Verstehen The German word for "understanding" or "insight"; used by Max Weber to stress the need for sociologists to take into account people's emotions, thoughts, beliefs, and attitudes. (12)

ADDITIONAL READINGS

Berger, Peter L. *Invitation to Sociology: A Humanistic Perspective.* New York: Anchor, 1963. Berger takes a thoughtful and whimsical look at the discipline ("There are very few jokes about sociologists"). He argues that sociology has a special responsibility because it focuses so often on human ideals and passions.

Borgatta, Edgar F., and Marie L. Borgatta (eds.). *Encyclopedia of Sociology.* New York: Macmillan, 1992. A four-volume work that includes more than 350 signed essays on subjects ranging from "adulthood" to "work orientation." This encyclopedia is a good place to begin further reading or research.

Chafetz, Janet Saltzman. *Feminist Sociology: An Overview of Contemporary Theories.* Itasca, Ill.: Peacock, 1988. An overview of the major feminist theories in sociology or theories useful to sociologists that have emerged in the last two decades, including Marxist-feminist theories, feminist neo-Freudian theories, and everyday life approaches.

Collins, Randall. *Sociological Insight: An Introduction to Nonobvious Sociology.* New York: Oxford University Press, 1982. A concise book that offers striking and "nonobvious" insights regarding religion, power, crime, love, and reason.

Huber, Bettina J. *Employment Patterns in Sociology: Recent Trends and Future Prospects.* Washington, D.C.: American Sociological Association, 1985. A factual and frank appraisal of employment opportunities; available from the ASA at 1722 N St., NW, Washington, D.C. 20036.

Kohn, Melvin L. (ed.). *Cross-National Research in Sociology.* Newbury Park, Calif.: Sage, 1989. This anthology includes 17 essays which present comparative and historical sociological research.

Lee, Alfred McClung. *Sociology for Whom?* New York: Oxford University Press, 1978. Lee, a former president of the American Sociological Association, argues that sociologists are responsible and accountable to the highest scientific and ethical ideals. In his view, sociologists must not compromise these ideals in an effort to serve the interests of administrators, business leaders, publishers, or the political establishment.

Sills, David L., and Robert K. Merton (eds.). *Social Science Quotations.* New York: Macmillan, 1991. The editors list and cross-index quotations from all the social science disciplines.

Smelser, Neil J. (ed.). *Handbook of Sociology.* Newbury Park, Calif.: Sage, 1988. This collection examines the state of the discipline and various sociological areas.

Straus, Roger (ed.). *Using Sociology.* Bayside, N.Y.: General Hall, 1985. Straus offers an illuminating view of clinical and applied sociology.

Journals

Journals and periodicals are an important resource for reviewing the latest sociological research. The major sociological journals that cover all areas of the discipline are the *American Journal of Sociology* (founded in 1895), *American Sociological Review* (1936), *Canadian Review of Sociology and Anthropology* (1984), *Critical Sociology* (formerly *The Insurgent Sociologist,* 1969), *Free Inquiry in Creative Sociology* (1972), *Qualitative Sociology* (1978), *Social Forces* (1922), *Social Problems* (1951), *Society* (1963), *Sociological Quarterly* (1960), and *Sociological Review* (1908).

2

METHODS OF SOCIOLOGICAL RESEARCH

WHAT IS THE SCIENTIFIC METHOD?
Defining the Problem
Reviewing the Literature
Formulating the Hypothesis
Collecting and Analyzing Data
　Selecting the Sample
　Creating Scales and Indices
　Ensuring Validity and Reliability
Developing the Conclusion
　Supporting Hypotheses
　Controlling for Other Factors
In Summary: The Scientific Method

**RESEARCH DESIGNS
FOR COLLECTING DATA**
Surveys
Observation
Experiments
Use of Existing Sources

ETHICS OF RESEARCH
Case Studies of Ethical Controversies
　Tearoom Trade
　Accident or Suicide?
Neutrality and Politics in Research

**APPENDIX I: WRITING A LIBRARY
RESEARCH REPORT**

**APPENDIX II: UNDERSTANDING
TABLES AND GRAPHS**

BOXES
2-1　Current Research: Racial "Eye Work"
　　on the Street
2-2　Speaking Out: Preserving
　　Confidentiality—One Sociologist's
　　View

LOOKING AHEAD

* How do sociologists use the scientific method?
* How can researchers study the impact of Black demands for equal rights on corporate hiring and promotion policies?
* Why does the conclusion of a sociological study invariably point the way to new research?
* What are the practical and ethical challenges faced by sociologists who wish to conduct observation research?
* How can sociologists use secondary measures to study social phenomena indirectly?
* Why is it valuable for sociologists to have a code of ethics?

How do sociologists study human behavior and institutions? Is it accurate to consider sociology a science? What ethical standards guide sociologists in conducting research? As a way of beginning our examination of the principles and methods of sociological research, let us look briefly at an interesting study of magazine advertisements.

In recent decades, women in the United States have increasingly entered occupations and careers that traditionally were reserved for men. As this change in the workplace evolved, the media persisted in typically portraying women in such traditional roles as mother and homemaker. Sociologists Penny Belknap and Wilbert Leonard, II (1991), devised a study to examine whether the media continue to show women primarily in these conventional roles. Their focus was sexual stereotyping in print advertisements appearing in major magazines.

The researchers suspected that advertisements in traditional magazines (*Good Housekeeping, Sports Illustrated,* and *Time*) would be more likely to portray women in subordinate positions (for example, being childlike and deferential) than would ads in modern magazines (*Gentlemen's Quarterly, Ms.,* and *Rolling Stone*). They examined approximately 170 print advertisements that appeared in 1985 in each of the "traditional" and "modern" magazines.

Belknap and Leonard found that advertisements in all six magazines tended to show women in subordinate positions. (It should be noted that this research was conducted *before Ms.* magazine stopped accepting advertising in 1990, in part because women continued to be treated as subordinate by many advertisers.) There was no substantial difference between the portrayal of women in traditional and modern magazine advertisements; both types of magazines perpetuated the sexual stereotyping that has long characterized the media's portrayal of women.

Many questions may come to mind as you consider this example of sociological research. Why did Belknap and Leonard use advertisements in studying magazines' portrayal of women, rather than focusing on the photographs on magazine covers and those that accompany articles? Indeed, why did the researchers choose to study magazines, as opposed to newspapers, television, movies, or music videos? Given their selection of subject matter, would Belknap and Leonard have found more dramatic changes in media images of women if they had compared current advertisements in these six magazines with print advertisements from the 1970s or even the 1950s?

Effective sociological research can be quite thought-provoking. It may interest us in many new questions about social interactions that require further study. On the other hand, effective research is not always dramatic. In some cases, rather than raising additional questions, a study will confirm previous beliefs and findings.

This chapter, building on what was considered in Chapter 1, will examine sociology as a social science. The basic principles and stages of the scientific method will be described. A number of techniques commonly used in sociological research, such as experiments, observations, and surveys, will be presented. Particular attention will be given to the practical and ethical challenges that sociologists face in studying human behavior and to the debate raised by Max Weber's call for "value neutrality" in social science research.

These themes form the core of Chapter 2, and they will also be reflected throughout this textbook. Whatever the area of sociological inquiry—whether culture or organizational behavior, the economy or education—and whatever the perspective of the sociologist—whether functionalist, conflict, interactionist, or any other—there is one crucial requirement. Within the discipline of sociology, all branches of specialization and all theoretical approaches depend on imaginative, responsible research which meets the highest scientific and ethical standards.

WHAT IS THE SCIENTIFIC METHOD?

Like the typical woman or man on the street, the sociologist is interested in the central questions of our time. Are we lagging behind in our ability to feed the world population? Is the family falling apart? Why is there so much crime in the United States? Such issues concern most people, whether or not they have academic training. However, unlike the typical citizen, the sociologist has a commitment to the use of the scientific method in studying society. The *scientific method* is a systematic, organized series of steps that ensures

Photo Works

Sociologists Penny Belknap and Wilbert Leonard, II, analyzed sexual stereotyping in print advertisements appearing in major magazines so that they could better understand the images that the media are conveying to women and men in the United States.

maximum objectivity and consistency in researching a problem.

Many of us will never actually conduct scientific research. Nonetheless, it is important that we understand the scientific method, for it plays a major role in the workings of our society. People in the United States are constantly being bombarded with "facts" or "data." Almost daily, advertisers cite supposedly scientific studies to prove that their products are superior. Such claims may be accurate or exaggerated. We can make better evaluations of such information—and will not be fooled so easily—if we are familiar with the standards of scientific research. As this chapter will indicate, the scientific method is stringent and demands that researchers adhere as strictly as possible to its basic principles.

The scientific method requires precise preparation in developing useful research. If investigators are not careful, research data that they collect may prove to be unacceptable for purposes of sociological study. There are five basic steps in the scientific method that sociologists and other researchers follow. These are (1) defining the problem, (2) reviewing the literature, (3) formulating the hypothesis, (4) selecting the research design and then collecting and analyzing data, and (5) developing the conclusion. An actual example will illustrate the workings of the scientific method.

At least 25 percent of African Americans are now members of the middle class (Schaefer, 1993:233). Yet has the relative success of certain Blacks included entry into and acceptance among the nation's corporate elite? How might sociologists use the scientific method to study Blacks' status as corporate executives? How might they move from a broad question (Have Black executives been accepted within corporate circles in the United States?) to a researchable problem?

A sociologist's approach to a research problem is influenced in important ways by his or her theoretical orientation. Thus, functionalists would view the presence of Blacks in management positions as a reflection of business firms' need to attract Black customers or clients to maintain stability and prosperity. Conflict theorists would raise the issue of tokenism, questioning whether a small number of African Americans were being placed in highly visible positions to provide the *appearance* of change—while the rest of corporate management remained White. Interactionists would focus on the nature of social relations between the few Black executives and their many White counterparts.

Defining the Problem

The first step in any sociological research project is to state as clearly as possible what you hope to investigate. Drawing on the conflict perspective, sociologist Sharon Collins (1983) had initially relied on census data to study the employment patterns of more affluent Blacks. Collins then wondered: "Did the progress of these individuals represent a genuine restructuring of society that allowed for the entry of Blacks into top executive positions in White-owned corporations?" Or, instead, was it a token response to civil rights pressures? Were African American executives being placed primarily in highly visible personnel and public relations posts

Drawing on the conflict perspective, sociologist Sharon Collins wondered if Black executives were being placed primarily in highly visible personnel and public relations posts that had little likelihood of leading to key policymaking positions in the corporate world.

that had little likelihood of leading to key policymaking positions in the corporate world?

Early in their research, sociologists face the task of developing an operational definition of each concept being studied. An *operational definition* is an explanation of an abstract concept that is specific enough to allow a researcher to measure the concept. For example, a sociologist interested in status might use membership in exclusive social clubs or professional organizations as an operational definition of high status. A sociologist who intended to examine prejudice might rely on responses to a series of questions concerning willingness to hire or work alongside members of racial and ethnic minority groups.

Whenever researchers wish to study an abstract

concept—such as intelligence, sexuality, prejudice, love, or liberalism—they must develop workable and valid operational definitions. Even when studying a particular group of people, it is necessary to decide how the group will be distinguished. Thus, in her study of Blacks in corporate management positions, Sharon Collins (1989:318; 1993) needed to develop an operational definition of "top executives." She classified private-sector positions as being "high-level" if a person's major job responsibilities involved planning or implementation of company policy decisions. Collins operationalized this conception by examining job titles; subjects were considered "top executives" if they held titles such as president, chief executive officer, director, vice president, and department manager.

Reviewing the Literature

By conducting a review of the literature—the relevant scholarly studies and information—researchers refine the problem under study, clarify possible techniques to be used in collecting data, and eliminate or reduce the number of avoidable mistakes they make. Thus, in addition to drawing on her earlier research, which relied on census data, Sharon Collins reviewed descriptive studies of college-educated African Americans and gave special attention to studies of African American business executives and professionals. Until rather recently, most Blacks who have achieved great success have done so in professions such as law and medicine or in the government sector. The corporate world has not been so open to Black executives, a fact that underscores the importance of studies such as Collins's.

Formulating the Hypothesis

After reviewing earlier research concerning Black executives and drawing upon the contributions of sociological theorists, the researcher may develop an intuitive guess about the relationship between Black demands for equal rights and corporate hiring and promotion policies. Such a speculative statement about the relationship between two or more factors is called a *hypothesis.*

A hypothesis essentially tells us what we are looking for in our research. In order to be meaningful, a hypothesis must be testable; that is, it must be capable of being evaluated. The statement "God exists" may or may not be true; it clearly cannot be scientifically confirmed. A research hypothesis must also be reasonably specific. "Young people have more fun" and "Florida is nicer than California" are statements that lack the kind of precision that sociologists need in order to collect suitable data.

As part of a study of African Americans in executive positions, one hypothesis might be: "In response to Black demands for equal rights, corporate hiring and promotion policies placed Black executives primarily in highly visible personnel and public relations posts." In formulating a hypothesis, we do not imply that it is correct. We merely suggest that it is worthy of study, that the hypothesis should be scientifically tested and confirmed, refuted, or revised, depending on the outcome of the study.

A hypothesis usually states how one aspect of human behavior influences or affects another. These aspects or factors are called *variables.* A **variable** is a measurable trait or characteristic that is subject to change under different conditions. Income, religion, occupation, and gender can all be variables in a study. In the hypothesis presented above, there are two variables: "Black demands for equal rights" and "corporate hiring and promotion policies."

In developing hypotheses, sociologists attempt to explain or account for the relationship between two or more variables. If one variable is hypothesized to cause or influence another one, social scientists call the first variable the **independent variable.** The second is termed the **dependent variable** because it is believed to be influenced by the independent variable. In her study of Black executives, Collins was interested in the effect that a particular variable (Black demands for equal rights) might have on corporate hiring and promotion policies. As the causal or influencing characteristic, "Black demands for equal rights" is the independent variable. The variable that Collins was trying to explain, "corporate hiring and promotion policies," is the dependent variable.

According to the hypothesis, Black demands for equal rights have a direct influence on corporate

FIGURE 2-1 Causal Logic

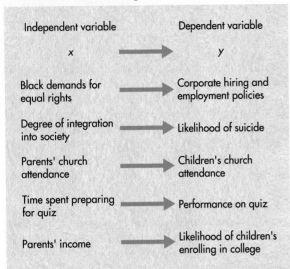

An independent variable is hypothesized to cause or influence another variable (a dependent variable). Causal logic involves the effect of an independent variable (often designated by the symbol x) on a dependent variable (generally designated as y) where x leads to y. For example, parents who attend church regularly (x) are more likely to have children who are regular churchgoers (y). Notice that the first two pairs of variables are taken from studies already described in this textbook.

hiring and promotion policies. As shown in Figure 2-1, *causal logic* involves the relationship between a condition or variable and a particular consequence, with one event leading to the other. Under causal logic, the degree of integration into society may be directly related to or produce a greater likelihood of suicide (refer back to Durkheim's study of suicide in Chapter 1). Similarly, the time students spend reviewing material for a quiz may be directly related to or produce a greater likelihood of getting a high score on the quiz.

A *correlation* exists when a change in one variable coincides with a change in the other. Correlations are an indication that causality *may* be present; they do not necessarily indicate causation. For

example, data indicate that working mothers are more likely to have delinquent children than are mothers who do not work outside the home. This correlation is actually caused by a third variable: family income. Lower-class households are more likely to have a full-time working mother; at the same time, reported rates of delinquency are higher in this class than in other economic levels. Consequently, while having a mother who works outside the home is correlated with delinquency, it does not *cause* delinquency. Sociologists seek to identify the causal link between variables; this causal link is generally advanced by researchers in their hypotheses.

Collecting and Analyzing Data

In order to test a hypothesis and determine if it is supported or refuted, researchers need to collect information. To do so, they must employ one of the research designs described later in the chapter. The research design guides them in collecting and analyzing data.

Selecting the Sample In most studies, social scientists must carefully select what is known as a *sample*. A *representative sample* is a selection from a larger population that is statistically found to be typical of that population. There are many kinds of samples, of which the *random sample* is frequently used by social scientists. For a *random sample,* every member of an entire population being studied has the same chance of being selected.

By using specialized sampling techniques, sociologists do not need to question everyone in a population in order to generalize. Thus, if researchers wanted to examine the opinions of people listed in a city directory (a book that, unlike the telephone directory, lists all households), they might contact every tenth or fiftieth or hundredth name listed. This would constitute a random sample.

If Sharon Collins had decided to conduct a survey of Blacks serving as top executives in corporations across the United States, she would have faced the problem of how to develop an appropriate sample of Black executives. Such a sample would have been essential, since the difficulty of questioning *all* Black executives would have been formidable. However, Collins chose instead to focus on a smaller target population: African Americans serving as top executives in White-owned corporations in the Chicago area. Still, she had to find a way of identifying her subjects, for there was no readily available list of Black executives in the region.

Collins (1989:318–319) studied corporate listings and identified 52 of the largest firms in Chicago. She then asked people familiar with the city's corporate community to name African American executives in these firms. Collins spoke to informants in these companies to see which Black managers served as top executives, and also asked participants in her study to refer her to other important Black managers. She found that almost one-third of the 52 firms lacked even one Black employee who met her operational definition of "top executive." Nevertheless, Collins identified 87 Blacks who qualified as top executives. Between May 1986 and January 1987 she was able to interview 76 of these men and women. Generally, researchers are unable to interview as high a proportion of a target population as Collins did.

Creating Scales and Indices It is relatively simple to measure certain characteristics statistically, such as level of education, income, and size of a community. However, it is far more difficult to measure attitudes and beliefs such as patriotism, respect, and tolerance. Sociologists create scales in order to assess aspects of social behavior that require judgments or subjective evaluations. The *scale* and *index* are indicators of attitudes, behavior, and characteristics of people or organizations.

A scale or index typically uses a series of questions to measure attitudes, knowledge of facts, events, objects, or behavior. For example, sociologists might want to learn not only whether respondents favor a constitutional amendment allowing prayer in public schools but also how knowledgeable they are about different alternatives such as a "silent time" for prayer or a daily ecumenical statement read by a teacher. In this type of situation, sociologists can develop a scale to measure citizens' awareness of the debate over school prayer.

Ensuring Validity and Reliability The scientific method requires that research results be both valid and reliable. *Validity* refers to the degree to which a measure or scale truly reflects the phenomenon

under study. A valid measure of workers' productivity would accurately indicate how much they had produced over a specified period of time. Similarly, in the study of Black executives, Collins used generally accepted business standards to identify major corporations. Had she included interviews with Black executives in charitable organizations and government agencies—or with African Americans who own small businesses—her research would lack validity as an examination of corporate behavior.

Reliability refers to the extent to which a measure provides consistent results. A reliable measure of workers' productivity would lead to the same results even when used by different researchers. The Chicago study provides detailed information concerning the research methods that Collins used, thereby allowing other social scientists to test the conclusions in other locales (or to repeat the study in Chicago at a later date).

Developing the Conclusion

Scientific studies, including those conducted by sociologists, do not aim to answer all the questions that can be raised about a particular subject. Therefore, the conclusion of a research study represents both an end and a beginning. It terminates a specific phase of the investigation, but it should also generate ideas for future study (see Figure 2-2 on page 38). This is true of the research on Black executives conducted by Sharon Collins, which raised important questions both about job segregation in corporations and the way in which certain employment gains by Blacks might lessen the pressure for further initiatives to assist minorities.

Supporting Hypotheses Sociological studies do not always generate data that support the original hypothesis. In many instances, a hypothesis is refuted, and researchers must reformulate their conclusions. Unexpected results may also lead sociologists to reexamine their methodology and make changes in the research design. In the study discussed above, however, the data supported the hypothesis: in response to Black demands for equal rights, corporate hiring and promotion policies in the Chicago area had indeed placed Black executives primarily in highly visible personnel and public relations posts.

FIGURE 2-2 The Scientific Method

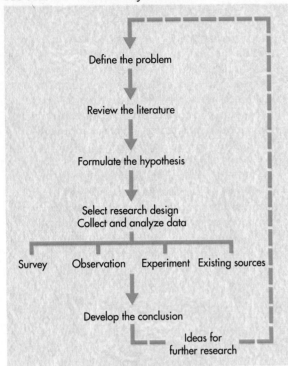

The scientific method allows sociologists to objectively and logically evaluate the facts collected. This can lead to further ideas for sociological research.

Collins found that 66 percent of the African American executives she interviewed had been tracked into corporate jobs focusing on the handling of "Black problems" or on dealings with a specifically Black consumer market. The vast majority of these executives held jobs involved with affirmative action and urban affairs. In discussing the limitations on Black managers, one executive, who had a master's degree and four years of experience in engineering when he was shifted to an affirmative action post, observed:

> When they would send me to some of those conferences about affirmative action . . . you'd walk in and there would be a room full of blacks. . . . It was a terrible misuse at that time of some black talent . . . (Collins, 1989:329).

Controlling for Other Factors The characteristics of Black executives are considered additional variables used in the study, and they are known as *control variables*. A **control variable** is a factor held constant to test the relative impact of the independent variable. If researchers wanted to know how adults in the United States feel about restrictions on smoking in public places, they would probably attempt to use a respondent's smoking behavior as a control variable. Consequently, the researchers would compile separate statistics on how smokers and nonsmokers feel about antismoking regulations.

By use of a control variable, the "time at which Black executives entered the labor force," Collins found support for the view that corporate hiring and promotion policies were significantly influenced by Blacks' demands for equal rights. As Figure 2-3 illustrates, respondents who entered the labor force before 1965 (the high point of the Black civil rights movement) were about equally likely to have found their first jobs in government or in the private sector. By contrast, the vast majority (70 percent) of African American executives who entered the labor force after 1965 found initial employment in the private sector. These data suggest that traditional corporate resistance to the hiring of Black managers began to decline in response to the civil rights movement of the 1960s (Collins, 1989:319–324).

Collins (1989:317) concludes that Blacks' demands for civil rights created a Black managerial elite that was highly visible, yet was "administratively marginal" and "economically vulnerable." In her view, the tracking of Black executives into racially linked jobs in such areas as affirmative action and urban affairs may reduce the likelihood of their advancing into mainstream top management posts. Moreover, in an era of growing economic uncertainty and widespread corporate mergers and takeovers, African American managers in personnel and public relations areas may find themselves the victims of staff reductions.

In Summary: The Scientific Method

Let us briefly summarize the process of the scientific method through a review of the example. Sharon Collins *defined a problem* (the relationship between Black civil rights protests and corporate

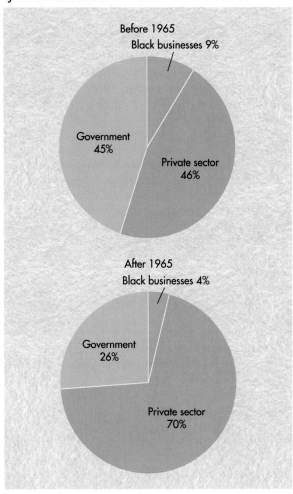

FIGURE 2-3 Initial Employment of Black Executives

Before 1965
Black businesses 9%

Government 45%

Private sector 46%

After 1965
Black businesses 4%

Government 26%

Private sector 70%

SOURCE: Based on S. Collins, 1989:320.

Before 1965, Black executives in the Chicago area were about equally likely to have found their first jobs in government or in the private sector. However, executives who entered the labor force after 1965 overwhelmingly began their careers in the corporate world.

employment policies). She *reviewed the literature* (other studies of Black executives) and *formulated a hypothesis* ("In response to Black demands for equal rights, corporate hiring and promotion policies placed Black executives primarily in highly vis-

ible personnel and public relations posts"). Collins identified a target population of Black executives in Chicago firms and then *collected and analyzed the data*. Finally, she *developed the conclusion:* Black activism did influence corporate decision making and lead to the creation of a highly visible (and yet economically vulnerable) Black managerial elite. Thus, through the systematic, organized application of the scientific method, this researcher studied a contemporary social issue and generated meaningful findings of interest to sociologists, civil rights leaders, business executives, and government policymakers.

RESEARCH DESIGNS FOR COLLECTING DATA

An important aspect of sociological research is deciding how data should be collected. A **research design** is a detailed plan or method for obtaining data scientifically. Selection of a research design is a critical step for sociologists and requires creativity and ingenuity. This choice will directly influence both the cost of the project and the amount of time needed to collect the results of the research.

Sociologists regularly use surveys, observation, experiments, and existing sources to generate data for their research. In her study of Black executives, Sharon Collins relied on interviews, which are a common form of survey research.

Surveys

Almost all of us have responded to surveys of one kind or another. We may have been asked what kind of detergent we use, which presidential candidate we intend to vote for, or what our favorite television program is. A **survey** is a study, generally in the form of an interview or questionnaire, which provides sociologists with information concerning how people think and act. Among our nation's best-known surveys of opinion are the Gallup poll and the Harris poll. As anyone who watches the news during presidential campaigns knows, these polls have become an important part of political life.

When you think of surveys, you may remember many "person on the street" interviews on local television news shows. While such interviews can be

Mimi Forsyth/Monkmeyer

Studies have shown that the gender (or race) of the researcher can have an impact on survey data.

at a certain location. Thus, such samples can be biased in favor of commuters, middle-class shoppers, or factory workers, depending on which street or area the newspeople select. Second, television interviews tend to attract outgoing people who are willing to appear on the air, while they frighten away others who may feel intimidated by a camera. A survey must be based on precise, representative sampling if it is to genuinely reflect a broad range of the population.

In preparing to conduct a survey, sociologists must exercise great care in the wording of questions (see Table 2-1). An effective survey question must be simple and clear enough for people to understand it. It must also be specific enough so that there are no problems in interpreting the results. Even questions that are less structured (What do you think of programming on educational television?) must be carefully phrased in order to solicit the type of information desired. Surveys can be indispensable sources of information, but only if the sampling is done properly and the questions are worded accurately.

There are two main forms of surveys: the **_interview_** and the **_questionnaire._** Each of these forms of survey research has its own advantages. An interviewer can obtain a high response rate because people find it more difficult to turn down a personal request for an interview than to throw away a written questionnaire. In addition, a skillful interviewer can go beyond written questions and

highly entertaining, they are not necessarily an accurate indication of public opinion. First, they reflect the opinions of only those people who appear

Doonesbury

BY GARRY TRUDEAU

TABLE 2-1	Asking the Correct Question	
POOR QUESTION	PROBLEM	BETTER QUESTION
Do you favor urban homesteading?	People may not understand the question.	Do you favor a government program which encourages families to improve inner-city housing?
Did your mother ever work?	Misleading	Did your mother ever work for pay outside the home?
Should it be possible for a woman to obtain a legal abortion?	Too general	Should it be possible for a woman to obtain a legal abortion if there is a strong chance of serious defect in her baby? If she became pregnant as a result of rape?
Do you favor making it legal for 18-year-olds to drink liquor and smoke marijuana?	Double-barreled (two questions in one)	Do you favor making it legal for 18-year-olds to drink liquor? Do you favor making it legal for 18-year-olds to smoke marijuana?
Don't you think that the press is slanted and that we should distrust whatever it says?	Biased question; leads people toward a particular response	Would you say that you have a great deal of confidence, some confidence, or very little confidence in the press?

"probe" for a subject's underlying feelings and reasons. On the other hand, questionnaires have the advantage of being cheaper, especially when large samples are used.

The gender (or race) of the researcher can have an impact on survey data. In 1990, the Eagleton Institute of Politics at Rutgers University confirmed that women were more likely to take strong "pro-choice" positions when questioned by a woman about the issue of abortion. For example, 84 percent of women interviewed by another woman agreed that the decision to have an abortion is a private matter that should be left to the woman to decide without government intervention. By contrast, only 64 percent of women interviewed by a man took the same position. Men's responses seemed unaffected by the gender of the researcher. Similarly, people's responses to questions about housing discrimination may be influenced by the racial and ethnic background of the interviewer. The findings of the Eagleton Institute study underscore the careful attention that sociologists must give to all elements of the research design (Morin, 1990).

Sociologists try to phrase questions carefully so that there will be no misunderstanding on the part of the respondents. If a question is improperly worded (or biased), the results are useless for the researchers.

Observation

When an investigator collects information through direct participation in and observation of a group, tribe, or community under study, he or she is engaged in *observation.* This method allows sociologists to examine certain behaviors and communities that could not be investigated through other research techniques. In some cases, the sociologist actually "joins" a group for a period of time to get an accurate sense of how it operates. This is called *participant observation.*

During the late 1930s, in a classic example of participant observation, William F. Whyte moved into a low-income Italian neighborhood in Boston. For nearly four years, he was a member of the social circle of "corner boys" that he describes in *Street Corner Society.* Whyte revealed his identity to these men

When an investigator collects information through direct participation in and observation of a group, tribe, or community, he or she is engaged in observation. *Shown are a photojournalist and Lotofaga villagers in Western Samoa.*

and joined in their conversations, bowling, and other leisure-time activities. His goal was to gain greater insight into the community that these men had established. As Whyte (1981:303) listened to Doc, the leader of the group, he "learned the answers to questions I would not even have had the sense to ask if I had been getting my information solely on an interviewing basis." Whyte's work was especially valuable, since, at the time, the academic world had little direct knowledge of the poor and tended to rely for information on the records of social service agencies, hospitals, and courts (Adler et al., 1992).

The initial challenge that Whyte faced—and that each observer must encounter if he or she actually participates in the group under study—was to gain acceptance into an unfamiliar group. It is no simple matter for a college-trained sociologist to win the trust of a religious cult, a youth gang, a poor Appalachian community, or skid row residents. It requires a great deal of patience and an accepting, nonthreatening type of person. Interestingly, as we saw earlier concerning surveys, the gender of the researcher can be a factor in the success of an observation study. Sociologist Terry Mizrahi (1986: 185) notes that female sociologists studying predominantly male environments can find it difficult to develop the cooperation and trust necessary for

effective observation. In her view, more attention must be given to the impact of gender of the data-gathering process itself.

Observers immediately face another question which has both practical and ethical implications: to whom (if anyone) should they reveal the ultimate purpose of their observations? In our society, many people resent the feeling of being "studied." Thus, if a group *sees* the researcher as an "outsider" and an observer—rather than as a member of the group—its members may feel uneasy and hide many thoughts and emotions. On the other hand, if the researcher disguises his or her identity or purpose, then the group has added a participant (and observer) who is being somewhat dishonest. This may well distort the group process. Moreover, it is not easy to maintain this type of masquerade for weeks or months while attempting to get to know strangers.

Observation is, in addition, a most time-consuming method of research. Systematic and thorough observations are essential; the sociologist cannot simply "drop by" the bowling alley or street corner every few weeks. Instead, the researcher may have to wait patiently for a particularly noteworthy or dramatic event. And in some instances, the deeper meanings of a seemingly trivial interaction may become clear to the observer only after months

BOX 2-1 • CURRENT RESEARCH

RACIAL "EYE WORK" ON THE STREET

How do African Americans and Whites interact on the street in racially mixed neighborhoods? In his book Streetwise, *sociologist Elijah Anderson (1990: 220–221) described the day-to-day interactions he observed in adjoining Philadelphia neighborhoods that he called the Village and Northton. Anderson systematically recorded social behavior on the street; in this excerpt, he focuses on how Whites maintain distance from Blacks through "eye work" and scowls:*

Many blacks perceive whites as tense or hostile to them in public. They pay attention to the amount of eye contact given. In general, black males get far less time in this regard than do white males. Whites tend not to "hold" the eyes of a black person. It is more common for black and white strangers to meet each other's eyes for only a few seconds, and then to avert their gaze abruptly. Such behavior seems to say, "I am aware of your presence," and no more. Women especially feel that eye contact invites unwanted advances, but some white men feel the same and want to be clear about what they intend. This eye work is a way to maintain distance, mainly for safety and social purposes. Consistent with this,

Elijah Anderson.

some blacks are very surprised to find a white person who holds their eyes longer than is normal according to the rules of the public sphere. As one middle-aged white female resident commented:

Just this morning, I saw a [black] guy when I went over to Mr. Chow's to get some milk at 7:15. You always greet people you see at 7:15, and I looked at him and smiled. And he said "Hello" or "Good morning" or something. I smiled again. It was clear that he saw this as surprising.

Many people, particularly those who see themselves as more economically privileged than others in the community, are careful not to let their eyes stray, in order to avoid an uncomfortable situation. As they walk down the street they pretend not to see other pedestrians, or they look right at them without speaking, a behavior many blacks find offensive.

Moreover, whites of the Village often scowl to keep young blacks at a social and physical distance. As they venture out on the streets of the Village and, to a lesser extent, of Northton, they may plant this look on their faces to ward off others who might mean them harm. Scowling by whites may be compared to gritting by blacks as a coping strategy. At times members of either group make such faces with little regard for circumstances, as if they were dressing for inclement weather. But on the Village streets it does not always storm, and such overcoats repel the sunshine as well as the rain, frustrating many attempts at spontaneous human communication.

---

of study. Finally, for this method to be effective, the sociologist must keep detailed records of events and behaviors, even when "nothing" seems to be happening.

Observation research poses other complex challenges for the investigator. Sociologists must be able to fully understand what they are observing. In a sense, then, researchers such as William F. Whyte or Elijah Anderson (see Box 2-1) must learn to see the world as the group sees it in order to fully comprehend the events taking place around them. This raises a delicate question regarding the effect of the group on the observer—and the observer on the group. The sociologist must retain a certain level of detachment from the group under study, even as he or she tries to understand how members feel.

If the research is to be successful, the observer cannot allow the close associations or even friendships that inevitably develop to influence the conclusions of the study. Anson Shupe and David Bromley (1980), two sociologists who have used participant observation, have likened this challenge to that of "walking a tightrope." Despite working so hard to gain acceptance from the group being studied, the participant observer *must* maintain some degree of detachment.

In addition to its use in basic research, observation studies may also be used to improve the policies and structures of organizations. William F. Whyte (1989), the researcher in the study of Boston corner boys described above, endorses the use of observation as a type of applied sociology. Whyte notes that when Norway's shipping industry was faced with severe cutbacks, a team of researchers worked aboard a merchant ship as part of an effort to improve the social organization and efficiency of Norway's fleet. Similarly, when faced with growing competition in the photocopying industry, Xerox Corporation employed a research team to propose cost-cutting measures to managers and union leaders. In each case, the methodology of participant observation proved useful in solving practical problems.

Experiments

When sociologists want to study a possible cause-and-effect relationship, they may conduct experiments. An *experiment* is an artificially created situation which allows the researcher to manipulate variables and introduce control variables.

In the classic method of conducting an experiment, two groups of people are selected and matched for similar characteristics such as age or education. The subjects are then assigned by researchers to one of two groups—the experimental or control group. The *experimental group* is exposed to an independent variable; the *control group* is not. Thus, if scientists were testing a new type of antibiotic drug, they would administer injections of that drug to an experimental group but not to a control group. While many experiments by medical researchers test the impact of drugs on human or animal subjects, a famous social science experiment examined how people are affected by pressures to conform to the views of others.

How many of us will "stick to our convictions" regardless of the feelings of others? Social psychologist Solomon Asch (1952:452–483) was interested in the effects of group pressure on people's opinions and tested this question in an experimental setting on a college campus. Asch pretested this experiment with control subjects not under any group pressure. The results of his investigation indicate that the pressure to conform in group situations can have a powerful impact on social behavior.

Asch brought groups of seven to nine male college students into a classroom and asked them to look at two white cards, one with a single line and one with three lines of varying lengths. All students were asked to state publicly which line on the second card most closely corresponded in length to the line on the first card. However, in each group of students, all but one were actually in league with the researchers and had been coached in advance to select wrong answers to some of the choices. Moreover, the uncoached students—the people who were the real targets of the study—were placed near the end of each group.

On a designated trial, the students coached by Asch all gave the *same* incorrect answer. Remarkably, many uncoached students ignored the evidence of their own senses—a different answer was clearly the correct one—and conformed to the behavior of the (deliberately incorrect) majority. Of Asch's 123 students put to this test, more than one-third followed the lead of the group and chose the wrong answer even without any explicit pressures to conform.

Conducting sociological research is more difficult, and therefore more costly, in the field than in a laboratory setting (often on a college campus). Consequently, as in the experiment described above, researchers must sometimes rely on samples composed entirely of college students. Such participants may or may not be representative of the larger public of the United States. There is an additional problem in using a laboratory setting: the responses of subjects in such settings may be different from their responses in less structured, real-life situations.

In an experiment, as in observation research, the presence of a social scientist or other observer may affect the behavior of the people being studied. The recognition of this phenomenon grew out of an experiment conducted during the 1920s and 1930s at

Courtesy AT&T

Sociologists are well aware that the presence of an observer may affect the behavior of the people being studied. Recognition of this phenomenon grew out of an experiment conducted during the 1920s and 1930s at the Hawthorne plant of the Western Electric Company.

the Hawthorne plant of the Western Electric Company. A group of researchers headed by Elton Mayo set out to determine how the productivity of workers at the plant could be improved. Investigators examined the impact on productivity of variations in the intensity of light and variations in working hours. To their surprise, they found that *all* steps they took seemed to increase productivity. Even measures that seemed likely to have the opposite effect, such as reducing the amount of lighting in the plant, led to higher productivity.

Why did the plant's employees work harder even under less favorable conditions? Their behavior apparently was influenced by the greater attention being paid them in the course of the research and by the novelty of being subjects in an experiment. Since that time, sociologists have used the term *Hawthorne effect* when subjects of research perform in a manner different from their typical behavior because they realize that they are under observation (S. Jones, 1992; Lang, 1992).

Use of Existing Sources

Sociologists do not necessarily have to collect new data in order to conduct research and test hypotheses. The term *secondary analysis* refers to a variety of research techniques that make use of publicly accessible information and data. Generally, in conducting secondary analysis, researchers utilize data in ways unintended by the initial collectors of information. For example, census data are compiled for specific uses by the federal government, but are valuable for marketing specialists in locating everything from bicycle stores to nursing homes.

Sociologists consider secondary analysis to be *nonreactive,* since people's behavior is not influenced. As an example, Émile Durkheim's statistical analysis of suicide neither increased nor decreased human self-destruction. Whereas subjects of an experiment or observation research are often aware that they are being watched—an awareness that can influence their behavior—this is not the case when secondary analysis is used. Consequently, researchers can avoid the Hawthorne effect by employing secondary analysis.

There is one inherent problem, however, in relying on data collected by someone else: the researcher may not find exactly what is needed. Social scientists studying family violence can use statistics from police and social service agencies on *reported* cases of spouse abuse and child abuse. Yet such government bodies have no precise data on *all* cases of abuse.

Many social scientists find it useful to study cultural, economic, and political documents, including newspapers, periodicals, radio and television tapes, scripts, diaries, songs, folklore, and legal papers, to name a few examples. In examining these sources, researchers employ a technique known as *content analysis,* which is the systematic coding

Using content analysis of television networks' coverage of the 1992 presidential election in their evening news broadcasts, researchers found that newscasters made more negative remarks concerning President George Bush than they did about challengers Bill Clinton and Ross Perot.

and objective recording of data, guided by some rationale. The study of sexual stereotyping discussed at the beginning of the chapter is an example of content analysis.

In another use of content analysis, researchers analyzed television networks' coverage of the 1992 presidential election in their evening news broadcasts. During the primaries, the conventions, and the general election campaign, newscasters made more negative remarks concerning President George Bush—whether in terms of his ability to govern, his record, or his proposals—than they did concerning challengers Bill Clinton and Ross Perot. While political partisans might insist that Bush *earned* these criticisms, content analysis nevertheless allows researchers to systematically analyze television coverage and assess possible biases (Kolbert, 1992).

These examples underscore the value of using existing sources in studying contemporary material. Researchers have learned, in addition, that such analysis can be essential in helping us to understand social behavior from the distant past. For example, sociologist Karen Barkey (1991) examined village court records from the seventeenth-century Ottoman Empire (centered in modern-day Turkey) to assess the extent of peasant rebellions against the empire and, more specifically, its tax policies. Barkey could hardly have relied on surveys, observations, or experiments to study the Ottoman Empire; like other scholars studying earlier civilizations, she turned to secondary analysis.

ETHICS OF RESEARCH

A biochemist cannot inject a serum into a human being unless it has been thoroughly tested. To do otherwise would be both unethical and illegal. Sociologists must also abide by certain specific standards in conducting research—a *code of ethics.* The professional society of the discipline, the American Sociological Association (ASA), first published the *Code of Ethics* in 1971 (most recently revised in 1989), which put forth the following basic principles:

1 Maintain objectivity and integrity in research.
2 Respect the subject's right to privacy and dignity.
3 Protect subjects from personal harm.
4 Preserve confidentiality.
5 Acknowledge research collaboration and assistance.
6 Disclose all sources of financial support (American Sociological Association, 1989).

In addition, in 1982 the Sociological Practice Association (SPA) introduced ethical standards for sociological practitioners in their clinical work with clients. Both the ASA and the SPA have emphasized that members have a responsibility to monitor not only their own behavior but also that of other sociologists.

On the surface, the basic principles of the ASA's *Code of Ethics* probably seem quite clear-cut. It may

BOX 2-2 • SPEAKING OUT

PRESERVING CONFIDENTIALITY— ONE SOCIOLOGIST'S VIEW

In his book Doomsday Cult, *sociologist John Lofland (1977:xi) analyzes the "first five years in America (1959–1964) of an obscure end-of-the-world religion that went on to become nationally and internationally famous in the 1970s." He explains that this cult, which he refers to as the "Divine Precepts," or "DPs," is led by a Korean man who arrived in the United States in 1971. Lofland adds that by the 1970s, the DPs had become widely viewed as a "powerful and nefarious social force that had to be countered."*

Many readers of Doomsday Cult *suspected that the DPs were, in fact, Reverend Sun Myung Moon's Unification church (see Chapter 14). However, after years of observation research, Lofland refused to break his initial promise of anonymity and reveal the real names of the DPs and their leader. At the end of the book, Lofland (1977: 345–346) explains why he maintained this position:*

... First, I continue to have a personal and private obligation to the members with whom I spent many months. I am determined that they will not suffer infamy on my account, despite the fact that some have achieved infamy by their own actions. Second, I am a sociologist rather than an investigative journalist . . . , muckraker or other moralist. . . .

Sociologists must agree to protect the people they study in ex-

John Lofland.

Lyn H. Lofland

change for permission to be privy to the secrets of social organization and social life. I made such an agreement with the group reported in this book, and although the fame of the group now makes it difficult to continue this protection, I must try. Anything less endangers the future of sociology itself, threatening to bring it into even more disrepute by giving credence to the charge that sociologists are merely one more breed of muckraker, whistle-blower, undercover agent, police spy, or worse. . . .

The position I offer above is not, of course, absolute. . . . There are a few circumstances in which I would not grant or continue the protections of anonymity. A prime one is if I believed that the DPs seriously threatened the pluralism of American society, that they had any serious chance of taking over the

United States government, I would try to stop them, and use personally identified information on members to do so. That is, a pluralistic and more or less free society is one indispensable condition of practicing sociology itself. I would not stand by and allow them to destroy my discipline (which they would do if they could) and the society that makes that discipline possible. In my judgment, they do not now nor are they ever likely to pose such a threat.

There is an interesting postscript to this story. Despite Lofland's firm efforts to protect the anonymity of the DPs and their leader, it was commonly assumed—and even flatly asserted in print by other scholars—that the DPs were indeed Moon's Unification church. By the early 1980s Lofland (1985: 120–121) finally concluded that "the 'secret' had become absurdly obvious, so obvious that continuing the 'cover' seemed pointless." Consequently, in 1983, he asked the president of the United States branch of the Unification church to release him from his 1962 agreement with church officials. This request was granted, but it was agreed that only the organization and its founder would be named by Lofland. He continues to protect the identities of the cult members whom he met during his years of observation research (see also R. Mitchell, 1993).

be difficult to imagine how they could lead to any disagreement or controversy. However, many delicate ethical questions cannot be resolved simply by reading the six points above. For example, should a sociologist engaged in participant-observation research *always* protect the confidentiality of subjects? What if the subjects are members of a religious cult allegedly engaged in unethical and possibly illegal activities? In Box 2-2, we consider this sensitive issue by examining the views of a sociologist who studied a highly controversial religious group (see also S. Heller, 1987; Shupe and Bromley, 1980).

While sociologists and other scholars may regard all information provided by interview subjects as confidential, courts do not always uphold this position. In May 1993, Rik Scarce, a doctoral candidate in sociology at Washington State University, was jailed for contempt of court. Scarce had declined to tell a federal grand jury what he knew—or even whether he knew anything—about a 1991 raid on a university research laboratory by animal rights activists. At the time, Scarce was conducting research for a book about environmental protestors and knew at least one suspect in the break-in. Curiously, although chastised by a federal judge, Scarce won respect from fellow prison inmates who regarded him as a man who "wouldn't snitch" (Monaghan, 1993:A8).

In press interviews, Scarce stated that he felt bound by the ASA's code of ethics, which says that scholars must maintain confidentiality even when the information involved enjoys no legal protection. In Scarce's (1993:38) view:

> Promising confidentiality is the norm in social-science research. . . . When journalists and scholars can no longer offer confidentiality to their sources in good faith—and the rulings in my case and others make it clear that they cannot—then society suffers, for the foundation of modern social-science research, and a crucial tool in reportage, is irreparably undermined.

The American Sociological Association supported Scarce's position as he appealed his sentence. Ultimately, Scarce maintained his silence, the judge ruled that nothing would be gained by further incarceration, and Scarce was released after serving 159 days in jail.

Case Studies of Ethical Controversies

Most sociological research uses *people* as sources of information—as respondents to survey questions, participants in experiments, or subjects of observation. In all cases, sociologists need to be certain that they are not invading the privacy of their subjects. Generally, this is handled by assuring those involved of anonymity and by guaranteeing that personal information disclosed will remain confidential. However, a study by Laud Humphreys raised important questions about the extent to which sociologists could threaten people's right to privacy.

Tearoom Trade Sociologist Laud Humphreys (1970a, 1970b, 1975) published a pioneering and controversial study of homosexual behavior in which he described the casual homosexual encounters between males meeting in public restrooms in parks. Such restrooms are sometimes called *tearooms* by homosexual men. As one consequence of this provocative research, the chancellor of the university where Humphreys was employed terminated his research grant and teaching contract.

In order to study the lifestyle of homosexual males in tearooms, Humphreys acted as a participant observer by serving as a "lookout," warning patrons when police or other strangers approached. While he was primarily interested in the behavior of these men, Humphreys also wanted to learn more about who they were and why they took such risks. Yet how could he obtain such information? Secrecy and silence were the norms of this sexual environment. None of the men under study knew of Humphreys's identity, and they would not have consented to standard sociological interviews.

As a result, Humphreys decided on a research technique that some social scientists later saw as a violation of professional ethics. He recorded the license plate numbers of tearoom patrons, waited a year, changed his appearance, and then interviewed them in their homes. The interviews were conducted as part of a larger survey, but they did provide information that Humphreys felt was necessary for his work. While Humphreys's subjects consented to be interviewed, their agreement fell short of *informed* consent, since they were unaware of the true purpose of the study.

Although the researcher recognized each of the men interviewed from his observations in the restrooms, there was no indication that they recognized him. Humphreys learned that most of his subjects were in their middle thirties and married. They had an average of two children and tended to have at least some years of college education. Family members appeared to be unaware of the men's visits to park restrooms for casual homosexual encounters.

Even before the public outcry over his research began, Humphreys (1970b:167–173, 1975:175–232) was aware of the ethical questions that his study would raise. He exerted great care in maintaining the confidentiality of his subjects. Their real identities were recorded only on a master list kept in a safe-deposit box. The list was destroyed by Humphreys after the research was conducted.

For social scientists, the ethical problem in this research was not Humphreys's choice of subject matter, but rather the deception involved. Patrons of the tearoom were not aware of Humphreys's purposes and were further misled about the real reasons for the household interviews. However, in the researcher's judgment, the value of his study justified the questionable means involved. Humphreys believed that, without the follow-up interviews, we would know little about the kinds of men who engage in tearoom sex and would be left with false stereotypes.

In addition, Humphreys believed that by describing such sexual interactions accurately, he would be able to dispel the myth that child molestation is a frequent practice in restrooms. One unintended consequence of the research was that it has been increasingly cited by attorneys seeking acquittal for clients arrested in public bathrooms. These lawyers have used the study to establish that such behavior is not unusual and typically involves consenting adults. A recent study of Canadian police records by sociologist Frederick Desroches (1990) supports Humphreys's earlier findings regarding tearoom sex. The majority of Canadian participants were married, and many of them had children. Of 190 males studied who were involved in such sexual activities, only three were teenagers (two of whom were participating in tearoom sex together), and none were children (see also J. Gray, 1991).

Do these gains in our knowledge and understanding offset Humphreys's actions of encroaching on people's private lives and deceiving them during interviews? Essentially, in reflecting on the study, we are left with a conflict between the right to know and the right to privacy. There is no easy resolution to this clash of principles. Yet we can certainly ask that sociologists be fully aware of the ethical implications of any such research techniques.

Accident or Suicide?   A similar ethical issue—with the right to know posed against the right to privacy—became apparent in research on automobile accidents in which fatalities occur. Sociologist William Zellner (1978) wished to learn if fatal car crashes are sometimes suicides that have been disguised as accidents in order to protect family and friends (and perhaps to collect otherwise unredeemable insurance benefits). These acts of "autocide" are by nature covert, even more so than the sexual behavior of Humphreys's subjects.

In his efforts to assess the frequency of such suicides, Zellner sought to interview the friends, coworkers, and family members of the deceased. He hoped to obtain information that would allow him to ascertain whether the deaths were accidental or purposeful. People approached for interviews were told that Zellner's goal was to contribute to a reduction of future accidents. For this reason (as they were falsely informed), Zellner wished to learn about the emotional characteristics of accident victims. No mention was made of the interviewer's suspicions of autocide, out of fear that potential respondents would refuse to meet with him.

Zellner eventually concluded that at least 12 percent of all fatal single-occupant crashes are suicides. This information could be valuable for society, particularly since some of the probable suicides actually killed or critically injured innocent bystanders in the process of taking their own lives. Yet the ethical questions still must be faced. Was Zellner's research unethical because he misrepresented the motives of his study and failed to obtain subjects' informed consent? Or was his deception justified by the social value of his findings?

As in the study of tearoom trade, the answers are

Are some people who die in single-occupant automobile crashes actually suicides? One sociological study of possible "autocides," which raised interesting ethical questions concerning the right to know and the right to privacy, concluded that at least 12 percent of such accident victims have in fact committed suicide.

not immediately apparent. Like Humphreys, Zellner appeared to have admirable motives and took great care in protecting confidentiality. Names of suspected suicides were not revealed to insurance companies, though Zellner did recommend that the insurance industry drop double indemnity (payment of twice the person's benefits in the event of accidental death) in the future.

Zellner's study raised an additional ethical issue: the possibility of harm to those who were interviewed. Subjects were asked if the deceased had "talked about suicide" and if they had spoken of how "bad or useless" they were. Could these questions have led people to guess the true intentions of the researcher? Perhaps, but according to Zellner, none of the informants voiced such suspicions. More seriously, might the study have caused the bereaved to *suspect* suicide—when before the survey they had accepted the deaths as accidental? Again, we have no evidence to suggest this, but we cannot be sure.

Given our uncertainty about this last question, was the research justified? Was Zellner taking too large a risk in asking the friends and families of the deceased victims if they had spoken of suicide before their death? Does the right to know outweigh the right to privacy in this type of situation? And who has the right to make such a judgment? In prac-

tice, as in Zellner's study, it is the *researcher,* not the subjects of inquiry, who makes the critical ethical decisions. Therefore, sociologists and other investigators bear the responsibility for establishing clear and sensitive boundaries for ethical scientific investigation.

Neutrality and Politics in Research

The ethical considerations of sociologists lie not only in the methods used, but in the way that results are interpreted. Max Weber (1949:1–49, original edition 1904) recognized that sociologists would be influenced by their own personal values in selecting questions for research. In his view, that was perfectly acceptable, but under no conditions could a researcher allow his or her personal feelings to influence the interpretation of data. In Weber's phrase, sociologists must practice **value neutrality** in their research.

As part of this neutrality, investigators have an ethical obligation to accept research findings even when the data run counter to their own personal views, to theoretically based explanations, or to widely accepted beliefs. Durkheim countered popular conceptions when he reported that social (rather than supernatural) forces were an important factor in suicide. Similarly, Humphreys chal-

J. Sohm/Image Works

Shown is a homeless woman who lives in Chicago. Sociologist Peter Rossi was attacked by the Chicago Coalition for the Homeless for hampering its efforts at social reform because his carefully researched estimate of the city's homeless population was far below that offered (with little firm documentation) by the coalition.

lenged traditional suspicions when he found that users of tearooms were not preying on adolescents or younger boys.

Some sociologists believe that it is impossible for scholars to prevent their personal values from influencing their work. As a result, Weber's call for a value-free sociology has been criticized by many advocates of the conflict perspective—among them African American and feminist scholars—on the grounds that it leads the public to accept sociological conclusions without exploring the biases of the researchers. Furthermore, Alvin Gouldner (1970: 439–440) has suggested, again drawing on the conflict perspective, that sociologists may use objectivity as a sacred justification for remaining uncritical of existing institutions and centers of power. These arguments are attacks not so much on Weber himself as on how his goals have been incorrectly interpreted. As we have seen, Weber was quite clear that sociologists may bring values to their subject matter. In his view, however, they must not confuse their own values with the social reality under study (Bendix, 1968:495).

Peter Rossi (1987:73) admits that "in my professional work as a sociologist, my liberal inclinations have led me to undertake applied social research in the hope that . . . my research might contribute to the general liberal aim of social reform. . . ." Yet,

in line with Weber's view of value neutrality, Rossi's commitment to rigorous research methods and objective interpretation of data has sometimes led him to controversial findings not necessarily supportive of his own liberal values. For example, when Rossi and a team of researchers carefully attempted to measure the extent of homelessness in Chicago in the mid-1980s, they arrived at estimates of the city's homeless population far below those offered (with little firm documentation) by the Chicago Coalition for the Homeless. As a result, Rossi was bitterly attacked by coalition members for hampering social reform efforts by minimizing the extent of homelessness. Having been through similar controversies before, Rossi (1987:79) concludes that "in the short term, good social research will often be greeted as a betrayal of one or another side to a particular controversy." But he insists that such applied research is exciting to do and can make important long-term contributions to our understanding of social problems.

Even the decision to conduct a study can spark partisan debate. In 1991, a challenge to a major research effort was partially fought off after the secretary of Health and Human Services announced that he was canceling funding for a five-year, $18 million national survey of teenage life in the United States. The survey had strong backing from the National Institutes of Health, but conservatives were troubled by the inclusion of questions on sexual behavior and pressured the Bush administration to kill the study. Intense debate followed, in which supporters of the research spoke of the need to better understand behavior in light of the prevalence of teenage pregnancy and sexually transmitted diseases (including AIDS). Eventually, researchers scaled down the sample size and successfully obtained private funding for the study. These developments underscored the fact that studying social behavior can generate serious controversy (COSSA, 1991; Lyon, 1992).

As this example illustrates, the issue of value neutrality becomes especially delicate when one considers the relationship of sociology to government. Indeed, in the United States, the federal government has become the major source of funding for sociological research. Yet Max Weber urged that sociology remain an autonomous discipline and not become unduly influenced by any one segment of society. According to his ideal of value neutrality, sociologists must remain free to reveal information that is embarrassing to government or, for that matter, is supportive of government institutions (L. Coser, 1977:219–222; Gouldner, 1962). Thus, re-

searchers investigating a prison riot must be ready to examine objectively not only the behavior of inmates but also the conduct of prison officials before and during the outbreak. This may be more difficult if sociologists fear that findings critical of governmental institutions will jeopardize their chances of obtaining federal support for new research projects.

Although the American Sociological Association's *Code of Ethics* expects sociologists to disclose all funding sources, the code does not address the issue of whether sociologists who accept funding from a particular agency may also accept their perspective on what needs to be studied. Lewis Coser (1956:27) has argued that as sociologists in the United States have increasingly turned from basic sociological research to applied research for government agencies and the private sector, "they have relinquished to a large extent the freedom to choose their own problems, substituting the problems of their clients for those which might have interested them on purely theoretical grounds." Viewed in this light, the importance of government funding for sociological studies raises troubling questions for those who cherish Weber's ideal of value neutrality in research.

APPENDIX I

WRITING A LIBRARY RESEARCH REPORT

In order to write a research report, students must follow procedures similar to those used by sociologists in conducting original research. Once a topic has been selected, you must define the problems that you wish to study. A review of the literature will generally require library research.

Where can you find information? The following steps will be helpful:

1 Check this textbook and other textbooks that you own. Do not forget to begin with the materials closest at hand.

2 Use the library catalog. Many libraries have abandoned *card* catalogs and now use computerized systems which access not only the college library's collection but also books and magazines

from other libraries which can be secured through interlibrary loans. These systems allow you to search for books by author or title. Title searches can be used to locate books by subject as well. For example, if you search the title base for the keyword "homeless," you will learn where books with that word somewhere in the title are located in the library's book stacks. Near these books will be other works on homelessness which may not happen to have that word in the title.

3 Locate useful articles that have appeared in periodicals. Three research guides found in most libraries will be especially valuable. The *Reader's Guide to Periodical Literature* indexes many popular magazines, including *Newsweek*, *Ebony*, and the *New Republic*. The *Social Sciences Index* lists articles in professional journals such as the *American Sociological Review*, the *American Journal of Sociology*, and *Social Problems*. A third index, entitled *Sociological Abstracts*, lists articles from appropriate journals and also provides brief summaries.

4 Investigate using computerized periodical indexes if available in your library. Sociofile covers all material in *Sociological Abstracts* since 1974, along with material from other periodicals. Expanded Academic Index covers general-interest periodicals (*Time, Ms., National Review, Atlantic Monthly,* and so forth) for the most recent four years; it also indexes the *New York Times* for the last six months. These electronic systems may be connected to a printer, thereby allowing you to produce your own printout complete with bibliographic information and sometimes even abstracts of articles.

5 Consult the *Encyclopedia of the Social Sciences,* which concentrates on material of interest to social scientists. Each article includes references for further information.

6 Examine government documents. The United States government, states and cities, and the United Nations publish information on virtually every subject of interest to social science researchers. Many university libraries have access to a wide range of government reports. Consult the librarian for assistance in locating such materials.

7 Use newspapers. Major newspapers publish indexes annually or even weekly that are useful in locating information about specific events or issues. Newspaper Abstracts Ondisc is a computerized index to eight major newspapers in the United States, with coverage beginning in 1985.

8 Ask people, organizations, and agencies concerned with the topic for information and assistance. Be as specific as possible in making requests.

9 If you run into difficulties, consult the instructor, teaching assistant, or librarian.

Once all research has been completed, the task of writing the report can begin. Here are a few tips:

- Be sure the topic you have chosen is not too broad. You must be able to cover it adequately in a reasonable amount of time and a reasonable number of pages.
- Develop an outline for your report. Be sure that you have an introduction and a conclusion that relate to each other—and that the discussion proceeds logically throughout the paper. Use headings within the paper if they will improve clarity and organization.
- Do not leave all the writing until the last minute. It is best to write a rough draft, let it sit for a few days, and then take a fresh look before beginning revisions.
- If possible, read your paper *aloud.* Doing so may be helpful in locating sections or phrases that do not make sense.

Remember that all information which you have obtained from other sources *must* be cited. If an author's exact words are used, it is essential that they be placed in quotation marks. Even if you reworked someone else's ideas, you must indicate the source of these ideas.

Some professors may require that students use footnotes in research reports. Others will allow students to employ the form of referencing used in this textbook, which follows the format of the American Sociological Association. If you see "(Merton, 1968:27)" listed after a statement or paragraph, it means that the material has been adapted from page 27 of a work published by Merton in 1968 and listed in the reference section at the back of this textbook. (See also Richlin-Klonsky and Strenski, 1994.)

Tables allow social scientists to summarize data and make it easier for them to develop conclusions. A *cross-tabulation* is a type of table that illustrates the relationship between two or more characteristics.

During 1992, the Gallup organization polled 1004 people in the United States, ages 18 and over, regarding the issue of whether the federal tax burden is distributed fairly. Each respondent was interviewed and asked: "Do you think that low income people are paying their fair share in federal taxes, are paying too much, or are paying too little?" There is no way that, without some type of summary, analysts in the Gallup organization could examine hundreds of individual responses and reach firm conclusions. However, through use of the cross-tabulation presented in the accompanying table, we can quickly see that the more affluent (and especially people with incomes of $50,000 a year and over) are less likely than those in lower-income groups to believe that lower-income people are paying too much in taxes.

Graphs, like tables, can be quite useful for sociologists. The accompanying illustration shows a type of pictorial graph that often appears in newspapers and magazines. It documents that in 1992 the state of New Jersey spent more than three times as much per student on elementary and secondary education as Utah did. However, this graph relies on a visual misrepresentation. Through use of two dimensions—length and width—the graph inflates the size of the expenditure level for New Jersey.

Direct Expenditures per Student for Elementary and Secondary Education, 1992

New Jersey

Utah

$10,219

$3,092

SOURCE: Bureau of the Census, 1993a:164.

Pictorial graphs, such as the one shown here, can be misleading. The money bag for New Jersey occupies about nine times the area on the page as the bag for Utah, thereby giving readers a false impression of the two states' comparative levels of funding for education. Actually, New Jersey spends more than three times as much per student.

Attitudes on Distribution of Federal Tax Burden

INCOME OF RESPONDENT	LOW-INCOME PEOPLE ARE PAYING THEIR FAIR SHARE, PERCENT	LOW-INCOME PEOPLE ARE PAYING TOO MUCH, PERCENT	LOW-INCOME PEOPLE ARE PAYING TOO LITTLE, PERCENT
$50,000 and over	50	40	9
$30,000–$49,999	30	59	6
$20,000–$29,999	26	59	9
Under $20,000	26	64	7

SOURCE: Hugick and Saad, 1992:34.

Although it should appear about three times as large as the Utah level, the New Jersey money bag actually appears about nine times as large. Thus, the graph misleads readers about the comparative spending levels of the two states.

This example underscores the fact that tables and graphs can be easily misunderstood and can even be deceptive. If you are reading a table, be sure to study carefully the title, the labels for variables, and any footnotes. If you are examining a pictorial graph, check to see if the visual representations seem to reflect accurately the statistics being illustrated (Huff, 1954:69; Lewandowsky and Spence, 1990).

SUMMARY

Sociologists are committed to the use of the scientific method in their research efforts. In this chapter, we examine the basic principles of the scientific method and study various techniques used by sociologists in conducting research.

1 There are five basic steps in the *scientific method:* defining the problem, reviewing the literature, formulating the hypothesis, selecting the research design and then collecting and analyzing data, and developing the conclusion.

2 Whenever researchers wish to study abstract concepts, such as intelligence or prejudice, they must develop workable *operational definitions.*

3 A *hypothesis* usually states a possible relationship between two or more variables.

4 By using specialized sampling techniques, sociologists avoid the necessity of testing everyone in a population.

5 According to the scientific method, research results must possess both *validity* and *reliability.*

6 The two principal forms of *survey* research are the *interview* and the *questionnaire.*

7 *Observation* allows sociologists to study certain behaviors and communities that cannot be investigated through other research methods.

8 When sociologists wish to study a cause-and-effect relationship, they may conduct an *experiment.*

9 In examining cultural, economic, and political documents (such as newspapers, songs, and folkways), researchers use a technique called *content analysis.*

10 The *Code of Ethics* of the American Sociological Association includes among its basic principles objectivity and integrity in research, respect for the subject's right to privacy, and preservation of confidentiality.

11 Max Weber urged sociologists to practice *value neutrality* in their research by ensuring that their personal feelings do not influence the interpretation of data.

CRITICAL THINKING QUESTIONS

1 According to the scientific method, the conclusion of a research study terminates a specific phase of the investigation, but should also generate ideas for future study. With this in mind, how would you expand on Sharon Collins's study of African American executives to continue researching the issues she raises?

2 Suppose that your sociology instructor has asked you to do a study of homelessness in the area where your college is located. Which research technique (surveys, observations, experiments, use of existing sources) would you find most useful in studying homelessness? How would you use that technique to complete your assignment?

3 Can a sociologist genuinely maintain value neutrality while studying a group that he or she finds repugnant (for example, a White supremacist organization, a satanic cult, or a group of prison inmates convicted of rape)?

KEY TERMS

Causal logic The relationship between a condition or variable and a particular consequence, with one event leading to the other. (page 36)

Code of ethics The standards of acceptable behavior developed by and for members of a profession. (46)

Content analysis The systematic coding and objective recording of data, guided by some rationale. (45)

Control group Subjects in an experiment who are not introduced to the independent variable by the researcher. (44)

Control variable A factor held constant to test the relative impact of an independent variable. (38)

Correlation A relationship between two variables whereby a change in one coincides with a change in the other. (36)

Cross-tabulation A table that shows the relationship between two or more variables. (54)

55

Dependent variable The variable in a causal relationship which is subject to the influence of another variable. (35)

Experiment An artificially created situation which allows the researcher to manipulate variables and introduce control variables. (44)

Experimental group Subjects in an experiment who are exposed to an independent variable introduced by a researcher. (44)

Hawthorne effect The unintended influence that observers or experiments can have on their subjects. (45)

Hypothesis A speculative statement about the relationship between two or more variables. (35)

Independent variable The variable in a causal relationship which, when altered, causes or influences a change in a second variable. (35)

Index An indicator of attitudes, behavior, or characteristics of people or organizations. (37)

Interview A face-to-face or telephone questioning of a respondent to obtain desired information. (40)

Observation A research technique in which an investigator collects information through direct involvement with and observation of a group, tribe, or community. (41)

Operational definition An explanation of an abstract concept that is specific enough to allow a researcher to measure the concept. (34)

Questionnaire A printed research instrument employed to obtain desired information from a respondent. (40)

Random sample A sample for which every member of the entire population has the same chance of being selected. (36)

Reliability The extent to which a measure provides consistent results. (37)

Representative sample A selection from a larger population that is statistically found to be typical of that population. (36)

Research design A detailed plan or method for obtaining data scientifically. (39)

Scale An indicator of attitudes, behavior, or characteristics of people or organizations. (37)

Scientific method A systematic, organized series of steps that ensures maximum objectivity and consistency in researching a problem. (33)

Secondary analysis A variety of research techniques that make use of publicly accessible information and data. (45)

Survey A study, generally in the form of interviews or questionnaires, which provides sociologists and other researchers with information concerning how people think and act. (39)

Validity The degree to which a scale or measure truly reflects the phenomenon under study. (37)

Value neutrality Max Weber's term for objectivity of sociologists in the interpretation of data. (50)

Variable A measurable trait or characteristic that is subject to change under different conditions. (35)

ADDITIONAL READINGS

Cuba, Lee J. *A Short Guide to Writing about Social Science.* Glenview, Ill.: Scott, Foresman, 1988. A concise (165-page) but thorough summary of the types of social science literature, with suggestions on writing a research paper and organizing an oral presentation.

Denisoff, R. Serge. *Inside MTV.* Rutgers, N.J.: Transaction, 1988. Known for his studies of popular culture, Denisoff employs the sociological perspective to examine a profitable 24-hour cable outlet.

Denzin, Norman K., and Yvonna S. Lincoln (eds.). *Handbook of Qualitative Research.* Thousand Oaks, Calif.: Sage, 1994. The 36 articles in this anthology cover newer techniques used in conducting observation and biographical research, as well as ethical issues facing researchers.

Gilbert, Nigel (ed.). *Researching Social Life.* Newbury Park, Calif.: Sage, 1993. Using actual studies, the contributors cover interviewing techniques, questionnaire design, and document review, and even discuss how to put collected data into written form.

Harding, Sue (ed.). *Feminism and Methodology.* Bloomington: Indiana University Press, 1987. A collection of essays which examine the ways in which conventional social scientific research fails to consider gender and draw upon the feminist perspective.

Huff, Darrell. *How to Lie with Statistics.* New York: Norton, 1954. "Figures don't lie, but liars do figure" is an adage that points to the way that statistics can be abused. Huff offers guidance to the reader unsophisticated in statistics as to how to better understand graphs and tables.

Lee, Raymond M. *Doing Research on Sensitive Topics.* Newbury Park, Calif.: Sage, 1993. Drawing on a variety of research techniques, the author considers how one can successfully study religious cults, child abuse, government policies, and other topics.

Miller, Delbert C. *Handbook of Research Design and Social*

Measurement (5th ed.). Newbury Park, Calif.: Sage, 1991. A veritable encyclopedia of scales, indexes, and measures used in sociological studies. Also includes guides to library research, writing of reports, and grant funding.

Reinharz, Shulamit. *Feminist Methods in Social Research.* New York: Oxford University Press, 1992. A feminist scholar offers a critique of established research techniques while examining alternative ways of conducting experiments, observations, content analysis, and oral history interviews.

Webb, Eugene J., Donald T. Campbell, Richard D. Schwartz, Lee Sechrest, and Janet Belew Grove. *Non-reactive Measures in the Social Sciences* (2d ed.). Boston: Houghton Mifflin, 1981. The authors identify unobtrusive methods of obtaining social science data other than questionnaires or interviews.

Journals

Among the journals that focus on methods of sociological and other social scientific research are the following: *Irb: A Review of Human Subjects Research* (founded in 1979), *Journal of Contemporary Ethnography* (1971), *Qualitative Sociology* (1977), *Social Science Research* (1972), and *Sociological Methods and Research* (1972).

PART TWO

ORGANIZING

SOCIAL

LIFE

Sociologist Peter Berger (1963:18–19) once observed that the "sociologist is a person intensively, endlessly, shamelessly interested" in the doings of people. In Part Two, we begin our study of the organization of social life within human communities and societies.

Chapter 3 examines the basic element of any society: its culture. It considers the development of culture, cultural universals, and variations among cultures. Chapter 4 presents the lifelong socialization process through which we acquire culture and are introduced to social structure. Chapter 5 examines social interaction and the major aspects of social structure: statuses, roles, groups, and institutions. Chapter 6 focuses on the impact of groups and organizations on social behavior. Chapter 7 examines attempts to enforce acceptance of social norms, as well as behavior that violates norms.

3

CULTURE

CULTURE AND SOCIETY

DEVELOPMENT OF CULTURE
Cultural Universals
Innovation
Diffusion

ELEMENTS OF CULTURE
Language
  Language as the Foundation of Culture
  Sapir-Whorf Hypothesis
  The Bilingualism Debate
Norms
  Types of Norms
  Acceptance of Norms
Sanctions
Values

CULTURAL INTEGRATION

CULTURAL VARIATION
Aspects of Cultural Variation
  Subcultures
  Countercultures
  Culture Shock
Attitudes toward Cultural Variation
  Ethnocentrism
  Cultural Relativism

**CULTURE AND THE DOMINANT
IDEOLOGY**

**SOCIAL POLICY AND CULTURE:
MULTICULTURALISM**

BOXES
3-1 Around the World: Sexism in
      Languages—English and Japanese
3-2 Around the World: The Skinhead
      Counterculture

LOOKING AHEAD

- How do aspects of a culture develop? How do they spread from one society to another?
- Why is language viewed by sociologists as the foundation of every culture?
- In what ways are norms and sanctions used to reward and penalize behavior?
- Why are test pilots, computer hackers, teenagers, and Appalachians all considered examples of subcultures?
- Should schools and colleges in the United States continue to focus on the traditions of western cultures? Or should they revise their curricula to give greater emphasis to African Americans, other racial and ethnic minorities, women, and nonwestern cultures?

While a graduate student in anthropology, George Esber, Jr. (1987) was hired to work with Apaches in Arizona and a group of architects to design a new community for the Apaches. The architects were expected to accommodate the distinctive traditions and customs of this Native American tribe; as a result, Esber was hired to obtain relevant information concerning the Apaches' housing needs and preferences. To do so, he reviewed written records of the Apaches (thereby engaging in use of existing sources) and conducted fieldwork (including observation research and interviews). Like many researchers, Esber had to overcome the Apaches' concerns about an outsider coming into their community, asking personal questions, and observing day-to-day interactions.

Esber ultimately was successful in discussing important issues with the Apaches and communicating to the architects those features of Apache life that should guide community design. Consequently, when the Apaches moved into their new homes in 1981, they entered a community that had been designed with their participation and with their specific traditions in mind. For example, it was essential that each new house have a large, open living space. The culture of the Apaches requires that all participants in a social situation remain in full view, so that each person can observe the behavior of all others and act appropriately (according to Apache norms and values).

The Apaches are also accustomed to major social gatherings at people's homes at which an offering of food precedes other social interactions. Consequently, based on Esber's findings, architects designed large kitchens (with extra-large sinks, cupboards, and worktables) that were conveniently near dining areas and living rooms. In these ways and others, the planners of this new community respected and took into account the unique cultural traditions of the Apaches.

CULTURE AND SOCIETY

Culture is the totality of learned, socially transmitted behavior. It includes the ideas, values, and customs (as well as the sailboats, comic books, and birth control devices) of groups of people. Therefore, patriotic attachment to the United States flag is an aspect of culture, as is the Apaches' preference for large, open living spaces where everyone can see one another or the tradition in Thailand that no one be allowed to touch their queen in public.

Sometimes people refer to a particular person as "very cultured" or to a city as having "lots of culture." That use of the term *culture* is different from our use in this textbook. In sociological terms, *culture* does not refer solely to the fine arts and refined intellectual taste. It consists of *all* objects and ideas within a society, including ice cream cones, rock music, and slang words. Sociologists consider both a portrait by Rembrandt and a portrait by a billboard painter to be aspects of a culture. A tribe that cultivates soil by hand has just as much of a culture as a people that relies on diesel-operated machinery. Thus, each people has a distinctive culture with its own characteristic ways of gathering and preparing food, constructing homes, structuring the family, and promoting standards of right and wrong.

Sharing a similar culture helps to define the group to which we belong. A fairly large number of people are said to constitute a *society* when they live in the same territory, are relatively independent of people outside their area, and participate in a common culture. The city of Los Angeles is more populous than many nations of the world, yet sociologists do not consider it a society in its own right. Rather, it is seen as part of—and dependent on—the larger society of the United States.

A society is the largest form of human group. It consists of people who share a common heritage and culture. Members of the society learn this culture and transmit it from one generation to the next. They even preserve their distinctive culture through literature, art, video recordings, and other means of expression. If it were not for the social transmission of culture, each generation would have to reinvent television, not to mention the wheel.

Having a common culture also simplifies many day-to-day interactions. For example, if you plan to go to a movie theater in the United States, you know that you will not need to bring along a chair. When you are part of a society, there are many small (as well as more important) cultural patterns that you take for granted. Just as you assume that theaters will provide seats for the audience, you also assume that physicians will not disclose confidential information, that banks will protect the money you deposit, and that parents will be careful when crossing the street with young children. All these assumptions reflect the basic values, beliefs, and customs of the culture of the United States.

Members of a society generally share a common language, and this fact also facilitates day-to-day exchanges with others. Language is a critical element of culture that sets humans apart from other species. When you ask a hardware store clerk for a flashlight, you do not need to draw a picture of the instrument. You share the same cultural term for a small, battery-operated, portable light. However, if you were in England and needed this item, you would have to ask for an "electric torch." Of course, even within the same society, a term can have a number of different meanings. In the United States, *grass* signifies both a plant eaten by grazing animals and an intoxicating drug.

The study of culture is an important part of contemporary sociological work. This chapter will examine the development of culture from its roots in the prehistoric human experience. The major aspects of culture—including language, norms, sanctions, and values—will be defined and explored. The discussion will focus both on general cultural practices found in all societies and on the wide variations that can distinguish one society from another. We will contrast the ways in which functionalist and conflict theorists view culture. The social policy section will look at the conflicts in cultural values which underlie current debates over the use of multicultural curricula in schools and colleges in the United States.

DEVELOPMENT OF CULTURE

Through advances in culture, human beings have come a long way from our prehistoric heritage. In the 1990s, we can send astronauts to the moon, split the atom, and prolong lives through heart transplants. The human species has produced such achievements as the ragtime compositions of Scott Joplin, the paintings of Vincent Van Gogh, the poetry of Emily Dickinson, the novels of Leo Tolstoy, and the films of Akira Kurosawa. We can even analyze our innermost feelings through the insights of Sigmund Freud and other pioneers of psychology. In all these ways, we are remarkably different from other species of the animal kingdom.

The process of expanding culture has already been under way for thousands of years and will continue in the future. The first archeological evidence of humanlike primates places our ancestors back many millions of years. Some 2.5 million years ago people used tools and had containers for storage. From 35,000 years ago we have evidence of paintings, jewelry, and statues. By that time, elaborate ceremonies had already been developed for marriages, births, deaths (Haviland, 1985).

Tracing the development of culture is not easy. Archeologists cannot "dig up" weddings, laws, or government, but they are able to locate items that point to the emergence of cultural traditions. Our early ancestors were primates that had characteristics of human beings. These curious and communicative creatures made important advances in the use of tools. Recent studies of chimpanzees in the wild have revealed that they frequently use sticks and other natural objects in ways learned from other members of the group. However, unlike chimpanzees, our ancestors gradually made tools from increasingly durable materials. As a result, the items could be reused and refined into more effective implements.

Cultural Universals

Throughout history, human beings have made dramatic cultural advances. Despite their differences, all societies have attempted to meet basic human needs by developing cultural universals. *Cultural universals,* such as language, are general practices found in every culture. Anthropologist George Murdock (1945:124) compiled a list of cultural universals. Some of the examples identified by Murdock include:

Athletic sports	Dream
Bodily adornment	interpretation
Calendars	Family
Cooking	Folklore
Courtship	Food habits
Dancing	Food taboos
Decorative art	Funeral ceremonies
Games	Myths
Gestures	Numerals
Gift giving	Personal names
Hairstyles	Property rights
Housing	Religion
Language	Sexual restrictions
Laws	Surgery
Marriage	Toolmaking
Medicine	Trade
Music	Visiting

Many cultural universals are, in fact, adaptations to meet essential human needs, such as people's need for food, shelter, and clothing. Yet although the cultural practices listed by Murdock may be universal, the manner in which they are expressed will vary from culture to culture. For example, one society may attempt to influence its weather by seeding clouds with dry ice particles to bring about rain. Another culture may offer sacrifices to the gods in order to end a long period of drought.

Like games, toys can be viewed as a cultural universal. However, as noted above, the manner in which cultural universals are expressed will vary. Thus, while it has expanded to international markets around the world, Toys "Я" Us sells porcelain dolls in Japan, wooden toys in Germany, and models of a high-speed train in France. Children in these countries may all want electronic games and stuffed animals, but their other toy preferences may differ significantly (A. Miller, 1992).

While all cultures share certain general practices—such as cooking, gift giving, and dancing—the expression of any cultural universal in a society may change dramatically over time. Thus, the most popular styles of dancing in the United States during the 1990s are sure to be different from the styles that were dominant in the 1950s or the 1970s. Each generation, and each year, most human cultures change and expand through the processes of innovation and diffusion.

Innovation

The process of introducing an idea or object that is new to culture is known as *innovation.* There are two forms of innovation: discovery and invention. A *discovery* involves making known or sharing the existence of an aspect of reality. The finding of the

Decorative art is a cultural universal. Shown are artworks from the island of Bali in Indonesia (top left), from Guatemala (top right), and from Aborigines in Australia (bottom).

DNA molecule and the identification of a new moon of Saturn are both acts of discovery. A significant factor in the process of discovery is the sharing of newfound knowledge with others. By contrast, an *invention* results when existing cultural items are combined into a form that did not exist before. The bow and arrow, the automobile, and the television are all examples of inventions, as are Protestantism and democracy.

Diffusion

One does not have to sample gourmet food to eat "foreign" foods. Breakfast cereal comes originally from Germany, candy from the Netherlands, chewing gum from Mexico, and the potato chip from the America of the Indians. The United States has also "exported" our foods to other lands. Residents of many nations enjoy pizza, which was popularized

The use of slogans on T shirts to make political statements originated in the United States during the 1960s. By the late 1980s, this practice had spread across the world through the process of diffusion. However, in 1987 the South African government banned such messages, most of which registered opposition to the enforced segregation (apartheid) that had existed at that time. The government's order was met with public ridicule and was soon rescinded, but many schools in South Africa continued to forbid "unacceptable" slogans.

in the United States. However, in Japan they add squid, in Australia it is eaten with pineapple, and in England people like kernels of corn with the cheese.

Just as a culture does not always discover or invent its foods, it may also adopt ideas, technology, and customs from other cultures. Sociologists use the term *diffusion* to refer to the process by which a cultural item is spread from group to group or society to society. Diffusion can occur through a variety of means, among them exploration, military conquest, missionary work, the influence of the mass media, and tourism.

Early in human history, culture changed rather slowly through discovery. As the number of discoveries in a culture increased, inventions became possible. The more inventions there were, the more rapidly further inventions could be created. In addition, as diverse cultures came into contact with one another, they could each take advantage of the other's innovations. Thus, when people in the United States read a newspaper, we look at characters invented by the ancient Semites, printed by a process invented in Germany, on a material invented in China (Linton, 1936:326–327).

Diffusion may take place over extremely long distances. The use of smoking tobacco began when Indian tribes in the Caribbean invented the habit of smoking the tobacco plant, where it grew wild. Over a period of hundreds of years, tobacco was acquired and cultivated by one neighboring tribe after another. Through diffusion, this practice traveled through Central America and across the North American continent (Kroeber, 1923:211–214).

Even within a society, diffusion occurs as innovations—discoveries and inventions—gain wider acceptance. For example, the practice of "rap" was evident among certain inner-city Blacks long before most people in the United States were aware of this form of singing. A 1985 music video by the Chicago Bears football team helped to popularize rap; partly as a result, rap singing groups like Run-D.M.C. became known outside central cities.

While these examples show that diffusion is common within the United States and from culture to culture, it must be emphasized that diffusion of cultural traits does not occur automatically. Groups and societies resist ideas which seem too foreign as well as those which are perceived as threatening to their own beliefs and values. Each culture tends to be somewhat selective in what it absorbs from competing cultures. Europe accepted silk, the magnetic compass, chess, and gunpowder from the Chinese but rejected the teachings of Confucius as an ideology. Many people in the United States have accepted the idea of *acupuncture,* the Chinese practice of puncturing the body with needles to cure disease or relieve pain, but few have committed themselves to the philosophy behind acupuncture, which involves the idea that the human body contains equal but opposite forces called *yin* and *yang.*

Sociologist William F. Ogburn (1922:202–203) made a useful distinction between elements of material and nonmaterial culture. **Material culture** refers to the physical or technological aspects of our daily lives, including food items, houses, factories, and raw materials. **Nonmaterial culture** refers to ways of using material objects and to customs, beliefs, philosophies, governments, and patterns of communication. Generally, the nonmaterial culture is more resistant to change than the material culture is. Therefore, as we have seen, foreign ideas are viewed as more threatening to a culture than foreign products are. This is true both for residents of the United States and for other peoples of the world. We are more willing to use technological innovations that make our lives easier than we are ideologies that change our way of seeing the world.

Just as our society has selectively absorbed certain practices and beliefs from China and other nonwestern cultures, so too have these cultures been on the receiving end of cultural diffusion. While Japan has only 800,000 practicing Christians in its population of 120 million people, *Kurisumasu* (the Japanese term for "Christmas") is nevertheless a major holiday. Although *Kurisumasu* is not a religious observance, it is a highly commercial occasion, reflecting obvious influences from the United States. The Japanese are encouraged to buy gifts as they pass through stores filled with tinseled Christmas trees and the sweet sounds of Bing Crosby singing "White Christmas" (R. Yates, 1985).

ELEMENTS OF CULTURE

Each culture considers its own distinctive ways of handling basic societal tasks as "natural." But, in fact, methods of education, marital ceremonies, religious doctrines, and other aspects of culture are learned and transmitted through human interactions within specific societies. Lifelong residents of Naples will consider it natural to speak Italian, whereas lifelong residents of Buenos Aires will feel the same way about Spanish. Clearly, the citizens of each country have been shaped by the culture in which they live.

Language

Language tells us a great deal about a culture. In the old west, words such as *gelding, stallion, mare, piebald,* and *sorrel* were all used to describe one animal—the horse. Even if we knew little of this period of history, we could conclude from the list of terms that horses were quite important in this culture. As a result, they received an unusual degree of linguistic attention.

In the contemporary culture of the United States, the terms *convertible, dune buggy, van, four-wheel drive, sedan,* and *station wagon* are all employed to describe the same mechanical form of transportation. Perhaps the car is as important to us as the horse was to the residents of the old west. Similarly, the Samal people of the southern Philippines—for whom fish are a main source of both food and income—have terms for more than 70 types of fishing and more than 250 different kinds of fish. The Slave Indians of northern Canada, who live in a rather frigid climate, have 14 terms to describe ice, including eight

The sign languages used by deaf people and others are an especially vivid example of communication without typical oral speech.

for different kinds of "solid ice" and others for "seamed ice," "cracked ice," and "floating ice." Clearly, the priorities of a culture are reflected in its language (Basso, 1972:35; J. Carroll, 1956).

Language as the Foundation of Culture Language is the foundation of every culture, though particular languages differ in striking ways. *Language* is an abstract system of word meanings and symbols for all aspects of culture. Language includes speech, written characters, numerals, symbols, and gestures of nonverbal communication.

The sign languages used by deaf people and others are an especially vivid example of communication without typical oral speech. At least 50 native sign languages are used in various cultures around the world, among them American Sign Language (ASL). In the past, ASL was not accepted as a language, but in 1965 educator Bill Stokoe published the first dictionary of American Sign Language based on linguistic principles. Stokoe's work underscores the fact that ASL users combine various hand and body movements to produce recognizable words and an understood language. Indeed,

Ursula Bellugi, a pioneering ASL researcher at the Salk Institute, contends that the "deaf *think* in signs. They *dream* in signs. And little children sign to themselves" (Wolkomir, 1992:32, 40; see also Dolnick, 1993; H. Lane, 1992).

Language, of course, is not an exclusively human attribute. Although they are incapable of human speech, chimpanzees have been able to use symbols to communicate. However, even at their most advanced level, animals operate with essentially a fixed set of signs with fixed meanings. By contrast, humans can manipulate symbols in order to express abstract concepts and rules and to expand human cultures.

In contrast to some other elements of culture, language permeates all parts of society. Certain cultural skills, such as cooking or carpentry, can be learned without the use of language through the process of imitation. However, it is impossible to transmit complex legal and religious systems to the next generation by watching to see how they are performed. You could bang a gavel as a judge does, but you would never be able to understand legal reasoning without language. Therefore, people invariably depend upon language for the use and transmission of the rest of a culture.

While language is a cultural universal, differences in the use of language are evident around the world. This is the case even when two countries use the same spoken language. For example, an English-speaking person from the United States who is visiting London may be puzzled the first time an English friend says she will "ring you up"; she means she will call you on the telephone. Similarly, the meanings of nonverbal gestures vary from one culture to another. Whereas residents of the United States commonly use and attach positive meanings to the "thumbs up" gesture, this gesture has only vulgar connotations in Greece (Ekman et al., 1984).

Sapir-Whorf Hypothesis Language does more than simply describe reality; it also serves to *shape* the reality of a culture. For example, people in the United States cannot easily make the verbal distinction about ice that are possible in the Slave Indian culture. As a result, we may be somewhat less likely to notice such differences.

The role of language in interpreting the world for us has been advanced in the *Sapir-Whorf hypothesis,* which is named for two linguists. According to Sapir and Whorf, since people can conceptualize the world only through language, language precedes thought. Thus, the word symbols and grammar of a language organize the world for us. The Sapir-Whorf hypothesis also holds that language is not a "given." Rather, it is culturally determined and leads to different interpretations of reality by focusing our attention on certain phenomena.

This hypothesis is considered so important that it has been reprinted by the State Department in its training programs to sensitize foreign service officers to the subtle uses of language. However, many social scientists challenge the Sapir-Whorf hypothesis and argue that language does not determine human thought and behavior patterns. As a result, the hypothesis has been moderated somewhat to suggest that language may *influence* (rather than determine) behavior and interpretations of social reality (J. Carroll, 1953:46; Kay and Kempton, 1984; Martyna, 1983:34; Sapir, 1929).

Berlin and Kay (1991) have noted that humans possess the physical ability to make millions of color distinctions, yet languages differ in the number of colors that are recognized. The English language distinguishes between yellow and orange, but some other languages do not. In the Dugum Dani language of New Guinea's West Highlands, there are only two basic color terms — *modla* for "white" and *mili* for "black." By contrast, there are 11 basic terms in English. Russian and Hungarian, though, have 12 color terms. Russians have terms for light blue and dark blue, while Hungarians have terms for two different shades of red. Thus, in a literal sense, language may color how we see the world.

Gender-related language can reflect — although in itself it will not determine — the traditional acceptance of men and women in certain occupations. Each time we use a term like *mailman, policeman,* or *fireman,* we are implying (especially to young children) that these occupations can be filled only by males. Yet many women work as *letter carriers, police officers,* and *firefighters* — a fact that is being increasingly recognized and legitimized through the use of nonsexist language (Martyna, 1983). Sexist biases of the English and Japanese languages are examined in Box 3-1 on page 70.

Just as language may encourage gender-related

stereotypes, it can also transmit stereotypes related to race. Dictionaries published in the United States list, among the meanings of the adjective *black:* "dismal, gloomy or forbidding," "destitute of moral light or goodness," "atrocious," "evil," "threatening," "clouded with anger." Dictionaries also list "pure" and "innocent" among the meanings of the adjective *white.* Through such patterns of language, our culture reinforces positive associations with the term (and skin color) *white* and a negative association with *black.* Therefore, it is not surprising that a list which prevents people from working in a profession is called a *blacklist,* while a lie that we think of as somewhat acceptable is called a *white lie.*

Language is of interest to all three sociological perspectives. Functionalists emphasize the important role of language in unifying members of a society. By contrast, conflict theorists focus on the use of language to perpetuate divisions between groups and societies — as in the subtle and not-so-subtle sexism and racism expressed in communication. Interactionists study how people rely upon shared definitions of phrases and expressions in both formal speech and everyday conversation.

Language can shape how we see, taste, smell, feel, and hear. It also influences the way we think about the people, ideas, and objects around us. A culture's most important norms, values, and sanctions are communicated to people through language. It is for these reasons that the introduction of new languages into a society is such a sensitive issue in many parts of the world.

The Bilingualism Debate According to a report released by the Bureau of the Census in 1993, almost 32 million residents of the United States — or about one out of every seven people — speak a language other than English. Indeed, 50 different languages are each spoken by at least 30,000 residents of this country. Over the period 1980 to 1990, there was a 38 percent increase in the number of people in the United States who speak a foreign language (Usdansky, 1993b).

These data are frequently cited as part of the passionate debate under way in the United States over bilingualism. *Bilingualism* is the use of two or more languages in workplaces or in educational facilities and the treatment of each language as equally

BOX 3-1 · AROUND THE WORLD

SEXISM IN LANGUAGES—ENGLISH AND JAPANESE

Nancy Henley, Mykol Hamilton, and Barrie Thorne (1985:169) suggest that the sexist bias of the English language takes three principal forms: "It ignores, it defines, it deprecates."

IGNORING

English ignores females by favoring the masculine form for all generic uses, as in the sentence: "Each entrant in the competition should do his best." According to the rules of English grammar, it is incorrect to use "their best" as the singular form in the previous sentence. Moreover, usage of the "he or she" form ("Each entrant in the competition should do his or her best") is often attacked as being clumsy. Nevertheless, feminists insist that common use of male forms as generic makes women and girls invisible and implicitly suggests that maleness and masculine values are the standard for humanity and normality. For this reason, there has been resistance to the use of terms like *mailman, policeman,* and *fireman* to represent the men and women who perform these occupations.

DEFINING

In the view of Henley and her colleagues (1985:170), "language both reflects and helps maintain women's secondary status in our society, by defining her and her 'place.'" The power to define through naming is especially significant in this process. Married women tradition-ally lose their own names and take their husbands', while children generally take the names of their fathers and not their mothers. These traditions of naming reflect western legal traditions under which children were viewed as the property of their fathers and married women as the property of their husbands. The view of females as possessions is also evident in the practice of using female names and pronouns to refer to material possessions such as cars, machines, and ships.

DEPRECATING

There are clear differences in the words that are applied to male and female things which reflect men's dominant position in English-speaking societies. For example, women's work may be patronized as "pretty" or "nice," whereas men's work is more often honored as "masterful" or "brilliant." In many instances, a woman's occupation or profession is trivialized with the feminine ending *-ess* or *-ette;* thus, even a distinguished writer may be given second-class status as a *poetess* or an *authoress.* In a clear manifestation of sexism, terms of sexual insult in the English language are applied overwhelmingly to women. One researcher found 220 terms for a sexually promiscuous woman but only 22 for a sexually promiscuous man (Stanley, 1977).

While the English language ignores, defines, and deprecates fe-males, the same is true of languages around the world. Indeed, in mid-1993, Japan's labor minister challenged that society's traditional practice of depicting women in government documents as always carrying brooms. The official term for women, *fujin,* is represented by two characters which literally mean "female person carrying broom" (Rafferty, 1993a).

The expressions commonly used by girls and boys in Japan underscore gender differences. A boy can refer to himself by using the word *boku,* which means "I." But a girl cannot assert her existence and identity that boldly and easily; she must instead refer to herself with the pronoun *watashi.* This term is viewed as more polite and can be used by either sex. Similarly, a boy can end a sentence assertively by stating "*Samui yo*" ("It's cold, I say!"). But a girl is expected to say "*Samui wa*" ("It's cold, don't you think?"). For girls, proper usage dictates ending with a gentle question rather than a strong declaration.

Ellen Rudolph (1991:8), a photographer from the United States who lives in Tokyo, reports that Japanese parents and teachers serve as "vigilant linguistic police" who remind children to use only those forms of speech deemed appropriate for their sex. Girls who violate these gender codes are told "*Onnanoko na no ni,*" which means, "You're a girl, don't forget."

legitimate. In an educational sense, bilingualism seemed one way of assisting millions of people who do not speak English as their first language, but who might want to *learn* English in order to function more efficiently within the United States. Bilingualism has been a particularly sensitive matter for millions of immigrants from Spanish-speaking nations.

In the last decade, bilingualism has become an increasingly controversial political issue. For example, a proposed constitutional amendment was introduced in the Senate in the mid-1980s to designate English as the "official language of the nation." A major force behind the proposed constitutional amendment and other efforts to restrict bilingualism is U.S. English, a nationwide organization which views the English language as the "social glue" that keeps the nation together. By contrast, Hispanic leaders see the U.S. English campaign as a veiled expression of racism (Perez, 1986, 1989).

While the United States remains resistant to official use of languages other than English, other societies experience the pervasiveness of the English language. The domination of other languages by English stems from such factors as the demands of world trade, where English is used to negotiate many international business deals. But the English language is not being enthusiastically welcomed in all countries. In 1990, several of India's largest states ordered that all government work be conducted in Hindi—the dominant language of northern India—and that letters not be answered if written to government offices in English (Crossette, 1990).

Norms

All societies have ways of encouraging and enforcing what they view as appropriate behavior while discouraging and punishing what they consider to be improper conduct. "Put on some clean clothes for dinner" and "Thou shalt not kill" are examples of norms found in the culture of the United States, just as respect for older people is a norm of Japanese culture. *Norms* are established standards of behavior maintained by a society.

In order for a norm to become significant, it must be widely shared and understood. For example, in movie theaters in the United States, we typically expect that people will be quiet while the film is showing. Because of this norm, an usher can tell a member of the audience to stop talking so loudly. Of course, the application of this norm can vary, de-

Fred Ward/Black Star

According to the informal norms of the United States, people may greet each other with a handshake or, in some cases, with a hug or a kiss. However, in the mountainous Asian kingdom of Bhutan, residents greet each other by extending their tongues and hands.

pending on the particular film and type of audience. People attending a serious artistic or political film will be more likely to insist on the norm of silence than those attending a slapstick comedy or horror movie.

Types of Norms Sociologists distinguish between norms in two ways. First, norms are classified as either formal or informal. *Formal norms* have generally been written down and involve strict rules for punishment of violators. In the United States, we often formalize norms into laws, which must be very precise in defining proper and improper behavior. In a political sense, *law* is the "body of rules, made by government for society, interpreted by the courts, and backed by the power of the state" (Cummings and Wise, 1993:491). Laws are an example of formal norms, although not the only type. The requirements for a college major and the rules of a card game are also considered formal norms.

By contrast, *informal norms* are generally understood but are not precisely recorded. Standards of proper dress are a common example of informal norms. Our society has no specific punishment or sanction for a person who comes to school or to college dressed quite differently from everyone else. Making fun of nonconforming students for their unusual choice of clothing is the most likely response (E. Gross and Stone, 1964; G. Stone, 1977).

Norms are also classified by their relative importance to society. When classified in this way, they are known as *mores* and *folkways.*

Mores (pronounced "MOR-ays") are norms deemed highly necessary to the welfare of a society, often because they embody the most cherished principles of a people. Each society demands obedience to its mores; violation can lead to severe penalties. Thus, the United States has strong mores against murder, treason, and child abuse that have been institutionalized into formal norms. *Folkways* are norms governing everyday behavior whose violation raises comparatively little concern. For example, walking up a "down" escalator in a department store challenges our standards of appropriate behavior, but it will not result in a fine or a jail sentence. Society is more likely to formalize mores than it is folkways. Nevertheless, folkways play an important role in shaping the daily behavior of members of a culture.

Like mores, folkways represent culturally learned patterns of behavior and can vary from one society to another. Even folkways concerning time are not universally shared. As an example, some cultures do not share the western concern with keeping appointments precisely. King Hassan II of Morocco is notorious for arriving late at meetings. In 1980, when Britain's Queen Elizabeth II paid a call, the king kept her waiting for 15 minutes. The queen was not amused, but the Moroccans could not understand why she and the British public were so upset. "The king could never have kept the queen or anybody else waiting," a Moroccan later remarked, "because the king cannot be late" (Levine, 1987:33).

In many societies around the world, folkways exist to reinforce patterns of male dominance. Men's hierarchical position above women within the traditional Buddhist areas of Southeast Asia is revealed in various folkways. In the sleeping cars of trains, women do not sleep in upper berths above men. In hospitals in which men are housed on the first floor, women patients will not be placed on the second floor. Even on clotheslines, folkways dictate male dominance: women's attire is hung lower than that of men (Bulle, 1987:4).

Acceptance of Norms Norms, whether mores or folkways, are not followed in all situations. In some cases, people evade a norm because they know it is weakly enforced. It is illegal in many states for teenagers to drink alcoholic beverages, yet drinking by minors is common throughout the nation. (In fact, teenage alcoholism is one of our country's most serious social problems.)

In some instances, behavior that appears to violate society's norms may actually represent adherence to the norms of one's particular group. Teenage drinkers often break the laws of a state government in order to conform to the standards of a peer group. Similarly, in 1993, after a deadly gun battle with federal officials, nearly 100 members of a religious cult associated with the Branch Davidians followed the dictates of the cult's leader, David Koresh, and defied government orders to abandon their compound near Waco, Texas. Eventually, after a 51-day standoff, the Department of Justice ordered an assault on the compound and 86 cult members (including Koresh) died.

Norms are violated in some instances because

one norm conflicts with another. For example, suppose that you live in an apartment building and one night hear the screams of the woman next door, who is being beaten by her husband. If you decide to intervene by ringing their doorbell or calling the police, you are *violating* the norm of "minding your own business" while, at the same time, *following* the norm of assisting a victim of violence.

Even when norms do not conflict, there are always exceptions to any norm. The same action, under different circumstances, can cause one to be viewed either as a hero or as a villain. Eavesdropping on telephone conversations is normally considered illegal and abhorrent. However, it can be done with a court order to obtain valid evidence for a criminal trial. A government agent who uses such methods to convict an organized crime baron may be praised. In our culture, even killing another human being is tolerated as a form of self-defense and is actually rewarded in warfare.

Some social norms are so widely accepted that they rarely need to be verbalized. They are implicitly taught by a society to its members, and there may be very little need to enforce them. An example of such a norm is the prohibition against cannibalism. It is unlikely that you can recall anyone telling you not to eat human flesh. Nevertheless, as members of the culture of the United States, we almost never consider doing so.

Acceptance of norms is subject to change, as the political, economic, and social conditions of a culture are transformed. For example, under traditional norms in the United States, a woman was expected to marry, rear children, and remain at home if her husband could support the family without her assistance. However, these norms have been changing in recent decades, in part as a result of the contemporary feminist movement (see Chapter 11). As support for traditional norms weakens, people will feel free to violate them more frequently and openly and will be less likely to receive serious negative sanctions for doing so.

Sanctions

What happens when people violate a widely shared and understood norm? Suppose that a football coach sends a twelfth player onto the field. Imagine a college graduate showing up in cutoffs for a

THE FAR SIDE By GARY LARSON

© 1987 FarWorks, Inc./Dist. by Universal Press Syndicate

The Far Side © Farworks, Inc./Dist. by Universal Press Syndicate. Reprinted with Permission. All Rights Reserved.

7-22

"You're sick, Jessy! ... Sick, sick, sick!"

The prohibition against cannibalism is an example of a social norm so widely accepted in the United States that it rarely needs to be verbalized.

job interview at a large bank. Or consider a driver who neglects to put any money in a parking meter. In each of these situations, the person will receive sanctions if his or her behavior is detected.

Sanctions are penalties and rewards for conduct concerning a social norm. Note that the concept of *reward* is included in this definition. Conformity to a norm can lead to positive sanctions such as a pay raise, a medal, a word of gratitude, or a pat on the back. Negative sanctions include fines, threats, imprisonment, and even stares of contempt.

In Table 3-1 on page 74, the relationship between norms and sanctions is summarized. As you can see in this table, the sanctions that are associated with formal norms (those written down and codified) tend to be formalized as well. If a coach sends too

TABLE 3-1	**Norms and Sanctions**	
	SANCTIONS	
NORMS	POSITIVE	NEGATIVE
Formal	Salary bonus	Demotion
	Testimonial dinner	Firing from a job
	Medal	Jail sentence
	Diploma	Expulsion
Informal	Smile	Frown
	Compliment	Humiliation
	Cheers	Ostracism

Sanctions serve to reinforce both formal and informal social norms.

many players onto the field, the team will be penalized 15 yards. The college graduate who comes to the bank interview in cutoff blue jeans will probably be treated with contempt by bank officials and will almost certainly lose any chance of getting the job. The driver who fails to put money in the parking meter will be given a ticket and expected to pay a fine.

Implicit in the application of sanctions is the detecting of norm violation or obedience. A person cannot be penalized or rewarded unless someone with the power to provide sanctions is aware of the person's actions. Therefore, if none of the officials in the football game realizes that there is an extra player on the field, there will be no penalty. If the police do not see the car which is illegally parked, there will be no fine or ticket. Furthermore, there can be *improper* application of sanctions in certain situations. The referee may make an error in counting the number of football players and levy an undeserved penalty on one team for "too many players on the field."

The entire fabric of norms and sanctions in a culture reflects that culture's values and priorities. The most cherished values will be most heavily sanctioned; matters regarded as less critical, on the other hand, will carry light and informal sanctions.

Values

Each individual develops his or her own personal goals and ambitions, yet each culture provides a general set of objectives for its members. *Values* are these collective conceptions of what is considered good, desirable, and proper—or bad, undesirable, and improper—in a culture. They indicate what people in a given culture prefer as well as what they find important and morally right (or wrong). Values may be specific, such as honoring one's parents and owning a home, or they may be more general, such as health, love, and democracy.

Values influence people's behavior and serve as criteria for evaluating the actions of others. There is often a direct relationship between the values, norms, and sanctions of a culture. For example, if a culture highly values the institution of marriage, it may have norms (and strict sanctions) which prohibit the act of adultery. If a culture views private property as a basic value, it will probably have laws against theft and vandalism.

The values of a culture may change, but most remain relatively stable during any one person's lifetime. Socially shared, intensely felt values are a fundamental part of our lives in the United States.

Obviously, not all of the 250 million people in this country agree on one set of goals. However, sociologist Robin Williams (1970:452–500) attempted to offer a list of basic values in the United States. His list included achievement, efficiency, material comfort, nationalism, equality, and the supremacy of science and reason over faith. Any such effort to describe our nation's values should be properly viewed as but a starting point in defining the national character. Nevertheless, a review of 27 different attempts to describe the "American value system," including the work of anthropologist Margaret Mead and sociologist Talcott Parsons, revealed an overall similarity to the values identified by Williams (Devine, 1972:185).

In his book *Continental Divide,* sociologist Seymour Martin Lipset (1990) contrasted the values of two superficially similar neighbors: the United States and Canada. According to survey data from many polls, people in the United States are more religious than Canadians and take more moralistic attitudes toward sex, pornography, and marriage. Whereas Canadians show greater concern for an orderly society and are more likely to favor a strong role for government, citizens of the United States show greater concern for liberty and are more supportive of limits on government power. In fact, people in the United States are more suspicious of "big-ness" than Canadians—whether in terms of big government or private economic power.

The issue of gays in the military reveals another example of the value differences in superficially similar cultures. In 1993, when President Bill Clinton announced his intention to lift the long-standing ban prohibiting lesbians and gay men from serving in the United States armed forces, there was strong opposition both inside and outside the military. Yet, only a year earlier, Canada had ended a similar ban. According to a review of 17 major allies of the United States by the General Accounting Office, only three (Great Britain, Greece, and Portugal) explicitly ban gays from their military forces. A Danish air force general was puzzled over the controversy in the United States, noting: "I don't understand why you have a debate on it. . . . Nobody cares about it" (J. Lancaster, 1992:14).

One commonly cited barometer of the values of the United States is an annual questionnaire survey of attitudes of more than 210,000 entering first-year college students at 404 two-year and four-year colleges. This survey focuses on an array of issues, beliefs, and life goals. For example, respondents are asked if various values are personally important to them. Over the last 25 years, the value of "being very well-off financially" has shown the strongest gain in popularity; the proportion of first-year college students who endorse this value as "essential" or "very important" rose from 44 percent in 1967 to 75 percent in 1993 (see Figure 3-1). By contrast, the value that has shown the most striking decline in endorsement by students is "developing a meaningful philosophy of life." While this value was the most popular in the 1967 survey, endorsed by more than 80 percent of the respondents, it had fallen to sixth place on the list by 1993 and was endorsed by only 45 percent of students entering college (Astin et al., 1987:97, 1993).

During the 1980s, there was growing support for values having to do with money, power, and status. At the same time, there was a decline in support for certain values having to do with social awareness and altruism, such as "helping others." However, by the 1990s there was evidence that college students were once again turning toward social concerns. According to the 1992 nationwide survey, 43 percent of first-year students stated that "influenc-

FIGURE 3-1 Life Goals of First-Year College Students in the United States, 1967–1993

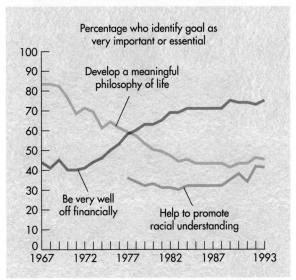

SOURCES: UCLA Higher Education Research Institute, as reported in Astin et al., 1987:97, 1993.

Over the last 25 years, entering first-year college students in the United States have become more concerned with becoming "very well-off financially" and less concerned with developing "a meaningful philosophy of life." There has been a recent increase in the proportion of students who value "helping to promote racial understanding."

ing social values" was an "essential" or a "very important" goal. Moreover, the proportion of students for whom "helping to promote racial understanding" was an essential or very important goal increased sharply to a record high of 42 percent (up from 34 percent in 1991). Clearly, like other aspects of culture, such as language and norms, a nation's values are not necessarily fixed (Dey et al., 1992:25).

It is important to emphasize that value systems can be quite different from that of our own culture. In Papua, New Guinea, much of what people in the United States would consider private property is shared. Different people may actually hold different rights on the same land. There is no "owner" in our terms; one person may hold ceremonial

In 1993, as Congress debated whether to lift the long-standing ban prohibiting lesbians and gay men from serving in the United States armed forces, gays currently in the military and gay veterans demonstrated in uniform to underscore their service to their country.

flicting cultural elements, resulting in a harmonious and cohesive whole. In a well-integrated culture, various norms, values, and customs will support one another and fit together well.

Traditionally, the Lapp people of Finland used the dogsled as a basic vehicle for transportation as well as a means of hunting and herding deer. However, in the early 1960s, snowmobiles became integrated into Lapp culture and, to some extent, reshaped the culture. These machines were not useful in hunting, since they made too much noise and frightened away deer. Nevertheless, the dogsled quickly became a thing of the past. Lapps used their new snowmobiles to haul goods and to escort tourists through the countryside.

This change in one element of material culture—the introduction of new technology—has had far-reaching consequences on both material and nonmaterial culture. The Lapps have quickly become much more dependent on their neighbors and the outside world. Whereas herding was traditionally a solitary occupation, a Lapp will now drive across the country with a second snowmobiler, who can drive him or her back to warmth and safety if the first snowmobile breaks down. New lines of work have emerged because of the need for fuel, for spare parts, and for mechanical servicing. In addition, the ease of travel afforded by the snowmobile has created a much wider network of friendships and family relationships among the Lapps. People can now visit each other much more frequently—despite the long, cold, snowy winters.

While the Lapps have successfully integrated the snowmobile into the rest of their culture, it has nevertheless transformed their culture in certain ways. Social rank has become more important among the Lapps than it was in the days when almost everyone owned reindeer herds of approximately equal size. The need for money to buy and maintain snowmobiles has caused some poor families to lose most of their herds and turn to government assistance. At the same time, those with greater wealth or mechanical ability have been able to keep their machines operating efficiently and to substantially enlarge their herds. Thus, while the coming of the snowmobile has brought Lapps together and into the larger social world, it has simultaneously created new social boundaries within the Lapp culture (Pelto, 1973).

rights, another fishing rights, another hunting rights, another dwelling rights, and so forth. In 1983, young men in one Papuan village were killed after developing export businesses for their own personal profit. These men were viewed as being too individualistic and as no longer contributing to the common good. This extreme example reminds us that what is valued in one society—"being very well-off financially"—may lead to a death sentence in a different culture (Ellis and Ellis, 1989).

CULTURAL INTEGRATION

As we have seen, the values and norms of every culture sometimes conflict with each other. *Cultural integration* refers to the bringing together of con-

Even relatively minor aspects of a culture can play a role in cultural integration. Children's games and nursery rhymes undoubtedly reinforce the norms and values of a culture, often ending with rather explicit "lessons" about appropriate and inappropriate behavior. Similarly, ceremonies such as weddings, funerals, and confirmations prepare participants for new social roles and reduce the shock of change which might threaten social continuity. Sociologists agree that no culture can be logically divided into separate parts for analysis and be truly understood. Every aspect of culture is intertwined with others and contributes to the culture as a whole (Arensberg and Neihoff, 1964:50–51).

Cultural integration is not always the result of agreement by all members of a culture. Often this process is enforced from the top; less powerful members of society have little choice but to accept the dictates and values of those in control. Conflict theorists emphasize that while cultural integration may exist in certain societies, the norms and values perpetuated are those favorable to the elites and the powerful (see also M. Archer, 1988).

CULTURAL VARIATION

Each culture has a unique character. Cultures adapt to meet specific sets of circumstances, such as climate, level of technology, population, and geography. This adaptation is evident in differences in all elements of culture, including norms, sanctions, values, and language. Thus, despite the presence of cultural universals such as courtship and religion, there is still great diversity among the world's many cultures. Moreover, even within a single nation, certain segments of the populace will develop cultural patterns which differ from those of the dominant society.

Aspects of Cultural Variation

Subcultures Older people living in housing for the elderly, workers in an offshore oil rig, rodeo cowboys, circus performers—all are examples of what sociologists refer to as *subcultures*. A *subculture* is a segment of society which shares a distinctive pattern of mores, folkways, and values which

differs from the pattern of the larger society. In a sense, a subculture can be thought of as a culture existing within a larger, dominant culture. The existence of many subcultures is characteristic of complex societies such as the United States. Conflict theorists argue that subcultures often emerge because the dominant society has unsuccessfully attempted to suppress a practice regarded as improper, such as use of illegal drugs.

The impact of subcultures within the United States is evident in the celebration of seasonal traditions. December is dominated by the religious and commercial celebration of the Christmas holiday—an event well-entrenched in the dominant culture of our society. However, the Jewish subculture observes Hanukkah, African Americans have begun to observe the relatively new holiday of Kwanzaa, and some atheists join in rituals celebrating the winter solstice (K. Peterson, 1992).

Aneal Vohra/Unicorn Stock Photos

Shown are members of the Star Trek *subculture dressed as Klingons. These "Trekkers" attend* Star Trek *conventions, subscribe to fan magazines and newsletters focused on* Star Trek, *and enjoy dressing in the distinctive attire of their favorite* Star Trek *characters.*

Members of a subculture participate in the dominant culture, while at the same time engaging in unique and distinctive forms of behavior. Frequently, a subculture will develop an **argot,** or specialized language, which distinguishes it from the wider society. Thus, the phrase "Smokey in a plain wrapper" has special meaning for truck drivers and others who listen to citizens' band radios (CBs). It indicates that a patrol officer is ahead on the road in an unmarked car. The phrase "bear in the woods giving out green stamps" means that the officer is giving out tickets, while "taking pictures" means that police are using a radar gun to monitor driving speeds.

Just as truck drivers have an unusual language for describing highway police, a subculture of prison inmates may create its own colorful argot. A study of men's prisons in California revealed that the term *jacketing* is used to refer to a guard's officially noting in an inmate's file that he is a suspected gang member. Often guards obtain this information about inmates through confidential informants (or "snitches"). By supplying such information to guards, a snitch develops a "juice card"—that is, a form of credit with the guard, which the guard will eventually have to repay with some type of favor (G. Hunt et al., 1993:401–402).

Even the names that people give to everyday objects and events may vary, depending on the argot of regional subcultures. For example, a study of 1002 communities across the United States revealed that 111 different terms are used to describe a type of sandwich in an unusually long bun that constitutes a meal in itself (Cassidy, 1985). Six names for this sandwich were especially popular: "poor boy" (primarily in the southeastern states and parts of California), "hoagie" (Pennsylvania and New Jersey), "grinder" (Connecticut and other New England states), "Dagwood" (Iowa, Minnesota, other midwestern states, and parts of southern California), "hero" (New York City and New Jersey), and "Cuban sandwich" (Florida).

Argot allows "insiders," the members of the subculture, to understand words with special meanings. It also establishes patterns of communication which cannot be understood by "outsiders." Sociologists associated with the interactionist perspective emphasize that language and symbols offer a powerful way for a subculture to maintain its identity. The

particular argot of a given subculture, therefore, provides a feeling of cohesion for members and contributes to the development of a group identity (Halliday, 1978).

Subcultures develop in a number of ways. Often a subculture emerges because a segment of society faces problems or even privileges unique to its position. Subcultures may be based on common age (teenagers or old people), region (Appalachians), ethnic heritage (Cuban Americans), or beliefs (a militant political group).

Occupations may also form subcultures. In his book *The Right Stuff,* subsequently made into a Hollywood film, Tom Wolfe examined the reclusive fraternity of test pilots who paved the way for United States exploration of space. According to Wolfe, members of this subculture shared distinctive norms and values governing their behavior in the air and on the ground. They were expected to pass continual tests of their flying skills, courage, and "righteous quality" in order to prove that they were the "elected and anointed ones who had *the right stuff*" (T. Wolfe, 1980:19).

Certain subcultures, such as that of computer "hackers," develop because of a shared interest or hobby. In still other subcultures, such as that of prison inmates, members have been excluded from normal society and are forced to develop alternative ways of living.

Countercultures Some subcultures conspicuously challenge the central norms and values of the prevailing culture. A *counterculture* is a subculture that rejects societal norms and values and seeks alternative lifestyles (J. Yinger, 1960, 1982). Countercultures are typically popular among the young, who have the least investment in the existing culture. In most cases, a person who is 20 years old can adjust to new cultural standards more easily than someone who has spent 60 years following the patterns of the dominant culture.

By the end of the 1960s, some writers claimed that an extensive counterculture had emerged in the United States, composed of young people who repudiated the technological orientation of our culture. This counterculture primarily included political radicals and "hippies" who had "dropped out" of mainstream social institutions. These young men and women rejected the pressure to accumulate

BOX 3-2 * AROUND THE WORLD

THE SKINHEAD COUNTERCULTURE

Beginning in about 1968, a new counterculture surfaced in Great Britain. The Skinheads were young people with shaved heads who often sported suspenders, tattoos, and steel-toed shoes. In part, Skinhead groups emerged as vocal and sometimes violent supporters of certain British soccer teams. These young people generally came from working-class backgrounds and had little expectation of "making it" in mainstream society. They listened to music that extolled violence and even racism, performed by such groups as Britain's Skrewdriver, France's Brutal Combat, and the United States' Tulsa Boot Boys.

Most seriously, some Skinhead groups championed racist and anti-Semitic ideologies and engaged in vandalism, violence, and even murder. Immigrants from India, Pakistan, and the West Indies became a common target of Skinhead attacks. (There were, however, other Skinhead groups that were explicitly *antiracist*.)

Throughout the 1970s, the Skinhead counterculture gradually spread from Britain to Europe, North America, and Australia. It is difficult to measure precisely the size of this counterculture, since Skinheads do not belong to a national or international organization. Nevertheless, according to one estimate, there were 3500 Skinheads in the United States in 1993, and their numbers appeared to be growing. Skinhead groups in this country were responsible for at least 28 killings over the period 1987 to 1993.

While some Skinheads around the world adopt only the distinctive dress and music associated with this counterculture, most seem to espouse White supremacy and racial hatred. In almost all the countries where Skinhead groups exist, they have committed acts of reckless violence against racial and ethnic minorities, including Jews. In the 1990s, lesbians, gay men, the homeless, and people with disabilities have also become targets of Skinhead attacks. It appears that Skinheads attack those viewed as "weaker" to bolster their own feelings of superiority.

Skinheads constitute a youthful counterculture which challenges the values of larger societies. While they claim an allegiance to history and to their (White) cultural heritage, their dress and music represent a symbolic rejection of the traditions of previous generations. Although Skinhead groups tolerate certain older adults—generally members of White supremacist and neo-Nazi organizations—this counterculture nevertheless is dominated by young males who project a tough, macho image.

SOURCES: Anti-Defamation League of B'nai B'rith, 1993; Came, 1989; *The Economist*, 1990b; Hamm, 1993; T. Post, 1992.

---

more and more cars, larger and larger homes, and an endless array of material goods. Instead, they expressed a desire to live in a culture based on more humanistic values, such as sharing, love, and coexistence with the environment. As a political force, the counterculture opposed the United States' involvement in the war in Vietnam and encouraged draft resistance (Flacks, 1971; Roszak, 1969). The Skinheads, a more recent counterculture with very different political values, are profiled in Box 3-2.

Culture Shock Maggie, born in 1946 of mixed ancestry, is fiercely proud of her Cree Indian heritage. She spent her early years on a reservation, but at the age of 16 moved to the Canadian city of Edmonton. There her uncle exposed her to the "white-man world":

> . . . it was all a push-button world. . . . I remember that first time when he plugged in the vacuum cleaner and it went "kaboom!" I was so scared. I just backed up in a corner because I had never seen a vacuum cleaner before in my life. . . . I didn't know what this monstrosity was.
>
> The phone. I had never ever saw a phone before in my life. I was sixteen, but . . . I hardly ever went to town because my dad was so strict with everything. . . . So it was really just mind-blowing. I went through cultural shock like you wouldn't believe when I came to the city (Shorten, 1991:166).

Owen Franken/Stock, Boston

A tourist from the United States who goes out to dinner in certain areas in China and learns that a local specialty is dog meat might well experience culture shock.

When immersed in an unfamiliar culture, a person may feel strangely disoriented, uncertain, out of place, even fearful. These are all indications that he or she may be experiencing what sociologists call **culture shock.** For example, a resident of the United States who visits certain areas in China and wants local meat for dinner may be stunned to learn that the specialty is dog meat. Similarly, someone from a strict Islamic culture may be shocked upon first seeing the comparatively provocative dress styles and open displays of affection that are common in the United States and various European cultures.

All of us, to some extent, take for granted the cultural practices of our society. As a result, it can be surprising and disturbing to realize that other cultures do not follow the "American way of life." In fact, customs that seem strange to us are considered normal and proper in other cultures, which may see *our* mores and folkways as odd.

Interestingly, members of certain cultures might experience culture shock simply by seeing people kiss. In many parts of the world, kissing is completely absent. Until recently, the Japanese viewed kissing as acceptable only between mother and child. Japanese poets wrote for centuries about the allure of the back of the neck, but were silent about the mouth. In fact, the Japanese had no word for kissing until they borrowed from English to create the term *kissu*. Similarly, until the arrival of westerners (and their motion pictures), kissing was unknown among the Balinese of Oceania, the Lepcha of Eurasia, and the Thonga of Africa. Among these peoples, the mouth-to-mouth kiss was considered dangerous, unhealthy, or disgusting. When the Thonga first saw Europeans kissing, they laughed and remarked: "Look at them! They eat each other's saliva and dirt!" (Ford and Beach, 1951; Tiefer, 1978).

Culture shock over conflicting value systems is not limited to contacts between traditional and modern societies. We can experience culture shock in our own society. A conservative, church-going older person might feel bewildered or horrified at a punk rock concert. Similarly, given traditional notions about gender roles in our culture, many men might be shocked by a women's martial arts class with a female instructor.

Attitudes toward Cultural Variation

Ethnocentrism Many everyday statements reflect our attitude that our culture is best. We use terms such as *underdeveloped, backward,* and *primitive* to refer to other societies. What "we" believe is a religion; what "they" believe is superstition and mythology (Spradley and McCurdy, 1980:28).

It is very tempting to evaluate the practices of other cultures on the basis of our own perspectives. Sociologist William Graham Sumner (1906:13–15) coined the term **ethnocentrism** to refer to the tendency to assume that one's culture and way of life are superior to all others. The ethnocentric person sees his or her own group as the center or defining

FIGURE 3-2 Mental Maps of the World

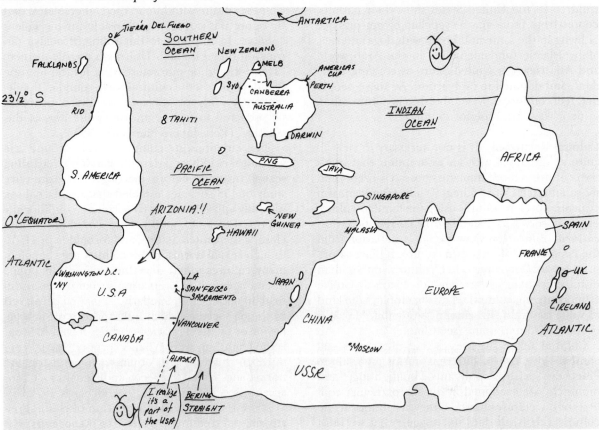

SOURCE: Saarinen, 1988:124.

How do we view the world? Do we see our own homeland in the center? In a map exercise, a student in the People's Republic of China saw China as central, while (as shown in this figure) an Australian student put Australia at the top.

point of culture and views all other cultures as deviations from what is "normal." As one manifestation of ethnocentrism, map exercises reveal that students in many nations draw maps in which their homelands are in the center of the world (see Figure 3-2).

The conflict approach to social behavior points out that ethnocentric value judgments serve to devalue groups and contribute to denial of equal opportunities. Psychologist Walter Stephan notes a typical example of ethnocentrism in New Mexico's schools. Both Hispanic and Native American cultures teach children to look down when they are being criticized by adults, yet many "Anglo" (non-Hispanic) teachers believe that you should look someone in the eye when you are being criticized. "Anglo teachers can feel that these students are be-

ing disrespectful," notes Stephan. "That's the kind of misunderstanding that can evolve into stereotype and prejudice" (Goleman, 1991:C8).

Functionalists note that ethnocentrism serves to maintain a sense of solidarity by promoting group pride. Yet this type of social stability is established at the expense of other peoples. Denigrating other nations and cultures can enhance our own patriotic feelings and belief that our way of life is superior. Of course, ethnocentrism is hardly limited to citizens of the United States. Visitors from many

African cultures are surprised at the disrespect that children in the United States show their parents. People from India may be repelled by our practice of living in the same household with dogs and cats. Many Islamic fundamentalists in the Arab world and Asia view the United States as corrupt, decadent, and doomed to destruction. All these people may feel comforted by membership in cultures that, in their view, are superior to ours.

Cultural Relativism   It is not necessary to view all cultural variations with an assumption that one's own culture is more humane, more "civilized," and more advanced than others. While ethnocentrism evaluates foreign cultures using the familiar culture of the observer as a standard of correct behavior, *cultural relativism* views people's behavior from the perspective of their own culture. It places a priority on *understanding* other cultures, rather than dismissing them as "strange" or "exotic." Unlike ethnocentrism, cultural relativism employs the kind of value neutrality in scientific study that Max Weber saw as so important (see Chapter 2).

Cultural relativism stresses that different social contexts give rise to different norms and values. Practices such as polygamy, bullfighting, and monarchy are examined within the particular contexts of the cultures in which they are found. While cultural relativism does not suggest that we must unquestioningly accept every form of behavior characteristic of a culture, it does require a serious and unbiased effort to evaluate norms, values, and customs in light of the distinctive culture of which they are a part.

In practice, of course, the application of cultural relativism can raise delicate questions. In 1989, a Chinese immigrant man was convicted in a New York court of bludgeoning his wife to death with a hammer. However, the man was acquitted of the most serious charges against him, and was sentenced only to five years' probation, when the judge ruled that cultural considerations warranted leniency. The deceased woman had confessed to having had an extramarital affair, and the judge revealed that he had been influenced by the testimony of an expert on Chinese culture that husbands in China often exact severe punishment on their wives in such situations. In posttrial hearings,

the judge declared that the defendant "took all his Chinese culture with him to the United States" and therefore was not fully responsible for his violent conduct. In response to this ruling, Brooklyn district attorney Elizabeth Holtzman angrily insisted: "There should be one standard of justice, not one that depends on the cultural background of the defendant. . . . Anyone who comes to this country must be prepared to live by and obey the laws of this country" (Rosario and Marcano, 1989:2).

The variations in cultural norms around the world are readily apparent in standards regarding sexual relations before marriage. An exhaustive study of 158 societies revealed that premarital sex was fully approved of in 65 societies, conditionally approved of in 43, mildly disapproved of in 6 (including the United States), and forbidden in 44. Although sexual norms in this country are changing, many cultures might nevertheless find our public discouragement of premarital sexual relations difficult to understand. Similarly, *we* may be perplexed by the 65 societies which fully approve of such behavior or by the 44 societies which forbid it. What is the "right" answer? What is "proper" sexual conduct? In this case and others, it depends on the norms and values that each individual or culture accepts as valid (Murdock, 1949; Richards, 1972:26).

There is an interesting extension of cultural relativism, referred to as *xenocentrism*. **Xenocentrism** is the belief that the products, styles, or ideas of one's society are inferior to those that originate elsewhere (W. Wilson et al., 1976). In a sense, it is a reverse ethnocentrism. For example, people in the United States often assume that French fashions or Japanese electronic devices are superior to our own. Are they, or are people unduly charmed by the lure of goods from exotic places? Such fascination with British china or Danish glassware can be damaging to competitors in the United States. Some companies have responded by creating products that *sound* European like Häagen-Dazs ice cream (made in Teaneck, New Jersey) or Nike shoes (produced in Beaverton, Oregon). Conflict theorists are most likely to be troubled by the economic impact of xenocentrism in the developing world. Consumers in developing nations frequently turn their backs on locally produced goods and instead purchase items imported from Europe or North America.

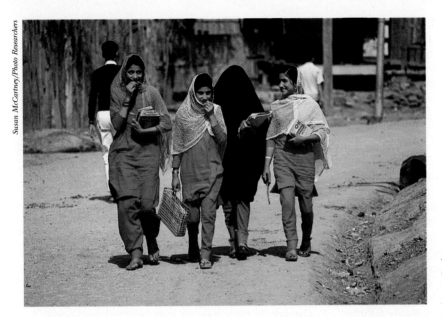

Susan McCartney/Photo Researchers

According to an exhaustive study of 158 societies, premarital sex is forbidden in 44, including many cultures where Islam is the dominant religion.

CULTURE AND THE DOMINANT IDEOLOGY

As is readily apparent, sociologists regard culture as a highly significant concept, since it embraces all learned and shared behavior. Nevertheless, there are important differences in the ways in which functionalist and conflict theorists view culture. We have seen that functionalists emphasize the role of language in unifying members of a society while conflict theorists focus on the use of language to perpetuate divisions between groups and societies. Similarly, functionalists stress that cultural integration reflects agreement among members of a society; conflict theorists counter that the norms and values perpetuated are those favorable to the elites and the powerful.

Both sociological perspectives agree that culture and society are in harmony with each other, but for different reasons. Functionalists maintain that stability requires a consensus and the support of society's members; consequently, there are strong central values and common norms. This view of culture became popular in sociology beginning in the 1950s, having been borrowed from British anthropologists who saw cultural traits as all working toward stabilizing a culture. As we learned in Chapter 1, the functionalist view of culture can be used to explain why widely condemned social practices such as prostitution continue to survive. From a functionalist perspective, a cultural trait or practice will persist if it performs functions that society seems to need or contributes to overall social stability and consensus.

Conflict theorists concur with functionalists that a common culture may exist, but they argue that it serves to maintain the privileges of some groups while keeping others in a subservient position. A culture, therefore, may offer "reasons" (justifications) for unequal social arrangements. As noted in Chapter 1, Karl Marx identified values in the culture of capitalist societies that justified the exploitation of the working class. Today, a society's culture may seek to explain why Protestants enjoy greater privileges than Catholics (Northern Ireland), why the separate economic development of Blacks is behind that of Whites (South Africa), or why women can be expected to earn less than men (the United States and elsewhere).

The term *dominant ideology* is used to describe a set of cultural beliefs and practices that help to maintain powerful social, economic, and political interests. This concept was first used by Hungarian Marxist Georg Lukacs (1923) and Italian Marxist

Antonio Gramsci (1929), but it did not gain an audience in the United States until the early 1970s. In Karl Marx's view, a capitalist society has a dominant ideology which serves the interests of the ruling class. Marx and Engels wrote in 1845:

> The ideas of the ruling class are in every age the ruling ideas; i.e. the class which is the dominant *material* force of society is at the same time its dominant *intellectual* force (Bottomore, 1983:431).

From a conflict perspective, the social significance of the dominant ideology is that a society's most powerful groups and institutions not only control wealth and property; even more important, they control the means of producing beliefs about reality through religion, education, and the media. For example, if all of a society's most important institutions tell women that they should be subservient to men, this dominant ideology will help to control women and keep them in a subordinate position (Abercrombie et al., 1980, 1990; R. Robertson, 1988).

Functionalist and conflict theorists agree, again for different reasons, that variation exists within a culture. Functionalists view subcultures as variations of particular social environments and as evidence that differences can exist within a common culture. However, conflict theorists suggest that variation often reflects the inequality of social arrangements within a society. Consequently, from a conflict perspective, the challenge to dominant social norms by African American activists, the feminist movement, and the disability rights movement can be seen as a reflection of inequality based on race, gender, and disability status.

A growing number of social scientists believe that a "core culture" cannot be easily identified in the United States. The lack of consensus on national values, the diffusion of cultural traits, the diversity of our many subcultures, and the changing views of young people (refer back to Figure 3-1) all are cited in support of this viewpoint. Yet there is no way of denying that certain expressions of values have greater influence than others even in so complex a society as the United States (Abercrombie et al., 1980, 1990; M. Archer, 1988; Wuthnow and Witten, 1988:52–53).

We see, then, that neither the functionalist nor the conflict perspective can be used exclusively to explain all aspects of a culture. For example, the custom of tossing rice at a bride and groom can be traced back to the wish to have children and to the view of rice as a symbol of fertility, rather than to the powerlessness of the proletariat. Nevertheless, there are cultural practices in our society and others that benefit some to the detriment of many. They may indeed promote social stability and consensus—but at whose expense?

SOCIAL POLICY AND CULTURE

MULTICULTURALISM

- How have changes in the population of the United States affected the debate over school and university curricula?
- What do scholars mean when they refer to the "canon"? What role should the canon play in the education of undergraduate students?
- How might functionalist and conflict theorists view the controversy over multiculturalism?

The culture of the United States can be compared to a kaleidoscope—the familiar optical device whose colors and patterns are formed by pieces of colored glass reflected from mirrors. As the viewer turns a set of mirrors in the kaleidoscope, he or she sees what appear to be an infinite variety of colorful images. Similarly, the culture of the United States is hardly static, especially with more than one million legal immigrants per year and a substantial number of illegal immigrants contributing to cultural diversity (Schaefer, 1992).

There is little doubt that the racial and ethnic makeup of the nation's schools and colleges is changing significantly. Sociologists have often been involved in documenting these changes and analyzing their social significance. In 1990, the enter-

There is little doubt that the racial and ethnic makeup of the nation's schools and colleges is changing significantly. Indeed, it is projected that by the year 2050, the combined Black, Hispanic, and Asian populations of the United States will account for 47 percent of the nation's population.

ing first-year class at the University of California at Berkeley was 34 percent White, 30 percent of Asian descent, 22 percent of Mexican or Latin American descent, and 7 percent African American. At Stanford University, more than 40 percent of entering undergraduates are from African American, Native American, Asian or Asian American, or Mexican American backgrounds. While these racial and ethnic ratios are not evident at all schools and colleges across the country, they nevertheless reflect long-range population trends. According to projections, by the year 2050 the combined Black, Hispanic, and Asian populations of the United States will account for 47 percent of the nation's population (Bureau of the Census, 1993b; Stimpson, 1992:52).

As the racial and ethnic profile of student populations has changed, there has been increasing debate over the proper curriculum materials that should be used in school and college classrooms. Traditionalists believe that it is essential to focus on what is often called the *canon* of the best books of western civilization, including famous works by Shakespeare, Hawthorne, Melville, Hemingway, Faulkner, and others. By contrast, troubled by the fact that this canon overwhelmingly consists of White male authors from United States or European backgrounds, advocates of **multiculturalism** insist that school and college curricula should be

revised to give greater emphasis to the contributions and experiences of African Americans, other racial and ethnic minorities, women, and nonwestern peoples. Catharine Stimpson (1992:43–44), a former president of the Modern Language Association, suggests that multiculturalism "most often . . . means treating society as the home of several valuable but distinct racial and ethnic groups." While sociologists have not uniformly endorsed multiculturalism, they have long argued against any type of ethnocentric world view.

Viewed from a functionalist perspective, the traditional canon of western culture promotes stability, social solidarity, and consensus by helping to define the common values of the United States. These "great books" are said to speak across barriers of gender, race, religion, and geography and to provide a cultural heritage that all of us share. By contrast, however, conflict theorists might view the western canon as central to a dominant ideology that serves the interests of society's most powerful groups and institutions. From a conflict perspective, the movement in support of multiculturalism represents a challenge to long-standing inequities based on gender, race, and ethnicity.

Intense debate has erupted across the United States in school systems, colleges, and universities regarding efforts to introduce or protest multicultural curricula. At Stanford University, a required one-year course on western culture for incoming students focused on the traditional western canon. When critics argued that non-European works should be added to the reading list and that substantial attention should be given to issues of gender, race, and class, a long battle resulted. At the University of Texas in Austin, a proposal for a required writing course, Writing about Difference, was bitterly attacked. Defenders of the proposal argued that students would sharpen their writing skills while learning (through required readings) about cultural diversity, especially as it pertains to issues of race and gender. Those opposed to the proposal derided it as "Oppression English" and insisted that it brought a loaded political agenda into the classroom (Rothenberg, 1992a; Searle, 1992: 106–108; Will, 1992).

In 1993, Hunter College—a part of the City University of New York—adopted a detailed and far-reaching multicultural curriculum. To receive a bachelor's degree, each student must satisfy a "pluralism and diversity requirement" by completing a three-credit course in each of four designated areas: non-European cultures, racial and ethnic minorities within the United States, women's studies and issues of gender and sexual orientation, and the intellectual traditions of Europe. The new multicultural requirement was adopted by the Hunter College Senate after two years of study, discussion, and debate (M. Newman, 1993).

At the elementary and secondary school levels, New York State has been one of the central battlegrounds concerning multiculturalism. In 1989, a task force appointed by the state commissioner of education released a controversial report entitled "A Curriculum of Inclusion." This examination of the state's history and social studies curriculum insisted that "African-Americans, Asian-Americans, Puerto Ricans/Latinos, and Native Americans have all been the victims of an intellectual and educational oppression that has characterized the culture and institutions of the United States and the European world for centuries" (Ravitch, 1992:291; Smoler, 1992).

In New York and elsewhere, some critics of traditional curricula have gone beyond a broad mul-

ticultural focus to advocate *Afrocentricity*. This term refers to the use of African cultures, rather than solely the European experience, to better understand human behaviors past and present. Afrocentricity would place the African and African American experiences at the heart of cultural study (Asante, 1992).

An important voice opposing multiculturalism and Afrocentricity has been the National Association of Scholars (NAS). Founded in 1987, this organization has 2500 members, most of them professors and many of them political conservatives. Like other critics of multiculturalism, the NAS (1992) argues that radicals are threatening intellectual inquiry and academic freedom by demanding "politically correct" curricula. Members of NAS and other defenders of the traditional canon (including conservative student newspapers on many campuses) insist that the classic western intellectual tradition must be taught in schools and colleges in the United States because this tradition largely shaped the development of our culture. Moreover, works by Plato, Shakespeare, and others are seen as of such high intellectual and artistic quality that they will have meaning for *all* students, regardless of gender, race, or ethnicity (Kimball, 1992:64; Searle, 1992:88; R. B. Smith, 1993:26).

Defenders of multiculturalism counter that the traditional canon reflects the interests and perspectives of privileged White European males while largely ignoring the contributions of women, men of color, and working people. Henry Louis Gates, Jr. (1992:197), one of the nation's most distinguished African American scholars, suggests that the "return of 'the' canon, the canon of Western masterpieces, represents the return of an order in which my people were the subjugated, the voiceless, the invisible. . . ." Critics of the canon charge that placing the western cultural and intellectual heritage in a preeminent position represents an example of ethnocentrism and racism. In their view, a genuinely multicultural approach to education will help to empower female and non-White students while broadening our appreciation of humanity's multifaceted cultural and intellectual history (Rothenberg, 1992a:265–266).

Sociologist Troy Duster (1991:B2) suggests that

the controversy over multiculturalism is actually a "struggle over who gets to define the idea of America." Duster asks:

> Are we essentially a nation with a common—or at least dominant—culture to which immigrants and "mi-norities" must adapt? Or is this a land in which ethnicity and difference are an accepted part of the whole; a land in which we affirm the richness of our differences and simultaneously try to forge agreement about basic values to guide public and social policy?

SUMMARY

Culture is the totality of learned, socially transmitted behavior. This chapter examines the basic elements which make up a culture, social practices which are common to all cultures, and variations which distinguish one culture from another.

1 If it were not for the social transmission of culture, each generation would have to reinvent television, not to mention the wheel.

2 Anthropologist George Murdock compiled a list of general practices found in every culture, including courtship, family, games, language, medicine, religion, and sexual restrictions.

3 Societies resist ideas which seem too foreign as well as those which are perceived as threatening to their own values and beliefs.

4 *Language* includes speech, written characters, numerals, symbols, and gestures and other forms of nonverbal communication.

5 Sociologists distinguish between *norms* in two ways. They are classified as either *formal* or *informal* norms and as *mores* or *folkways.*

6 The most cherished *values* of a culture will receive the heaviest *sanctions,* whereas matters regarded as less critical will carry light and informal sanctions.

7 Sociologist Robin Williams has offered a list of basic values of the United States, including achievement, efficiency, material comfort, nationalism, equality, and the supremacy of science and reason over faith.

8 In a well-integrated culture, various elements of culture will support one another and fit together well.

9 Generally, members of a *subculture* participate in the dominant culture, while at the same time engaging in unique and distinctive forms of behavior.

10 *Ethnocentric* people see their own culture as superior and view all other cultures as deviations from what is "normal."

11 *Cultural relativism* places priority on understanding other cultures rather than dismissing them as "strange" or "exotic."

12 From a conflict perspective, the social significance of the concept of the *dominant ideology* is that a society's most powerful groups and institutions control the means of producing beliefs about reality through religion, education, and the media.

13 Advocates of *multiculturalism* argue that the traditional curricula of schools and colleges in the United States should be revised to include more works by and about African Americans, other racial and ethnic minorities, and women.

CRITICAL THINKING QUESTIONS

1 Select three cultural universals from George Murdock's list and analyze them from a functionalist perspective. Why are these practices found in every culture? What functions do they serve?

2 Drawing on the theories and concepts presented in the chapter, apply sociological analysis to one subculture with which you are familiar. Describe the norms, values, argot, and sanctions evident in that subculture.

3 In what ways is the dominant ideology of the United States evident in the nation's literature, music, movies, television programs, and sporting events?

KEY TERMS

Afrocentricity The use of African cultures, rather than solely the European experience, to better understand human behaviors past and present. (page 86)

Argot Specialized language used by members of a group or subculture. (78)

Bilingualism The use of two or more languages in workplaces or educational facilities and the treatment of each language as equally legitimate. (69)

Counterculture A subculture that rejects societal norms and values and seeks an alternative lifestyle. (78)

Cultural integration The bringing together of conflicting cultural elements, resulting in a harmonious and cohesive whole. (76)

Cultural relativism The viewing of people's behavior from the perspective of their own culture. (82)

Cultural universals General practices found in every culture. (64)

Culture The totality of learned, socially transmitted behavior. (62)

Culture shock The feeling of surprise and disorientation that is experienced when people witness cultural practices different from their own. (80)

Diffusion The process by which a cultural item is spread from group to group or society to society. (66)

Discovery The process of making known or sharing the existence of an aspect of reality. (64)

Dominant ideology A set of cultural beliefs and practices that help to maintain powerful social, economic, and political interests. (83)

Ethnocentrism The tendency to assume that one's culture and way of life are superior to others. (80)

Folkways Norms governing everyday social behavior whose violation raises comparatively little concern. (72)

Formal norms Norms which have generally been written down and which involve strict rules for punishment of violators. (72)

Informal norms Norms which are generally understood but which are not precisely recorded. (72)

Innovation The process of introducing new elements into a culture through discovery or invention. (64)

Invention The combination of existing cultural items into a form that did not previously exist. (65)

Language An abstract system of word meanings and symbols for all aspects of culture. It also includes gestures and other nonverbal communication. (68)

Law In a political sense, the body of rules made by government for society, interpreted by the courts, and backed by the power of the state. (72)

Material culture The physical or technological aspects of our daily lives. (67)

Mores Norms deemed highly necessary to the welfare of a society. (72)

Multiculturalism The effort to revise school and college curricula to give greater emphasis to the contributions and experiences of African Americans, other racial and ethnic minorities, women, and nonwestern peoples. (85)

Nonmaterial culture Cultural adjustments to material conditions, such as customs, beliefs, patterns of communication, and ways of using material objects. (67)

Norms Established standards of behavior maintained by a society. (71)

Sanctions Penalties and rewards for conduct concerning a social norm. (73)

Sapir-Whorf hypothesis A hypothesis concerning the role of language in shaping cultures. It holds that language is culturally determined and serves to influence our mode of thought. (68)

Society A fairly large number of people who live in the same territory, are relatively independent of people outside it, and participate in a common culture. (63)

Subculture A segment of society which shares a distinctive pattern of mores, folkways, and values which differs from the pattern of the larger society. (77)

Values Collective conceptions of what is considered good, desirable, and proper—or bad, undesirable, and improper—in a culture. (74)

Xenocentrism The belief that the products, styles, or ideas of one's society are inferior to those that originate elsewhere. (82)

ADDITIONAL READINGS

Abercrombie, Nicholas, Stephen Hill, and Bryan S. Turner (eds.). *Dominant Ideologies*. Cambridge, Mass.: Unwin Hyman, 1990. A critique of the view that common cultures emerge as ideological systems.

Bellah, Robert N., Richard Madsden, Anne Swidler, William M. Sullivan, and Steven M. Tipton. *Habits of the Heart: Individualism and Commitment in American Life*. Berkeley: University of California Press, 1985. Several social scientists team up to summarize the contemporary philosophy of the people of the United States as reflected in such values as individualism and commitment.

Berman, Paul (ed.). *Debating P.C.: The Controversy over Political Correctness on College Campuses*. New York: Dell, 1992. This timely anthology explores many aspects of the debate over multiculturalism and includes selections by Henry Louis Gates, Jr., Edward Said, Catharine Stimpson, George Will, Dinesh D'Souza, Molefi Kete Asante, Irving Howe, and Diane Ravitch.

Featherstone, Mike (ed.). *Global Culture: Nationalism, Globalization, and Modernity*. London: Sage, 1990. In this anthology, social scientists from many nations analyze the extent to which we are witnessing a globalization of culture.

Hall, Edward T., and Mildred Reed Hall. *Understanding Cultural Differences.* Yarmouth, Me.: Intercultural Press, 1990. Two anthropologists review their lifelong work on cultural differences and focus on specific applications of how corporations operate in France, Germany, and the United States.

Imhoff, Gary (ed.). *Learning in Two Languages.* New Brunswick, N.J.: Transaction, 1990. This collection of essays brings together the research findings of those who advocate and those who are critical of bilingual education.

Kraybill, Donald B. *The Riddle of Amish Culture.* Baltimore: Johns Hopkins University Press, 1989. Drawing on observation research in Lancaster County, Pennsylvania, Kraybill seeks to clarify how the Amish continue to prosper despite their resistance to technological change.

Mascia-Lees, Francis E., and Patricia Sharpe (eds.). *Tattoo, Torture, Mutilation, and Adornment: The Denaturalization of the Body in Culture and Text.* Albany: State University of New York Press, 1992. Two professors of anthropology and women's studies consider the manner in which various cultures and subcultures deal with (and alter) the human body.

Wallerstein, Immanuel. *Geopolitics and Geoculture: Essays on the Changing World System.* Cambridge, Eng.: Cambridge University Press, 1991. Wallerstein argues that in light of the collapse of the iron curtain and the decline of the United States' dominance, a new world economy is emerging along with an accompanying "geoculture."

Weinstein, Deena. *Heavy Metal: A Cultural Sociology.* New York: Lexington, 1992. A sociologist examines the subculture associated with "heavy metal" music and efforts to curtail this subculture.

Journals

Among the journals that focus on issues of culture and language are *American Anthropologist* (founded in 1988), *Cross-Cultural Research* (1994), *Cultural Survival Quarterly* (1977), *Ethnology* (1962), *International Journal of the Sociology of Language* (1974), and *Theory, Culture, and Society* (1982).

4

SOCIALIZATION

THE ROLE OF SOCIALIZATION
Environment: The Impact of Isolation
The Influence of Heredity
Sociobiology

THE SELF AND SOCIALIZATION
Sociological Approaches to the Self
  Cooley: Looking-Glass Self
  Mead: Stages of the Self
  Goffman: Presentation of the Self
Psychological Approaches to the Self

SOCIALIZATION AND THE LIFE CYCLE
Stages of Socialization
Anticipatory Socialization and
  Resocialization

AGENTS OF SOCIALIZATION
Family
School
Peer Group
Mass Media
Workplace
The State

SOCIAL POLICY AND SOCIALIZATION: THE NEED FOR CHILD CARE

BOXES
4-1 Everyday Behavior: Impression
    Management by Students after Exams
4-2 Everyday Behavior: Socialization in
    Mexican American Families

LOOKING AHEAD

- What would happen if a child was reared in total isolation from other people?
- Will identical twins show similarities in personality traits, behavior, and intelligence if reared apart?
- How do we come to develop self-identity?
- What stages of socialization do we pass through during the life cycle?
- How do the family, the school, the peer group, the mass media, the workplace, and the state contribute to the socialization process?
- What are the social implications of placing young children in child care centers?

Jacob and his family are part of the Amish community in Lancaster County, Pennsylvania. The Amish live in a manner quite similar to their nineteenth-century ancestors. They reject most aspects of modernization and contemporary technology; consequently, they shun such conveniences as electricity, automobiles, radio, and television. The Amish maintain their own schools and do not want their children socialized into many norms and values of the dominant culture of the United States. As one example, they are pacifists who oppose all forms of war under any conditions.

As a 14-year-old Amish youth, Jacob is in the final year of his schooling. Over the next few years, he will become a full-time worker on his family's farm, taking breaks only for the three-hour religious services held each morning. On Sunday nights, Jacob will attend the community's "singings," where he will meet young Amish women, sing songs, and enjoy refreshments. (According to the norms of the Amish, however, there is no use of musical instruments or playing of recorded music at these singings.) When he is a bit older, Jacob may bring a date to a singing in his family's horse-drawn buggy. But he will be forbidden to date anyone outside his own Amish community and can marry only with the consent of his deacon.

Jacob is well-aware of the rather different way of life of the "English" (the Amish term for non-Amish people). One summer, he and his friends hitchhiked late at night to a nearby town and saw a movie. His parents learned of his adventure, but like most Amish they are confident that their son will choose to continue living in the Amish community. Indeed, more than 80 percent of Amish children choose the Amish way of life as adults. Given such data, it is likely that Jacob will grow increasingly uncomfortable with his "English" neighbors and will accept the Amish view of the dangers and evils of the outside world (Kephart and Zellner, 1994:28–31).

As was seen in Chapter 3, each culture and subculture has a unique character which shapes the values and behavior of its members. *Socialization* is the process whereby people learn the attitudes, values, and actions appropriate to individuals as members of a particular culture. Just as members of the dominant culture of the United States are socialized to accept use of electricity, automobiles, and television as "normal," Jacob and other members of

Amish families in Pennsylvania reject most aspects of modernization and contemporary technology. Consequently, they shun such conveniences as electricity, automobiles, radio, and television.

Amish subcultures are socialized to accept horse-drawn buggies as a common means of transportation and "singings" without recorded music or musical instruments as a familiar cultural event.

Socialization occurs through human interactions. We will, of course, learn a great deal from those people most important in our lives—immediate family members, best friends, and teachers. But we also learn from people we see on the street, on television, and in films and magazines. From a microsociological perspective, socialization helps us to discover how to behave "properly" and what to expect from others if we follow (or challenge) society's norms and values. From a macrosociological perspective, socialization provides for the passing on of a culture and thereby for the long-term continuance of a society.

Socialization affects the overall cultural practices of a society, and it also shapes our self-images. For example, in the United States, a person who is viewed as "too heavy" or "too short" does not conform to the ideal cultural standard. If he or she is therefore judged unattractive, the evaluation can significantly influence the person's self-esteem. In this sense, socialization experiences can have an impact on the shaping of people's personalities. In everyday speech, the term **personality** is used to refer to a person's typical patterns of attitudes, needs, characteristics, and behavior.

This chapter will examine the role of socialization in human development. It will begin by analyzing the debate concerning the interaction of heredity and environmental factors. Particular attention will be given to how people develop perceptions, feelings, and beliefs about themselves. The chapter will explore the lifelong nature of the socialization process, as well as important agents of socialization, among them the family, schools, and the media. Finally, the social policy section will focus on group child care for young children as a socialization experience.

THE ROLE OF SOCIALIZATION

Researchers have traditionally clashed over the relative importance of biological inheritance and environmental factors in human development. This conflict has been called the *nature versus nurture* (or *heredity versus environment*) debate. Today, most social scientists have moved beyond this debate, acknowledging instead the *interaction* of these variables in shaping human development. However, we can better appreciate how hereditary and environmental factors interact and influence the socialization process if we first examine situations in which one factor operates almost entirely without the other (Homans, 1979).

Environment: The Impact of Isolation

For the first six years of her life, Isabelle lived in almost total seclusion in a darkened room. She had little contact with other people with the exception of her mother, who could neither speak nor hear. Isabelle's mother's parents had been so deeply ashamed of Isabelle's illegitimate birth that they kept her hidden away from the world. Ohio authorities finally discovered the child in 1938 when Isabelle's mother escaped from her parents' home, taking her daughter with her.

When she was discovered, despite being more than 6 years old, Isabelle could not speak. Her only communications with her mother had been by simple gestures. Verbally, Isabelle could merely make various croaking sounds. Marie Mason (1942:299), a speech specialist who worked closely with the child, observed that Isabelle

> . . . was apparently unaware of relationships of any kind. When presented with a ball, she held it in the palm of her hand, then reached out and stroked my face with it. Such behavior is comparable to that of a child of six months. She made no attempt to squeeze it, throw it, or bounce it.

Isabelle had been largely deprived of the typical interactions and socialization experiences of childhood. Since she had actually seen few people, she initially showed a strong fear of strangers and reacted almost like a wild animal when confronted with an unfamiliar person. As she became accustomed to seeing certain individuals, her reaction changed to one of extreme apathy. At first, it was believed that Isabelle was deaf, but she soon began to react to nearby sounds. On tests of maturity, she scored at the level of an infant rather than a 6-year-old.

Specialists developed a systematic training program to help Isabelle adapt to human relationships and socialization. After a few days of training, she made her first attempt to verbalize. Although she started slowly, Isabelle quickly passed through six years of development. In a little over two months, she was speaking in complete sentences. Nine months later, she could identify both words and sentences. Before Isabelle reached the age of 9, she was ready to attend school with other children. By her fourteenth year, she was in sixth grade, doing well in school, and was emotionally well adjusted.

Yet, without an opportunity to experience socialization in her first six years, Isabelle had been hardly human in the social sense when she was first discovered (K. Davis, 1940, 1947:435–437).

Isabelle's experience is important because there are relatively few cases of children deliberately reared in isolation. Her inability to communicate at the time of her discovery—despite her physical and cognitive potential to learn—and her remarkable progress over the next few years underscore the impact of socialization on human development.

Unfortunately, in other cases in which children have been locked away or severely neglected, they have not fared so well as Isabelle. In many instances, the consequences of social isolation have proved to be much more damaging. For example, in 1970 a 13-year-old Californian named Genie was discovered in a room where she had been confined since

FIGURE 4-1 Genie's Sketches

SOURCE: Curtiss, 1977:274.

This sketch was made in 1975 by Genie—a girl who had been isolated for most of her first 14 years until she was discovered by authorities in 1970. In her drawing, her linguist friend (on the left) plays the piano while Genie listens. Genie was 18 when she drew this picture.

Rhesus monkeys display a need for social interaction when they cling to warm, terry cloth "substitute mothers." The monkey here is reaching for milk on a "mother" made of bare wire while remaining on the cloth "mother."

the age of 20 months. During her years of isolation, no family member had spoken to her, nor could she hear anything other than swearing. Since there was no television or radio in her home, she had never listened to the sounds of normal human speech. One year after beginning extensive therapy, Genie's grammar resembled that of a typical 18-month-old child. She made further advances as her therapy continued, but was unable to achieve full language ability (Curtiss, 1977:274, 1981, 1982, 1985:108–109; Pines, 1981; Rigler, 1993; Rymer, 1992a, 1992b, 1993).

The case studies of Isabelle and Genie document the adverse impact of extreme deprivation. Increasingly, researchers are emphasizing the importance of early socialization experiences for humans who grow up in more normal environments. It is now recognized that it is not enough to care for an infant's physical needs; parents must also concern themselves with children's social development. If children are discouraged from having friends, they will be deprived of social interactions with peers that are critical in their emotional growth.

Studies of animals raised in isolation also support the importance of socialization on development. Harry Harlow (1971), a researcher at the primate laboratory of the University of Wisconsin, conducted tests with rhesus monkeys that had been raised away from their mothers and away from contact with other monkeys. As was the case with Isabelle, the rhesus monkeys raised in isolation were found to be fearful and easily frightened. They did not mate, and the females who were artificially inseminated became abusive mothers. Apparently, isolation had had a damaging effect on the monkeys.

A creative aspect of Harlow's experimentation was his use of "artificial mothers." In one such experiment, Harlow presented monkeys raised in isolation with two substitute mothers—one cloth-covered replica and one covered with wire which had the ability to offer milk. Monkey after monkey went to the wire mother for the life-giving milk, yet spent much more time clinging to the more motherlike cloth model. In this study, artificial mothers who provided a comforting physical sensation (conveyed by the terry cloth) were more highly valued than those who provided food. As a result, the infant monkeys developed greater social attachments from their need for warmth, comfort, and intimacy than from their need for milk.

Harlow found that the ill effects of being raised

Drawing by Chas. Addams; ©1981 The New Yorker Magazine, Inc.

"Separated at birth, the Mallifert twins meet accidentally."

in isolation were often irreversible. However, we need to be cautious about drawing parallels between animal and human behavior. Human parents are not covered with cloth (or fur); they use more behavioral means of showing affection for their offspring. Nonetheless, Harlow's research suggests that the harmful consequences of isolation can apply to other primates besides humans (R. W. Brown, 1965:39).

The Influence of Heredity

The isolation studies discussed above may seem to suggest that inheritance can be dismissed as a factor in the social development of humans and animals. However, the interplay between hereditary and environmental factors is evident in a fascinating study involving pairs of twins.

Researchers at the Minnesota Center for Twin and Adoption Research are studying pairs of identical twins reared apart to determine what similarities, if any, they show in personality traits, behavior, and intelligence. Thus far, the preliminary results from the available twin studies indicate that both genetic factors and socialization experiences are influential in human development. Certain characteristics, such as twins' temperaments, voice patterns, and nervous habits, appear to be strikingly similar even in twins reared apart, thereby suggesting that these qualities may be linked to hereditary causes. However, there are far greater differences between identical twins reared apart in terms of attitudes, values, types of mates chosen, and even drinking habits. In examining clusters of personality traits among such twins, the Minnesota studies have found marked similarities in their tendency toward leadership or dominance, but significant differences in their need for intimacy, comfort, and assistance.

Researchers have also been impressed with the similar scores on intelligence tests of twins reared apart, although in roughly similar social settings. Most of the identical twins register scores even closer than those that would be expected if the same person took a test twice. At the same time, however, identical twins brought up in *dramatically different* social environments score quite differently on intelligence tests—a finding that supports the impact of socialization on human development (Bailey et al., 1993; Bouchard, 1991; Byne and Parsons, 1993; Horgan, 1993).

In reviewing the studies of twin pairs and other relevant research, one should proceed with a significant degree of caution. Widely broadcast findings have often been based on extremely small samples and preliminary analysis. For example, one study (not involving twin pairs) was frequently cited as confirming genetic links with behavior. Yet the researchers had to retract their conclusions after the sample was increased from 81 to 91 cases and two of the original 81 cases were reclassified. After these changes in the study were completed, the initial findings were no longer valid. Critics add that the studies on twin pairs have not provided satisfactory information concerning the extent to which these separated identical twins may have had contact with each other, even though they were "raised apart." Such interactions—especially if they were extensive—could call into question the validity of the twin studies (Kelsoe et al., 1989).

Psychologist Leon Kamin fears that overgeneralizing from the Minnesota twin results—and granting too much importance to the impact of heredity—may be used to blame the poor and downtrodden for their unfortunate condition. As the debate over nature versus nurture continues, we can certainly anticipate numerous replication research efforts to clarify the interplay between hereditary and environmental factors in human development (Horgan, 1993; Leo, 1987; Plomin, 1989; Wallis, 1987:67).

Sociobiology

As part of the continuing debate on the relative influences of heredity and the environment, there has been renewed interest in sociobiology in recent years. *Sociobiology* is the systematic study of the biological bases of social behavior. Sociobiologists basically apply naturalist Charles Darwin's principles of natural selection to the study of social behavior.

They assume that particular forms of behavior become genetically linked to a species if they contribute to its fitness to survive (van den Berghe, 1978:20). In its extreme form, sociobiology resembles biological determinism by suggesting that all behavior is totally the result of genetic or biological factors and that social interactions play no role in shaping people's conduct.

Sociobiology does not seek to describe individual behavior on the level of "Why is Fred more aggressive than Jim?" Rather, sociobiologists focus on how human nature is affected by the genetic composition of a group of people who share certain characteristics (such as men or women, or members of isolated tribal bands). In general, sociobiologists have stressed the basic genetic heritage that is shared by all humans and have shown little interest in speculating about alleged differences between racial groups or nationalities.

Many social scientists have strongly attacked the main tenets of sociobiology as expressed by Edward O. Wilson (1975, 1977, 1978), a zoologist at Harvard University. Some researchers insist that intellectual interest in sociobiology will only deflect serious study of the more significant factor influencing human behavior—socialization. Yet Lois Wladis Hoffman (1985), in her presidential address to the Society for the Psychological Study of Social Issues, argued that sociobiology poses a valuable challenge to social scientists to better document their own research. Interactionists, for example, could show how social behavior is not programmed by human biology but instead adjusts continually to the attitudes and responses of others.

The conflict perspective shares with sociobiology a recognition that human beings do not like to be dominated, yet there the similarity ends. Conflict theorists (like functionalists and interactionists) believe that social reality is defined by people's behavior rather than by their genetic structure. Consequently, conflict theorists fear that the sociobiological approach could be used as an argument against efforts to assist disadvantaged people, such as schoolchildren who are not competing successfully (A. Caplan, 1978; M. Harris, 1980:514).

Wilson has argued that there should be parallel studies of human behavior with a focus on both genetic and social causes. Certainly most social scientists would agree that there is a biological basis for social behavior. But there is less support for the more extreme positions taken by certain advocates of sociobiology (Gove, 1987; see also A. Fisher, 1992; Lopreato, 1992).

THE SELF AND SOCIALIZATION

We all have various perceptions, feelings, and beliefs about who we are and what we are like. How do we come to develop these? Do they change as we age? We were not born with these understandings. Building on the work of George Herbert Mead (1964b), sociobiologists recognize that we create our own designation: the self. The *self* represents the sum total of people's conscious perception of their own identity as distinct from others. It is not a static phenomenon, but continues to develop and change throughout our lives.

Sociologists and psychologists alike have expressed interest in how the individual develops and modifies a sense of self because of social interaction. The work of sociologists Charles Horton Cooley and George Herbert Mead, pioneers of the interactionist approach, has been especially useful in furthering our understanding of these important issues (Gecas, 1982).

Sociological Approaches to the Self

Cooley: Looking-Glass Self In the early 1900s, Charles Horton Cooley advanced the belief that we learn who we are by interacting with others. Our view of ourselves, then, comes not only from direct contemplation of our personal qualities, but also from our impressions of how others perceive us. Cooley used the phrase *looking-glass self* to emphasize that the self is the product of our social interactions with other people.

The process of developing a self-identity or self-concept has three phases. First, we imagine how we present ourselves to others—to relatives, friends, even strangers on the street. Then we imagine how others evaluate us (attractive, intelligent, shy, or strange). Finally, we develop some sort of feeling about ourselves, such as respect or shame, as a result of these impressions (Cooley, 1902:152; M. Howard, 1989:249).

A critical but subtle aspect of Cooley's looking-glass self is that the self results from an individual's "imagination" of how others view him or her. As a result, we can develop self-identities based on incorrect perceptions of how others see us. A student may react strongly to a teacher's criticism and decide (wrongly) that the instructor views the student as stupid. This misperception can easily be converted into a negative self-identity through the following process: (1) the teacher criticized me, (2) the teacher must think that I'm stupid, (3) I *am* stupid. Yet self-identities are also subject to change. If the student above received an "A" at the end of the course, he or she might no longer feel stupid.

Mead: Stages of the Self George Herbert Mead (1930:706) acknowledged to Charles Horton Cooley that he was "profoundly indebted" to Cooley's "insight and constructive thought." We are in turn indebted to Mead for continuing Cooley's exploration of interactionist theory and for his contributions to sociological understanding of the self. Mead (1934, 1964a) developed a useful model of the process by which the self emerges, defined by three distinct stages.

During the *preparatory stage,* children merely imitate the people around them, especially family members with whom they continually interact. Thus, a small child will bang on a piece of wood while a parent is engaged in carpentry work or will try to throw a ball if an older sibling is doing so nearby.

As they grow older, children become more adept at using symbols to communicate with others. *Symbols* are the gestures, objects, and language which form the basis of human communication. By interacting with relatives and friends, as well as by watching cartoons on television and looking at picture books, children begin to understand the use of symbols. Like spoken languages, symbols vary from culture to culture and even between subcultures. "Thumbs up" is not always a positive gesture; nodding the head up and down does *not* always mean "yes." As part of the socialization process, children learn the symbols of their particular culture (Ekman et al., 1984).

Mead was among the first to analyze the relationship of symbols to socialization. As children develop skill in communicating through symbols, they gradually become more aware of social relation-

During the preparatory stage *described by George Herbert Mead, children imitate the people around them, especially family members with whom they continually interact.*

ships. As a result, during the *play stage,* the child becomes able to imitate the actions of others, including adults. Just as an actor "becomes" a character, a child becomes a doctor, parent, superhero, or ship captain.

Mead noted that an important aspect of the play stage is role taking. ***Role taking*** is the process of mentally assuming the perspective of another, thereby enabling one to respond from that imagined viewpoint. For example, a young child will gradually learn when it is best to ask a parent for favors. If the parent usually comes home from work in a bad mood, the child will wait until after dinner when the parent is more relaxed and approachable. Although for children role taking may involve conforming to the behavior of others, for adolescents and adults role taking is more selective and creative (R. Turner, 1962).

In Mead's third stage, the *game stage,* the child of about 8 or 9 years old begins to consider several tasks and relationships simultaneously. At this point in development, children grasp not only their own social positions, but also those of others around them. Consider a girl or boy of this age who is part of a scout troop out on a weekend hike in the mountains. The child must understand what he or she is expected to do, but also must recognize the responsibilities of other scouts (as well as the leaders). This is the final stage of development under

Mead's model; the child can now respond to numerous members of the social environment.

Mead uses the term ***generalized others*** to refer to the child's awareness of the attitudes, viewpoints, and expectations of society as a whole. Simply put, this concept suggests that when an individual acts, he or she takes into account an entire group of people. For example, a child who reaches this level of development will not act courteously merely to please a particular parent. Rather, the child comes to understand that courtesy is a widespread social value endorsed by parents, teachers, and religious leaders.

At this developmental stage, children can take a more sophisticated view of people and the social environment. They now understand what specific occupations and social positions are and no longer equate Mr. Williams only with the role of "librarian" or Ms. Franks only with "principal." It has become clear to the child that Mr. Williams can be a librarian, a parent, and a marathon runner at the same time and that Ms. Franks is but one of many principals in our society. Thus, the child has reached a new level of sophistication in his or her observations of individuals and institutions.

Mead is best known for this theory of the self. According to Mead (1964b), the self begins as a privileged, central position in a person's world. Young children picture themselves as the focus of everything around them and find it difficult to consider the perspectives of others. For example, when shown a mountain scene and asked to describe what an observer on the opposite side of the mountain sees (such as a lake or hikers), young children nevertheless describe only objects visible from their own vantage point. This childhood tendency to place ourselves at the center of events never entirely disappears. When an instructor is ready to return term papers or examinations and mentions that certain students did exceptionally well, we often assume that we fall into that select group (Fenigstein, 1984).

As people mature, the self changes and begins to reflect greater concern about the reactions of others. Parents, friends, coworkers, coaches, and teachers are often among those who play a major role in shaping a person's self. Mead used the term *significant others* to refer to those individuals who are most important in the development of the self (Schlenker, 1985:12–13).

In some instances, studies concerning significant others have generated controversy among researchers. For example, it has often been argued that African American adolescents are more "peer-oriented" than their White counterparts because of presumed weaknesses in Black families. However, recent investigations indicate that these hasty conclusions were based on limited studies focusing on less affluent Blacks. Indeed, there appears to be little difference in who African Americans and Whites from similar economic backgrounds regard as their significant others (Giordano et al., 1993; Juhasz, 1989).

Courtesy American Sociological Association

Erving Goffman (1922–1982) made a distinctive contribution to sociology by popularizing a particular type of interactionist method known as the dramaturgical approach.

Goffman: Presentation of the Self   As was seen in Chapter 1, the interactionist approach, which owes a great deal to both Cooley and Mead, emphasizes the micro (or small-scale) level of analysis. Thus, this sociological perspective is especially suited to an examination of how the self develops. Erving Goffman, a recent sociologist associated with the interactionist perspective, suggested that many of our daily activities involve attempts to convey impressions of who we are.

Early in life, the individual learns to slant his or her presentation of the self in order to create distinctive appearances and to satisfy particular audiences. Goffman (1959) refers to this altering of the presentation of the self as *impression management*. Box 4-1 provides an everyday example of this concept by describing how students engage in impression management after examination grades have been awarded.

In examining such everyday social interactions, Goffman makes so many explicit parallels to the theater that his view has been termed the *dramaturgical approach*. According to this perspective, people can be seen as resembling performers in action. For example, clerks may try to appear busier than they actually are if a supervisor happens to be watching them. Waiters and waitresses may "not see" a customer who wants more coffee if they are on a break.

Face-work is another aspect of the self to which Goffman (1959) has drawn attention. Maintaining the proper image can be essential to continued social interaction; face-saving behavior must be initiated if the self suffers because of embarrassment or some form of rejection. Thus, in response to a rejection at a singles' bar, a person may engage in face-work by saying, "I really wasn't feeling well anyway" or "There isn't an interesting person in this entire crowd."

Goffman's approach is generally regarded as an insightful perspective on everyday life, but it is not without its critics. Writing from a conflict perspective, sociologist Alvin Gouldner (1970) sees Goffman's work as implicitly reaffirming the status quo, including social class inequalities. Using Gouldner's critique, one might ask if women and minorities are expected to deceive both themselves and others while paying homage to those in power.

Sociologists Daniel Albas and Cheryl Albas (1988) drew upon Erving Goffman's concept of impression management to examine the strategies that college students employ to create desired appearances after grades have been awarded and examination papers returned. Albas and Albas divide these encounters into three categories: those between students who have all received high grades (Ace-Ace encounters), those between students who have received high grades and those who have received low or even failing grades (Ace-Bomber encounters), and those between students who have all received low grades (Bomber-Bomber encounters).

Ace-Ace encounters occur in a rather open atmosphere because there is comfort in sharing one's high mark with another high achiever. It is even acceptable to violate the norm of modesty and brag when among other Aces, since, as one student admitted, "It's much easier to admit a high mark to someone who has done better than you, or at least as well."

Ace-Bomber encounters are often sensitive. Bombers generally attempt to avoid such exchanges because "you . . . emerge looking like the dumb one" or "feel like you are lazy or unreliable." When forced into interactions with Aces, Bombers work to appear gracious and congratulatory. For their part, Aces offer sympathy and support for the dissatisfied Bombers and even rationalize their own "lucky" high scores. To help Bombers save face, Aces may emphasize the difficulty of the course and unfairness of the exam.

Bomber-Bomber encounters tend to be closed, reflecting the group effort to wall off the feared disdain of others. Yet, within the safety of these encounters, Bombers openly share their disappointment and engage in expressions of mutual self-pity that they themselves call "pity parties." Face-saving excuses are developed for the Bombers' poor performances, such as "I wasn't feeling well all week" or "I had four exams and two papers due that week." If the grade distribution in a class included particularly low scores, Bombers may engage in scapegoating the professor, who will be attacked as a sadist, a slave driver, or simply an incompetent teacher.

As is evident from these descriptions, students' impression-management strategies are constrained by society's informal norms regarding modesty and consideration for less successful peers. In classroom settings, as in the workplace and in other types of human interactions, efforts at impression management are most intense when status differentials are most pronounced—as in encounters between the high-scoring Aces and the low-scoring Bombers.

Moreover, as discussed in Box 1-2 (refer back to page 24), sociologist Carol Brooks Gardner (1989) has suggested that Goffman's view of interactions in public places gives insufficient attention to women's well-founded fear of the sexual harassment, assault, and rape that can occur there. In considering impression management and the other concepts developed by Goffman, sociologists must remember that by *describing* social reality one is not necessarily endorsing its harsh impact on many individuals and groups (S. Williams, 1986:357–358).

Goffman's work represents a logical progression of the sociological efforts begun by Cooley and Mead on how personality is acquired through socialization and how we manage the presentation of our self to others. Cooley stressed the process by which we come to create a self; Mead focused on how the self develops as we learn to interact with others; Goffman emphasized the ways in which we consciously create images of ourselves for others.

Psychological Approaches to the Self

Psychologists have shared the interest of Cooley, Mead, and other sociologists in the development of the self. Early work in psychology, such as that of Sigmund Freud (1856–1939), stressed the role of inborn drives—among them the drive for sexual gratification—in channeling human behavior.

Other psychologists, such as Jean Piaget and Lawrence Kohlberg, have emphasized the stages through which human beings progress as the self develops.

Like Charles Horton Cooley and George Herbert Mead, Freud believed that the self is a social product and that aspects of one's personality are influenced by others (especially one's parents). However, unlike Cooley and Mead, he suggested that the self has components that are always fighting with each other. According to Freud, people are in constant conflict between their natural impulsive instincts and societal constraints. Part of us seeks limitless pleasure, while another part seeks out rational behavior. By interacting with others, we learn the expectations of society and then select behavior most appropriate to our own culture. (Of course, as Freud was well-aware, we sometimes distort reality and behave irrationally.)

Research on newborn babies by the Swiss child psychologist Jean Piaget (1896–1980) has underscored the importance of social interactions in developing a sense of self. Piaget found that newborns have no self in the sense of a looking-glass image. Ironically, though, they are quite self-centered; they demand that all attention be directed toward them. Newborns have not yet separated themselves from the universe of which they are a part. For these babies, the phrase "you and me" has no meaning; they understand only "me." However, as they mature, children are gradually socialized into social relationships even within their rather self-centered world.

In his well-known *cognitive theory of development,* Piaget (1954) identifies four stages in the development of children's thought processes. In the first, or *sensorimotor,* stage, young children use their senses to make discoveries. For example, through touching they discover that their hands are actually a part of themselves. During the second, or *preoperational,* stage, children begin to use words and symbols to distinguish objects and ideas. The milestone in the third, or *concrete operational,* stage is that children engage in abstract thinking. They learn that if a formless lump of clay is shaped into a snake, it is still the same clay. Finally, in the fourth, or *formal operational,* stage, adolescents are capable of sophisticated abstract thought and can deal with ideas and values in a logical manner.

Piaget has suggested that moral development becomes an important part of socialization as children become able to think more abstractly. When children learn the rules of a game such as checkers or jacks, they are learning to obey societal norms. Those under 8 years old display a rather basic level of morality: rules are rules, and there is no concept of "extenuating circumstances." However, as they mature, children become capable of greater autonomy and begin to experience moral dilemmas as to what constitutes proper behavior.

According to Jean Piaget, children's development is based on social interaction. As they grow older, children give increasing attention to how other people think and why they act in particular ways. In order to develop a distinctive personality, each of us needs opportunities to interact with others. As we saw earlier, both Isabelle and Genie were deprived of the chance for normal social interactions (Kitchener, 1991).

SOCIALIZATION AND THE LIFE CYCLE

Stages of Socialization

The socialization process continues throughout all stages of the human life cycle. In cultures less complex than our own, stages of development are marked by specific ceremonies. Many societies have definite *rites of passage* that dramatize and validate changes in a person's status. For example, a young Aboriginal woman in Australia will be honored at a ceremony at the time of her first menstruation. During these festivities, her first, unborn daughter is betrothed to a grown man. Hence the expression is heard that "there is no such thing as an unmarried woman" (Goodale, 1971). For the Aborigines, there is a sharp dividing line between childhood and the responsibilities of adult life.

This is not the case within our culture, but several psychologists and sociologists have nonetheless assigned particular labels to various periods of socialization. In examining the socialization process in the United States, it is important to understand that we do not necessarily move from one stage to another in the clear-cut way that we are promoted from one grade in school to another. This may lead to some ambiguity and confusion as we develop ourselves: At a certain age and level of maturity, are we children or adolescents? At another, are we adolescents or adults?

The United States does bear some resemblance to simpler societies such as that of the Aborigines in that we have events marking the assumption of new roles and statuses. The wedding represents a rite of passage in our society; yet, there is no one ceremony that clearly marks the shift from childhood to adulthood. Instead, we go through a prolonged period of transition known as *adolescence*.

This transition varies depending on certain social factors, especially social class. A person from a poor background may not have any alternatives but to work full time at a rather early age. Because of the need to contribute to the family income or to become financially self-supporting, such a young person may not have the luxury of delaying entry into the labor force by continuing his or her education.

Even after the attainment of adulthood, a person will pass through a series of developmental stages. On the basis of research involving males in the United States, psychologist Daniel Levinson (1978) identified three major transitional periods that occur during men's lifetimes. One of these begins at about age 40. Men in the United States often experience a stressful period of self-evaluation, commonly known as the **midlife crisis,** in which they realize that they have not achieved basic goals and ambitions and have little time left to do so. Thus, Levinson (1978:199) found that 80 percent of men surveyed experienced tumultuous midlife conflicts within the self and with the external world.

Levinson's formulation was developed to describe the life cycle of *men* in the United States. While his conclusions are relevant for some women—especially those who follow the traditional career patterns of men—they do not necessarily reflect the typical life cycle for women. A key aspect of Levinson's work is the notion that, as youths, men have a dream of what the adult world is like—a vision that creates excitement and a sense of possibility. Yet, until recently, most women were socialized into visions of the future centering on marriage and children rather than achievements in the paid labor force. Moreover, most women carry the role of "mother" throughout their lives; this role

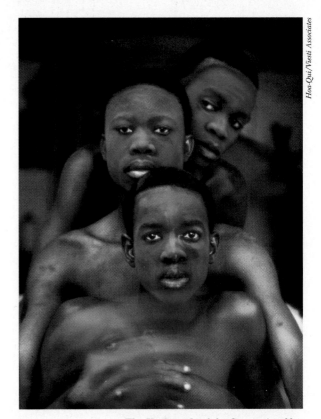

The Kota people of the Congo view blue as the color of death. As a traditional rite of passage into adulthood, adolescent males paint themselves blue to symbolize the death of childhood. Villagers may pretend not to recognize these "dead" youths until they have journeyed into the bush and completed a ritual transformation into adults. Interestingly, as an accommodation to modern life in Africa, this Kota rite of passage now takes place somewhat later in life so that young males can complete their public schooling.

has traditionally been viewed as more time-consuming and more important than the role of "father" is for men. While such patterns are changing, as we will see in Chapters 11 and 13, expectations at different stages of socialization are not yet the same for men and women (Baruch et al., 1983; see also P. Brown, 1987).

Some researchers maintain that the midlife crisis is clearly evident in *both* sexes. In her books *Passages* and *Pathfinders,* Gail Sheehy (1976, 1981:63) found that women in the United States experience fear and confusion in their midlife years as they encounter gaps between their youthful illusions and their day-to-day lives. Sheehy's studies suggest that midlife turmoil may begin somewhat earlier for women than for men, often at about age 35. An important factor in the midlife crises of women is the fact that they typically outlive male contemporaries, including their husbands. Consequently, as she reaches midlife, a woman faces a future in which she may eventually live alone and may become dependent on her children (Baruch et al., 1983:238–241; Rosenfeld and Stark, 1987:64, 66).

Is the phenomenon of the midlife crisis unique to the United States? In some cultures, people are given specific goals during childhood which they are able to achieve early in life. However, in our society people have unusual flexibility in selecting objectives and aspirations. This has an unintended consequence: it leaves a great deal of room for indecision or even failure.

Some of the most difficult socialization challenges (and rites of passage) are encountered in the later years of life. Assessing one's accomplishments, coping with declining physical abilities, experiencing retirement, and facing the inevitability of death may lead to painful adjustments. Old age is further complicated by the negative way in which the elderly are viewed and treated in many societies, including the United States. Older people's self-image may weaken if they are influenced by the common stereotype of the elderly as helpless and dependent. However, as we will explore more fully in Chapter 12, many older people continue to lead active, productive, fulfilled lives—whether within the paid labor force or as part of retirement.

Anticipatory Socialization and Resocialization

The development of a social self is literally a life-long transformation which begins in the crib and continues as one prepares for death. Two types of socialization occur at many points throughout the life cycle: anticipatory socialization and resocialization.

Preparation for many aspects of adult life begins with anticipatory socialization during childhood and adolescence and continues throughout our lives as we prepare for new responsibilities. *Anticipatory socialization* refers to the processes of socialization in which a person "rehearses" for future positions, occupations, and social relationships. A culture can function more efficiently and smoothly if members become acquainted with the norms, values, and behavior associated with a social position before actually assuming that status.

The process of anticipatory socialization is evident in the families of snakers (a term they prefer to *snake charmers*) in India. At the age of 5 or 6, the son of a snaker will begin to touch the snakes he has observed all his life. The boy will soon learn how to catch snakes and will become familiar with the habits of each species. In snaker families, it is a matter of intense pride when a boy follows in the footsteps of his father, his grandfather, and earlier male ancestors (Skafte, 1979).

Occasionally, as we assume new social and occupational positions, we find it necessary to unlearn our previous orientation. *Resocialization* refers to the process of discarding former behavior patterns and accepting new ones as part of a transition in one's life. Often resocialization occurs when there is an explicit effort to transform an individual, as is true in reform schools, therapy groups, prisons, political indoctrination camps, and religious conversion settings. Much more so than socialization in general or even anticipatory socialization, the process of resocialization typically involves considerable stress for the individual (Gecas, 1992:1869).

Resocialization is particularly effective when it occurs within a total institution. Erving Goffman (1961) coined the term *total institutions* to refer to institutions, such as prisons, the military, mental hospitals, and convents, which regulate all aspects of a person's life under a single authority. The total institution is generally cut off from the rest of society and therefore provides for all the needs of its members. Quite literally, the crew of a merchant vessel at sea becomes part of a total institution. So elaborate are its requirements, so all-encompassing are its activities, that a total institution often represents a miniature society.

Goffman (1961) has identified four common traits of total institutions. First, all aspects of life are conducted in the same place and are under the control of a single authority. Second, any activities within the institution are conducted in the com-

A prison "boot camp" is an example of a total institution which regulates all aspects of a person's life. In this military-style "boot camp" for first-time offenders in California, young men live under tough, "no-nonsense" discipline.

pany of others in the same circumstances—for example, novices in a convent or army recruits. Third, the authorities devise rules and schedule activities without consulting participants. Finally, all aspects of life within a total institution are designed to fulfill the purpose of the organization. Thus, all activities in a monastery are centered on prayer and communion with God (Davies, 1989; P. Rose et al., 1979:321–322).

Individuality is often lost within total institutions. For example, upon entering prison to begin "doing time," a person may experience the humiliation of a ***degradation ceremony*** as he or she is stripped of clothing, jewelry, and other personal possessions (H. Garfinkel, 1956). Even the person's self is taken away to some extent; the prison inmate loses his or her name and becomes known to authorities as No. 72716. From this point on, daily routines are scheduled with little or no room for personal initiative. The institution is experienced as an overbearing social environment; the individual becomes secondary and rather invisible.

AGENTS OF SOCIALIZATION

As we have seen, the culture of the United States is defined by rather gradual movements from one stage of socialization to the next. The continuing and lifelong socialization process involves many different social forces which influence our lives and alter our self-images. The family is the most important agent of socialization in the United States, especially for children. Five other agents of socialization will be given particular attention in this chapter: the school, the peer group, the mass media, the workplace, and the state. The role of religion in socializing young people into society's norms and values will be explored in Chapter 14.

Family

The family is the institution most closely associated with the process of socialization. Obviously, one of its primary functions is the care and rearing of children. We experience socialization first as babies and infants living in families; it is here that we develop an initial sense of self. Most parents seek to help their children become competent adolescents and self-sufficient adults, which means socializing them into the norms and values of both the family and the larger society. In this process, adults themselves experience socialization as they adjust to becoming spouses, parents, and in-laws (Gecas, 1981).

The lifelong process of learning begins shortly after birth. Since newborns can hear, see, smell, taste, and feel heat, cold, and pain, they orient themselves to the surrounding world. Human beings, especially family members, constitute an important part of the social environment of the newborn. People minister to the baby's needs by feeding, cleansing, and carrying the baby.

The family of a newborn and other caretakers are not concerned with teaching social skills per se. Nevertheless, babies are hardly asocial. An infant enters an organized society, becomes part of a generation, and typically enters into a family. Depending on how they are treated, infants can develop strong social attachments and dependency on others.

Most infants go through a relatively formal period of socialization generally called *habit training*. Schedules are imposed for eating and sleeping, the termination of breast or bottle feeding, and the acceptance of new foods. In these and other ways, infants can be viewed as objects of socialization, yet they also function as socializers. Even as the behavior of a baby is being modified by interactions with people and the environment, the baby is causing others to change their behavior patterns. He or she converts adults into mothers and fathers, who, in turn, assist the baby in progressing into childhood (Rheingold, 1969).

As both Charles Horton Cooley and George Herbert Mead noted, the development of the self is a critical aspect of the early years of one's life. In the United States, such social development includes exposure to cultural assumptions regarding gender and race. African American parents, for example, have learned that children as young as 2 years old can absorb negative messages about Blacks in children's books, toys, and television shows—all of which are designed primarily for White consumers (J. White, 1993).

Children also are influenced by cultural messages regarding gender. The term **gender roles** refers to expectations regarding the proper behavior, attitudes, and activities of males and females. For example, "toughness" has been traditionally seen as masculine—and desirable only in men—while "tenderness" has been viewed as feminine. As we will see in Chapter 11, other cultures do not necessarily assign these qualities to each gender in the way that our culture does.

As the primary agents of childhood socialization, parents play a critical role in guiding children into those gender roles deemed appropriate in a society. Other adults, older siblings, the mass media, and religious and educational institutions also have noticeable impact on a child's socialization into feminine and masculine norms. A culture or subculture may require that one sex or the other take primary responsibility for socialization of children, economic support of the family, or religious or intellectual leadership. Socialization within Mexican American families—including socialization into traditional gender roles—is examined in Box 4-2.

Psychologist Shirley Weitz (1977:60–110) has suggested that differential treatment of children by adults is an influential aspect of gender-role socialization. Let us consider a hypothetical example of differential treatment of children which begins in the family. Ron and Louise are twins who both show an unusual interest in science at an early age. For his birthdays, Ron is given chemistry sets, telescopes, microscopes, and the like; however, despite asking for similar gifts, Louise is given miniature dollhouses, beautiful dresses, and dancing lessons.

When the twins are in junior high school, teachers take note of Ron's love for science. They encourage him to do special projects, to help with their laboratory work, and to join the science club. Louise is given no such encouragement; in fact, one teacher considers her fascination with astronomy "strange" for a girl. By the twins' high school years, Ron is known as a "science whiz." The guidance counselor suggests that he attend a college with a strong science program in order to achieve his goal of becoming a biologist. Louise has realized that she would like to become an astronomer, but the counselor and her parents pressure her into preparing for a career as an early childhood teacher—a career which they see as more suitable for a woman.

During their college years, Ron and Louise might develop self-images as "scientist" and "teacher," respectively. On the other hand, Louise might get to college, switch her major, and become an astronomer despite everyone's opposition. Neither of these young people is a passive actor who will inevitably follow the traditional gender roles of the United States. Yet it can be extremely difficult to pursue a career, or any other type of life choice, if one's parents, teachers, and society as a whole seem to be telling you that you are "unmasculine" or "unfeminine" for doing so.

Without question, differential socialization has a powerful impact on the development of females

BOX 4-2 · EVERYDAY BEHAVIOR

SOCIALIZATION IN MEXICAN AMERICAN FAMILIES

In 1987, San Antonio mayor Henry Cisneros, the first Hispanic ever to serve as chief executive of a major city in the United States, announced that he was dropping out of the race for governor of Texas. His new son was ailing from birth defects, and Cisneros felt that his family responsibilities precluded staying active in politics. Many observers saw Cisneros's decision as typical of the high value that Mexican Americans (also known as *Chicanos*) place on the family (Schaefer, 1993:293).

The Mexican American subculture has long emphasized traditional gender-role socialization, with boys being socialized to expect male dominance while girls prepare to focus on the needs of their future families. An important rite of passage for Mexican American girls is known as the *quinceañera*. While some traditions of Mexican culture have been discarded by Chicanos, this ceremony—marking the transition from girl to woman—has become more popular over the last 30 years. Although there are variations in the quinceañera, Mexican American girls typically participate in a daylong religious retreat, a mass, and an elaborate (and sometimes very expensive) dance or cotillion. The weekends before the dance are filled with prepara-

tory rehearsals involving many family members. During the dance itself, a Catholic bishop often will make an appearance and accept contributions from the girl's father (Garza, 1993).

In socializing male children, Mexican culture and the Mexican American subculture emphasize ***machismo,*** a term which refers to a sense of virility, personal worth, and pride in one's maleness. Machismo may be demonstrated in many differing ways. For some men, bold challenges or success in fights may establish virility; others may simply attempt to be attractive to women. Mexican Americans are also believed to be more familistic than other subcultures. ***Familism*** refers to pride in the extended family expressed through the maintenance of close ties and strong obligations to kinfolk outside the immediate family (S. Wallace, 1984). Neither machismo nor familism is unique to Mexican Americans and both may be found in other cultures and subcultures.

Research data now suggest that machismo and familism are in decline among Mexican Americans. The feminist movement in both the United States and Latin America has challenged traditional gender-role socialization and has changed the ways in which men and women

interact. Feminists argue that Chicano males have falsely glorified machismo, thereby giving this aspect of Mexican culture more attention than it deserves. Moreover, as a result of industrialization, urbanization, upward mobility, and assimilation, the traditional values of machismo and familism are likely to become more of a historical footnote with each passing generation. Like other immigrants from Europe and Asia, Mexican Americans can be expected to gradually adopt the norms of the dominant culture of the United States regarding family life (Becerra, 1988; J. Moore and Pachon, 1985:96–98).

The distinctive socialization experience of Mexican American children also includes an unfortunate and sometimes bitter aspect. Like girls and boys from other racial and ethnic minorities, Mexican American youths will experience resentment, prejudice, and discrimination because of their appearance, language, accent, and customs. Along with participation in school, religious activities, sports, and dating, young Mexican Americans will learn how to confront, manage, and cope with the particular difficulties of being part of an identifiable minority within the dominant culture of the United States.

and males in the United States. Indeed, the gender roles first encountered in early childhood are often a factor in defining a child's popularity. Sociologist Patricia Adler and her colleagues (P. Adler et al., 1992) observed elementary school children and found that boys typically achieved high status on

the basis of their athletic ability, "coolness," toughness, social skills, and success in relationships with girls. By contrast, girls gained popularity owing to their parents' economic background and their own physical appearance, social skills, and academic success.

As an example of reverse socialization, many children and adolescents teach parents how to play video games or— even more broadly—how to use computers.

Like other elements of culture, socialization patterns are not fixed. In the last 20 years, for example, there has been a sustained challenge to traditional gender-role socialization in the United States, due in good part to the efforts of the feminist movement (see Chapter 11). Nevertheless, despite such changes, children growing up in the 1990s are hardly free of traditional gender roles. As Letty Cottin Pogrebin (1981:380), a founder and editor of *Ms.* magazine, wondered, how many parents would move a 6-year-old girl's toy chest into the room of their 6-year-old boy with confidence that he would enjoy its contents?

Interactionists remind us that socialization concerning not only masculinity and femininity, but also marriage and parenthood, begins in childhood as a part of family life. Children observe their parents as they express affection, deal with finances, quarrel, complain about in-laws, and so forth. This represents an informal process of anticipatory socialization. The child develops a tentative model of what being married and being a parent are like. We will explore socialization for marriage and parenthood more fully in Chapter 13.

As noted earlier, children function within the family as agents of socialization themselves. The term *reverse socialization* refers to the process whereby people normally being socialized are at the same time socializing their socializers. For example, young people may affect the way their parents (and other adults) dress, eat, and even think. Sociologist John Peters (1985) studied reverse socialization by surveying the parents of his college students in Canada. Peters found that these parents had been influenced by their children in such areas as sports, politics, clothing, physical appearance, and sexuality (see also Thorne, 1987:95). Anthropologist Margaret Mead (1970:65–91) has suggested that reverse socialization is greatest in societies undergoing rapid social change; in such societies, the young socialize the old to new customs and values.

School

Like the family, schools have an explicit mandate to socialize people in the United States—and especially children—into the norms and values of our cultures. As conflict theorists Samuel Bowles and Herbert Gintis (1976) have observed, schools in this country foster competition through built-in systems of reward and punishment, such as grades and evaluations by teachers. Consequently, a child who is working intently to learn a new skill can nevertheless come to feel stupid and unsuccessful. However, as the self matures, children become capable of increasingly realistic assessments of their intellectual, physical, and social abilities.

Functionalists point out that, as agents of socialization, schools fulfill the function of teaching recruits the values and customs of the larger society. Conflict theorists concur with this observation, but add that schools can reinforce the divisive aspects of society, especially those of social class. For example, higher education in the United States is quite costly despite the existence of financial aid programs. Students from affluent backgrounds thus have an advantage in gaining access to universities and professional training. At the same time, less affluent young people may never receive the preparation that would qualify them for our society's best-paying and most prestigious jobs. The contrast between the functionalist and conflict views of education will be discussed in more detail in Chapter 16.

In teaching students the values and customs of the larger society, schools in the United States have traditionally socialized children into conventional gender roles. Professors of education Myra Sadker and David Sadker (1985:54, 1994) note that "although many believe that classroom sexism disappeared in the early '70s, it hasn't." Indeed, a report released in 1992 by the American Association of University Women—which summarized 1331 studies of girls in school—concludes that schools in the United States favor boys over girls.

According to this report, girls show a disturbing pattern of *downward* intellectual mobility compared with boys, resulting from differential treatment based on gender. Teachers praise boys more than girls and offer boys more academic assistance. Boys receive praise for the intellectual content of their work, whereas girls are more likely to be praised for being neat. Teachers reward boys for assertiveness (for example, calling out answers without raising their hands) while reprimanding girls for similar behavior. Finally, girls often are not expected or encouraged to pursue higher-level mathematics or science courses. The report concludes that girls are less likely than boys to reach their academic potential and insists that the "system must change" (American Association of University Women, 1992:84).

In other cultures as well, schools serve socialization functions. During the 1980s, for example, Japanese parents and educators were distressed to realize that children were gradually losing the knack of eating with chopsticks (which seemed to symbolize a failure to socialize a new generation into the nation's traditional norms and values). Having been seduced by spoons and cheeseburgers, some children could not use *hashi* (chopsticks) at all. Consequently, schools were chosen as the proper institution to remedy the situation. Whereas only 10 percent of school lunch programs provided chopsticks in 1975, this figure had risen to 69 percent in 1983 and to 90 percent by the end of the decade (Hiatt, 1988).

Peer Group

As a child grows older, the family becomes somewhat less important in his or her social development. Instead, peer groups increasingly assume the role of George Herbert Mead's significant others. Within the peer group, young people associate with others who are approximately their own age and who often enjoy a similar social status.

Peer groups, such as friendship cliques, youth gangs, and special-interest clubs, frequently assist adolescents in gaining some degree of independence from parents and other authority figures. As we will study in more detail in Chapter 7, conforming to peers' behavior is an example of the socialization process at work. If all of one's friends have successfully battled for the right to stay out until midnight on a Saturday night, it may seem essential to fight for the same privilege. Peer groups also provide for anticipatory socialization into new roles that the young person will later assume.

Teenagers imitate their friends in part because the peer group maintains a meaningful system of rewards and punishments. The group may encourage a young person to follow pursuits that society considers admirable, as in a school club engaged in volunteer work in hospitals and nursing homes. On the other hand, the group may encourage someone to violate the culture's norms and values by driving recklessly, shoplifting, engaging in acts of vandalism, and the like.

Gender differences are noteworthy in the social world of adolescents. Males are more likely to spend time in groups of males, while females are more likely to interact with a single other female. This pattern reflects differences in levels of emotional intimacy; teenage males are less likely to develop strong emotional ties than are females. Instead, males are more inclined to share in group activities. These patterns are evident among adolescents in many societies besides the United States (Dornbusch, 1989:248).

Peer groups serve a valuable function by assisting the transition to adult responsibilities. At home, parents tend to dominate; at school, the teenager must contend with teachers and administrators. But, within the peer group, each member can assert himself or herself in a way that may not be possible elsewhere. Nevertheless, almost all adolescents in our culture remain economically dependent on their parents, and most are emotionally dependent as well.

Mass Media

In the last 75 years, such technological innovations as radio, motion pictures, recorded music, and television have become important agents of socialization. Television, in particular, is a critical force in the socialization of children in the United States. Many parents in essence allow the television set to become a child's favorite "playmate"; consequently, children in our society typically watch over three hours of television per day. Remarkably, between the ages of 6 and 18, the average young person spends more time watching the "tube" (15,000 to 16,000 hours) than working in school (13,000 hours). Apart from sleeping, watching television is the most time-consuming activity of young people.

Relative to other agents of socialization discussed earlier—such as family members, schools, and peers—television has certain distinctive characteristics. It permits imitation and role playing but does not encourage more complex forms of learning. Watching television is, above all, a passive experience; one sits back and waits to be entertained. Critics of television are further alarmed by the programming that children view as they sit for hours in front of a television set. It is generally agreed that children (as well as adults) are exposed to a great deal of violence on television. By age 16, the average television viewer has witnessed some 200,000 acts of television violence, including 33,000 fictional murders (Murphree, 1991; Waters, 1993).

Like other agents of socialization, television has traditionally portrayed and promoted conventional gender roles. A content analysis of child characters on prime-time television revealed that boys are shown as significantly more active, aggressive, and rational than girls. The two sexes are also shown as differing substantially in the types of activities in which they participate. Young girls on prime-time television talk on the telephone, read, and help with housework, whereas boys play sports, go on excursions, and get into mischief. In terms of socialization, television's portrayal of child characters is especially significant, since these characters may be the most meaningful for younger viewers (Peirce, 1989). The ways in which television misrepresents

the realities of day-to-day life in the United States are explored in Table 4-1.

Even critics of the medium generally concede that television is not always a negative socializing influence. Creative programming such as *Sesame Street* can assist children in developing basic skills essential for schooling. In addition, television programs and even commercials expose young people to lifestyles and cultures of which they are unaware. This entails not only children in the United States learning about life in "faraway lands," but also inner-city children learning about the lives of farm children and vice versa.

TABLE 4-1	Distorted Viewing: Television Characters versus Reality	
	PROPORTION OF ALL PRIME-TIME TELEVISION CHARACTERS	PROPORTION OF U.S. POPULATION
Male	63%	49%
Female	37	51
Children, ages 0–12	4	19
Older people, ages 60 and over	8	17
White	84	76
Hispanic	2	9
Wear glasses	14	38
Are overweight	10	68
Drink alcoholic beverages	7	61
Smoke cigarettes	2	26
Have been crime victims	18	5

NOTE: Data adapted from *USA Today* study of television, Bureau of the Census, NIDA Household Survey, National Association to Advance Fat Acceptance, and Roper Survey.
SOURCES: Adapted from Gable, 1993a, 1993b.

Content analysis of prime-time television programs has found significant discrepancies between the representation of various groups on television and their actual size within the general population of the United States. For example, White males are overrepresented on prime-time television, while women, Hispanics, young children, and older people are underrepresented.

Not only does television educate viewers about members of other cultures and subcultures, it may even influence changes in self-identity. Researchers have long documented the strong differences between Puerto Ricans, Mexican Americans, Cuban Americans, and other Hispanic peoples. Yet the emergence of two nationwide Spanish-language television networks, Univision and Telemundo—watched in 1989 by three-fourths of all Hispanics—has blurred these distinctions somewhat and strengthened the common identity of these minorities as Hispanics. While minimizing certain subcultural differences, television appears to be having a unifying influence on the nation's growing Hispanic population (Mydans, 1989).

Recognizing the powerful impact of television, soap operas in developing countries have attempted to convey specific social messages. For example, Nigeria's *Cock Crow at Dawn* encourages villagers to adopt modern agricultural practices, while India's *Hum Log* (*O We People*) has promoted family planning and higher status for women. One survey revealed that three-fourths of Indian viewers approved of the messages being dramatized in *Hum Log* (W. Brown and Cody, 1991).

While we have focused on television as an agent of socialization, it is important to note that similar issues have been raised regarding the content of popular music (especially rock music and "rap"), music videos, and motion pictures. These forms of entertainment, like television, serve as powerful agents of socialization for many young people in the United States and elsewhere. There has been continuing controversy about the content of music, music videos, and films—sometimes leading to celebrated court battles—as certain parents' organizations and religious groups challenge the intrusion of these media into the lives of children and adolescents.

Workplace

A fundamental aspect of human socialization involves learning to behave appropriately within an occupation. In the United States, working full time serves to confirm adult status; it is an indication to all that one has passed out of adolescence. In a sense, socialization into an occupation can represent both a harsh reality ("I have to work in order

A unique feminist example of occupational socialization took place in April 1993. On a "Take Our Daughters to Work Day," organized by the Ms. Foundation for Women, mothers across the nation took their daughters to their workplaces to help them better understand their mothers' occupations and careers. Shown are a New York City emergency services operator (who screens 911 calls) and her daughter.

to buy food and pay the rent") and the realization of an ambition ("I've always wanted to be an airline pilot") (W. Moore, 1968:862).

Occupational socialization cannot be separated from the socialization experiences that occur during childhood and adolescence. We are most fully exposed to occupational roles through observing the work of our parents, of people whom we meet while they are performing their duties (doctors or firefighters, for example), and of people portrayed in the media (presidents, professional athletes, and so forth). These observations, along with the subtle messages we receive within a culture, help to shape—and often limit—the type of work we may consider.

Wilbert Moore (1968:871–880) has divided occupational socialization into four phases. The first phase is *career choice,* which involves selection of academic or vocational training appropriate for the desired job. If one hopes to become a physician, one must take certain courses, such as biology and chemistry, which are required of applicants to medical school. If one's goal is to become a violin maker, it will be useful to work as an apprentice for an expert practicing that craft.

The next phase identified by Moore is *anticipatory socialization,* which may last only a few months or extend for a period of years. Some children in the United States "inherit" their occupations because their parents run farms or "ma and pa" stores. In a sense, these young people are experiencing anticipatory socialization throughout childhood and adolescence as they observe their parents at work. In addition, some people *decide* on occupational goals at relatively early ages and never waver from their choices. A young woman or man may resolve to become a dancer at the age of 11 or 12; the entire adolescent period may focus on training for that future.

The third phase of occupational socialization—*conditioning and commitment*—occurs while one actually occupies the work-related role. *Conditioning* consists of reluctantly adjusting to the more unpleasant aspects of one's job. Most people find that the novelty of a new daily schedule quickly wears off and then realize that parts of the work experience are rather tedious. Moore uses the term *commitment* to refer to the enthusiastic acceptance of pleasurable duties that comes as the recruit identifies the positive tasks of an occupation.

In Moore's view, if a job proves to be satisfactory, the person will enter a fourth stage of socialization, which he calls *continuous commitment.* At this point, the job becomes an indistinguishable part of the person's self-identity. Violation of proper conduct becomes unthinkable. A person may choose to join professional associations, unions, or other groups which represent his or her occupation in the larger society.

Occupational socialization can be most intense immediately after one makes the transition from school to the job, but it continues through one's work history. Technological advances may alter the requirements of the position and necessitate some degree of resocialization. Thus, after years of working at typewriters, secretaries may find themselves adjusting to sophisticated word-processing equipment. In addition, many people change occupations, employers, or places of work during their adult years. Therefore, occupational socialization continues throughout a person's years in the labor market (Mortimer and Simmons, 1978:440–441; see also Becker et al., 1961; Ritzer, 1977).

The State

Social scientists have increasingly recognized the importance of the state—or government at all levels—as an agent of socialization because of its growing impact on the life cycle. Traditionally, family members have served as the primary caregivers in our culture, but in the twentieth century the family's protective function has steadily been transferred to outside agencies such as hospitals, mental health clinics, and insurance companies (Ogburn and Tibbits, 1934:661–778). Many of these agencies are run by the government; the rest are licensed and regulated by governmental bodies. In the social policy section of this chapter, we will see that the state is under pressure to become a provider of child care, which would give it a new and direct role in the socialization of infants and young children.

In the past, the life cycle was influenced most significantly by heads of households and by local groups such as religious organizations. However, in the 1990s the individual as a citizen and an economic actor is influenced by national interests. For example, labor unions and political parties serve as intermediaries between the individual and the state.

The state has had a noteworthy impact on the life cycle by reinstituting the rites of passage that had disappeared in agricultural societies and in periods of early industrialization. For example, government regulations stipulate the ages at which a person may drive a car, drink alcohol, vote in elections, marry without parental permission, work overtime, and retire. These regulations do not constitute strict rites of passage: most 21-year-olds do not vote and most people choose their age of retirement without reference to government dictates. Still, by regulating the life cycle to some degree, the state shapes the socialization process by influencing our views of appropriate behavior at particular ages (Mayer and Schoepflin, 1989).

• Is it desirable to expose young children to the socializing influence of day care?
• In the view of conflict theorists, why does child care receive little government support?
• Should the costs of day care programs be paid by government, by the private sector, or entirely by parents?

The rise in single-parent families, increased job opportunities for women, and the need for additional family income have all propelled an increasing number of mothers of young children into the paid labor force of the United States (see Chapter 11).

In 1993, 57 percent of all mothers with children under the age of 6 were found in the paid labor force, and the number either working or looking for a job is expected to reach 70 percent by the year 2000. Who, then, will take care of the children of these women during work hours? For two-thirds of all 3-to-5-year-olds for whom national data are now available, the solution has become group child care programs. Day care centers have become the functional equivalent of the nuclear family, performing some of the nurturing and socialization functions previously handled only by family members (Beck, 1993; Holmes, 1990b).

Studies indicate that children placed in high-quality child care centers are not adversely affected by such experiences; in fact, good day care benefits children. The value of preschool programs was documented in a comparison of full-time Milwaukee preschoolers with a "non-nursery" group. Those children attending the preschool program from ages 3 to 6 years showed significantly greater language development and greater gains on achievement tests than children in the non-nursery control group did. In addition, research conducted in the last few years indicates that children in day care or preschool programs are more self-sufficient. They react well to separation from their parents and tend to have more stimulating interactions when together. Finally, it appears from recent studies that children may be better off in centers with well-trained caregivers than cared for full time by those mothers who are depressed and frustrated because they wish to work outside the home (Galinsky, 1986; Garber and Herber, 1977; Shell, 1988).

Even if policymakers decide that publicly funded child care is desirable, they must determine the degree to which taxpayers should subsidize it. A number of European nations, including the Netherlands and Sweden, provide preschool care at minimal or no cost. In 1991, about half of all Danish children under the age of 3 and 70 percent of children ages 3 to 6 attended public child care pro-

Carol Simpson Productions ©1990

grams. Parents pay a maximum of 30 percent of day care costs. In France, virtually all children ages 3 to 5 attend free schooling, and free after-school care is widely available. However, providing first-rate child care in the United States is anything but cheap, with a cost of $4000 per year not unusual in urban areas. Thus, a nationally financed system of child care could lead to staggering costs (*New York Times*, 1993b; Topolnicki, 1993).

Feminists echo the concern of conflict theorists that high-quality child care receives little governmental support because it is regarded as "merely a way to let women work." Nearly all child care workers (94 percent) are women; many find themselves in low-status, minimum wage jobs. The average salary of child care workers in the United States in 1992 was only $15,488, and there are few fringe benefits. A child care teacher with a college degree earns only 45 percent as much as a similarly educated woman working in other occupations and only 27 percent as much as a similarly educated man. Although parents may complain of child care costs, the staff are, in effect, subsidizing children's care by working for low wages. Not surprisingly, there is high turnover among child care teachers. In 1992 alone, 25 percent of all day care teachers (and more than 40 percent in metropolitan areas) left their jobs (D. Blau, 1993; N. Carroll, 1993).

Thus far, few local communities have passed ordinances to encourage child care. What about the private sector? Companies are increasingly recognizing that child care can be good for business, since many employees view it as an important fringe benefit. Between 1984 and 1987, there was an increase of 50 percent in the number of companies that offered subsidized child care. Still, even with this increase, as of 1990, only 13 percent of major corporations sponsored child care centers at or near their job sites. Even fewer companies offered discounts or vouchers for child care (F. Chapman, 1987; P. Taylor, 1991).

Many policymakers believe that parents—rather than government or the private sector—should be solely responsible for the costs of day care programs. Yet parents often rely on child care because they are attempting to increase family income. Unless fees are kept to a minimum, the expenses of day care will wipe out the additional wages earned.

As limited as child care is across the United States, it is not equally available to all families. Parents in wealthy neighborhoods have an easier time finding day care than those in poor or working-class communities. In a study covering 36 states, Harvard researchers Bruce Fuller and Xiaoyan Liang (1993) found wide disparities in the availability of child care. In the richest communities, there is one preschool teacher for every 45 children ages 3 to 5; in the poorest communities, there is one teacher for every 77 children.

Viewed from a conflict perspective, child care costs are an especially serious burden for lower-class families, who already find it hard to take advantage of limited job opportunities. Moreover, the difficulty of finding affordable child care has particularly serious implications for mothers who work (or wish to work) outside the home. Even if they enter the paid labor force, mothers may find their work performance and opportunities for advancement hindered by child care difficulties. Since child care is commonly viewed as a woman's responsibility (given the persistence of traditional gender roles), working mothers rather than working fathers are especially likely to bear the burden of these problems.

Public support for child care has risen markedly in the last two decades. In 1987, national surveys showed that 80 percent of adults favored the establishment of more day care services for children (compared with only 56 percent in 1970). In a 1989 survey, two-thirds of parents with children under 14 years of age agreed that government has an obligation to provide child care assistance, and 57 percent of these parents stated that employers have a similar responsibility. But, to date, most government officials and leaders of private enterprise continue to give low priority to the issue of child care. This is ironic given the importance of early childhood socialization to the intellectual and social development of future generations in the United States (Morin, 1989; S. Rebell, 1987).

In 1987, the Act for Better Child Care (known as the *ABC bill*) was introduced in Congress to make child care more affordable for low-income families and to increase the accessibility of high-quality child care for *all* families. The ABC bill continued to be a focal point of discussion for policymakers and finally was approved in greatly modified form in 1990 as the Child Care Act. Consisting of two parts, this act provided for both grants and tax credits to support child care. A total of $2.5 billion was authorized for grants to the states over the years 1991–1993, with most of this funding intended to assist low-income families in obtaining child care services. The new tax credits would allow parents to deduct out-of-pocket child care expenses from their income taxes. While this legislation provides much less financial support for child care than had been proposed years earlier, it nevertheless establishes a precedent for direct federal subsidies through the states for child care programs (Holmes, 1990a; Rovner, 1990).

SUMMARY

Socialization is the process whereby people learn the attitudes, values, and actions appropriate to individuals as members of a particular culture. This chapter examines the role of socialization in human development; the way in which people develop perceptions, feelings, and beliefs about themselves; and the lifelong nature of the socialization process.

1 Socialization affects the overall cultural practices of a society, and it also shapes the images that we hold of ourselves.

2 In the early 1900s, Charles Horton Cooley advanced the belief that we learn who we are by interacting with others.

3 George Herbert Mead is best known for his theory of the *self.* He proposed that as people mature, their selves begin to reflect their concern about reactions from others.

4 Erving Goffman has shown that many of our daily activities involve attempts to convey distinct impressions of who we are.

5 The family is the most important agent of socialization in the United States, especially for children.

6 As the primary agents of socialization, parents play a critical role in guiding children into those *gender roles* deemed appropriate in a society.

7 Like the family, schools have an explicit mandate to socialize people in the United States—and especially children—into the norms and values of our culture.

8 Peer groups frequently assist adolescents in gaining some degree of independence from parents and other authority figures.

9 Television has been criticized as an agent of socialization because it encourages children to forsake human interaction for passive viewing.

10 We are most fully exposed to occupational roles through observing the work of our parents, of people whom we meet while they are performing their duties, and of people portrayed in the media.

11 By regulating the life cycle, the state shapes the socialization process by influencing our views of appropriate behavior at particular ages.

12 As more and more mothers of young children have entered the labor market of the United States, the demand for child care has increased dramatically.

CRITICAL THINKING QUESTIONS

1 Should social research in areas such as sociobiology be conducted even though many investigators believe that this analysis is potentially detrimental to large numbers of people?

2 Drawing on Erving Goffman's dramaturgical approach, discuss how the following groups engage in impression management: athletes, college instructors, parents, physicians, politicians?

3 How would functionalists and conflict theorists differ in their analyses of the mass media?

KEY TERMS

Anticipatory socialization Processes of socialization in which a person "rehearses" for future positions, occupations, and social relationships. (page 104)

Cognitive theory of development Jean Piaget's theory explaining how children's thought progresses through four stages. (102)

Degradation ceremony An aspect of the socialization process within total institutions, in which people are subjected to humiliating rituals. (105)

Dramaturgical approach A view of social interaction, popularized by Erving Goffman, under which people are examined as if they were theatrical performers. (100)

Face-work A term used by Erving Goffman to refer to people's efforts to maintain the proper image and avoid embarrassment in public. (100)

Familism Pride in the extended family, expressed

through the maintenance of close ties and strong obligations to kinfolk. (107)

Gender roles Expectations regarding the proper behavior, attitudes, and activities of males and females. (106)

Generalized others A term used by George Herbert Mead to refer to the child's awareness of the attitudes, viewpoints, and expectations of society as a whole. (99)

Impression management A term used by Erving Goffman to refer to the altering of the presentation of the self in order to create distinctive appearances and satisfy particular audiences. (100)

Looking-glass self A phrase used by Charles Horton Cooley to emphasize that the self is the product of our social interactions with others. (98)

Machismo A sense of virility, personal worth, and pride in one's maleness. (107)

Midlife crisis A stressful period of self-evaluation, often occurring between the ages of 35 and 50, in which a person realizes that he or she has not achieved certain personal goals and aspirations and that time is running out. (103)

Personality In everyday speech, a person's typical patterns of attitudes, needs, characteristics, and behavior. (93)

Resocialization The process of discarding former behavior patterns and accepting new ones as part of a transition in one's life. (104)

Reverse socialization The process whereby people normally being socialized are at the same time socializing their socializers. (108)

Rites of passage Rituals marking the symbolic transition from one social position to another. (102)

Role taking The process of mentally assuming the perspective of another, thereby enabling one to respond from that imagined viewpoint. (99)

Self According to George Herbert Mead, the sum total of people's conscious perception of their identity as distinct from others. (98)

Significant others A term used by George Herbert Mead to refer to those individuals who are most important in the development of the self, such as parents, friends, and teachers. (100)

Socialization The process whereby people learn the attitudes, values, and actions appropriate to individuals as members of a particular culture. (92)

Sociobiology The systematic study of the biological bases of social behavior. (97)

Symbols The gestures, objects, and language which form the basis of human communication. (98)

Total institutions A term coined by Erving Goffman to refer to institutions which regulate all aspects of a person's life under a single authority, such as prisons, the military, mental hospitals, and convents. (104)

ADDITIONAL READINGS

Elkin, Frederick, and Gerald Handel. *The Child and Society: The Process of Socialization* (5th ed.). New York: Random House, 1989. This book reviews the social science literature on socialization, examines agents of socialization, and gives special emphasis to gender-role socialization.

Goffman, Erving. *The Presentation of Self in Everyday Life.* New York: Doubleday, 1959. Goffman demonstrates his interactionist theory that the self is managed in everyday situations in much the same way that a theatrical performer carries out a stage role.

Harlow, Harry F. *Learning to Love.* New York: Ballantine, 1971. This heavily illustrated book describes the landmark studies of behavior conducted at the Primate Research Center at the University of Wisconsin.

Klein, Abbie Gordon. *The Debate over Child Care, 1969–1990: A Sociohistorical Analysis.* Albany: State University of New York Press, 1992. A background view of child care services in the United States.

Lott, Bernice. *Women's Lives: Themes and Variations in Gender Learning.* Monterey, Calif.: Brooks/Cole, 1987. An overview of the socialization experiences of women in the United States.

Schlenker, Barry R. (ed.). *The Self and Social Life.* New York: McGraw-Hill, 1985. Social scientists, primarily psychologists, examine the concept of the self as an explanation of behavior.

Tobin, Joseph J., David Y. H. Wu, and Dana H. Davidson. *Preschool in Three Cultures: Japan, China, and the United States.* New Haven, Conn.: Yale University Press, 1989. A comparative look at formal early childhood education in three nations, drawing upon the views of parents, teachers, and administrators.

Journals

Among the journals that deal with socialization issues are *Adolescence* (founded in 1966), *Journal of Personality and Social Psychology* (1965), and *Young Children* (1945).

5

SOCIAL INTERACTION AND SOCIAL STRUCTURE

SOCIAL INTERACTION AND REALITY
Defining and Reconstructing Reality
Negotiated Order

ELEMENTS OF SOCIAL STRUCTURE
Statuses
    Ascribed and Achieved Status
    Master Status
Social Roles
    What Are Social Roles?
    Role Conflict
Groups
Social Institutions
    Functionalist View
    Conflict View
    Interactionist View

**SOCIAL STRUCTURE
AND MODERN SOCIETY**
Durkheim's Mechanical and Organic
    Solidarity
Tönnies's *Gemeinschaft* and *Gesellschaft*

**SOCIAL POLICY AND SOCIAL
STRUCTURE: THE AIDS CRISIS**

BOXES
5-1 Current Research: The Process
    of Role Exit
5-2 Speaking Out: Savage Inequalities
    in Public Education

LOOKING AHEAD

- How do we redefine reality through social interaction?
- How do sociologists use the terms *status* and *role?*
- Why are social roles a significant component of social structure?
- How is "networking" helpful in finding employment?
- How do the family, religion, and government contribute to a society's survival?
- How do social interactions in a preindustrial village differ from those in a modern urban center?
- How has the social structure of the United States been affected by the spread of AIDS?

Seventy male students at Stanford University were asked to participate in an experiment designed by social psychologist Philip Zimbardo (1992; Haney et al., 1973). The students were paid to give up their vacation time and become part of a simulated prison experience in the basement corridor of a classroom building. By a flip of a coin, half were arbitrarily designated as prisoners, the others as guards. The guards were instructed to establish their own rules for maintaining law, order, and discipline.

Within a short time, the guards began to act "guardlike." Some attempted to be tough but fair and held strictly to the prison rules. But about one-third of the student guards became cruel and abusive in their treatment of prisoners. They shouted commands, took pleasure in imposing arbitrary rules, and treated the prisoners like animals. In one case, a guard ordered a prisoner into "solitary confinement" and forced him to stay overnight in a small closet.

Soon after the experiment began, the prisoners became depressed, apathetic, and helpless—or else rebellious and angry. Some cried hysterically. The situation became so intolerable that Zimbardo and his colleagues were forced to abandon the mock prison study after only six days. It seemed unethical to continue because of the anxiety and distress evident among the student prisoners.

Zimbardo's study demonstrated that college students adopted predictable patterns of social interaction (those expected of guards and prisoners) when placed in a mock prison. Sociologists use the term *social interaction* to refer to the ways in which people respond to one another. These interactions need not be face to face; friends talking over the telephone and coworkers communicating over a computer are engaged in social interaction. In the mock prison experiment, social interactions between prisoners and guards were highly impersonal. Prisoners were not addressed by name but instead by their prison number. Guards wore reflector sunglasses which made eye contact impossible.

As in many real-life prisons, the simulated prison at Stanford University had a social structure in which guards held virtually total control over prisoners. The term *social structure* refers to the way in which a society is organized into predictable relationships. The social structure of Zimbardo's mock prison influenced the interactions between the guards and prisoners. Zimbardo (1992:576) notes that it was a real prison "in the minds of the jailers and their captives." His simulated prison experiment was first conducted 20 years ago but has subsequently been repeated (with similar findings) both in the United States and in other countries.

The concepts of social interaction and social structure, which are closely linked to each other, are central to sociological study. Sociologists observe patterns of behavior closely to understand and accurately describe the social interactions of a community or society and the social structure of which this behavior is a part.

This chapter begins by considering how social interaction shapes the way we view the world around us. Interactions involve negotiation, which results in ever-changing forms of social organization. The chapter will focus on the four basic elements of social structure: statuses, social roles, groups, and institutions. Since much of our behavior occurs in groups, the vital part that groups play in a society's social structure will be emphasized. Social institutions such as the family, religion, and government are a fundamental aspect of social structure. The chapter will contrast the functionalist, conflict, and interactionist approaches to the study of social in-

stitutions. It will also examine the typologies developed by sociologists Émile Durkheim and Ferdinand Tönnies for comparing modern societies with simpler forms of social structure. The social policy section will consider the AIDS crisis and its implications for the social institutions of the United States.

SOCIAL INTERACTION AND REALITY

According to sociologist Herbert Blumer (1969:79), the distinctive characteristic of social interaction among people is that "human beings interpret or 'define' each other's actions instead of merely reacting to each other's actions." In other words, our response to someone's behavior is based on the *meaning* we attach to his or her actions. Reality is shaped by our perceptions, evaluations, and definitions. These meanings typically reflect the norms and values of the dominant culture and our socialization experiences within that culture.

Defining and Reconstructing Reality

How do we define our social reality? As an example, let us examine how abortion clinics attempt to present themselves to their clients. Two different

Philip G. Zimbardo, Stanford University

In Philip Zimbardo's famous mock prison experiment, 70 male students at Stanford University were arbitrarily designated as prisoners or guards. The study had to be abandoned after only six days because of some guards' cruel treatment of prisoners. As one example, guards required prisoners to sleep on cots without blankets.

sociologists examined abortion clinics: one in the 1960s, when abortion was illegal, the other in the late 1970s after the Supreme Court's landmark 1973 decision assuring a right to abortion under most circumstances (see Chapter 11). Before abortion was legal, clinics attempted to reassure women by emphasizing medical professionalism and creating an intentionally sterile atmosphere—much like that of a doctor's office or a hospital. However, by the late 1970s, clinics had begun to deemphasize this clinical focus and instead to stress that they were offering "personalized," nontraditional care. Attention turned to relaxing the client, offering her emotional support, and encouraging discussion of any doubts or fears. In each time period, abortion clinics—influenced by the prevailing social structure—attempted to project and define a particular social reality that would help women to feel more comfortable in seeking out their services (Ball, 1967; Charon, 1985:154; P. M. Hall, 1987:6–7; M. Zimmerman, 1981:151).

By the 1990s, however, opponents of abortion were portraying clinics as killing centers. The militant group Operation Rescue tried to shut down abortion clinics through picketing and harassment of health care professionals and patients. In 1989, for example, 11,800 people were arrested across the United States for blocking access to clinics (Hancock, 1990). Despite the explosive atmosphere outside many abortion clinics, the clinics continued to emphasize that they offered a supportive environment for their clients.

The ability to define social reality clearly reflects a group's power within a society. Indeed, one of the most crucial aspects of the relationship between dominant and subordinate groups is the ability of the dominant or majority group to define a society's values. Sociologist William I. Thomas (1923: 41–44), an early critic of theories of racial and gender differences, saw that the "definition of the situation" could mold the thinking and personality of the individual. Writing from an interactionist perspective, Thomas observed that people respond not only to the objective features of a person or situation but also to the meaning that the person or situation has for them. For example, in Philip Zimbardo's mock prison experiment, student "guards" and "prisoners" accepted the definition of the situation (including the traditional roles and behavior associated with being a guard or prisoner) and acted accordingly.

As we have seen throughout the last 30 years—first in the civil rights movement of the 1960s and since then among such groups as women, the elderly, gays and lesbians, and people with disabilities—an important aspect of the process of social change involves redefining or reconstructing social reality. Members of subordinate groups begin to challenge traditional definitions and instead perceive and experience reality in a new way. For example, the Black activist Malcolm X (1925–1965), an eloquent and controversial advocate of Black power and Black pride in the early 1960s, recalled that his feelings and perspective changed dramatically while in eighth grade. His English teacher advised him that his goal of becoming a lawyer was "no realistic goal for a nigger" and encouraged him instead to become a carpenter. In Malcolm X's (1964:37) words:

> It was then that I began to change—inside. I drew away from white people. I came to class, and I answered when called upon. It became a physical strain simply to sit in Mr. Ostrowski's class. Where "nigger" had slipped off my back before, wherever I heard it now, I stopped and looked at whoever said it. And they looked surprised that I did.

Viewed from a sociological perspective, Malcolm X was redefining social reality by looking much more critically at the racist thinking and terminology that restricted him and other African Americans (Charon, 1985:4).

Negotiated Order

As we have seen, people can reconstruct social reality through a process of internal change as they take a different view of everyday behavior. Yet people also reshape reality by negotiating changes in patterns of social interaction. The term *negotiation* refers to the attempt to reach agreement with others concerning some objective. Negotiation does not involve coercion; it goes by many names, including *bargaining, compromising, trading off, mediating, exchanging, "wheeling and dealing,"* and *collusion* (A. Strauss, 1977:2; see also G. Fine, 1984).

Viewed from a sociological perspective, the Black activist Malcolm X redefined social reality by looking much more critically at the racist thinking and terminology that restricted him and other African Americans.

Negotiation occurs in many ways. Some social situations, such as buying groceries, involve no mediation, while other situations require significant amounts of negotiation. For example, we may negotiate with others regarding time ("When should we arrive?"), space ("Can we have a meeting at your house?"), or even assignment of places while waiting for concert tickets. Burglars commonly bargain with tipsters about how much the tipsters should be paid for the information that they provide—usually a flat 10 percent of the gross proceeds of a "score" (Shover, 1973).

In traditional societies, impending marriages often lead to negotiations between the families of the husband and wife. For example, anthropologist Ray

Abrahams (1968) has described how the Labwor people of Africa arrange for an amount of property to go from the groom's to the bride's family at the time of marriage. In the view of the Labwor, such bargaining over an exchange of cows and sheep culminates not only in a marriage but, more important, in the linking of two clans or families.

While such family-to-family bargaining is common in traditional cultures, negotiation can take much more elaborate forms in modern industrial societies. Consider the tax laws of the United States. From a sociological perspective, such laws are formal norms (reflected in federal and state codes) that constitute the framework in which negotiations take place concerning legitimate tax deductions. If audited, taxpayers will mediate with agents of the Internal Revenue Service. Changes in the taxpayers' individual situations will occur through such negotiations. On a broader level, however, the entire tax code undergoes revision through negotiated outcomes involving many competing interests, including big business, foreign nations, and political action committees (see Chapter 15). The tax structure of the United States can hardly be viewed as fixed; rather, it reflects the sum of negotiations for change at any time (Maines, 1977:242–244; 1982; J. Thomas, 1984).

It is important to understand that negotiations are not merely an aspect of social interaction; they underlie much of our social behavior. Most elements of social structure are not static and are therefore subject to change through bargaining and exchanging. For this reason, sociologists use the term *negotiated order* to underscore the fact that the social order is continually being constructed and altered through negotiation. **Negotiated order** refers to a social structure that derives its existence from the social interactions through which people define and redefine its character.

We can add negotiation to our list of cultural universals (see Chapter 3) because all societies provide guidelines or norms in which negotiations take place. Not all behavior involves negotiated order; after all, there are social orders involving coercion. Nevertheless, the recurring role of negotiation in social interaction and social structure will be apparent as we examine statuses, social roles, groups, and institutions (Strauss, 1977:234–236, 262).

ELEMENTS OF SOCIAL STRUCTURE

Predictable social relationships can be examined in terms of four elements: statuses, social roles, groups, and social institutions. These elements make up social structure just as a foundation, walls, and ceilings make up a building's structure. The elements of social structure are developed through the lifelong process of socialization described in Chapter 4.

Statuses

When we speak of a person's "status" in casual conversation, the term usually conveys connotations of influence, wealth, and fame. However, sociologists use *status* to refer to any of the full range of socially defined positions within a large group or society—from the lowest to the highest position. Within our society, a person can occupy the status of president of the United States, fruit picker, son or daughter, violinist, teenager, resident of Minneapolis, dental technician, or neighbor. Clearly, a person holds more than one status simultaneously.

Ascribed and Achieved Status Some of the statuses we hold are viewed by sociologists as *ascribed*, while others are categorized as *achieved* (see Figure 5-1). An **ascribed status** is "assigned" to a person by society without regard for the person's unique talents or characteristics. Generally, this assignment takes place at birth; thus, a person's racial background, gender, and age are all considered ascribed statuses. These characteristics are biological in origin but are significant mainly because of the social meanings that they have in our culture. Conflict theorists are especially interested in ascribed statuses, since these statuses often confer privileges or reflect a person's membership in a subordinate group. The social meanings of race and ethnicity, gender, and age will be analyzed more fully in Chapters 10, 11, and 12, respectively.

In most cases, there is little that people can do to change an ascribed status. But we can attempt to change the traditional constraints associated with such statuses. As an example, the Gray Panthers hope to restructure social reality by modifying society's negative and confining stereotypes regarding older people (see Chapter 12). If they are suc-

FIGURE 5-1 Social Statuses

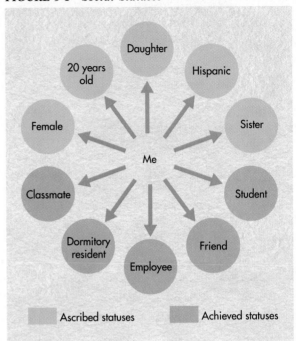

The person in this figure— "me"— occupies many positions in society, each of which involves distinct statuses.

cessful, the ascribed status of "senior citizen" will not be as difficult for millions of older people in the United States.

It is important to emphasize that an ascribed status does not necessarily have the same social meaning in every society. In a cross-cultural study, sociologist Gary Huang (1988) confirmed the long-held view that respect for the elderly is an important cultural norm in China. In many cases, the prefix "old" will be used respectfully: calling someone "old teacher" or "old person" has a similar meaning to calling a judge in the United States "your honor." Huang points out that positive age-seniority distinctions in language are absent in the United States; consequently, the term *old man* is viewed as more of an insult than a celebration of seniority and wisdom.

Unlike ascribed statuses, an **achieved status** is attained by a person largely through his or her own effort. Both "bank president" and "prison guard" are achieved statuses, as are "lawyer," "pianist," "advertising executive," and "social worker." One must do something to acquire an achieved status—go to school, learn a skill, establish a friendship, or invent a new product.

Master Status Each person holds many different statuses; some may connote higher social positions and some, lower positions. How is one's overall position viewed by others in light of these conflicting statuses? Sociologist Everett Hughes (1945) observed that societies deal with such inconsistencies by agreeing that certain statuses are more important than others. A *master status* is a status that dominates others and thereby determines a person's general position within society. For example, Arthur Ashe, who died of AIDS in 1993, had a remarkable career as a tennis star; but at the end of his life, his status as a person with AIDS may have outweighed his statuses as a retired athlete, an author, and a political activist. As we will see in Chapter 20, many people with disabilities find that their status as "disabled" is given undue weight and overshadows their actual ability to perform successfully in meaningful employment.

Race and gender are given such importance in our society that they often dominate one's life. Indeed, such ascribed statuses influence achieved status. As we have seen, Malcolm X found that his position as a Black man (ascribed status) was an obstacle to his dream of becoming a lawyer (achieved status). In the United States, ascribed statuses of race and gender can function as master statuses that have an important impact on one's potential to achieve a desired professional and social status.

Social Roles

What Are Social Roles? Throughout our lives, we are acquiring what sociologists call *social roles*. A *social role* is a set of expectations for people who occupy a given social position or status. Thus, in the United States, we expect that cab drivers will know how to get around a city, that secretaries will be reliable in handling phone messages, and that police officers will take action if they see a citizen being threatened. With each distinctive social status—whether ascribed or achieved—come particular role expectations. However, actual performance varies from individual to individual. One secretary may assume extensive administrative responsibilities, while another may focus on clerical duties. Similarly, in Philip Zimbardo's mock prison experiment, some students were brutal and sadistic as guards, but others were not.

Roles are a significant component of social structure. Viewed from a functionalist perspective, roles contribute to a society's stability by enabling members to anticipate the behavior of others and to pattern their own actions accordingly. Yet social roles can also be dysfunctional by restricting people's interactions and relationships. If we view a person *only* as a "police officer" or a "supervisor," it will be difficult to relate to this person as a friend or neighbor. The demands and restrictions of certain roles contribute to the process of disengagement known as *role exit* (see Box 5-1 on page 126).

In the quotation at the beginning of the chapter, Shakespeare uses the theater as an analogy for the world as a whole and for the human experience. Actors obviously take on roles, but so do the rest of us. We learn how to fulfill a social role by observing the behavior and interactions of others.

Role Conflict Imagine the delicate situation of a woman who has worked for a decade on an assembly line in an electrical plant and has recently been named supervisor of the unit she worked in. How is this woman expected to relate to her longtime friends and coworkers? Should she still go out to lunch with them, as she has done almost daily for years? How should she deal with the workers' resentment of an arrogant supervisor who is now her equal and colleague? Is it her responsibility to recommend the firing of an old friend who cannot keep up with the demands of the assembly line?

Role conflict occurs when incompatible expectations arise from two or more social positions held by the same person. Fulfillment of the roles associated with one status may directly violate the roles linked to a second status. In the example above, the newly promoted supervisor will experience a serious conflict between certain social and occupational roles. As a friend, she should try to protect her former coworker; as a supervisor, she should report an unsatisfactory employee.

Role conflicts call for important ethical choices.

BOX 5-1 · CURRENT RESEARCH

THE PROCESS OF ROLE EXIT

Often when we think of assuming a social role, we focus on the preparation and anticipatory socialization that a person undergoes in becoming ready for that role. This is true if a person is about to become an attorney, a chef, a spouse, or a parent. Yet, until recently, social scientists have given less attention to the adjustments involved in *leaving* social roles.

Sociologist Helen Rose Fuchs Ebaugh (1988) developed the term *role exit* to describe the process of disengagement from a role that is central to one's self-identity and reestablishment of an identity in a new role. Drawing on interviews with 185 people—among them ex-convicts, divorced men and women, recovering alcoholics, ex-nuns, former doctors, retirees, and transsexuals—Ebaugh studied the process of voluntarily exiting from significant social roles.

Ebaugh's interest in role exit grew out of her own background as an ex-nun. She recalls: "I grew up in a small Catholic, German community in Olfen, Texas, where at 18 women had the choice of getting married or joining the convent.

The nuns were unwitting feminists back then in that they were the only educated role models we had." She spent 11 years as Sister Helen Rose, but while working on her doctorate at Columbia University, she began questioning her religious life and realized she felt a strong desire to be married and have children (Bartlett, 1988:C1).

Ebaugh has offered a four-stage model of role exit. The first stage begins with doubt—as the person experiences frustration, burnout, or simply unhappiness with an accustomed status and the roles associated with this social position. This doubt leads to what Ebaugh calls *unconscious cueing*, which was evident in the convent in the hairstyles of nuns. In Ebaugh's view, those nuns who let their hair grow longer and turned to fashionable hairstyles were in the initial stage of role exit.

The second stage involves a search for alternatives. A person unhappy with his or her career may take a leave of absence; an unhappily married couple may begin what they see as a temporary separation. Then comes the third stage of role exit: the action stage or departure. Ebaugh found that the vast majority of her respondents identified a clear turning point which made them feel it was essential to take final action and leave their jobs, end their marriages, or engage in other types of role exit. However, 20 percent of respondents saw their role exits as a gradual, evolutionary process that had no single turning point.

The last stage of role exit involves the creation of a new identity. Ebaugh points out: "It is important to maintain contact with some people in the old role, to keep some bridges. . . . It's also important to be able to talk to someone about who one used to be." Consequently, while she is now a sociologist, wife, and mother of two children, Ebaugh has not blocked out her memories of her years in the convent. In fact, in 1988 she attended what would have been her twenty-fifth anniversary as a nun, had she remained in her religious order. "It was a wonderful kind of closure for me," says Ebaugh (Bartlett, 1988:C1).

In the example just given, the new supervisor has to make a difficult decision about how much allegiance she owes her friend. Our culture tells us that success is more important than friendship. If friends are holding us back, we should leave them and pursue our ambitions. Yet, at the same time, we are told that abandoning our friends is contemptible. The supervisor must decide whether she will risk her promotion out of concern for her friend.

During the Second World War, Christians living in Nazi Germany had to choose between trying to protect Jewish friends and associates and turning them in to the authorities. Remember that the Third Reich had defined Jews as enemies of the state. Protecting such people was considered treason and was dangerous for the person who offered protection. On the other hand, the policies of the Nazi regime, notably its bitter and irrational hatred of Jews, violated humanitarian values. If German

Christians did not act to assist Jewish friends—and instead decided to turn them in—the Jews were likely to be murdered. Clearly, if they wished to fulfill the social roles of friendship or being "good neighbors," non-Jews in Germany would be expected to assist innocent victims of the Nazi terror.

Sociologists are particularly interested in how a society and culture inform the individual about conflicting ethical choices. Hitler's Third Reich devised propaganda campaigns to discredit and slander Jews and to encourage citizens to support the regime's persecution of Jews. Despite such propaganda, some individuals (such as Oskar Schindler) resolved their role conflict by making brave and dangerous choices: they opposed the Nazis openly or helped to protect and hide Jews. However, most German Christians supported the nation's leaders and their attacks on European Jews. In the process, these non-Jews turned their backs on the roles associated with being friends and good neighbors (see also Oliner and Oliner, 1989).

In some instances, changing gender roles have contributed to role conflict. Sociologist Tracey Watson (1987) studied the ways in which female athletes in college sports programs resolve the conflicts raised by two traditionally incongruent identities: being a woman and being an athlete. On the basketball court, the identity of "athlete" is clearly dominant for these college students. According to an unwritten norm, no makeup is worn during games, much less jewelry; knee pads and Ace bandages are the more likely attire. By contrast, when dressing for a dinner honoring college athletes, these women present a conventional feminine image with notable adornment and makeup.

Clearly, these women resorted to impression management (described by Erving Goffman in Chapter 4) to resolve the role conflicts of women athletes. Nevertheless, as Tracey Watson observed, the general college population took little notice of such impression management and instead stereotyped these athletes as decidedly unfeminine. This stereotyping serves as a reminder that while there has been a significant change in gender roles in the United States—as is evident in the dramatic increase in girls' and women's participation in sports—traditional assumptions about femininity and masculinity remain an influential part of our culture.

Groups

In sociological terms, a **group** is any number of people with similar norms, values, and expectations who regularly and consciously interact. The members of a women's college basketball team, of a hospital's business office, or of a symphony orchestra constitute a group. However, the entire staff of a large hospital would not be considered a group, since the staff members rarely interact with one another at one time. Perhaps the only point at which they all come together is the annual winter party.

Every society is composed of many groups in which daily social interaction takes place. We seek out groups to establish friendships, to accomplish certain goals, and to fulfill social roles that we have acquired. The various types of groups in which people interact will be explored in detail in Chapter 6, where sociological investigations of group behavior will also be examined.

Groups play a vital part in a society's social structure. Much of our social interaction takes place within groups and is influenced by the norms and sanctions established by groups. Being a teenager or a retired person takes on special meanings as individuals interact within groups designed for people with that particular status. The expectations associated with many social roles, including those accompanying the statuses of brother, sister, and student, become most clearly defined in the context of a group.

Groups do not merely serve to define other elements of the social structure, such as roles and statuses; they also are an intermediate link between the individual and the larger society. For example, members of occupational or social groups may be acquaintances rather than close friends; consequently, they are likely to connect other members to people in different social circles. This connection is known as a **social network**—that is, a series of social relationships that link a person directly to others and therefore indirectly to still more people. Social networks may constrain people by limiting the range of their interactions, yet these networks may empower people by making available vast resources (Marsden, 1992).

Involvement in social networks—commonly known as *networking*—provides a vital social resource in such tasks as finding employment. For ex-

In the United States, groups take all forms. Shown are members of the Polar Bear Club taking a winter dip in the icy waters of the Atlantic Ocean, members of a widowers' club, and the "sisters" of an African American sorority.

ample, while looking for a job one year after finishing school, Albert Einstein was successful only when the father of a classmate put him in touch with his future employer. These kinds of contacts, even weak and distant contacts, can be crucial in establishing social networks and facilitating transmission of information. According to one 1989 survey, 70 percent of respondents learned about employment opportunities through personal contacts and social networks, while only 14 percent did so through advertisements. Yet, as conflict theorists have emphasized, networking is not so easy for some individuals or groups as for others. In comparison with women, men tend to have longer job histories, a fact which leads to larger networks which can be used in locating employment opportunities. Men are better able to utilize what is literally an "old boy network" (K. Carter, 1989; J. Montgomery, 1992).

Sociologist Melvin Oliver (1988) used the concept of *social network* to better understand life in African American urban neighborhoods, which are often stigmatized as chaotic. Oliver interviewed Black adults in three areas of metropolitan Los Angeles to study their friendship and kinfolk ties. Respondents were *not* found to be socially isolated; they generally had little difficulty identifying mem-

bers of their social networks. Oliver's data contradict the stereotype of such neighborhoods as being "disorganized" or even "pathological." Instead, a picture unfolds of an elaborate organization of personal social networks that tie people together within and outside the Black community in bonds of concern and support.

A very different type of African American social network is evident in the U.S. Army. In 1975, a group of African American senior officers founded Rocks, an association named after Brigadier General Roscoe Cartwright, who had been killed in an airplane crash the year before. Cartwright, better known as "Rock," was an esteemed role model and mentor for many Black officers who entered the Army during the 1960s. Rocks does not view itself as a pressure group; it is dedicated to mentoring junior Black officers. Unlike African American associations outside the military, Rocks and its members tend to distance themselves from any social agenda that views recognition of past discrimination as central to Black achievement. In their political conservatism and discomfort with viewing Blacks as victims, senior African American army officers differ in an important way from the types of mentors and social networks found among Blacks' civilian leadership (Moskos, 1991).

Courtesy the Air Force Cadet Officer Action Program

Founded in 1975 by a group of African American senior officers, Rocks is an association dedicated to mentoring junior Black officers in the U.S. military.

Social Institutions

The mass media, the government, the economy, the family, and the health care system are all examples of social institutions found in our society. *Social institutions* are organized patterns of beliefs and behavior centered on basic social needs. Institutions are organized in response to particular needs, such as replacing personnel (the family) and preserving order (the government).

By studying social institutions, sociologists gain insight into the structure of a society. For example, the institution of religion adapts to the segment of society that it serves. Church work has a very different meaning for ministers who serve a skid row area, a naval base, and a suburban middle-class community. Religious leaders assigned to a skid row mission will focus on tending to the ill and providing food and shelter. By contrast, clergy in affluent suburbs will be occupied with counseling those considering marriage and divorce, arranging youth activities, and overseeing cultural events.

Functionalist View   One way to understand social institutions is to see how they fulfill essential functions. Anthropologist David F. Aberle and his colleagues (1950) and sociologists Raymond Mack and Calvin Bradford (1979:12–22) have identified five major tasks, or functional prerequisites, that a society or relatively permanent group must accomplish if it is to survive (see Table 5-1).

1   *Replacing personnel.* Any society or group must replace personnel when they die, leave, or become incapacitated. This is accomplished through immigration, annexation of neighboring groups of people, acquisition of slaves, or normal sexual reproduction of members. The Shakers, a religious sect found in the United States, are a conspicuous example of a group that failed to replace personnel. The Shakers' religious doctrines forbade any physical contact between the sexes; therefore, the group's survival depended on recruiting new members. At first, the Shakers proved quite effective in attracting members; however, their recruitment subsequently declined dramatically. Despite this fact, the Shakers maintained their commitment to celibacy, and their numbers have eventually dwindled to only a few members today (Riddle, 1988).

TABLE 5-1	Functions and Institutions
FUNCTIONAL PREREQUISITE	**SOCIAL INSTITUTIONS**
Replacing personnel	Family Government (immigration)
Teaching new recruits	Family (basic skills) Economy (occupations) Education (schools) Religion (sacred teachings)
Producing and distributing goods and services	Family (food preparation) Economy Government (regulations regarding commerce) Health care system
Preserving order	Family (child rearing, regulation of sexuality) Government Religion (morals)
Providing and maintaining a sense of purpose	Government (patriotism) Religion

Social institutions are organized patterns of beliefs and behavior which perform functions necessary for a society's survival.

2   *Teaching new recruits.* No group can survive if many of its members reject the established behavior and responsibilities of the group. As a result, finding or producing new members is not sufficient. The group must encourage recruits to learn and accept its values and customs. This learning can take place formally within schools (where learning is a manifest function) or informally through interaction and negotiation in peer groups (where instruction is a latent function).

3   *Producing and distributing goods and services.* Any relatively permanent group or society must provide and distribute desired goods and services for its members. Each society establishes a set of rules for the allocation of financial and other resources. The group must satisfy the needs of most members at least to some extent, or it will risk the possibility of discontent and, ultimately, disorder.

4   *Preserving order.* The native people of Tasmania, a large island just south of Australia, are now extinct. During the 1800s, they were destroyed by the hunting parties of European conquerors, who looked upon the Tasmanians as half-human. This annihilation underscores a critical function of every group or society—preserving order and protecting itself from attack. When faced with the more developed European technology of warfare, the Tasmanians were unable to defend themselves and an entire people was wiped out.

5 *Providing and maintaining a sense of purpose.* People must feel motivated to continue as members of a society in order to fulfill the previous four requirements. The behavior of United States prisoners of war (POWs) while in confinement during the war in Vietnam is a testament to the importance of maintaining a sense of purpose. While in prison camps, some of these men mentally made elaborate plans for marriage, family, children, reunions, and new careers. A few even built houses in their minds—right down to the last doorknob or water faucet. By holding on to a sense of purpose—their intense desire to return to their homeland and live normal lives—the POWs refused to allow the agony of confinement to destroy their mental health.

Many aspects of a society can assist people in developing and maintaining a sense of purpose. For some people, religious values or personal moral codes are most crucial; for others, national or tribal identities are especially meaningful. Whatever these differences, in any society there remains one common and critical reality. If an individual does not have a sense of purpose, he or she has little reason to contribute to a society's survival.

This list of functional prerequisites does not specify how a society and its corresponding social institutions will perform each task. For example, one society may protect itself from external attack by maintaining a frightening arsenal of weaponry, while another may make determined efforts to remain neutral in world politics and to promote cooperative relationships with its neighbors. No matter what its particular strategy, any society or relatively permanent group must attempt to satisfy all these functional prerequisites for survival. If it fails on even one condition, as the Tasmanians did, the society runs the risk of extinction.

Conflict View Conflict theorists do not concur with the functionalist approach to social institu-

Shown is Eldress Bertha Lindsay of the Shaker community in Canterbury, New Hampshire. The Shakers' continuing commitment to celibacy has limited their recruitment, and today there are few Shakers left in the United States.

tions. While both perspectives agree that institutions are organized to meet basic social needs, conflict theorists object to the implication inherent in the functionalist view that the outcome is necessarily efficient and desirable. Conflict theorists concede the presence of a negotiated order, but they add that many segments of our society—among them the homeless, the disabled, and people with AIDS—are not in a position to negotiate effectively, because they lack sufficient power and resources.

From a conflict perspective, the present organization of social institutions is no accident. Major institutions, such as education, help to maintain the privileges of the most powerful individuals and groups within a society, while contributing to the powerlessness of others. As one example, public schools in the United States are financed largely through property taxes. This allows more affluent

131

BOX 5-2 · SPEAKING OUT

SAVAGE INEQUALITIES IN PUBLIC EDUCATION

Educator Jonathan Kozol toured the United States and found that many public schools across the nation are literally falling apart. Kozol emphasizes that while many students in affluent school districts receive a high-quality public education, the same is hardly true for students in low-income areas. In the following excerpt, Kozol (1991: 158–159) describes the conditions in New Jersey's public schools:

. . . Overcrowding in New Jersey, as in Harlem and the Bronx, is a constant feature of the schools that serve the poorest children. In low-income Irvington, for instance, where 94 percent of students are nonwhite, 11 classes in one school don't even have the luxury of classrooms. They share an auditorium in which they occupy adjacent sections of the stage and backstage areas. "It's very difficult," says the music teacher, "to have concert rehearsals with the choir" while ten other classes try to study in the same space. "Obviously," she says, "there is a problem with sound. . . ."

"I'm housed in a coat room," says

Jonathan Kozol.

a reading teacher at another school in Irvington. "I teach," says a music teacher, "in a storage room." Two other classes, their teachers say, are in converted coal bins. A guidance counselor says she holds her parent meetings in a closet. "My problem," says a compensatory-reading teacher, "is that I work in a

pantry. . . . It's very difficult to teach in these conditions."

At Irvington High School, where gym students have no showers, the gym is used by up to seven classes at a time. To shoot one basketball, according to the coach, a student waits for 20 minutes. There are no working lockers. Children lack opportunities to bathe. They fight over items left in lockers they can't lock. They fight for their eight minutes on the floor. Again, the scarcity of things that other children take for granted in America—showers, lockers, space and time to exercise—creates the overheated mood that also causes trouble in the streets. The students perspire. They grow dirty and impatient. They dislike who they are and what they have become.

The crowding of the school reflects the crowding of the streets. "It becomes striking," says a parent in another urban district, "how closely these schools reflect their communities, as if the duty of the school were to prepare a child for the life he's born to. . . . It hardly seems fair."

areas to provide their children with better-equipped schools and better-paid teachers than low-income areas can afford. Children from prosperous communities will therefore be better prepared to compete academically than children from impoverished communities. The structure of the nation's educational system permits and even promotes such unequal treatment of schoolchildren. In Box 5-2, we are reminded that children in underfinanced schools are defenseless against the inequities of society.

Conflict theorists argue that social institutions such as education have an inherently conservative

nature. Without question, it has been difficult to implement educational reforms that promote equal opportunity—whether in the area of bilingual education, school desegregation, or mainstreaming of students with disabilities (see Chapter 16). From a functionalist perspective, social change can be dysfunctional, since it often leads to instability. However, from a conflict view, why should we preserve the existing social structure if it is unfair and discriminatory?

Sociologist D. Stanley Eitzen notes a basic paradox of all institutions: they are absolutely necessary, yet they are a source of social problems. He adds that it has become fashionable to attack social institutions, such as the family and the government, in recent years. In Eitzen's view, we should not forget that people depend on institutions for "stability and guarantees against chaos" (1978:545). We must recognize that social institutions are essential yet must not regard permanence as a justification for inequality and injustice.

Interactionist View Social institutions affect our daily lives. Whether we are driving down the street or standing in a long shopping line, our everyday behavior is governed by social institutions. For example, in her fascinating account of behavior within large organizations, *Men and Women of the Corporation,* sociologist Rosabeth Moss Kanter (1977a:36) describes how an impulsive statement by a top executive is routinely viewed as an order and often leads to immediate and unnecessary action by subordinates. For example, when the vice chairman of a corporation mentioned at a luncheon that he was looking for a car for his daughter, a lower-level executive instructed a purchasing agent to take on the job. The vice chairman had no idea that this was happening; had he known, he probably would not have approved. But an innocent remark by someone at the top of an organization's hierarchy can easily be seen as an ultimatum.

Drawing on the interactionist perspective, sociologist William Thompson studied the day-to-day activities of assembly line workers by conducting nine weeks of observation research in the slaughter division of a beef processing plant in the midwest. Thompson (1983:215) notes that "working in the beef plant is 'dirty' work, not only in the literal sense of being drenched with perspiration and beef blood, but also in the figurative sense of performing a low status, routine, and demeaning job." In addition to being "dirty," work in this plant is monotonous and exhausting. Thompson and his coworkers had to hang, brand, and bag between 1350 and 1500 beef tongues in an eight-hour shift.

Thompson emphasizes that a subtle sense of unity exists among the "beefers," as they call themselves. It is almost impossible for workers to speak with one another while on the assembly line because of excessive noise, the need for earplugs, and the isolation of certain work areas. Nevertheless, workers communicate through an extensive system of nonverbal symbols, including exaggerated gestures, shrill whistles, "thumbs up" and "thumbs down" signs, and the clanging of knives against stainless steel tables and tubs. Thompson (1983:233) suggests that "in a setting which would apparently eliminate it, the workers' desire for social interaction won out and interaction flourished."

Interactionist theorists emphasize that our social behavior is conditioned by the roles and statuses which we accept, the groups to which we belong, and the institutions within which we function. For example, the social roles associated with being a judge occur within the larger context of the criminal justice system. The status of "judge" stands in relation to other statuses, such as attorney, plaintiff, defendant, and witness, as well as to the social institution of government. While the symbolic aspects of courts and jails, for example, are awesome, the judicial system derives continued significance from the roles people carry out in social interactions (P. Berger and Luckmann, 1966:74–76).

SOCIAL STRUCTURE AND MODERN SOCIETY

A common feature of modern societies when contrasted with earlier social arrangements is the greater complexity of contemporary life. Sociologists Émile Durkheim and Ferdinand Tönnies offered typologies for contrasting modern societies with simpler forms of social structure.

Durkheim's Mechanical and Organic Solidarity

In his *Division of Labor* (1933, original edition 1893), Durkheim argued that social structure depends on the level of division of labor in a society—in other words, on the manner in which tasks are performed. Thus, a task such as providing food can be carried out almost totally by one individual or can be divided among many people. The latter pattern typically occurs in modern societies; cultivation, processing, distribution, and retailing of a single food item are performed by literally hundreds of people.

In societies in which there is minimal division of labor, a collective consciousness develops with an emphasis on group solidarity. Durkheim termed this *mechanical solidarity,* implying that all individuals perform the same tasks. No one needs to ask, "What do your parents do?" since all are engaged in similar work. Each person prepares food, hunts, makes clothing, builds homes, and so forth. People have few options regarding what to do with their lives, so there is little concern for individual needs. Instead, the group will is the dominating force in society. Both social interaction and negotiation are based on close, intimate, face-to-face social contacts. Since there is little specialization, there are few social roles.

As societies become more advanced technologically, greater division of labor takes place. The person who cuts down timber is not the same person who puts up your roof. With increasing specialization, many different tasks must be performed by different individuals—even in manufacturing one item such as a radio or stove. In general, social interactions become less personal than in societies characterized by mechanical solidarity. We begin relating to others on the basis of their social positions ("butcher," "nurse") rather than their distinctive

human qualities. Statuses and social roles are in perpetual flux as the overall social structure of the society continues to change.

In Durkheim's terms, *organic solidarity* involves a collective consciousness resting on the need a society's members have for one another. Once society becomes more complex and there is greater division of labor, no individual can go it alone. Dependence on others becomes essential for group survival. Durkheim chose the term *organic solidarity,* since, in his view, individuals become interdependent in much the same way as organs of the human body.

Tönnies's *Gemeinschaft* and *Gesellschaft*

Sociologist Ferdinand Tönnies (1855–1936) was appalled by the rise of an industrial city in his native Germany during the late 1800s. In his view, this marked a dramatic change from the ideal type of a close-knit community, which Tönnies (1988, original edition 1887) termed *Gemeinschaft,* to that of an impersonal mass society known as *Gesellschaft.*

The *Gemeinschaft* ("guh-MINE-shoft") community is typical of rural life. It is a small community in which people have similar backgrounds and life

"I'd like to think of you as a person, David, but it's my job to think of you as personnel."

In a Gesellschaft, *people are likely to relate to one another in terms of their roles rather than their individual backgrounds.*

TABLE 5-2	Comparison of *Gemeinschaft* and *Gesellschaft*	
GEMEINSCHAFT		**GESELLSCHAFT**
Rural life typifies this form.		Urban life typifies this form.
People share a feeling of community which results from their similar backgrounds and life experiences.		People perceive little sense of commonality. Their differences in background appear more striking than their similarities.
Social interactions, including negotiations, are intimate and familiar.		Social interactions, including negotiations, are more likely to be task-specific.
There is a spirit of cooperation and unity of will.		Self-interests dominate.
Tasks and personal relationships cannot be separated.		The task being performed is paramount; relationships are subordinate.
There is little emphasis on individual privacy.		Privacy is valued.
Informal social control predominates.		Formal social control is evident.
There is less tolerance of deviance.		There is greater tolerance of deviance.
Emphasis is on ascribed statuses.		There is more emphasis on achieved statuses.
Social change is relatively limited.		Social change is very evident—even within a generation.

experiences. Virtually everyone knows one another, and social interactions (including negotiations) are intimate and familiar, almost as one might find among kinfolk. There is a commitment to the larger social group and a sense of togetherness among community members. Therefore, in dealing with people, one relates to them not merely as "clerk" or "manager" but, rather, in a more personal way. With this more personal interaction comes less privacy: we know more about everyone.

Social control in the *Gemeinschaft* community is maintained through informal means such as moral persuasion, gossip, and even gestures. These techniques work effectively because people are genuinely concerned about how others feel toward them. Social change is relatively limited in the *Gemeinschaft;* the lives of members of one generation may be quite similar to those of their grandparents.

By contrast, the **Gesellschaft** ("guh-ZELL-shoft") is an ideal type characteristic of modern urban life. Most people are strangers and perceive little sense of commonality with other community residents. Relationships are governed by social roles which grow out of immediate tasks, such as purchasing a product or arranging a business meeting. Self-interests dominate, and there is generally little con-

Writing in 1887, Ferdinand Tönnies described two contrasting types of social structure: Gemeinschaft *and* Gesellschaft.

sensus concerning values or commitment to the group. As a result, social control must rely on more formal techniques, such as laws and legally defined punishments. Social change is an important aspect of life in the *Gesellschaft;* it can be strikingly evident even within a single generation.

Table 5-2 summarizes the differences between the *Gemeinschaft* and the *Gesellschaft* as described by Tönnies. Sociologists have used these terms to compare social structures stressing close relationships with those that emphasize less personal ties. It is easy to view *Gemeinschaft* with nostalgia as a far better way of life than the "rat race" of contemporary existence. However, with the more intimate relationships of the *Gemeinschaft* comes a price. The prejudice and discrimination found within *Gemeinschaft* can be quite confining; more emphasis is placed on such ascribed statuses as family background than on people's unique talents and achievements. In addition, *Gemeinschaft* tends to be distrustful of the individual who seeks to be creative or just to be different.

The work of Émile Durkheim and Ferdinand Tönnies shows that a major focus of sociology has been to identify changes in social structure and the consequences for human behavior. At the macro level, they both offer descriptions of societies shifting to more advanced forms of technology. In addition, they identify the impact of these societywide changes at the micro level in terms of the nature of social interactions between people. Durkheim emphasizes the degree to which people carry out the same tasks. Tönnies directs our attention to whether people look out for their own interests or for the well-being of the larger group. Nevertheless, there is a great deal of similarity between the typologies of these European sociologists. They agree that as social structure becomes more complex, people's relationships tend to become more impersonal, transient, and fragmented. In the social policy section which follows, we will examine how the AIDS crisis has transformed the social structure of our complex society.

SOCIAL POLICY AND SOCIAL JUSTICE

THE AIDS CRISIS

- How has AIDS affected the normal functioning of social institutions in the United States?
- Why is there such a strong stigma attached to infection with the HIV virus and to AIDS?
- How might sociologists influence research on AIDS and AIDS-related issues?

In his novel *The Plague,* Albert Camus (1948) wrote: "There have been as many plagues as wars in history, yet always plagues and wars take people equally by surprise." Regarded by many as the distinctive plague of the modern era, AIDS certainly caught major social institutions—particularly the government, the health care system, and the economy—by surprise.

The first cases of AIDS in the United States were reported in 1981. By 1987, 50,000 cases had been reported; by mid-1989, 100,000 cases. As of September 30, 1992, 242,000 cases of AIDS had been reported in the United States, and more than 160,000 people had died of AIDS-related causes. Around the world, about 350,000 cases had been formally reported as of 1992, but it is estimated that more than 1 million people actually have AIDS (R. Anderson and May, 1992; Centers for Disease Control, 1992b, 1992c; see Table 5-3).

AIDS is the acronym for *acquired immune deficiency syndrome.* Rather than being a distinct disease, AIDS is actually a predisposition to disease caused by a virus, the human immunodeficiency virus (HIV), that destroys the body's immune system, thereby leaving the carrier vulnerable to infections such as pneumonia that those with healthy immune systems can generally resist. AIDS is not transmitted through touching, shaking hands, sharing meals, drinking from the same cup, or other types of routine, nonintimate contact in the home or the workplace. Transmission from one person to another appears to require either intimate sexual contact or exchange of blood or bodily fluids (whether from contaminated hypodermic needles or syringes, transfusions of infected blood, or transmission from an infected mother to her child before or during birth). The attention given by health practitioners to methods of transmitting the HIV virus is the direct result of the absence of a vaccine or cure for AIDS. Since there is currently no way to eradicate AIDS medically, it is essential to reduce the transmission of the virus.

TABLE 5-3	Total AIDS Cases in Ohio, 1981–1995
1981	2
1983	35
1987	797
1990	2417
1993	5060
1995	7288

NOTE: Data for 1993 and 1995 are projections.
SOURCE: Gould and Kabel, 1993:90–91.

This table shows the continuing and dramatic rise in AIDS cases in the state of Ohio over the period 1981 to 1995.

As has been well publicized, the high-risk groups most in danger of contracting AIDS in the United States are homosexual and bisexual men (who account for about 60 percent of all cases), intravenous (IV) drug users (who account for about 30 percent of all cases), and their sexual partners. Recently, there has been increasing evidence that AIDS is a particular danger for the urban poor, in good part because of transmission via IV drug use. Whereas Blacks and Hispanics represent about 20 percent of the nation's population, they constitute 48 percent of all adults in the United States who have been found to have AIDS in the last two years. Around the world, women are becoming infected with HIV about as often as men. According to Dr. Michael Merson, head of the World Health Organization's global program on AIDS, the "AIDS epidemic is becoming heterosexual everywhere" (L. Altman, 1992a:C3; Centers for Disease Control, 1992b; *New York Times*, 1991b).

As of 1993, more than two-thirds of all companies in the United States with at least 2500 employees—as well as nearly one out of every ten small companies—have had an employee with HIV infection or AIDS (Pogash, 1992). The staggering rise in AIDS cases has affected the nation in a profound way. Harvey Fineberg (1988:128), dean of the Harvard School of Public Health, has observed: "Its reach extends to every social institution, from families, schools and communities to businesses, courts of law, the military and Federal, state, and local governments." The strain on the health care system has become increasingly obvious, as hospitals are being overwhelmed by the demands of caring for AIDS patients and the desperate need for more beds to meet the rising AIDS caseload.

On the micro level of social interaction, it has been widely forecast that AIDS will lead to a more conservative sexual climate—among both homosexuals and heterosexuals—in which people will be much more cautious about involvement with new partners. Yet it appears that many sexually active people in the United States have not heeded precautions about "safer sex." According to the 1990 nationwide Youth Risk Behavior Survey, only half of males questioned and only 40 percent of females reported that they or their partner used a condom during their last experience of sexual intercourse (Centers for Disease Control, 1992a).

AIDS activist organizations bitterly charge that public health efforts and government funding for AIDS-related research have been grossly inadequate. Especially visible and outspoken in this effort is the AIDS Coalition to Unleash Power (ACT-UP), shown here in a "lie-in" to dramatize deaths from AIDS.

In the 1990s, the label of "person with AIDS" or "HIV-positive" often functions as a master status. Indeed, people with AIDS or infected with the HIV virus face a powerful dual stigma. Not only are they associated with a lethal and contagious disease; they have a disease which is disproportionately evident in already stigmatized groups, such as gay males and drug users. This linkage with stigmatized groups delayed recognition of the severity of the AIDS epidemic; the media took little interest in the disease until it seemed to be spreading beyond the gay community. Viewed from a conflict perspective, policymakers have been slow to respond to the AIDS crisis because those in high-risk groups—gay men and IV drug users—are comparatively powerless. As one health care consultant pointedly asked: "Who speaks for the drug abuser in our society? Who's in favor of them?" (J. Gross, 1987:A16; Herek and Glunt, 1988; Shilts, 1987).

Polling data show how the stigma associated with high-risk groups affects people's feelings about AIDS. According to a national survey in 1991, 85 percent of respondents said they had a "lot of sympathy" or "some sympathy" for people with AIDS—an increase from the 75 percent who answered the same question this way in a 1988 survey. Yet only 39 percent of those questioned in 1991 indicated that they had a lot of sympathy or some sympathy for "people who get AIDS from homosexual activity," while only 30 percent expressed such sympathy for "people who get AIDS from sharing needles while using illegal drugs." The discrepancy in these data reflects a tendency to blame members of high-risk groups for contracting AIDS. Indeed, those who got AIDS without engaging in homosexual behavior or drug use, such as teenage hemophiliacs, are often spoken of as "innocent victims"—with the implication that others with AIDS are "blamable victims" (Herek and Glunt, 1988:888; Kagay, 1991:C3).

In this climate of fear and blame, there has been increasing harassment of homosexual males. Gay rights leaders believe that the concept of homosexuals as "disease carriers" has contributed to violent incidents directed at people known or suspected to be gay. "What AIDS has done," argues Kevin Berrill of the National Lesbian and Gay Task Force, "is simply give bigots and bashers the justification to attack gays" (D. Altman, 1986:58–70; D. Johnson, 1987:A12).

Fears about AIDS have led to growing discrimination within major social institutions of the United States. For example, people with AIDS have faced discrimination in employment, housing, and insurance. Yet the legal system has hardly taken the lead in fighting such discrimination. According to a report issued in 1992 by the National AIDS Program Office, which coordinates the work of all federal agencies dealing with the disease, the courts seem guided more by stereotypes and fears than by scientific evidence when they rule on AIDS-related cases. Larry Gostin, a professor of health law and a coauthor of the report, points out that some courts have exacerbated public fears of the disease by placing "Do Not Touch" signs on AIDS-related evidence, by having defendants with HIV wear rubber gloves, and by levying harsh penalties on people with AIDS for biting or spitting at others. Gostin insists that these situations pose minimal risks of transmission and that the court decisions "fly in the face of all the public health wisdom about AIDS" (Margolick, 1992:16).

Any such dramatic crisis is likely to bring about certain transformations in a society's social structure. From a functionalist perspective, if established social institutions cannot meet a crucial need, new social networks are likely to emerge to fulfill that function. In the case of AIDS, self-help groups—especially in the gay communities of major cities—have been established to care for the sick, educate the healthy, and lobby for more responsive public policies. By 1993, Gay Men's Health Crisis (GMHC), New York City's largest private organization providing AIDS services, had a paid staff of 250 and more than 2300 volunteers typically working in a "buddy system" with those afflicted with AIDS. Although initially GMHC's clients were almost exclusively White homosexual men, today 10 percent of clients are female, 44 percent are non-White, and many are heterosexual. GMHC operates a telephone hot line, sends advocates to hospitals to insist on better care for patients, and runs legal and financial clinics as well as therapy and support groups for people with AIDS and their loved ones (Navarro, 1993).

GMHC and other groups concerned with AIDS argue that the proper societal response to this deadly disease includes testing of new drugs to combat AIDS, massive public education campaigns regarding the need for "safer sex," wide distribution and proper use of condoms, and effective counseling and support services for those with AIDS and HIV infection. AIDS activist organizations bitterly charge that there has been grossly inadequate governmental funding for AIDS-related research and public health efforts. Especially visible and outspoken in this effort is the AIDS Coalition to Unleash Power (ACT-UP), which has conducted controversial protests, sit-ins, and "zaps" in the halls of government, at scientific conferences concerned with AIDS, at New York City's St. Patrick's Cathedral, and on Wall Street. ACT-UP has popularized the slogan it views as the crucial message of the AIDS crisis:

"Silence = Death" (France, 1988; J. Gamson, 1989; Shilts, 1989).

How can sociologists use their expertise to assist in responding to the AIDS crisis? In an address before the American Sociological Association, Canadian sociologist Barry Adam (1992:5–15) expressed concern that research on AIDS has been largely conducted by biomedical scientists. Adam argued that sociologists can make an important contribution to AIDS-related research; he outlined four directions for such sociological research:

• How is information about AIDS produced and distributed? Is the distribution of information about how to have "safer sex" being limited or even censored?

• How does an AIDS "folklore" emerge, and how does it become integrated into a community? Why do certain communities and individuals resist or ignore scientific information about the dangers of AIDS?

• How are medical and social services made available to people with AIDS? Why are these services often denied to the poorest patients?

• How is *homophobia* (fear of and prejudice against homosexuality) related to fears concerning AIDS? In what ways does homophobia correlate with other forms of bias?

SUMMARY

Social interaction refers to the ways in which people respond to one another. *Social structure* refers to the way in which a society is organized into predictable relationships. This chapter examines these concepts, which are central to sociological study.

1 Our response to people's behavior is based on the *meaning* we attach to their actions.

2 The ability to define social reality clearly reflects a group's power within a society.

3 An *ascribed status* is generally assigned to a person at birth, whereas an *achieved status* is attained largely through one's own effort.

4 In the United States, ascribed statuses of race and gender can function as *master statuses* that have an important impact on one's potential to achieve a desired professional and social status.

5 With each distinctive status—whether ascribed or achieved—come particular *social roles.*

6 Much of our patterned behavior takes place within *groups* and is influenced by the norms and sanctions established by groups.

7 The mass media, the government, the economy, the family, and the health care system are all examples of *social institutions* found in the United States.

8 One way to understand social institutions is to see how they fulfill essential functions, such as replacing personnel, training new recruits, and preserving order.

9 The conflict perspective argues that social institutions help to maintain the privileges of the powerful while contributing to the powerlessness of others.

10 Interactionist theorists emphasize that our social behavior is conditioned by the roles and statuses that we accept, the groups to which we belong, and the institutions within which we function.

11 Ferdinand Tönnies distinguished the close-knit community of *Gemeinschaft* from the impersonal mass society known as *Gesellschaft.*

12 The AIDS crisis has affected every social institution in the United States, including the family, the schools, the health care system, the economy, and government.

CRITICAL THINKING QUESTIONS

1 Analyze your college community as an example of a negotiated order. What types of negotiations are common in the day-to-day interactions in this social institution?

2 People in certain professions seem particularly susceptible to role conflict. For example, journalists commonly experience role conflict during disasters, crimes, and other distressing situations. Should they offer assistance to the needy or cover breaking news as reporters? Select two other professions and discuss the types of role conflict they might experience.

3 The functionalist, conflict, and interactionist perspectives can all be used in analyzing social institutions. What are the strengths or weaknesses in each perspective's analysis of social institutions?

KEY TERMS

Achieved status A social position attained by a person largely through his or her own effort. (page 124)

Ascribed status A social position "assigned" to a person by society without regard for the person's unique talents or characteristics. (124)

Gemeinschaft A term used by Ferdinand Tönnies to describe close-knit communities, often found in rural areas, in which strong personal bonds unite members. (134)

Gesellschaft A term used by Ferdinand Tönnies to describe communities, often urban, that are large and impersonal, with little commitment to the group or consensus on values. (135)

Group Any number of people with similar norms, values, and expectations who regularly and consciously interact. (127)

Homophobia Fear of and prejudice against homosexuality. (139)

Master status A status that dominates others and thereby determines a person's general position within society. (125)

Mechanical solidarity A term used by Émile Durkheim to describe a society in which people generally all perform the same tasks and in which relationships are close and intimate. (134)

Negotiated order A social structure that derives its existence from the social interactions through which people define and redefine its character. (123)

Negotiation The attempt to reach agreement with others concerning some objective. (122)

Organic solidarity A term used by Émile Durkheim to describe a society in which members are mutually dependent and in which a complex division of labor exists. (134)

Role conflict Difficulties that occur when incompatible expectations arise from two or more social positions held by the same person. (125)

Role exit The process of disengagement from a role that is central to one's self-identity, and reestablishment of an identity in a new role. (126)

Social institutions Organized patterns of beliefs and behavior centered on basic social needs. (130)

Social interaction The ways in which people respond to one another. (120)

Social network A series of social relationships that link a person directly to others and therefore indirectly to still more people. (127)

Social role A set of expectations of people who occupy a given social position or status. (125)

Social structure The way in which a society is organized into predictable relationships. (120)

Status A term used by sociologists to refer to any of the full range of socially defined positions within a large group or society. (124)

ADDITIONAL READINGS

Deegan, Mary Jo, and Michael Hill (eds.). *Women and Symbolic Interaction.* Winchester, Mass.: Allen and Unwin, 1987. A varied and useful collection of writings drawing on the interactionist perspective to examine the role of gender in everyday life.

Duneier, Mitchell. *Slim's Table: Race, Respectability, and Masculinity.* Chicago: University of Chicago Press, 1992. This study describes everyday social interactions and relationships between Whites and African Americans in a small diner on Chicago's Southside.

Ebaugh, Helen Rose Fuchs. *Becoming an Ex: The Process of Role Exit.* Chicago: University of Chicago Press, 1988. As described in Box 5-1, sociologist Ebaugh examines the process of disengaging from a significant social role and establishing a new identity.

Huber, Joan, and Beth E. Schneider (eds.). *The Social Context of AIDS.* Newbury Park, Calif.: Sage, 1992. This anthology addresses a variety of issues as they relate to AIDS, including race, gender stratification, education, and persistent poverty.

Kephart, William M., and William M. Zellner. *Extraordinary Groups: An Examination of Unconventional Life-Styles* (5th ed.). New York: St. Martin's, 1994. Among the groups described in this very readable book are the Amish, the Oneida community, the Mormons, Hasidic Jews, Jehovah's Witnesses, and the Romani (commonly known as *Gypsies).*

Majors, Richard, and Janet Mancini Bellson. *Cool Pose: The Dilemmas of Black Manhood in America.* New York: Lexington, 1992. An African American psychologist and a White sociologist analyze the ways in which African American adolescent males present themselves in everyday life.

Scheff, Thomas J. *Microsociology: Discourse, Emotion, and Structure*. Chicago: University of Chicago Press, 1992. An examination of sociological treatment of self and society.

Tannen, Deborah. *You Just Don't Understand: Women and Men in Conversation*. New York: Ballantine, 1990. A popularly written book that provides an overview of how men and women in the United States differ in their styles of communication.

Journals

Among the journals that focus on issues of social interaction and social structure are *Journal of Contemporary Ethnography* (formerly *Urban Life*, founded 1971) and *Symbolic Interaction* (1977). Several relevant publications have devoted special issues to the behavioral implications of AIDS, including *American Psychologist* (September 1988), *Scientific American* (October 1988), and *Social Problems* (October 1989).

6

GROUPS AND ORGANIZATIONS

UNDERSTANDING GROUPS
Types of Groups
  Primary and Secondary Groups
  In-Groups and Out-Groups
  Reference Groups
Studying Small Groups
  Size of a Group
  Coalitions
  Physical Environment

UNDERSTANDING ORGANIZATIONS
Formal Organizations and Bureaucracies
  Development of Formal Organizations
  Characteristics of a Bureaucracy
    1 Division of Labor
    2 Hierarchy of Authority
    3 Written Rules and Regulations
    4 Impersonality

*5 Employment Based on Technical
    Qualifications*
  Bureaucratization as a Process
  Oligarchy: Rule by a Few
  Bureaucracy's Other Face
Voluntary Associations
Organizational Change
  Goal Multiplication
  Goal Succession

**SOCIAL POLICY AND
ORGANIZATIONS:
SEXUAL HARASSMENT**

BOXES
6-1 Current Research: Multicultural Small
    Groups
6-2 Everyday Behavior: Self-Help Groups

LOOKING AHEAD

- How do sociologists distinguish between various types of groups?
- How does cultural diversity affect the performance of small groups in the workplace?
- What are some of the positive and negative consequences of bureaucracy?
- How important are informal structures within formal organizations?
- Why do so many people in the United States join voluntary associations?
- How common is sexual harassment within organizations in the United States?

Many of us know or have been visited by someone employed by a direct-selling organization (DSO) such as Amway, Tupperware, Shaklee, or Mary Kay Cosmetics. These salespeople often go door to door or arrange house parties in an attempt to reach potential customers. Involvement in DSO work is an intense experience; the gatherings of DSO employees have been compared to religious revival meetings. After conducting a study of 42 DSOs, sociologist Nicole Woolsey Biggart (1989) characterized DSOs as "charismatic" because of the awe they arouse in employees.

The strong personal appeal of DSO founders accounts in good part for the intense and passionate tone of gatherings. DSO employees speak of their companies' founders in terms not usually applied to corporate chief executive officers (CEOs):

[Shaklee was] a remarkable man. He was far ahead of his time. He developed Vita-Line minerals, the first product, a year before the word "vitamin" was even coined. He's [had] a special place in my heart (Biggart, 1989:142).

Even watching [Mary Kay] on TV is real hard for me. I just get this knot in my stomach whenever I see her or listen to her talk or anything (Biggart, 1989:143).

These founders are successful in promoting organizational ideologies that are missionary in character. DSO employees genuinely believe that their clients will be better people and enjoy happier lives by using DSO products.

In most DSOs, the sales force is overwhelmingly female, and many of these salespeople are homemakers. Sociologist Paul DiMaggio points out that DSOs provide these homemakers with income, enhance their marital power, and offer a sense of community. Nevertheless, DiMaggio (1990:210) concludes that DSOs are "prefeminist" because their ideologies are supportive of male dominance: "women should view selling as not quite a job, seek husbands' permission to enroll, place family before career, or, when firms recruit spouses as teams, take backstage roles."

People in the United States are joiners, whether they join direct-selling organizations, chamber music groups, street gangs, athletic teams, religious institutions, or professional organizations. Many of us ask, "When is the next meeting?" almost as often as we ask, "What should we have for dinner?" As was pointed out in the earlier chapters, social interaction is necessary for the transmission of culture and

In most direct-selling organizations (DSOs), the sales force is overwhelmingly female, and many of these salespeople are homemakers. Shown is an Avon sales representative visiting a home in Budapest, Hungary.

the survival of a society. Our lives are filled with relatively random and inconsequential interactions, such as conversations with cashiers in stores and supermarkets. However, many social interactions are planned or anticipated. We relate to certain people because we like them, they have something to offer us, they are working to accomplish a goal we share, or we have no other choice.

This chapter will consider the impact of groups and organizations on social interaction. It will begin by noting the distinctions between various types of groups. Particular attention will be given to small groups and to the analysis of interactionist theorists regarding the dynamics of small groups. How and why formal organizations came into existence will be examined, and Max Weber's model of the modern bureaucracy will be described. The tendency of people in the United States to join voluntary associations, as noted by Alexis de Tocqueville, will be discussed. The social policy section will focus on the issue of sexual harassment, which has become a major concern of both governmental and private-sector organizations.

UNDERSTANDING GROUPS

In everyday speech, people use the term *group* to describe any collection of individuals, whether three strangers sharing an elevator or hundreds at a meeting of the Tupperware sales force. However,

as we noted in Chapter 5, in sociological terms a *group* is any number of people with similar norms, values, and expectations who regularly and consciously interact. College sororities and fraternities, dance companies, tenants' associations, and chess clubs are all considered examples of groups. It is important to emphasize that members of a group share some sense of belonging. This characteristic distinguishes groups from mere *aggregates* of people, such as passengers who happen to be together on an airplane flight, or from *categories* who share a common feature (such as being retired) but otherwise do not act together.

A college debating society is typical of groups found in the United States. It has agreed-upon values and social norms. All members want to improve their public speaking skills and believe that informed debate on issues of public policy is an essential aspect of democracy. In addition, like many groups, the society has both a formal and an informal structure. It has monthly meetings, run by elected officers, in a student union building. At the same time, unofficial leadership roles are held by the club's most experienced debaters, who often coach new members regarding debating strategies and techniques.

Types of Groups

The study of groups has become an important part of sociological investigation because they play such

In sociological terms, a group is any number of people with similar norms, values, and expectations who regularly and consciously interact. Shown are members of the Full Gospel Motor Association in Plano, Texas. The members of this group typically join hands before setting out to change tires, help stranded motorists, and preach the gospel. The bikers initially talk with motorists about their motorcycles but then steer the conversation to loftier topics, such as how to "reverse direction from the highway to hell to the highway to heaven."

a key role in the transmission of culture. Sociologists have made a number of useful distinctions between types of groups (see Table 6-1).

Primary and Secondary Groups   Charles Horton Cooley (1902:23–57) coined the term *primary*

TABLE 6-1	Comparison of Primary and Secondary Groups
PRIMARY GROUP	SECONDARY GROUP
Generally small	Usually large
Relatively long period of interaction	Short duration, temporary
Intimate, face-to-face association	Little social intimacy or mutual understanding
Some emotional depth in relationships	Relationships generally superficial
Cooperative, friendly	More formal and impersonal

In distinguishing between types of groups, sociologists have noted the differences between primary and secondary groups.

group to refer to a small group characterized by intimate, face-to-face association and cooperation. The members of a street gang constitute a primary group; so do members of a family living in the same household, as well as "sisters" in a college sorority.

Primary groups play a pivotal role both in the socialization process (see Chapter 4) and in the development of roles and statuses (see Chapter 5). Indeed, primary groups can be instrumental in a person's day-to-day existence. Studies have shown, for example, that neighbors, close friends, and especially kinfolk play a vital role in assisting people to follow complicated schedules for taking prescription medicines (Kail and Litwak, 1989).

When we find ourselves identifying closely with a group, it is probably a primary group. However, people in the United States participate in many groups which are not characterized by close bonds of friendship, such as large college classes and business associations. The term *secondary group* refers to a formal, impersonal group in which there is little social intimacy or mutual understanding (see Table 6-1). The distinction between primary and secondary groups is not always clear-cut. Some fraternities or social clubs become so large and impersonal that they no longer function as primary groups.

In-Groups and Out-Groups A group can hold special meaning for members because of its relationship to other groups. People sometimes feel antagonistic to or threatened by another group, especially if the group is perceived as being different culturally or racially. Sociologists identify these "we" and "they" feelings by using two terms first employed by William Graham Sumner (1906:12–13): *in-group* and *out-group*.

An **in-group** can be defined as any group or category to which people feel they belong. Simply put, it comprises everyone who is regarded as "we" or "us." The in-group may be as narrow as one's family or as broad as an entire society. The very existence of an in-group implies that there is an out-group viewed as "they" or "them." More formally, an **out-group** is a group or category to which people feel they do not belong.

People in the United States tend to see the world in terms of in-groups and out-groups, a perception often fostered by the very groups to which we belong. "*Our* generation does not have those sexual hangups." "*We* Christians go to church every week." "*We* have to support *our* troops in the Persian Gulf." Although not explicit, each of these declarations suggests who the in-groups and out-groups are.

One typical consequence of in-group membership is a feeling of distinctiveness and superiority among members, who see themselves as better than people in the out-group. This sense of superiority can be enhanced by a double standard maintained by members of the in-group. Proper behavior for the in-group is simultaneously viewed as unacceptable behavior for the out-group. Sociologist Robert Merton (1968:480–488) describes this process as the conversion of "in-group virtues" into "out-group vices."

The attitudes of certain Christians toward Jews illustrate such a double standard. If Christians take their faith seriously, it is seen as "commendable"; if Jews do the same, it is a sign of "backwardness" and a refusal to enter the twentieth century. If Christians prefer other Christians as friends, it is "understandable"; if Jews prefer other Jews as friends, they are attacked for being "clannish." This view of "us and them" can be destructive, as conflict theorists have suggested. At the same time, it promotes in-group solidarity and a sense of belonging (Karlins et al., 1969).

"So long, Bill. This is my club. You can't come in."

Reference Groups Both in-groups and primary groups can dramatically influence the way an individual thinks and behaves. Sociologists use the term **reference group** when speaking of any group that individuals use as a standard for evaluating themselves and their own behavior. For example, a high school student who aspires to join a social circle of punk rock devotees will pattern his or her behavior after that of the group. The student will begin dressing like these peers, listening to the same record albums and CDs, and hanging out at the same stores and clubs.

Reference groups have two basic purposes. They serve a normative function by setting and enforcing standards of conduct and belief. Thus, the high school student who wants the approval of the punk rock crowd will have to follow the group's dictates to at least some extent. Reference groups also perform a comparison function by serving as a standard against which people can measure themselves and others. A law student will evaluate himself or herself against a reference group composed of lawyers, law professors, and judges (Merton and Kitt, 1950).

BOX 6-1 · CURRENT RESEARCH

MULTICULTURAL SMALL GROUPS

The growing diversity of the paid labor force, especially in Europe and North America, is well documented. What impact will this diversity have on decision making within organizations? How does cultural diversity affect the performance of small groups in the workplace? Since policies and procedures are typically developed in meetings of relatively modest size, small-group research can be especially useful in helping us understand the impact of diversity within organizations.

In many experimental studies, a small group is created and then assigned a task or problem to resolve. The overall conclusion of such research is that heterogeneous small groups (including culturally diverse groups) produce solutions of higher quality than do homogeneous groups. In fact, as a group's composition becomes more diverse, additional alternatives are proposed that enhance the quality

of decision making. The likelihood that a group will offer many ideas and proposals is particularly attractive in light of the current demands on many organizations to be more innovative and creative (Kirchmeyer, 1993; Ruhe and Eatman, 1977).

This general finding about the advantages of diversity in small groups has been tempered by the fact that such groups often fail to benefit from the unique perspectives of members from racial and ethnic minorities. Researchers report that minorities are less active participants within small groups and are slightly less committed to the groups' efforts than are other members.

For example, one Canadian study focused on 45 small groups in which most minority participants were from Asian backgrounds. In 34 of these 45 groups (76 percent), the member who contributed least frequently was a minority group

member (Kirchmeyer and Cohen, 1992; see also Kirchmeyer, 1993). Such studies raise two sobering questions for organizations: (1) How do the dynamics of small groups impede minority participation and (2) how can organizations assist and benefit from employees who may be reluctant to participate in small-group decision making?

Viewed from a conflict perspective, the apparently subordinate role of racial and ethnic minorities within small groups—like the subordinate role of females in conversations with males (see Chapter 11)—reminds us that the power relations of the larger society influence members of small groups within an organization. So long as inequality based on gender, race, and ethnicity is evident throughout our society, it will influence people's self-confidence and their ability to exercise leadership within a small group.

In many cases, people model their behavior after groups to which they do not belong. For example, a college student majoring in finance may read the *Wall Street Journal,* study the annual reports of corporations, and listen to midday stock market news on the radio. The student is engaging in the process of anticipatory socialization (see Chapter 4) by using financial experts as a reference group to which he or she aspires.

It is important to recognize that individuals are often influenced by two or more reference groups at the same time. One's family members, neighbors, and coworkers shape different aspects of a person's self-evaluation. In addition, certain reference group attachments change during the life cycle. A corpo-

rate executive who quits the rat race at age 45 to become a social worker will find new reference groups to use as standards for evaluation. We shift reference groups as we take on different statuses during our lives.

Studying Small Groups

In an unusual example of small-group research, social scientists examined the communications processes and social interactions between members of airline flight crews. One study conducted for the federal government found that 70 percent of all civil-aviation incidents during a five-year period were attributable to human error, primarily where information was improperly transmitted from one crew member to another or was not transmitted at all. According to psychologist Robert Helmrich, a substantial number of airline accidents arise from the flight crews' failure to work well as a team. Yet close cooperation is difficult to achieve in large airlines because pilots and copilots frequently fly with crew members whom they have never met before (Burrows, 1982).

Studying small groups is an important aspect of sociological research (see Box 6-1). The term *small group* is used to refer to a group small enough for all members to interact simultaneously, that is, to talk with one another or at least be acquainted. Certain primary groups, such as families, may also be classified as small groups. However, many small groups differ from primary groups in that they do not necessarily offer the intimate personal relationships characteristic of primary groups. For example, a manufacturer may bring together its seven-member regional sales staff twice a year for an intensive sales conference. The salespeople, who live in different cities and rarely see one another, constitute a small secondary group, not a primary group.

We may think of small groups as being informal and unpatterned; yet, interactionist researchers have revealed that there are distinct and predictable processes at work in the functioning of small groups. As sociologist Cecilia Ridgeway (1987) has shown, even nonverbal behavior plays a role in a person's dominance or influence in a group. People who employ direct eye contact and an upright, forward-leaning posture are able to be more persuasive without speaking louder or seeming threatening. Moreover, like formal organizations—which will be examined later in the chapter—small groups have a definite structure (Back, 1981; Nixon, 1979).

Size of a Group It is not exactly clear at what point a collection of people becomes too large to be called a *small group*. If there are more than 20 members, it is difficult for individuals to interact regularly in a direct and intimate manner. Even within a range of 2 to 20 people, group size can substantially alter the quality of social relationships. For example, as the number of group participants increases, the most active communicators become even more active relative to others. Therefore, a

German sociologist Georg Simmel (1858–1918) pioneered in the study of small-group behavior and developed approaches to the formation of coalitions which are still used today.

person who dominates a group of 3 or 4 members will be relatively more dominant in a 15-person group.

Group size also has noticeable social implications for members who do not assume leadership roles. In a larger group, each member has less time to speak, more points of view to absorb, and a more elaborate structure within which to function. At the same time, an individual has greater freedom to ignore certain members or viewpoints than he or she would in a smaller group. Clearly, it is harder to disregard someone in a 4-person work force than in an office with 30 employees or a high school band with 50 members.

German sociologist Georg Simmel (1858–1918) is credited as the first sociologist to emphasize the importance of interaction processes within groups. Reflecting on group size, Simmel (1950:87, original edition 1917) suggested that smaller groups have distinctive qualities and patterns of interaction which inevitably disappear as they expand in size.

Larger groups, in Simmel's view, develop particular forms of interaction which are unnecessary in small groups.

Subsequent research has clarified the social significance of group size on behavior. Researchers in the United States have given special attention to comparisons of 6-person and 12-person juries. State legislatures have shown an interest in reducing jury size to save money and expedite courtroom proceedings; social scientists have explored how this might affect a jury's decision making. In one study of criminal cases, the size of a jury had no impact on the likelihood of conviction when the defendant appeared not to be guilty. However, when the defendant's guilt seemed more obvious, 12-person juries were more reluctant to convict than 6-person juries (Hare, 1992).

The simplest of all social groups or relationships is the **dyad,** or two-member group. The conventional marital relationship between a wife and a husband is an example of a dyad, as is a business partnership or a singing team. In a dyad, one is able to achieve a special level of intimacy that cannot be duplicated in larger groups. However, as Simmel (1950) noted, a dyad, unlike any other group, can be destroyed by the loss of a single member. Therefore, the thought of termination hangs over a dyadic relationship perhaps more than over any other type.

Obviously, the introduction of one additional person to a dyad dramatically transforms the character of the small group. The dyad now becomes a three-member group, or **triad.** The new member has at least three basic ways of interacting with and influencing the dynamics of the group. The new person may play a *unifying* role within a triad. When a married couple has its first child, the baby may serve to bind the group closer together. A newcomer may also play a *mediating* role within a three-person group. If two roommates in an apartment are perpetually sniping at each other, the third roommate may attempt to remain on good terms with each and arrange compromise solutions to problems. Finally, a member of a triad can choose to employ a *divide-and-rule* strategy. This is the case, for example, with a coach who hopes to gain greater control over two assistants by making them rivals (Nixon, 1979:9–13).

Coalitions As groups become the size of triads or larger, coalitions can be expected to develop. A **coalition** is a temporary or permanent alliance toward a common goal. For example, in 1993, the Congressional Black Caucus in the House of Representatives—first organized in 1970—included 38 Democrats and 1 Republican. In that year, this coalition used its voting power to block spending cuts in programs that benefit poor and

A coalition *is a temporary or permanent alliance toward a common goal. The Congressional Black Caucus in the House of Representatives, first organized in 1970, is an example of a coalition.*

working-class families, including many African American families (Cunningham, 1993).

How do coalitions work within a small group? Imagine that Elena Rivera, Frank DiStefano, and Alex Smith are all hoping to become editor-in-chief of their college newspaper. The editor-in-chief is selected by a majority vote of the 15 outgoing editors. A few days before the election, it appears that Rivera is a strong favorite. She is estimated to have seven supporters, while DiStefano has five, and Smith only three.

DiStefano and Smith have the option of forming a coalition to stop Rivera. For example, Smith could drop out of the contest and urge his supporters to vote for DiStefano. In return, DiStefano might promise to appoint Smith as his assistant or to some other prestigious job. Such a coalition might be particularly likely if these two candidates have some personal or ideological bond or some common reason for wanting to keep Rivera from becoming editor-in-chief.

On the other hand, a different type of coalition could be developed. In order to assure her victory, Rivera could try to make a deal with Smith. If she receives the support of his three backers, her election would be assured. Thus, in any political, organizational, or small-group setting, there are numerous ways in which coalitions can be created. Repeated experiments by social scientists confirm the complex nature of coalition formation (Caplow, 1969; M. Shaw, 1981:107–114).

Physical Environment Small groups do not function in isolation. They meet and interact within physical environments which have implications for group dynamics. Rooms, chairs (as opposed to benches), and even the shape of a table can influence a group's performance and exchanges in important ways. For example, if a group is seated at a rectangular table and is allowed to discuss a topic freely, members across the table from each other will direct comments to one another more than they will to those on either side.

Seating arrangements can also influence leadership status. One controlled experiment involved five-person groups seated at a rectangular table, with three members on one side of the table and two on the other. Since interactions are more likely to occur across the table, researchers expected that more leaders would emerge from the two-person side. This was because participants on the two-person side would have easy access to three group members across the table; those on the three-person side would have easy access to only two group members. The data later confirmed these predictions: 70 percent of the leaders emerged from the two-seat side, even though it accounted for only 40 percent of the participants. Thus, physical environment can have a clear impact on the dynamics of small groups (M. Shaw, 1981).

The effects of group size, coalition, and physical environment on group dynamics are but three of the many aspects of the small group which have been studied by sociologists. Another area, conformity and deviance, is given particular attention in Chapter 7. Of course, while it is clear that small-group encounters have a considerable influence on our lives, we are also deeply affected by much larger groupings of people.

UNDERSTANDING ORGANIZATIONS

Formal Organizations and Bureaucracies

One poignant message of recent decades has been the power and pervasiveness of large organizations. Statements such as "You can't fight city hall" have underscored the frustrations and despair of the lonely individual in opposing the towering structures of government or big business. In a mock commercial, the telephone operator Ernestine—a character created by the comedian Lily Tomlin—proclaims: "We don't care; we don't have to. We're the phone company!"

Our lives are increasingly dominated by large secondary groups which take the form of formal organizations designed for a specific purpose. A *formal organization* is a special-purpose group designed and structured in the interests of maximum efficiency. Organizations vary in their size, specificity of goals, and degree of efficiency, but are structured in such a way as to facilitate the management of large-scale operations. They also have a bureaucratic form of organization, which will be described later in the chapter. The United States Postal Service, the Boston Pops orchestra, and the college you attend are all examples of formal organizations.

In our society, formal organizations fulfill an enormous variety of personal and societal needs and shape the lives of every person. In fact, formal organizations have become such a dominant force that we must create organizations to supervise other organizations, such as the Securities and Exchange Commission (SEC) and other federal regulatory agencies. It sounds much more exciting to say that we live in the "space age" than that we live in the "age of formal organizations"; however, the latter is probably a more accurate description of the 1990s (Azumi and Hage, 1972:1; Etzioni, 1964:1–2).

Development of Formal Organizations   How and why have formal organizations come into existence? The first large-scale formal organizations seem to have emerged as central governments became more complex. Formal organizations became inevitable in societies which had state-controlled irrigation networks, such as Egypt, Mesopotamia, India, China, and Peru under the Incas. Centralized decisions had to be made about water distribution, and networks for carrying out such policies had to be established.

The growth of formal organizations has been closely tied to the emergence of industrial societies. Earlier societies had not developed large-scale organizations to their fullest extent because their technology was relatively underdeveloped. Consequently, there was no need to accumulate profits to invest in machinery. As mechanical innovations evolved, more sophisticated management emerged to maximize production in order to serve new markets brought about by improved transportation networks and increased consumer demand.

To see how a formal organization can develop, let us consider the example of a carpenter in colonial New England, whom we call James Wooley. Wooley began his adult life as a self-employed artisan who personally performed all the tasks of his trade. He cut the lumber, sawed it, made furniture, and sold his products himself. Generally, he worked alone in the building that served as his shop, store, and home.

As his village and business grew, Wooley concluded that he had more customers than he could personally serve. At first, he hired a single assistant. A few years later, as he was able to respond to demand in neighboring areas, he began to employ a small group of workers. Each of them specialized in a specific aspect of furniture making and took advantage of new tools and innovative carpentry techniques. One worker cut the wood, one made bedposts, one was in charge of staining, and another ran the store. Before long, a carpenter had become the manager of a small furniture factory (Stark et al., 1973:145).

Wooley discovered that by coordinating the work of several assistants efficiently, he could produce furniture more quickly and with less expense. However, this conversion from a one-person operation to a small assembly line illustrates more than simply a change in production techniques. It reflects the emergence of a dramatically different form of organization, known as *bureaucracy*, that has special significance for people's interactions and their relationship to work. A **bureaucracy** is a component of formal organization in which rules and hierarchical ranking are used to achieve efficiency.

Characteristics of a Bureaucracy   When we think of the term *bureaucracy*, a variety of images—mostly unpleasant—come to mind. Rows of desks staffed by seemingly faceless people, endless lines and forms, impossibly complex language (see Table 6-2), and frustrating encounters with red tape—all these have combined to make *bureaucracy* a dirty word and an easy target in political campaigns. As a result, few people want to identify their occupation as "bureaucrat" despite the fact that all of us perform various bureaucratic tasks. Elements of bureaucracy are found in almost every occupation in an industrial society such as the United States.

It is important to emphasize that complaints about bureaucracy are not limited to the United States. In 1993, the bureaucratic nature of the United Nations' humanitarian efforts in Somalia came under attack. Critics noted that the five international agencies designated to run relief efforts in Somalia had more than 12,000 employees, of whom only 116 were serving in the impoverished, war-torn African nation. Moreover, like many bureaucracies, the relief apparatus was slow in dealing with a drastic problem. In the words of a former United Nations worker in

TABLE 6-2	Bureaucratic "Doublespeak"	
BUREAUCRACY	**EVENT**	**DOUBLESPEAK**
Sunset Publishing Company	Laying off of 20 percent of work force	Workers were declared "duplicative"
EJV Partners	Laying off of 19 officials	Called a "refocusing of the company's skills set"
Roberts Lincoln of Pennsylvania	Advertisement of used cars	Calls these cars "pre-enjoyed" cars
Domino's Pizza	Institution of new job title for drivers who deliver pizza	Drivers now called "delivery ambassadors"
Federal Aviation Agency	Collision of two planes on the ground	Called a "runway incursion"
Hospital in Philadelphia	Death of a patient as a result of medical malpractice	A "diagnostic misadventure of a high magnitude"

SOURCES: National Council of Teachers of English, 1989, 1991, 1993.

Somalia: "The average U.N. person takes 15 days to reply to a fax. . . . 3,000 people can die in 15 days" (Longworth, 1993:9).

In order to develop a more useful and objective definition of bureaucracy, let us consider the writings of Max Weber (1947:333–340, original edition 1922). This pioneer of sociology, who was introduced in Chapter 1, first directed researchers to the significance of bureaucratic structure. In an important sociological advance, Weber emphasized the basic similarity of structure and process found in the otherwise dissimilar enterprises of religion, government, education, and business.

Weber viewed bureaucracy as a form of organization quite different from the family-run business. He developed an ideal type of bureaucracy, which reflects the most characteristic aspects of all human organizations. Since perfect bureaucracies are never achieved, no actual organization will correspond exactly to Weber's ideal type (Blau and Meyer, 1987:19–22). Nevertheless, Weber argued that every bureaucracy—whether its purpose is to run a day care center, corporation, or army—will have five basic characteristics. These characteristics, as well as *dysfunctions* (or potential negative consequences) of bureaucracy, are discussed below and summarized in Table 6-3 on page 154.

1 Division of Labor Specialized experts are employed in each position to perform specific tasks. Thus, the president of the United States need not

The Quarterly Review of Doublespeak, *a publication of the National Council of Teachers of English, regularly fights language pollution by publishing examples of bureaucratic "doublespeak" designed to mislead people and manipulate social reality.*

be a good typist. A lawyer need not be able to complete an income tax form. By working at a specific task, people are more likely to become highly skilled and carry out a job with maximum efficiency. This emphasis on specialization is so basic a part of our lives that we may not realize that it is a fairly recent development in western culture.

Analysis of division of labor by interactionist researchers has led to scrutiny of how various employees at a workplace interact with one another. For example, after a cardiac patient is brought into a surgical recovery room, nurses and technicians independently make 10 to 20 connections between the patient and various monitoring devices. Later procedures, by contrast, are more likely to involve the cooperative efforts of two or more workers. Through these tasks, medical personnel gain proficiency in delicate and essential procedures (Strauss, 1985:2).

Although division of labor has certainly been beneficial in the performance of many complex bureaucracies, in some cases it can lead to *trained incapacity;* that is, workers become so specialized that they develop blind spots and fail to notice ob-

TABLE 6-3   Characteristics of a Bureaucracy

CHARACTERISTIC	POSITIVE CONSEQUENCE	NEGATIVE CONSEQUENCE	
		FOR THE INDIVIDUAL	FOR THE ORGANIZATION
Division of labor	Produces efficiency in large-scale corporation	Produces trained incapacity	Produces a narrow perspective
Hierarchy of authority	Clarifies who is in command	Deprives employees of a voice in decision making	Permits concealment of mistakes
Written rules and regulations	Let workers know what is expected of them	Stifle initiative and imagination	Lead to goal displacement
Impersonality	Reduces bias	Contributes to feelings of alienation	Discourages loyalty to company
Employment based on technical qualifications	Discourages favoritism and reduces petty rivalries	Discourages ambition to improve oneself elsewhere	Allows Peter principle to operate

vious problems. Even worse, they may not *care* about what is happening next to them on the assembly line. Some observers believe that, through such developments, workers have become much less productive on the job.

Although trained incapacity has negative implications for the smooth running of organizations, it is especially disastrous for the person who loses a job during a layoff. An unemployed worker may have spent years becoming proficient at highly technical work and yet may be totally unsuited for other positions, even those which are directly related to his or her former job. As an example, an automotive machinist who pushes buttons on an automobile assembly line in Michigan will lack the proper training and skill to work as an oil industry machinist in Texas (Wallis, 1981).

In some instances, the division of labor (as reflected in the fragmentation of job titles) may actually contribute to sex discrimination by creating unnecessary and inappropriate distinctions between female and male employees. In a study of 368 businesses in California, sociologist James Baron and William Bielby (1986) found that proliferation of job titles tended to increase as men and women reached parity in their level of employment. Apparently, separate job titles—ostensibly designed to reflect a division of labor—were actually being used to preserve traditional occupational segregation by gender.

Max Weber introduced the concept of bureaucracy but tended to emphasize its positive aspects. More recently, social scientists have described the negative consequences (or dysfunctions) of bureaucracy both for the individual within the organization and for the bureaucracy itself.

2 Hierarchy of Authority Bureaucracies follow the principle of hierarchy; that is, each position is under the supervision of a higher authority (see Figure 6-1). A professional baseball team is run by an owner, who hires a general manager, who in turn hires a manager. Beneath the manager come the coaches and last the players. In the Roman Catholic church, the pope is the supreme authority; under him are cardinals, bishops, and so forth. Even large medical group practices have boards of directors, executive committees, and administrators (Kralewski et al., 1985).

Social science research suggests that bureaucracies may be a positive environment for women at the lower but not the upper echelons of the hierarchy. Political scientist Kathy Ferguson (1983, 1984) observes that many traits traditionally associated with the feminine gender role—such as valuing warm, supportive, cooperative relationships— are conducive to participation in a bureaucratic

FIGURE 6-1 *Organization Chart of a Government Agency*

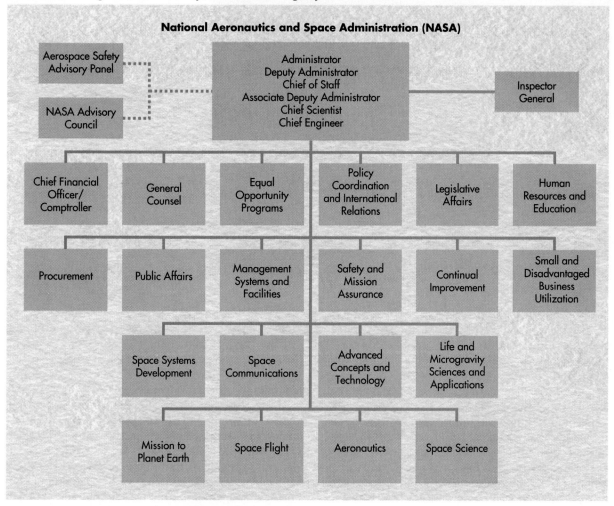

National Aeronautics and Space Administration (NASA)

SOURCE: Adapted from Office of the Federal Register, 1993:648.

The formal structure of a government agency is fairly easy to ascertain. Equally important, but less apparent, is the informal chain of command.

organization. However, upwardly mobile women may find their career progress hindered because they function more as facilitators than as innovators, and then are not viewed as aggressive enough to serve in higher management posts. Consequently, although traditional feminine values may be functional for women in the lower levels of bureaucratic structure, they appear to become dysfunctional as women aspire to greater power and prestige.

3 Written Rules and Regulations Wouldn't it be

nice if a bank teller cashed your check for $100 and deliberately handed you six $20 bills, saying; "You have such a friendly smile; here's an extra $20"? It would certainly be a pleasant surprise, but it would also be "against the rules."

Rules and regulations, as we all know, are an important characteristic of bureaucracies. Ideally, through such procedures, a bureaucracy ensures

As an example of goal displacement, London's transport workers can quickly cause chaos in the subway system by strictly adhering to all safety check regulations and thereby preventing the use of any subway car that has even a trivial defect.

uniform performance of every task. This prohibits us from receiving an extra $20 at the bank, but it also guarantees us that we will receive essentially the same treatment as other customers. If the bank provides them with special services, such as monthly statements or investment advice, it will also provide us with those services.

Through written rules and regulations, bureaucracies generally offer employees clear standards as to what is considered an adequate (or exceptional) performance. In addition, procedures provide a valuable sense of continuity in a bureaucracy. Individual workers will come and go, but the structure and past records give the organization a life of its own that outlives the services of any one bureaucrat. Thus, if you are brought in to work as the new manager of a bookstore, you do not have to start from scratch. Instead, you can study the store's records and accounting books to learn about the payroll, financial dealings with distributors, discount policies on "sale" books, and other procedures.

Of course, rules and regulations can overshadow the larger goals of an organization and become dysfunctional. If blindly applied, they will no longer serve as a means to achieving an objective but instead will become important (and perhaps too important) in their own right. This would certainly be the case if a hospital emergency room physician failed to treat a seriously injured person because he or she had no valid proof of United States citizenship. Robert Merton (1968:254–256) has used the term *goal displacement* to refer to overzealous conformity to official regulations.

In some instances, rather than blindly applying rules and regulations, employees may *consciously* engage in goal displacement. Sociologist Mike O'Donnell (1992:275) observes that British labor unions often have their members "work to rule" (perform all tasks strictly by the regulations) to bring management to the bargaining table. For example, London's transport workers can quickly cause chaos in the subway system by strictly adhering to all safety check regulations and thereby preventing the use of any subway car that has even a trivial defect.

It is widely believed that the rules and regulations of bureaucracy tend to suppress or destroy the individuality of employees. However, studies conducted by Melvin Kohn (1978) suggest that bureaucracies often encourage intellectual flexibility, tolerance for nonconformity, and willingness to accept change. The complexity and diversified responsibilities of most bureaucratic jobs appear to play an important role in promoting flexibility and openness to change.

4 Impersonality Max Weber wrote that in a bureaucracy, work is carried out *sine ira et studio*, "without hatred or passion." Bureaucratic norms dictate that officials perform their duties without the personal consideration of people as individuals. This is intended to guarantee equal treatment for each person; however, it also contributes to the often cold and uncaring feeling associated with modern organizations.

We typically think of big government and big business when we think of impersonal bureaucracies. Interestingly, during the most turbulent years of the 1960s, student activists around the world bitterly protested the bureaucratic nature of the university. One of the symbols of the free speech movement at the University of California at Berkeley was an IBM computer card which stated: "Student at U.C.: Do not bend, fold, or mutilate." In the view of dissidents, the university had become one more giant, faceless, unfeeling bureaucracy which cared little for the uniqueness of the individual (P. Jacobs and Landau, 1966:216–219).

5 Employment Based on Technical Qualifications Within a bureaucracy, hiring is based on technical qualifications rather than on favoritism, and performance is measured against specific standards. This is designed to protect bureaucrats against arbitrary dismissal and to provide a measure of security. Promotions are dictated by written personnel policies, and people often have a right to appeal if they believe that particular rules have been violated. Such procedures encourage loyalty to the organization.

In this sense, the "impersonal" bureaucracy can be an improvement over nonbureaucratic organizations. A federal bureaucrat in a civil service position, for example, has ideally been selected on the basis of merit, not because he or she did favors for a political machine. Above all, the bureaucracy is expected to value technical and professional competence, which is essential in the day-to-day functioning of a complex, industrial society such as the United States.

Unfortunately, personnel decisions within a bureaucracy do not always follow this ideal pattern. Dysfunctions within bureaucracy have become well publicized, particularly because of the work of Lawrence J. Peter. According to the **Peter principle,** every employee within a hierarchy tends to rise to his or her level of incompetence (Peter and Hull, 1969:25). This hypothesis, which has not been directly or systematically tested, reflects a possible dysfunctional outcome of structuring advancement on the basis of merit. Talented people receive promotion after promotion until, sadly, they finally achieve positions that they cannot handle (Blau and Meyer, 1987:21; Chinoy, 1954:40–41).

Bureaucratization as a Process As stated earlier, Weber's characteristics of bureaucracy should be seen as describing an ideal type rather than as offering a precise definition of an actual bureaucracy. Sociologist Alvin Gouldner (1950:53–54) notes that not every formal organization will possess all of Weber's characteristics. In fact, there can be wide variation among actual bureaucratic organizations.

Stanley Udy (1959) compared the structure of formal organizations in 150 nonindustrial societies. Like their counterparts in modern industrial nations, these organizations possessed many of—but not necessarily all—the bureaucratic characteristics identified by Weber. Similarly, Richard Hall (1963) tested Weber's ideal type against 10 formal organizations within the United States, including a hotel and a stock brokerage firm. His findings concurred with those of Udy: bureaucracy must be viewed as a matter of degree, that is, as more, or less, bureaucratic. Therefore, in describing organizations, we need to apply the Weberian model carefully, with the understanding that an organization can be more or less rule-oriented, more or less hierarchical, and so forth (Nickinovich, 1992).

Sociologists have used the term **bureaucratization** to refer to the process by which a group, organization, or social movement becomes increasingly bureaucratic. Earlier in the chapter, we saw the beginnings of this process as carpenter James Wooley became the manager of a small furniture factory in colonial America. Wooley's factory, even early in its operation, took on at least two of Weber's characteristics of bureaucracy: division of labor and hierarchical authority. If the factory continued to grow—and Wooley took on more and more employees—his organization would undoubtedly become more impersonal and he would probably develop more rules and regulations to ensure efficiency.

Normally, we think of bureaucratization in terms of large organizations. In a typical citizen's nightmare, one may have to speak to 10 or 12 individuals in a corporation or government agency to find out which official has jurisdiction over a particular problem. Callers can get transferred from one department to another until they finally hang up in disgust. Bureaucratization also takes place within small-group settings. Children organizing a school club may elect as many officers as there are club members and may develop various rules for meetings.

In addition to varying from society to society, bureaucratization also serves as an independent (or causal) variable affecting social change. Conflict theorists have argued that bureaucratic organizations tend to inhibit change because of their emphasis on regulations and security for officeholders. As one example, some public assistance (or welfare) caseworkers are so preoccupied with the required forms for clients that they forget to see whether people's basic needs are being satisfied. Paper becomes more meaningful than people; numbers take precedence over needs.

Oligarchy: Rule by a Few   The bureaucratizing influence on social movements has also been a concern of conflict theorists. German sociologist Robert Michels (1915), in studying socialist parties and labor unions in Europe before World War I, found that such organizations were becoming increasingly bureaucratic. The emerging leaders of these organizations—even some of the most radical—had a vested interest in clinging to power. If they lost their leadership posts, they would have to return to full-time work as manual laborers.

Similarly, a team of sociologists studied bureaucratization in "crisis centers." These organizations, born in the counterculture of the 1960s (see Chapter 3), were established to offer counseling and support to people experiencing divorce, death of a family member, drug and alcohol problems, and other types of emotional crisis. Despite their initial commitment to less bureaucratic, nonhierarchical structures, crisis centers increasingly turned to written job descriptions, organization charts, and written policies regarding treatment of cases and clients

(Senter et al., 1983; for a different view, see Rothschild-Whitt, 1979).

Through his research, Michels originated the idea of the *iron law of oligarchy,* under which even a democratic organization will develop into a bureaucracy ruled by a few (the oligarchy). Why do oligarchies emerge? People who achieve leadership roles usually have the skills, knowledge, or charismatic appeal (as Weber noted) to direct, if not control, others. Michels argues that the rank and file of a movement or organization look to leaders for direction and thereby reinforce the process of rule by a few. In addition, members of an oligarchy are strongly motivated to maintain their leadership roles, privileges, and power.

Michels' insights continue to be relevant in the 1990s. Contemporary labor unions in the United States and western Europe bear little resemblance to those organized after spontaneous activity by exploited workers. Conflict theorists have expressed concern about the longevity of union leaders, who are not always responsive to the needs and demands of membership. As Michels noted in his iron law of oligarchy, leaders may become more concerned with maintaining their own positions and power.

At least one recent study, however, raises questions about Michels' views. On the basis of her research on organizations active in the "pro-choice" social movement, which endorses the right to legal abortions, sociologist Suzanne Staggenborg (1988) disputes the assertion that formal organizations with professional leaders inevitably become conservative and oligarchical. Indeed, she notes that many formal organizations in the pro-choice movement appear to be more democratic than informal groups; the routinized procedures that they follow make it more difficult for leaders to achieve excessive power (see also E. Scott, 1993).

It should be added that bureaucracies are not always a conservative force within a society. Political scientist Gregory Kasza (1987) studied military regimes in Japan (in the period 1937–1945), Peru (1968–1975), and Egypt (1952–1970). He found that the civilian bureaucracies serving these military governments actually *promoted* radical policies. For example, Egyptian bureaucrats introduced sweeping land reforms that redistributed 20 percent of all land suitable for cultivation to the country's peasants. In criticizing previous work on bu-

Planning based on the human relations perspective focuses on workers' feelings, frustrations, and emotional need for job satisfaction.

reaucratic conservatism, Kasza emphasizes that different types of regimes may encourage radical, liberal, or conservative bureaucratic policies.

While the "iron law" may sometimes help us to understand the concentration of formal authority within organizations, sociologists recognize that there are a number of checks on leadership. Groups often compete for power within a formal organization, as in an automotive corporation in which divisions manufacturing heavy machinery and passenger cars compete against each other for limited research and development funds. Moreover, informal channels of communication and control can undercut the power of top officials of an organization. This is bureaucracy's "other face."

Bureaucracy's Other Face How does bureaucratization affect the average individual who works in an organization? The early theorists of formal organizations tended to neglect this question. Max Weber, for example, focused on management personnel within bureaucracies, but he had little to say about workers in industry or clerks in government agencies.

According to the ***classical theory*** of formal organizations, also known as the ***scientific management approach,*** workers are motivated almost entirely by economic rewards. This theory stresses that productivity is limited only by the physical constraints of workers. Therefore, workers are treated as a resource, much like the machines that have begun to replace them in the twentieth century. Management attempts to achieve maximum work efficiency through scientific planning, established performance standards, and careful supervision of workers and production. Planning under the scientific management approach involves time and motion studies but not studies of workers' attitudes or feelings of job satisfaction.

It was not until workers organized unions—and forced management to recognize that they were not objects—that theorists of formal organizations began to revise the classical approach. Along with management and administrators, social scientists became aware that informal groups of workers have an important impact on organizations (Perrow, 1986:79–118). One result was an alternative way of considering bureaucratic dynamics, the ***human relations approach,*** which emphasizes the role of people, communication, and participation within a bureaucracy. This type of analysis reflects the interest of interactionist theorists in small-group behavior. Unlike planning under the scientific management approach, planning based on the human relations perspective focuses on workers' feelings, frustrations, and emotional need for job satisfaction.

The gradual move away from a sole focus on physical aspects of getting the job done—and toward the concerns and needs of workers—led advocates of the human relations approach to stress the less formal aspects of bureaucratic structure. Informal structures and social networks within organizations develop partly as a result of people's ability to create more direct forms of communication than the formal structures mandate. Charles Page (1946) has used the term *bureaucracy's other face* to refer to the unofficial activities and interactions which are such a basic part of daily organizational life. Two studies—one of a factory, the other of a law enforcement agency—illustrate the value of the human relations approach.

In Chapter 2, we looked at the Hawthorne studies, which alerted sociologists to the fact that research subjects may alter their behavior to match the experimenter's expectations. This methodological finding notwithstanding, the major focus of the Hawthorne studies was the role of social factors in workers' productivity. As one aspect of the research, an investigation was made of the switchboard-bank wiring room, where 14 men were making parts of switches for telephone equipment. These men were found to be producing far below their physical capabilities. This was especially surprising because they would earn more money if they produced more parts.

Why was there such an unexpected restriction of output? According to the classical theory, productivity should be maximized, since workers had been given a financial incentive. However, in practice the men were carefully subverting this scheme to boost productivity. They feared that if they produced switch parts at a faster rate, their pay rate might be reduced or some might lose their jobs.

As a result, this group of workers established their own (unofficial) norm for a proper day's work. They created informal rules, sanctions, and argot terms to enforce this standard. Workers who produced "too much" were called "speed kings" and "rate busters," while those judged to be "too slow" were "chiselers." Workers who violated this agreement were "binged" (slugged on the shoulder) by coworkers. Yet management was unaware of such practices and had actually come to believe that the men were working as hard as they could (Etzioni, 1964:33–34; Roethlisberger and Dickson, 1939).

In another study of interactions within bureaucracy, Peter Blau (1963) observed agents working in a federal law enforcement agency. Their work involved auditing books and records and also interviewing employees and employers. If agents encountered a problem or procedure that they could not handle, they were required to consult their superior (a staff attorney) rather than ask each other. However, many were reluctant to follow this established policy for fear that it would adversely affect their job ratings. Therefore, they usually sought guidance from other agents—even though this clearly violated the official rules.

How does one get advice without asking for it? To put it another way, how does one officially respect a policy while in fact subverting it? Typically, when faced with this problem, an agent would describe an "interesting case" to colleagues, slowly allowing them to interrupt. Listeners would remind the agent of new data that might be helpful or suggest other ways of approaching the problem. Yet, of course, the agent had never asked—at least directly—for assistance. These maneuvers permitted law enforcement agents to maintain face, in Goffman's terms (see Chapter 4), with both their coworkers and their superiors.

Both the Hawthorne studies and Blau's research testify to the importance of informal structures within formal organizations. Whenever we examine sufficiently small segments of such organizations, we discover patterns of interaction that cannot be accounted for by the official structure. Thus, while a bureaucracy may establish a clear hierarchy and well-defined rules and standards, people can always get around their superiors. Informal understandings among workers can redefine official policies of a bureaucracy.

Recent research has underscored the impact of informal structures within organizations. Sociologist James Tucker (1993) studied everyday forms of resistance by temporary employees working in short-term positions. Tucker points out that informal social networks can offer advice to a temporary employee on how to pursue a grievance. For example, a female receptionist working for an automobile dealer was being sexually harassed both physically and verbally by a male supervisor. She consulted other female employees, who were aware of the supervisor's behavior and suggested that she complain to the manager of the dealership. Although the manager said that there was little that he could do, he apparently spoke with the supervisor and the harassment stopped. We will examine sexual harassment within organizations in the social policy section at the end of the chapter.

Voluntary Associations

In April 1992, independent presidential candidate Ross Perot appeared on *Larry King Live* and was asked by a caller if he belonged to any social clubs that excluded Jews or Blacks. Perot replied, "Yes, I do. All my Jewish friends in Dallas, they've had a great deal of fun with me over this. If it bothers people, I'll quit immediately." Perot's membership in restrictive voluntary associations—the Brook Hollow Country Club and the Dallas Country Club—offended Blacks and Jews on his staff. Within a few days of the telecast, he resigned his memberships in these clubs (Cerio, 1992).

By 1992, there were more than 23,000 voluntary associations in the United States—an increase of 44 percent over the 1980 figure. *Voluntary associations* are organizations established on the basis of common interest, whose members volunteer or even pay to participate. The Girl Scouts of America, the American Jewish Congress, the Kiwanis Club, and the League of Women Voters are all considered voluntary associations; so, too, are the American Association of Aardvark Aficionados, the Cats on Stamps Study Group, the Mikes of America, the New York Corset Club, and the William Shatner Fellowship. The nation's largest voluntary association, the American Automobile Association, has 32 million members; the smallest, the School Bus Manufacturers Institute, has only 5 (Burek, 1992).

The categories of "formal organization" and "voluntary association" are not mutually exclusive. Large voluntary associations such as the Lions Club and the Masons have structures similar to those of profit-making corporations. At the same time, certain formal organizations, such as the Young Men's Christian Association (YMCA) and the Peace Corps, have philanthropic and educational goals usually found in voluntary associations. Interestingly, the Democratic party and the United Farm Workers union are considered examples of voluntary asso-

The Samba clubs or "schools" of Rio de Janeiro, Brazil, are voluntary associations that compete during carnival time in the Sambadrome before hundreds of thousands of spectators. To become champion is like winning the World Series or the Super Bowl in the United States.

ciations. In a sense, belonging to a political party or a union can be a condition of employment and not genuinely voluntary; nevertheless, political parties and unions are usually included in discussions of voluntary associations.

Participation in voluntary associations is not unique to the United States. This textbook's senior author attended a carnival in London featuring bungee-jumping, at which participants were expected to jump from a height of 180 feet. Skeptics were given assurances of the attraction's safety by being told that the proprietor belonged to a voluntary association: the British Elastic Rope Sports Association. In a cross-cultural study, three Canadian sociologists examined membership in voluntary associations in 15 countries. Religious memberships were found to be prominent in the United States, Canada, the Netherlands, Ireland, and Northern Ireland. By contrast, union participation was highest in Great Britain, Norway, and Sweden. While people's country of residence may influence the types of voluntary associations they join, membership in such organizations is clearly a common social pattern (Curtis et al., 1992).

Voluntary associations can provide support to people in preindustrial societies. During the post-World War II period, migration from rural areas of Africa to the cities was accompanied by a growth in voluntary associations, including trade unions, occupational societies, and mutual aid organizations developed along old tribal ties. As people moved from the *Gemeinschaft* of the countryside to the *Gesellschaft* of the city (refer back to Chapter 5), these voluntary associations provided immigrants with substitutes for the extended groups of kinfolk that they had had in their villages (Little, 1988).

A common voluntary association in nonindustrial societies is the military association, which may be compared to our own American Legion or Veterans of Foreign Wars posts. These associations unite members through their experiences in the military, glorify the activities of war, and perform certain services for the community. Membership in such associations is usually voluntary and based on the achieved criterion of participation in a war. Among the North American Plains Indians, such military societies were common. The Cheyenne Indians, for example, originally had five military associations: the Fox, the Dog, the Shield, the Elk, and the Bowstring. Although these associations featured distinctive costumes, songs, and dances, they were alike in their internal organization. Each was headed by four leaders, who were among the Cheyenne's most important war chiefs (Ember and Ember, 1993:359–360).

Residents of the United States belong to voluntary associations for a remarkable variety of reasons. Some join to share in activities, such as members of a college debating society or a senior citizens' hiking club. For others, voluntary associations serve as a potent political force, and they may join national lobbying groups such as the American Civil Liberties Union, or the National Right to Life Committee. Finally, many people join "self-help groups" to deal with personal problems that they cannot handle alone (see Box 6-2). Clearly, there is no typ-ical voluntary association; the size and complexity of such groups vary dramatically.

Membership in voluntary associations is not random. The most consistent predictor of participation is socioeconomic status—that is, a person's income, education, and occupation. People of higher socioeconomic status are more likely to belong to and participate actively in such organizations. Partly, this reflects the cost of group memberships, which may exclude people with limited income from joining (Sills, 1968:365–366; J. Williams et al., 1973).

Reflecting the occupational patterns of the larger society, voluntary associations in the United States are largely segregated by gender. Half of them are exclusively female, and one-fifth are all-male. The exclusively male associations tend to be larger and more heterogeneous in terms of background of members. As noted in Chapter 5, membership in all-male associations holds more promise for making desirable business contacts than membership in all-female groups (McPherson and Smith-Lovin, 1986). Although participation varies across the population of the United States, most people belong to at least one voluntary association (see Figure 6-2),

FIGURE 6-2 *Membership in Voluntary Associations, 1993*

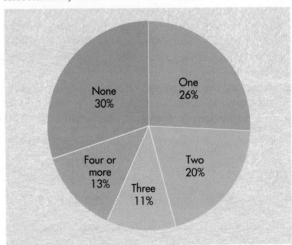

SOURCE: NORC, 1993:373.

Most people in the United States belong to at least one voluntary association; about one-fourth maintain three or more memberships.

BOX 6-2 · EVERYDAY BEHAVIOR

SELF-HELP GROUPS

Overeaters Anonymous, Women Who Love Too Much, Compulsive Shoppers, Children of Aging Parents, Fundamentalists Anonymous, Incest Survivors—these are but six of thousands of self-help groups in which about 15 million people in the United States participate. A *self-help group* is a mutual aid group "in which people who face a common concern or condition come together voluntarily for emotional support and practical assistance." These groups, known for their near-religious fervor, generally meet without any professional supervision, instead assisting members through peer support (P. Brown, 1988:1).

The nation's oldest and best-known self-help group, Alcoholics Anonymous (AA), was established in 1935 by heavy drinkers who felt that sharing feelings and experiences with other alcoholics was an essential part of recovery. Currently, AA has a worldwide membership of about 1.7 million. Its famous Twelve Step program for recovery emphasizes acceptance of one's addiction, the need for honesty and support, and the acknowledgment of a "higher power" in the universe.

In its early years in the United States, AA was almost exclusively White, male, middle-aged, and middle-class. However, the AA of the 1990s is increasingly multiracial, multiethnic, and diverse in terms of members' social class backgrounds. Women represent perhaps half of all members in large cities, and AA has become much more accepting of openly gay members than it was in the past. Although it maintains a national headquarters, AA is remarkably decentralized and basically consists of rather autonomous local groups. The AA model of group process includes few rules, little hierarchy except for nominal group leaders, and a common purpose of recovery which overcomes any traditional division of labor (Leehrsen, 1990; N. Robertson, 1988).

Sociologist Norman Denzin (1987, 1990) has drawn upon the interactionist approach in his examination of the "self story telling" that takes place in AA and other self-help groups. Denzin suggests that a person who becomes active in AA is socialized into the group's norms, values, and distinctive argot; as a result, the individual learns to view and express his or her life story in a manner structured by the group. As an example, Denzin (1987:145) quotes a man who had been in AA for two years:

Never thought I'd make it. Remember when I first came here. Couldn't talk. Scared to death. Alone. Not that way today. I can talk. I got the Steps. I got the Program. I got my meetings to go to. I got my *Big Book*. Found my story in there. Talk to my mom now. Got my old job back. You people gave me back my life. Thanks.

The success of AA in assisting many recovering alcoholics has unquestionably contributed to the increase in self-help groups, many of which have borrowed from AA's model. In the last decade, the number of self-help organizations in the United States has more than quadrupled. Alfred Katz, an expert on public health and social welfare, points out that the dramatic rise in these mutual aid efforts reflects a profound dissatisfaction with existing medical and counseling services. "People are dissatisfied with impersonality and bureaucratic runarounds," notes Katz. "They do not want to be dependent on outside professionals. They want to have more of a say" (P. Brown, 1988:7; Leehrsen, 1990).

While unquestionably popular, the self-help movement also has its critics. Wendy Kaminer (1992), an attorney and journalist, has condemned the recovery movement for its anti-intellectualism, its therapeutic and evangelical oversimplifications, and its infatuation with charismatic authority. Kaminer adds that many self-help groups place excessive focus on the need to "get in touch with one's feelings" at the expense of rational discourse concerning such injustices as sexism and racism. In her view, because of the insularity that the recovery movement encourages, "it becomes more important to focus on your own problems than on larger social issues" (Graber, 1992:43).

while about one-fourth maintain three or more memberships.

Sociologists have applied functionalist analysis to the study of voluntary associations. David Sills (1968:373–376) has identified several key functions that these groups serve within our society. First, they mediate between individuals and government. Professional associations such as the American Medical Association mediate between their members and government in such matters as licensing and legislation. Second, voluntary associations give people training in organizational skills that is invaluable for future officeholders—and for better performance within most jobs. Third, organizations such as the National Association for the Advancement of Colored People (NAACP), the National Women's Political Caucus, and the American Association of Retired Persons (AARP) help to bring traditionally disadvantaged and underrepresented groups into the political mainstream. Finally, voluntary associations assist in governing. During the influx of Indochinese and Cuban refugees in the late 1970s and early 1980s, religious and charitable groups became deeply involved in helping the federal government resettle refugees.

The importance of voluntary associations—and especially of their unpaid workers (or volunteers)—is increasingly being recognized. Traditionally, unpaid work has been devalued in the United States, even though the skill levels, experience, and training demands are often comparable with those of wage labor. Viewed from a conflict perspective, the critical difference has been that a substantial amount of volunteer work is performed by women. Feminists and conflict theorists agree that, like the unpaid child care and household labor of homemakers, the effort of volunteers has been too often ignored by scholars—and awarded too little respect by the larger society—because it is viewed as "women's work." Failure to recognize women's volunteerism thereby obscures a critical contribution women make to a society's social structure (A. Daniels, 1987, 1988).

Curiously, although membership in voluntary associations in the United States is high, people tend to add and drop affiliations rather quickly. This reflects the fact that a decision to enter a voluntary association typically involves only limited personal objectives (Babchuk and Booth, 1969). As de Tocqueville wrote, people in the United States are "forever forming associations."

Organizational Change

Just as individuals and relationships change, so too do organizations, both formal and voluntary. The most obvious changes often involve personnel: a new president of the United States is elected, an executive is fired, a star athlete retires. However, sociologists are most interested in how the organization itself changes.

These changes often relate to other social institutions, particularly the government. Its regulatory statutes, licensing procedures, tax laws, and contracting for goods and services directly influence the structure of formal organizations. Government policies relating to affirmative action (see Chapter 15) or disability rights (see Chapter 20) influence the internal decisions of organizations and may even require the hiring of new personnel.

In addition, an organization's goals may change over time along with its leaders and structure. A church starts a basketball league; an oil company purchases a movie studio; a chewing tobacco firm begins to manufacture ballpoint pens. Such actions take place when an organization decides that its traditional goals are no longer adequate. It must then modify its previous objectives or cease to exist.

Goal Multiplication If an organization concludes that its goals must change, it will typically establish additional goals or expand upon its traditional objectives. For example, in the 1970s many colleges began continuing education programs to meet the needs of potential students holding full-time jobs and wishing to take classes at night. In the 1980s, the Elderhostel movement opened college campuses in the United States to older people who could live and learn along with much younger college students.

Goal multiplication takes place when an organization expands its purposes. Generally, this is the result of changing social or economic conditions which threaten the organization's survival. The YMCA has practiced such goal multiplication. Reflecting its name, the Young Men's Christian Association had a strong evangelistic focus during its beginnings in the United States in the 1850s. Bible

The Young Men's Christian Association (YMCA) has experienced goal multiplication in recent decades. Its range of activities currently includes social service programs for the disabled, day care centers, fitness classes for office workers, residence dormitories for college students and single adults, and senior citizens' facilities.

study and tent revival meetings were provided by the early YMCAs. However, in the early 1900s, the YMCA began to diversify its appeal. It attempted to interest members by offering gymnasium facilities and residence quarters. Gradually, women, Lutherans, Roman Catholics, Jews, and the "unchurched" were accepted and even recruited as members.

The most recent phase of goal multiplication at the YMCA began in the 1960s. In larger urban areas, the organization became involved in providing employment training and juvenile delinquency programs. As a result, the YMCA received substantial funding from the federal government. This was a dramatic change for an organization whose income had previously come solely from membership fees and charitable contributions.

In the 1980s, the YMCA continued to serve the poor, as evidenced by the building of a new facility in 1984 in the Watts section of Los Angeles—the first major private construction in the area since the riots of 1965. Yet the organization also maintains a lucrative branch in Beverly Hills and has expanded rapidly to serve middle-class residents of cities and suburbs. The YMCA's impressive range of activities currently includes social service programs for the disabled, day care centers, fitness classes for office workers, residence dormitories for college students and single adults, "learning for living" classes for

adults, and senior citizens' facilities (Schmidt, 1990).

These transitions in the YMCA were not always smooth. At times, major contributors and board members withdrew support because of opposition to organizational changes; they preferred the YMCA to remain as it had been. However, the YMCA has survived and grown by expanding its goals from evangelism to general community service (Etzioni, 1964:13; Zald, 1970).

Goal Succession   Unlike goal multiplication, *goal succession* occurs when a group or organization has either realized or been denied its goal. It must then identify an entirely new objective that can justify its existence. Cases of goal succession are rare because most organizations never fully achieve their goals. If they do, as in the case of a committee supporting a victorious candidate for public office, they usually dissolve.

Sociologist Peter Blau (1964:241–246), who coined the term *succession of goals,* noted that organizations do not necessarily behave in a rigid manner when their goals are achieved or become irrelevant. Rather, they may shift toward new objectives. A case in point is the Foundation for Infantile Paralysis, popularly known for its annual March of Dimes campaign. For some time, the

Some organizations may actually have a stake in avoiding goal succession. For example, government agencies responsible for enforcing drug laws continue to exist because they fail to put drug pushers out of business.

foundation's major goals were to support medical research on polio and to provide assistance for victims of the disease. However, in 1955 the Salk vaccine was found to be an effective protection against paralytic polio. This left the foundation, so to speak, "unemployed." A vast network of committed staff members and volunteers was suddenly left without a clear rationale for existence. The group might have disbanded at this point, but instead it selected a new goal—combating arthritis and birth defects—and took on a new name. Like many bureaucracies, it simply refused to die (Etzioni, 1964:13; Sills, 1957:253–271).

Ironically, some organizations may have a stake in avoiding goal succession. Through his observation research in "skid row" missions, sociologist James Rooney (1990) has shown that program failure is necessary for the maintenance of certain bureaucracies. Rooney worked as a migratory farm worker and casual laborer as part of his research. Through these work experiences, he routinely interacted with skid row residents with whom he visited more than 200 rescue missions throughout the United States. These missions hope to convert visitors; they urge them to accept Christ, to attend church services, to abstain from liquor, and to accept regular employment. By controlling the distribution of food and shelter, the missions' man-

agers are able to force skid row residents to attend gospel services.

Rooney found that only a very small portion of skid row residents ever came forward to make a profession of faith. In his view, if the missions actually became more successful and quickly converted a much higher proportion of skid row visitors, a very few rescue missions would be able to handle the relatively small number of "newly fallen" individuals. Consequently, the majority of missions would have to cease operations. Contrary to the usual view that organizations perpetuate themselves by accomplishing their stated objectives, Rooney suggests that skid row missions continue to exist because of their ongoing failure.

Rescue missions, of course, are hardly the only example of programs that succeed through failure. Government agencies responsible for enforcing drug laws continue to exist because they fail to put drug pushers out of business. Prisons fail to rehabilitate inmates, thereby guaranteeing a steady return of many clients. With such paradoxes in mind, Rooney concludes by examining the policymaking implications of his study. In an example of applied sociology (refer back to Chapter 2), he questions giving continued support to organizations which directly benefit from their own failure, and wonders if other treatment options might be more effective.

- Viewed from a conflict perspective, how do the data on sexual harassment reflect inequalities based on gender and race?
- In what ways do organizational structures encourage or permit sexual harassment?
- How have women's concerns about sexual harassment influenced the political system of the United States?

In 1991, the issue of sexual harassment received unprecedented attention in the United States, as Supreme Court nominee (now Associate Justice) Clarence Thomas was accused of repeatedly harassing a former aide, law professor Anita Hill, over a period of years. But Anita Hill is far from alone in making such a complaint about a coworker. Whether they hold managerial or clerical positions, whether they work in a voluntary association or a Fortune 500 corporation, women report being victimized by sexual harassment.

Under evolving legal standards, *sexual harassment* is recognized as any unwanted and unwelcome sexual advances that interfere with a person's ability to perform a job and enjoy the benefits of a job. The most blatant example is the boss who tells a subordinate: "Put out or get out!" However, the unwelcome advances which constitute sexual harassment may take the form of subtle pressures regarding sexual activity, inappropriate sexual language, inappropriate touching, attempted kissing or fondling, demands for sexual favors, or sexual assault. Indeed, in the computer age, there is growing concern that sexually harassing messages are being sent anonymously over computer networks through E-mail (Price, 1993).

Women of all ages and racial and ethnic groups—and men as well—have been the victims of sexual harassment. Such harassment may occur as a single encounter or as a repeated pattern of behavior. In a national survey in the United States conducted in December 1992, 32 percent of women indicated that they had been sexually harassed in their work outside the home, compared with 23 percent in a similar survey in October 1991. These numbers may at first suggest that there has been a dramatic increase in sexual harassment, but in fact they may simply represent a shift in attitudes concerning such abuses. Martha Burt, director of social services research at the Urban Institute, observes: "People now are more willing to label these behaviors as being sexual harassment, people are more willing to talk about it, and people are more [angry] about it" (R. Morin, 1993a:37).

Obviously, experiencing sexual harassment can have a shattering impact on an employee's satisfaction on the job. In the 1986 case of *Meritor Savings Bank v. Vinson,* the Supreme Court unanimously held that sexual harassment by a supervisor violates federal law against sex discrimination in the workplace, as outlined in the 1964 Civil Rights Act. If sufficiently severe, sexual harassment constitutes a violation of the law even if the unwelcome sexual demands are not linked to concrete employment benefits such as a raise or a promotion. The justices ruled that the existence of a hostile or abusive work environment—in which a woman feels degraded as the result of unwelcome flirtation or obscene joking—may in itself constitute illegal sex discrimination. In 1991, a federal judge ruled that the public display of photographs of nude and partly nude women at a workplace constitutes sexual harassment (T. Lewin, 1991a; Withers and Benaroya, 1989:6–7).

Sexual harassment has been commonly reported not only in the workplace but also in colleges and universities. A variety of studies involving both undergraduate and graduate students show that 20 to 40 percent of students are the victims of sexual harassment by faculty members. Women are by far the main targets of such harassment, but most incidents are not reported to college administrators. Even the hallways of high schools are dangerous territory for female students. According to a 1993 national survey, 65 percent of female students in grades 8 through 11 reported that they were "touched, grabbed, or pinched in a sexual way." Because of these experiences and other forms of sexual harassment, 33 percent of those female students stated that they wanted to avoid going to school and were less inclined to speak in class (Barringer, 1993:B7; McKinney, 1990:424).

In the United States, sexual harassment must be

Law professor Anita Hill is shown during her 1991 testimony before the Senate Judiciary Committee, in which she accused Supreme Court nominee (now Associate Justice) Clarence Thomas of repeatedly sexually harassing her over a period of years.

understood in the context of continuing prejudice and discrimination against women (see Chapter 11). Whether it occurs in the federal bureaucracy, in the corporate world, or in universities, sexual harassment generally takes place in organizations in which the hierarchy of authority finds White males at the top and in which women's work is valued less than men's. One survey in the private sector found that African American women were three times more likely than White women to experience sexual harassment. From a conflict perspective, it is not surprising that women—and especially women of color—are most likely to become victims of sexual harassment. These groups are typically an organization's most vulnerable employees in terms of job security (J. Jones, 1988).

While it is agreed that sexual harassment is widespread in the United States, it is nevertheless clear that most victims do not report these abuses to proper authorities. For example, in a survey of federal government employees conducted in 1988, only 5 percent of those who had been harassed stated that they had filed complaints. "It takes a lot of self-confidence to fight," suggests Catherine Broderick, a lawyer for the Securities and Exchange Commission (SEC) who won a sexual harassment complaint against the agency's Washington office. Broderick had refused her supervisor's advances

and then had been repeatedly denied promotions. After a nine-year legal battle, Broderick was victorious in court and won a promotion and years of back pay. Still, her experience is a reminder that pursuing justice against those guilty of sexual harassment can be costly and draining (Havemann, 1988; Saltzman, 1988:56–57).

Even if the victim does have the will to fight, the process of making a sexual harassment complaint in the courts or in most bureaucracies is slow and burdensome. In 1992, Evan Kemp, head of the federal Equal Employment Opportunity Commission (EEOC), admitted that a woman who has filed a complaint of sexual harassment may have to wait as long as *four years* to get a hearing before the EEOC. The agency has a huge caseload; it receives 60,000 complaints of discrimination each year and also oversees 50,000 others that are handled by state fair-employment agencies. Yet EEOC's funding is clearly inadequate to investigate all these cases (Hentoff, 1992:20–21).

Money, however, is not the only problem. In many organizations, written procedures for handling complaints of sexual harassment lead to goal displacement by those in positions of power. There is more concern for following the regulations than for dealing with and preventing harassment. Part of the problem is that many organizations do not have personnel who are adequately trained to deal with such complaints. This responsibility is often handed to a personnel officer whose only background for the task is a two-day seminar on sexual harassment.

Many bureaucracies have traditionally given little attention to the pervasive sexual harassment in their midst; the emotional costs of this discrimination suffered by (largely female) employees have not been a major concern. However, more regulations prohibiting sexual harassment have been issued as managers and executives have been forced to confront the costs of sexual harassment *for the organization*. After calculating losses linked to absenteeism, low productivity, and employee turnover, a 1988 study of 160 Fortune 500 business firms concluded that sexual harassment costs the average large company (with 23,750 employees) about $6.7 million per year. This figure, high as it is, does not include the costs of legal defense and damages when an employee sues a company because of sexual harassment on the job (Crawford, 1993:F17).

In the aftermath of Anita Hill's testimony before the Senate Judiciary Committee, the political system of the United States is responding to allegations of sexual abuse in ways that were hardly common earlier. In a recent example, the secretary of the Navy resigned in 1992—and Congress delayed hundreds of Navy and Marine Corps promotions— in reaction to a scandal that erupted after at least 80 naval women were harassed by 175 or more naval officers at their annual Tailhook convention (M. R.

Gordon, 1993). Some observers believe that public officials are taking the issue of sexual harassment more seriously because they believe their political futures are at stake. Indeed, spurred by the intense anger of many women about what they viewed as the (all-male) Judiciary Committee's mistreatment of Anita Hill, four female candidates critical of the committee defeated male opponents in 1992 Democratic senatorial primaries—and three were subsequently elected to office.

The battle against sexual harassment is being fought not only in the United States but around the world. In 1991, the European Economic Community established a code of conduct which holds employers ultimately responsible for combating such behavior. In 1992, France joined many European countries in banning sexual harassment. That same year, in an important victory for Japan's feminist movement, a district court ruled that a small publishing company and one of its male employees had violated the rights of a female employee because of crude remarks that led her to quit her job. The complainant had charged that her male supervisor had spread rumors about her, telling others that she was promiscuous. When she attempted to get him to stop making such comments, she was advised to quit her job. In the view of Yukido Tsunoda, a lawyer for the complainant: "Sexual harassment is a big problem in Japan, and we hope this will send a signal to men that they have to be more careful" (Riding, 1992; Weisman, 1992:A3).

SUMMARY

Social interaction among human beings is necessary to the transmission of culture and the survival of every society. This chapter examines the impact of small groups, formal organizations, and voluntary associations on social behavior.

1 When we find ourselves identifying closely with a group, it is probably a *primary group*.

2 People in the United States tend to see the world in terms of *in-groups* and *out-groups*, a perception often fostered by the very groups to which we belong.

3 *Reference groups* set and enforce standards of conduct and perform a comparison function for people's evaluations of themselves and others.

4 Interactionist researchers have revealed that there are distinct and predictable processes at work in the functioning of *small groups*.

5 One poignant and recurring message of recent decades has been the power and pervasiveness of large organizations.

6 Max Weber argued that, in its ideal form, every *bureaucracy* will share these five basic characteristics: division of labor, hierarchical authority, written rules and regulations, impersonality, and employment based on technical qualifications.

7 Bureaucracy can be understood as a process and as a matter of degree; thus, an organization is more or less bureaucratic than other organizations.

8 The informal structure of an organization can undermine and redefine official bureaucratic policies.

9 People belong to *voluntary associations* for a variety of purposes—for example, to share in joint activities or to get help with personal problems.

10 Change is an important element in organizational life. An organization may need to change its goals if its original objectives are fully realized or are no longer adequate.

11 Sexual harassment has been commonly reported not only in the federal workplace and in private-sector organizations, but also in institutions of higher learning.

CRITICAL THINKING QUESTIONS

1 Within a formal organization, are you likely to find primary groups, secondary groups, in-groups, out-groups, and reference groups? What functions do these groups serve for the formal organization? What dysfunctions might occur as a result of their presence?

2 Max Weber identified five basic characteristics of bureaucracy. Select an actual organization with which you are familiar (for example, your college, a business at which you work, a religious institution or civic association to which you belong) and apply Weber's analysis to that organization. To what degree does it correspond to Weber's ideal type of bureaucracy?

3 How might sociologists draw on surveys, observation research, experiments, and existing sources to better understand voluntary associations?

KEY TERMS

Bureaucracy A component of formal organization in which rules and hierarchical ranking are used to achieve efficiency. (page 152)

Bureaucratization The process by which a group, organization, or social movement becomes increasingly bureaucratic. (157)

Classical theory An approach to the study of formal organizations which views workers as being motivated almost entirely by economic rewards. (159)

Coalition A temporary or permanent alliance toward a common goal. (150)

Dyad A two-member group. (150)

Dysfunction An element or a process of society that may disrupt a social system or lead to a decrease in stability. (153)

Formal organization A special-purpose group designed and structured in the interests of maximum efficiency. (151)

Goal displacement Overzealous conformity to official regulations within a bureaucracy. (156)

Goal multiplication The process through which an organization expands its purpose. (164)

Goal succession The process through which an organization identifies an entirely new objective because its traditional goals have been either realized or denied. (165)

Group Any number of people with similar norms, values, and expectations who regularly and consciously interact. (145)

Human relations approach An approach to the study of formal organizations which emphasizes the role of people, communication, and participation within a bureaucracy and tends to focus on the informal structure of the organization. (159)

In-group Any group or category to which people feel they belong. (147)

Iron law of oligarchy A principle of organizational life developed by Robert Michels under which even democratic organizations will become bureaucracies ruled by a few individuals. (158)

Out-group A group or category to which people feel they do not belong. (147)

Peter principle A principle of organizational life, originated by Laurence J. Peter, according to which each individual within a hierarchy tends to rise to his or her level of incompetence. (157)

Primary group A small group characterized by intimate, face-to-face association and cooperation. (146)

Reference group A term used when speaking of any group that individuals use as a standard in evaluating themselves and their own behavior. (147)

Scientific management approach Another name for the *classical theory* of formal organizations. (159)

Secondary group A formal, impersonal group in which there is little social intimacy or mutual understanding. (146)

Self-help group A mutual aid group in which people who face a common concern or condition come together voluntarily for emotional support and practical assistance. (163)

Sexual harassment Any unwanted and unwelcome sexual advances that interfere with a person's ability to perform a job and enjoy the benefits of a job. (167)

Small group   A group small enough for all members to interact simultaneously, that is, to talk with one another or at least be acquainted. (149)

Trained incapacity   The tendency of workers in a bureaucracy to become so specialized that they develop blind spots and cannot notice obvious problems. (153)

Triad   A three-member group. (150)

Voluntary associations   Organizations established on the basis of common interest whose members volunteer or even pay to participate. (161)

ADDITIONAL READINGS

Biggart, Nicole Woolsey. *Charismatic Capitalism: Direct Selling Organizations in America.* Chicago: University of Chicago Press, 1989. Biggart details the social and cultural factors that have given rise to direct-selling organizations (DSOs) and explores the dynamics of organizational life in these groups.

Blee, Kathleen M. *Women of the Klan: Racism and Gender in the 1920s.* Berkeley: University of California Press, 1991. Although White men dominated the Ku Klux Klan in the 1920s, women joined this voluntary association in large numbers.

Daniels, Arlene Kaplan. *Invisible Careers.* Chicago: University of Chicago Press, 1988. A critical look at how work is viewed in the United States, noting the widespread failure to include the unpaid labor disproportionately performed by women.

Ferguson, Kathy E. *The Feminist Case against Bureaucracy.* Philadelphia: Temple University Press, 1984. Ferguson draws on a broad range of social science literature to document how women are at a comparative disadvantage in contemporary bureaucracies.

Fisher, B. Aubrey, and Donald G. Ellis. *Small Group Decision Making: Communication and the Group Process* (3d ed.). New York: McGraw-Hill, 1990. Communication specialist Donald G. Ellis has revised the examination of group structure, decision making, and conflict resolution by renowned authority B. Aubrey Fisher.

Jacoby, Henry. *The Bureaucratization of the World.* Berkeley: University of California Press, 1973. Jacoby, a German sociologist, offers a historical perspective on bureaucracies and focuses on the impact of bureaucratization on democratic ideals.

Janis, Irving. *Victims of Groupthink.* Boston: Houghton Mifflin, 1967. A presentation concerning the power that small-group dynamics has over decision making.

Kaminer, Wendy. *Women Volunteering: The Pleasure, Pain, and Politics of Unpaid Work from 1830 to the Present.* Garden City, N.Y.: Anchor, 1984. A historical examination of the prominent role women have played within voluntary associations.

Matyko, Alexander J. *The Self-Defeating Organization: A Critique of Bureaucracy.* New York: Praeger, 1986. Matyko argues that traditional, hierarchical organizations face a crisis because people are less willing to accept such authoritarian arrangements.

Zald, Mayer N. *Organizational Change: The Political Economy of the YMCA.* Chicago: University of Chicago Press, 1970. This sociological study traces the YMCA's transformation from an evangelistic association to a service organization heavily dependent on federal funding.

Journals

Among the journals that focus on the study of groups and organizations are *Administration and Society* (founded in 1969), *Administrative Science Quarterly* (1956), *Clinical Sociology Review* (1981), *Quarterly Review of Doublespeak* (1974), *Small Group Research* (formerly *Small Group Behavior,* 1970), and *Social Psychology Review* (1948).

7

DEVIANCE AND SOCIAL CONTROL

SOCIAL CONTROL
Conformity and Obedience
  Conformity to Prejudice
  Obedience to Authority
Informal and Formal Social Control
Law and Society

DEVIANCE
What Is Deviance?
Explaining Deviance
  Functionalist Perspective
  Durkheim's Legacy
  Merton's Theory of Deviance
  Interactionist Perspective: Differential
    Association
  Labeling Theory
  Conflict Theory

CRIME
Types of Crime
  Professional Crime
  Organized Crime
  White-Collar Crime
  Victimless Crimes
Crime Statistics
  International Crime Rates
  Use and Meaning of Crime Statistics

**SOCIAL POLICY AND CRIMINAL
JUSTICE: GUN CONTROL**

BOXES
7-1 Current Research: Neutralization
    of Deviance and Female Bodybuilders
7-2 Around the World: Police Power
    in Japan

LOOKING AHEAD

- How does a society bring about acceptance of social norms?
- How does obedience differ from conformity?
- How do sociologists view the creation of laws?
- Can we learn deviant behavior from others?
- Why is certain behavior evaluated as "deviant" while other behavior is not?
- Why is there so little crime in Japan?
- Should Congress and state legislatures adopt stronger gun control measures?

Why would a person alter his or her appearance—and challenge traditional social norms—by choosing unusual forms of body piercing or deciding to be tattooed? Body piercing is common in numerous cultures around the world and has become increasingly popular in the United States. Men have joined women in piercing their earlobes to wear earrings, and members of both sexes have begun piercing their nipples, their noses, and other body parts. Some enthusiasts of body piercing read magazines focusing on this practice or gather at social activities organized for like-minded individuals. While scorned by many members of the dominant culture, people engaged in body piercing view their behavior as merely part of a continuum of altering one's appearance that includes use of lipstick, painted nails, false eyelashes, cosmetic dental work, hair coloring and replacement, and even plastic surgery (Caniglia, 1993; J. Myers, 1992).

Sociologist Clinton Sanders (1989) studied the practice of tattooing by engaging in participant-observation research. Sanders not only chose to be tattooed himself; he worked for a time as an assistant to a tattooist, stretching the skin of those being tattooed, and calming the anxieties of men and women receiving their first tattoos. Sanders found that while those electing to be tattooed were deviating from broad social norms, they were at the same time conforming to the views and behavior of significant others, including family members and close friends who had already been tattooed. One subject noted: "My father got one when he was in the war and I always wanted one, too" (Sanders, 1989:42). For others, however, tattoos allow them to participate in an unconventional subculture which flaunts authority and to establish immediate bonding with strangers whose values are obviously compatible. Veterans, members of motorcycle gangs, and others can identify like-minded people based on the kind of tattoos they display (see also Mascia-Lees and Sharpe, 1992).

Of course, like those with unusual types of body piercing, men and women with easily visible tattoos often face disapproval and even hostility from people committed to traditional norms regarding appearance. For women in particular, having a tattoo may be regarded as a departure from conventional gender roles. One woman interviewed by Sanders (1989:55) recalls:

My father's reaction was just one of disgust because women who get tattoos to him are . . . I don't know . . . they just aren't nice girls. They aren't the type of girl he wants his daughter to be. He let me know that. He let me have it right between the eyes. He said, "Do you know what kind of girls get tattoos?" and just walked out of the room.

People maintain distinctive standards regarding the proper appearance of physicians, military officers, members of the clergy, and even sociologists. (Many colleagues and students would at least be surprised to meet a sociologist with visible tattoos.) As we will see in this chapter, conformity, obedience, and deviance can be understood only within a given social context. If people disrobe publicly, they are violating widely held social norms. However, if the same people disrobe within a "naturist" (or nudist) camp, they are obeying the rules and conforming to the behavior of peers. Clearly, then, what is deviant in one setting may be common and accepted in another.

Conformity and deviance are two responses to real or imagined pressures from others. In the United States, people are socialized to have mixed feelings about both conforming and nonconforming behavior. The term *conformity* can conjure up images of mindless imitation of one's peer group—whether a circle of teenagers wearing punk rock garb or a group of business people dressed in similar gray suits. Yet the same term can also suggest that an individual is cooperative or a "team player." What about those who do not conform? They may be respected as individualists, leaders, or creative thinkers who break new ground. Or they may be labeled as "troublemakers" and "weirdos" (Aronson, 1972:14–15).

This chapter will examine the relationship between conformity, deviance, and social control. It begins by distinguishing between conformity and obedience and then looks at two experiments regarding conforming behavior and obedience to authority. The informal and formal mechanisms used by societies to encourage conformity and discourage deviance are analyzed. Particular attention is given to the legal order and how it reflects underlying social values.

The second part of the chapter focuses on theoretical explanations for deviance, including the functionalist approaches employed by Émile Durkheim and Robert Merton, the interactionist-based differential association theory of Edwin Sutherland, and labeling theory, which draws upon both the interactionist and the conflict perspectives.

While scorned by many members of the dominant culture, people engaged in tattooing and body piercing view their behavior as merely part of a continuum of altering one's appearance that includes use of lipstick, painted nails, false eyelashes, cosmetic dental work, hair coloring and replacement, and even plastic surgery.

The third part of the chapter focuses on crime. As a form of deviance subject to official, written norms, crime has been a special concern of policymakers and the public in general. Various types of crime found in the United States, and the ways in which crime is measured, are discussed. Finally, the social policy section at the end of the chapter considers a controversy highly influenced by people's perceptions of crime: the debate over gun control.

SOCIAL CONTROL

As was seen in Chapter 3, every culture, subculture, and group has distinctive norms governing what it deems appropriate behavior. Laws, dress codes, by-laws of organizations, course requirements, and rules of sports and games all express social norms. Functionalists contend that people must respect such norms if any group or society is to survive. In their view, societies literally could not function if massive numbers of people defied standards of appropriate conduct. By contrast, conflict theorists are concerned that "successful functioning" of a society will consistently benefit the powerful and work to the disadvantage of other groups. They point out, for example, that widespread resistance to social norms was necessary in order to overturn the institution of slavery in the United States.

How does a society bring about acceptance of basic norms? The term *social control* refers to the "techniques and strategies for regulating human behavior in any society" (R. Roberts, 1991:274). Social control occurs on all levels of society. In the family, we are socialized to obey our parents simply because they are our parents. In peer groups, we are introduced to informal norms such as dress codes that govern the behavior of members. In bureaucratic organizations, workers must cope with a formal system of rules and regulations. Finally, the government of every society legislates and enforces social norms—including norms regarding "proper" and "improper" expressions of sexual intimacy.

Most of us respect and accept basic social norms and assume that others will do the same. Even without thinking, we obey the instructions of police officers, follow the day-to-day rules at our jobs, and move to the rear of elevators when people enter. Such behavior reflects an effective process of socialization to the dominant standards of a culture. At the same time, we are well-aware that individuals, groups, and institutions *expect* us to act "properly." If we fail to do so, we may face punishment through informal *sanctions* such as fear and ridicule, or formal sanctions such as jail sentences or fines (see Chapter 3).

Conformity and Obedience

Techniques for social control can be viewed on both the group level and the societal level. People whom we regard as our peers or as our equals influence us to act in particular ways; the same is true of people who hold authority over us or occupy positions which we view with some awe. Stanley Milgram (1975:113–115) made a useful distinction between these two important levels of social control.

Milgram defined *conformity* as going along with one's peers—individuals of a person's own status, who have no special right to direct that person's behavior. By contrast, *obedience* is defined as compliance with higher authorities in a hierarchical structure. Thus, a recruit entering military service will typically *conform* to the habits and language of other recruits and will *obey* the orders of superior officers.

Conformity to Prejudice   We often think of conformity in terms of rather harmless situations, such as members of an expensive health club who work out in elaborate and costly sportswear. But researchers have found that people may conform to the attitudes and behavior of their peers even when such conformity means expressing intolerance toward others. Amidst concerns about growing racial tension in the United States, Fletcher Blanchard, Teri Lilly, and Leigh Ann Vaughn (1991) conducted an experiment at Smith College and found that overheard statements by others influence expressions of opinion on the issue of racism.

The researchers had a student who said she was conducting an opinion poll for a class approach 72 White students as each was walking across the campus. Each time she did so, she also stopped a second White student—actually a confederate working with the researchers—and asked her to participate in the survey as well. Both students were asked how Smith College should respond to anonymous racist notes actually sent to four African American students in 1989. However, the confederate was always instructed to answer first. In some cases, she condemned the notes; in others, she justified them.

Blanchard and his colleagues (1991:102–103) concluded that "hearing at least one other person express strongly antiracist opinions produced dramatically more strongly antiracist public reactions to racism than hearing others express equivocal opinions or opinions more accepting of racism." However, a second experiment demonstrated that when the confederate expressed sentiments justifying racism, subjects were much *less* likely to express antiracist opinions than were those who heard no one else offer opinions. In this experiment, social control (through the process of conformity) influenced people's attitudes and the expression of those attitudes. In the next section, we will see that social control (through the process of obedience) can alter people's behavior.

Obedience to Authority If ordered to do so, would you comply with an experimenter's instruction to give people increasingly painful electric shocks? Most people would say no; yet, the research of social psychologist Stanley Milgram (1963, 1975; B. Allen, 1978:34–63) suggests that most of us will obey such orders. In Milgram's words (1975:xi): "Behavior that is unthinkable in an individual . . . acting on his own may be executed without hesitation when carried out under orders."

Milgram placed advertisements in New Haven, Connecticut, newspapers to recruit subjects for what was announced as a learning experiment at Yale University. Participants included postal clerks, engineers, high school teachers, and laborers. They were told that the purpose of the research was to investigate the effects of punishment on learning. The experimenter, dressed in a gray technician's coat, explained that in each testing, one subject would be randomly selected as the "learner" while the other would function as the "teacher." However, this lottery was rigged so that the "real" subject would always be the teacher while an associate of Milgram's served as the learner.

At this point, the learner's hand was strapped to an electric apparatus. The teacher was taken to an electronic "shock generator" with 30 lever switches. Each switch was labeled with graduated voltage designations from 15 to 450 volts. Before beginning the experiment, subjects were given sample shocks of 45 volts, which convinced them of the authenticity of the experiment.

The teacher was instructed by the experimenter to apply shocks of increasing voltage each time the learner gave an incorrect answer on a memory test (recalling paired words such as *blue sky* and *wild duck*). Teachers were told that "although the shocks can be extremely painful, they cause no permanent tissue damage." In reality, the learner did not receive actual shocks; however, subjects in the role of teacher believed that the procedure was genuine.

The learner deliberately gave incorrect answers and acted out a prearranged script. For example,

In one of Stanley Milgram's experiments concerning obedience to authority, a supposed "victim" received an electric shock when his hand rested on a shock plate. At the 150-volt level, the "victim" demanded to be released and refused to place his hand on the shock plate. The experimenter then ordered the actual subject to force the "victim's" hand onto the plate (as shown in the photo). While 40 percent of the true subjects immediately ended compliance at this point, 30 percent did force the "victim's" hand onto the shock plate, even through the 450-volt level, despite his pretended agony.

at 150 volts, the learner would cry out, "Experimenter, get me out of here! I won't be in the experiment any more!" At 270 volts, the learner would scream in agony. When the shock level reached 350 volts, the learner would fall silent. If the teacher wanted to stop the experiment, the experimenter would insist that the teacher continue, using such statements as "The experiment requires that you continue" and "You have no other choice; you *must* go on" (Milgram, 1975:19–23).

The results of this unusual experiment stunned and dismayed Milgram (1975:31) and other social scientists. A sample of psychiatrists had predicted that virtually all subjects would refuse to shock innocent victims. In their view, only a "pathological fringe" of less than 2 percent would continue administering shocks up to the maximum level. Yet almost *two-thirds* of participants fell into the category of "obedient subjects." As Milgram (1975:5) observed: "Despite the fact that many subjects . . . protest to the experimenter, a substantial proportion continue to the last shock on the generator."

Why did these subjects obey? Why were they willing to inflict seemingly painful shocks on innocent victims who had never done them any harm? There is no evidence to suggest that these subjects were unusually sadistic; few seemed to enjoy administering the shocks. Instead, in Milgram's view, the key to obedience was the experimenter's social role as a "scientist" and "seeker of knowledge."

Milgram pointed out that in the modern industrial world we are accustomed to submitting to impersonal authority figures whose status is indicated by a title (professor, lieutenant, doctor) or by a uniform (the technician's coat). The authority is viewed as larger and more important than the individual; consequently, the obedient individual shifts responsibility for his or her behavior to the authority figure. Milgram's subjects frequently stated: "If it were up to me, I would not have administered shocks." They saw themselves as merely doing their duty (Milgram, 1975:xii, 7–8, 137, 144–146).

Viewed from an interactionist perspective, one important aspect of Milgram's findings is the fact that subjects in follow-up studies were less likely to inflict the supposed shocks as they were moved physically closer to their victims. Moreover, interactionists emphasize that teachers assumed responsibility for punishment by *incrementally* administering additional dosages of 15 volts. In effect, the experimenter negotiated with the teacher (see Chapter 5) and convinced the teacher to continue inflicting higher levels of punishment. It is doubtful that anywhere near the two-thirds rate of obedience would have been reached had the experimenter told the teachers to administer 450 volts immediately to the learners (Allen, 1978:42–43; Katovich, 1987).

Milgram launched his experimental study of obedience to better understand the involvement of Germans in the annihilation of 6 million Jews and millions of other people during World War II. In an interview conducted long after the publication of his study, he suggested that "if a system of death camps were set up in the United States of the sort we had seen in Nazi Germany, one would be able to find sufficient personnel for those camps in any medium-sized American town" (CBS News, 1979: 7–8).

Informal and Formal Social Control

The sanctions used to encourage conformity and obedience—and to discourage violation of social norms—are carried out through informal and formal social control. *Informal social control,* as the term implies, is used by people casually. Norms are enforced through the use of the informal sanctions described in Chapter 3. Examples of informal social control include smiles, laughter, raising of an eyebrow, and ridicule.

Techniques of informal control are typically employed within primary groups such as families. Individuals learn such techniques early in their childhood socialization to cultural norms. Since these mechanisms of social control are not formalized, there can be great variation in their use even within the same society. For example, imagine that a teenager is seated on a crowded bus in a seat reserved for elderly and disabled people. A rather frail-looking elderly man gets on the bus and has nowhere to sit, yet the teenager does not move. One nearby passenger may scowl at the teenager, another may stare until the teenager becomes uncomfortable, while a third may verbalize the control mechanism by telling the teenager to get up.

In some cases, informal methods of social control are not adequate in enforcing conforming or obedient behavior. In the example above, the teenager might look away from the scowling and staring passengers and might tell the third person, "Mind your own business!" At this point, passengers might enlist the aid of the bus driver—whose occupational role carries with it a certain authority—in an attempt to force the teenager to give up the seat. *Formal social control* is carried out by authorized agents, such as police officers, physicians, school administrators, employers, military officers, and managers of movie theaters. As we have seen, it can serve as a last resort when socialization and informal sanctions do not bring about desired behavior.

Societies vary in deciding which behaviors will be subjected to formal social control and how severe the sanctions will be. In the nation of Singapore, there are fines of $625 for littering, $312 for eating on the subway, and $94 for failing to flush a public toilet. In 1992, Singapore banned the sale of chewing gum, and 514 people were convicted of illegally smoking in public. Although a law has not yet been passed, Singapore's government has officially criticized people who come fashionably late for dinner parties; such behavior is viewed as a "growing problem with wide implications for national productivity" (Branegan, 1993:36).

It is important to emphasize that formal social control is not always carried out only by government officials in response to violations of the law. Certain subcultures within a society exercise formal social control to maintain adherence to their distinctive social norms. For example, if a member of the Amish religious minority (refer back to Chapter 4) violates the community's standards, he or she will initially be verbally chastised by a member (informal social control). However, if an Amish person commits an especially serious transgression or repeatedly violates accepted norms, the community may invoke its most severe means of formal social control, known as *Meidung,* or "shunning." Within the close-knit Amish community, a formal decision to shun a member amounts to "social death": the person is totally ignored, even by family members. Generally, the shunned member chooses to leave the community rather than endure this painful technique of formal social control (Kephart and Zellner, 1994:27).

Law and Society

Some norms are considered so important by a society that they are formalized into laws controlling people's behavior. In a political sense, *law* is the "body of rules made by government for society, interpreted by the courts, and backed by the power of the state" (Cummings and Wise, 1993:491). Some laws, such as the prohibition against murder, are directed at all members of society. Others, such as fishing and hunting regulations, are aimed primarily at particular categories of people. Still others govern the behavior of social institutions (corporation law and laws regarding the taxing of nonprofit enterprises). Despite such differences, all types of laws are considered examples of formal social norms (Chambliss and Seidman, 1971:8).

Sociologists have become increasingly interested in the creation of laws as a social process. Laws are created in response to perceived needs for formal social control. Sociologists have sought to explain how and why such perceptions are manifested. In their view, law is not merely a static body of rules handed down from generation to generation. Rather, it reflects continually changing standards of what is right and wrong, of how violations are to be determined, and of what sanctions are to be applied (Schur, 1968:39–43).

Sociologists representing varying theoretical perspectives agree that the legal order reflects underlying social values. Therefore, the creation of criminal law can be a most controversial matter. Should it be against the law to employ illegal immigrants in a factory (see Chapter 10), to have an abortion (see Chapter 11), or to smoke on an airplane? Such issues have been bitterly debated because they require a choice among competing values. Not surprisingly, laws that are unpopular—such as the prohibition of the manufacture and sale of intoxicating liquors under the Eighteenth Amendment in 1919 and the establishment of a national 55 mile per hour speed limit on highways in 1973—become difficult to enforce owing to lack of consensus supporting the norms.

It is important to underscore the fact that socialization is the primary source of conforming and obedient behavior, including obedience to law. Generally, it is not external pressure from a peer group or authority figure that makes us go along with social norms. Rather, we have internalized such norms as valid and desirable and are committed to observing them. In a profound sense, we *want* to see ourselves (and to be seen) as loyal, cooperative, responsible, and respectful of others. In the United States and other societies around the world, people are socialized both to want to belong and to fear being viewed as different or deviant.

DEVIANCE

What Is Deviance?

For sociologists, the term *deviance* does not mean perversion or depravity. *Deviance* is behavior that violates the standards of conduct or expectations of

Left, Ted Streshinsky/Photo 20-20; right, courtesy Isolar Enterprises, Inc.

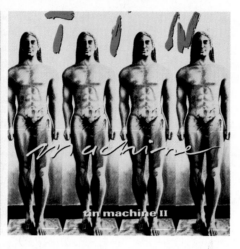

Deviance is often a highly relative matter. People may consider it acceptable to view nude statues in a museum, but are shocked by seeing nude statues on a record album cover. The resulting controversy caused by Tin Machine's album forced their record company to remove the male genitalia from the statues featured on the cover.

a group or society (Wickman, 1991:85). In the United States, alcoholics, people with tattoos, compulsive gamblers, and the mentally ill would all be classified as deviants. Being late for class is categorized as a deviant act; the same is true of dressing too casually for a formal wedding. On the basis of the sociological definition, we are all deviant from time to time. Each of us violates common social norms in certain situations.

Deviance involves the violation of group norms which may or may not be formalized into law. It is a comprehensive concept that includes not only criminal behavior but also many actions not subject to prosecution. The public official who takes a bribe has defied social norms, but so has the high school student who refuses to sit in an assigned seat or cuts class. Of course, deviation from norms is not always negative, let alone criminal. A member of an exclusive social club who speaks out against its traditional policy of excluding women, Blacks, and Jews from admittance is deviating from the club's norms. So is a police officer who "blows the whistle" on corruption or brutality within the department.

As we noted earlier, deviance can be understood only within its social context. A nude photograph of a woman or man may be perfectly appropriate in an art museum but would be regarded as out of place in an elementary school classroom. A pharmacist is expected to sell prescription drugs only to people who have explicit instructions from medical authorities. If the pharmacist sells the same drugs to a narcotics dealer, he or she has committed deviant (and criminal) behavior.

Standards of deviance vary from one group (or subculture) to another. In the United States, it is generally considered acceptable to sing along at a folk or rock concert, but not at the opera. Just as deviance is defined by the social situation, so too is it relative to time. For instance, having an alcoholic drink at 6:00 P.M. is a common practice in our society, but engaging in the same behavior upon arising at 8:00 A.M. is viewed as a deviant act and as symptomatic of a drinking problem. In Table 7-1, we offer additional examples of untimely acts that are regarded as deviant in the United States.

Deviance, then, is a highly relative matter. Peo-

TABLE 7-1	Untimely Acts
Ringing a doorbell at 2 A.M.	
Working on New Year's eve	
Having sex on a first date	
Playing a stereo loudly in early morning hours	
Having an alcoholic drink with breakfast	
An instructor's ending a college class after 15 minutes	
Getting married after having been engaged for only a few days	
Taking five years or more to complete high school	

SOURCE: Reese and Katovich, 1989.

Society may regard certain acts as deviant simply because of the time element involved.

ple in the United States may consider it strange for a person to fight a bull in an arena, before an audience of screaming fans. Yet we are not nearly so shocked by the practice of two humans fighting *each other* with boxing gloves in front of a similar audience.

Explaining Deviance

Why do people violate social norms? We have seen that deviant acts are subject to both informal and formal sanctions of social control. The nonconforming or disobedient person may face disapproval, loss of friends, fines, or even imprisonment. Why, then, does deviance occur?

Early explanations for deviance identified supernatural causes or genetic factors (such as "bad blood" or evolutionary throwbacks to primitive ancestors). By the 1800s, there were substantial research efforts to identify biological factors that lead to deviance and especially to criminal activity. While such research has been discredited in the twentieth century, contemporary studies, primarily by biochemists, have sought to isolate genetic factors leading to a likelihood of certain personality traits. Although criminality (much less deviance) is hardly a personality characteristic, researchers have focused on traits that might lead to crime, such as aggression. Of course, aggression can also lead to success in the corporate world, professional sports, or other areas of life.

The contemporary study of possible biological roots of criminality is but one aspect of the larger sociobiology debate discussed in Chapter 4. In general, sociologists reject any emphasis on genetic roots of crime and deviance. The limitations of current knowledge are so significant, the likelihood of reinforcing racist and sexist assumptions so clear, and the implications for rehabilitation of criminals so disturbing, that sociologists have largely drawn upon other approaches to explain deviance (Sagarin and Sanchez, 1988).

Functionalist Perspective According to functionalists, deviance is a common part of human existence, with positive (as well as negative) consequences for social stability. Deviance helps to define the limits of proper behavior. Children who see one parent scold the other for belching at the dinner table learn about approved conduct. The same is true of the driver who receives a speeding ticket, the department store cashier who is fired for yelling at a customer, and the college student who is penalized for handing in papers weeks overdue.

Durkheim's Legacy Émile Durkheim (1964:67, original edition 1895) focused his sociological investigations mainly on criminal acts, yet his conclusions have implications for all types of deviant behavior. In Durkheim's view, the punishments established within a culture (including what we have identified as formal and informal mechanisms of social control) help to define acceptable behavior and thus contribute to stability. If improper acts were not committed and then sanctioned, people

On the basis of his study of the Puritans of seventeenth-century New England, sociologist Kai Erikson suggested that the Puritans' persecution of Quakers and execution of women as witches represented continuing attempts to define and redefine the boundaries of their community.

might extend their standards as to what constitutes appropriate conduct.

Kai Erikson (1966) illustrated this boundary-maintenance function of deviance in his study of the Puritans of seventeenth-century New England. By today's standards, the Puritans placed tremendous emphasis upon conventional morals. Their persecution of Quakers and execution of women as witches represented continuing attempts to define and redefine the boundaries of their community. In effect, changing social norms created "crime waves," as people whose behavior was previously acceptable suddenly faced punishment for being deviant (Abrahamson, 1978:78–79; N. Davis, 1975: 85–87).

Unexpectedly, boundary maintenance reemerged in the same area some 300 years later. The town of Salem, Massachusetts, draws (and profits from) 1 million visitors per year who come to see the sites of the witch trials and executions. At the urging of descendants of 20 innocent victims who had been executed, a statue was designed to commemorate the slain women. However, protests blocked the public installation of the statue, owing to concern that such a prominent memorial to the *victims* would dampen tourists' interest in witch lore (Driscoll, 1988).

Durkheim (1951, original edition 1897) also introduced the term *anomie* in sociological literature to describe a loss of direction felt in a society when social control of individual behavior has become ineffective. As was noted in Chapter 1, anomie is a state of normlessness which typically occurs during a period of profound social change and disorder, such as a time of economic collapse. People become more aggressive or depressed, and this results in higher rates of violent crime or suicide. Since there is much less agreement on what constitutes proper behavior during times of revolution, sudden prosperity, or economic depression, conformity and obedience become less significant as social forces. It also becomes much more difficult to state exactly what constitutes deviance.

Merton's Theory of Deviance A mugger and a secretary do not seem at first to have a great deal in common. Yet, in fact, each is "working" to obtain money which can then be exchanged for desired goods. As this example illustrates, behavior that violates accepted norms (such as mugging) may be performed with the same basic objectives in mind as those of people who pursue more conventional lifestyles.

Using the above analysis, sociologist Robert Merton of Columbia University (1968:185–214) adapted Durkheim's notion of anomie to explain why people accept or reject the goals of a society, the socially approved means to fulfill their aspirations, or both. Merton maintained that one important cultural goal in the United States is success, measured largely in terms of money. In addition to providing this goal for people, our society offers specific instructions on how to pursue success—go to school, work hard, do not quit, take advantage of opportunities, and so forth.

What happens to individuals in a society with a heavy emphasis on wealth as a basic symbol of success? Merton reasoned that people adapt in certain ways, either by conforming to or by deviating from such cultural expectations. Consequently, he developed the ***anomie theory of deviance,*** which posits five basic forms of adaptation (see Table 7-2).

Conformity to social norms, the most common adaptation in Merton's typology, is the opposite of deviance. It involves acceptance of both the overall societal goal ("become affluent") and the approved means ("work hard"). In Merton's view, there must

TABLE 7-2	**Modes of Individual Adaptation**	
MODE	INSTITUTIONALIZED MEANS (HARD WORK)	SOCIETAL GOAL (ACQUISITION OF WEALTH)
Nondeviant		
Conformity	+	+
Deviant		
Innovation	−	+
Ritualism	+	−
Retreatism	−	−
Rebellion	±	±

NOTE: + indicates acceptance; − indicates rejection; ± indicates replacement with new means and goals.

Robert Merton's typology (1968:194) shows that, in many cases, those whose form of adaptation is deviant still accept either the work ethic or the desire for material wealth widely valued by "conformists."

be some consensus regarding accepted cultural goals and legitimate means for attaining them. With~~~~~ ~ch consensus, societies could exist only ~~~~~~~~~~ ~ of people—rather than as unified cultures—and might function in continual chaos.

Of course, in a society such as that of the United States, conformity is not universal. For example, the means for realizing objectives are not equally distributed. People in the lower social classes often identify with the same goals as those of more powerful and affluent citizens yet lack equal access to high-quality education and training for skilled work. Even within a society, institutionalized means for realizing objectives vary. For instance, it is legal to gain money through roulette or poker in Nevada, but not in neighboring California.

The other four types of behavior represented in Table 7-2 all involve some departure from conformity. The "innovator" accepts the goals of a society but pursues them with means regarded as improper. For example, Harry King—a professional thief who specialized in safecracking for 40 years—gave a lecture to a sociology class and was asked if he had minded spending time in prison. King responded:

> I didn't exactly like it. But it was one of the necessary things about the life I had chosen. Do you like to come here and teach this class? I bet if the students had their wishes they'd be somewhere else, maybe out stealing, instead of sitting in this dumpy room. But they do it because it gets them something they want. The same with me. If I had to go to prison from time to time, well, that was the price you pay (Chambliss, 1972:x).

Harry King saw his criminal lifestyle as an adaptation to the goal of material success or "getting something you want." According to Merton's anomie theory of deviance, if a society largely denies people the opportunity to achieve success through socially approved avenues, some individuals (like King) will turn to illegitimate paths of upward mobility.

In Merton's typology, the "ritualist" has abandoned the goal of material success and become compulsively committed to the institutional means. Therefore, work becomes a way of life rather than a means to the goal of success. In discussing goal displacement within bureaucracy in Chapter 6, we noted that officials can blindly apply rules and reg-

In Robert Merton's typology, the "retreatist" has basically withdrawn from both the goals and means of a society. In the United States, there is growing concern about adolescents addicted to alcohol who become retreatists at an early age.

ulations without remembering the larger goals of an organization. Certainly this would be true of a welfare caseworker who refuses to assist a homeless family because their last apartment was in another district. People who overzealously and rigidly enforce bureaucratic regulations can be classified as "ritualists."

The "retreatist," as described by Merton, has basically withdrawn (or "retreated") from both the goals and the means of a society. In the United States, while drug addicts and residents of skid row are typically portrayed as retreatists, there is growing concern about adolescents addicted to alcohol who become retreatists at an early age.

The final adaptation identified by Merton reflects

people's attempts to create a new social structure. The "rebel" is assumed to have a sense of alienation from dominant means and goals and to be seeking a dramatically different social order. Members of a revolutionary political organization, such as the Irish Republican Army (IRA) or the Puerto Rican nationalist group Fuerzas Armadas de Liberación Nacional (FALN), can be categorized as rebels according to Merton's model.

Merton has stressed that he was not attempting to describe five types of individuals. Rather, he offered a typology to explain the actions that people *usually* take. Thus, leaders of organized crime syndicates will be categorized as innovators, since they do not pursue success through socially approved means. Yet they may also attend church and send their children to medical school. Conversely, "respectable" people may occasionally cheat on their taxes or violate traffic laws. According to Merton, the same person will move back and forth from one mode of adaptation to another, depending on the demands of a particular situation.

Despite its popularity, Merton's theory of deviance has had relatively few applications. Little effort has been made to determine how comprehensive the five modes of adaptation are—in other words, to what extent all acts of deviance can be accounted for by innovation, ritualism, retreatism, and rebellion. Moreover, while Merton's theory is useful in examining certain types of behavior, such as illegal gambling by disadvantaged people functioning as innovators, his formulation fails to explain key differences in rates. Why, for example, do some disadvantaged groups have lower rates of reported crime than others? Why is criminal behavior not viewed as a viable alternative by many people faced with adversity? Such questions are not easily answered by Merton's theory of deviance (Cloward, 1959; Hartjen, 1978).

Nevertheless, Merton has made a key contribution to sociological understanding of deviance by pointing out that deviants (such as innovators and ritualists) share a great deal with conforming people. The convicted felon may hold many of the same aspirations that people with no criminal background have. Therefore, deviance can be understood as socially created behavior, rather than as the result of momentary pathological impulses.

Interactionist Perspective: Differential Association

The functionalist approaches to deviance explain why rule violation continues to exist in societies despite pressures to conform and obey. However, functionalists do not indicate how a given person comes to commit a deviant act. The theory of differential association draws upon the interactionist perspective to offer just such an explanation.

There is no natural, innate manner in which people interact with one another. Rather, humans *learn* how to behave in social situations—whether properly or improperly. These simple ideas are not disputed today, but this was not the case when sociologist Edwin Sutherland (1883–1950) advanced the argument that an individual undergoes the same basic socialization process whether learning conforming or deviant acts.

Sutherland's ideas have been the dominating force in criminology. He drew upon the **cultural transmission** school, which emphasizes that criminal behavior is learned through interactions with others. Such learning includes not only techniques of lawbreaking (for example, how to break into a car quickly and quietly) but also the motives, drives, and rationalizations of criminals. The cultural transmission approach can also be used to explain the behavior of people who engage in habitual—and ultimately life-threatening—use of alcohol or drugs.

Sutherland maintained that through interactions with a primary group and significant others, people acquire definitions of behavior that are deemed proper and improper. He used the term **differential association** to describe the process through which exposure to attitudes favorable to criminal acts leads to violation of rules. Recent research suggests that this view of differential association can be applied to such noncriminal deviant acts as sitting down during the singing of the National Anthem or lying to a spouse or friend (E. Jackson et al., 1986).

To what extent will a given person engage in activity regarded as proper or improper? For each individual, it will depend on the frequency, duration, and importance of two types of social interaction experiences—those which endorse deviant behavior and those which promote acceptance of social norms. Deviant behavior, including criminal activ-

Edwin Sutherland used the term differential association *to describe the process through which exposure to attitudes favorable to criminal acts leads to violation of rules. In a scandal which erupted in Lakewood, California in 1993, members of a teenage clique known as the "Spur Posse" were convicted of a series of burglaries, assaults, and an auto theft. In addition, there were allegations that Posse members had committed rapes and had devised a "scoring system" to keep track of their sexual conquests.*

ity, is selected by those who acquire more sentiments in favor of violation of norms. People are more likely to engage in norm-defying behavior if they are part of a group or subculture that stresses deviant values.

Sutherland offers the example of a boy who is sociable, outgoing, and athletic and who lives in an area with a high rate of delinquency. The youth is very likely to come into contact with peers who commit acts of vandalism, fail to attend school, and so forth, and may, thus, adopt such behavior. However, an introverted boy living in the same neighborhood may stay away from his peers and avoid delinquency. In another community, an outgoing and athletic boy may join a Little League baseball team or a scout troop because of his interactions with peers. Thus, Sutherland views learning improper behavior as the result of the types of groups to which one belongs and the kinds of friendships one has with others (Sutherland and Cressey, 1978:82).

In an empirical study of differential association theory, sociologists Mark Warr and Mark Stafford (1991) examined the attitudes and behavior of 11- to 17-year-olds. The researchers found that young people's attitudes and especially their behavior influenced the behavior of their peers. Indeed, the young people studied by Warr and Stafford were likely to imitate their friends' behavior even when it involved delinquent conduct, such as cheating in school, using marijuana, or committing acts of larceny.

According to its critics, however, the differential association approach fails to explain the deviant behavior of the first-time impulsive shoplifter or the impoverished person who steals out of necessity. While not a precise statement of the process through which one becomes a criminal, differential association does direct our attention to the paramount role of social interaction in increasing a person's motivation to engage in deviant behavior (Cressey, 1960:53–54; E. Jackson et al., 1986; Sutherland and Cressey, 1978:80–82).

The differential association approach deals not only with the process by which criminal techniques are learned, but also with the content that is actually passed on from one person to another. This content includes methods of committing a crime as well as ways of justifying criminal behavior. The concept of "techniques of neutralization," as described in Box 7-1 on page 186, illustrates how criminal and other norm-defying sentiments are defined by the deviant person to justify his or her conduct.

Labeling Theory The Saints and Roughnecks were two groups of high school males who were constantly occupied with drinking, wild driving, tru-

BOX 7-1 • CURRENT RESEARCH

NEUTRALIZATION OF DEVIANCE AND FEMALE BODYBUILDERS

When we have been observed in an action that others regard as improper, a common response is, "But I didn't do anything wrong." Gresham Sykes and David Matza (1957) clarified the various explanations for wrongdoing that we use in such situations by offering a five-part model of justifications of deviant behavior which they call *techniques of neutralization*:

1 *Denying responsibility.* We argue that larger forces—such as poverty, poor academic preparation, or the bad example of others—drove us to the misdeed.

2 *Denying the injury.* Crimes such as vandalism or obstruction of traffic near a college campus are called *pranks* or *mischief.* Such terminology suggests that these actions are not serious violations.

3 *Blaming the victim.* We admit that we hurt someone else but maintain that the victim "had it coming" or provoked the incident.

4 *Condemning the authorities.* Lawbreakers often insist that police or government leaders are the true guilty parties. The alleged stupidity, brutality, and corruption of authority figures are used to justify deviant or criminal behavior.

5 *Appealing to higher principles or authorities.* People rationalize actions by asserting that they are adhering to standards more important than the law—whether the unwritten criminal code of "never squeal on a friend" or moral and religious beliefs said to justify acts of civil disobedience.

By using these five techniques of neutralization, people who break the law are able to defend their conduct. But how useful is this model in understanding justifications of *noncriminal* deviance? Sociologists Robert Duff and Lawrence Hong (1986, 1988) applied neutralization theory in studying impression management among participants in a relatively new sport: women's bodybuilding. Female bodybuilders are sometimes treated favorably in the media, but they have also been socially stigmatized—partly because of allegations that they use steroids, but primarily because they represent a blatant departure from traditional gender-role expectations for women.

Drawing upon the results of a mail survey by the International Federation of Bodybuilders, Duff and Hong suggest that female bodybuilders respond to negative feedback from the public and the media by use of three more neutralization techniques:

1 *Claiming benefits.* Women defend their participation in the sport of bodybuilding by claiming that they have developed healthy, strong, and attractive bodies and improved mental health. Such "claims of benefit" have been employed by people engaged in other roles and activities viewed as deviant (N. Friedman, 1974; L. Hong and R. Duff, 1977).

2 *Blasting.* "Blasting" is an attack on critics in order to enhance one's own status (K. Richardson and Cialdini, 1981). Female bodybuilders typically "blast" their critics by portraying them as ignorant, jealous, unhealthy, fat, and lazy.

3 *Basking in reflected glory.* Out of sensitivity to the criticism that women bodybuilders are not "feminine," some participants in the sport "bask in the reflected glory" of a few less muscular, more lithe and slender bodybuilders who have been glamorized in the electronic and print media.

Duff and Hong suggest that both women's and men's bodybuilding may be viewed as a form of "positive deviance" whereby the approved societal emphasis on health and fitness is carried to an extreme. Apparently, in comparison with the neutralization of "negative deviance" (such as crime), neutralization of positive deviance requires fewer techniques and allows for greater reliance on direct and aggressive strategies of justification for one's behavior.

---

ancy, petty theft, and vandalism. There the similarity ended. None of the Saints was ever arrested, but every Roughneck was continually in trouble with police and townspeople. Why the disparity in their treatment? On the basis of his observation research in their high school, William Chambliss (1973) concluded that social class standing played an important role in the varying fortunes of the two groups.

The Saints effectively produced a facade of respectability. They came from "good families," were active in school organizations, expressed the intention of attending college, and received good grades. Their delinquent acts were generally viewed as a few isolated cases of "sowing wild oats." By contrast, the Roughnecks had no such aura of respectability. They drove around town in beaten-up cars, were generally unsuccessful in school, and were viewed with suspicion no matter what they did.

The Roughnecks were labeled as "troublemakers," where the Saints were seen merely as "fun-loving kids." Both groups were gangs of delinquents, yet only one came to be treated that way. More recently, Chambliss's observations concerning juveniles have been confirmed in research using self-reports of delinquents and police records in Seattle, Washington. Sociologist Robert Sampson (1986) found that juveniles from the lower classes who came into contact with the Seattle police because of delinquent behavior were more likely to be arrested and then indicted than were their middle-class counterparts engaged in similar activities.

Such discrepancies can be understood by use of an approach to deviance known as **labeling theory.** Unlike Sutherland's work, labeling theory does not focus on why some individuals come to commit deviant acts. Instead, it attempts to explain why certain people (such as the Roughnecks) are *viewed* as deviants, delinquents, "bad kids," and criminals, while others whose behavior is similar (such as the Saints) are not seen in such harsh terms.

Reflecting the contribution of interactionist theorists, labeling theory emphasizes how a person comes to be labeled as deviant or to accept that label. Sociologist Howard Becker (1963:9; 1964), who popularized this approach, summed it up with the statement: "Deviant behavior is behavior that people so label." Labeling theory is also called the **societal-reaction approach,** reminding us that it is the *response* to an act and not the behavior that determines deviance. For example, studies have shown that some school personnel and therapists expand educational programs designed for learning-disabled students to include those with behavioral problems. Consequently, a "trouble-maker" can be improperly labeled as learning-disabled, and vice versa (Osborne et al., 1985).

Drawing on labeling theory, a recent study of mental illness in the United States suggests that while the labeling process does not *produce* mental illness, it nevertheless has negative effects for those individuals labeled as "mentally ill." Through socialization into the norms and values of our culture, we are all exposed to fears and prejudices concerning the mentally ill. Consequently, when people enter mental hospitals as patients, they may expect that others will devalue them, shun them, and even discriminate against them. With this in mind, former mental patients may be secretive about their problems and may avoid interactions with those who they fear will reject them. Thus, as people accept the label of "mentally ill," they often experience a decline in self-esteem and isolation from social networks (Link et al., 1989).

Labeling theory can also help us to understand that while some people routinely and often cruelly label severely disabled people as "vegetables" (see Chapter 20), there are many nondisabled people who do not stigmatize, stereotype, or reject those with severe and obvious disabilities. Robert Bogdan and Steven Taylor (1989) conducted observation studies over a 20-year period at settings in the community that support people with severe disabilities. The researchers supplemented their observations by interviewing agency administrators and caregivers. Bogdan and Taylor found that many family members, friends, and helpers of the disabled are caring and accepting of people with severe disabilities. These nondisabled people assume that the severely disabled have rational thought processes, see individuality in them, view them as reciprocating, and define them as actors in a social environment. Rather than adhering to negative labeling based on obvious "deviant" behavior, the nondisabled accept the severely disabled as valued and loved human beings.

Traditionally, research on deviance has focused on those individuals who violate social norms. In contrast, labeling theory focuses on police, probation officers, psychiatrists, judges, teachers, employers, school officials, and other regulators of social control. These agents, it is argued, play a significant role in creating the deviant identity by designating certain people (and not others) as "deviant." An important aspect of labeling theory is the recognition that some individuals or groups have the power to *define* labels and apply them to others. This view recalls the conflict perspective's emphasis on the social significance of power.

Should it be against the law to sell or use marijuana? In the 1930s, the Federal Bureau of Narcotics launched a campaign to have marijuana viewed as a dangerous drug rather than as a pleasure-conducting substance. From a conflict perspective, lawmaking is often an attempt by the powerful to coerce others into their own brand of morality. Marijuana is outlawed because it is alleged to be harmful to users, yet cigarettes and alcohol are sold legally almost everywhere.

The labeling approach does not fully explain why certain people accept a label and others are able to reject its application. In fact, this perspective may exaggerate the ease with which our self-images can be altered by societal judgments. Labeling theorists do suggest, however, that differential power is important in determining a person's ability to resist an undesirable label. Competing approaches (including those of both Merton and Sutherland) fail

to explain why some deviants continue to be viewed as conformists rather than as violators of rules. According to Howard Becker (1973:179–180), labeling theory was not conceived as the *sole* explanation for deviance; its proponents merely hoped to focus more attention on the undeniably important actions of those people officially in charge of defining deviance (N. Davis, 1975:172; compare with Cullen and Cullen, 1978:36–37).

Conflict Theory Why is certain behavior evaluated as deviant while other behavior is not? According to conflict theorists, it is because people with power protect their own interests and define deviance to suit their own needs. For decades, laws against rape reflected the overwhelmingly male composition of state legislatures. As one consequence, the legal definitions of rape pertained only to sexual relations between people not married to each other. It was legally acceptable for a husband to have forcible sexual intercourse with his wife—without her consent and against her will. However, repeated protests by feminist organizations finally led to changes in the criminal law. By 1991, husbands in all 50 states could be prosecuted under certain circumstances for the rape of their wives (although 34 states still required a higher standard for conviction if an accused rapist was the victim's husband). In this instance, the rise of the women's liberation movement (see Chapter 11) led to important changes in societal notions of criminality—as it has in educating judges, legislators, and police officers to view wife battering and other forms of domestic violence as serious crimes (National Center on Women and Family Law, 1991).

Sociologist Richard Quinney (1974, 1979, 1980) is a leading exponent of the view that the criminal justice system serves the interests of the powerful. Crime, according to Quinney (1970:15–23), is a definition of human conduct created by authorized agents of social control—such as legislators and law enforcement officials—in a politically organized society. He and other conflict theorists argue that lawmaking is often an attempt by the powerful to coerce others into their own morality.

This helps to explain why our society has laws against gambling, drug usage, and prostitution which are violated on a massive scale (we will examine these "victimless crimes" later in the chapter). According to the conflict school, criminal law does not represent a consistent application of societal values, but instead reflects competing values and interests. Thus, marijuana is outlawed in the United States because it is alleged to be harmful to users, yet cigarettes and alcohol are sold legally almost everywhere.

The conflict perspective reminds us that while the basic purpose of law may be to maintain stability and order, this can actually mean perpetuating inequality. For example, researchers have found that African Americans and Hispanics receive stiffer prison sentences and serve longer terms than Whites convicted of similar felonies. A 1991 study reported by the United States Sentencing Commission reported that Blacks and Hispanics are more likely than Whites to receive mandatory minimum sentences in federal courts. Ironically, Congress had adopted such mandatory minimums for certain federal crimes in order to end discrimination based on gender, race, and age. Yet, whereas 68 percent of African Americans facing mandatory minimum sentences actually get them, the same is true for 57 percent of Hispanics and only 54 percent of Whites. According to the commission, Whites are more likely to enter into plea bargains which lead to the dropping of those charges that require mandatory minimum sentences. Consequently, Whites are more likely to receive short sentences than are Hispanics or Blacks (Cauchon, 1991:8A).

On the whole, conflict theorists contend that the criminal justice system of the United States treats suspects and offenders differently, on the basis of racial, ethnic, and social class backgrounds. In commenting on the exercise of discretion in the courts (see Table 7-3). Justice Lois Forer (1984:9) of Philadelphia suggests that there are:

TABLE 7-3	Discretion within the Criminal Justice System
CRIMINAL JUSTICE OFFICIALS	**DISCRETIONARY POWERS**
Police	Enforce specific laws Investigate specific crimes Search people, vicinities, buildings Arrest or detain people
Prosecutors	File charges or petitions for judicial decision Seek indictments Drop cases Reduce charges Recommend sentences
Judges or magistrates	Set bail or conditions for release Accept pleas Determine delinquency Dismiss charges Impose sentences Revoke probation
Probation officers	File presentence reports Recommend sentences
Correctional officials	Assign people to type of correctional facility Award privileges Punish for disciplinary infractions
Parole authorities	Determine date and conditions of parole Revoke parole

SOURCE: Adapted from Department of Justice, 1988:59.

Conflict theorist Richard Quinney contends that social control is applied differentially to suspects because of their social class backgrounds. In a 1988 report by the Bureau of Justice Statistics, discretionary practices were outlined at various levels of the criminal justice system.

. . . two separate and unequal systems of justice: one for the rich in which the courts take limitless time to examine, ponder, consider, and deliberate over hundreds of thousands of bits of evidence, . . . and hear elaborate, endless appeals; the other for the poor, in which hasty guilty pleas and brief hearings are the rule and appeals are the exception.

Quinney (1974) argues that, through such differential applications of social control, the criminal justice system helps to keep the poor and oppressed in their deprived position. In his view, disadvantaged individuals and groups who represent a threat to those with power become the primary targets of criminal law. Yet the real criminals in poor neighborhoods are not the people arrested for vandalism and theft, but rather absentee landlords and exploitative store owners. Even if we do not accept this challenging argument, we cannot ignore the role of the powerful in creating a social structure that perpetuates suffering.

The perspective advanced by labeling and conflict theorists forms quite a contrast to the functionalist approach to deviance. Functionalists view standards of deviant behavior as merely reflecting cultural norms, whereas conflict and labeling theorists point out that the most powerful groups in a society can *shape* laws and standards and determine who is (or is not) prosecuted as a criminal. Thus, the label "deviant" is rarely applied to the corporate executive whose decisions lead to large-scale environmental pollution. In the opinion of conflict theorists, agents of social control and powerful groups can generally impose their own self-serving definitions of deviance on the general public.

CRIME

Crime is a violation of criminal law for which formal penalties are applied by some governmental authority. It represents some type of deviation from formal social norms administered by the state. Crimes are divided by law into various categories, depending on the severity of the offense, the age of the offender, the potential punishment that can be levied, and the court which holds jurisdiction over the case.

The term *index crimes* refers to the eight types of crime that are reported annually by the Federal Bureau of Investigation (FBI) in its *Uniform Crime Reports*. This category of criminal behavior generally consists of those serious offenses that people think of when they express concern about the nation's crime problem. Index crimes include murder, rape, robbery, and assault—all of which are violent crimes committed against people—as well as the property crimes of burglary, theft, motor vehicle theft, and arson.

There are almost 2 million violent crimes reported each year in the United States, including more than 22,000 homicides. The key ingredients in the high incidence of street crime appear to be drug use and the widespread presence of firearms. (The controversy over gun control will be examined in the social policy section at the end of the chapter.) Given projections that the number of people in the United States in the crime-prone ages of 15 to 19 will rise 23 percent between 1993 and 2005, there is little reason to expect any decline in the level of street crime or violent crime (Department of Justice, 1993; Meddis, 1993).

Types of Crime

Rather than relying solely on legal categories, sociologists classify crimes in terms of how they are committed and how the offenses are viewed by society. In this section, we will examine four types of crime as differentiated by sociologists: professional crime, organized crime, white-collar crime, and "victimless crimes."

Professional Crime Although the adage "crime doesn't pay" is familiar, many people do make a career of illegal activities. A *professional criminal* is a person who pursues crime as a day-to-day occupation, developing skilled techniques and enjoying a certain degree of status among other criminals. Some professional criminals specialize in burglary, safecracking, hijacking of cargo, pickpocketing, and shoplifting. Such people can reduce the likelihood of arrest, conviction, and imprisonment through their skill. As a result, they may have long careers in their chosen "professions."

Edwin Sutherland (1937) offered pioneering insights regarding professional criminals by publishing an annotated account written by a professional thief. Unlike the person who engages in crime only once or twice, professional thieves make a business of stealing. These professional criminals devote their entire working time to planning and executing crimes and sometimes travel across the nation to pursue their "professional duties." Like people in regular occupations, professional thieves consult with their colleagues concerning the demands of work, thus becoming part of a subculture of similarly occupied individuals. They exchange information on possible places to burglarize, on outlets for unloading stolen goods, and on ways of securing bail bonds if arrested.

Learning technical skills is an important aspect of working as a professional criminal. Sociologist Peter Letkemann (1973:117–136) makes a distinction between two types of criminal skills: those which are extensions of the legitimate social order but are sharpened and refined (such as the ability to detect when homeowners are away) and those skills not easily available to the average citizen (such as opening a safe). The latter are learned in the manner suggested by Sutherland in his cultural transmission approach. It is a norm among professional criminals that the chief areas for the exchange of criminal skills are the streets and prisons. Although such skills are not *systematically* taught in either place, they are nonetheless communicated

effectively (Chambliss and Seidman, 1971:487; McCaghy, 1980:180–192).

Organized Crime The term *organized crime* has many meanings, as is evident from a 1978 government report that uses three pages to define the term. For our purposes, we will consider **organized crime** to be the work of a group that regulates relations between various criminal enterprises involved in smuggling and sale of drugs, prostitution, gambling, and other activities. Organized crime dominates the world of illegal business just as large corporations dominate the conventional business world. It allocates territory, sets prices for illegal goods and services, and acts as an arbitrator in internal disputes (Blakey et al., 1978:107–109).

Organized crime is a secret, conspiratorial activity that generally evades law enforcement. Organized crime takes over legitimate businesses, gains influence over labor unions, corrupts public officials, intimidates witnesses in criminal trials, and even "taxes" merchants in exchange for "protection" (National Advisory Commission on Criminal Justice, 1976).

Through its success, organized crime has served as a means of mobility for groups of people struggling to escape poverty. Daniel Bell (1953:127–150) used the term *ethnic succession* to describe the

Alon Reininger/Woodfin Camp

Organized crime in the United States has traditionally served as a means of mobility for groups of people struggling to escape poverty. Shown are Cambodian Americans in California who are believed to be involved in illegal activities.

process during which leadership of organized crime, held by Irish Americans in the early part of the twentieth century, was transferred in the 1920s to Jewish Americans. In the early 1930s, Jewish crime leaders were in turn replaced by Italian Americans. More recently, ethnic succession has become more complex, reflecting the diversity of the nation's latest immigrants. Colombian, Mexican, Pakistani, and Nigerian immigrants are among those who have begun to play a significant role in organized crime activities.

White-Collar Crime Edwin Sutherland, who popularized the differential association theory discussed earlier, noted that certain crimes are committed by affluent, "respectable" people in the course of their daily business activities. Sutherland (1949, 1983) likened these crimes to organized crime because they are often perpetrated through the roles of one's occupation (Hagan and Parker, 1985). In his 1939 presidential address to the American Sociological Society, Sutherland (1940) referred to such offenses as *white-collar crimes.* More recently, the term *white-collar crime* has been broadened to include offenses by businesses and corporations as well as by individuals. A wide variety of offenses are now classified as white-collar crimes, such as income tax evasion, stock manipulation, consumer fraud, bribery and extraction of "kickbacks," embezzlement, and misrepresentation in advertising.

A new type of white-collar crime has emerged since Sutherland first wrote on this topic: computer crime. The use of such "high technology" allows one to carry out embezzlement or electronic fraud without leaving a trace, or to gain access to a company's inventory without leaving one's home. An adept programmer can gain access to a firm's computer by telephone and then copy valuable files. It is virtually impossible to track such people unless they are foolish enough to call from the same phone each time. According to a 1990 estimate, the cost of computer crimes in the United States has reached $3 to $5 billion annually (Conly and McEwen, 1990:2).

In the last 20 years, the concept of white-collar crime has also been expanded to include *corporate crime,* or any act by a corporation that is punishable by the government. Corporate crime takes many forms and includes individuals, organizations, and institutions among its victims. Corporations may engage in anticompetitive behavior, acts that lead to environmental pollution, stock fraud and manipulation, the production of unsafe goods, bribery and corruption, and worker health and safety violations. In addition, they may be found guilty of more common behaviors that violate criminal law, such as tax fraud (Simpson, 1993).

An often-cited example of corporate crime concerns asbestos. Although the dangers of working with asbestos have been known since Roman times and were scientifically documented as early as 1935, Johns Manville and other companies in the asbestos industry maintain that the risks were unknown to them until 1964. Yet, in a series of cover-ups dating back to the 1930s, the industry suppressed research that documented the links between exposure to asbestos and lung diseases (including lung cancer). At Johns Manville, company physicians were instructed not to inform employees about asbestos-related health dangers—even when workers were displaying symptoms of such diseases. Eventually, in 1982, with thousands of lawsuits pending because of the company's alleged responsibility in asbestos poisoning cases, Johns Manville filed for bankruptcy reorganization. While this scheme saved the company millions of dollars, victims of asbestos poisoning and their families were left with little protection, because the act of filing for bankruptcy voids all pending litigation (Brodeur, 1985; Mokhiber, 1988; Simpson, 1993).

In a survey of business practices in the United States in the period 1975 to 1984, sociologist Amitai Etzioni (1990) found that 62 percent of *Fortune's* 500 largest industrial corporations were involved in one or more illegal incidents, such as price-fixing, overcharging, fraud, and falsification of tax records. Indeed, the top 100 corporations were guilty of more such crimes than all the other firms combined. Since Etzioni's study was limited to those white-collar crimes *detected* by the government, his findings must be regarded as an underestimate of the prevalence of white-collar crime in the corporate world (Department of Justice, 1987; Reiman, 1984).

In addition to the financial costs of this form of crime, which run into billions of dollars per year, white-collar crime has distinctive social costs, including a decline in the quality of life and a weakening of the social order (Conklin, 1981:50). If those at the top of the nation's economic and social structure feel free to violate the law, less privileged citizens can certainly be expected to follow suit. Ralph Nader (1985:F3), director of the Corporate Accountability Research Group, suggests that "by almost any measure, crime in the suites takes far more money and produces far more casualties and diseases than crime in the streets—bad as that situation is."

Given the economic and social costs of white-collar crime, one might expect this problem to be taken quite seriously by the criminal justice system of the United States. Yet white-collar offenders are more likely to receive fines than prison sentences. In federal courts—where most white-collar cases are considered—probation is granted to 40 percent of those who have violated antitrust laws, 61 percent of those convicted of fraud, and 70 percent of convicted embezzlers (Gest, 1985). In Etzioni's study (1985, 1990), he found that in 43 percent of the incidents either no penalty was imposed or the company was required merely to cease engaging in the illegal practice and to return any funds gained through illegal means (for a different view, see Manson, 1986).

Moreover, conviction for such illegal acts does not generally harm a person's reputation and career aspirations nearly so much as conviction for an index crime would. Apparently, the label "white-collar criminal" does not carry the stigma of the label "felon convicted of a violent crime." In the view of conflict theorists, such differential labeling and treatment are not surprising. The conflict perspective argues that the criminal justice system largely disregards the white-collar crimes of the affluent, while focusing on index crimes often committed by the poor. Thus, if an offender holds a position of status and influence, his or her crime is treated as less serious and the sanction is much more lenient (Maguire, 1988).

Victimless Crimes   In white-collar or index crimes, people's economic or personal well-being is endangered against their will (or without their direct knowledge). By contrast, sociologists use the term *victimless crimes* to describe the willing exchange among adults of widely desired, but illegal, goods

Shown is a wanted poster for a New Hampshire judge who fled the state in 1989 after being indicted on charges that he had stolen $1.8 million from clients. While such white-collar criminals are sometimes prosecuted and imprisoned, the conflict perspective nevertheless argues that the criminal justice system of the United States largely disregards the white-collar crimes of the affluent.

and services (Schur, 1965:169; 1985). Despite the social costs to families and friends of those engaged in such behavior, many people in the United States continue to view gambling, prostitution, public drunkenness, and use of marijuana as victimless crimes in which there is no "victim" other than the offender. As a result, there has been pressure from some groups to decriminalize various activities which fall into the category of victimless crimes.

Supporters of decriminalization are troubled by the attempt to legislate a moral code of behavior for adults. In their view, it is impossible to prevent prostitution, gambling, and other victimless crimes. The already overburdened criminal justice system should instead devote its resources to "street crimes" and other offenses which have obvious victims. However, opponents of decriminalization insist that such offenses do indeed bring harm to innocent victims. For example, a person with a drinking problem can become abusive to a spouse or children; a compulsive gambler or drug user may steal in order to pursue this obsession. Therefore, according to critics of decriminalization, society must not give tacit approval to conduct which has such harmful consequences (National Advisory Commission on Criminal Justice, 1976:216–248; Schur, 1968, 1985).

The controversy over decriminalization reminds us of the important insights of labeling and conflict theories presented earlier. Underlying this debate are two interesting questions: Who has the power to define gambling, prostitution, and public drunkenness as "crimes"? And who has the power to label such behaviors as "victimless"? It is generally the state legislatures and, in some cases, the police and the courts.

Again, we can see that criminal law is not simply a universal standard of behavior agreed upon by all members of society. Rather, it reflects the struggle among competing individuals and groups to gain governmental support for their particular moral and social values. For example, such organizations as Mothers Against Drunk Driving (MADD) and Students Against Drunk Driving (SADD) have had success in recent years in shifting public attitudes toward drunkenness. Rather than being viewed as a "victimless crime," drunkenness is increasingly being associated with the potential dangers of driving while under the influence of alcohol. As a result, the mass media are giving greater attention to people guilty of drunk driving, while many states have instituted more severe fines and jail terms for a wide variety of alcohol-related offenses.

Crime Statistics

Crime statistics are not as accurate as social scientists would like. However, since they deal with an issue of grave concern to the people of the United States, they are frequently cited as if they are completely reliable. Such data do serve as an indicator of police activity, as well as an approximate indication of the level of certain crimes. Yet it would be a mistake to interpret these data as an exact representation of the incidence of crime.

International Crime Rates   Given the difficulties of developing reliable crime data in the United States, it is still more difficult to make useful cross-national comparisons. Nevertheless, with some care, we can offer preliminary conclusions about how crime rates differ around the world.

During the 1980s, violent crimes were far more common in the United States than in western Europe. Murders, rapes, and robberies were reported to police at rates four to nine times higher in the United States. Rates for other violent crimes were also higher in this country than in western Europe, but the difference in rates of property crimes was not so great. For example, in 1984, the most recent year for which comparative data are available, the burglary rate in the United States was about 20 percent higher than that of western Europe, while rates of auto theft and larceny were twice as high.

Rates of violent crime in the United States were also higher than in Canada, Australia, and New Zealand, while rates of burglary and automobile theft were comparable in these four countries. A 1990 report by the National Center for Health Statistics compared homicide rates for young males in the United States with rates in 21 other countries. The homicide rate for young males in the United States was four times higher than that of any other nation studied and was at least 20 times as high as the homicide rate for young males in such diverse nations as France, Poland, and Japan (Clines, 1989; Fingerhut and Kleinman, 1990). In Box 7-2, we examine the reasons for Japan's low crime rate.

Why are rates of violent crime so much higher in the United States? While there is no simple answer to this question, sociologist Elliot Currie (1985) has suggested that our society places greater emphasis on individual economic achievement than do other societies. At the same time, many observers have noted that the culture of the United States has long tolerated, if not condoned, many forms of violence. When coupled with sharp disparities between poor and affluent citizens, significant unemployment, and substantial alcohol and drug abuse, these factors combine to produce a climate conducive to crime. Finally, the comparatively easy availability of firearms in the United States makes crime relatively more lethal than in other countries (Fingerhut and Kleinman, 1990).

BOX 7-2 • AROUND THE WORLD

POLICE POWER IN JAPAN

It is midnight in Tokyo. Downtown streets are filled with pedestrians, strollers abound in the park, bikes sit unchained on the street, many front doors are unlocked, and children under 8 years old are even seen riding alone on the subway. As much of a culture shock as this may be to a visitor from the United States, an additional surprise comes the next morning when virtually no crimes are reported.

"As a woman, I feel safest here in all the world," reports Wakako Hironaka, who lived in the United States and France before being elected as a member of the upper house of Japan's parliament (I. Williams, 1991:25). Indeed, Tokyo has the lowest rates of murder, rape, robbery, and theft of any major city in the world. In comparison with Japan, the murder rate of the United States is seven times greater, the rate of rape 30 times greater, and the rate of robbery 200 times greater. Yet Japan has fewer police officers per capita: 1 for each 557 residents, compared with 1 for each 357 residents in the United States.

Why is there so little crime in Japan? The answer seems to center on the absolute trust that people have in the police. Outside observers believe that people's faith in the police results in good part from their extraordinary 99.83 percent conviction rate. It is also suggested that people's confidence in police is a cultural artifact dating back to the 400-year period before the beginning of the nation's modernization in 1868. In that era of Japanese history, samurai had the shogun's authority to enforce justice instantly against criminals by cutting off their hands or even beheading them.

But an examination of police-community interactions in Japan offers quite a different explanation for the power of the police and the low rate of crime. Once or twice a year, the police knock on every door in Japan to speak with residents or business owners about conditions in the building and neighborhood. Japanese people do not regard this as harassment, but rather as an example of the police taking personal interest in their welfare.

Small police boxes, known as *kobans*, are located in all urban neighborhoods and are staffed by two officers at all times. These 1250 *kobans* report to Tokyo's 99 police stations, which in turn report to 9 district headquarters. The *koban* officials are the first line of police response to a crime or crisis, yet they more often function as information brokers, providing information about locations and addresses in Tokyo's confusing maze of houses and businesses. When a person seeks police assistance, he or she typically goes to a *koban*. Consequently, the Japanese tend to look favorably on the *koban* system, rather than fearing its social control functions.

Other factors, as well, contribute to the low rate of crime in Japan. The cultural values of the Japanese help to promote law-abiding behavior and cooperation with police officers. There is persistent community disapproval of wrongdoing, and socially deviant behavior is not excused. Consequently, as part of their early socialization, children are encouraged to respect authority figures and place great value on self-discipline. In schools, young people are taught to accept codes of responsible behavior associated with citizenship. It is not surprising, therefore, that Japanese adults often belong to or support crime prevention programs.

In recent years the power of Japan's police has come under fire. International human rights groups criticize the police for such practices as conducting investigations without allowing suspects access to a lawyer and jailing suspects for up to 23 days without filing criminal charges. Yet there are no broad public demands for curtailing the power of the police. Indeed, even in death penalty cases, the Japanese seem to completely trust the police. When convicted criminals are executed, the police make no announcement and the media offer no coverage. These executions come to light only at the end of each year when the police release crime data.

SOURCES: Braithwaite, 1989; Shelley, 1992; R. Thornton and Endo, 1990; I. Williams, 1991; see also Miyazawa, 1992.

TABLE 7-4	National Crime Rates and Percent Change				
CRIME INDEX OFFENSES IN 1992	NUMBER REPORTED	RATE PER 100,000 INHABITANTS	PERCENT CHANGE IN RATE	
			SINCE 1988	SINCE 1983
Violent crime				
Murder	23,760	9	+11	+12
Forcible rape	109,060	43	+14	+27
Robbery	672,480	264	+19	+22
Aggravated assault	1,126,970	442	+19	+58
Total	1,932,270	758	+19	+41
Property crime				
Burglary	2,979,900	1,168	−11	−13
Larceny-theft	7,915,200	3,103	−1	+8
Motor vehicle theft	1,610,800	632	−8	+47
Total	12,505,900	4,902	−3	+6
Total index crime	14,438,200	5,660	−0.1	+9

NOTE: Arson was designated an index offense beginning in 1979; data on arson are still incomplete as of 1992. Because of rounding, some offenses listed may not add to totals.
SOURCE: Department of Justice, 1993:58.

The crime index, published annually by the FBI, is the major source of information on crime in the United States (although victimization surveys are increasingly being used).

Shelly Katz/Black Star

Use and Meaning of Crime Statistics Typically, the crime data used in the United States are based on the index crimes described earlier in the chapter. The crime index, published annually by the FBI as part of the *Uniform Crime Reports,* includes statistics on murder, rape, robbery, assault, burglary, larceny-theft, motor vehicle theft, and arson (see Table 7-4). Obviously many serious offenses, such as those referred to as *white-collar crimes,* are not included in this index (although they are recorded elsewhere). In addition, the crime index is disproportionately devoted to property crimes, whereas most citizens are more worried about violent crimes against people. Thus, a significant decrease in the

The comparatively easy availability of firearms in the United States makes crime relatively more lethal than in other countries.

number of rapes and robberies could be overshadowed by a slightly larger increase in the number of automobiles stolen, thereby leading to the mistaken impression that *personal* safety is more at risk than before.

The most serious limitation of such official crime statistics is that they include only those crimes actually *reported* to law enforcement agencies. As is clear in Figure 7-1, many crimes are not reported, including about half of all assaults and robberies. In these instances, victims typically feel that the experience has been too personal to reveal to police officers and other strangers or that the crime is "not important enough."

Use of official police statistics clearly presents major methodological problems for sociologists and other researchers in understanding crime. Partly because of the deficiencies of police data, the *National Crime Survey* was introduced in 1972 as a means of learning how much crime actually takes place in the United States. The Bureau of Justice Statistics, in compiling this report, seeks information from law enforcement agencies but also interviews members of 100,000 households annually and asks if they have been victims of a specific set of crimes during the preceding year. In general, **victimization surveys** question ordinary people, not police officers, to learn how much crime occurs.

The FBI has noted that forcible rape is one of the nation's most underreported crimes, owing primarily to the victims' feelings of fear, embarrassment, or both. Using victimization surveys, we can better assess the underreporting of rape in the United States. As we noted earlier, the feminist movement has spoken out strongly regarding the way in which the frequency of rape reflects the high level of misogyny (woman hating) in our society. The media have paid increasing attention to this offense—with a recent focus on date and acquaintance rape (see Chapter 13)—and law enforcement agencies have sensitized their officers to the plight of victims.

Partly as a result, victimization surveys showed an increase in the reporting of rapes from 41 percent in 1980 to 59 percent in 1991 (although the figure had reached as high as 61 percent in 1985). Thus, victimization data document the fact that while many rapes are still not reported, the proportion of rapes that *are* reported is somewhat higher than

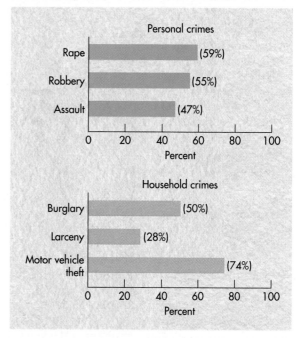

FIGURE 7-1 *Percent of Crimes Reported to the Police, 1991*

SOURCE: Department of Justice, 1992:102.

It is estimated that a large proportion of serious crimes go unreported. Less than 60 percent of all rapes and robberies and less than half of all assaults are reported to the police.

it was in the past. Moreover, victimization data reveal that virtually no rape victim fails to report this crime because she feels she does not have evidence. The most common reason, offered by 25 percent of those who fail to report rapes, is that the assault is regarded as a "private or personal matter." However, another 11 percent of rape victims remain silent because they fear further reprisal from the offender (Department of Justice, 1992:110–111).

Unfortunately, like other crime data, victimization surveys have particular limitations. They require first that victims understand what has happened to them and also that victims disclose such information to interviewers. Fraud, income tax evasion, and blackmail are examples of crimes that are unlikely to be reported in victimization studies. Nevertheless, virtually all households have been willing to cooperate with investigators for the *National Crime Survey* (Blumstein et al., 1991).

- What are the main approaches open to policy-makers who favor some form of gun control legislation?
- In what way has social science research offered some support for gun control advocates?
- How do conflict theorists view the power of the National Rifle Association and other strong lobbying groups?

Firearms have achieved an almost inevitable place in the United States. The right to bear arms stems in part from the nation's gun-ridden frontier heritage. In addition, the Second Amendment to the Constitution guarantees that the "right of the people to keep and bear arms shall not be infringed." Currently, the population of the United States has an estimated arsenal of 60 to 70 million automatic weapons and revolvers (Mackenzie, 1991:25). Clearly, owning a gun is not an act of deviance in our society. Informal gun clubs of both a primary- and secondary-group nature exist across the country, while, as we shall see, formal organizations promoting gun ownership exist on a national basis.

Many index crimes in the United States involve the use of a firearm. According to the FBI, in the year 1992, 24 percent of all reported aggravated assaults, 40 percent of reported robberies, and 66 percent of reported murders involved a firearm. More than 15,000 people died in 1992 through homicides committed with a firearm. Gunshot wounds have become the second-leading cause of death among high school–age youths, while 60 percent of deaths among teenage African American males result from a firearm injury. Since 1963, there have been more than 400,000 gun-related deaths in the United States—a figure which exceeds the number of the nation's troops who died in World War II (Department of Justice, 1993; Fingerhut, 1993; Hilts, 1992).

These deaths—along with the assassinations of such public figures as President John F. Kennedy, Senator Robert Kennedy, Dr. Martin Luther King, Jr., and singer John Lennon—have forced legislators to consider gun control measures. Although handgun owners frequently insist that they need to own firearms in order to protect themselves and their loved ones from violent criminals, studies have shown that gun owners kill themselves and members of their families 43 times as often as they shoot a criminal who has entered the home. According to a study released in late 1993, keeping a handgun in a home almost triples the likelihood that someone will be killed there. Moreover, in a society where domestic violence is all too common (see Chapter 13), use of firearms in domestic quarrels is 12 times more likely to result in death than use of other weapons (Hilts, 1992; Kellermann et al., 1993).

As noted earlier in the chapter, society's laws are not a static body of rules but reflect changing standards of right and wrong. There are four main approaches open to policymakers who favor some form of gun control legislation:

1 *Requiring registration of handguns.* This option is already in use in states across the nation. However, experts agree that registration of handguns has only a limited impact in reducing crime.
2 *Requiring a waiting period before a person can purchase a gun.* As of 1991, 14 states had waiting periods ranging from 48 hours to 15 days (Police Foundation, 1992).
3 *Allowing unrestricted ownership of firearms, but toughening criminal penalties for illegal use of guns.* This approach is favored by opponents of other gun control measures, such as the National Rifle Association (NRA).
4 *Banning handguns altogether.* This could include prohibiting the manufacture, sale, and possession of such weaponry. Yet, even if Congress were to pass such a law, the enormous nationwide reserve of guns would mean that many firearms would still be available illegally, and these could, of course, contribute to many violent crimes.

Social science research offers some support for gun control advocates. According to a study com-

SENATOR, HAS YOUR POSITION ON GUN CONTROL CHANGED?

NO, I GET HUNDREDS OF LETTERS A WEEK OPPOSING IT

WHAT ABOUT THE 10,000 PEOPLE KILLED EACH YEAR WITH HANDGUNS?

THEY SEEM TO BE MUCH LESS VOCAL

WASSERMAN © '81

In 1991, when this cartoon was first published, about 10,000 people in the United States were dying every year through homicides committed with a firearm. By 1992, that figure had risen to more than 15,000 killings with handguns each year.

paring crime rates in Seattle and Vancouver, Canada, gun control measures may reduce a community's homicide rate. A team of researchers studied crime data in the two cities over the period 1980 to 1986. These port cities are only 140 miles apart, and residents were found to have comparable levels of schooling, median annual incomes, and rates of unemployment. During the period under study, Seattle and Vancouver had similar rates of burglary and robbery, while Seattle's rate of assault was only slightly higher than that of Vancouver. Yet the risk of being killed with a firearm was nearly three times as high in Seattle as in Vancouver—which has more restrictive regulation of handguns (Sloan et al., 1988).

While the people of the United States have consistently favored gun control legislation in recent decades, the nation's major anti-gun control lobbying group, the National Rifle Association (NRA), has wielded impressive power in blocking or diluting such measures. Conflict theorists contend that powerful groups like the NRA can dominate the decision-making process because of their ability to mobilize resources and exert influence—even in opposition to the will of the majority. Founded in

1871, the NRA has 3 million members; in addition, 4 to 5 million members of state rifle associations support many of the NRA's goals. These figures compare with only 350,000 members of Handgun Control, a key organization in the gun control lobby. Whereas the NRA has a formidable war chest, Handgun Control has less than $7 million per year (Mackenzie, 1991; McLean, 1992).

Despite opposition from the NRA and its allies, some communities have passed gun control measures. Morton Grove, a Chicago suburb of 24,000 people, made the mere possession of a handgun a crime beginning in 1982. Violators are subject to up to six months in jail and a $500 fine. This statute, the nation's most stringent gun control law, has had little practical impact, since town police have not launched an enforcement drive. Nevertheless, the Morton Grove law has symbolic value, as was recognized by the NRA, which unsuccessfully attempted to have the statute ruled unconstitutional. Spurred in part by the Morton Grove measure, the city of Chicago passed a law prohibiting the registration of any new handguns. Yet, while four suburbs followed suit, such legislation has not been passed by any other city in the United States (McRoberts and Kuczka, 1992; *Time,* 1982).

The crucial problem in assessing the effectiveness of any state or local gun law is that weapons can be imported from localities in which laws are more lax. Consequently, advocates of handgun control insist that stringent *federal* gun control legislation is essential. In recent years, congressional debate on this issue centered on the so-called Brady bill. This bill was named after one of its chief advocates, former White House press secretary James Brady, who was shot and paralyzed in 1981 by John Hinckley during Hinckley's attempt to assassinate President Ronald Reagan. The Brady bill proposed a compulsory seven-day waiting period on all handgun purchases to allow for background checks of those who wish to buy guns and to permit impulse purchasers to "cool off."

While the NRA predictably opposed the Brady bill—noting that it would not have deterred Hinckley, who obtained his firearm six months before the assassination attempt—a 1993 national survey revealed that 85 percent of respondents favored such a seven-day waiting period. In late 1993, Congress passed and President Clinton signed into law a modified version of the Brady bill which requires the buyer of a handgun to wait five days before taking possession of it. Gun control advocates also won major victories in New Jersey and Virginia in 1993. New Jersey upheld its ban on the purchase of assault weapons, while Virginia restricted handgun purchases to one per month and outlawed gun possession by minors (Eckholm, 1993; *Newsweek,* 1993).

In the aftermath of the Los Angeles riots of 1992—which erupted after the acquittal of four White police officers charged with the (videotaped) beating of suspect Rodney King—gun control advocates and opponents found still another way of debating this controversial issue. California has a 15-day waiting period for gun purchases, which helped reduce impulse buying during the riots. However, after the disturbances, in the first 11 days of May 1992, gun sales in the state were 50 percent higher than in the same period in 1991. Supporters of gun control argue that, had such impulse purchases of guns occurred on a large scale *during* the riots, many more people would have died. NRA officials counter that while rioters stole thousands of weapons during the riots, law-abiding citizens were not able to buy guns to protect themselves (Eckholm, 1992).

This debate recalls a controversy that erupted in 1991, when the Chicago Housing Authority began to enforce a 20-year-old rule forbidding tenants to keep guns on the premises. This action was taken primarily because in 1990 alone, 72 murders had occurred in the city's public housing projects. While the Housing Authority's tenants, many of them African American, supported this ban on guns, the National Rifle Association did not. The NRA insisted that the Housing Authority was infringing on the tenants' constitutional right to bear arms and that this action would have disproportionate and unfair impact on the rights of Blacks living in public housing. Critics of the NRA charged that the NRA's sudden concern for the rights of African Americans was rather transparent and added that the ban on guns would disproportionately *save the lives* of Blacks (Prud'homme, 1991).

SUMMARY

Conformity and deviance are two ways in which people respond to real pressures or to imagined pressures from others. In this chapter, we examine the relationships between conformity, deviance, and mechanisms of social control.

1 A society uses *social control* to bring about acceptance of basic norms.

2 Stanley Milgram defined *conformity* as going along with one's peers, whereas *obedience* is defined as compliance with higher authorities in a hierarchical structure.

3 Examples of *informal social control* include smiles, laughter, raising of an eyebrow, and ridicule.

4 Some norms are considered so important that they are formalized into *laws* controlling people's behavior.

5 Socialization is the primary source for effecting conforming and obedient behavior, including obedience to law.

6 For functionalist theorists, deviance helps to define the limits of proper behavior.

7 The theory of *differential association* holds that deviance results from exposure to attitudes favorable to criminal acts.

8 An important aspect of **labeling theory** is the recognition that some people are *viewed* as deviant while others engaged in the same behavior are not.

9 The conflict perspective views laws and punishments as reflecting the interests of the powerful.

10 The category of **index crimes** includes murder, rape, assault, and other serious offenses that people think of when they express concern about crime.

11 **White-collar crimes** have serious economic and social costs for the United States.

12 The power of the National Rifle Association (NRA) has been a major factor in preventing the passage of strong gun control legislation.

CRITICAL THINKING QUESTIONS

1 What mechanisms of formal and informal social control are evident in your college classes and in day-to-day life and social interactions at your school?

2 Which approach to deviance do you find most persuasive: that of functionalists, conflict theorists, interactionists, or labeling theorists? Why is this approach more convincing than the other three? What are the main weaknesses of each approach?

3 As is discussed in the chapter, rates of violent crime are much higher in the United States than in western Europe, Canada, Australia, New Zealand, or Japan. Draw on as many of the theories discussed in the chapter as possible to explain why the United States is such a comparatively violent society.

KEY TERMS

Anomie Durkheim's term for the loss of direction felt in a society when social control of individual behavior has become ineffective. (page 182)

Anomie theory of deviance A theory developed by Robert Merton which explains deviance as an adaptation either of socially prescribed goals or of the norms governing their attainment. (182)

Conformity Going along with one's peers, individuals of a person's own status, who have no special right to direct that person's behavior. (176)

Crime A violation of criminal law for which formal penalties are applied by some governmental authority. (190)

Cultural transmission A school of criminology which argues that criminal behavior is learned through social interactions. (184)

Deviance Behavior that violates the standards of conduct or expectations of a group or society. (179)

Differential association A theory of deviance proposed by Edwin Sutherland which holds that violation of rules results from exposure to attitudes favorable to criminal acts. (184)

Formal social control Social control carried out by authorized agents, such as police officers, judges, school administrators, and employers. (178)

Index crimes The eight types of crime reported annually by the FBI in the *United Crime Reports*. These are murder, rape, robbery, assault, burglary, theft, motor vehicle theft, and arson. (190)

Informal social control Social control carried out by people casually through such means as laughter, smiles, and ridicule. (178)

Labeling theory An approach to deviance popularized by Howard S. Becker which attempts to explain why certain people are *viewed* as deviants while others engaging in the same behavior are not. (187)

Law In a political sense, the body of rules made by government for society, interpreted by the courts, and backed by the power of the state. (179)

Obedience Compliance with higher authorities in a hierarchical structure. (176)

Organized crime The work of a group that regulates relations between various criminal enterprises involved in smuggling and sale of drugs, prostitution, gambling, and other activities. (191)

Professional criminal A person who pursues crime as a day-to-day occupation, developing skilled techniques and enjoying a certain degree of status among other criminals. (190)

Sanctions Penalties and rewards for conduct concerning a social norm. (176)

Social control The techniques and strategies for regulating human behavior in any society. (176)

Societal-reaction approach Another name for *labeling theory*. (187)

Techniques of neutralization Justifications for deviant behavior. (186)

Victimization surveys Questionnaires or interviews used to determine whether people have been victims of crime. (197)

Victimless crimes A term used by sociologists to describe the willing exchange among adults of widely desired, but illegal, goods and services. (193)

White-collar crimes Crimes committed by affluent individuals or corporations in the course of their daily business activities. (192)

ADDITIONAL READINGS

Barak, Gregg (ed.). *Crimes by the Capitalist State: An Introduction to State Criminality*. Albany: State University of New York Press, 1991. An examination of how governments initiate or facilitate crimes, covering such topics as deaths of Aborigines in Australian prisons, responses to prison riots, and indifference to Canada's sexual assault laws.

Gaylord, Mark S., and John F. Galliher. *The Criminology of Edwin Sutherland*. Rutgers, N.J.: Transaction, 1987. An intellectual biography of Sutherland which places the development of differential association theory into its social context.

Hirschi, Travis, and Michael Gottfredson (eds.). *The Generality of Deviance*. Rutgers, N.J.: Transaction, 1994. This anthology advances the argument that all forms of deviant and criminal behavior share in common the pursuit of immediate benefits without concern for long-term costs.

Miyazawa, Setsuo. *Policing in Japan: A Study on Making Crime*. Albany: State University of New York Press, 1992. A professor of law in Japan reviews the nation's legal environment and criminal justice system in a work translated into English.

Paternoster, Raymond. *Capital Punishment in America*. New York: Lexington, 1991. A criminologist examines the social implications of replacing the death penalty with life sentences without parole and mandatory financial restitution.

Sanders, Clinton R. *Customizing the Body: The Art and Culture of Tattooing*. Philadelphia: Temple University Press, 1989. Sanders offers a brief history of the practice of tattooing and discusses his participant observation of those who work as tattooists.

Schur, Edwin M. *Labeling Women Deviant: Gender, Stigma, and Social Control*. Philadelphia: Temple University Press, 1983. An examination of the criminal justice system in its broadest context as it applies to women. Includes coverage of sexual harassment, rape, family violence, and mental illness.

Vachss, Alice. *Sex Crimes*. New York: Random House, 1993. A former New York City prosecutor assesses the way in which sex crimes—and especially rape—are handled by the criminal justice system.

Weisburd, David, Stanton Wheeler, Elin Waring, and Nancy Bode. *Crimes of the Middle Classes: White-Collar Offenders in the Federal Courts*. New Haven, Conn.: Yale University Press, 1991. An analysis of the handling of cases of securities fraud, antitrust violation, and tax fraud.

Wilson, James Q., and Richard J. Hernstein. *Crime and Human Nature*. New York: Simon and Schuster, 1986. A challenging, controversial approach to crime that examines the relationship of law-abiding behavior to intelligence, personality, and even body type.

Journals

Among the journals which focus on issues of deviance, crime, and social control are *Crime and Delinquency* (founded in 1955), *Criminology* (1961), and *Law and Society Review* (1966).

PART THREE

SOCIAL

INEQUALITY

PART THREE

SOCIAL

INEQUALITY

Part Three focuses on the structure and processes of social inequality. Chapter 8 examines the important sociological concepts of stratification and social mobility, as well as inequality based on social class, with special emphasis on the United States. In Chapter 9, we consider stratification and mobility abroad and give particular attention to the inequality evident in the world's developing nations. Chapter 10 deals with inequality based on racial and ethnic background and focuses on prejudice and discrimination against minority groups. Chapter 11 discusses inequality based on gender and the position of women as an oppressed majority. In Chapter 12, sociological analysis of the aging process is presented, and inequality based on age is examined.

8

STRATIFICATION AND SOCIAL MOBILITY

UNDERSTANDING STRATIFICATION
Systems of Stratification
    Slavery
    Castes
    Estates
    Social Classes
Perspectives on Stratification
    Karl Marx's View of Class
      Differentiation
    Max Weber's View of Stratification
Is Stratification Universal?
    Functionalist View
    Conflict View

STRATIFICATION BY SOCIAL CLASS
Measuring Social Class
Consequences of Social Class in the
   United States
    Wealth and Income

Poverty
   The Underclass
   Studying Poverty
   Unemployment
   Stratification and Life Chances

SOCIAL MOBILITY
Open versus Closed Class Systems
Types of Social Mobility
Social Mobility in the United States

**SOCIAL POLICY AND
STRATIFICATION:
RETHINKING WELFARE**

BOXES
8-1 Around the World: Slavery
    in the 1990s
8-2 Speaking Out: Blaming the Victim

> *A*ll animals are equal.
> But some animals are more equal than others.
>
> *George Orwell*
> *Animal Farm, 1945*

LOOKING AHEAD

- How are societies organized to deny privileges to some members while extending them to others?
- How did Karl Marx and Max Weber contribute to our understanding of social class?
- Can life be organized without structured inequality?
- How do sociologists measure social class?
- How is the ideology of "blaming the victim" used to minimize the problems of poverty in the United States?
- How likely are people in the United States either to move into or to rise out of poverty?
- Should there be major cuts in welfare programs in the United States?

In 1990, the United Nations began issuing a *Human Development Report* as a means of assessing the quality of life of peoples around the world. The 1993 report painted a bleak picture for much of the world's population, including significant segments of the population of the United States. In an especially striking finding, Blacks and Hispanics in this country appear to have a quality of life comparable to the residents of many developing countries in the Third World (Beals, 1993).

To assess the quality of life in a given country, the *Human Development Report* relies on an index that combines indicators of real purchasing power, ed-ucation, and health. In 1993, the United States ranked sixth-highest among the 173 nations studied, yet Whites in the United States enjoyed a quality of life higher than the people of top-ranked Japan. By contrast, the quality of life for African Americans was comparable to that in the Caribbean nations of Trinidad and Tobago, which ranked thirty-first, while Hispanics' quality of life was comparable to that in Estonia (which until recent years was part of the Soviet Union), which ranked thirty-fourth. The quality of life for Blacks and Hispanics was slightly higher than in Russia and Costa Rica but was slightly lower than in Hungary and Uruguay.

All around the world, there are substantial differences in people's quality of life. By contrasting the extremes, we see that residents of the lowest-ranked nation of Guinea, a former French colony in Africa ranked 173, have a life expectancy at birth of 44 years, compared with nearly 79 years in top-ranked Japan. In Guinea, only 24 percent of adults are literate, compared with 99 percent in Japan, and Guinea's annual level of production per capita is one-tenth that of Japan (United Nations Development Programme, 1993).

Ever since people began to speculate about the nature of human society, their attention has been drawn to the differences that can be readily observed between individuals and groups within any society. The term *social inequality* describes a condition in which members of a society have different amounts of wealth, prestige, or power. All societies are characterized by some degree of social inequality.

When a system of social inequality is based on a hierarchy of groups, sociologists refer to it as *stratification:* a structured ranking of entire groups of people that perpetuates unequal economic rewards and power in a society. These unequal rewards are evident not only in the distribution of wealth and income, but also in the distressing life expectancy data in Guinea and other developing countries. Stratification involves the ways in which social inequalities are passed on from one generation to the next, thereby producing groups of people arranged in rank order from low to high.

Stratification is one of the most important and complex subjects of sociological investigation because of its pervasive influence on human interactions and institutions. Social inequality is an inevitable result of stratification in that certain groups of people stand higher in social rankings, control scarce resources, wield power, and receive special treatment. As we will see in this chapter, the consequences of stratification are evident in the unequal distribution of wealth and income within industrial societies. The term *income* refers to salaries and wages. By contrast, *wealth* is an inclusive term encompassing all of a person's material assets, including land and other types of property.

Of course, each of us wants a "fair share" of society's rewards, and we often come into conflict over how these rewards should be divided. Family members argue over who should be given money to buy new clothing or take a vacation; nations go to war over precious resources such as oil or minerals. As a result, sociologists have directed their attention to the implications of stratification in ranking members of a society.

This chapter will focus on the unequal distribution of socially valued rewards within human societies. It begins with an examination of four general systems of stratification. Particular attention will be given to Karl Marx's theories of class and to Max Weber's analysis of the components of stratification. In addition, functionalist and conflict theorists' explanations for the existence of stratification will be considered and contrasted.

The second part of the chapter will explain how sociologists measure social class. The consequences

To assess the quality of life in a given country, the Human Development Report—issued annually by the United Nations—relies on an index that combines indicators of real purchasing power, education, and health. In 1993, the lowest-ranked nation in terms of people's quality of life was Guinea, a former French colony in Africa. Residents of Guinea have a life expectancy at birth of only 44 years.

of stratification in terms of wealth and income, health, educational opportunities, and other aspects of life will be discussed. In the third part of the chapter, the movement of individuals up and down the social hierarchies of the United States will be examined. Finally, in the social policy section, we will address the controversy over the welfare system of the United States.

Systems of Stratification

This section will examine four general systems of stratification—systems of slavery, castes, estates, and social classes. These should be viewed as ideal types useful for purposes of analysis. Any stratification system may include elements of more than one type. For example, the southern states of the United States had social classes dividing Whites as well as institutionalized enslavement of Blacks.

Slavery The most extreme form of legalized social inequality for individuals or groups is *slavery.* The distinguishing characteristic of this oppressive system of stratification is that enslaved individuals are owned by other people. These human beings are treated as property, just as if they were equivalent to household pets or appliances.

Slavery has varied in the way it has been practiced. In ancient Greece, the main source of slaves consisted of captives of war and piracy. Although slave status could be inherited by succeeding generations, it was not necessarily permanent. A person's status might change depending on which city-state happened to triumph in a military conflict. In effect, all citizens had the potential of becoming slaves or of being granted freedom, depending on the circumstances of history. By contrast, in the United States and Latin America, racial and legal barriers were established to prevent the freeing of slaves. As we will see in Box 8-1, millions of people around the world continue to live as slaves.

Whenever and wherever it has existed, slavery has required extensive coercion in order to maintain the privileges and rewards of slave owners. For example, it is estimated that as many as 9000 Blacks were involved in an 1822 slave revolt in Charleston, South Carolina, led by a carpenter and former slave named Denmark Vesey. Imagine the resources that must have been needed to crush such a massive rebellion. This is but one reflection of the commitment to social control required to keep people trapped in lives of involuntary servitude (Franklin and Moss, 1988; Schaefer, 1993).

Castes *Castes* are hereditary systems of rank, usually religiously dictated, that tend to be fixed and immobile. The caste system is generally associated with Hinduism in India and other countries. In India there are four major castes, called *varnas.* A fifth category of outcastes, referred to as *untouchables,* is considered to be so lowly and unclean as to have no place within this system of stratification. There are also many minor castes. Caste membership is established at birth, since children automatically assume the same position as their parents. Each caste is quite sharply defined, and members are expected to marry within that caste.

Caste membership generally determines one's occupation or social roles. An example of a lower caste is the *Dons,* whose main work is the undesirable job of cremating bodies. The caste system promotes a remarkable degree of differentiation. Thus, the single caste of chauffeurs has been split into two separate subcastes: drivers of luxury cars have a higher status than drivers of economy cars.

In recent decades, industrialization and urbanization have taken their toll on India's rigid caste system. Many villagers have moved to urban areas where their low-caste status is unknown. Schools, hospitals, factories, and public transportation facilitate contacts between different castes that were previously avoided at all costs. In addition, there have been governmental efforts to reform the caste system. India's constitution, adopted in 1950, includes a provision abolishing discrimination against untouchables, who had traditionally been excluded from temples, schools, and most forms of employment. Today, untouchables constitute about 15 percent of India's population and are eligible for certain reserved governmental jobs. This situation has created resentment among people just above the untouchables in the caste system and therefore deemed ineligible for these special jobs (*Economist,* 1991:22–23).

Sociologists have also used the term *caste* to describe stratification systems that emphasize racial distinctions. The type of differential treatment given to White, "Colored," Asian, and Black people in the Republic of South Africa, and to a lesser extent to racial groups in the United States (see Chapter 10), brings to mind certain aspects of India's caste system.

Estates A third type of stratification system, called *estates,* was associated with feudal societies during

BOX 8-1 ★ AROUND THE WORLD

SLAVERY IN THE 1990s

According to the 1948 Universal Declaration of Human Rights, which is supposedly binding on all members of the United Nations: "No one shall be held in slavery or servitude; slavery and the slave trade shall be prohibited in all their forms" (Masland, 1992:30, 32). Yet Britain's Anti-Slavery International, the world's oldest human rights organization, estimates that more than 100 million people around the world are still enslaved.

It is estimated that at least 300,000 (and perhaps 1 million) children work as rug weavers in northern India. They work 12 to 16 hours a day, 7 days a week, 52 weeks a year, creating carpets sold in the United States and other countries. Many of these children come from Bihar, India's most impoverished state, and are sold by their parents to agents for the loom owners at the going rate of $50 to $66 for an 8-year-old boy. A 10-year-old who escaped with three friends after 18 months working in and confined to a red adobe hut recalls: "No money was paid to me. All day we had to weave, even up until midnight. We were not allowed to rest during the day. If we became slow, . . . we were beaten with sticks" (Gargan, 1992a:A8).

The Islamic Republic of Mauritania, an Arabic state in northwest Africa, is another country in which slavery is all too common. Although Mauritania outlawed slavery upon achieving independence in 1960 and passed a similar measure in 1980, the government never passed legislation setting punishment for slave owners and never informed most of its population that slavery had become illegal. Consequently, more than 100,000 of Mauritania's residents of African descent are still believed to be living as slaves. Dada Ould Mbarek, a 25-year-old man who lives on a date plantation, declares: "I am a slave, my whole family are slaves." When asked about the emancipation of Mauritania's slaves, he says: "I never heard of it. And what's more, I don't believe it. Slaves free? Never here" (Masland, 1992:32).

The United States considers any person a slave who is unable to withdraw his or her labor voluntarily from an employer. Yet, in many parts of the world, "bonded laborers" are imprisoned in virtual lifetime employment as they struggle to repay small debts. As of 1991, India alone had an estimated 5 million bonded laborers working in road-building gangs, in quarries and brickworks, on plantations, and in sweatshops. In many cases, bonded laborers endure beatings and torture while repaying debts incurred by their parents or other ancestors. Indeed, the Bonded Labor Liberation Front has found workers paying off debts that are eight centuries old.

Exploitation of children is often an aspect of slavery in the 1990s, as in the case of the Indian rug weavers described earlier. On the Indian-Bangladeshi border, girls are commonly sold at an exchange rate of six cows; these girls may later surface as child prostitutes in Calcutta or Bombay. In some parts of Asia, young females are abducted and then sold at auctions reminiscent of the southern United States during the plantation era.

While contemporary slavery may be most obvious in Third World countries, it is also present in the industrialized nations of the west. Throughout Europe, guest workers and maids are employed by "masters" who hold their passports, subject them to degrading working conditions, and threaten them with deportation if they protest. Similar tactics are used to essentially imprison young women from eastern Europe who have been brought (through deceptive promises) to work in the sex industries of Belgium, France, Germany, Greece, the Netherlands, and Switzerland. Within the United States, illegal immigrants are forced to labor for years under terrible conditions to pay off debts as high as $30,000 to the smugglers who brought them into the country. In 1992, for example, 300 Mexicans were found living in enslaved conditions on a California ranch; in mid-1993, a decrepit freighter carrying nearly 300 illegal immigrants from China ran aground in New York City's harbor. Eight of the immigrants died, primarily from drowning.

SOURCES: *Economist*, 1990a; Gargan, 1992a; Masland, 1992; S. Myers, 1993; *New York Times*, 1992a; Pringle, 1993; Simons, 1993a; C. Tyler, 1991.

the Middle Ages. The **estate system,** or feudalism, required peasants to work land leased to them by nobles in exchange for military protection and other services. The basis for the system was the nobles' ownership of land, which was critical to their superior and privileged status. As in systems based on slavery and caste, inheritance of one's position largely defined the estate system. The nobles inherited their titles and property, whereas the peasants were born into a subservient position within an agrarian society.

As the estate system developed, it became more differentiated. Nobles began to achieve varying degrees of authority. By the twelfth century, a priesthood emerged in most of Europe, as did classes of merchants and artisans. For the first time, there were groups of people whose wealth did not depend on land ownership or agriculture. This economic change had profound social consequences as the estate system ended and a class system of stratification came into existence.

Social Classes A *class system* is a social ranking based primarily on economic position in which achieved characteristics can influence mobility. In contrast to slavery, caste, and estate systems, the boundaries between classes are less precisely defined, and there is much greater movement from one stratum, or level, of society to another. Yet class systems maintain stable stratification hierarchies and patterns of class divisions. Consequently, like the other systems of stratification described thus far, class systems are marked by unequal distribution of wealth and power.

Income inequality is also a basic characteristic of a class system. In 1991, the median family income in the United States was $35,939. In other words, half of all families had higher incomes in that year and half had lower incomes. Yet this fact may not fully convey the income disparities in our society. In 1991, about 61,000 tax returns reported incomes in excess of $1 million. At the same time, some 4.6 million households reported incomes under $5000 (Bureau of the Census, 1993a:340, 459). Table 8-1 offers a picture of the relative number of people in the United States earning various levels of income.

Sociologist Daniel Rossides (1990:404–416) has conceptualized the class system of the United States

TABLE 8-1	Family Income in the United States, 1991
INCOME LEVEL	PERCENT DISTRIBUTION
$50,000 and over	31.9
$35,000 to $49,999	19.5
$25,000 to $34,999	15.6
$15,000 to $24,999	16.0
$10,000 to $14,999	7.2
$ 5,000 to $ 9,999	6.1
Under $5,000	3.6

SOURCE: Bureau of the Census, 1993a:46.

In 1991, half of all families in the United States earned more than $35,939 in income; half of all families earned less than that amount.

using a five-class model. While the lines separating social classes in his model are not so sharp as the divisions between castes, he shows that members of the five classes differ significantly in ways other than their levels of income.

About 1 to 3 percent of the people of the United States are categorized by Rossides as upper-class, a group limited to the very wealthy. These people form intimate associations with one another in exclusive clubs and social circles. By contrast, the lower class, consisting of approximately 20 percent of the population, disproportionately consists of Blacks, Hispanics, single mothers with dependent children, and people who cannot find regular work. This class lacks both wealth and income and is too weak politically to exercise significant power.

Both of these classes, at opposite ends of the nation's social hierarchy, reflect the importance of **ascribed status,** which is a social position "assigned" to a person without regard for the person's unique characteristics or talents. (By contrast, **achieved status** is a social position attained by a person largely through his or her own effort.) While privilege and deprivation are not guaranteed in the United States, those born into extreme wealth or poverty will often remain in the same class position they inherited from their parents.

The nation's most affluent families generally inherit wealth and status, while many members of racial and ethnic minorities inherit disadvantaged status. Age and gender, as well, are ascribed statuses that influence a person's wealth and social position.

Sociologist Richard Jenkins (1991) has researched how the ascribed status of being disabled marginalizes a person in the labor market of the United States. People with disabilities are particularly vulnerable to unemployment, are often poorly paid, and in many cases are on the lower end of occupational ladders. Regardless of their actual performance on the job, the disabled are stigmatized as not "earning their keep." Such are the effects of ascribed status.

Between the upper and lower classes in Rossides' model are the upper middle class, the lower middle class, and the working class. The upper middle class, numbering about 10 percent of the population, is composed of professionals such as doctors, lawyers, and architects. They participate extensively in politics and exercise leadership roles in the types of voluntary associations described in Chapter 6. The lower middle class, which accounts for approximately 30 percent of the population, includes less affluent professionals (such as elementary school teachers and nurses), owners of small businesses, and a sizable number of clerical workers. While not all members of this varied class hold college degrees, they share the goal of sending their children to institutions of higher education.

Rossides describes the working class—about 40 percent of the population—as people holding regular manual or blue-collar jobs. Certain members of this class, such as electricians, may have higher incomes than people in the lower middle class. Yet, even if they have achieved some degree of economic security, they tend to identify with manual workers and their long history of involvement in the labor movement of the United States. Of the five classes identified in Rossides' model, the working class is noticeably declining in size. In the economy of the United States, service and technical jobs are replacing positions involved in the actual manufacturing or transportation of goods.

Class is seen by sociologists as a key determinant of people's values, attitudes, and behavior. For example, studies have found that working-class young people are likely to engage in sexual intercourse before the age of 17, whereas middle-class young people typically wait until 19 and become intimate with fewer partners before marriage. Theorists suggest that the less successful, less satisfying nature of life in the lower classes encourages people to seek

G. Schachmes/Sygma

Achieved status *is a social position attained by a person largely through his or her own effort. The stardom reached by a popular entertainer, such as Tina Turner, is an example of achieved status.*

emotional fulfillment through sexual relationships. At the same time, the values of middle- and upper-class families discourage early sexual behavior (B. Miller and Moore, 1990:1030; Weinberg and Williams, 1980).

Social class is one of the independent or explanatory variables most frequently used by social scientists. The chapters to follow will analyze the relationships between social class and divorce patterns (Chapter 13), religious behavior (Chapter 14), formal schooling (Chapter 16), and residence and housing (Chapter 18), as well as other relationships in which social class is a variable.

Perspectives on Stratification

As sociologists have examined the subject of stratification and attempted to describe and explain social inequality, they have engaged in heated debates and reached varying conclusions. No theorist stressed the significance of class for society—and for social change—more strongly than Karl Marx. Marx viewed class differentiation as the crucial determinant of social, economic, and political inequality. By contrast, Max Weber questioned Marx's emphasis on the overriding importance of the economic sector and argued that stratification should be viewed as a multidimensional phenomenon.

Karl Marx's View of Class Differentiation   Sociologist Leonard Beeghley (1978:1) aptly noted that "Karl Marx was both a revolutionary and a social scientist." Marx was concerned with stratification in all types of human societies, beginning with primitive agricultural tribes and continuing into feudalism. But his main focus was on the effects of class on all aspects of nineteenth-century Europe. Marx focused on the plight of the working class and felt it imperative to strive for changes in the class structure of society.

In Marx's view, social relations during any period of history depend on who controls the primary mode of economic production. His analysis centered on how the relationships between various groups were shaped by differential access to scarce resources. Thus, under the estate system, most production was agricultural, and the land was owned by the nobility. Peasants had little choice but to work according to terms dictated by those who owned land.

Using this type of analysis, Marx examined social relations within *capitalism*—an economic system in which the means of production are largely in private hands and the main incentive for economic activity is the accumulation of profits (D. Rosenberg, 1991). Marx focused on the two classes that began to emerge as the estate system declined—the bourgeoisie and the proletariat. The *bourgeoisie*, or capitalist class, owns the means of production, such as factories and machinery, while the *proletariat* is the working class. In capitalist societies, the bourgeois maximize profit in competition with other firms. In the process, they exploit workers, who must exchange their labor for subsistence wages. In Marx's view, members of each class share a distinctive culture. He was most interested in the culture of the proletariat, but also examined the ideology of the bourgeoisie, through which it justifies its dominance over workers.

According to Marx, exploitation of the prole-

In his analysis of capitalism, Karl Marx argued that the bourgeoisie owns the means of production, such as factories and machinery; and that while attempting to maximize profit, the bourgeoisie exploits workers, who must exchange their labor for subsistence wages.

tariat will inevitably lead to the destruction of the capitalist system. But, for this to occur, the working class must first develop *class consciousness*—a subjective awareness held by members of a class regarding their common vested interests and the need for collective political action to bring about social change. Workers must often overcome what Marx termed *false consciousness*, or an attitude held by members of a class that does not accurately reflect its objective position. A worker with false consciousness may feel that he or she is being treated fairly by the bourgeoisie or may adopt an individualistic viewpoint toward capitalist exploitation ("*I* am being exploited by *my* boss"). By contrast, the class-conscious worker realizes that *all* workers are being exploited by the bourgeoisie and have a common stake in revolution (Vanneman and Cannon, 1987).

For Karl Marx, the development of class consciousness is part of a collective process whereby the proletariat comes to identify the bourgeoisie as the source of its oppression. Through the guidance of revolutionary leaders, the working class will become committed to class struggle. Ultimately, the proletariat will overthrow the rule of the bourgeoisie and the government (which Marx saw as representing the interests of capitalists) and will eliminate private ownership of the means of production. In his rather utopian view, classes and oppression will cease to exist in the postrevolutionary workers' state.

Many of Marx's predictions regarding the future of capitalism have not been borne out. Marx failed to anticipate the emergence of labor unions, whose power in collective bargaining weakens the stranglehold that capitalists maintain over workers. Moreover, as contemporary conflict theorists note, he did not foresee the extent to which the political liberties present in western democracies and the relative prosperity achieved by the working and middle classes could contribute to what he called *false consciousness*. Many people have come to view themselves as individuals striving for improvement within "free" societies with substantial mobility—rather than as members of social classes facing a collective fate. Finally, Marx did not predict that Communist party rule would be established and later overthrown in the former Soviet Union and throughout eastern Europe. Despite these limitations, the Marxist approach to the study of class is useful in stressing the importance of stratification as a determinant of social behavior and the fundamental separation in many societies between two distinct groups, the rich and the poor.

Max Weber's View of Stratification Unlike Karl Marx, Max Weber insisted that no single characteristic (such as class) totally defines a person's position within the stratification system. Instead, writing in 1916, he identified three analytically distinct components of stratification: class, status, and power (Gerth and Mills, 1958).

Weber used the term *class* to refer to people who have a similar level of wealth and income. For example, certain workers in the United States provide the sole financial support for their families through jobs which pay the federal minimum wage. According to Weber's definition, these wage earners constitute a class, because they have the same economic position and fate. In this conception, Weber agreed with Marx regarding the importance of the economic dimension of stratification. Yet Weber argued that the actions of individuals and groups could not be understood solely in economic terms.

Weber used the term *status group* to refer to people who have the same prestige or lifestyle, independent of their class positions. In his analysis, status is a cultural dimension that involves the ranking of groups in terms of the degree of prestige they possess. An individual gains status through membership in a desirable group, such as the medical profession. Weber further suggested that status is subjectively determined by people's lifestyles and therefore can diverge from economic class standing. In our culture, a successful pickpocket may be in the same income class as a college professor. Yet the thief is widely regarded as a member of a low-status group, while the professor holds high status.

For Weber, the third major component of stratification, power, reflects a political dimension. *Power* is the ability to exercise one's will over others. In the United States, power stems from membership in particularly influential groups, such as corporate boards of directors, government bodies, and interest groups. As we will explore more fully in Chapter 15, conflict theorists generally agree that two major sources of power—big business and government—are closely interrelated.

AP/Wide World

In Max Weber's analysis, status *is a cultural dimension that involves ranking groups in terms of the degree of prestige they possess. The members of President Bill Clinton's cabinet, shown here, are unquestionably a high-status group in our society.*

In Weber's view, then, each of us has not one rank in society but three. A person's position in a stratification system reflects some combination of his or her class, status, and power. Each factor influences the other two, and in fact the rankings on these three dimensions tend to coincide. Thus, John F. Kennedy came from an extremely wealthy family, attended exclusive preparatory schools, graduated from Harvard University, and went on to become president of the United States. Like Kennedy, many people from affluent backgrounds achieve impressive status and power.

At the same time, these dimensions of stratification may operate somewhat independently in determining a person's position. A widely published poet may achieve high status while earning a relatively modest income. Successful professional athletes have little power, but enjoy a relatively high position in terms of class and status. In order to understand the workings of a culture more fully, sociologists must carefully evaluate the ways in which it distributes its most valued rewards, including wealth and income, status, and power (Duberman, 1976:35–40; Gerth and Mills, 1958:180–195).

Is Stratification Universal?

Is it necessary that some members of society receive greater rewards than others? Can social life be organized without structured inequality? Do people need to feel socially and economically superior to others? These questions have been debated by social theorists (and by the "average" woman and man) for centuries. Such issues of stratification have also been of deep concern to political activists. Utopian socialists, religious minorities, and members of recent countercultures have all attempted to establish communities which, to some extent or other, would abolish inequality in social relationships.

Social scientific research has revealed that inequality exists in all societies—even the simplest of cultures. For example, when anthropologist Gunnar Landtman (1968, original edition 1938) studied the Kiwai Papuans of New Guinea, he initially noticed little differentiation among them. Every man in the village performed the same work and lived in similar housing. However, upon closer inspection, Landtman observed that certain Papuans—the men who were warriors, harpooners, and sorcerers—were described as "a little more high" than others. By contrast, villagers who were female, unemployed, or unmarried were considered "down a little bit" and were barred from owning land.

Stratification is universal in that all societies maintain some form of differentiation among members. Depending on its values, a society may assign people to distinctive ranks based on their religious knowledge, skill in hunting, beauty, trading expertise, or ability to provide health care. But why has such inequality developed in human societies? How much differentiation among people, if any, is actually essential?

Functionalist and conflict sociologists offer contrasting explanations for the existence and necessity of social stratification. Functionalists maintain that a differential system of rewards and punishments is necessary for the efficient operation of society. Conflict theorists argue that competition for scarce resources results in significant political, economic, and social inequality.

Functionalist View   Would people go to school for many years to become physicians if they could make as much money and gain as much respect working as street cleaners? Functionalists reply in the negative, which is partly why they believe that a stratified society is universal.

In the view of Kingsley Davis and Wilbert Moore (1945), society must distribute its members among a variety of social positions. It must not only make sure that these positions are filled but also see that they are staffed by people with the appropriate talents and abilities. Thus, rewards, including money and prestige, are based on the importance of a position and the relative scarcity of qualified personnel. Yet this assessment often devalues work performed by certain segments of society, such as

women's work as homemakers or in occupations traditionally filled by women.

Davis and Moore argue that stratification is universal and that social inequality is necessary so that people will be motivated to fill functionally important positions. One critique of this functionalist explanation of stratification holds that unequal rewards are not the only means of encouraging people to fill critical positions and occupations. Personal pleasure, intrinsic satisfaction, and value orientations motivate people to enter particular careers. Functionalists agree but note that society must use *some* type of rewards to motivate people to enter unpleasant or dangerous jobs, as well as jobs that require a long training period. However, this response does not justify stratification systems such as slave or caste societies in which status is largely inherited. Similarly, it is difficult to explain the high salaries our society offers to professional athletes or entertainers on the basis of importance of these jobs to the survival of society (R. Collins, 1975; Kerbo, 1991:129–134; Tumin, 1953, 1985: 16–17).

Even if stratification is inevitable, the functionalist explanation for differential rewards does not explain the wide disparity between the rich and the poor. Critics of the functionalist approach point out that the richest 10 percent of households account for 21 percent of the nation's income in Sweden,

Functionalists argue that rewards, including money and prestige, are based on the importance of a position and the relative scarcity of qualified personnel. In line with this view, highly skilled employees in the oil industry (such as these workers shown putting out oil fires in Kuwait) generally receive generous compensation.

Peter Menzel/Stock, Boston

25 percent in the United States, and 32 percent in Switzerland. In their view, the level of income inequality found in contemporary industrial societies cannot be defended—even though these societies have a legitimate need to fill certain key occupations (World Bank, 1992:277).

Conflict View As was noted in Chapter 1, the intellectual tradition at the heart of conflict theory begins principally with the writings of Karl Marx. Marx viewed history as a continuous struggle between the oppressors and the oppressed which would ultimately culminate in an egalitarian, classless society. In terms of stratification, he argued that the dominant class under capitalism—the bourgeoisie—manipulated the economic and political systems in order to maintain control over the exploited proletariat. Marx did not believe that stratification was inevitable, but he did see inequality and oppression as inherent in capitalism (E. Wright et al., 1982).

Contemporary conflict theorists believe that human beings are prone to conflict over such scarce resources as wealth, status, and power. However, where Marx focused primarily on class conflict, more recent theorists have extended this analysis to include conflicts based on gender, race, age, and other dimensions. Sociologist Ralf Dahrendorf, formerly president of the respected London School of Economics and now at Oxford University, is one of the most influential contributors to the conflict approach.

Dahrendorf (1959) has argued that while Marx's analysis of capitalist society was basically correct, it must be modified if it is to be applied to *modern* capitalist societies. For Dahrendorf, social classes are groups of people who share common interests resulting from authority relationships. In identifying the most powerful groups in society, he includes not only the bourgeoisie—the owners of the means of production—but also the managers of industry, legislators, the judiciary, heads of the government bureaucracy, and others. In one respect, Dahrendorf has merged Marx's emphasis on class conflict with Weber's recognition that power is an important element of stratification (Cuff and Payne, 1979:81–84).

Conflict theorists, including Dahrendorf, contend that the powerful of today, like the bourgeois of Marx's time, want society to run smoothly so that they can enjoy their privileged positions. The status quo is satisfactory to those with wealth, status, and power; thus, they have a clear interest in preventing, minimizing, or controlling societal conflict.

One means through which the powerful maintain the status quo is defining and disseminating the society's dominant ideology. In Chapter 3, we noted that the term **dominant ideology** is used to describe a set of cultural beliefs and practices that help to maintain powerful social, economic, and

Conflict theorists contend that the powerful of today, like the bourgeois of Marx's time, want society to run smoothly so that they can enjoy their privileged positions.

political interests. In Karl Marx's view, a capitalist society has a dominant ideology which serves the interests of the ruling class. From a conflict perspective, the social significance of the dominant ideology is that a society's most powerful groups and institutions not only control wealth and property; even more important, they control the means of producing beliefs about reality through religion, education, and the media (Abercrombie et al., 1980, 1990; R. Robertson, 1988).

The powerful, such as leaders of government, also use limited social reforms to buy off the oppressed and reduce the danger of challenges to their dominance. For example, minimum wage laws and unemployment compensation unquestionably give some valuable assistance to needy men and women. Yet these reforms may pacify those who might otherwise become disgruntled and rebellious. Of course, in the view of conflict theorists, such maneuvers can never eliminate conflict, since workers will continue to demand equality and the powerful will not give up their control of society.

Conflict theorists see stratification as a major source of societal tension and conflict. They do not agree with Davis and Moore that stratification is functional for a society or that it serves as a source of stability. Rather, conflict sociologists argue that stratification will inevitably lead to instability and to social change (R. Collins, 1975:62; L. Coser, 1977:580–581).

We now return to the question posed earlier—"Is stratification universal?"—and consider the sociological response. Some form of differentiation is found in every culture, including the advanced industrial societies of our time. Sociologist Gerhard Lenski, Jr. (1966; Lenski et al., 1991) has suggested that as a society advances in terms of technology, it becomes capable of producing a considerable surplus of goods—more than enough to attract members to valued occupations. The allocation of these surplus goods and services—controlled by those with wealth, status, and power—reinforces the social inequality which accompanies stratification systems. While this reward system may once have served the overall purposes of society, as functionalists contend, the same cannot be said for present disparities separating the "haves" of current societies from the "have-nots."

Measuring Social Class

In everyday life, people in the United States are continually judging relative amounts of wealth and income by assessing the cars people drive, the neighborhoods in which they live, the clothing they wear, and so forth. Yet it is not so easy to locate an individual within our social hierarchies as it would be in caste or estate systems of stratification, where placement is determined by religious dogma or legal documents. In order to determine someone's class position, sociologists generally rely on the objective method.

The ***objective method*** of measuring social class views class largely as a statistical category. Individuals are assigned to social classes on the basis of criteria such as occupation, education, income, and residence. The key to the objective method is that the *researcher,* rather than the person being classified, makes a determination about an individual's class position.

The first step in using this method is to decide what indicators or causal factors will be measured objectively, whether wealth, income, education, or occupation. The prestige ranking of occupations has proved to be a useful indicator in determining a person's class position. The term ***prestige*** refers to the respect and admiration with which an occupation is regarded by society. "My daughter, the physicist" has a very different connotation from "my daughter, the waitress." Prestige is independent of the particular individual who occupies a job, a characteristic which distinguishes it from esteem. ***Esteem*** refers to the reputation that a specific person has within an occupation. Therefore, one can say that the position of president of the United States has high prestige, even though it has been occupied by people with varying degrees of esteem.

Table 8-2 on page 220 illustrates the results of an effort to assign prestige to a number of well-known occupations. In a series of national surveys from 1972 to 1991, sociologists drawing on earlier survey responses assigned prestige rankings to about 500 occupations, ranging from physician to janitor. The highest possible prestige score was 100, the lowest was 0. As the data indicate, physician and college professor were among the most highly regarded oc-

OCCUPATION	SCORE	OCCUPATION	SCORE
Physician	86	Painter and sculptor	52
College professor	78	Electrician	49
Dentist	74	Funeral director	49
Lawyer	72	Military person	49
Airline pilot	70	Police officer	48
Clergy	69	Insurance agent	47
High school teacher	66	Secretary	46
Athlete	65	Bank teller	43
Prekindergarten teacher	64	Farmer	40
Registered nurse	62	Auto mechanic	40
Pharmacist	61	Baker	34
Elementary school teacher	60	Bus driver	32
Actor	58	Sales clerk	29
Accountant	57	Hunter and trapper	23
Librarian	54	Waiter and waitress	20
Firefighter	53	Garbage collector	17
Postmaster	53	Janitor	16

TABLE 8-2   Prestige Ranking of Occupations

SOURCES: Nakao and Treas, 1990a, 1990b; see also NORC, 1993:927–945.

In a national survey conducted in 1989, occupations were ranked in terms of prestige. The highest possible score was 100, the lowest 0. Some of the results are presented above.

cupations. Sociologists have used such data to assign prestige rankings to virtually all jobs and have found a stability in rankings from 1925 to 1991. Similar studies in other countries have also developed useful prestige rankings of occupations (Hodge and Rossi, 1964; Lin and Xie, 1988; NORC, 1993; Treiman, 1977).

Sociologists have become increasingly aware that studies of social class tend to neglect the occupations and incomes of women as determinants of social rank. In an exhaustive study of 589 occupations, sociologists Mary Powers and Joan Holmberg (1978) examined the impact of women's participation in the paid labor force on occupational status. Since women tend to dominate the relatively low-paying occupations, such as bookkeepers and secretaries, their participation in the work force leads to a general upgrading of the status of most male-dominated occupations.

The objective method of measuring social class has traditionally focused on the occupation and education of the husband in measuring the class position of two-income families. With more than half of all married women now working outside the home (see Chapter 11), this represents a serious omission. Furthermore, how is class or status to be judged in dual-career families—by the occupation

regarded as having greater prestige, the average, or some other combination of the two occupations?

Research in the area of women and social class is just beginning, because until recently few sociologists had raised such methodological questions. One study found that over the last 20 years married men have typically used their own occupations to define their class positions—whether or not their wives worked outside the home. By contrast, there has been a noticeable change in how married women define their class positions. Whereas in the 1970s married women tended to attach more weight to their husbands' occupations than to their own in defining their class positions, by the 1980s they began to attach equal weight to their own occupations and those of their husbands (N. Davis and Robinson, 1988).

Sociologists—and, in particular, feminist sociologists in Great Britain—are drawing on new approaches in assessing women's social class standing. One approach is to focus on the individual (rather than the family or household) as the basis of categorizing a woman's class position. Thus, a woman would be classified based on her own occupational status rather than that of her spouse. Still another approach is to use a *joint* classification of a couple's class standing, drawing on both partners' occupations (rather than that of the "head of the household," often the man). These approaches have been helpful in examining the area of women and social class, but as yet there is not wide agreement among researchers about which approach to use (O'Donnell, 1992:124–126).

Advances in statistical methods and computer technology have also multiplied the factors used to define class under the objective method. No longer are sociologists limited to annual income and education in evaluating a person's class position. Today, studies are published which use as criteria the value of homes, sources of income, assets, years in present occupations, neighborhoods, and considerations regarding dual careers. While the addition of these variables will not necessarily lead to a different picture of class differentiation in the United States, it does allow sociologists to measure class in a more complex and multidimensional way.

Whatever the technique used to measure class, the sociologist is interested in real and often dramatic differences in power, privilege, and opportu-

nity in a society. The study of stratification is a study of inequality. Nowhere is this more evident than in the distribution of wealth and income.

Consequences of Social Class in the United States

Wealth and Income By all measures, income in the United States is distributed unevenly. Nobel prize–winning economist Paul Samuelson has described the situation in the following words: "If we made an income pyramid out of a child's blocks, with each layer portraying $500 of income, the peak would be far higher than Mount Everest, but most people would be within a few feet of the ground" (Samuelson and Nordhaus, 1992:355).

Samuelson's analogy is certainly supported by recent data on incomes. In 1991, the top fifth (or 20 percent) of the nation—earning $62,991 or more—accounted for more than 44 percent of total wages and salaries. By contrast, the bottom fifth of the population—earning $17,000 or less—accounted for less than 5 percent of income (Bureau of the Census, 1993a:463).

As Figure 8-1 shows, there has been modest re-

"And just why do we always call my *income the second income?"*

Studies of social class tend to ignore the occupations and incomes of wives and focus on the incomes of husbands in determining social rank or measuring the class position of two-income families.

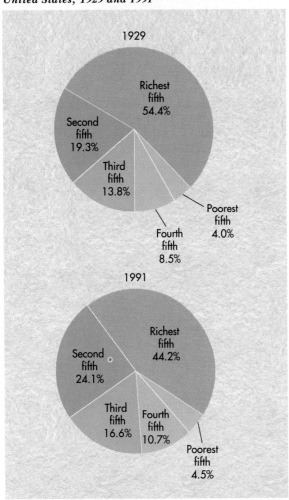

FIGURE 8-1 Distribution of Income in the United States, 1929 and 1991

1929

Richest fifth 54.4%

Second fifth 19.3%

Third fifth 13.8%

Fourth fifth 8.5%

Poorest fifth 4.0%

1991

Richest fifth 44.2%

Second fifth 24.1%

Third fifth 16.6%

Fourth fifth 10.7%

Poorest fifth 4.5%

NOTE: 1929 data for the bottom two-fifths are an estimate by the authors based on data from Bureau of the Census, 1975a.
SOURCES: Bureau of the Census, 1975a:301, 1993a:463.

From 1929 to 1970, there was some redistribution of income in the United States to the less affluent. But over the last 20 years this trend has reversed, with the distribution of income shifting in favor of the most affluent.

distribution of income in the United States over the past 60 years. From 1929 through 1970, the government's economic and tax policies seemed to shift income somewhat to the poor. However, in the last 20 years—especially during the 1980s—federal budgetary policies favored the affluent. Moreover, while the salaries of highly skilled workers and professionals have continued to rise, the wages of less skilled workers have *decreased* when controlled for inflation.

As a result, the income gap between the richest and poorest groups in the United States has increased over the last two decades. According to data compiled by the Congressional Budget Office, the wealthiest 1 percent of families in the United States were the main beneficiaries of the prosperity of the late 1970s and 1980s. In the period 1977 to 1989, about 60 percent of the growth in after-tax income among all families in the nation went to the wealthiest 660,000 families. The average before-tax income of these families rose from $315,000 to $560,000—a staggering 77 percent increase. By contrast, in this same period the bottom 40 percent of families experienced actual declines in income (Nasar, 1992; see also Mishel and Frankel, 1991).

As concentrated as income is in the United States, wealth is much more unevenly distributed. As Figure 8-2 shows, in 1983 (the latest year for which such data are available), the richest fifth of the population held almost 80 percent of the wealth. A study by the Bureau of the Census (1986:10) found that more than 1.6 million households had assets over $500,000, while 9.6 million households were in debt (had a negative net worth).

As one consequence of this growing inequality in terms of wealth and income, observers have spoken of the "disappearance of the middle class." Some households have moved out of the middle class to upper-class positions in the stratification system, but a larger proportion have fallen from the middle class into poverty. In the 1980s, for every 7 families in the United States that rose from the middle to the upper class, 10 families declined from the middle to the lower class (Krugman, 1992).

No single factor explains this shrinking of the middle class, yet it must be understood in terms of broad historical changes in the nation's economy. Traditionally, through the efforts of strong labor unions, workers in heavy industries achieved mid-

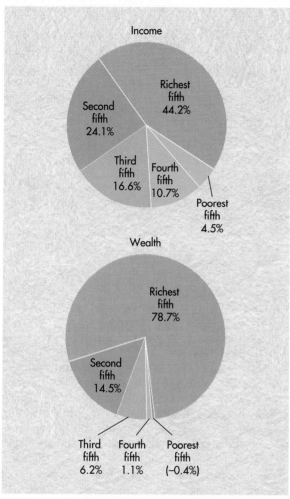

SOURCES: Income data are for 1991 and are from Bureau of the Census, 1993a:463. Data on wealth are from 1983 and are from Kerbo, 1991:40; and J. Smith, 1986.

As these data illustrate, wealth in the United States is distributed much less evenly than income. The richest 20 percent of the population hold close to 80 percent of all wealth. By contrast, the poorest fifth are, as a group, in debt to an amount equivalent to −0.4 percent of the nation's wealth.

dle-class incomes and financial security. These industries offered immigrants and members of minority groups an opportunity to rise out of poverty. In recent decades, however, the manufacturing sector of the economy has suffered, while there has been a significant boom in the service sector. Many of these service jobs (for example, in discount stores or fast-food restaurants) are part-time, low-paying, nonunionized positions without benefits such as health insurance. Even in newer, "high-tech" industries such as microelectronics, many employees work as low-wage assemblers. Consequently, because of the nature of the service jobs that are available, upward mobility into the middle class has become much more difficult than in earlier periods of the nation's history. Other factors which contribute to the shrinking of the middle class include the effects of extended periods of unemployment, the impact of governmental tax policies, and the rise in single-mother households.

Poverty What are the consequences of this uneven distribution of wealth and income? Approximately one out of every nine people in the United States lives below the poverty line established by the federal government. Indeed, in 1992, the number of people living in poverty rose by 1.2 million, to a total of 36.9 million. This represented the highest number of poor people in the United States since 1964, when President Lyndon Johnson declared a national "war on poverty" (Bureau of the Census, 1993c).

However, the category of the "poor" defies any simple definition—and counters common stereotypes about "poor people." For example, many people in the United States believe that the vast majority of the poor are able to work but will not. Yet, as of 1989, only about 60 percent of poor adults did not work, primarily because they were ill or disabled, were maintaining a home, or were retired. Fully 40 percent of the poor did work outside the home, although only a small portion (9 percent of all low-income adults) worked full time throughout the year (Bureau of the Census, 1990b:65).

A sizable number of the poor live in urban slums, but a majority live outside these poverty areas. Included among the poor of the United States are elderly people, children living in single-parent fami-

TABLE 8-3	Who Are the Poor in the United States?	
GROUP	PERCENT OF THE POPULATION OF THE UNITED STATES	PERCENT OF THE POOR OF THE UNITED STATES
Under 16 years old	23	37
16 to 65 years old	65	52
Over 65 years old	12	11
Whites	84	67
Blacks	12	29
Hispanics	8	18
People in families with male heads of households	84	48
People in families with female heads of households	16	52

In 1991, the poverty level for a family of four was a combined income of $12,812 or less.

NOTE: Percentages in the racial and ethnic category exceed 100 percent, since Hispanic people can be either Black or White.
SOURCE: Bureau of the Census, 1993a: 16, 470–471, 474.

lies with their mothers, and over 10,000 men in military service who cannot adequately support their large families. Table 8-3 provides additional statistical information regarding these low-income people in the United States. The situation of the nation's homeless people will be examined in the social policy section of Chapter 18.

Since World War II, an increasing proportion of the nation's poor have been women—many of whom are divorced or never-married mothers. Currently, two out of three adults classified as "poor" by the federal government are women. In 1959, female-headed households accounted for 26 percent of the nation's poor; by 1991, that figure had risen to 52 percent (Bureau of the Census, 1993a: 471). This alarming trend, known as the *feminization of poverty,* is evident not only in the United States but also around the world.

About half of all women in the United States living in poverty are in "transition," coping with an economic crisis caused by the departure, disability, or death of a husband. The other half tend to be economically dependent either on the welfare system or on friends and relatives living nearby. A key factor in the feminization of poverty has been the increase in families with women as single heads of the household (see Chapter 13). In the view of conflict theorists, the higher rates of poverty among

women can be traced to three distinct factors: the difficulty in finding affordable child care (see Chapter 4), sexual harassment (see Chapter 6), and sex discrimination on the job (see Chapter 11).

While policymakers in the United States attempt to address the problem of the feminization of poverty, this distressing phenomenon has become evident around the world. During the last 15 years, female-headed families have become an increasing proportion of Canada's low-income population. This trend is also noticeable throughout Europe, in developing countries, and even in three widely differing nations whose legislation on behalf of women is the most advanced in the world: Israel, Sweden, and Russia. In these countries, national health care programs, housing subsidies, and other forms of government assistance cushion the impact of poverty somewhat, yet the feminization of poverty advances nevertheless (Abowitz, 1986; Rodgers, 1987:95–111; H. Scott, 1985).

The Underclass In 1990, 43 percent of poor people in the United States were living in central cities. These urban residents have the greatest visibility among low-income people and are the focus of most governmental efforts to alleviate poverty. According to many observers, the plight of the urban poor is growing worse, owing to the devastating interplay of inadequate education and limited employment prospects. Traditional employment opportunities in the industrial sector are largely closed to the unskilled poor. For low-income urban residents who are Black and Hispanic, these problems have been heightened by past and present discrimination.

Sociologist William Julius Wilson (1980, 1987a, 1987b, 1988:15, 1989, 1991) and other social scientists have used the term ***underclass*** to describe long-term poor people who lack training and skills. While estimates vary depending on the definition, in 1990 the underclass comprised more than 3 million adults in the United States, not including the elderly. In central cities, about 49 percent of the underclass are African American, 29 percent are Hispanic, 17 percent are White, and 5 percent are "Other" (W. O'Hare and Curry-White, 1992).

Conflict theorists, among others, have expressed alarm at the portion of the nation's population living on this lower rung of the stratification hierarchy and at society's reluctance to address the lack of economic opportunities for these people. Often portraits of the underclass seem to "blame the victims" for their own plight (this phenomenon will be explored in Box 8-2 later in the chapter). Yet Wilson and other scholars insist that the core of the problem is not the antisocial behavior of some members of the underclass, but rather structural factors (such as the loss of manufacturing jobs in cities) which have had a devastating impact on low-income neighborhoods. Moreover, members of the underclass experience social isolation; they lack contact and sustained interaction with individuals and institutions that are part of the legitimate and profit-making economy. In the view of many scholars concerned about the problems of the underclass, it is the economy, not the poor, that needs reforming (Kornblum, 1991; Morris, 1989; Schaefer, 1993:72–75; S. Wright, 1993).

Poverty, of course, is not a new phenomenon. Yet the concept of the underclass describes a chilling development: individuals and families, whether employed or unemployed, who are beyond the reach of any safety net provided by existing social programs. In addition, membership in the underclass is not an intermittent condition but a long-term attribute. The underclass is understandably alienated from the larger society and engages sporadically in illegal behavior. Not surprisingly, these illegal acts hardly encourage society to genuinely address the long-term problems of the underclass.

Studying Poverty The efforts of sociologists and other social scientists to better understand poverty are complicated by the difficulty of developing a

The problem of the feminization of poverty is evident not only in the United States but throughout Europe and in many developing countries. Shown is a mother begging on the street in Rome, Italy.

satisfactory operational definition of poverty. This problem is evident even in government programs which conceive of poverty in either absolute or relative terms. **Absolute poverty** refers to a minimum level of subsistence below which families should not be expected to exist. This standard theoretically remains unchanged from year to year. Policies concerning minimum wages, housing standards, or school lunch programs for the poor imply a need to bring citizens up to some predetermined level of existence.

By contrast **relative poverty** is a floating standard of deprivation by which people at the bottom of a society, whatever their lifestyles, are judged to be disadvantaged in comparison with the nation as a whole. Most of our country's current social programs view poverty in relative terms. Therefore, even if the poor of the 1990s are better off in absolute terms than the poor of the 1930s or 1960s, they are still seen as deserving special assistance from government.

One commonly used measure of relative poverty is the federal government's *poverty line,* a money income figure adjusted annually to reflect the consumption requirements of families based on their size and composition. The poverty line serves as an official definition of which people are poor. In 1991, for example, any family of four with a combined income of $12,812 or less fell below the poverty line. This definition determines which individuals and families will be eligible for certain governmental benefits.

In the 1990s, there was growing debate over the validity of the poverty line as a measure of poverty and a standard for allocating government benefits. Some critics charge that the poverty line is too low; they note that the federal government continues to use 20-year-old nutritional standards in assessing people's level of poverty. If the poverty line is too low, then government data will underestimate the extent of poverty in the United States, while many deserving poor citizens will fail to receive benefits. Yet other observers dispute this view and argue that the poverty line may actually overestimate the number of low-income people because it fails to consider noncash benefits (such as Medicare, Medicaid, food stamps, public housing, and health care and other fringe benefits provided by some employers). In response, the Bureau of the Census considered 15 different definitions of poverty; they *all* showed that between 1979 and 1991 median household income in the United States had decreased (after accounting for inflation) while the number of people living in poverty had increased (Cloward and Piven, 1992; Pollard, 1992).

Analyses of the poor reveal that they are not a static social class. Instead, the composition of the poor changes continually, with some individuals and families moving above the poverty level after a year or two, while others slip below it. Depending on definitions, a significant segment of the people of the United States are "persistently poor." At any given time, some 40 to 60 percent of the poor can be expected to remain in a state of poverty for at least eight consecutive years. African Americans and Hispanics are more likely than Whites to be found among the persistent poor (Bureau of the Census, 1990d; Ruggles, 1991).

Why does such pervasive poverty continue within a nation of vast wealth? Sociologist Herbert Gans (1991:263–270) has applied functionalist analysis to the existence of poverty and has identified various social, economic, and political functions that the poor perform for society. Among these are the following:

- The presence of poor people means that society's "dirty work"—physically dirty or dangerous, dead-end and underpaid, undignified and menial jobs—will be performed at low cost.
- Poverty creates jobs for occupations and professions which "service" the poor. It creates both legal employment (public health experts, welfare caseworkers) and illegal jobs (drug dealers, numbers "runners").
- The identification and punishment of the poor as deviants uphold the legitimacy of conventional social norms regarding hard work, thrift, and honesty (see Chapter 7).
- The poor serve as a measuring rod for status comparisons. Within a relatively hierarchical society, they guarantee the higher status of more affluent people. Indeed, as is described in Box 8-2, the affluent may justify inequality (and gain a measure of satisfaction) by "blaming the victims" of poverty for their disadvantaged conditions.
- Because of their lack of political power, the poor

BOX 8-2 ★ SPEAKING OUT

BLAMING THE VICTIM

Psychologist William Ryan struck a vulnerable chord in 1971 when he coined the phrase "blaming the victim" to describe how some people essentially justify inequality by finding defects in the victims rather than examining the social and economic factors that contribute to poverty, racism, and other national problems. In the following selection, Ryan (1976:3–8) explains the process of "blaming the victim" and notes that this process is aimed not only at disadvantaged people in the United States but also at residents of the world's less developed nations:

William Ryan.

Courtesy William Ryan, photo by Carillo

. . . Consider some victims. One is the miseducated child in the slum school. He is blamed for his own miseducation. He is said to contain within himself the causes of his inability to read and write well. The shorthand phrase is "cultural deprivation," which, to those in the know, conveys what they allege to be inside information: that the poor child carries a scanty pack of intellectual baggage as he enters school. He doesn't know about books and magazines, they say. . . . They say if he talks at all . . . he certainly doesn't talk correctly. . . . In a word, he is "disadvantaged" and "socially deprived," they say, and this, of course, accounts for his failure (*his* failure, they say) to learn much in school. . . .

What is the culturally deprived child *doing* in the school? What is wrong with the victim? In pursuing

this logic, no one remembers to ask questions about the collapsing buildings and torn textbooks; the frightened, insensitive teachers; the six additional desks in the room; the blustering, frightened principals; the relentless segregation; the callous administrator; the irrelevant curriculum; the bigoted or cowardly members of the school board; the insulting history book; the stingy taxpayers; the fairy-tale readers; or the self-serving faculty of the local teachers' college. We are encouraged to confine our attention to the child and to dwell on all his alleged defects. Cultural deprivation becomes an omnibus explanation for the educational disaster area known as the inner-city school. This is Blaming the Victim. . . .

The generic process of Blaming the Victim is applied to almost every American problem. The miserable health care of the poor is explained away on the grounds that the victim has poor motivation and lacks health information. The problems of slum housing are traced to the characteristics of tenants who are labeled as "Southern rural migrants" not yet "acculturated" to life in the big city. . . . It would be possible for me to venture into other areas—one finds a perfect example in literature about the underdeveloped countries of the Third World, in which the lack of prosperity and technological progress is attributed to some aspect of the national character of the people, such as lack of "achievement motivation." . . .

Blaming the Victim is, of course, quite different from old-fashioned conservative ideologies. . . . The new ideology attributes defect and inadequacy to the malignant nature of poverty, injustice, slum life, and racial difficulties. The stigma that marks the victim and accounts for his victimization is an acquired stigma, a stigma of social, rather than genetic, origin. But the stigma, the defect, the fatal difference. . . is still located *within* the victim, inside his skin. . . . It is a brilliant ideology for justifying a perverse form of social action designated to change, not society, as one might expect, but rather society's victim.

often absorb the costs of social change. Under the policy of deinstitutionalization, released mental patients have been "dumped" primarily into low-income communities and neighborhoods. Urban renewal projects to restore central cities have typically pushed out the poor in the name of "progress."

Consequently, in Gans's view, poverty and the poor actually satisfy positive functions for many nonpoor groups in the United States.

Unemployment　As we have seen in our discussion of poverty, a substantial portion of poor people experience intermittent or long-term unemployment. As sociological research points out, unemployment affects the entire society and has far-reaching consequences on both the macro and the micro levels. On the societal, or macro, level, unemployment leads to a reduced demand for goods and services. Sales by retail firms and other businesses are affected adversely, and this can lead to further layoffs. Wage earners must contribute to unemployment insurance and welfare programs that assist those without jobs.

From the micro level, the unemployed person and his or her family must adjust to a loss of spending power. Both marital happiness and family cohesion may suffer as a result. In addition, there is an accompanying loss of self-image and social status, since our society and others view unemployment as a kind of personal failure. According to one estimate, a 1.4 percent increase in the unemployment rate of the United States is associated with a 5.7 percent increase in suicide, a 4.7 percent increase in admissions to state mental hospitals, and an 8.0 percent increase in homicides (Tipps and Gordon, 1983).

The unemployment rate of the United States is traditionally represented as a percentage; for example, it was about 7 percent in 1992. Such statistics can minimize the problem; it is more revealing to point out that in 1992, over 8 million people across the nation were unemployed at any one time. But even this latter figure may disguise the severity of unemployment. The federal government's Bureau of Labor Statistics regards as unemployed only those people *actively* seeking employment. Thus, in order to be counted as unemployed, a person must not hold a full-time job, must be registered with a government unemployment agency, and must be seeking a job. Quite simply, the official unemployment rate leaves out millions of people who are effectively unemployed but have given up and are not seeking work.

The burden of unemployment in the United States is unevenly distributed throughout the nation's labor force. Women are about 20 percent more likely than men to be unemployed and are less likely to be rehired following layoffs. Racial minorities and teenagers have unemployment rates twice that of adult White males. The unemployment rate for Black teenagers in urban areas is about 43 percent, well above the rate for the nation as a whole during the Depression of the 1930s, which was 25 percent. Again, such statistics do not include those who have dropped out of the system—who are not at school, not at work, and not looking for a job. If we add discouraged job seekers to the official statistics, the rate of unemployment and underemployment for Black teenagers in central-city areas climbs to 90 percent (Gordus and Yamakawa, 1988; Swinton, 1987).

While the chronically unemployed understandably receive the attention of policymakers, a growing portion of the nation's unemployed people have previously enjoyed long careers as relatively well-paid executives. According to Warren Boeker, a professor of management, during the 1970s, 90 percent of laid-off white-collar workers soon found similar jobs. By the late 1980s, only 50 percent of such individuals did so, and by 1992 the figure had decreased to only 25 percent. Even if they eventually regain the types of positions they lost, these white-collar workers are unlikely to view the future with the sense of security they once had (A. Cowan and Barron, 1992).

Stratification and Life Chances　Poverty and unemployment unquestionably have a marked influence on people's lives. Max Weber saw class as closely related to people's *life chances*—that is, their opportunities to provide themselves with material goods, positive living conditions, and favorable life experiences (Gerth and Mills, 1958:181). Life chances are reflected in such measures as housing, education, and health. Occupying a higher position in a society will improve one's life chances and bring greater access to social rewards. By contrast, people in the lower social classes are forced to devote a larger proportion of their limited resources to the necessities of life.

The affluent and powerful not only have more material possessions than others; they also benefit in many nonmaterial ways. For example, as is shown in Figure 8-3, children from higher-income families in the United States are much more likely to attend college than are children from less affluent families. In 1990, 79 percent of all unmarried high school graduates ages 18 to 24 from families earning $60,388 and over were enrolled in or had attended college. For families earning less than $20,436, the comparable figure was 44 percent. This gap in educational opportunities has remained significant and fairly constant over the last 20 years (Mortenson, 1992).

As is true of educational opportunities, a person's health is affected in important ways by his or her class position (see Chapter 17). The chances of a child's dying during the first year of life are approximately 70 percent higher in poor families than for the middle class. This higher infant mortality rate results in part from the inadequate nutrition received by low-income expectant mothers. Even when they survive infancy, the poor are more likely than the affluent to suffer from serious, chronic illnesses such as arthritis, bronchitis, diabetes, and heart disease. In addition, the poor are less likely to be protected from the high costs of illness by private health insurance. They may be employed in jobs in which health insurance is not a fringe benefit; may not be employed full time and, thus, may be ineligible for employee health benefits; or may simply be unable to afford the premiums. Moreover, the occupations of the nation's lower classes tend to be more dangerous than those of more affluent citizens (J. Erickson and Bjerkedal, 1982; R. Kessler et al., 1989; Paneth, 1982; Szymanski, 1983: 301–314).

All these factors contribute to differences in the death rates of the poor and the affluent. A study published in mid-1993, which drew on data on death rates in the United States in 1986, documents the impact of class (as well as gender and race) on mortality. Among people whose family incomes were less than $9000, the death rates per 1000 people 25 to 64 years old were as follows: Black men,

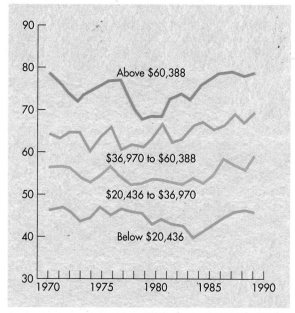

FIGURE 8-3 College Participation Rates by Family Income, 1970 to 1990

SOURCE: Mortenson, 1992.

This figure shows the college participation rates of unmarried 18- to 24-year-old high school graduates over the last 20 years. Despite the existence of financial aid programs to assist the college-bound from lower-income backgrounds, a poor young person in the United States continues to be much less likely to go to college than a more affluent young person.

19.5; White men, 16.0; Black women, 7.6; White women, 6.5. By contrast, among people whose family incomes were $25,000 or more, the comparable death rates were Black men, 3.6; White men, 2.4; Black women, 2.3; White women, 1.6. The researchers add that the gap in the death rate between Blacks and Whites is *widening* (Pappas et al., 1993:103–109; see also Guralnik et al., 1993).

Like disease, crime can be particularly devastating when it affects the poor. Lower-income people, who can hardly afford to lose any of their limited funds, are more likely to be assaulted or raped than are more affluent citizens (Langan and Innes, 1985). Furthermore, if accused of a crime, a person with low income and status is likely to be represented by an overworked public defender. Whether innocent or guilty, such a person may sit in jail for months because of an inability to raise the money for bail.

Even in the armed forces, social class standing in civilian life can be crucial to determining a person's fortunes. Members of lower classes were more likely to be drafted when the military draft was in operation. Once in the service, people from low- and moderate-income backgrounds are more likely to die in combat. Research indicates that during the wars in Korea and Vietnam, soldiers from the lower social classes suffered a higher casualty rate than the more affluent, who tended to be officers (F. Peterson, 1987; J. Willis, 1975; Zeitlin et al., 1973: 328).

Differences in life chances based on race and ethnicity were evident in 1991 during the war in the Persian Gulf. Only two members of Congress (one of whom was Hispanic) had children serving in Operation Desert Storm. Although Blacks and Hispanics together constitute only 20 percent of all young adults in the United States, about 36 percent of the nation's military personnel in the Gulf were Black or Hispanic. In some respects, these data reflect the irony that the all-volunteer armed forces offer more career options for many minority citizens than are available to them in civilian life (Howlett and Keen, 1991).

Even the administration of state lotteries underscores differences in life chances. A lottery participant is six times more likely to be struck by lightning than to win the jackpot, yet states target low-income residents in their lottery promotions. Lottery terminals are more heavily concentrated in poor neighborhoods than in wealthy communities. Lottery advertisements are most frequent at the beginning of each month, when Social Security and public assistance checks arrive. Apparently, state lottery executives believe that the poor are more likely than the affluent to spend a high portion of their earnings for the very unlikely chance of becoming an instant millionaire (Mangalmurti and Cooke, 1991; Smothers, 1992a).

Wealth, status, and power may not ensure happiness, but they certainly provide additional ways of coping with one's problems and disappointments. For this reason, the opportunity for advancement is of special significance to those who are on the bottom of society looking up. These people want the rewards and privileges that are granted to high-ranking members of a culture.

SOCIAL MOBILITY

It is clear that stratification matters, that class position quietly influences one's life chances. It can be important that people have the feeling that they can hold on to or even improve upon their class position. But how significant—how frequent, how

Even the administration of state lotteries underscores differences in life chances. Lottery terminals are more heavily concentrated in poor neighborhoods than in wealthy communities.

dramatic—is mobility in a class society such as the United States? Ronald Reagan's father was a barber, and Jimmy Carter began as a peanut farmer, yet each man eventually achieved the most powerful and prestigious position in our country.

Does this mean that the United States is a genuinely open society in which any parent's child can become president? Thus far, no woman has served in the nation's highest office, nor has any man who was African American, Hispanic, Asian American, or Jewish. Moreover, despite the examples of Carter and Reagan, class remains a critical factor in one's likelihood of becoming president. The vast majority of the nation's presidents (82 percent) were born into upper-middle-class or upper-class families. Even Abraham Lincoln, famous for his days in a log cabin, came from a family that belonged to the community's richest 15 percent of taxpaying property owners by the time young Abraham reached the age of 5 (Baltzell and Schneiderman, 1988).

The rise of a child from a poor background to the presidency—or to some other position of great prestige, power, or financial reward—is an example of social mobility. The term *social mobility* refers to movement of individuals or groups from one position of a society's stratification system to another.

Open versus Closed Class Systems

Sociologists use the terms *open class system* and *closed class system* to distinguish between two ideal types of class system in terms of social mobility. An *open system* implies that the position of each individual is influenced by the person's achieved status. In an open class system, competition between members of society is encouraged. The United States is moving toward this ideal type as it attempts to reduce barriers to mobility faced by women, racial and ethnic minorities, and people born in lower social classes.

At the other extreme in terms of social mobility is the *closed system,* in which there is little or no possibility of individual mobility. The slavery and caste systems of stratification, and to a lesser extent the estate system, are examples of closed systems. In such societies, social placement is based on ascribed statuses, such as race or family background, which cannot be changed.

Types of Social Mobility

Following the lead of Pitirim Sorokin (1959, original edition 1927), contemporary sociologists distinguish between horizontal and vertical mobility. *Horizontal mobility* refers to the movement of a person from one social position to another of the same rank. If we use the prestige rankings presented earlier in Table 8-2, an electrician who becomes a funeral director would be experiencing horizontal mobility. Each occupation has the same prestige ranking: 49 on a scale ranging from a low of 0 to a high of 100. If the funeral director later leaves a Los Angeles establishment for a similar job at a funeral parlor in New York, he or she would once again experience horizontal mobility.

Most sociological analysis, however, focuses on vertical rather than horizontal mobility. *Vertical mobility* refers to the movement of a person from one social position to another of a different rank. An electrician who becomes a lawyer (prestige ranking of 72) would experience vertical mobility. So, too, would an electrician who becomes a sales clerk (prestige ranking of 29). Thus, vertical mobility can involve moving upward or downward in a society's stratification system.

One way of examining vertical social mobility is to contrast intergenerational and intragenerational mobility. *Intergenerational mobility* involves changes in the social position of children relative to their parents. Thus, a plumber whose father was a physician provides an example of downward intergenerational mobility. A film star whose parents were both factory workers illustrates upward intergenerational mobility.

Intragenerational mobility involves changes in a person's social position within his or her adult life. A woman who enters the paid labor force as a teacher's aide and eventually becomes superintendent of the school district has experienced upward intragenerational mobility. A man who becomes a taxicab driver after his accounting firm goes bankrupt has undergone downward intragenerational mobility.

Another type of vertical mobility is *structural,* or *stratum, mobility.* These terms refer to the vertical movement of a specific group, class, or occupation relative to others in the stratification system. For example, historical circumstances or changes in the labor market may lead to the rise or decline of an occupational group within the social hierarchy. Military officers and strategists are likely to be regarded highly in times of war or foreign policy crises. As our information retrieval systems rely increasingly on machines, computer technicians are receiving respect previously reserved for lawyers and scientists. An influx of immigrants may also alter class alignments—especially if the new arrivals are disproportionately highly skilled or unskilled.

Efforts at structural mobility may be consciously undertaken by the groups themselves. Thus, in an effort to generate more dignified and prestigious images of their work, garbage collectors have begun to call themselves "sanitation engineers" and maids have selected the label "household technicians."

Even in the rigid caste systems of India, one low-status group, the subcaste of "toddy tappers," attempted to improve itself through structural mobility. Toddy tappers, also known as *Nadars,* had the historic task of climbing palmyra palm trees to collect the sap, known as *toddy.* Often these people would become deformed or physically disabled after a lifetime of climbing; some even fell to their deaths. However, during the 1700s, the Nadars became dissatisfied with their oppressive work and low status and organized a movement to raise their collective status within the caste system. Gradually, more and more Nadars refused to tap the palms, and some began to learn mercantile skills. Members of the caste became vegetarians—a practice associated with higher castes. There was strong resistance to the Nadars' effort to improve their social standing, including riots protesting their actions at the end of the nineteenth century. Today, Nadars in rural areas still work as toddy tappers, but those in cities are more prosperous and are viewed as higher in rank. While the Nadars have not fully succeeded in achieving upward structural mobility, they have gained a deeper sense of self-respect and have widened their options within a generally restrictive caste system (Hardgrave, 1969; Spradley and McCurdy, 1980:161–166).

Social Mobility in the United States

The belief in upward mobility is an important aspect of our society. Does this mean that the United States is indeed the land of opportunity? Not if the phrase "land of opportunity" implies that such ascriptive characteristics as race, gender, and family background have ceased to be significant in determining one's future prospects.

Two sociological studies conducted a decade apart offer insight into the degree of mobility in the nation's occupational structure. The highly regarded work of Peter Blau and Otis Duncan (1967) was followed by the research of David Featherman and Robert Hauser (1978), two of Duncan's students, who replicated the earlier study. Taken together, these investigations led to several noteworthy conclusions. First, occupational mobility (which can be intergenerational or intragenerational) has been common among males. Approximately 60 to 70 percent of sons are employed in different and higher-ranked occupations than their fathers.

Second, although there is a great deal of mobility in the United States, much of it covers a very "short distance." By this, researchers mean that people who reach an occupational level different from that of their parents usually advance or fall back only one or two out of a possible eight occupational levels. Thus, the child of a laborer may become an artisan or a technician, but he or she is less likely to become a manager or professional. The odds against reaching the top, then, are extremely high unless one begins from a relatively privileged position.

Third, as the later study by Featherman and Hauser (1978:381–384) documents, occupational mobility among African Americans remains sharply limited by racial discrimination (see Chapter 10). Even when the researchers compared Black and White males who had similar levels of schooling, parental background, and early career experience, the achievement levels of Blacks were less than those of Whites. The researchers have also noted that Blacks are more likely than Whites to be downwardly mobile and less likely to be upwardly mobile. Featherman and Hauser offer evidence that there is a modest decline in the significance of race; yet, their conclusions must be regarded with some caution, since they did not consider households with no adult male present or individuals who were not counted in the labor force.

A final conclusion of both studies is that education plays a critical role in social mobility. The im-

In the United States, education continues to play a critical role in social mobility. The impact of formal schooling on adult status is even greater than that of family background.

pact of formal schooling on adult status is even greater than that of family background (although, as we saw in our discussion of stratification and life chances, family background influences the likelihood that one will receive a higher education). Furthermore, education represents an important way of effecting intergenerational mobility. Three-fourths of college-educated men achieved some upward mobility, compared with only 12 percent of those who received no schooling (see also J. Davis, 1982).

It should be noted, however, that the impact of education on mobility has diminished somewhat in the last decade. While completing a college education remains essential for occupational success, an undergraduate degree—a B.A. or B.S.—serves less as a guarantee of upward mobility than it did in the past—simply because more and more entrants into the job market now hold such a degree. Moreover, intergenerational mobility is declining, since there is no longer such a stark difference between generations. Whereas in earlier decades many high school–educated parents successfully sent their children to college, today's college students are increasingly likely to have college-educated parents (Hout, 1988).

Thus far, although we have given some consideration to the impact of race on mobility, we have dealt primarily with social mobility as a monolithic phenomenon. However, gender, like race, is an important factor in one's mobility. Earlier we noted that studies of class have only recently given serious consideration to the occupations and incomes of women as determinants of social rank. Studies of mobility, even more than those of class, have traditionally ignored the significance of gender, but some research findings are now available which explore the relationship between gender and mobility.

As we will discuss in more detail in Chapter 11, women's employment opportunities are much more limited than men's. According to recent research, women are more likely than men to withdraw entirely from the paid labor force when faced with downward mobility because of a substantial gap between their employment skills and the jobs being offered them. This withdrawal violates an assumption common to traditional mobility studies: that most people will aspire to upward mobility and seek to make the most of their opportunities.

In contrast to men, women have a rather large range of clerical occupations open to them. Yet many of these positions have modest salary ranges and limited prospects for advancement, thereby severely restricting the possibility of upward mobility. Moreover, self-employment as shopkeepers, entrepreneurs, independent professionals, and the like—an important road to upward mobility for men—has often been closed to women. Although sons commonly follow in the footsteps of their fathers, women are unlikely to move into these areas even when their fathers held such positions. Consequently, gender remains an important factor in shaping social mobility within the United States.

To what degree do women (and men) on welfare experience upward mobility? Do they find jobs that allow them to leave the welfare system, or do they remain trapped in persistent poverty year after year? These questions will be examined in the social policy section on rethinking welfare which follows.

- How does the level of spending for social services in the United States compare with that of European countries?
- How do conflict theorists view the backlash against welfare recipients in the United States?
- How do welfare mothers draw on social networks to supplement their incomes?

While stratification is evident around the world, countries differ substantially in their commitment to social service programs that will assist the needy. It is difficult to develop cross-national comparisons of welfare programs, since there is such variance from nation to nation. Nevertheless, the World Bank (1992:238–239) has calculated the proportion of central-government expenditures in various countries that are devoted to housing, Social Security, welfare, and unemployment compensation. In 1990, the figure for the United States stood at 28 percent, but no European nation had a proportion that low. In Great Britain, 35 percent of central-government spending went to these social service areas; in Spain, 38 percent; in France, 46 percent. In good part, this is because the United States has such a comparatively high level of military spending. In 1990, the United States spent 23 percent of its central budget on defense, as compared with 12 percent in Britain, 7 percent in France, and only 6 percent in Spain.

As noted earlier in the chapter, fully 40 percent of poor adults in the United States work outside the home. The 60 percent of poor adults who do not work outside the home include many who are ill or disabled, are taking care of young children, or are retired. Despite such data, in 1992, many political candidates reflected the public mood by offering "tough talk" commercials concerning welfare. President George Bush used advertisements pledging that he would "change welfare and make the able-bodied work," while Governor Bill Clinton's commercials showed him insisting that "those on welfare move into the workplace." Such "welfare scapegoating," as it has been labeled by Governor Mario Cuomo of New York, unfairly blames the nation's serious economic problems on welfare spending and the poor. Viewed from a conflict perspective, this backlash against welfare recipients reflects deep fears and hostility toward the nation's urban, and predominantly Black and Hispanic, underclass (Bureau of the Census, 1990b:65; Sack, 1992:24).

"Welfare scapegoating" also conveniently overlooks the lucrative federal handouts that go to affluent individuals and families. For example, the most affluent 4 percent of the nation's families (with earnings of more than $100,000 a year) collect more than 8 percent of all federal subsidies for retirement—or about $30 billion annually. During the 1980s, while federal housing aid to the poor was being cut drastically, the amount of deductions for mortgage interest and property taxes more than doubled, reaching $47 billion a year. These deductions generally benefit affluent taxpayers who own their own homes. According to estimates, the United States could save more than $60 billion each year by reducing these and other programs and tax breaks that primarily benefit the wealthiest 10 percent of the nation (Goodgame, 1993).

Stereotypes about lavish welfare spending mask well-documented realities. The average state in the United States spends only 3.4 percent of its budget on welfare programs. Moreover, such spending is being *cut* by federal, state, and local governments. According to a report by the Center on Budget and Policy Priorities, states slashed welfare programs more extensively in 1991 than at any time since 1901. In 1991, 40 states froze or cut funds for families with children, 27 of the 30 states with welfare for single adults and childless couples cut or froze such benefits, 12 states cut emergency aid to prevent homelessness, and 9 states decreased funding for those already homeless (DeParle, 1992a; A. Stone, 1991).

The best-publicized and most controversial part of the welfare system is Aid to Families with Dependent Children (AFDC), a public assistance program which provides aid to low-income families with children. Currently, about 13.2 million people in the United States receive AFDC benefits, of whom about 9 million are children. (In contrast to stereotypes, the size of the average welfare family has decreased substantially in the last 20 years, and only 10 percent of such families have three or more children.) Overall, the number of AFDC recipients in the United States increased by more than 20 percent in the early 1990s—a sharp increase undoubtedly fueled by the nation's economic recession and the rise in families headed by single mothers (DeParle, 1992a; 1992b:A11).

Of families that receive AFDC assistance, 40 percent are Black, while 38 percent are White, and 16 percent are of Hispanic descent. More than half the women who enter the welfare system stay on the rolls for less than four years and do not return once they leave welfare. However, only 15 percent of welfare recipients remain on the rolls for 5 to 10 years and only 7 percent remain for more than 10 years. It is this *minority* of recipients that most closely fits the picture of a permanent underclass trapped in persistent poverty (Welch, 1994).

Many states have instituted welfare reform programs in recent years, often with the stated goal of "cracking down" on abuses of the system. Many reform proposals assume that small incentives, such as cuts or bonuses of $50 or $100 per month, will lead recipients to make major behavioral changes. The state of Ohio offers a $62-per-month bonus to teenage parents who continue in school, while Wisconsin's Learnfare program has cut aid to hundreds of families when their teenage children miss too many school days. In Maryland, families can lose

Reprinted by permission of Mike Luckovich and Creators Syndicate.

The majority of people in the United States below the government's poverty line are under 18 years of age. Of the more than 13 million people receiving Aid to Families with Dependent Children (AFDC) benefits in 1992, about 9 million were children.

their AFDC benefits if they fail to see a doctor regularly or fail to pay the rent on time. Yet, after studying such welfare reform experiments, David Ellwood, a professor of public policy, concludes: "There's absolutely no evidence that small changes have more than a tiny, tiny impact" (Conniff, 1992; DeParle, 1992a:E3).

Sociologists Richard Cloward and Frances Fox Piven (1993) have joined many researchers in criticizing "workfare programs." They emphasize that, given the state of the nation's economy, participants in workfare experiments will find it highly difficult to find full-time jobs that pay more than welfare. Indeed, studies show that one in every seven year-round, full-time jobs pays less than is required to keep a family of four above the poverty line. Cloward and Piven add that well-run, well-administered training programs will cost more than policymakers are likely to appropriate.

On the federal level, the Family Support Act, passed by Congress in 1988, was hailed as the most sweeping welfare reform in 50 years. Under this law, states must require some welfare recipients to look for jobs or enter educational and training programs. However, about half the women on welfare

CHAPTER 8 • STRATIFICATION AND SOCIAL MOBILITY

are exempt from the provisions of this measure because they lack transportation and child care. While a 1993 report showed that the law had raised the earnings of people on welfare in California and had reduced the amount they received in public assistance, analysts disagree on whether the California data suggest that the program has made a significant contribution in reducing welfare dependency (DeParle, 1993).

It is important to emphasize that inflation has substantially eroded the purchasing power of welfare payments. As of 1992, the average monthly payment for a family of three was only $402; even adding in the value of food stamps, the monthly average rose to only $623. These combined payments will allow the typical welfare family to buy 27 percent less (in terms of value of goods) than the average grant did in 1972. Thus, welfare does not encourage dependency, simply because welfare benefits are too low to live on (DeParle, 1992a).

Kathryn Edin (1991) of the Russell Sage Foundation conducted in-depth interviews with 50 welfare mothers in the Chicago area and questioned them intensively about their family finances. She reports that the total income of the women in her sample averaged $897 per month, of which 58 percent ($521) came from AFDC benefits and food stamps. About half of the remaining 42 percent came from unreported work in regular or illegal jobs, while the other half (also unreported) came from social networks consisting of family members, friends, boyfriends, absent fathers, churches, and community organizations. Although these welfare recipients generally felt guilty about concealing this additional income from caseworkers, they did conceal it because they needed the income to survive and would lose their benefits if they reported the extra income.

On the basis of her research, Edin challenges the stereotypes that welfare mothers do not work, do not want to work, and hold values different from those of mainstream society. Indeed, many of her interview subjects wanted to work outside the home but could not find jobs that would pay them more than welfare did—especially when the added costs of child care, clothing, and transportation were considered. Edin (1991:472) concludes:

> In a society where single mothers must provide financially for their children, where women are economically marginalized into unreliable jobs that pay little more than the minimum wage, where child support is inadequate or nonexistent, and where day care costs and health insurance (usually not provided by employers) are unaffordable for most, it should surprise no one that half the mothers supporting children on their own choose welfare over reported work.

By 1994, the Clinton administration had certainly recognized the challenges of reforming the nation's welfare system. Despite a ringing campaign pledge by Bill Clinton to "end welfare as we know it," welfare reform had not been initiated during the administration's first year. As a presidential candidate, Clinton had envisioned setting a two-year limit on AFDC benefits—while at the same time offering welfare recipients job training, education, child care, health care, and other forms of support. Ideally, this ambitious plan would reduce the number of people on the AFDC rolls by 25 percent, but it is far from becoming federal policy (Welch and Nichols, 1993).

SUMMARY

Stratification is structured ranking of entire groups of people that perpetuates unequal economic rewards and power in a society. In this chapter, we examine four general systems of stratification, various components of stratification, the explanations offered by functionalist and conflict sociologists for the existence of social inequality, and the relationship between stratification and social mobility.

1 All cultures are characterized by some degree of *social inequality.*

2 The most extreme form of legalized social inequality for individuals or groups is *slavery.*

3 In contrast to other systems of stratification, the boundaries between social classes are less precisely defined.

4 Karl Marx viewed class differentiation as the crucial determinant of social, economic, and political inequality.

5 Max Weber identified three analytically distinct components of stratification: class, status, and power.

6 Functionalists argue that stratification is necessary so that people will be motivated to fill society's important positions; conflict theorists see stratification as a major source of societal tension and conflict.

7 The category of the "poor" defies any simple definition and counters common stereotypes about low-income people.

8 The affluent and powerful not only have more material possessions than others; they also benefit in terms of educational opportunities, health, and even casualty rates while in the armed forces.

9 *Social mobility* is more likely to be found in an *open system* that emphasizes *achieved status* than in a *closed system* that focuses on *ascribed status.*

10 Despite prevailing beliefs about the possibilities of upward mobility in the United States, our society places significant restrictions on the mobility of individuals and groups.

11 Much of the debate over the welfare system of the United States has focused on Aid to Families with Dependent Children (AFDC), a public assistance program that provides aid for low-income families.

CRITICAL THINKING QUESTIONS

1 Sociologist Daniel Rossides has conceptualized the class system of the United States using a five-class model. According to Rossides, the upper middle class and the lower middle class together account for about 40 percent of the nation's population. Yet studies suggest that a higher proportion of respondents identify themselves as "middle class." Drawing on the model presented by Rossides, suggest why members of the upper class and the working class might prefer to identify themselves as "middle class."

2 Sociological study of stratification generally is conducted at the macro level and draws most heavily on the functionalist and conflict perspectives. How might sociologists use the interactionist perspective to examine social class inequalities within a college community?

3 In Box 8-2, psychologist William Ryan examines the process of "blaming the victim." Ryan focuses on the problems experienced by children in inner-city schools, poor people living in slum housing, and developing countries of the Third World. All these situations, in Ryan's view, commonly lead to the ideology of blaming the victim. How might Ryan's model be applied in ex-

amining the problems faced by women who experience rape, domestic violence, or sexual harassment?

KEY TERMS

Absolute poverty A standard of poverty based on a minimum level of subsistence below which families should not be expected to exist. (page 226)

Achieved status A social position attained by a person largely through his or her own effort. (212)

Ascribed status A social position "assigned" to a person by society without regard for the person's unique talents or characteristics. (212)

Bourgeoisie Karl Marx's term for the capitalist class, comprising the owners of the means of production. (214)

Capitalism An economic system in which the means of production are largely in private hands, and the main incentive for economic activity is the accumulation of profits. (214)

Castes Hereditary systems of rank, usually religiously dictated, that are relatively fixed and immobile. (210)

Class A term used by Max Weber to refer to people who have a similar level of wealth and income. (215)

Class consciousness In Karl Marx's view, a subjective awareness held by members of a class regarding their common vested interests and need for collective political action to bring about social change. (215)

Class system A social ranking based primarily on economic position in which achieved characteristics can influence mobility. (212)

Closed system A social system in which there is little or no possibility of individual mobility. (231)

Dominant ideology A set of cultural beliefs and practices that help to maintain powerful social, economic, and political interests. (218)

Estate system A system of stratification under which peasants were required to work land leased to them by nobles in exchange for military protection and other services. Also known as *feudalism.* (212)

Esteem The reputation that a particular individual has within an occupation. (219)

False consciousness A term used by Karl Marx to describe an attitude held by members of a class that does not accurately reflect its objective position. (215)

Horizontal mobility The movement of an individual from one social position to another of the same rank. (231)

Income Salaries and wages. (209)

Intergenerational mobility Changes in the social position of children relative to their parents. (231)

Intragenerational mobility Changes in a person's social position within his or her adult life. (231)

Life chances Max Weber's term for people's opportunities to provide themselves with material goods, positive living conditions, and favorable life experiences. (228)

Objective method A technique for measuring social class that assigns individuals to classes on the basis of criteria such as occupation, education, income, and place of residence. (219)

Open system A social system in which the position of each individual is influenced by his or her achieved status. (231)

Power The ability to exercise one's will over others. (215)

Prestige The respect and admiration with which an occupation is regarded by society. (219)

Proletariat Karl Marx's term for the working class in a capitalist society. (214)

Relative poverty A floating standard of deprivation by which people at the bottom of a society, whatever their lifestyles, are judged to be disadvantaged in comparison with the nation as a whole. (226)

Slavery A system of enforced servitude in which people are owned by others and in which enslaved status is transferred from parents to children. (210)

Social inequality A condition in which members of a society have different amounts of wealth, prestige, or power. (208)

Social mobility Movement of individuals or groups from one position of a society's stratification system to another. (231)

Status group A term used by Max Weber to refer to people who have the same prestige or lifestyle, independent of their class positions. (215)

Stratification A structured ranking of entire groups of people that perpetuates unequal economic rewards and power in a society. (209)

Stratum mobility Another name for *structural mobility*. (231)

Structural mobility The vertical movement of a specific group, class, or occupation relative to others in the stratification system. (231)

Underclass Long-term poor people who lack training and skills. (225)

Vertical mobility The movement of a person from one social position to another of a different rank. (231)

Wealth An inclusive term encompassing all of a person's material assets, including land and other types of property. (209)

ADDITIONAL READINGS

Dahrendorf, Ralf. *Reflections on the Revolution in Europe.* New York: Random House, 1990. A noted sociologist views recent events in this region as a vote for an open society over a closed society, but warns that the continuing challenge will be to sustain economic growth.

Lamont, Michéle, and Marcel Fournier. *Cultivating Differences: Symbolic Boundaries and the Making of Inequality.* Chicago: University of Chicago Press, 1993. A sociological analysis of how cultural tastes and practices vary according to social class.

McGuire, Randall M., and Robert Paynter (eds.). *The Archaeology of Inequality.* Oxford, Eng.: Basil Blackwell, 1991. An archaeologist draws on primary sources to examine racial, gender, and class-based inequality both among and within Native American, African American, and European peoples living on the North American continent.

Piven, Frances Fox, and Richard A. Cloward. *Regulating the Poor: The Functions of Public Welfare.* New York: Pantheon, 1993. A critical look at how the welfare policies of the United States fail to seriously address the problems of the poor, but merely keep the underclass and others quiet.

Rodgers, Harrell R., Jr. *Poor Women, Poor Families.* Armonk, N.Y.: Sharpe, 1987. This book analyzes data on the changing profile of low-income families over the last 30 years and provides a clear view of poverty among women.

Sidel, Ruth. *Women and Children Lost: The Plight of Poor Women in Affluent America,* rev. ed. New York: Penguin, 1992. An overview of the societal treatment of women and children in the United States, with consideration of the feminization of poverty, child care, the situation of older women, and the impact of government policies.

Voydanoff, Patricia, and Linda C. Majka (eds.). *Families and Economic Distress.* Newbury Park, Calif.: Sage, 1988. Published in cooperation with the National Council on Family Relations, this volume documents the effects of unemployment and economic dislocation on the family.

Wilson, William Julius (ed.). *The Ghetto Underclass: Social Science Perspectives.* Newbury Park, Calif.: Sage, 1989. This book examines the use of the term *underclass* by social scientists and the applicability of this concept to the poor of the United States.

Journals

Among the journals focusing on issues of stratification, social class, and social mobility are *American Journal of Economics and Sociology* (founded in 1941), *Humanity and Society* (1977), and *Review of Black Political Economy* (1970). See also the *Current Population Reports* series published by the Bureau of the Census.

9

SOCIAL
INEQUALITY
WORLDWIDE

**STRATIFICATION IN THE WORLD
SYSTEM: A GLOBAL PERSPECTIVE**
Colonialism, Neocolonialism, and World
   Systems Theory
Modernization
Multinational Corporations
Consequences of Stratification for
   Developing Nations

**STRATIFICATION WITHIN NATIONS:
A COMPARATIVE PERSPECTIVE**
Distribution of Wealth and Income
Prestige
Social Mobility

**STRATIFICATION IN BRAZIL:
A CASE STUDY**
Race Relations in Brazil: The Legacy of
   Slavery
The Status of Brazilian Women
Brazil's Economy and Environment

**SOCIAL POLICY AND WORLDWIDE
INEQUALITY: UNIVERSAL HUMAN
RIGHTS**

BOXES
9-1 Around the World: The Informal
   Economy
9-2 Around the World: Inequality in Japan

> *For any state, however small, is in fact divided into two, one the state of the poor, the other of the rich; these are at war with one another.*
>
> Plato
> *The Republic, ca. 290 B.C.*

LOOKING AHEAD

- How are former colonies kept dependent on their past colonial masters through the process of neocolonialism?
- What impact do multinational corporations have on the world's developing nations?
- Which nations have the highest and lowest levels of income inequality?
- How are women and racial minorities treated in Japan?
- How does immigration affect social mobility?
- How has the legacy of slavery shaped race relations in Brazil?
- What has the term *ethnic cleansing* meant in Bosnia and other parts of the former Yugoslavia?

In an article published in 1993 in the *Washington Post*, journalist Julia Preston (1993:8) used the story of a woman in Santa Rita, Brazil, to illustrate the struggles of life in poor villages in the Third World:

> Somewhere under the sun-hardened ground of this village's cemetery lie the remains of 13 babies born to one mother, a farm woman whose life, in flatlands seared by chronic drought, has been edged with thirst and hunger.
>
> The woman, named Geni Sequiera Gomes, says without regret that she does not mourn her dead children and cannot even recall their faces, since they died as infants of afflictions she summarized as "weak blood." She does not know precisely

where they are buried; village tradition mandates that mothers stay home during funerals of tiny offspring, and the little wooden crosses that marked their graves have long since fallen down.

Sequiera, now 42, has given birth 18 times—not an unusual number for the Brazilian interior. Playing the steep odds of rural survival, she has seen only five of her 18 children grow—a record that might seem abysmal in the developed world but by standards here is nothing less than success.

Despite the changes that have swept the globe in the past two decades, the miseries endured by countless millions of rural women in the developing world remain unameliorated. In this arid back-country village of Brazil's Northeast, poverty is the great oppressor, skewing women's lives and their relationships with their children in ways that are mirrored throughout Latin America, Africa, and Asia.

The poverty of rural families in Brazil must be understood in broader perspective. Alan Durning, a global environmental researcher, points out that while the world has 157 billionaires and perhaps as many as 2 million millionaires, some 100 million people live on city streets, in garbage dumps, and under bridges. More than half the world's population lacks sanitary toilets. Durning (1990:22) adds that "in 1988 the world's nations devoted $1 trillion—$200 for each person on the planet—to the means of warfare, but failed to scrape together the $5 per child it would have cost to eradicate the diseases that killed 14 million that year."

As Durning reminds us, worldwide stratification is evident in the gap between those enjoying lavish wealth and those suffering from overwhelming poverty. This chapter will focus on stratification around the world, beginning with an examination of who controls the world marketplace. The impact of colonialism and neocolonialism on social inequality will be studied, as will world systems theory and the immense power of multinational corporations. After this macro-level examination of the disparity between rich and poor countries, we will focus on stratification *within* the nations of the world through discussions of the distribution of wealth and income, comparative perspectives on prestige, and comparative social mobility. To better understand inequality in another country, we will present a case study of stratification in Brazil. Finally, in the social policy section, we will address the issue of international human rights and the violations of human rights evident around the world.

STRATIFICATION IN THE WORLD SYSTEM: A GLOBAL PERSPECTIVE

While the world marketplace is gradually being unified in terms of space and tastes, the profits of business are not equally shared. There remains a substantial disparity between the world's "have" and "have not" nations. For example, in 1993 the average value of goods and services produced per citizen (per capita gross national product) in the United States, Japan, Switzerland, and Norway was more than $22,000. By contrast, the figure was $200 in several poorer countries. The 140 developing nations accounted for 78 percent of the world's population but possessed only 16 percent of all wealth (Haub and Yanagishita, 1993). These contrasts are vividly illustrated in Figure 9-1 (page 244). Two forces discussed below are particularly responsible for the domination of the world marketplace by a few nations: the legacy of colonialism and the advent of multinational corporations.

Colonialism, Neocolonialism, and World Systems Theory

Colonialism is the maintenance of political, social, economic, and cultural domination over a people by a foreign power for an extended period of time

Geni Sequiera Gomes, a 42-year-old Brazilian farm woman who has been pregnant 18 times, is shown with her husband, their five surviving children, and a grandchild.

Julia Preston for Washington Post National Weekly Edition, March 29–April 4, 1993, p. 8

(W. Bell, 1981b). In simple terms, it is rule by outsiders. The long reign of the British Empire over much of North America, parts of Africa, and India is an example of colonial domination. The same can be said of French rule over Algeria, Tunisia, and other parts of north Africa. Relations between the colonial nation and the colonized people are similar to those between the dominant capitalist class and the proletariat as described by Karl Marx.

By the 1980s, colonialism had largely become a phenomenon of the past; most of the world's nations that were colonies before World War I had achieved political independence and established their own governments. However, for many of these countries, the transition to genuine self-rule was not yet complete. Colonial domination had established patterns of economic exploitation that con-

FIGURE 9-1 Worldwide Gross National Product Per Capita, 1991

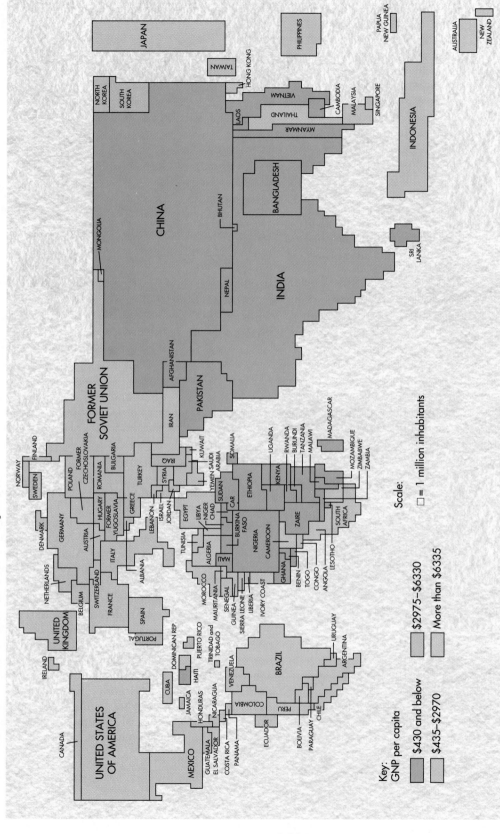

SOURCES: Crow and Thomas, 1983:14; Haub and Yanagishita, 1993.

This stylized map reflects the different sizes in populations of the world's nations. The color for each country shows the gross national product (the total value of goods and services produced by the nation in a given year) per capita. As the map shows, some of the world's most populous nations—such as the People's Republic of China, India, Indonesia, Bangladesh, and Pakistan—are among the countries with the lowest standard of living as measured by per capita gross national product.

tinued even after nationhood was achieved—in part because former colonies were unable to develop their own industry and technology. Their dependence on more industrialized nations, including their former colonial masters, for managerial and technical expertise, investment capital, and manufactured goods kept former colonies in a subservient position. Such continuing dependence and foreign domination is known as **neocolonialism.**

The economic and political consequences of colonialism and neocolonialism are quite evident. Drawing on the conflict perspective, sociologist Immanuel Wallerstein (1974, 1979) views the global economic system as divided between nations who control wealth and those from whom capital is taken. Neocolonialism is one means by which industrialized societies accumulate even more capital. Wallerstein has advanced a **world systems theory** of unequal economic and political relationships in which certain industrialized nations (among them, the United States, Japan, and Germany) and their multinational corporations are in a dominant position at the *core* of the system. Found at the *semiperiphery* of the system are countries with marginal economic status, such as Israel, Ireland, and South Korea. Wallerstein suggests that the poor developing countries of Asia, Africa, and Latin America are on the *periphery* of the world economic system. Their economies are controlled and exploited by core nations and corporations much as the old colonial empires ruled their colonies (Kerbo, 1991: 495–498).

In addition to their political and economic impact, colonialism and neocolonialism have an important cultural component. The colonized people lose their native values and begin to identify with the culture of the colonial power. The native language of the country is discarded and even hidden as people attempt to emulate the colonizers. Therefore, in the view of opponents of contemporary neocolonialism, every consumer product, film, or television program designed by a colonial nation is an attack on the traditions and cultural autonomy of the dependent people. Even the popularity of *Batman* or *Beverly Hills 90210* may be viewed as a threat to native cultures when such programs dominate their media at the expense of local art forms. In reflecting on the dangers posed by television, Sembene Ousmane, one of Africa's most prominent writers and filmmakers, noted: "[Today] we are more familiar with European fairy tales than with our own traditional stories" (R. Emerson, 1968; T. McPhail, 1981:244–245; Memmi, 1967:105–108; Schramm et al., 1981; World Development Forum, 1990:4).

Modernization

For millions of people around the world, the introduction of television into their cultures is but one symbol of a revolutionary transition in day-to-day life. Contemporary sociologists use the term **modernization** to describe the far-reaching process by which a society moves from traditional or less developed institutions to those characteristic of more developed societies.

Wendell Bell (1981a), whose definition of modernization we are using, notes that modern societies tend to be urban, literate, and industrial. They have sophisticated transportation and media systems. Families tend to be organized within the nuclear family unit rather than the extended-family model (see Chapter 13). On the individual level, members of societies which have undergone modernization shift allegiance from such traditional sources of authority as parents and priests to newer authorities such as government officials.

Many sociologists are quick to note that terms such as *modernization* and even *development* contain an ethnocentric bias. The unstated assumptions behind these terms are that "they" (people living in developing countries) are struggling to become more like "us" (in the core industrialized nations). Viewed from a conflict perspective, such use of *modernization* and *development* perpetuates the dominant ideology of capitalist societies.

By contrast, contemporary sociologists emphasize that both industrialized and developing countries are "modern." (Indeed, developing countries are inextricably linked to the economies of core nations through colonialism, neocolonialism, and the activities of multinational corporations.) Current researchers are increasingly viewing modernization as movement along a series of social indicators—among them, degree of urbanization, energy use, literacy, political democracy, and use of birth control. Clearly, these are often subjective indicators; even in industrialized nations, not all ob-

Although Kenya is over 78 percent rural, modernization is clearly underway in Nairobi and other Kenyan cities.

servers would agree that wider use of birth control represents an example of "progress" (Armer and Katsillis, 1992; Hedley, 1992).

Contemporary modernization studies generally take a convergence perspective. Using the indicators noted above, researchers focus on how societies are moving closer together despite traditional differences. Initially, such modernization studies emphasized the convergence between the United States and the (former) Soviet Union or between capitalist North America and the socialist democracies of western Europe. Now, however, this convergence perspective increasingly includes the developing countries of the Third World. Researchers recognize the interdependence of core industrialized nations and the developing world—as well as the continuing exploitation of the latter countries by the former (C. Kerr, 1960; O'Donnell, 1992: 472–473).

We can apply the modernization approach (as it has been refined) to a case study of Kenya, an African nation of 28 million people. Kenya remained a British colony until 1962, and its people exercised little authority, as European settlers clung to their privileges and power. For Kenya and most other developing nations, colonialism stimulated the use of modern technology, but it also delayed the development of new leaders.

Initially, the impact of technological and institutional changes can be quite unsettling. For example, the introduction of improved health measures in Kenya led to a rise in the birthrate, a decline in the death rate, and an overall increase in population growth. Yet, at first, there were not adequate food supplies or school facilities to cope with the larger population.

Upon independence in 1962, Kenyans turned to the charismatic Jomo Kenyatta, longtime organizer against colonial rule, for political leadership. Popularly elected and in office until his death in 1978, Kenyatta maintained a model of *harambee,* a Swahili term which means "let us all pull together." This motto symbolized his effort to bring together Kenyans—rural and urban, Black and White, of various tribes and groups. As one indicator of Kenyatta's effectiveness, presidential succession occurred peacefully following his death.

However, Kenya remains at the periphery of the global economy. According to the United Nations' Human Development Index for 1993, Kenya ranked 127 out of 173 nations studied. While a small, privileged African elite holds disproportionate wealth and power, the World Bank has estimated per capita income at $370. According to United Nations' studies, about 30 percent of the nation's population is malnourished (Barnet, 1990; Perlez,

1991; United Nations Development Programme, 1993).

The political situation in Kenya had been characterized in the early 1990s as a retreat from democracy. In 1991, western countries suspended hundreds of millions of dollars in aid to Kenya as a means of forcing economic and political changes. Consequently, in late 1992, Kenya held multiparty elections for the first time in 26 years. Nevertheless, as of mid-1993, Kenya was experiencing severe economic problems, including inflation rates as high as 45 percent per month, repeated fuel shortages, unprecedented price increases for basic goods, and declines in food production (Lorch, 1993).

From a conflict perspective, modernization in developing countries such as Kenya often perpetuates their dependence on and continued exploitation by more industrialized nations. For example, in recent decades Kenya has been the second-largest recipient of United States assistance in sub-Saharan Africa, owing in good part to Kenya's anticommunist posture (more of a factor during the cold war) and to a 1980 defense agreement that gives the United States access to its airports and seaports. Conflict theorists view such a continuing dependence on foreign powers as an example of contemporary neocolonialism. In the case of Kenya, however, the dissolution of the Soviet Union and the resulting reduction in cold war tensions led to a significant decline in foreign aid from the United States.

Sociologist York Bradshaw (1988) has modified Immanuel Wallerstein's world system analysis as it relates to Kenya. After examining changes in the economy and the role of foreign capital since 1963, Bradshaw concluded that while multinational corporations obviously find it profitable to invest in Kenya, they do not completely dominate the nation's economy. These corporations are heavily taxed and are required by law to form joint ventures with local business people. However, as noted earlier, a small, privileged elite benefits from such foreign investment—while most Kenyans gain little from economic development.

Multinational Corporations

A key role in the neocolonialism of the 1990s is played by worldwide corporate giants. The term *multinational corporations* refers to commercial organizations which, while headquartered in one country, own or control other corporations and subsidiaries throughout the world. Such private trade and lending relationships are not new; merchants have conducted business abroad for hundreds of years, trading gems, spices, garments, and other goods. However, today's multinational giants are not merely buying and selling overseas; they are also *producing* goods all over the world (I. Wallerstein, 1974).

Moreover, today's "global factory" (the factories throughout the developing world run by multinational corporations) now has alongside it the "global office." Multinationals based in core countries are beginning to establish reservations services, centers to process insurance claims, and data processing centers in the periphery nations. As service industries become a more important part of the international marketplace, many companies have concluded that the low costs of overseas operations more than offset the expense of transmitting information around the world (J. Burgess, 1989).

Traditionally, a high percentage of multinationals have been based in the United States, but this pattern has changed significantly in recent decades (see Table 9-1 on page 248). The size of these global corporations should not be underestimated. For example, Unilever, only the twentieth-largest multinational, had 1992 sales of $43.9 billion—a figure which exceeded the final value of goods and services of Nigeria and Sri Lanka combined for the year. Even more striking is the fact that the sales of the top 500 multinationals account for almost one-fourth of the gross *world* product (Hadjian and Tritto, 1993; Haub and Yanagishita, 1993).

Foreign sales represent an important source of profit for multinational corporations. For example, foreign subsidiaries account for about 40 percent of all sales of larger multinationals headquartered in the United States. In general, foreign sales have grown more rapidly than domestic sales for such corporations, a fact which encourages them to expand into other countries (in many cases, the developing nations). The economy of the United States is heavily dependent on foreign commerce, much of which is conducted by multinationals. According to a 1991 report by the Bureau of the Cen-

TABLE 9-1	The 20 Largest Industrial Companies in the World				
RANK	COMPANY	HEADQUARTERS	INDUSTRY	SALES IN BILLIONS OF DOLLARS	PROFITS IN MILLIONS OF DOLLARS
1	General Motors	Detroit	Motor vehicles	132.8	−23,498
2	Exxon	Irving, Tex.	Petroleum refining	103.5	4,770
3	Ford Motor	Dearborn, Mich.	Motor vehicles	100.8	−7,385
4	Royal Dutch/Shell Group	London/The Hague	Petroleum refining	98.9	5,408
5	Toyota Motor	Toyota City, Japan	Motor vehicles	79.1	1,812
6	IRI	Rome	Metals	67.5	−3,811
7	International Business Machines	Armonk, N.Y.	Computers	65.1	−4,965
8	Daimler-Benz	Stuttgart, Germany	Motor vehicles	63.3	929
9	General Electric	Fairfield, Conn.	Electronics	62.2	4,725
10	Hitachi	Tokyo	Electronics	61.5	619
11	British Petroleum	London	Petroleum refining	59.2	−808
12	Matsushita Electric Industrial	Osaka, Japan	Electronics	57.4	308
13	Mobil	Fairfax, Va.	Petroleum refining	57.4	862
14	Volkswagen	Wolfsburg, Germany	Motor vehicles	56.7	50
15	Siemens	Munich	Electronics	51.4	1,136
16	Nissan Motor	Tokyo	Motor vehicles	50.2	449
17	Philip Morris	New York	Food, tobacco	50.2	4,939
18	Samsung	Seoul, South Korea	Electronics	49.6	374
19	Fiat	Turin, Italy	Motor vehicles	47.9	447
20	Unilever	London/Rotterdam	Food	43.9	2,279

SOURCE: Hadjian and Tritto, 1993:191.

In 1993, 14 of the world's 50 largest industrial firms ranked by sales had their headquarters in the United States. By contrast, such firms had accounted for 42 of the 50 leaders in the year 1960.

sus (1991a), one out of seven manufacturing jobs in the United States had to do with the export of goods to foreign countries.

Multinational corporations can have a positive impact on the developing nations of the world. They bring jobs and industry to areas where subsistence agriculture previously served as the only means of survival. Multinationals promote rapid development through diffusion of inventions and innovations from industrial nations. Viewed from a functionalist perspective, the combination of skilled technology and management provided by multinationals and the relatively cheap labor available in developing nations is ideal for a global enterprise. Multinationals can thus take maximum advantage of technology while reducing costs and boosting profits.

The international ties of multinational corporations also facilitate the exchange of ideas and technology around the world. Their worldwide influence contributes to interdependence among nations, which may prevent certain disputes from reaching the point of serious conflict. A country cannot afford to sever diplomatic relations, or engage in warfare, with a nation that is the headquarters for its main business suppliers or is a key outlet for exports.

Conflict theorists challenge this favorable evaluation of the impact of multinational corporations and emphasize that multinationals exploit local workers to maximize profits. They point out that when business firms build plants in places such as South Korea, residents (including those as young as 13 years old) may work seven days a week, 10 hours a day, for as little as 62 cents an hour. More than 80 percent of the low-skilled assembly jobs in these plants are held by women, many of whom earn only $5 *per day*. These women perform monotonous, painstaking work under stressful and hazardous working conditions. For example, a study in South Korea found that most electronics assembly workers developed severe eye problems after one year of employment (Ehrenreich and Fuentes, 1981; Gittelsohn, 1987).

Because there is a pool of cheap labor available in the developing world, multinationals are able to move factories out of countries such as the United States, where organized labor insists on decent wages and humane working conditions, thereby increasing unemployment in core nations. Moreover, in the developing world it is difficult to build strong trade unions in factories run by multinational corporations. The ever-present danger exists that if labor's demands become threatening, the firm will simply move its plant elsewhere. As a result, governments seeking to attract or keep multinationals may develop a "climate for investment" which includes repressive antilabor laws restricting union activity and collective bargaining. Conflict theorists therefore conclude that, on the whole, multinational corporations have a negative social impact on workers in both industrialized and developing nations (Bluestone and Harrison, 1982; Harrison and Bluestone, 1988).

Several sociologists have surveyed the effects of foreign investment and concluded that although it may initially contribute to a host nation's wealth, it eventually increases economic inequality within developing nations. This is true in terms of both income and ownership of land. The upper and middle classes of such countries benefit most from economic expansion, while the lower classes are less likely to benefit. Such disparities result from the peculiarly uneven economic development which results from foreign investment. Multinationals invest in limited areas of an economy and in restricted regions of a nation. Although certain sectors of the host nation's economy expand, such as hotels and expensive restaurants, this very expansion appears to retard growth in agriculture and other economic sectors. Moreover, multinational corporations often buy out or force out local entrepreneurs and companies, thereby increasing economic and cultural dependence (Bornschier et al., 1978; P. Evans, 1979; Wallerstein, 1979).

Recent studies suggest that multinationals tend to generate income for a developing nation's elite, while at the same time undermining the market for goods produced by the poor. Moreover, multinationals consciously act to prevent reductions in inequality in host countries. For example, foreign corporations oppose increases in minimum wage levels and issue grants to support legislation that would restrict labor union activity. While the relationship between foreign investment and economic inequality needs further research, the best data currently available point directly to the conclusion that

Sergio Dorantes/Sygma

Many multinational corporations based in the United States have opened factories in the developing world to take advantage of this pool of cheap labor. Shown are workers at a Reebok factory in Indonesia.

multinational corporations intensify inequality in the developing world (Moran, 1978).

Sociologist Dale Wimberley (1990) studied the impact of foreign investment on the infant mortality rates of 63 developing nations, among them Brazil, Egypt, India, and the Philippines. (The *infant mortality rate*—the number of deaths of infants under 1 year of age per 1000 live births in a given year—is widely regarded as an effective measure of general health care in a society.) Wimberley found that a reduction in the infant mortality rate was most likely to occur when there was *less* penetration by multinational corporations into the local economy. How could outside investment be detrimental to a society's level of health? Wimberley concluded that foreign investment promotes low-wage labor and therefore income inequality within developing countries—which, in turn, retards advances in health care (Bornschier and Chase-Dunn, 1985; Bradshaw, 1988).

In many respects, the rise of multinational corporations has become a threat to national sovereignty. One of the most flagrant illustrations of the power of multinationals took place in Chile. In 1970, International Telephone and Telegraph (ITT) attempted to stop a Marxist politician, Salvador Allende, from coming to power—even though he was running for the Chilean presidency in a free and democratic election. After Allende was victorious, ITT and the Central Intelligence Agency (CIA) participated in the overthrow of the legally constituted government. In 1973, Allende and many of his supporters died during a bloody military coup. The elected regime was then replaced by a military dictatorship which was widely denounced for its violations of human rights (A. Sampson, 1973; see also Barnet and Müller, 1974; Michalowski and Kramer, 1987; R. Vernon, 1977). We will examine the issue of universal human rights in more detail in the social policy section at the end of the chapter.

Consequences of Stratification for Developing Nations

As discussed above, colonialism, neocolonialism, and foreign investment by multinationals have often had unfortunate consequences for residents of developing nations. From 1950 to 1980, the gap between the world's rich and poor nations continued to grow, primarily because the rich nations got even richer. As for the decade of the 1980s, it is estimated that more than 40 Third World countries finished the decade poorer in per capita terms than they started it. The world's 14 most-devastated nations—including Zambia, Bolivia, and Nigeria—saw per capita income plummet as dramatically as it did in the United States during the Great Depression of the 1930s. With these trends in mind, researcher Alan Durning (1990:26) observed that the term "developing nation" has become a cruel misnomer; many of the world's less affluent nations are disintegrating rather than developing.

The day-to-day impact of the economic backslide in Africa, Latin America, and parts of Asia during the 1980s was tragic. Malnutrition rose in Burma, Burundi, the Gambia, Guinea-Bissau, Jamaica, Niger, Nigeria, Paraguay, the Philippines, Nicaragua, El Salvador, and Peru. According to the World Bank, life expectancy declined in nine African countries over the period 1979 to 1983. Today, more than 100 million Africans are believed to lack sufficient food to sustain themselves in good health (Durning, 1990:26; World Bank, 1990).

The 1980s were a particularly cruel decade for Latin America. El Salvador, Nicaragua, and Peru, all torn by war, went into economic tailspins. According to Peru's government, one-third of the country's children are malnourished to the extent that they have stunted growth. The per capita income of the average Latin American—only about $3500 in 1980—declined by 9 percent over the next eight years (Durning, 1990:26–27). Faced with soaring unemployment and desperate poverty, many residents were forced to participate in, and were often exploited within, their countries' underground economies (see Box 9-1).

Like Geni Sequiera Gomes, the Brazilian woman profiled at the beginning of the chapter, women in developing countries find life especially difficult. "Women are the most exploited among the oppressed," notes Karuna Chanana Ahmed, an anthropologist from India who has studied the position of women in developing nations. In addition to the debilitating poverty experienced by many men in these countries, women face sex discrimination beginning at birth. They are commonly fed

BOX 9-1 · AROUND THE WORLD

THE INFORMAL ECONOMY

Goods and services do not have to be produced and consumed in officially recognized and registered businesses. Instead, they can be made, sold, and traded by members of informal social networks. Anthropologists studying developing nations and preindustrial societies have long acknowledged such networks, but only recently have these networks been identified as common to all societies (Ferman et al., 1987).

The term *informal economy* refers to transfers of money, goods, or services that are not reported to the government. Participants in this economy avoid taxes, regulations, and minimum wage provisions, as well as certain expenses incurred in bookkeeping and financial reporting. In industrial societies, the informal economy embraces transactions that are individually quite small but which can be quite significant when taken together. One major segment of this economy involves illegal transactions—such as prostitution, sale of illegal drugs, gambling, and bribery—leading some observers to describe it as an "underground economy." Yet the informal economy also includes unregulated child care services, garage sales, and the unreported income of craftspeople, street vendors, and

employees who receive substantial tips. According to estimates, the informal economy may account for as much as 10 to 20 percent of all economic activity in the United States. In 1993, it was estimated that New York City's underground economy had increased to $54 billion per year, or about 20 percent of the city's economy (Hershey, 1988; Sontag, 1993a:42).

Although these informal economic transactions take place in virtually all societies—both capitalist and socialist—the pattern in developing countries differs somewhat from the informal economy of industrialized nations. In the developing world, government bureaucracies are often unable to respond to increased requests for licenses or services, thereby forcing legitimate entrepreneurs to go "underground." Informal industrial enterprises, such as textile factories and repair shops, tend to be labor-intensive. Underground entrepreneurs cannot rely on advanced machinery, since a firm's assets can be confiscated for failure to operate within the open economy.

Viewed from a functionalist perspective, the burdensome bureaucratic regulations of developing societies have contributed to the rise of an efficient informal economy in certain countries. Nevertheless,

these regulatory systems are dysfunctional to overall political and economic well-being. Since informal firms typically operate in remote locations to avoid detection, they cannot easily expand even when they become profitable. Given the limited protection for their property and contractual rights, participants in the informal economy are less likely to save and invest their income.

Informal economies have also been criticized for promoting highly unfair and dangerous working conditions. In his study of the underground economy of Spain, sociologist Louis Lemkow (1987) found that workers' incomes were low, there was little job security, and safety and health standards were rarely enforced. Both the Spanish government and the nation's trade unions seemed to ignore the exploitation of participants in the informal economy. Yet, especially in the developing world, the existence of a substantial underground economy—estimated, for example, to account for about one-third of the gross domestic product of Peru—reflects the absence of an economic system accessible to all residents (Fiola, 1990; Portes et al., 1989; Weigard, 1992; World Bank, 1987:74–75).

---

less than male children, are denied educational opportunities, and are often hospitalized only when critically ill. Whether inside or outside the home, women's work is devalued.

There are disturbing reports of sex discrimination

all through the developing world (and also, of course, from core industrialized nations such as the United States and Japan). Surveys show a significant degree of *female infanticide* (the killing of baby girls) in China and rural areas of India. Only one-third of Pakistan's

Sex discrimination is evident across the world. In Saudi Arabia, women are prohibited from driving, walking alone in public, and socializing with men outside their families.

sexually segregated schools are for women, and one-third of these schools have no buildings. In Kenya and Tanzania, it is illegal for a woman to own a house. In Saudi Arabia, women are prohibited from driving, walking alone in public, and socializing with men outside their families (J. Anderson and Moore, 1993:6–7; C. Murphy, 1993:10–11). We will explore women's second-class status throughout the world more fully in Chapter 11.

What factors have contributed to the recent difficulties of developing nations? Certainly runaway population growth has hurt the standard of living of many Third World peoples. So, too, has the accelerating environmental decline evident in the quality of air, water, and other natural resources. (We will examine population growth and environmental decline in more detail in Chapter 19.) Still another factor has been the developing nations' collective debt of $1.3 trillion. Today, poor nations are paying rich countries $50 billion each year in debt and interest payments beyond what they receive in new loans. If we add to this figure the estimates of capital flight involving wealthy citizens of poor nations, the annual outflow of funds may reach $100 billion (Durning, 1990:25–26; Kerbo, 1991:498).

Viewed from a world systems approach, a growing share of the human and natural resources of developing countries is being redistributed to the core industrialized nations. Consequently, the global debt crisis has intensified the Third World dependency begun under colonialism, neocolonialism, and multinational investment. International financial institutions are pressuring indebted countries to adopt austerity measures in order to more easily meet their interest payments. Developing nations may be forced to devalue their currencies, freeze workers' wages, increase privatization of industry, and reduce government services and employment. These policies often lead to high inflation, reduced purchasing power, substantial layoffs of government workers, and higher unemployment—all of which are harmful to a nation's overall economic development (Bradshaw and Huang, 1991; George, 1988:77–85; Roddick, 1988:81–104).

World systems theorists add that the policies dictated by international financial institutions are destructive to the quality of life in developing countries. For example, in 1990, as part of an austerity program designed to ease debt repayment, the African nation of Zambia ended governmental subsidies which had reduced citizens' costs in buying food. Once the "free market" determined food prices, these prices increased dramatically, quickly leading to intense antigovernment riots. At least 23 people died during the unrest, which included an unsuccessful attempt to overthrow Zambia's government. Such an explosive response to austerity measures is not unusual; since 1976, Third World countries have witnessed more than 85 protests directed toward austerity programs intended to facilitate international debt payments (Bradshaw and Huang, 1991; Walton and Ragin, 1988, 1989).

Unfortunately, the massive exodus of money from poorer regions of the world only intensifies their destruction of natural resources. From a conflict view, less affluent nations are being forced to exploit their mineral deposits, forests, and fisheries in order to meet their debt obligations while offering subsistence labor to local workers. The poor turn to the only means of survival available to them: marginal lands. They plow mountain slopes, burn plots in tropical forests, and overgraze grasslands—often knowing that their actions are destructive to the environment. But they see no alternative in their agonizing fight for simple survival (Durning, 1990:26; Waring, 1988).

STRATIFICATION WITHIN NATIONS: A COMPARATIVE PERSPECTIVE

The world marketplace is highly stratified, with affluent, industrialized nations well in control while poorer developing countries face desperate problems. Worldwide stratification is evident not only in the disparity between rich and poor nations (in Wallerstein's terms, between countries at the core and at the periphery of the world economic system) but also *within* nations in the substantial gap between rich and poor citizens.

Stratification in developing nations is closely related to their relatively weak and dependent position in the world economic system. As discussed earlier, local elites work hand in hand with multinational corporations and prosper from such alliances, while the exploitation of industrial and agricultural workers is created and perpetuated by the economic system and prevailing developmental values. Consequently, foreign investment in developing countries tends to increase economic inequality (Bornschier et al., 1978; Kerbo, 1991: 507–511).

Distribution of Wealth and Income

In Chapter 8, we noted that in 1991, the top fifth (or 20 percent) of the U.S. population—earning

$62,991 or more—accounted for more than 44 percent of total wages and salaries in the nation. By contrast, the bottom fifth of the population—earning $17,000 or less—accounted for less than 5 percent of income (Bureau of the Census, 1993a:463).

As Figure 9-2 on page 254 shows, the degree of income inequality varies markedly around the world. Of the seven nations studied that are contrasted in the figure, Brazil had the greatest gap between its most affluent and least affluent residents. The top fifth in Brazil received 68 percent of total wages and salaries, while the bottom fifth accounted for only 2 percent of income. Similar disparities are found in many developing countries, where small elites control a large portion of the nation's income. There are 10 countries around the globe in which the most affluent 10 percent receive at least 40 percent of income, and they are all developing countries: Brazil (the leader at 51 percent), Kenya, Sri Lanka, Botswana, Guatemala, Chile, Panama, Tanzania, Honduras, and Lesotho.

Workers are shown cutting down a forest in Papua, New Guinea. From a conflict perspective, less affluent nations are being forced to exploit their mineral deposits, forests, and fisheries in order to meet their debt obligations while offering subsistence labor to local workers.

FIGURE 9-2 Distribution of Income in Seven Nations

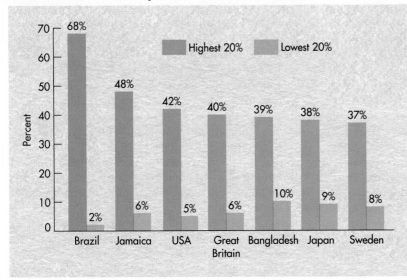

This figure shows the distribution of household income by population fifths in seven countries. Data were collected by the World Bank and by United Nations agencies. As the figure shows, the proportion of income held by the most affluent 20 percent of the population is highest in Brazil (68 percent) and Jamaica (48 percent) and lowest in Sweden (37 percent). By comparing the bars for the poorest and richest quintiles (a quintile is 20 percent of the population), we can see that the gap between the highest and lowest quintiles is smallest in Bangladesh, Japan, and Sweden. Consequently, of the seven countries pictured, these nations have the lowest level of income inequality.

NOTE: Data are considered comparable although based on statistics covering 1979 to 1990.
SOURCE: World Bank, 1993:296–297.

In examining the world's advanced industrial economies, researchers have found the *least* income inequality in Sweden, Japan, and Belgium. The *highest* income inequality is evident in the United States, Switzerland, and Australia. Redistributive tax policies have reduced income inequality in many European nations; the factors which contribute to Japan's comparatively low level of income inequality are explored in Box 9-2 on page 256 (World Bank, 1992:262–263; see also P. Nolan, 1992).

As we saw in Chapter 8, wealth in the United States is much more unevenly distributed than income. The richest fifth of the population holds almost 80 percent of the nation's wealth (refer back to Figure 8-2 on page 223). This extreme concentration of wealth is evident in most industrial societies. In Great Britain, for example, the distribution of wealth is even more lopsided than in the United States. In good part, this is because in the United States many people with rather modest incomes own automobiles or homes, whereas ownership of automobiles or homes is less common among poorer residents of Great Britain (Samuelson and Nordhaus, 1992:355–358).

Prestige

Sociologists have recognized that comparative research is essential in determining whether observed patterns of stratification are unique to a single nation, are restricted to a particular type of society (such as industrial or developing nations), or are applicable to a wide range of societies (Kalleberg, 1988). We have seen that societies as different as Brazil, Bangladesh, the United States, and Japan all share a marked inequality in the distribution of income (refer back to Figure 9-2). But, as we saw in Chapter 8, a person's class position, defined largely in economic terms and reflecting his or her level of wealth and income, is but one component of stratification.

By ranking the prestige of various occupations, sociologists can gain a deeper understanding of another aspect of inequality. How do perceptions in the United States regarding the prestige of occupations compare with those held in other societies? In an effort to study stratification from a cross-cultural perspective, sociologist Donald Treiman (1977) examined the reputation that certain jobs had in 53 different nations. People were asked to

TABLE 9-2	**Comparative Ranking of Occupations**					
	NATION					
OCCUPATION	USA	CANADA	NIGERIA	POLAND	THAILAND	SOVIET UNION
Physician or medical officer	78	83	70	81	73	77
Captain	63	67	66	44	69	60
High school teacher	63	63	58	70	70	57
Bank manager	53	67	58	49	54	NA
Truck driver	32	31	49	44	29	45

NOTE: People in the Soviet Union were not asked to rank bankers; hence, this category is marked "NA" (data not available).
SOURCE: Treiman, 1977:318–405.

The table above presents a sampling of data collected by sociologist Donald Treiman regarding the ranking of various occupations throughout the world. The findings reveal a striking similarity of ratings in the six nations.

rate occupations, and the results were tabulated along a scale ranging from 0 to 100, with higher scores being more prestigious. As the data presented in Table 9-2 illustrate, Treiman found a high degree of correlation or similarity in all contemporary societies, including both industrialized and nonindustrialized nations.

Treiman's pioneering research inspired subsequent efforts to gather and compare data from many societies using the objective method of measuring stratification differences. In one important study, sociologists Nan Lin and Wen Xie (1988) interviewed a random sample of residents of Beijing, the capital of the People's Republic of China, to study occupational prestige. The researchers recognized the potential bias of sampling those who live in one of China's most cosmopolitan cities. They found that 47 percent of the 1774 respondents questioned were professionals, managers, or administrators—whereas this was true of only 23 percent of residents of other urban areas. Nevertheless, given the constraints on acquiring social scientific data, this study offers unique insights regarding stratification in the world's most populous nation.

Lin and Xie found that physicians were near the top of the occupational hierarchy in terms of prestige, while police officers were near the middle, and garbage collectors were close to the bottom—a finding similar to the results of surveys in the United States (refer back to Table 8-2 on page 220). Interestingly, however, teachers and professors received much lower prestige ratings in China,

reflecting the comparatively limited economic rewards they receive relative to other occupations. The Chinese respondents gave a much higher prestige rating to textile workers than did respondents in the United States. In explaining this finding, Lin and Xie point out that textile workers in China fare much better relative to other workers than they do in the United States or Europe.

As one part of their analysis, the researchers compared the prestige rankings of male and female respondents. Although China has officially maintained a national policy of gender equality since 1949, occupational segregation by gender has not been completely eliminated. Partly as a result, the prestige rankings of Chinese men and women seemed to reflect the structure of occupational opportunity. Males, for example, gave higher ratings than females to such occupations as natural scientist, athlete, driver, and mechanic—all of which are more likely to be held by males. Each gender showed a tendency to rate more highly those occupations most open to it.

Treiman's cross-cultural research reminds us that prestige distinctions are universal; the study of China by Lin and Xie underscores this finding. Even a society that has experienced revolutionary movements and decades of Communist party rule

BOX 9-2 ⋆ AROUND THE WORLD

INEQUALITY IN JAPAN

A tourist visiting Japan may at first experience a bit of culture shock after noticing the degree to which everything in Japanese life is ranked: corporations, universities, even educational programs. These rankings are widely reported and accepted. Moreover, day-to-day social interactions are shaped by rankings: Japanese find it difficult to sit, talk, or eat together unless the relative rankings of those present have been established, often through the practice of *meishi* (the exchange of business cards).

This apparent preoccupation with ranking and formality suggests an exceptional degree of stratification. Yet researchers have determined that Japan's level of income inequality is among the lowest of major industrial societies (refer back to Figure 9-2). Whereas the pay gap between Japan's top corporate executives and the nation's lowest-paid workers is about 8 to 1, the comparable figure for the United States would be 37 to 1. In addition, the lucrative stock options received by top executives of U.S. corporations are actually prohibited by law in Japan (Abegglen and Stalk, 1985:187, 192; Kerbo, 1991:421–423; Nakane, 1970:30).

This relative level of equality in Japanese society is rather recent; it dates back to post–World War II economic changes, including ex-

Charles Gupton/Stock, Boston

While women constitute more than 40 percent of Japan's work force, they are generally restricted to subordinate positions.

tensive land reform and the breakup of powerful holding companies. Among the factors contributing to a lower level of inequality in Japan have been an expanding economy combined with a labor shortage, an educational system that treats students alike regardless of family background at least through their junior high school years, restraints on excessively high incomes, relatively little discrimination against male heads of households, and certain governmental policies that serve to redistribute income (Kerbo, 1991:431–432, 454–457).

Still another factor that works against inequality is that Japan is

rather homogeneous—certainly when compared with the United States—in terms of race, ethnicity, nationality, and language. Japan's population, racially and ethnically, is 98 percent Japanese, but there is discrimination against the nation's Chinese and Korean minorities, and the *Buraku* constitute a low-status subculture who encounter extensive prejudice (Hirasawa, 1992).

There has been growing controversy concerning Japan's treatment of its Korean minority. About 675,000 Koreans live in Japan, of whom more than 85 percent were born there. It is not easy for Koreans to obtain Japanese citizenship; without citizenship, they cannot vote, cannot work as teachers or government officials, and must carry alien registration cards at all times (a practice that has been likened to the South African requirement that Blacks carry passbooks).

Koreans in Japan disproportionately work for low wages, without safety standards, and without any real hope of advancement. Moreover, because discrimination is so common, less than 5 percent of Koreans use their own names in business circles; similarly, many young Koreans use Japanese aliases to conceal their heritage in schools. In 1992, after years of bitter debate, Japan's parliament agreed to end the mandatory fingerprinting of most Koreans and other foreign residents required under the nation's Alien Registration Law. Nevertheless, Korean residents—many of whose families have lived in Japan for generations—still have no right to vote, to work in government jobs, or to learn about their heritage in public schools (Makihara, 1990; *New York Times,* 1991a; Sterngold, 1992).

Gender discrimination and in-equality are deep-rooted. Japanese girls do not receive the same encouragement to achieve in education that boys do (refer back to Box 3-1 on page 70). Not surprisingly, therefore, Japanese women occupy a subordinate position in higher education. Whereas 80 percent of the nation's male college students are in four-year universities, two-thirds of female students are in women's junior colleges which promote traditional domestic roles for women. Even when Japanese women enter four-year universities, they often major in home economics, nutrition, or literature.

Women constitute more than 40 percent of Japan's work force, and 70 percent of married women with teenage children work outside the home. But, whether in terms of income, status, or power, women occupy a secondary position in Japan's paid labor force. Less than 10 percent of Japanese women in the work force hold management positions; overall, women earn only 50.3 percent of men's wages (Watanabe, 1991:18–22).

In 1985, Japan's parliament—at the time, 97 percent male—passed an Equal Employment bill which encourages employers to end sex discrimination in hiring, assignment, and promotion policies. But feminist organizations remain dissatisfied because the law lacks strong sanctions to prevent continued discrimination against women. Michiko Nakajima, a lawyer who has argued many discrimination cases, notes: "The only way to make the equal opportunity law work is to give it power to punish companies." Employment data concerning Japan's largest and most prestigious trading companies underscore the law's ineffectiveness. In 1992, Mitsubishi hired 4 women and 213 men, C. Itoh hired 5 women and 198 men, and Nissho Iwai hired 3 women and 127 men (Sanger, 1992:A10).

There has, however, been progress on the political front for Japanese women. In 1991, Harue Kitamura of Ashiya City became the nation's first female mayor. More women were elected that year to local government posts in cities, towns, and villages than ever before. Moreover, as was noted in the social policy section in Chapter 6, in 1992 a Japanese district court issued an important ruling against sexual harassment in the workplace. The court held that a small publishing company and one of its male employees had violated the rights of a female employee because of crude remarks that led her to quit her job. This ruling was a dramatic victory for Japan's feminist movement (Watanabe, 1991; Weisman, 1992; see also Brinton, 1992).

still exhibits noticeable stratification in rating some occupations as most prestigious and others as less desirable.

Social Mobility

In Chapter 8, we saw that the amount of social movement in a society—both upward and downward—is rather limited in societies characterized by slavery, caste, and estate systems of stratification. For example, a study of agricultural households in central India between 1975 and 1983 found that, on average, 84 percent of those who were poor in any year had been poor in the previous year. Over the nine-year period of study, 44 percent of households had been poor for six or more years, and 19 percent were poor in all nine years (World Bank, 1990:135).

More recent studies of intergenerational mobility in industrialized nations have found that (1) there are substantial similarities in the ways that parents' positions in stratification systems are transmitted to their children; (2) as in the United States, mobility opportunities in other nations have been influenced by structural factors, such as labor market changes which lead to the rise or decline of an occupational group within the social hierarchy; (3) immigration continues to be a significant factor shaping a society's level of intergenerational mobility (Ganzeboom et al., 1991; Haller et al., 1990; Hauser and Grusky, 1988).

Cross-cultural studies suggest that intergenerational mobility has been increasing in recent decades, at least among men. Dutch sociologists Harry Ganzeboom and Ruud Luijkx joined by sociologist Donald Treiman of the United States (1989) examined surveys of mobility in 35 industrial and developing nations; they found that almost all the countries studied had witnessed increased intergenerational mobility between the 1950s and 1980s. In particular, there was a common pattern of movement away from agriculture-based occupations.

Mobility patterns in industrialized countries are usually associated with intergenerational or intragenerational mobility. However, within developing nations, micro-level movement from one occupation to another is often overshadowed by macro-level social and economic changes. For example, there is typically a substantial wage differential between rural and urban areas, which leads to high levels of migration to the cities. Yet the urban industrial sectors of developing countries generally cannot provide sufficient employment for all those seeking work. Consequently, such internal migration contributes to an expansion of the informal economies described earlier in Box 9-1 (Thirlwall, 1989:103).

Recent research on social mobility has persua-

Greenlar/Images Works

Haitian immigrants are shown working in a potato field in New York State. Sociological research suggests that high rates of immigration contribute to an expansion of job opportunities and therefore facilitate social mobility.

sively pursued a conflict view that cross-national differences in mobility are influenced by the differing relations of countries to the world economy. Drawing on Wallerstein's world systems theory, researchers argue that there is likely to be greater inequality and less mobility in the developing countries than in the core industrialized nations. Further studies examining this thesis can be anticipated (Ries, 1992:187).

Only recently have researchers begun to investigate the impact of gender differences on the mobility patterns of developing nations. Many aspects of the development process—especially modernization in rural areas and the rural-to-urban migration described above—may result in the modification or abandonment of traditional cultural practices and even marital systems. The effects on women's social standing and mobility are not necessarily positive. Through development and modernization, women's vital role in food production deteriorates, thereby jeopardizing both their autonomy and their material well-being. The movement of families to the cities weakens women's ties to relatives who can provide food, financial assistance, and social support (Alam, 1985; Boserup, 1977; Tiano, 1987).

One recent effort to investigate gender and mobility took place in Sri Lanka (formerly known as Ceylon). Researchers examined the impact of foreign aid—in the form of plans to improve agricultural production, irrigation, and rural electrification—on the local population. Virtually all the foreign aid programs were more successful in increasing the incomes of men than of women. Where women's incomes did rise, it was usually in such occupations as rubber and tea cultivation, in which women earn almost 40 percent less than their male counterparts. Overall, foreign aid in Sri Lanka had the unintended consequence of increasing income inequality between male and female workers; similar conclusions were reached in studies conducted in India and Malaysia (Stoeckel and Sirisena, 1988).

Our examination of the distribution of wealth and income within various countries, of comparative studies of prestige, and of cross-cultural research on mobility consistently reveals that stratification based on class, gender, and other factors is evident within a wide range of societies. Clearly, a worldwide view of stratification must involve not only the sharp contrast between wealthy and impoverished nations but also the stratification hierarchies within industrialized societies and developing countries.

STRATIFICATION IN BRAZIL: A CASE STUDY

Thus far in the chapter, our discussion of stratification, inequality, and mobility has examined many diverse societies. In illustrating the dynamics of stratification outside the United States, it will be helpful to study one country in somewhat more detail.

Brazil is an economic giant; it has the world's tenth-largest economy. Brazil's 150 million people constitute a majority of all South Americans. As in the United States, race relations in Brazil reflect the legacy of European colonization and the slave trade. As in many developing countries, women in Brazil are speaking out against their traditional second-class status. Moreover, in recent years, Brazil has been the focus of considerable international attention, both because of the destruction of the Amazon rain forest and the nation's serious debt problems. For these reasons, Brazil seems an ideal choice for such a case study.

The gap between Brazil's richest and poorest citizens is one of the widest in the world—and it has grown since 1960 (refer back to Figure 9-2). According to Brazil's 1991 census, the richest 10 percent of the population held 49 percent of the nation's wealth. By contrast, the poorest 10 percent of the population held less than 1 percent of all wealth. Data from the World Bank indicate that in the 1980s about 41 percent of all Brazilians survived on less than $2 per day (Brooke, 1993b).

In contrast to the upper class in the United States, the Brazilian upper class (the top 1 percent in terms of income) is composed primarily of large landowners and successful immigrant industrialists. Reflecting the continuing impact of colonialism and neocolonialism, less than one in five of Brazil's leading industrialists is a child or even grandchild of Brazilians. The upper middle class, comprising about 2 percent of the population, includes professionals, civil servants, and military officers, while

The lives of poor people in Brazil are often bleak, especially when they are confronted with the lavish wealth of the nation's elite.

the middle class (about 24 percent of the population) is composed of craftspeople, white-collar workers, government employees, and workers in service occupations. Finally, at the bottom of Brazil's stratification hierarchy are the rural and urban poor, who together constitute an overwhelming majority (73 percent) of the nation's people (Fiechter, 1975:15–17).

As we saw at the beginning of the chapter in our discussion of the rural woman who had lost 13 children, the lives of poor people in Brazil are often bleak. Indeed, in 1992, there were more than 16,000 documented cases of people falling victim to slavery practices, such as the imprisonment of indebted rural workers by employers (refer back to Box 8-1 on page 211, which focuses on slavery in the 1990s). In the cities, poor people are confronted with the lavish wealth of the nation's elite.

A poster on the waiting room in the only medical station in Rocinha, the largest slum neighborhood in Rio de Janeiro, warns of an outbreak of leprosy. "Everybody's suffering here," explains a nurse, "but we all have views. We see their mansions, but they don't see us" (Brooke, 1993b; Dabrowski et al., 1989:64; Wood and de Carvalho, 1988).

Race Relations in Brazil: The Legacy of Slavery

To someone knowledgeable in racial and ethnic relations in the United States, Brazil seems familiar in a number of respects. Like the United States, Brazil was colonized by Europeans (in Brazil's case, the Portuguese) who overwhelmed the native population. Like the United States, Brazil imported Black Africans as slaves to meet the demand for laborers. Even today, excluding nations on the African continent, Brazil is second only to the United States in number of people of African descent.

Brazil depended much more on slave trade than the United States did, even though at the height of slavery each nation had approximately 4 to 4.5 million slaves. Brazil's reliance on a continual influx of slaves from Africa meant that typical Brazilian slaves had closer ties to Africa than did their counterparts in the United States. Revolts and escapes were more common among slaves in Brazil. The most dramatic example was the slave *quilombo* (or hideaway) of Palmores, where 20,000 inhabitants repeatedly fought off Portuguese assaults until 1698. In 1888, Brazil reluctantly became the last nation in the western hemisphere to abolish slavery—though, as we have seen, slavery remains a bitter reality in contemporary Brazil (Brooke, 1993b; Degler, 1971:7–8, 47–52).

Today, rather than being classified simply as "Black" or "White" (as is typical in the United States) Brazil's racial groupings constitute a type of color gradient on a continuum from light to dark skin color. Consequently, Mulattos (people of mixed racial ancestry) are viewed as an identifiable social group. According to the 1980 census, Brazil's population was 55 percent *Branco* (White), 38 percent Mulatto, 6 percent *Preto* (Black), and 1 percent other. Over the last 50 years, the proportion of Mulattos has grown, while the proportion of both

Brancos and *Pretos* has declined (Brazil, 1981; Wood and de Carvalho, 1988:135–153).

Historian Carl Degler (1971) has suggested that the key difference between race relations in Brazil and race relations in the United States is Brazil's "Mulatto escape hatch," under which Mulattos are not classified with Blacks. But, while lighter skin color does appear to enhance status in Brazil, the impact of this escape hatch has been exaggerated. Income data show that Mulattos earn 42 percent more income than Blacks, but this difference is not especially remarkable, given that Mulattos have more formal schooling. More striking is the finding that Whites earn 98 percent more income than Mulattos. As a result, the most significant distinction appears to be that between Whites and all Brazilian "people of color," rather than that between the country's Blacks and Mulattos (Dzidzienyo, 1987; Silva, 1985).

In 1988, Brazil marked as a national holiday the hundredth anniversary of the abolition of slavery, but for 40 to 50 percent of Brazil's people of color there was little rejoicing. Zézé Motta, Brazil's leading Black actress and a longtime campaigner for Black civil rights, observed: "We have gone from the hold of the ship to the basements of society." As of late 1992, fewer than 10 members of Brazil's 584-member Congress considered themselves Black. Whites are still many times more likely to graduate from college than Blacks, while job advertisements continue to seek individuals of "good appearance" (a euphemism for light skin). According to census data released in 1993, the average Black man in Brazil earns $163 per month, or 41 percent that of his White male counterpart (Brooke, 1992, 1993a; Simons, 1988:1).

The Status of Brazilian Women

The position of women in Brazil is typical of that of women in many developing nations. While Brazil is more industrialized than most developing countries, it still has a labor surplus and high rates of unemployment. These factors contribute to the exclusion of large numbers of women from the Brazilian work force. Consequently, many women in Brazil's cities, especially migrant women, must seek income within the informal economy (which accounts for 40 percent of Brazil's gross national product) in such jobs as domestic servants and street vendors. Domestic service is still the leading form of employment for Brazilian women. Factory work is generally reserved for those women who have grown up in cities and have more education than migrants from rural areas (Fiola, 1990; Sarti, 1989:76).

Although women's participation in Brazil's informal economy is accepted, traditional views of women's role in society discourage married women's employment in full-time jobs outside the family. With many children working, a large family means more wage earners—but having a large family reduces women's employment options. Finally, factory owners are reluctant to hire married women because of the maternity benefits to which permanently employed pregnant women are entitled (Patai, 1988; Safa, 1983:96; Wood and de Carvalho, 1988:174–175).

In 1932, Brazilian women won the right to vote and became the first women in Latin America to gain suffrage. In recent decades, women have emphasized their identities as mothers and homemakers in protesting shortages in food and other necessities. Moreover, women have taken the lead in demonstrating against human rights violations, including the "disappearances" of loved ones. In many of these protests, women have attacked the violence of their nation's male leaders (Patai, 1988).

Feminist initiatives are evident in contemporary Brazil, but have been met with resistance. Often, in working for social change, women's groups must present issues in a way that will be less threatening to the larger, male-dominated Brazilian society. For example, in order to receive broad public support, feminists defend the need for child care centers as a "workers' issue," a "children's issue," or a "health issue," rather than as a "women's issue" (Alvarez, 1989).

In 1985, the National Council for Women's Rights was established within the Ministry of Justice. This was the first time that the Brazilian government had formally recognized the existence of sexual inequality in the country and had taken steps to guarantee full equality for women. Among the council's goals are the elimination of sexism within the criminal justice system and the reduction of violence against women (Sarti, 1989:88).

As one response to feminist protests regarding violence against women, Brazil has created more than 185 women's police stations run by all-female staffs at which policewomen take all statements and make arrests. These stations are intended to provide a "secure and sympathetic atmosphere" in which women can report crimes such as rape, incest, and battering. If they are injured, they can receive immediate medical treatment at these stations. Unfortunately, the women's police stations are hampered by inadequate government funding. In addition, there are only three shelters for battered women in all of Brazil (Corral, 1993).

Brazilian feminists won an important victory in 1991, when the nation's Supreme Court ruled that a husband who kills his wife can no longer be acquitted on the grounds of "legitimate defense of honor" because of her alleged adultery. This defense had been used by attorneys to win acquittals for thousands of husbands on trial for killing their wives. Brazilian women had rallied against it throughout the 1980s, using the slogan "Lovers Don't Kill." The Supreme Court majority declared that such killings defend "not honor, but vanity, exaggerated self-importance, and the pride of a lord who sees a woman as his personal property" (Brooke, 1991a:B16).

Just as violence against heterosexual women is common in Brazil, so too are attacks against lesbians and gay men. One gay rights organization in Brazil has listed 1200 killings of gays since 1980 and estimates that the actual number of killings is twice as high. In early 1993, a town councilman in Alagoas State publicly revealed his bisexuality; six weeks later, he was kidnapped, tortured, and killed. With such events in mind, in mid-1993 an immigration judge in California granted political asylum to a 30-year-old Brazilian housepainter who himself had been badly beaten outside a gay bar in Rio de Janeiro. This marked the first time that an openly gay person had won asylum in the United States on the ground that homosexuals were a persecuted social group in the individual's country of origin (Brooke, 1993d).

Brazil's Economy and Environment

By the 1990s, Brazil's economy had reached a state of crisis. The rate of inflation had risen as high as 2700 percent in 1989, meaning that workers could get a raise every week and still not stay ahead of inflation. At the same time, Brazil's foreign debt of $130 billion was the largest of any developing nation. Brazil has found itself unable to pay the principal or interest on its debt since 1989; as a result, the United States Export-Import Bank demoted Brazil to its riskiest loan category.

In response to this crisis, President Fernando Collor de Mello—the country's first directly elected civilian president in 29 years—announced a startling economic plan in early 1990. In an effort to modernize the Brazilian economy and to "liquidate" inflation, the president proposed declaring a moratorium on internal debt, privatizing state-controlled companies, imposing new taxes, loosening foreign exchange controls, establishing a new currency, and streamlining the government bureaucracy. The president's program provoked controversy as soon as it was introduced. By late 1990, unions had called hundreds of strikes to protest the dismissals of 250,000 public employees and many private-sector workers (Brooke, 1990b, 1990c; Silverstein, 1990).

Throughout 1991 and 1992, there was little evidence that the president's bold economic plan was achieving success. Eventually, in late 1992, Collor de Mello was forced to resign in the face of impeachment charges of bribery and influence peddling. His successor, Vice President Itamar Franco, appeared to have little popular support. By mid-1993, the nation's inflation rate was 360 percent per year; unemployment in São Paolo, Brazil's business capital, stood at 16 percent; and Brazil's largest denomination bill, the 500,000-*cruziero* note, was worth only $10 (Brooke, 1993c).

Brazil's severe economic troubles have contributed to environmental destruction in the mineral-rich areas surrounding the Amazon River. This destruction has become a global concern. Each year, some 12,000 square miles of the Amazon rain forest are cleared for crops and livestock through burning—an area larger than Belgium. It is believed that the elimination of the rain forest affects worldwide weather patterns and heightens the gradual warming of the earth in a process known as the *greenhouse effect*. This destruction is additionally unfortunate in that the Amazon region represents a potential source of important pharmaceutical advances, including drugs that might cure diseases (Linden, 1989).

The burning of the rain forests is not the only aspect of Brazil's environmental troubles. By 1990, environmental activists around the world were expressing concern about the conflict between mining companies and the Yanomani Indians, considered to be the last major isolated Indian tribe in the Americas. More than 40,000 illegal gold prospectors have been mining in the traditional lands of the Yanomani in recent years. The miners are primarily poor Brazilians who move from gold rush to gold rush—all the while destroying forests and polluting rivers with chemicals used in purifying gold. In the view of Fernando César Mesquita, president of the Brazilian Institute of Environment and Renewable Resources, "the miners leave a trail of devastation wherever they go. They level nature around the mines. They leave the rivers useless" (Brooke, 1990a:3; Schmink and Wood, 1989).

The miners' presence in the Amazon lands has been a disaster not only for the environment, but also for the Yanomani. As a result of their contact with miners, more than half the 9000 Yanomani Indians in northern Brazil have contracted malaria and other deadly diseases. Yet the Yanomani have been largely without medical care since Funai (Brazil's national agency for Indian affairs) closed two health posts in their territory in 1988. In 1990, Indian rights organizations as far away as London launched demonstrations to protest the mistreatment of the Yanomani by the mining companies and the Brazilian government (Brooke, 1990a; Rabben, 1990a).

Worldwide protests concerning the Yanomani influenced government policy. In 1991, President Collor de Mello signed a decree reserving a stretch of 68,331 square miles of the Amazon rain forest as a homeland for the nation's 9000 members of the Yanomani tribe. The reserve will be linked to a slightly smaller park across the border in Venezuela. International supporters of the Yanomani cause were ecstatic; anthropologist Napoleon Chagnon of the United States said that "this will go a long way to making cultural survival of the Yanomani a real possibility" (Brooke, 1991b:A3).

Sygma

More than 40,000 illegal gold prospectors have been mining in the traditional lands of Brazil's Yanomani Indians. The miners destroy forests and pollute rivers with chemicals used in purifying gold.

The conflict over the Yanomani lands is but one of many in Brazil in which multinational mining companies and the government are pitted against Indian tribes and environmentalists. Underlying these disputes is overt racism against Indians, whose concern for their traditional lands is disparaged by land speculators and developers. However, in contrast to the miners in the Yanomani territories, thousands of Indians and other forest residents have learned to conduct extensive activities without devastating the environment (Rabben, 1990a, 1990b).

- Why did violence in the former Yugoslavia become a concern of the world community during the early 1990s?
- Is there an inherent conflict between a commitment to international human rights and a respect for the distinctive traditions and practices of each culture?
- How have feminist groups broadened the debate over universal human rights?

The final decade of the twentieth century began with great promise, but in a short time the world was reminded of how quickly peoples and their rights can be trampled. After the reunification of Germany was joyously celebrated in the former East and West Germanys, street gangs revived Nazi-style rhetoric and launched ugly attacks on Turkish residents and foreign immigrants. The end of Soviet dominance of eastern Europe set off bitter and sometimes violent clashes between racial, ethnic, and religious groups in the former Czechoslovakia, the former Yugoslavia, and the former Soviet Union itself (Auchincloss, 1993).

The most gripping of these tragedies brought the term *ethnic cleansing* into the world's vocabulary. Within the former Yugoslavia, ethnic Serbs instituted a policy intended to "cleanse" Muslims from parts of Bosnia-Herzegovina. According to one report:

> Hundreds, probably thousands, of civilians and captured or wounded combatants were deliberately and arbitrarily killed in the course of armed conflict. Tens of thousands of people were detained in connection with the fighting, in most cases solely because of their ethnic origin, sometimes as hostages for exchange. Torture or other ill-treatment of detainees, including rape, was common. Although all sides in the conflict were responsible for abuses, the majority of victims were Muslims and the main perpetrators were local Serbian armed forces (Amnesty International, 1993b:70).

As of August 1993, as many as 670,000 people had been killed in fighting in the former Yugoslavia, while an equal number had been uprooted from their homes and forced to become refugees. Moreover, there have been reports of substantial numbers of rapes of Muslim and Croatian women by Serbian soldiers. In a war crime trial in Sarajevo in early 1993, a Serbian soldier testified that the rapes he committed had been ordered for "Serbian morale." A 28-year-old Croatian and Muslim woman recalls that soldiers would invite their friends to come and watch the rapes, as if they were in a movie theater. In late 1993, a United Nations war crimes commission suggested that there were indications that the Serbs had used rape as a weapon of terror in their campaign to drive Muslims out of Bosnia and Herzegovina (Binder and Crossette, 1993; P. Lewis, 1993; MacKinnon, 1993:27, 29; Ottaway, 1993).

To many observers, Serbia's policy of ethnic cleansing is a blatant violation of people's human rights. The term **human rights** refers to universal moral rights belonging to all people because they are human. The most important elaboration of these rights appears in the Universal Declaration of Human Rights, adopted by the United Nations in 1948. This declaration prohibits slavery, torture, and degrading punishment; grants everyone the right to a nationality and its culture; affirms freedom of religion and the right to vote; proclaims the right to seek asylum in other countries to escape persecution; and prohibits arbitrary interference with one's privacy and arbitrary taking of a person's property. It also emphasizes that motherhood and childhood are entitled to special care and assistance. Each year, the United Nations receives between 20,000 and 30,000 complaints about human rights violations (Selby, 1987:8, 58).

In 1992, the United Nations condemned Serbia for driving non-Serbs from its territories as part of its policy of ethnic cleansing. Twenty-two countries, especially Iran and Cuba, were cited for human rights abuses. The United Nations also suggested that the United States might be violating the human rights of Haitian refugees by returning them to Haiti without allowing them to appeal for protection and asylum (Swift, 1993). The issue of Haitian refugees will be examined in more detail in the social policy section in Chapter 10.

Morin /The Miami Herald

Initially, the United States was opposed to a precise and binding obligation to the Universal Declaration of Human Rights. At the time that this declaration was adopted by the United Nations, the United States feared international scrutiny of the nation's domestic civil rights controversies (since racial segregation by law was still common). Consequently, the United States worked to limit the budget for the United Nations' Human Rights Commission.

In the early 1960s, the United States briefly began to use the Universal Declaration of Human Rights to promote democracy abroad, but during the Vietnam War era relations between the United States and the United Nations deteriorated. After Vietnam, the Carter administration emphasized international human rights concerns and initiated an embargo of South Africa, yet it deferred action against friends like the Shah of Iran who were guilty of serious human rights abuses. During the Reagan-Bush years, the cry of "human rights" was commonly invoked when criticizing "totalitarian" communist adversaries, while "authoritarian" allies of the United States were not held to a similar standard (Forsythe, 1990).

In 1993, President Bill Clinton began his administration by taking a more aggressive stance on international human rights. He has pressed the United Nations for the appointment of a High Commissioner for Human Rights as well as a special envoy to investigate abuses against women. (Both Ronald Reagan and George Bush had opposed having such a commissioner.) While many observers welcome these changes, skeptics wonder if this administration (like its predecessors) will ignore human rights violations committed by allies of the United States (S. Holmes, 1993).

By its very title, the Universal Declaration of Human Rights emphasizes that such rights should be *universal*. In some situations, however, conflicts arise between international human rights standards and local social practices that rest on alternative views of human dignity. Is India's caste system (refer back to Chapter 8) an inherent violation of human rights? What about the many cultures of the world that view the subordinate status of women as an essential element in their traditions?

As we saw in Chapter 3, cultural relativism encourages understanding and respecting the distinctive norms, values, and customs of each culture.

TABLE 9-3	Populations in Danger

Azerbaijanis and Armenians in the Caucasus (former Soviet Union)

Muslims in Bosnia-Herzegovina (former Yugoslavia) besieged by Serbian and Croatian forces

Kurds oppressed in Turkey, Iraq, Iran, and the former Soviet Union

Mozambicans suffering from a 15-year civil war

Peruvians caught between Maoist Shining Path rebels and the government

Rohingyas, a Muslim group in Burma

Somalis threatened by starvation, drought, and clan warfare

Sri Lankans caught between Tamil rebels and government forces

South Sudanese victims of a government attempt to crush a revolt by starving the entire area

Tuaregs, a nomadic group of the Sahara Desert, who are endangered by clashes in Mali, Niger, Algeria, and Burkina Faso

SOURCE: Jean, 1992.

Médecins Sans Frontièrer (Doctors Without Borders) has identified 10 peoples around the world who are the most severely threatened by warfare and oppression.

Does this mean that human rights should be interpreted differently in different parts of the world? In mid-1993, in a major speech at the first World Conference on Human Rights in 25 years, the United States' Secretary of State, Warren Christopher, rejected such a view. Christopher insisted that the Universal Declaration of Human Rights sets a single standard for acceptable behavior around the world. He warned that the United States would oppose any attempt to cite religious or cultural traditions as a rationale for weakening the standard of universal human rights. Christopher concluded that "we cannot let cultural relativism become the last refuge of repression" (Donnelly, 1989; Sciolino, 1993:A1).

The most far-reaching denial of universal human rights is evident when an entire group faces annihilation. Médecins Sans Frontièrer (Doctors Without Borders), the world's largest independent emergency medical aid organization, has identified 10 minorities and nationalities who are the most severely threatened by warfare and oppression (see

Table 9-3). Founded in 1971 and based in Paris, the organization has 5000 doctors and nurses working in 80 countries. "Our intention is to highlight current upheavals, to bear witness to foreign tragedies and reflect on the principles of humanitarian aid," explains Dr. Rony Brauman, the president of Médecins Sans Frontièrer (Jean, 1992; Spielmann, 1992:12).

Among the endangered peoples of the world are many indigenous (or native or tribal) peoples whose settlement precedes immigration from other societies and colonialism. They include nomadic Bedouins of the Arabic peninsula, the Inuit (Eskimo) of North America, the Sami (or Lapp) of northern Scandinavia, the Ainu of Japan, the Aborigines of Australia, and Brazil's Yanomani Indians (discussed earlier in the chapter). Indigenous peoples are organizing themselves to defend their way of life; their efforts are being assisted by voluntary associations of supporters in the core industrialized nations. As one result of this activism, the United Nations has established a working group to draft a Universal Declaration on the Rights of Indigenous Peoples (Durning, 1993).

Like Médecins Sans Frontièrer, Amnesty International is concerned with human rights violations around the world. Founded in 1966, Amnesty International has chapters in many countries and 400,000 members in the United States alone. It works for the release of men and women detained anywhere for their conscientiously held beliefs, their color, ethnic origin, sex, religion, or language—provided that they have neither used nor advocated violence. The winner of the 1977 Nobel Prize for Peace, Amnesty International opposes all forms of torture and capital punishment and advocates prompt trials for all political prisoners. In its 1993 annual report, Amnesty International (1993a) documents human rights violations in 163 countries—ranging alphabetically from Afghanistan (where a new government inflicted cruel and inhuman punishment on thousands of political prisoners) to Zimbabwe (where mass graves were uncovered of prisoners executed without trial by the army during the 1980s).

Interestingly, the traditional view of universal human rights—long accepted by the United Nations, Amnesty International, and others—is being reexamined in light of contemporary feminist activism.

In mid-1993, the *New York Times* noted that women's groups had emerged as "easily the strongest and most effective lobby" at the World Conference on Human Rights in Vienna. Some 950 women's organizations from around the world had joined in a coalition to back what they called the Global Campaign for Women's Human Rights. An all-day tribunal on violence against women was held at the Vienna conference, with more than 20 women offering personal testimony about abuse they had suffered from husbands, boyfriends, and fathers, as well as from governments, national armies, and guerrilla groups. Charlotte Bunch, director of the Center for Women's Global Leadership (based at Rutgers University in New Jersey), concluded: "Women are tearing down the wall of silence that has prevented the world from recognizing our human rights" (Flanders, 1993:175; Riding, 1993).

SUMMARY

Worldwide stratification can be seen both in the gap between rich and poor nations and in the inequality within countries around the world. This chapter examines stratification within the world economic system, modernization, the impact of multinational corporations on developing countries, and the distribution of wealth and income in various nations.

1 While the world has 157 billionaires, some 100 million people are homeless.
2 Former colonized nations are kept in a subservient position, subject to foreign domination, through the process of *neocolonialism.*
3 Drawing on the conflict perspective, sociologist Immanuel Wallerstein views the global economic system as divided between nations who control wealth (*core nations*) and those from whom capital is taken (*periphery nations*).
4 Many sociologists are quick to note that terms such as *modernization* and even *development* contain an ethnocentric bias.
5 Conflict theorists argue that *multinational corporations* have a negative social impact on workers in both industrialized and developing nations.
6 The day-to-day impact of the economic backslide in Africa, Latin America, and parts of Asia during the 1980s was tragic.
7 Of the world's advanced industrial economies, Sweden and Japan have the lowest degree of income inequality.
8 Social mobility is especially likely to be high in nations which share a recent history of having received large numbers of immigrants.
9 In contrast to the upper class of the United States, the Brazilian upper class is composed primarily of large landowners and successful immigrant industrialists.
10 Brazil's severe economic troubles have contributed to environmental destruction in the mineral-rich areas surrounding the Amazon River.
11 To many observers, Serbia's policy of "ethnic cleansing" is a blatant violation of people's *human rights.*

CRITICAL THINKING QUESTIONS

1 Analyze the war in the Persian Gulf, drawing on the concepts and issues in the chapter (especially colonialism, neocolonialism, world systems theory, modernization, and multinational corporations).
2 In what ways is the informal economy evident in your college community and in the city or town where you grew up? Drawing on the functionalist, conflict, and interactionist perspectives, analyze the informal economy as you have seen it in these communities.
3 Imagine that you had the opportunity to spend a year in Brazil studying inequality in that nation. How would you draw on the research designs of sociology (surveys, observation, experiments, existing sources) to better understand and document stratification in Brazil?

KEY TERMS

Colonialism The maintenance of political, social, economic, and cultural dominance over a people by a foreign power for an extended period of time. (page 243)
Human rights Universal moral rights belonging to all people because they are human. (264)
Infant mortality rate The number of deaths of infants under 1 year of age per 1000 live births in a given year. (250)

Informal economy Transfers of money, goods, or services that are not reported to the government. (251)

Modernization The far-reaching process by which a society moves from traditional or less developed institutions to those characteristic of more developed societies. (245)

Multinational corporations Commercial organizations which, while headquartered in one country, own or control other corporations and subsidiaries throughout the world. (247)

Neocolonialism Continuing dependence of former colonies on foreign countries. (245)

World systems theory Immanuel Wallerstein's view of the global economic system as divided between certain industrialized nations who control wealth and developing countries who are controlled and exploited. (245)

ADDITIONAL READINGS

Bornschier, Volker, and Christopher Chase-Dunn. *Transnational Corporations and Underdevelopment.* New York: Praeger, 1985. A detailed analysis of the impact of multinational corporations on developing nations.

Braun, Denny. *The Rich Get Richer.* Chicago: Nelson-Hall, 1991. Sociologist Braun looks at growing inequality within the United States, as well as throughout the world, with a special focus on the rise of multinational corporations.

Ferman, Louis A., Stuart Henry, and Michele Hoyman (eds.). *The Informal Economy.* Newbury Park, Calif.: Sage, 1987. Published as the September 1987 issue of the *Annals of the American Academy of Political and Social Science,* this volume provides an overview of the informal economy in both industrial and developing nations.

Fontaine, Pierre-Michel (ed.). *Race, Class, and Power in Brazil.* Los Angeles: UCLA Center for Afro-American Studies, 1986. A collection of essays examining the lives of Black Brazilians.

Simon, John L. *Population and Development in Poor Countries.* Princeton, N.J.: Princeton University Press, 1992.

A collection of essays by a well-known economist, including both theoretical treatments and empirical studies.

Third World Institute (Instituto del Tercer Mundo). *Third World Guide 93/94.* Toronto, Can.: Garamond, 1993. A Third World perspective on developing countries, with a nation-by-nation examination of protest groups, evidence of discrimination, the status of women, and the situation of indigenous peoples.

Tinker, Irene (ed.). *Persistent Inequalities: Women and World Development.* New York: Oxford University Press, 1990. Tinker's anthology offers an overview of past and current debates regarding the role of women in world development and the impact of development on women.

Waring, Marilyn. *If Women Counted: A New Feminist Economics.* San Francisco: Harper and Row, 1988. Waring, a social scientist from New Zealand, considers how women's labor is overlooked in the global economy.

Weigard, Bruce. *Off the Books: A Theory and Critique of the Underground Economy.* Dix Hills, N.Y.: General-Hall, 1992. An examination of the social consequences of people's participation in activities outside the mainstream economy.

The World Bank. *World Development Report.* New York: Oxford University Press. Published annually by the International Bank for Reconstruction and Development (the United Nations agency more commonly referred to as the World Bank), this volume provides a vast array of social and economic indicators regarding world development.

Journals

Among those journals that consider issues of worldwide stratification, uneven development, and universal human rights are *Holocaust and Genocide Studies* (founded in 1987), *Human Rights Quarterly* (1978), *International Journal of Urban and Regional Research* (1976), *International Labor Review* (1921), *Journal of Developing Areas* (1965), *Latin American Research Review* (1956), *Review of Income and Wealth* (1954), and *World Development* (1973).

10

RACIAL AND ETHNIC INEQUALITY

10

RACIAL AND ETHNIC INEQUALITY

MINORITY, RACIAL, AND ETHNIC GROUPS
Minority Groups
Race
   Biological Significance of Race
   Social Significance of Race
Ethnicity

STUDYING RACE AND ETHNICITY
Functionalist Perspective
Conflict Perspective
Interactionist Perspective

PREJUDICE AND DISCRIMINATION
The Structural Component
Discriminatory Behavior
Institutional Discrimination

PATTERNS OF INTERGROUP RELATIONS
Amalgamation
Assimilation
Segregation
Pluralism

RACE AND ETHNICITY IN THE UNITED STATES
Racial Groups
   Black Americans
   Native Americans
   Chinese Americans
   Japanese Americans
   Korean Americans
Ethnic Groups
   Hispanics: Mexican Americans and
     Puerto Ricans
   Jewish Americans
   White Ethnics

SOCIAL POLICY AND RACE AND ETHNICITY: REGULATING IMMIGRATION

BOXES
10-1 Speaking Out: Hispanics as an
     Invisible Minority
10-2 Current Research: Asian Americans
     and the "Model Minority" Stereotype

> Once riding in old Baltimore,
> Heart-filled, head-filled with glee,
> I saw a Baltimorean
> Keep looking straight at me.
> Now I was eight and very small,
> And he was no whit bigger,
> And so I smiled, but he poked out
> His tongue, and called me, "Nigger."
> I saw the whole of Baltimore
> From May until December;
> Of all the things that happened there
> That's all that I remember.
>
> Countee Cullen
> Incident, 1925

LOOKING AHEAD

- In sociological terms, why are Blacks, Native Americans, and Jews considered minority groups?
- Why are stereotypes harmful to members of racial and ethnic minorities?
- How does the Marxist perspective view race relations?
- What types of interracial contact can foster tolerance between dominant and subordinate groups?
- Is it harmful to Asian Americans to view them as a "model minority"?
- What challenges does the United States face from contemporary immigration?

In 1991, Rodney King, a Black construction worker, was beaten by Los Angeles Police Department officers after a high-speed car chase. A shocking videotape, shown repeatedly on television in subsequent months, captured the police administering 56 blows to King in 81 seconds as he lay on the ground. A year later, four White officers were charged in connection with the beatings, but they were found not guilty by a jury of 10 Whites, one Hispanic, and one Asian American. For many Blacks, the acquittal of these officers was an outrageous reminder of the historic persecution of African Americans. Even though White officers had been shown on videotape repeatedly beating a defenseless Black man, they were not initially convicted of a crime, although they were subsequently found guilty of violating King's civil rights.

The jury's verdict touched off rioting in Los Angeles and other cities across the United States. The Los Angeles riots became the nation's worst in the twentieth century, leading to 58 deaths, 2283 injuries, 13,505 arrests, and about 1 billion dollars in property damage. Ironically, the South-Central neighborhood where the most serious disturbances took place borders Watts, the area where rioting had occurred in 1965. As in Watts 27 years earlier, South-Central was shattered by fires and looting. Small businesses owned by Koreans were a particular target, reflecting continuing anger about a light sentence given in 1991 to a Korean grocer who had shot and killed a 15-year-old Black woman in a dispute over a bottle of orange juice (M. Davis, 1992; Kwong, 1992; *Los Angeles Times*, 1992).

Media coverage of the riots was typified by a cover story in *U.S. News and World Report* entitled "Black vs. White." As journalist Peter Kwong (1992:29–32) points out, this overly simplistic view ignores the important role of Koreans and Hispanics in the events in Los Angeles. More than 1800 Korean businesses—many of them groceries and liquor stores—were looted or burned. Together, Korean establishments suffered $347 million in property damage—more than one-third of all such losses from the riots.

Hispanics constitute about half the population of south Los Angeles—although there are no Hispanic elected officials from this area. At least 1000 of those arrested during the disturbances (primarily for violating curfew) were undocumented Hispanic immigrants who were turned over to the Immigration and Naturalization Service for immediate deportation. As for the victims of the riots, more than one-third of those killed were Hispanic. Between 30 and 40 percent of businesses wiped out during the riots were owned by Hispanics, mostly Mexican Americans and Cubans. Yet content analysis of 6000 references to racial and ethnic groups in six major newspapers in the two weeks following the riots revealed that only 11 percent of these references were to Hispanics. Moreover, negative descriptions of Hispanics outnumbered positive descriptions by a five to one ratio (NALEO, 1993).

African Americans, Hispanic Americans, Asian Americans, and many other racial and ethnic minorities in the United States have experienced the often bitter contrast between the "American dream" of freedom, equality, and success and the grim realities of poverty, prejudice, and discrimination. The social definitions of race and ethnicity—like class—affect people's place and status in a stratification system. This is true not only in this country but throughout the world.

By the 1990s, as one result of the successful revolts against communist rule in the Soviet Union and eastern Europe, traditional and long-suppressed ethnic rivalries had once again erupted into open conflict in many areas. The Soviet Union officially dissolved in 1991 along boundaries reflecting its many nationalities, while Yugoslavia's republics entered into a long and bloody civil war. In 1992, Czechoslovakia divided (much more peacefully) along ethnic lines into the Czech and Slovak republics. Protests against mistreatment by dominant groups came from national, racial, and ethnic minorities throughout the region—among them, Hungarians living in Rumania and Turks living in Bulgaria. Moreover, long-standing prejudices against Jews and Romani (better known as Gypsies) were being expressed more openly in many of these nations.

This chapter will focus primarily on the meaning of race and ethnicity in the United States. It will begin by identifying the basic characteristics of a minority group and distinguishing between racial and ethnic groups; then it will consider the functionalist, conflict, and interactionist perspectives on race and ethnicity. The next sections of the chapter will examine the dynamics of prejudice and discrimination and their impact on intergroup relations. Particular attention will then be given to the experiences of racial and ethnic minorities in the United States. Finally, the social policy section will explore the immigration policy of the United States.

MINORITY, RACIAL, AND ETHNIC GROUPS

Sociologists frequently distinguish between racial and ethnic groups. The term *racial group* is used to describe a group which is set apart from others because of obvious physical differences. Whites, Blacks, and Asian Americans are all considered racial groups in the United States. Unlike racial groups, an *ethnic group* is set apart from others primarily because of its national origin or distinctive cultural patterns. In the United States, Puerto Ricans, Jews, and Polish Americans are all categorized as ethnic groups.

Minority Groups

A numerical minority is a group that makes up less than half of some larger population. The population of the United States includes thousands of numerical minorities, including television actors, green-eyed people, tax lawyers, and descendants of the Pilgrims who arrived on the *Mayflower.* How-

Members of a minority group have a strong sense of group solidarity, which develops partly as a result of the prejudice and discrimination they experience. Korean Americans are shown demonstrating after the 1992 riots in Los Angeles.

ever, these numerical minorities are not considered to be minorities in the sociological sense; in fact, the number of people in a group does not necessarily determine its status as a social minority (or dominant group). When sociologists define a minority group, they are primarily concerned with the economic and political power, or powerlessness, of that group. A ***minority group*** is a subordinate group whose members have significantly less control or power over their own lives than the members of a dominant or majority group have over theirs.

Sociologists have identified five basic properties of a minority group—physical or cultural traits, unequal treatment, ascribed status, solidarity, and ingroup marriage (Wagley and Harris, 1958:4–11):

1 Members of a minority group share physical or cultural characteristics that distinguish them from the dominant group. Each society has its own arbitrary standard for determining which characteristics are most important in defining dominant and minority groups.

2 Members of a minority experience unequal treatment and have less power over their lives than members of a dominant group have over theirs. For example, the management of an apartment complex may refuse to rent to African Americans, Hispanics, or Jews. Social inequality may be created or maintained by prejudice, discrimination, segregation, or even extermination.

3 Membership in a minority (or dominant) group is not voluntary; people are born into the group. Thus, race and ethnicity are considered *ascribed* statuses (see Chapter 5).

4 Minority group members have a strong sense of group solidarity. William Graham Sumner, writing in 1906, noted that individuals make distinctions between members of their own group (the *in-group*) and everyone else (the *out-group*). In-groups and out-groups were discussed in Chapter 6. When a group is the object of long-term prejudice and discrimination, the feeling of "us versus them" can and often does become extremely intense.

5 Members of a minority generally marry others from the same group. A member of a dominant group is often unwilling to join a supposedly inferior minority by marrying one of its members. In addition, the minority group's sense of solidarity encourages marriages within the group and discourages marriages to outsiders.

Race

As already suggested, the term *racial group* is reserved for those minorities (and the corresponding dominant groups) set apart from others by obvious physical differences. But what is an "obvious" physical difference? Each society determines which differences are important while ignoring other characteristics that could serve as a basis for social differentiation. In the United States, differences in both skin color and hair color are generally quite obvious. Yet people learn informally that differences in skin color have a dramatic social and political meaning, while differences in hair color are not nearly so socially significant.

When observing skin color, Americans tend to lump people rather casually into such general categories as "Black," "White," and "Asian." More subtle differences in skin color often go unnoticed. However, this is not the case in other societies. Many nations of Central America and South America have color gradients distinguishing people on a continuum from light to dark skin color. African slaves were brought to almost all these countries; these people intermarried, to varying degrees, with each other or with indigenous Indians. Consequently, as noted in Chapter 9, Brazil has approximately 40 racial groupings, while in other countries people may be described as "Mestizo Hondurans," "Mulatto Colombians," or "African Panamanians." Viewed in this light, residents of the United States must recognize that what we see as "obvious" differences are subject to each society's social definitions.

The largest racial minorities in the United States are Blacks (or African Americans), Native Americans, Japanese Americans, Chinese Americans, and other Asian peoples. Information about the population and distribution of racial groups in this country is presented in Table 10-1.

Biological Significance of Race Viewed from a biological perspective, the term *race* would refer to a genetically isolated group with distinctive gene frequencies. It is impossible to scientifically define or identify such a group. Consequently, contrary to popular belief, there are no "pure races." Nor are there physical traits—whether skin color or baldness—that can be used to describe one group to the exclusion of all others. If scientists examine a smear of human blood under a microscope, they cannot tell whether it came from a Chinese or a Navajo, a Hawaiian or an African American.

Migration, exploration, and invasion have further compromised the maintenance of pure races and led to increased racial intermingling. Scientific investigations suggest that the percentage of North American Blacks with White ancestry ranges from 20 percent to as much as 75 percent. Such statistics undermine a fundamental assumption of life in the United States: that we can accurately

TABLE 10-1	Racial and Ethnic Groups in the United States, 1990	
CLASSIFICATION	NUMBER, IN THOUSANDS	PERCENT OF TOTAL POPULATION
Racial groups		
Whites	199,686	80.3
Blacks/African Americans	29,986	12.1
Native Americans, Eskimos, Aleuts	1,959	0.8
Chinese	1,645	0.7
Filipinos	1,407	0.6
Japanese	848	0.3
Asian Indians	815	0.3
Koreans	799	0.3
Vietnamese	615	0.2
Laotians	149	0.1
Cambodians	147	0.1
Ethnic groups		
White ancestry (single or mixed)		
Germans	57,986	23.3
Irish	38,740	15.6
English	32,656	13.1
Italians	14,715	5.9
French	10,321	4.1
Poles	9,366	3.8
Jews	5,935	2.6
Hispanics (or Latinos)	22,354	9.0
Mexican Americans	13,496	5.4
Puerto Ricans	2,728	1.0
Cubans	1,044	0.4
Other	5,086	2.2
Total (all groups)	248,710	

NOTE: Percentages do not total 100 percent, and subheads do not add up to figures in major heads, since overlap between groups exists (e.g., Polish American Jews or people of mixed ancestry, such as Irish and Italian). Therefore, numbers and percentages should be considered approximations. Data on Jews are for 1989.
SOURCE: Bureau of the Census, 1992:24–25; 1993a:18, 51.

categorize individuals as "Black" or "White" (Herskovits, 1930:15; D. Roberts, 1975).

Some people would like to find biological explanations which could help us to understand why certain peoples of the world have come to dominate others (refer back to the discussion of sociobiology in Chapter 4). Given the absence of pure racial groups, there can be no satisfactory biological answers for such social and political questions.

Social Significance of Race One of the most crucial aspects of the relationship between dominant and subordinate groups is the ability of the dominant or majority groups to define a society's values. Sociologist William I. Thomas (1923:41–44), an early critic of theories of racial and gender differences, saw that the "definition of the situation" could mold the personality of the individual. To put it another way, Thomas, writing from the interactionist perspective, observed that people respond not only to the objective features of a situation or person but also to the meaning that situation or person has for them. Thus we can create false images or stereotypes that become real in their consequences. *Stereotypes* are unreliable generalizations about all members of a group that do not recognize individual differences within the group.

In the last 25 years, there has been growing awareness of the power of the mass media to introduce stereotypes into everyday life. As one result, stereotyping of racial and ethnic minorities in Hollywood films, on television, and in Broadway shows has come under increasing fire. For example, in mid-1993 Asian American groups in several cities picketed outside movie theaters showing *Rising Sun*. They charged that the film reinforced traditional "yellow peril" stereotypes concerning Japan and would lead to increasing attacks on Asian Ameri-

cans. Hispanics note that Hollywood has generally presented them as vicious bandits, lazy peasants, or humorous buffoons; the media's treatment of Hispanics is examined in Box 10-1. In a striking example of stereotyping in the print media, *Newsweek* used two photos of African American robbers to illustrate a 1991 article entitled "The Bank Robbery Boom"—even though the article stated that the modern bank robber is "usually White." While the use of stereotyping can promote in-group solidarity, conflict theorists point out that stereotypes contribute to prejudice and thereby assist the subordination of minority groups (Kaplan, 1991:63; Schaefer, 1993:46–49).

In certain situations, we may respond to stereotypes and act on them, with the result that false definitions become accurate. This is known as the *self-fulfilling prophecy*. A person or group is described as having particular characteristics and then begins to display the very traits that were said to exist. In assessing the impact of self-fulfilling prophecies, we can refer back to labeling theory (see Chapter 7), which emphasizes how a person comes to be labeled as deviant and even to accept a self-image of deviance.

Self-fulfilling prophecies can be especially devastating for minority groups (see Figure 10-1). Such groups often find that they are allowed to hold only

FIGURE 10-1 Self-Fulfilling Prophecy

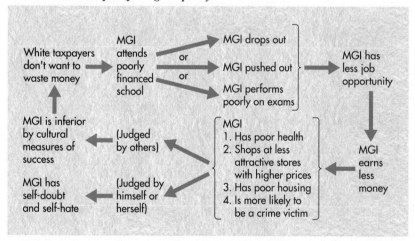

The self-validating effects of definitions made by the dominant group are shown in this figure. A minority-group person attends a poorly financed school and is left unequipped to perform jobs which offer high status and high pay. He or she then gets a low-paying job and must settle for a lifestyle far short of society's standards. Since the person shares these standards, he or she may begin to feel self-doubt and self-hatred. This last aspect of the cycle has been called into question in recent research.

NOTE: MGI stands for "minority group individual." Arrows represent direction of negative cumulative effect.
SOURCE: Schaefer, 1993:19.

BOX 10-1 · SPEAKING OUT

HISPANICS AS AN INVISIBLE MINORITY

The news media and the entertainment industry have traditionally either ignored Hispanics or portrayed them in a negative light. In the following selection, Raul Yzaguirre (1993:11A), president of the National Council of La Raza—a national umbrella organization of 150 groups working for civil rights and economic opportunities for Hispanics—challenges the media to cover the Hispanic community with balance and fairness:

A recent night of television viewing led me to conduct my own totally unscientific survey. As I flipped through the channels, I watched several minutes of an economic-plan discussion on C-SPAN, sat through a couple of newscasts, caught a few glimpses of movies on the premium channels and even glanced at a few sitcoms.

As I watched, the questions grew in my mind. Where are the Hispanics? Are Latinos not interested in or affected by the economy? Are Hispanics not making news? Are we neither talented nor funny?

Then I turned to one of the late-night, "real life" cop shows that are becoming popular. And, finally, I saw some Hispanics! The screen was filled with images of dark, swarthy people with strong accents being arrested for everything from selling drugs to abusing their spouses.

"My God," I thought, "is this what the public thinks about my people?" I slept fitfully that night.

We may be nearly 30 million

Raul Yzaguirre.

Courtesy National Council of La Raza

strong in this country, but you would never know it by watching television or listening to policy debates. America's soon-to-be largest minority is also, to most Americans, its most invisible minority.

Just last month, my own scientific observations were confirmed by a Screen Actors Guild study that showed the almost complete absence of Hispanics in films and on television.

Another study, by the Center for Media and Public Affairs, confirmed the other aspect of my own unscientific survey. It found that the few media portrayals that do exist focus principally on Hispanics as "problems"—as rioters, looters, gang members, drug dealers, criminals or "illegals."

Because the media play such a crucial role in influencing public opinion, this situation has a devastating effect both on the public's perception of Hispanics and on our community's ability to participate effectively in shaping public-policy debates.

Pick any front-burner issue and, in most cases, portrayals of Latinos in the policy process resemble those in the entertainment industry. Hispanics are either absent from the discussion or are negatively portrayed. . . .

All the Hispanic community wants—and deserves—is balance and fairness. For the media, that means programming and news coverage that fully includes Hispanics in positive as well as negative roles.

It means making the effort to include Hispanic spokespersons, not just on bilingual education and immigration, but on issues like the economy and trade policy.

Maybe the next time I do another unscientific television survey, I'll get to see the Hispanic community I know: the doctors, lawyers, farm workers and janitors; the business people struggling to make a payroll and housewives struggling to raise a family; the native-born citizen as well as the recent immigrant; the rich and the poor; the liberal and the conservative.

If nothing else, I'll sleep better at night.

low-paying jobs with little prestige or opportunity for advancement. The rationale of the dominant society is that these members of a minority lack the ability to perform in more important and lucrative positions. Minority group members are then denied the training needed to become scientists, executives, or physicians and are locked into society's inferior jobs. As a result, the false definition has become real: in terms of employment, the minority has become inferior because it was originally defined as inferior and was prevented from achieving equality.

Because of this vicious circle, talented people from minority groups may come to see the worlds of entertainment and professional sports as their only hope for achieving wealth and fame. Thus, it is no accident that successive waves of Irish, Jewish, Italian, Black, and Hispanic performers and athletes have made their mark on our society. Unfortunately, these very successes may convince the dominant group that its original stereotypes are valid—that these are the only areas of society in which minorities can excel. Furthermore, athletics and the arts are well known in our society as highly competitive arenas. For every Gloria Estefan, Michael Jordan, Jose Canseco, or Oprah Winfrey who "makes it," many, many more will end up disappointed (Allport, 1979:189–205; Merton, 1968).

Sociologist Harry Edwards (1984:8–13) agrees that the self-fulfilling prophecy of "innate Black athletic superiority" can have damaging consequences. Edwards points out that although this perception of athletic prowess may cause many African Americans to be channeled into sports, at best, only about 2500 of them currently make a living in professional sports as players, coaches, trainers, team doctors, and executives. In his view, Blacks should no longer put football playbooks ahead of textbooks, and the Black community should abandon its "blind belief in sport as an extraordinary route to social and economic salvation" (see also Gates, 1991).

African Americans and other minorities do not always passively accept harmful stereotypes and self-fulfilling prophecies. In the 1960s and 1970s, many subordinate minorities in the United States rejected traditional definitions and replaced them with feelings of pride, power, and strength. "Black is beautiful" and "Red power" movements among Blacks and Native Americans were efforts to take control of their own lives and self-images. However, although a minority can make a determined effort to redefine a situation and resist stereotypes, the definition that remains most important is the one used by a society's most powerful groups. In this sense, the historic White, Anglo-Saxon, Protestant norms

In the United States, many racial and ethnic minorities hold parades and celebrations to preserve and display their unique cultural and artistic traditions. Shown is a West Indian Day parade in New York City.

of the United States still shape the definitions and stereotypes of racial and ethnic minorities.

Ethnicity

An ethnic group, unlike a racial group, is set apart from others because of its national origin or distinctive cultural patterns. Among the ethnic groups in the United States are peoples referred to collectively as *Hispanics*, such as Puerto Ricans, Mexican Americans, Cubans, and other Latin Americans (refer back to Table 10-1). Other ethnic groups in this country include Jewish, Irish, Polish, Italian, and Norwegian Americans.

The distinction between racial and ethnic minorities is not always clear-cut. Some members of racial minorities, such as Asian Americans, may have significant cultural differences from other groups. At the same time, certain ethnic minorities, such as Hispanics, may have obvious physical differences which set them apart from other residents of the United States.

Despite such problems of categorization, sociologists continue to feel that the distinction between racial groups and ethnic groups is socially significant. In most societies, including the United States, physical differences tend to be more visible than ethnic differences. Partly as a result of this fact, stratification along racial lines is less subject to change than stratification along ethnic lines. Members of an ethnic minority sometimes can, over time, become indistinguishable from the majority—although this process may take generations and may never include all members of the group. By contrast, members of a racial minority find it much more difficult to blend in with the larger society and to gain acceptance from the majority.

STUDYING RACE AND ETHNICITY

Relations among racial and ethnic groups have lent themselves to analysis from the three major perspectives of sociology. Viewing race from the macro level, functionalists observe that racial prejudice and discrimination serve positive functions for dominant groups, whereas conflict theorists see the economic structure as a central factor in the exploitation of minorities. The micro-level analysis of interactionist researchers stresses the manner in which everyday contact between people from different racial and ethnic backgrounds contributes to tolerance or leads to hostility.

Functionalist Perspective

It would seem reasonable to assume that racial bigotry offers no essential benefits for society. Why, then, does it exist? Functionalist theorists, while agreeing that racial hostility is hardly to be admired, point out that it indeed serves positive functions for those practicing discrimination.

Anthropologist Manning Nash (1962) has identified three functions that racially prejudiced beliefs have for the dominant group. First, such views provide a moral justification for maintaining an unequal society that routinely deprives a minority of its rights and privileges. Southern Whites justified slavery by believing that Africans were physically and spiritually subhuman and devoid of souls (Hoebel, 1949:85–86). Second, racist beliefs discourage the subordinate minority from attempting to question its lowly status, since to do so is to question the very foundations of society. Finally, racial myths encourage support for the existing order by introducing the argument that if there were any major societal change (such as an end to discrimination), the minority would experience greater poverty and the majority would see its standard of living lowered. As a result, Nash suggests, racial prejudice grows when a society's value system (for example, that underlying a colonial empire or a regime perpetuating slavery) is being threatened.

Although racial prejudice and discrimination may serve the interests of the powerful, such unequal treatment can also be dysfunctional to a society and even to its dominant group. Sociologist Arnold Rose (1951:19–24) outlines four dysfunctions associated with racism:

1 A society which practices discrimination fails to use the resources of all individuals. Discrimination limits the search for talent and leadership to the dominant group.
2 Discrimination aggravates social problems such as poverty, delinquency, and crime and places the financial burden to alleviate these problems on the dominant group.

3 Society must invest a good deal of time and money to defend its barriers to full participation of all members.

4 Goodwill and friendly diplomatic relations between nations are often undercut by racial prejudice and discrimination.

Conflict Perspective

Conflict theorists would certainly agree with Arnold Rose that racial prejudice and discrimination have many harmful consequences for society. Sociologists such as Oliver Cox (1948) and Robert Blauner (1972) have used the **exploitation theory** (or *Marxist class theory*) to explain the basis of racial subordination in the United States. As we saw in Chapter 8, Karl Marx viewed the exploitation of the lower class as a basic part of the capitalist economic system. Under a Marxist approach, racism keeps minorities in low-paying jobs, thereby supplying the capitalist ruling class with a pool of cheap labor. Moreover, by forcing racial minorities to accept low wages, capitalists can restrict the wages of *all* members of the proletariat. Workers from the dominant group who demand higher wages can always be replaced by minorities who have no choice but to accept low-paying jobs (O. Cox, 1976; H. Hunter and Abraham, 1987; C. Johnson, 1939).

This Marxist perspective seems persuasive in a number of instances. Japanese Americans were the object of little prejudice until they began to enter jobs that brought them into competition with Whites. The movement to keep Chinese immigrants out of the United States became most fervent during the latter half of the nineteenth century, when Chinese and Whites fought over dwindling work opportunities. Both the enslavement of Blacks and the removal westward of Native Americans were, to a significant extent, economically motivated (McWilliams, 1951:144–150).

However, though some examples support the exploitation theory of race relations, it is too limited to explain prejudice in its many forms. Not all minority groups have been economically exploited to the same extent. In addition, many groups (among them the Quakers and Mormons) have been victimized by prejudice for reasons other than economic ones. Still, as Gordon Allport (1979:210) concludes, the exploitation theory correctly "points a sure finger at one of the factors involved in preju-

dice, . . . rationalized self-interest of the upper classes."

Interactionist Perspective

A Black woman is transferred from a job on an assembly line to a similar position working next to a White man. At first, he is patronizing, assuming she must be incompetent. She is cold and resentful; even when she needs assistance, she refuses to admit it. After a week, the growing tension between the two leads to a bitter quarrel. Yet, over time, each slowly comes to appreciate the other's strengths and talents. A year after they begin working together, these two workers become respectful friends. This is an example of what interactionists call the *contact hypothesis* in action.

The **contact hypothesis** states that interracial contact of people with equal status in cooperative circumstances will cause them to become less prejudiced and to abandon previous stereotypes. The factors of *equal status* and a *pleasant, noncompetitive atmosphere* must be underscored. In the example above, if the two workers had been competing for one vacancy as a supervisor, the racial hostility between them might have worsened (Allport, 1979: 261–282; Schaefer, 1993:63–64).

As African Americans and other minorities slowly gain access to better-paying and more responsible jobs in the United States, the contact hypothesis may take on even greater significance. The trend in our society is toward increasing contact between individuals from dominant and subordinate groups. This may be one hope of eliminating—or at least reducing—racial and ethnic stereotyping and prejudice.

PREJUDICE AND DISCRIMINATION

False definitions of individuals and groups are perpetuated by prejudice. **Prejudice** is a negative attitude toward an entire category of people, often an ethnic or racial minority. If you resent your roommate because he or she is sloppy, you are not necessarily guilty of prejudice. However, if you immediately stereotype your roommate on the basis of such characteristics as race, ethnicity, or religion, that is a form of prejudice.

In recent years, college campuses across the

In recent years, college campuses across the United States have been the scene of bias-related incidents. At the same time, racial and ethnic minorities on campus have spoken out against racism and in support of a multicultural education. In this photograph, Mexican American students at the University of California at Los Angeles are shown in a protest aimed at establishing a Chicano Studies program.

United States have been the scene of bias-related incidents. Student-run newspapers and radio stations have ridiculed racial and ethnic minorities; threatening literature has been stuffed under the doors of minority students; graffiti endorsing the views of White supremacist organizations such as the Ku Klux Klan have been scrawled on university walls. In some cases, there have even been violent clashes between groups of White and Black students. These distressing incidents serve as a reminder that prejudice is evident among both educated and uneducated members of our society (Bunzel, 1992; Hively, 1990).

Prejudice can result from *ethnocentrism*—the tendency to assume that one's culture and way of life are superior to all others (see Chapter 3). Ethnocentric people judge other cultures by the standards of their own group, which leads quite easily to prejudice against cultures viewed as inferior.

One important and widespread form of prejudice is *racism,* the belief that one race is supreme and all others are innately inferior. When racism prevails in a society, members of subordinate groups generally experience prejudice, discrimination, and exploitation. In 1990, as concern mounted about racist attacks in the United States, Congress passed and President George Bush signed into law the Hate Crimes Statistics Act. This law directs the Department of Justice to gather data on crimes motivated by the victim's race, religion, ethnicity, or sexual orientation. In 1992, a total of 4755 hate crimes were reported to authorities, an increase of

4 percent over the previous year. Some 62 percent of these crimes involved racial bias (with African Americans the targets in more than half of such cases), while 19 percent reflected religious bias, 9 percent ethnic bias, and 9 percent bias based on sexual orientation (Mauro, 1993a).

The Structural Component

While cultural factors are important contributors to prejudice, structural factors must also be given serious consideration. Societies develop social norms that dictate—for example—not only what foods are desirable (or forbidden), but also which racial and ethnic groups are to be favored (or despised). These norms are often reinforced by the social institutions of a society's social structure, such as government, religion, education, and the economy.

Social psychologist Thomas Pettigrew (1981) collected data that substantiated the importance of such social norms in encouraging or discouraging prejudice. Pettigrew found that Whites in the southern states were more anti-Black than Whites in the northern states and that Whites in the United States were not so prejudiced against Blacks as were Whites in the Republic of South Africa. He concluded that structural factors explain differences in the levels of prejudice between these regions and countries.

A more recent study by psychologist J. Louw-Potgieter (1988) supports this view. Typically, personality studies have maintained that White South

Africans rear their children in a strict, disciplined, and patriarchal manner. These studies tend to ascribe authoritarianism particularly to the Afrikaners, who are the leaders of government and the architects of rule by the nation's White minority. Yet Louw-Potgieter finds that empirical research does not support these assumptions. Indeed, previous work in South Africa shows evidence in one sample that Black students are more authoritarian than White students (Heaven and Niewoudt, 1981).

Louw-Potgieter points to studies showing intergroup variability in the levels of prejudice that can be explained only by the kinds of structural variables first described by Pettigrew. Consequently, in explaining prejudice in South Africa, both personality and structural factors need to be considered. The structural factors identified by Louw-Potgieter include group membership, group position, peer pressure, ideology, and the media.

The personality and structural approaches to prejudice should not be viewed as mutually exclusive. Social circumstances provide cues for a person's attitudes; personality determines the extent to which people follow social cues and the likelihood that they will encourage others to do the same through social interaction. Societal norms may promote or deter tolerance; personality traits suggest the degree to which a person will conform to norms of intolerance (Allport, 1962).

Discriminatory Behavior

The biased attitudes of the prejudiced person often lead to discriminatory behavior. *Discrimination* is the process of denying opportunities and equal rights to individuals and groups because of prejudice or other arbitrary reasons. Imagine that a White corporate president with a stereotyped view of Asian Americans has an executive position to fill. The most qualified candidate for the job is a Vietnamese American. If the president refuses to hire this candidate and instead selects an inferior White candidate, he or she is engaging in an act of racial discrimination.

Prejudiced *attitudes* should not be equated with discriminatory *behavior*. Although the two are generally related, they are not identical, and either condition can be present without the other. For example, a prejudiced person does not always act on his or her biases. In the situation described above, the White president might choose—despite his or her stereotypes—to hire the Vietnamese American. This would be prejudice without discrimination. On the other hand, a White corporate president with a completely respectful view of Vietnamese Americans might refuse to hire them for executive posts out of fear that biased clients would take their business elsewhere. In this case, the president's action would constitute discrimination without prejudice.

Institutional Discrimination

Discrimination is practiced not only by individuals in one-to-one encounters but also by institutions in their daily operations. Social scientists are particularly concerned with the ways in which structural factors such as employment, housing, health care, and government operations maintain the social significance of race and ethnicity. *Institutional discrimination* refers to the denial of opportunities and equal rights to individuals or groups which results from the normal operations of a society.

Institutional discrimination continuously imposes more hindrances on—and awards fewer benefits to—certain racial and ethnic groups than it does others. In some cases, even ostensibly neutral institutional standards can turn out to have discriminatory effects. In 1992, African American students at a midwestern state university protested a policy under which fraternities and sororities who wished to use campus facilities for a dance were required to post $150 security deposits to cover possible damages. The Black students complained that this policy had a discriminatory impact on minority student organizations. Campus police countered that the university's policy applied to *all* student groups interested in using these facilities. However, since overwhelmingly White fraternities and sororities at the school had their own houses that they used for dances, the policy indeed affected only African American and other minority organizations.

The U.S. Commission on Civil Rights (1981: 9–10) has identified various forms of institutional discrimination, including:

- Rules requiring that only English be spoken at a place of work, even when it is not a business necessity to restrict the use of other languages
- Preferences shown by law and medical schools in

the admission of children of wealthy and influential alumni, nearly all of whom are White
• Restrictive employment-leave policies, coupled with prohibitions on part-time work, that make it difficult for the heads of single-parent families (most of whom are women) to obtain and keep jobs

The social policy section on affirmative action in Chapter 15 will examine legal prohibitions against institutional discrimination.

Discrimination in the United States has proved difficult to eradicate. The 1960s saw the passage of many pioneering civil rights laws, including the landmark 1964 Civil Rights Act (which prohibits discrimination in public accommodations and publicly owned facilities on the basis of race, color, creed, national origin, and gender). In two important rulings in 1987, the Supreme Court held that federal prohibitions against racial discrimination protect members of all ethnic minorities—including Hispanics, Jews, and Arab Americans—even though they may be considered White. Yet discriminatory practices continue to pervade nearly all areas of life in the United States today.

In part, this is because—as Manning Nash's functionalist analysis suggests—various individuals and groups actually *benefit* from racial and ethnic discrimination in terms of money, status, and influence. Discrimination permits members of the majority to enhance their wealth, power, and prestige at the expense of others. Less qualified people are hired and promoted simply because they are members of the dominant group. Such individuals and groups will not surrender these advantages easily.

A member of a racial or ethnic minority in the United States is likely to face various forms of prejudice and discrimination from dominant group members and from important institutions of our society. This is the underlying and painful context of intergroup relations in this country.

PATTERNS OF INTERGROUP RELATIONS

Racial and ethnic groups can relate to one another in a wide variety of desirable and undesirable ways, ranging from friendships and intermarriages that require mutual approval to behaviors imposed on the subordinate group by the dominant group.

Undesirable patterns include *genocide*—the deliberate, systematic killing of an entire people or nation. This term has been used in reference to the killing of 1 million Armenians by Turkey beginning in 1915 (Melson, 1986:64–66). It is most commonly applied to Nazi Germany's extermination of 6 million European Jews, as well as members of other ethnic minorities, during World War II. However, the term *genocide* is also appropriate in describing the United States' policies toward Native Americans in the nineteenth century. In 1800, the Native American (or American Indian) population of the United States was about 600,000; by 1850, it had been reduced to 250,000 through warfare with the cavalry, disease, and forced relocation to inhospitable environments.

The *expulsion* of a people is another extreme means of acting out racial or ethnic prejudice. In 1979, Vietnam expelled nearly 1 million ethnic Chinese, partly as a result of centuries of hostility between Vietnam and neighboring China. These Chinese "boat people" were abruptly eliminated as a minority within Vietnamese society. In a more recent example of expulsion (which had aspects of genocide), Serbian forces began a program of "ethnic cleansing" in 1991 in the newly independent states of Bosnia and Herzegovina. Throughout the former nation of Yugoslavia, the Serbs drove more than 1 million Croats and Muslims from their homes. Some were tortured and killed, others abused and terrorized, in an attempt to "purify" the land for the remaining ethnic Serbs (refer back to Chapter 9).

There are four identifiable patterns that describe typical intergroup relations as they occur in North America and throughout the world: (1) amalgamation, (2) assimilation, (3) segregation, and (4) pluralism. Each pattern defines the dominant group's actions and the minority group's responses. Intergroup relations are rarely restricted to only one of the four patterns, although invariably one does tend to dominate. Therefore, these patterns should be viewed primarily as ideal types.

Amalgamation

Amalgamation describes the end result when a majority group and a minority group combine to form a new group. Through intermarriage over several generations, various groups in the society combine

Shown is a "Shogun Santa" in the Little Tokyo neighborhood of Los Angeles. The popularity of this "Shogun Santa" can be viewed as an example of Japanese Americans' assimilation into the norms and values of the dominant culture of the United States.

to form a new group. This can be expressed as A + B + C = D, where A, B, and C represent different groups present in a society, and D signifies the end result, a unique cultural-racial group unlike any of the initial groups (W. Newman, 1973).

The belief in the United States as a "melting pot" became very compelling in the first part of the twentieth century, particularly since it suggested that the nation had an almost divine mission to amalgamate various groups into one people. However, in actuality many residents were not willing to have Native Americans, Jews, African Americans, Asian Americans, and Irish Roman Catholics as a part of the melting pot. Therefore, this pattern does not adequately describe dominant-subordinate relations existing in the United States.

Assimilation

Many Hindus in India complain about Indian citizens who copy the traditions and customs of the British. In Australia, Aborigines who have become part of the dominant society refuse to acknowledge their darker-skinned grandparents on the street. In the United States, there are Italian Americans, Polish Americans, Hispanics, and Jews who have changed their ethnic-sounding family names to names typically found among White, Protestant families.

Assimilation is the process by which a person forsakes his or her own cultural tradition to become part of a different culture. Generally, it is practiced by a minority group member who wants to conform to the standards of the dominant group. Assimilation can be described as an ideology in which A + B + C = A. The majority A dominates in such a way that members of minorities B and C imitate A and attempt to become indistinguishable from the dominant group (W. Newman, 1973).

Assimilation can strike at the very roots of a person's identity as he or she seeks to gain full acceptance as an "American." Hence, Alphonso D'Abruzzo changed his name to Alan Alda and Cherilyn LaPiere Sarkisian shortened hers to Cher. (This process is not unique to the United States: Joyce Frankenberg of Great Britain changed her name to Jane Seymour.) Despite such efforts, assimilation does not necessarily bring acceptance for the minority group individual. A Chinese American may speak flawless English, go faithfully to a Protestant church, and know the names of all members of the Baseball Hall of Fame. Yet he or she is still *seen* as different and may therefore be rejected as a business associate, a neighbor, or a marriage partner.

Segregation

Segregation refers to the physical separation of two groups of people in terms of residence, workplace, and social functions. Generally, it is imposed by a dominant group on a minority group. However, segregation is rarely complete; intergroup contact inevitably occurs even in the most segregated societies.

In the 1990s, the Republic of South Africa finally began to lift the severe restrictions on the movement of Blacks and other non-Whites that had been historically enforced through a wide-ranging system of segregation known as **aparteid.** Apartheid has involved many forms of segregation, including the creation of homelands where Blacks are expected to live. Moreover, as of 1993, Blacks were still not allowed to vote in elections for the South African parliament. From a conflict perspective, apartheid can perhaps best be understood as a twentieth-century effort to reestablish the form of race relations typified by the master-slave relationship.

South Africa is far from the only country in which segregation is common. Housing practices in the United States have often forced subordinate racial and ethnic groups into certain neighborhoods, usually undesirable ones. In addition, members of a minority group may voluntarily seek to separate themselves from the dominant majority because they fear reprisals. This is not, however, the primary factor contributing to segregation. The central causes of residential segregation in the United States appear to be the prejudices of Whites and the resulting discriminatory practices in the housing and lending markets. Data consistently show that Blacks, Hispanics, and (to a somewhat lesser extent) Asians face segregation in the nation's metropolitan areas. Such housing segregation is evident around the world: studies in Sweden, for example, document that migrants from Chile, Greece, and Turkey are confined to segregated areas of Swedish cities (Andersson-Brolin, 1988; Doig et al., 1993).

Pluralism

In a pluralistic society, a subordinate group will not have to forsake its lifestyle and traditions. **Pluralism** is based on mutual respect between various groups in a society for one another's cultures. It allows a minority group to express its own culture and still to participate without prejudice in the larger society. Earlier, amalgamation was described as A + B + C = D, and assimilation as A + B + C = A. Using this same approach, we can conceive of pluralism as A + B + C = A + B + C. All the groups are able to coexist in the same society (W. Newman, 1973).

In the United States, pluralism is more of an ideal than a reality. There are distinct instances of pluralism: the ethnic neighborhoods in major cities, such as Koreatown, Little Tokyo, Andersonville (Swedish Americans), and Spanish Harlem. Yet there are also limits to such cultural freedom. In order to survive, a society must promote a certain consensus among its members regarding basic ideals, values, and beliefs. Thus, if a Rumanian migrating to the United States wants to move up the occupational ladder, he or she cannot avoid learning the English language.

Several authors argue persuasively that Switzerland exemplifies a modern pluralistic state. The absence both of a national language and of a dominant religious faith leads to a tolerance for cultural diversity. In addition, various political devices have

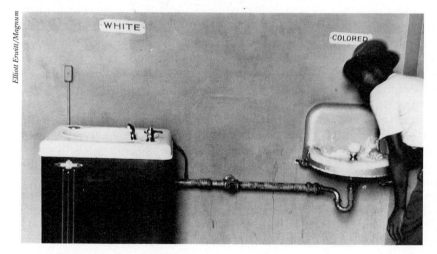

Elliott Erwitt/Magnum

When segregation was common in the southern states, "Jim Crow" laws enforced official segregation of the races. In a blatant example of institutional discrimination in North Carolina in 1950, Blacks were not allowed to use a water fountain reserved for Whites. Instead, Blacks had to drink out of a nearby sink.

been adopted to safeguard the interests of ethnic groups in a way that has no parallel in the United States. By contrast, Great Britain has found it difficult to achieve cultural pluralism in a multiracial society. East Indians, Pakistanis, and Blacks from the Caribbean and Africa are experiencing prejudice and discrimination within the dominant White British society. There is increasing pressure to cut off all Asian and Black immigration and to expel those non-Whites currently living in Britain.

RACE AND ETHNICITY IN THE UNITED STATES

Few societies have a more diverse population than the United States does; the nation is truly a multiracial, multiethnic society. Of course, this has not always been true. The different groups listed in Table 10-1 have come to the United States as a result of immigration, colonialism, and, in the case of Blacks, the institution of slavery.

Racial Groups

The largest racial minorities in the United States include Black Americans, Native Americans, Chinese Americans, Japanese Americans, and Korean Americans.

Black Americans   "I am an invisible man," wrote Black author Ralph Ellison in his novel *Invisible Man* (1952:3). "I am a man of substance, of flesh and bone, fiber and liquids—and I might even be said to possess a mind. I am invisible, understand, simply because people refuse to see me."

Over four decades later, many Blacks (or African Americans) still feel invisible. Despite their large numbers, African Americans have long been treated as second-class citizens. Currently, by the standards of the federal government, nearly 1 out of every 3 Blacks—as opposed to 1 out of every 9 Whites—is poor (Bureau of the Census, 1993a:469).

Contemporary institutional discrimination and individual prejudice against African Americans are rooted in the history of slavery in the United States. Even in bondage, the Africans were forced to assimilate and were stripped of much of their African tribal heritage. Yet the destruction of African cultures was not complete; some aspects survived in oral literature, religious customs, and music. Black resistance to slavery included many slave revolts, such as those led by Denmark Vesey in South Carolina in 1822 and Nat Turner in Virginia in 1831. Still, most Blacks remained subject to the arbitrary and often cruel actions of their White owners (Du Bois, 1909; Herskovits, 1941, 1943).

The end of the Civil War did not bring genuine freedom and equality for Blacks. The "Jim Crow" laws of the south, which were designed to enforce official segregation, were upheld as constitutional by the Supreme Court in 1896. In addition, Blacks faced the danger of lynching campaigns, often led by the Ku Klux Klan, during the late nineteenth and early twentieth centuries. From a conflict perspective, the dominance of Whites was maintained formally through legalized segregation and maintained informally by means of vigilante terror and violence (Franklin and Moss, 1988).

A turning point in the struggle for Black equality came in the unanimous Supreme Court decision in the 1954 case of *Brown v. Board of Education of Topeka, Kansas.* The Court outlawed segregation of public school students, ruling that "separate educational facilities are inherently unequal." In the wake of the *Brown* decision, there was a surge of activism on behalf of Black civil rights, including boycotts of segregated bus companies and sit-ins at restaurants and lunch counters which refused to serve Blacks.

During the decade of the 1960s, a vast civil rights movement emerged, with many competing factions and strategies for change. The Southern Christian Leadership Conference (SCLC), founded by Dr. Martin Luther King, Jr., used nonviolent civil disobedience to oppose segregation. The National Association for the Advancement of Colored People (NAACP) favored use of the courts to press for equality for African Americans. But many younger Black leaders, most notably Malcolm X, turned toward an ideology of Black power. Proponents of **Black power** rejected the goal of assimilation into White, middle-class society. They defended the beauty and dignity of Black and African cultures and supported the creation of Black-controlled political and economic institutions (Carmichael and Hamilton, 1967).

Although numerous courageous actions have

During the 1950s and 1960s, Blacks were inspired by the leadership of Dr. Martin Luther King, Jr., who led numerous boycotts and marches on behalf of civil rights. More recently, Blacks have been inspired by Nelson Mandela, leader of the African National Congress. Mandela, who spent almost 28 years in South African prisons, was released in 1990 and toured the United States later that year.

taken place to achieve Black civil rights, Black and White America are still separate, still unequal. From birth to death, Blacks suffer in terms of the life chances described in Chapter 8. Life remains quite difficult for millions of poor Blacks, who must attempt to survive in ghetto areas shattered by high unemployment and abandoned housing. The economic position of Blacks is shown in Table 10-2. As the table illustrates, the median income of Blacks is only 57 percent that of Whites, and the unemployment rate among Blacks is more than twice that of Whites (Bennett, 1993).

The economic position of African American women and their children is particularly critical. Two-thirds of households headed by Black females are below the poverty line. Economist Bernard Anderson of the Rockefeller Foundation observes: "You cannot discuss Black poverty without discussing the dreadful condition of life and opportunity among Black women who are poor and raising children" (Bennett, 1993:68; Noble, 1984:E20).

There have been economic gains for *some* Blacks—especially middle-class Blacks—over the last 35 years. For example, data compiled by the Department of Labor show that Blacks in management areas of the labor market increased nationally from 2.4 percent of the total in 1958 to 6.3 percent in 1991. Yet African Americans still represent only 4 percent or less of all physicians, engineers, scientists, lawyers, judges, and marketing and financial managers. Moreover, with regard to an area that is especially important for developing role models, Blacks and Hispanics together account for less than 7.3 percent of all editors and reporters in the United States (Bureau of the Census, 1992:392).

In many respects, the civil rights movement of the 1960s left institutionalized discrimination against Blacks untouched. Consequently, in the 1980s, Black leaders worked to mobilize Black political power as a force for social change. Between 1969 and 1986, the number of African American elected officials increased by more than fivefold (Joint Center for Political Studies, 1992).

Native Americans There are approximately 2 million Native Americans (or American Indians). They represent a diverse array of cultures, distinguishable by language, family organization, religion, and livelihood. To the outsiders who came to the United States—European settlers and their descendants—the native people came to be known as "American Indians." By the time that the Bureau of Indian Affairs (BIA) was organized as part of the *War* Department in 1824, Indian-White relations had already included three centuries of mutual misunderstanding (Berg, 1975). As we saw earlier, many bloody wars took place during the nineteenth century in which a significant part of the nation's Indian population was wiped out. By the end of the nineteenth century, schools for Indians operated by the BIA or church missions prohibited the practice of Native American cultures. Yet such schools did little to make the children effective competitors in White society.

Today, Native Americans are an impoverished people; life is difficult, whether they live in cities or on the reservations. For example, the death rate of Navajo babies over 18 weeks old is 2 times that of the overall population of the United States. One Native American teenager in six has attempted sui-

TABLE 10-2	Relative Economic Positions of Blacks and Whites, 1991–1992		
CHARACTERISTIC	BLACKS	WHITES	RATIO, BLACK TO WHITE
Four-year college education, people 25 and over	12%	22%	.55
Median family money income	$21,548	$37,782	.57
Unemployment rate	14.1%	7.4%	1.91
People below the poverty line	32.7%	11.3%	2.84

SOURCE: Bennett, 1993:8–9, 12, 16.

Despite some progress among Blacks in the 1960s and 1970s, there remains a wide gap in the economic positions of African Americans and Whites in the United States.

cide—a rate four times higher than the rate for other teenagers. In 1987, the National Urban Indian Council estimated that 60 to 80 percent of Native Americans living in cities were unemployed (Giago and Illoway, 1982; D. Martin, 1987:46; *New York Times,* 1992b:D24).

In 1972, a regional director of the Commission on Civil Rights characterized government policy toward American Indians as "assimilate—or starve!" Native Americans who choose to abandon all vestiges of their tribal cultures may escape certain forms of prejudice. Native Americans who remain on the reservation and cherish their cultural heritage will suffer the consequences of their choice (Muskrat, 1972).

Nevertheless, an increasing number of people in the United States are openly claiming an identity as Native American. Since 1960, the federal government's count of Native Americans has tripled, to an estimated 1.8 million. According to the 1990 census, there has been a 38 percent increase in Native Americans over the last 10 years. Demographers believe that more and more Native Americans who previously concealed their identity are no longer pretending to be White. Russell Thornton, a sociologist and member of the Cherokee nation of Oklahoma, notes: "There were many people who were ashamed of their Indian past, so they hid it." But, today, many Indian tribes have reported sharp increases in applications for membership, and there has been a noticeable rise in participation in Native American cultural events (D. Johnson, 1991).

Native American activists have bitterly protested the mistreatment of their people in the United States. The latest battleground—not only in the United States, but also in Brazil and other societies—has been land and natural resources. Reservations typically contain a wealth of resources. In the past, Indian tribes have lacked the technical knowledge to negotiate beneficial agreements successfully with private corporations; when they had such ability, the federal government often stepped in and made the final agreements more favorable to corporations than to residents of the reservations. More recently, however, a coalition of Native American tribes has had impressive results in its bargaining efforts. An Atlantic Richfield Company (ARCO) offer of $300,000 for an oil pipeline right-of-way on a Navajo reservation was converted

By Daniel M. Wasserman. © 1992 Boston Globe. Distributed by Los Angeles Times Syndicate. Reprinted with permission.

The riots in Los Angeles and other cities following the acquittal of four White police officers in the videotaped beating of Black construction worker Rodney King reminded people that the nation's historic racial problems have not been resolved.

through skillful negotiating into a contract that will bring the tribe $78 million over 20 years (Schaefer, 1993:179–181).

Chinese Americans   Unlike African slaves and Native Americans, the Chinese were initially encouraged to immigrate to the United States. From 1850 to 1880, over 200,000 Chinese immigrated to this country, lured by job opportunities created by the discovery of gold. However, as employment possibilities decreased and competition for mining grew, the Chinese became the target of a bitter campaign to limit their numbers and restrict their rights. Chinese laborers were exploited, then discarded.

In 1882 Congress enacted the Chinese Exclusion Act, which prevented Chinese immigration and even forbade Chinese in the United States to send for their families. As a result, there was a steady decline in the Chinese population until after World War II. More recently, the descendants of the nineteenth-century immigrants have been joined by a new influx from Hong Kong and Taiwan. The groups of immigrants sometimes form sharp contrasts in their degree of assimilation, desire to live in Chinatowns, and feelings about this country's relations with the People's Republic of China (Kwong and Lum, 1988).

There are currently about 1.65 million Chinese Americans in the United States. Some Chinese Americans have entered lucrative occupations. This has led to the popular concept that the strides made by Chinese Americans (and other Asian Americans) constitute a success story. We examine the consequences of this "model minority" image in Box 10-2.

Many Chinese immigrants struggle to survive under living and working conditions that belie the "model minority" stereotype. New York City's Chinatown district is filled with illegal sweatshops in which recent immigrants—many of them Chinese women—work for minimal wages. Even in "legal" factories in the garment industry, hours are long and rewards are limited. A seamstress typically works 11 hours per day, six days a week, and earns about $10,000 a year. Other workers, such as hemmers and cutters, earn only $5000 per year (Lum and Kwong, 1989).

Japanese Americans There are approximately 800,000 Japanese Americans in the United States. As a people, they are relatively recent arrivals to this nation. In 1880 there were only 148 Japanese in the United States, but by 1920 there were over 110,000. The early Japanese immigrants—who are called the *Issei*—were usually males seeking employment opportunities. Along with Chinese immigrants, they were seen as a "yellow peril" by many Whites, and they were subjected to widespread prejudice and discrimination.

In 1941, the attack on Pearl Harbor by Japan—by then allied with Hitler's Germany—had severe repercussions for Japanese Americans. The federal government decreed that all Japanese Americans on the west coast must leave their homes and report to "evacuation camps." They became, in effect, scapegoats for the anger that other people in the United States felt concerning Japan's role in World War II. By August 1943, in an unprecedented application of guilt by virtue of ancestry, 113,000 Japanese Americans were forced to live in hastily built camps (Hosokawa, 1969).

Financially, the Federal Reserve Board placed the losses entailed by evacuation for Japanese Americans at nearly half a billion dollars, or more than $4500 per person. Accounting for inflation, this figure represents a loss of about $27,000 per person today. Moreover, the psychological effect on these citizens—including the humiliation of being la-

Shown is Gene Sogioka's watercolor, "FBI Takes Father Away." Born in California, Sogioka worked as a background artist for Walt Disney studios and taught art part-time. During World War II, he was taken (along with his wife Mini and their very young daughter) to an evacuation camp for Japanese Americans in Poston, Arizona. The camp was located on a deserted Indian reservation near the Colorado River. Sogioka was later hired by the wartime Bureau of Sociological Research to document the lives of the confined Japanese Americans through his artwork (Gesensway and Roseman, 1987:166).

BOX 10-2 · CURRENT RESEARCH

ASIAN AMERICANS AND THE "MODEL MINORITY" STEREOTYPE

It is commonly believed that Asian Americans constitute a model or ideal minority group, supposedly because, despite past suffering from prejudice and discrimination, they have succeeded economically, socially, and educationally without resorting to political and violent confrontations with Whites. Some observers see the existence of a model minority as a reaffirmation that anyone can get ahead in the United States with talent and hard work.

Indeed, there is an implicit critique of Blacks, Hispanics, and others for failing to succeed as well as the model minority has. Viewed from a conflict perspective, this becomes yet another instance of "blaming the victim" (refer back to Box 8-2 on page 227), for the hidden allegation is that any minorities who have been less successful than Asian Americans are completely responsible for their own failures. Proponents of the model minority view add that because Asian Americans have achieved success, they have ceased to be a disadvantaged minority (Hurh and Kim, 1989).

The concept of a model minority ignores the diversity among Asian Americans: there are rich and poor Japanese Americans, rich and poor Filipino Americans, and so forth. Moreover, even when certain Asian Americans are clustered at the higher-paying end of the stratification system, there may nevertheless be limits on how far they can advance. A study conducted in 1988 showed that only 8 percent of Asian Americans were classified as "officials" and "managers," compared with 12 percent for all groups (Takaki, 1990).

The dramatic success of Asian Americans in the educational system has undoubtedly contributed to the model minority stereotype. In comparison with their numbers in the population of the United States, Asian Americans are overrepresented by far as students in the nation's most prestigious public and private universities. Their success can be attributed, in part, to the belief in many Asian cultures in the value of education, family pressures to succeed, and the desire to use academic achievement as a means of escaping discrimination.

Even the positive stereotype of Asian American students as "academic stars" can be dysfunctional. Asian Americans who do only modestly well in school may face criticism from parents or teachers for their failure to conform to the "whiz kid" image. In fact, despite the model minority label, the high school dropout rate for Asian Americans is increasing rapidly. California's special program for low-income, academically disadvantaged students has a 30 percent Asian American clientele, and the proportion of Asian students in the program is on the rise (Tachibana, 1990).

A study of the California state university system, released in 1991, casts further doubt on the model minority stereotype of Asian Americans. According to the report, while Asian Americans are often viewed as successful overachievers, they suffer from unrecognized and overlooked needs, discomfort, and harassment on campus—as well as from a shortage of Asian faculty and staff members to whom they can turn for support. The report noted that an "alarming number" of Asian American students appear to be experiencing intense stress and alienation—problems which have often been "exacerbated by racial harassment" (Ohnuma, 1991: 5; Takagi, 1993).

Ben Fong-Torres (1986:7) worries that while reports of successes achieved by Asian Americans may inspire pride within this minority, they may also intensify fear and envy in the dominant White majority and even in other minorities. Combined with resentment about the growing economic dominance of Japan, such jealousy may contribute not only to racial slurs and biases against Asian Americans but to violent attacks against this identifiable minority.

Viewed from a conflict perspective, the model minority stereotype is likely to provoke further prejudice and discrimination against a racial minority quite easily viewed as "different." Full social acceptance of Asian Americans may be hindered if they are resented for becoming "too successful too fast." Ginger Lew, a Washington attorney and former State Department official, concludes that the "'model minority' myth is just that. It's not true in terms of income or status. Stereotypes, whether positive or negative, are a disservice to the community" (Commission on Civil Rights, 1992; Oxnam, 1986:89, 92; Schaefer, 1993:340–350).

beled as "disloyal"—was immeasurable. Eventually, the Japanese born in the United States, the *Nisei,* were allowed to enlist in the Army and serve in a segregated combat unit in Europe. Others resettled in the east and midwest to work in factories.

In 1983, the federal Commission on Wartime Relocation and Internment of Civilians recommended government payments to all surviving Japanese Americans held in detention camps during World War II. The commission reported that the detention was motivated by "race prejudice, war hysteria, and a failure of political leadership." It added that "no documented acts of espionage, sabotage, or fifth-column activity were shown to have been committed" by Japanese Americans (Pear, 1983).

In 1988, President Ronald Reagan signed unprecedented legislation, entitled the Civil Liberties Act, in which the United States government apologized for the forced relocation of 120,000 Japanese Americans and established a $1.25 billion trust fund to pay reparations to those placed in detention camps. Under the new law, the federal government was to issue individual apologies for all violations of Japanese Americans' constitutional rights. Beginning in 1990, awards of $20,000 were to be given to each of the approximately 77,500 surviving Japanese Americans who had been interned by the federal government.

Korean Americans The population of Korean Americans is now nearly as large as that of Japanese Americans. Yet Korean Americans are often overlooked in favor of the larger groups from Asia.

Today's Korean American community is the result of three waves of immigration. The initial wave, of a little more than 7000 immigrants, came to the United States between 1903 and 1910, when laborers migrated to Hawaii. The second wave followed the end of the Korean war, accounting for about 14,000 immigrants from 1951 through 1964. Most of these immigrants were wives of U.S. servicemen and war orphans. The third wave, continuing to the present, has reflected the admissions priorities set up in the 1965 Immigration Act. These immigrants have been well educated and have arrived in the United States with professional skills. However, because of language difficulties and discrimination, many must settle at least initially for positions of lower responsibility than those they held in Korea

and must suffer through a period of disenchantment. Some may experience stress, loneliness, and family strife as part of the pain of adjustment (Hurh and Kim, 1994).

Today's young Korean Americans face many of the cultural conflicts common to any first generation born in a new country. Their parents may speak the native Korean tongue, but the road to opportunity for the younger generation involves adapting to the English language and the dominant culture of the United States. It is difficult to maintain a sense of Korean culture within the United States; the host society is far from helpful. Indeed, the few studies of attitudes toward Korean Americans indicate that other residents of the United States respond with vague, negative attitudes or simply lump Korean Americans with other Asian groups.

Korean American women commonly participate in the paid labor force, as do many Asian American women. About 60 percent of native-born Korean American women and half of those born abroad work in the labor force. These figures may not seem striking compared with data for White women, but the cultural differences make the figures more significant. Korean women immigrate from a family system that establishes well-defined marital roles; the woman is expected to serve as mother and homemaker only. Although these roles are carried over to the United States, women are pressed to support their families because of their husbands' struggles to establish themselves financially. Many Korean American men begin small service or retail businesses and gradually involve their wives in the business. Wages do not matter as the household mobilizes to make a profitable enterprise out of a marginal business. The situation is made more difficult by the hostility Korean American–run businesses often encounter from their prospective customers (K. Kim and Hurh, 1985).

In the early 1990s, the apparent friction between Korean Americans and another subordinate racial group, African Americans, attracted nationwide attention. In New York City, Los Angeles, and Chicago, the scene was replayed where a Korean American merchant confronted a Black person allegedly threatening or robbing a store. The Black neighborhood responded with hostility to what they perceived as the disrespect and arrogance of the

Korean American entrepreneur. Such friction is not new; earlier generations of Jewish, Italian, and Arab merchants encountered similar hostility from what to outsiders seems an unlikely source—another oppressed minority. The contemporary conflict was even dramatized in Spike Lee's 1989 movie *Do the Right Thing*, in which African Americans and Korean Americans clashed. The situation stems from Korean Americans' being the latest immigrant group to cater to the needs of inner-city populations abandoned by those who moved up the economic ladder.

The tension that can arise between subordinate groups gained national attention during the 1992 South-Central Los Angeles riots. In that city's poor areas, the only shops in which to buy groceries, liquor, or gasoline are owned by Korean immigrants. They have largely replaced the White business people who left the ghetto area after the 1965 Watts riot. African Americans were well-aware of the dominant role that Korean Americans play in their local retail market. As noted earlier in the chapter, Black resentment had been fueled by the light sentence given to a Korean grocer after the fatal shooting of a young Black woman in 1991. More than 1800 Korean businesses were looted or burned during the 1992 riots; Korean establishments suffered $347 million in property damage (Commission on Civil Rights, 1992; McIntosh, 1992; Mydans, 1992).

Among Korean Americans the most visible organization holding the community together is the church. Half the immigrants were affiliated with Christian churches before immigrating. One study of Koreans in Chicago and Los Angeles found that 70 percent were affiliated with Korean ethnic churches, mostly Presbyterian, with small numbers of Roman Catholics or Methodists. The church performs an important function, apart from the manifest religious one, by giving Korean Americans a sense of community attachment and a practical way to meet other Korean Americans (Hurh and Kim, 1990; I. Kim, 1981).

Ethnic Groups

Unlike racial minorities, members of subordinate ethnic groups are generally not hindered by physical differences from assimilating into the dominant culture of the United States. However, members of

Taken together, the various groups which are included under the general term Hispanics (or Latinos) represent the largest ethnic minority in the United States.

ethnic minority groups still face many forms of prejudice and discrimination. This will be apparent as we examine the situations of the country's largest ethnic groups—Hispanics, Jews, and White ethnics.

Hispanics: Mexican Americans and Puerto Ricans

Taken together, the various groups which are included under the general term *Hispanics* (or *Latinos*) represent the largest ethnic minority in the United States. It is estimated that there are more than 20 million Hispanics in this country, including 13 million Mexican Americans, over 2 million Puerto Ricans, and smaller numbers of Cubans and people of Central or South American origin.

The various Hispanic groups share a heritage of Spanish language and culture. Yet people whose first language is Spanish have serious problems with assimilation in the United States. An intelligent student for whom English is a second language may be presumed slow or even unruly by English-speaking schoolchildren, and frequently by English-speaking teachers as well. This self-fulfilling prophecy can lead to the immediate labeling of Hispanic children as being underachievers, as having learning disabilities, or as suffering from emotional problems—all labels which some of the children may then fulfill. Bilingual education has been introduced in many school districts as a means of easing the educational difficulties experienced by Hispanic children and others whose first language is not English.

The educational difficulties of Hispanic students certainly contribute to the generally low economic status of Hispanics. By 1991, only 10 percent of Hispanic adults had completed college, compared with 22 percent of Whites. At the same time, the median family income of Hispanics was only 63 percent that of Whites. In 1991, 6.3 million Hispanics (or 29 percent of all Hispanics in the United States) lived below the poverty line (Bureau of the Census, 1993a:469).

Despite common problems, there is considerable diversity among the various Hispanic groups found in the United States. The largest Hispanic population comprises Mexican Americans, who can be further subdivided into those descended from the residents of the territories annexed after the Mexican-American War of 1848 and those who have immigrated from Mexico to the United States. The opportunity for a Mexican to earn in one hour what it would take an entire day to earn in Mexico has motivated millions of legal and illegal immigrants to come north.

The second-largest segment of Hispanics in the United States is composed of Puerto Ricans. Since 1917, residents of Puerto Rico have held the status of American citizens. Many have migrated to New York and other eastern cities. Unfortunately, Puerto Ricans experience serious poverty both in the United States and on the island. Those living in the continental United States have barely half the family income of Whites. As a result, a reverse migration began in the 1970s; more Puerto Ricans began leaving for the island than were coming to the mainland (Lemann, 1991).

Politically, Puerto Ricans in the United States have not been so successful as Mexican Americans in organizing for their rights. For many mainland Puerto Ricans—as for many residents of the island—the paramount political issue is the destiny of Puerto Rico itself. Should it continue in its present commonwealth status, petition for admission to the United States as the fifty-first state, or attempt to become an independent nation? This question has divided Puerto Rico for decades and remains a central issue in Puerto Rican elections. In November 1993, a referendum was held on Puerto Rico's future and voters narrowly favored continuing the commonwealth status over statehood, with little support for independence.

The fastest-growing segment, by far, of the Hispanic community consists of people from Central or South America. Until recently, this group has not been closely studied; government data have rarely differentiated these people by nationality and have instead lumped them together as "other." Yet people from Chile and Costa Rica may have little in common except their hemisphere of origin and the Spanish language. Moreover, immigrants from Brazil speak Portuguese, those from Surinam speak Dutch, and those from French Guiana speak French. In recent years, increasing numbers of Central Americans and South Americans have fled to the United States to escape political unrest. Many have had difficulty gaining official status as refugees. The arrival of immigrants and refugees from countries in Central and South America has contributed to changes in the racial and ethnic balance of the population of the United States.

Jewish Americans   Jews constitute almost 3 percent of the population of the United States. They play a prominent role in the worldwide Jewish community because the United States has the world's largest concentration of Jews. Like the Japanese, many Jewish immigrants came to this country and became white-collar professionals. But again, as in the case of the Japanese, Jewish achievements have come despite prejudice and discrimination.

Anti-Semitism—that is, anti-Jewish prejudice—in the United States has often been vicious, although rarely so widespread and never so formalized as in Europe. In many cases, Jews have been used as scapegoats for other people's failures. This was clearly indicated in a study of World War II veterans by Bettelheim and Janowitz (1964). The researchers found that men who had experienced downward mobility (for example, job failure) were more likely to blame their setbacks on Jewish Americans than on their own shortcomings.

Jews have not achieved equality in the United States. Despite high levels of education and professional training, they are still conspicuously absent from the top management of large corporations (except for the few firms founded by Jews). Until the late 1960s, many prestigious universities maintained restrictive quotas that limited Jewish enrollment. Social clubs and fraternal groups frequently limit membership to gentiles (non-Jews), a practice upheld by the Supreme Court in the 1964 case of *Bell v. Maryland.*

One recent study suggests that anti-Semitism in the corporate world may be declining. In 1985 and 1986, sociologist Samuel Klausner (1988) and his colleagues questioned 444 people with Master of Business Administration (M.B.A.) degrees from three business schools. The purpose of the study was to compare the experiences of Jewish and non-Jewish executives who began their careers at the same business schools. Researchers tested seven indicators of discrimination and, in each case, *failed* to find evidence of discrimination against Jewish executives. (The same study, however, did detect substantial discrimination against Black and female executives.)

As is true for other minorities discussed in this chapter, Jewish Americans face the choice of maintaining ties to their long religious and cultural heritage or becoming as indistinguishable as possible from gentiles. Many Jews have tended to assimilate, as is evident from the rise in marriages between Jews and Christians. Indeed, a study conducted for the Council of Jewish Federations reported that since 1985 slightly more than half of Jews who married chose to marry a non-Jew. Moreover, of those children of intermarriages who receive religious instruction, 72 percent are reared in faiths other than Judaism. These trends worry Jewish leaders, some of whom fear that the long-term future of the Jewish people is in question (*Religion Watch,* 1991). We will examine Jewish religious life in greater detail in Chapter 14.

In the 1980s, there were disturbing increases in acts of violence against Jews and Jewish institutions.

In the year 1993, the Anti-Defamation League (ADL) of B'nai B'rith reported the second-highest number of anti-Semitic incidents in the United States in the 15 years that ADL has published its annual audit.

This same period was marked by a wave of cross burnings and bombings directed at Blacks living in predominantly White neighborhoods. These actions seemed to coincide with renewed activity among anti-Semitic White supremacist groups such as the Ku Klux Klan and the Aryan Nation. The Anti-Defamation League of B'nai B'rith (1994) reported that in 1993 anti-Semitic incidents reached the second-highest level since the organization began collecting statistics 15 years earlier. Such threatening behavior only underscores the fears of many Jewish Americans, who find it difficult to forget the Holocaust—the extermination of 6 million European Jews by the Nazi Third Reich during the late 1930s and 1940s.

White Ethnics A significant segment of the population of the United States is made up of White ethnics whose ancestors have come from Europe within the last 100 years. In terms of ancestry, the nation's White ethnic population includes about 58 million people who claim at least partial German ancestry, 39 million Irish Americans, 15 million Italian Americans, and 9 million Polish Americans, as well as immigrants from other European nations. Some of these people continue to live in close-knit ethnic neighborhoods, while others have largely assimilated and have left the "old ways" behind (Bureau of the Census, 1993a:51).

	WHITE ANGLO-SAXON PROTESTANTS, %	OTHER WHITE PROTESTANTS, %	IRISH CATHOLICS, %	OTHER WHITE CATHOLICS, %	JEWS, %	BLACKS, HISPANICS, ASIANS, NATIVE AMERICANS, %
National population						
Men born before 1932	22.9	22.5	4.2	17.2	2.9	14.4
College-educated men born before 1932	31.0	19.8	6.0	15.5	8.9	5.2
Overall elite	43.0	19.5	8.5	8.7	11.3	3.9
Business	57.3	22.1	5.3	6.1	6.9	0.0
Labor	23.9	15.2	37.0	13.0	4.3	2.2
Political parties	44.0	18.0	14.0	4.0	8.0	4.0
Voluntary associations	32.7	13.5	1.9	7.7	17.3	19.2
Mass media	37.1	11.3	4.8	9.7	25.8	0.0
Congress	53.4	19.0	6.9	8.6	3.4	3.4
Political appointees	39.4	28.8	1.5	13.6	10.6	3.0
Civil servants	35.8	22.6	9.4	9.4	15.1	3.8

SOURCE: Alba and Moore, 1982.

To what extent are White ethnics found among the nation's top decision makers? Sociologists Richard Alba and Gwen Moore (1982) conducted interviews with 545 people who held important positions in powerful social, economic, and political institutions. Table 10-3 compares the representation of White Anglo-Saxon Protestants in these positions with that of certain minorities. It shows that White Anglo-Saxon Protestants are overrepresented among the nation's elite, while White ethnics are underrepresented (although not so dramatically as are Blacks, Hispanics, Asians, and Native Americans). Some ethnic minorities appear to have risen to key positions in particular areas of the elite structure. Irish Catholics are well represented among labor leaders; Jews and racial minorities compare favorably among leaders of voluntary associations.

White ethnics and racial minorities have often been antagonistic to one another because of economic competition—an interpretation in line with

This table shows the representation of White Anglo-Saxon Protestants, Irish Catholics, and others among the leaders of powerful social, economic, and political institutions of the United States. The representation of each group within the nation's overall elite and within particular types of positions is compared with the percentage of group members who are men born before 1932 or college-educated men born before 1932. These comparative data are offered because older males and college-educated males have traditionally been the groups from which members of the elite emerge.

the conflict approach to sociology. As Blacks, Hispanics, and Native Americans emerge from the lower class, they will initially be competing with working-class Whites for jobs, housing, and educational opportunities. In times of high unemployment or inflation, any such competition can easily generate intense intergroup conflict.

In many respects, the plight of White ethnics raises the same basic issues as that of other subordinate people in the United States. How ethnic can people be—how much can they deviate from an essentially White, Anglo-Saxon, Protestant norm—before society punishes them for a willingness to be different? Our society does seem to reward people for assimilating. Yet, as we have seen, assimilation is no guarantee of equality or freedom from discrimination. In the social policy section which follows, we will focus on people who inevitably face the question of whether to strive for assimilation: immigrants and refugees who come to the United States.

SOCIAL POLICY AND RACE AND ETHNICITY

REGULATING IMMIGRATION

- Why are immigrants "pulled" and "pushed" to the United States?
- From a conflict perspective, how does the nation's treatment of illegal immigrants reinforce stratification based on class, race, and ethnicity?
- In what way does the debate over immigration and refugee policy reflect the deep value conflicts in the culture of the United States?

The words of poet Emma Lazarus—"Give us your tired, your poor, your huddled masses yearning to breathe free . . ."—are inscribed on the Statue of Liberty, long the symbol of hope for those who wanted to come to the United States. Yet, by the beginning of the twentieth century, this country had begun to turn its back on some of the huddled masses. As early as 1882, people of Chinese descent were prohibited from establishing permanent residence in the United States. Campaigns soon began to limit entry of other peoples regarded as "undesirable."

In the 1920s, the United States instituted an immigration policy that gave preference to people from western Europe, while making it difficult for residents of southern and eastern Europe, Asia, and Africa to enter the country. Then, during the late 1930s and early 1940s, the federal government refused to lift or loosen restrictive immigration quotas in order to allow Jewish refugees to escape the terror of the Nazi regime. In line with this policy, the *S.S. St. Louis,* with more than 900 Jewish refugees on board, was denied permission to land in the United States in 1939. This ship was forced to sail back to Europe, where it is estimated that at least a few hundred of its passengers later died at the hands of the Nazis (Morse, 1967; G. Thomas and Witts, 1974).

As in the past, immigration remains a controversial part of U.S. public policy. According to the Immigration and Naturalization Service (INS), as of mid-1993 some 8.9 million people had immigrated legally into the United States during the previous decade, while an estimated 3 million more had entered the country illegally. In 1992, there was almost one immigrant entering the United States for every two new births. While national attention is largely focused on legal and illegal immigrants from Mexico, the immigrant population of the United States is rather varied. For example, a study released in late 1993 of illegal immigrants in New York State—second only to California in the number of illegal immigrants it absorbs each year—found that the three major groups coming to New York are from Ecuador, Italy, and Poland (Mydans, 1993; Sontag, 1993b).

As substantial numbers of Hispanic and Asian immigrants enter the United States, the proportion of residents with European origins continues to decline and the nation becomes much more diverse. This trend is enhanced by the fact that families with European origins have comparatively lower birthrates than Hispanic or Asian immigrants. As is evident in Figure 10-2 on page 298, in the coming decades Hispanics will overtake African Americans as the nation's largest racial or ethnic minority group. However, Asian immigrants will have a cultural influence well beyond their numbers because they are especially likely to be *recent* immigrants (and therefore less assimilated into the dominant culture of the United States). According to popu-

FIGURE 10-2 *Population of the United States by Race and Ethnicity, 1993 and 2050 (Projected)*

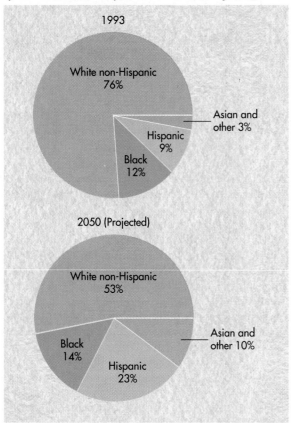

1993

White non-Hispanic
76%

Asian and other 3%

Hispanic 9%

Black 12%

2050 (Projected)

White non-Hispanic
53%

Asian and other 10%

Black 14%

Hispanic 23%

SOURCE: Bureau of the Census, 1993b.

According to projections by the Bureau of the Census, the proportion of residents of the United States who are White and non-Hispanic will decrease significantly by the year 2050. By contrast, there will be a striking rise in the proportion of both Hispanics and Asian Americans.

lation projections, by the middle of the twenty-first century approximately 86 percent of Asian Americans will be foreign-born or children of a foreign-born parent, compared with 66 percent of Hispanics (Edmonston and Passel, 1993).

Since the mid-1980s, public opinion polls have shown that people in the United States are increasingly unhappy about high rates of immigra-tion. In a national telephone survey conducted in mid-1993, 61 percent of those questioned felt that immigration into the United States should be de-creased (as compared with 49 percent who favored such a decrease in a 1986 poll). Beneath this grow-ing opposition to immigration is a bias against His-panic and Asian immigrants. For example, in 1993, 64 percent of respondents (in a different survey) said that there were too many immigrants from Asia and the Middle East, and 62 percent said there were too many from Latin America. But only 33 percent felt that there were too many immigrants from Eu-rope (Mydans, 1993; Puente, 1993a).

Survey data demonstrate that many people in the United States adhere to the stereotype that immi-grants wind up on welfare and thereby cause in-creases in taxes. However, social scientific studies underscore how false this stereotype can be. For ex-ample, a team of researchers from the University of Michigan explored the mobility patterns of south-east Asian immigrant families and found that they had succeeded extraordinarily well despite major economic and language obstacles. While not *all* these immigrants achieved success, many did—in good part because of parents' support of teachers and their active involvement in structuring a sup-portive learning environment at home (N. Caplan et al., 1992).

Perhaps the greatest controversy over immigra-tion has resulted from the federal government's ap-parent inability to control illegal or undocumented immigration. Illegal immigrants are commonly known as *illegal aliens* and are sometimes referred to as *undocumented workers*. They come to the United States in search of higher-paying jobs than are avail-able in their home countries. The immigrants are pulled here by the lure of prosperity and better lives for their children, while they are pushed out of their native lands by unemployment and poverty. Despite fears to the contrary, immigrants—whether legal or illegal—have had only a slight impact on the em-ployment prospects of longtime United States citi-zens. In general, immigrants are employed in jobs that employers find difficult to fill and that many residents do not want (Borjas, 1990).

Throughout the 1980s, there was a growing per-ception that the United States had lost control of its borders and simply was no longer able to pre-vent illegal immigrants from entering. With public pressure for immigration control on the rise, Congress ended a decade of debate by approving the Immigration Reform and Control Act of 1986. The act marked a historic change in immigration policy. For the first time, hiring of illegal aliens was outlawed, and employers caught doing so became subject to fines and even prison sentences. Just as significant a change was the extension of legal status to many illegal immigrants already living in the United States.

It appears that the 1986 immigration law has had mixed results. According to data compiled by the U.S. Border Patrol, arrests along the Mexican border declined substantially in the first three years after the law took effect. However, in the fiscal year ending in September 1992, more than 1.2 million illegal immigrants were arrested crossing the border. As of 1993, it was estimated that 3.2 million illegal immigrants continued to live in the United States (Frankel, 1993; Puente, 1993b).

Although the Immigration Reform and Control Act prohibited employers from discriminating against legal aliens because they were not U.S. citizens, a 1990 report by the General Accounting Office revealed that the law had produced a "widespread pattern of discrimination" against people who looked or sounded like foreigners. The report estimates that some 890,000 employers initiated one or more discriminatory practices in response to the 1986 immigration law. Although these firms employ nearly 7 million workers, fewer than 1000 complaints of discrimination have been filed with government agencies—in good part because most employees are unaware of the protections included in the Immigration Reform and Control Act (C. Brown, 1990:3).

Critics of the new immigration law emphasize that while it has been extremely beneficial for many immigrants who qualified for amnesty, it has had a devastating impact on those who could not qualify. Many aliens in this situation are being overworked or underpaid by unscrupulous employers, who are well-aware that these workers have few options. Consequently, millions of illegal immigrants continue to live in fear and hiding, subject to even more severe harassment and discrimination than before.

© Mark Bolton© 1992 The Clarion Ledger

"NEXT TIME, READ THE FINE PRINT!!!"

From a conflict perspective, these immigrants—primarily poor and Hispanic—are being firmly entrenched at the bottom of the nation's social and economic hierarchies.

Just as the United States has traditionally presented itself as a haven for immigrants, so too has the nation taken pride in its history of welcoming political refugees. Despite periodic public opposition, the United States government is committed to accepting about 130,000 additional refugees per year as part of an agreement to relieve the pressure on international refugee camps. Under the Refugee Act of 1980, aliens may qualify for political asylum in the United States if they have a "well-founded fear of persecution" in their homelands "on account of race, religion, nationality, membership in a particular social group, or political opinion."

In recent years, U.S. policy toward refugees from Haiti has received much publicity. Haitians have been fleeing their country, often on small boats, ever since a military coup in 1991 overthrew the elected government of President Jean-Bertrand Aristide. The Coast Guard interdicts (or intercepts) many Haitians at sea, which saves some of these "boat people" from death due to their rickety and overcrowded wooden ships.

The Haitians fear detentions, beatings, torture, and execution if they remain in Haiti. However, the Bush administration viewed most of the Haitian exiles as economic migrants rather than political refugees and opposed granting them asylum and permission to enter the United States. During the 1992 presidential campaign, candidate Bill Clinton denounced the policy of interdiction as "cruel" and illegal, yet after assuming the presidency in 1993 he kept this policy in place. In 1993, the Supreme Court, by an 8-1 vote, upheld the government's right to intercept Haitian refugees at sea and return them to their homeland without asylum hearings. Steven Forester, an attorney at the Haitian Refugee Center in Miami, wondered how the justices could uphold a policy of forcibly returning Haitian refugees to "their military persecutors, . . . who the State Department condemns for their horrendous human rights practices" (Greenhouse, 1993b; Rohter, 1993:18; refer back to the social policy section on universal human rights in Chapter 9).

In 1992, more than 103,000 people from 154 countries sought political asylum in the United States, with the greatest number coming from Guatemala, El Salvador, the former Soviet Union, and Haiti. However, as of mid-1993, more than 250,000 people were waiting for hearings regarding their petitions for political asylum; some had been waiting for years. The federal government had only 150 asylum officers available to hear these cases. The logjam of asylum seekers became especially controversial in 1993 when it was discovered that one of the suspects in the bombing of New York City's World Trade Center had entered the United States by pleading for asylum. Partly with this in mind, in mid-1993 President Clinton asked Congress for additional funds and new laws to combat illegal immigration and to speed interviews for those asking for political asylum (Friedman, 1993; Weiner, 1993).

Throughout the history of the United States, as we have seen, there has been intense debate over the nation's immigration and refugee policies. In a sense, this debate reflects the deep value conflicts in the culture of the United States and parallels the "American dilemma" identified by Swedish social economist Gunnar Myrdal (1944). One strand of our culture—well epitomized by Emma Lazarus's words, "Give us your tired, your poor, your huddled masses yearning to breathe free . . ." has emphasized egalitarian principles and a desire to help people in their time of need. At the same time, however, hostility to potential immigrants and refugees—whether Chinese in the 1880s, European Jews in the 1930s and 1940s, or Mexicans, Haitians, and Arabs today—reflects not only racial, ethnic, and religious prejudice, but also a desire to maintain the dominant culture of the in-group by keeping out those viewed as outsiders. The conflict between these cultural values is central to the "American dilemma" of the 1990s.

The social dimensions of race and ethnicity are important factors in shaping people's lives in the United States and other countries. In this chapter, we examine the meaning of race and ethnicity and study the major racial and ethnic minorities of the United States.

1 A *racial group* is set apart from others by obvious physical differences, whereas an *ethnic group* is set apart primarily because of national origin or distinctive cultural patterns.

2 When sociologists define a *minority group*, they are primarily concerned with the economic and political power, or powerlessness, of the group.

3 In a biological sense, there are no "pure races" and no physical traits that can be used to describe one group to the exclusion of all others.

4 Prejudiced attitudes often lead to *discrimination*, but the two are not identical, and each can be present without the other.

5 *Institutional discrimination* results from the normal operations of a society.

6 Four patterns describe typical intergroup relations in North America and elsewhere: *amalgamation, assimilation, segregation,* and *pluralism.*

7 In the United States, the most highly rewarded pattern of intergroup relations is assimilation. Pluralism remains more of an ideal than a reality.

8 Contemporary prejudice and discrimination against African Americans are rooted in the history of slavery in the United States.

9 Asian Americans are commonly viewed as a "model minority," a stereotype not necessarily beneficial to members of this group.

10 The various groups included under the general term *Hispanics* represent the largest ethnic minority in the United States.

11 Much of the debate in the United States concerning immigration has centered on the federal government's apparent inability to control illegal or undocumented immigration.

CRITICAL THINKING QUESTIONS

1 Which sociological perspective would be most helpful in discussing the riots in Los Angeles in 1992? Apply this perspective in exploring the causes of the rioting and the implications of these events for racial and ethnic relations in the United States.

2 The text states that "in the United States, pluralism is more of an ideal than a reality." Can the community in which you grew up and the college you attend be viewed as genuine examples of pluralism? Examine the relations between dominant and subordinate racial and ethnic groups in your hometown and your college.

3 What are some of the similarities and differences in the position of African Americans and Hispanics as minorities in the United States? What are some of the similarities and differences in the position of Asian Americans and Jewish Americans?

KEY TERMS

Amalgamation The process by which a majority group and a minority group combine through intermarriage to form a new group. (page 283)

Anti-Semitism Anti-Jewish prejudice. (294)

Apartheid The policy of the South African government designed to maintain the separation of Blacks, Coloureds, and Asians from the dominant Whites. (285)

Assimilation The process by which a person forsakes his or her own cultural tradition to become part of a different culture. (284)

Black power A political philosophy promoted by many younger Blacks in the 1960s which supported the creation of Black-controlled political and economic institutions. (286)

Contact hypothesis An interactionist perspective which states that interracial contact of people with equal status in noncompetitive circumstances will reduce prejudice. (280)

Discrimination The process of denying opportunities and equal rights to individuals and groups because of prejudice or for other arbitrary reasons. (282)

Ethnic group A group which is set apart from others because of its national origin or distinctive cultural patterns. (273)

Ethnocentrism The tendency to assume that one's culture and way of life are superior to all others. (281)

Exploitation theory A Marxist theory which views racial subordination in the United States as a manifestation of the class system inherent in capitalism. (280)

Genocide The deliberate, systematic killing of an entire people or nation. (283)

Institutional discrimination The denial of opportunities and equal rights to individuals or groups which results from the normal operation of a society. (282)

Issei The early Japanese immigrants to the United States. (290)

Minority group A subordinate group whose members have significantly less control or power over their own lives than the members of a dominant or majority group have over theirs. (274)

Nisei Japanese born in the United States who were descendants of the Issei. (292)

Pluralism Mutual respect between the various groups in a society for one another's cultures, which allows minorities to express their own cultures without experiencing prejudice. (285)

Prejudice A negative attitude toward an entire category of people, such as a racial or ethnic minority. (280)

Racial group A group which is set apart from others because of obvious physical differences. (273)

Racism The belief that one race is supreme and all others are innately inferior. (281)

Segregation The act of physically separating two groups; often imposed on a minority group by a dominant group. (284)

Self-fulfilling prophecy The tendency of people to respond to and act on the basis of stereotypes, a predisposition which can lead to validation of false definitions. (276)

Stereotypes Unreliable generalizations about all members of a group that do not recognize individual differences within the group. (276)

ADDITIONAL READINGS

Alba, Richard D. *Ethnic Identity: The Transformation of White America.* New Haven, Conn.: Yale University Press, 1990. A sociologist looks at the changing patterns of ethnic identity in the United States and focuses on the myths that today's White ethnics hold about their place in the nation's history.

Bunzel, John H. *Race Relations on Campus: Stanford Students Speak.* Stanford, Calif.: Portable Stanford, 1992. Bunzel, a former president of Stanford University and member of the U.S. Commission on Civil Rights, analyzes campus racial tensions and draws heavily on interviews with students.

Cowan, Neil M., and Ruth Schwartz Cowan. *Our Parents' Lives: The Americanization of Eastern European Jews.* New York: Basic Books, 1989. Drawing on oral histories, the authors explore the assimilation of eastern European Jews and the implications this had for Jewish identity.

Hacker, Andrew. *Two Nations: Black and White, Separate, Hostile, Unequal.* New York: Scribner, 1992. A political scientist analyzes the relative status of African Americans in terms of family, income, employment, education, criminal justice, and government.

Jaimes, M. Annette (ed.). *The State of Native America.* Boston: South End, 1992. Drawing mostly on Native American writers, Jaimes—a member of the Juaneño and Yaqui Indian tribes—explores the various circumstances confronted by Native Americans in the United States.

Massey, Douglas S., and Nancy A. Denton. *American Apartheid: Segregation and the Making of the Underclass.* Cambridge, Mass.: Harvard University Press, 1993. In the view of the authors, the persistence of the ghetto is no accident, and is a significant factor in perpetuating poverty among African Americans.

Moore, Joan, and Harry Pachon. *Hispanics in the United States.* Englewood Cliffs, N.J.: Prentice-Hall, 1985. A concise sociological examination of Hispanic Americans.

Schaefer, Richard T. *Racial and Ethnic Groups* (5th ed.). New York: HarperCollins, 1993. Comprehensive in its coverage of race and ethnicity, this text also discusses women as a social minority and examines minority relations in Great Britain, Northern Ireland, Israeli-occupied territories, Brazil, and South Africa.

Takaki, Ronald. *A Different Mirror: A History of Multicultural America.* Boston: Little, Brown, 1993. An overview of the history of the United States as seen from the perspective of numerous racial and ethnic minorities.

West, Cornel. *Race Matters.* Boston: Beacon, 1993. The director of Afro-American Studies at Princeton University examines the basic racial problems confronting the United States.

Journals

Among the journals that focus on issues of race and ethnicity are *Amerasian Journal* (founded in 1971), *The Black Scholar* (1969), *Contemporary Jewry* (1978), *Ethnic and Racial Studies* (1978), *Hispanic Journal of Behavioral Studies* (1979), and *Journal of Refugee Studies* (1988). Local publications produced by racial and ethnic communities are also useful.

11

STRATIFICATION
BY GENDER

11

STRATIFICATION BY GENDER

GENDER IDENTITY AND GENDER ROLES
Gender Roles in the United States
   Gender-Role Socialization
   Men's Gender Role
Cross-Cultural Perspective

EXPLAINING STRATIFICATION BY GENDER
The Functionalist View
The Conflict Response
The Interactionist Approach

WOMEN: THE OPPRESSED MAJORITY
The Global Perspective

Women in the Work Force of the United States
   A Statistical Overview
   Social Consequences of Women's Employment
Women: Emergence of a Collective Consciousness
Minority Women: Double Jeopardy

SOCIAL POLICY AND GENDER STRATIFICATION: THE BATTLE OVER ABORTION

BOXES
11-1 Current Research: Gendered Spaces
11-2 Current Research: Male Nurses in a Traditional "Women's Job"

> *I really think that women ought to have representatives, instead of being arbitrarily governed without having any direct share allowed them in the deliberations of government.*
>
> Mary Wollstonecraft
> *A Vindication of the Rights of Woman, 1792*

LOOKING AHEAD

- How are girls socialized to be "feminine" and boys to be "masculine"?
- How are gender roles apparent in everyday conversations between men and women?
- Why is it that, despite outnumbering men, women are viewed as a subordinate minority by sociologists?
- How pervasive is sex-typing of jobs? Are there many jobs viewed either as "men's work" or as "women's work"?
- When married women work outside the home, do their husbands assume equal responsibility for housework and child care?
- Why is it said that women from racial and ethnic minorities face a kind of "double jeopardy"?
- How does the world view of feminists involved in defending abortion rights differ from that of antiabortion activists?

Among the significant events in Japan during 1993 were the marriage of the crown prince and the summit meetings of seven major industrial nations in Tokyo. In June, Crown Prince Naruhito, the future emperor of Japan, took as his wife Masako Owada. The Japanese were definitely impressed by this Harvard- and Oxford-educated woman who had held a series of important positions in the Ministry of Foreign Affairs. While some feminists applauded the role model she would provide for Japanese girls, others were troubled by her entering a new life defined by her husband's status. Indeed, at precisely the moment she exchanged vows with the crown prince in a traditional Shinto ceremony, the name of Masako Owada was literally removed from the birth registry in her hometown of Murakami City. She had ceased to exist as Masako Owada, since she was now Japan's crown princess (Rafferty, 1993b).

The following month, Hillary Rodham Clinton attracted as much press attention at the Tokyo Summit as did her husband, the president of the United States. The Japanese were curious to see the woman who until 1993 had earned more money than her spouse. But they saw the first lady of the United States rather than the nation's new health care czar. Hillary Rodham Clinton toured Tokyo's landmarks and museums along with the wives of other heads of state; she didn't speak a word in public. Asked by reporters whether his wife had been "muzzled," Bill Clinton responded with a straight face: "No, she did what she wanted to. She thought about it quite a lot" (R. Thomas, 1993:19).

Differentiation based on gender is evident in virtually every human society about which we have information. We saw in Chapters 8, 9, and 10 that most societies establish hierarchies based on social class, race, and ethnicity. This chapter will examine the ways in which societies stratify their members on the basis of gender. It will begin by looking at how various cultures, including our own, assign women and men to particular social roles. Then it will consider sociological explanations for gender stratification.

Two women who attracted significant attention in Japan in 1993 were Hillary Rodham Clinton (who visited during the summit meetings of seven industrial nations in Tokyo) and Masako Owada (a former official in the Ministry of Foreign Affairs who became Japan's crown princess through her marriage to Crown Prince Naruhito).

Next, Chapter 11 will focus on the unique situation of women as an oppressed majority within the United States. Particular attention will be given to the social, economic, and political aspects of women's subordinate position and to the consequences of gender stratification for men. The chapter will also examine the emergence of the contemporary feminist movement. Finally, the social policy section will analyze the intense and continuing controversy over abortion.

GENDER IDENTITY AND GENDER ROLES

There are obvious biological differences between the sexes. Most important, women have the capacity to bear children, whereas men do not. These biological differences contribute to the development of *gender identity,* the self-concept of a person as being male or female. Gender identity is one of the first and most far-reaching identities that a human being learns. Typically, a child learns that she is a girl or he is a boy between the ages of 18 months and 3 years (Cahill, 1986).

Many societies have established social distinctions between the sexes which do not inevitably result from biological differences. This largely reflects the impact of conventional gender-role socialization. In Chapter 4, *gender roles* were defined as expectations regarding the proper behavior, attitudes, and activities of males and females. The application of traditional gender roles leads to many forms of differentiation between women and men. Both sexes are physically capable of learning to cook and type, yet most western societies determine that these tasks should be performed by women. Both men and women are capable of learning to weld and fly airplanes, but these functions are generally assigned to males.

It is important to stress that gender identity and gender roles are distinct concepts. Gender identity is based on a sense of oneself as male or female; gender roles involve socialization into norms regarding masculinity and femininity. Yet being male does not necessarily mean being "masculine" in a traditional sense; being female does not necessar-

ily mean being "feminine." Thus, a woman who enters a historically male occupation such as welding, and who displays such traditionally masculine qualities as physical strength and assertiveness, may have a positive and highly secure gender identity. She may feel quite comfortable about being female—and, in fact, proud to be a woman—without feeling "feminine" as *femininity* has conventionally been defined. Similarly, a gentle, sensitive man who rejects the traditional view of masculinity may be quite secure in his gender identity as a man (Bem, 1978: 20–21; L. Hoffman, 1977; C. West and Zimmerman, 1987).

Gender Roles in the United States

Gender-Role Socialization All of us can describe the traditional gender-role patterns which have been influential in the socialization of children in the United States. Male babies get blue blankets, while females get pink ones. Boys are expected to play with trucks, blocks, and toy soldiers; girls are given dolls and kitchen goods. Boys must be masculine—active, aggressive, tough, daring, and dominant—whereas girls must be feminine—soft, emotional, sweet, and submissive.

It is *adults,* of course, who play a critical role in guiding children into those gender roles deemed appropriate in a society. Parents are normally the first and most crucial agents of socialization (see Chapter 4). But other adults, older siblings, the mass media, and religious and educational institu-

tions also exert an important influence on gender-role socialization in the United States.

Psychologist Shirley Weitz (1977:60–110) has pointed to two mechanisms which are primarily responsible for gender-role socialization: differential treatment and identification. In an illuminating study of differential treatment, a baby was sometimes dressed in pink and called "Beth" and at other times dressed in blue and called "Adam." Adults who played with the baby indicated that, without question, they *knew* whether the child was male or female from its behavior. They remarked on how sweet and feminine *she* had been, and on how sturdy and vigorous *he* had been. Clearly, these adults perceived the baby's behavior on the basis of their understanding of its sex. Such gender-related assumptions commonly lead to differential treatment of girls and boys (J. Will et al., 1976).

The process of identification noted by Weitz is more complex. How does a boy come to develop a masculine self-image whereas a girl develops one that is feminine? In part, they do so by identifying with females and males in their families and neighborhoods and in the media. If a young girl regularly sees female characters on television working as defense attorneys and judges, she may believe that she herself can become a lawyer. And it will not hurt if women that she knows—her mother, sister, parents' friends, or neighbors—are lawyers. By contrast, if this young girl sees women portrayed in the media only as models, nurses, and secretaries, her identification and self-image will be quite different.

The portrayal of women and men on television has tended to reinforce conventional gender roles. A cross-cultural content analysis of television advertising in the United States, Mexico, and Australia found sexual stereotyping common in all three countries. Australia was found to have the lowest level of stereotyping, but even in that country, feminist groups were working to eliminate the "use of the woman's body to sell products" (Courtney and Whipple, 1983:183; Gilly, 1988).

Television is far from alone in its stereotyping of women. Studies of children's books published in the United States in the 1940s, 1950s, and 1960s found that females were significantly underrepresented in central roles and illustrations. Virtually all female characters were portrayed as helpless, passive, incompetent, and in need of a strong male caretaker. Even books that had been awarded the celebrated Caldecott Medal were found to have stereotyped girls and women. By the 1980s, there was somewhat less stereotyping in children's books, with some female characters shown to be active. Nevertheless, boys are still shown engaged in active play three times as often as girls are (Kortenhaus and Demarest, 1993).

Females have been most severely restricted by traditional gender roles. Throughout this chapter, we will see how women have been confined to subordinate roles within the political and economic institutions of the United States. Yet it is also true that gender roles have restricted males.

Men's Gender Role Boys are socialized to think that they should be invulnerable, fearless, decisive, and even emotionless in some situations (Cicone and Ruble, 1978). These are difficult standards to meet; yet, for boys who do not "measure up," life can be trying. This is especially true for boys who show an interest in activities thought of as feminine (such as cooking) or for those who do not enjoy traditional masculine activities (such as competitive sports). Following are one man's recollections of his childhood, when he disliked sports, dreaded gym classes, and had particular problems with baseball:

During the game I always played the outfield. Right field. Far right field. And there I would stand in the hot sun wishing I was anyplace else in the world. Every

so often a ball looked like it was coming up in my direction and I prayed to God that it wouldn't happen. If it did come, I promised God to be good for the next 37 years if he let me catch it—especially if it was a fly ball (Fager et al., 1971:36).

Boys who do not conform to the designated male gender role, like the right fielder quoted above, face constant criticism and even humiliation both from other children and from adults. It can be agonizing to be treated as a "chicken" or a "sissy"—particularly if such remarks come from one's father or brothers. At the same time, boys who successfully adapt to cultural standards of masculinity may grow up to be inexpressive men who cannot share their feelings with others. They remain forceful and tough—but as a result they are also closed and isolated (Balswick and Peek, 1971).

In the last 25 years, inspired in good part by the contemporary feminist movement (which will be examined later in the chapter), increasing numbers of men in the United States have criticized the restrictive aspects of the traditional male gender role. Some men have taken strong public positions in support of women's struggle for full equality, among them members of the National Organization for Men Against Sexism (NOMAS).

Accounts in the mass media commonly indicate that a "new man" emerged in the 1980s. Journalist Anthony Astrachan (1986:402) defined this "new man" as:

. . . one who has abandoned or transcended most traditional male sex roles and the male attempt to monopolize power. He doesn't insist on being the sole or dominant earner of family income and he resists being a slave to his job even though he prizes competence and achievement. He believes that men are just as emotional as women and should learn to express their feelings, and he can talk about his own problems and weaknesses. The new man supports women's quest for independence and equality with more than lip service.

However, after an extensive study of men in the United States, Astrachan estimated that only 5 to 10 percent of men come close to (or are moving toward) this ideal definition. Apparently, then, the traditional male gender role remains well entrenched as an influential element of our culture

Although major institutions socialize youngsters into conventional gender roles, every society has women and men who resist and successfully oppose traditional gender stereotypes: strong women who become leaders or professionals, gentle men who care for children, and so forth.

(see also Craig, 1992; Kimmel, 1987; Lamm, 1977; Pleck, 1981, 1985).

Cross-Cultural Perspective

To what extent do the actual biological differences between the sexes contribute to the cultural differences associated with gender? This question brings us back to the debate over "nature versus nurture" presented in Chapter 4. In assessing the alleged and real differences between men and women, it is useful to examine cross-cultural data.

The research of anthropologist Margaret Mead points to the importance of cultural conditioning—as opposed to biological factors—in defining the social roles of males and females. In her book *Sex*

and Temperament, Mead (1963, original edition 1935; 1973) describes the typical behaviors of members of each sex in three different cultures within New Guinea:

> In one [the Arapesh], both men and women act as we expect women to act—in a mild parental responsive way; in the second [the Mundugumor], both act as we expect men to act—in a fierce initiating fashion; and in the third [the Tchambuli], the men act according to our stereotypes for women—are catty, wear curls, and go shopping—while the women are energetic, managerial, unadorned partners (Mead, 1963: preface to 1950 ed.).

As is evident, Mead found two societies (the Arapesh and the Mundugumor) in which there was no dramatic gender-role differentiation between women and men. From the perspective of western society, we might say that these cultures created women and men who are both feminine (the Arapesh) or both masculine (the Mundugumor). In the third culture analyzed by Mead, the Tchambuli, expectations for each sex were almost the reverse of those found in the United States.

Mead (1963:260, original edition 1935) concludes:

> The material suggests that . . . many, if not all, of the personality traits which we have called masculine or feminine are as lightly linked to sex as are the clothing, the manners, and the form of headdress that a society at a given period of time assigns to either sex.

If all differences between the sexes were determined by biology, then cross-cultural differences, such as those described by Mead, would not exist. Her findings therefore confirm the influential role of culture and socialization in shaping gender-role differentiation. There appears to be no innate or biological reason to designate completely different gender roles for men and women.

In any society, gender stratification requires not only individual socialization into traditional gender roles within the family, but also the promotion and support of these traditional roles by other social institutions such as religion and education. Moreover, even with all major institutions socializing the young into conventional gender roles, every society has women and men who resist and successfully oppose these stereotypes: strong women who become leaders or professionals, gentle men who care for children, and so forth. With these realities in mind, it seems clear that differences between the sexes are not dictated by biology. Indeed, the maintenance of traditional gender roles requires constant social controls—and these controls are not always effective.

EXPLAINING STRATIFICATION BY GENDER

As we will consider further in Chapter 13, cross-cultural studies indicate that societies dominated by men are much more common than those in which women play the decisive role. Sociologists have turned to all the major theoretical perspectives to understand how and why social distinctions between males and females are established. Each approach focuses on culture, rather than biology, as the primary determinant of gender differences. Yet, in other respects, there are wide disagreements between advocates of these sociological perspectives.

The Functionalist View

Within the general framework of their theory, functionalists maintain that gender differentiation has contributed to overall social stability. Sociologists Talcott Parsons and Robert Bales (1955:13–15, 22–26) argue that in order to function most efficiently, the family requires adults who will specialize in particular roles. They view the current arrangement of gender roles as arising out of this earlier need to establish a division of labor between marital partners.

Parsons and Bales contend that women take the expressive, emotionally supportive role and men the instrumental, practical role, with the two complementing each other. *Instrumentality* refers to emphasis on tasks, focus on more distant goals, and a concern for the external relationship between one's family and other social institutions. *Expressiveness* denotes concern for maintenance of harmony and the internal emotional affairs of the family. According to this theory, women's interest in

expressive goals frees men for instrumental tasks, and vice versa. Women become "anchored" in the family as wives, mothers, and household managers, whereas men are anchored in the occupational world outside the home. Parsons and Bales do not explicitly endorse traditional gender roles, but they imply that a division of tasks between spouses is functional for the family unit.

Given the typical socialization of women and men in the United States, the functionalist view is initially persuasive. However, it would lead us to expect girls and women with no interest in children to become baby-sitters and mothers. Similarly, males who love spending time with children might be "programmed" into careers in the business world. Clearly, such differentiation between the sexes can have harmful consequences for the individual who does not fit into prescribed roles, while also depriving society of the contributions of many talented individuals who are confined owing to stereotyping by gender. Even if it were considered ideal for one marital partner to play an instrumental role and the other an expressive role, the functionalist approach does not convincingly explain why men should be categorically assigned to the instrumental role and women to the expressive role.

Viewed from a conflict perspective, this functionalist approach masks underlying power relations between men and women. Parsons and Bales never explicitly present the expressive and instrumental tasks as unequally valued by society, yet this inequality is quite evident. Although social institutions may pay lip service to women's expressive skills, it is men's instrumental skills that are most highly rewarded—whether in terms of money or prestige. Consequently, according to feminists and conflict theorists, any division of labor by gender into instrumental and expressive tasks is far from neutral in its impact on women.

The Conflict Response

Conflict theorists contend that the relationship between females and males has been one of unequal power, with men in a dominant position over women. Men may originally have become powerful in preindustrial times because their size, physical strength, and freedom from childbearing duties al-

Conflict theorists emphasize that men's work is uniformly valued, while women's work (whether unpaid labor in the home or wage labor) is devalued. Shown are workers making tents for camping in a factory in Binghamton, New York.

lowed them to dominate women physically. In contemporary societies, such considerations are not so important, yet cultural beliefs about the sexes are now long established. Such beliefs support a social structure which places males in controlling positions.

In this sense, traditional gender roles do not simply assign various qualities and behaviors to females and males. Feminist author Letty Cottin Pogrebin (1981:40) suggests that the two crucial messages of gender-role stereotypes are that "boys are better" and "girls are meant to be mothers." In order for a system of male dominance to maintain itself, she argues, children must be socialized to accept traditional gender-role divisions as natural and just. Sociologist Barbara Bovee Polk (1974:418), in describing the "conflicting cultures approach" to gender differences, observes that "masculine values have higher status and constitute the dominant and visible culture of the society. They . . . provide the standard for adulthood and normality." According to this view, women are oppressed because they constitute an alternative subculture which deviates from the prevailing masculine value system.

Thus, conflict theorists see gender differences as a reflection of the subjugation of one group (women) by another group (men). If we use an analogy to Marx's analysis of class conflict (see Chapters 1 and 8), we can say that males are like the bourgeois, or capitalists; they control most of the society's wealth, prestige, and power. Females

are like the proletarians, or workers; they can acquire valuable resources only by following the dictates of their "bosses." Men's work is uniformly valued, while women's work (whether unpaid labor in the home or wage labor) is devalued.

A significant component of the conflict approach to gender stratification draws on feminist theory. While use of that term is comparatively recent, the critique of women's position in society and culture goes back to some of the earliest works that have influenced sociology. Among the most important are Mary Wollstonecraft's *A Vindication of the Rights of Woman* (originally published in 1792 and from which the chapter-opening quote is taken), John Stuart Mill's *The Subjection of Women* (originally published in 1869), and Friedrich Engels's *The Origin of Private Property, the Family, and the State* (originally published in 1884).

Engels, a close associate of Karl Marx, argued that women's subjugation coincided with the rise of private property during industrialization. Only when people moved beyond an agrarian economy could males "enjoy" the luxury of leisure and withhold rewards and privileges from women. Drawing on the work of Marx and Engels, contemporary feminist theorists often view women's subordination as part of the overall exploitation and injustice that they see as inherent in capitalist societies. Some radical feminist theorists, however, view the oppression of women as inevitable in *all* male-dominated societies, including those labeled as "capitalist," "socialist," and "communist" (Feuer, 1959: 393–394; Tuchman, 1992).

From a conflict perspective, political and economic power in western industrial societies is concentrated in male hands, and there is substantial social differentiation between the sexes. Yet conflict theorists (including feminist theorists) emphasize that male dominance of the United States goes far beyond the economic sphere. Throughout this textbook, we examine disturbing aspects of men's behavior toward women. The ugly realities of rape (refer back to Chapter 7), wife battering (see Chapter 13), sexual harassment (refer back to Chapter 6), and street harassment (refer back to Box 1-2 on page 24) all illustrate and intensify women's subordinate position. Even if women reach economic parity with men, even if women win equal representation in government, genuine equality between the sexes cannot be achieved if these attacks remain as common as they are today.

Both functionalist and conflict theorists acknowledge that it is not possible to change gender roles drastically without dramatic revisions in a culture's social structure. For functionalists, there is potential for social disorder, or at least unknown social consequences, if all aspects of traditional gender stratification are disturbed. Yet, for conflict theorists, no social structure is ultimately desirable if it is maintained by oppressing a majority of its citizens. These theorists argue that gender stratification may be functional for men—who hold power and privilege—but it is hardly in the interests of women (R. Collins, 1975:228–259; Schmid, 1980).

The Interactionist Approach

Sociologists associated with the interactionist perspective generally agree with conflict theorists that men hold a dominant position over women. For example, recalling the Marxist view that the man is like the bourgeoisie within the home whereas the woman is like the proletariat, Erving Goffman (1977:315) has observed:

> A man may spend his day suffering under those who have power over him . . . and yet on returning home each night regain a sphere in which he dominates. . . . Wherever the male goes, apparently, he can carry a sexual division of labor with him.

While conflict theorists studying gender stratification typically focus on macro-level social forces and institutions, interactionist researchers often examine gender stratification on the micro level of everyday behavior (see Box 11-1 on page 314). As an example, studies show that up to 96 percent of all interruptions in cross-sex (male-female) conversations are initiated by men. Men are more likely than women to change topics of conversation, to ignore topics chosen by members of the opposite sex, to minimize the contributions and ideas of members of the opposite sex, and to validate their own contributions. These patterns reflect the conversational (and, in a sense, political) dominance of males. Moreover, even when women occupy a prestigious position, such as that of physician, they are more likely to be interrupted than their male counterparts are (A. Kohn, 1988; Tannen, 1990; C. West and Zimmerman, 1983).

In certain studies, all participants are advised in advance of the overall finding that males are more likely than females to interrupt during a cross-sex conversation. After learning this information, men reduce the frequency of their interruptions, yet they continue to verbally dominate conversations with women. At the same time, women reduce their already low frequency of interruption and other conversationally dominant behaviors after they are told of the general patterns of male dominance (Hoyenga and Hoyenga, 1993).

These findings regarding cross-sex conversations have been frequently replicated. They have striking implications when one considers the power dynamics underlying likely cross-sex interactions—employer and job seeker, college professor and student, husband and wife, to name only a few. From an interactionist perspective, these simple, day-to-day exchanges are one more battleground in the struggle for sexual equality—as women try to "get a word in edgewise" in the midst of men's interruptions and verbal dominance.

WOMEN: THE OPPRESSED MAJORITY

Many people—both male and female—find it difficult to conceive of women as a subordinate and oppressed group. Yet, when one looks at the political structure of the United States, one has to look

BOX 11-1 · CURRENT RESEARCH

GENDERED SPACES

After dinner, the women gather in one group, perhaps in the kitchen, while the men sit together elsewhere in the house, perhaps watching a televised sporting event. Is this an accurate picture of day-to-day social life in the United States? According to architect Daphne Spain (1992), it certainly is. Indeed, the physical separation of men and women has been common whether in the Mongolian *ger* (or hut), the longhouses of the Iroquois tribes of North America, or recreational facilities on contemporary college campuses.

Spain notes that gendered spaces in workplaces in the United States reflect our society's traditional division of labor into "men's work" and "women's work." But, as with historic patterns of racial segregation, the spatial segregation of women and men does not lead to "separate but equal" status. Instead, it serves to reinforce the dominant position of men in the workplace in terms of financial rewards, status, and power.

Drawing on her own research and on studies in a variety of disciplines, Spain concludes that:

- Women are more likely than men to supervise employees who share the same workspace or work in adjoining areas. Men tend to supervise people who work elsewhere. These differences are evident even when both men and women have the same job descriptions.
- Women in the workplace are often grouped in open spaces (in the "secretarial pool") or are without offices altogether (nurses and schoolteachers). By contrast, men are more likely to work in "private" offices. These spatial arrangements have obvious implications in terms of status and power.
- Even when women have private offices, the spatial characteristics of these offices often underscore their subordinate position in the workplace. Higher-status jobs within an organization—usually held by men—are accompanied by greater control of space. This is evident when an office has an entrance with a door that closes and locks, a back exit, no glass partition, soundproofing, a private telephone line, and so forth.

In summary, Spain (1992:227) found that "women typically engage in highly visible work—to colleagues, clients, and supervisors—subject to repeated interruptions." Viewed from an interactionist perspective, these spatial conditions reflect and reinforce women's subordinate status relative to men. The closed doors of men's offices in managerial and professional jobs not only protect their privacy and limit other employees' access to knowledge; they also symbolize men's dominant position in the workplace.

---

hard to find many women. In 1993, there were only 54 women in Congress. They accounted for 47 of the 435 members of the House of Representatives and 7 of the 100 members of the Senate. Similarly, in 1993, only 3 of the nation's 50 states had female governors.

In October 1981, Justice Sandra Day O'Connor of the Arizona Court of Appeals was sworn in as the nation's first female Supreme Court justice. In 1993, women achieved two significant breakthroughs: Janet Reno became the nation's first female attorney general, and Judge Ruth Bader Ginsburg joined Justice O'Connor on the Supreme Court (the first time the Court had ever had two female justices). Still, no woman has ever served as president of the United States, vice president, speaker of the House of Representatives, or chief justice of the Supreme Court. (We will examine women's involvement in politics and government in more detail in Chapter 15.)

This lack of women in decision-making positions is evidence of women's powerlessness in the United States. In Chapter 10, five basic properties which define a minority or subordinate group were identified. If we apply this model to the situation of women in this country, we find that a numerical majority group fits our definition of a subordinate minority (Dworkin, 1982; Hochschild, 1973: 118–120):

1 Women obviously share physical and cultural characteristics that distinguish them from the dominant group (men).
2 Women experience unequal treatment. In the year 1991, the median income for year-round, male workers was $30,332; for comparable female workers, it was only $21,245 (Bureau of the Census, 1993a:465). Though they are not segregated from men, women are the victims of prejudice and discrimination in the paid labor force, in the legal system, and in other areas of society. Moreover, as we saw in Chapter 8, women are increasingly dominating the ranks of the impoverished, leading to what has been called the *feminization of poverty*.
3 Membership in this subordinate group is involuntary.
4 Through the rise of contemporary feminism, women are developing a greater sense of group solidarity. (The women's movement will be studied later in the chapter.)
5 Women are not forced to marry within the group, yet many women feel that their subordinate status is most irrevocably defined within the institution of marriage (Bernard, 1972).

The most common analogy used for purposes of analysis is that of the positions of women and African Americans. Many scholars (H. Hacker, 1951, 1974; Myrdal, 1944; A. Rich, 1979; Stimpson, 1971) have drawn attention to striking parallels between the two groups, among them the following:

- Both are limited by ascribed characteristics (Blacks' skin color and women's gender).
- Both were denied suffrage when the Constitution of the United States was first drafted in 1787.
- Both have historically been treated as property within the legal system of the United States (Black slaves as the property of their masters, women as the property of their husbands).
- Women and Blacks, despite intense struggles for equal rights, remain significantly underrepresented in the political system of the United States.
- Both groups are subject to negative and prejudicial stereotypes.
- Both are generally given menial jobs with low pay and few prospects for advancement.
- Women and Blacks have traditionally been ignored in the writing of U.S. history.

Of course, there are also many differences. Perhaps most important, Blacks have faced widespread patterns of segregation, whereas women frequently live in intimate relationships with members of the dominant male sex.

Ralf-Finn Hestoft/SABA

After the 1992 elections, women held six seats in the United States Senate—an all-time high which increased to seven in 1993. Among the new senators elected in 1992 was Carol Moseley Braun, Democrat of Illinois, who became the first African American woman ever elected to the Senate.

Just as African Americans are victimized by racism, women in the United States suffer from sexism. *Sexism* is the ideology that one sex is superior to the other. The term is generally used to refer to male prejudice and discrimination against women. In Chapter 10 it was noted that Blacks can suffer from both individual acts of racism and institutional discrimination. *Institutional discrimination* was defined as the denial of opportunities and equal rights to individuals or groups which results from the normal operations of a society. In the same sense, women can be said to suffer both from individual acts of sexism (such as sexist remarks and acts of violence) and from institutional sexism.

It is not simply that particular men are biased in their treatment of women. All the major institutions of our society—including the armed forces, large corporations, the media, the universities, and the medical establishment—are controlled by men. These institutions, in their "normal" day-to-day operations, often discriminate against women and perpetuate sexism. Consequently, if the central office of a nationwide bank sets a policy that single women are a bad risk for loans—regardless of their incomes and investments—the *institution* will discriminate against women in state after state. It will do so even at bank branches in which loan officers hold no personal biases concerning women, but are merely "following orders." We will examine institutional discrimination against women within the educational system in Chapter 16.

Why is there sexism in the United States? Why do individual males, and male-dominated institutions, discriminate against women? Barbara Bovee Polk (1974:419) has summarized the "power analysis" of sex differentiation, which holds that it is in men's interest to maintain power and privilege over women:

> Power over women in personal relationships gives men what they want, whether that be sex, smiles, chores, admiration, increased leisure, or control itself. Men occupy and actively exclude women from positions of economic and political power in society. These positions give men a heavily disproportionate share of the rewards of society, especially economic rewards.

Yet with the power that comes to men comes responsibility. And with increased responsibility can come increased stress. Men have higher reported rates of certain types of mental illness than women do and greater likelihood of death due to heart attack or strokes (see Chapter 17). The pressure on men to succeed—and then to remain on top in a competitive work world—can be especially intense. This is not to suggest that gender stratification is as damaging to men as it is to women. But it is clear that the power and privilege which men enjoy are no guarantee of mental and physical well-being. Jimmy Carter, shortly after becoming president of the United States, summed up the potential problems of the male role: "If you're a woman doing more than your mother did, you feel successful. If you're a man and you're not president, you feel like a failure" (E. Goodman, 1977; Pogrebin, 1981:63–64).

Thus far, we have focused primarily on the social and political aspect of women's subordinate position in the United States. Before we turn to the economic situation of women within the nation's work force, we will first look briefly at the situation of women around the world.

The Global Perspective

In mid-1993, Canada and Turkey elected women as their prime ministers. These countries joined Bangladesh, Dominica, Nicaragua, Norway, and Poland in having women as heads of government. Nevertheless, women continue to experience second-class status throughout the world. It is estimated that women grow half the world's food, but they rarely own land. They constitute one-third of the world's paid labor force but are generally found in the lowest-paying jobs. Single-parent households headed by women—which appear to be on the increase in many nations—are typically found in the poorest sections of the population. Indeed, the feminization of poverty has become a global phenomenon.

According to a United Nations report on women's lives around the world, the majority of women still lag far behind men in terms of wealth, power, and opportunity. A 120-page book, entitled *The World's Women: Trends and Statistics 1970–1990*, was released by the United Nations in 1991. This report represents the first global attempt to evaluate women's place statistically. Among the report's findings were the following:

Women have second-class status throughout the world. Shown are women planting potatoes in the Tatra Mountains of Poland.

- In almost all countries, the workplace is segregated by gender, with women found in less prestigious and lower-paying jobs. Among the countries with the lowest women's wages—about half those of men—were Japan, South Korea, and Cyprus.
- Women are poorly represented in the higher ranks of power, policy, and decision making in politics, government, unions, and business.
- The number of illiterate women in the world rose from 543 million in 1970 to 597 million in 1985. By contrast, in 1985 there were 352 million illiterate men in the world (United Nations Department of International Economic and Social Affairs, 1991).

A study by the Population Crisis Committee (1988), a nonprofit group which promotes international family planning programs, attempted to assess and compare the status of women in five major areas: health, control over childbearing, education, employment, and legal protection. In general, the richer the country, the greater the measure of women's equality found by researchers. Western industrialized countries tended to rank high: Sweden scored 87 points (this was the highest score) out of a possible 100, while the United States ranked third with 82.5 points. By contrast, African, middle eastern, and south Asian countries clustered at the bottom of the list, with Bangladesh ranking last at 21.5 points.

In reviewing the global perspective on women's equality, two conclusions can be offered. First, as anthropologist Laura Nader (1986:383) has observed, even in the relatively more egalitarian nations of the west, women's subordination is "institutionally structured and culturally rationalized, exposing them to conditions of deference, dependency, powerlessness, and poverty." While the situation of women in Sweden and the United States is significantly better than in Saudi Arabia and Bangladesh, women nevertheless remain in a second-class position in the world's most affluent and developed countries.

Second, as was discussed in Chapter 9, there is a link between the wealth of industrialized nations and the poverty of the developing countries. Viewed from a conflict perspective, the economies of developing nations are controlled and exploited by industrialized countries and multinational corporations based in those countries. Much of the exploited labor in developing nations, especially in the nonindustrial sector, is performed by women. Women workers typically toil long hours for low pay, but contribute significantly to their families' incomes. Consequently, the affluence of western nations has come, in part, at the expense of women in Third World countries (Jacobson, 1993).

Women in the Work Force of the United States

"Does your mother work?" "No, she's just a housewife." This familiar exchange reminds us of women's traditional role in the United States, and it reminds us that women's work has generally been viewed as unimportant. The United States Commission on Civil Rights (1976:1) concluded that the passage in the Declaration of Independence proclaiming that "all men are created equal" has been taken too literally for too long. This is especially true with respect to employment.

A Statistical Overview Women's participation in the paid labor force of the United States has increased steadily throughout the twentieth century. No longer is the adult woman associated solely with the role of homemaker. Instead, millions of women—married and single, with and without children—are working outside the home. In fact, a greater proportion of women are seeking and obtaining paid employment than ever before in our country's history. In 1992, more than 58 percent of

adult women held jobs outside the home, compared with 43 percent in 1970. A majority of women are now members of the paid labor force, not full-time homemakers (Bureau of the Census, 1993a:395).

The most dramatic rise in the female work force has been among married women (see Figure 11-1). In 1992, 59 percent of married women worked outside the home, compared with less than 5 percent in 1890; and more than half the married women with children under 6 years old were in the labor force. Yet this change in women's work lives is not a recent revolution. Women's participation in the paid labor force has increased steadily throughout the twentieth century.

Unfortunately, women entering the job market find their options restricted in important ways. Particularly damaging to women workers is occupational segregation, or confinement to sex-typed "women's jobs." For example, in 1991 women accounted for 99 percent of all secretaries, 96 percent of all private household workers, and 94 percent of all registered nurses. Entering such sex-typed occupations places women in "service" roles which parallel the traditional gender-role standard under which housewives "serve" their husbands.

By contrast, women are underrepresented in occupations historically defined as "men's jobs,"

FIGURE 11-1   Trends in Women's Participation in the Paid Labor Force, 1890–1992

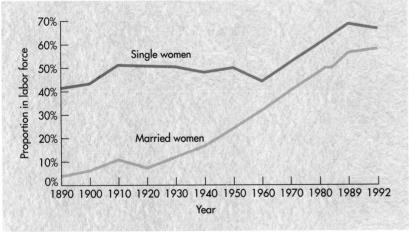

In 1992, 66 percent of single women and 59 percent of married women were found in the paid labor force of the United States.

SOURCE: Bureau of the Census, 1975b, 1993a:399.

TABLE 11-1	Employment of Women in Selected Occupations, 1950 and 1992	

	WOMEN AS PERCENT OF ALL WORKERS IN THE OCCUPATION	
OCCUPATION	1950	1992
Professional workers	40	52
Engineers	1	9
Lawyers and judges	4	21
Physicians	7	20
Registered nurses	98	94
College teachers	23	41
Other teachers	75	75
Managers	14	42
Sales workers	35	48
Clerical workers	62	79
Machine operators	34	40
Transport operatives	1	9
Service workers	57	60

Although strides have been made in some areas, many occupations continue to be filled routinely by members of one sex.

SOURCES: Bureau of the Census, 1993a:405; Department of Labor, 1980:10–11.

which often carry much greater financial rewards and prestige than women's jobs do. For example, in 1992 women accounted for approximately 46 percent of the paid labor force of the United States. Yet they constituted only 9 percent of all engineers, 9 percent of all dentists, 20 percent of all physicians, and 21 percent of all lawyers and judges (Bureau of the Census, 1993a:393, 405–407). A general picture of women's employment in various occupations appears in Table 11-1.

According to a study released in 1991 by the Feminist Majority Foundation, women continue to be dramatically underrepresented in top positions at Fortune 500 companies. As of 1990, of 6502 jobs at the vice presidential level or higher in these corporations, only 175 (or 2.6 percent) were held by women. Only five women were chief executives at Fortune 500 companies. However, women appear to be making progress in gaining middle-management jobs. In 1990, women held 40 percent of all executive, management, and administrative positions at Fortune 500 companies—compared with 24 percent in 1976 (*USA Today*, 1991).

Key roles in the mass media and the entertainment industry have similarly been regarded as "men's jobs." According to studies released in 1989, women hold only 6 percent of top management

jobs in the news media, compared with 25 percent of middle-management jobs and 57 percent of entry-level jobs. The researchers suggest that women face biases in salaries and promotions, and are segregated into "dead-end jobs" with little decision-making authority. Hollywood studios have also been reluctant to place women in positions of authority. In 1990, women directors—who account for 20 percent of the membership of the Directors Guild of America—received assignments for 5 percent of all feature films, less than 3 percent of television movies, and 0 percent of television miniseries (Rasky, 1989a; Rohter, 1991).

How pervasive is sex-typing of occupations? In one study, researchers compiled a "segregation index" to estimate the percentage of women who would have to change their jobs to make the distribution of men and women in each occupation mirror the relative percentage in the adult working population. This study showed that 58 percent of women workers would need to switch jobs in order to create a paid labor force without sex segregation (J. Jacobs, 1990; Reskin and Blau, 1990). In Box 11-2 (page 321), we examine the entry of men into the traditionally female profession of nursing.

The result of the workplace patterns described throughout this section is that women earn much

Photofest

Despite the successes of female directors such as Jodie Foster, Hollywood studios have been reluctant to place women in positions of authority.

less money than men do in the paid labor force of the United States. In 1992, the median income of full-time female workers was 70 percent that of full-time male workers. Given these data, it is hardly surprising to learn that many women are living in poverty, particularly when they must function as heads of households. In the discussion of poverty in Chapter 8, it was noted that by 1991 female heads of households and their children accounted for 52 percent of the nation's poor. Yet not all women are in equal danger of experiencing poverty. As will be discussed more fully later in the chapter, women who are members of racial and ethnic minorities suffer from "double jeopardy": stratification by race and ethnicity as well as by gender (Bureau of the Census, 1993a:465, 471).

There are certain encouraging trends in women's employment patterns. Despite traditional gender-role socialization and sexist attitudes that have limited their employment opportunities, women *are* moving into at least some jobs that have generally been held by men. For example, between 1960 and 1990, the proportion of medical school graduates who were female rose more than fivefold, from 6 percent in 1960 to 34 percent in 1990. Nevertheless, even as more women have entered the medical profession, women physicians still have disproportionately low pay and status. In 1988, for ex-

ample, women doctors earned 63 cents for each dollar earned by a male doctor (Bureau of the Census, 1993a:85; Hilts, 1991).

Social Consequences of Women's Employment
There have already been many obvious consequences of women's increasing involvement in the paid labor force. As was seen in Chapter 4, the need for child care facilities has grown, and there have been pressures for greater public financing of day care. Even the rise of fast-food chains partially reflects the fact that many women are no longer home and cooking during the day.

In theory at least, women should gain in self-esteem and power within the family as they move outside the home and function as productive wage earners. In an ongoing study of women between the ages of 35 and 55, researchers have found that "for employed women, a high-prestige job, rather than a husband, is the best predictor of well-being" (Baruch et al., 1980:199; 1983). Holding this type of position appears to be the factor most influential in a woman's self-esteem. Of course, as we have seen in this chapter, the number of women employed in high-prestige jobs is rather small.

In terms of power dynamics, women clearly gain some degree of power by earning their own incomes. Studies indicate that when a woman pro-

BOX 11-2 · CURRENT RESEARCH

MALE NURSES IN A TRADITIONAL "WOMEN'S JOB"

In her important book *Men and Women of the Corporation,* sociologist Rosabeth Moss Kanter (1977a) identified characteristics that were present when women entered traditionally male occupations. Sociologist E. Joel Heikes (1991) wondered if male nurses exhibit similar characteristics when entering a traditionally female occupation; consequently, he conducted in-depth interviews with male registered nurses employed in hospital settings in Austin, Texas. Nationally, less than 4 percent of all nurses are male; in Austin, the comparable figure is 7.7 percent.

In Kanter's view (1977a, 1977b), an important determinant of workplace interactions between members of a dominant group and a subordinate group is the ratio of majority to minority employees. The smaller the minority group, the less successful they tend to be relative to group standards. When few members of a minority are present in a workplace, they are viewed as "tokens," since they are typically treated as symbols or representatives of their group rather than as distinct individuals.

According to Kanter, tokens operate under a number of disadvantages in the workplace. First, their high visibility creates increased performance pressure, which may result in either overachievement or underachievement. Performance pressure makes it more hazardous for tokens to make mistakes and therefore allows them fewer options in doing their jobs. Second, the presence of tokens leads to polarization at the workplace; tokens experience social isolation which

may exclude them from situations in which important information is shared about job-related tasks and procedures. Third, individual characteristics of tokens are perceived as fitting into preexisting stereotypes about the minority group and often result in further stereotyping.

Heikes reports that male nurses in Austin feel more visible than female nurses and typically respond by overachieving. There was not any clear polarization between Austin's female and male nurses, but the male nurses did experience social isolation. Typically, they were excluded from traditionally female gatherings, such as female nurses' baby and bridal showers. Such social isolation did not reduce the male nurses' skills training, but it excluded them from informal interactions in which they could have "networked" with female nurses and learned more about the day-to-day workings of the hospital.

The stereotyping discussed by Kanter was also evident in Austin: male nurses were commonly mistaken for physicians. Even though being mistaken for someone of higher status may appear to be advantageous, it can often have negative connotations for the male nurse. It is a constant reminder of his deviant position in a traditionally female occupation, with the implicit message that men should be doctors rather than nurses. Indeed, when correctly identified as nurses, men face a much more serious form of stereotyping. Because of the persistence of traditional gender roles, it is assumed that all male nurses must be gay. Many male nurses told Heikes that they felt a

need to deny this stigmatized identity.

While Heikes's research on male nurses confirmed many of Kanter's findings about tokenism, the Austin study suggests that the social context in which tokenism dynamics take place may influence whether the effects on individual tokens are positive or negative.

One year after Heikes's study was published, sociologist Christine Williams (1992) examined the underrepresentation of men in four predominantly female professions: nursing, elementary school teaching, librarianship, and social work. Drawing on in-depth interviews with 99 men and women in these professions in four cities in the United States, Williams found that the experience of tokenism is very different for women and men.

Whereas Kanter had offered a more "gender neutral" view of tokenism, Williams emphasizes that the crucial factor in the experience of being a token is the social status of the minority group rather than its numerical rarity. Indeed, Williams emphasizes that while men in these traditionally female professions commonly experience negative stereotyping, they nevertheless benefit from hidden *advantages* stemming from their status as men, such as receiving early and disproportionate encouragement to become administrators. By contrast, women in traditionally male professions often find that their advancement is limited and their token status is hardly an asset (see also Zimmer, 1988).

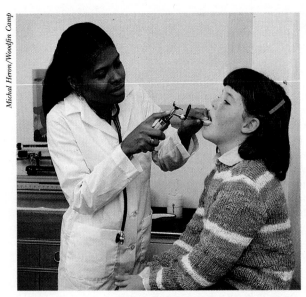

In the last 25 years, there has been a striking increase in the proportion of women students in medical schools in the United States.

vides sole support for her family, employment even in a low-status occupation has a positive effect on her self-esteem (Hoffman and Nye, 1975). For married women, such income from employment can be effective security in case of separation or divorce. In the past, many full-time homemakers had little confidence in their ability to make a living. As a result, some remained in unsatisfying marriages, believing that they had no alternative way to survive. This is still the case for a considerable number of women in the United States and around the world.

As women become increasingly involved in employment outside the home, men will have an opportunity to become more involved in the care and socialization of children. In industrial societies, the demands on men as primary wage earners have traditionally contributed to a deemphasis on the social roles of being a father. Freda Rebelsky and Cheryl Hanks (1973) examined interactions between fathers and babies and found that the longest time period any father in the sample devoted to his infant was 10 minutes 26 seconds. The average period of verbal interaction between father and baby was only *38 seconds per day.* More recently, psychologist Wade Mackey (1987) conducted a cross-cultural study of 17 societies—including Morocco, Hong Kong, Ireland, and Mexico—and found that the limited father-child interactions in the United States were typical of all the societies surveyed.

The division of household and child care duties is far from trivial in defining power relations within the family. Heidi Hartmann (1981:377) argues that "time spent on housework, as well as other indications of household labor, can be fruitfully used as a measure of power relationships in the home." Hartmann points out that as women spend more hours per week working for wages, the amount of time they devote to housework decreases, yet their overall "workweek" increases.

Studies indicate that there is a clear gender gap in the performance of housework (Zick and McCullough, 1991). Drawing on data from a 1985 national survey, sociologist John Robinson (1988) reports that while men have increased their share of some household duties—among them, caring for pets and paying bills—women in the United States continue to perform two hours of housework for each hour done by men. In 1985, not including time spent on child care, women averaged 19.5 hours of housework each week, compared with only 9.8 hours for men. Data from a 1989 national survey underscore the common sex segregation evident in the performance of household tasks (see Figure 11-2). For example, 78 percent of women report that they do all or most of their families' meal preparation, and 72 percent say they do all or most of the child care. By contrast, 74 percent of men indicate that they do all or most of the minor home repairs (DeStefano and Colasanto, 1990:28–29, 31).

A study of Canadian married couples by sociologist Susan Shaw (1988) offers insight into the rather different ways in which men and women view housework. Specifically, men are more likely than women to view these activities as "leisure"—and are less likely to see them as "work." The reason for this is that these tasks continue to be seen as women's work. Consequently, men perceive themselves as having more freedom of choice in engaging in housework and child care; they are more likely than women to report that cooking, home chores, shopping, and child care are, in fact, leisure. Confirming earlier research, Shaw found that the employment status of women had little effect on this gender difference.

FIGURE 11-2   Division of Household Tasks by Gender

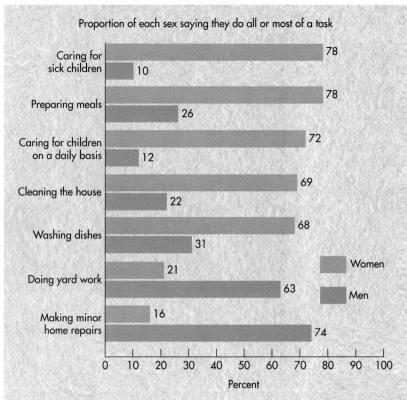

Proportion of each sex saying they do all or most of a task

In a national survey conducted in 1989, men and women indicated who they felt did all or most of a variety of household tasks. Segregation of housework and child care was evident, and other studies indicate that women spend more than twice as much time on housework as men—even when child care is not included.

NOTE: Questions regarding child care were asked only of respondents with children living at home.
SOURCE: DeStefano and Colasanto, 1990:31.

The continuing disparity in household labor has a rather striking meaning in terms of power relationships within the family (a subject which will be examined more fully in Chapter 13). As married women have taken on more and more hours of paid employment, they have been only partially successful in getting their husbands to assume a greater role in needed homemaking duties, including child care. Sociologist Arlie Hochschild (1989, 1990) has used the phrase "second shift" to describe the double burden—work outside the home followed by child care and housework—that many women face and few men share equitably.

On the basis of interviews with and observations of 52 couples over an eight-year period, Hochschild reports that the wives (and not their husbands) drive home from the office while planning domestic schedules and play dates for children—and then begin their second shift. Drawing on national studies, she concludes that women spend 15 fewer hours in leisure activities each week than their husbands do. In a year, these women work an extra month of 24-hour days because of the "second shift"; over a dozen years, they work an extra year of 24-hour days. Hochschild found that the married couples she studied were fraying at the edges, and so were their careers and their marriages. With such reports in mind, many feminists have advocated greater governmental and corporate support for child care (refer back to Chapter 4), more flexible family leave policies, and other reforms designed to ease the burden on the nation's families.

The continuing difficulties faced by professional women are evident in a recent survey of 902 female graduates of Harvard University's business, law, and medical schools. When asked if they felt they have been successful in combining career and family, 85 percent of respondents answered affirmatively. Yet 53 percent of the women questioned said that they had changed their jobs or specialties as a result of family obligations, while 25 percent of those with M.B.A. degrees had left the paid labor force completely. Apparently, even professional women with all the advantages of advanced degrees from Harvard still encounter significant problems in combining careers and family life (Swiss and Walker, 1993).

Women: Emergence of a Collective Consciousness

Many people believe that the feminist movement is a new and recent development in the history of the United States. But, in fact, the fight for women's rights dates back at least as far as colonial times. On March 31, 1776, months before the signing of the Declaration of Independence, Abigail Adams wrote to her husband John Adams, later the nation's second president:

> . . . I desire you would remember the Ladies, and be more favourable and generous to them than your ancestors. Do not put such unlimited power in the hands of Husbands. Remember all Men would be tyrants if they could. If particular care and attention is not paid to the Ladies, we are determined to foment a Rebellion, and will not hold ourselves bound by any Laws in which we have no voice, or representation (A. Rossi, 1973:10–11).

In a formal sense, the feminist movement in the United States was born in upstate New York, in a town called Seneca Falls, in the summer of 1848. On July 19, the first women's rights convention began, attended by Elizabeth Cady Santon, Lucretia Mott, and other pioneers in the struggle for women's rights. This first wave of *feminists,* as they are currently known, battled ridicule and scorn as they fought for legal and political equality for women. They were not afraid to risk controversy on behalf of their cause; in 1872 Susan B. Anthony was arrested for attempting to vote in that year's presidential election.

After many decades of struggle, women gained the right to vote in national elections beginning in 1920. However, women's suffrage did not dramatically change the position of women within the United States.

Ultimately, the early feminists won many victories, among them the passage and ratification of the Nineteenth Amendment to the Constitution, which granted women the right to vote in national elections beginning in 1920. But suffrage did not lead to other reforms in women's social and economic position, and the women's movement became a much less powerful force for social change in the early and middle twentieth century.

The second wave of feminism in the United States emerged in the 1960s and came into full force in the 1970s. In part, the movement was inspired by three pioneering books arguing for women's rights: Simone de Beauvoir's *The Second Sex,* Betty Friedan's *The Feminine Mystique,* and Kate Millett's *Sexual Politics.* In addition, the general political activism of the 1960s led women—many of whom were working for Black civil rights or against the war in Vietnam—to reexamine their own powerlessness as women. The sexism often found within allegedly progressive and radical political circles made many women decide that they needed to establish their own movement for "women's liberation" (S. Evans, 1980; Firestone, 1970:15–40; J. Freeman, 1973, 1975).

Sometimes, it was very simple, day-to-day situations that made women aware of their subordinate status. Feminist writer Jane O'Reilly (1972:55) described such an occurrence:

> In suburban Chicago, the party consisted of three couples. The women were a writer, a doctor, and a teacher. The men were all lawyers. As the last couple arrived, the host said, jovially, "With a room full of lawyers, we ought to have a good evening." Silence. Click! "What are we?" asked the teacher. "Invisible?"

More and more women became aware of sexist attitudes and practices—including attitudes they themselves had accepted through socialization into traditional gender roles—and began to challenge male dominance. A sense of "sisterhood," much like the class consciousness that Marx hoped would emerge in the proletariat (see Chapter 8), became evident. Individual women identified their interests with those of the collectivity *women*. No longer were they "happy" in submissive, subordinate roles ("false consciousness" in Marxist terms).

This new sense of group solidarity and loyalty was fostered within feminist consciousness-raising groups. In these small discussion groups, women shared their personal feelings, experiences, and conflicts. Many discovered that their "individual" problems were shared by other women and often reflected sexist conditioning and powerlessness. Such awareness of common oppression is a precondition for social change. Consciousness does not always lead to efforts to transform social conditions, but it is essential in mobilizing a group for collective action.

Through the strength gained in consciousness raising, the women's movement has undertaken public protests on a wide range of issues. Feminists have endorsed passage of the equal rights amendment, government subsidies for child care (see Chapter 4), greater representation of women in government (see Chapter 15), affirmative action for women and minorities (see Chapter 15), federal legislation outlawing sex discrimination in education (see Chapter 16), and the right to legal abortions (which will be discussed later in this chap-

ter). Feminists have condemned violence against women in the family (see Chapter 13), sexual harassment in organizations (see Chapter 6), forced sterilization of poor and minority women, sexist advertising and pornography, and discrimination against lesbians and gay men (see Chapter 13).

In an overview of the feminist campaign for social change, Barbara Bovee Polk (1974:422–430) distinguishes a number of basic approaches:

1 Attempts by women to resocialize themselves and overcome traditional gender conditioning
2 Efforts to change day-to-day personal interactions with men and other women and to avoid conventional sexist patterns
3 Use of the media and academic world to combat sexism and resocialize others to more egalitarian values and greater respect for women
4 Challenges to male dominance of social institutions through demonstrations, boycotts, lawsuits, and other tactics
5 Creation of alternative institutions, such as women's self-help medical clinics (see Chapter 17), publishing houses, and communes

The women's movement has employed all these approaches simultaneously in its efforts to transform the United States and promote women's rights.

Minority Women: Double Jeopardy

We have seen that the historical oppression of women limits them by tradition and law to specific roles. Many women experience differential treatment not only because of gender but because of race and ethnicity as well. These citizens face a "double jeopardy"—that of subordinate status twice defined. A disproportionate share of this low-status group are also impoverished, so that the double jeopardy effectively becomes a triple jeopardy. The litany of social ills continues for many if we consider old age, ill health, disabilities, and the like.

Feminists have addressed themselves to the particular needs of minority women, but overshadowing the oppression of these women because of gender is the subordinate status imposed because of race and ethnicity. The question for African American women, Chicanas (Mexican American women), Asian American women, and others appears to be whether they should unify with their "brothers" against racism or challenge them for their sexism. One answer is that, in a truly just society, both sexism and racism must be eradicated.

The discussion of gender roles among African Americans has always provoked controversy. Advocates of Black nationalism contend that feminism only distracts women from full participation in the Black struggle. The existence of feminist groups among Blacks, in their view, simply divides the Black community and thereby serves the dominant White society.

By contrast, Black feminists such as Florynce Kennedy argue that little is to be gained by adopting or maintaining the gender-role divisions that place women in a subservient position. African American journalist Patricia Raybon (1989) has noted that the media commonly portray Black women in a negative light: as illiterate, as welfare mothers, as prostitutes, and so forth. Black feminists emphasize that it is not solely Whites and White-dominated media that focus on these negative images; Black men (most recently, Black male rap artists) have been criticized for the way they portray African American women. In the view of Black feminists, African American women deserve and clearly stand to gain from increased employment and educational opportunities (Giddings, 1984; Ladner, 1986).

The plight of Chicanas is usually considered part of either the Chicano or the feminist movement, ignoring the distinctive experience of Chicanas. In the past, these women have been excluded from decision making in the two institutions that most directly affect their daily lives: the family and the church. The Mexican American family, especially in the lower class, feels the pervasive tradition of male domination (refer back to Box 4-2 on page 107). The Roman Catholic church relegates women to supportive roles while reserving the leadership positions for men (Burciaga et al., 1977; Rosaldo, 1985:415).

Activists among minority women do not agree on whether priority should be granted to equalizing the sexes or to eliminating inequality among racial and ethnic groups. Chicana feminist Enriqueta Longauex y Vasquez (1970:384), while acknowledging the importance of the Chicano movement, believes in stressing sexual equality: "When a man can look upon a woman as human, then, and only then, can he feel the true meaning of liberation and equality."

We can see that there is disagreement among minority women activists on whether priority should be granted to fighting for sexual equality or to eliminating inequality among racial and ethnic groups. Perhaps it would be most useful to conclude that neither component of inequality can be ignored. Helen Mayer Hacker (1973:11), who pioneered research on both Blacks and women, stated before the American Sociological Association: "As a partisan observer, it is my fervent hope that in fighting the twin battles of sexism and racism, Black women and Black men will [create] the outlines of the good society for all Americans" (see also Zia, 1993).

- Why has the issue of abortion rights been a fundamental concern of the feminist movement?
- From a conflict perspective, how are the factors of race, class, and ethnicity an important part of the abortion controversy?
- How do pro-choice and pro-life activists view the issues of parental consent and parental notification regarding abortions for teenagers?

Few issues seem to stir as much intense conflict as abortion. Until about 25 years ago, it was very difficult for a woman to terminate a pregnancy legally in the United States and most other industrial nations. Beginning in the late 1960s, a few state governments reformed statutes and made it easier for a woman to obtain a legal abortion. However, with abortion permissible only in a small minority of states, and only under certain conditions, a large number of women continued to have illegal abortions (Conover and Gray, 1983).

The fight for the right to safe, inexpensive, and legal abortions was a key priority of the feminist movement of the late 1960s and early 1970s. Feminists argued that the right to abortion was fundamental to women's sexual and reproductive freedom. In their view, women—not legislators or judges—should have an unconditional right to decide whether, and under what circumstances, they would bear children. Feminists further insisted that no law would ever prevent women from obtaining abortions. The issue was simply whether these abortions would be performed safely by doctors, or dangerously by "back room" abortionists or by the pregnant women themselves (Petchesky, 1990; E. Willis, 1980).

The critical victory in the struggle for legalized abortion came in the 1973 Supreme Court decision of *Roe v. Wade.* The justices held, by a 7-2 margin, that the "right to privacy . . . founded in the Fourteenth Amendment's concept of personal liberty . . . is broad enough to encompass a woman's decision whether or not to terminate a pregnancy." How-

ever, the Court did set certain limits on a woman's right to abortion. During the last three months of pregnancy, the fetus was ruled capable of life outside the womb. Therefore, states were granted the right to prohibit all abortions in the third trimester except those needed to preserve the life, physical health, or mental health of the mother. In subsequent decisions in the 1970s, the Supreme Court upheld the right of a woman to terminate pregnancy without the consent of her husband or (in the case of younger, unmarried women) her parents.

The Court's decision in *Roe v. Wade,* while generally applauded by "pro-choice" groups, which support the right to legal abortions, was bitterly condemned by those opposed to abortion. For people who call themselves "pro-life," abortion is a moral and often a religious issue. In their view, human life actually begins at the moment of conception rather than at the moment of a baby's delivery. On the basis of this judgment, the fetus is a human life, not a potential person. Termination of this life, even before it has left the womb, is viewed as essentially an act of murder. Consequently, antiabortion activists were alarmed by the fact that by 1989, over 22 million legal abortions had taken place in the United States in the years since the Supreme Court decision in *Roe v. Wade* (Bureau of the Census, 1993a:83; Luker, 1984:126–157).

In the mid-1970s, the antiabortion movement focused not only on legislative initiatives to prevent abortions but also on termination of government funding of abortions. In 1976, Congress passed the Hyde amendment, which prohibited use of Medicaid funds to pay for abortions except when the woman's life was in danger or when she was the victim of rape or incest. The effects of the Hyde amendment were dramatic: federally funded abortions were reduced by 99 percent. Moreover, as of 1992, only 13 states paid for abortions for low-income women. Consequently, for 3 million women of childbearing age relying on Medicaid, many of them teenagers, it became much more difficult to exercise the right to a legal abortion (Lewin, 1992; Schultz, 1977).

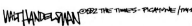

Both "pro-choice" and "pro-life" activists were disappointed with the Supreme Court's 1992 ruling in the key case of Planned Parenthood v. Casey. *The Court seemed to uphold* Roe v. Wade *in principle but allowed restrictions on the right to an abortion.*

For at least some low-income women, the results of these policies have been fatal. In 1977, Rosaura Jimenez of Texas became the first woman known to die of complications following an illegal abortion after implementation of the Hyde amendment. Viewing the issue from a conflict perspective, it was not surprising that the first group to lose access to legal abortions comprised poor women, of whom a significant number are Black and Hispanic (*Washington Post*, 1984).

In recent years, influenced by the votes of conservative justices appointed by Ronald Reagan and George Bush, the Supreme Court has increasingly restricted the right to an abortion. In the 1989 case of *Webster v. Reproductive Health Services,* the Court upheld, by a 5-4 vote, the state of Missouri's right to prohibit public hospitals from performing abortions and to prohibit public employees from performing or assisting in abortions not necessary to save a woman's life.

In 1992, in the case of *Planned Parenthood v. Casey,* a narrow 5-4 majority ruled that the "essential holding of *Roe v. Wade* should be retained and once again reaffirmed" but nevertheless allowed restrictions on the right to an abortion. The Court upheld the state of Pennsylvania's right to require a woman to wait 24 hours before having an abortion and to first hear a presentation intended to persuade her to change her mind. The majority also upheld Pennsylvania's right to require a teenager seeking an abortion to get the consent of one parent or a judge. These restrictions appeared likely to make access to abortion extremely difficult for low-income women and teenagers (Greenhouse, 1992).

Parental notification and parental consent have become especially sensitive issues in the debate over abortion. The respected Alan Guttmacher Institute estimates that over 1 million teenagers in the United States become pregnant each year and that 42 percent of them decide to have abortions. Pro-life activists argue that the parents of these teenagers should have the right to be notified about—and to permit or prohibit—these abortions. In their view, parental authority deserves full support at a time when the traditional nuclear family is embattled. However, pro-choice activists counter that many pregnant teenagers come from troubled families where they have been abused. These young women may have good reason to avoid discussing such explosive issues with their parents (Salholz, 1990).

In 1991, in another controversial ruling that pleased pro-life activists, the Supreme Court upheld federal regulations that prohibited employees of federally funded family planning clinics from discussing abortion with their patients. Under these regulations, 4500 clinics serving almost 4 million women each year were not permitted to offer basic medical information about abortion. The clinics were prohibited from assisting women to find doctors who would perform abortions (Greenhouse, 1991).

However, the election of Bill Clinton as president in 1992 delighted pro-choice activists and led to an immediate and dramatic change in federal policies concerning abortion. In early 1993, only days after his inauguration, and on the twentieth anniversary of the landmark *Roe v. Wade* ruling, President Clinton issued a series of memorandums which reversed the pro-life policies of the Reagan and Bush administrations. The president lifted the ban on abortion counseling at federally funded clinics, eased government policy concerning abortions in military hospitals, and ended a prohibition on aid to international family planning programs involved in abortion-related activities.

As of 1993, the people of the United States appeared to support the right to legal abortion in principle, but some were ambivalent concerning certain applications of that right. In a Gallup national survey, 32 percent of respondents stated that abortion should remain legal in all cases, while 55 percent said that it should be legal only in some cases or were unsure. Only 13 percent of respondents stated that abortion should be illegal in all cases. In the same survey, 47 percent of respondents indicated that they had an unfavorable view of pro-choice activists, 61 percent held an unfavorable view of pro-life activists, and 83 percent said that it was inappropriate for protestors to block access to abortion clinics (M. Hall, 1993).

Public opinion on the issue of abortion has been influenced by the extreme tactics of certain pro-life activists. In March 1993, Dr. David Gunn, a physician who performed abortions in Alabama and Florida, was shot and killed by an abortion opponent during a demonstration outside a clinic in Pensacola, Florida. The murder of Dr. Gunn occurred within a context of growing violence against abortion clinics, including an increasing number of personal attacks on clinic workers and even their families. From 1991 to 1992, the number of reported incidents of vandalism at clinics doubled; among the 186 attacks in 1992 were 13 acts of arson and at least 50 chemical attacks (Warner, 1993).

By the 1990s, abortions had also become a controversial issue in western Europe. As in the United States, many European nations bowed to public opinion and liberalized abortion laws in the 1970s. While Ireland, Belgium, and Malta continue to prohibit abortion, it is legal in other western European countries. Austria, Denmark, Greece, the Netherlands, Norway, and Sweden have laws that allow a woman to have an abortion on request. Other countries have much more restrictive legislation, especially concerning abortions in the later stages of pregnancy. Inspired by their counterparts in the United States, antiabortion activists have become more outspoken in Great Britain, France, Spain, Italy, and Germany. In a victory for antiabortion forces, Germany's highest court ruled in mid-1993 that a liberal abortion law passed in 1992 was unconstitutional because the state was required to protect human life (Kinzer, 1993; Simons, 1989).

In both western Europe and the United States, rural women experience difficulty in finding a physician who will perform an abortion. Currently, 83 percent of all counties in the United States lack a single abortion provider; 31 percent of women of childbearing age live in counties which have no clinic or hospital which provides abortions. Since only 12 percent of the nation's residency programs in obstetrics-gynecology even teach this procedure, the situation is likely to get worse before it improves. The inability to find a physician, clinic, or hospital that will perform an abortion forces rural women in the United States and Europe to travel long distances to get an abortion. Viewed from a conflict perspective, this is one more financial burden that falls especially heavily on low-income women (Bush, 1993; Lewin, 1992).

The intense conflict over abortion reflects broader differences over women's position in society. Sociologist Kristin Luker (1984:158–191) has offered a detailed study of activists in the pro-choice and pro-life movements. Luker interviewed 212 activists in California, overwhelmingly women, who spent at least five hours a week working for one of these movements. According to Luker, each group has a "consistent, coherent view of the world." Feminists involved in defending abortion rights typically believe that men and women are essentially similar; they support women's full participation in work outside the home and oppose all forms of sex discrimination. By contrast, most antiabortion activists believe that men and women are fundamentally different. In their view, men are best-suited for the public world of work, whereas women are best-suited for the demanding and crucial task of rearing children. These activists are troubled by women's growing participation in work outside the home, which they view as destructive to the family and ultimately to society as a whole.

SUMMARY

Differentiation based on gender is evident in virtually every human society about which we have information. As with race, the biological fact of gender is given a distinct social significance by society.

1 *Gender identity* is one of the first and most far-reaching identities that a human being holds.

2 Members of the female sex have been more severely restricted by traditional gender roles, but these roles have also restricted males.

3 The research of anthropologist Margaret Mead points to the importance of cultural conditioning in defining the social roles of males and females.

4 Functionalists maintain that sex differentiation contributes to overall social stability, whereas conflict theorists contend that the relationship between females and males has been one of unequal power, with men in a dominant position over women.

5 As one example of their micro-level approach to the study of gender stratification, interactionists have analyzed men's verbal dominance over women through conversational interruptions.

6 Although numerically a majority, in many respects women fit the definition of a subordinate minority group within the United States.

7 In terms of power dynamics, women clearly gain some additional degree of power by earning their own incomes.

8 As women have taken on more and more hours of paid employment outside the home, they have been only partially successful in getting their husbands to take a greater role in homemaking duties, including child care.

9 The fight for women's rights in the United States dates back as far as colonial times.

10 Minority women experience double jeopardy through differential treatment based not only on gender but also on race and ethnicity.

11 The issue of abortion has bitterly divided the United States and pitted pro-choice activists against pro-life activists.

CRITICAL THINKING QUESTIONS

1 Sociologist Barbara Bovee Polk suggests that women are oppressed because they constitute an alternative subculture which deviates from the prevailing masculine value system. Does it seem valid to view women as an "alternative subculture"? In what ways do women support and deviate from the prevailing masculine value system evident in the United States?

2 Imagine that you receive a grant to spend one year studying the status of women in any country outside the United States. What country would you choose? How would you draw on the functionalist, conflict, and interactionist perspectives to guide your study? In what ways would you make use of surveys, observations, experiments, and existing sources? What steps would you take to counteract any possible ethnocentrism in your study?

3 In what ways is the position of White women in the United States similar to that of African American women, Hispanic women, and Asian American women? In what ways is a woman's social position markedly different, given her racial and ethnic status?

KEY TERMS

Expressiveness A term used by Parsons and Bales to refer to concern for maintenance of harmony and the internal emotional affairs of the family. (page 311)

Gender identity The self-concept of a person as being male or female. (307)

Gender roles Expectations regarding the proper behavior, attitudes, and activities of males and females. (307)

Institutional discrimination The denial of opportunities and of equal rights to individuals or groups which results from the normal operations of a society. (316)

Instrumentality A term used by Parsons and Bales to refer to emphasis on tasks, focus on more distant goals, and a concern for the external relationship between one's family and other social institutions. (311)

Sexism The ideology that one sex is superior to the other. (316)

ADDITIONAL READINGS

Bem, Sandra Lipsitz. *The Lenses of Gender: Transforming the Debate on Sexual Inequality.* New Haven, Conn.: Yale University Press, 1993. An examination of how women and gays are subordinated in a culture defined by three "lenses": male-centeredness, gender polarization, and biological determinism.

Brinton, Mary C. *Women and the Economic Miracle: Gender and Work in Postwar Japan.* Berkeley: University of California Press, 1992. A sociological analysis of women's education and employment in contemporary Japan.

Craig, Steve (ed.). *Men, Masculinity, and the Media.* Newbury Park, Calif.: Sage, 1992. An overview of men's roles as portrayed in music, advertisements, films, and television.

Epstein, Cynthia Fuchs. *Deceptive Distinctions: Sex, Gender, and the Social Order.* New Haven, Conn.: Yale University Press, 1988. A feminist sociologist surveys social scientific research on gender.

Faludi, Susan. *Backlash: The Undeclared War against Women.* New York: Crown, 1991. A Pulitzer prize–winning journalist examines the growing backlash against women and against feminism, with a special focus on how the media have spread the backlash message.

Goldin, Claudia. *Understanding the Gender Gap: An Economic History of American Women.* New York: Oxford University Press, 1990. Goldin presents a historical framework for understanding how women have been assigned to particular occupations with lower pay than those held by men.

Hochschild, Arlie Russell, with Anne Machung. *The Second Shift: Working Parents and the Revolution at Home.* New York: Viking Penguin, 1989. A critical look at housework in dual-career couples, in which Hochschild observes that women's duties at home constitute a "second shift" after their work in the paid labor force.

Hoyenga, Katharine Blick, and Kermit T. Hoyenga. *Gender-Related Differences: Origins and Outcomes.* Boston: Allyn and Bacon, 1993. An overview of biological and psychological research on women and men.

Richardson, Laurel, and Verta Taylor. *Feminist Frontiers II: Rethinking Sex, Gender, and Society.* New York: Random House, 1989. This revised work summarizes the social perspective on gender in the United States.

Rothenberg, Paula S. *Race, Class, and Gender in the United States: An Integrated Study* (2d ed.). New York: St. Martin's, 1992. A collection of more than 70 articles focusing on the experiences and difficulties faced by women of color.

Schwartz, Felice N., with Jean Zimmerman. *Breaking with Tradition: Women and Work, the New Facts of Life.* New York: Warner, 1992. This book focuses on changing gender roles in the workplace and includes a full discussion of Schwartz's controversial concept, the "mommy track."

Thorne, Barrie. *Gender Play: Girls and Boys in School.* New Brunswick, N.J.: Rutgers University Press, 1993. An examination of how gender identity develops and is encouraged among 10- to 11-year olds.

Journals

Among the journals that focus on issues of gender stratification are *Changing Men* (founded in 1981), *Gender and Society* (1987), *Journeymen* (1991), *Sex Roles* (1975), *Signs: Journal of Women in Culture and Society* (1975), *Women: A Cultural Review* (1990), *Women's Studies* (1972), and *Women's Studies International Forum* (1978).

12

STRATIFICATION BY AGE

AGING AND SOCIETY

AGING WORLDWIDE

EXPLAINING THE AGING PROCESS
Functionalist Approach: Disengagement
   Theory
Interactionist Approach: Activity Theory
The Conflict Response

**AGE STRATIFICATION
IN THE UNITED STATES**
The "Graying of America"
Ageism
Competition in the Labor Force

The Elderly: Emergence of a Collective
   Consciousness

ROLE TRANSITIONS IN LATER LIFE
Adjusting to Retirement
Death and Dying

**SOCIAL POLICY AND AGE
STRATIFICATION: THE RIGHT
TO DIE**

BOXES
12-1 Around the World: The Elderly
    in !Kung Society
12-2 Speaking Out: An Older Person
    Speaks to Younger Generations

LOOKING AHEAD

- Why are the elderly considered a minority or subordinate group?
- Why does the aging of the world's peoples represent a major success story of the late twentieth century?
- In what ways do functionalists and interactionists take opposing views of the aging process?
- Do people in the United States tend to accept negative stereotypes of the elderly?
- How does the experience of retirement differ based on such factors as gender and race?
- How have voters in the United States responded to initiatives that would permit physician-assisted suicide?

"Does this person appear to you to be competent or incompetent? Generous or selfish?" Sociologist William Levin (1988) asked such questions of college students in California, Massachusetts, and Tennessee after showing them photographs of men who appeared to be about 25, 52, and 73 years old. Levin's findings confirmed the widespread age bias against the elderly evident across the United States.

The students questioned in Levin's experiment were *not* told that the three photographs were of the same man at different stages of his life. Special care was taken to select old photographs that had a contemporary look. All three photos were then professionally reproduced to equalize their tone qualities and screening counts. Levin initially intended to do a similar experiment using three photographs of the same woman, but changes in clothing and hairstyles made it much more difficult to pass off a 1940 photo of a young woman as a contemporary shot.

Levin asked the college students to evaluate the "three men" for a job using 19 measures. The 25-year-old man was found to be active, powerful, healthy, fast, attractive, energetic, involved, and in possession of a good memory. Students thought that the 52-year-old man had a high IQ and was reliable. By contrast, the 73-year-old man was evaluated as inactive, weak, sickly, slow, ugly, unreliable, lazy, socially isolated, and possessing a low IQ and a poor memory. Clearly, these findings suggest strong and consistent age stereotyping; the negative stereotypes of the elderly evident in this study could contribute to discrimination in the paid labor force and other areas of our society.

In contrast to the United States, the Sherpas—a Tibetan-speaking, Buddhist people in Nepal—live in a culture that idealizes old age. The Sherpas are a mountaineering people who engage in subsistence agriculture and cultivate land by hand. Almost all elderly members of the Sherpa culture own their own homes, and most are in relatively good physical condition. Typically, older Sherpas value their independence and prefer not to live with their children (M. C. Goldstein and Beall, 1981).

Although this chapter examines aging around

Sociologist William Levin showed college students these photographs (without telling them the photos were all of the same man at different stages of his life) and asked them to evaluate these "three men" as job candidates. The results of this experiment confirmed that age stereotyping of the elderly is common.

the world, it focuses primarily on the position of older people within the age-stratification system of the United States. It presents various theories developed to explain the impact of aging on the individual and society, including disengagement theory and activity theory. The effects of prejudice and discrimination on older people and the rise of a growing political consciousness among the elderly are discussed. Particular attention is given to older people's adjustment to retirement and to the experiences of death and dying. In the social policy section, we explore the controversy over whether people in the United States should have a "right to die" through mercy killings or even physician-assisted suicide.

AGING AND SOCIETY

Like gender stratification, age stratification varies from culture to culture. One society may treat older people with great reverence, while another sees them as "unproductive" and "difficult." Societies differ, as well, in their commitment to providing social services for older citizens. Sweden, Denmark, and Finland have pioneered an approach to aging known as "open old-age care," under which older citizens are encouraged and helped to live their later years in dignity in their own homes. "Home helpers" paid by local governments visit the elderly and perform such chores as housekeeping, cleaning, shopping, and cooking. But while Sweden had 1500 home helpers per 100,000 older people in need of such aid in 1987, the United States had

only 66 helpers per 100,000 older people (Szulc, 1988).

The elderly were highly regarded in the culture of traditional China. The period beginning at about age 55 was probably the most secure and comfortable time for men and women. As the closest living contact with people's ancestors, older family members received deference from younger kin and had first claim on all family resources. As China has become more urbanized and less traditional, older people without children have been given special assistance by trade unions and have also been granted limited welfare benefits (Foner, 1984; P. Olson, 1987, 1988).

Not all societies have traditions of caring for the elderly. Among the Fulani of Africa, older men and women move to the edge of the family homestead. Since this is where people are buried, the elderly sleep over their own graves, for they are already viewed as socially dead. Among the Mardudjara, a hunting-and-gathering culture of Australia, disabled older members are given food; however, when frequent travel becomes unavoidable, some are left behind to perish (Stenning, 1958; Tonkinson, 1978:83).

Some 25 societies are known to have practiced *senilicide*—the killing of the aged—because of extreme difficulties in providing basic necessities such as food and shelter. In the past, Eskimo culture encouraged elderly members to leave the settlement and die quietly in the cold. The social policy section at the end of the chapter will present a more detailed discussion of the killing, abandoning, or "death hastening" of the elderly in nonindustrial

Drawing by Ed Fisher; © 1983 The New Yorker Magazine, Inc.

"That was back then. I now espouse gerontocracy."

societies—as well as the acceptance of physician-assisted suicide in the Netherlands.

At the opposite extreme from societies practicing senilicide are the people of the Andaman Islands off Australia. In their culture, older members hold dominant positions in the social structure. They get the best available food, and their judgments are valued highly in their communities' informal decision making. Anthropologists have classified Andaman society as an example of **gerontocracy,** or rule by the elderly. This term is derived from the Greek word *geras,* meaning "old age" (Guemple, 1969; Radcliffe-Brown, 1964:44).

It is understandable that all societies have some system of age stratification and associate certain social roles with distinct periods in one's life. Some of this age differentiation seems inevitable; it would make little sense to send young children off to war or to expect most older citizens to handle physically demanding tasks such as loading goods at shipyards. However, as is the case with stratification by gender (see Chapter 11), age stratification in the United States goes far beyond the physical constraints of human beings at different ages (Babbie, 1980:299–300).

"Being old," in particular, is a master status that commonly overshadows all others in the United States. We can draw upon the insights of labeling theory (see Chapter 7) in sociological analysis of the consequences of aging. Once people are labeled "old" in the United States, this designation will have a major impact on how they are perceived and even on how they view themselves. As will be discussed more fully later in the chapter, negative stereotypes of the elderly contribute to their position as a minority group subject to discrimination.

Chapter 10 introduced five basic properties of a minority group. This model may be applied to older people in the United States in order to clarify the subordinate status of the elderly:

1 The elderly share physical characteristics that distinguish them from younger people. In addition, their cultural preferences and leisure-time activities are often at variance with those of the rest of society.
2 As we will show later in the chapter, the elderly experience unequal treatment in employment and may face prejudice and discrimination.
3 Membership in this disadvantaged group is involuntary.
4 Older people have a strong sense of group solidarity, as is reflected in the growth of senior citizens' centers, housing projects, and advocacy organizations.
5 When married (or when they marry later in life), older people generally are married to others of comparable age.

In analyzing the elderly as a minority, we find one crucial difference between older people and other subordinate groups, such as racial and ethnic minorities or women. All of us who live long enough will eventually assume the ascribed status of being an older person (M. Barron, 1953; Wagley and Harris, 1958:4–11; J. Levin and Levin, 1980).

AGING WORLDWIDE

Around the world, there are more than 330 million people aged 65 or over; they represent about 6 percent of the world's population. In an important sense, the aging of the world's population repre-

PART THREE • SOCIAL INEQUALITY

sents a major success story which has unfolded during the later stages of the twentieth century. Through the efforts of both national governments and international agencies, many societies have drastically reduced the incidence of diseases and their rates of death. Consequently, these nations—especially the industrialized countries of Europe and North America—have increasingly higher proportions of older members. This does not mean, however, that such nations have aged gracefully. Belated recognition of the demographic and socioeconomic changes associated with aging has often resulted in suffering (Haub and Yanagishita, 1993; Kinsella, 1988).

The overall population of Europe is older than that of any other continent. With this in mind, the European Economic Community (EEC) designated 1993 as the European Year of Older People and sponsored seminars, conferences, and studies examining issues of aging and age discrimination. Nevertheless, as the proportion of older people in Europe continues to rise, many governments that have long prided themselves on their social welfare programs are examining ways to shift a larger share of the costs of caring for the elderly to the private sector and charities. Germany, Italy, France, and Great Britain have instituted or are weighing plans to raise the age at which retirees will qualify for pensions (Schmidt, 1993).

Japan's population is aging faster than that of any other country as a result of falling birth- and death rates. Japan has traditionally honored its older citizens and even has a national holiday, Honor the Aged Day, on September 15. Yet the proportion of elderly people living with adult children has decreased substantially in recent decades. Changing attitudes in Japanese culture seem to include a decline in the belief that children are obligated to support their aging parents. Indeed, older people are singled out for criticism if they make what are viewed as excessive demands. Policymakers are worried that the Japanese government will be expected to provide financial and emotional support for the nation's growing population of older residents (C. Kiefer, 1990; L. Martin, 1989).

In most developing countries, aging has not yet emerged as a dominant social phenomenon. Rarely are special resources directed to meet the needs of people over 60, even though they are likely to be in poorer health than their counterparts in industrialized nations. Since many younger adults in developing nations immigrate to the cities, rural areas have higher proportions of older people. Formal social support mechanisms are less likely to exist in rural areas, yet at least family caregivers are present (see Box 12-1 on page 338). In the cities, these caregivers enter the work force, which makes it more difficult for them to care for elderly family members. At the same time, urban housing in developing countries is often poorly suited to traditional extended-family arrangements (Kinsella, 1988; Neysmith and Edwardh, 1984).

In industrialized nations, governmental social programs, such as Social Security, are the primary source of income for older citizens. However, given the economic difficulties of developing countries (refer back to Chapter 9), few of these nations are in a position to offer extensive financial support to the elderly. Regionally, South American countries provide the most substantial benefits, often assisting older people in both urban and rural areas. By contrast, such government support is nonexistent in many African states (Heisel, 1985; Kinsella, 1988).

Ironically, modernization in the developing world, while bringing with it many social and economic advances, has at the same time undercut the traditionally high status of the elderly. In many cultures, the earning power of younger adults now exceeds that of older family members. Consequently, the leadership role of the elderly has come into question, just as the notion of retirement has been introduced in the cultures of developing nations (Cowgill, 1986).

EXPLAINING THE AGING PROCESS

Aging is one important aspect of socialization—the lifelong process through which an individual learns the cultural norms and values of a particular society. As we saw in Chapter 4, there are no clear-cut definitions for different periods of the aging cycle in the United States. The term *age grades* refers to cultural categories that identify the stages of biological maturation. The ambiguity found in our culture about exactly when these age grades begin and end reflects the ambivalence with which we ap-

BOX 12-1 AROUND THE WORLD

THE ELDERLY IN !KUNG SOCIETY

It is not always easy to accurately interpret the treatment of the elderly in another culture. For example, long-term observation research has focused on the !Kung, a nomadic hunting-and-gathering tribe in southern Africa. In the culture of the !Kung, sharp and constant complaints are commonplace. For example, Kasupe, a 74-year-old man and a skilled storyteller, charges:

My own children do not look after me. See the clothes I am wearing — these rags I'm wearing — I get them from my own work, my own sweat. None of them have done anything for me. Because they do not look after me, I, their parent, say they are *kwara n* (without sense) (H. Rosenberg, 1990:25).

In fact, by North American standards, the treatment of older people in !Kung society is rather favorable. The tribe's elders are involved in their community's social, economic, political, and spiritual life. Most of the respected healers — the crucial health care providers for the !Kung — are elders. In general, older people in this culture enjoy personal autonomy, respect, and a significant degree of control over their day-to-day lives.

Care-giving is an integral part of the culture of the !Kung. Incapacitated elders are scrupulously cared for by relatives and the larger community. Only 10 percent of !Kung report that they have ever heard of an older person's being abandoned. Moreover, the elderly are not made to feel that they are a burden on younger generations. They do not need to negotiate care as if it were a favor; instead, it is perceived as a right. If older people can no longer produce enough to feed themselves, they will be given the basics of life in this nomadic culture: firewood, water, and food.

Why, then, are complaints like those of Kasupe so common among the !Kung? The community appears to set such high standards of care-giving — with each person ideally obligated to meet the needs of everyone else at all times — that no one can possibly meet this standard. Moreover, the !Kung, described by one researcher as "cranky, funny, and loud," love a captivating story — even if it is a passionate, elaborate complaint that is not fully justified. Thus, when Kasupe denounced his uncaring children, another tribal member observed that it was a "big story" (in other words, totally untrue). Rather than reacting angrily to this charge, Kasupe laughed, for he knew he had spun an enchanting tale which had captured the attention of listeners.

SOURCE H. Rosenberg, 1990.

---

proach the aging process, especially at its end point. Thus, while *old age* has typically been regarded as beginning at 65, which corresponds to the retirement age for many workers, this definition of old age is not universally accepted in the United States. Indeed, with life expectancy being extended, writers are beginning to refer to people in their sixties as the "young old" to distinguish them from those in their mid-eighties and beyond (the "old old").

The particular problems of the elderly have become the focus for a specialized area of research and inquiry known as gerontology. *Gerontology* is the scientific study of the sociological and psychological aspects of aging and the problems of the aged. It originally developed in the 1930s, as an increasing number of social scientists became aware of the plight of the elderly.

Gerontologists rely heavily on sociological principles and theories to explain the impact of aging on the individual and society. They also draw upon the disciplines of psychology, anthropology, physical education, counseling, and medicine in their study of the aging process. Two influential views of aging — disengagement theory and activity theory — can be best understood in terms of the sociological perspectives of functionalism and interactionism, respectively. The conflict perspective can also contribute to our sociological understanding of aging.

Functionalist Approach: Disengagement Theory

Elaine Cumming and William Henry (1961) introduced an explanation of the impact of aging known as *disengagement theory*. This theory, based on a study of elderly people in good health and relatively comfortable economic circumstances, contends that society and the aging individual mutually sever many of their relationships. In keeping with the functionalist perspective, disengagement theory emphasizes that a society's stability is assured when social roles are passed on from one generation to another.

According to this theory, the approach of death forces people to drop most of their social roles—including those of worker, volunteer, spouse, hobby enthusiast, and even reader. These functions are then undertaken by younger members of society. The aging person, it is held, withdraws into an increasing state of inactivity while preparing for death. At the same time, society withdraws from the elderly by segregating them residentially (retirement homes and communities), educationally (programs designed solely for senior citizens), and recreationally (senior citizens' social centers). Implicit in disengagement theory is the view that society should *help* older people to withdraw from their accustomed social roles.

Since it was first outlined more than three decades ago, disengagement theory has generated considerable controversy. Some gerontologists have objected to the implication that older people want to be ignored and "put away"—and even more to the idea that they should be encouraged to withdraw from meaningful social roles. Critics of disengagement theory insist that society *forces* the elderly into an involuntary and painful withdrawal from the paid labor force and from meaningful social relationships. Rather than seeking to disengage, older employees are pushed out of their jobs—in many instances, even before they are entitled to maximum retirement benefits (Boaz, 1987).

Although functionalist in its approach, disengagement theory ignores the fact that postretirement employment has been *increasing* in recent decades. In the United States, less than half of all employees actually retire from their career jobs.

Most instead move from a longtime career job into a "bridge job"—employment that bridges the period between the end of a person's longest job and his or her retirement (Doeringer, 1990; Hayward et al., 1987). Unfortunately, the elderly can easily be victimized in such "bridge jobs." Psychologist Kathleen Christensen (1990) warns of "bridges over troubled water" and emphasizes that older employees do not want to end their working days as minimum-wage jobholders engaged in activities unrelated to their career jobs.

Studies of other age groups suggest that disengagement is not exclusively associated with any particular age grade. For example, sociologist Helen Rose Fuchs Ebaugh (1988) uses the concept of disengagement to help describe the larger process of role exit (refer back to Box 5-1 on page 126). In some instances, disengagement from a social role is gradual and minimal, while in others it may be rapid and complete. Currently, sociologists agree with the assumption implicit in disengagement theory that aging should not be viewed simply as a personal process, but rather as a social phenomenon interrelated with the social structure and institutions of any particular society. Nevertheless, most sociologists and gerontologists do not regard disengagement theory as a valid explanation of aging (Pillemer, 1992).

Interactionist Approach: Activity Theory

Often seen as an opposing approach to disengagement theory, *activity theory* argues that the elderly person who remains active will be best-adjusted. Proponents of this perspective acknowledge that a 70-year-old person may not have the ability or desire to perform various social roles that he or she had at age 40. Yet they contend that old people have essentially the same need for social interaction as any other group.

The improved health of older people—sometimes overlooked by social scientists—has strengthened the arguments of activity theorists. Illness and chronic disease are no longer quite the scourge of the elderly that they once were. The recent emphasis on fitness, the availability of better medical

David Wells/Image Works

The recent emphasis on fitness has helped to mitigate the traumas of growing old in the United States and has strengthened the arguments of activity theorists.

care, greater control of infectious diseases, and the reduction of fatal strokes and heart attacks have combined to mitigate the traumas of growing old. Accumulating medical research also points to the importance of remaining socially involved. Among those who decline in their mental capacities later in life, deterioration is most rapid in old people who withdraw from social relationships and activities.

Admittedly, many activities open to the elderly involve unpaid labor—even though younger adults may receive salaries for the same work. Such unpaid workers include hospital volunteers (versus aides and orderlies), drivers for charities such as the Red Cross (versus chauffeurs), tutors (as opposed to teachers), and craftspeople for charity bazaars (as opposed to carpenters and dressmakers). However, some companies have recently initiated programs to hire retirees for full-time or part-time work. For example, about 130 of the 600 reservationists at the Days Inn motel chain are over 60 years of age (T. Lewin, 1990).

Disengagement theory suggests that older people find satisfaction in withdrawal from society. Functionally speaking, they conveniently recede into the background and allow the next generation to take over. Proponents of activity theory view such withdrawal as harmful for both the elderly and society and focus on the potential contributions of older

people to the maintenance of society. In their opinion, aging citizens will feel satisfied only when they can be useful and productive in *society's* terms—primarily by working for wages (Dowd, 1980:6–7; Quadagno, 1980:70–71).

Thus far, research findings have not provided consistent support for either disengagement or activity theory. Disengagement does not appear to be inevitable, universal, or commonly sought by older people. Rather than being a natural by-product of old age, disengagement seems more related to such factors as poor health, widowhood, retirement, and poverty. In terms of activity theory, one study found that people's feelings about their lives were *not* significantly affected by their level of activity. Moreover, research on mortality among 508 older Mexican Americans and Whites revealed that there was no relationship between how active they had been and how long they lived—once such factors as gender, age, and health were considered (D. Lee and Markides, 1990; Maddox, 1968; Okun et al., 1984; Reichard et al., 1962).

The Conflict Response

Conflict theorists have criticized both disengagement theory and activity theory for failing to consider the impact of social structure on patterns of aging. Neither approach attempts to question why social interaction "must" change or decrease in old age. In addition, these perspectives often ignore the impact of social class on the lives of the elderly.

The privileged position of the upper class generally leads to better health and vigor and to less likelihood of facing dependency in old age. Affluence cannot forestall aging indefinitely, but it can soften the economic hardships faced in later years. By contrast, working-class jobs often carry greater hazards to health and a greater risk of disability; aging will be particularly difficult for those who suffer job-related injuries or illnesses. Working-class people also depend more heavily on Social Security benefits and private pension programs. During inflationary times, their relatively fixed incomes from these sources hardly keep pace with the escalating costs of food, housing, utilities, and other necessities (Atchley, 1985).

Conflict theorists have noted that the transition from agricultural economies to industrialization and capitalism has not always been beneficial for the elderly. As a society's production methods change, the traditionally valued role of older people within the economy tends to erode. Although pension plans, retirement packages, and insurance benefits may be developed to assist older people, those whose wealth allows them access to investment funds can generate the greatest income for their later years (Dowd, 1980:75; Hendricks, 1982; L. Olson, 1982).

The conflict approach views the treatment of older people in the United States as reflective of the many divisions in our society. From a conflict perspective, the low status of older people is reflected in prejudice and discrimination against them and unfair job practices—none of which are directly addressed by either disengagement or activity theory.

AGE STRATIFICATION IN THE UNITED STATES

The "Graying of America"

As is evident in Figure 12-1, an increasing proportion of the population of the United States is composed of older people. Men and women aged 65 years and over constituted only 4 percent of the na-

FIGURE 12-1   Actual and Projected Growth of the Elderly Population

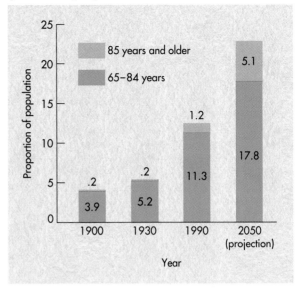

SOURCE: Taeuber, 1992:2–3.

An increasing proportion of the population of the United States is aged 65 and over. It is projected that by the year 2050, this group will constitute almost 23 percent of the nation's population. Moreover, projections point to a dramatic rise in the proportion of the "old old" (people aged 85 and over).

tion's population in the year 1900, but by 1990 this figure had reached 12.5 percent. It is currently projected that by the year 2050, almost 23 percent of people in the United States will be 65 and older. Moreover, while the elderly population continues to rise, the "old old" segment of the population (that is, people 85 years old and over) is growing at an ever-faster rate. By 2050, the proportion of the population 85 and over will reach 5.1 percent, compared with only 0.2 percent in 1930 (Taeuber, 1992:2–3).

It should be noted that the "graying of America" is not a uniform trend. As Figure 12-2 on page 342 shows, the highest proportion of older people is found in Florida, Arkansas, Pennsylvania, Rhode Island, West Virginia, and five midwestern states. Two different migratory movements with different social consequences have tended to concentrate older

FIGURE 12-2   People 65 Years and Over as a Percentage of Total Population, 1992

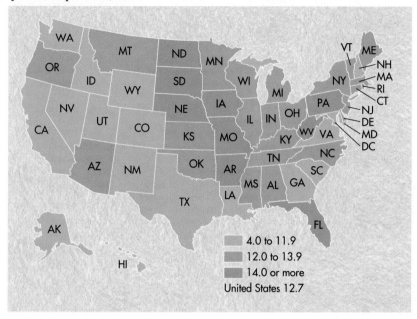

4.0 to 11.9
12.0 to 13.9
14.0 or more
United States 12.7

The highest proportion of older people live in Florida, Arkansas, Pennsylvania, Rhode Island, West Virginia, and five midwestern states.

SOURCE: Bureau of the Census, 1993a:33.

people in certain areas: retirement into magnet areas (primarily in the South) and the exodus of younger and middle-aged adults from economically declining areas (primarily in the North). Migrating retirees tend to be relatively well-off financially and therefore bring with them buying power and consumer demand. By contrast, where individuals and families have left an area owing to a lack of jobs, the resulting concentration of older residents may be viewed as a sign of malaise—a harbinger of a rising demand for government services coupled with a shrinking tax base to support those services (Frey, 1993).

While the United States is noticeably graying, the nation's older citizens are in a sense getting younger, owing to improved health and nutrition. As psychologist Sylvia Mertz told a symposium on aging in 1986, the activities of a contemporary 70-year-old "are equivalent to those of a 50-year-old a decade or two ago" (Horn and Meer, 1987:76). From the perspective of activity theory, this is obviously a welcome change which should be encouraged.

There is significant variation in wealth and poverty among the nation's older people. Some individuals and couples find themselves poor in part because of fixed pensions and skyrocketing health care costs (see Chapter 17). Nevertheless, as a group, older people in the United States are neither homogeneous nor poor. The typical elderly person enjoys a standard of living that is much higher than at any point in the nation's past. Class differences among the elderly remain evident but tend to narrow somewhat: those older people who enjoyed middle-class incomes while younger tend to remain better off after retirement than those who previously had lower incomes, but the financial gap lessens a bit (Arber, 1990; Duncan and Smith, 1989).

While part of the overall improved standard of living for older people stems from a greater accumulation of wealth—in the form of home ownership, private pensions, and other financial assets—much of the improvement is due to more generous Social Security benefits. While modest when compared with other countries' pension programs, Social Security nevertheless provides 38 percent of all income received by older people in the United States. Currently, about one-eighth of the nation's elderly population is below the poverty line; without Social Security, that figure would rise to half (Duncan and Smith, 1989; J. Hess, 1990:453). At the extremes of poverty are those groups who were more likely to be poor at earlier points in the life cycle: female-headed households and racial and ethnic minorities.

Women account for 60 percent of people in the United States 65 years old and over and 72 percent of those 85 and over. Older women experience a double burden: they are female in a society which favors males, and they are elderly in a society which values youth. The social inequities that women experience throughout their lifetimes (refer back to Chapter 11) only intensify as they age. As a result, in 1990 about half of older women living alone received some form of public assistance—whether Medicaid, food stamps, or subsidized or public housing (Taeuber, 1992).

The double burden of older women is evident around the world. Social workers Martin Tracy and Roxanne Ward (1986) studied women's pensions compared with men's for a period of 20 years in 10 industrialized nations. In *none* of these countries did women's benefits improve compared with men's, while in five nations (the United States, France, Switzerland, Finland, and Sweden) women's benefits not only were lower to begin with but fell even further behind those of men.

Viewed from a conflict perspective, it is not surprising that older women experience a double burden; the same is true of elderly members of racial and ethnic minorities. For example, in 1991 the proportion of older Hispanics with incomes below the poverty line (20.8 percent) was more than twice as large as the proportion of older Whites (10.3 percent) in this condition. The median income of an older White man was about $7400, or about $2800 more than that of an older Hispanic man and about $3300 more than that of an older African American man (Bureau of the Census, 1993a:470).

Clearly, the graying of the United States is a phenomenon that can no longer be ignored—either by social scientists or by government policymakers. Advocacy groups on behalf of the elderly have emerged and spoken out on a wide range of issues (as we will see later in the chapter). Politicians are often found courting the votes of older people, since they constitute a powerful and growing voting bloc. The elderly are much more likely to vote than younger age groups, a fact which tends to enhance their political clout. In 1992, 70 percent of people 65 years old and over reported voting, com-

Viewed from a conflict perspective, older women experience a double burden; the same is true of elderly members of racial and ethnic minorities.

343

pared with 61 percent of the total population and only 43 percent of people ages 18 to 20 (Jennings, 1993).

Ageism

In 1968, physician Robert Butler, the founding director of the National Institute on Aging, coined the term *ageism* to refer to prejudice and discrimination against the elderly. Ageism reflects a deep uneasiness among young and middle-aged people about growing old. For many, old age symbolizes disease, disability, and death; seeing the elderly serves as a reminder that *they* may someday become old and infirm. Ageism is so common that Butler (1990:178) noted that it "knows no one century, nor culture, and is not likely to go away any time soon."

With ageism all too common in the United States, it is hardly surprising that older people are barely visible on television. A recent content analysis of 1446 fictional television characters revealed that only 2 percent were age 65 and over—even though this age group accounts for more than 12 percent of the nation's population. In a second study, older women were found to be particularly underrepresented on television (J. D. Robinson and Skill, 1993; J. Vernon et al., 1990).

Even trained professionals are guilty of ageism, as in the case of medical personnel who too quickly diagnose patients as senile or view their ailments as imaginary or "nothing but old age." The consequences of ageism among physicians and other health care professionals can be especially serious. For example, a 1987 study revealed that older women with breast cancer frequently receive less medical treatment than they should, because of their age (Greenfield et al., 1987).

As one reflection of ageism, many people in the United States hold negative stereotypes of the elderly. The study discussed at the beginning of the chapter documented such stereotyping by college undergraduates; other studies of college students report widespread perceptions of older people as stubborn, touchy, quarrelsome, bossy, and meddlesome. Not surprisingly, the elderly resent such negative and patronizing stereotypes. As Irene Paull, the author of *Everybody's Studying Us,* a biting commentary on mistreatment of older people, pointed out: "Not only is our age not respected; in some mysterious way it is supposed to undermine our faculties and reduce us to the infantile" (B. Hess and Markson, 1980; Paull and Bülbül, 1976:7).

In contrast to negative stereotypes, researchers have found that older workers can be an asset for employers. According to a study issued in 1991, older workers can be retrained in new technologies, have lower rates of absenteeism than younger employees, and are often more effective salespeople. The study focused on two corporations based in the United States (the hotel chain Days Inns of America and the holding company Travelers Corporation of Hartford) and a British retail chain—all of which have long-term experience in hiring workers age 50 and over. Thomas Moloney, senior vice president of the Commonwealth Fund, a private foundation which commissioned the study, concluded: "We have here the first systematic hardnosed economic analysis showing older workers are good investments" (Telsch, 1991:A16).

Competition in the Labor Force

In the United States in the year 1900, fully two-thirds of men aged 65 and over were found in the paid labor force, working either full time or part time. Even as recently as 1950, 46 percent of older men were in the labor force, but by 1990 this figure had dropped to 16 percent. Even among the "young old" (those 65 to 69 years of age), labor force participation has declined from 60 percent in 1950 to less than 30 percent today (Taeuber, 1992). Nevertheless, younger adults continue to view older workers as "job stealers," a biased judgment similar to that directed against illegal immigrants (see Chapter 10). This belief not only intensifies age conflict but leads to age discrimination.

Although age discrimination (defined as discrimination against people 40 years old and over) has been illegal in the United States since 1968, it still persists within our society. In the words of the late U.S. representative Claude Pepper, the chief congressional advocate for the elderly during the 1970s and 1980s:

Age discrimination has oozed into every pore of the workplace. It stalks mature workers and severs them from their livelihoods, often at the peak of their careers. . . . Those who lose their jobs because of age discrimination often never recover from the shock of the experience (Weaver, 1982:A12).

In the last decade, age discrimination has been increasingly evident in the disproportionate firing of older employees (often in their fifties and sometimes in their forties) during layoffs. For example, when a new owner took over the *New York Daily News* in early 1993, 182 of the 544 members of the newspaper's editorial staff lost their jobs. Of those fired, 24 percent were under 40 years of age, 27 percent were between 40 and 50, and 49 percent were over 50. The termination of older workers—evident in such industries as securities, advertising, and publishing—allows employers to drop longtime employees with high salaries and to reduce their pension expenses. "It doesn't matter what company or what industry you work in these days," noted an employee of a Wall Street securities firm who asked to remain anonymous. "If you're over 40, you're old. Does it worry me? You bet" (M. Webb, 1993:67).

According to a report released in 1991 by the Older Women's League, middle-aged and older women are especially likely to face discrimination in the workplace. In 1989, the median annual earnings of women 45 to 54 years of age were $20,466, compared with $34,684 for men of that age group. Women 55 to 64 years of age had median annual earnings of $18,727, compared with $32,476 for men of that age. According to the report, less than half these wage differentials result from differences in education or work experience. Segregation of the work force by gender is viewed as a key factor in earning differentials (refer back to Chapter 11); such segregation is particularly severe among older women. For example, 62 percent of working women over age 55 are found in low-paying sales, clerical, and service jobs (T. Lewin, 1991b:8).

Like older people, the young feel that they are victimized within the job market because of their age. For example, in the 1980s Congress debated a law setting a lower minimum wage for teenagers in order to encourage increased employment of young people. Canada, the Netherlands, New Zealand, and Sweden all have instituted such subminimum wage programs for younger workers. Economists critical of the congressional proposal insisted that it would lead to exploitation of

N. Rowan/Image Works

The termination of older workers— evident in such industries as securities, advertising, and publishing—allows employers to drop longtime employees with high salaries and to reduce their pension benefits. Shown are young stockbrokers working in the World Trade Center in New York City.

teenagers at low wages; older employees feared that they would lose their jobs to those who could be hired at this lower minimum wage rate.

The Social Security system has also provoked age conflict within the paid labor force of the United States. Younger people are increasingly unhappy about paying Social Security taxes, especially since they worry that they themselves will never receive benefits from the fiscally insecure program. Reflecting such concerns, Americans for Generational Equity (AGE) was established in 1984 to represent the interests of "younger and future generations of Americans."

Backed by contributions from banks, insurance companies, and corporations offering health care services—all of which are private-sector competitors of Social Security and Medicare—AGE argues that the poor and the young suffer because society misappropriates too much funding for older people. AGE activists emphasize that while health care costs for the elderly continue to rise, there is inadequate funding for schools and younger generations are being saddled with an increasing national debt. However, critics of this voluntary association counter that AGE incorrectly and unfairly targets social services for older people as the cause of other problems. Moreover, critics point out that in the early 1990s AGE openly lobbied to reduce Social Security benefits yet was silent when social programs to benefit younger people were being debated (Hewitt and Howe, 1988; Quadagno, 1989, 1991).

The Elderly: Emergence of a Collective Consciousness

During the 1960s, students at colleges and universities across the country became concerned about "student power" and demanded a role in the governance of educational institutions. In the following decade, the 1970s, many older people became aware that they were being treated as second-class citizens. Just as the National Organization for Women (NOW) had been established to bring about equal rights for women, the Gray Panthers

organization was founded in 1971 to work for the rights of the elderly. Moreover, as NOW has enlisted the aid of male allies, the Gray Panthers have actively sought and received aid from younger generations.

In order to combat prejudice and discrimination against older people, the Gray Panthers issue publications and monitor industries particularly important to the elderly, such as health care and housing. For example, the condition of nursing homes in the United States prompted Gray Panther leader Maggie Kuhn to declare: "We throw away people, and before we throw them away, we warehouse them in institutions. We make them vegetables. . . ." (G. Collins, 1987:C8).

The growing collective consciousness among older people also contributed to the establishment of the Older Women's League (OWL) in 1980. OWL focuses on access to health insurance, Social Security benefits, and pension reform. OWL leaders and the group's 20,000 members hope that the organization will serve as a critical link between the feminist movement and activists for "gray power" (Hillebrand, 1992).

Still another manifestation of the new awareness of older people is the formation of organizations for elderly homosexuals. One such group, New York City's Senior Action in a Gay Environment

Paul Conklin/Monkmeyer

The Gray Panthers organization, founded in 1971, is dedicated to the fight against ageism.

(SAGE), has 3500 members. Like more traditional senior citizens' groups, SAGE sponsors workshops, classes, dances, and food deliveries to the homebound. At the same time, SAGE's activities provide a supportive gay environment where older lesbians and gay men can share their experiences. The vitality of such organizations helps to dispel the stereotype of aging homosexuals as inevitably isolated, lonely, and bitter (R. Alexander, 1988).

The largest organization representing the nation's elderly is the American Association of Retired Persons (AARP), founded in 1958 by a retired school principal who was having difficulty getting insurance because of age prejudice. Many of AARP's services involve discounts and insurance for its 33 million members, but the organization also functions as a powerful lobbying group which works for legislation that will benefit the elderly. For example, AARP has backed passage of a uniform mandatory-reporting law for cases of abuse of the elderly, which would be accompanied by enough federal funds to guarantee enforcement and support services.

The potential power of AARP is enormous: it is the second-largest voluntary association in the United States (behind only the Roman Catholic church) and represents one out of every four registered voters in the United States. While criticized for its lack of minority membership (the group is 97 percent White), AARP has endorsed voter registration campaigns, nursing home reforms, and pension reforms (Georges, 1992; Hornblower, 1988; Ornstein and Schmitt, 1990).

While such organizations as the Gray Panthers, OWL, SAGE, and AARP are undoubtedly valuable, the diversity of the nation's older population requires many different responses. For example, older African Americans and Hispanics tend to rely more on family members, friends, and informal social networks than on organizational support systems. Owing to their comparatively lower incomes and higher levels of incapacity resulting from poor health, older Blacks and Hispanics are more likely to need substantial assistance from family members than are older Whites. Representative Edward Roybal (1992:13A), chair of the House Committee on Aging, notes: "The minority elderly face difficulties not unlike the majority of the population. But their daily survival is made more difficult by economic, cultural, and language barriers which have confronted them throughout most of their lives."

There are several reasons why the influence of older people is expected to grow in coming decades. As noted earlier, their numbers are increasing substantially in the United States, and the elderly are more likely to go to the polls than other age groups are. In addition, through the efforts of many senior citizens' groups, including those described above, the elderly have become much more forceful in demanding their rights (see Box 12-2 on page 348).

ROLE TRANSITIONS IN LATER LIFE

As we have emphasized in Chapter 4 and throughout this textbook, socialization is a lifelong process. As a consequence of aging, people experience many dramatic changes in their day-to-day lives, including a loss of the primary parenting role and widowhood. In the following sections, we will focus on two major transitions associated with the later stages of the human life cycle: retirement and death and dying.

Adjusting to Retirement

Retirement is a rite of passage that marks a critical transition from one phase of a person's life to another. Typically, there are symbolic events associated with this rite of passage, such as retirement gifts, a retirement party, and special moments on the "last day on the job." The preretirement period itself can be emotionally charged, especially if the retiree is expected to train his or her successor (Atchley, 1976).

For both men and women in the United States, the average age of retirement has declined since 1950, while at the same time longevity has increased. Consequently, not only are more people reaching retirement age than ever before; they are also living longer after retirement. Typically, a man will live more than 16 years after retirement, while a woman will live more than 20 years (Gendell and Siegel, 1993).

Gerontologist Robert Atchley (1976) has identified several phases of the retirement experience:

AN OLDER PERSON SPEAKS TO YOUNGER GENERATIONS

Irene Paull, a fiction writer and long-time activist in civil rights, antiwar, and gray power causes, offered the following message to younger people (Paull and Bülbül:1976:79):

We are not a special interest group. We are simply your mothers, fathers, and grandparents. We are not asking you for a handout. We ran the world until you came along. Operated the factories. Tilled the soil. Bore the children. Taught them. Tended the sick. Built freeways and railroads, dug subways. We are simply the generation or two that preceded you. When we are gone you will move up to the vanguard and another generation will wonder what to do with you short of pushing you off a cliff.

© 1986 by Bülbül and Irene Paull

Irene Paull.

We are asking you, our children and grandchildren, for nothing that is not due us. At the cost of great sacrifice, and many casualties, we built the labor unions and the farm unions; won the eight-hour day; eliminated child labor; won Social Security and the concept that health care is a human right, not an act of someone's charity.

Millions of us fought all our lives for a peaceful world. We did not achieve it. Do not indict us for our failure. We leave it to you to wage that struggle not in millions but in tens of millions.

When we ask for a chance to live our old age in comfort, creativity, and usefulness, we ask it not for ourselves only, but for you. We are not a special interest group. We are your parents and grandparents. We are your roots. You are our continuity. What we gain is your inheritance.

- *Preretirement,* a period of anticipatory socialization as the person prepares for retirement.
- *The near phase,* when the person establishes a specific departure date from his or her job.
- *The honeymoon phase,* an often-euphoric period in which the person pursues activities that he or she never had time for before.
- *The disenchantment phase,* in which retirees feel a sense of letdown or even depression as they cope with their new lives, which may include illness or poverty.
- *The reorientation phase,* which involves the development of a more realistic view of retirement alternatives.
- *The stability phase,* a period in which the person has learned to deal with life after retirement in a reasonable and comfortable fashion.
- *The termination phase,* which begins when the person can no longer engage in basic, day-to-day activities such as self-care and housework.

As this analysis demonstrates, retirement is not a single transition but rather a series of adjustments that vary from one person to another. The length and timing of each phase will vary for each individual, depending on such factors as his or her financial and health status. In fact, a person will not necessarily go through all the phases identified by Atchley. For example, people who were forced to retire or who face financial difficulties may never experience a "honeymoon phase." Indeed, a significant number of retirees continue to be part of the paid labor force of the United States, often taking part-time jobs to supplement their pension income (M. Morrison, 1988; Quadagno, 1993).

Like other aspects of life in the United States, the experience of retirement varies according to gender, race, and ethnicity. White males are most likely to benefit from a structure of retirement wages as well as to have participated in a formal retirement preparation program. As a result, anticipatory socialization for retirement is most systematic for White men. By contrast, members of racial and ethnic minority groups—especially African Americans—

are more likely to exit the paid labor force through disability than through retirement. Because of their comparatively lower incomes and smaller savings, men and women from racial and ethnic minority groups work intermittently after retirement more often than do older Whites (M. Hardy, 1992; Quadagno, 1993).

In 1992, a special committee of the House of Representatives examined how well women fare under the nation's retirement policies. While at face value the retirement system does not discriminate against women, the Social Security program is still designed to serve the traditional nuclear family of the 1930s. Because women enter and exit the paid labor force more frequently than men, women often earn lower benefits than the spousal or survivors' benefits that married women would earn based on their husbands' earning records. Moreover, private pension plans generally fail to consider the particular work patterns of women in calculating benefits. Finally, women in the paid labor force are especially likely to work in low-wage, part-time, nonunion service jobs in small firms without pension coverage. For these reasons, women are not well served by retirement policies in the United States (Select Committee on Aging, 1992).

No matter what a person's gender, race, or income, the postretirement years typically involve difficult adjustments to aging and declining health. People who enter later life proud of their independence and who live full and active lives for a decade or two may nevertheless experience a chronic illness or disability that severely restricts them. Consequently, relationships between aging parents and their adult children may need to be redefined; the children may need to decide how much time and money they will devote to caring for ailing parents. Later life, of course, is not the only period in which an adult can become more dependent on other family members, but it is certainly the most likely time that this will occur (Koch, 1990).

Death and Dying

Among the role transitions that typically (but not always) come later in life is death. Until recently, death was viewed as a taboo topic in the United States. However, open discussion of the process of dying was greatly encouraged by psychologist Elis-abeth Kübler-Ross (1969) through her pioneering book *On Death and Dying.*

Drawing on her work with 200 cancer patients, Kübler-Ross identified five stages of the experience of dying that a person may undergo. When people finally realize that they are dying, they first *deny* the truth to themselves, their families, and their friends. When denial can no longer be maintained, it is followed by a period of *anger,* which can be directed at almost anyone or anything. Next comes a stage of *bargaining*—often relatively brief—in which people talk about the unfulfilled goals they will pursue if they somehow recover. In effect, they are hoping to bargain with God for additional time. When people realize that these deals are not realistic, they enter a stage of *depression* and experience a pervasive sense of loss. The final stage, *acceptance,* is not always reached by the dying patient. Those who accept death are not happy about the prospect, but have come to terms with their fate and are ready to die in peace. As Kübler-Ross (1969:113) notes: "It is as if the pain had gone, the struggle is over, and there comes a time for 'the final rest before the long journey' as one patient phrased it."

Despite its continued popular appeal, the Kübler-Ross five-stage theory of dying has been challenged. Efforts by researchers to substantiate these stages have often proved unsuccessful. Moreover, this model relies on an assumption that the dying person can clearly recognize that death is nearing, yet more than 20 percent of people in the United States age 65 and over die in nursing homes; for them and many others, death can be masked by an array of chronic, debilitative, degenerative diseases. Finally, critics of Kübler-Ross emphasize that even if this five-stage model is accurate for the United States, it does not apply to other cultures which deal with death quite differently (Marshall and Levy, 1990; Retsinas, 1988).

Viewed from a functionalist perspective, those who are dying must fulfill distinct social functions. Gerontologist Richard Kalish (1985) lists among the tasks of the dying: completing unfinished business, such as settling insurance and legacy matters; restoring harmony to social relationships and saying farewell to friends and family; dealing with medical care needs; and making funeral plans and other arrangements for survivors after death occurs. In accomplishing these tasks, the dying person actively contributes to meeting society's needs for smooth intergenerational transitions, role continuity, compliance with medical procedures, and minimal disruption of the social system despite loss of one of its members.

This functionalist analysis brings to mind the cherished yet controversial concept of a "good death." One researcher described a "good death" among the Kaliai, a people of the South Pacific, in which the dying person "called all his kinsmen to gather around him, disposed of his possessions after repaying the obligations owed by him and forgiving any obligations of others to him, and then informed those gathered that it was time for him to die" (Counts, 1977:370).

The "good death" among the Kaliai has its parallel in western societies, where we may refer to a "natural death," an "appropriate death," or a "death with dignity." In the western ideal of a "good death," a dying person is surrounded by friends and family, there is minimal technological interference with the dying process, the dying person's pain and discomfort are controlled, and there is an orderly and meaningful closure for the dying person and his or her loved ones. While this ideal makes the experience of dying as positive as possible, some critics fear that acceptance of the "good death" concept may direct individual efforts and social resources away from attempts to extend life. Indeed, arguments have been made that fatally ill older people should not only passively accept death but should forgo further treatment in order to reduce health care expenditures. As we will see in the social policy section later in the chapter, such issues are at the heart of current debates over the "right to die" and physician-assisted suicide (Kearl, 1989; Marshall and Levy, 1990).

Recent studies in the United States suggest that, in many varied ways, people have broken through the historic taboos about death and are attempting to arrange certain aspects of the idealized "good death." For example, bereavement practices—once highly socially structured—are becoming increasingly varied and therapeutic. More and more people are actively addressing the inevitability of death by making wills, leaving "living wills" (health care proxies which explain their feelings about the use of life-support equipment), and providing instructions for family members about funerals, cremations, and burials. Given medical and technological advances and a breakthrough in open discussion and negotiation regarding death and dying, it is more possible than ever that "good deaths" can become a social norm in the United States (Riley, 1992:414).

SOCIAL POLICY AND AGE STRATIFICATION

THE RIGHT TO DIE

- How common is "death-hastening" behavior in nonindustrialized societies?
- What positions have voluntary associations and professional associations taken regarding the "right to die"?
- In what ways are conflict theory and disengagement theory relevant in the debate over the "right to die"?

On August 4, 1993, Dr. Jack Kevorkian, a 64-year-old retired pathologist, helped a 30-year-old Michigan man with Lou Gehrig's disease commit suicide in a van. Thomas Hyde, Jr., died after inhaling carbon monoxide through a mask designed by Dr. Kevorkian; in doing so, he became the seventeenth person to commit suicide with Kevorkian's assistance. In aiding Hyde's suicide, Kevorkian openly challenged a Michigan law adopted in early 1993 (and aimed at him) which makes it a felony crime—punishable by up to four years in jail—to assist in a suicide. Michigan authorities had attempted to prosecute Kevorkian for murder three times since he began assisting people to kill themselves in 1990, but each time the charges were dismissed (Terry, 1993).

The issue of physician-assisted suicide—first brought into national focus by Kevorkian during a 1989 television appearance on the *Donahue* show—is but one aspect of the larger debate in the United States and other countries over the ethics of suicide and euthanasia. The term *euthanasia* has been de-

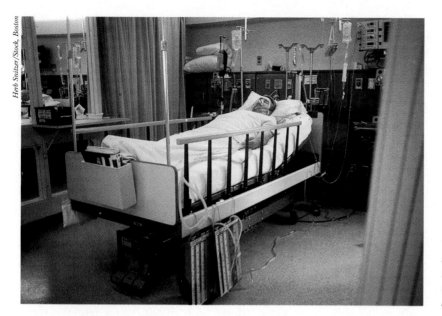

While active euthanasia remains illegal across the United States, there is greater legal tolerance for passive euthanasia (such as disconnecting life-support equipment when a patient is comatose).

fined as the "act of bringing about the death of a hopelessly ill and suffering person in a relatively quick and painless way for reasons of mercy" (Council on Ethical and Judicial Affairs, American Medical Association, 1992:2229). This type of mercy killing reminds us of the ideal of "good death" discussed earlier in the chapter. The debate over euthanasia and assisted suicide often focuses on cases involving older people, though it can involve younger adults with terminal and degenerative diseases (as in the case of Thomas Hyde, Jr.) or even children.

As discussed earlier, many societies are known to have practiced senilicide because of extreme difficulties in providing basic necessities such as food and shelter. In a study of the treatment of the elderly in 41 nonindustrialized societies, Anthony Glascock (1990) found that some form of "death-hastening" behavior was present in 21 of them. Killing of the elderly was evident in 14 of these societies, while abandoning of older people was evident in 8 societies. Typically, such death hastening occurs when older people become decrepit and are viewed as "already dead." Death hastening in these nonindustrialized cultures is open and socially approved; decisions are generally made by family members, often after open consultation with those about to die.

In the industrialized world, euthanasia is widely accepted only in the Netherlands. Since 1970, many Dutch physicians have violated prohibitions against euthanasia, and court rulings have appeared to tolerate this practice. According to a government report released in 1991, there are more than 25,000 cases of euthanasia each year—accounting for nearly 20 percent of all deaths in the nation—including some 1000 cases per year of people killed without their consent (that is, involuntarily) by physicians in acts intended as euthanasia. As of early 1993, the Dutch parliament was close to adopting the world's least restrictive euthanasia policy, with specific guidelines permitting a physician to assist in a suicide or kill a terminally ill patient at the patient's request. Legislators were also considering permitting euthanasia for those unable to request it, among them severely disabled newborns and mentally disabled adults. But Dr. Karel Gunning, a member of a Dutch antieuthanasia group, warned: "It is exactly like what Hitler started to do in the 1930s" (Kass, 1991; *New York Times*, 1993c:A3; Simons, 1993b; see also Battin, 1992; McCord, 1993).

Currently, public policy in the United States does not permit *active euthanasia* (such as a physician's deliberately administering a lethal injection to a terminally ill patient) or physician-assisted suicide. Although suicide itself is no longer a crime, assisting suicide is illegal in at least 29 states. In 1991, by a 54 to 46 percent margin, voters in the state of Washington rejected an initiative that asked: "Shall adult patients who are in a medically terminal condition be permitted to request and receive from a physician aid-in-dying?" The following year, by a similar margin, California's voters turned down a "death with dignity" initiative (Margolick, 1993; Martinez, 1993; McCord, 1993:26).

While active euthanasia remains illegal across the United States, there is greater legal tolerance for *passive euthanasia* (such as disconnecting life-support equipment when a patient is comatose). In a historic ruling in 1975, the New Jersey Supreme Court held that the parents of Karen Ann Quinlan (who had lapsed into a substance-abuse coma) could have her disconnected from a respirator so that she might die "with grace and dignity." In a 1990 case focusing on Nancy Cruzan, who existed on a feeding tube, the U.S. Supreme Court upheld a person's constitutional right to the discontinuance of life-support treatment. By 1991, 28 states had declared that patients have the right to refuse life-sustaining medical treatment; as of early 1993, 9 states specifically allowed the withdrawal of feeding tubes from patients in a vegetative state, thereby allowing these patients to starve to death (Kearl, 1989:431–432; Martinez, 1993:68; McCord, 1993:26).

While formal norms concerning euthanasia may be in flux, informal norms seem to exist which permit mercy killings. According to an estimate by the American Hospital Association, as many as 70 percent of all deaths in the United States are quietly negotiated with patients, family members, and physicians agreeing not to use life-support technology. In an informal poll of internists, one in five reported that he or she had assisted or helped cause the death of a patient. In a period in which AIDS-related deaths are common (refer back to Chapter 5), an AIDS underground is known to share information and assistance regarding suicide (Gibbs, 1993:37; Martinez, 1993:69).

Survey data reveal growing support for the "right to die." In a 1975 Gallup poll, 41 percent of respondents believed that someone in great pain, with "no hope of improvement," had the moral right to commit suicide; by 1990, this figure had risen to 66 percent. An analysis of 1991 survey data revealed that younger people are more likely than older people to favor permitting withdrawal of life support and euthanasia. Interestingly, acceptance of withdrawal of life support was found to be strong and steady among all major religious groups in the United States, including fundamentalists and born-again Christians (Ames et al., 1991; Blendon et al., 1992:2659–2660; McCord, 1993:27).

Voluntary associations have been established in the United States (and various European countries) to work for legalization of voluntary euthanasia and physician-assisted suicide. The Hemlock Society, the best known of these groups, doubled its membership in the United States to 33,000 over the period 1987 to 1992. In mid-1993, Compassion in Dying was founded in Seattle; it is the nation's first organization established to provide professionals who will help terminally ill people kill themselves. The National Organization for Women (NOW) supports "death with dignity" as a feminist issue, noting that the courts have upheld 60 percent of men's request to die but only 14 percent of women's (Council on Ethical and Judicial Affairs, 1992:2232; Martinez, 1993:66; *New York Times*, 1993c; see also Belkin, 1993).

By contrast, professional associations such as the American Bar Association and the American Medical Association (AMA) remain opposed to physician-assisted suicide and most forms of euthanasia. While the AMA has approved disconnecting life-support equipment when a patient's coma is irreversible, it emphasizes that the proper role of doctors (and the health care system as a social institution) is to care for patients and preserve their lives. "Medicine is a profession dedicated to healing," says the AMA. "Its tools should not be used to kill people" (Gibbs, 1993:38).

Defenders of the right to die see what they call "rational suicide" as a noble and uniquely human decision. Summarizing this position, sociologist William McCord (1993:27) writes:

A death with dignity is a final proof that we are not merely pawns to be swept from the board by an unknown hand. As a courageous assertion of independence and self-control, suicide can serve as an affirmation of our ultimate liberty, our last infusion of meaning into a formless reality.

Other supporters of the right to die emphasize that

euthanasia and physician-assisted suicide will end horrible and needless suffering. A Los Angeles physician who works with AIDS patients suggests: "You have to understand what it is I see. I see people in agony. . . . By God, if someone is dying, far be it for me to say 'Hey, tough it out'" (Gibbs, 1993:37).

Some opponents of the "right to die" draw on religious traditions and argue that suicide and euthanasia are morally wrong under any circumstances. But other critics of "rational suicide" fear that granting legitimacy to even limited types of euthanasia and assisted suicide will open the way to many dangerous abuses. These critics note with horror the proliferation of *involuntary* euthanasia in the Netherlands. Reflecting the conflict perspective, gerontologist Elizabeth Markson (1992:6) argues that the "powerless, poor or undesirable are at special risk of being 'encouraged' to choose assisted death."

Critics of euthanasia charge that many of its supporters are guilty of ageism and other forms of bias. In a society that commonly discriminates against the elderly and people with disabilities (see Chapter 20), medical authorities and even family members may decide too quickly that such people should die "for their own good" or (in a view somewhat reminiscent of disengagement theory) "for the good of society." It is feared that society may use euthanasia to reduce health care costs—rather than striving to make life better for those near the end. Indeed, older people may feel compelled to (prematurely) end their lives to ease the emotional and financial burdens on family members and friends (Glascock, 1990:45; *New York Times,* 1993d; Richman, 1992).

For many opponents of euthanasia, hospice care for the terminally ill serves as a preferred alternative. The first hospice in the United States was established in 1974; by 1992, some 1700 hospices were serving 200,000 patients per year. The hospice movement encourages people to "live until they die" and believes that they can die peacefully, painlessly, and with dignity in small, caring institutions or at home. Ideally, the hospice provides a meaningful social network, allowing the dying person to share his or her feelings with others in the same situation—as well as with trained hospice professionals. Unfortunately, hospice care is not economically feasible for many terminally ill people—and overcrowded hospitals have little room for those who are slowly dying and cannot be saved (Conley, 1992:14–15; Guillemin, 1992:32; R. Miller, 1992:128–129).

Through advances in technology, we can now prolong life in ways that were unimaginable decades ago. But medical and technological advances cannot provide answers to the complex ethical, legal, and political questions raised by active and passive euthanasia and physician-assisted suicide.

SUMMARY

Age, like gender and race, is an ascribed status that forms the basis for social differentiation. This chapter examines theories regarding the aging process, age stratification in the United States, and the growing political activism of the nation's elderly population.

1 Like other forms of stratification, age stratification varies from culture to culture.

2 "Being old" is a master status that seems to overshadow all others in the United States.

3 The aging of the world's populations represents a major success story which has unfolded during the later stages of the twentieth century.

4 The particular problems of the aged have become the focus for a specialized area of research and inquiry known as **gerontology.**

5 **Disengagement theory** implicitly suggests that society should help older people withdraw from their accustomed social roles, whereas **activity theory** argues that the elderly person who remains active will be best-adjusted.

6 From a conflict perspective, the low status of older people is reflected in prejudice and discrimination against them and unfair job practices.

7 An increasing proportion of the population of the United States is composed of older people.

8 There is considerable adherence to negative stereotypes about the elderly in the United States.

9 The American Association of Retired Persons (AARP) works as a powerful lobbying group backing legislation that will benefit senior citizens.

10 Retirement is a rite of passage that marks a critical transition in the life of a person from one phase to another.

11 The controversy over physician-assisted suicides, such as those performed by Dr. Jack Kevorkian, is but one aspect of the larger debate in the United States over the right to die.

CRITICAL THINKING QUESTIONS

1 Are there elderly students at your college or university? How are they treated by younger students and by faculty members? Is there a subculture of older students? How do younger students view faculty members in their fifties and sixties?

2 Is age segregation functional or dysfunctional for older people in the United States? Is it functional or dysfunctional for society as a whole? What are the manifest functions, the latent functions, and the dysfunctions of age segregation?

3 Imagine that you were asked to study political activism among older people. How might you employ surveys, observations, experiments, and existing sources to better understand such activism?

KEY TERMS

Activity theory   An interactionist theory of aging which argues that elderly people who remain active will be best-adjusted. (page 339)

Age grades   Cultural categories that identify the stages of biological maturation. (337)

Ageism   A term coined by Robert Butler to refer to prejudice and discrimination against the elderly. (344)

Disengagement theory   A functionalist theory of aging introduced by Cumming and Henry which contends that society and the aging individual mutually sever many of their relationships. (339)

Euthanasia   The act of bringing about the death of a hopelessly ill and suffering person in a relatively quick and painless way for reasons of mercy. (350)

Gerontocracy   Rule by the elderly. (336)

Gerontology   The scientific study of the sociological and psychological aspects of aging and the problems of the aged. (338)

Senilicide   The killing of the aged. (335)

ADDITIONAL READINGS

Binstock, Robert M., and Linda K. George (eds.). *Handbook of Aging and the Social Sciences* (3d ed.). New York: Van Nostrand Reinhold, 1990. This collection of 23 articles views aging from the perspective of many academic disciplines, among them geography, economics, and epidemiology.

Butler, Robert N. *Why Survive? Being Old in America.* New York: Harper and Row, 1975. The now-classic, Pulitzer prize–winning study that introduced the term *ageism* to our understanding of older people.

Chudacoff, Howard P. *How Old Are You?* Princeton, N.J.: Princeton University Press, 1989. A historian examines how age became such a dominant status in the United States.

Doeringer, Peter B. (ed.). *Bridges to Retirement: Older Workers in a Changing Labor Market.* Ithaca, N.Y.: ILR Press, 1990. An analysis of labor market opportunities for older people, including flexible retirement policies.

Dychtwald, Ken, with Joe Flower. *Age Wave: The Challenges and Opportunities of an Aging America.* Los Angeles: Tarcher, 1989. Psychologist Dychtwald presents a rapid-paced, journalistic account of aging in the United States. He emphasizes the benefits of an aging nation both for the individual and for the larger society.

Hess, Beth B., and Elizabeth W. Markson (eds.). *Growing Old in America* (4th ed.). New Brunswick, N.J.: Transaction, 1991. This book views aging from the life course and political economy perspectives.

Howe, Neil, and Bill Strauss. *13th Gen: Abort, Retry, Ignore, Fail?* New York: Vintage, 1993. A heavily illustrated view of the lifestyles and beliefs of the thirteenth generation in the United States (people born between 1961 and 1981).

Olson, Laura Katz. *The Political Economy of Aging: The State, Private Power, and Social Welfare.* New York: Columbia University Press, 1982. Drawing on the conflict perspective, Olson argues that capitalistic societies are structured to deprive those outside the privileged core (such as older people) of wealth and power.

Palmer, John L., Timothy Smeeding, and Barbara Boyle Torrey (eds.). *The Vulnerable.* Washington, D.C.: Urban Institute, 1988. This study focuses on the changes in well-being among the nation's two largest dependent groups—children and the elderly—and the potential implications for public policies.

Sokolovsky, Jay (ed.). *The Cultural Context of Aging: Worldwide Perspectives.* New York: Bergin and Garvey, 1990. A series of descriptions of aging and the position of the elderly in cultures throughout the world.

Journals

Among the journals that focus on issues of aging and age stratification are *Ageing International* (founded in 1994), *Aging and Society* (1981), *Contemporary Gerontology* (1994), *Death Studies* (1976), *Generations* (1976), *The Gerontologist* (1961), *Journal of Gerontology* (1946), *Research on Aging* (1979), and *Youth and Society* (1968).

PART FOUR

SOCIAL

INSTITUTIONS

*Part Four will consider sociological analysis of major institutions, including the family, religion, government, the economy, education, and health care. As noted earlier in the text, **social institutions** are organized patterns of beliefs and behavior centered on basic social needs.*

Chapter 13 focuses on the functions of the family and its importance as a cultural universal. Chapter 14 discusses the dimensions, functions, and organization of religion. Chapter 15 looks at government and the economy, with particular emphasis on types of governments and economic systems. Chapter 16 considers the functions of education, schools as social organizations, and recent trends in education. Chapter 17 analyzes sociological perspectives on health and illness, the health care system of the United States, and mental illness.

13

THE FAMILY

THE FAMILY: UNIVERSAL BUT VARIED
Composition: What Is the Family?
Descent Patterns: To Whom Are
  We Related?
Family Residence: Where Do We Live?
Authority Patterns: Who Rules?

FUNCTIONS OF THE FAMILY

MARRIAGE AND FAMILY IN THE UNITED STATES
Courtship and Mate Selection
  Aspects of Mate Selection
  The Love Relationship
Parenthood and Grandparenthood
Adoption
Dual-Career Families
Variations in Family Life
  Social Class Differences
  Racial and Ethnic Differences

DIVORCE IN THE UNITED STATES
Statistical Trends in Divorce
Factors Associated with Divorce

ALTERNATIVE LIFESTYLES
Cohabitation
Remaining Single
Gay Relationships
Marriage without Children
Single-Parent Families

SOCIAL POLICY AND THE FAMILY: DOMESTIC VIOLENCE

BOXES
13-1 Everyday Behavior: Marital Power
13-2 Current Research: The Effects
     of Divorce on Female and
     Male Children

> *T*he couple is a basic unit of society. It is the unit of reproduction, the wellspring of the family, and most often the precinct of love, romance, and sexuality.
>
> Philip Blumstein and Pepper Schwartz,
> American Couples, 1983

LOOKING AHEAD

- Are all families necessarily composed of a husband, a wife, and their children?
- What functions does the family perform for society?
- Do married women who work outside the home have greater marital power than full-time homemakers?
- What factors influence our selection of a mate?
- Does divorce have a more detrimental effect on boys than on girls?
- Should gay couples and unmarried heterosexual couples have the same legal protections and benefits as married couples?
- What can be done to prevent violence between family members?

In the 1950s and the early 1960s, television programs in the United States—among them *Ozzie and Harriet, Leave It to Beaver,* and *Father Knows Best*—inevitably presented a single (and idealized) model of family life. All families seemingly were stable and peaceful two-parent families with children. This never-ending television image masked less pleasant realities: divorce was on the rise, an increasing number of children were living with a single parent, and domestic violence was far from uncommon (Coontz, 1992).

In the last 25 years, family life in the United States (and other industrialized nations) has moved further and further away from the idealized model of the 1950s and 1960s. Consider the following data concerning family patterns:

- In the period 1970 to 1990, the marriage rate of the United States decreased by almost 30 percent.
- During this same period, the nation's divorce rate increased by nearly 40 percent.
- In 1990, more than one-fourth of all births in the United States were to unmarried mothers, compared with only one-tenth in 1970.
- Currently, about half of all children born in the United States are expected to spend some part of their childhood in single-parent homes (Ahlburg and De Vita, 1992:4).

While politicians and religious leaders are debating the meaning of "family values," an increasing proportion of people in the United States are living in nontraditional types of family arrangements such as single-parent families, stepfamilies, and foster families.

In this chapter, we will see how family patterns differ from one culture to another and even within the same culture. In the Toda culture of southern India, a woman may be simultaneously married to several men. Fatherhood is not always connected with actual biological facts; any husband may establish paternity by presenting a pregnant woman with a toy bow and arrow. The Balinese of Indonesia permit twins to marry each other because they believe that twins have already been intimate in the womb. In the Banaro culture of New Guinea, the husband is forbidden to have intercourse with his wife until she has first borne a child by another man chosen for that purpose. Once the wife has proved that she can bear children, the husband is allowed to have sexual relations with her (Leslie and Korman, 1989:15, 30, 39).

In this chapter, we will see that the family is uni-

As we will see in this chapter, most households in the United States do not have two parents living with their unmarried children.

versal—found in every culture—though varied in its organization. A *family* can be defined as a set of people related by blood, marriage (or some other agreed-upon relationship), or adoption who share the primary responsibility for reproduction and caring for members of society. We will look at the primary functions of the family and the variations in marital patterns and family life in the United States. Particular attention will be given to the increasing number of people who are living in dual-career or single-parent families. The social policy section will examine the distressing prevalence of domestic violence in the United States.

THE FAMILY: UNIVERSAL BUT VARIED

The family as a social institution is present in all cultures. Although the organization of the family can vary greatly, there are certain general principles concerning its composition, descent patterns, residence patterns, and authority patterns.

Composition: What Is the Family?

In the United States, the family has traditionally been viewed in very narrow terms—as a married couple and their unmarried children living together. However, this is but one type of family, what

sociologists refer to as a *nuclear family.* The term *nuclear family* is well-chosen, since this type of family serves as the nucleus, or core, upon which larger family groups are built. People in the United States see the nuclear family as the preferred family arrangement. Yet, as is shown in Figure 13-1, by 1990 only about one-quarter of the nation's households fit this model. (The term *household* is used by the Bureau of the Census to refer to related or unrelated individuals sharing a residence as well as to people who live alone.)

As Figure 13-1 (page 362) illustrates, the proportion of households in the United States composed of married couples with children at home has decreased steadily over the last 30 years. At the same time, there have been substantial increases in the number of single-person and single-parent households. Similar trends are evident in other industrialized nations, including Canada, Great Britain, and Japan (see Figure 13-2 on page 363).

A family in which relatives in addition to parents and children—such as grandparents, aunts, or uncles—live in the same home is known as an *extended family.* While not common, such living arrangements do exist in the United States. The structure of the extended family offers certain advantages over that of the nuclear family. Crises such as death, divorce, and illness involve less strain for family members, since there are more people who can provide assistance and emotional support. In

FIGURE 13-1 *Types of Households in the United States, 1970, 1980, and 1990*

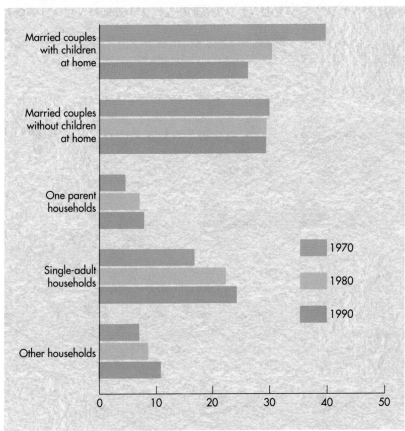

The proportion of households in the United States composed of married couples continues to decline, and the proportion of single-adult households rose from about 17 percent in 1970 to almost 25 percent in 1990.

NOTE: "Children" refers to children under 18. "Other households" includes people living together who may be related (but not married) with no children present. Because of rounding, numbers may not total 100 percent.
SOURCE: Bureau of the Census, 1990c:2.

addition, the extended family constitutes a larger economic unit than the nuclear family. If the family is engaged in a common enterprise—for example, a farm or a small business—the additional family members may represent the difference between prosperity and failure.

In considering these differing family types, we have limited ourselves to the form of marriage that is characteristic of the United States—monogamy. The term *monogamy* describes a form of marriage in which one woman and one man are married only to each other. Some observers, noting the high rate of divorce in the United States, have suggested that "serial monogamy" is a more accurate description of the form that monogamy takes in the United States. Under *serial monogamy,* a person is allowed to have several spouses in his or her life but can have only one spouse at a time.

Some cultures allow an individual to have several husbands or wives simultaneously. This form of marriage is known as *polygamy.* You may be surprised to learn that most societies throughout the world, past and present, have preferred polygamy, not monogamy. Anthropologist George Murdock

(1949, 1957) sampled 565 societies and found that over 80 percent had some type of polygamy as their preferred form.

There are two basic types of polygamy. According to Murdock, the most common—endorsed by the majority of cultures he sampled—was polygyny. *Polygyny* refers to the marriage of a man to more than one woman at the same time. The various wives are often sisters, who are expected to hold similar values and have already had experience sharing a household. In polygynous societies, relatively few men actually have multiple spouses. Most individuals live in typical monogamous families; having multiple wives is viewed as a mark of status.

The other principal variation of polygamy is *polyandry,* under which a woman can have several husbands at the same time. As we saw earlier in the chapter, this was the case in the culture of the Todas of southern India. Yet, despite such examples, polyandry tends to be exceedingly rare. It has been accepted by some extremely poor societies which practice female infanticide (the killing of baby girls) and thus have a relatively small number of women. Like many other societies, polyandrous cultures devalue the social worth of women.

Descent Patterns: To Whom Are We Related?

In the late 1970s, many people in the United States were deeply moved by Alex Haley's successful quest for his family tree, which was documented in his book *Roots* and later popularized on network television. Beginning with stories passed down by his grandmother, Haley was able to trace his heritage back to Africa—to a man named Kunta Kinte who lived in Gambia, West Africa, and was brought to the United States in chains by slave traders.

Many of us, like Alex Haley, have retraced our roots by listening to elderly family members tell us

FIGURE 13-2   *Married-Couple Households with Children in Industrialized Nations, 1960 and 1990*

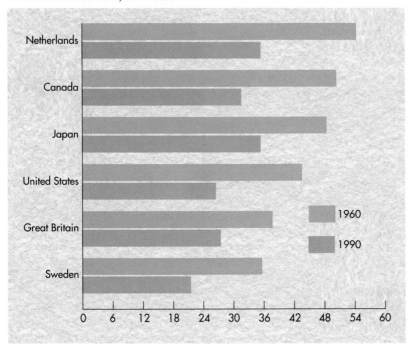

As in the United States, the proportion of all households consisting of a married couple with children is declining in many other industrialized nations.

SOURCE: Bureau of Labor Statistics data in Sorrentino, 1990:46–47; and authors' estimates.

The state of being related to others is called kinship. *Kin groups include aunts, uncles, cousins, in-laws, and so forth.*

about their lives—and about the lives of ancestors who died long before we were even born. Yet a person's lineage is more than simply a personal history; it also reflects societal patterns that govern descent. In every culture, children are introduced to relatives to whom they are expected to show an emotional attachment. The state of being related to others is called **kinship.** Kinship is culturally learned and is not totally determined by biological or marital ties. For example, adoption creates a kinship tie which is legally acknowledged and socially accepted.

The family and the kin group are not necessarily the same. While the family is a household unit, kin do not always live together or function as a collective body on a daily basis. Kin groups include aunts, uncles, cousins, in-laws, and so forth. In a society such as the United States, the kinship group may come together only rarely, as for a wedding or funeral. However, kinship ties frequently create obligations and responsibilities. We may feel compelled to assist our kin and feel free to call upon relatives for many types of aid, including loans and baby-sitting.

How are kinship groups identified? The principle of descent assigns people to kinship groups according to their relationship to an individual's mother or father. There are three principal ways of determining descent. In the United States, the system of **bilateral descent** is followed, which means that both sides of a person's family are regarded as equally important. No higher value is given to the brothers of one's father as opposed to the brothers of one's mother.

Most societies—according to Murdock, 64 percent—give preference to one side of the family or the other in tracing descent. **Patrilineal** (from Latin *pater,* "father") **descent** indicates that only the father's relatives are important in terms of property, inheritance, and the establishment of emotional ties. Conversely, in societies which favor **matrilineal** (from Latin *mater,* "mother") **descent,** only the mother's relatives are significant; the relatives of the father are considered unimportant.

Family Residence: Where Do We Live?

In every society, there are social norms concerning the appropriate residence of a newly created family. Under the **neolocal** pattern of residence, which is prevalent in the United States, a married couple is expected to establish a separate household. However, if we take a cross-cultural view, it becomes clear that the ideal type of neolocal residence is relatively uncommon. In many societies, the bride and groom live either with his parents (the **patrilocal** pattern) or with her parents (the **matrilocal** pattern). In such cultures, it is felt that the new couples need the emotional support and especially the economic support of kinfolk.

Authority Patterns: Who Rules?

Imagine that you have recently married and must begin to make decisions about the future of your new family. You and your spouse face many questions. Where will you live? How will you furnish your place of residence? Who will do the cooking, the shopping, the cleaning? Whose friends will be invited to dinner? Each time a decision must be made, an issue is raised: "Who has the power to make the decision?" In simple terms, who rules the family? From a conflict perspective, these questions must be examined in light of traditional gender stratification (see Chapter 11), under which men have held a dominant position over women.

Societies vary in the way that power within the family is distributed. If a society expects males to dominate in all family decision making, it is termed a *patriarchy*. Frequently, in patriarchal societies, the eldest male wields the greatest power. Women hold low status in such societies and rarely are granted full and equal rights within the legal system. It may be more difficult, for example, for a woman to obtain a divorce than it is for a man. By contrast, in a *matriarchy*, women have greater authority than men. Matriarchies may have emerged among Native American tribal societies and in nations in which men were absent for long periods of time for warfare or food gathering.

Some marital relationships may be neither male-dominated nor female-dominated. The third type of authority pattern, the *egalitarian family*, is one in which spouses are regarded as equals. This does not mean, however, that each decision is shared in such families. Mothers may hold authority in some spheres, fathers in others. In the view of many sociologists, the egalitarian family has begun to replace the patriarchal family as the social norm. A study of Detroit families by Robert Blood, Jr., and Donald Wolfe (1960) supports this contention (see Box 13-1 on page 366).

FUNCTIONS OF THE FAMILY

Do we really need the family? A century ago, Friedrich Engels (1884), a colleague of Karl Marx, described the family as the ultimate source of social inequality because of its role in the transfer of power, property, and privilege. More recently, conflict theorists have argued that the family contributes to societal injustice, denies opportunities to women that are extended to men, and limits freedom in sexual expression and selection of a mate.

In order to evaluate such issues, it is helpful to use the tools provided by the functionalist perspective, which encourages us to examine the ways in which an institution gratifies the needs of its members and contributes to the stability of society. The family fulfills a number of functions, such as providing religious training, education, and recreational outlets. Yet there are six paramount functions performed by the family; these functions were first outlined 60 years ago by sociologist William F. Ogburn (Ogburn and Tibbits, 1934):

1 *Reproduction.* For a society to maintain itself, it must replace dying members. In this sense, the family contributes to human survival through its function of reproduction.

2 *Protection.* Unlike the young of other animal species, human infants need constant care and economic security. Infants and children experience an extremely long period of dependency, which places special demands on older family members. In all cultures, it is the family that assumes ultimate responsibility for the protection and upbringing of children.

3 *Socialization.* Parents and other kin monitor a child's behavior and transmit the norms, values, and language of a culture to the child (see Chapters 3 and 4). Of course, as conflict theorists point out, the social class of couples and their children significantly influences the socialization experiences to which they are exposed and the protection they receive.

4 *Regulation of sexual behavior.* Sexual norms are subject to change over time (for instance, changes in customs for dating) and across cultures (Islamic Saudi Arabia compared with more permissive Denmark). However, whatever the time period or cultural values in a society, standards of sexual behavior are most clearly defined within the family circle. The structure of society influences these standards so that, characteristically in male-dominated societies, formal and informal norms permit men to express and enjoy their sexual desires more freely than women may.

BOX 13-1 · EVERYDAY BEHAVIOR

MARITAL POWER

Sociologists Robert Blood, Jr., and Donald Wolfe (1960) developed the concept of **marital power** to describe the manner in which decision making is distributed within families. They defined power by examining who makes the final decision in each of eight important areas that, the researchers argue, traditionally have been reserved entirely for the husband or for the wife. These areas include what job the husband should take, what house or apartment to live in, where to go on vacation, and which doctor to use if there is an illness in the family.

Recent research suggests that money plays a central role in determining marital power. Money has different meanings for members of each sex: for men it typically represents identity and power; for women, security and autonomy. Apparently, money establishes the balance of power not only for married couples but also for unmarried heterosexual couples who are living together. Married women with paying work outside the home enjoy greater marital power than full-time

homemakers do (Blumstein and Schwartz, 1983; Godwin and Scanzoni, 1989; G. Kaufman, 1985).

Labor not only enhances women's self-esteem but also increases their marital power, because some men have greater respect for women who work at paying jobs. Sociologist Isik Aytac (1987) studied a national sample of households in the United States and found that husbands of women holding management positions share more of the domestic chores than other husbands. In addition, as a wife's proportional contribution to the family income increases, her husband's share of meal preparation increases. Aytac's research supports the contention that the traditional division of labor at home can change as women's position in the labor force improves and women gain greater marital power.

Comparative studies have revealed the complexity of marital power issues in other cultures. For example, anthropologist David Gilmore (1990) examined decision making in two rural towns in southern Spain. These communities—

one with 8000 residents and the other with 4000—have an agricultural economy based on olives, wheat, and sunflowers. Gilmore studied a variety of decision-making situations, including prenuptial decisions over household location, administration of domestic finances, and major household purchases. He found that working-class women in these communities—often united with their mothers—are able to prevail in many decisions despite opposition from their husbands.

Interestingly, wives' control over finances in these towns appears to lessen with affluence. Among the wealthier peasants, husbands retain more rights over the family purse strings, especially in terms of bank accounts and investments. In some cases, they make investments without their wives' knowledge. By contrast, in the working class—where surplus cash is uncommon and household finances are often based on borrowing and buying on credit because of the uncertainties of household employment—the wife "rules" the household economy, and the husband accepts her rule.

---

5 *Affection and companionship.* Ideally, the family provides members with warm and intimate relationships and helps them feel satisfied and secure. Of course, a family member may find such rewards outside the family—from peers, in school, at work—and may perceive the home as an unpleasant place. Nevertheless, unlike other institutions, the family is obligated to serve the emotional needs of its members. We *expect* our relatives to understand us, to care for us, and to be there for us when we need them.

6 *Providing of social status.* We inherit a social position because of the "family background" and reputation of our parents and siblings. The family unit presents the newborn child with an ascribed status of race and ethnicity that helps to determine his or her place within a society's stratification system. Moreover, family resources affect children's ability to pursue certain opportunities such as higher education and specialized lessons.

It is apparent, then, that the family has been assigned at least six vital functions in human societies. However, one might ask if the family can effectively fulfill these weighty responsibilities. To answer this question, we must begin a more detailed examination of marital and family life in the United States of the 1990s.

MARRIAGE AND FAMILY IN THE UNITED STATES

Currently, close to 90 percent of all men and women in the United States marry at least once during their lifetimes. Historically, the most consistent aspect of family life in this country has been the high rate of marriage.

In this part of the chapter, we will examine various aspects of love, marriage, and parenthood in the United States. Many of us are accustomed to viewing such phenomena as romance and mate selection as influenced primarily, if not exclusively, by individual preferences. Yet, as we will see, sociological analysis emphasizes that such behavior is influenced in important ways by social institutions and by the distinctive norms and values of each culture.

Courtship and Mate Selection

In certain traditional cultures, arranged marriages are common, and courtship practices are severely restricted. For example, some Japanese traditionalists favor arranged marriages for their children. A go-between will often take a young man to a public place for a *kagemi* (a hidden look) at a young woman viewed as a likely candidate for marriage. The woman is unaware that her appearance is being evaluated (Hendry, 1981:116–123). Similarly, "secret looks" are common in rural Egypt. A boy from a village observes:

> One favorite place for us to get a glimpse of girls is at the village water source. The girls know that and like to linger there. If we see one we like and think she might be suitable, we ask our parents to try to arrange a marriage, but usually not before we have some sign from the girl that she might be interested (Rugh, 1984:137).

As is true in this Egyptian village, courtship in the United States requires people to rely heavily on intricate games, gestures, and signals. For example, how do you act when you have met an attractive stranger in a bookstore, in a supermarket, or at a party? Do you come right out and say, "I'd really like to see you again," after just meeting the person? Or do you find elaborate and slightly disguised ways of showing your interest and testing how the other person feels about you?

An important aspect of the courtship process is labeling. Sociologist Robert Lewis (1973) reports that early labeling as a couple by family and friends results in a greater likelihood that the relationship will be maintained over time. By contrast, the absence of such labeling—or a negative reaction from people termed *significant others* by George Herbert Mead (see Chapter 4)—can weaken the couple's relationship.

Courtship is clearly influenced by the values of our society. But what about our *choice* of a mate? Why are we drawn to a particular person in the first place? To what extent are such judgments shaped by the society around us?

Aspects of Mate Selection Many societies have explicit or unstated rules which define potential mates as acceptable or unacceptable. These norms can be distinguished in terms of endogamy and exogamy. *Endogamy* (from the Greek *endon*, "within") specifies the groups within which a spouse must be found and prohibits marriage with others. For example, in the United States, many people are expected to marry within their own racial, ethnic, or religious group and are prohibited from marrying outside the group. Endogamy is intended to reinforce the cohesiveness of the group by suggesting to the young that they should marry someone "of our own kind."

By contrast, *exogamy* (from the Greek *exō*, "outside") requires mate selection outside certain groups, usually one's own family or certain kinfolk. The *incest taboo*, a social norm common to virtually all societies, prohibits sexual relationships between certain culturally specified relatives. For people in the United States, this taboo means that we must marry outside the nuclear family. We cannot marry our siblings, and in most states we cannot marry our first cousins.

Endogamous restrictions may be seen as prefer-

Marriages that are exogamous with respect to race are increasing but still account for only a small minority of marriages in the United States.

ences for one group over another. In the United States, such preferences are most obvious in racial barriers. Until the 1960s, some states outlawed interracial marriages. This practice was challenged by Richard Loving (a White man) and Mildred Jeter Loving (a part-Black, part-Native American woman), who married in 1958. Eventually, in 1967, the Supreme Court ruled that it was unconstitutional to prohibit marriage solely on the basis of race. The decision struck down statutes in Virginia and 16 other states.

According to the Bureau of the Census, the number of marriages between Blacks and Whites in the United States has more than tripled in recent decades, jumping from 65,000 in 1970 to 231,000 in 1991. One of the nation's interracial couples, Tom and Yvette Weatherly, grew up in different parts of Atlanta and first met when she was bused to his overwhelmingly White high school and sat behind him in English class. "We are a segregationist's worst nightmare," notes Tom Weatherly. "But, to other people, we're the perfect example" (Wilkerson, 1991:B6).

Survey data show that many Whites still oppose interracial marriages. According to the General Social Survey, an annual poll of 1500 people in the United States, 66 percent of Whites state that they would oppose a close relative's marrying a Black person. About 45 percent would oppose such a marriage to an Asian or Hispanic person. Moreover, one in five Whites believes that interracial marriage should be illegal (as it was in some states until the Supreme Court's 1967 ruling). By contrast, Blacks were found to be indifferent on the subject of intermarriage; nearly two-thirds of respondents stated that they would neither favor nor oppose a close relative's marrying someone from another race (Wilkerson, 1991).

The Love Relationship Love and mate selection do not necessarily coincide. For example, feelings of love are not a prerequisite for marriage among the Yaruros of inland Venezuela or in other cultures where there is little freedom for mate selection. As Linton Freeman (1958:27–30) has shown, the Yaruro male of marriageable age does not engage in the kind of dating behavior so typical of young people in the United States. Rather, he knows that, under the traditions of his culture, he must marry one of his mother's brothers' daughters or one of his father's sisters' daughters. The young man's choice is further limited because one of his uncles selects the eligible cousin that he must marry.

Many of the world's cultures give priority in mate selection to factors other than romantic feelings. In some societies, marriages are arranged, often by parents or religious authorities. The newly married couple is expected to develop a feeling of love *after* the legal union is formalized. Economic considerations also play a significant role in mate selection in certain societies.

In the United States, love is important in the courtship process. Neolocal residence places added importance on the affectional bond between husband and wife. The couple is able to develop its own emotional ties, free of the demands of other household members for affection. Sociologist William Goode (1959) observed that spouses in a nuclear family have to rely heavily on each other for the companionship and support that might be provided by other relatives in an extended-family situation.

Parents in the United States value love highly as a rationale for marriage, and they encourage love to develop between young people. In addition, the theme of romantic love is reinforced in songs, films, books, magazines, television shows, and even cartoons and comic books. At the same time, our society expects parents and peers to help a person confine his or her search for a mate to "socially acceptable" members of the opposite sex.

Traditional gender-role socialization has made it easier for women to express love and other feelings of social intimacy than it is for men. The qualities identified with intimacy—emotional warmth, expressiveness, vulnerability, and sensitivity—are associated with the female but not the male gender role. Studies show that men are more likely than women to base their perceptions of love and intimacy on sex, on providing practical help, and on simply being in the presence of a loved one (Cancian, 1986; L. Thompson and Walker, 1989:847).

Parenthood and Grandparenthood

Caring for children is a universal function of the family, yet societies vary in assigning this function to family members. Among the Nayars of southern India, the biological role of fathers is acknowledged, but the mother's eldest brother is responsible for her children (Gough, 1974). By contrast, uncles play only a peripheral role in child care in the United States.

Despite such differences, the socialization of children is essential to the maintenance of any culture.

Consequently, as we saw in Chapter 4, parenthood is one of the most important (and most demanding) social roles in the United States. Sociologist Alice Rossi (1968, 1984:5–10) has pointed to four factors related to socialization that complicate the transition to parenthood. First, there is little anticipatory socialization for the social roles of caregiver. Subjects most relevant to successful family life—such as child care and home maintenance—are given little attention in the normal school curriculum. Second, only limited learning occurs during the period of pregnancy itself. Third, the transition to parenthood is quite abrupt. Unlike adolescence, it is not prolonged; unlike socialization for work, one cannot gradually take on the duties of caregiving. Finally, in Rossi's view, our society lacks clear and helpful guidelines concerning successful parenthood. There is little consensus on how parents can produce happy and well-adjusted offspring—or even on what it means to be "well-adjusted." For these reasons, socialization for parenthood involves difficult challenges for most men and women in the United States.

One recent development in family life in the United States has been the extension of parenthood, as adult children continue to (or return to) live at home. Currently, more than half of all children ages 20 to 24 and one out of four of those ages 25 to 34 live with their parents. Some of these adult children are still pursuing an education, but in many instances financial difficulties are at the heart of these living arrangements. While rents and real estate prices skyrocketed in the 1980s, salaries for younger workers did not keep pace and many found themselves unable to afford their own homes. Moreover, with many marriages now ending in divorce—most commonly in the first seven years of marriage—divorced sons and daughters are now returning to live with their parents, sometimes with their own children (Bureau of the Census, 1993a:59).

Is this living arrangement a positive development for family members? Social scientists have just begun to examine this phenomenon, sometimes called the "boomerang generation" in the popular press. One survey in Virginia seemed to show that neither the parents nor their adult children were happy about continuing to live together. The children often felt resentful and isolated, but the par-

Parenthood is one of the most important social roles. Shown here are a mother from the United States with her children, a Tibetan family going to a religious festival, and a family from a rural village in Slovakia.

ents also suffered, since learning to live without children in the home can be viewed as an essential stage of adult life and indeed may be a significant turning point for a marriage (*Berkeley Wellness Letter,* 1990:1–2).

As life expectancy increases in the United States, more and more parents are becoming grandparents and even great-grandparents. After interviewing many grandparents, sociologists Andrew Cherlin and Frank Furstenberg, Jr. (1986) identified three principal styles of grandparenting:

• More than half (55 percent) of grandparents surveyed functioned as "specialists in recreational care-giving." They enriched their grandchildren's lives through recreational outings and other special activities.
• More than one-fourth (29 percent) carried on a "ritualistic" (primarily symbolic) relationship with their grandchildren. In some instances, this was because the grandparents lived far away from their grandchildren and could see them only occasionally.
• About one-sixth (16 percent) of grandparents surveyed were actively involved in everyday routine care of their grandchildren and exercised substantial authority over them.

Divorce (which will be discussed more fully later in the chapter) affects a child's relationships with his or her grandparents in significant ways. The child often becomes more deeply involved with the custodial parent's (generally the mother's) parents and relatives. Consequently, maternal grandparents of children of divorce are more likely to live with the child or see the child almost every day. By contrast, the child may lose contact altogether with paternal grandparents. In some cases, the effects of a divorce have led grandparents to go to court in order to establish visitation rights with their grandchildren. Maintaining cross-generational ties may have particular value as the United States increasingly shifts toward small, single-parent families (Ahlburg and De Vita, 1992).

Adoption

In a legal sense, **adoption** is a "process that allows for the transfer of the legal rights, responsibilities, and privileges of parenting from legal parents to new legal parents" (E. Cole, 1985:638). In many cases, these rights are transferred from biological parents (often called *birth parents*) to adoptive parents. Viewed from a functionalist perspective, government has a strong interest in encouraging adop-

© Harley Schwadron

" I'M LOOKING FORWARD to GETTING OUT OF THE DORM AND ON MY OWN. BY THE WAY, IS MY OLD ROOM READY FOR ME?"

The term "boomerang generation" is being used in the popular press to refer to the increasing proportion of adults in the United States who are returning (sometimes after divorce) to live with their parents.

tion. Kenneth Watson (1986:5) of the Chicago Child Care Society notes: "Adoption is seen as a neat solution to three of society's vexing problems: unplanned pregnancy outside of marriage, children in need of families to rear them, and infertile couples unable to have children."

Policymakers have both a humanitarian and a financial stake in promoting adoption. In theory, adoption offers a stable family environment for children who otherwise might not receive satisfactory care. Moreover, government data show that unwed mothers who keep their babies tend to be of lower socioeconomic status and often require public assistance to support their children (C. Bachrach, 1986). Consequently, various levels of government may lower their social welfare expenses if children are transferred to economically self-sufficient families. From a conflict perspective, such financial considerations raise the ugly specter of adoption's serving as a means whereby affluent (often infertile) couples are allowed to "buy" the children of the poor.

The largest single category of adoption in the United States is adoption by relatives. In most cases, a stepparent adopts the children of a spouse. There are two legal methods of adopting an unrelated person: adoptions arranged by licensed agencies and private agreements sanctioned by the courts (E. Cole, 1985:639–640,662–663; Salvatore,1986:60).

According to the National Committee for Adoption, an association of private adoption agencies, the number of adoptions between unrelated people in the United States decreased from 89,200 in 1970 to 51,157 in 1986 (the last year for which complete data are available). This change was due largely to a decline in the number of children available for adoption. Key factors contributing to this diminishing pool of children include wider use of contraceptives, an increase in the number of abortions (see Chapter 11), and a lessening of the social stigma faced by single parents who keep their babies (Bureau of the Census, 1992:373).

According to a study by the National Center for Health Statistics, about 200,000 women in the United States sought to adopt children in 1988. The alleged "parent surplus" often described in the mass media reflects an abundance of childless couples anxious to adopt White, nondisabled babies. Ironically, at the same time that these parents wait for babies, many children and adolescents from minority group backgrounds or with disabilities live in group homes or in foster-care situations (M. Harris, 1988; Hilts, 1990b).

Dual-Career Families

In the traditional nuclear family, the husband serves as the sole breadwinner, while the wife fills the roles of mother and homemaker. However, an increasing proportion of couples in the United States today are rejecting this traditional model for a "dual-career" lifestyle. Currently, the majority of all married couples have two partners active in the paid labor force. In one-fourth of couples, both partners are "permanently committed" to their careers in that they have worked for at least five years.

Why has there been such a rise in the number of dual-career couples? A major factor, especially among less affluent families, is economic need. In 1990, the median income for married-couple families with both partners employed was $48,169, compared with $30,075 (or 38 percent less) in families in which only the husband was working outside the home. Sociologists have noted, however, that not all of a family's second wage is genuine additional income because of such work-related costs as child care. Other factors contributing to the rise of the dual-career model include the nation's declining birthrate (see Chapter 19), the increase in the proportion of women with a college education, the shift in the economy of the United States from manufacturing to service industries, and the impact of the feminist movement in changing women's consciousness (Bureau of the Census, 1993a:467).

In a sense, members of dual-career couples must undergo a process of resocialization (see Chapter 4). A newly married couple may intend to have a "two-career household" and share child care in an egalitarian manner. Their parents, however, may have followed the conventional nuclear family pattern described earlier. Thus, neither of the newlyweds may have had useful role models for a dual-career lifestyle. Each may have had to overcome previous socialization into traditional expectations regarding marriage and the "proper" roles of husbands and wives. As was discussed in Chapter 11, sociologist Arlie Hochschild (1989, 1990) has used the phrase "second shift" to describe the double

An increasing proportion of couples in the United States are rejecting the traditional nuclear family model for a "dual-career" lifestyle.

burden—work outside the home followed by child care and housework—that many women carry and few men share equitably.

Some dual-career couples actually come to resemble single-parent families because of their reliance on jobs with evening or weekend hours. These couples split work and parenthood shifts as a means of coping with the pressures of the dual-career lifestyle. Approximately one out of every six dual-income couples with children under the age of 6 has work hours that do not overlap at all (McEnroe, 1991).

The rise in dual-career couples increased pressure on policymakers to consider family leave legislation. According to a 1989 survey by the Bureau of Labor Statistics, 37 percent of workers at companies with 100 or more employees were eligible for unpaid maternity leave, while 17 percent could take unpaid paternity leave, 2 percent could take paid maternity leave, and only 1 percent could take paid paternity leave. (These disparities reflect the continuing impact of traditional gender roles regarding which parent should care for infants.) Parental leaves are even less common in smaller firms; policies allowing leave time for adoption or the care of sick family members are rare in both large and small businesses (Holmes, 1990c; Meisenheimer, 1989:20–22).

By 1990, a broad national coalition had come together to support federal family and medical leave legislation. Among the diverse organizations joined in this effort were the Service Employees International Union, the National Organization for Women, the U.S. Catholic Conference, the Gray Panthers (refer back to Chapter 12), and the Nine to Five National Association of Working Women. Proponents of family leave measures argued that they would strengthen family life by allowing parents time with infants or adopted children at crucial points of the life cycle, by giving parents a better opportunity to adjust to their new roles, and by providing job security for employees facing stressful life changes or crises. Supporters of family leave added that such policies would assist business firms by reducing job turnover, especially of female employees who are most likely to suffer from role strain. Given the lack of affordable, high-quality child care (refer back to Chapter 4), family leave was viewed as essential for both single-parent and dual-career families.

In early 1993, Congress passed and President Bill Clinton signed into law the Family and Medical Leave Act. This legislation—vetoed twice by President George Bush—requires employers to give workers up to 12 weeks of unpaid leave to deal with birth, adoption, or a serious illness affecting them-

In some lower-class families, children must return home from school alone and wait there without adult supervision until a parent returns from work. These children are known as "latchkey children."

umented the differences in family organization among social classes in the United States. In the upper class, there is a particular emphasis on lineage and maintenance of family position. One is considered not simply a member of a nuclear family but rather a member of a larger family tradition ("the Rockefellers" or "the Kennedys"). As a result, upper-class families are quite concerned about what they see as "proper training" for children.

Lower-class families do not often have the luxury of worrying about the "family name"; they must first struggle to pay their bills and survive the crises often associated with life in poverty. Such families are more likely to have only one parent in the home, a situation which presents special challenges in terms of child care and financial needs. Children in lower-class families typically assume adult responsibilities—including marriage and parenthood—at an earlier age than children of affluent homes. In part, this is because they may lack the money needed to remain in school.

Social class differences in family life may not be as striking as they once were. In the past, family specialists agreed that there were pronounced contrasts in child-rearing practices. Lower-class families were found to be more authoritarian in rearing children and more inclined to use physical punishment. Middle-class families were more permissive and more restrained in punishing their children. However, these differences may have narrowed as more and more families from all social classes have turned to the same books, magazines, and even television talk shows for advice on rearing children (M. Kohn, 1970; Luster et al., 1989).

Among the poor, women often play a significant role in the economic support of the family. Men may earn low wages, may be unemployed, or may be absent from the family. In 1991, 46 percent of all families headed by women with no husband present were below the government poverty line. This compared with only 7 percent for all traditional dual-parent families (Bureau of the Census, 1993a:473).

Many racial and ethnic groups appear to have distinctive family characteristics. However, racial and class factors are often closely related. In examining family life among racial and ethnic minorities, we must remember that certain patterns may result from class as well as cultural factors.

selves or members of their immediate families. The act covers about half the paid labor force of the United States, including employees of companies with 50 or more workers as well as federal, state, and local government employees (Clymer, 1993).

Variations in Family Life

Within the United States, there are many variations in family life associated with distinctions of social class, race, and ethnicity. An examination of such variations will give us a more sophisticated understanding of contemporary family styles in our country.

Social Class Differences Various studies have doc-

Racial and Ethnic Differences Family life among racial and ethnic minorities in the United States has been profoundly affected by the subordinate status of these minority groups. For example, African American families continue to be influenced by the legacy of slavery, during which conventional family units were discouraged and separated. Native American families were forcibly removed from their tribal homelands and resettled on reservations with limited economic and educational opportunities. The immigration policy of the United States has complicated the successful relocation of intact families from Asia and Latin America (Doob, 1993).

In examining minority families, political leaders and the media have tended not only to emphasize the problems of such families but to "blame the victims" (refer back to Box 8-2 on page 227), thereby ignoring the impact of generations of prejudice and discrimination. For example, in the aftermath of the 1992 riots in Los Angeles, observers generally focused on such structural sources of unrest as the declining employment opportunities in central-city neighborhoods, the lack of available health care, and the rise of organized gang activity. Yet (then) Vice President Dan Quayle instead pointed to the breakdown of family values, especially among African Americans (as evidenced by the absence of adult males in many Black families). He criticized the media for presenting in a positive fashion a television character (Murphy Brown) who chose to have a child while remaining unmarried. Quayle's message was clear: the cause of the riots was within Los Angeles, and its Black and Hispanic residents were at fault (Schaefer, 1993).

There are many negative and inaccurate stereotypes in the United States regarding the African American family. It is true that a significantly higher proportion of Black than of White families have no husband present in the home (see Figure 13-3). Yet Black single mothers are often part of stable, functioning kin networks, despite the pressures of sexism and racism. Members of these networks—predominantly female kin such as mothers, grandmothers, and aunts—share goods and services and thereby ease financial strains. In addition to these strong kinship bonds, Black family life has emphasized deep religious commitment and high aspirations for achievement. The strengths of the Black family were evident during slavery, when Blacks demonstrated a

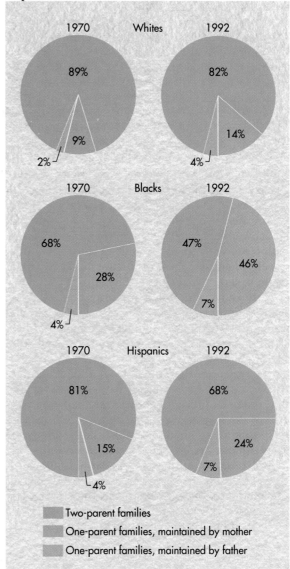

FIGURE 13-3 One-Parent Families among Blacks, Hispanics, and Whites, 1970 and 1992

Two-parent families

One-parent families, maintained by mother

One-parent families, maintained by father

SOURCE: Bureau of the Census, 1993a:56.

In 1992, 46 percent of Black families, 24 percent of Hispanic families, and only 14 percent of White families were maintained by the mother with no husband in the home.

remarkable ability to maintain family ties despite the fact that they enjoyed no legal protections (R. Hill, 1972, 1987; Hudgins, 1992).

In Box 4-2 on page 107, we examined socialization in Mexican American families. Distinctive family patterns are also evident among the more than 2 million Greek Americans—especially those who have migrated to the United States in recent years. Generally, Greek families have left agricultural areas in their homelands to settle in urban centers where there is already a Greek American community. This community is typically centered on a Greek Orthodox church that helps to maintain the traditional old world culture. Gender roles are sharply defined within a patriarchal and close-knit community. Even as adolescents, young Greek Americans are closely watched by parents, who play an active role in mate selection. However, as assimilation proceeds among second- or third-generation Greek Americans, these distinctive family dynamics begin to fade (Kourvetaris, 1988; Moskos, 1980).

Within a racial or ethnic minority, family ties can serve as an economic boost. For example, Korean immigrants to the United States generally begin small service or retail businesses involving all adult family members. To obtain the funds needed to begin a business, they often pool their resources through a *kye* (pronounced KAY)—an association that grants money to members on a rotating basis so they can gain access to even more additional capital. While not limited to kinfolk, the *kye* allows Korean Americans to start small businesses long before other minorities in similar economic circumstances. Such rotating credit associations are not unique to Korean Americans; they have been used as well by West Indians living in the United States (I. Kim, 1988; Light and Bonacich, 1988).

DIVORCE IN THE UNITED STATES

"Do you promise to love, honor, and cherish . . . until death do you part?" Every year, people of all social classes and racial and ethnic groups make such legally binding agreements. Yet an increasing number of these promises are apparently not realistic, given our rising divorce rate.

Statistical Trends in Divorce

Just how common is divorce? Surprisingly, this is not a simple question; divorce statistics are difficult to interpret.

The media frequently report that one out of every two marriages ends in divorce. However, this figure is misleading, since it is based on a comparison of all divorces which occur in a single year (regardless of when the couples were married) against the number of new marriages in the same year. As the second column of Table 13-1 indicates, there were 51.4 divorces in the United States in 1992 for every 100 new marriages. But that could, in fact, represent 51.4 divorces for every 3000 marriages in the decades leading up to 1992.

A more accurate perspective on divorce can be obtained if we examine the number of divorces per married women ages 15 to 44 (see the third column in Table 13-1). Using these statistics, we can see that the number of divorces per 1000 married women in this age group has more than doubled over the past 30 years. Nevertheless, about 4 out of 10 first marriages remain intact; about 70 percent of those who obtain a divorce before age 35 later remarry, half of those within three years after a first

TABLE 13-1	Divorce Rates in the United States	
YEAR	DIVORCES PER 100 MARRIAGES PERFORMED	DIVORCES PER 1000 MARRIED WOMEN, 15 TO 44 YEARS OLD
1920	13.4	10.0
1930	17.0	10.0
1940	16.9	14.0
1950	23.1	17.0
1960	25.8	16.0
1970	32.8	26.0
1980	49.7	40.0
1992	51.4	37.0[a]

[a]Data for 1989.
SOURCES: National Center for Health Statistics, 1974, 1990, 1993b; Norton and Miller, 1992:2.

Divorce rates have fluctuated since World War II, but represent a two- to threefold increase from pre-1940 levels.

divorce (Bumpass et al., 1990; Norton and Miller, 1992; J. Sweet and Bumpass, 1987).

While the nation's high rate of remarriage is regarded as an endorsement of the institution of marriage, it does lead to the new challenges of a remarriage kin network composed of current and prior marital relationships. This network can be particularly complex if children are involved or if an ex-spouse remarries. As is shown in Figure 13-4, by 1990 about 15 percent of children in the United States lived with a parent and a stepparent.

The current high divorce rate of the United States is not the result of a sudden explosion; rather, signs of such a tendency can be seen early in the nation's history. Residents of colonial America could receive divorces more easily than their counterparts anywhere in the western world. The divorce rate in the United States doubled between 1900 and 1920 and rose steadily until 1980, when it began to level off. Furthermore, the country's *teenage* divorce rate is more than twice the overall national average (Bureau of the Census, 1993a:100).

Divorce is a complex and difficult experience for all family members. Anthropologist Paul Bohannan (1970) has identified six overlapping experiences which arise from divorce and which vary in intensity depending on the couple. The "six stations of divorce," as Bohannan calls them, include:

1 *Emotional divorce,* which represents the problem of the deteriorating marriage
2 *Legal divorce,* based on the grounds on which the marriage will be dissolved
3 *Economic divorce,* which deals with the division of money and property
4 *Coparental divorce,* which includes decisions having to do with child custody and visitation rights
5 *Community divorce,* or the changes in friendships and institutional ties that a divorced person experiences
6 *Psychic divorce,* focused on the person's attempt to regain autonomy and self-esteem

As Bohannan has observed, "undivorced" people rarely appreciate the difficulties that the divorced person experiences in mastering these "stations of divorce" (Gerstel, 1987). The impact of divorce on girls and boys is examined in Box 13-2 (page 378).

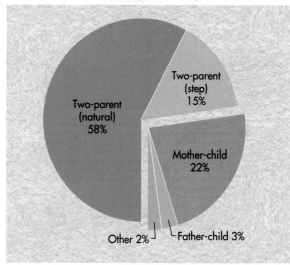

FIGURE 13-4 Living Arrangements of Children in the United States by Type of Family, 1990

SOURCE: Bureau of the Census, 1991c; and authors' estimates.

As of 1990, less than 60 percent of children under 18 years old in the United States lived in two-parent families with both biological parents.

An increasing number of families in the United States are coping with the traumas of divorce by experimenting with joint or shared custody arrangements. Joint custody has become popular, since it allows each parent meaningful time with children and promotes an egalitarian sharing of decision-making authority. However, adults unable to live together as husband and wife may find it difficult to cooperate in resolving important issues of parenthood. Three studies by psychologist Judith Wallerstein and her colleagues suggest that joint custody arrangements do not benefit all children whose parents have separated or divorced and, in certain instances, may be harmful for these children (J. Wallerstein and Blakeslee, 1989).

Factors Associated with Divorce

Why does the United States have such a high frequency of divorce? There is no fully satisfactory an-

BOX 13-2 · CURRENT RESEARCH

THE EFFECTS OF DIVORCE ON FEMALE AND MALE CHILDREN

Traditionally, family researchers have suggested that divorce has a more detrimental effect on boys than on girls. These researchers have often written that the absence of fathers is more harmful for the development of boys than for girls and that girls receive greater emotional support from custodial mothers. However, more recent studies have led to a reexamination of these long-held assumptions (Hetherington, 1979; Zaslow, 1988, 1989).

Psychologist Neil Kalter (1989) and his associates supervised clinical work with more than 600 children of divorce over a 10-year period. In addition, they interviewed and tested about 500 research subjects and conducted preventive intervention programs for about 2000 children in public schools. Kalter's work shows that boys and girls react differently to divorce, but that traditional views concerning their reactions are not necessarily accurate.

Boys from divorced families are often angry and combative and may develop delinquent behavior. They frequently resist the authority of their mothers and teachers, become involved in fights at school or in the neighborhood, and underachieve at school relative to their abilities. The reduced interaction with their fathers which typically results from divorce has a clear and negative impact on sons.

For girls, the harmful effects of divorce emerge somewhat later than for boys, sometimes only in adolescence or even in adulthood. When compared with daughters from intact families, daughters of divorce are more likely to have feelings of lowered self-worth. The absence of a caring father leads many daughters to wonder if they can be loved by a man; indeed, these girls may believe that their fathers left home because their daughters were not attractive or lovable enough.

In suggesting that divorce has a more detrimental impact on boys than on girls, many researchers maintain that custodial mothers develop closer relationships with their daughters than with their sons. However, for the adolescent female, this may be a mixed blessing. A daughter of divorce may find it difficult to achieve a healthy separation and independence from her mother. Moreover, as she struggles with her emerging sexuality during her adolescence, a young woman may face additional complications if she is sharing a home with a stepfather or a close male friend of her mother.

Kalter's studies show that the detrimental effect of divorce often appears *earlier* in boys than in girls —and that this detrimental effect is sometimes more obvious and more dramatic in boys because of their greater tendency toward aggressiveness and antisocial behavior. Nevertheless, these studies remind us that we should not underestimate the harmful impact of divorce on girls.

While divorce can obviously be a painful experience for both female and male children, it is important to avoid labeling young people as "children of divorce" as if this *parental* experience is the singular event defining the life of a girl or boy. Large-scale studies in the United States and Great Britain have shown that some of the alleged negative effects of divorce actually resulted from conditions (such as poverty) that existed before the parental separation. Moreover, if divorce does not lower children's access to resources and does not increase stress, its impact on children may be neutral or even positive. Divorce does not ruin the life of every child it touches, though its effect on a child is not always benign (K. Allen, 1993; Amato, 1993; Cherlin et al., 1991).

swer to this question. Table 13-2 indicates factors which are associated with a higher probability of divorce among married couples. In addition to these strains in each individual relationship, however, there are overall social changes which have contributed to the nation's rising divorce rate.

Perhaps the most important factor in the increase in divorce throughout the twentieth century has been the greater social acceptance of divorce. In particular, this increased tolerance has resulted from a relaxation of negative attitudes toward divorce among various religious denominations. Al-

TABLE 13-2	Factors Associated with Higher Probability of Divorce

Marriage at a very young age (15 to 19 years old)
Short acquaintanceship before marriage (less than two years)
Short engagement (under six months) or no engagement
Parents with unhappy marriages
Disapproval of marriage expressed by kin and friends
General dissimilarity of background
Membership in different religious faiths
Failure to attend religious services
Incomplete education (leaving school before getting diploma or degree)
Disagreement of husband and wife on role obligations
Urban background

Research has shown that many factors are associated with greater probability of divorce.

SOURCES: Adapted from Goode, 1976:537–538; Norton and Miller, 1992. See also Fergusson et al., 1984.

though divorce is still seen as unfortunate, it is no longer treated as a sin by most religious leaders (Gerstel, 1987; A. Thornton, 1985).

A few other factors deserve mention. Many states have adopted more liberal divorce laws in the last two decades. Divorce has become a more practical option in newly formed families, since they now tend to have fewer children than in the past. A general increase in family incomes, coupled with the availability of free legal aid for some poor people, has meant that more couples can afford the traditionally high legal costs of divorce proceedings. Finally, as society provides greater opportunities for women, more and more wives are becoming less dependent on their husbands—both economically and emotionally. They may then feel more able to leave if the marriage seems hopeless.

The most extreme cause of marital breakdown is domestic violence—an issue that will be discussed in the social policy section at the end of the chapter.

Photo by Walter Grey © California Dreamers

"Congratulations on your divorce!" exclaims this greeting card. The greater acceptance of marital dissolution in the United States has led to a new custom—sending cards to people congratulating them on their divorce.

ALTERNATIVE LIFESTYLES

In the 1990s, it is clear that family life in the United States has undergone many changes. Teenagers have babies, children return to live at home as adults, and an increasing number of adults and children live in stepfamily arrangements. As we will see in the following discussions, many people have chosen alternative lifestyles rather than the traditional nuclear family norm.

Cohabitation

Saint Paul once wrote: "It is better to marry than to burn." However, as journalist Tom Ferrell (1979) has suggested, more people than ever "prefer combustible to connubial bliss." One of the most dramatic trends of recent years has been the tremendous increase in male-female couples who choose to live together without marrying, thereby engaging in what is commonly called *cohabitation.*

The number of such households in the United States rose sixfold in the 1960s and increased another sixfold between 1970 and 1991. The dramatic rise in cohabitation has been linked to greater acceptance of premarital sex and delayed entry into marriage. According to a 1988 national survey, 11 percent of women who had never married were cohabiting while 44 percent of women who had married in the early 1980s had cohabited at some time (Bouvier and De Vita, 1991:18; Thomson and Colella, 1992).

Increases in cohabitation have also been found in Canada, France, Sweden, Denmark, and Australia. Data released in Great Britain indicate that more than 12 percent of people ages 18 to 24 are cohabiting. One report notes that in Sweden it is almost universal for couples to live together before marriage. Demographers in Denmark call the practice of living together *marriage without papers.* In Australia, these couples are known as *de factos* (Blanc, 1984; A. Levinson, 1984; O'Donnell, 1992:66; Thomson and Colella, 1992).

For some people in the United States, living together may represent a kind of trial marriage that will eventually lead to a traditional marriage with their current partner (or some other person). Margaret Mead (1966) gave the idea of trial marriage her support when she suggested that marriage be contracted in two stages. The *individual marriage* would involve a minimal legal commitment but would become a legally binding *parental marriage* once a child was expected. Mead's formulation has not yet won wide acceptance. However, in many instances, a couple engaged in extended cohabitation comes to view the relationship as a partnership somewhat like marriage — but with unresolved legal implications.

It would be incorrect, however, to associate cohabitation only with college campuses, sexual experimentation, or trial marriages. According to a study in Los Angeles, working couples are almost twice as likely to cohabit as college students are. At the same time, census data show that 28 percent of unmarried couples have one or more children present in the household. These cohabitants can be regarded as more similar to spouses than to dating partners. Moreover, in contrast to the common perception that people engaged in cohabitation have never married, researchers report that about half of all people involved in cohabitation in the United States have been previously married. Indeed, cohabitation serves as a temporary or permanent alternative to matrimony for many men and women who have experienced marital disruption. Clearly, cohabitation should not be regarded as a pastime limited to the unmarried and the inexperienced (London, 1991; Spanier, 1983).

Remaining Single

Current data indicate that more people in the United States are postponing entry into first marriages than was true in the past. In 1992, 66 percent of all women 20 to 24 years of age had never married, compared with only 36 percent in 1970. Indeed, as of 1992, one out of every four households in the United States (accounting for 23 million people) was a single-member household. Still, less than 10 percent of women and men in the United States are likely to remain single throughout their lives (Bureau of the Census, 1993a:54–55; Seligmann, 1993).

The trend toward maintaining an unmarried lifestyle is related to the growing economic independence of young people. This is especially significant for women. In 1890, women accounted for only one-sixth of the paid labor force; they are now approximately half of it (see Chapter 11). From a financial point of view, it is often no longer necessary for a woman to marry in order to enjoy a satisfying life.

There are many reasons why a person may choose not to marry (see Table 13-3). Singleness is an attractive option for those who do not want to limit their sexual intimacy to one lifetime partner. Also, some men and women do not want to become highly dependent on any one person — and do not want anyone depending heavily on them. In a society which values individuality and self-fulfillment,

TABLE 13-3	Singleness: An Alternative to Marriage

ATTRACTIONS OF BEING SINGLE	ATTRACTIONS OF BEING MARRIED
Career opportunities	Economic security
Sexual availability	Regular sex
Exciting lifestyle	Desire for family
Self-sufficiency	Sustained love
Freedom to change and experiment	Security in personal relationships

SOURCE: Adapted from P. Stein, 1975. Also appears in P. Stein, 1981:18.

More people in the United States are making a conscious choice to remain single. As the balance sheet above indicates, there are attractions to being single as well as to being married.

the single lifestyle can offer certain freedoms that married couples may not enjoy.

Remaining single represents a clear departure from societal expectations; indeed, it has been likened to "being single on Noah's Ark." A single adult must confront the inaccurate view that he or she is always lonely, is a workaholic, is immature, and is automatically affluent. These stereotypes help support the traditional assumption in the United States and most other societies that to be truly happy and fulfilled, a person must get married and raise a family (Cargan and Melko, 1991).

Gay Relationships

According to estimates, lesbians and gay men together constitute perhaps 10 percent of the nation's population. Their lifestyles vary greatly. Some live alone, others with roommates. Some live in long-term, monogamous relationships with a lover and with children from former marriages. Others remain married and have not publicly acknowledged their homosexuality.

The 1990 census was the first that attempted to calculate the number of gay households in the United States. Some 88,200 gay male couples and 69,200 lesbian couples self-identified as living together, but census officials acknowledge that these figures underreport the actual numbers of gay and lesbian couples. These census respondents were found to have more years of formal schooling and higher incomes than their heterosexual counterparts (Usdansky, 1993a).

The contemporary gay liberation movement has given an increasing number of lesbians and gay males the support to proclaim their sexual and affectional orientation. Gay activists were distressed in 1986 when a divided Supreme Court ruled, by a 5-4 vote, that the Constitution does not protect homosexual relations between consenting adults, even within the privacy of their own homes. Nevertheless, as of mid-1993, at least 19 states (8 through legislation and 11 through executive orders or interpretations of civil service rules), the District of Columbia, and 119 cities and counties had adopted laws or policies that provide varying degrees of civil rights protection for lesbians and gay men (*Harvard Law Review*, 1993:1908).

Gay activist organizations emphasize that lesbian and gay male couples are prohibited from marrying—and therefore from gaining traditional partnership benefits—in all 50 states. Consequently, with such inequities in mind, certain municipalities have been encouraged to pass legislation or adopt executive orders to provide benefits to "domestic partners." Under such policies, a ***domestic partnership*** may be defined as "two unrelated adults who have chosen to share one another's lives in a relationship of mutual caring, who reside together, and agree to be jointly responsible for their dependents, basic living expenses, and other common necessities." While the most passionate support for domestic partnership legislation has come from lesbian and gay activists, only about 40 percent of those whose long-term relationships would qualify them as domestic partners are gay. The vast majority of those eligible for such benefits would be cohabiting heterosexual couples (Dittersdorf, 1990:6; Isaacson, 1989).

While various municipalities have passed domestic partnership legislation, such proposals continue to face strong opposition from conservative religious and political groups. In the view of opponents, support for domestic partnership undermines the historic societal preference for the nuclear family. Advocates of domestic partnership counter that such relationships fulfill the same functions for the individuals involved and for society as the traditional family and should enjoy the same legal protections and benefits. As one mea-

Some lesbian and gay couples have joined in formal "commitment ceremonies." Elaine Ashari and Galen Ellis, shown together in this photograph, exchanged vows and rings and cut a wedding cake before 100 friends and family members in a park in Oakland, California.

sure of the continuing controversy, a domestic partnership ordinance passed in San Francisco in 1989 was narrowly overturned by voters in a referendum later that year.

During the massive 1993 gay rights march in Washington, D.C.—involving hundreds of thousands of gay men, lesbians, and their supporters—some 1500 homosexual couples participated in a mass wedding. While these vows were not legally binding, many participants clearly viewed their relationships as lifelong commitments. "My parents were together for 30 years. Patrick's have been together almost as long," noted Craig Dean, who established the Equal Marriage Rights Fund with his lover, Patrick Gill, after they were denied a marriage license in 1991. "We want to continue to live our lives that way," concluded Dean. Not long after this march, the prospects for legalization of gay marriages improved somewhat. In May 1993, Hawaii's highest court ruled that the state's ban on same-sex unions probably violates the state constitution. This decision could pave the way for lesbian and gay couples to legally marry in Hawaii and other states (Salholz, 1993).

Marriage without Children

There has been a modest increase in childlessness in the United States. According to data from the 1990 census, about 16 percent of women in their 40s will complete their childbearing years without having borne any children. As many as 20 percent of women in their thirties expect to remain childless (Bureau of the Census, 1991e:12).

Childlessness within marriage has generally been viewed as a problem that can be solved through such means as adoption and artificial insemination. Some couples, however, *choose* not to have children and regard themselves as child-free, not childless. They do not believe that having children automatically follows from marriage, nor do they feel that reproduction is the duty of all married couples.

Economic considerations have contributed to this shift in attitudes; having children has become quite expensive. According to a government estimate in 1992, the average middle-class family will spend $128,670 to feed, clothe, and shelter a child from birth to age 17. If the child attends college, that amount could double, depending on the college chosen. With such financial pressures in mind, some couples are having fewer children than they otherwise might, and others are weighing the advantages of a child-free marriage (Department of Agriculture, 1992).

Single-Parent Families

Single-parent families, in which there is only one parent present to care for the children, can hardly be viewed as a rarity in the United States. As noted earlier in the chapter, as of 1992, about 18 percent of White families, 31 percent of Hispanic families, and 53 percent of African American families were headed by a single parent. Recent data show a sharp decline in the proportion of women who marry to avoid an out-of-wedlock first birth, from 52 percent in the early 1960s to 27 percent in the early 1990s (Bureau of the Census, 1993a:56; Norton and Miller, 1992:4).

Whether judged in economic or emotional terms, the lives of single parents and their children are not inevitably more difficult than life in a traditional nuclear family. It is as inaccurate to assume that a single-parent family is necessarily "deprived" as it is to assume that a two-parent family is always secure and happy. Nevertheless, life in a single-parent family can be extremely stressful. Ronald Haskins, director of the Child Development Institute at the University of North Carolina, observes: "It's a big and risky undertaking when so many parents try to raise so many children alone" (Mann, 1983:62).

There is a clear association between the increase in families headed by single mothers and the feminization of poverty (see Chapter 8). Families headed by divorced or never-married mothers represent the fastest-growing segment of the female poor. The economic problems of single mothers result from such factors as sex discrimination in the paid labor force, the high costs of child care, inadequate welfare benefits, and fathers' failure to pay court-ordered child support.

A family headed by a single mother faces especially difficult problems when the mother is a teenager. According to a study released in 1985 and updated in 1989 by the Alan Guttmacher Institute, teenagers in the United States become pregnant, give birth, and have abortions at much higher rates than adolescents in almost any other industrialized nation. And the United States is the only developed country in which pregnancy among teenagers has been on the rise in recent years. Many adults with traditional attitudes toward sexuality and family life have suspected that the availability of birth control and sex education in the United States and other developed countries leads to increases in pregnancy among teenagers. However, the researchers point out that the *lowest* rates of pregnancy among teenagers are found in countries with liberal attitudes toward sex, easily accessible birth control services for young people, and comprehensive sex education programs (Brozan, 1985; Henshaw and Van Vort, 1989; E. Jones et al., 1985, 1986).

Why might low-income teenage women wish to have children and face the obvious financial difficulties of motherhood? Viewed from an interactionist perspective, these women tend to have low self-esteem and limited options; a child may pro-

In the United States, a growing proportion of single mothers are educated women with enough financial resources to support a child without assistance from a husband.

vide a sense of motivation and purpose for a teenager whose economic worth in our society is limited at best. Given the barriers that many young women face because of their gender, race, ethnicity, and class, many teenagers may believe that they have little to lose and much to gain by having a child. In a 1988 survey of 13,000 high school sophomores from varied economic backgrounds, one out of four said that she would consider having a child if she became pregnant while unmarried. A follow-up study showed that these respondents were two to three times more likely than their reluctant peers to actually have become mothers (Abrahamse et al., 1988; V. Alexander et al., 1987; Gimenez, 1987; Zelnick and Young, 1982).

It should be noted, however, that single mothers in the United States are not necessarily young or poor. A small but growing proportion of single mothers are educated women with enough financial resources to support a child without assistance from a husband. By 1993, more than 6 percent of single mothers were college-educated and more than 8 percent were employed in professional jobs;

both figures were double those of only 10 years earlier. While these percentages remain small, it nevertheless appears that marriage and motherhood are no longer inevitably linked in the minds of affluent women. Consequently, sociologist Larry Bumpass has asked: "What is uniquely associated with being married? In our culture it was sexual privilege, co-residence, having children. We're seeing each of those traditional benefits of marriage being progressively separated" (Ingrassia, 1993:58).

While 86 percent of single parents in the United States are mothers, the number of households headed by single fathers has doubled over the period 1980 to 1992. The stereotypes of single fathers are that they raise only boys or only older children. In fact, about 44 percent of children living in such households are girls, while almost one-third of single fathers care for preschoolers. Whereas single mothers often develop social networks, single fathers are typically more isolated. In addition, they must deal with schools and social service agencies more accustomed to women as custodial parents (D. Johnson, 1993).

- Why is it difficult to measure precisely the prevalence of domestic violence in the United States?
- How do conflict theorists view domestic violence?
- In what ways may intervention in cases of domestic violence draw on an interactionist approach?

A television reporter wears long-sleeved, high-collared blouses to hide her bruises. Her husband, a businessman, frequently batters her body but never touches her face. The reporter once filed charges against him but later dropped them out of fear that the beating might become public knowledge.

Deidre still has painful flashbacks about her abusive stepfather. The smell of a country barn or the scent of the aftershave he used to wear brings it all back: how he forced her to have sex with him at

the family's rural home. Deidre's mother was sick; her stepfather made the child believe that her mother would die if she told her the truth (*Changing Times*, 1981; R. Watson, 1984:32).

Wife battering, child abuse, abuse of the elderly, and other forms of domestic violence are an ugly reality of family life in the United States. In a sense, domestic violence begins even before marriage in the form of violent behavior within dating and courtship relationships. According to a 1990 review of recent research, while there has been great variance from survey to survey, as many as 67 percent of high school and college students have reported that they have been the victims of such attacks. As with other forms of abuse, victims of courtship violence are reluctant to tell others about their experiences; if they do, they typically tell their peers rather than their parents or teachers. This lack of early intervention is especially regrettable, since studies of battered women in shelters indicate that 51 percent have been physically abused in earlier dating relationships (Gelles and Cornell, 1990:65–66).

Violence during dating resembles other assaults in that it may involve pushing, slapping, punching, hitting with a weapon, and choking. Yet its consequences differ in one important respect: assaults or rapes by strangers leave victims wary of being alone, but rape by an acquaintance often causes the victim to become fearful of trusting someone again or forming close relationships. According to victimization surveys, one-third of victims of reported rapes identify the attacker as an acquaintance or date (Makepeace, 1986).

It is difficult to measure precisely the prevalence of domestic violence, since many victims are reluctant to call the police or bring charges against family members. With so many cases remaining unreported, researchers find it difficult to determine whether the level of domestic violence in the United States is increasing or decreasing. Studies find that 20 to 40 percent of couples seeking divorce cite "physical abuse" as their major complaint, while married couples who are not contemplating divorce report a similar incidence of violence. Moreover, consistently throughout the 1970s and 1980s, 34 percent of all female murder victims in the United States—more than 2800 a year—were killed by members of their own families. Family violence, of course, is a worldwide problem; it can be especially harsh in societies that devalue particular members of the family circle, such as children born outside of marriage, stepchildren, disabled children, female babies, or wives in general (Gelles and Cornell, 1990:28–31, 67–68; Gelles et al., 1988; T. Randall, 1990b:940; Stocks, 1988).

As of 1992, researchers offered the following generalizations concerning domestic violence in the United States (*Psychology Today*, 1992:22):

- Domestic violence is evident among every racial and ethnic group and socioeconomic class.
- Physical abuse is the leading cause of injury to women.
- One out of every two women will find herself in a battering relationship at some time in her life.
- In 70 percent of cases involving wife battering, it is the abuser—the husband—who is granted custody of the children.

Shown is Carolyn Suzanne Sapp of Hawaii, Miss America of 1992, as she is being crowned by a former Miss America. After becoming Miss America, Sapp spoke out strongly against domestic violence and revealed that she herself had been battered by a former lover.

- A person is nine times more likely to be killed in a family relationship than on the streets.

The situation of battered women is so intolerable that it has been compared to that of prison inmates. Criminologist Noga Avni (1991) interviewed battered women at a shelter in Israel and found that their day-to-day lives with their husbands or lovers had many elements of life in an oppressive total institution, as described by Erving Goffman (1961). Physical barriers are placed upon these women; compulsory confinement to their homes damages their self-esteem and limits their ability to cope with repeated abuse. Moreover, as in a total institution (refer back to Chapter 4), battered women are cut off from external sources of physical and emotional

TABLE 13-4	Five Steps to Prevent Domestic Violence

1. *Eliminate the norms that legitimize violence in society and the family.* The elimination of spanking as a child-raising technique, gun control to get deadly weapons out of the home, the elimination of the death penalty, the elimination of corporal punishment in schools, and the elimination of media violence are all necessary steps.

2. *Reduce violence-provoking stress created by society.* Reducing poverty, inequality, and unemployment and providing adequate housing, nutrition, medical and dental care, and educational opportunities could reduce stress in families.

3. *Integrate families into a network of families and the community.* Reducing social isolation could reduce stress and increase the ability of families to manage stress.

4. *Change the sexist character of society.* Sexual inequality, perhaps more than economic inequality, makes violence possible in the home. The elimination of the separation of men's work from women's work would be a major step toward equality inside and outside the home.

5. *Break the cycle of violence in the family.* Violence cannot be prevented as long as we are taught that it is acceptable to hit the people we love. Physical punishment of children is perhaps the most effective means of teaching violence, and eliminating it would be an important step in violence prevention.

SOURCE: Gelles, 1993:568; see also M. Straus et al., 1980.

In 1993, sociologist Richard Gelles reaffirmed five important ways to prevent domestic violence. This model was first presented in 1980 by Gelles and his colleagues Murray Straus and Suzanne Steinmetz.

assistance and moral support. In Avni's view, society could more effectively aid victims of domestic violence if the essential imprisonment of these women were better understood.

In the United States, the family can be a dangerous place not only for women but also for children and the elderly. In 1992, 2.9 million cases of child abuse were reported to state and local authorities. According to the National Committee for Prevention of Child Abuse (1993), about 1300 children in the United States die annually as a result of abuse or neglect.

It is estimated that between 4 and 10 percent of older people in the United States have suffered from physical abuse, verbal abuse, or neglect. If these findings are generalized across the nation, by 1995 there will be about 1.3 to 3.4 million abused elderly people in the United States. In general, as is true of wife beating and child abuse, the number of reported cases of abuse of the elderly is undoubtedly well below the actual incidence. As a result of growing public concern, legislation in many states has redefined the concept of "domestic violence" to include abuse of the elderly as well as child abuse and violence between spouses or lovers (Gelles and Cornell, 1990:102; Rosado, 1991).

Viewed from a conflict perspective, domestic violence should be seen in terms of dominance and control. It is one means by which men reinforce their power over women and adults reinforce their power over children. Nevertheless, despite the obvious in-

equities in domestic violence cases, victims of such assaults are often accused of "asking for" or provoking the abusive behavior. This is a classic example of "blaming the victim" for the misdeeds of others (refer back to Box 8–2 on page 227). In the case of wife beating, for example, feminists and conflict theorists emphasize that blaming the victim is but another reflection of men's power over women (K. Quinn et al., 1984:2; Stets and Pirog-Good, 1987).

Intervention in cases of domestic violence may draw on an interactionist approach by attempting to bolster the self-esteem of victims. Existing programs dealing with wife beating avoid telling the women what to do; instead, they help them to assess their internal strengths, and they provide information about available resources. Counselors typically believe that the female victim should not blame herself or excuse the offender. When working with men who are batterers, counselors encourage them to accept responsibility for their violent behavior and to learn other, nonabusive ways of communicating their feelings (C. Anderson and Rouse, 1988:139).

What can be done to prevent domestic violence? Some sociologists argue that a basic attack on courtship and family violence must involve a challenge to the glorification of violence which pervades our society (see Table 13-4). This could include reducing the number of television programs and motion pictures with violent themes, as well as outlawing use of corporal punishment in schools (Jaffe et al., 1990; McCormick, 1992).

Numerous decisions by federal courts have held that the domestic relations of husband and wife, as well as parent and child, are not a matter of federal jurisdiction. Consequently, in terms of social policy, domestic violence has been addressed primarily on the state and local levels. Over the past 20 years, spurred in good part by the activism of the feminist movement, there has been increasing pressure on police officers, judges, and other criminal justice officials to treat domestic violence as a serious crime. Many state and local governments have increased funding for shelters for battered women, telephone "hot lines" to assist victims of rape and domestic violence, and other social services that will reduce assaults within the family (Malinowski, 1990).

Despite such advances, the magnitude of the problem remains distressing. Sociologist Murray Straus has estimated that at least 8 million people in the United States are assaulted every year by family members. Some form of violence occurs in 25 percent of all marriages. Of those women needing emergency surgery procedures, at least one in every five—and perhaps one in every three—is a victim of domestic violence (Kantrowitz, 1988:59; T. Randall, 1990a:939; see also M. Straus and Gelles, 1990).

With such data in mind, in 1992 the American Medical Association (1992) recommended that physicians routinely screen their female patients for indications of domestic violence. Noting the widespread denial and apathy concerning assaults within the family, Dr. Antonia Novello, then surgeon general of the United States, stated: "I think the time has come to take the issue of domestic violence out of the shadows and out of the closet" (*New York Times*, 1992c:A26).

SUMMARY

The *family*, although it has many varying forms, is present in all human cultures. This chapter examines the state of marriage and the family in the United States and considers alternatives to the traditional nuclear family.

1 There are many variations in the family from culture to culture and even within the same culture.
2 The structure of the *extended family* can offer certain advantages over that of the *nuclear family*.
3 Sociologists are not agreed on whether the *egalitarian family* has replaced the *patriarchal family* as the social norm in the United States.
4 Sociologists have identified six basic functions of the family: reproduction, protection, socialization, regulation of sexual behavior, companionship, and the providing of social status.
5 Currently, the majority of all married couples in the United States have two partners active in the paid labor force.
6 In the United States, there is considerable variation in family life associated with social class, racial, and ethnic differences.
7 Among the factors which contribute to the rising divorce rate in the United States are the greater social ac-

ceptance of divorce and the liberalization of divorce laws in many states.
8 More and more people are living together without marrying, thereby engaging in what is called *cohabitation*.
9 It is difficult to measure precisely the prevalence of domestic violence, since many victims are reluctant to call police or bring charges against family members.

CRITICAL THINKING QUESTIONS

1 During the 1992 presidential campaign, there was substantial discussion of "family values." What does this term mean to you? Why was it used by candidates during an election year? Are there ways in which government should act to strengthen family life in the United States? Should government act to promote the traditional nuclear family model? Or should it give equal support to all types of families, including single-parent households and families headed by gay and lesbian parents?
2 An increasing proportion of couples in the United States are adopting a dual-career lifestyle. What are the advantages and disadvantages of the dual-career model for women, for men, for children, and for the society as a whole?
3 Given the high rate of divorce in the United States,

is it more appropriate to view divorce as dysfunctional or as a "normal" part of our marriage system? What are the implications of viewing divorce as normal rather than as dysfunctional?

KEY TERMS

Adoption In a legal sense, a process that allows for the transfer of the legal rights, responsibilities, and privileges of parenthood from legal parents to new legal parents. (page 371)

Bilateral descent A kinship system in which both sides of a person's family are regarded as equally important. (364)

Cohabitation The practice of living together as a male-female couple without marrying. (380)

Domestic partnership Two unrelated adults who have chosen to share one another's lives in a relationship of mutual caring, who reside together, and agree to be jointly responsible for their dependents, basic living expenses, and other common necessities. (381)

Egalitarian family An authority pattern in which the adult members of the family are regarded as equals. (365)

Endogamy The restriction of mate selection to people within the same group. (367)

Exogamy The requirement that people select mates outside certain groups. (367)

Extended family A family in which relatives in addition to parents and children—such as grandparents, aunts, or uncles—live in the same home. (361)

Family A set of people related by blood, marriage (or some other agreed-upon relationship), or adoption who share the responsibility for reproducing and caring for members of society. (361)

Incest taboo The prohibition of sexual relationships between certain culturally specified relatives. (367)

Kinship The state of being related to others. (364)

Marital power A term used by Blood and Wolfe to describe the manner in which decision making is distributed within families. (366)

Matriarchy A society in which women dominate in family decision making. (365)

Matrilineal descent A kinship system which favors the relatives of the mother. (364)

Matrilocal A pattern of residence in which a married couple lives with the wife's parents. (364)

Monogamy A form of marriage in which one woman and one man are married only to each other. (362)

Neolocal A pattern of residence in which a married couple establishes a separate residence. (364)

Nuclear family A married couple and their unmarried children living together. (361)

Patriarchy A society in which men are expected to dominate family decision making. (365)

Patrilineal descent A kinship system which favors the relatives of the father. (364)

Patrilocal A pattern of residence in which a married couple lives with the husband's parents. (364)

Polyandry A form of polygamy in which a woman can have several husbands at the same time. (363)

Polygamy A form of marriage in which an individual can have several husbands or wives simultaneously. (362)

Polygyny A form of polygamy in which a husband can have several wives at the same time. (363)

Serial monogamy A form of marriage in which a person can have several spouses in his or her lifetime but can have only one spouse at a time. (362)

Single-parent families Families in which there is only one parent present to care for children. (382)

Social institutions Organized patterns of beliefs and behavior centered on basic social needs. (357)

ADDITIONAL READINGS

Blumstein, Philip, and Pepper Schwartz. *American Couples: Money, Work, Sex.* New York: Morrow, 1983. An ambitious examination of couples in the United States: married, cohabiting, lesbian, and gay male.

Cherlin, Andrew (ed.). *The Changing American Family and Public Policy.* Washington, D.C.: Urban Institute Press, 1988. A collection of articles considering the link between public policy and family-related issues in the United States.

Gelles, Richard J., and Claire Pedrick Cornell. *Intimate Violence in Families* (2d ed.). Newbury Park, Calif.: Sage, 1990. An examination of all aspects of domestic violence, including reviews of research on incidence. For a similar analysis, see M. Straus and Gelles, 1990.

Goode, William J. *World Changes in Divorce Patterns.* New Haven, Conn.: Yale University Press, 1993. An examination of current trends in divorce in Arab and Asian countries and eastern Europe, as well as Latin America and western Europe.

Greil, Arthur L. *Not Yet Pregnant.* New Brunswick, N.J.: Rutgers University Press, 1991. A sociological analysis of the impact of infertility on a couple's marriage and their relationships with relatives and friends.

Hertz, Rosanna. *More Equal Than Others: Women and Men in Dual-Career Marriages.* Berkeley: University of California Press, 1986. A study of the lives of dual-career corporate couples in 34 different organizations in the Chicago metropolitan area.

Lewis, Suzan, Dafna N. Izraeli, and Helen Hootsmans. *Dual-Earner Families: International Perspectives.* Newbury Park, Calif.: Sage, 1991. A concise examination of dual-earner families in the United States, Great Britain, the Netherlands, and Japan.

Mindel, Charles H., Robert W. Habenstein, and Roosevelt Wright, Jr. (eds.). *Ethnic Families in America: Patterns and Variations* (3d ed.). New York: Elsevier, 1988. A collection of articles on the family lives of various racial and ethnic groups in the United States, including Italian Americans, Greek Americans, and Irish Americans.

Mintz, Steven, and Susan Kellogg. *Domestic Revolutions: A Social History of American Family Life.* New York: Free Press, 1988. A historian and an anthropologist look at changes in family life in the United States over the last four centuries; they conclude that this social institution has changed dramatically in its structure, role, and conception.

Weitzman, Lenore J. *The Divorce Revolution: The Unexpected Social and Economic Consequences for Women and Children in America.* New York: Free Press, 1985. A sociological examination of the impact of no-fault divorce laws on custody arrangements and property settlements.

Journals

Among the journals focusing on the family are *Family Planning Perspectives* (founded in 1969), *Family Relations* (1951), *International Family Planning Perspectives* (1975), *Journal of Family Issues* (1980), and *Journal of Marriage and the Family* (1938).

14

RELIGION

**DURKHEIM AND THE
SOCIOLOGICAL APPROACH
TO RELIGION**

FUNCTIONS OF RELIGION
The Integrative Function of Religion
Religion and Social Control: The
    Marxist Critique
Religion and Social Support
Religion and Social Change:
    The Weberian Thesis

DIMENSIONS OF RELIGION
Belief
Ritual
Experience

**ORGANIZATION OF RELIGIOUS
BEHAVIOR**
Ecclesiae

Denominations
Sects
Cults
Comparing Forms of Religious
    Organization

RELIGION IN THE UNITED STATES
Beliefs and Practices
Resurgent Fundamentalism
Jews in the United States
Sects and Cults in the United States

**SOCIAL POLICY AND RELIGION:
RELIGION IN THE SCHOOLS**

BOXES
14-1 Around the World: Liberation
    Theology
14-2 Everyday Behavior: Women
    in the Clergy

> *Congress shall make no law respecting an establishment of religion, or prohibiting the free exercise thereof.*
>
> First Amendment
> Constitution of the United States, 1787
>
> *Religion is the sigh of the oppressed creature, the feelings of a heartless world. . . . It is the opiate of the people.*
>
> Karl Marx
> Introduction to the Critique of the Hegelian
> Philosophy of Right, 1844

LOOKING AHEAD

- What are the manifest and latent functions of religion?
- Why did Karl Marx view religion as a form of social control within an oppressive society?
- What did Max Weber mean when he referred to the "Protestant ethic"?
- What are the basic forms of religious organization?
- Are women being accepted into the clergy of the United States?
- Why is religious fundamentalism on the rise in the United States and in other countries?
- How has the Supreme Court ruled regarding religion in the nation's public schools?

At noon, the school day comes to a temporary halt at the Clara Muhammad School in Corona, a neighborhood in New York City. The loudspeaker announces: "Allah is great. . . . Come to prayer." All classwork stops, books and pencils are put away, and students and teachers walk silently in their stocking feet to the second-floor mosque. There they face east, fall on bended knees, put their heads to the ground, and pray to Allah.

Across the United States, there are now more than 60 Muslim day schools, in such cities as New York, Boston, Philadelphia, Atlanta, Chicago, Detroit, and Los Angeles. These full-day private schools teach required subjects such as English, history, science, and mathematics—but they also teach the Arabic language and offer religious instruction. The Muslim schools serve a mosaic of students, including African American children and immigrant children from such countries as Egypt, Uganda, Bermuda, Pakistan, Turkey, and Yugoslavia. A significant number of teachers are immigrants who previously worked as engineers, technicians, or college instructors in their native lands.

Many parents send their children to Muslim schools because they view the order and discipline preached in these schools as an important alternative to the drugs, alcohol, and violence found in troubled urban neighborhoods. Moreover, like earlier generations of Catholic and Jewish immigrants to the United States, Islamic parents hope that religious day schools will help to preserve their cherished traditions. "We want to keep Islam alive for us and our children," notes Imam Quasim Bakiridin, the religious director of the Clara Muhammad School (Goldman, 1992:26).

Since the overthrow of communist rule in the Soviet Union and eastern Europe, there has been a dramatic resurgence of religious activity in that part of the world. The traditionally dominant Russian Orthodox church remains Russia's largest religious

392

organization, with an estimated 60 million believers. In the last three years, it has reopened more than 6000 churches and monasteries. At the same time, as many as 1000 foreign missionaries and 50 foreign religious organizations have come to Russia to recruit new adherents. In Hungary, 95 percent of the population is now baptized; in the former Czechoslovakia, nearly 80 percent are (Bezilla, 1993:70–71; Schmemann, 1993).

In Chapter 3 various *cultural universals* were identified—general practices found in every culture—such as dancing, food preparation, the family, and personal names. Religion is clearly such a cultural universal; religious institutions are evident in all societies. At present, an estimated 4 billion people belong to the world's many religious faiths (see Figure 14-1).

Religion is found throughout the world because it offers answers to such ultimate questions as why we exist, why we succeed or fail, and why we die. It is difficult to determine with certainty when religious behavior began, but anthropological evidence suggests that such behavior was evident at least 100,000 years ago. The remains of early people in Europe reveal ceremonial burials with artifacts placed near the deceased, which implies that they believed in an afterlife. Apparently, the human species has long been preoccupied with spiritual concerns (Elaide, 1978; A. Wallace, 1966:224–227).

In contemporary industrial societies, scientific and technological advances have increasingly affected all aspects of life, including the social institution of religion. The term *secularization* refers to the process through which religion's influence on other social institutions diminishes. When this process occurs, religion will survive in the private sphere of individual and family life; indeed, it may thrive on a personal level. At the same time, other social institutions—such as the economy, the government, and education—maintain their own sets of norms independent of religious guidance (Stark and Iannaccone, 1992).

This chapter will focus on religion as it has emerged in modern industrial societies. It will begin with a brief overview of the approaches that Émile Durkheim first introduced and those that later sociologists have used in studying religion. The basic functions of religion as a source of societal integration and social control and as a means of providing social support will be explored. Particular attention will be given to the insights of Karl Marx and Max Weber regarding the relationship between religion and social change. Three important dimensions of religious behavior—belief, ritual, and experience—will be examined, as will the basic forms of religious organization.

The remainder of the chapter will analyze the increasing influence of religion on contemporary life in the United States. Even within the same society, people turn to a variety of religions for answers to the ultimate questions of existence. Therefore, the discussion examines not only the dominant religious beliefs and practices of organized Christian faiths but also the rich spiritual and cultural tradition of Jewish Americans. The revival of a conservative approach to religion, termed *resurgent fundamentalism*, will be studied. Finally, the social policy section of the chapter will examine the controversy over religion in the public schools of the United States.

FIGURE 14-1 Proportion of the World Population by Religion

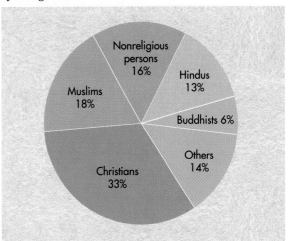

NOTE: The category "nonreligious persons" includes atheists and others who profess no religion.
SOURCE: Based on data from *Encyclopedia Britannica Book of the Year*, 1993:270.

The world's two largest religious faiths are Christianity (accounting for 33 percent of the world population) and Islam (18 percent).

Religion can take many forms. Shown are adherents of the Zoroastrian religion in the United States, Buddhists in Japan meditating on television images of happiness, and a family in India worshipping Lord Krishna in their home.

DURKHEIM AND THE SOCIOLOGICAL APPROACH TO RELIGION

Sociologists are interested in the social impact of religion on individuals and institutions. Consequently, if a group believes that it is being directed by a "vision from God," a sociologist will not attempt to prove or disprove this "revelation." Instead, he or she will assess the effects of the religious experience on the group (M. McGuire, 1981:1–2).

Émile Durkheim was perhaps the first sociologist to recognize the critical importance of religion in human societies. He saw its appeal for the individual but—more important—he stressed that religion is socially constructed. In Durkheim's view, religion is a collective act and includes many forms of behavior in which people interact with others. As in his work on suicide (see Chapter 1), Durkheim was not so interested in the personalities of religious believers as he was in understanding religious behavior within a social context.

Durkheim initiated sociological analysis of religion by defining *religion* as a "unified system of beliefs and practices relative to sacred things." In his formulation, religion involves a set of beliefs and practices that are uniquely the property of religion—as opposed to other social institutions and ways of thinking. Durkheim (1947:37, original edition 1912) argued that religious faiths distinguish between the everyday world and certain events that transcend the ordinary. He referred to these realms as the *sacred* and the *profane*.

The *sacred* encompasses those elements beyond everyday life which inspire awe, respect, and even fear. People become a part of the sacred realm only by completing some ritual, such as prayer or sacrifice. Believers have faith in the sacred; this faith allows them to accept what they cannot understand. By contrast, the *profane* includes the ordinary and commonplace. Interestingly, the same object can be either sacred or profane depending on how it is viewed. A table is profane, but it becomes sacred to Christians if it bears the elements of a communion as an altar. For Confucians and Taoists, incense sticks are not mere decorative items; they are highly valued offerings to the gods in religious ceremonies marking new and full moons.

Following the direction established by Durkheim

Émile Durkheim's distinction between the sacred and the profane is evident in this poster distributed by the Tokyo subway system. A sorrowful figure of Jesus urges absentminded riders not to leave umbrellas in subway cars. While an image of Jesus is sacred for Christians, it is used in a profane manner in Japan—a nation whose dominant faiths are Shintō and Buddhism.

almost a century ago, contemporary sociologists evaluate religions in two different ways. The norms and values of religious faiths can be studied through examination of their substantive religious beliefs. For example, we can compare the degree to which Christian faiths literally interpret the Bible, or Muslim groups follow the Qur'an (or Koran), the sacred book of Islam. At the same time, religions can be evaluated in terms of the social functions they fulfill, such as providing social support or reinforcing the social norms. By exploring both the beliefs and the functions of religion, we can better understand its impact on the individual, on groups, and on society as a whole.

FUNCTIONS OF RELIGION

Since religion is a cultural universal, it is not surprising that it fulfills several basic functions within human societies. In sociological terms, these include both manifest and latent functions (see Chapter 1). Among the manifest (open and stated) functions of religion are defining the spiritual world and giving meaning to the divine. Because of its beliefs concerning people's relationships to a beyond, religion provides an explanation for events that seem difficult to understand.

By contrast, latent functions of religion are unintended or hidden. Church services provide a manifest function by offering a forum for religious worship; at the same time, they fulfill a latent function as a meeting ground for unattached members.

In viewing religion as a social institution, functionalists evaluate its impact on human societies. The first two functions of religion that will be discussed in this section—integration and social control—are oriented toward the larger society. Thus, they are best understood from a macro-level viewpoint in terms of the relationship between religion and society as a whole. The third function—providing social support—is more oriented toward the individual and can be understood more effectively from a micro-level viewpoint. The fourth function, promoting social change, is illustrated using Max Weber's macro-level concept of the Protestant ethic.

The Integrative Function of Religion

Émile Durkheim viewed religion as an integrative power in human society—a perspective reflected in functionalist thought today. Durkheim was concerned with a perplexing question: "How can human societies be held together when they are generally composed of individuals and social groups with diverse interests and aspirations?" In his view, religious bonds often transcend these personal and divisive forces. Durkheim acknowledged that religion is not the only integrative force—nationalism or patriotism may serve the same end.

Why should religion provide this "societal glue"? Religion, whether it be Buddhism, Christianity, or Judaism, offers people meaning and purpose for their lives. It gives them certain ultimate values and ends to hold in common. Although subjective and not always fully accepted, these values and ends help a society to function as an integrated social system. For example, the Christian ritual of communion not only celebrates a historical event in the life of Jesus (the last supper) but also represents a participation in the group of believers. Similarly, funerals, weddings, bar and bat mitzvahs, and confirmations serve to integrate people into larger communities by providing shared beliefs and values about the ultimate questions of life.

The integrative function of religion is particularly apparent in traditional, preindustrial societies. In these cultures, gathering of crops, exercise of authority by leaders, relationships between kinfolk, and artistic expression are all governed by religious beliefs and rituals. In industrial societies, religion helps to integrate newcomers by providing a source of identity. For example, Italian American immigrants, after settling in their new social environment, came to identify strongly with the local Catholic church. Many Italian Catholic congregations in cities became neighborhood centers that helped members preserve their ethnic heritage while adjusting to an unfamiliar culture. In a rapidly changing world, religious faith can provide an important sense of belonging. Later in this chapter, we shall see that the failure of traditional religions to satisfy people's need for identity has contributed to the rise of religious cults in the United States (Greeley, 1972:108–126; K. Roberts, 1984:57–58).

There is probably no better example of a nationally unifying religious symbol than the Virgin of Guadalupe of Mexico. According to the accepted account, the Virgin Mary appeared in 1531 to Juan Diego, a Christianized Indian, and commanded him to inform church officials of her desire to see a church built in her honor in Guadalupe. Diego failed at first to gain approval for the new church, but then, on the direction of the Virgin Mary, placed some roses in a cloak and presented this cloak to the archbishop. Astonished, the archbishop opened the cloak to find the Virgin's image stamped on it. The church was subsequently built, and Diego's cloak still hangs on the central altar with the miraculous image.

This story and church are accepted in Mexico as symbols of salvation and success. It gives Indians a unique role in the history of Christianity in Mexico—both in terms of their place in society and in heaven. The account of Diego and his vision is also integrative from a historical perspective, since the site of his vision was a shrine to Tonantzin, a much-loved Aztec goddess of earth and maize. The names of Guadalupe and Tonantzin are still used interchangeably by some Indians living in central Mexico (W. Johnson, 1961:136; Wolf, 1979).

Although the integrative impact of religion has been emphasized here, it should be noted that religion is not the *dominant* force maintaining social cohesion in contemporary industrial societies. People are also bound together by patterns of consumption, laws, nationalistic feelings, and other forces. Moreover, in some instances religious loyalties are dysfunctional; they contribute to tension and even conflict between groups or nations. During the Second World War, the Nazis attempted to exterminate the Jewish people, and approximately 6 million European Jews were killed. In modern times, nations such as Lebanon (Muslims versus Christians), Northern Ireland (Roman Catholics versus Protestants), and India (Hindus versus Muslims and, more recently, Sikhs) have been torn by clashes that are in part based on religion.

In the 1990s, the bloody conflict in the former Yugoslavia (refer back to the discussion of "ethnic cleansing" in the social policy section of Chapter 9) has been exacerbated by related religious and ethnic tensions. Serbia, Macedonia, and Montenegro are dominated by the Orthodox church, and Croatia and Slovenia by the Catholic church; the embattled republic of Bosnia-Herzegovina has a 40 percent Islamic plurality. In many of these areas, the dominant political party is tied into the most influential church.

Religious conflict (though on a less violent level) has been increasingly evident in the United States as well. In a speech before the 1992 Republican National Convention, conservative presidential candidate Patrick Buchanan warned that there was a "religious war going on for the soul of America" (Galloway, 1992:1). Sociologist James Davison

In recent years, Lebanon has been the scene of bitter clashes between native Christians and Muslims, as well as fighting involving Israelis, Palestinians, and Syrians. The soldier shown in the foreground is a Lebanese Christian who carries the image of a madonna on his rifle.

Hunter (1991) has referred to the "cultural war" taking place in the United States: Christian fundamentalists, conservative Catholics, and Orthodox Jews have joined forces in many communities in a battle against their progressive counterparts for control of the secular culture. The battlefield is an array of familiar social issues, among them multiculturalism (see Chapter 3), child care (see Chapter 4), abortion (see Chapter 11), gay rights (see Chapter 13), and funding for the arts.

Religion and Social Control: The Marxist Critique

As we saw in the quotation beginning the chapter, Karl Marx described religion as an "opiate" particularly harmful to oppressed peoples. In his view, religion often drugged the masses into submission by offering a consolation for their harsh lives on earth: the hope of salvation in an ideal afterlife. For example, during the period of slavery in the United States, White masters forbade Blacks to practice native African religions, while encouraging them to adopt the Christian religion. Through Christianity, slaves were prodded to obey their masters; they were told that obedience would lead to salvation and eternal happiness in the hereafter. Viewed from a conflict perspective, Christianity may have pacified certain slaves and blunted the rage that often fueled rebellion (M. McGuire, 1981:186; J. Yinger, 1970:598).

Marx acknowledged that religion plays an important role in legitimating the existing social structure. The values of religion, as already noted, reinforce other social institutions and the social order as a whole. From Marx's perspective, religion promotes stability within society and therefore helps to perpetuate patterns of social inequality. In a society with several religious faiths, the dominant religion will represent the ruling economic and political class.

Marx concurred with Durkheim's emphasis on the collective and socially shared nature of religious behavior. At the same time, he was concerned that religion would reinforce social control within an oppressive society. Marx argued that religion's focus on otherworldly concerns diverted attention from earthly problems and from needless suffering created by unequal distribution of valued resources (Harap, 1982).

Religion reinforces the interests of those in power. For example, India's traditional caste system defined the social structure of that society, at least among the Hindu majority (see Chapter 8). The caste system was almost certainly the creation of the priesthood, but it also served the interests of India's political rulers by granting a certain religious legitimacy to social inequality.

Even in societies not as visibly ruled by religious dogma, religion legitimates the political sector. Military chaplains work to maintain the morale of combat troops during warfare; they do not counsel that taking a human life is morally wrong. The Dutch Reformed church in South Africa—the church of most South African governmental leaders—has traditionally insisted that the regime's policy of apartheid reflects God's intention that certain racial groups be kept separate (refer back to Chapter 10). This "legitimating function of religion," as Max Weber called it, may be used to explain, justify, or rationalize the exercise of power. Whether through the divine right of a monarch or the administration of an oath of office on a Bible, religion provides legitimacy for political rulers and leaders (P. Berger, 1973:311; Marty, 1987).

In the view of Karl Marx and later conflict theorists, religion is not necessarily a beneficial or admirable force for social control. For example, contemporary Christianity, like the Hindu faith, reinforces traditional patterns of behavior that call for the subordination of the powerless. Assumptions about gender roles leave women in a subservient position both within Christian churches and at home. In fact, women find it as difficult to achieve leadership positions in many churches as they do in large corporations (see Box 14-2 on page 410). While women play a significant role as volunteers in community churches, men continue to make the major theological and financial judgments for nationwide church organizations. Conflict theorists argue that to whatever extent religion actually does influence social behavior, it reinforces existing patterns of dominance and inequality.

From a Marxist perspective, religion functions as an "agent of de-politicization" (J. Wilson, 1978: 355–356). In simpler terms, religion keeps people from seeing their lives and societal conditions in political terms—for example, by obscuring the overriding significance of conflicting economic interests. Marxists suggest that by inducing a "false consciousness" among the disadvantaged (see Chapter 8), religion lessens the possibility of collective political action that can end capitalist oppression and transform society.

It should be noted, however, that religious leaders have sometimes been in the forefront of movements for social change. During the 1960s, Dr. Martin Luther King, Jr., supported by numerous ministers, priests, and rabbis, fought for civil rights

BOX 14-1 • AROUND THE WORLD

LIBERATION THEOLOGY

Many religious activists, especially in Latin America, support *liberation theology*, which refers to use of a church in a political effort to eliminate poverty, discrimination, and other forms of injustice evident in secular society. Advocates of this religious movement sometimes display a sympathy for Marxism. Many believe that radical liberation, rather than economic development in itself, is the only acceptable solution to the desperation of the masses in impoverished developing countries. Indeed, the deteriorating social conditions of the last two decades have nurtured this ideology of change.

A significant portion of worshippers are unaffected by this radical mood, but religious leaders are well-aware of liberation theology. The official position of Pope John Paul II and others in the hierarchy of the Catholic church is that clergy should adhere to traditional pastoral duties and keep a distance from radical politics. However, activists associated with liberation theology believe that organized religion has a moral responsibility to take a strong public stand against the oppression of the poor, racial and ethnic minorities, and women (C. Smith, 1991).

The term *liberation theology* has a recent origin, dating back to the 1973 publication of the English translation of *A Theology of Liberation*. This book was written by a Peruvian priest, Gustavo Gutiérrez, who lived in a slum area of Lima during the early 1960s. After years of exposure to the vast poverty around him, Gutiérrez concluded: "The poverty was a destructive thing, something to be fought against and destroyed. . . . It became crystal clear that in order to serve the poor, one had to move into political action" (R. M. Brown, 1980:23).

Gutiérrez's discoveries took place during a time of increasing radicalization among Latin American intellectuals and students. An important element in their radicalization was the theory of *dependencia*, developed by Brazilian and Chilean social scientists. According to this theory, the reason for Latin America's continued underdevelopment was its dependence on industrialized nations (first Spain, then Great Britain, and, most recently, the United States). A related approach shared by most social scientists in Latin America was a Marxist-influenced class analysis that viewed the domination of capitalism and multinational corporations as central to

the problems of the hemisphere. As these perspectives became more influential, a social network emerged among politically committed Latin American theologians who shared experiences and insights. One result was a new approach to theology which rejected the models developed in Europe and the United States and instead built on the cultural and religious traditions of Latin America (Sigmund, 1990:32).

In the 1970s, many advocates of liberation theology expressed strong Marxist views and saw revolutionary struggle to overthrow capitalism as essential to ending the suffering of Latin America's poor. More recently, liberation theology seems to have moved away from orthodox Marxism and endorsement of armed struggle. As an example, Gutiérrez (1990:214, 222) has written that one does not need to accept Marxism as an "all-embracing view of life and thus exclude the Christian faith and its requirements." Gutiérrez adds that the proper concerns of a theology of liberation are not simply the world's "exploited classes," but also "races discriminated against," "despised cultures," and the "condition of women, especially in those sectors of society where women are doubly oppressed and marginalized."

---

for Blacks. In the 1980s, the *sanctuary movement* of loosely connected organizations began offering asylum, often in churches, to those who seek refugee status but are regarded by the Immigration and Naturalization Service as illegal aliens (refer back to Chapter 10). By giving shelter in homes, offices, or religious institutions to those refused asylum, participants in the sanctuary movement are violating the law and become subject to stiff fines and jail sentences. Nevertheless, movement activists (including many members of the clergy) believe that such humanitarian assistance is fully justified. The efforts of religious groups to promote social change extend beyond the United States; in Box 14-1 we focus on religious activism in Latin America.

In times of tragedy, religion provides social support and helps people cope with their problems.

Religion and Social Support

Most of us find it difficult to accept the stressful events of life—death of a loved one, serious injury, bankruptcy, divorce, and so forth. This is especially true when something "senseless" happens. How can family and friends come to terms with the death of a talented college student, not even 20 years old, from a terminal disease?

Through its emphasis on the divine and supernatural, religion allows us to "do something" about the calamities we face. In some faiths, one can offer sacrifices or pray to a deity with the belief that it will change one's earthly condition. At a more basic level, religion encourages us to view our personal misfortunes as relatively unimportant in the broader perspective of human history—or even as part of an undisclosed divine purpose. Friends and relatives of the deceased college student may see this death as being "God's will" and as having some ultimate benefit that we cannot understand. This perspective may be much more comforting than the terrifying feeling that any of us can die senselessly at any moment—and that there is no divine "answer" as to why one person lives a long and full life whereas another dies tragically at a relatively early age.

As we saw earlier, religion offers consolation to oppressed peoples by giving them hope that they can achieve salvation and eternal happiness in an afterlife. Similarly, during times of national tragedy (assassinations, invasions, and natural disasters), people attend religious services as a means of coping with problems that demand political and technological as well as spiritual solutions. On more of a micro level, clergy are often the first source of aid sought out by people faced with a crisis. In a 1990 survey in Texas, respondents were asked to whom they would go first to discuss personal problems. The highest percentage, 41 percent, stated that they would turn to clergy, as contrasted with 29 percent who would choose medical doctors and 21 percent who would go to psychiatrists or psychologists (Chalfant et al., 1990; M. McGuire, 1981: 186; J. Yinger, 1970:598).

Religion and Social Change: The Weberian Thesis

For Karl Marx, the relationship between religion and social change was clear: religion impeded change by encouraging oppressed people to focus on otherworldly concerns rather than on their immediate poverty or exploitation. However, Max Weber (1958a, original edition 1904) was unconvinced by Marx's argument and carefully examined the connection between religious allegiance and capitalist development. His findings appeared in his pioneering work *The Protestant Ethic and the Spirit of Capitalism,* first published in 1904.

Weber noted that in European nations with both Protestant and Catholic citizens, an overwhelming number of business leaders, owners of capital, and skilled workers were Protestant. In his view, this was no mere coincidence. Weber pointed out that the followers of John Calvin (1509–1564), a leader of the Protestant Reformation, emphasized a disciplined work ethic, this-worldly concern, and rational orientation to life that has become known as the **Protestant ethic.** One by-product of the Protestant ethic was a drive to accumulate savings that could be used for future investment. This "spirit of capitalism," to use Weber's phrase, contrasted with the moderate work hours, leisurely work habits, and lack of ambition that he saw as typical of the times (Winter, 1977; J. Yinger, 1974).

What were the Calvinist religious principles that Weber saw as so conducive to capitalism? Calvinism believed in the doctrine of **predestination,** which holds that people either will be among the elect, who are rewarded in heaven, or will be condemned to hell. One's predestined future was not dependent on being righteous or sinful while on earth. Nevertheless, many Calvinists viewed hard work at a vocation as an outward sign of one's inner Christianity and as an indication that one would be rewarded in the afterlife. In addition, hard work served as a means of reducing anxiety over one's possible future in hell. For these reasons, Weber argued, Calvinism and, to a lesser degree, other branches of Protestant religion initiated change in society favorable to capitalistic behavior. Whereas Marx had seen religion as a consequence of the economy, Weber believed that religion helped to shape a new economic system.

Few books in the sociology of religion have aroused as much commentary and criticism as *The Protestant Ethic and the Spirit of Capitalism.* It has been hailed as one of the most important theoretical works in the field and as an excellent example of macro-level analysis. Like Durkheim, Weber demonstrated that religion is not solely a matter of intimate personal beliefs. He stressed that the collective nature of religion has social consequences for society as a whole.

Despite this insight, some casual readers of Weber have found it difficult to accept his ideas. A common but misguided criticism is that Weber naively assigned too much significance to the effects of Calvinism. However, he never argued that the Protestant ethic was *necessary* for the development of capitalism. In Weber's own words (1958a: 91, original edition 1904):

> . . . We have no intention whatever of maintaining such a foolish and doctrinaire thesis as that . . . capitalism as an economic system is a creation of the Reformation.

It is clear that capitalism has flourished in Japan without Calvinism (or, for that matter, Christianity). In an interesting application of the Weberian thesis, sociologist Robert Bellah (1957) examined the relationship between Japanese religious faiths and capitalism. Bellah determined that, as was true of Calvinism, these faiths stressed values of hard work and success and thus paved the way for the rise of Japanese capitalism.

Conflict theorists caution that Weber's theory—even if it is accepted—should not be regarded as an analysis of mature capitalism as reflected in the rise of large corporations which transcend national boundaries (see Chapter 9). The primary disagreement between Karl Marx and Max Weber concerned not the origins of capitalism, but rather its future. Unlike Marx, Weber believed that capitalism could endure indefinitely as an economic system. He added, however, that the decline of religion as an overriding force in society opened the way for workers to express their discomfort more vocally (R. Collins, 1980).

We can conclude that, although Weber provides a convincing description of the origins of European capitalism, this economic system has subsequently been adopted by non-Calvinists in many parts of the world. Contemporary studies in the United States show little or no difference in achievement orientation between Roman Catholics and Protestants. Apparently, the "spirit of capitalism" has become a generalized cultural trait rather than a specific religious tenet (Greeley, 1989a).

DIMENSIONS OF RELIGION

All religions have certain elements in common, yet these elements are expressed in the distinctive manner of each faith. The dimensions of religion, like other patterns of social behavior, are of great interest to sociologists, since they underscore the relationship between religion and society. Religious beliefs, religious rituals, and religious experience all help to define what is sacred and to differentiate the sacred from the profane.

Belief

Some people believe in life after death, in supreme beings with unlimited powers, or in supernatural forces. **Religious beliefs** are statements to which members of a particular religion adhere. These views vary dramatically from religion to religion.

Religious beliefs can be subdivided into values and cosmology. *Religious values* are shared conceptions of what is good, desirable, and proper that arise out of religious faith. These values govern personal conduct and may have direct impact on other social institutions. For example, religious values regarding marriage will influence patterns of family life in a society—perhaps by discouraging couples from seeking divorce. Even the economy can be reinforced by religious values. The sacred character of the child Jesus for Christians promotes the seasonal exchange of gifts as an expression of caring for others. Retailing establishments encourage this form of interaction, and an entire society (including non-Christians and nonbelievers) is affected by the gift exchange (Young, 1981).

The term *cosmology* refers to a general theory of the universe. The cosmology of a religion explains the ultimate questions; offers a divinity or hierarchy of gods and goddesses; and describes heaven, hell, life, and death. Several North American Indian accounts of creation tell of a succession of animals that dove into a flood of waters. The animals emerged with bits of mud or sand, and from this the earth was formed. Among some Asian and African peoples and some Indian tribes, it is believed that, in antiquity, a spider spun the earth. The same spider laid an egg out of which the first male and female human beings developed (Dundes, 1962).

The account of the creation found in Genesis, the first book of the Old Testament, is also part of a cosmology. Many people strongly adhere to the biblical explanation of creation and insist that this view be taught in public schools. These people, known as *creationists,* are worried by the secularization of society and oppose educational curricula which directly or indirectly question biblical scripture.

Ritual

Religious rituals are practices required or expected of members of a faith. Rituals usually honor the divine power (or powers) worshipped by believers; they also remind adherents of their religious duties and responsibilities. Rituals and beliefs can be interdependent; rituals generally involve the affirmation of beliefs, as in a public or private statement confessing a sin (K. Roberts, 1984:96–107).

Like any social institution, religion develops distinctive normative patterns to structure people's behavior. Moreover, there are sanctions attached to religious rituals, whether rewards (pins for excellence at church schools) or penalties (expulsion from a religious institution for violation of norms).

In the United States, rituals may be very simple, such as saying grace at a meal and observing a moment of silence to commemorate someone's death. Yet certain rituals, such as the process of canonizing a saint, are quite elaborate. Most religious rituals in our culture focus on services conducted at houses of worship. Thus, attendance at a service, silent and spoken reading of prayers, and singing of spiritual hymns and chants are common forms of ritual behavior that generally take place in group settings. From an interactionist perspective, these rituals serve as important face-to-face encounters in which people reinforce their religious beliefs and their commitment to their faith.

Some rituals actually induce an almost trancelike state. The Plains Indians eat or drink peyote, a cactus containing the powerful hallucinogenic drug mescaline. Similarly, the ancient Greek followers of the god Pan chewed intoxicating leaves of ivy in order to become more ecstatic during their celebrations. Of course, artificial stimulants are not necessary to achieve a religious "high." Devout believers, such as those who practice the pentecostal Christian ritual of "speaking in tongues," can reach a state of ecstasy simply through spiritual passion.

Sacrifice is a rather widespread ritual. It is generally based on the hope that if a person gives up something of value to honor a supreme being, he or she will receive a divine blessing. A common sacrificial custom within industrial societies is making a contribution to a religious institution, as in the practice of tithing (giving one-tenth of one's income to a church). Other examples of religious sacrifice include fasting on holy days (such as Yom Kippur, the Day of Atonement for Jews) and giving up worldly pleasures (as Christians do for Lent). Yet the most ancient form of sacrifice—still commonly found throughout the world in the 1990s—is the burial of goods with a corpse. Such artifacts as food, clothing, money, and weapons are intended to provide the soul of the deceased with whatever will be needed during an afterlife. In the United States, the provision of comfortable coffins for well-dressed corpses and the regular placement of flowers near a grave are forms of sacrifice offered in a similar spirit.

Are there limits to the free exercise of religious rituals? Today, tens of thousands of members of the Native American church believe that ingestion of the powerful drug peyote is a sacrament and that those who partake of peyote will enter into direct contact with God. In 1990, the Supreme Court ruled that prosecuting people who use illegal drugs as part of religious rituals is *not* a violation of the First Amendment guarantee of religious freedom. The case arose because two members of the Native American church were dismissed from their jobs for religious use of peyote and then were refused unemployment benefits by the state of Oregon's employment division. In 1991, however, Oregon enacted a new law permitting the sacramental use of peyote by Native Americans (*New York Times*, 1991c:A14).

In another ruling on the exercise of religious rituals, in 1993 the Supreme Court unanimously overturned a local ordinance in Florida which banned ritual animal sacrifice. The high court held that this law violated the free-exercise rights of adherents of the Santeria religion, in which the sacrifice of animals (including goats, chickens, and other birds) plays a central role (Greenhouse, 1993a).

Experience

In sociological study of religion, the term *religious experience* refers to the feeling or perception of being in direct contact with the ultimate reality, such as a divine being, or of being overcome with religious emotion. A religious experience may be rather slight, such as the feeling of exaltation a person receives from hearing a choir sing Handel's "Hallelujah Chorus." But many religious experiences are more profound, among them the act of being "born again"—that is, having a turning point in life during which one makes a personal commitment to Jesus.

According to a 1993 national survey, more than 40 percent of people in the United States claimed that they had had a born-again Christian experience at some time in their lives—a figure which translates into nearly 70 million adults. An earlier survey found that Baptists (61 percent) were the

most likely to report such experiences; by contrast, only 18 percent of Catholics and 11 percent of Episcopalians stated that they had been born again. The collective nature of religion, as emphasized by Durkheim, is evident in these statistics. The beliefs and rituals of a particular faith can create an atmosphere either friendly or hostile to this type of religious experience. Thus, a Baptist would be encouraged to come forward and share such experiences with others, whereas an Episcopalian would receive much less support if he or she claimed to have been born again (Gallup Opinion Index, 1978; Princeton Religion Research Center, 1993b).

ORGANIZATION OF RELIGIOUS BEHAVIOR

The collective nature of religion has led to many forms of religious association. In modern societies, religion has become increasingly formalized. Specific structures such as churches and synagogues are constructed for religious worship; individuals are trained for occupational roles within various fields. These developments make it possible to distinguish between the sacred and secular parts of one's life—a distinction that could not be made in earlier societies in which religion was largely a family activity carried out in the home.

Sociologists find it useful to distinguish between four basic forms of organization: the ecclesia, the denomination, the sect, and the cult. As is the case with other typologies used by social scientists, this system of classification can help us to appreciate the variety of organizational forms found among religious faiths. Distinctions are made between these types of organizations on the basis of such factors as size, power, degree of commitment expected from members, and historical ties to other faiths.

Ecclesiae

An *ecclesia* (plural, *ecclesiae*) is a religious organization that claims to include most of or all the members of a society and is recognized as the national or official religion. Since virtually everyone belongs to the faith, membership is by birth rather than conscious decision. Examples of ecclesiae include the Lutheran church in Sweden, the Catholic church

In Saudi Arabia's Islamic regime, leaders of the ecclesia hold vast power over actions of the state.

beliefs, a defined system of authority, and a generally respected position in society (Doress and Porter, 1977). Denominations count among their members large segments of a population. Generally, children accept the denomination of their parents and give little thought to membership in other faiths. Denominations also resemble ecclesiae in that few demands are made on members. However, there is a critical difference between these two forms of religious organization. Although the denomination is considered respectable and is not viewed as a challenge to the secular government, it lacks the official recognition and power held by an ecclesia.

No nation of the world has more denominations than the United States. In good measure, this is a result of our nation's immigrant heritage. Many settlers in the "new world" brought with them the religious commitments native to their homelands. As a result, some denominations of Christianity, such as those of the Roman Catholics, Episcopalians, and Lutherans, were the outgrowth of ecclesiae established in Europe. In addition, new Christian denominations emerged in the United States, including the Mormons and Christian Scientists.

in Spain, Islam in Saudi Arabia, and Buddhism in Thailand. However, there can be significant differences even within the category of *ecclesia*. In Saudi Arabia's Islamic regime, leaders of the ecclesia hold vast power over actions of the state. By contrast, the Lutheran church in contemporary Sweden has no such power over the Riksdag (parliament) or the prime minister.

Generally, ecclesiae are conservative in that they do not challenge the leaders or policies of a secular government. In a society with an ecclesia, the political and religious institutions often act in harmony and mutually reinforce each other's power over their relative spheres of influence. Within the modern world, ecclesiae tend to be declining in power.

Denominations

A *denomination* is a large, organized religion that is not officially linked with the state or government. Like an ecclesia, it tends to have an explicit set of

Sects

In contrast to the denomination is the sect, which Max Weber (1958b:114, original edition 1916) termed a "believer's church," because affiliation is based on conscious acceptance of a specific religious dogma. A *sect* can be defined as a relatively small religious group that has broken away from some other religious organization to renew what it views as the original vision of the faith. Many sects, such as that led by Martin Luther during the Reformation, claim to be the "true church" by seeking to cleanse the established faith of what they regard as innovative beliefs and rituals (Stark and Bainbridge, 1985).

Sects are in a high state of tension with society and do not seek to become established national religions. Unlike ecclesiae, sects require intensive commitments and demonstrations of belief by members. Partly owing to their "outsider" status in society, sects frequently exhibit a higher degree of religious fervor and loyalty than more established religious groups do. Recruitment is focused mainly on adults; as a result, acceptance comes through conversion.

Sects are often short-lived; however, if able to survive, they may become less antagonistic to society and begin to resemble denominations. In a few instances, sects have been able to endure over several generations while remaining fairly separate from society. Sociologist J. Milton Yinger (1970:226–273) uses the term **established sect** to describe a religious group that is the outgrowth of a sect, yet remains isolated from society. The Hutterites, Jehovah's Witnesses, Seventh-Day Adventists, and Amish are contemporary examples of established sects in the United States.

Cults

International attention focused on religious cults in 1993 as a result of the violence at the Branch Davidians' compound near Waco, Texas. The Davidians began as a sect of the Seventh-Day Adventists church in 1934 and based their beliefs largely on the biblical book of Revelation and its doomsday prophecies. In 1984, the Davidians' sect split, with one group emerging as a cult under the leadership of David Koresh. After a 51-day standoff against federal authorities in early 1993, Koresh and 85 of

his followers died when the Federal Bureau of Investigation (FBI) attempted to seize control of the Davidians' compound (Barkun, 1993).

As psychotherapist Irvin Doress and sociologist Jack Nusan Porter (1977:3–4) have suggested, the word *cult* has taken on a negative meaning in the United States and is used more as a means of discrediting religious minorities than as a way of categorizing them. They note that some groups, such as the Hare Krishnas, are labeled as "cults" because they seem to come from foreign (often nonwestern) lands and have customs perceived as "strange." This reflects people's ethnocentric evaluations of that which differs from the commonplace. James Richardson, a sociologist of religion, does not like the term *cult* and prefers to call such groups *new*, *minority*, or *exotic* religions. "We forget that 99 percent of minority religious groups are benign and peaceful and just want to be left alone," says Richardson (Goldman, 1993:11).

It is difficult to distinguish sects from cults. A **cult** is a generally small, secretive religious group that represents either a new religion or a major innovation of an existing faith. Cults are similar to sects in that they tend to be small and are often viewed as less respectable than more established faiths. However, unlike sects, cults normally do not re-

Alan Carey/Image Works

The Hutterites are a contemporary example of an established sect found in the United States. Shown is a Hutterite community in Rifton, New York.

TABLE 14-1	Characteristics of Ecclesiae, Denominations, Sects, and Cults			
CHARACTERISTIC	ECCLESIA	DENOMINATION	SECT	CULT
Size	Very large	Large	Small	Small
Wealth	Extensive	Extensive	Limited	Variable
Religious services	Formal, little participation	Formal, little participation	Informal, emotional	Variable
Doctrines	Specific, but interpretation may be tolerated	Specific, but interpretation may be tolerated	Specific, purity of doctrine emphasized	Innovative, pathbreaking
Clergy	Well-trained, full-time	Well-trained, full-time	Trained to some degree	Unspecialized
Membership	By virtue of being a member of society	By acceptance of doctrine	By acceptance of doctrine	By an emotional commitment
Relationship to the state	Recognized, closely aligned	Tolerated	Not encouraged	Ignored

SOURCE: Adapted from G. Vernon, 1962; see also Chalfant et al., 1987:91–92.

sult from schisms or breaks with established ecclesiae or denominations. Some cults, such as contemporary cults focused on UFO sightings or expectations of colonizing outer space, may be totally unrelated to the existing faiths in a culture. Even when a cult does accept certain fundamental tenets of a dominant faith—such as belief in the divinity of Jesus or Muhammad—it will offer new revelations or new insights to justify its claim to be a more advanced religion (Doress and Porter, 1977:3; 1981; Stark and Bainbridge, 1979, 1985:27).

As is true of sects, cults may undergo transformation over time into other types of religious organizations. An example is the Christian Science church, which began as a cult under the leadership of Mary Baker Eddy. Today, this church exhibits the characteristics of a denomination (Johnstone, 1988:88).

Comparing Forms of Religious Organization

Clearly, it is no simple matter to determine whether a particular religious group falls into the sociological category of ecclesia, denomination, sect, or cult. Yet, as we have seen, these ideal types of religious organizations have somewhat different relationships to society. Ecclesiae are recognized as national churches; denominations, although not

Ecclesiae, denominations, and sects are best viewed as ideal types along a continuum; cults are outside the continuum because they generally define themselves as a new view of life rather than in terms of existing religious faiths.

officially approved, are generally respected. By contrast, sects as well as cults are much more likely to be at odds with the larger culture.

Ecclesiae, denominations, and sects are best viewed as ideal types along a continuum rather than as mutually exclusive categories. Some of the primary characteristics of these ideal types are summarized in Table 14-1. Since the United States has no ecclesia, sociologists studying this nation's religions have naturally focused on the denomination and the sect. These religious forms have been pictured on either end of a continuum, with denominations accommodating to the secular world and sects making a protest against established religions. Cults have also been included in Table 14-1 but are outside the continuum because they generally define themselves as a new view of life rather than in terms of existing religious faiths (Chalfant et al., 1987:89–99).

Advances in electronic communications have led to still another form of religious organization: the electronic church. Facilitated by cable television and satellite transmissions, *televangelists* (as they are called) direct their messages to more people—especially in the United States—than are served by all but the largest denominations. While some televangelists are affiliated with religious denominations, most give viewers the impression that they are disassociated from established faiths.

The programming of the electronic church is not solely religious. There is particular focus on issues concerning marriage and the family, death and dying, and education; yet more overtly political topics such as foreign and military policy are also discussed (Abelman and Nevendorf, 1985). Although many television ministries in the United States avoid political positions, others have been quite outspoken. Most noteworthy in this regard is pentecostal minister Pat Robertson, a strong conservative. Robertson founded the Christian Broadcasting Network in 1961, served for many years as host of CBN's syndicated religious talk show *The 700 Club*, and took leave of his television posts in 1986 to seek the 1988 Republican nomination for president. He has continued his political activism through his leadership of the Christian Coalition, which will be discussed later in the chapter.

RELIGION IN THE UNITED STATES

As mentioned earlier, the United States includes a wide variety of religious denominations. Figure 14-2 (on page 408) illustrates the fact that particular Christian faiths dominate certain areas of the country in terms of membership. Of course, for most nations of the world, such a "religious map" would hardly be useful, since one faith accounts for virtually all the religious followers. The diversity of beliefs, rituals, and experiences that characterize religious life in the United States reflects both the nation's immigrant heritage and the First Amendment prohibition against establishment of an ecclesia.

By far the largest single denomination in the United States is Roman Catholicism, yet at least 23 other religious faiths have 1 million or more members. These particular statistics are conservative, since other faiths are growing in size. For example, there are close to 5 million Muslims in the United States. Protestants collectively accounted for about 56 percent of the nation's adult population in 1991, compared with 25 percent for Catholics and almost 3 percent for Jews (Bezilla, 1993:37). The United States also includes a smaller number of people who adhere to such eastern faiths as Hinduism, Confucianism, Buddhism, and Taoism. As Figure 14-3 (on page 409) reveals, certain faiths, such as Episcopalianism and Judaism, have a higher proportion of affluent members. Adherents of other faiths, including Baptists and Methodists, are comparatively less affluent.

Beliefs and Practices

At present, religion continues to be an important influence on the United States. According to surveys, only 4 percent of the adults in this country can be described as "totally nonreligious." (These people have no religious preference, are not members of a congregation, and state that religion is either "not very important" or "not at all important" in their lives.) By contrast, more than 81 percent of adults surveyed in the United States consider themselves "religious persons"—compared with less than 60 percent in Great Britain and Germany. Among 20 nations surveyed during the period 1989 to 1991, only Spain had a higher proportion of respondents who considered themselves religious (83 percent) than did the United States (Bezilla, 1993:70).

Studies suggest, however, that religion is not uniformly on the upswing in the United States. There is a great deal of switching of denominations and, as in the past, considerable interest in new ways of expressing spirituality. It would be incorrect to conclude either that religion is slowly being abandoned or that people in the United States are turning to religion with the zeal of new converts. The future may well bring periods of religious revivalism but also times of decline in religious fervor (Chalfant et al., 1987:312–315; Princeton Religion Research Center, 1993a).

One of the most common religious rituals in the Protestant and Catholic churches is church attendance. The Gallup poll has provided the only regular measurement of such attendance. In 1992, it reported that during an average week, 42 percent of adults in the United States attended church (Princeton Religion Research Center, 1993a).

FIGURE 14-2 *Predominant Christian Faiths by Counties of the United States, 1990*

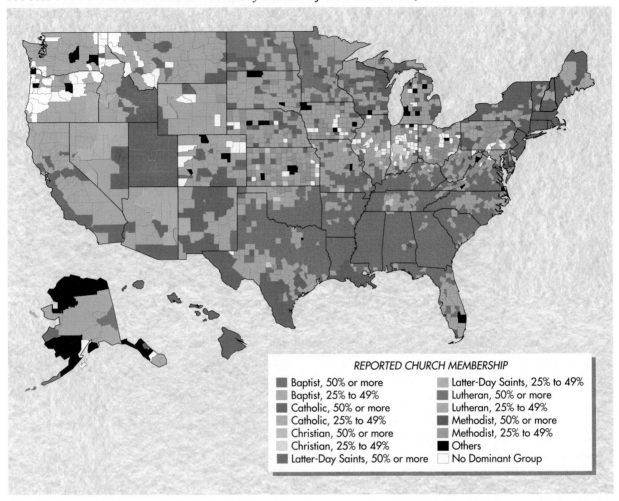

SOURCE: M. Bradley et al., 1992.

The diversity of Christian religious life in the United States is apparent here. Many different Christian faiths account for 25 percent or more of the church members in a county. Among non-Christian faiths, only Judaism may figure so significantly—in New York County (Manhattan) of New York City and in Palm County, Florida (north of Miami).

A significant change in religious practices in the United States has been the increase in the number of women in the clergy (see Box 14-2 on page 410). Although the nation's religions pay tribute to saintly and wise women, women have been traditionally represented in religious beliefs and rituals as a weaker sex, less capable than men of handling religious authority. In recent decades, however, there has been increasing resistance to beliefs and practices which relegate women to second-class status within organized religion (Carmody, 1989).

FIGURE 14-3 Income and Denominations

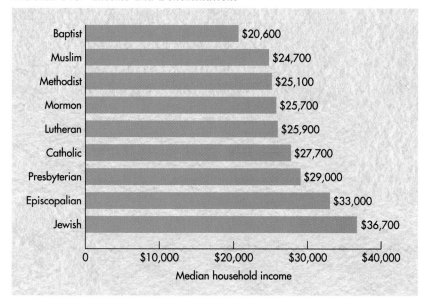

Baptist — $20,600
Muslim — $24,700
Methodist — $25,100
Mormon — $25,700
Lutheran — $25,900
Catholic — $27,700
Presbyterian — $29,000
Episcopalian — $33,000
Jewish — $36,700

Median household income

This figure—based on a survey of 114,000 adults in 1989–1990—reveals the different income groups that denominations attract. All denominations have both affluent and poor members, yet some have a higher proportion of affluent members (as measured by income) while others are less affluent.

SOURCE: Kosmin and Lachman, 1993:260.

Resurgent Fundamentalism

In the late 1960s, something rather remarkable took place in the world of organized religion. For the first time in the nation's history, most of the major Christian denominations began to shrink in size. The Presbyterians, Lutherans, Methodists, and Episcopalians all decreased in membership, while Roman Catholics remained stable primarily because of an influx of practicing Catholics from Latin America. However, not all religious faiths were in decline. During this same period, groups such as the Southern Baptist Convention, the Assemblies of God, the Mormons, the Jehovah's Witnesses, and the Seventh-Day Adventists began overflowing with vitality. These fundamentalist groups share a conservative, "back-to-basics" approach to religion and stress strict interpretation of the Bible. The term *fundamentalism* refers to adherence to earlier-accepted religious doctrines and often is accompanied by a literal application of historical beliefs and scriptures to today's world.

This religious revival, called *resurgent fundamentalism* by theologian Martin Marty (1980), has been accompanied by noticeable growth among evangelical and pentacostal faiths. *Evangelical faiths* are Christian faiths which place great emphasis on a personal relationship between the individual and God and believe that each adherent must spread the faith and bear personal witness by openly declaring the religion to nonbelievers. *Pentecostal faiths* hold many of the same values but also believe in the infusion of the Holy Spirit into services and in such religious experiences as faith healing and "speaking in tongues." Fundamentalists are not necessarily evangelical or pentecostal; they may seek to restore doctrine and literal interpretations within the structure of established faiths such as Catholicism or Islam.

Sociologists Dean Hoge and David A. Roozen (1979) offered statistical support for Marty's conceptualization of resurgent fundamentalism. They found that in recent decades, denominations experiencing the most growth tended to emphasize local evangelism, maintain a lifestyle and morality apart from mainstream culture, and deemphasize social action and religious universalism.

BOX 14-2 • EVERYDAY BEHAVIOR

WOMEN IN THE CLERGY

Throughout history and in many diverse cultures, the highest positions of spiritual leadership within organized religion have been reserved for men. Even today, the largest denomination in the United States, Roman Catholicism, does not permit women to be priests. A 1993 Gallup survey found that 63 percent of Roman Catholics in this country favor the ordination of women, compared with only 29 percent in 1974, but the church has continued to maintain its long-standing teaching that priests should be male.

The largest Protestant denomination, the Southern Baptist Convention, has voted against ordaining women (even though some of its autonomous churches have women ministers). Other religious faiths that do not allow women clergy include the Lutheran Church–Missouri Synod, the Greek Orthodox Archdiocese of North and South America, the Orthodox Church in America, the Church of God in Christ, the Church of Jesus Christ of Latter-Day Saints, and Orthodox Judaism.

Despite these restrictions, there has been a notable rise in female clergy in the last 20 years. Female enrollment in seminaries in the United States has steadily increased since the early 1970s. For example, in 1973 women accounted for 10 percent of Protestant theological students; by 1992 the proportion of women had risen to almost 33 percent. Of 190 students in Reform Judaism's rabbinical school in the 1992–1993 school year, 43 percent were female. Of 32 students who entered Conservative Judaism's rabbinical school in late 1991, 15 were women. Nevertheless, as of 1992, 92 percent of all clergy in the United States were male.

Clearly, many branches of Protestantism and Judaism have been convinced that women have the right to be ordained as spiritual leaders. Yet a lingering question remains: once ordained, will these female ministers and rabbis be *accepted* by congregations? Will they advance in their calling as easily as male counterparts, or will they face blatant or subtle discrimination in their efforts to secure desirable posts within their faiths?

It is too early to offer any definitive answers to these questions, but thus far women clergy continue to face lingering sexism after ordination. According to a 1986 random sampling of 800 lay and ordained leaders of the United Church of Christ, women find it difficult to secure jobs in larger, more prestigious congregations. Women ministers in other Protestant faiths have encountered similar problems. Although they may be accepted as junior clergy or as co-pastors, women may fail to receive senior clergy appointments. In both Reform and Conservative Judaism, women rabbis are rarely hired by the largest and best-known congregations. Consequently, women clergy in many denominations appear restricted to the low end of clerical pay scales and hierarchies.

Women clergy are well-aware that their struggle for equality is far from over. The Reverend Joan Forsberg, an administrator at the Yale Divinity School, tells women graduates that they must view their efforts as part of a larger, long-term process of change. "Even if you don't see change overnight," she notes, "you must remind yourself that you *are* making a difference for future generations."

SOURCES: Brooks, 1987:15; Bureau of the Census, 1993a:405; Cohen, 1991; Ostling, 1992; Princeton Religion Research Center, 1993c.

Martin Marty points out that this fundamentalist revival has surprised many observers of religious life in the United States. It had been widely assumed that, in the face of increasing secularization, the only religions likely to survive would be those which were least demanding and most tolerant of differences in religious interpretation. Instead, people seem anxious to return to traditional sources of collective religious feeling that Durkheim viewed as fundamental to religion's role in society.

What has led to this dramatic change in religious life? Sociologist Wade Clark Roof (1976, 1978), in a North Carolina survey, found that religious commitment was strongly associated with local community attachment. Since the evangelical and pentecostal churches are more likely to support local values—as opposed to a world view tolerant of non-traditional lifestyles—it is not surprising that such faiths have grown in popularity. In addition, the intense commitment and proselytizing spirit of members of fundamentalist churches serve as key factors in their success. Dean Kelley (1979), an executive with the National Council of Churches and an authority on religious behavior, points out that "strict" churches which expect members to practice what they preach have proved to be more effective recruiters than more liberal churches have (see also J. Hunter, 1985).

The resurgence of Christian fundamentalism has led to intense debate regarding an otherwise secular area of life in the United States—the school system. Beginning in the 1980s, the fundamentalist movement has pursued three main goals regarding public schools: pressuring Congress and the courts to permit school prayer, revising school curricula to give the biblical explanation of creation equal weight with scientific theories of evolution, and generally increasing fundamentalist content in school textbooks while blocking the study of material viewed as reflecting an antireligious point of view (Stevens, 1987b:6).

As one part of its effort to influence the nation's school systems, Christian fundamentalists have begun running candidates in school board elections who are sympathetic to conservative Christian values. Especially influential in this strategy has been the Christian Coalition, an organization headed by the Reverend Pat Robertson. In 1990, thanks to a "stealth campaign" in which office seekers allied with the Christian Coalition avoided debates and forums and concealed their affiliations, 60 of the Coalition's 90 candidates won election to school boards in San Diego, California. According to estimates, some 3000 conservative Christians have been elected to school boards across the United States (L. Anderson, 1993; Porteous, 1993:21). We will discuss the controversy over religion in the schools in more detail in the social policy section at the end of the chapter.

The United States is not the only country in which fundamentalism has become more popular in recent decades. In a troubled secular and technological age, many people around the world are turning to well-ordered, even authoritarian, explanations of religious matters. Protestant fundamen-talism has become a significant force in Northern Ireland, a nation torn by religious strife between Protestants and Catholics. Fundamentalist Ashkenazic Jews have emerged as an increasingly important political bloc within the state of Israel; in Jerusalem, they have clashed with secular Jews over public showings of movies during the Sabbath hours. In India, Hindu fundamentalists have become a strong political force and have expressed growing hostility toward other religions. In Iran and other Islamic nations, there has been a dramatic return to literal interpretation of the sacred book, the Qur'an. Egypt's Coptic Christians, the largest religious minority in the middle east, have become a target of attacks by roving bands of Islamic fundamentalists (Gargan, 1992b; Ibrahim, 1993).

This renewed interest in fundamentalist faiths reflects the integrative function of religion—as individuals seek to affirm a religious identity in a manner they find difficult within established denominations. While the United States remains largely secular, members of religious institutions are choosing faiths that place greater emphasis on strict religious teachings and public declaration of religious experience.

Jews in the United States

Outside the Christian faith, the largest single religious group in the United States is Jews. As noted earlier, Jews constitute almost 3 percent of the nation's population. Interestingly, Jews in the United States can be viewed both as an ethnic minority (see Chapter 10) and as a religious denomination. Many people in the United States consider themselves to be culturally Jewish—and are seen by others as Jewish—even though they do not participate in Jewish religious life. Available data suggest that about 60 to 70 percent of Jewish Americans are affiliated with a temple or synagogue, but only 20 to 30 percent attend services more frequently than once a month (Kleinman, 1983).

The diversity of religious faiths in the United States is manifested not only in the variety of denominations, but also in the diversity within the same faith. For example, Judaism can be divided into three major branches or denominations: Orthodox, Conservative, and Reform. No precise data exist on the number of Jews in each category. How-

Judaism is one of many religions that are reaching out to people with disabilities. Rabbi Douglas Goldhammer (right) communicates in sign language to a group of senior citizens at Congregation Bene Shalom in Skokie, Illinois. This synagogue for the deaf serves more than 300 hearing-impaired Jews.

ever, through data obtained in the 1990 National Jewish Population Survey, it appears that Reform Jews constitute 42 to 49 percent of the Jewish community, Conservative Jews 31 to 38 percent, Orthodox Jews 6 to 7 percent, and other Jews 13 to 14 percent. These ranges depend on whether the estimates include only those people who were born Jewish or also include those who have converted to Judaism (Kosmin et al., 1991).

The differences in religious beliefs and practices between Orthodox, Conservative, and Reform Jews are based on their relationships to traditional religious codes and rituals. All three faiths embrace a philosophy founded on the Torah, the first five books of the Old Testament. Orthodox Jews are the most strict in following religious law. For example, they observe *kashrut,* a detailed set of religious restrictions governing food preparation and consumption. By contrast, Reform Jews have altered many traditional religious rituals, conduct services largely in English (rather than Hebrew), and have ordained a growing number of women as rabbis. Such practices are unacceptable and disturbing to many Orthodox Jews. Conservative Judaism can be seen as a kind of middle ground between the traditionalism of the Orthodox and the more "modernized" practices of Reform Judaism.

As is true of Protestant denominations, there are distinct social class differences between Jewish faiths. Reform Jews have the highest proportion of wealthy and well-educated adherents, whereas Orthodox Jews have the lowest proportion. Once again, Conservative Jews fall in between the other major Jewish denominations in terms of social class. In some cases, poor Jews from immigrant backgrounds strictly follow traditional Jewish law, but their grandchildren move into the middle class and turn to Reform Judaism. This reflects, at least in part, the process of assimilation to the norms of the dominant culture (Goldscheider, 1986; Lazerwitz and Harrison, 1979; Liebman, 1973:84).

Sects and Cults in the United States

Since the arrival of the Puritans in colonial Massachusetts, the United States has been a fertile ground for new faiths. In fact, religious dissent, like political dissent, has been viewed as a basic element in the nation's ideal of freedom. However, people's feelings concerning religious sects and cults have been badly shaken by reports of violence, questionable business practices, and undue pressures to hold on to their followers. Indeed, when a 1989 survey asked people in the United States what groups they did not want as neighbors, members of religious sects and cults scored highest—well ahead of racial and ethnic minorities. Fully 62 percent of respondents did not want sect and cult members as neighbors, as compared with only 5 percent for Jews, 5 percent for Protestants, and 3 percent for Roman Catholics (Princeton Religion Research Center, 1989).

It has been estimated that as many as 2 to 3 million people in the United States—primarily between the ages of 18 and 25—belong to religious sects and cults. One study of cults in the United States counted about 600 such groups in 1983. Older cults are generally based on more established forms of Christianity; more recent sects and cults reflect the influence of Hinduism and Buddhism in the United States. The majority of the newer cults are less than 20 years old, and, lacking the dogma, ritual, and validation that come from association with more established religions, many may therefore depend for survival on the emotional appeal of a charismatic leader (Lindsey, 1987).

Why do young people join religious cults? Irwin Doress and Jack Nusan Porter (1977) note several reasons that lead people to become members of such religious organizations. Many have come from families beset by problems and conflicts and have had difficulties coping with a world filled with violence, drugs, and sexual permissiveness. For these young people, a cult may offer a new, seemingly secure and appreciative "family" filled with love, caring, and acceptance. The puritanical aspects of cults—the rigid discipline, enforced celibacy, and banning of drugs and alcohol—may represent a welcome change from the responsibilities of adult life in a rapidly changing society.

In addition, cults appeal to the political idealism and spiritual longings of recruits and offer an opportunity to commit their entire lives to the search for a better world. Even the names of cults—the Children of God, the Family, and so forth—may seem attractive to troubled people who feel a deep need to belong to *something* and feel connected to *someone*. Consequently, cults provide the feeling of identity and sense of community that some people find difficult to achieve within more traditional religious groups.

Perhaps no contemporary sect or cult has aroused so much controversy in the United States as has the Unification church (refer back to Box 2-2 on page 47). The Unification church was founded in South Korea in the mid-1950s by the Reverend Sun Myung Moon, an ex-Presbyterian evangelist born in Korea in 1920. Moon's theology is a distinctive blend of Buddhism, Taoism, and his own interpretations of the Old and New Testaments. For example, the church teaches that Jesus failed to complete his mission of salvation; people need to be restored to God's divine grace through the advent of a new messiah (Moon himself). Followers call him "Father" or acknowledge him with such grand terms as "Lord of the Second Advent" and "Master of Mankind" (Coughlin, 1983).

The Unification church has come under strong attack for its deceptive methods of luring young people to weekend retreats and for its alleged brainwashing of them once they arrive. In 1982, Moon was convicted of filing false income tax returns and was sentenced to an 18-month prison term. Upon leaving prison in 1985, however, Moon found his religious and financial empire still intact. Individuals and organizations associated with Moon currently control a global web of businesses, including a major daily newspaper in the United States, the *Washington Times* (Lamm, 1983; Ridgeway, 1988; Rothmyer, 1984).

- Is promoting religious observance a legitimate function of the social institution of education?
- How might organized school prayer be viewed from a conflict perspective?
- Why are advocates of a liberal education frightened by the effort to promote creationism in public schools?

Although most people in the United States support the general principle of separation of church and state as enunciated by Thomas Jefferson, legislative actions and judicial decisions concerning religion in the schools continue to provoke intense controversy. The Supreme Court has consistently interpreted the Constitution's First Amendment to mean that government should attempt to maximize religious freedom by maintaining a policy of neutrality. Thus government may not assist religion by financing a new church building, but it cannot obstruct religion by denying a church or synagogue adequate police and fire protection. In this section, we will focus on two issues involving religion in the schools that continue to provoke passionate debate: school prayer and creationism.

Should organized prayer be allowed in the public schools of the United States? In the key case of *Engel v. Vitale,* the Supreme Court ruled in 1962 that the use of nondenominational prayer in New York schools was "wholly inconsistent" with the First Amendment's prohibition against government establishment of religion. In finding that such organized school prayer violated the Constitution—even when no student was required to participate—the Court argued, in effect, that promoting religious observance was not a legitimate function of government or education.

Critics of this ruling insist that school prayer is a harmless ritual—although admittedly a religious ritual—that should be permitted to begin a school day. Prohibiting school prayer, in their view, forces too great a separation between what Émile Durkheim called the *sacred* and the *profane.* Moreover, supporters of school prayer insist that use of nonde-

nominational prayer can in no way lead to the establishment of an ecclesia in the United States. Nevertheless, subsequent Supreme Court rulings overturned state laws requiring Bible reading in public schools, requiring recitation of the Lord's Prayer, and permitting a daily one-minute period of silent meditation or prayer.

In 1992, the Supreme Court ruled, by a narrow 5–4 vote, that a rabbi's invocation and dedication at a junior high school graduation in Providence, Rhode Island, violated the constitutional separation of church and state. The rabbi had given thanks to God for the "legacy of America, where diversity is celebrated and the rights of minorities are protected." The Bush administration had encouraged the Supreme Court to permit a greater role for religion in public schools, but the majority ruling emphasized that students were coerced into joining in these prayers. While this decision continues to allow *voluntary* school prayer by students, it forbids school officials to sponsor any prayer or religious observance at school events (Aikman, 1991:62; Elsasser, 1992).

Despite such judicial pronouncements, children in many public schools in the United States are led in regular prayer recitations or Bible reading. Many communities believe that schools should transmit the dominant culture of the United States by encouraging prayer. In a 1985 survey (the most recent available), 15 percent of school administrators (including 42 percent of school administrators in the south) reported that prayers are said in at least one of their schools. Moreover, according to a 1993 survey, 69 percent of adults in the United States favor a constitutional amendment that would permit organized prayer in public schools (J. Bacon, 1987; Mauro, 1993b).

Troubled by what they see as the growing secularization of our society, Christian fundamentalists have become the leading proponents of school prayer. Along with certain lay Catholic and Orthodox Jewish groups, they have advocated a constitutional amendment permitting organized prayer in public schools and other public institutions. Supporters of school prayer charge that, in outlawing any religious expression in public schools, the Supreme Court has violated the First Amendment clause protecting the "free exercise" of religion.

Opponents of organized school prayer include the mainline Christian denominations, represented by the National Council of Churches; most Jewish organizations; and secular groups, notably the American Civil Liberties Union (ACLU). They stress that no child is currently prevented from praying in school when eating lunch in the cafeteria, awaiting an examination, or preparing for a foul shot on the basketball court. What is prohibited—properly, in the view of these critics—is prayer *organized* by public officials. Opponents of such rituals insist that organizing prayer is not a legitimate function of the social institution of education.

Critics dismiss as unrealistic the argument that school prayer can remain truly voluntary. Drawing on the interactionist perspective and small-group research, they suggest that children will face enormous social pressure to conform to the beliefs and practices of a religious majority. Opponents of school prayer add that a religious majority in a community might impose a prayer specific to its faith, at the expense of religious minorities. Viewed from a conflict perspective, organized school prayer could reinforce the religious beliefs, rituals, and interests of the powerful; violate the rights of the powerless; increase religious dissension; and threaten the cultural and religious pluralism of the United States.

A second area of continuing controversy regarding religion in the schools has been over whether the biblical account of creation should be presented in school curricula. As discussed earlier, *creationists* support a literal interpretation of the book of Genesis regarding the origin of the universe and argue that evolution should not be presented as established scientific fact. Their efforts recall the famous "monkey trial" of 1925, in which high school biology teacher John T. Scopes was convicted of violating a Tennessee law making it a crime to teach the scientific theory of evolution in public schools. However, contemporary creationists have gone beyond espousing fundamentalist religious doctrine; they attempt to reinforce their position regarding the origins of the universe with quasi-scientific data (Chalfant et al., 1987:236).

In 1968, the Supreme Court overturned an

"TODAY'S AGENDA IS A TOUGH ONE, DEALING PRIMARILY WITH RELIGION IN THE PUBLIC SCHOOLS. BUT FIRST, LET US PRAY."

Arkansas law which barred any teaching of evolution in the state's public schools. This led creationists to a new strategy: they endorsed "balanced-treatment legislation" under which school systems would be forced to give the biblical account of creation equal weight in their curricula with scientific theories of evolution. However, in 1982, a federal district court judge ruled that an Arkansas balanced-treatment law violated the First Amendment guarantee of separation of church and state. Judge William Ray Overton declared that "creation science . . . has no scientific merit or educational value." Then, in 1987, the Supreme Court, by a 7–2 vote, held that states may not require the teaching of creationism alongside evolution in public schools if the primary purpose of such legislation is to promote a religious viewpoint (Stuart, 1982; S. Taylor, 1987; see also Eve and Harrold, 1991).

The effort to promote creationist views is directly related to the rise of Christian fundamentalist belief and practice within the United States and the worldwide fundamentalist resurgence. Underlying this controversy is a more general question: "Whose ideas and values deserve a hearing in the nation's classrooms?" Critics of creationism see this campaign as one step toward sectarian religious control of public education. They worry that, at some point in the future, teachers may not be able to use books, or make statements, that conflict with fundamentalist interpretations of the Bible. For advocates of a liberal education, who are deeply committed to intellectual (and religious) diversity, this is a genuinely frightening prospect.

SUMMARY

Religion is found throughout the world because it offers answers to such ultimate questions as why we exist, why we succeed or fail, and why we die. This chapter examines the dimensions and functions of religion, types of religious organizations, and the role of religion in the United States.

1   In contemporary industrial societies, scientific and technological advances have increasingly affected all aspects of life, including the social institution of religion.

2   Émile Durkheim stressed the social aspect of religion and attempted to understand individual religious behavior within the context of the larger society.

3   Religion can provide values and ends which help a society to function as an integrated social system.

4   From a Marxist point of view, religion lessens the possibility of collective political action that can end capitalist oppression and transform society.

5   Max Weber argued that Calvinism (and, to a lesser degree, other branches of Protestant religion) produced a type of person more likely to engage in capitalistic behavior.

6   *Religious beliefs, religious rituals,* and *religious experiences* are interrelated and help to reinforce one another.

7   Sociologists have identified four ideal types of religious organizations: the *ecclesia,* the *denomination,* the *sect,* and the *cult.*

8   By far the largest single denomination in the United States is Roman Catholicism, although Protestant faiths collectively accounted for about 56 percent of the nation's adult population in 1991.

9   Despite the restrictions that exist against ordaining women in certain faiths, there has been a noticeable rise in female clergy in the United States over the last 15 years.

10   In the late 1960s, while major Christian denominations were beginning to shrink in size, a resurgence of *fundamentalism* began in the United States.

11   The issues of school prayer and *creationism* continue to provoke passionate debate regarding the proper role of religion in public schools.

CRITICAL THINKING QUESTIONS

1   Should atheists and agnostics be viewed as religious minorities in the United States? Do they have religious beliefs, rituals, or experiences? Are their rights protected —or even considered—in the many religious controversies evident across the country? How can the text material on the functions of religion be used to better understand the position of atheists and agnostics in the United States?

2   What role does religion play in the life of your college community? To what extent do students, faculty members, and administrators reveal (or promote) their religious preferences and affiliations? Is the study of religion a part of the college's curriculum? Are there religious subcultures on campus?

3   How might functionalists, conflict theorists, and interactionists view the rise of religious fundamentalism in the United States and around the world?

KEY TERMS

Cosmology   A general theory of the universe advanced by a religion. (page 402)

Creationists   People who support a literal interpretation of the book of Genesis regarding the origins of the universe and argue that evolution should not be presented as established scientific fact. (402)

Cult   A generally small, secretive religious group that represents either a new religion or a major innovation of an existing faith. (405)

Cultural universals   General practices found in every culture. (393)

Denomination   A large, organized religion not officially linked with the state or government. (404)

Ecclesia   A religious organization that claims to include most of or all the members of a society and is recognized as the national or official religion. (403)

Established sect   J. Milton Yinger's term for a religious group that is the outgrowth of a sect, yet remains isolated from society. (405)

Evangelical faiths   Christian faiths which place great

emphasis on a personal relationship between the individual and God and believe that each adherent must spread the faith and bear personal witness by openly declaring the religion to nonbelievers. (409)

Fundamentalism Adherence to earlier-accepted religious doctrines, often accompanied by a literal application of historical beliefs and scriptures to today's world. (409)

Liberation theology Use of a church, primarily Roman Catholicism, in a political effort to eliminate poverty, discrimination, and other forms of injustice evident in secular society. (399)

Pentecostal faiths Religious groups similar in many respects to evangelical faiths, which in addition believe in the infusion of the Holy Spirit into services and in religious experiences such as faith healing and "speaking in tongues." (409)

Predestination A Calvinist doctrine which holds that people either will be among the elect, who are rewarded in heaven, or will be condemned to hell and that their futures are not dependent on being righteous or sinful while on earth. (401)

Profane The ordinary and commonplace elements of life, as distinguished from the sacred. (395)

Protestant ethic Max Weber's term for the disciplined work ethic, this-worldly concerns, and rational orientation to life emphasized by John Calvin and his followers. (400)

Religion According to Émile Durkheim, a unified system of beliefs and practices relative to sacred things. (395)

Religious beliefs Statements to which members of a particular religion adhere. (401)

Religious experience The feeling or perception of being in direct contact with the ultimate reality, such as a divine being, or of being overcome with religious emotion. (403)

Religious rituals Practices required or expected of members of a faith. (402)

Religious values Shared conceptions of what is good, desirable, and proper that arise out of religious faith. (402)

Sacred Those elements beyond everyday life which inspire awe, respect, and even fear. (395)

Sanctuary movement A movement of loosely connected organizations that offers asylum, often in churches, to those who seek refugee status but are regarded by the Immigration and Naturalization Service as illegal aliens. (399)

Sect A relatively small religious group that has broken away from some other religious organization to renew what it views as the original vision of the faith. (404)

Secularization The process through which religion's influence on other social institutions diminishes. (393)

ADDITIONAL READINGS

Carmody, Denise Lardner. *Women and World Religions* (2d ed.). Englewood Cliffs, N.J.: Prentice-Hall, 1989. A feminist examination of world religions and women's religious experiences.

Davidman, Lynn. *Tradition in a Rootless World: Women Turn to Orthodox Judaism.* Berkeley: University of California Press, 1991. Using participant observation, Davidman follows the conversion of young, secular Jewish women into Orthodox Judaism.

Eve, Raymond A., and Francis B. Harrold. *The Creationist Movement in Modern America.* Boston: Twayne, 1991. The authors present a nonjudgmental analysis of the creationists' effort to control school curricula.

Greeley, Andrew M. *Religious Change in America.* Cambridge, Mass.: Harvard University Press, 1989. Examines social trends in religious doctrine, church attendance, financial contributions, and social attitudes.

Shupe, Anson, and Jeffrey K. Hadden (eds.). *The Politics of Religion and Social Change.* New York: Paragon House, 1988. This volume considers religion throughout the world and its interplay with politics, focusing on such topics as religion in South Africa, the experiences of Muslims in communist nations, the impact of Zionism on the mideast, and liberation theology.

Sigmund, Paul E. *Liberation Theology at the Crossroads: Democracy or Revolution?* New York: Oxford University Press, 1990. A careful look at liberation theology, with appendixes reprinting some of the writings of Gustavo Gutiérrez.

Smith, Christian. *The Emergence of Liberation Theology: Radical Religion and Social Movement Theory.* Chicago: University of Chicago Press, 1991. A sociologist provides a brief history and an analysis of the liberation theology movement in Latin America.

Swatos, William H., Jr. (ed.). *Gender and Religion.* New Brunswick, N.J.: Transaction, 1993. This anthology considers women's involvement in religious roles and the impact of religion on women's lives.

Journals

The sociological study of religion is reflected in the *Journal for the Scientific Study of Religion* (founded in 1961), *Religion Watch* (monthly newsletter, 1986), *Review of Religious Research* (1958), *Social Compass* (1954), and *Sociological Analysis* (1940).

15

GOVERNMENT AND THE ECONOMY

ECONOMIC SYSTEMS
Preindustrial Societies
Industrial Societies
   Capitalism
   Socialism
Postindustrial and Postmodern Societies

POLITICS AND GOVERNMENT
Power
Types of Authority
   Traditional Authority
   Legal-Rational Authority
   Charismatic Authority

**POLITICAL BEHAVIOR IN THE
UNITED STATES**
Political Socialization
Participation and Apathy
Women in Politics
Interest Groups

**MODELS OF POWER STRUCTURE
IN THE UNITED STATES**
Elite Model
   The Power Elite
   The Ruling Class
Pluralist Model
   Veto Groups
   Dahl's Study of Pluralism

ASPECTS OF THE ECONOMY
Occupations and Professions
Work and Alienation: Marx's View

**SOCIAL POLICY, GOVERNMENT, AND
THE ECONOMY: AFFIRMATIVE
ACTION**

BOXES
15-1 Speaking Out: Martin Luther King
    on War and Peace
15-2 Everyday Behavior: Farm Workers
    and the Abolition of the Short-
    Handled Hoe

> *Every course of rational political action is economically oriented.*
>
> Max Weber
> *The Theory of Social and Economic Organization, 1913–1922*

LOOKING AHEAD

- How do capitalism, socialism, and communism differ as ideal types?
- How are systems of power and authority organized?
- Can people in the United States be considered apathetic in their political behavior?
- Is the United States run by a small ruling elite?
- How does a profession differ from an occupation?
- Have affirmative action programs gone too far—or not far enough—in an effort to combat discrimination against women and minorities?

On January 20, 1993, Bill Clinton was administered the oath of office and became president of the United States. In the months after he assumed the presidency, the stock market slowly went up. As of mid-1993, many analysts forecast that the market would drop during Clinton's second year in office, but would register a slow but steady increase during 1995 and 1996. The basis for this view is that a newly elected president wishes to fulfill a social, economic, and political agenda—but also wants to be reelected. Analysis of the record of every first-term president since 1900 reveals a predictable pattern: initial economic optimism, followed by a negative reaction as the president fights for controversial aspects of his agenda, ultimately followed by two years of economic good news as the president prepares for a reelection campaign (Sivy, 1993).

It is difficult to imagine two social institutions as intertwined as government and the economy. In addition to being the largest employer in the United States, government at all levels regulates commerce and entry into many occupations. At the same time,

the economy generates the revenue to support government services, while lobbying groups representing industries and labor unions rally behind political candidates and attempt to influence public policy.

The term *economic system* refers to the social institution through which goods and services are produced, distributed, and consumed. As with social institutions such as the family, religion, and government, the economic system shapes other aspects of the social order and is, in turn, influenced by them. Throughout this textbook, we have been reminded of the economy's impact on social behavior—for example, individual and group behavior in factories and offices. We have studied the work of Karl Marx and Friedrich Engels (see Chapters 1 and 8), who emphasized that the economic system of a society can promote social inequality. And we learned (in Chapter 9) that foreign investment in developing countries can intensify inequality among residents.

The term *political system* refers to the social institution which relies on a recognized set of procedures for implementing and achieving the goals of a group. Each society must have a political system in order to maintain recognized procedures for allocating valued resources. Thus, like religion and the family, the economic and political systems are cultural universals; they are social institutions found in every society. In the United States, the political system holds ultimate responsibility for addressing the social policy issues examined in this textbook: child care, the AIDS crisis, sexual harassment, gun control, and all the rest.

Chapter 15 will present sociological analysis of the impact of government and the economy on people's lives. We will begin with macro-level analysis of the variety of economic systems used by preindustrial and industrial societies to handle tasks of production and distribution. Next we will examine the sources of power in a political system and will describe three types of authority identified by Max Weber. In studying government and politics in the United States, we will give particular attention to political socialization, citizens' participation in political life, the changing role of women in politics, and the influence of interest groups on decision making. The question "Who really rules the United States?" will be posed, and the elite and pluralist models of power will be contrasted. Then, using micro-level sociological analysis, we will consider work and the workplace. Finally, the social policy section will focus on the intense debate over affirmative action—an issue which underscores the way in which government and the economy are intertwined.

ECONOMIC SYSTEMS

Preindustrial Societies

The earliest written documents known to exist, clay tablets from about 3000 B.C., were found in 1981 in Iran, Iraq, and Syria. It is fitting commentary on the importance of the economic sector that these tablets record units of land and agricultural products such as grain. Of course, economic life has grown exceedingly complex during the intervening 5000 years. One key factor in this change has been the development of increasingly sophisticated technology for tasks of production and distribution.

The term *technology* refers to the application of knowledge to the making of tools and the utilization of natural resources. The form that a particular economic system takes is not totally defined by the available technology. Nevertheless, the level of technology will limit, for example, the degree to which a society can depend on irrigation or complex machinery.

Preindustrial societies can be categorized on the basis of their economic systems. The first type to emerge is the *hunting-and-gathering society,* in which people simply rely on whatever foods and fiber are readily available. Technology in such societies is minimal. People are constantly on the move in search of food, and there is little division of labor into specialized tasks (Lenski et al., 1991).

Bill Clinton is shown in a May 1993 "town meeting" held in the Rose Garden of the White House.

Hunting-and-gathering societies are composed of small, widely dispersed groups. Each group consists almost entirely of people related to one another. As a result, kinship ties are the source of authority and influence, and the family takes on a particularly important role. Since resources are scarce, there is relatively little inequality in terms of material goods. Social differentiation within the hunting-and-gathering society is based on such ascribed characteristics as gender, age, and family background.

Horticultural societies, in which people plant seeds and crops rather than subsist merely on available foods, emerged perhaps 9000 years ago. In contrast to the hunters and gatherers, members of horticultural societies are much less nomadic. Consequently, they place greater emphasis on the production of tools and household objects. Yet technology within horticultural societies remains rather limited. Cultivation of crops is performed with the aid of digging sticks or hoes.

Loren McIntyre/Woodfin Camp

Preindustrial economic systems still exist in the 1990s. Shown are villagers in Brazil who live near the Amazon River.

As farming in horticultural societies gradually becomes more efficient, a social surplus is created. The term *social surplus* refers to the production by a group of people of enough goods to cover their own needs, while at the same time sustaining other people who are not engaged in agricultural tasks. As a result of the emergence of a surplus, some individuals in horticultural societies begin to specialize in such tasks as governance, military defense, and leadership of religious observance. As was noted in Chapter 8, increasing division of labor can lead to a hierarchical social order and to differential rewards and power.

The last stage of preindustrial development is the *agrarian society.* As in horticultural societies, members of agrarian societies are primarily engaged in the production of food. However, because of the introduction of new technological innovations such as the plow, farmers dramatically increase their crop yield. It becomes possible to cultivate the same fields over generations, thereby allowing the emergence of still larger settlements.

The technology of the agrarian society continues to rely on the physical power of humans and animals. Nevertheless, there is more extensive division of labor than in horticultural societies. Individuals focus on specialized tasks, such as repair of fishing

nets or work as a blacksmith. As human settlements become more established and stable, political institutions become more elaborate and concepts of property rights take on growing importance. The comparative permanence and greater surpluses of agrarian society make it more feasible to create artifacts such as statues, public monuments, and art objects and to pass them on from one generation to the next.

Industrial Societies

Although the industrial revolution did not topple monarchs, it produced changes as significant as those resulting from political revolutions. The *industrial revolution,* which took place largely in England during the period 1760 to 1830, was a scientific revolution focused on the application of nonanimal sources of power to labor tasks. It involved changes in the social organization of the workplace, as people left the homestead and began working in central locations such as factories.

As the industrial revolution proceeded, societies relied on new inventions that facilitated agricultural and industrial production and on new sources of energy such as steam. Many societies underwent an irrevocable shift from an agrarian-oriented economy to an industrial base. No longer did an individual or family typically make an entire product. Instead, the division of labor became increasingly complex, especially as manufacturing of goods became more common (Lenski et al., 1991).

The process of industrialization had distinctive social consequences. Families and communities could not continue to function as self-sufficient units. Individuals, villages, and regions began to exchange goods and services and become interdependent. As people came to rely on the labor of members of other communities, the family lost its unique position as the source of power and authority. The need for specialized knowledge led to more formalized education, and education emerged as a social institution distinct from the family.

In general terms, an *industrial society* can be defined as a "society that relies chiefly on mechanization for the production of its economic goods and services" (Dushkin, 1991:283–284). There are two basic types of economic systems which distinguish contemporary industrial societies: capitalism and socialism. As described in the following sections, capitalism and socialism serve as ideal types of economic systems. No nation precisely fits either model. Instead, the economy of each industrial state represents a mixture of capitalism and socialism, although one type or the other will generally be more useful in describing a society's economic structure.

Capitalism   In the preindustrial societies described earlier, land functioned as the source of virtually all wealth. However, the industrial revolution required that certain individuals and institutions be willing to take substantial risks in order to finance new inventions, machinery, and business enterprises. Consequently, bankers, industrialists, and other holders of large sums of money replaced landowners as the most powerful economic force. These people invested their funds in the hope of realizing even greater profits and thereby became owners of property and business firms.

The transition to private ownership of business was accompanied by the emergence of the capitalist economic system. As we saw in Chapter 8, *capitalism* is an economic system in which the means of production are largely in private hands and the main incentive for economic activity is the accumulation of profits (D. Rosenberg, 1991). In practice, capitalist systems vary in the degree to which private ownership and economic activity are regulated by government.

During the period immediately following the industrial revolution, the prevailing form of capitalism was what is termed *laissez-faire* ("let them do"). Under the principle of laissez-faire, as expounded and endorsed by British economist Adam Smith (1723–1790), people could compete freely with minimal government intervention in the economy. Business retained the right to regulate itself and essentially operated without fear of government regulation (Smelser, 1963:6–7).

Two centuries later, capitalism has taken on a somewhat different form. Private ownership and maximization of profits remain the most significant characteristics of capitalist economic systems. However, in contrast to the era of laissez-faire, contemporary capitalism features extensive government regulation of economic relations. Without restrictions, business firms can mislead consumers, endanger the safety of their workers, and even defraud the companies' investors—all in the pursuit of greater profits. As a result, the government of a capitalist nation often monitors prices, sets safety standards for industries, passes legislation to protect the rights of consumers, and regulates collective bargaining between labor unions and management. Yet, under capitalism as an ideal type, government rarely takes over ownership of an entire industry.

Contemporary capitalism also differs from laissez-faire in another important respect: the tolerance of monopolistic practices. A *monopoly* exists in a market when it is controlled by a single business firm. Domination of an industry allows the firm to effectively control a commodity so that it can dictate pricing, standards of quality, and availability. Buyers have little choice but to yield to the firm's decision; there is no other place to purchase the product or service. Clearly, monopolistic practices violate the ideal of free competition cherished by Adam Smith and other supporters of laissez-faire capitalism.

As is true in the United States, the government of a capitalist nation can outlaw monopolies

Despite an official commitment to building a classless communist society, China's rulers have allowed elements of a free market economy—and even McDonald's—to do business in the nation's cities.

through antitrust legislation. Such laws prevent any business from taking over so much of the competition in an industry that it gains control of the market. The federal government allows monopolies to exist only in certain exceptional cases, such as the utility and transportation industries. Even then, regulatory agencies are established to scrutinize these officially approved monopolies and protect the public. Yet, as conflict theorists point out, while *pure* monopolies are not a basic element of the economy of the United States, competition is much more restricted than one might expect in what is called a *free enterprise system.* In numerous industries, a few companies largely dominate the field and exclude new enterprises from entering the marketplace.

An *oligopoly* is a market with relatively few sellers. In the United States, three cereal companies account for 80 percent of the market. Moreover, control of the domestic production of 98 percent of locomotives, 96 percent of automobiles, 88 percent of chewing gum, and 81 percent of cigarettes is held by no more than four firms in each of these respective industries. The nation's economy has remained concentrated in the hands of a small number of companies. Indeed, the principle of free competition has been seriously compromised in contemporary capitalist societies (Galbraith, 1978:189–196; Nader et al., 1976:209).

Socialism Socialist theory was refined in the writings of Karl Marx and Friedrich Engels (see Chapter 1). These European radicals were disturbed by the exploitation of the working class as it emerged during the industrial revolution. In their view, capitalism forced large numbers of people to exchange their labor for wages. As was detailed in Chapter 8, the owners of an industry profit from the labor of their workers, primarily because they pay workers less than the value of the goods produced.

As an ideal type, a socialist economic system represents an attempt to eliminate such economic exploitation. Under *socialism,* the means of production and distribution in a society are collectively rather than privately owned. The basic objective of the economic system is to meet people's needs rather than to maximize profits. Socialists reject the laissez-faire philosophy that free competition benefits the general public. Instead, they believe that basic economic decisions should be made by the central government, which acts as the representative of the people. Therefore, government ownership of all major industries—including steel production, automobile manufacturing, and agriculture—is a major feature of socialism as an ideal type.

In practice, socialist economic systems vary in the extent to which private ownership is tolerated. For example, in Great Britain, a nation with certain aspects of both a socialist and a capitalist economy, passenger airline service is concentrated in the government-owned corporation British Airways. Yet private airline companies are allowed to compete with it.

Socialist societies also differ from capitalist nations in their commitment to social service programs. For example, the United States government provides health care and health insurance for the elderly and destitute through the Medicare and Medicaid programs. As we shall see in the social policy section of Chapter 17, in 1993 the Clinton administration proposed a broad program to reform the nation's health care system. By contrast, socialist countries typically offer *government-financed* medical care for all citizens. In theory, the wealth of the people as a collectivity is used to provide health care, housing, education, and other key services for each individual and family.

In recent decades, the Soviet Union, the People's Republic of China, Vietnam, Cuba, and the nations of eastern Europe were popularly thought of as examples of communist economic systems. However, this is actually an incorrect usage of a term with sensitive political connotations. As an ideal type, **communism** refers to an economic system under which all property is communally owned and no social distinctions are made on the basis of people's ability to produce. In Marx's view, communist societies will naturally evolve out of the stage of socialism. The socialist state or government of each nation will eventually "wither away," as will all inequality and social class differentiation. Although the leaders of many twentieth-century revolutions—including the Russian Revolution of 1917 and the Chinese Revolution of 1949–1950—have proclaimed the goal of achieving a classless communist society, all nations known as *communist* in the twentieth century have remained far from this ideal.

By the early 1990s, Communist parties were no longer ruling the nations of eastern Europe. The first major challenge to Communist rule came in 1980 when Poland's Solidarity movement—led by Lech Walesa and backed by many workers—questioned the injustices of that society. While martial law initially forced Solidarity underground, it eventually negotiated the end of Communist party rule in 1989. Over the next two years, dominant communist parties were overthrown after popular up-

risings in the Soviet Union and throughout eastern Europe. The former Soviet Union, Czechoslovakia, and Yugoslavia were subdivided to more closely approximate the ethnic, linguistic, and religious differences within these areas. However, as of 1993, China, Cuba, and Vietnam remained socialist societies ruled by Communist parties (M. Kennedy, 1993).

As we have seen, capitalism and socialism serve as ideal types of economic systems. In reality, the economy of each industrial society—including the United States, Great Britain, and Japan—includes certain elements of both capitalism and socialism. Whatever the differences, whether they more closely fit the ideal type of capitalism or socialism, all industrial societies rely chiefly on mechanization in the production of goods and services.

Postindustrial and Postmodern Societies

The significant changes in the occupational structure of industrial societies as their focus shifts from manufacturing to service industries have led social scientists to call technologically advanced nations *postindustrial societies.* Sociologist Daniel Bell (1973, 1989:168) defines **postindustrial society** as a society whose economic system is engaged in the processing and control of information. The primary output of a postindustrial society is services rather than manufactured goods. Large numbers of people become involved in occupations devoted to the teaching, generation, or dissemination of ideas.

Taking a functionalist perspective, Bell views this transition from industrial to postindustrial society as a positive development. He sees a general decline in organized working-class groups and a rise in interest groups concerned with such national issues as health, education, and the environment. Bell's outlook is functionalist because he portrays postindustrial society as basically consensual. Organizations and interest groups will engage in an open and competitive process of decision making. The level of conflict between diverse groups will diminish, and there will be much greater social stability.

Conflict theorists take issue with Bell's analysis of postindustrial society. For example, Michael Harrington (1980:125–126), who alerted the nation to the problems of the poor in his book *The Other America,* was critical of the significance that Bell attached to the growing class of white-collar workers. Harrington conceded that scientists, engineers, and economists are involved in important political and economic decisions, but he disagreed with Bell's claim that they have a free hand in decision making, independent of the interests of the rich. Harrington followed in the tradition of Marx by arguing that conflict between social classes will continue in postindustrial society.

More recent analysts have gone beyond discussion of postindustrial societies to the ideal type of postmodern society. A ***postmodern society*** is a technologically sophisticated society that is preoccupied with consumer goods and media images (Fiala, 1992:1516). In such societies, goods and information are consumed on a mass scale that facilitates social tastes and requires wide spread appreciation and participation by the masses of people.

Postmodern theorists take a global perspective and give attention to the ways in which aspects of culture are shared across national boundaries (refer back to Chapter 9). For example, residents of the United States may listen to reggae music from Jamaica, wear perfume or cologne from Paris, go to museums to see African art, and eat sushi and other types of Japanese food. At the same time, people around the world enjoy Hollywood action films and television programs (Lyotard, 1993).

The emphasis of postmodern theorists is on observing and describing newly emerging cultural forms and patterns of social interaction. In the academic world, postmodernism contributes to a breakdown of boundaries between disciplines; there is encouragement for drawing on the contributions of historians, economists, psychologists, biologists, anthropologists, sociologists, and others. Within sociology, the postmodern view offers support for integrating the insights of various theoretical perspectives—functionalism, conflict theory, interactionism, and labeling theory—while incorporating feminist theories and other contemporary approaches. Indeed, feminist sociologists argue optimistically that, with its indifference to hierarchies and distinctions, postmodernism will discard traditional values of male dominance in favor of gender equality (Ritzer, 1992b:493–497; Smart, 1990; B. Turner, 1990; van Vucht Tijssen, 1990).

POLITICS AND GOVERNMENT

A cultural universal common to all economic systems is the exercise of power and authority. The struggle for power and authority inevitably involves *politics,* which political scientist Harold Lasswell (1936) defined as "who gets what, when, and how." In their study of politics and government, sociologists are concerned with social interactions among individuals and groups and their impact on the larger political and economic order.

Power

Power is at the heart of a political system. In Chapter 8, Max Weber's concept of power was examined, and ***power*** was defined as the ability to exercise one's will over others. To put it another way, if one party in a relationship can control the behavior of the other, that individual or group is exercising power. Power relations can involve large organizations, small groups, or even people in an intimate association. As we saw in Chapter 13, Blood and Wolfe (1960) devised the concept of ***marital power*** to describe the manner in which decision making is distributed within families (refer back to Box 13-1 on page 366).

There are three basic sources of power within any political system—force, influence, and authority. ***Force*** is the actual or threatened use of coercion to impose one's will on others. When leaders imprison or even execute political dissidents, they are applying force; so, too, are terrorists when they seize an embassy or assassinate a political leader. ***Influence,*** on the other hand, refers to the exercise of power through a process of persuasion. A citizen may change his or her position regarding a Supreme Court nominee because of a newspaper editorial, the expert testimony of a law school dean before the Senate Judiciary Committee, or a stirring speech at a rally by a political activist. In each case, sociologists would view such efforts to persuade people as examples of influence. The third source of power, *authority,* will be discussed in the next section of this chapter.

Types of Authority

The term ***authority*** refers to power that has been institutionalized and is recognized by the people

Shown are a Yoruba king and elders in Nigeria. The king's young attendants carry his ceremonial swords, symbols of traditional authority.

over whom it is exercised. Sociologists commonly use the term in connection with those who hold legitimate power through elected or publicly acknowledged positions. It is important to stress that a person's authority is limited by the constraints of a particular social position. Thus, a referee has the authority to decide whether a penalty should be called during a football game but has no authority over the price of tickets to the game.

Max Weber (1947, original edition 1913) developed a classification system regarding authority that has become one of the most useful and frequently cited contributions of early sociology. He identified three ideal types of authority; traditional, legal-rational, and charismatic. Weber did not insist that only one type is accepted in a given society or organization. Rather, all can be present, but their relative importance will vary. Sociologists have found Weber's typology valuable in understanding different manifestations of legitimate power within a society.

Traditional Authority In a political system based on ***traditional authority***, legitimate power is conferred by custom and accepted practice. The orders of one's superiors are felt to be legitimate because "this is how things have always been done." For example, a king or queen is accepted as ruler of a nation simply by virtue of inheriting the crown. The monarch may be loved or hated, competent or destructive; in terms of legitimacy, that does not matter. For the traditional leader, authority rests in custom, not in personal characteristics, technical competence, or even written law. Traditional authority is absolute in many instances because the ruler has the ability to determine laws and policies.

Legal-Rational Authority Power made legitimate by law is known as ***legal-rational authority***. Leaders derive their legal-rational authority from the written rules and regulations of political systems. For example, the authority of the president of the United States and the Congress is legitimized by the Constitution. Generally, in societies that are based on legal-rational authority, leaders are conceived of as having specific areas of competence and authority. They are not viewed as having divine inspiration, as are the heads of certain societies with traditional forms of authority.

Charismatic Authority Weber also observed that power can be legitimized by the charisma of an individual. The term *charismatic authority* refers to power made legitimate by a leader's exceptional personal or emotional appeal to his or her followers. Charisma lets a person lead or inspire without relying on set rules or traditions. Interestingly, charismatic authority is derived more from the beliefs of followers than from the actual qualities of leaders. So long as people *perceive* a leader as having qualities setting him or her apart from ordinary citizens, that leader's authority will remain secure and often unquestioned.

Unlike traditional rulers, charismatic leaders often become well known by breaking with established institutions and advocating dramatic changes in the social structure and the economic system. Their strong hold over their followers makes it easier to build protest movements which challenge the dominant norms and values of a society. Thus, charismatic leaders such as Jesus, Joan of Arc, Mahatma Gandhi, Malcolm X, and Martin Luther King (see Box 15-1) all used their power to press for changes in accepted social behavior. But so did Adolf Hitler, whose charismatic appeal turned people toward violent and destructive ends.

Observing from an interactionist perspective, sociologist Carl Couch (1990) points out that the growth of the electronic media has facilitated the development of charismatic authority. During the 1930s, the heads of state of the United States, Great Britain, and Germany all used radio to issue direct appeals to citizens. In recent decades, television has allowed leaders to "visit" people's homes and communicate with them. In 1950, for example, President Harry Truman announced the outbreak of the Korean war on television. By 1990, Iraq's president, Saddam Hussein, was posing with foreign "guests" (actually, hostages) to convey a particular message to an international audience (see also Wasielewski, 1985).

As was noted earlier, Weber used traditional, legal-rational, and charismatic authority as ideal types. In reality, particular leaders and political systems com-bine elements of two or more of these forms. Presidents Franklin D. Roosevelt, John F. Kennedy, and Ronald Reagan wielded power largely through the legal-rational basis of their authority. At the same time, they were unusually charismatic leaders who commanded the personal loyalty of large numbers of citizens.

POLITICAL BEHAVIOR IN THE UNITED STATES

As citizens of the United States, we take for granted many aspects of our political system. We are accustomed to living in a nation with a Bill of Rights, two major political parties, voting by secret ballot, an elected president, state and local governments distinct from the national government, and so forth. Yet, of course, each society has its own ways of governing itself and making decisions. Just as we expect Democratic and Republican candidates to compete for public offices, residents of the People's Republic of China and Cuba are accustomed to the domination of the Communist party. In this section, we will examine a number of important aspects of political behavior within the United States.

Political Socialization

In Chapter 5, five functional prerequisites that a society must fulfill in order to survive were identified. Among these was the need to teach recruits to accept the values and customs of the group. In a political sense, this function is crucial; each succeeding generation must be encouraged to accept a society's basic political values and its particular methods of decision making.

Political socialization is the process by which individuals acquire political attitudes and develop patterns of political behavior. This involves not only learning the prevailing beliefs of a society but also coming to accept the surrounding political system despite its limitations and problems (Marger, 1981:321–323). In the United States, people are socialized to view representative democracy as the best form of government and to cherish such values as freedom, equality, patriotism, and the right of dissent.

The principal institutions of political socializa-

BOX 15-1 • SPEAKING OUT

MARTIN LUTHER KING ON WAR AND PEACE

One source of charismatic appeal is the eloquence of a political or religious leader. Certainly this was true of Dr. Martin Luther King, Jr., whose famed "I have a dream" speech during the 1963 march on Washington for civil rights inspired many people of all races. King was well-aware of the ways in which political decisions on the world scene influenced domestic issues. In the following selection, excerpted from the conclusion of his last book, Where Do We Go from Here: Chaos or Community? *King (1968:181, 185–186, 191) addresses the danger of nuclear weapons and the need to cherish peace:*

Dr. Martin Luther King, Jr.

Flip Schulke/Black Star

. . . A final problem that mankind must solve in order to survive in the world house that we have inherited is finding an alternative to war and human destruction. Recent events have vividly reminded us that nations are not reducing but rather increasing their arsenals of weapons of mass destruction. The best brains in the highly developed nations of the world are devoted to military technology. The proliferation of nuclear weapons has not been halted, in spite of the limited-test-ban treaty [of 1963]. . . .

It is not enough to say, "We must not wage war." It is necessary to love peace and sacrifice for it. We must concentrate not merely on the eradication of war but on the affirmation of peace. A fascinating story about Ulysses and the Sirens is pre-

served for us in Greek literature. The Sirens had the ability to sing so sweetly that sailors could not resist steering toward their island. Many ships were lured upon the rocks, and men forgot home, duty and honor as they flung themselves into the sea to be embraced by arms that drew them down to death. Ulysses, determined not to succumb to the Sirens, first decided to tie himself tightly to the mast of his boat and his crew stuffed their ears with wax. But finally he and his crew learned a better way to save themselves: They took on board the beautiful singer Orpheus, whose melodies were sweeter than the music of the Sirens. When Orpheus sang, who would bother to listen to the Sirens?

So we must see that peace represents a sweeter music, a cosmic melody that is far superior to the discords of war. Somehow we must transform the dynamics of the world power struggle from the nuclear arms race, which no one can

win, to a creative contest to harness man's genius for the purpose of making peace and prosperity a reality for all the nations of the world. In short, we must shift the arms race into a "peace race." If we have the will and determination to mount such a peace offensive, we will unlock hitherto tightly sealed doors of hope and bring new light into the dark chambers of pessimism. . . .

We are now faced with the fact that tomorrow is today. We are confronted with the fierce urgency of *now.* In this unfolding conundrum of life and history there is such a thing as being too late. Procrastination is still the thief of time. Life often leaves us standing bare, naked and dejected with a lost opportunity. The "tide in the affairs of men" does not remain at the flood; it ebbs. We may cry out desperately for time to pause in her passage, but time is deaf to every plea and rushes on. Over the bleached bones and jumbled residues of numerous civilizations are written the pathetic words: "Too late." There is an invisible book of life that faithfully records our vigilance or our neglect. "The moving finger writes, and having writ moves on. . . ." We still have a choice today: nonviolent coexistence or violent coannihilation. This may well be mankind's last chance to choose between chaos and community.

429

In the United States, children are socialized to view representative democracy as the best form of government. One part of this socialization process is encouraging schoolchildren to vote in "mock elections."

tion are those which also socialize us to other cultural norms—including the family, schools, and the media. Many observers see the family as playing a particularly significant role in the process. "The family incubates political man," observed political scientist Robert Lane (1959:204). In fact, parents pass on their political attitudes and evaluations to their sons and daughters through discussions at the dinner table and also through the example of their political involvement or apathy. Early socialization does not always *determine* a person's political orientation; there are changes over time and between generations. Yet research on political socialization continues to show that parents' views have an important impact on their children's outlook (M. Jennings and Niemi, 1981:384).

The schools can be influential in political socialization, since they provide young people with information and analysis of the political world. Unlike the family and peer groups, schools are easily susceptible to centralized and uniform control; consequently, totalitarian societies commonly use educational institutions for purposes of indoctrination. Yet, even in democracies, where local schools are not under the pervasive control of the national government, political education will generally reflect the norms and values of the prevailing political order.

In the view of conflict theorists, students in the United States learn much more than factual information about our political and economic way of life. They are socialized to view capitalism and representative democracy as the "normal" and most desirable ways of organizing a nation. At the same time, competing values and forms of government are often presented in a most negative fashion or are ignored. From a conflict perspective this type of political education serves the interests of the powerful and ignores the significance of the social divisions found within the United States (Marger, 1981:324–325).

Like the family and schools, the mass media can have obvious effects on people's thinking and political behavior—this is one reason why the media were included among the agents of socialization discussed in Chapter 4. Beginning with the Kennedy-Nixon presidential debates of 1960, television has given increasing exposure to political candidates. During the 1992 campaign, Democratic candidate Bill Clinton appeared on MTV and the *Arsenio Hall Show,* while independent challenger Ross Perot advocated use of electronic "town meetings." Today, many speeches given by our nation's leaders are designed not for immediate listeners but for the larger television audience.

Political socialization can take different forms in different types of societies. Using observation research, sociologist Benigno Aguirre (1984) concluded that certain types of crowd behavior were encouraged by the Cuban government to reinforce its legitimacy. The Committees for the Defense of the Revolution—which functioned much like the Communist party did when it ruled the Soviet Union—mobilized Cubans for parades, celebrations, protests, and testimonials on behalf of deceased revolutionary leaders. Through these mobilizations, Cuba's rulers hoped to convey the political message that Fidel Castro's government had and deserved widespread popular support.

Participation and Apathy

In theory, a representative democracy will function most effectively and fairly if there is an informed and active electorate communicating its views to government leaders. Unfortunately, this is hardly the case in the United States. Virtually all citizens are familiar with the basics of the political process, and most tend to identify to some extent with a political party (see Table 15-1), but only a small minority (often members of the higher social classes) actually participate in political organizations on a local or national level. Studies reveal that only 8 percent of people in the United States belong to a political club or organization. Not more than one in five has *ever* contacted an official of national, state, or local government about a political issue or problem (Orum, 1989:249).

The failure of most citizens to become involved in political parties has serious implications for the functioning of our democracy. Within the political system of the United States, the political party serves as an intermediary between people and government. Through competition in regularly scheduled elections, the two-party system provides for challenges to public policies and for an orderly transfer of power. An individual dissatisfied with the state of the nation or a local community can become involved in the political party process in many ways, such as by joining a political club supporting candidates for public office, or working to change the party's position on controversial issues. If, however, people do not take interest in the decisions of major political parties, public officials in a "representative" democracy will be chosen from two unrepresentative lists of candidates.

In the 1980s, it became clear that many people in the United States were turned off by political parties, politicians, and the specter of big government. The most dramatic indication of this growing alienation comes from voting statistics. Voters of all ages and races appear to be less enthusiastic than ever about elections, even presidential contests. For example, almost 80 percent of eligible voters in the United States went to the polls in the presidential election of 1896. Yet by the 1992 election, turnout had fallen to less than 61 percent of all eligible voters. By contrast, elections in the late 1980s brought out 84 percent or more of the voting-age population in Australia, Great Britain, France, Italy, and New Zealand (Cummings and Wise, 1993:309; J. Jennings, 1993; Piven and Cloward, 1988).

Declining political participation allows institutions of government to operate with less of a sense of accountability to society. This issue is most serious for the least powerful individuals and groups within the United States. Voter turnout has been particularly low among younger adults and members of racial and ethnic minorities. In 1992, only 43 percent of eligible voters ages 18 to 24 went to the polls. According to a postelection survey, only 54 percent of Black voters and 28.9 percent of Hispanics reported that they had actually voted (see

TABLE 15-1	Political Party Preferences in the United States, 1993
PARTY IDENTIFICATION	PERCENTAGE OF POPULATION
Strong Democrat	15
Not very strong Democrat	20
Independent, close to Democrat	12
Independent	13
Independent, close to Republican	10
Not very strong Republican	19
Strong Republican	11

SOURCE: NORC, 1993:104.

According to the results of a national survey conducted in 1993, 47 percent of respondents in the United States identify to some extent with the Democratic party, while 40 percent identify with the Republican party.

TABLE 15-2	Surveys of Voter Participation in the Presidential Elections of 1972 and 1992			
	1972 (NIXON-McGOVERN)		1992 (CLINTON-BUSH-PEROT)	
GROUP	PERCENT REGISTERED	PERCENT WHO VOTED	PERCENT REGISTERED	PERCENT WHO VOTED
Total U.S. population	72.3	63.0	68.2	61.3
Whites	73.4	64.5	70.1	63.6
Blacks	65.5	52.1	63.9	54.0
Hispanics	44.4	37.4	35.0	28.9

SOURCE: J. Jennings, 1993:v, viii.

Table 15-2). Moreover, the poor—whose focus understandably is on survival—are traditionally underrepresented among voters as well. The low turnout found among these groups is explained, at least in part, by their common feeling of powerlessness. Yet such voting statistics encourage political power brokers to continue to ignore the interests of the young, the less affluent, and the nation's minorities.

Cross-national comparisons, while confirming the relatively low level of voting in the United States, also suggest that we are *more* likely than citizens of other nations to be active at the community level, to contact local officials on behalf of ourselves or others, and to have worked for a political party. Perhaps this contrast reflects how unusual it is for people to be directly involved in national political decision making in the modern world. Nevertheless, it is possible that if tens of millions of people did not stay home on Election Day—and instead became more active in the nation's political life—the outcome of the political process might be somewhat different.

Women in Politics

In 1984, women in the United States achieved an unprecedented political breakthrough when Representative Geraldine Ferraro of New York became the Democratic nominee for vice president of the United States. Never before had a woman received the nomination of a major party for such high office.

Nevertheless, women continue to be dramatically underrepresented in the halls of government. In

According to data obtained in federal postelection surveys, in which voters were questioned two weeks after the 1972 and 1992 presidential elections, there was a relatively light turnout among Black and Hispanic voters in both years. The percentage of Blacks who voted in 1992 was a bit higher than the 1972 figure, whereas there was less voting among Whites and a substantial decline among Hispanics.

1993, there were only 54 women in Congress. They accounted for 47 of the 435 members of the House of Representatives and 7 of the 100 members of the United States Senate. While the number of women in state legislatures in 1993 was more than four times larger than it was 20 years ago, only three states had women governors. As of 1993, women held no more than 18 percent of the available positions at any level of public office. Moreover, of 121 U.S. ambassadors to other countries, only 11 (9 percent) were women (Carey and Parker, 1993; Center for the American Woman and Politics, 1992a).

Sexism (see Chapter 11) has been the most serious barrier to women interested in holding office. Female candidates have had to overcome the prejudices of both men and women regarding women's fitness for leadership. Not until 1955 did a majority of people state that they would vote for a qualified woman for president. Moreover, women often encounter prejudice, discrimination, and abuse after they are elected.

Despite these problems, more women are being elected and more of them are identifying themselves as feminists. The traditional woman in politics was a widow who took office after her husband's death to continue his work and policies. However, women being elected in the 1990s are much more likely to view politics as their own career rather than as an afterthought. These trends are not restricted to the United States; Figure 15-1 (page 434) shows the representation of women in the governments of several nations around the world. In no nation do women account for 50 percent of the legislators.

A new dimension of women and politics emerged beginning in the 1980s. Surveys detected a "gender gap" in the political preferences and activities of males and females. Women were more likely to register as Democrats than as Republicans and were also more critical of the policies of the Reagan and Bush administrations. According to political analysts, the Democratic party's continued support for the right to choose a legal abortion is attracting women voters (Center for the American Woman and Politics, 1992b).

Politicians have begun to watch voting trends among women carefully, since women voters can prove decisive in close elections. In the 1990 elections for the House of Representatives, Election Day voter polls showed that women voted for Democratic candidates by a margin of 54 to 46 percent, while men split their votes evenly between Republican and Democratic candidates. Similarly, a gender gap was evident in the 1992 presidential race.

Data from exit polls revealed that Bill Clinton won 45 percent of women's votes compared with 41 percent of men's votes. George Bush received 37 percent of women's votes and 38 percent of men's; independent candidate Ross Perot garnered 17 percent of women's votes and 21 percent of men's (S. Carroll, 1993; *New York Times*, 1990).

At the same time, surveys show that women who hold public office are more feminist and more liberal than their male colleagues. While female officeholders are more likely to give priority to women's rights policies than are men, they are also more likely than men to show a distinctive concern for such areas as health care, children and the family, education, housing, and the elderly. Moreover, there are apparent gender differences among legislators even in addressing the same issue. Lynn Kathlene studied Colorado's House of Representatives in 1989, when 33 percent of its members were women. On the issue of crime, she found that both Republican and Democratic women tended to emphasize the societal link to crime and therefore to sponsor anticrime bills that included long-term preventative strategies. By contrast, male legislators from both parties generally focused on the individual's criminal conduct rather than underlying social causes of crime. Kathlene concluded that women were more likely than men to sponsor "in-

In 1993, in a historic breakthrough for women in the United States, Judge Ruth Bader Ginsburg (back row, right) joined Justice Sandra Day O'Connor (front row, left) on the Supreme Court—the first time the Court had ever had two female justices.

© National Geographic Society, Courtesy The Supreme Court Historical Society

FIGURE 15-1 Women in National Legislatures

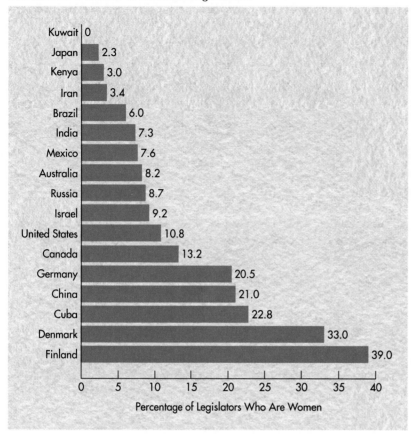

Globally, an average of only 10.1 percentage of seats in all national legislatures were occupied by women as of June 30, 1993.

NOTE: Where the national legislature is formed of two chambers, as in the United States, the percentages are based on the lower chamber or parliament such as the House of Representatives.
SOURCE: Inter-Parliamentary Union, 1993.

novative" bills targeting new areas for public legislation or offering new solutions to old problems (Center for American Woman and Politics, 1992b; Halperin, 1993).

Interest Groups

This discussion of political behavior has focused primarily on individual participation (and nonparticipation) in decision-making processes of government and on involvement in the nation's political parties. However, there are other important ways that citizens can play a role in a nation's political arena. Because of common needs or common frustrations, people may band together in social movements such as the civil rights movement of the 1960s or the anti-nuclear power movement of the 1980s (Sherman and Kolker, 1987:17). We will consider social movements in more detail in Chapter 20. People can also influence the political process through membership in interest groups (some of which, in fact, may be part of larger social movements).

An *interest group* is a voluntary association of citizens who attempt to influence public policy. The National Organization for Women (NOW) is considered an interest group; so, too, are the Juvenile Diabetes Foundation and the National Rifle Association (NRA). Such groups are a vital part of the political process of the United States. Many interest groups (often known as *lobbies*) are national in scope and address a wide array of social, economic, and political issues.

One way in which interest groups influence the political process is through their political action committees. A **political action committee** (or **PAC**) is a political committee established by an interest group—a national bank, corporation, trade association, or cooperative or membership association—to accept voluntary contributions for candidates or political parties.

Political action committees distribute substantial funds to candidates for public office. In the 1992 elections, for example, PACs gave congressional candidates about $189 million; the biggest contributors were PACs representing real estate agents, physicians, and members of the Teamsters union. The power of well-heeled PACs established by interest groups threatens the independence of lawmakers and, therefore, the integrity of the democratic process (Babcock, 1993).

Interest groups are occasionally referred to as **pressure groups**—a term which implies that they attempt to force their will on a resistant public. In the view of functionalists, however, such groups play a constructive role in decision making by allowing orderly expression of public opinion and by increasing political participation. They also provide legislators with a useful flow of information.

Conflict theorists stress that although a very few organizations do work on behalf of the poor and disadvantaged, most interest groups in the United States represent affluent White professionals and business leaders. Studies show that Blacks running for public office receive substantially less money from PACs than do White candidates. From a conflict perspective, the overwhelming political clout of these powerful lobbies discourages participation by the individual citizen and raises serious questions about who actually rules a supposedly democratic nation (Wilhite and Theilmann, 1986).

MODELS OF POWER STRUCTURE IN THE UNITED STATES

Who really holds power in the United States? Do "we the people" genuinely run the country through elected representatives? Or is it true that, behind the scenes, a small elite controls both the government and the economic system? It is difficult to determine the location of power in a society as complex as the United States. In exploring this critical question, social scientists have developed two basic views of our nation's power structure: the elite and the pluralist models.

© Mike Peters/Tribune Media

WHAT DO I DO? THIS CONGRESSMAN SAYS HE ALREADY SOLD HIS SOUL TO A POLITICAL ACTION COMMITTEE.

Elite Model

Karl Marx essentially believed that nineteenth-century representative democracy was a sham. He argued that industrial societies were dominated by relatively small numbers of people who owned factories and controlled natural resources. In Marx's view, government officials and military leaders were essentially servants of the capitalist class and followed their wishes. Therefore, any key decisions made by politicians inevitably reflected the interests of the dominant bourgeoisie. Like others who hold an *elite model* of power relations, Marx thus believed that society is ruled by a small group of individuals who share a common set of political and economic interests.

The Power Elite   In his pioneering work *The Power Elite*, sociologist C. Wright Mills described a small ruling elite of military, industrial, and governmental leaders who controlled the fate of the United States. Power rested in the hands of a few, both inside and outside government—the *power elite*. In Mills's words:

> The power elite is composed of men whose positions enable them to transcend the ordinary environments of ordinary men and women; they are in positions to make decisions having major consequences. . . . They are in command of the major hierarchies and organizations of modern society (1956:3–4).

In Mills's model, the power structure of the United States can be illustrated by the use of a pyramid (see Figure 15-2). At the top are the corporate rich, leaders of the executive branch of government, and heads of the military (whom Mills called the "warlords"). Below this triumvirate are local opinion leaders, members of the legislative branch of government, and leaders of special-interest groups. Mills contended that such individuals and groups would basically follow the wishes of the dominant power elite. At the bottom of society are the unorganized, exploited masses.

This power elite model is, in many respects, similar to the work of Karl Marx. The most striking difference is that Mills felt that the economically powerful coordinate their maneuvers with the military and political establishments in order to serve their common interests. Yet, reminiscent of Marx, Mills

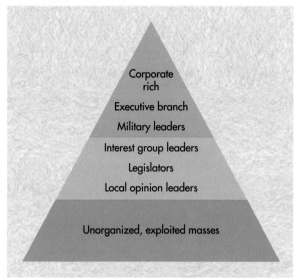

FIGURE 15-2 *C. Wright Mills's Model of the Power Structure of the United States*

Corporate rich

Executive branch

Military leaders

Interest group leaders

Legislators

Local opinion leaders

Unorganized, exploited masses

SOURCE: Adapted from Kornhauser, 1961:253.

In the view of sociologist C. Wright Mills, power rests in the hands of big business, the federal government, and the military. All other members of society play a secondary and largely irrelevant role in decision making.

argued that the corporate rich were perhaps the most powerful element of the power elite (first among "equals"). And, of course, there is a further dramatic parallel between the work of these conflict theorists. The powerless masses at the bottom of Mills's power elite model certainly bring to mind Marx's portrait of the oppressed workers of the world, who have "nothing to lose but their chains."

A fundamental element in Mills's thesis is that the power elite not only has relatively few members but also operates as a self-conscious, cohesive unit. Although not necessarily diabolical or ruthless, the elite comprises similar types of people who regularly interact with one another and have essentially the same political and economic interests. Mills's power elite is not a conspiracy but rather a community of interest and sentiment among a small number of influential people (A. Hacker, 1964).

Admittedly, Mills failed to clarify when the elite acts against protests and when it tolerates them; he also failed to provide detailed case studies which would substantiate the interrelationship between members of the power elite. Nevertheless, his challenging theories forced scholars to look more critically at the "democratic" political system of the United States.

The Ruling Class Sociologist G. William Domhoff (1967, 1970) agreed with Mills that the United States is run by a powerful elite. But, rather than fully accepting Mills's power elite model, Domhoff (1993:836) maintains that "wealthy elites who own income-producing property—corporations, real estate, plantations, and agribusiness—set the rules by which policy battles are waged in this country." He estimates that this ruling class includes less than 1 percent of the population of the United States, but nevertheless receives 10 to 13 percent of the nation's yearly income and owns up to 30 percent of all wealth.

In Domhoff's view, the ruling class should not be seen in a conspiratorial way, as "sinister men lurking behind the throne." On the contrary they tend to hold public positions of authority. Almost all important appointive government posts—including those of diplomats and cabinet members—are filled by members of the social upper class. Domhoff contends that members of this elite dominate powerful corporations, foundations, universities, and the executive branch of government. They control presidential nominations and the political party process through campaign contributions. In addition, the ruling class exerts a significant (though not absolute) influence within Congress and units of state and local government (Domhoff, 1983:116–156; see also Steiber, 1979).

Perhaps the major difference between the elite models of Mills and Domhoff is that Mills insisted on the relative autonomy of the political elite and attached great significance to the independent power of the military. By contrast, Domhoff suggests that high-level government leaders and military leaders serve the interests of the ruling class. Both theorists, in line with a Marxian approach, assume that the rich are interested only in what benefits them financially. Furthermore, as advocates of elite models of power, Mills and Domhoff argue that the masses of people in the United States have no real influence on the decisions of the powerful (Eitzen, 1988:565–573).

Pluralist Model

Several social scientists have questioned the elite models of power relations proposed by Marx, Mills, Domhoff, and other conflict theorists. Quite simply, the critics insist that power in the United States is more widely shared than the elite model indicates. In their view, a pluralist model more accurately describes the nation's political system. According to the *pluralist model,* "many conflicting groups within the community have access to government officials and compete with one another in an effort to influence policy decisions" (Cummings and Wise, 1993:206).

Veto Groups David Riesman's *The Lonely Crowd* (Riesman et al., 1961) suggested that the political system of the United States could best be understood through examination of the power of veto groups. The term *veto groups* refers to interest groups that have the capacity to prevent the exercise of power by others. Functionally, they serve to increase political participation by preventing the concentration of political power. Examples cited by Riesman include farm groups, labor unions, professional associations, and racial and ethnic groups. Whereas Mills pointed to the dangers of rule by an undemocratic power elite, Riesman insisted that veto groups could effectively paralyze the nation's political processes by blocking *anyone* from exercising needed leadership functions. In Riesman's words, "The only leaders of national scope left in the United States are those who can placate the veto groups" (Riesman et al., 1961:247). A more detailed contrast between the models of the power structure of the United States proposed by Mills and Riesman can be found in Table 15-3 (page 438).

Dahl's Study of Pluralism Community studies of power have also supported the pluralist model. One of the most famous—an investigation of decision making in New Haven, Connecticut—was reported by Robert Dahl in his book *Who Governs?* (1961). Dahl found that while the number of people involved in any important decision was rather small, community power was nonetheless diffuse. Few political actors exercised decision-making power on all issues. Therefore, one individual or group might be influential in a battle over urban renewal but at the same time might have little impact over educa-

TABLE 15-3 TWO PORTRAITS OF THE POWER STRUCTURE OF THE UNITED STATES

ASPECTS	MILLS	RIESMAN
Levels	a Unified power elite b Diversified and balanced plurality of interest groups c Mass of unorganized people who have practically no power over elite	a No dominant power elite b Diversified and balanced plurality of interest groups c Mass of unorganized people who have some power over interest groups
Changes	a Increasing concentration of power	a Increasing dispersion of power
Operation	a One group determines all major policies b Manipulation of people at the bottom by group at the top	a Policymakers shift with the issue b Monopolistic competition among organized groups
Bases	a Coincidence of interests among major institutions (economic, military, governmental)	a Diversity of interests among major organized groups b Sense of weakness and dependence among those in higher as well as lower status
Consequences	a Enhancement of interests of corporations, armed forces, and executive branch of government b Decline of politics as public debate c Decline of responsible and accountable power—loss of democracy	a No one group or class is favored significantly over others b Decline of politics as duty and self-interest c Decline of capacity for effective leadership

SOURCE: Kornhauser, 1961.

Sociologists C. Wright Mills and David Riesman differ as to the degree of consolidation of power in the United States. Mills argues that a power elite of highly concentrated and overlapping bases of power exists, whereas Riesman sees power dispersed among competing groups.

tional policy. Several other studies of local politics, in such communities as Chicago and Oberlin, Ohio, further document that monolithic power structures do not operate on the level of local government.

Just as the elite model has been challenged on political and methodological grounds, the pluralist model has been subjected to serious questioning. Domhoff (1978) reexamined Dahl's study of decision making in New Haven and argued that Dahl and other pluralists had failed to trace how local elites prominent in decision making were part of a larger national ruling class. In addition, studies of community power, such as Dahl's work in New Haven, examine decision making only on issues which become part of the political agenda. This focus fails to address the possible power of elites to keep certain matters entirely out of the realm of government debate. Conflict theorists contend that these elites will not allow any outcome of the political process which threatens their dominance.

They may even be strong enough to block *discussion* of such measures by policymakers (P. Bachrach and Baratz, 1962:947–952; Sherman and Kolker, 1987:169–170).

Dianne Pinderhughes (1987) has further criticized the pluralist model for its failure to account for the exclusion of African Americans from the political process. Drawing on her studies of Chicago politics, Pinderhughes points out that the residential and occupational segregation of Blacks and their long political disenfranchisement violated the logic of pluralism—according to which such a substantial minority should have always been influential in community decision making. The critique offered by Pinderhughes is relevant in many cities across the United States in assessing the relative political powerlessness of other racial and ethnic minorities, among them Asian Americans, Puerto Ricans, and Mexican Americans (J. Watts, 1990).

We can end this discussion by reinforcing the one common point of the elite and pluralist perspectives—power in the political system of the United States is unequally distributed. All citizens may be equal in theory, yet those high in the nation's power structure are "more equal."

ASPECTS OF THE ECONOMY

Occupations and Professions

Whatever we call it—*job, work, occupation, gig, stint, position, duty,* or *vocation*—it is what we do for pay. The labor for which we are financially rewarded relates to our social behavior in a number of ways. As we saw in Chapter 4, preparation for work is a critical aspect of the socialization process. In addition, our social identities, or what Charles Horton Cooley termed the *looking-glass self,* are influenced by our work. A person who asks, "What do you do?" expects us to indicate our occupation. This underscores the importance of our work in defining who we are for others and, indeed, for ourselves. Of course, work has more than a symbolic significance; our positions in the stratification system are determined in good part by our occupations or those of the primary wage earners in our families.

In the United States and other contemporary societies, the majority of the paid labor force is involved in the service sector of the economy—providing health care, education, selling of goods, banking, and government. Along with the shift from manufacturing toward service industries, there has been a rise in the number of occupations that are viewed as professions. There is no single characteristic that defines a profession. In popular usage, the term *profession* is frequently used to convey a positive evaluation of work ("She's a real professional") or to denote full-time paid performance in a vocation (as in "professional golfer").

Sociologists use the term *profession* to describe an occupation requiring extensive knowledge which is governed by a code of ethics. Professionals tend to have a great degree of autonomy; they are not responsible to a supervisor for every action, nor do they have to respond to the customer's wishes. In general, professionals are their own authority in determining what is best for their clients.

It is widely agreed that medicine and law are professions, whereas driving a taxi is an occupation. However, when one considers such jobs as funeral director, firefighter, and pharmacist, it is not clear where "occupations" end and "professions" begin. Moreover, in recent decades, a growing number of occupational groups have claimed and even demanded professional status—often in an attempt to gain greater prestige and financial rewards. In certain instances, existing professions may object to

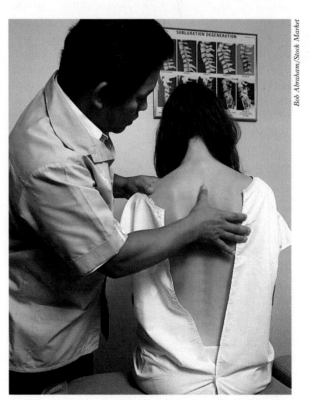

The hostility of the medical profession toward chiropractors is an example of a conflict between an established profession and an occupation aspiring to professional status.

the efforts of a related vocation to achieve designation as a profession. They may fear that a loss in business or clientele will result or that the status of their profession will be downgraded if still more occupations are included. As we will see in Chapter 17, the hostility of the medical profession toward chiropractors is an example of such a conflict between an established profession and an occupation which has aspired to professional status.

In Chapter 6, it was noted that our society is increasingly dominated by large formal organizations with bureaucratic structures. Since autonomy is an important characteristic of professions, there is an inherent conflict in serving as a professional within a bureaucracy, such as being a staff physician in a hospital or a scientist in a corporation. The organization follows the principle of hierarchy and expects loyalty and obedience. Yet professionalism demands the individual responsibility of the practitioner. Bureaucracy fosters impersonality, yet professions emphasize close relations with one's professional colleagues. Consequently, working in a large organization represents a kind of trade-off for most professionals. While they resent limitations on their freedom and individual initiative, they appreciate the security that the organization provides (Pavalko, 1971:188–192; 1972:250–293).

Work and Alienation: Marx's View

For millions of men and women, work is a central activity of day-to-day life. Work may be satisfying or deadening; the workplace may be relatively democratic or totally authoritarian. Although the conditions and demands of people's work lives vary, there can be little doubt of the importance of work and workplace interactions in our society and others.

All the pioneers of sociological thought were concerned that changes in the workplace resulting from the industrial revolution would have a negative impact on workers. Émile Durkheim (1933, original edition 1893) argued that as labor becomes more and more differentiated, individual workers will experience *anomie,* or a loss of direction. Workers cannot feel the same fulfillment from performing one specialized task in a factory as they did when they were totally responsible for creating a product. As was noted in Chapter 6, Max Weber suggested that impersonality is a fundamental characteristic of bureaucratic organizations. One result is the cold and uncaring feeling often associated with contemporary bureaucracies. But the most penetrating analysis of the dehumanizing aspects of industrialization was offered by Karl Marx.

Marx believed that as the process of industrialization advanced within capitalist societies, people's lives became increasingly devoid of meaning. While Marx expressed concern about the damaging effects of many social institutions, he focused his attention on what he saw as a person's most important activity: labor. For Marx, the emphasis of the industrial revolution on specialization of factory tasks contributed to a growing sense of alienation among industrial workers (Erikson, 1986).

The term *alienation* refers to the situation of being estranged or disassociated from the surrounding society. The division of labor increased alienation because workers were channeled into monotonous, meaningless repetition of the same tasks. However, in Marx's view, an even deeper cause of alienation is the powerlessness of workers in a capitalist economic system. Workers have no control over their occupational duties, the products of their labor, or the distribution of profits. The very existence of private property within capitalism accelerates and intensifies the alienation of members of the working class, since they are constantly producing property which is owned by others (members of the capitalist class).

The solution to the problem of workers' alienation, according to Marx, is to give workers greater control over the workplace and the products of their labor. Of course, Marx did not focus on limited reforms of factory life within the general framework of capitalist economic systems. Rather, he envisioned a revolutionary overthrow of capitalist oppression and a transition to collective ownership of the means of production (socialism) and eventually to the ideal of communism.

Yet the trend in capitalist societies has been toward concentration of ownership by giant corporations (refer back to Chapter 9). In 1990, 45 percent of the paid labor force of the United States (excluding U.S. government workers) was em-

BOX 15-2 · EVERYDAY BEHAVIOR

FARM WORKERS AND THE ABOLITION OF THE SHORT-HANDLED HOE

Workers' dissatisfaction with a job often results from conditions unique to that industry. For farm workers in California, a hated implement, the short-handled hoe, was a central part of their dissatisfaction. Sociologist Douglas Murray (1982) studied the successful battle of farm workers to abolish use of this type of hoe.

Known to the overwhelmingly Mexican and Mexican American farm workers as *el cortito* (the "short one"), the short-handled hoe came to symbolize the oppressive working conditions of California farm labor. Growers claimed that the short-handled hoe enabled workers to achieve greater accuracy and efficiency than the long-handled hoe. However, farm workers believed that the true reason for growers' enthusiasm was that the short-handled hoe facilitated supervision of workers. One supervisor noted:

With the long-handled hoe I can't tell whether they are working or just leaning on their hoes. With the short-handled hoe I know when they are not working by how often they stand up (Murray, 1982:28).

While the short-handled hoe may have been preferable for supervisors, workers quickly learned that use of this tool over a prolonged period could result in degeneration of the spine and permanent disabilities. Hector de la Rosa, a farm worker, said of *el cortito*:

When I used the short-handled hoe my head would ache and my eyes hurt because of the pressure of bending down so long. My back would hurt whenever I stood up or bent over. I moved down the rows as fast as I could so I could get to the end and rest my back for a moment (Murray, 1982:29).

In hearings before California's Industrial Safety Board, physicians and medical specialists testified that use of the short-handled hoe had a damaging impact on a worker's spine. Nevertheless, growers continued to defend *el cortito*, in part because it increased turnover among farm workers. The growers found it beneficial to rely on a steady (and steadily changing) supply of cheap labor from Mexico, along with Mexican Americans living in California.

Beginning in 1969, attorneys from California Rural Legal Assistance campaigned to prohibit the use of the short-handled hoe. They were supported by Cesar Chavez and the United Farm Workers union (UFW) and were opposed by growers and other agribusiness interests. After Jerry Brown, an ally of the UFW, became governor of California in 1975, the state's Division of Industrial Safety quickly issued a ruling banning use of the short-handled hoe.

The abolition of *el cortito* led to an important improvement in the working conditions of farm workers; some growers reported substantial decreases in workers' compensation claims for back injuries after the state ruling. Moreover, the farm workers' victory encouraged activism on other health-related issues, among them the hazards of workers' exposure to pesticides.

---

ployed in business firms with more than 100 employees. Through mergers and acquisitions, such corporations become even larger, and individual workers find themselves the employees of firms with overwhelming size and power. For example, there were 4168 mergers in 1990 alone, involving $172 billion in business. This was three times the number of mergers that had occurred in 1980; the mergers in 1990 accounted for five times as much economic activity (Bureau of the Census, 1993a:538, 543).

In the 1980s, the term *burnout* was increasingly being used to describe the stress experienced by a wide variety of workers, including professionals, self-employed people, and even unpaid volunteers. Whereas Marx had focused on alienation among the proletarians, whom he viewed as powerless to effect change within capitalist institutions, the

For both men and women in blue-collar jobs, the repetitive nature of the work can be particularly unsatisfying.

broader concept of work-related anxiety now covers alienation among more affluent workers with a greater degree of control over their working conditions. From a conflict perspective, we have masked the fact that alienation falls most heavily on the lower and working classes by making it appear to be endemic from the boardroom to the shop floor (Walker, 1986).

For both men and women working in blue-collar jobs, the repetitive nature of work can be particularly unsatisfying. Moreover, as is discussed in Box 15-2, the strain of day-to-day work in certain occupations not only alienates workers but can also lead to significant health hazards.

SOCIAL POLICY, GOVERNMENT, AND THE ECONOMY

AFFIRMATIVE ACTION

- How has the Supreme Court ruled regarding the constitutionality of affirmative action programs adopted by local governments and universities?
- How do the people of the United States view preferential treatment for women and members of racial minorities?
- What does sociological research reveal regarding the impact of affirmative action programs?

The term *affirmative action* first appeared in an executive order issued by President John F. Kennedy in 1963. That order called for contractors to "take affirmative action to ensure that applicants are employed, and that employees are treated during employment, without regard to their race, creed, color, or national origin." Four year later, the order was amended to prohibit discrimination on the basis of sex, but affirmative action remained a vague concept. Currently, ***affirmative action*** refers to positive efforts to recruit minority group members or women for jobs, promotions, and educational opportunities.

A variety of court decisions and executive branch statements have outlawed certain forms of job discrimination based on race, sex, or both, including (1) word-of-mouth recruitment among all-White or all-male work forces, (2) recruitment exclusively in schools or colleges that are limited to one sex or are predominantly White, (3) discrimination against married women or forced retirement of pregnant women, (4) advertising in male and female "help wanted" columns when gender is not a legitimate occupational qualification, and (5) job qualifications and tests that are not substantially related to the job. Also, the lack of minority (Black, Asian, Native American, or Hispanic) or female employees may in itself represent evidence of unlawful exclusion (Commission on Civil Rights, 1981).

In the late 1970s, a number of bitterly debated cases on affirmative action reached the Supreme Court. In 1978, in the *Bakke* case, by a narrow 5–4 vote, the Supreme Court ordered the medical school of the University of California at Davis to admit Allen Bakke, a White engineer who originally had been denied admission. The justices ruled that the school had violated Bakke's constitutional rights by establishing a fixed quota system for minority students. The Court added, however, that it was constitutional for universities to adopt flexible admissions programs that use race as one factor in decision making.

Defenders of affirmative action insist that it is needed to counter continuing discrimination against women and minorities. White males still hold the overwhelming majority of prestigious and high-paying jobs. In fact, despite affirmative action, the gap in earning power between White males and others has remained unchanged over the last 20 years. The contemporary earnings gap is illustrated in Figure 15-3.

Even if they acknowledge the disparity in earnings between White males and others, the majority of people in the United States doubt that everything done in the name of affirmative action is desirable. Public opinion appears united against hiring or admissions programs that offer preferential treatment to women and racial minorities. Surveys conducted throughout the 1980s consistently showed that very few people favored such preferential efforts. Many respondents insisted that these programs unfairly penalize White males and should properly be viewed as "reverse discrimination" (Colasanto, 1989; L. Harris, 1987:188–193).

In recent years, the Supreme Court, increasingly dominated by a conservative majority, has issued many critical rulings concerning affirmative action programs. In a key case in 1989, the Court invalidated, by a 6–3 vote, a Richmond, Virginia, law that had guaranteed 30 percent of public works funds to construction companies owned by minorities. In ruling that the Richmond statute violated the constitutional right of White contractors to equal protection under the law, the Court held that affirma-

FIGURE 15-3 Median Income by Race, Ethnicity, and Gender, 1992

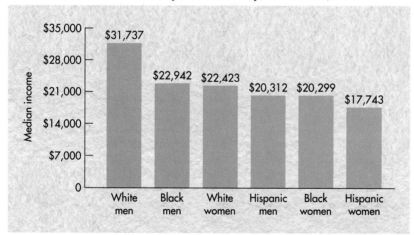

Even a brief glance reveals striking differences in earning power between White men in the United States and other groups.

NOTE: Median income is from all sources and is limited to year-round, full-time workers over 15 years of age.
SOURCE: Bureau of the Census, 1993d:94–95.

tive action programs are constitutional only when they serve the "compelling state interest" of redressing "identified discrimination" by the government or private parties.

Has affirmative action actually helped to alleviate employment inequality on the basis of race and gender? Sociologist Dula Espinosa (1992) studied the impact of affirmative action on a California municipal work force whose hiring practices were traced from 1975 through 1985. As a federal contractor, the city was required to comply with federal guidelines regarding employment practices, including making "good faith efforts" to increase employment opportunities for women and minorities. Espinosa found that employment inequality by gender and ethnicity did indeed decrease during the 10-year period studied.

Espinosa adds, however, that most of the reduction in the city's level of employment inequality occurred just after the affirmative action policy was introduced. In Espinosa's view, once immediate progress can be seen, an organization may then be-

come less inclined to continue to implement an affirmative action policy. Moreover, while high levels of inequality may be relatively easy to address initially, sustaining positive results may take longer because of institutional discrimination. Espinosa concludes that affirmative action was successful to some degree in reducing employment inequality in the city studied, but clearly had its limitations as well.

Sociologists In Soo Son, Suzanne Model, and Gene Fisher (1989) studied income data and occupational mobility among Black male and White male workers in the period 1974 to 1981 to examine possible class polarization among Blacks. The researchers found that while Black college graduates made substantial gains as a result of affirmative action, less advantaged Blacks apparently did not benefit from it. The researchers (1989:325) conclude that the "racial parity achieved by young college-educated blacks in the 1970s will be maintained only if the government's commitment to affirmative action does not slacken."

In the early 1990s, affirmative action emerged as

an increasingly important issue in state and national political campaigns. Generally, discussion focused on the use of quotas (or the "Q word," as it came to be known) in hiring practices. Supporters of affirmative action argue that hiring goals establish "floors" for minority inclusion but do not exclude truly qualified candidates from any group. Opponents insist that these "targets" are, in fact, quotas that lead to reverse discrimination. However, research efforts do not show that any significant reverse discrimination actually occurs. For example, a 1991 survey of employers in Chicago and Washington, D.C.—using similarly skilled African American and White applicants—found that 15 percent of the Whites and only 5 percent of the Blacks received job offers. Despite such studies, confusion continues about the merits of affirmative action—owing in part to the bewildering array of Supreme Court decisions and the often contradictory pronouncements of various administrations (B. Cohn, 1991; M. Turner et al., 1991).

SUMMARY

The *economic system* of a society has an important influence on social behavior and on other social institutions. Each society must have a *political system* in order to have recognized procedures for the allocation of valued resources. This chapter examines the economic systems found in preindustrial and *industrial societies;* it also examines the dimensions of the political system of the United States, and the social nature of the workplace.

1 Preindustrial societies are categorized as *hunting-and-gathering societies, horticultural societies,* and *agrarian societies.*

2 Economic systems of *capitalism* vary in the degree to which private ownership and economic activity are regulated by government, but all emphasize the profit motive.

3 In a *postindustrial society,* large numbers of people become involved in teaching and disseminating ideas.

4 There are three basic sources of *power* within any political system: these sources are *force, influence,* and *authority.*

5 Max Weber provided one of the most useful and frequently cited contributions of early sociology by identifying three ideal types of authority: *traditional, legal-rational,* and *charismatic.*

6 The principal institutions of *political socialization* in the United States are the family, schools, and media.

7 Women are becoming more successful at winning election to public office.

8 Advocates of the *elite model* of the power structure of the United States see the nation as being ruled by a small group of individuals who share common political and economic interests, whereas advocates of a *pluralist model* believe that power is more widely shared among conflicting groups.

9 In comparison with other occupations, *professions* tend to have a great deal of autonomy.

10 Karl Marx believed that the powerlessness of workers under capitalism was a primary cause of *alienation.*

11 Despite recent *affirmative action* programs, White males continue to hold the overwhelming majority of prestigious and high-paying jobs in the United States.

CRITICAL THINKING QUESTIONS

1 The United States has long been put forward as the model of a capitalist society. Drawing on material in earlier chapters of the textbook, discuss the values and beliefs that have led people in the United States to cherish a laissez-faire, capitalist economy. To what degree have these values and beliefs changed during the twentieth century? What aspects of socialism are now evident in the nation's economy? Have there been basic changes in our values and beliefs to support certain principles traditionally associated with socialist societies?

2 During the 1992 elections in the United States, many commentators referred to that year as the "Year of the Woman." How could you use experiments, observation research, surveys, and existing sources to study public attitudes toward electing women to high governmental office?

3 Who really holds power in the college or university that you attend? Describe the distribution of power at your school, drawing on the elite and pluralist models where they are relevant.

Affirmative action   Positive efforts to recruit minority group members or women for jobs, promotions, and educational opportunities. (page 442)

Agrarian society   The most technologically advanced form of preindustrial society. Members are primarily engaged in the production of food but increase their crop yield through such innovations as the plow. (422)

Alienation   The situation of being estranged or disassociated from the surrounding society. (440)

Authority   Power that has been institutionalized and is recognized by the people over whom it is exercised. (426)

Capitalism   An economic system in which the means of production are largely in private hands, and the main incentive for economic activity is the accumulation of profits. (423)

Charismatic authority   Max Weber's term for power made legitimate by a leader's exceptional personal or emotional appeal to his or her followers. (428)

Communism   As an ideal type, an economic system under which all property is communally owned and no social distinctions are made on the basis of people's ability to produce. (425)

Economic system   The social institution through which goods and services are produced, distributed, and consumed. (420)

Elite model   A view of society as ruled by a small group of individuals who share a common set of political and economic interests. (436)

Force   The actual or threatened use of coercion to impose one's will on others. (426)

Horticultural societies   Preindustrial societies in which people plant seeds and crops rather than subsist merely on available foods. (421)

Hunting-and-gathering society   A preindustrial society in which people rely on whatever foods and fiber are readily available in order to live. (421)

Industrial revolution   A scientific revolution, largely occurring in England between 1760 and 1830, which focused on the application of nonanimal sources of power to labor tasks. (422)

Industrial society   A society which relies chiefly on mechanization for the production of its economic goods and services. (423)

Influence   The exercise of power through a process of persuasion. (426)

Interest group   A voluntary association of citizens who attempt to influence public policy. (434)

Laissez-faire   A form of capitalism under which people compete freely, with minimal government intervention in the economy. (423)

Legal-rational authority   Max Weber's term for power made legitimate by law. (427)

Marital power   A term used by Blood and Wolfe to describe the manner in which decision making is distributed within families. (426)

Monopoly   Control of a market by a single business firm. (423)

Oligopoly   A market with relatively few sellers. (424)

Pluralist model   A view of society in which many conflicting groups within a community have access to governmental officials and compete with one another in an attempt to influence policy decisions. (437)

Political action committee (PAC)   A political committee established by an interest group—a national bank, corporation, trade association, or cooperative or membership association—to accept voluntary contributions for candidates or political parties. (435)

Political socialization   The process by which individuals acquire political attitudes and develop patterns of political behavior. (428)

Political system   The social institution which relies on a recognized set of procedures for implementing and achieving the goals of a group. (420)

Politics   In Harold D. Lasswell's words, "who gets what, when, how." (426)

Postindustrial society   A society whose economic system is engaged in the processing and control of information. (425)

Postmodern society   A technologically sophisticated society that is preoccupied with consumer goods and media images. (426)

Power   The ability to exercise one's will over others. (426)

Power elite   A term used by C. Wright Mills for a small group of military, industrial, and government leaders who control the fate of the United States. (437)

Pressure groups   A term sometimes used to refer to interest groups. (435)

Profession   An occupation requiring extensive knowledge and governed by a code of ethics. (439)

Socialism   An economic system under which the means of production and distribution are collectively owned. (424)

Social surplus   The production by a group of people of enough goods to cover their own needs, while at the same time sustaining people who are not engaged in agricultural tasks. (422)

Technology   The application of knowledge to the making of tools and the utilization of natural resources. (421)

Traditional authority Legitimate power conferred by custom and accepted practice. (427)

Veto groups David Riesman's term for interest groups that have the capacity to prevent the exercise of power by others. (437)

ADDITIONAL READINGS

Bensman, David, and Roberta Lynch. *Rusted Dreams: Hard Times in a Steel Community*. New York: McGraw-Hill, 1987. An analysis of a southeast Chicago neighborhood hit hard by plant closings that threw half the local labor force out of work.

DeVault, Marjorie L. *Feeding the Family: The Social Organization of Caring as Gendered Work*. Chicago: University of Chicago Press, 1991. On the basis of interviews in the United States, a sociologist explores the role of women in providing food for their families and the ways this single activity defines their lives.

Domhoff, G. William. *Who Rules America Now? A View for the '80s*. Englewood Cliffs, N.J.: Prentice-Hall, 1983. Updating his earlier classic, *Who Rules America?* Domhoff argues that the United States is run by a socially cohesive ruling class which dominates the political process.

Enloe, Cynthia. *Bananas, Beaches, and Bases: Making Feminist Sense of International Politics*. Berkeley: University of California Press, 1990. Enloe studied the lives of women on military bases and diplomatic wives as part of her examination of the male-determined agenda of international politics.

Lyotard, Jean-François. *The Postmodern Explained: Correspondence 1982–1985*. Minneapolis: University of Minnesota Press, 1993. A French philosopher explores the term *postmodern*, which he popularized in discussions in the humanities and social sciences.

Orum, Anthony M. *Introduction to Political Sociology: The Social Anatomy of the Body Politic* (3d ed.). Englewood Cliffs, N.J.: Prentice-Hall, 1989. A fine sociological overview of the political system. Orum presents a detailed account of the relevant work of Karl Marx, Max Weber, and Talcott Parsons.

Randall, Vicky. *Women in Politics: An International Perspective* (2d ed.). Chicago: University of Chicago Press, 1987. An examination of women in politics and their relationship to men in both industrialized western nations and developing nations.

Statham, Anne, Eleanor M. Miller, and Hans O. Mauksch (eds.). *The Worth of Women's Work*. Albany: State University of New York Press, 1988. An examination of women's work both inside and outside the home.

Woronoff, Jon. *The Japan Syndrome: Symptoms, Ailments, and Remedies*. New Brunswick, N.J.: Transaction, 1986. A sociological examination of the workplace in contemporary Japan.

Zwerdling, Daniel. *Workplace Democracy*. New York: Harper and Row, 1980. A fascinating account of workers' control and self-management in the United States, Great Britain, Spain, and Yugoslavia.

Journals

Among the journals focusing on issues of government and the economy are the *American Political Science Review* (founded in 1906), *Congressional Digest* (1921), *Congressional Quarterly Weekly Report* (1943), *Industrial and Labor Relations Review* (1947), *Insurgent Sociologist* (1969), *Social Policy* (1970), *Terrorism* (1988), and *Work and Occupations* (1974).

16

EDUCATION

SOCIOLOGICAL PERSPECTIVES ON EDUCATION
Functionalist View
  Transmitting Culture
  Promoting Social and Political
    Integration
  Maintaining Social Control
  Serving as an Agent of Change
Conflict View
  Credentialism
  Bestowal of Status
  Private versus Public Schools
Interactionist View

SCHOOLS AS FORMAL ORGANIZATIONS
Bureaucratization of Schools
Teachers: Employees and Instructors

The Student Subculture

EDUCATION IN THE UNITED STATES: CURRENT TRENDS
Minimum-Competency Testing
Mainstreaming and Inclusion
Women in Education
Adult Education

SOCIAL POLICY AND EDUCATION: SCHOOL CHOICE PROGRAMS

BOXES
16-1 Around the World:
    Inequality in Education
16-2 Everyday Behavior:
    Violence in the Schools

> *Excellence costs, . . . but in the long run mediocrity costs far more.*
>
> National Commission on Excellence in Education
> *A Nation at Risk*, 1983

LOOKING AHEAD

- How does education transmit the norms and values of a culture?
- In what ways do schools function as agents of social control?
- Does tracking of students serve to maintain social class differences across generations?
- In what ways is a school like a bureaucracy?
- What types of subcultures exist on college campuses?
- Should government provide financial assistance to families that send children to private or parochial schools?

Education does not have a single face. Vietnam has a literacy rate of 80 percent, one of the highest rates among developing countries. Although the government supports the principle of free education, only the first three years of a child's schooling are actually free. After that, families must pay fees for textbooks and for a part of teachers' salaries. Because many children and adults in Vietnam are chronically malnourished—often eating nothing but rice—day care centers in rural areas maintain their own gardens and provide nutritional training for parents (Jarvis, 1990).

Deborah Fallows, a citizen of the United States, lived with her family in Japan and southeast Asia for four years. In reflecting on the differences in education in Japan and the United States, Fallows recalls her initial shock and embarrassment when she attended the first two after-school meetings of parents with their children's sixth-grade teacher— only to discover that the main focus of discussion each time was the impact of having her son Tommy join the class. Eventually, Fallows came to realize that Japanese students acquire a keen sense of how to function as part of a group. Consequently, these Japanese parents had a personal stake in a foreign child's adjustment to his new classmates. "How the group dealt with him," Fallows (1990:25) concludes, "was part of their children's lessons in group behavior."

In a sense, education is an important aspect of *socialization*—the lifelong process of learning the attitudes, values, and behavior appropriate to individuals as members of a particular culture. In their years in Japan, Deborah Fallows' two sons were exposed to the socialization process in that nation's schools—where young girls and boys learn to make group decisions, to value the welfare of the group, and to assess success or failure based on the performance of the group. By contrast, schoolchildren in the United States are socialized into our culture's emphasis on the importance of the individual.

Socialization may occur in a classroom, but, as we learned in Chapter 4, it may also take place through interactions with parents, friends, and even strangers. Socialization results as well from exposure to books, films, television, and other forms of communication. When such learning is explicit and formalized —when people consciously teach while others adopt the social role of learner—this process is called **education.**

Until the 1830s, education in the United States was totally administered by localities, and the quality of education differed dramatically throughout

Schoolchildren in Japan acquire a keen sense of how to function as part of a group.

the nation. However, reforms during the middle of the nineteenth century widened educational opportunities and helped to provide the United States with a skilled labor force needed in a time of growing industrialization. During the late nineteenth and early twentieth centuries, schools also assumed the function of assimilating immigrants into the dominant culture and values of the nation.

In the last 50 years, an increasing proportion of people in the United States have obtained high school diplomas, college degrees, and advanced professional degrees. As is shown in Figure 16-1, the proportion of people 25 to 29 years old with a high school diploma has increased from 38 percent in 1940 to 85 percent in 1991. Similarly, the proportion of 25- to 29-year-olds with a college degree has

FIGURE 16-1 Educational Attainment in the United States, People 25 to 29 Years Old, 1940–1991

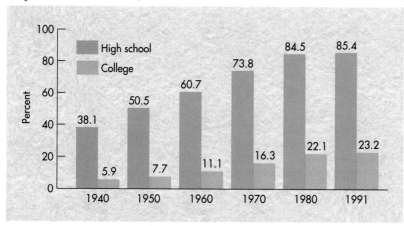

SOURCE: Bureau of the Census, 1991b:138, 1992:143.

Since 1940, the proportion of people in the United States 25 to 29 years old with a high school diploma has more than doubled; the proportion with a college degree has nearly quadrupled.

risen from less than 6 percent in 1940 to more than 23 percent in 1991 (Bureau of the Census, 1991b: 138; 1992:143).

Currently, nearly 59 million people in the United States attend public or private schools—or about 25 percent of the nation's population. As a result, education has become a major industry in the United States. More than 3 million people are employed as teachers, clerical staff, food service workers, grounds keepers, and full-time administrators.

Clearly, education has become a vast and complex social institution throughout the world. It prepares citizens for the various roles demanded by other social institutions, such as the family, government, and the economy. This chapter contrasts the functionalist and conflict analyses of the educational system of the United States. Functionalists stress the importance of education in transmitting culture, maintaining social control, and promoting social change. To conflict theorists, however, education preserves social class distinctions instead of promoting equality. Interactionists generally focus on micro-level classroom dynamics, such as how teachers' expectations about students affect the students' actual achievements.

This chapter also analyzes schools as formal organizations. Particular attention is given to the bureaucratization of schools, the role of teachers as employees, and the student subculture. Current trends in education in the United States—among them, minimum-competency testing and mainstreaming of students with disabilities—are discussed. Finally, the social policy section examines the controversy over school choice programs in the United States.

SOCIOLOGICAL PERSPECTIVES ON EDUCATION

Functionalist View

Like other social institutions, education has both manifest (open, stated) and latent (hidden) functions. The most basic *manifest* function of education is the transmission of knowledge. Schools teach students how to read, speak foreign languages, and repair automobiles. Education has another important manifest function: bestowing status. Owing to widespread criticism of the differential way in which this function is performed, it will be considered later, in the section on the conflict view of education.

In addition to these manifest functions, schools perform a number of *latent* functions. Among these are transmitting culture, promoting social and political integration, maintaining social control, and serving as agents of change.

Transmitting Culture As a social institution, education performs a rather conservative function—transmitting the dominant culture. Through schooling, each generation of young people is exposed to the existing beliefs, norms, and values of our culture. We learn respect for social control and reverence for established institutions, such as religion, the family, and the presidency. Of course, this is true in many other cultures as well. While schoolchildren in the United States are hearing about the greatness of George Washington and Abraham Lincoln, British children are hearing about the greatness of Queen Elizabeth I and Winston Churchill.

A dispute over Japanese textbooks provides an interesting case study of the transmission of culture through education. In 1982, Japanese newspapers reported that high school social studies textbooks dealing with the nation's wartime aggression and atrocities had been "watered down" by Japan's Ministry of Education. For example, where the expansion into Manchuria in the 1930s had previously been termed an "invasion," it was now to be called an "advance." Japanese atrocities in Korea in 1919 and later in Manchuria were rationalized as a "response to local resistance." Critics charged that these changes not only distorted history but might contribute to a revival of Japanese militarism. Despite vehement protests from China and South Korea, the revised language was retained, but teachers were instructed to take these criticisms into account as they prepared their lessons (K. Greenfield, 1993; Seddon, 1987).

Debates over school curricula have become common in the United States in the last decade. Such distinguished works of literature as Alice Walker's Pulitzer prize–winning novel *The Color Purple*, John Steinbeck's *Of Mice and Men*, J. D. Salinger's *The Catcher in the Rye*, and Arthur Miller's *Death of a Salesman* have been the target of censorship efforts within local school districts; so, too, have "Little Red

Through schooling, each generation of young people in the United States is exposed to the existing beliefs, norms, and values of our culture. Socialization regarding Thanksgiving and other national holidays is a part of this process.

Riding Hood," "Sleeping Beauty," and "Snow White."

In its annual report on *Attacks on the Freedom to Learn,* People for the American Way (1993) noted that during the 1992–1993 school year there were 395 challenges to school materials, the highest total in the 11-year history of the report. These challenges included 347 incidents of attempted censorship, where demands were made to remove or restrict curricular or library materials for all students. In 41 percent of these cases, challenged materials were removed or were restricted to some degree. According to the report, more than 20 percent of all challenges to school materials came from right-wing (and often religious right-wing) organizations and individuals working at the national or local level (refer back to the discussion of religion in the schools in the social policy section of Chapter 14).

On the college level, there has been growing controversy over the general education or basic curriculum requirements of colleges and universities. Critics charge that standard academic curricula have failed to represent the important contributions of women and people of color to history, literature, and other fields of study. The underlying question raised by this debate, still to be resolved, is which ideas and values are essential for instruction. What culture should be transmitted by the schools and colleges of the United States? (Refer back to the social policy section on multiculturalism in Chapter 3.)

Promoting Social and Political Integration Education serves the latent function of promoting social and political integration by transforming a population composed of diverse racial, ethnic, and religious groups into a society whose members share—to some extent—a common identity (Touraine, 1974:115). As noted earlier, U.S. schools have historically played an important role in socializing the children of immigrants into the norms, values, and beliefs of the dominant culture. From a functionalist perspective, the common identity and social integration fostered by education contribute to societal stability and consensus.

In the past, the integrative function of education was most obvious through its emphasis on promoting a common language. As was discussed in Chapter 3, immigrant children were expected to learn English. In some instances, they were even forbidden to speak their native languages on school grounds. More recently, bilingualism has been defended both for its educational value and as a means of encouraging cultural diversity. However, in the view of its critics, bilingualism undermines the social and political integration that education has traditionally promoted.

Ole the Viking serves as a reminder of the ethnic heritage of Augustana College, in Sioux Falls, South Dakota. This popular statue is often a site for student gatherings and celebrations.

The debate over bilingualism underscores the fact that not everyone may want to be integrated into the dominant culture of the United States. For example, members of Amish communities (refer back to Chapter 4) shun most modern conveniences, such as electricity, automobiles, radio, and television. The Amish maintain their own schools, which end at the eighth grade, and do not want their children socialized into many norms and values of the dominant culture. In some states, Amish parents have been prosecuted for violating compulsory education laws which require education beyond eighth grade. However, in 1972, the Supreme Court upheld a lower court ruling that Wisconsin's compulsory education law violated the First Amendment rights of the Amish to free exercise of religion (Kephart and Zellner, 1994:36).

Maintaining Social Control In performing the manifest function of transmitting knowledge, schools go far beyond teaching such skills as reading, writing, and mathematics. Schoolchildren are introduced to standards of proper conduct in public life which are quite different from the rules of behavior in their families. Like other social institutions such as the family and religion, education prepares young people to lead productive and orderly lives as adults by introducing them to the norms, values, and sanctions of the larger society.

Through the exercise of social control, students are taught various skills and values which will be essential in their future positions within the labor force. They learn punctuality, discipline, scheduling, and responsible work habits, as well as how to negotiate their way through the complexities of a bureaucratic organization. In effect, then, schools serve as a transitional agent of social control—between parents and employers in the life cycle of most individuals. As a social institution, education reflects the interests of the family and in turn prepares young people for their participation in yet another social institution—the economy. Students are being trained for what is ahead, whether it be the assembly line or the office (Bowles and Gintis, 1976; M. Cole, 1988).

From a functionalist perspective, social control socializes students to the impersonal rules of society. This function is undertaken by schools not only through transmitting the existing culture but also by re-creating within their walls the social control found in other institutions such as government and the economy. A national survey in the United States in 1989 asked adults what qualities were important in the development of a child. Nearly as many responded with "the ability to get along with others" as with the more academically related answer "learning to think for oneself" (Elam and Gallup, 1989).

As will be discussed more fully later in the chapter, schools are highly bureaucratic organizations. Many teachers rely on the rules and regulations of schools in order to maintain order. Unfortunately, the need for control and discipline can take precedence over the learning process. Teachers may focus on obedience to the rules as an end in itself—a shift in priorities which reflects the type of goal displacement that was considered in Chapter 6. If this occurs, students and teachers alike become victims of what Philip Jackson (1968) has called the *hidden curriculum.*

The term **hidden curriculum** refers to standards of behavior that are deemed proper by society and are taught subtly in schools. According to this "curriculum," children must wait before speaking until the teacher calls on them and must regulate their activities according to the clock or bells. In addition, they are expected to concentrate on their own work rather than assist other students who learn more slowly. A hidden curriculum is evident in schools around the world. For example, Japanese schools offer guidance sessions during lunch which seek to improve the classroom experience but also to develop "healthy living skills." In effect, these sessions instill values and encourage behavior useful for the Japanese business world, such as self-discipline and openness to group problem solving and decision making (Tsuneyoshi, 1992).

In a classroom overly focused on obedience, value is placed on pleasing the teacher and remaining quiet—rather than on creative thought and academic learning (Leacock, 1969:59–61). If students become accustomed to habitual obedience to authority, the type of distressing behavior which was documented by Stanley Milgram in his class obedience studies (see Chapter 7) may result.

The social-control function of education is not limited to patterns of rules and behavior. Schools direct and even restrict students' aspirations in a manner that reflects societal values and prejudices. School administrators may allocate substantial educational funds for athletic programs while giving much less support to music, art, and dance. Moreover, as we saw in Chapter 4, teachers and guidance counselors may encourage male students to pursue careers in the sciences but steer equally talented female students into careers as early childhood teachers. Such socialization into traditional gender roles can be viewed as a form of social control.

Serving as an Agent of Change Thus far, this discussion has focused on conservative functions of education—on its role in transmitting the existing culture, promoting social and political integration, and maintaining social control. Yet education can

stimulate or bring about desired social change. Sex education classes were introduced in public schools in response to the soaring pregnancy rate among teenagers. Affirmative action in education has been endorsed as a means of countering racial and sexual discrimination (see Chapter 15). Project Head Start—an early childhood program serving 400,000 children annually—has sought to compensate for the disadvantages in school readiness experienced by children from low-income families.

Education also promotes social change by serving as a meeting ground where each society's distinctive beliefs and traditions can be shared. In 1992, there were 420,000 foreign students in the United States, of whom about 72 percent were from developing nations (Watkins, 1992). Cross-cultural exchanges between these visitors and citizens of the United States ultimately broaden the perspective of both the hosts and their guests. The same is certainly true when students from the United States attend schools in Europe, Latin America, Africa, or the far east.

Numerous sociological studies have revealed that increased years of formal schooling are associated with openness to new ideas and more liberal social and political viewpoints. Sociologist Robin Williams (R. Williams et al., 1964:374–375) points out that better-educated people tend to have greater access to factual information, a diversity of opinion, and subtle distinctions of analysis. Formal education stresses both the importance of qualifying statements and the need at least to question (rather than simply accept) established "truths" and practices. As we saw in Chapter 2, scientific method relies on *testing* hypotheses and reflects the questioning spirit that characterizes modern education. For these reasons, education can make one less likely to champion outmoded beliefs and prejudices and more likely to promote and accept social change (Schaefer, 1976:127; 1995).

Conflict View

Sociologist Christopher Hurn (1985:48–76) has compared the functionalist and conflict views of schooling. According to Hurn, the functionalist perspective portrays the major features of contemporary education in fundamentally benign terms.

Education can stimulate or bring about desired social change. For example, sex education classes have been introduced in many schools to combat the soaring pregnancy rate among teenagers. In recent years, controversy has arisen over the distribution of condoms in schools, which defenders argue is necessary to prevent the spread of AIDS.

For example, it argues that schools rationally sort and select students for future high-status positions, thereby meeting society's need for talented and expert personnel. By contrast, the conflict perspective views education as an instrument of elite domination. Schools convince subordinate groups of their inferiority, reinforce existing social class inequality, and discourage alternative and more democratic visions of society.

Conflict theorists take a critical view of the social institution of education. They argue that the educational system socializes students into values dictated by the powerful, that schools stifle individualism and creativity in the name of maintaining order, and that the level of change promoted by education is relatively insignificant. From a conflict perspective, the inhibiting effects of education are particularly apparent in the creation of standards for entry into occupations, the differential way in which status is bestowed, and the existence of a dual system of private and public schools.

Credentialism Today, a college diploma has become virtually a minimum requirement for entry into the paid labor force of the United States, just as a high school diploma was 50 years ago. This change reflects the process of *credentialism*—a term used to describe the increase in the lowest level of education needed to enter a field.

The discussion of the economy in Chapter 15 looked at the growing trend of professionalization of occupations. Credentialism is one symptom of this trend. Employers and occupational associations typically contend that such changes are a logical response to the increasing complexity of many jobs (R. Collins, 1979:5; Dore, 1976:5; Hurn, 1985:95). However, in many cases, employers raise degree requirements for a position simply because all applicants have achieved the existing minimum credential.

Conflict theorists have observed that credentialism may reinforce social inequality. They note that applicants from poor and minority backgrounds are especially likely to suffer from the escalation of qualifications, since they lack the financial resources needed to obtain degree after degree. In addition, upgrading credentials serves the self-interest of the two groups most responsible for this trend. Educational institutions have a vested interest in prolonging the investment of time and money that people make by staying in school. Moreover, as Christopher Hurn (1985:56–57) has suggested, current jobholders have a stake in raising occupational requirements. Credentialism can increase the status of an occupation and is crucial to demands for higher pay. Max Weber anticipated such possibilities as far back as 1916, concluding that the "universal clamor for the creation of educational certificates in all fields makes for the formation of a privileged stratum in businesses and in offices" (Gerth and Mills, 1958:240–241).

Bestowal of Status Both functionalist and conflict theorists agree that education performs the important function of bestowing status. As noted earlier, an increasing proportion of people in the United States are obtaining high school diplomas, college degrees, and advanced professional degrees (refer back to Figure 16-1). From a functionalist perspective, this widening bestowal of status is beneficial not only to particular recipients but to the society as a whole. In our discussion of stratification in Chapter 8, we noted the view of Kingsley Davis and Wilbert Moore (1945) that society must distribute its members among a variety of social positions. Education can contribute to this process by sorting people into appropriate levels and courses of study that will prepare them for appropriate positions within the labor force.

Conflict sociologists are far more critical of the differential way education bestows status; they stress that schools sort pupils according to social class background. Although the educational system helps certain poor children to move into middle-class professional positions, it denies most disadvantaged children the same educational opportunities afforded children of the affluent. In this way, schools tend to preserve social class inequalities in each new generation (Labaree, 1986; Mingle, 1987).

Money contributes to this disparity. In all but a few cases, public schools in the United States have been financed through local property taxes. Since the total value of property tends to be lower in areas with many low-income families, these school districts generally have less money available for education. Studies conducted since 1987 suggest that the funding inequities between richer and poorer districts have actually widened in recent years. While educational expenses have increased across the nation, less affluent districts have been unable to keep pace (refer back to Box 5-2 on page 132). In recent years, there have been a growing number of legal challenges to the district-by-district school financing inequities within various states (Glaub, 1990).

Class differences can also be reinforced within a single school. Working-class children are much

Bob Daemmrich/Image Works

Shown is a high school cosmetology class. Working-class students may be placed in vocational tracks as part of the general practice of tracking.

more likely to be viewed as destined for subordinate positions and therefore placed in high school vocational or general tracks. The term *tracking* refers to the practice of placing students in specific curriculum groups on the basis of test scores and other criteria. Tracking begins very early in the classroom, often in reading groups during first grade. These tracks can reinforce the disadvantages that children from less affluent families may have if they have not been exposed to reading materials and writing instruments in their homes during early childhood years. It is estimated that about 60 percent of elementary schools in the United States and about 80 percent of secondary schools retain some form of tracking (Strum, 1993).

Sociologists Glenna Colclough and E. M. Beck (1986) considered three factors that contribute to the role of education in maintaining social class differences: public versus private schooling, economic disparities between school communities, and tracking of students into curriculum groups. The researchers found that tracking was the most significant mechanism for sorting and channeling students into desirable or subordinate positions in society. To put it another way, the placement of a student into either a college-bound or a vocational track will have more of an influence on his or her future than sending the student to a private school, a public school, a school in an affluent community, or a school in a low-income neighborhood. Moreover, as noted above, tracking is related to students' social class backgrounds and therefore serves to maintain class inequalities across generations.

A national study released in 1992 found that ability grouping worsens the academic prospects of lower-achieving students while it fails to improve the prospects of higher-achieving students. Moreover, tracking appears to lessen the likelihood that students will learn about and interact with others from different racial backgrounds, since ability grouping often contributes to segregation within schools. For example, 35 percent of White eighth-graders are in high-ability mathematics groupings, compared with only 15 percent of African American eighth-graders (Mansnerus, 1992; Braddock and Slavin, 1993; see also Oakes, 1985).

Tracking and differential access to higher education are evident not only in the United States but also in many nations around the world (see Box 16-1). For example, Japan's educational system mandates equality in school funding and insists that all schools use the same textbooks. Nevertheless, it is the more affluent Japanese families who can afford to send their children to *juku,* or cram schools. These afternoon schools assist high school students in preparing for examinations which determine admission into prestigious colleges (McGrath, 1983: 66; Rohlen, 1983; M. White, 1987).

According to a study of teachers' attitudes toward students in the "outback" in rural Australia—an area where sheep vastly outnumber people—students are being prepared to stay in the "bush." Indeed, only a small minority seek out electives geared toward preparation for college. However, beginning in the 1980s, parents questioned this agriculture-oriented curriculum in view of rural Australia's declining employment base (M. Henry, 1989).

Conflict theorists hold that the educational inequalities resulting from funding disparities and tracking are designed to meet the needs of modern capitalist societies. Samuel Bowles and Herbert Gintis (1976:131–148) argue that capitalism requires a skilled, disciplined labor force and that the educational system of the United States is structured with this objective in mind. Citing numerous studies, they offer support for what they call the *correspondence principle.*

According to this approach, schools attended by different social classes promote the values expected of individuals in each class and perpetuate social class divisions from one generation to the next. Thus, working-class children, assumed to be destined for subordinate positions, are more likely to be placed in high school vocational and general tracks which emphasize close supervision and compliance with authority. By contrast, young people from more affluent families are largely directed to college preparatory tracks which stress leadership and decision-making skills—corresponding to their likely futures. While the correspondence principle continues to be persuasive, researchers have noted that the impact of race and gender on students' educational experiences may even overshadow that of class (M. Cole, 1988).

Private versus Public Schools For every child in the United States who attends a private school, six children go to public schools. It was hardly surpris-

BOX 16-1 • AROUND THE WORLD

INEQUALITY IN EDUCATION

As was discussed in Chapter 8, educational achievements play a critical role in social mobility. Consequently, concern has been expressed that subordinate minorities in the United States—such as Blacks, Hispanics, and Native Americans—do not have positive experiences in schools that will assist them in later competition in the job market. This country's minorities, however, are not alone in this experience.

The anthropologist John Ogbu (1978) looked at educational opportunities and achievements in six societies and found group inequality in all of them. In Great Britain, for example, Black West Indian immigrants and their descendants (many of whom are born in Britain) perform poorly in school. By contrast, in New Zealand it is the native Maori people—the original islanders now outnumbered and dominated by White Europeans—who have the greatest difficulty in the educational system. Whites are 350 times more likely than Maori to attend college.

In these societies, race was the critical factor differentiating successful and unsuccessful educational performance. However, in studying other societies, Ogbu found that inequality was evident even when racial distinctions were absent. In India, people from lower-caste backgrounds (refer back to Chapter 8) are physically indistinguishable from other residents. Yet children from the lower castes are much less likely to attend the private schools that launch Indians toward better careers. While lower-caste children account for more than 15 percent of India's population, they constitute only about 5 percent of those attending college.

Ogbu found certain common themes in all the societies he studied (one of which was the United States). The dominant groups in each society agree on the importance of education and the key role of educational attainment in shaping one's position in adult life. At the same time, however, folk explanations in many societies contribute to prejudice and discrimination by ascribing failure in school to the alleged inferiority of subordinate minorities.

More recent studies have demonstrated that educational inequalities persist around the world:

• A study of educational attainment in Taiwan found a substantial difference between the "mainlanders" (those who immigrated to Taiwan from mainland China in the 1940s) and the native Taiwanese. The latter are much less likely to continue schooling than are the mainlanders (Tsai and Chiu, 1993).

• Researchers have found a significant gap in educational attainment between Jews and Arabs living in Israel. In part, this has resulted from the government's failure to apply compulsory school attendance laws to Arabs as forcefully as it has to Jews (Shavit, 1993).

• According to a 1992 report by the World Bank, children from poor and rural families around the world are less likely to attend primary schools than children from affluent and urban families. Moreover, girls from *all* types of families are less likely to attend primary schools than boys. The report urges governments to ensure greater access to education for these underrepresented groups (Lockheed et al., 1991).

ing, then, that a storm of protest followed a study by sociologist James S. Coleman and his associates (J. S. Coleman et al., 1982) which concluded that private high schools provide a better education than public high schools. This project used data from more than 1000 public and private high schools. It was the most extensive examination of nonpublic schools ever conducted in the United States.

Coleman found, even when controlling for such important factors as parents' social class and education, that private school students do better than their public school counterparts on tests of reading and mathematical ability and measures of self-esteem. The gains in test performance from sophomore to senior year are also greater among private school students. The study suggests that private

Shown is the lavish campus of the Deerfield Academy, an elite prep school in Massachusetts. From a conflict perspective, private schools can be seen as promoting religious and social class divisions.

schools have fewer absences, instances of cutting classes, and fights, along with more homework, smaller classes, and greater participation in athletics. In line with Coleman's findings, more recent research by sociologists Barbara Falsey and Barbara Heyns (1984) indicates that students who graduate from private schools are much more likely to enroll in college than public school graduates are. These differences persist even when ability levels, students' aspirations, and social class backgrounds are controlled (see also Bryk et al., 1993).

The study by Coleman of public and private schools has been criticized on various methodological grounds. Some researchers have questioned the sampling procedures and tests of ability used by Coleman and his staff. Others have noted that this study made no attempt to examine measures of actual academic achievement, such as class ranking or grade point average. Perhaps most seriously, critics have suggested that Coleman's research may actually be measuring the earlier educational performance of public and private elementary and junior high schools more than that of high schools (Fiske, 1981:1; L. Middleton, 1981; E. West, 1984:16–18).

Viewed from a conflict perspective, private schools can be seen as promoting division along lines of religion and social class. About two-thirds of private school students are in schools affiliated with religious denominations. In addition, although private high schools include students from all income levels, they have a greater proportion from higher social classes than public high schools do. Using a conflict approach, one can argue that Coleman's study may weaken the already negative image of public education and encourage more affluent parents to send their children to private schools. This could accelerate the trend toward a dual school system: public schools for the disadvantaged, private schools for the privileged.

Interactionist View

In George Bernard Shaw's play *Pygmalion*, later adapted into the hit Broadway musical *My Fair Lady*, flower girl Eliza Doolittle is transformed into a "lady" by Professor Henry Higgins. He changes her manner of speech and teaches her the etiquette of "high society."

Is it actually possible to change someone's behavior simply by treating the person differently? Because of their focus on micro-level classroom dynamics, interactionist researchers have been particularly interested in this question. The labeling approach (see Chapter 7) and the concept of the self-fulfilling prophecy (see Chapter 10) suggest that if we treat people in particular ways, they may fulfill our expectations. Children labeled as "troublemakers" come to view themselves as delinquents. A dominant group's stereotyping of racial minorities may limit their opportunities to break away from expected roles.

Can this labeling process operate in the classroom? Howard Becker (1952) studied public schools in low-income and more affluent areas of Chicago. He noticed that administrators expected less of students from poor neighborhoods, and he wondered if this view was being accepted by teachers. Subsequently, in *Pygmalion in the Classroom*, psychologist Robert Rosenthal and school principal Lenore Jacobson (1968) documented what they referred to as a *teacher-expectancy effect*—the impact that a teacher's expectations about a student's performance may have on the student's actual achievements.

Between 1965 and 1966, children in a San Francisco elementary school were administered a verbal and reasoning pretest. The researchers then randomly selected 20 percent of the sample and designated them as "spurters"—children of whom teachers could expect superior performance. On a later verbal and reasoning test, the spurters were found to score significantly higher than before. Moreover, teachers evaluated them as more interesting, more curious, and better-adjusted than their classmates. These results were quite striking, since the spurters—unbeknownst to the teachers—had been *arbitrarily* classified in the "superior" group. Apparently, teachers' perceptions that these students were exceptional led to noticeable improvements in performance.

Studies in the United States have revealed that teachers wait longer for an answer from a student believed to be a high achiever and are more likely to give such children a second chance. In one experiment, teachers' expectations were even shown to have an impact on students' athletic achievements. Teachers obtained better athletic performance—as measured in the number of sit-ups or push-ups performed—from those students of whom they expected higher numbers (R. Rosenthal and Babad, 1985).

The teacher-expectancy effect has been confirmed in a rather surprising setting: a training base for the Israeli army. Instructors for a combat command course were purposely given incorrect information about the "command potential" of 105 men about four days before the trainees arrived. Once the course began, the trainees who had been labeled "high in potential" did indeed learn more than others. These trainees also developed more favorable attitudes toward the combat command course (Eden and Shani, 1982).

Despite these findings, some researchers continue to question the validity of this self-fulfilling prophecy because of the difficulties in defining and measuring teacher expectancy (S. Chow et al., 1990). Further studies are also needed to clarify the relationship between teacher expectations and actual student performance. Interestingly, an experiment by mathematician Urie Treisman underscores how social realities—including a teacher's expectations and encouragement—can influence students' performance.

Treisman (1989) observed the study habits of mathematics students at the University of California, Berkeley. He found that Asian Americans (a high-achieving population in mathematics classes) often studied in groups; by contrast, African Americans (whose grades in mathematics tended to be lower) generally studied alone. Treisman persuaded a group of first-year African American students to participate in a special mathematics honors program that required group study. He closely monitored the students' progress and provided consistent encouragement. The results of this experiment were dramatic: African American students in the honors program performed at the same high level as students from other racial and ethnic groups.

SCHOOLS AS FORMAL ORGANIZATIONS

Nineteenth-century educators would be amazed at the scale of schools in the United States as we head toward the end of the twentieth century. For example, California's school system, the largest in the nation, currently enrolls as many children as there were in the entire country's secondary schools in 1930 (Bureau of the Census, 1975a:368; 1993a:159).

In many respects, today's schools, when viewed as an example of a formal organization, are similar to factories, hospitals, and business firms. Like these organizations, schools do not operate autonomously; they are influenced by the market of potential students. This is especially true of private schools, but could have broader impact if acceptance of school choice programs increases. (Voucher plans and other types of school choice programs will be examined in the social policy section at the end of the chapter.) The parallels between schools and other types of formal organizations will become more apparent as we examine the bureaucratic nature of schools, teaching as an occupational role, and the student subculture (Dougherty and Hammack, 1992).

Bureaucratization of Schools

The bureaucratization of schools in the United States has resulted not only from the growing number of students being served by individual schools and school systems but also from the greater degree of specialization required within a technologically complex society. It is simply not possible for a single teacher to transmit culture and skills to children of varying ages who will enter many diverse occupations.

Chapter 6 examined Max Weber's insights on bureaucracy as an ideal type. Weber noted five basic characteristics of bureaucracy, all of which are evident in the vast majority of schools, whether at the elementary, secondary, or even college level.

1 *Division of labor.* Specialized experts are employed to teach particular age levels of students and specific subjects. Public schools now employ instructors whose sole responsibility is to work with children who have learning disabilities or physical impairments. In a college sociology department, one professor may specialize in sociology of religion, another in marriage and the family, and a third in industrial sociology.

2 *Hierarchy of authority.* Each employee of a school system is responsible to a higher authority. Teachers must report to principals and assistant principals and may also be supervised by department heads. Principals are answerable to a superintendent of schools, and the superintendent is hired and fired by a board of education. Even the students are hierarchically organized by grade and within clubs and organizations.

3 *Written rules and regulations.* Teachers and administrators must conform to numerous rules and regulations in the performance of their duties. This bureaucratic trait can become dysfunctional; the time invested in completing required forms could instead be spent in preparing lessons or conferring with students.

The bureaucratic characteristics of division of labor (specialization), written rules and regulations, and employment based on technical qualifications (lifelong job security through tenure for many employees) contribute to resistance to educational reform — especially if the reforms are proposed from outside the organization.

4 *Impersonality.* As was noted in Chapter 6, the university has been portrayed as a giant, faceless bureaucracy which cares little for the uniqueness of the individual. As class sizes have increased at schools and universities, it has become more difficult for teachers to give personal attention to each student. In fact, bureaucratic norms may actually encourage teachers to treat all students in the same way despite the fact that students have distinctive personalities and learning needs.

5 *Employment based on technical qualifications.* At least in theory, the hiring of teachers and college professors is based on professional competence and expertise. Promotions are normally dictated by written personnel policies; people who excel may be granted lifelong job security through tenure. Teachers have achieved these protections partly because of the bargaining power of unions (Borman and Spring, 1984; W. Tyler, 1985).

Functionalists take a generally positive view of the bureaucratization of education. Teachers can master the skills needed to work with a specialized clientele, since they no longer are expected to cover a broad range of instruction. The chain of command within schools is clear; students are presumably treated in an unbiased fashion because of uniformly applied rules. Finally, security of office protects teachers from unjustified dismissal. In general, then, functionalists observe that bureaucratization of education increases the likelihood that students, teachers, and administrators will be dealt with fairly—that is, on the basis of rational and equitable criteria.

By contrast, conflict theorists argue that the trend toward more centralized education has harmful consequences for disadvantaged people. The standardization of educational curricula, including textbooks, will generally reflect the values, interests, and lifestyles of the most powerful groups in our society and may ignore those of racial and ethnic minorities. In addition, the disadvantaged, more so than the affluent, will find it difficult to sort through complex educational bureaucracies and to organize effective lobbying groups. Therefore, in the view of conflict theorists, low-income and minority parents will have even less influence over citywide and statewide educational administrators than they have over local school officials (Bowles and Gintis, 1976; Katz, 1971).

Teachers: Employees and Instructors

Whether they serve as instructors of preschoolers or graduate students, teachers are employees of formal organizations with bureaucratic structures. In Chapter 15, it was noted that there is an inherent conflict in serving as a professional within a bureaucracy. The organization follows the principle of hierarchy and expects adherence to its rules; professionalism demands the individual responsibility of the practitioner. This conflict is very real for teachers, who experience all the positive and negative consequences of working in bureaucracies (refer back to Table 6-3 on page 154).

On a day-to-day level, the occupational status of *teacher* brings with it many perplexing stresses. While teachers' academic assignments have become more specialized as a result of the increasing division of labor within education, the demands on their time remain diverse and contradictory. In analyzing the work of schoolteachers, sociologist C. Wayne Gordon (1955) noted the conflicts inherent in serving as an instructor, a disciplinarian, and an employee of a school district at the same time. For college professors, different types of role strain arise. While formally employed as teachers, they are expected to work on committees and are encouraged to conduct scholarly research. In many colleges and universities, security of position (tenure) is based primarily on the publication of original scholarship. As a result, instructors must fulfill goals that compete for time.

College professors rarely have to occupy themselves with the role of disciplinarian, but this task has become a major focus of schoolteachers' work in the United States. Clearly, maintenance of order is essential in establishing an educational environment in which students can actually learn. Yet the nation's schools have been the scene of increasingly violent misbehavior in recent years (see Box 16-2 on page 464).

Given these difficulties, does teaching remain an attractive profession in the United States? In 1969, when teachers were already having difficulty finding jobs because of growing educational cutbacks, fully 75 percent of parents indicated that they would like their children to become public school teachers. By 1993, that figure had fallen to 67 percent. In the minds of parents, the status of teaching as a career for their children had declined

BOX 16-2 • EVERYDAY BEHAVIOR

VIOLENCE IN THE SCHOOLS

Lorain, Ohio, a community of 70,000 people, was shaken in early 1993 by the arrests of two seventh-grade girls allegedly involved in a plot to kill their English teacher. Encouraged by $200 in lunch money wagered by dozens of students aware of the conspiracy, a 13-year-old honor student admitted she had brought a 12-inch kitchen knife from home to stab her teacher in the heart. According to their plan, her 12-year-old accomplice would hold the teacher down. However, just minutes before the class bell sounded—the signal for the attack—an assistant principal passing by the classroom noticed how tense the 13-year-old was. After investigating, the assistant principal uncovered the conspiracy and prevented the attack (J. Hull, 1993).

The data on school violence in the United States are horrifying. An estimated 100,000 pupils across the nation carry guns to school each day. Some 3 million incidents of street crime (assault, rape, robbery, or theft) take place each year inside schools or on school property. Nearly 300,000 high school students are physically attacked each month. According to a 1993 report by the National Center for Education Statistics, 16 percent of public school teachers have been threatened with injury, and 7 percent report they have actually been physically attacked. School violence is not an urban phenomenon alone. For example, according to a 1993 survey, 12 percent of rural schools in the United States had witnessed an increase in guns on school grounds during the previous year (D. W. Hayes, 1993; Ostling, 1989; Sharp, 1993).

Even these distressing data probably underreport the extent of violence in the nation's schools. Especially in suburban and rural areas, schools do not want to be *labeled* as unsafe or violent and therefore may remain silent about violent incidents whenever possible. Moreover, there are indications that school administrators take a "not in my district" attitude when assessing the nationwide rise in school-related violence. In a 1993 survey by the National School Board Association, 39 percent of school administrators said that violence had increased in their own districts, 63 percent believed it had risen in neighboring school districts, and 97 percent suggested that there was more school violence across the United States than was the case five years ago (Lawton, 1993a).

What explanations have been offered for the increase in violence in the schools? Among the factors contributing to this rise in violence are increasing use of drugs and alcohol by students (even on school property); the decline in family supervision of children and adolescents; young people's daily exposure to violence in the media; the rise in organized gang activity (a phenomenon evident in urban, suburban, and rural areas and among young people from all social classes and racial and ethnic backgrounds); and the increased use of guns and knives during disputes (refer back to the social policy section on gun control in Chapter 7). This last factor is especially noteworthy; while there have always been conflicts between students, they have now become increasingly life-threatening because many students carry dangerous weapons (Bastian and Taylor, 1991; Celis, 1993; D. W. Hayes, 1993).

Increasingly, efforts to prevent school violence are focusing on the ways in which the socialization of young people in the United States contributes to violence. In early 1993, the National Education Association called on the federal government to spend $100 million over a five-year period to assist the nation's school districts in efforts to combat violence. Such funding, if allocated, could be used to introduce programs designed to prevent chronic aggressive behavior. For example, a pilot program known as Fast Track (Families and Schools Together) is funded by the National Institute of Mental Health. It is an early-intervention anger management program which works with children beginning in the first grade. Fast Track socializes children to sensitivity to others, the damaging effects of violence, and the importance of nonviolent resolution of conflicts. The program uses games and exercises and relies on active parental involvement. Contemporary research both inside and outside schools suggests that attention to socialization and anger management of children is essential in reducing violence (Celis, 1993; Lawton, 1993b; Marklein, 1992; Terrell, 1992).

somewhat. In 1992, 4.4 percent of first-year male college students and 13 percent of first-year female students indicated that they were interested in becoming teachers. While these figures reflect a modest upturn in the appeal of teaching in recent years, they are dramatically lower than the 12.7 percent of first-year male students and 37.5 percent of first-year female students who had such occupational aspirations in 1968 (Astin et al., 1987:46, 70; Elam et al., 1993:148).

Undoubtedly, students' feelings about the attractiveness of teaching have been influenced by the economics of the profession. In 1993, the average salary for all public elementary and secondary school teachers in the United States was $35,104. This salary places teachers somewhere near the average of all wage earners in the nation. (In private industry, workers with professional responsibilities and educational qualifications comparable with teachers earn salaries ranging from $29,000 to $60,000.) By contrast, university students in Japan line up for coveted teaching jobs. By law, Japanese teachers are paid 10 percent more than employees in the top-level civil service job, which places them among the top 10 percent of wage earners in the country (T. Henry, 1993; Richburg, 1985).

As was noted in Chapter 8, the status of any job reflects several factors, including the level of education required, financial compensation, and the respect given the occupation within society. Teaching is feeling pressure in all three areas: the amount of formal schooling required for this profession remains high, but the public has begun to call for new competency examinations for teachers; the statistics cited above demonstrate that teachers' salaries are significantly lower than those of many professionals and skilled workers; finally, as we have seen, the prestige of the teaching profession has declined in the last decade. It is not surprising, then, to find that many teachers become disappointed and frustrated and leave the educational world for other careers. Many are simply "burned out" by the severe demands, limited rewards, and general sense of alienation that they experience on the job (see Chapter 15).

In 1987, a Rand Corporation report estimated attrition among teachers in the United States at 9 percent annually. The researchers noted that the "teacher burnout" rate had been as high as 17 per-

cent per year in the 1960s. However, although the current rate is much lower, it has raised even greater concern among educators because the profession is no longer attracting a sufficient number of college graduates. Until 20 years ago, a steady supply of women and minority group members entered teaching. However, as career options have widened for these groups in recent decades (refer back to Chapters 10 and 11), many people have chosen to enter higher-paying occupations, rather than teaching (Grissmer and Kirby, 1987; Solórzano, 1986).

The Student Subculture

Earlier, various functions of education, such as transmitting culture, maintaining social control, and promoting social change, were described. An additional latent function which relates directly to student life can be identified: schools provide for students' social and recreational needs. Education helps toddlers and young children develop interpersonal skills that are essential during adolescence and adulthood. During high school and college years, students may meet future husbands and wives and may establish lifelong friendships (J. W. Coleman and Cressey, 1980:96).

When people observe high schools, community colleges, or universities from the outside, students appear to constitute a cohesive, uniform group. However, the student subculture is actually much more complex and diverse. High school cliques and social groups may be established on the basis of race, social class, physical attractiveness, placement in courses, athletic ability, and leadership roles in the school and community. Remarkably, in his study of Elmtown, allowing for the fact that an individual could belong to more than one social group, August Hollingshead (1975:154) found some 259 distinct cliques in a single high school. These cliques, whose average size was five, were centered on the school itself, on recreational activities, and on religious and community groups.

A similar diversity can be found at the college level. Burton Clark and Martin Trow (1966) — and, more recently, Helen Lefkowitz Horowitz (1987) — have identified distinctive subcultures among college students. Looking at their analyses together, we can present four ideal types of subcultures.

Social cliques consisting of athletes are one aspect of the larger student subculture of a high school.

The *collegiate* subculture focuses on having fun and socializing. These students define what constitutes a "reasonable" amount of academic work (and what amount of work is "excessive" and leads to being labeled as a "grind"). Members of the collegiate subculture have little commitment to academic pursuits. By contrast, the *academic* subculture identifies with the intellectual concerns of the faculty and values knowledge for its own sake. The *vocational* subculture is primarily interested in career prospects and views college as a means of obtaining degrees which are essential for advancement. Finally, the *nonconformist* subculture is hostile to the college environment and seeks out ideas that may or may not relate to studies. Indeed, it may be removed from the dominant college culture but may find outlets through campus publications or issue-oriented groups. Each college student is eventually exposed to these competing subcultures and must determine which (if any) seem most in line with his or her feelings and interests.

The typology used by these researchers reminds us that school is a complex social organization—almost like a community with different neighborhoods. However, it is important to note that these four subcultures are not the only ones evident on college campuses in the United States. For example, one might find subcultures of Vietnam veterans or former full-time homemakers at community colleges and four-year commuter institutions. The striking increase in older college students will be discussed more fully later in the chapter.

Sociologist Joe Feagin has studied a distinctive collegiate subculture: Black students at predominantly White universities. These students must function academically and socially within universities where there are few Black faculty members or Black administrators, where harassment of Blacks by campus police is common, and where the curricula place little emphasis on Black contributions. Indeed, Feagin (1989:11) suggests that "for minority students life at a predominantly white college or university means long-term encounters with *pervasive whiteness.*" In Feagin's view, African American students at such institutions experience blatant and subtle racial discrimination which has a cumulative impact that can seriously damage students' confidence.

EDUCATION IN THE UNITED STATES: CURRENT TRENDS

Most of this chapter has focused on the basic processes and social structure of educational institutions in the United States. This section will examine a number of important educational innovations that have been proposed or implemented within the last 20 years.

It is worth noting that people in the United States believe that change is needed in the nation's educational system. A 1990 survey revealed that only 18 percent of respondents were prepared to give a grade of "A" to their communities' elementary schools. Only 2 percent were willing to give this top grade to the public schools in the nation as a whole. But such dissatisfaction is hardly unique to the United States. In a comparative analysis of more than 3500 policymakers and organization leaders in the United States, Great Britain, and West Germany, researchers found agreement that each country's educational system was not functioning well and that reforms were essential (Elam, 1990:52; Landsberger et al., 1988).

No matter what the public sentiment, the constraints against change in education can be formidable. Educators may resist theories or techniques that seem "untested" or "too experimental." Taxpayers are reluctant to spend more money on unproven programs. Nevertheless, our educational system is badly in need of change, and certain proposals to fundamentally reshape this institution have attracted considerable attention.

Minimum-Competency Testing

Over the last three decades, standard procedure in schools in the United States was to pass children from one grade to the next on the basis of age rather than actual educational attainment. This practice was called *social promotion;* it stemmed from a belief that the stigma of being left back might cripple motivation and self-esteem and further impede learning. Educators thus recognized the importance of the student subculture in academic success and failure. However, in the 1970s, more and more people—both inside and outside the educational world—became upset about the number of students graduating from high school who had never mastered basic skills. As a result, a nationwide movement emerged in support of *minimum-competency tests (MCTs),* which measure the knowledge that a child possesses in such areas as reading, writing, and mathematics.

Currently, school districts in 33 states require that some test be passed before a student can graduate from high school. Those who fail must enter a remedial program to prepare for retesting. However, a minimum-competency test does not grade students or place them at some level or percentile. Instead, it simply indicates whether the student has or has not achieved a minimum level of proficiency in a subject or skill. While the manifest function of the MCT is to certify the learner, the latent effect is to restore the credibility of the high school diploma in the minds of employers.

Minimum-competency testing is not without its critics. The MCT has been attacked on the grounds that it does not genuinely represent students' abilities. In addition, concern has been expressed that teachers may train students to pass the MCT, rather than educate them in a broader manner. Again, the social role of the teacher is made more difficult. Teachers may resent the pressure to focus their educational efforts on MCTs and may feel that they too have "failed" if their students do not pass the tests. Indeed, a 1990 Gallup survey of teachers found that 78 percent believe that the emphasis on standardized tests has increased in the last decade and 73 percent report that they are being pressured to spend more time preparing students for tests (Kelly, 1990).

The debate over minimum-competency testing raises a fundamental question about the functions of education. Communities and policymakers must resolve whether schools should concentrate on the manifest function of teaching skills—by stressing reading, writing, and mathematics—or should take a broader view of education which embraces the arts, the humanities, and the social sciences. A move toward certifying abilities represents a further step toward credentialism. To date, while parents strongly support the general principle of going "back to the basics," they have been reluctant to sacrifice the alleged frills of a more rounded educational approach.

Mainstreaming and Inclusion

Perhaps no area of contemporary education is as widely misunderstood as education for students with disabilities. Disagreement even exists as to who should (and should not) be considered "handicapped," but for the most part educators agree that this category includes those who are mentally

According to federal legislation which took effect in 1980, children with disabilities must be educated in the atmosphere most similar to a regular classroom that is suitable for them. Shown is a child with Down's syndrome who has been "mainstreamed" into a class of nondisabled students.

disabled, hearing-handicapped (or acoustically disabled), visually impaired, speech-handicapped, emotionally disturbed (or socially maladjusted), learning-disabled, and physically handicapped. Of course, each of these classifications is subject to varying definitions and further subdivisions. In addition, many children are multiply handicapped, experiencing two or more of these conditions.

Current policy in the United States regarding schoolchildren with disabilities was shaped by the passage in 1975 of Public Law 94-142 (Education of All Handicapped Children Act), which took full effect in 1980. With a few exceptions, this law calls for local school districts to provide an individualized education plan (IEP) for every handicapped child. In addition, Public Law 94-142 holds that states wishing to receive federal funds to educate disabled students must place these students within the "least restrictive environment." In other words, children with disabilities must be educated in the atmosphere most similar to a regular classroom that is suitable for them. The practice of promoting maximum integration of handicapped children with nonhandicapped children is referred to as *mainstreaming.*

By 1991, the federal government had spent more than $16 billion to implement mainstreaming through the provisions of Public Law 94-142. One student in nine in the nation's public schools is now covered by this law. According to the Department of Education, 69 percent of all students with disabilities are participating in regular classes and receiving only support services. Most of the rest are in separate classes in regular school buildings (Gartner and Lipsky, 1987; see also A. Asch, 1989; P. Ferguson and Asch, 1989).

An important goal of mainstreaming is to break down societal prejudices regarding disabled people. Viewed from the perspective of labeling theory (see Chapter 7), mainstreaming is an attempt to remove the stigma attached to children with disabilities. It is hoped that, through day-to-day interactions with disabled children, nondisabled peers (as well as parents and teachers) will become more accepting of those with disabilities. Student life will be altered as young people with and without disabilities share classroom experiences. Yet, despite this rather humane objective, mainstreaming has not been received with enthusiasm by teachers or by parents of nondisabled children.

In particular, such parents fear that integration of disabled students into classrooms will make it more difficult for their own children to receive a high-quality education. Actually, mainstreaming does not dictate that *all* disabled children be placed in regular classrooms. Only those able to function in traditional school settings are affected. But this distinction is sometimes ignored by an apprehensive public.

Beginning in the late 1980s, a few school districts across the United States moved far beyond mainstreaming to an approach known as *inclusion.* Under this educational experiment, all children—even those with severe disabilities—are taught in regular public school classrooms. In the 1989–1990 school year (the last for which data are available), 6 percent of children with multiple disabilities and 6.7 percent of mentally disabled children were included in regular classrooms.

Unlike mainstreaming, inclusion is not mandated by Public Law 94-142 or other federal educational guidelines. It is even more controversial than mainstreaming, since inclusion requires additional special education teachers and classroom aides to modify lessons and offer teacher training. Thus far, early research on the impact of inclusion has been unclear, with some studies suggesting that it benefits both disabled and nondisabled children and other studies indicating that it is harmful to students with disabilities. As a result, inclusion programs have aroused both praise and criticism from educators and parents of disabled children (Chira, 1993).

The issues of mainstreaming students with disabilities and inclusion are not simply educational issues. They are viewed by many, including members of a growing movement for disability rights, as civil rights efforts designed to end unjust segregation of disabled students. As we will explore further in our discussion of the Americans with Disabilities Act (ADA) in Chapter 20, the goal of integrating disabled people into educational and other institutions is a challenge to the national credo of equality and justice for all.

Women in Education

The educational system of the United States, like many other social institutions, has long been characterized by discriminatory treatment of women. In 1833, Oberlin College became the first institution of higher learning to admit female students—some 200 years after the first men's college was established. But Oberlin believed that women should aspire to become wives and mothers, not lawyers and intellectuals. Female students washed men's clothing, cared for their rooms, and served them at meals. In the 1840s Lucy Stone, then an Oberlin undergraduate and later one of the nation's most outspoken feminist leaders, refused to write a commencement address because it would have had to

be read to the audience by a male student (Fletcher, 1943; Flexner, 1972:29–30, 342).

In the twentieth century, sexism in education has been manifested in many ways—in textbooks with negative stereotypes of women, counselors' pressure on female students to prepare for "women's work," and unequal funding for women's and men's recreational programs. But perhaps nowhere has educational discrimination been more evident than in the employment of teachers. The positions of university professor and college administrator, which hold relatively high status in the United States, have generally been reserved for men. Yet public school teachers, who have much lower status, are largely female.

According to data compiled by the federal government, as of 1992 about 85 percent of grade school teachers in the nation were women. By contrast, as of 1991, women accounted for only 12 percent of all full professors at colleges and universities. Moreover, according to a study by the American Association of University Women, as of 1991 women accounted for only 5 percent of the nation's school superintendents and held fewer than 350 of the 3000 college and university presidencies. Even when they hold the same degree as men, women academics often receive lower salaries. According to federal data for 1991, female full professors typically received $49,700, compared with $56,500 for their male counterparts (Bureau of the Census, 1993a:405; Department of Education, 1992:224, 229–230; Hicks, 1991:19).

There has, however, been an increase in the proportion of women continuing their schooling (see Figure 16-2 on page 470). Whereas in the past, women were underrepresented in college enrollment, today 55 percent of the nation's undergraduate students are female. Access to graduate education for women has also increased dramatically; for example, the percentage of doctoral degrees awarded to women rose from 14 percent in 1950 to 44 percent in 1992. Professional schools, as well, have become much more open to women. The proportion of women graduates from medical schools has increased from 6 percent in 1960 to 34 percent in 1990. Thirty-one percent of all dental school graduates are now female, compared with less than one percent in 1960. Similarly, 42 percent of all law school graduates are women, compared

FIGURE 16-2 *Proportion of High School Graduates That Enroll in College, by Gender and Race, 1960–1991*

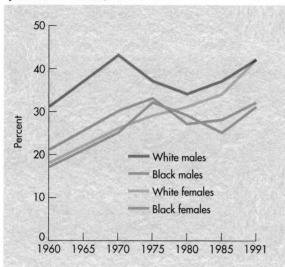

SOURCE: Bureau of the Census, 1993a:173.

Enrollment of White women in higher education in the United States has continued to grow since 1960, while enrollment of African American women has fluctuated. Enrollment of White and African American men increased substantially during the war in Vietnam, declined in the late 1970s, and rose again in the 1980s.

with less than 3 percent in 1960. Pressure from the feminist movement (see Chapter 11) played a major role in opening the doors of these institutions (Bureau of the Census, 1993a:183, 185; Manegold, 1994).

Adult Education

Picture a "college student." Most likely, you will imagine someone under 25 years of age. This reflects the belief that education is something experienced and completed during the first two or three decades of life and rarely supplemented after that. However, many colleges and universities have witnessed a dramatic increase in the number of older students pursuing two-year, four-year, and graduate degrees. These older students are more likely to be female—and are more likely to be Black or Hispanic—than is the typical 19- or 20-year-old college student. Viewed from a conflict perspective, it is not surprising that women and minorities are overrepresented among older students; members of these groups are the most likely to miss out on higher education the first time around (F. Best and Eberhard, 1990).

In 1970, only one-quarter of all students taking credit courses in colleges in the United States were 25 years old or older. However, by the early 1990s, this figure had risen to more than 40 percent (see Figure 16-3). Obviously, sociological models of the collegiate subculture will have to be revised significantly in light of such changes. Moreover, as the age of the "typical" college student increases, there will

Many colleges and universities have witnessed a dramatic increase in the number of older students pursuing two-year, four-year, and graduate degrees.

be a growing need for on-campus child care (refer back to Chapter 4). This is especially true in community colleges, where the median age of students is already 31.

It should be noted that the nation's colleges *need* older students. Given the expected decrease in population in the age group 18 to 24 years old over the period 1983 to 1995, institutions of higher learning will have to find new consumers for their services in order to survive financially. This need has led colleges across the United States to develop adult education programs. Currently, about half of all adults take part in some type of adult education.

One aspect of the adult education boom involves the rapidly changing nature of the business world in an age of technological innovation. Business firms have come to accept the view of education as lifelong and may encourage (or require) employees to learn job-related skills. Thus, secretaries are sent to special schools to be trained to use word-processing systems and video display units. Realtors attend classes to learn about alternative forms of financing for home buyers. In occupation after occupation, longtime workers and professionals are going back to school to adapt to the new demands of their jobs. So, too, are younger employees: a national survey in 1993 showed that one out of four

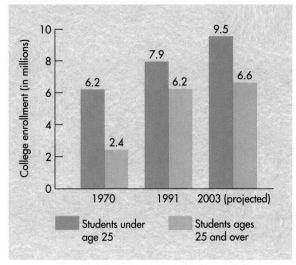

FIGURE 16-3 *Age Distribution of College Students in the United States, 1970–2003*

SOURCE: Bureau of the Census, 1993a:173.

By the mid-1990s, older students will account for 40 percent of all students in colleges in the United States.

workers ages 21 to 29 received such job-related education (Department of Labor, 1993).

SOCIAL POLICY AND EDUCATION

SCHOOL CHOICE PROGRAMS

- How do advocates of school choice programs draw on an analogy to "free-market" business competition to support their views?
- Viewed from a conflict perspective, why is there concern over the social class and religious implications of school choice programs?
- Viewed from a functionalist perspective, how would school choice programs affect the role of education in promoting social and political integration?

In January 1993, Chelsea Clinton began attending Sidwell Friends School, a respected private school in Washington, D.C. Chelsea's parents—President Bill Clinton and Hillary Rodham Clinton—explained that they remain strong supporters of the nation's public schools. Yet their decision meant that they would begin paying $10,000 a year (nearly double the amount that the average public school is able to spend per student) on their daughter's junior high school education. Many observers insisted that the Clintons' choice of a school for Chelsea should be regarded as a private family decision. But critics noted the irony that Bill Clinton has opposed school choice programs that would assist parents in sending their children to private schools, yet the Clintons are affluent enough that they can send Chelsea to Sidwell Friends School without any government aid (Doerr, 1993).

The term *school choice programs* refers to various types of educational experiments under which par-

About two-thirds of private school students in the United States attend institutions with religious affiliations.

ents can choose where to send their children. Such plans often attempt to stimulate better performance from local schools by mandating that some type of financial reward will follow students as they move to new schools. For example, choice programs may use vouchers or tuition tax credits, which provide for the transfer of public funds to the public or private school of parents' choice.

The use of school vouchers was first advanced by economist Milton Friedman in his book *Capitalism and Freedom* (1962). Proponents of school choice often rely on the work of economists for support (J. A. Tucker, 1993). In the view of journalist Billy Tashman (1992:9):

> They dream of a free-market education system in which parents shop for schools the way they shop for toothpaste. Every student would be handed their portion of the school budget (about $6000 in New York City) in the form of vouchers to present to the school of their choice. Schools picked the most would grow rich and thrive. Schools not picked, presumably "bad" schools, would be forced to compete or go out of business.

Sociologist James S. Coleman (1992:260), a supporter of school choice programs, believes that they will benefit the "consumers of education, that is, parents and children."

Currently, 13 states allow students to cross district lines and take with them their share of state and lo-

cal educational funds. At least 12 other states are actively considering various types of school choice programs. Only the city of Milwaukee allows private schools to compete for students. Under an experimental program, $2600 tuition grants were given to students from low-income families; these grants could be used for tuition at private schools which participated in the program (Chira, 1992; Kelly, 1993; Tashman, 1992).

Many criticisms have been voiced concerning school choice programs. The analogy to business competition within a free-market economy has been challenged as deceptive. Opponents of school choice argue that while a successful business such as Coca-Cola can expand into new markets across the United States and indeed around the world, an elementary school has a limited potential for expanding its clientele. Rather than expanding, an outstanding public school will instead become more selective as parents compete to enroll their children (Bracey, 1993).

Critics add that voucher or tuition tax credit programs involving private schools give these schools an unfair advantage in attracting students and funding. Private schools can exclude prospective students who may be difficult to educate, whereas public schools are obligated to serve any and all students. This issue has been raised as well in assessing school choice programs within public high schools. A study of alternative high school (or "magnet school") placement programs in New York City, Chicago, Boston, and Philadelphia found that these programs often operated to the detriment of "students at risk." The typical high school admissions process in these programs works against those families who are poor, who do not speak English, or with parents who failed in school. The magnet schools generally admit students with high basic skills and test scores, good attendance and behavior records, a mastery of English, and no special learning problems or disabilities (D. Moore and Davenport, 1988).

Viewed from a conflict perspective, the social class and religious implications of school choice programs are a matter of concern—especially when such programs provide financial support for families to send children to private and parochial schools. Studies of existing choice programs suggest that the more affluent households and those with highly educated parents are especially likely to take advantage of these experiments. (In part, this is because vouchers and tuition tax credits may not cover the full cost of private school and therefore may not be useful for less affluent families.) Consequently, there is a danger that expansion of school choice programs would accelerate the flight of affluent families out of the nation's public school systems (Chira, 1992).

Critics of choice programs are also troubled by the divisive religious issue underlying this policy. About two-thirds of private school students in the United States attend institutions with religious affiliations. For opponents of vouchers and tuition tax credits, any federal aid to parochial education —whether direct (payments to parochial schools) or indirect (tuition grants to students or tax credits)—threatens the nation's historic separation between church and state. Moreover, drawing on the functionalist perspective, critics of school choice point out that education in the United States has traditionally promoted social and political integration. Such integration is undermined when students attend private and parochial schools and do not interact with peers across class, racial, ethnic, and religious lines (Bracey, 1993; Lines, 1985). This aspect of the controversy over school choice programs recalls the battles over religion in the schools discussed in the social policy section in Chapter 14.

A report issued in 1992 by the Carnegie Foun-

dation for the Advancement of Teaching, a leading educational research group, casts doubt on the value of school choice programs. Researchers visited choice programs across the United States and surveyed more than 1000 parents. Despite finding certain bright spots, such as innovative programs run by rural schools in Minnesota, the researchers found that no statewide choice program had demonstrated a clear link between school choice and improvement in student achievement. Moreover, because of their finding that the parents who take advantage of choice programs are better educated, the Carnegie researchers expressed concern that children from less educated families may be the losers in an educational "free market" and may end up in the worst schools (Chira, 1992).

The Carnegie report is also critical of Milwaukee's two-year experiment with vouchers. Of the 341 students who used vouchers to enroll in private schools, 54 percent dropped out of the program after one year, primarily due to problems related to their families' poverty. One of the private schools participating in the experiment closed in the middle of the first year, stranding 63 children. Moreover, 13 eligible private schools in the Milwaukee area exercised their "school choice" by deciding *not* to participate in the voucher program—thereby limiting the available choices for (primarily less affluent) families seeking a better education for their children (Chira, 1992; Tashman, 1992).

In 1992, a Gallup national survey found that 70 percent of adults in the United States (and 78 percent of parents with school-age children) favored a voucher system that would allow parents to send children to any school they chose. However, other surveys, using questions with different wording, have produced quite different results. For example, a poll conducted in 1992 by the Carnegie Foundation found that 62 percent of respondents opposed giving parents a voucher "which they could use toward enrolling their child in a private school at public expense," while 32 percent of respondents favored this policy (Chira, 1992:B8; Lawton, 1992).

In the 1993 elections, more than 70 percent of California's voters rejected a major initiative that would have provided $2600 in vouchers for each of the state's 5.8 million schoolchildren. The measure had been supported primarily by political conservatives (among them former vice president Dan

Quayle, television evangelist Pat Robertson, and former cabinet members Jack Kemp and William Bennett) and had been opposed by President Bill Clinton, California governor Pete Wilson, the California Teachers Association, and the National Education Association (NEA). A similar initiative had been voted down in Colorado in 1992 by a nearly two-to-one margin (Egan, 1993; Schrag, 1993).

SUMMARY

Education is a process of learning in which some people consciously and formally teach while others adopt the social role of learner. This chapter examines the functionalist, conflict, and interactionist views of education; assesses schools as an example of formal organizations; and discusses current trends in education in the United States.

1 Transmission of knowledge and bestowal of status are manifest functions of education.

2 As a social institution, education has as its primary purpose a rather conservative function—transmitting the existing culture.

3 Schools perform a latent function as agents of social control by attempting to regulate the behavior of students.

4 Education can be a major force for bringing about or stimulating social change.

5 In the view of conflict theorists, schools "track" pupils according to their social class backgrounds, thus preserving class-related inequalities.

6 Teacher expectations about a student's performance can sometimes have an impact on the student's actual achievements.

7 Today, most schools in the United States are organized in a bureaucratic fashion. Weber's five basic characteristics of bureaucracy are all evident in schools.

8 Many teachers are leaving the educational world and moving into other occupations, owing in part to such factors as inadequate salaries and violence in the schools.

9 Public policy toward students with disabilities was dramatically reshaped by Public Law 94-142, which calls for local school districts to place these children in the "least restrictive environment."

10 The positions of university professor and college administrator, which hold relatively high status in the United States, have generally been reserved for men.

11 School choice programs often attempt to stimulate better performance from local schools by mandating that some type of financial reward will follow students as they move to new schools.

CRITICAL THINKING QUESTIONS

1 What are the functions and dysfunctions of tracking? Viewed from an interactionist perspective, how would tracking of high school students influence the interactions between students and teachers? In what ways might tracking have positive and negative impacts on the self-concepts of various students?

2 Are the student subcultures identified in the text evident on your college campus? What other student subcultures are present? Which subcultures have the highest (and the lowest) social status? How might functionalists, conflict theorists, and interactionists view the existence of student subcultures on a college campus?

3 How might sociologists draw on surveys, observation research, experiments, and existing sources to study the position of women within higher education in the United States?

KEY TERMS

Correspondence principle A term used by Bowles and Gintis to refer to the tendency of schools to promote the values expected of individuals in each social class and to prepare students for the types of jobs typically held by members of their class. (page 458)

Credentialism An increase in the lowest level of education required to enter a field. (456)

Education A formal process of learning in which some people consciously teach while others adopt the social role of learner. (450)

Hidden curriculum Standards of behavior that are deemed proper by society and are taught subtly in schools. (455)

Inclusion An educational experiment under which all children—even those with severe disabilities—are taught in regular public school classrooms. (468)

Mainstreaming The practice, mandated by Public Law 94-142, of integrating handicapped children into "regular" classrooms whenever possible by placing each child in the "least restrictive environment." (468)

Minimum-competency tests (MCTs) Tests which measure a child's knowledge of basic skills, such as reading, writing, and mathematics. (467)

Social promotion The practice of passing children from one grade to the next on the basis of age rather than actual educational achievement. (467)

Teacher-expectancy effect The impact that a teacher's expectations about a student's performance may have on the student's actual achievements. (461)

Tracking The practice of placing students in specific curriculum groups on the basis of test scores and other criteria. (458)

ADDITIONAL READINGS

Bowles, Samuel, and Herbert Gintis. *Schooling in Capitalist America: Educational Reforms and the Contradictions of Economic Life.* New York: Basic Books, 1976. An insightful critical examination of educational reform from a conflict perspective.

Crouse, James, and Dale Trusheim. *The Case against the S.A.T.* Chicago: University of Chicago Press, 1988. A critique of the well-known standardized test which outlines the adverse impact it has on poor and minority students and questions whether the SAT genuinely is useful in the college admissions process.

Dworkin, Anthony Gary. *Teacher Burnout in the Public Schools: Structural Causes and Consequences for Children.* Albany: State University of New York Press, 1987. Rather than focusing on the impact of burnout on teachers, Dworkin considers the negative consequences of teachers' burnout for *students.*

Hurn, Christopher J. *The Limits and Possibilities of Schooling* (2d ed.). Boston: Allyn and Bacon, 1985. Hurn provides a useful analysis of controversial methodological issues in education, such as IQ testing, teacher-expectancy effect, and equality of opportunity.

Meier, Kenneth J., and Joseph Stewart, Jr. *The Politics of Hispanic Education.* Albany: State University of New York Press, 1991. A concentrated analysis of Hispanic education in the United States, ranging from local school board politics to federal bilingual programs.

Moffatt, Michael. *Coming of Age in New Jersey: College and American Culture.* New Brunswick, N.J.: Rutgers University Press, 1989. An anthropologist draws on surveys and observation research to describe contemporary life on college campuses.

Oakes, Jeannie. *Keeping Track: How High Schools Structure Inequality.* New Haven, Conn.: Yale University Press, 1985. An explanation of how tracking promotes social inequality.

Powell, Arthur G., Eleanor Farrar, and David K. Cohen. *The Shopping Mall High School: Winners and Losers in the Educational Marketplace.* Boston: Houghton Mifflin, 1985. On the basis of their study of 15 secondary schools, the authors argue that the "losers" in the high school marketplace are the majority of students not served by special programs.

Sowell, Thomas. *Inside American Education: The Decline, the Deception, the Dogmas.* New York: Free Press, 1993. The author, a noted conservative columnist, contends that schools in the United States are deteriorating despite having sufficient financial resources.

White, Merry. *The Japanese Educational Challenge: A Commitment to Children.* New York: Free Press, 1987. A look at the strengths and weaknesses of the Japanese educational system, with an emphasis on the early years.

Journals

The sociology of education is reflected in *Educational Record* (founded in 1920), *Education and Urban Society* (1968), the *Harvard Educational Review* (1974), *Journal of Educational Finance* (1975), *Phi Delta Kappan* (1915), and *Sociology of Education* (1927).

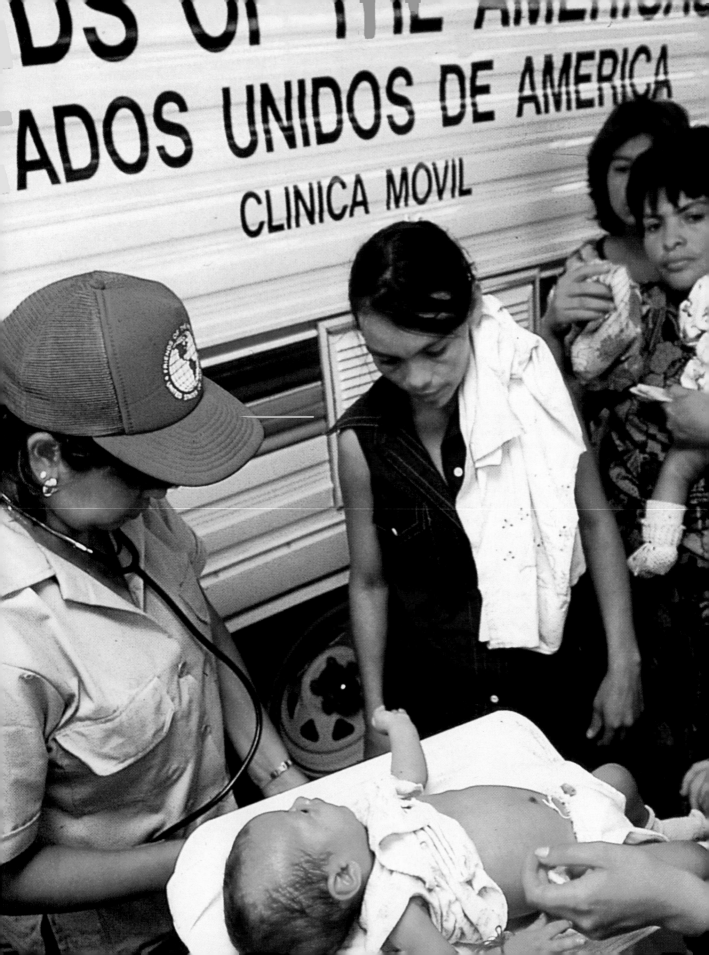

17

HEALTH AND MEDICINE

**SOCIOLOGICAL PERSPECTIVES
ON HEALTH AND ILLNESS**
Functionalist Approach
Conflict Approach
Interactionist Approach
Labeling Approach
An Overview

**SOCIAL EPIDEMIOLOGY AND
HEALTH**
Gender
Social Class
Race and Ethnicity

**HEALTH CARE IN THE
UNITED STATES**
A Historical View
Physicians, Nurses, and Patients

The Role of Government
Alternatives to Traditional Health Care

**MENTAL ILLNESS IN THE
UNITED STATES**
Theoretical Models of Mental Disorders
Patterns of Care

**SOCIAL POLICY AND HEALTH:
NATIONAL HEALTH INSURANCE**

BOXES
17-1 Around the World: Bitter Pills—
 Prescription Drugs in the Third
 World
17-2 Current Research: Sexism in Medical
 Research

> *G*ive me health and a day, and I will make the pomp of emperors ridiculous.
>
> *Ralph Waldo Emerson*
> *Nature, Addresses, and Lectures, 1836*

LOOKING AHEAD

- In what ways are health and illness socially defined?
- In the United States, what behavior is required of people considered to be sick?
- How does medicine function as a mechanism of social control?
- Does gender, social class, race, or ethnicity influence a person's likelihood of experiencing illness, disease, and disability?
- How do functionalists and interactionists view the professional socialization of physicians as it relates to patient care?
- How do sociologists apply labeling theory to the study of mental illness?
- Should the United States institute a program of national health insurance for all citizens?

*A*ll of us would agree that the general health of individuals should be viewed as an important factor in assessing a society's quality of life. Yet *health*—like such related terms as *wellness, sickness,* and *disease*—is actually an elusive concept. Although these terms may initially appear to belong in the realm of the physical sciences, their meanings are clearly shaped by social definitions of behavior.

As a reflection of the relativistic nature of health, certain ailments are found only in one or a few societies. The term *culture-bound syndrome* refers to a disease or illness that cannot be understood apart from its specific social context (C. Cassidy, 1982: 326). For example, in the last 20 years, a culture-bound syndrome quite evident in the United States, anorexia nervosa, has received increasing attention. First described in England in the 1860s, this condition is characterized by an intense fear of becoming obese and a distorted image of one's body. Those suffering from anorexia nervosa (primarily young women in their teenage years or twenties) drastically reduce their body weight through self-induced semistarvation and self-induced vomiting. Anorexia nervosa is best understood in the context of western culture, which typically views the slim, youthful body as healthy and beautiful, whereas the fat person is viewed as ugly and lacking in self-discipline (Chernin, 1981; R. Hahn, 1985; Prince, 1985; Swartz, 1985).

Other societies have their own culture-bound syndromes. For example, dyschromic spirochetosis—a disease characterized by spots of various colors on the skin—is so common in a particular South American Indian tribe that people who do not have it are regarded as abnormal. Indeed, the few single men who do not suffer from this disease are excluded from many of the tribe's social activities because they are viewed as "strange." In a 1982 study conducted in Nigeria, at least half of all students questioned reported suffering from "brain fog," with symptoms including burning or crawling sensations. In 1993, hundreds of girls in Egypt broke out in sobs and complained of unpleasant smells and nausea. Many of them fainted and dozens of schools subsequently closed. Although investigators

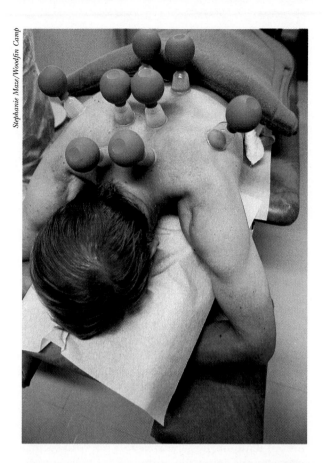

Stephanie Maze/Woodfin Camp

David Austen/Stock, Boston

Jim Pozarik/Gamma Liaison

Health care takes many forms around the world. Cupping—a traditional practice used in ancient China, India, Egypt, and Greece—survives in modern Finland. Physiotherapists use suction cups to draw out blood in order to lower blood pressure, improve circulation, and relieve muscular pain. The Malaitan people of Laulasi Island—one of the Solomon Islands of the western Pacific—believe that there are medicinal properties which reduce swelling in a leaf called raralu. In the photograph, a boy has twisted and squeezed a raralu leaf to release its juices as a remedy for his broken finger. In China, a man is shown being covered with sand to reap the healing benefits of sand therapy.

could not find any clinical reasons for this outbreak, similar incidents had occurred in Europe but are unknown in North America (Hedges, 1993; Prince, 1985; Zola, 1983:39).

Throughout this book, we have repeatedly seen that the same actions can be defined differently, depending on the social actors and the larger social context. How, then, can we define health? We can imagine a continuum with health on one end and death on the other. In the preamble to its 1946 constitution, the World Health Organization defined **health** as a "state of complete physical, mental, and social well-being, and not merely the absence of disease and infirmity" (Leavell and Clark, 1965:14). With this definition in mind, the "healthy" end of our continuum represents an ideal toward which we are oriented rather than a precise condition that we expect to attain. Along the continuum, people define themselves as "healthy" or "sick" on the basis of criteria established by each individual, relatives, friends, coworkers, and medical practitioners. This relativistic approach to health allows us to view it in a social context and to consider how it varies in different situations or cultures (Twaddle, 1974; Wolinsky, 1980:64–98).

In this chapter, we will consider a sociological overview of health, illness, health care, and medicine as a social institution. We will begin by examining how functionalists, conflict theorists, interactionists, and labeling theorists look at health-related issues. Then we will study the distribution of diseases in a society by gender, social class, and race and ethnicity. Particular attention will be given to the evolution of the health care system of the United States. Sociologists are interested in the roles that people play within the health care system and the organizations that deal with issues of health and sickness. Therefore, we will analyze the interactions among doctors, nurses, and patients; the role of government in providing health services to the needy; and alternatives to traditional health care. The chapter continues with an examination of mental illness in which we contrast the medical and labeling approaches to mental disorders. Finally, the social policy section will consider whether the United States should follow the lead of other western democracies by establishing a national health care system or providing national health insurance.

SOCIOLOGICAL PERSPECTIVES ON HEALTH AND ILLNESS

Why is it that we may consider ourselves sick or well when others do not agree? Who controls definitions of health and illness in our society, and for what ends? What are the consequences of viewing oneself (or being viewed) as ill or disabled? Drawing on four sociological perspectives—functionalism, conflict theory, interactionism, and labeling theory—we can gain greater insight into the social context shaping definitions of health and treatment of illness.

Functionalist Approach

Although illness is a phenomenon evident in all societies, functionalists contend that an overly broad definition of illness would impose serious difficulties on the workings of a society. Illness entails at least a temporary disruption in a person's social interactions both at work and at home. Consequently, from a functionalist perspective, "being sick" must be controlled so as to ensure that not too many people are released from their societal responsibilities at any one time.

"Sickness" requires that one take on a social role, even if temporarily. The **sick role** refers to societal expectations about the attitudes and behavior of a person viewed as being ill (S. H. King, 1972). Sociologist Talcott Parsons (1951:428–479, 1972, 1975), well known for his contributions to functionalist theory (see Chapter 1), has outlined the behavior required of people considered "sick." They are exempted from their normal, day-to-day responsibilities and generally are not blamed for their condition. Yet they are obligated to try to get well, and this may include seeking competent professional care. Attempting to get well is particularly important in the world's developing countries. In modern automated industrial societies, we can absorb a greater degree of illness or disability, but in horticultural or agrarian societies the issue of workers' availability is a much more critical concern (Mechanic, 1978:84–85; H. Schwartz, 1987:23–24).

According to Parsons' theory, physicians function as "gatekeepers" for the sick role, either verifying a patient's condition as "illness" or designating the patient as "recovered." The ill person becomes dependent on the doctor, because the latter can control valued rewards (not only treatment of illness, but also excused absences from work and school). Parsons suggests that the doctor-patient relationship is somewhat like that between parent and child. Like a parent, the physician grants the patient the privilege of returning to society as a full and functioning adult (Bloom and Wilson, 1979; Freidson, 1970:206; Parsons and Fox, 1952).

There have been a number of criticisms of the concept of the sick role. In the view of some observers, patients' judgments regarding their own state of health may be related to their gender, age, social class, and ethnic group. The sick role may be more applicable to people experiencing short-term illnesses than those with recurring, long-term illnesses. Even simple factors such as whether a person is employed or not seem to affect willingness to assume the sick role—as does the impact of socialization into a particular occupation or activity. For example, beginning in childhood, athletes learn to define certain ailments as "sports injuries" and therefore do not regard themselves as "sick" (Curry, 1993). Nonetheless, sociologists continue to rely on Parsons' model for functionalist analysis of the relationship between illness and societal expectations for the sick.

Conflict Approach

Whereas functionalists seek to explain how health care systems meet the needs of society as well as those of individual patients and medical practitioners, conflict theorists take issue with this view. They express concern that the profession of medicine has assumed a preeminence that extends well beyond whether to excuse a student from school or an employee from work. Sociologist Eliot Freidson (1970:5) has likened the position of medicine today "to that of state religions yesterday—it has an officially approved monopoly of the right to define health and illness and to treat illness." Conflict theorists use the term *medicalization of society* to refer to the growing role of medicine as a major institution of social control (Conrad and Schneider, 1992; McKinlay and McKinlay, 1977; Zola, 1972, 1983).

What is the significance of medicine as a mechanism of social control? In Chapter 7, we learned that social control involves techniques and strategies for regulating behavior in order to enforce the distinctive norms and values of a culture. Typically, we think of informal social control as occurring within families and peer groups, whereas formal social control is carried out by authorized agents such as police officers, judges, school administrators, and employers. However, viewed from a conflict perspective, medicine is not simply a "healing profession"; it is a regulating mechanism as well.

How is such social control manifested? First, medicine has greatly expanded its domain of expertise in recent decades. Society tolerates such expansion of the boundaries of medicine because we hope that these experts can bring new "miracle cures" to complex human problems as they have to the control of certain infectious diseases. Consequently, as the medicalization of society has proceeded in the twentieth century, physicians have become much more involved in examining a wide range of issues, among them sexuality (including homosexuality), old age, anxiety, obesity, child development, alcoholism, and drug addiction. The social significance of medicalization is that once a problem is viewed using a *medical model*—once medical experts become influential in proposing and assessing relevant public policies—it becomes more difficult for "common people" to join the discussion and to exert influence on decision making. It also becomes more difficult to view these issues as being shaped by social, cultural, or psychological factors, rather than by physical or medical factors (R. Caplan, 1989; Conrad and Kern, 1986:378; Conrad and Schneider, 1992; Starr, 1982).

Second, medicine serves as an agent of social control by retaining absolute jurisdiction over many health care procedures. It has even attempted to guard its jurisdiction by placing health care professionals such as chiropractors and nurse-midwives outside the realm of acceptable medicine. Despite the fact that midwives first brought professionalism to child delivery, they have been portrayed as having invaded the "legitimate" field of obstetrics. Nurse-midwives have sought licensing as a means of achieving professional respectability, but physicians continue to exert power to ensure that midwifery remains a subordinate occupation (M. Radosh, 1984; P. Radosh, 1986; Zia, 1990; Zola, 1972).

The medicalization of society is but one concern of conflict theorists as they assess the workings of

Nurse-midwives have sought licensing to achieve professional respectability, but physicians continue to exert power to ensure that midwifery remains a subordinate occupation.

health care institutions. As we have seen throughout this textbook, when analyzing any issue, conflict theorists seek to determine who benefits, who suffers, and who dominates at the expense of others. Viewed from a conflict perspective, there are glaring inequities in health care delivery within the United States. For example, there is an unequal distribution of medical services on the basis of both income and geographical location of facilities and personnel, leaving poor and rural areas underserved.

Similarly, from a global perspective, there are obvious inequities in health care delivery. There are 470 people per physician in the United States, while African nations have 26,000 to 80,000 people per physician. This situation is only worsened by the "brain drain"—the immigration to the United States and other industrialized nations of skilled workers, professionals, and technicians who are des-

perately needed by their home countries. As part of this brain drain, physicians and other health care professionals have come to the United States from developing countries such as India, Pakistan, and various African states. Conflict theorists view such emigration out of the Third World as yet another way in which the world's core industrialized nations gain a better quality of life at the expense of developing countries. Similarly, as is discussed in Box 17-1 (page 484), multinational corporations based in industrialized countries have reaped significant profits by "dumping" unapproved drugs on unsuspecting Third World consumers (Schaefer, 1993: 103–104; World Bank, 1992:272–273).

Conflict theorists emphasize that such inequities in health care resources can have clear life-and-death consequences. For example, in 1992 the **infant mortality rate** (the number of deaths of infants under 1 year of age per 1000 live births in a given year) ranged as high as 168 per 1000 live births in Afghanistan and 127 in Ethiopia (see Figure 17-1). By contrast, Iceland's infant mortality rate was only 5.5 infant deaths per 1000 live births and Japan's was only 4.4.

In 1992 the United States had a rate of 8.6 infant deaths per 1000 live births (although it is estimated that the rate in some poor, inner-city neighborhoods exceeds 30 deaths per 1000 live births). Yet, despite the wealth of the United States, at least 25 nations have lower infant mortality rates, among them Great Britain and Canada. Conflict theorists point out that, unlike the United States, many of these 25 countries offer some form of government-supported health care for all citizens, which typically leads to greater availability and use of prenatal care than in this country (Haub and Yanagishita, 1993).

Interactionist Approach

In examining health, illness, and medicine as a social institution, interactionists generally focus on micro-level study of the roles played by health care professionals and patients. They emphasize that the patient should not always be viewed as passive, but instead as an actor who often shows a powerful intent to see the physician (Alonzo, 1989; Zola, 1983:59).

One way in which patients sometimes play an active role in health care is by failing to follow a physician's advice. For example, despite physicians' instructions, nearly half of all patients stop taking medications long before they should. Also, some patients take an incorrect dosage on purpose, and others never even fill their prescriptions. Such noncompliance results in part from the prevalence of self-medication: in our society, many people are accustomed to self-diagnosis and self-treatment.

In their studies of the roles played by physicians and patients, interactionists point out that the same symptoms may be presented differently by different groups of people. In one study, for example, patients were interviewed while they were waiting to see physicians; the symptoms these patients presented were compared with the eventual diagnosis and an evaluation of the urgency of the condition. The researchers found that first-generation Irish

American patients had a tendency to understate their symptoms, whereas first-generation Italian American patients were more likely to generalize and overstate their symptoms. Such results remind us that health care interactions occur within a larger social context and are influenced by the norms and values of distinctive subcultures. Indeed, a greater sensitivity to cultural differences by physicians would, in all likelihood, increase patients' compliance with medical advice (Zola, 1966; see also Wolinsky, 1980:67–68).

Labeling Approach

In studying deviance, we used labeling theory to understand why certain people are *viewed* as deviants, "bad kids," or criminals whereas others whose behavior is similar are not (see Chapter 7). Labeling

FIGURE 17-1   Infant Mortality Rates, 1992

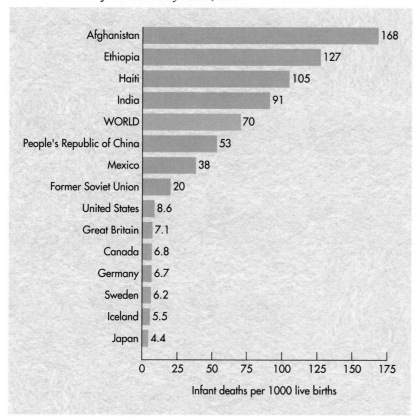

Infant mortality rates vary dramatically from nation to nation. The United States has a comparatively low rate, but several other nations have even lower rates.

SOURCE: Haub and Yanagishita, 1993.

BOX 17-1 • AROUND THE WORLD

BITTER PILLS—PRESCRIPTION DRUGS IN THE THIRD WORLD

People in the United States are familiar with controversies concerning prescription medicine—among them, the high cost of drugs, abuse of prescription drugs by patients, and the government's slow approval process for new medications. Yet many more people are affected by these problems in Asia, Africa, and Latin America. In addition, developing countries in the Third World face the following difficulties concerning prescription drugs:

• *Drug labeling.* Although there have been improvements, the information available to physicians and patients in developing countries is less likely to include warnings of health hazards and more likely to include undocumented testimonials than in industrialized nations (Silverman, 1976).

• *Lack of sales regulation.* The distinction in industrialized nations between prescription and "over-the-counter" drugs is largely absent in the Third World. Apart from a very few strong medications, virtually all drugs are available to the general public without a prescription. One result is widespread misuse of antibiotics.

• *Lack of access to generic drugs.* Even more than in the United States, people in developing countries need the money they would save by purchasing generic drugs. However, the multinational corporations (refer back to Chapter 9) that manufacture prescription drugs strongly resist any efforts to market their patented drugs at lower costs. When they cannot block the manufacture of generic drugs, multinationals sometimes turn to orchestrated public relations campaigns to convince Third World consumers that generics may be ineffective, impure, or even contaminated.

• *"Dumping" of unapproved drugs.* Drug companies based in western Europe, Japan, and (until 1986) the United States have made substantial profits by selling drugs to foreign countries which have not been approved in their own homelands. Often Third World nations are the main dumping ground for these unapproved drugs.

• *Sale of counterfeit drugs.* In a practice virtually unknown in industrialized nations, fraudulent capsules and tablets are manufactured and marketed as established products in the Third World. These "medications" contain useless ingredients or perhaps one-tenth of the needed dosage of a genuine medication. In some cases, they are sold at low prices as "bargains," but in other instances they are priced as high as legitimate prescription drugs. In 1988, a study in Indonesia found that 30 percent of all drugs in circulation were fraudulent; an investigation in Brazil in the late 1980s found that 20 percent of drugs sold in non-hospital pharmacies were counterfeit (Masland and Marshall, 1990; Silverman et al., 1990).

These problems are now being addressed by international organizations and voluntary associations. The World Health Organization and consumer groups in various nations are working with government agencies, medical associations, and industry groups to bring an end to the use of "bitter pills" in the Third World (Silverman et al., 1992).

---

theorists also suggest that the designation "healthy" or "ill" generally involves social definition by significant others. Just as police, judges, and other regulators of social control have the power to define certain people as criminals, health care professionals (especially physicians) have the power to define certain people as "sick." Moreover, like labels that suggest nonconformity or criminality, labels associated with illness commonly reshape how we are treated by others and how we see ourselves. In our society serious consequences are attached to labels which suggest less than perfect physical or mental health (Becker, 1963; C. Clark, 1983; H. Schwartz, 1987:82–84).

Perhaps the ultimate extreme in labeling social behavior as a sickness can be seen from a historical example. As enslavement of Africans in the United States came under increasing attack in the nineteenth century, medical authorities provided new rationalizations for this oppressive practice. Noted physicians published articles stating that the skin color of Africans deviated from "healthy" white skin coloring because Africans suffered from congenital leprosy. Moreover, the continuing efforts of enslaved Africans to escape from their White masters were classified as an example of the "disease" of drapetomania (or "crazy runaways"). The prestigious *New Orleans Medical and Surgical Journal* suggested that the remedy for this "disease" was to treat slaves kindly as one might treat children. Apparently, these medical authorities would not entertain the view that it was quite healthy and sane to run away from slavery or join in a slave revolt (Szasz, 1971).

The power of labeling was poignantly revealed by British sociologist Ann Holohan in describing a vivid personal experience. Holohan visited a physician for treatment of what she believed to be a routine breast infection arising from an earlier injury. However, the physician found a lump, told her that she might have cancer, and recommended that she enter the hospital for a biopsy. Holohan (1977:88) relates the shock she felt as she left the clinic and returned to the "outside world":

> It seemed incredible that nothing had changed — the sun was still shining, the road sweeper gathering the leaves. I sat in my car and immense waves of panic engulfed me. I drove blindly home and recall very little of the actual journey. . . . Yet I was no "sicker" than before my consultation. All that had changed was the possibility of a medical label for my symptom.

Upon returning home, Holohan attempted to deny the seriousness of her illness. She rationalized that since she could still perform household chores, she could not possibly have cancer. Eventually, Holohan did enter the hospital and undergo a biopsy; the results showed that she did not have a malignant tumor.

By the late 1980s, the power of another label — "person with AIDS" — had become quite evident. Once someone is told by a physician that he or she has tested positive for HIV, the virus associated with AIDS, the patient must deal with the possibility that death may not be far away. Immediate and difficult questions must then be faced: should one tell one's family members, one's spouse or lover, one's friends, one's coworkers, one's employer? How will

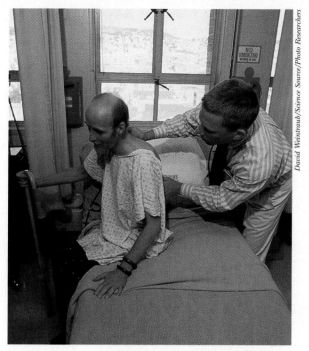

A person who has AIDS must deal not only with the devastating medical consequences of the disease itself but also with the distressing social consequences of a feared label.

each of them respond? As discussed in the social policy section of Chapter 5, people's intense fear of this deadly disease has led to prejudice and discrimination — even social ostracism — against those who have (or are suspected of having) AIDS. Consequently, a person who has AIDS must deal not only with the devastating medical consequences of the disease but also with the distressing social consequences associated with this feared label.

Labeling theorists argue that even physical traits can, in a sense, be socially "created" through labels. Applying labeling theory to treatment of the blind, health statistician Marc Berk (1985) examined rates of reported blindness throughout New York State — where physicians and optometrists are required by law to report the names of blind patients. Berk found that in counties with a higher proportion of physicians and optometrists, a higher proportion of residents are classified as blind. He found no similar pattern involving the distribution of health care professionals and reported rates of infectious diseases. Berk's research suggests that deviance is indeed in the "eye of the beholder" (or, more accurately, in the "perceptions of the beholder," whether sighted or not). The prevalence of a condition such as blindness apparently depends in part on the number of official beholders available to apply this label. In the social policy section of Chapter 20, we will examine prejudice and discrimination against people with disabilities.

An Overview

As has been noted throughout this book, the four sociological approaches described above should not be regarded as mutually exclusive. In the study of health-related issues, they share certain common themes. First, any person's health or illness is more than an organic condition, since it is subject to the interpretation of others. Owing to the impact of culture, family and friends, and the medical profession, health and illness are not purely biological occurrences but are sociological occurrences as well. Second, since members of a society (especially industrial societies) share the same health delivery system, health is a group and societal concern. Although health may be defined as the complete well-being of an individual, it is also the result of his or her social environment. As we shall see in the next section, such factors as a person's gender, social class, race, and ethnicity can influence the likelihood of contracting a particular disease (Cockerham, 1989:171).

SOCIAL EPIDEMIOLOGY AND HEALTH

Social epidemiology is the study of the distribution of disease, impairment, and general health status across a population. In its earliest period, epidemiology concentrated on the scientific study of epidemics, focusing on how they started and spread. Contemporary social epidemiology is much broader in scope and is concerned not only with epidemics but also with nonepidemic diseases, injuries, drug addiction and alcoholism, suicide, and mental illness. Epidemiology draws on the work of a wide variety of scientists and researchers, among

them physicians, sociologists, public health officials, biologists, veterinarians, demographers (see Chapter 19), anthropologists, psychologists, and (in studies of air pollution) meteorologists.

In social epidemiology, as well as in studies of population and crime victimization, two concepts are commonly employed: incidence and prevalence. *Incidence* refers to the number of new cases of a specific disorder occurring within a given population during a stated period of time, usually a year. For example, the incidence of AIDS in the United States in 1992 was 45,472 cases. By contrast, *prevalence* refers to the total number of cases of a specific disorder that exist at a given time. The prevalence of AIDS in 1992 was close to 242,000 cases (Bureau of the Census, 1993a:134; *New York Times*, 1993a).

When incidence figures are presented as rates, or as the number of reports per 100,000 people, they are called *morbidity rates.* Sociologists find morbidity rates useful because they reveal that a specific disease occurs more frequently among one segment of a population than another. The term *mortality rate* refers to the incidence of death in a given population. We will examine mortality rates in greater detail when we consider population issues in Chapter 19.

Gender

A large body of research indicates that, in comparison with men, women experience a higher prevalence of many illnesses. There are variations—for example, men are more likely to have parasitic diseases whereas women are more likely to become diabetic—but, as a group, women appear to be in poorer health than men.

This seems noteworthy and surprising, especially in view of women's greater longevity rates and lower mortality rates at all ages. Sociologist Lois Verbrugge (1985:162–163) observes:

In sum, women have more frequent illness and disability, but the problems are typically not serious (life threatening) ones. In contrast, men suffer more from life threatening diseases, and these cause more permanent disability and earlier death for them. One sex is "sicker" in the short run, and the other in the long run.

The apparent inconsistency between the "short-run" ill health of women and their greater longevity deserves an explanation, and researchers have advanced a theory. Women's lower rate of cigarette smoking (which reduces their risk of heart disease, lung cancer, and emphysema), lower consumption of alcohol (which reduces the risk of auto accidents and cirrhosis of the liver), and lower rates of employment in dangerous occupations explain about one-third of their greater longevity than men—despite women's otherwise poorer health record. Moreover, some clinical studies suggest that the genuine differences in morbidity between women and men may be less pronounced than is evident in the data on morbidity. Researchers argue that women are much more likely than men to seek treatment, to be diagnosed as having diseases, and thus to have their illnesses reflected in data examined by epidemiologists.

According to a national survey released in mid-1993 by Louis Harris (1993), women in the United States have less health insurance coverage than men and receive less medical care annually. They are more likely than men to depend on public health care programs such as Medicaid. Partially as a result of inadequate coverage, women are less likely to have access to needed medical care. For example, one-third of the women surveyed indicated that in the previous year they had not had such preventive care as a breast exam, a Pap smear, a pelvic exam, or a mammogram.

From a conflict perspective, women have been particularly vulnerable to the medicalization of society, with everything from birth to beauty treated in an increasingly medical context. Such medicalization may contribute to women's higher morbidity rates as compared with those of men (Conrad and Kern, 1986:25–26; Riessman, 1983; for a different view, see Gove and Hughes, 1979). Ironically, while women have been especially affected by medicalization, medical researchers often exclude women from clinical studies. The controversy over this issue is discussed in Box 17-2 (page 488).

Social Class

Social class is clearly associated with differences in morbidity and mortality rates. Studies in the United States and other countries have consistently shown

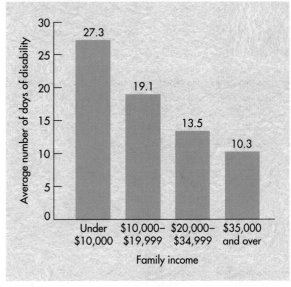

FIGURE 17-2 Days of Disability by Family Income, 1990

SOURCE: Bureau of the Census, 1993a:132.

The lower a family's income, the higher its incidence of disabling illness, as measured by days of disability per person.

that people in the lower classes have higher rates of mortality and disability (see Figure 17-2). Moreover, as was discussed in Chapter 8, a study published in mid-1993, which drew on data on death rates in the United States in 1986, documents the impact of class (as well as gender and race) on mortality. Among people whose family incomes were less than $9000, the death rates per 1000 people 25 to 64 years old were as follows: Black men, 19.5; White men, 16.0; Black women, 7.6; White women, 6.5. By contrast, among people whose family incomes were $25,000 or more, the comparable death rates were: Black men, 3.6; White men, 2.4; Black women, 2.3; White women, 1.6. The researchers add that the gap in the death rate between Blacks and Whites is *widening;* apparently, the strides being made in improved health care are reaching Whites but not African Americans (Pappas et al., 1993:103–109; see also Guralnik et al., 1993).

Although people in the United States from higher social classes have greater life expectancy

BOX 17-2 • CURRENT RESEARCH

SEXISM IN MEDICAL RESEARCH

One study, using 22,071 volunteer subjects, found that taking small doses of aspirin can reduce the risk of a heart attack. These results, reported in 1988, gave physicians in the United States a valuable piece of information. But there was a major problem: not one of the 22,071 subjects was a woman. Consequently, older women—the women most likely to experience heart problems—had no way of knowing if the results of the study would be applicable to them.

This male-only study is not unprecedented. A study designed to learn whether smoking increases the risk of getting cataracts involved 838 male subjects and no women. A research project exploring the links between heart disease and high cholesterol, lack of exercise, and smoking used 12,866 male subjects and, again, no women. Representative Patricia Schroeder, noting the absence of women in many medical studies, concludes: "At this point, doctors just aren't getting the kind of guidance they need when they try to prescribe to women" (Purvis, 1990:59–60).

Female physicians and researchers charge that sexism is at the heart of such research practices. "White men control these things," insists Dr. Kathy Anastos, a New York City internist. "When, for scientific reasons, they have to limit diversity, they choose to study themselves. Then when they get the results, they apply them to everyone. It's very unscientific" (Berney, 1990:27).

Even when women *are* the subjects of medical research, conclusions may be drawn and widely popularized despite fragmentary data. In 1990, the prestigious *New England Journal of Medicine* ran an editorial focusing on the relative inability of the female digestive system to metabolize alcohol as effectively as that of the male. This conclusion was based on a study of only 20 men and 23 women; moreover, 12 of the women were alcoholics, and all 23 had been hospitalized for surgery for gastric dysfunction. In criticizing this editorial, Jeanne Mager Stellman (1990:A23), a professor of clinical public health, and Joan E. Bertin, an executive of the Women's Rights Project of the American Civil Liberties Union, ask: "Where was the usual caution and prudence of the New England Journal in the overextrapolation of data from hospitalized patients to the healthy population, and why was this story front-page news?"

Critics of current medical research practices insist that there is a desperate need for studies with women subjects. Estelle Ramey, a recently retired physiology researcher, points out that researchers have far too little information on the impact of cholesterol and diet on women's health. Ramey adds that the lack of research on women and heart disease is especially shocking, since heart disease is the number one killer of women. There is also a shortage of data on women with AIDS—even though the proportion of AIDS patients who are female has increased. With such issues in mind, in 1992 the National Institutes of Health (NIH) established an Office of Research on Women. This office is charged with ensuring that adequate numbers of women serve both as researchers and as participants in taxpayer-supported studies (Berney, 1990: 26–27; Cotton, 1990:1050; Painter, 1992).

The federal government has also launched a 15-year, $625 million study of the health of 160,000 women ages 50 to 79. Among the focal points of the study will be the causes of heart disease, cancer, and osteoporosis among these older women. Researchers expect that the results of this study will provide scientifically valid information for older women and their physicians and will ultimately be relevant to all women in the United States. Efforts will be made to examine medically underserved areas and to target African American, Hispanic, and Native American women to take part in this research.

This research on older women will constitute the largest medical study ever undertaken in the United States. In announcing the program, Dr. Bernadine Healy, director of the National Institutes of Health (1993:1), declared: "In terms of medical research, women have been ignored too long.... Today, we are entering a new age in women's health research" (see also Angell, 1993; Wheeler, 1993).

The occupations of people in the lower classes of the United States tend to be more dangerous than those of the more affluent.

than the less affluent, they are more likely to experience peptic ulcers. The lower classes, by contrast, are more likely to suffer from certain forms of cancer, as well as from problems related to alcoholism and drug abuse. In general, there appears to be two to three times as much serious illness among low-income people as among the nation's population as a whole (Graham and Reeder, 1979:76; see also Lemkow, 1986).

Why is class linked to health? Crowded living conditions, substandard housing, poor diet, and stress all contribute to the ill health of many low-income people in the United States. In certain instances, poor education may lead to a lack of awareness of measures necessary to maintaining good health. Yet financial strains are certainly a major factor in the health problems of less affluent people in the United States. Given the high costs of quality medical care—which we will explore more fully later in the chapter—the poor have significantly less access to health care resources.

The differential delivery of health care by social class is apparent from a 1993 national survey. Of those respondents earning $75,000 or more, 79 percent were satisfied with the quality of their medical coverage, compared with only 47 percent of those earning less than $15,000. Similarly, 51 percent of affluent respondents expressed satisfaction with the cost of medical care, compared with only 25 percent of low-income respondents (Berke, 1993:E6).

Another factor in the link between class and health is evident at the workplace: the occupations of people in the lower classes of the United States tend to be more dangerous than those of more affluent citizens. Miners, for example, must face the possibility of injury or death due to explosions and cave-ins; they are also likely to develop respiratory diseases such as black lung. Workers in textile mills may contract a variety of illnesses caused by exposure to toxic substances, including one disease commonly known as *brown lung disease* (R. Hall, 1982). In recent years, the nation has learned of the perils of asbestos poisoning, which is a particular worry for construction workers.

In the view of Karl Marx and contemporary conflict theorists, capitalist societies such as the United States care more about maximizing profits than they do about the health and safety of industrial workers. As a result, government agencies do not take forceful action to regulate conditions in the workplace, and workers suffer many preventable, job-related injuries and illnesses.

According to a 1988 analysis by health specialists in Great Britain, almost 40,000 adult deaths *each year* in that nation can be attributed to class differences. Members of the lower social classes experience higher mortality because of their greater vulnerability to such factors as dangerous jobs and inadequate housing. It is little wonder, then, that the World Health Organization has asked countries to reduce differences in health status due to economic advantages by at least 25 percent by the year 2000 (Scott-Samuel and Blackburn, 1988).

Race and Ethnicity

Health profiles of many racial and ethnic minorities reflect the social inequality evident in the United States. The poor economic and environmental conditions of groups such as African Americans, Hispanics, and Native Americans are manifested in high morbidity and mortality rates for these groups. Some afflictions, such as sickle-cell anemia among Blacks, have a clear genetic basis. But, in most instances, environmental factors contribute to differential rates of disease.

Compared with Whites, Hispanics are more likely to live in poverty, to be unemployed, and to have little education. These factors contribute to Hispanics' increased risk of contracting a variety of diseases. For example, Hispanics are four times more likely than Whites to suffer from tuberculosis, are three times more likely to contract diabetes, and are also more likely to have cancer of the stomach, pancreas, and cervix. Hispanic children suffer disproportionately from lead poisoning and measles. Although Hispanics constitute only about 8 percent of the population of the United States, they account for 14 percent of reported cases of AIDS, including nearly 21 percent of AIDS cases among women and 22 percent among children (Council on Scientific Affairs, 1991; Novello et al., 1991).

The morbidity rates and mortality rates for Blacks are also distressing. Compared with Whites, Blacks have higher death rates from diseases of the heart, pneumonia, diabetes, and cancer. The death rate from strokes is twice as high among African Americans as it is among Whites. Such epidemiological findings reflect in part the fact that a higher proportion of Blacks are found among the nation's lower classes. According to a study released in 1992 by the National Center for Health Statistics (1992), Whites can expect to live 76.0 years. By contrast, life expectancy for Blacks is 69.2 years; indeed, for Black men life expectancy is only 64.8 years and has been *decreasing* since 1984.

What accounts for these racial differences? According to a national survey conducted in 1986, Blacks of all income levels are substantially worse off than Whites in terms of access to physicians. For example, African Americans had a lower rate of visits to physicians; this finding is especially disturbing, since rates of serious illness are higher among Blacks than Whites. The survey points to significantly less use of medical care by Blacks, and adds that Blacks are less likely than Whites to have medical insurance. Finally, in comparison with Whites, Blacks were found to be less satisfied with the health care they received from physicians and from hospital personnel (Blendon et al., 1989).

A study of health care in Veterans Affairs hospitals found that substantial racial inequalities exist in the provision of cardiac care. Researchers drew on records of hospitalizations in these hospitals over a five-year period. They found that Whites admitted with heart problems were significantly more likely (sometimes twice as likely) to undergo cardiac surgery than were African Americans. These results were especially troubling, since patients at Veterans Affairs hospitals are not billed for medical services, and physicians are salaried; consequently, financial considerations should not be influencing medical decisions. Racial bias appears to be the only explanation for the differences in treatment of patients hospitalized with serious heart problems (Whittle et al., 1993).

Moreover, drawing on the conflict perspective, sociologist Howard Waitzkin (1986) suggests that racial tensions contribute to the medical problems of Blacks. In his view, the stress resulting from racial prejudice and discrimination helps to explain the higher rates of hypertension found among African Americans (and Hispanics) compared with Whites. Hypertension is twice as common in Blacks as in Whites; it is believed to be a critical factor in Blacks' high mortality rates from heart disease, kidney disease, and stroke. Although there is disagreement among medical experts, some argue that the stress resulting from racism and suppressed hostility exacerbates hypertension among Blacks (Goleman, 1990).

Just how significant is the impact of poorer health on the lives of the nation's less educated people, less affluent classes, and minorities? Drawing on a variety of research studies, population specialist Evelyn Kitagawa (1972) estimated the "excess mortality rate" to be 20 percent. In other words, 20 per-

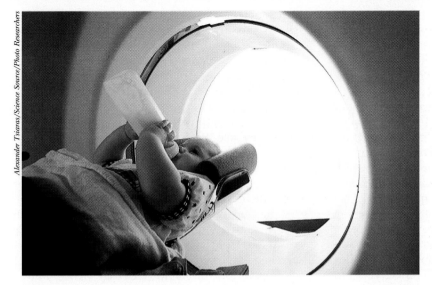

Health costs in the United States have escalated in part because of increasing use of expensive technology. The CAT scanner, a direct descendant of the X-ray machine, uses a computer to integrate pictures shot from various angles into a single, multidimensional image of a toddler's (or an adult's) skull.

cent more people were dying than otherwise might have, because of differentially poor health linked to race and class. Using Kitagawa's model, we can calculate that if every person in the United States were White and had at least one year of college education, some 458,000 fewer people would die in 1995 (Bureau of the Census, 1993a:19).

HEALTH CARE IN THE UNITED STATES

As the entire nation is well-aware, the costs of health care have skyrocketed in the last 20 years. For example, in 1991 total expenditures for health care in the United States reached $809 billion, almost twice the 1985 figure (see Figure 17-3). The amount we now spend on health care equals that spent on education, defense, prisons, farm subsidies, food stamps, and foreign aid combined. Moreover, it is estimated that by the year 2000, total expenditures for health care in the United States will rise to $1.5 to $2 *trillion* (K. Anderson, 1991; Hasson, 1992; Welch, 1993).

The rising costs of medical care are especially apparent in the event of catastrophic illnesses or confinement in a nursing home. Bills of tens of thousands of dollars are not unusual in the treatment of cancer, Alzheimer's disease, and other chronic diseases requiring custodial care. Moreover, ac-

cording to a statement by a federal health official in 1992, the lifetime cost of treating an AIDS patient in the United States has reached $102,000, compared with $57,000 in 1988. At the same time,

FIGURE 17-3   Total Health Care Expenditures in the United States, 1975–2000

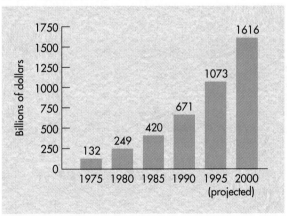

SOURCE: Hasson, 1992.

Expenditures for health care in the United States have continued to rise, reaching an all-time high of $809 billion in 1991. According to projections, expenditures for health care will reach $1.6 trillion by the year 2000.

however, even treatment of short-term illnesses for patients of all ages has come to involve greater reliance on specialists and new medical technologies —which has contributed significantly to escalating health care costs (L. Altman, 1992b:B8).

The "graying of America" (see Chapter 12) is clearly a factor in rising health care costs. Older people typically have longer stays in the hospital than younger patients, and the elderly obviously account for an overwhelming percentage of nursing home expenditures. Insurance coverage and existing federal assistance programs, such as Medicare, provide reimbursement for not quite half of all medical costs. For example, a 70-year-old person who enters the hospital four times for heart problems and surgery can easily spend $6000 that will not be covered by Medicare. Proposals to fill this "medigap," as it has been called, reflect concern about such unknown and potentially staggering costs (Mechanic, 1986; W. Stevens, 1987a).

Clearly, the health care system of the United States has moved far beyond the days when general practitioners living in a neighborhood or community typically made house calls and charged modest fees for their services. How did health care become big business involving nationwide hospital chains and marketing campaigns? How have these changes reshaped typical interactions between doctors, nurses, and patients? We will address these questions in the next section of the chapter.

A Historical View

According to sociologist Paul Starr (1982), writing in his critically acclaimed book, *The Social Transformation of American Medicine,* the authority of medical professionals rests on a system of standardized educational licensing. The establishment of such a system maintains authority from one generation to the next and transmits authority from the profession as a whole to its individual members. However, health care in the United States has not always followed this model.

The "popular health movement" of the 1830s and 1840s emphasized preventive care and what is termed "self-help." There was strong criticism of "doctoring" as a paid occupation. New medical philosophies or sects established their own medical schools and challenged the authority and methods of more traditional doctors. By the 1840s, most states had repealed medical licensing laws. However, through the leadership of the American Medical Association (AMA), founded in 1848, "regular" doctors attacked lay practitioners, sectarian doctors, and female physicians in general. (For a different view, see V. Navarro, 1984.)

The emergence of massive, organized philanthropy in the early twentieth century—administered by such organizations as the Rockefeller and Carnegie foundations—had a critical impact in reshaping and centralizing medicine. Beginning in 1903, extensive foundation support was allocated to create a respectable medical profession. A researcher employed by the Carnegie Corporation was sent to tour the nation in order to determine which medical schools should receive funding. After the publication of the Flexner report in 1910, numerous medical schools that he found unworthy of financial aid were forced to close. Among them were six of the nation's eight Black medical schools and most of the alternative schools which had been open to female students. In state after state, tough licensing laws were adopted to restrict medical practice to traditional doctors from approved institutions. As one result, babies could no longer be delivered by midwives in most states; the practice of obstetrics were restricted to physicians (Ehrenreich and English, 1973).

Once authority was institutionalized through standardized programs of education and licensing, it was conferred upon all who successfully completed these programs. Recognition became relatively unambiguous. The authority of the physician no longer depended on lay attitudes or the person occupying the sick role; it was increasingly built into the structure of the medical profession and the health care system. As the institutionalization of health care proceeded, the medical profession gained control over both the market for its services and the various organizational hierarchies that govern medical practice, financing, and policymaking. By the 1920s, physicians controlled hospital technology, the division of labor of health personnel and, indirectly, other professional practices such as nursing and pharmacy (R. Coser, 1984).

Physicians, Nurses, and Patients

The preeminence of physicians within the health care system of the United States has traditionally given them a position of dominance in their dealings with both patients and nurses. The functionalist and interactionist perspectives combine to offer a framework for understanding the professional socialization of physicians as it relates to patient care. Functionalists suggest that established physicians and medical school professors serve as mentors or role models who transmit knowledge, skills, and values to the passive learner—the medical student. Interactionists emphasize that students are molded by the medical school environment as they interact with their classmates. Both approaches argue that the typical training of physicians in the United States leads to rather dehumanizing physician-patient encounters. Despite many efforts to formally introduce a humanistic dimension of patient care into medical school curricula, patient overload and cost-containment efforts of hospitals tend to reduce positive relations. Moreover, widespread publicity concerning malpractice suits and high medical costs has further strained the physician-patient dyad (Becker et al., 1961; Merton et al., 1957; Mizrahi, 1986:14).

These problems in medicine have taken their toll on contemporary physicians. A survey conducted for the American Medical Association in 1989 revealed that 39 percent of doctors either definitely or probably would not go into medicine today if they were in college and knew what they now know about the field. This disenchantment is somewhat similar to the "burnout" experienced by teachers (refer back to Chapter 16), yet it is nevertheless surprising because physicians (unlike schoolteachers) enjoy substantial incomes and high prestige. Despite these benefits, the physicians surveyed report that they are disillusioned by the growing competition for patients, increased government regulation of medicine, and worrisome malpractice litigation (L. Altman and Rosenthal, 1990).

Interactionists have closely examined how compliance and negotiation occur between physician and patient. They concur with Talcott Parsons' view that the relationship is generally asymmetrical, with doctors holding a position of dominance and control of rewards. Just as physicians have maintained dominance in their interactions with patients, doctors have similarly controlled interactions with nurses. Despite their training and professional status, nurses commonly take orders from physicians. Traditionally, the relationship between doctors and nurses has paralleled the male dominance of the United States: most physicians have been male, whereas virtually all nurses have been female (refer back to Box 11-2 on page 321, which focuses on male nurses within a traditionally female profession).

Like other women in subordinate roles, nurses have been expected to perform their duties without challenging the authority of men. Psychiatrist Leonard Stein (1967:699–700) refers to this process as the *doctor-nurse game*. According to the rules of this "game," the nurse must never disagree openly with the physician. When she has recommendations concerning a patient's care, she must communicate them indirectly in a deferential tone. For example, if asked by a hospital's medical resident, "What sleeping medication has been helpful to Mrs. Brown in the past?" (an indirect request for a recommendation), the nurse will respond with a disguised recommendation statement, such as "Pentobarbital mg 100 was quite effective night before last." Her careful response allows the physician to authoritatively restate the same prescription as if it were *his* idea.

By the 1980s nurses in the United States were increasingly speaking out, engaging in political action, walking picket lines, and joining lawsuits—all with the goals of better pay, more respect for their professional expertise, and transformation of the health care system. Margretta Styles, president of the American Nurses Association (ANA), notes: "Nursing is 97 percent female, and the problems we face are typical of those faced in women's professions, especially low pay and low status." Both inside the hospital and in the larger political system, nurses have organized to battle for autonomy, an improved image, and fair compensation for their skill and dedication (Holcomb, 1988:74).

Like nurses, female physicians find themselves in a subordinate position due to gender. According to a report issued in 1991 by the Feminist Majority Foundation and the American Medical Women's

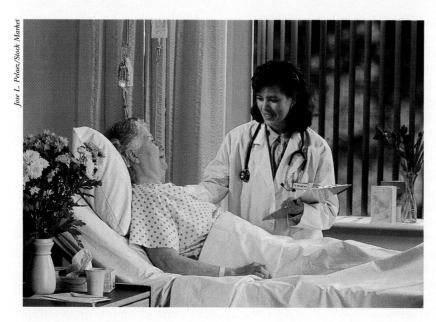

Women still receive disproportionately low pay and status within the medical profession.

Association, women still receive disproportionately low pay and status within the medical profession. In 1988, for example, women doctors earned 63 cents for each dollar earned by a male doctor. This gap in earnings is not simply the result of differing levels of experience. The American Medical Association reports that in 1987, male doctors with one to four years' experience earned an average net income of $110,600, compared with $74,000 for women doctors with comparable experience. Male physicians with 10 to 20 years' experience earned an average net income of $158,000, compared with $99,400 for female physicians with similar experience.

The 1991 report noted that although 36 percent of all medical students in the United States were female, 79 percent of medical school faculty members, 98 percent of medical school chairpersons, and *all* medical school deans were male. The American Medical Association (AMA) has never had a woman as chief executive officer in its 144-year history (J. Gross, 1991b:10; Hilts, 1991:C7).

The Role of Government

Cindy Martin died in 1990 at age 26, after four months of surgery and intensive care at Presbyterian University Hospital in Pittsburgh. In the after-

math of her death, her husband's insurance company received a bill for $1.25 million. While accountants attempted to untangle the costs of seven surgical procedures performed on Cindy Martin—including heart, liver, and kidney transplants—this case underscored troubling issues regarding the high cost of health care. Who should pay for the expensive medical procedures of the 1990s? What role, if any, should government play in providing medical care and health insurance for U.S. citizens (Freudenheim, 1990)?

The first significant involvement of the federal government in the financing of health care came with the 1946 Hill-Burton Act, which provided subsidies for building and improving hospitals, especially in rural areas. An even more important change came with the enactment of two wide-ranging government assistance programs: Medicare, which is essentially a compulsory health insurance plan for the elderly; and Medicaid, which is a noncontributory federal and state insurance plan for the poor. These programs greatly expanded federal involvement in health care financing for needy men, women, and children. In addition, over 1000 government-subsidized community health centers are located in low-income, medically underserved communities (Blendon, 1986).

Given rates of illness and disability among elderly

Jose L. Pelaez/Stock Market

people, Medicare has had a particularly noteworthy impact on the health care system of the United States. Initially, Medicare simply reimbursed health care providers such as physicians and hospitals for the costs of their services. However, as the overall costs of Medicare increased dramatically, the federal government introduced a price-control system in 1983. All illnesses were classified into 468 diagnostic-related groups (DRGs); a reimbursement rate was set for each condition and remained fixed regardless of the individual needs of any patient.

In effect, the federal government told hospitals and doctors that it would no longer be concerned with their costs in treating Medicare patients; it would reimburse them only to a designated level. If a patient is sicker than average (that is, the average set for a particular illness) and requires extra care, the hospital must absorb any expenses beyond its DRG allowance. However, if the patient is less ill than average for an illness, the hospital can essentially make a profit from the fixed level of reimbursement (Downs, 1987; Easterbrook, 1987:49).

The DRG system of reimbursement has contributed to the controversial practice of "dumping," under which patients whose treatment may be unprofitable are transferred by private hospitals to public facilities. Many private hospitals in the United States have begun to conduct routine "wallet biopsies" to investigate the financial status of potential patients; those judged as undesirable are then refused admission or are dumped. Since the introduction of DRGs, some urban public hospitals have reported 400 to 500 percent increases in the number of patients transferred from private hospitals (Feinglass, 1987).

Such dumping can have grave consequences for patients. In 1984, a Harvard Medical School team analyzed records of 458 patients transferred during a six-month period to a public hospital in Oakland, California. Researchers found that in 7.2 percent of cases, the patients were transferred before being stabilized medically; their care suffered as a result. Viewed from a conflict perspective, such practices are especially likely to hurt those people at the bottom of stratification hierarchies based on social class, race and ethnicity, gender, and age (P. Taylor, 1985:9).

During the twentieth century, one European nation after another has adopted government-sponsored national health insurance or created a national health service. By contrast, the United States government has been much less active in providing health care for its citizens. The social policy section at the end of the chapter will examine the issue of national health care insurance, which in 1993 became a major legislative focus for the Clinton administration.

Alternatives to Traditional Health Care

Thus far, we have concentrated exclusively on traditional forms of health care—particularly, reliance on physicians and hospitals for treatment of illness. Yet at least one out of every three adults in the United States attempts to maintain good health or respond to illness through use of alternative health care techniques. For example, in recent decades there has been growing interest in *holistic* (this term is also spelled *wholistic*) medical principles first developed in China. **Holistic medicine** is a means of health maintenance which views the person as an integration of body, mind, and spirit (Sirott and Waitzkin, 1984:246). The individual is regarded as a totality, rather than as a collection of interrelated organ systems. Treatment methodologies include massage, chiropractic medicine, acupuncture (which involves the insertion of fine needles into surface points), respiratory exercises, and the use of herbs as remedies. Nutrition, exercise, and "talking therapy" may also be used to treat ailments generally treated through medication or hospitalization (E. Chow, 1984; Eisenberg et al., 1993; M. Goldstein et al., 1987).

Practitioners of holistic medicine do not necessarily function totally outside the health care system. Some have medical degrees and rely on x-rays and EKG machines for diagnostic assistance. Other holistic clinics, often referred to as *wellness clinics,* reject the use of medical technology. The recent resurgence of holistic medicine comes amidst a widespread recognition of the value of nutrition and the dangers of overreliance on prescription drugs (especially those used to reduce stress, such as valium).

The medical establishment—professional organizations, research hospitals, and medical schools—has generally served as a stern protector of traditionally accepted health care techniques. How-

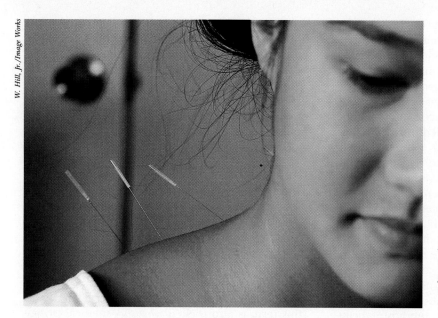

Acupuncture, which involves the insertion of fine needles into surface points, is one common treatment methodology associated with holistic medicine.

ever, a major breakthrough occurred in 1993 when the federal government's National Institutes of Health—the nation's major funding source for biomedical research—opened an Office of Alternative Medicine, empowered to accept grant requests. Potential areas of study include herbal medicine, mind-body control techniques, and the use of electromagnetism to heal bones. The director of this office, Dr. Joe Jacobs, is a Yale-trained pediatrician who became familiar with the work of Native American healers through his Mohawk mother and later through serving as a doctor on a Navajo reservation. Although the Office of Alternative Medicine was initially given only $2 million of the Institutes' $10.3 billion budget, its establishment nevertheless represents the first official recognition of alternative health care treatments (Angier, 1993a, 1993b).

In some cases, movements for political change have generated health care alternatives. For example, as part of the larger feminist movement beginning in the 1960s, women became more vocal in their dissatisfaction with the traditional health care system. Marked by the appearance of the book *Our Bodies, Ourselves* (Boston Women's Health Book Collective, 1969, 1984), the contemporary women's health movement emerged out of the realization that women are by far the most frequent users of health services for themselves, their children, and

other dependent family members. Activists agree that women should assume more responsibility for decisions concerning their health. The movement therefore has taken many forms, including organizations working for changes in the health care system, women's clinics, and birth and "self-help" groups.

Although the women's health movement supports greater access to health care for all people in the United States, it focuses on specific women's health issues such as menstruation, childbirth, abortion rights (see Chapter 11), and menopause. Women's health groups have expressed concern about the hazards of oral contraceptives and the intrauterine device (IUD)—hazards which they feel have been concealed by drug companies and the medical establishment. Activists generally favor a greater voice for women in maternity care, the establishment of midwifery centers, and full representation of female consumers on health policy-making boards. Partly in the name of equal opportunity, but also in the hope of increasing sensitivity to women within the health care establishment, the women's health movement has demanded increased entry of women into medical school and hospital administration positions. Some activists have gone so far as to endorse the exclusion of male medical students from obstetrics and gynecological specialties. Clearly, feminists are resisting the social-control aspects of the male-dominated medical hierarchy (Corea, 1977:252–266; Ruzek, 1978; Sherwin, 1992; M. Zimmerman, 1987; Zola, 1983:282).

The goals of the women's health movement are ambitious, but the health care system has proved to be fairly resistant to change. Conflict theorists point out that physicians, medical schools, hospitals, and drug companies all have a vested interest in keeping women in a rather dependent and uninformed position as health care consumers. Although there has been an increase in female doctors, women remain underrepresented in key positions in the health care system of the United States (R. Sidel and Sidel, 1984:268).

MENTAL ILLNESS IN THE UNITED STATES

Terms such as *mental illness* and *insanity* evoke dramatic and often inaccurate images of emotional problems. The media routinely emphasize the most violent behavior of those with disturbances, but mental health and mental illness can more appropriately be viewed as a continuum of behavior that we ourselves move along. Using a less sensational definition, a person can be considered to have a mental disorder "if he or she is so disturbed that coping with routine, everyday life is difficult or impossible" (J. W. Coleman and Cressey, 1980:315).

How prevalent is mental illness in the United States? In the largest study of its kind conducted in this country, Darrell Regier (1988) and his colleagues at the National Institute of Mental Health interviewed 18,571 adults. They found that, in the previous month, 15.4 percent of respondents had suffered from at least one mental disorder. The most common disorders included anxiety disorders (affecting 7 percent of those surveyed) and mood disorders (5 percent). According to Regier, the relative absence of high-quality mental health care is confirmed by the finding that only one-third of the respondents with mental disorders reported receiving treatment during the previous six months.

People in the United States have traditionally maintained a negative and suspicious view of those with mental disorders. Holding the status of "mental patient" or even "former mental patient" can have unfortunate and undeserved consequences. For example, during the 1972 election campaign, it was learned that the Democratic vice presidential nominee, Senator Thomas Eagleton of Missouri, had once received treatment for depression. Public reaction was so strong that presidential nominee George McGovern was forced to drop Eagleton from the Democratic ticket.

Politics is not the only arena where people viewed as mentally ill experience second-class treatment. Voting rights are denied in some instances, acceptance for jury duty is problematic, and past emotional problems are an issue in divorce and custody cases. Moreover, content analysis of network television programs shows mentally ill characters uniformly portrayed in a demeaning and derogatory fashion; many are labeled as "criminally insane," "wackos," or "psychos." From an interactionist perspective, a key social institution is shaping social behavior by manipulating symbols and thereby intensifying people's fears about the mentally ill (Burton, 1990; DeFleur and Dennis, 1981; Link, 1987).

Theoretical Models of Mental Disorders

In studying mental illness, we can draw on both a medical model and a more sociological approach derived from labeling theory. Each model offers distinctive assumptions regarding treatment of people with mental disorders.

The *medical model* views mental illness as a disease derived from biological causes that can be treated through medical intervention. All mental dysfunctions are attributed to physical causes—whether physiological, biochemical, or genetic. In the view of its critics, the medical model relies too heavily on chemical intervention in treating people with mental disorders. Psychologist Albert Bandura (1969:16) argues that this approach has led to the "unremitting search for drugs as quick remedies for interpersonal problems, and long-term neglect of social variables as influential determinants of deviant response patterns." Nonetheless, the medical model continues to be persuasive in treatment of mental illness—in good part because all psychiatrists are first trained as medical doctors (Cockerham, 1989; Conrad, 1975).

In contrast to the medical model, labeling theory suggests that mental illness is not really an "illness," since the individual's problems arise from living in society and not from physical maladies. Psychiatrist Thomas Szasz (1974), in his book *The Myth of Mental Illness*, which first appeared in 1961, advanced the view that numerous personality disorders are not "diseases" but simply patterns of conduct labeled as disorders by significant others. The response to Szasz's challenging thesis was sharp: the commissioner of the New York State Department of Hygiene demanded his dismissal from his university position because Szasz did not "believe" in mental illness. By contrast, many sociologists embraced his model as a logical extension of examining individual behavior in a social context. As we have noted throughout this textbook, a given behavior may be viewed as normal in one society, disapproved of but tolerated in a second, and labeled as "sick" and heavily sanctioned in a third.

Although labeling will not typically "make sane people insane," it undoubtedly causes mentally ill patients to feel that they are devalued by the larger society. And the more they believe they are being negatively labeled, the more difficult they will find it to interact with others. Some mentally ill people may keep their problems and treatment a secret and may withdraw from social contacts. Such coping strategies to deal with labeling can lead to negative consequences in terms of employment, social support networks, and self-esteem (Cockerham, 1989:252–256; for a different view, see Gove, 1970, 1975, 1980:103; Link et al., 1989).

In reviewing the medical and labeling models of mental illness, we can conclude that neither model offers a satisfactory overall explanation. The medical model is persuasive because it pinpoints causes of mental illness and treatments for disorders. Yet proponents of the labeling perspective maintain that mental illness is a distinctively social process, whatever other processes are involved. From a sociological perspective, the ideal approach to mental illness integrates the insights of labeling theory with those of the medical approach (Scheff, 1975a, 1975b:256–257; see also Meile, 1986; Thoits, 1985).

Patterns of Care

For most of human history, those suffering from mental disorders were deemed the responsibility of their families. Yet mental illness has been a matter of governmental concern much longer than physical illness has. This is because severe emotional disorders threaten stable social relationships and entail prolonged incapacitation (Clausen, 1979:105). As early as the 1600s, European cities began to confine the insane in public facilities along with the poor and criminals. This development brought resistance from prisoners, who were indignant at being forced to live with "lunatics." The isolation of the mentally ill from others in the same facility and from the larger society made physicians the central and ultimate authority for their welfare.

In the United States, the period of the 1840s and 1850s was the "age of the asylum." Before 1810, only a few states had institutions for the mentally ill, but by 1860, 28 of the nation's 33 states had such public facilities. The asylum was put forward as a humanitarian and even utopian institution which would rehabilitate the suffering and serve as a model facility for the rest of society. Its social structure emphasized discipline, neatness, fixed schedules, and work assignments for patients. Existing relationships were deemphasized; families were discouraged from visiting with patients because they would disrupt hospital routines (Perrucci, 1974; Rothman, 1971).

As noted in Chapter 4, the residential mental hospital is an example of a total institution in which people are removed from the larger society for an appreciable period of time. Drawing on the work of Erving Goffman, Harold Garfinkel (1956) revealed that people in total institutions undergo "degradation ceremonies" which strip them of their identities, destroy personal dignity, and often lead to confusion and distress. From a functionalist perspective, the crowding and depersonalization inherent in mental hospitals are dysfunctional to society's resolving emotional problems.

A major policy development in caring for those with mental disorders came with the passage of the 1963 Community Mental Health Centers Act. The CMHC program, as it is known, was significant in increasing federal government involvement in the treatment of the mentally ill. It also marked acceptance of the view that community-based mental health centers (which treat clients on an outpatient basis, thereby allowing them to continue working and living at home) provide more effective treat-

Patients in residential mental hospitals undergo "degradation ceremonies" which strip them of identity and destroy personal dignity.

ment than the institutionalized programs of state and county mental hospitals do.

The expansion of the federally funded CMHC program decreased inpatient care. Consequently, by the 1980s, community-based mental health care replaced hospitalization as the typical form of treatment. The deinstitutionalization of the mentally ill reached dramatic proportions across the United States. Whereas state mental hospitals had held almost 560,000 long-term patients in 1955, by 1993 they held fewer than 100,000 patients (Sack, 1993).

Deinstitutionalization was often defended as a social reform which would effectively reintegrate the mentally ill into the outside world. However, the authentic humanitarian concern behind deinstitutionalization proved to be convenient for politicians whose goal was simply cost cutting. Sociologist P. R. Dingman (1974:48) has argued that the principal factor in getting rid of state mental hospitals was the rising cost of maintaining such institutions.

Moreover, because of severe financial cutbacks fueled by the recessions of the 1970s and 1980s, community care is far from adequate, especially in major cities and rural areas. Although the CMHC program was originally intended to include some 2000 community centers, only 760 are currently in operation (Bureau of the Census, 1993a:130; Elshtain, 1981).

A report released in 1990 by the Public Citizen Research Group and the National Alliance for the Mentally Ill reveals that more than 250,000 people with serious mental illnesses (schizophrenia or manic-depressive illness) are living untreated in public shelters, on the streets, or in jails. By contrast, only 68,000 people with such illnesses are in mental hospitals. In the view of Dr. E. Fuller Torrey, a psychiatrist who served as lead author of this report, there has been a "near total breakdown in public psychiatric services in the United States" (Hilts, 1990a:A28).

- Which people are especially likely to be without health insurance coverage?
- If the United States adopted nationalized health care, how would it change the position of physicians within the health care system?
- Viewed from a conflict perspective, why is it difficult to achieve basic change within the health care system of the United States?

Each year, people in the United States spend about $800 billion on health care, and that figure continues to rise dramatically (refer back to Figure 17-3). Health care has become a serious economic issue for many individuals and families, who fear (with reason) that illness can lead to economic catastrophe. Because of the skyrocketing costs of all medical services—but particularly hospitalization—the issue of health insurance is on the minds of many citizens and legislators in the United States. Indeed, a national survey in 1993 found that 79 percent of respondents (and 94 percent of African Americans and Hispanics) endorsed the general concept of a national health care policy (Clements, 1993).

At present, the United States remains the only western industrial democracy that does not treat health care as a basic right. Conflict theorists argue that this difference reflects an underlying and disturbing aspect of capitalism: illness may be exploited for profit. While other western democracies have adopted government-sponsored national health insurance or created a national health service, the American Medical Association (AMA) has played a major role in blocking such measures in the United States. The AMA has exacerbated fears about "socialized medicine" and has encouraged the public to believe that the "sacred doctor-patient relationship" would become less personal and intimate in any governmental health system. Yet even the editors of the *Journal of the American Medical Association,* writing of the institutional racism of the nation's health care system, have concluded that "it is not a coincidence that the United States of America and the Republic of South Africa . . ." are the only developed, institutionalized countries that do not ensure access to basic health care for all citizens (Lundberg, 1991:2566).

Most people in the United States currently hold some form of private health insurance, such as Blue Cross (which covers many hospital costs), Blue Shield (which covers doctors' fees during hospitalization), or both. Hundreds of firms supply such insurance to the public and reap substantial profits. In addition, millions of people are covered by Medicare and Medicaid, two programs passed by Congress in the 1960s to assist senior citizens and the poor in paying their health care bills.

According to the National Center for Health Statistics (1993a), as of 1992 some 37 million people in the United States had no health insurance. The uninsured typically include self-employed people with limited incomes, illegal immigrants, and single and divorced mothers who are the sole providers for their families. Blacks and especially Hispanics are less likely than Whites to carry private health insurance. In 1992, 32 percent of Hispanics were uninsured, compared with 21 percent of African Americans and 11 percent of Whites. Currently, the segment of the nation's population without health insurance remains high, both because the costs of private coverage are rising sharply and because many private insurers now refuse to create policies for individuals and groups viewed as "high risks" because of their medical histories.

People without health insurance may be vulnerable to a lower quality of medical care than those who are covered. According to a study of nearly 600,000 patients hospitalized in 1987 in a national sample of hospitals, patients without health insurance are significantly more likely to die than are patients who have private health insurance. Moreover, a study released in 1992—which analyzed more than 30,000 medical records in city hospitals in New York City—found that uninsured patients had more than twice the risk of receiving substandard care than did privately insured patients. This was true regardless of the gender, race, or income of the patients (Burstin et al., 1992; Hadley et al., 1991:374–379).

With such disturbing inequities in mind, policymakers have expressed renewed interest in the pos-

The American Medical Association (AMA) has played a major role in blocking national health insurance or the creation of a national health service in the United States.

sibility of national health insurance. *National health insurance* is a general term for legislative proposals that focus on ways to provide the entire population with health care services. First discussed by government officials in the 1930s, it has come to mean many different things, ranging from narrow health insurance coverage with minimal federal subsidies to broad coverage with large-scale federal funding. As of mid-1994, at least 20 health care bills were pending in Congress. Experts divide these proposals into four basic categories:

- *"Pay or play."* Employers either would provide basic health coverage for all workers or would be required to pay into a fund to assist government in extending coverage to those who are currently uninsured.
- *Tax credits and vouchers.* Each person would receive either a full tax credit to buy health coverage, a partial tax credit, or (in the case of the poor) a tax-supported voucher.
- *A managed market.* Employers and government would bargain with existing health care plans and with networks of physicians and hospitals to ensure affordable care for all and more effective control of health care costs.
- *Universal health care.* All residents would be entitled to health care funded primarily through tax revenues. People would choose their physicians,

who would be paid by government (V. Cohn, 1992:7).

Opponents of broad national health insurance insist that any of these proposals would be extremely costly and would lead to significant tax increases. Defenders of the proposals counter that other countries have maintained broad governmental health coverage for decades:

- Great Britain's National Health Service is almost totally tax-supported, and health care services (including medical visits and hospitalization) are free to all citizens.
- Under Sweden's national health system, medical care is delivered primarily by publicly funded hospitals and clinics, while a national health insurance system sets fees for health care services and reimburses providers of health care.
- Although Canadians rely on private physicians and hospitals for day-to-day treatment, health care is guaranteed as a right for all citizens. Income taxes are used to finance public medical insurance, medical fees are set by the government, and private health insurance is prohibited.
- Australia has universal health coverage provided by the government and supplemented by private insurance companies. The government sets basic fees for medical services, but patients can choose their own physicians.

Ironically, while these countries offer extensive health coverage for all citizens, the United States has higher health care costs than any other nation: an average annual cost of $2566 per person, compared with $1770 in Canada and only $972 in Great Britain (Farnsworth, 1993; Marmor and Godfrey, 1992; Ridgeway, 1993; Rodell, 1993; Twaddle and Hessler, 1987).

Critics point out that if the United States were to move in the direction of nationalized health care as in Great Britain or Sweden, there would be a marked transformation in the health care system as a social institution. With medicine under tight control by the federal government (which would own and operate all hospitals), the doctor-patient relationship would be altered, since an individual would not necessarily have a "family doctor." Physicians and dentists would no longer be self-employed professionals who would set their own fees. Instead, they would become salaried professionals working for the government. As one consequence, the dominant role of doctors in the health care system might be diminished somewhat. Under such a national health care service, physicians, nurses, technicians, and other health care staff would all work for a common "boss" in Washington.

In late 1993, after seven months of secret deliberations by a health care advisory group headed by Hillary Rodham Clinton, President Bill Clinton unveiled a bold plan to guarantee health insurance coverage for all people in the United States by 1998 while dramatically expanding the federal government's power to control health care costs. Under this plan, everyone would have to carry health insurance and contribute to its cost, but government subsidies would be extended to the poor. Officials estimate that the average premium for a basic benefits package would be $1800 per year for an individual and $4200 for a two-parent family; employers would pay 80 percent of these costs, while the employee would pay 20 percent. Children's dental care, increased mental health coverage, and pregnancy services (including abortions) would be included in the benefits package. Cost controls would come through a system of "managed competition," since regional health alliances would purchase care from competing networks of physicians, hospitals, and insurance companies. The ensuing competition between these networks ideally would restrict health care costs and improve the quality of care. As of mid-1994, there was fierce debate in Congress about the Clinton health plan and competing legislative proposals.

As conflict theorists suggest, the health care system, like other social institutions, resists basic change. In general, those who receive substantial wealth and power through the workings of an existing institution will have a strong incentive to keep things as they are. As explained earlier, private insurance companies are benefiting financially from the current system and have a clear interest in opposing certain forms of national health insurance. In addition, the American Medical Association, one of Washington's most powerful lobbying groups, has been successfully fighting national health insurance since the 1930s. Overall, there are more than 200 political action committees (PACs) which represent the medical, pharmaceutical, and insurance industries. These PACs contribute millions of dollars each year to members of Congress and use their influence to block any legislation that would threaten their interests (Dolbeare, 1982; Kemper and Novak, 1991).

SUMMARY

The meanings of **health,** wellness, sickness, and disease are shaped by social definitions of behavior. This chapter considers sociological perspectives on health and illness, the distribution of diseases in a society, the evolution of the health care system as a social institution, and mental illness in the United States.

1 A relativistic approach to healthy status allows us to view health in a social context and to consider how health varies in different situations or cultures.

2 According to Talcott Parsons, physicians function as "gatekeepers" for the **sick role,** either verifying a person's condition as "ill" or designating the person as "recovered."

3 Conflict theorists use the term *medicalization of society* to refer to medicine's growing role as a major institution of social control.

4 Interactionists emphasize that the patient should not always be viewed as a passive actor within the health care system.

5 Labeling theorists suggest that the designation of a person as "healthy" or "ill" generally involves social definition by significant others.

6 Contemporary *social epidemiology* is concerned not only with epidemics but also with nonepidemic diseases, injuries, drug addiction and alcoholism, suicide, and mental illness.

7 Studies have consistently shown that people in the lower classes have higher rates of mortality and disability.

8 The preeminent role of physicians within the health care system has given them a position of dominance in their dealings with nurses and patients.

9 The DRG system of reimbursement has contributed to the controversial practice of "dumping," under which patients whose treatment may be unprofitable are transferred by private hospitals to public facilities.

10 People in the United States have traditionally maintained a negative and suspicious view of those with mental disorders.

11 At present, the United States remains the only western industrial democracy that does not treat health care as a basic right.

CRITICAL THINKING QUESTIONS

1 Sociologist Talcott Parsons has argued that the doctor-patient relationship is somewhat like that between parent and child. Does this view seem accurate? Should the doctor-patient relationship become more egalitarian? How might functionalist and conflict theorists differ in their views of the power of physicians within the health care system of the United States?

2 In the 1990s, what does it mean to carry a label associated with a disability, such as "blind," "deaf," or "wheelchair user"? Are there strong stigmata attached to labels which suggest physical or mental disabilities? Are students with disabilities generally accepted in your college and your community? Are there explicit challenges to negative labeling of such students?

3 Imagine that your instructor has asked you to develop a survey concerning people's attitudes toward alternatives to traditional health care, such as acupuncture and chiropractic medicine. How would you select a sample for this study? What kinds of questions would you ask?

KEY TERMS

Culture-bound syndrome A disease or illness that cannot be understood apart from its specific social context. (page 478)

Health As defined by the World Health Organization, a state of complete physical, mental, and social well-being, and not merely the absence of disease and infirmity. (480)

Holistic medicine A means of health maintenance which views the person as an integration of body, mind, and spirit, rather than as a collection of interrelated organ systems. (495)

Incidence The number of new cases of a specific disorder occurring within a given population during a stated period of time. (486)

Infant mortality rate The number of deaths of infants under 1 year of age per 1000 live births in a given year. (482)

Morbidity rates The incidence of diseases in a given population. (486)

Mortality rate   The incidence of death in a given population. (486)

Prevalence   The total number of cases of a specific disorder that exist at a given time. (486)

Sick role   Societal expectations about the attitudes and behavior of a person viewed as being ill. (480)

Social epidemiology   The study of the distribution of disease, impairment, and general health status across a population. (486)

ADDITIONAL READINGS

Bosk, Charles L. *All God's Mistakes: Genetic Counseling in a Pediatric Hospital.* Chicago: University of Chicago Press, 1992. Drawing on observation research, Bosk provides an inside look at how a genetic counseling team interacts with parents and with one another.

Conrad, Peter, and Joseph W. Schneider. *Deviance and Medicalization: From Badness to Sickness* (expanded ed.). Philadelphia: Temple University Press, 1992. In examining such topics as drug use, mental illness, and child abuse, the authors weigh the fine line between defining cases as deviance or as medical problems.

Fox, Renee C., and Judith P. Swazey. *Spare Parts: Organ Replacement in American Society.* New York: Oxford University Press, 1992. The authors argue that the concept of organ donation as a gift is gradually being replaced by the view that human organs required for transplants are a special type of commodity.

McBride, David. *From TB to AIDS: Epidemics among Urban Blacks since 1900.* Albany: State University of New York Press, 1991. An unusual book which focuses on the public health of African Americans and how the relative prevalence of tuberculosis and AIDS among Blacks created health care crises.

Payer, Lynn. *Medicine and Culture: Varieties of Treatment in the United States, England, West Germany, and France.* New York: Holt, 1988. A medical journalist examines the ways in which culture contributes to differences in medical care in four industrialized nations.

Sherwin, Susan. *No Longer Patient: Feminist Ethics and Health Care.* Philadelphia: Temple University Press, 1992. An introduction to the feminist perspective on ethical judgments made in medicine.

Smolan, Rick, Phillip Moffit, and Matthew Naythons (eds.). *The Power to Heal: Ancient Arts and Modern Medicine.* Englewood Cliffs, N.J.: Prentice-Hall, 1990. An illustrated look at medicine as it is practiced throughout the world.

Waitzkin, Howard. *The Second Sickness: Contradictions of Capitalist Health Care.* Chicago: University of Chicago Press, 1986. This indictment of medical care delivery in the United States offers interesting comparisons with health care in Cuba and the People's Republic of China.

World Bank. *World Development Report 1993: Investing in Health.* New York: Oxford University Press, 1993. This international agency's annual report examines health care policies worldwide and analyzes their relative success in improving health and limiting health spending.

Zussman, Robert. *Intensive Care: Medical Ethics and the Medical Profession.* Chicago: University of Chicago Press, 1992. Intensive care units in hospitals—filled with critically ill patients and expensive technology—are testing grounds for fundamental ethical questions. Zussman examines the processes through which these questions are negotiated.

Journals

Among the journals dealing with issues of health, illness, and health care are *Journal of Health and Social Behavior* (founded in 1965), *Milbank Memorial Quarterly* (1923), and *Social Science and Medicine* (1967).

PART FIVE

CHANGING

SOCIETY

CHANGING

SOCIETY

Throughout this textbook, we have been reminded that sociologists are vitally concerned with changes in cultures, social institutions, and social behavior. Part Five will focus more directly on change as a characteristic aspect of human societies.

Chapter 18 describes changes in human communities, with particular emphasis on urban and metropolitan growth. The diversity of suburban and rural communities will also be demonstrated. Chapter 19 considers changing patterns of population growth and their social consequences in the United States and throughout the world. The chapter also focuses on the environmental issues that confront our planet as we move toward the twenty-first century. Chapter 20 offers sociological analysis of social change as reflected in collective behavior and social movements. In the book's epilogue, we offer a sociological view of technological changes and the ways in which they are reshaping our future.

18

COMMUNITIES

HOW DID COMMUNITIES ORIGINATE?
Early Communities
Preindustrial Cities
Industrial Cities

SOCIOLOGICAL APPROACHES TO COMMUNITIES
Ecological Views of Urban Growth
Conflict View of Urban Growth
Models of Community Attachment
  Linear-Development Model
  Systemic Model

TYPES OF COMMUNITIES
Central Cities

Who Lives in the Cities?
  Social Problems of Cities
Suburbs
  Suburban Expansion
  Diversity in the Suburbs
Rural Communities

SOCIAL POLICY AND COMMUNITIES: HOMELESSNESS

BOXES
18-1 Current Research: Urban Apartheid in the United States
18-2 Speaking Out: The Death of a Family Farm

> *The city is rooted in the habits and customs of the people who inhabit it.*
>
> Robert E. Park and Ernest W. Burgess
> *The City,* 1925

LOOKING AHEAD

- How do industrial cities differ from earlier forms of human communities?
- What theories have social scientists proposed to explain the process of urban growth?
- What effect does the size of a community have on people's feelings of identity and belonging?
- What types of people tend to be found in cities?
- What factors have contributed to suburban expansion?
- Why have rural communities experienced increasing economic problems in recent decades?
- How has the profile of homeless people in the United States changed in the last 15 years?

Today, the suburban mall is a significant retailing and social center for communities across the United States. For parents caring for young children during weekday shopping hours—for teenagers after school or on weekends—the mall may be a comfortable place to interact with peers. Nevertheless, while malls serve positive social functions for many people, malls do not necessarily welcome everyone.

This was evident in 1987 when the manager of a mall in South Bend, Indiana, opposed a "holiday shopper" shuttle bus service. This service would have provided additional buses to enable poor and primarily African American residents to come to the mall during the busy Christmas season. Even though retail businesses normally want as many customers as possible, mall officials regarded these bus riders—in the words of the manager—as "downtowners" and "westsiders" who would be "undesirable" at the mall. It was easier, of course, to use such code words than to explicitly state that the mall viewed low-income and Black consumers as "undesirable" (Rochberg-Halton, 1991:6).

As we will see in this chapter, neighborhoods and even suburban malls play an important role in people's lives. They do so by giving people the feeling that they are part of a community (although sometimes this community feeling is based in part on the exclusion of others viewed as different and "undesirable"). In sociological terms, a **community** is a spatial or territorial unit of social organization in which people have a sense of identity and a feeling of belonging (Dotson, 1991).

Communities influence who our friends will be, since it is difficult to maintain more than a few friendships over long distances. Communities also have an impact on the types of occupations that people seek to enter. A member of an Israeli *kibbutz*—a collective society in which all members share in ownership of community assets and governance—may decide to study irrigation or some other aspect of farming in order to best serve the larger group. Perhaps most important, communities define social standards and exercise formal and informal social control. In 1973, the United States Supreme Court identified "community standards" as appropriate criteria for evaluating whether a book or film is pornographic and can be prohibited from sale.

Anthropologist George Murdock (1949:79) has observed that there are only two truly universal units of human social organization: the family and the community. This chapter will explore the importance of communities from a sociological perspective. It will begin by examining the successive development of early communities, preindustrial cities, and industrial cities. A number of theories used by social scientists to explain urban growth will be presented, including ecological perspectives and conflict theory. Then, the three basic types of communities found in the United States—central cities, suburbs, and rural areas—will be contrasted. Finally, in the social policy section, we will analyze the distressing phenomenon of homelessness in the United States.

HOW DID COMMUNITIES ORIGINATE?

Early Communities

For most of human history, people used *subsistence technology*—the tools, processes, and knowledge that a society requires to meet its basic needs for survival. Thus, the need for an adequate food supply was satisfied through hunting, foraging for fruits or vegetables, fishing, and herding. In comparison with later industrial societies, early civilizations were much more dependent on the physical environment and much less able to alter that environment to their advantage. As we saw in Chapter 15, the emergence of horticultural societies, in which people actually cultivated food rather than merely gathered fruits and vegetables, led to many dramatic changes in human social organization.

Significantly, people no longer had to move from place to place in search of food. In fact, group cultivation required that people remain in specific locations and thereby encouraged the development of more stable and enduring communities. Ultimately, as agricultural techniques became more and more sophisticated, a cooperative division of labor involving both family members and others developed. It gradually became possible for people to produce more food than they actually needed for themselves. Consequently, food could be given, perhaps as part of an exchange, to others who might

be involved in nonagricultural labor. This transition from subsistence to surplus represented a critical step in the emergence of cities.

The term *social surplus* refers to the production by a group of people of enough goods to cover their own needs, while at the same time sustaining people who are not engaged in agricultural tasks. Initially, the social surplus of early communities was limited to agricultural products, but it gradually evolved to include all types of goods and services. Residents of a city came to rely on community members who provided crafts products and means of transportation, gathered information, and so forth (Lenski et al., 1991; F. Wilson, 1984:297–298).

With this social surplus came a more elaborate division of labor, as well as a greater opportunity for differential rewards and privileges. So long as everyone was engaged in the same tasks, stratification was limited to such factors as gender, age, and perhaps the ability to perform the task (a skillful hunter could win unusual respect from the community). However, the social surplus allowed for expansion of goods and services, which ironically can lead to greater differentiation, a hierarchy of occupations, and social inequality. Therefore, social surplus was a precondition not only for the establishment of cities but also for the division of members of a community into social classes (see Chapter 8). The emergence of social surplus marked a fundamental shift in human social organization.

Preindustrial Cities

It is estimated that, beginning about 10,000 B.C., permanent settlements free from dependence on crop cultivation emerged. Yet, by today's standards of population, these early communities would barely qualify as cities. The *preindustrial city,* as it is termed, had only a few thousand people living within its borders. These residents relied on perhaps 100,000 farmers and their own part-time farming to provide them with the needed agricultural surplus. The Mesopotamian city of Ur had a population of about 10,000 and was limited to roughly 220 acres of land, including the canals, the temple, and the harbor.

Why were these early cities so small and relatively few in number? Urbanization was restricted by a number of key factors:

1 *Reliance on animal power (both humans and beasts of burden) as a source of energy for economic production.* This limited the ability of humans to make use of and alter the physical environment.

2 *Modest levels of surplus produced by the agricultural sector.* Sociologist Kingsley Davis (1949) has estimated that between 50 and 90 farmers were required to support 1 city resident.

3 *Problems in transportation and storage of food and other goods.* Even an excellent crop could easily be lost as a result of such difficulties.

4 *Hardships of migration to the city.* For many peasants, migration was both physically and economically impossible. A few weeks of travel was out of the question without more sophisticated techniques of food storage.

5 *Dangers of city life.* Concentrating a society's population in a small area left a society open to attack from outsiders, as well as more susceptible to extreme damages from plagues and fires.

Gideon Sjoberg (1960:27–31) examined the available information on early urban settlements of medieval Europe, India, and China. He identified three preconditions of city life: advanced technology in both agricultural and nonagricultural areas

(that is, the creation of a social surplus), a favorable physical environment, and a well-developed social organization.

For Sjoberg, the criteria for defining a "favorable" physical environment are variable. Proximity to coal and iron will be helpful only if a society has the technological expertise to use these natural resources. Similarly, proximity to a river will be particularly beneficial if a culture has the means to transport water efficiently to the fields for irrigation and to the cities for consumption.

A sophisticated social organization is also an essential precondition for urban existence. Specialized social roles emerge more fully in industrial societies than in earlier communities. These roles bring people together in new ways through the exchange of goods and services. A well-developed social organization ensures that these relationships are clearly defined and generally acceptable to all parties. This function becomes even more crucial as cities become larger and more industrialized.

Industrial Cities

Advances in agricultural technology led to dramatic changes in community life, but so did the process of industrialization. As was noted in Chapter 15, the *industrial revolution,* which began in the middle of the eighteenth century, focused on the application of nonanimal sources of power to labor tasks. Industrialization had a wide range of effects on people's lifestyles as well as on the structure of communities. Emerging urban settlements became centers not only of industry but also of banking, finance, and industrial management.

The factory system which developed during the industrial revolution led to a much more refined division of labor than was evident in early preindustrial cities. Many new occupations were created, and one by-product was a much more complex set of relationships among workers. Thus, the *industrial city* was not merely more populous than its preindustrial predecessors; it was also based on very different principles of social organization. Contrasts between preindustrial and industrial cities were outlined by Sjoberg (1960:323–328) and are summarized in Table 18-1.

In comparison with industrial cities, preindustrial cities had relatively closed class systems and limited social mobility as well as a much more rigid division of labor by gender. Status in these early cities was based on ascribed characteristics such as family background. Education was limited to members of the elite. However, in industrial cities, formal education gradually became available to many children from poor and working-class families. While ascribed characteristics such as gender, race, and ethnicity remained important, there was a greater opportunity for a talented or skilled individual to better his or her social position. In these and other respects, the industrial city is genuinely a "different world" from the preindustrial urban community.

SOCIOLOGICAL APPROACHES TO COMMUNITIES

Ecological Views of Urban Growth

Human ecology is concerned with the interrelationships among people in their spatial setting and physical environment. Human ecologists have long been interested in how the physical environment shapes people's lives (rivers can serve as a barrier to residential expansion) and also how people influence the surrounding environment (the advent of air-conditioning has played a critical role in the growth of major metropolitan areas in the southwest). *Urban ecology* focuses on such interrelationships as they emerge in urban areas.

Early urban ecologists such as Robert Park (1916, 1936) and Ernest Burgess (1925) concentrated on city life but drew on the approaches used by ecologists in studying plant and animal communities. With few exceptions, urban ecologists trace their work back to the *concentric-zone theory* devised in the 1920s by Burgess (see Figure 18-1 on page 514). Using the city of Chicago as an example, Burgess offered a framework for describing land use in industrial cities. At the center, or nucleus, of such a city is the central business district. Large department stores, hotels, theaters, and financial institutions occupy this highly valued land. Surrounding this urban center are succeeding zones that contain other types of land use and that illustrate the growth of the urban area over time.

Encircling the central business district is the "zone of transition," which has a temporary character, since its residents are in the immediate path

TABLE 18-1	Comparing Preindustrial and Industrial Cities
PREINDUSTRIAL CITIES	INDUSTRIAL CITIES
Closed class system— pervasive influence of social class at birth	Open class system— mobility based on achieved characteristics
Economic realm controlled by guilds and a few families	Relatively open competition
Beginnings of division of labor in creation of goods	Elaborate specialization in manufacturing of goods
Pervasive influence of religion on social norms	Influence of religion limited to certain areas as society becomes more secularized
Little standardization of prices, weights, and measures	Standardization enforced by custom and law
Population largely illiterate, communication by word of mouth	Emergence of communication through posters, bulletins, and newspapers
Schools limited to elites and designed to perpetuate their privileged status	Formal schooling open to the masses and viewed as a means of advancing the social order

SOURCE: Based on G. Sjoberg, 1960:323–328.

Industrial cities differed from their preindustrial forerunners in many important respects. They not only were larger but also had open class systems, relatively open competition, and elaborate specialization in the manufacturing of goods.

FIGURE 18-1 *Burgess's Concentric-Zone Theory*

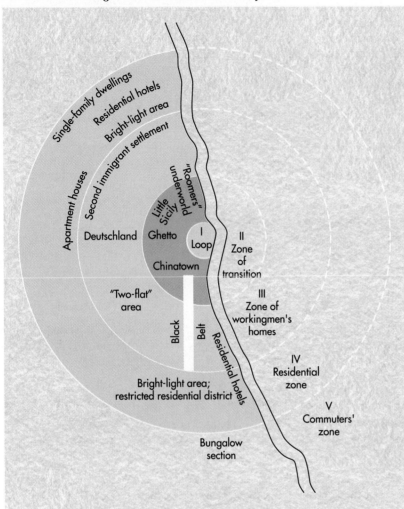

Single-family dwellings

Residential hotels

Bright-light area

Second immigrant settlement

Apartment houses

Deutschland

Little Sicily

Ghetto

"Roomers" underworld

I
Loop

II
Zone
of
transition

Chinatown

"Two-flat"
area

Black

Belt

Residential hotels

III
Zone of
workingmen's
homes

IV
Residential
zone

Bright-light area;
restricted residential district

V
Commuters'
zone

Bungalow
section

The concentric-zone hypothesis was developed by Ernest Burgess to describe housing and social characteristics of Chicago. However, the model proved to have wider applications.

SOURCE:: E. Burgess, 1925:55.

of business and industrial expansion. Homes in this area are generally unpopular; most people do not wish to live next to a factory. The zone of transition is populated by those at the bottom of the nation's social hierarchies, including recent immigrants and the poor. When people living in this zone achieve upward mobility, they frequently move to the outer zones of residential housing.

It must be stressed that the creation of zones is a *social* process, not the result of nature alone. Families and business firms compete for the most valuable land; those possessing the most wealth and power are generally the winners. The concentric-zone theory proposed by Burgess also represented a dynamic model of urban growth. As urban growth proceeded, each zone would move even further from the central business district.

By the middle of the twentieth century, urban populations had spilled beyond the traditional city limits. No longer could urban ecologists focus exclusively on *growth* in the central city, for large numbers of urban residents were abandoning the cities to live in suburban areas. As a response to the emergence of more than one focal point in some metropolitan areas, C. D. Harris and Edward L. Ullman (1945) presented the ***multiple-nuclei theory.*** In their view, all urban growth does not radiate outward from a central business district. Instead, a metropolitan area may have many centers of development, each of which reflects a particular urban need or activity. Thus, a city may have a financial district, a manufacturing zone, a waterfront area, an entertainment center, and so forth. Certain types of business firms and certain types of housing will naturally cluster around each distinctive nucleus.

The rise of suburban shopping malls is a vivid example of the phenomenon of multiple nuclei within metropolitan areas. Initially, all major retailing in cities was located in the central business district. Each residential neighborhood had its own grocers, bakers, and butchers, but people traveled to the center of the city to make major purchases at department stores. However, as major metropolitan areas expanded and the suburbs became more populous, an increasing number of people began to shop nearer their homes. Today, the suburban mall is a significant retailing and social center for communities across the United States.

In a refinement of multiple-nuclei theory, contemporary urban ecologists have begun to study what journalist Joel Garreau (1991) has called "edge cities." These communities, which have grown up on the outskirts of major metropolitan areas, are economic and social centers with identities of their own. (The edge cities surrounding Phoenix, Arizona, are shown in Figure 18-2 on page 516.) By any standard of measurement—height of buildings, amount of office space, presence of medical facilities, presence of leisure-time facilities, or, of course, population—edge cities qualify as urban areas rather than as large suburbs (B. O'Hare, 1992).

The 1990 census was the first to demonstrate that more than half the population of the United States lives in 39 metropolitan areas—each with 1 million or more residents. In only three states (Mississippi, Vermont, and West Virginia) do more than half the residents live in rural areas. Clearly, urbanization has become a central aspect of life in the United States (Bureau of the Census, 1991d).

It is important to emphasize that urbanization is evident not only in the United States but throughout the world. In 1920, only 14 percent of the world's people lived in urban areas, but by 1990 that proportion had risen to 43 percent and by the year 2025 it is expected to be as high as 61 percent (see Figure 18-3 on page 517). During the nineteenth and early twentieth centuries, rapid urbanization occurred primarily in European and North

Shown is a squatter settlement in Mexico City. Residents of squatter settlements generally have substandard housing and receive few public services.

Dagmar Fabricius/Stock, Boston

FIGURE 18-2 Edge Cities Near Phoenix, Arizona

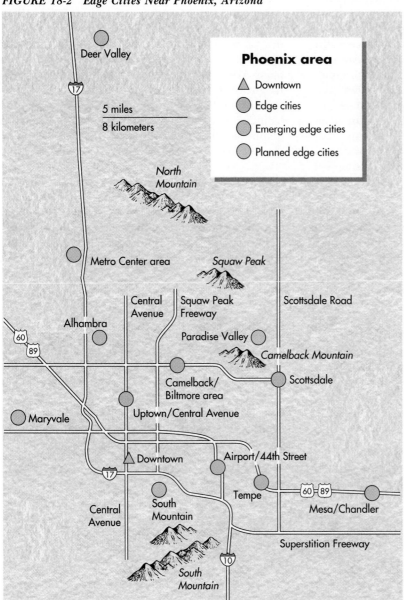

SOURCE: Garreau, 1991:181.

This figure shows the downtown area of Phoenix, Arizona, along with edge cities, emerging edge cities, and planned edge cities. Edge cities are economic and social centers with identities of their own which have grown up on the outskirts of major metropolitan areas.

The figure on the opposite page, based on consumer graphics prepared by the Los Alamos Laboratory, shows the astonishing changes that are occurring in major metropolitan areas across the world. In 1950, only ten cities had 5 million or more inhabitants. However, according to projections made by the United Nations, 48 cities will have 5 million or more people by the year 2000.

FIGURE 18-3   Urban Population Worldwide

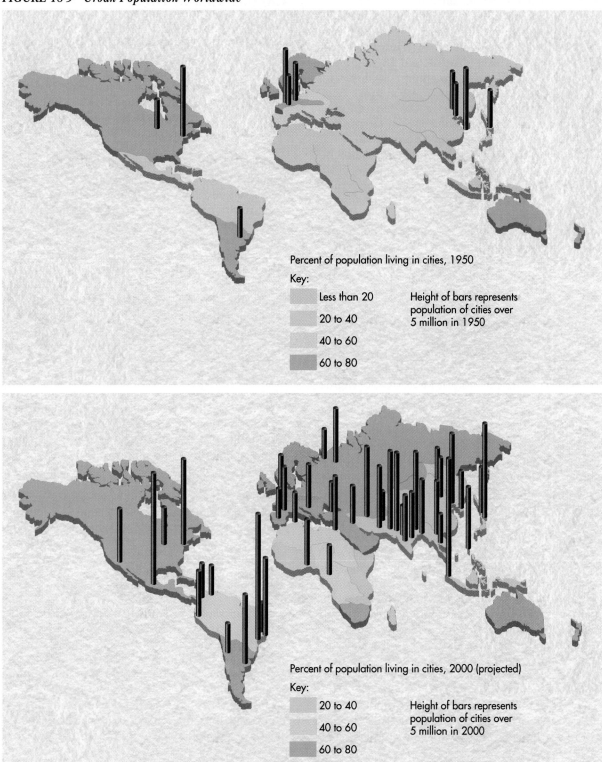

Percent of population living in cities, 1950

Key:

Less than 20

20 to 40   Height of bars represents
                 population of cities over
40 to 60   5 million in 1950

60 to 80

Percent of population living in cities, 2000 (projected)

Key:

20 to 40

40 to 60   Height of bars represents
                  population of cities over
60 to 80   5 million in 2000

Over 80

SOURCE: R. FOX, 1987:10–13.

American cities; however, since World War II, there has been an urban "explosion" in the world's developing countries. The dramatic growth in urban populations has been fueled by natural increase (excess of births over deaths) and by migration. In Mexico, for example, migration accounts for one-fourth of the expansion of urban areas. Visually, this growth is obvious in the expansion of "squatter settlements" on the edges of Mexico City (R. Fox, 1987:32–33; United Nations, 1993).

The term *squatter settlements* refers to areas occupied by the very poor on the fringe of cities. Their housing, which is more accurately called "shelter," is constructed by the settlers themselves from discarded material, including crates from loading docks and loose lumber from completed building projects. A thriving "informal economy" (refer back to Box 9-1 on page 251) typically develops; residents establish small, home-based businesses such as grocery stores, jewelry shops, and the like.

Squatter settlements are not commonly found in the industrialized nations of North America and Europe but rather in cities in the world's developing countries. Indeed, such settlements hold 30 to 60 percent of the population of many developing nations in the Third World. The existence of these communities reminds us that respected theoretical models of social science developed in the United States may not be directly applicable to other cultures. Ecological models of urban growth, for example, would not explain metropolitan expansion that locates the poorest people on the urban fringes (Castells, 1983:173–212; Lowe, 1992; Patton, 1988).

As part of the worldwide urban expansion, some metropolitan areas have spread so far that they have connected with other urban centers. Such a densely populated area, containing two or more cities and their suburbs, has become known as a *megalopolis.* An example is the 500-mile corridor stretching from Boston south to Washington, D.C., and including New York City, Philadelphia, and Baltimore, which accounts for one-sixth of the total population of the United States. Even when it is divided into autonomous political jurisdictions, the megalopolis can be viewed as a single economic entity. The megalopolis is not evident solely in the United States; such areas are now seen in Great Britain, Germany, Italy, Egypt, India, Japan, and China.

Conflict View of Urban Growth

While acknowledging the descriptive value of urban ecological models, conflict theorists insist that metropolitan growth is not governed by waterways and rail lines, as a purely ecological interpretation might suggest. From a conflict perspective, communities are human creations that reflect people's needs, choices, and decisions—but some people have more influence over these decisions than others.

Conflict theorists argue that ecological approaches typically avoid examining the social forces, largely economic in nature, that guide urban growth. For example, central business districts may be upgraded or abandoned depending on whether urban policymakers grant substantial tax exemptions to developers. The suburban boom was fueled by federal housing policies that channeled investment capital into the construction of single-family homes rather than to affordable rental housing in the cities. Similarly, while some observers suggest that the growth of sun belt cities is due to a "good business climate," conflict theorists counter that this term is actually a euphemism for hefty government subsidies and antilabor policies (Gottdiener and Feagin, 1988; M. Smith, 1988:183).

Sociologist Joe Feagin has likened urban development to a game in which powerful elites play Monopoly with real money. Feagin (1983:2) notes that class conflict has always been part of the dynamics of urban life:

> On the one side we have the progressive city councils and the urban grass-roots people's movements opposing unbridled growth and development. On the other side, we have the class of profit-oriented developers, bankers, landowners, and industrial executives who buy, sell, and develop land and buildings in cities just like they do with other for-profit commodities.

In the view of conflict theorists, developers, builders, and investment bankers are not especially interested in urban growth when it means providing housing for middle- or low-income people. This lack of interest contributes to the problem of homelessness, which will be discussed in the social policy section at the end of the chapter. These urban elites counter that the nation's housing shortage and the plight of the homeless are not their fault—and in-

Viewed from a conflict perspective, urban developers, builders, and investment bankers are primarily concerned with maximizing profit, not with solving social problems such as homelessness.

ing, a home. But for developers and investors—many of them large corporations—an apartment is simply a housing investment. These financiers and owners are primarily concerned with maximizing profit, not with solving social problems (Feagin, 1983:192).

Models of Community Attachment

What effect does the size of a community have on people's feelings of identity and belonging? Do residents of Phoenix feel as deep a sense of community as people who live in the much smaller locality of Tempe, Arizona? What is the impact of one's neighbors' moving in and out on feelings of community attachment?

Two models have been advanced by sociologists to assess the influence of the size of a community's population and its geographical mobility on social behavior: these are the linear-development model and the systemic model. Let's consider each of them in turn.

Linear-Development Model The linear-development model is illustrated by Ferdinand Tönnies's (1988, original edition 1887) use of the concepts of *Gemeinschaft* and *Gesellschaft*. As we saw in Chapter 5, *Gemeinschaft* describes close-knit communities where social interaction among people is intimate and familiar. By contrast, the ideal type of *Gesellschaft* describes modern urban life; there is little sense of commonality, and social relationships often develop as a result of interactions focused on immediate tasks, such as purchasing a product.

Tönnies and other sociologists contend that as a community grows in size, the nature of relationships between its members changes accordingly. This is termed the *linear-development model*, since a change in one variable (population size) is hypothesized to lead to a direct change in a second variable (feelings of community attachment). Furthermore, it is argued that population size is the primary factor affecting patterns of social behavior in a community. This is somewhat like saying that "people behave differently in cities because they live in cities."

Several decades after Tönnies's work, an American sociologist came to similar conclusions. Louis

sist that they do not have the capital needed to construct and support such housing. But affluent people *are* interested in growth, and *can* somehow find capital, to build new shopping centers, office towers, and business parks.

Why, then, can't they provide capital for affordable housing, ask conflict theorists? Part of the answer is that developers, bankers, and other powerful real estate interests view housing in quite a different manner from tenants and most homeowners. For a tenant, an apartment is shelter, hous-

Shown is "The Subway" (1950), a painting by George Tooker. According to sociologist Georg Simmel, urban residents (such as these subway passengers) cannot have social relationships with all the people they encounter. Indeed, as is evident in the painting, urban life can sometimes be intimidating and alienating.

Wirth (1928), while a graduate student in sociology at the University of Chicago, researched and wrote about a Jewish area in that city. His study was later published as a book entitled *The Ghetto;* it focused attention on the unique lifestyle found among residents of urban areas. Wirth later expanded on this theme in his notable article "Urbanism as a Way of Life" (1938).

Like Tönnies, Wirth argued that a relatively large and permanent settlement leads to distinctive patterns of behavior, which he called **urbanism.** He identified three critical factors contributing to urbanism: the size of the population, population density, and the heterogeneity (variety) of the population. Each of these factors has particular implications for the nature of relations between people within an urban environment. Size prevents residents from getting to know most of the people in the community. It also facilitates spatial (or physical) segregation based on race, ethnicity, social class, and lifestyle ("singles" versus elderly couples).

A frequent result of urbanism, according to Wirth, is that we become insensitive to events around us and restrict our attention to primary groups to which we are emotionally attached. Thus, residents of large cities may walk past alcoholics passed out on the street without offering help.

As early as 1902, German sociologist Georg Simmel (1950:409–424) observed in a lecture that it is impossible to carry on a social relationship with each person one encounters in an urban area. If someone attempted this, he or she might "be completely atomized internally and come to an unimaginable psychic state."

Therefore, the size of an industrial city contributes to a certain distancing in personal relationships outside one's primary groups. On the other hand, there are advantages to living in highly populated areas. C. R. Creekmore (1985) suggests that, in certain respects, city life is healthier than life in rural areas. For example, cities have better medical care, water supplies, sewage systems, and emergency services. Moreover, the greater the number of individuals in a community, the greater the possible range of occupations, ideas, values, and lifestyles. In Wirth's (1938:15) words, the city can become a "mosaic of social worlds."

Systemic Model Some of Wirth's colleagues at the University of Chicago shared his interest in the effects of urbanization on behavior but came to somewhat different conclusions. William I. Thomas (1927), along with Robert Park and Ernest Burgess (1921, 1925), asked if a *Gemeinschaft* was ever truly characteristic of preindustrial societies. They proposed a ***systemic model*** of urbanism as resulting from a variety of factors, of which population size was only one. In their view, in order to understand urbanism fully it is essential to examine the entire social system, including people's interactions, their participation in social institutions, and the influence of societal norms and values. For example, if one is a recent arrival to a city—or if one's neighbors are constantly changing as people move into and out of the city—one's sense of community attachment and belonging will be reduced. The systemic model tends to emphasize geographic mobility, rather than community size, as a crucial determinant of community attachment. Family ties and friendships can overcome the anonymity of densely populated urban areas—but only if people have enough time to get acquainted and to maintain stable and supportive relationships.

The research of sociologists John Kasarda and Morris Janowitz (1974) offers support for the systemic model. Over 2000 adults in England were interviewed and asked if they felt "at home" in their communities, if they would be disappointed if they had to move away, and so forth. The researchers found that length of residence was a better predictor of community attachment than other factors were, including the size of a community's population. Subsequent study of 50 northern California communities by Claude Fischer (1982) also suggested that population size was not the central factor leading to feelings of alienation from friends and neighbors.

We can better understand the evidence for the systemic model if we use the analogy of the classroom. Generally, educators argue that smaller classes promote a more personal relationship among students and faculty—an academic *Gemeinschaft*, in a sense. But suppose that in a 25-member

seminar, 4 or 5 new students join the class every week, while a similar number drop the course. It will be difficult to develop any sense of community attachment. On the other hand, if a larger class of 60 students remains together for two years, everyone (including the instructor) will get to know each other fairly well. Thus, length of contact, as well as size or density, can be a crucial determinant of social relationships.

The data developed by Kasarda and Janowitz as well as by Fischer appear to lend greater support to the systemic model than to the linear-development model. For both Tönnies and Wirth, large industrial cities are characterized by anonymity and impersonality. However, these researchers may have given insufficient emphasis to the effects of large-scale migration on community attachment within urban centers. Therefore, if we wish to identify key factors which affect urbanism, we need to add mobility to size, density, and heterogeneity of population (Tittle, 1989).

TYPES OF COMMUNITIES

The following sections will examine different types of communities found in the United States, focusing on the distinctive characteristics and problems of central cities, suburbs, and rural communities.

Central Cities

In terms of both land and population, the United States is the fourth-largest nation in the world. Yet three-quarters of the population is concentrated in a mere 1.5 percent of the nation's land area. In 1990, some 197 million people—accounting for 79 percent of the nation's people—lived in metropolitan areas. Even those people who live outside central cities, such as residents of suburban and rural communities, find that their lifestyles are heavily influenced by urban centers (Bureau of the Census, 1993a:35).

Who Lives in the Cities? Many urban residents are the descendants of European immigrants—Irish, Italians, Jews, Poles, and others—who came to the United States in the nineteenth and early twentieth centuries. The cities socialized these newcomers to

According to sociologist Herbert J. Gans, urban life is noteworthy for its diversity. One category of urban residents, whom Gans calls cosmopolites, *remain in the city to take advantage of its unique cultural and intellectual benefits.*

the norms, values, and language of their new homeland and gave them an opportunity to work their way up the economic ladder. In addition, a substantial number of low-income Blacks and Whites came to the cities from rural areas in the period following World War II.

Even today, cities in the United States are the destinations of immigrants from around the world—including Mexico, Ireland, Cuba, Vietnam, and Haiti—as well as migrants from the United States commonwealth of Puerto Rico (refer back to Chapter 10). Yet, unlike those who came to this country 75 or 100 years ago, current immigrants are arriving at a time of growing urban decay. This makes it more difficult for them to find employment and decent housing.

Urban life is noteworthy for its diversity; it would be a serious mistake to see all city residents as being alike. Sociologist Herbert J. Gans (1991:54–56) has distinguished between five types of people found in our cities:

1 *Cosmopolites.* Such residents remain in cities to take advantage of the unique cultural and intellectual benefits. Writers, artists, and scholars fall into this category.
2 *Unmarried and childless people.* Such people choose to live in cities because of the active nightlife and varied recreational opportunities.
3 *Ethnic villagers.* These urban residents prefer to live in their own tight-knit communities. Typically, immigrant groups isolate themselves in such neighborhoods in order to avoid resentment from well-established urban dwellers.
4 *The deprived.* Very poor people and families have little choice but to live in low-rent, and often run-down, neighborhoods.
5 *The trapped.* Some city residents wish to leave urban centers but cannot because of their limited economic resources and prospects. Gans includes the "downward mobiles" in this category—people who once held higher social positions but who are forced to live in less prestigious neighborhoods owing to loss of a job, death of a wage earner, or old age. Both elderly individuals living alone and families may feel "trapped" in part because they resent changes in their communities. Their desire to live elsewhere may reflect their uneasiness with unfamiliar immigrant groups who have become their neighbors.

From the categories first devised by Gans in 1962, we are reminded that the city represents a choice (even a dream) for certain people and a nightmare for others. Gans's work underscores the importance of neighborhoods in contemporary urban life. Ernest Burgess, in his study of life in Chicago during the 1920s, had given special attention to the ethnic neighborhoods of that city (refer back to Figure 18-1). Many decades later, residents in such districts as Chinatowns or Greektowns continue to feel attached to their own ethnic communities rather than to the larger unit of a city. Even outside such ethnic enclaves, a special sense of belonging can take hold in a neighborhood.

In a more recent study of Chicago, Gerald Suttles (1972:21–43) coined the term *defended neighborhood* to refer to people's definitions of their community boundaries. Neighborhoods acquire unique identities because they are viewed by residents as geographically separate—and socially different—from adjacent areas. The defended neighborhood, in effect, becomes a sentimental union of similar people. Neighborhood phone directories, community newspapers, school and parish boundaries, and business advertisements all serve to define an area and distinguish it from nearby communities.

In some cases, a neighborhood must literally defend itself. Plans for urban renewal or a superhighway may threaten to destroy an area's unique character and sense of attachment. In resisting such changes, a neighborhood may employ the strategies and tactics of community organization developed by pioneering organizer Saul Alinsky (1909–1972). Like many conflict sociologists, Alinsky was concerned with the ways in which society's most powerful institutions act to maintain the privileges of certain groups (such as real estate developers), while helping to keep other groups (such as slum dwellers) in a subservient position. Alinsky (1946:29) emphasized the need for community residents to fight for power in their localities. In his view, it was "only through the achievement and constructive use of power" that people could better themselves (Horwitt, 1989).

Of course, the possibility exists that a defended neighborhood will acquire its distinctive identity by excluding those who are deemed different or threatening. In 1981 the Supreme Court upheld the right of the city of Memphis, Tennessee, to erect a barrier and close a street connecting an all-White and all-Black neighborhood. White residents requested the closure, claiming that there was too much "undesirable traffic" coming through their own community. In a dissenting opinion, Justice Thurgood Marshall, the first African American to serve on the Supreme Court, called the barrier a "badge of slavery."

In some cases, neighborhoods use more subtle methods to exclude those viewed as "outsiders." Sociologist Judith DeSena (1987) found that White, non-Hispanic residents of the Brooklyn neighborhood of Greenpoint sold or rented apartments and homes only by "word of mouth." Their goal was to keep vacant housing from falling into the hands of minority families. Although Suttles tends to stress that strategies of neighborhood defense are episodic, studies by DeSena and others indicate that such social networks aimed at maintaining housing segregation may be constantly active. Memphis and Greenpoint serve as a reminder that some communities unite to fight off developers and their bulldozers, but others come together to exclude racial and ethnic minorities.

Social Problems of Cities   There can be great variance in the types of people and neighborhoods found in a city in the United States. Yet all residents of a central city—regardless of their social class, racial, and ethnic differences—face certain common problems. Crime, air pollution, noise, unemployment, overcrowded schools, inadequate public transportation—these unpleasant realities and many more are an increasing feature of contemporary urban life. They are particularly evident in the nation's older cities, such as New York, Philadelphia, Boston, and Washington, D.C.

Perhaps the single most dramatic reflection of the nation's urban ills has been the apparent "death" of entire neighborhoods. In some urban districts, business activity seems virtually nonexistent. One can walk for blocks and find little more than a devastating array of deteriorating, boarded-up, abandoned, and burned-out buildings. Some observers have gone so far as to compare such neighborhoods to parts of European cities which suffered intense aerial bombing during World War II. Such urban devastation has greatly contributed to the growing problem of homelessness, which will be discussed in the social policy section at the end of the chapter.

In some urban districts in the United States, one can walk for blocks and find little more than a devastating array of deteriorating, boarded-up, abandoned, and burned-out buildings.

Another critical problem for the cities has been mass transportation. Since 1950, the number of cars in the United States has multiplied twice as fast as the number of people. As a result, there has been growing traffic congestion in metropolitan areas, and many cities have recognized a need for safe, efficient, and inexpensive mass transit systems. However, the federal government has traditionally given much more assistance to highway programs than to public transportation. Proponents of the conflict perspective note that such a bias favors the relatively affluent (automobile owners) as well as corporations such as auto manufacturers, tire makers, and oil companies. Meanwhile, poor residents of metropolitan areas, who are much less likely to own cars than members of the middle and upper classes, face higher fares on public transit along with deteriorating service (Lazare, 1990, 1991).

This disproportionate funding of highways began to change somewhat only in the 1970s, as Congress passed a number of laws designed to aid the nation's mass transportation efforts. Yet federal funding for mass transit has fallen to less than half the 1960 level of spending. Consequently, few new transit systems have been built in the last two decades. Some, such as those in Portland, Oregon, and Bal-

timore, have enjoyed success; others, such as Miami's Metrorail, have failed to attract the expected ridership. In fact, the Miami system has been sarcastically labeled "Metrofail" by its critics (Work et al., 1987).

Money—or, more accurately, lack of money—is at the heart of many of our nation's urban problems. It clearly limits each city's ability to rebuild burned-out neighborhoods, to provide housing for homeless individuals and families, and to improve mass transit facilities. Moreover, in the 1970s and early 1980s, certain cities came near to financial default, while others were forced to close their school systems before the end of the academic year because they could not afford to meet their payrolls. During 1979, Cleveland became the first major city to default since the Depression of the 1930s.

The conventional explanation for the fiscal (in other words, financial) crises of New York and other cities was excessive municipal services. Advocates of this view noted that in an era of urban decline, the cities simply could not afford substantial public subsidies for city colleges, municipal hospitals, welfare programs, the arts, and so forth. However, conflict sociologists have rightly questioned this explanation. French urbanologist Manuel

BOX 18-1 · CURRENT RESEARCH

URBAN APARTHEID IN THE UNITED STATES

In a provocative column in the *New York Times* on "America's Urban Apartheid," David Rusk (1992), a former mayor of Albuquerque, New Mexico, noted a distressing pattern evident in the nation's communities. According to census data, in two-thirds of the 200 largest metropolitan areas in the United States, inner-city populations—primarily poor Blacks and Hispanics—are surrounded by suburbs that are 90 percent White. With the exception of certain commercial and residential city neighborhoods tailored for the affluent, the cities are decaying while suburbs and communities beyond the suburbs prosper.

Data from the 1990 census concerning South Central Los Angeles—the neighborhood which became the center of that city's tragic rioting in 1992 (refer back to Chapter 10)—underscore the grim realities of life in the inner city. This predominantly African American and Hispanic community—where Whites constitute less than 3 percent of residents—had a median household income of only $19,382. For Los Angeles as a whole, the comparable figure was $30,925; for the United States as a whole, $34,995. In 1990, one out of every four South Central residents was on welfare; 55 percent of adults were unemployed or were not in the paid labor force (Hubler, 1992).

In some cities, conditions have become so desperate that low-income and homeless residents have erected "shantytowns" reminiscent of the squatter settlements found in many Third World cities. In New York City, an estimated 15,000 makeshift dwellings have been built on marginal property (for example, under approaches to bridges). Encampments for the homeless have become evident in many other communities, among them Los Angeles, Dallas, Santa Monica, California, and Aurora, Illinois. These contemporary shantytowns are reminiscent of the "Hoovervilles" established across the United States during the Depression of the 1930s (P. Brown, 1993; I. Fisher, 1993).

The critical factor in the varying fortunes of financially troubled inner-city neighborhoods and prospering suburban communities has been the transformation in the economy of the United States resulting from the postindustrial revolution (refer back to Chapter 15). There has been a significant decline in the number of manufacturing jobs—traditionally the staple of the urban work force. At the same time, the growth in service- and information-related jobs has required an educated and skilled labor force that most cities find difficult to provide. Consequently, while job growth in cities has been negligible, suburbs have benefited from the opening of new "technology corridors," many of which were begun with substantial government assistance.

Given the persistence of housing segregation in the United States, African Americans and Hispanics are increasingly trapped in cities where employment opportunities are shrinking and where many of the available jobs are low-wage service positions (such as work in a fast-food restaurant). Yet, in relatively distant locales, suburban Whites are holding important jobs in the industries of the future. This is the nation's "urban apartheid" as we approach the twenty-first century (Massey and Denton, 1993; Sassen, 1990).

Castells (1976, 1977:415–420) argues that New York's "bankruptcy" resulted from the failure of big business to pay additional taxes which would support needed services.

Despite these financial stresses, some cities have revitalized themselves in the last decade. Well before its default, Cleveland had become a national subject for jokes in 1969 when its polluted Cuyahoga River caught fire. Yet today this same river is lined with pleasure boats, bars, and restaurants, while new downtown stores and luxury hotels have been opened. But who really benefits from this brick and mortar? As in many other cities that have invested heavily in downtown redevelopment, Cleveland's impoverished neighborhoods have barely seen any financial gain from downtown re-

Shown is an "office park" in Newport Beach, California. Many suburbs— filled with new skyscrapers and high-tech industries—have evolved into "outer cities" that rival traditional big-city downtown areas as economic centers.

vitalization. Indeed, while employment in the Cleveland metropolitan area is increasing, most of the new jobs are in suburban industrial parks and few are in inner-city neighborhoods (Turque, 1991). In Box 18-1, we examine the disparity between affluent, predominantly White suburbs and financially deteriorating cities that are increasingly populated by African Americans and Hispanics.

Suburbs

There are various definitions of suburban areas. The term *suburb* derives from the Latin *sub urbe,* meaning "under the city." Until recent times, most suburbs were just that—tiny communities totally dependent on urban centers for jobs, recreation, and even water.

Today, the **suburb** defies any simple definition. The term generally refers to any community near a large city—or, as the Census Bureau would say, any territory within a metropolitan area that is not included in the central city. By that definition, more than 119 million people, or about 48 percent of the population of the United States, lived in the suburbs in 1990. However, as we will see, suburbs often have little in common, apart from their classification as "suburban." For example, the city of

Yonkers, New York, borders on parts of New York City. As of 1990, Yonkers had a population of 188,000 and was the eighty-fourth-largest city in the nation. Yet many consider Yonkers to be a suburb of New York City (Baldassare, 1992; Bureau of the Census, 1993a:44).

It can also be difficult to distinguish between suburbs and rural areas. Certain criteria are generally used to define suburbs: most people work at urban (as opposed to rural) jobs, and local governments provide services such as water supply, sewage disposal, and fire protection. In rural areas, such services are less common, and a greater proportion of residents are employed in farming and related activities (Baldassare, 1992).

Suburban Expansion Whatever the precise definition of a suburb, it is clear that suburbs have expanded. In fact, suburbanization has been the most dramatic population trend in the United States throughout the twentieth century. Suburban areas grew at first along railroad lines, then at the termini of streetcar tracks, and by the 1950s along the nation's growing systems of freeways and expressways. The suburban boom has been especially evident in the period since World War II.

Suburbanization—or metropolitanization, as the process has also been called—is not necessarily prompted by expansion of transportation services to the fringe of a city. The 1923 earthquake that devastated Tokyo encouraged decentralization of the city. Until the 1970s, dwellings were limited to a height of 102 feet. Initially, the poor were relegated to areas outside municipal boundaries in their search for housing; many chose to live in squatter-type settlements. With the advent of a rail network and rising land costs in the central city, middle-class Japanese began moving to the suburbs after World War II (P. Hall, 1977:225–226).

In the United States, people moved to the suburbs for a variety of reasons. Sociologist Peter Rossi (1955) divided these causes for moving to suburbia into what he called "push" and "pull" factors. People were pushed toward the suburbs by the difficulties associated with life in central cities: crime, pollution, overcrowding, and the like. At the same time, they were pulled toward suburbia by a desire to live in smaller communities, to own their own homes and gardens, to find better schools for their children, or simply to enjoy the status linked to life in an affluent suburb.

In recent decades, large corporations and other businesses are increasingly being pushed away from the cities and pulled toward suburbia. In 1980, less than half of all office construction in the United States was in the suburbs; by 1985, the figure had risen to about two-thirds of all construction. As a result, many suburbs—filled with new skyscrapers, office parks, and high tech industries—have evolved into "outer cities" that rival traditional big-city downtown areas as economic centers. This new development in suburban expansion provides additional support for the multiple-nuclei theory of urban growth (Dentzer, 1986:61; W. Stevens, 1987c).

Diversity in the Suburbs   In the United States, race and ethnicity remain the most important factors distinguishing cities from suburbs. After studying 44 central cities and 128 suburbs, Patricia Gober and Michelle Behr (1982) concluded that the size of the minority population—more than other variables such as age of population or social class—was the critical distinguishing factor between these two types of communities. Nevertheless, the common assumption that suburbia includes only prosperous Whites is far from correct.

The proportion of African Americans living in suburban areas in the United States has increased from 26 percent in 1980 to 32 percent in 1990. (In the suburbs of Chicago, while the number of Whites increased by only 2 percent during the 1980s, there was a 45 percent increase among Blacks, a 72 percent increase among Asian Americans, and an 84 percent increase among Hispanics.) Yet the most significant growth in the percentage of suburban African Americans has come from movement into suburbs that are predominantly Black or are adjacent to predominantly Black areas. In many in-

Shown is a suburban mall which serves many Asian American customers. The suburbs have become home to many immigrants from foreign countries, including an increasing number of Asian Americans.

stances, these suburbs are isolated from surrounding White communities and have less satisfactory housing and municipal services (Dent, 1992; Dunn, 1987; Massey and Denton, 1993; Reardon, 1991; Stahura, 1987).

Again in contrast to prevailing stereotypes, the suburbs include a surprising number of low-income people from White, Black, and Hispanic backgrounds. Poverty is not conventionally associated with the suburbs, partly because the suburban poor tend to be scattered amongst more affluent people. In some instances, however, suburban communities intentionally hide social problems in order to maintain a "respectable" image. Sociologist J. Jeff McConnell has studied homelessness in suburban communities on Long Island, near New York City. He found an unstated contract between these communities and their homeless residents. Shopkeepers, police officers, and public officials tolerate and even assist homeless people—so long as they stay away from central business districts, sleep out of sight of casual observers, and allow suburban communities to pretend that homelessness is only a problem somewhere else (Henneberger, 1993).

Surprisingly, the suburbs have also become home to many immigrants from foreign countries. Traditionally, immigrants entering the United States have become entrenched in central-city neighborhoods, many of which have taken on the distinctive culture and ethnic flavor of the newcomers. However, according to population surveys conducted by the Census Bureau between 1975 and 1985, almost half the 4.7 million Asian, Hispanic, and Black immigrants who moved to the United States during that period chose to settle in suburban and nonmetropolitan areas rather than in central cities. Many of these immigrants—especially those from affluent, professional backgrounds—have settled in largely White neighborhoods (Herbers, 1986).

Regarding age distribution, the suburbs are "graying" like the rest of the United States (see Chapter 12). For example, Levittown, Long Island —named for its developer, Bill Levitt—had only a three-room country schoolhouse in 1947. The community experienced dramatic growth in the decades after World War II; by 1972, Levittown Memorial High School alone had a senior class of 400 students. Yet, by the early 1980s, the school's graduating class had decreased to 200, and Levit-

town was attempting to identify locations for indoor pools and community centers that would cater to the growing proportion of elderly residents (J. Barron, 1983).

Suburban settlements have become so diverse that even the collective term *suburbs* gives undue support to the stereotype of suburban uniformity. Pollster Louis Harris has divided suburbs into four distinct categories based on income level and rate of growth. Higher-income suburbs are categorized as either *affluent bedroom* or *affluent settled. Affluent bedroom communities* rank at the highest levels in terms of income, proportion of people employed in professional and managerial occupations, and percentage of homeowners. *Affluent settled communities* tend to be older, and perhaps even declining in population. They are more likely to house business firms and do not serve mainly as a place of residence for commuters.

Harris has recognized that certain suburban areas are composed of individuals and families with low or moderate incomes. *Low-income growing communities* serve as the home of upwardly mobile blue-collar workers who have moved from the central cities. *Low-income stagnant communities* are among the oldest suburbs and are experiencing the full range of social problems characteristic of the central cities. As is true of Gans's model of city residents, Harris emphasizes the diversity found within the general category of *suburbia* (*Time*, 1971; see also Palen, 1994).

Clearly, not all suburban residents appreciate the diversity of the suburbs—especially if it means that less affluent families, or members of racial and ethnic minorities, will be moving into their communities. When the Ford Motor Company moved from Richmond, California, to Milpitas, California, the union attempted to build housing for the firm's employees—many of whom were Black. The local government of Milpitas promptly rezoned the area for industrial use (Larson and Nikkel, 1979:235–236).

Zoning laws, in theory, are enacted to ensure that certain standards of housing construction are satisfied. These laws can also separate industrial and commercial enterprises from residential areas. Thus, a suburb might wish to prevent a factory from moving to a quiet residential neighborhood. However, some zoning laws have served as thinly veiled efforts to keep low-income people out of a suburb and have been attacked as "snob statutes." By requiring that a person own a certain number of square feet of land before he or she can build a home—or by prohibiting prefabricated or modular housing—a community can effectively prevent the construction of any homes that lower-class families might be able to afford. The courts have generally let such exclusionary zoning laws stand, even when charges have been made that their enactment was designed to keep out racial minorities.

According to a study by researchers at the University of Chicago's Population Research Center, African Americans are more likely than other minority groups to face residential segregation in the suburbs. The study compared suburban settlement patterns for African Americans, Hispanics, and Asians in 59 cities in the United States. Asians were most likely to be accepted in traditionally White suburbs. Hispanics were likely to be accepted if they were perceived as White, but were likely to experience discrimination if they were perceived as Black. The director of the Population Research Center, Douglas Massey, concludes that "strong penalties" for being Black were evident in the Center's findings (Hays, 1988:A16; Massey and Denton, 1993).

Rural Communities

As we have seen, the people of the United States live mainly in urban areas. Yet one-fourth of the population lives in towns of 2500 people or less which are not adjacent to a city. As is true of the suburbs, it would be a mistake to view rural communities as fitting into one set image. Turkey farms, coal mining towns, cattle ranches, and gas stations along interstate highways are all part of the rural United States.

In contrast to the historic stereotype of the farmer as a White male, African Americans and women have long played a significant role in agriculture in the United States. Women actively participate in farming across the country—in large and small farms, in profitable and failing family businesses. Farming women are almost always married and generally have large families. Segregation by gender is typical of farm labor: men are more likely to be engaged in field work, while women serve as their farms' accountants, personnel and equipment managers, and purchasing agents. Many studies have documented the high degree of stress experienced by farming women as they attempt to

Karen Kasmauski/Woodfin Camp

In contrast to the historic stereotype of the farmer as a White male, African Americans and women have long played a significant role in agriculture in the United States.

fulfill many demanding social roles (Hennon and Marotz-Baden, 1987; Keating and Munro, 1988; Lofflin, 1988).

Whereas women are involved in farming in all regions of the United States, 90 percent of African American farmers work in the south. Their farms tend to be small—only an average of about 100 acres compared with the national average of 4400 acres. Moreover, Black farmers are concentrated in areas of the country with severe economic difficulties, including limited job opportunities and few supportive services for residents. In 1960, 11 percent of people running farms in the United States were African American, but by 1990 this figure had fallen to only 1.5 percent. In good part, this was not a voluntary withdrawal from farming; farm displacement and loss of land among African Americans occurs at a rate 2½ times higher than the rate among White farmers (Banks, 1987; Hoppe and Bluestone, 1987; Smothers, 1992b).

In the United States, people have traditionally maintained a rather idyllic image of life in rural communities. When asked about their living preferences for a 1989 Gallup poll, 56 percent of respondents indicated that they would prefer to live in a small town or a rural farming area. By contrast, only 24 percent chose a suburb, and only 19 percent favored a city—despite the fact that four out of five respondents lived in metropolitan areas (D. Johnson, 1990).

This idyllic image of rural life tends to mask serious problems. In small towns, for example, many retail and service stores are closing—among them, badly needed auto repair outlets. Public services such as fire protection, road maintenance, hospital and medical services, and waste facilities are often inadequate. One study reported that 60 percent of midwestern towns have no public water systems. Although homelessness is not so serious a problem as in central cities, substandard housing conditions are all too common in rural communities (J. Reid, 1984).

The recent difficulties of the nation's farmers have been well documented in the mass media. Although the federal government spends billions of dollars annually to subsidize farm prices, bankruptcies and foreclosures have increased in farming areas across the United States (see Box 18-2). The decline of family farms is especially evident, as smaller farms are rapidly being swallowed up by larger ones. It has become more and more difficult to maintain a family grain farm with 350 to 400 acres; moreover, anyone who thinks of *beginning* a family farm now faces start-up costs as high as $200,000. Consequently, since 1980, the number of farmers under the age of 25 has dropped by 50 percent. Today, only 25 percent of members of the Future Farmers of America (and only 7 percent in Illinois) say that they plan to go into farming (Gunset, 1992; D. Johnson, 1992).

The postindustrial revolution has been far from kind to the rural communities of the United States. Despite the images portrayed in the media, agriculture accounts for only 9 percent of employment in nonurban counties. Yet mining and logging—the two nonagricultural staples of the rural economy—have been in decline along with farming. At the same time, the manufacturing base of such areas has been slow to participate in the growth of high technology industries.

Consequently, with rural economies faltering and poverty on the rise, data on internal migration in the 1980s showed a shift away from rural communities toward metropolitan areas. Whereas in 1975 rural communities had experienced a net gain of 1.6 million people, in 1988 rural areas suffered a net loss of 150,000 people to metropolitan areas. This decline reduced the number of farmers in the United States below the 5 million mark—the first time this had been true since 1920, when the United States had only 9.6 million inhabitants. Indeed, in 1993, the Census Bureau calculated that farm residents accounted for only 2 percent of the nation's population—compared with 95 percent in 1790—and therefore announced that it would no longer conduct its special farm surveys (Bureau of the Census, 1990e; Vobejda, 1993).

One consequence of this rural decline is that policymakers have been confronted with a most unpleasant responsibility: deciding which ailing towns and counties will be supported with funds for economic development and which will, in effect, be allowed to die. New schools, bridges, and roads can help to save a declining area, but state governments are not in a position to support every area in need. At present, there are no precise data on how many small towns across the United States vanish each decade. Still, Mark Drabensott, an executive with

BOX 18-2 · SPEAKING OUT

THE DEATH OF A FAMILY FARM

It is becoming more and more difficult to maintain a family farm in the United States. In the following selection, Amy Jo Keifer (1991:E15) of Bangor, Pennsylvania—a student at American University—speaks of how her family's farm is dying and how difficult it is to watch:

I am a farmer's daughter. I am also a 4-H member, breeder and showman of sheep and showman of cattle. My family's farm is dying and I have watched it, and my family, suffer.

Our eastern Pennsylvania farm is a mere 60 acres. The green rolling hills and forested land are worth a minimum of $200,000 to developers, but no longer provide my family with the means to survive. It's a condition called asset rich and cash poor, and it's a hard way of life.

My grandfather bought our farm when he and my grandmother were first married. He raised dairy cattle and harvested the land full time for more than 20 years. When he died, my father took over and changed the farm to beef cattle, horses and pigs, and kept the crops. But it wasn't enough to provide for a young family, so he took on a full time job, too.

I can remember, when I was young, sitting on the fence with my sister and picking out a new name for each calf. My sister's favorite cow was named Flower, and so we named

Amy Jo Keifer.

her calves Buttercup, Daisy, Rose, and Violet. Flower was the leader of a herd of more than 20. The only cattle left on our farm now are my younger sister's and brother's 4-H projects.

I can remember a huge tractor-trailer backed into the loading chute of our barn on days when more than 200 pigs had to be taken to market. That was before the prices went down and my father let the barn go empty rather than take on more debt.

I can remember my father riding on the tractor, larger than life, bailing hay or planting corn. When

prices started dropping, we began to rent some land to other farmers, so they could harvest from it. But prices have dropped so low this year there are no takers. The land will go unused; the tractor and the equipment have long since been sold off.

I don't remember the horses. I've seen a few pictures in which my father, slim and dark, is holding his newborn daughter on horseback amid a small herd. And I've heard stories of his delivering hay to farms all over the state, but I can't ever remember his loading up a truck to do it.

Piece by piece, our farm has deteriorated. We started breeding sheep and now have about 25 head, but they yield little revenue. My mother, who works as a registered nurse, once said something that will remain with me forever: "Your father works full time to support the farm. I work full time to support the family."

I've seen movies like "The River" and "Places in the Heart." They tell the real struggle. But people can leave a movie theater, and there's a happy ending for them. There aren't many happy endings in a real farmer's life. I was reared hearing that hard work paid off, while seeing that it didn't. My younger brother would like to take over the farm some day, but I'm not sure it will hold on much longer. Its final breath is near.

the Federal Reserve Bank in Kansas City, predicts: "There are going to be some rural communities that prosper at the expense of dying neighbors, and I fully expect the trend to continue" (Lapping et al., 1989; Wilkerson, 1990:A16).

Faced with declines in agriculture, mining, and manufacturing, more than 200 rural communities across the United States have developed marketing campaigns to lure elderly migrants. For example, North Dakota's state legislature has begun Operation Back Home Again, which helps small towns trace their high school graduates as far back as 1950 and encourage them to return home for their later years. Guntersville, Alabama, a town of 7000, has attracted 250 retired couples over a three-year period through advertisements in retirement publications and television commercials on fishing programs shown on ESPN (the cable sports network). Ideally, these retirees will bring with them substantial assets and spending while placing few demands on costly services such as public schools. Indeed, according to one estimate, retired couples who have migrated to Alabama have annual incomes of $35,000 and assets of more than $250,000 (Kerr, 1991).

SOCIAL POLICY AND COMMUNITIES

HOMELESSNESS

- Is it correct to assert that the vast majority of homeless people are isolated individuals with no sense of community?
- In what ways has gentrification exacerbated the problem of homelessness?
- Are the people of the United States concerned about or indifferent to the plight of the homeless?

O n the evening of November 29, 1993, despite near-freezing temperature, Yetta Adams apparently went to sleep on a bus bench in Washington, D.C. The next morning, this 43-year-old mother of three grown children was found dead on the bench, surrounded by shopping bags and covered only by an old blanket. Adams had been a familiar face to office workers and homeless people in the neighborhood. Once an employee of a preschool, she had long battled severe depression and an addiction to painkilling drugs (M. Hall, 1993b).

Every winter, homeless people like Yetta Adams die on the streets during cold nights. Typically, there is little publicity attached to their deaths, and in some cases authorities can never even identify the deceased. However, Yetta Adams' death received nationwide attention because of *where* she died: right across from the U.S. Department of Housing and Urban Development (HUD). Well aware of the bitter irony, secretary of Housing and Urban Development Henry Cisneros (1993:23) noted: "She died across the street from my office, just weeks after I said that relieving homelessness would be HUD's top priority."

Yetta Adams was but one of many people in the United States who live on city or suburban streets, in abandoned buildings, in subway stations and train yards, in public parks, or in shelters. According to a 1993 estimate, the nation's homeless population is at least 700,000 and may be as high as 3 million. Given the limited space in public shelters, at a minimum hundreds of thousands of people in this country are homeless and without shelter (Lim, 1993).

Homelessness is evident in both industrialized and developing countries. In Great Britain, some 175,000 households accounting for about 400,000 people are accepted as homeless by the government and are given housing. An even larger number, perhaps 1 million people, are turned away from government assistance or are sharing a household with relatives or acquaintances but want separate accommodations. While an accurate figure is not available, it is estimated that 1 percent of western Europeans are homeless; they sleep in the streets, depend on night shelters and hostels, or live in precarious accommodations. In Third World countries, rapid population growth has outpaced the expansion of housing by a wide margin, leading to a rise in homelessness (B. Lee, 1992; Platt, 1993; Stearn, 1993).

The master status of being homeless carries a serious stigma and can lead to prejudice and discrimination.

Both in the United States and around the world, being homeless functions as a master status (refer back to Chapter 5) that largely defines a person's position within society. In this case, homelessness tends to mean that in many important respects, the individual is *outside* society. Indeed, the master status of being homeless carries a serious stigma and can lead to prejudice and discrimination. Many communities have reported acts of random violence against homeless people. In New York City, there were 21 incidents in 1992 alone in which young people tried to set fire to men and women sleeping in subway stations. Two of these victims burned to death; in 13 of the 21 attacks, the perpetrators were not found (M. Kaufman, 1993).

There has been a significant change in the profile of homelessness during the last 15 years. In the past, homeless people were primarily older White males living as alcoholics in skid row areas. However, today's homeless are comparatively younger —with an average age in the low thirties. Overall, an estimated 44 percent of homeless people in the United States are from racial and ethnic minority groups. Moreover, a 1992 survey in Los Angeles of shelters that accepted only homeless adults found that 46 percent were African American, 25 percent were Hispanic, 23 percent were White, 2 percent

were Native American, and 1 percent were Asian American (Ford Foundation, 1989:20; Heffernan, 1992; R. Rosenthal, 1987; see also Burt and Cohen, 1989).

Although the mass media present the homeless primarily as mentally ill, a study of homeless people in Austin, Texas, concluded that the "linkage between homelessness and mental illness has been overstated." In contrast to the stereotype of homeless people as isolated individuals, recent research suggests that a growing proportion of homeless people are *families* without homes (often a woman and her children). According to a report issued in late 1993 by the U.S. Conference of Mayors, families with children accounted for 33 percent of those seeking food and shelter in 1992 and 43 percent of those seeking such aid in 1993 (*New York Times*, 1993e; Snow et al., 1986:421).

Homeless women often have additional problems that distinguish them from homeless men. In comparison with homeless men, homeless women report more recent injuries or acute illnesses, as well as more chronic health problems. Moreover, homeless women have experienced more disruptions in their families and social networks than homeless men. For many homeless women, having a child represents an important source of support.

Homeless women with children who live in shelters are less likely than homeless women in single-adult shelters to have mental health symptoms and to have drinking problems; homeless women with children are also less likely to have been homeless over a long period of time (Milburn and D'Ercole, 1991).

Studies of homelessness point to a wide variety of causes of this condition, among them unemployment, cutbacks in public assistance, deinstitutionalization of the mentally ill (refer back to Chapter 17), and the decline in affordable housing in metropolitan areas. By the late 1980s, it had become clear that the nation's low-income renters and homeowners were being increasingly priced out of the housing market. Studies show that half of the poorest households (those with incomes below $3000) were paying more than 72 percent of their incomes for rent, leaving them with an average of only $71 per month for all other daily needs. Yet the federal budget for housing had fallen from $30 billion in 1980 to less than $8 billion in 1988 (P. Kerr, 1986; McBride, 1987; Morganthau, 1988:18).

In recent decades, the process of urban renewal has included a noticeable boom in *gentrification.* This term refers to the resettlement of low-income city neighborhoods by prosperous families and business firms. In some instances, city governments have promoted gentrification by granting lucrative tax breaks to developers who convert low-cost rental units into luxury apartments and condominiums. Conflict theorists note that although the affluent may derive both financial and emotional benefits from gentrification and redevelopment, the poor often end up being thrown out on the street.

There is an undeniable connection between the nation's growing shortage of affordable housing and the rise in homelessness (Elliott and Krivo, 1991). Yet sociologist Peter Rossi (1989, 1990) cautions that it would be incorrect to focus too narrowly on lack of shelter while ignoring the decline in the demand for manual labor in cities, the increasing prevalence of chronically unemployed young men among the homeless, and other structural factors. Rossi contends that structural changes have put everyone in extreme poverty at higher risk of becoming homeless—especially poor people who exhibit an accumulation of disabilities (such as drug abuse, bad health, unemployment, and criminal records). Being disabled in *this* manner forces the individual to rely on a social network of family and friends for support, often for a prolonged period. If the strain on this support network is so great that it collapses, homelessness may result. While Rossi's theory has been accepted by many researchers, the general public often prefers to "blame the victim" (refer back to Box 8-2 on page 227) for becoming homeless (B. Lee, 1992).

Thus far, policymakers have often been content to steer the homeless toward large, overcrowded, unhealthy shelters. Many neighborhoods and communities have resisted plans to open large shelters or even smaller residences for the homeless, often raising the familiar cry of "Not in my backyard!" The major federal program intended to assist the homeless is the McKinney Homeless Assistance Act, passed in 1987. This act authorizes federal aid for emergency food, shelter, health, mental health care, job training, and education for homeless children and adults. Approximately $1 billion in funds is distributed annually to about 100 community-based service organizations (Doblin et al., 1992).

Survey data suggest that the public favors strong action to address the needs of the homeless. A 1990 analysis of both national and local polling data found nearly 60 percent of respondents willing to pay higher taxes to support programs that would attack the root causes of homelessness. This finding runs counter to people's typically negative feeling about taxes and stands in sharp contrast to the public's harsh view of welfare recipients and the poor (Raymond, 1990).

While policymakers struggle about how to deal with the growing problem of homelessness, homeless people themselves sometimes join forces to better their lives. As discussed earlier in the chapter, many homeless people construct shantytowns that provide them with both makeshift housing and a sense of community. Most studies emphasize that homeless people are disempowered and disenfranchised. However, drawing on interviews and participant-observation research with homeless people in Maine, David Wagner and Marcia Cohen (1991:543) conclude that "with just minimal resources and organizational structure, homeless and very poor people can achieve considerable success in affecting resource distribution on a local level.

Moreover, . . . engagement in protest movements can have a dramatic impact on the lives of participants in movements for the poor."

Wagner and Cohen conducted a follow-up study of homeless activists in Portland, Maine, who had lived in a "tent city" for almost one month in 1987 as a protest against the closing of two emergency homeless shelters. Over a six-month period in 1990, the researchers were able to interview 65 of some 105 tent city participants. They found that strong social ties and social networks were evident among the survey respondents.

Whether in terms of housing or social welfare benefits, the situation of the tent city activists was better in 1990 than at the time of the protest. For example, as of mid-1990, 50 of the 65 participants interviewed were housed rather than homeless. While the tent city participants seemed to have gained the most from their protests, their activism led to positive changes for *all* homeless people in Portland. Protestors left the tent city only after the city government agreed to the opening of several year-round shelters and other social welfare reforms, including assuring the homeless direct representation on certain city boards. By the following winter, the number of shelter beds available in Portland had increased by 50 percent (Wagner and Cohen, 1991:543–561).

SUMMARY

A *community* is a spatial or territorial unit of social organization in which people have a sense of identity and a feeling of belonging. This chapter examines the three basic types of communities that are found in the United States: central cities, suburbs, and rural areas.

1 Anthropologist George Murdock has observed that there are only two truly universal units of human social organization: the family and the community.

2 The single most significant precondition for the emergence of a relatively large and stable community was the creation of a *social surplus* of agricultural production.

3 Gideon Sjoberg identified three preconditions of city life: advanced technology in both agricultural and nonagricultural areas, a favorable physical environment, and a well-developed social organization.

4 An *industrial city* is based on very different principles of social organization than a *preindustrial city* is.

5 Whereas ecological theories of urban growth focus on the impact of waterways, railroads, and the like on settlement patterns, conflict theorists emphasize that urban elites exert significant control over the process of growth.

6 Many urban residents are recent immigrants from other nations or are the descendants of earlier immigrants.

7 In the last two decades, cities have confronted an overwhelming array of economic and social problems, including the possibility of financial default.

8 Suburbanization has been the most dramatic population trend in the United States throughout the twentieth century.

9 The nation's rural economy is growing more diverse; new industrial, service, and mining jobs are being created in areas previously restricted to farming.

10 In contrast to the stereotype of homeless people as isolated individuals, recent research suggests that a growing proportion of homeless people are *families* without homes.

CRITICAL THINKING QUESTIONS

1 This chapter gives special attention to the conflict view of urban growth. How might functionalist theorists view urban growth? Should ecological views of urban growth, such as concentric-zone theory and multiple-nuclei theory, be properly viewed as functionalist?

2 In the United States, there has long been a fear and suspicion concerning life in cities. Imagine that your instructor has assigned you to conduct a survey of attitudes toward cities in your community. How might you develop a representative sample for this study? What types of questions would you ask? How would you attempt to ensure that your questions are unbiased? What would be the advantages and disadvantages of using in-person interviews, telephone interviews, and mailed questionnaires for this research?

3 How has your home community (your city, town, or neighborhood) changed over the years you have lived there? Have there been significant changes in the community's economic base and in its racial and ethnic profile? Have the community's social problems intensified or lessened over time? Is homelessness currently a major problem? What are the community's future prospects as it approaches the twenty-first century?

KEY TERMS

Community A spatial or territorial unit of social organization in which people have a sense of identity and a feeling of belonging. (page 510)

Concentric-zone theory A theory of urban growth devised by Ernest Burgess which sees growth in terms of a series of rings radiating from the central business district. (513)

Defended neighborhood Suttles's formulation that area residents identify their neighborhood through defined community borders and through a perception that adjacent areas are geographically separate and socially different. (523)

Gentrification The resettlement of low-income city neighborhoods by prosperous families and business firms. (534)

Human ecology An area of study concerned with the interrelationships among people in their spatial setting and physical environment. (513)

Industrial city A city characterized by relatively large size, open competition, an open class system, and elaborate specialization in the manufacturing of goods. (512)

Industrial revolution A scientific revolution, largely occurring in England between 1760 and 1830, which focused on the application of nonanimal sources of power to labor tasks. (512)

Linear-development model A view of community attachment which points to population size as the primary factor influencing patterns of behavior in a community. (519)

Megalopolis A densely populated area containing two or more cities and their surrounding suburbs. (518)

Multiple-nuclei theory A theory of urban growth developed by Harris and Ullman, which views growth as emerging from many centers of development, each of which may reflect a particular urban need or activity. (515)

Preindustrial city A city with only a few thousand people living within its borders and characterized by a relatively closed class system and limited mobility. (512)

Social surplus The production by a group of people of enough goods to cover their own needs, while at the same time sustaining people who are not engaged in agricultural tasks. (511)

Squatter settlements Areas occupied by the very poor on the fringes of cities, in which housing is often constructed by the settlers themselves from discarded material. (518)

Subsistence technology The tools, processes, and knowledge that a society requires to meet its basic needs for survival. (511)

Suburb According to the Census Bureau, any territory within a metropolitan area that is not included in the central city. (526)

Systemic model A model of community attachment proposed by Thomas, Park, and Burgess which emphasizes geographical mobility, rather than population size, as a crucial factor in influencing patterns of behavior. (521)

Urban ecology An area of study which focuses on the interrelationships between people and their environment as they emerge in urban areas. (513)

Urbanism A term used by Wirth to describe distinctive patterns of social behavior evident among city residents. (520)

Zoning laws Legal provisions stipulating land use and architectural design of housing and often employed as a means of keeping racial minorities and low-income people out of suburban areas. (528)

ADDITIONAL READINGS

Anderson, Elijah. *Streetwise: Race, Class, and Change in an Urban Community.* Chicago: University of Chicago Press, 1990. An African American sociologist draws on participant-observation research to provide insight into a lower-class Black community and an adjoining gentrified neighborhood (refer back to Box 2-1 on page 43, which is derived from this book).

Castells, Manuel. *The Informational City.* Oxford, England: Basil Blackwell, 1989. A conflict theorist considers how the nature of space, place, and distance has changed fundamentally as a result of recent technological change.

Frey, William H. *Metropolitan America: Beyond the Transition.* Washington, D.C.: Population Reference Bureau, 1990. This concise (52-page) work looks at recent changes in metropolitan areas, including minority population, suburban growth, income distribution, and age of residents.

Glazer, Nathan, and Mark Lilla (eds.). *The Public Face of Architecture: Civic Culture and Public Spaces.* New York: Free Press, 1987. This collection, drawn from a variety of academic disciplines, shows how buildings can shape social life and are, in turn, affected by governmental action.

Jackson, Kenneth T. *Crabgrass Frontier: The Suburbanization of the United States.* New York: Oxford University Press, 1986. A historian describes the development of outlying areas from the eighteenth century to the present.

Kling, Rob, Spencer Olin, and Mark Poster (eds.). *Postsuburban California: The Transformation of Orange County since World War II.* Berkeley: University of California Press, 1991. This collection of 10 articles covers the latest developments in edge cities, from taxpayers' revolts to industrial development.

Kozol, Jonathan. *Rachel and Her Children: Homeless Families in America.* New York: Ballantine, 1988. The noted educator records the desperate voices of the men, women, and especially children who are homeless and struggling for survival.

Nyden, Phillip W., and Wim Wiewel. *Challenging Uneven Development: An Urban Agenda for the 1990s.* New Brunswick, N.J.: Rutgers University Press, 1991. A critical analysis of proposals to deal with the problems of central cities, with special emphasis on Chicago.

Rossi, Peter H. *Down and Out in America: The Origins of Homelessness.* Chicago: University of Chicago Press, 1989. Rossi analyzes the problems faced both by homeless people and by "precariously domiciled" people who are vulnerable to becoming homeless.

Waterfield, Larry W. *Conflict and Crisis in Rural America.* New York: Praeger, 1986. A journalistic account of the challenges facing rural areas of the United States.

Journals

Among the journals focusing on community issues are *Journal of Urban Affairs* (founded in 1979), *Rural Sociology* (1936), *Urban Affairs Quarterly* (1965), *Urban Anthropology* (1972), and *Urban Studies* (1964).

19

POPULATION AND THE ENVIRONMENT

DEMOGRAPHY: THE STUDY OF POPULATION
Malthus's Thesis and Marx's Response
Studying Population Today
Elements of Demography

WORLD POPULATION HISTORY
Demographic Transition
The Population Explosion

FERTILITY PATTERNS IN THE UNITED STATES
The Baby Boom
Stable Population Growth

POPULATION AND MIGRATION
International Migration
Internal Migration

THE ENVIRONMENT
Environmental Problems: An Overview
 Air Pollution
 Water Pollution
 Contamination of Land
Functionalism and Human Ecology
Conflict View of Environmental Issues

SOCIAL POLICY AND THE ENVIRONMENT: OPPOSITION TO LANDFILLS

BOXES
19-1 Around the World: Japan's Declining Fertility
19-2 Current Research: The Demography of Islamic Nations

LOOKING AHEAD

- Why is it important to study population issues?
- Why did Karl Marx disagree with Thomas Robert Malthus's view that rising world population was the cause of social ills?
- Why is there such concern in Japan about the nation's low fertility rate?
- If the United States maintains stable population growth, what will be the social implications for our society?
- How can the functionalist and conflict perspectives be applied in studying the environment?
- Why is there so much community opposition to locating landfills nearby?

In 1977 the Population Reference Bureau proclaimed the "discovery" of a minicontinent in the Pacific Ocean about the size of California. Since then, the Bureau has used this imaginary land mass, which it named "Populandia," to illustrate the growth of world population. We are to imagine that from January 1, 1978, onward, all the world's natural increase—that is, all people born above the number needed to replace those who die—has been transplanted to Populandia.

According to the Bureau, a jumbo jet arrives at Populandia International Airport every two minutes, carrying at least 280 more children. By the end of the first day (January 1, 1978), there were already 200,677 people in Populandia—about as many as currently live in Mobile, Alabama. By the beginning of 1994, after only 16 years of "existence," the population of the island was more than 1.3 billion. This made Populandia the world's largest nation—more populous than China by over 100 million (Haub and Yanagishita, 1993).

World population growth—as symbolized by the striking growth of Populandia—vitally concerns anyone confronting the social problems of the 1990s. For example, since 1975 Mexico has made notable strides in increasing agricultural production through a rise in the amount of land under cultivation, greater reliance on machinery, and improved uses of fertilizer. At the same time, however, Mexico's population has increased dramatically, from 50 million in 1970 to 86 million in 1990. Consequently, even though the nation's agricultural production has become more sophisticated and efficient, the actual amount of food production per person in Mexico is less than it was decades ago (Haub and Yanagishita, 1993; Weeks, 1994:400).

In the United States as well, there is a relationship between population growth and social issues. Indeed, the size, composition, and distribution of the population of the United States have an important influence on many of the policy issues discussed in this book. For example, significant levels of immigration from Latin America and Asia have contributed to what some observers see as a need for multiculturalism (see Chapter 3). The clustering of people in metropolitan areas has intensified the nation's housing problems (see Chapter 18).

Many natural and social scientists are involved in the study of population-related issues. The biologist explores the nature of reproduction and casts light on factors that affect *fertility* (the amount of reproduction among women of childbearing age). The medical pathologist examines and analyzes trends in the causes of death. Geographers, historians, and psychologists also have distinctive contributions to make to our understanding of population (Wrong, 1977:6). Sociologists, more than these other researchers, focus on the *social* factors that influence population rates and trends.

In their study of population issues, sociologists are keenly aware that various elements of population—such as fertility, *mortality* (the amount of death), and migration—are profoundly affected by the norms, values, and social patterns of a society. Fertility is influenced by people's age of entry into sexual unions and by their use of contraception—both of which, in turn, reflect the social and religious values that guide a particular culture. Mortality is shaped by a nation's level of nutrition, acceptance of immunization, and provisions for sanitation, as well as its general commitment to health care and health education. Migration from one country to another can depend on marital and kinship ties, the relative degree of racial and religious tolerance in various societies, and people's evaluations of employment opportunities (Heer, 1975).

This chapter will consider certain aspects of population as studied by sociologists. It will begin by examining the controversial analysis of population trends presented by Thomas Robert Malthus and the critical response of Karl Marx. The special terminology used in population research will be detailed, and a brief overview of world population history will be offered. Particular attention will be given to the current problem of overpopulation and to the prospects for and potential social consequences of stable population growth in the United States.

Later in the chapter, we will examine the environmental problems facing the world as we enter the twenty-first century, and will draw on the functionalist and conflict perspectives to better understand environmental issues. It is important not to oversimplify the relationship between population and the environment. Rising population, in itself, does not necessarily destroy the environment, while stable population growth alone is no guarantee of healthy air, water, or land. Nevertheless, as will be evident in the social policy section on opposition to landfills, increases in population can strain our environmental resources and present difficult choices for policymakers.

DEMOGRAPHY: THE STUDY OF POPULATION

Demography is the scientific study of population. It draws upon several components of population, including size, composition, and territorial distribution, in order to understand the social consequences of population. Demographers study migration patterns, geographical variations, and historical trends in an effort to develop population forecasts. In addition, they analyze the structure of a population in terms of such factors as the age, gender, race, and ethnicity of its members.

One of the earliest demographers was Edmond Halley (1656–1742), an English astronomer who became well known through his association with the comet visible most recently during 1985–1986. Halley applied his mathematical skills to outlining the mortality records of the German town of Breslau and eventually developed a table showing death rates by age. Although Halley's statistical techniques have been questioned by later scholars, his analysis does represent the first simulation of the lifetime mortality experiences of a population. Halley was the first scientist to use death statistics in different age groups to determine a person's likelihood of death as he or she passed through each age group (*Population Today*, 1986).

Despite such early contributions, demography has emerged as a science only in the last 200 years. Demographer Judah Matras (1973:10–11) has shown that the scientific study of population could not begin until there were sophisticated systems for reporting vital events (births, deaths, marriages, and divorces) for purposes of taxation and governmental administration. Such systematic compilation of data began on a large scale in nineteenth-century Europe. Moreover, the science of demography required theorists who would offer generalizations concerning the relationship between population factors and social change. A key figure in undertaking this type of analysis was Thomas Malthus.

The Reverend Thomas Robert Malthus (1766–1834) suggested that the world's population was growing more rapidly than the available food supply.

Malthus's Thesis and Marx's Response

The Reverend Thomas Robert Malthus (1766–1834) was educated at Cambridge University and spent his life teaching history and political economy. His written work contains strong criticisms of two major institutions of his time—the church and slavery—yet, the most significant legacy of Malthus for contemporary scholars is his still-controversial work *Essays on the Principle of Population,* first published in 1798.

Essentially, Malthus suggested that the world's population was growing more rapidly than the available food supply. Malthus argued that the food supply increases in an arithmetic progression (1, 2, 3, 4, and so on), whereas the population expands by a geometric progression (1, 2, 4, 8, and so on). According to his analysis, the gap between the food supply and the population will continue to grow over time. Even though the food supply will increase, it will not increase nearly enough to meet the needs of an expanding world population.

Malthus proposed population control as an answer to the gap between rising population and food supply, yet he explicitly denounced artificial means of birth control because they were not sanctioned by religion. For Malthus, the appropriate way to control population was to postpone marriage. He argued that couples must take responsibility for the number of children they choose to bear; without such restraint, the world would face widespread hunger, poverty, and misery (Malthus et al., 1960, original edition 1824; Petersen, 1979:192–194; Rashid, 1987).

Karl Marx strongly criticized Malthus's views on population. Marx saw the nature of economic relations in Europe's industrial societies as the central problem. He could not accept the Malthusian notion that rising world population, rather than capitalism, was the cause of social ills. In Marx's opinion, there was no special relationship between world population figures and the supply of resources (including food). If society were well-ordered, increases in population should lead to greater wealth, not to hunger and misery.

Of course, Marx did not believe that capitalism operated under these ideal conditions. He maintained that capitalism devoted its resources to the financing of buildings and tools rather than to more equitable distribution of food, housing, and other necessities of life. Marx's work is important to the study of population because he linked overpopulation to the distribution of resources—a topic that will be taken up again later in this chapter. His concern with the writings of Malthus also testifies to the importance of population in political and economic affairs (Hawley, 1950; Meek, 1954; Petersen, 1975:165, 1979:74–77).

The insights of Malthus and Marx regarding population issues have come together in what is termed the *neo-Malthusian view.* Best exemplified by the work of Paul Ehrlich (1968; Ehrlich and Ehrlich, 1990), author of *The Population Bomb,* neo-Malthusians agree with Malthus that world population growth is outstretching natural resources. However, in contrast to the British theorist, they insist that birth control measures are needed to regulate population increases. Neo-Malthusians have a Marxist flavor in their condemnation of developed nations which, despite their low birthrates, consume a disproportionately large share of world resources.

While rather pessimistic about the future, these theorists stress that birth control and sensible use of resources are essential responses to rising world population (J. Tierney, 1990; Weeks, 1994; for a critique, see Commoner, 1971).

Studying Population Today

The relative balance of births and deaths is no less important in the 1990s than it was during the lifetime of Malthus and Marx. The suffering that Malthus spoke of is certainly a reality for many people of the world who are hungry and poor. Malnutrition remains the largest contributing factor to illness and death among children in the developing countries. Almost 15 percent of these children will die before age 5—a rate nearly 14 times higher than in developed nations. Furthermore, warfare and large-scale migration have exacerbated the relationship between population and food supply. In order to combat world hunger, it may be necessary to reduce human births, to dramatically increase the world's food supply, or perhaps to do both at the same time. With this in mind, it seems essential to study population-related issues (World Bank, 1993:202–203).

In the United States and most other countries, the census is the primary mechanism for collecting population information. A *census* is an enumeration or counting of a population. The Constitution of the United States requires that a census be held every 10 years in order to determine congressional representation. This periodic investigation is supplemented by *vital statistics;* these records of births, deaths, marriages, and divorces are gathered through a registration system maintained by government units. In addition, other governmental surveys provide up-to-date information on commercial developments, educational trends, industrial expansion, agricultural practices, and the status of such groups as children, the elderly, racial minorities, and single parents.

In administering a nationwide census and conducting other types of research, demographers employ many of the skills and techniques described in Chapter 2, including questionnaires, interviews, and sampling. The precision of population projections is contingent on the accuracy of a series of assumptions that demographers must make. First, they must determine past population trends and establish a base population as of the date for which the forecast began. Next, birth- and death rates must be established, along with estimates of future fluctuations. In making projections for a nation's population trends, demographers must consider migration as well, since a significant number of individuals may enter and leave the country.

Because of the difficulties of estimating future

In the United States and most other countries, the census is the primary mechanism for collecting information about the population.

R. Sidney/Image Works

births, deaths, and migration, demographers usually specify a range of projections—from "high" through "medium" to "low." These statistical forecasts are useful to a wide range of concerned parties, including planners, public administrators, economists, and commercial interests.

Elements of Demography

Demographers employ the distinctive terminology of their science in analyzing and projecting population trends. Population facts are communicated with a language derived from the basic elements of human life—birth and death. The ***birthrate*** (or, more specifically, the *crude birthrate*) is the number of live births per 1000 population in a given year. In 1993, for example, there were 16 live births per 1000 people in the United States. The birthrate provides information on the actual reproductive patterns of a society.

One way demography can project future growth in a society is to make use of the ***total fertility rate (TFR)***. The TFR is the average number of children born alive to any woman, assuming that she conforms to current fertility rates. The TFR reported for the United States in 1993 was 2.0 births per woman, as compared with over 7.3 births per woman in such developing countries as Ethiopia and Yemen. In Box 19-1, we examine the concern in Japan over the nation's low total fertility rate.

Mortality, like fertility, is measured in several different ways. The ***death rate*** (also known as the *crude death rate*) is the number of deaths per 1000 population in a given year. In 1993 the United States had a death rate of 9.0 per 1000 population. The ***infant mortality rate*** is the number of deaths of infants under 1 year of age per 1000 live births in a given year. This particular measure serves as an important indicator of a society's level of health care; it reflects prenatal nutrition, delivery procedures, and infant screening measures. The infant mortality rate also functions as a useful indicator of future population growth, since additional infants who survive to adulthood will contribute to further population increases.

There is a wide disparity among nations in the rate of death of newborn children. In 1992, the infant mortality rate for the United States was 8.6 deaths per 1000 live births, whereas for the world as a whole it was an estimated 70.0 births. At least 25 nations have lower rates of infant mortality than the United States, including Great Britain, Canada, and Sweden (refer back to Figure 17-1 on page 483). In 1992, Japan's infant mortality rate was only 4.4 deaths per 1000 live births—slightly less than half the rate of infant deaths in the United States (Haub and Yanagishita, 1993).

A general measure of health used by demographers is ***life expectancy***, which is the average number of years a person can be expected to live under current mortality conditions. Usually the figure is reported as life expectancy *at birth*. At present, Japan reports a life expectancy at birth of 76 years and Iceland reports 75 years, both slightly higher than the United States' figure of 72 years. By contrast, life expectancy at birth is less than 45 years in many developing nations, including The Gambia, Sierra Leone, and Afghanistan.

The ***growth rate*** of a society is the difference between births and deaths, plus the difference between *immigrants* (those who enter a country to establish permanent residence) and *emigrants* (those who leave a country permanently) per 1000 population. For the world as a whole, the growth rate is simply the difference between births and deaths per 1000 population, since worldwide immigration and emigration must of necessity be equal. In 1992, the United States had a growth rate of 1.1 percent, compared with an estimated 1.6 percent for the entire world (Bureau of the Census, 1993a:8–9; Haub and Yanagishita, 1993).

WORLD POPULATION HISTORY

One important aspect of demographic work involves study of the history of population. However, this is made difficult by the lack of reliable information for all but the modern era. For example, official national censuses were relatively rare before 1850. Researchers interested in early population therefore turn to archeological remains of settlements, burial sites, baptismal and tax records, and oral history sources.

We think of the world as having a large population—some 5.5 billion in 1993. Yet until modern times, there were relatively few humans living on this planet. One estimate placed the world popu-

BOX 19-1 ⋆ AROUND THE WORLD

JAPAN'S DECLINING FERTILITY

Beginning in 1990, Japanese newspapers, magazines, and television newscasts gave increasing attention to a phenomenon they called the "1.57 shock." This phrase captured the widespread sense of disbelief over the fact that Japan's total fertility rate (TFR) had fallen to 1.57 births; Japanese women were averaging only slightly above 1 and one-half children per lifetime. And the shocks kept coming. By 1993, Japan's TFR was down to 1.5 births and was projected to fall to 1.37 births by 2000 (Haub and Yanagishita, 1993; Yanagishita, 1992, 1993).

To put Japan's total fertility rate in perspective, the lowest TFR reached in the United States was 1.74 births in 1976. The lowest figure ever reported was 1.28 births in West Germany in 1985. Conversely, the Hutterites, a North American religious sect, averaged 12 children per woman in the 1930s by promoting early and universal mar-

riage and by discouraging use of birth control measures (McFalls, 1991:4, 7).

According to official population estimates, Japan's annual growth rate fell to its lowest postwar level between 1989 and 1990—just 0.33 percent per year. Population projections released in 1992 suggest that its population will actually begin to decline after 2011. Japan is already experiencing some of the demographic consequences typically associated with low fertility, among them a shortage of younger workers and rises in the cost of health care for the elderly. Indeed, Tokyo Shoko Research reports that whereas only 1 percent of successful Japanese businesses had to close in 1988 owing to a shortage of labor, this figure had increased to 6 percent by 1990.

Why has there been such a continuing decline in Japan's total fertility rate? While Japanese men continue to favor traditional gender

roles both in the workplace and within marriage, an increasing proportion of Japanese women resent male dominance and view marriage as a "raw deal" that denies them opportunities available to men. In 1970, only 18 percent of women 25 to 29 years old were single, but by 1989, 38 percent of women in this age group were single (Yanagishita, 1992:3, 1993).

Even among couples that do marry, work and financial pressures have contributed to lower fertility. "People feel so much pressure on the job that they work until nine, ten o'clock at night," observes Kunio Kitamura, a Tokyo obstetrician. "Then they have another hour and a half home on the train, because most people can't afford a house anywhere near the office. You probably can't get a seat, and the train is full of drunks, singing and throwing up. After all that, who has the strength to get in bed and make a baby?" (J. Schwartz, 1991:20).

---

lation of a million years ago at only 125,000 people. As Table 19-1 (page 546) indicates, the population has exploded in the last 200 years and continues to accelerate rapidly. Merely in the time it has taken you to read this far in this one paragraph, the world population has increased by 97 people!

Demographic Transition

The phenomenal growth of world population in recent times can be accounted for by changing patterns of births and deaths. Beginning in the late 1700s—and continuing until the middle 1900s—there was a gradual reduction in death rates in northern and western Europe. People were able to

live longer because of advances in food production, sanitation, nutrition, and public health care. While death rates fell, birthrates remained high; as a result, there was unprecedented population growth during this period of European history. However, by the late 1800s, the birthrates of many European countries began to decline, and the rate of population growth also decreased (Matras, 1977:38–44; McKeown, 1976).

The changes in birth- and death rates in nineteenth-century Europe serve as an example of demographic transition. Demographers use this term to describe an observed pattern in changing vital statistics. Specifically, *demographic transition* is the change from high birthrates and death rates to rel-

TABLE 19-1	For World Population, Estimated Time for Each Successive Increase of 1 Billion People	
POPULATION LEVEL	TIME TAKEN TO REACH NEW POPULATION LEVEL	YEAR OF ATTAINMENT
First billion	Human history before 1800	About A.D. 1800
Second billion	Approximately 130 years	1930
Third billion	30 years	1960
Fourth billion	15 years	1975
Fifth billion	12 years	1987
Sixth billion	10 years	1997
Seventh billion	11 years	2008
Eighth billion	11 years	2019
Ninth billion	13 years	2032
Tenth billion	18 years	2050
Eleventh billion	34 years	2084

During the twentieth century, the world population has grown at a much faster rate than in earlier periods of history. Whereas it took roughly 130 years to reach the second billion in world population, it took only 30 years to reach the third billion and 12 years to reach the fifth billion.

NOTE: Data for 1997 through 2050 are projections.
SOURCE: Population Reference Bureau, 1993.

atively low birthrates and death rates. This concept, which was introduced in the 1920s, is now widely used in the study of population trends.

As illustrated in Figure 19-1, demographic transition is typically viewed as a three-stage process:

1 High birth- and death rates with little population growth
2 Declining death rates, primarily the result of reductions in infant deaths, along with high to medium fertility—resulting in significant population growth
3 Low birth- and death rates with little population growth

Demographic transition should be regarded not as a "law of population growth," but rather as a generalization of the population history of industrial nations. Through use of this concept, we can better understand the growth problems faced by the world in the 1990s. About two-thirds of the world's nations have yet to pass fully through the second stage of demographic transition, among them, many countries in which Islam is the dominant religion (see Box 19-2 on page 548). Even if such nations make dramatic advances in fertility control, their populations will nevertheless increase seriously because of the large base of people already at prime childbearing age.

The pattern of demographic transition varies

from nation to nation. One particularly useful distinction is the contrast between the transition now occurring in developing nations—which include about two-thirds of the world's population—and that which occurred over almost a century in more industrialized countries. Demographic transition in developing nations has involved a rapid decline in death rates without adjustments in birthrates. Specifically, until the end of World War II, there was a very gradual decrease in the death rates of developing countries, due primarily to improved water supplies and other public sanitary measures. Yet the birthrates of these countries remained very high—about 30 per 1000 population in the 1940s (as compared with under 19 per 1000 in the United States during the same period).

In the post–World War II period, the death rates of developing nations began a sharp decline. This revolution in "death control" was triggered by antibiotics, immunization, insecticides (such as DDT, used to strike at malaria-bearing mosquitoes), and largely successful campaigns against such fatal diseases as smallpox. Substantial medical and public health technology was imported almost overnight from more developed nations. As a result, the drop in death rates that had taken a century in Europe was telescoped into two decades in many developing countries.

Birthrates scarcely had time to adjust. Cultural beliefs about the proper size of families could not

FIGURE 19-1 Demographic Transition

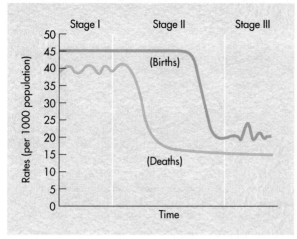

Demographers use the concept of demographic transition *to describe changes in birthrates and death rates during stages of a nation's development. This graph shows the pattern that took place in presently developed nations. In the first stage, both birthrates and death rates were high, so that there was little population growth. In the second stage, the birthrate remained high, while the death rate declined sharply, which led to rapid growth. By the last stage, which many developing nations have yet to enter, the birthrate also declined, and there was again little population growth.*

possibly change as quickly as the falling death rates. For centuries, couples had given birth to as many as eight or more children with the realization that perhaps two or three would survive to adulthood. Consequently, whereas Europeans had had several generations to restrict their birthrates, peoples of developing nations needed to do the same in less than a lifetime. Many did not, as is evident from the astronomical "population explosion" that was already under way by the middle 1900s. Clearly, families were more willing to accept technological advances that prolonged life than to abandon fertility patterns which reflected centuries of tradition and religious training (Almgren, 1992).

The Population Explosion

Apart from war, rapid population growth has been perhaps the dominant international social problem of the past 30 years. Often this issue is referred to in emotional terms as the "population bomb" or "population explosion." Such striking language is not surprising, given the staggering increases in world population during the last two centuries. As was detailed in Table 19-1, the population of our planet rose from 1 billion around the year 1800 to 5.5 billion by 1993. The United Nations projects that world population could rise as high as 6.4 billion by 2000 (Haub and Yanagishita, 1993; Haupt, 1990).

Shown is a family planning class in Pakistan. Family planning efforts in developing countries not only reduce unwanted population growth but can improve maternal health by helping women to time and space pregnancies.

BOX 19-2 · CURRENT RESEARCH

THE DEMOGRAPHY OF ISLAMIC NATIONS

The 47 nations in which Islam is the dominant religion are the fastest-growing group of countries in the world. Currently, nearly one in every five human beings is Muslim. At present rates of growth, the world's Islamic population of about 980 million in 1988 could almost double to 1.9 billion before the year 2020.

Sociologist and demographer John Weeks (1988:5) points out that "although Islam is a proselytizing religion, its proportionate increase in the modern world is much more a result of natural increase (the excess of births over deaths) than it is the conversion of non-Moslems to the Islamic faith." The Islamic nations report higher-than-average fertility, higher-than-average mortality, and rapid rates of population growth. These countries are viewed as being in the early stages of demographic transition from high to low birth- and death rates.

The total fertility rate (TFR) of the Islamic nations is 6.0 projected births per woman, compared with 4.5 births in other developing nations and only 1.7 births per woman in the developed nations. Islamic countries are growing at an average of 2.8 percent per year, or 22 percent faster than the world's other developing nations (Weeks, 1988: 12–13).

Weeks (1988:47) reviewed the population policies of these Islamic countries and found that there was considerable diversity in their positions regarding reproductive behavior and population growth. About half the governments of the Islamic nations reported that they were satisfied with their current rates of population growth; 40 percent stated that their current rates of growth were too high, whereas 10 percent indicated that their growth rates were too low.

Certain Islamic nations have implemented "pronatalist" policies to increase population. For example, Iraq, which has the highest natural increase rate (3.9 percent) of any country in the world, grants allowances and benefits to families. Women receive paid maternity leave at 100 percent of earnings for the first 10 weeks of pregnancy. The government's explicit goal is to encourage each woman to have a minimum of four children. By contrast, many Islamic countries either directly implement family planning programs or allow voluntary family planning associations to operate health care facilities and distribute contraceptive methods.

The diversity in the positions of Islamic nations regarding population growth is underscored in a report issued in 1992 by the Population Crisis Committee. Saudi Arabia was ranked as one of five countries with the worst family planning records for 1991 (as was the United States), while Morocco was praised for achieving dramatic increases in contraceptive use. Other studies have included Indonesia, Turkey, Egypt, and Tunisia among the Islamic nations that have made substantial progress in promoting contraceptive use and reducing fertility rates (de Sherbinin, 1990; *Ms.,* 1992; Omran and Roudi, 1993; Weeks, 1988:47).

By the middle 1970s, demographers had observed a slight decline in the growth rate of many developing nations. These countries were still experiencing population increases, yet their rates of increase had declined as death rates could not go much lower and birthrates began to fall. It appears that family planning efforts have been instrumental in this demographic change. Beginning in the 1960s, governments in certain developing nations sponsored or supported campaigns to encourage family planning. For example, in good part as the result of government-sponsored birth control campaigns, Thailand's total fertility rate fell from 6.1 births per woman in 1970 to only 2.6 in 1990. As noted in Box 19-2, Indonesia, Tunisia, and Egypt are among the other countries which have made substantial progress in promoting contraceptive use and reducing fertility rates (Haub and Yanagishita, 1993; *Ms.,* 1992; Weeks, 1988).

Through the efforts of many governments (among them the United States) and private agencies (among them Planned Parenthood), the fertility rates of many developing countries have declined. Supporters of international family planning efforts applauded in 1993 when President Bill Clinton signed an executive order resuming U.S. fund-

FIGURE 19-2 Population Structure of Mexico and the United States

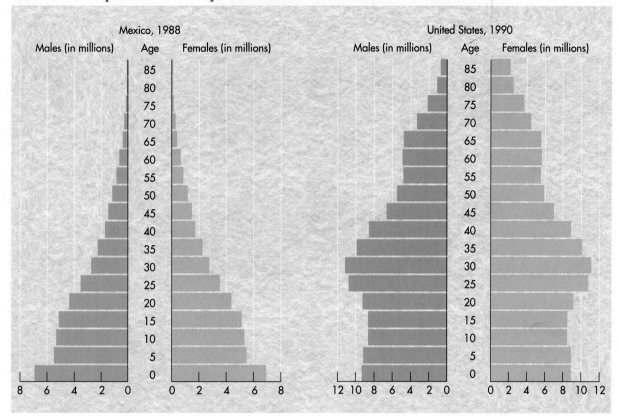

SOURCE: Weeks, 1994:230.

This figure shows the population pyramids of Mexico and the United States. Developing countries like Mexico have high birthrates, but mortality takes its toll over the life cycle and there are relatively few people over the age of 65. By contrast, the United States continues to display the bulge of the "baby boom" of the 1950s and shows serious mortality only at older ages.

ing of organizations within the nation and overseas that support or promote abortion as a method of family planning. However, some critics, reflecting a conflict orientation, have questioned why the United States and other industrialized nations are so enthusiastic about population control in the developing world. In line with Marx's response to Malthus, they argue that large families and even population growth are not the causes of hunger and misery. Rather, the unjust economic domination by the developed states of the world results in an unequal distribution of world resources and in widespread poverty in exploited developing nations (Rowen, 1993:5).

Even if family planning efforts are successful in reducing fertility rates, the momentum toward growing world population is well established. The developing nations face the prospect of continued population growth, since a substantial portion of their population is approaching childbearing years. This is evident in Figure 19-2, in which the population pyramids of the United States and Mexico are compared.

A ***population pyramid*** is a special type of bar chart that shows the distribution of population by gender and age; it is generally used to illustrate the

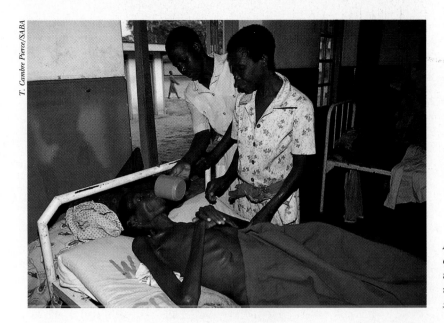

According to estimates, as many as one-quarter to one-third of all adults in urban areas carry the HIV virus which destroys the body's immune system.

population structure of a society. As Figure 19-2 illustrates, a substantial portion of the population of Mexico consists of children who are under the age of 15, with their childbearing years still to come. Thus, the built-in momentum for population growth is much greater in Mexico (and other developing countries) than it is in the United States.

This is evident in an examination of population data for India, which in 1993 had a population of 897 million. Demographer Leon Bouvier (1984:25) has projected that, even if India's fertility rates level off to rates near those of North America and Europe, the nation's population will still reach 1.4 billion by the year 2025. That figure is higher than the current combined total for all of North America, South America, Africa, and Europe. Thus, because of the substantial momentum for growth built into India's age structure, the nation will face a staggering increase in population in the coming decades—even if its birthrate declines sharply.

By 1993, population specialists and policymakers, worried about the population explosion, were facing certain disturbing facts, among them the following:

• The world population rose by 93 million between mid-1988 and mid-1989, an all-time record increase.

• According to projections of the United Nations Food and Agriculture Organization, as many as 64 nations will experience critical food problems in the future. India now produces less food grain per person than it did in 1900 (Haub, 1988).

• Developing nations are not experiencing the declines in fertility that had been predicted earlier by researchers. Most seriously, a report published in late 1992 by the Population Crisis Committee suggests that neither China nor India is likely to stabilize growth until well into the next century, owing to serious shortcomings in these countries' family planning programs. China and India are the world's two most populous nations, and continued growth in these two countries is likely to result in substantial environmental damage, including soil and water depletion (Crossette, 1992).

Population growth is not a problem in all industrialized nations. Indeed, a handful of countries are adopting policies which *encourage* growth—among them, Japan, which is considering offering benefits to families which have children and is upgrading child care services. Nevertheless, a global perspective underscores the dire consequences that could result from continued population growth (T. Reid, 1990).

A tragic new factor has emerged in the last decade which will restrict worldwide population growth: the spread of AIDS (refer back to the social policy section in Chapter 5). According to estimates, in certain African nations, as many as one-quarter to one-third of all adults in urban areas carry the HIV virus which destroys the body's immune system. It is projected that at least 10 million people in Asia will be infected with the HIV virus by the year 2000. Given the grim forecasts offered by researchers, the AIDS epidemic is likely to have increasing impact on world population patterns (Shenon, 1992).

FERTILITY PATTERNS IN THE UNITED STATES

During the last four decades, the United States and other industrial nations have passed through two different patterns of population growth—the first marked by high fertility and rapid growth (stage II in the theory of demographic transition), the second marked by decline in fertility and little growth (stage III). Sociologists are keenly aware of the social impact of these fertility patterns.

The Baby Boom

The most recent period of high fertility in the United States has often been referred to as the *baby boom*. After World War II—during which large numbers of military personnel were separated from their spouses—the annual number of births began to rise dramatically. Yet the baby boom was not a return to the large families common in the 1800s. In fact, there was only a slight increase in the proportion of couples having three or more children. The boom resulted from a striking decrease in the number of childless marriages and one-child families. Although a peak was reached in 1957, the nation maintained a relatively high birthrate of over 20 live births per 1000 population until 1964. (In 1993, by contrast, the birthrate was 16 live births per 1000 population—or 20 percent lower than in 1964.)

It would be a mistake to attribute the baby boom solely to the return home of large numbers of soldiers. High wages and general prosperity during the post-World War II period encouraged many married couples to have children and purchase homes. In addition, several sociologists—as well as feminist author Betty Friedan (1963)—have noted that there were pervasive pressures on women during the 1950s for marriage, homemaking, and motherhood (Bouvier, 1980).

Stable Population Growth

Although the total fertility rate of the United States has remained low over the last two decades, the nation continues to grow in size because of two factors: the momentum built into our age structure by the postwar population boom, and the continued high rates of immigration. Because of the upsurge of births in the 1950s, there are now many more people in their childbearing years than in older age groups (where most deaths occur). This growth of population represents a "demographic echo" of the baby boom generation, many of whom are now parents. Consequently, the number of people born each year in the United States continues to exceed the number who die. In addition, the nation allows a large number of immigrants to enter each year; these immigrants currently account for between one-fourth and one-third of annual growth.

However, assuming relatively low fertility levels and moderate net migration in the coming decades, the United States may reach *zero population growth (ZPG)*. ZPG is the state of a population where the number of births plus immigrants equals the number of deaths plus emigrants. For more than 99 percent of its history, humanity remained in the first stage of demographic transition and had little or no population growth (McFalls, 1991; McFalls et al., 1984; Population Reference Bureau, 1978).

The United States is not alone in approaching zero population growth. Other countries, especially in Europe, are at or are approaching ZPG. In the recent past, although some nations have achieved ZPG, it has been relatively short-lived. However, given the current international concern over world population, more nations may attempt to maintain ZPG in the early twenty-first century. Demographers estimate that it will probably take until the year 2200 for demographic transition to run its course worldwide, with the world's population

As the United States approaches zero population growth (ZPG), the median age of the population continues to rise.

reaching a peak of 12 to 14 billion (McNamara, 1992).

What will a society with stable population growth be like? In demographic terms, it will be quite different from the United States of the 1990s. By the year 2040, there will be relatively equal numbers of people in each age group, and the median age of the population will be 37 (compared with 33 in 1991). As a result, the population pyramid will look more like a rectangle. Yet stable growth does not necessarily mean that people will be nonmobile. Internal migrations—whether "back to the city" or "back to the farm"—are still possible in a ZPG society (Bureau of the Census, 1993a:16; Day, 1978).

The impact of zero population growth goes far beyond demographic statistics. Day-to-day life will be somewhat different as countries cease to grow and the relative proportions of the population in various age groups remain constant. By itself, ZPG is no guarantee either of bounty or of economic ruin. There will be a much larger proportion of older people, especially aged 75 and over, a fact which will place a greater demand on the nation's social service programs and health care institutions. On a more positive note, the economy will be less volatile under ZPG, since the number of entrants to the labor market will be more stable (Spengler, 1978:187).

In industrial societies such as the United States, power and position in the work force have traditionally been determined in part by length of service. With ZPG, there will be less opportunity for promotion based on time of service, since a large part of the population will be older. For example, in 1988 the United States had 40 percent fewer people aged 50 to 55 than aged 20 to 25. By contrast, if the nation reaches ZPG, there will be only 5 to 10 percent fewer adults of age 50 than of age 20. Consequently, many more people with 20 to 30 years of work experience will be competing for the same desirable positions.

ZPG will also lead to changes in family life. Clearly, as fertility rates continue to decline, women will devote fewer years to childbearing and to the social roles of motherhood. The proportion of married women entering the paid labor force can be expected to rise (see Chapter 11). In addition, there may be further increases in the divorce rate in a ZPG society. As families have fewer children, unhappy couples may feel freer to seek separation and divorce (Day, 1978; McFalls, 1981; Weeks, 1994:249).

POPULATION AND MIGRATION

Along with births and deaths, migration is one of the three factors affecting population growth or decline. The term *migration* refers to relatively permanent movement of people with the purpose of changing their place of residence (Prehn, 1991). Migration usually describes movement over a sizable distance, rather than from one side of a city to another.

As a social phenomenon, migration is fairly complex and results from a variety of factors. The most important tend to be economic—financial failure in the "old country" and a perception of greater economic opportunities and prosperity in the new homeland. Other factors which contribute to migration include racial and religious bigotry, dislike for prevailing political regimes, and desire to reunite one's family. All these forces combine to *push* some individuals out of their homelands and to *pull* them to areas believed to be more attractive.

International Migration

International migration—changes of residence across national boundaries—has been a significant force in redistributing the world's population dur-ing certain periods of history. For example, the composition of the United States has been significantly altered by immigrants who have come here in the nineteenth and twentieth centuries. Their entry was encouraged or restricted by various immigration policies. The immigration policy of the United States was examined in detail in the social policy section of Chapter 10.

In the last decade, immigration has become a controversial issue throughout much of Europe. Western Europe, in particular, has become a desirable destination for many individuals and families from former colonies or former communist-bloc countries who are fleeing the poverty, persecution, and warfare of their native lands. Currently, there are 20 million legal immigrants in western Europe, along with an estimated 2 million illegal immigrants. With the number of immigrants and refugees increasing at a time of widespread unemployment and housing shortages, there has been a striking rise in antiforeign (and often openly racist) sentiment in Germany, France, and other countries. Right-wing forces in Germany (including members of the skinhead counterculture examined in Chapter 3) have mounted more than 3500 attacks on foreigners in recent years. Gypsies from eastern Europe and immigrants from Asia are often the tar-

Young neo-Nazis are shown in late 1991 in a march through the city of Halle, Germany. Right-wing forces in Germany (including members of the skinhead counterculture) have mounted more than 3500 attacks on foreigners in recent years.

DPA/Photoreporters

553

gets, and there have been attacks as well on Germany's small Jewish community (Range, 1993).

Developing countries in Asia and Africa are also encountering difficulties as thousands of displaced people seek assistance and asylum. For example, as of 1992, Bangladesh had received more than 300,000 refugees from Myanmar's Rohingya Muslim community; Jordan had taken in 250,000 to 300,000 Palestinians who had fled or been expelled from Kuwait; and Kenya had accepted more than 230,000 refugees fleeing war and famine in Ethiopia and Somalia. The political and economic problems of developing nations (refer back to Chapter 9) are only intensified by such massive migration under desperate conditions (Kushnick, 1993:252).

Internal Migration

Migratory movements within societies can vary in important ways. In traditional societies, migration often represents a way of life, as people move to accommodate the changing availability of fertile soil or wild game. In industrial societies, people may relocate as a result of job transfers or because they believe that a particular region has better employment opportunities or a more desirable climate.

Although nations typically have laws and policies governing movement across their borders, the same is not true of internal movement. Generally, residents of a country are legally free to migrate from one locality to another. Of course, this is not the case in all nations; the Republic of South Africa has historically restricted the movement of Blacks and other non-Whites through the system of segregation known as *apartheid* (see Chapter 10).

We can identify two distinctive trends of recent internal migration within the United States:

1 *Suburbanization.* During the period 1980–1990, suburban counties grew in population by 14 percent while the total population of the United States rose by 10 percent. The proportion of the population living in central cities stayed constant at about one-third over the preceding 40 years. Meanwhile, the share of the population living in nonmetropolitan areas declined from 44 percent in 1950 to 20 percent in 1992 (Bureau of the Census, 1994).
2 *"Sunning of America."* There has been significant

internal migration from the "snow belt" of the north central and northeastern states to the "sun belt" in the south and west. Since 1970, the sun belt has absorbed almost two-thirds of the population growth of the United States. Individuals and families move to the sun belt because of its expanding economy and desirable climate. Businesses are attracted by the comparatively inexpensive energy supplies, increased availability of labor, and relative weakness of labor unions. Since 1988, however, while internal migration to the south has remained high, migration to the west has lessened as the job boom in that region has ended (Dunn, 1991; Gober, 1993).

THE ENVIRONMENT

In 1962, in her pioneering book *Silent Spring,* Rachel Carson warned about the health hazards resulting from the widespread use of insecticides and other pesticides. Carson pointed to the dangers of the insecticide DDT, later banned by the Environmental Protection Agency after it was found to cause cancer in test animals. In warning of the domination of society by industry and the profit motive, Carson concluded: "We shall have no relief from this poisoning of the environment until our officials have the courage and integrity to declare that the public welfare is more important than dollars, and to enforce this point of view in the face of all pressures and all protests, even from the public itself" (Brodeur, 1993:114).

By the 1970s, the environment had become a major concern across the United States. An estimated 25 million people participated in the nation's first Earth Day on April 22, 1970. Some 2000 communities held planned Earth Day celebrations, while there were environmental teach-ins at more than 2000 colleges and 10,000 schools. Protest marches on behalf of environmental causes were held in many parts of the nation. In the early 1970s, a major movement on behalf of environmental concerns emerged, while Congress established the Environmental Protection Agency in 1970 and passed the Clean Air and Clean Water Acts (D. Hayes, 1990).

In the 1990s, people around the planet are worried about the continuing deterioration of the environment. In 1992, some 106 heads of government

—the largest gathering of the world's political leaders in history—met in Rio de Janeiro to attend the United Nations Conference on Environment and Development (commonly known as the "Earth Summit"). Indeed, more than 35,000 people, including 9000 journalists, participated in the official meetings and nongovernmental events in Rio.

The Earth Summit occurred within a climate of grave concern. In 1992, the United States National Academy of Sciences and the Royal Society of London (1992:1) issued a report that began: "If current predictions of population growth prove accurate and patterns of human activity on the planet remain unchanged, science and technology may not be able to prevent either irreversible degradation of the environment or continued poverty for much of the world." The report represented a remarkable admission by two of the world's leading scientific bodies that science and technology can no longer ensure a better future unless population growth is checked and the world economy is restructured (L. Brown, 1993:3).

Within the United States, concern about environmental issues has grown steadily since Rachel Carson published *Silent Spring* in 1962 and the first Earth Day was held in 1970. A diversified social movement has arisen to address environmental issues. It is estimated that 14 million people in the United States belong to one of the 150 nationwide environmental organizations or to one of the 12,000 grass-roots groups. The best known of the national organizations include the Sierra Club (established in 1892), the Natural Resources Defense Council (founded in 1970), and the controversial activist group Greenpeace. By 1990, a national survey revealed that 76 percent of adults in the United States view themselves as environmentalists. When Democratic presidential nominee Bill Clinton chose Senator Albert Gore of Tennessee as his running mate in 1992, an important reason was Gore's record as an outspoken environmentalist (Sale, 1993; J. Schwartz, 1990; see also Cable and Benson, 1993).

Like any social movement, the environmental movement has aroused opposition. Opponents argue that we must balance our need for clean air, unspoiled offshore waters, and pristine wilderness areas with our need for jobs, energy, and tourist sites. At the same time, some observers who support environmentalist goals are troubled by the fact that the most powerful nationwide environmental organizations are predominantly White and affluent. Viewed from a conflict perspective, it is significant that these organizations accept funding from oil companies, chemical giants, and other powerful corporations. Perhaps as a result, the environmentalist movement has often emphasized limited reforms rather than profound structural changes—for example, requiring cars to be more energy-efficient rather than drastically reducing the number of automobiles (Burke, 1993; Sale, 1993).

What is ahead in confronting the world's environmental problems? Environmentalist Lester Brown (1993:21), president of the Worldwatch Institute—a nonprofit organization concerned with worldwide social and physical environmental issues—concludes:

> We know what we have to do. And we know how to do it. If we fail to convert our self-destructing economy into one that is environmentally sustainable, future generations will be overwhelmed by environmental degradation and social disintegration. Simply stated, if our generation does not turn things around, our children may not have the option of doing so.

Environmental Problems: An Overview

With each passing year, we are learning more about the environmental damage caused by present population levels and production and consumption patterns. The superficial signs are visible almost everywhere. Our air and water are being polluted, whether we live in St. Louis, Mexico City, or Lagos, Nigeria. As we will explore more fully in the social policy section, disposal of both toxic and nontoxic wastes is a nationwide and worldwide problem (McNamara, 1992).

In recent decades, the world has witnessed serious environmental disasters. For example, Love Canal, near Niagara Falls in New York State, was declared a disaster area in 1978 because of chemical contamination. In the 1940s and 1950s, the site had been used by a chemical company to dispose of waste products, but later a housing development and a school were built there. The metal drums which held the chemical wastes eventually rusted out and toxic chemicals with noxious odors began seeping into the residents' yards and basements. Subsequent investigations revealed that the chemical company knew as early as 1958 that toxic chemicals were seeping into homes and a school playground. After repeated protests in the late 1970s, 239 families living in Love Canal had to be relocated.

In 1986, a series of explosions set off a catastrophic nuclear reactor accident at Chernobyl, a part of the Ukraine (in what was then the Soviet Union). As a result of this accident, at least 500 and perhaps as many as 10,000 people died. Some

F. Hibon/Sygma

At least 500 and perhaps as many as 10,000 people died as a result of the catastrophic 1986 nuclear reactor accident at Chernobyl, a part of the Ukraine (in what was then the Soviet Union).

300,000 residents had to be evacuated, and the area became uninhabitable for 19 miles in any direction. Continuing levels of high radiation were found as far as 30 miles from the reactor site, while radioactivity levels were well above normal as far away as Sweden and Japan. According to one estimate, the Chernobyl accident and the resulting nuclear fallout may ultimately result in 5000 to 150,000 excess cases of cancer worldwide (Bharadwaj, 1992; Bogert, 1990).

While Love Canal, Chernobyl, and other environmental disasters understandably grab headlines, it is the silent, day-to-day deterioration of the environment that ultimately poses a devastating threat to humanity. It is impossible to examine all our environmental problems in detail, but three broad areas of concern stand out: air pollution, water pollution, and contamination of land.

Air Pollution According to a study by the United Nations Environment Programme and the World Health Organization (1988), more than 1 billion people on the planet are exposed to potentially health-damaging levels of air pollution. Indeed, in cities around the world, residents have come to accept smog and polluted air as "normal." Air pollution in urban areas is caused primarily by emissions from automobiles and secondarily by emissions from electric power plants and heavy industries. Urban smog not only limits visibility; it can lead to health problems as uncomfortable as eye irritation and as deadly as lung cancer. It is estimated that air pollution may cost the United States as much as $40 billion per year in health care expenses and lost productivity. Studies in Bulgaria have documented that, compared with other residents, people living near heavy industrial complexes have asthma rates nine times as high, rates of skin disease seven times as high, and rates of liver disease four times as high (L. Brown, 1993; Cannon, 1985; J. Friedman, 1990).

Water Pollution Throughout the United States, streams, rivers, and lakes have been polluted through dumping of waste materials by both industries and local governments. Consequently, many bodies of water have become unsafe for drinking, fishing, and swimming. Around the world, the pollution of the oceans has become a growing concern. Such pollution results regularly from waste dumping and is exacerbated by fuel leakage from shipping and occasional oil spills. In a dramatic accident, the oil tanker *Exxon Valdez* ran aground in Prince William Sound, Alaska, in 1989. The tanker's cargo of 11 million gallons of crude oil was lost in the sound or washed onto the shore, thereby contaminating 1285 miles of shoreline. About 11,000 people had to join in a cleanup effort which ultimately cost over $2 billion.

Recent data from Russia, the largest country in Europe, underscore the problems caused by water pollution. With half the nation's drinking water and one-tenth of its food supply contaminated, 55 percent of school-age children experience health problems, and Russia's life expectancy is now declining (Freeland, 1992; see also L. Brown, 1993:9–10).

Contamination of Land As was evident in Love Canal, land can be seriously contaminated by industrial dumping of hazardous wastes and chemicals. In another noteworthy case of contamination, unpaved roads in Times Beach, Missouri, were sprayed to control dust in 1971 with an oil that contained dioxin. This highly toxic chemical is produced as a by-product of the manufacture of herbicides and other chemicals. After the health dangers of dioxin became evident, the entire community of 2800 people was relocated (at a cost of $33 million) and the town of Times Beach was fully shut down in 1985.

What are the basic causes of our growing environmental problems? Neo-Malthusians such as Paul Ehrlich (1968; Ehrlich and Ehrlich, 1990) see world population growth as the central factor in environmental deterioration and argue that population control is essential in preventing widespread starvation and environmental decay. Barry Commoner (1971), a biologist, counters that the primary cause of environmental ills is the increasing use of technological innovations that are destructive to the environment—among them, plastics, detergents, synthetic fibers, pesticides, herbicides, and chemical fertilizers. Sociologist Allan Schnaiberg (1980) is critical of both these approaches. He argues that those who own and control the means of production in advanced capitalist societies have ultimate responsibility for our environmental problems because of their need to constantly generate greater

W. Eastep/Stock Market

Shown is a dam in Tampa, Florida. Human ecologists emphasize that the environment provides the resources essential for life.

profits no matter what their environmental consequences (Dunlap, 1993; McNamara, 1992). In the following sections, we will contrast the functionalist and conflict approaches to the study of environmental issues.

Functionalism and Human Ecology

In Chapter 18, we noted that *human ecology* is concerned with the interrelationships among people in their spatial setting and physical environment. Environmentalist Barry Commoner (1971:39) has stated that "everything is connected to everything else." With this in mind, human ecologists focus on how the physical environment shapes people's lives and also on how people influence the surrounding environment.

In an application of the human ecological perspective, sociologist Riley Dunlap (1993:711–712; Dunlap and Catton, 1983) suggests that the natural environment serves three basic functions for humans, as it does for the many animal species:

1 *The environment provides the resources essential for life.* These include air, water, and materials used to create shelter, transportation, and needed products. If human societies exhaust these resources—for example, by polluting the water supply or cut-

ting down rain forests—the consequences can be most serious.

2 *The environment serves as a waste repository.* More so than other living species, humans produce a huge quantity and variety of waste products, including bodily wastes, garbage, and sewage. Various types of pollution have become more common because human societies are generating more wastes than the environment can safely absorb.

3 *The environment "houses" our species.* It is our home, our living space, the place where we reside, play, and work. At times, we take this for granted, but not when day-to-day living conditions become unpleasant and difficult. If our air is "heavy," if our tap water turns brown, if our neighborhood is overcrowded, we remember why it is vital to live in a healthy environment.

Dunlap (1993:712–713) points out that these three functions of the environment actually compete with one another. Human use of the environment for one of these functions will often strain its ability to fulfill the other two. For example, with world population continuing to rise, we have an increasing need to raze forests or farmland and build housing developments. But each time we do so, we are reducing the amount of land providing food, lumber, or habitat for wildlife.

This tension between the three essential functions of the environment brings us back to the human ecologists' view that "everything is connected to everything else." In facing the environmental challenges of the twenty-first century, government policymakers and environmentalists must determine how they can fulfill human societies' pressing needs (for example, for food, clothing, and shelter) while at the same time preserving the environment as a source of resources, as a waste repository, and as our home.

Conflict View of Environmental Issues

As was discussed earlier, some theorists view overpopulation as the central cause of environmental problems, while others emphasize the role of harmful technological innovations. From a conflict perspective, however, neither of these approaches is satisfactory. Like Allan Schnaiberg, many sociologists draw on the conflict perspective and blame the dominant social paradigm of advanced capitalist societies for threatening our environment (Bharadwaj, 1992).

In Chapter 9, we drew on world systems theory to show how a growing share of the human and natural resources of the developing countries is being redistributed to the core industrialized nations. This process only intensifies the destruction of natural resources in poorer regions of the world. From a conflict perspective, less affluent nations are being forced to exploit their mineral deposits, forests, and fisheries in order to meet their debt obligations. The poor turn to the only means of survival available to them: they plow mountain slopes, burn plots in tropical forests, and overgraze grasslands (Durning, 1990:26; Waring, 1988).

This interplay between economic troubles and environmental destruction has been quite evident in Brazil, where each year thousands of square miles of the Amazon rain forest are cleared for crops and livestock through burning. (As was discussed in Chapter 9, the elimination of the rain forest affects worldwide weather patterns and heightens the gradual warming of the earth in a process known as the *greenhouse effect*.) Similarly, Susan Stonich (1989) suggests that environmental destruction in southern Honduras is intricately connected to problems of poverty, unemployment, and land

tenure. Stonich found that the policies of multinational corporations and international aid organizations encourage an export-oriented agriculture that relies on intensive land use. In her view, such policies are likely to lead to destruction of the remaining rain forests in Central America, while increasing inequality, malnutrition, and conflicts within and between nations.

These socioeconomic patterns, with harmful environmental consequences, are evident not only in Latin America but also in many regions of Africa and Asia. Nevertheless, while well-aware of the en-

FIGURE 19-3 *Global Concern for the Environment*

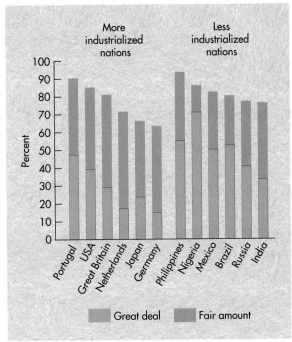

SOURCE: Adapted from Dunlap et al., 1993:8.

A 1992 survey conducted by The Gallup International Institute in 24 nations showed that people around the world worried about the environment. A higher proportion of people in the Philippines, Nigeria, Mexico, and Brazil said that they had a "great deal" of personal concern about environmental problems than did people in the United States, Great Britain, Japan, and Germany.

vironmental implications of land use policies in the Third World, conflict theorists contend that such a focus on the developing countries can contain an element of ethnocentrism. Who, they ask, is more to blame for environmental deterioration: the poverty-stricken and "food-hungry" populations of the world or the "energy-hungry" industrialized nations (G. Miller, 1972:117)?

Conventional wisdom holds that concern for environmental quality is limited to the world's wealthy industrialized nations. However, the results of the 1992 Health of the Planet survey conducted in 24 countries by The Gallup International Institute show that there is *widespread* environmental concern around the planet. Indeed, as is shown in Figure 19-3, a higher proportion of people in the Philippines, Nigeria, Mexico, and Brazil said that they had a "great deal" of personal concern about environmental problems than did people in the United States, Great Britain, Japan, and Germany (Dunlap et al., 1993:8).

In challenging the ethnocentrism inherent in blaming environmental ills on poor and developing nations, conflict theorists point out that western industrialized nations account for only 25 percent of the world's population but are responsible for 85 percent of worldwide consumption. Looking at the United States alone, a mere 6 percent of the world's people consume more than half the world's nonrenewable resources and more than one-third of all the raw materials produced. With such data in mind, conflict theorists charge that the most serious threat to the environment comes from "affluent megaconsumers and megapolluters" (Bharadwaj, 1992:853; G. Miller, 1972:122).

Allan Schnaiberg (1980) further refines this analysis by criticizing the focus on affluent *consumers* as the cause of environmental troubles. In his view, a capitalist system has a "treadmill of production" because of its inherent need to build ever-expanding profits. This treadmill necessitates *creating* an increasing demand for products, obtaining natural resources at minimal cost, and manufacturing products as quickly and cheaply as possible—no matter what the long-range environmental consequences of this treadmill. In Schnaiberg's view, drawing on the work of Karl Marx, it is those who own and control the means of production who are ultimately responsible for the effects of this treadmill of production and the ever-expanding consumption that results (see also K. Zimmerman et al., 1986). As we will see in the social policy section that follows, this insatiable production and consumption contribute directly to the demand for more and more landfills.

SOCIAL POLICY AND THE ENVIRONMENT

OPPOSITION TO LANDFILLS

- How can community opposition to a landfill or another public project be viewed from a conflict perspective?
- According to sociological research, how is a community's exposure to hazardous waste sites and pollution affected by the race, ethnicity, and social class standing of its members?
- Why are environmentalists somewhat divided on the issue of landfills and waste disposal?

The small town of Canadea, New York, seemed an unlikely setting for a riot. Nestled in the hills near the Pennsylvania border, this town of 2300 people had never been the site of a major demonstration, much less a violent one. But in April 1990, protestors charged local police, and 39 residents were arrested. The issue at stake was not civil rights, unemployment, workers' wages, or other traditional political and economic flashpoints. Rather, it was an issue posed by a major governmental body which raised long-range questions of public policy: the disposal of waste. According to a survey, 91 percent of Canadea residents were opposed to a proposed landfill in their community. Public opposition was so intense that the local prosecutor was unable to indict the rioters even though the violence had been witnessed by many bystanders and captured on videotape (Inhaber, 1992a, 1992b).

Many of us have heard the commonsense notion

A man is shown being arrested after committing civil disobedience as part of a 1990 protest against a proposed landfill in Canadea, New York.

that the United States is running out of safe places to locate landfills. While it is true that there is a shortage of such sites in the northeastern states, there are many acceptable locations across the country. Nevertheless, policymakers face significant financial strains in funding expensive landfills. Even more important, as we saw in the Canadea example, landfills arouse strong opposition from local residents (Rathje and Murphy, 1992:118–120).

The controversies over landfills in many states and communities have led social scientists to apply the labels of "NIMBY" and "NIMTOO." Community activists often respond to proposed landfills by declaring "not in my back yard" (NIMBY). Legislators then respond to the political climate by supporting studies and environmental impact statements as a delaying tactic and a way of implicitly saying "not in my term of office" (NIMTOO). Proponents of NIMBY and NIMTOO do not necessarily challenge the need for a proposed landfill; they simply insist "not here" and "not now." These cries are heard as well when people protest proposals for prisons, nuclear power facilities, sewage treatment plants, drug rehabilitation clinics, hospices for AIDS patients, and group homes for people with developmental disabilities (see Chapter 20).

Urban planner Michael Dear (1992) has identified the stages of a NIMBY battle against a landfill or another targeted facility. First, news of the proposal spreads, leading to strong and blunt community opposition. Residents seem unwilling to compromise. Second, battle lines are drawn as the debate moves from private complaints to public forums. Consequently, despite heated moments, the debate gradually becomes more rational and objective. In the third (and generally the longest) stage, political and legal debates continue, and concessions are made on both sides. Victory frequently goes to those with the political and economic resources, as well as the persistence and stamina, to continue the fight.

The NIMBY phenomenon has been viewed both positively and critically in sociological literature. The more positive assessments emphasize that citizens have a fairly good grasp of local issues and a reasonable concern for genuine risks to a community's health and welfare. But critics counter that it is becoming impossible to find locations for essential public projects. From a conflict perspective, NIMBY politics can be a reflection of direct prejudices (communities not wanting mentally disabled people or critically ill AIDS patients in their midst) or of less direct forms of bias (perhaps the controversial facility can be relocated to a poor or minority community that will not have the political power to veto it). Certainly those areas with the greatest wealth, prestige, and power will have the most success in declaring "not in my back yard" (Kraft and Clary, 1991).

Sociologist Robert Bullard (1990) has shown that low-income communities and areas with significant minority populations are more likely to be adjacent to waste sites than are affluent White communities. In a pioneering 1979 study of Houston, Bullard showed that since the 1920s, all the city-owned landfills and six of the eight garbage incinerators had been located in Black neighborhoods (Suro, 1993). Similarly, sociologist Timothy Maher (1991) examined the locations of all hazardous waste sites identified by the Indiana Department of Environmental Management. He found that these sites are especially likely to be found near communities with many working-class residents or with substantial African American populations.

A landmark study published in 1987 by the United Church of Christ's Commission for Racial Justice (1987) found that a large minority population—even more than poverty—was the distinguishing characteristic of communities exposed to toxic wastes. According to this study, three of every five Blacks and Hispanics in the nation live in areas with uncontrolled toxic waste sites. Moreover, a report issued in mid-1992 by the Environmental Protection Agency suggested that racial and ethnic minorities suffer disproportionate exposure to dust, soot, carbon monoxide, ozone, sulfur, sulfur dioxide, and lead, along with disproportionate emissions from hazardous waste dumps. In line with a conflict perspective, activists in African American, Hispanic, Asian American, and Native American communities draw on such data to challenge what they call "environmental racism." In the view of these activists, because their neighborhoods are poor and powerless, they have become industrial dumping grounds—with the results evident in disproportionate rates of birth defects, lead poisoning, and cancer (Bryant and Mohai, 1992; P. Davis, 1992; Elson, 1990; Suro, 1993; see also Kirby, 1982).

With opposition to landfills intensifying in both non-White and White communities, waste disposal and waste transport companies are turning to Congress in search of a federal solution to the waste problem. Garbage is increasingly being shipped across state lines, leading to tensions between those states that export garbage (primarily New York and New Jersey) and those that have been inundated with out-of-state trash (including Alabama, New Mexico, Ohio, Pennsylvania, Michigan, and West Virginia). The latter states have been largely frustrated in their efforts to ban out-of-state waste because of a Supreme Court decision that the Constitution protects interstate shipping of garbage. Nevertheless, some states have attempted to discourage imports by imposing moratoriums on new landfills, by taxing waste disposal, or by allowing counties to prohibit outside garbage from being dumped within their jurisdictions.

Environmentalists appear somewhat divided on the issue of landfills and waste disposal. For example, the Citizens Clearinghouse for Hazardous Wastes, which is affiliated with some 6300 community groups, strongly opposes new landfills and garbage incinerators. Their strategy is to prevent waste facilities from being established, thereby (they hope) forcing cutbacks in the amount of waste that is generated and dumped. But a representative of the Sierra Club insists that waste will continue to be dumped *somewhere*—even if new and safer facilities are not constructed (Pytte, 1990:174).

For many environmentalists, recycling is an essential element in a long-range solution to the waste disposal problem. Whereas in 1989, there were 600 curbside collection programs in the United States, by 1992 there were 4000 (van Voorst, 1992). Indeed, Germany, Japan, and other nations have achieved recycling levels far ahead of those in this country. A study of recycling in the Canadian province of Alberta by sociologists Linda Derksen and John Gartrell (1993) suggests that the critical factor in the success of recycling programs is easy accessibility, rather than individual attitudes toward recycling.

Even at best, recycling seems only *part* of the solution to the landfill crisis. "There are some utopians out there who think we can handle all waste through source reduction and recycling," notes John Arlington, senior counsel to a House of Representatives Subcommittee on Hazardous Materials. "State and local officials who have to deal with the real problems think that's pie in the sky" (Pytte, 1990:174).

SUMMARY

The size, composition, and distribution of the population of the United States have an important influence on many of the policy issues that we have studied in this book. This chapter examines various elements of population, the current problem of overpopulation, the possibility of zero population growth, and the environmental problems facing our planet.

1 Demographers study geographical variations and historical trends which are useful in developing population forecasts.

2 Thomas Robert Malthus suggested that the world's population was growing more rapidly than the available food supply and that this gap would increase over time. However, Karl Marx was critical of Malthus and saw capitalism rather than rising world population as the cause of social ills.

3 The primary mechanism for obtaining population information in the United States and most other countries is the *census*.

4 Roughly two-thirds of the world's nations have yet to pass fully through the second stage of *demographic transition,* and thus they continue to experience significant population growth.

5 The United Nations projects that world population could rise as high as 6.4 billion by the year 2000.

6 By 2040, when most people born in the United States will be entering retirement age, the nation will be approaching *zero population growth (ZPG)*.

7 The most important factors in *migration* tend to be economic—financial failure in the "old country" and a perception of greater economic opportunities elsewhere.

8 In 1992, an "Earth Summit" took place in Rio de Janeiro with some 106 heads of government in attendance.

9 Three broad areas of environmental concern are air pollution, water pollution, and contamination of land.

10 Community residents often respond to proposals for landfills by declaring NIMBY: "Not in My Back Yard."

CRITICAL THINKING QUESTIONS

1 Select one of the social policy issues examined in this textbook and analyze in detail how the size, composition, and distribution of the population of the United States have an important influence on that issue.

2 Some European nations are now experiencing population declines. Their death rates are low and their birthrates are even lower than in stage III of the demographic transition model. Does this pattern suggest that there is now a fourth stage in the demographic transition? Even more important, what are the implications of negative population growth for an industrialized nation approaching the twenty-first century?

3 Imagine that you have been asked to study the issue of air pollution in the largest city in your state. How might you draw on surveys, observation research, experiments, and existing sources to help you study this issue?

KEY TERMS

Birthrate The number of live births per 1000 population in a given year. Also known as the *crude birthrate*. (page 544)

Census An enumeration or counting of a population. (543)

Death rate The number of deaths per 1000 population in a given year. Also known as the *crude death rate.* (544)

Demographic transition A term used to describe the change from high birthrates and death rates to relatively low birthrates and death rates. (545)

Demography The scientific study of population. (541)

Fertility The amount of reproduction among women of childbearing age. (541)

Growth rate The difference between births and deaths, plus the difference between immigrants and emigrants, per 1000 population. (544)

Human ecology An area of study concerned with the interrelationships among people in their spatial setting and physical environment. (558)

Infant mortality rate The number of deaths of infants under 1 year of age per 1000 live births in a given year. (544)

Life expectancy The average number of years a person can be expected to live under current mortality conditions. (544)

Migration Relatively permanent movement of people with the purpose of changing their place of residence. (553)

Population pyramid A special type of bar chart that shows the distribution of population by gender and age. (549)

Total fertility rate (TFR) The average number of children born alive to a woman, assuming that she conforms to current fertility rates. (544)

Vital statistics Records of births, deaths, marriages, and divorces gathered through a registration system maintained by governmental units. (543)

Zero population growth (ZPG) The state of a population with a growth rate of zero, which is achieved when the number of births plus immigrants is equal to the number of deaths plus emigrants. (551)

ADDITIONAL READINGS

Brown, Lester R. (ed.). *State of the World, 1993*. New York: Norton, 1993. Brown offers an annual assessment of the environment and people's impact (both positive and negative) on it.

Bryant, Bunyan, and Paul Mohai (eds.). *Race and the Incidence of Environmental Hazards: A Time for Discourse*. Boulder, Colo.: Westview, 1992. A critical view of environmental hazards and how they have disproportionate negative impact on racial minorities.

Ehrlich, Paul R., and Anne H. Ehrlich. *The Population Explosion*. New York: Simon and Schuster, 1990. Two biologists advance the neo-Malthusian thesis that unless interventionist policies are adopted to deal with the population bomb, the world will be subjected to natural forces (perhaps massive increases in death rates) that will bring world population back into balance.

Jones, Landon Y. *Great Expectations: America and the Baby Boom Generation*. New York: Ballantine, 1980. This book provides a readable account of the social consequences of the baby boom cohort (1946 to 1964) and the baby bust cohort which followed.

Menard, Scott W., and Elizabeth W. Moen (eds.). *Perspectives on Population: An Introduction to Concepts and Issues*. New York: Oxford University Press, 1987. A collection of classic and contemporary essays covering the scientific study of population.

Menken, Jane (ed.). *World Population and U.S. Policy*. New York: Norton, 1986. A collection of articles dealing with the impact of American policies on other countries' efforts to deal with the problem of population growth.

Rubin, Charles T. *The Green Crusade: A History of the Environmental Idea*. New Brunswick, N.J.: Transaction, 1994. A political scientist traces the emergence of the environment as a social issue in the United States.

Russell, Cheryl. "The Business of Demographics." Washington, D.C.: Population Reference Bureau, 1984. Russell, a demographic researcher, describes the applications of the study of population in the marketplace. Published as the June 1984 issue of *Population Bulletin*.

Weeks, John R. *Population: An Introduction to Concepts and Issues* (updated 5th ed.). Belmont, Calif.: Wadsworth, 1994. A sociological treatment of demography with consideration of such social issues as aging, urbanization, economic development, and food supply.

Journals

The Population Reference Bureau (777 14th St., NW, Suite 800, Washington, D.C. 20005) publishes *Population Bulletin* (quarterly), *Population Today* (11 times annually), *Interchange* (quarterly), and occasionally *Teaching Modules*. These publications provide up-to-date information on population trends. The Bureau of the Census issues *Current Population Reports* which are helpful to researchers. Other journals focusing on demographic issues include *American Demographics* (founded in 1979), *Demography* (1964), and *International Migration Review* (1964).

20

COLLECTIVE
BEHAVIOR AND
SOCIAL CHANGE

20

COLLECTIVE BEHAVIOR AND SOCIAL CHANGE

THEORIES OF COLLECTIVE BEHAVIOR
Emergent-Norm Perspective
Value-Added Perspective
Assembling Perspective

FORMS OF COLLECTIVE BEHAVIOR
Crowds
Disaster Behavior
Fads and Fashions
Panics and Crazes
Rumors
Publics and Public Opinion
Social Movements
    Relative Deprivation
    Resource Mobilization

THEORIES OF SOCIAL CHANGE
Evolutionary Theory
Functionalist Theory
Conflict Theory

RESISTANCE TO SOCIAL CHANGE

SOCIAL POLICY AND SOCIAL MOVEMENTS: DISABILITY RIGHTS

BOXES
20-1 Around the World: Exit Polling in the Former Soviet Union
20-2 Everyday Behavior: The Social Movement for Prostitutes' Rights

LOOKING AHEAD

- How do contemporary sociological theorists view collective behavior?
- What functions do rumors perform for a society?
- What impact have social movements had on the course of history and the evolution of social structure?
- How have theorists analyzed the process of social change?
- Why are efforts to promote social change likely to be met with resistance?
- How has the disability rights movement contributed to societal changes in treatment of people with disabilities?

The year 1989 brought tumultuous change in East Germany. That summer, both Hungary and Czechoslovakia began allowing visiting East Germans to continue on to the west. Tens of thousands began to use this escape route; by autumn, as many as 1 million East Germans had applied to emigrate. There were weekly demonstrations against Communist party rule; one demand of protestors was that all restrictions on travel be eliminated.

On October 18, East Germany's ruling Politburo responded to growing pressures for reform by removing Erich Honecker as head of state and replacing him with Egon Krenz. But protests against the Communist regime continued to intensify. Finally, on November 9, a government official announced a new travel decree, under which people who wished to travel to the west could do so if they obtained visas from their local police stations. As word of the new policy spread that evening via radio and television, thousands of East Germans—most of whom had no visas—surged excitedly to the borders by car and by foot. With the approval of Krenz, the gates which had long separated the two Germanys, among them the hated Berlin Wall, were opened. Waves of East Germans were allowed to cross into the west, and West Germans were allowed to cross to the east (Moseley, 1990).

The norms, values, and social structure of Germany were forever altered that November as East and West Germans crossed the borders to see friends and relatives (and, in the case of many East Germans, to begin new lives). Indeed, the entire world was deeply affected by photographs and television coverage of the celebrations at the Berlin Wall. Less than a year later, the world's superpowers consented to the reunification of Germany. The dramatic events of November 9 and 10—the rumors that the borders were open, the gathering of huge crowds, the capitulation of the Communist leadership to social forces they could no longer control—represent an example of both collective behavior and social change, the two focal points of this chapter.

Practically all group activity can be thought of as collective behavior, but sociologists have given distinct meaning to the term. Neil Smelser (1981:431), a sociologist who specializes in this field of study, has defined **collective behavior** as the "relatively spontaneous and unstructured behavior of a group of people who are reacting to a common influence in an ambiguous situation." The crowd behavior evident in the joyous celebrations at the Berlin Wall is but one example of collective behavior.

Social change has been defined by sociologist Wilbert Moore (1967:3) as significant alteration over time in behavior patterns and culture, including norms and values. But what constitutes a "significant" alteration? Certainly the dramatic rise in formal education documented in Chapter 16 represents a change that has had profound social consequences. Other social changes that have had long-term and important consequences include the emergence of slavery as a system of stratification (see Chapter 8), the industrial revolution (Chapters 8 and 15), the greatly increased participation of women in the paid labor force of the United States and Europe (Chapter 11), and the worldwide population explosion (Chapter 19).

This chapter begins with an examination of a number of theories used by sociologists to better understand collective behavior, including the emergent-norm, value-added, and assembling perspectives. Particular attention is given to certain types of collective behavior, among them crowd behavior, disaster behavior, fads and fashions, panics and crazes, rumors, public opinion, and social movements. Contemporary sociology acknowledges the crucial role that social movements can play in mobilizing discontented members of a society and initiating social change.

Efforts to explain long-term social changes have led to the development of theories of change, which are examined in the second half of the chapter. All theories of social change recognize that there will be resistance to variations in social interactions, norms, and values. This chapter reviews the manner in which vested interests can block changes that they perceive as threatening. Finally, in the social policy section, we focus on changing societal treatment of people with disabilities and on the growing disability rights movement.

THEORIES OF COLLECTIVE BEHAVIOR

As Neil Smelser's definition suggests, collective behavior is usually unstructured and spontaneous. This fluidity makes it more difficult for sociologists to generalize about people's behavior in such situ-

In late 1989, the Berlin Wall separating West Germany from East Germany was opened (leading to the reunification of Germany in 1990). Jubilant Germans celebrated atop the Wall and some attempted to destroy this hated structure.

ations. Nevertheless, sociologists have developed various theoretical perspectives which can help us to study—and deal with in a constructive manner —crowds, riots, fads, and other types of collective behavior.

Emergent-Norm Perspective

The early writings on collective behavior imply that crowds are basically ungovernable. However, this is not always the case. In many situations, crowds are effectively governed by norms and procedures and may even engage in such practices as queuing, or waiting in line. We routinely encounter queues when we await service, as in a fast-food restaurant

Shown is the stairwell of a gymnasium at New York City's City College. Nine young men and women died and 29 were injured in late 1991 when a crowd surged through this stairwell to gain entrance to a charity basketball game. Many of the victims were crushed against locked metal doors or concrete walls.

or bank; or when we wish to enter or exit, as in a movie theater or football stadium. Normally, physical barriers, such as guardrails and checkout counters, help to regulate queuing. When massive crowds are involved, ushers or security personnel may also be present to assist in the orderly movement of the crowd.

On December 28, 1991, people began gathering outside a building at City College in New York City to see a heavily promoted charity basketball game involving rap stars and other celebrities. By late afternoon, more than 5000 people had gathered for the 6:00 P.M. game, even though the gym could accommodate only 2730 spectators. Although the crowd was divided into separate lines for ticket holders and those wishing to buy tickets at the door, restlessness and discontent swept through both lines and sporadic fights broke out. The arrival of celebrities only added to the commotion and the crowd's tension.

Doors to the gymnasium were finally opened one hour before game time, but only 50 people were admitted to the lobby at a time. Once their tickets had been taken, spectators proceeded down two flights of stairs, through a single unlocked entrance, and into the gym. Those further back in the crowd experienced the disconcerting feeling of moving forward, then stopping for a period of time, then repeating this process again and again. Well past the publicized starting time, huge crowds were still outside, pressing to gain entrance to the building.

Finally, with the arena more than full, the doors to the gym were closed. As rumors spread outside the building that the game was beginning, more than 1000 frustrated fans, many with valid tickets, surged through the glass doors into the building and headed for the stairs. Soon the stairwell became a horrifying mass of people surging against locked metal doors to the gym and crushed against concrete walls. The result was a tragedy: nine young men and women eventually died, and 29 were injured through the sheer pressure of bodies pressing against one another and against walls and doors (Mollen, 1992).

This was not the first time that violent crowding had led to tragedy. In 1979, 11 rock fans died of suffocation after a crowd outside Cincinnati's Riverfront Stadium pushed to gain entrance to a concert by The Who. In 1989, when thousands of soccer fans forced their way into a stadium to see the semifinals of the English Cup, more than 90 people were trampled to death or smothered. In 1991, three young people died of suffocation *inside* an arena in Salt Lake City as a crowd surged forward to get the best vantage point to hear the heavy metal group AC/DC (J. Gross, 1991a; D. L. Miller, 1988:46–47).

Sociologists Ralph Turner and Lewis Killian (1987) have offered a view of collective behavior which is helpful in assessing these tragic events. Their emergent-norm perspective begins with the assumption that a large crowd, such as a group of rock or soccer fans, is governed by expectations of proper behavior just as much as four people playing doubles tennis. The **emergent-norm perspective** states that a collective definition of appropriate and inappropriate behavior emerges during episodes of collective behavior. Like other social norms, the emergent norm reflects shared convictions held by members of the group and is enforced through sanctions (see Chapter 3). These new norms of proper behavior may arise in what seem at first as ambiguous situations. There is latitude for a wide range of acts, yet within a general framework established by the emergent norms (for a critique of this perspective, see McPhail, 1991:71–103).

Using the emergent-norm perspective, we can see that fans outside the charity basketball game at City College found themselves in an ambiguous situation. Normal procedures of crowd control, such as orderly queues, were rapidly dissolving. A new norm was simultaneously emerging: it is acceptable to push forward, even if people in front protest. Some members of the crowd—especially those with valid tickets—may have felt that this push forward was justified as a way of ensuring that they would get to see the game. Others pushed forward simply to relieve the physical pressure of those pushing behind them. Even individuals who rejected the emergent norm may have felt afraid to oppose it, fearing ridicule or injury. Thus, conforming behavior, which we usually associate with highly structured situations (see Chapter 7), was evident in this rather chaotic crowd, as it had been earlier at the concerts by The Who and AC/DC and at the soccer game in England. It would be misleading to assume that these fans acted simply as a united, collective unit in creating a dangerous situation.

Value-Added Perspective

Neil Smelser (1963) continued the sociological effort to analyze collective behavior with his value-added theory. He uses the **value-added model** to explain how broad social conditions are transformed in a definite pattern into some form of collective behavior. This model outlines six important determinants of collective behavior.

Initially, in Smelser's view, certain elements must be present for an incident of collective behavior to take place. He uses the term *structural conduciveness* to indicate that the organization of society can facilitate the emergence of conflicting interests. Structural conduciveness makes collective behavior possible, though not inevitable.

The second determinant of collective behavior, *structural strain,* occurs when the conduciveness of the social structure to potential conflict gives way to a perception that conflicting interests do, in fact, exist. This type of strain was evident in East Germany in 1989: the intense desire of many East Germans to travel to or emigrate to the west placed great strain on the social control exercised by the ruling Communist party. Such structural strain contributes to what Smelser calls a *generalized belief*—a shared view of reality that redefines social action and serves to guide behavior. The overthrow of Communist rule in East Germany and other Soviet-bloc nations occurred in part as a result of a generalized belief that the Communist regimes were oppressive and that popular resistance *could* lead to social change.

Smelser suggests that a specific event or incident, known as a *precipitating factor,* triggers collective behavior. The event may grow out of the social structure, but whatever its origins, it contributes to the strains and beliefs shared by a group or community. For example, studies of race riots have found that interracial fights or arrests and searches of minority individuals by police officers often precede disturbances. The 1992 riots in South Central Los Angeles, during which 58 people were killed, were sparked by the acquittal of four White police officers charged after the videotaped beating of Rodney King, a Black construction worker.

According to Smelser, the presence of the four determinants identified above is necessary for collective behavior to occur. Nevertheless, the group must be *mobilized for action.* An extended thundershower or severe snowstorm may preclude such a mobilization. People are more likely to come together on weekends than on weekdays, in the evening rather than during the daytime.

The manner in which *social control is exercised*—both formally and informally—can be significant

The 1992 riots in South Central Los Angeles, during which 58 people were killed, were sparked by the acquittal of four White police officers charged after the videotaped beating of Rodney King, a Black construction worker.

in determining whether the preceding factors will end in collective behavior. Stated simply, social control may prevent, delay, or interrupt a collective outburst. In some instances, forces of social control may be guilty of misjudgments that intensify the severity of an outbreak. In the view of many observers, the Los Angeles police did not respond fast enough as the initial rioting began in 1992, thereby creating a vacuum that allowed the level of violence to escalate.

Sociologists have questioned the validity of both the emergent-norm and value-added perspectives because of their imprecise definitions and the difficulty of testing them empirically. For example, they have criticized the emergent-norm perspective for being too vague in defining what constitutes a norm and have challenged the value-added model for its lack of specificity in defining generalized belief and structural strain. Of these two theories, the emergent-norm perspective appears to offer a more useful explanation of societywide episodes of collective behavior, such as crazes and fashions, than the value-added approach (M. Brown and Goldin, 1973; Quarantelli and Hundley, 1975; K. Tierney, 1980).

Nevertheless, Smelser's value-added model has been persuasive for many sociologists involved in the study of collective behavior. His perspective represents an advance over earlier theories that treated

gatherings as dominated by irrational, extreme impulses. The value-added approach firmly relates episodes of collective behavior to the overall social structure of a society (for a critique, see McPhail, 1994).

Assembling Perspective

As we have seen, one of the key determinants of collective behavior is mobilization for action. Some sociologists have paid particular attention to the question of how people come together to undertake collective action. Clark McPhail, perhaps the most prolific researcher of collective behavior in the last 20 years, sees such behavior as involving people and organizations consciously responding to one another's actions. Drawing upon the interactionist approach to sociology, McPhail (1994) has observed that organized interactions occur during such diverse events as celebrations and revolutions. People may chant, sing, or gesture with respect to a common object. In the midst of waiting in line outside a rock concert, as we have already seen, they may accept an emergent norm and begin to push forward toward the doors.

Building on the interactionist approach, McPhail and Miller (1973) introduced the concept of the assembling process. Earlier theorists of collective behavior had been content to explain events such as riots without concerning themselves with how gatherings of people actually came together. However, the *assembling perspective* sought for the first time to examine how and why people move from different points in space to a common location.

For example, sociologists David Snow, Louis Zurcher, and Robert Peters (1981) studied a series of football victory celebrations at the University of Texas that spilled over into the main streets of Austin. Some participants actively tried to recruit passersby for the celebrations by thrusting out open palms "to get five" or by yelling at drivers to honk their horns. In fact, encouraging still further assembling became a preoccupation of the celebrators. Whenever spectators were absent, those celebrating were relatively quiet.

A basic distinction has been made between two types of assemblies. *Periodic assemblies* include recurring, relatively routine gatherings of people such as work groups, college classes, and season ticket holders of an athletic series. These assemblies are characterized by advance scheduling and recurring attendance of the majority of participants. Thus, most members of an introductory sociology class may gather together for lectures every Monday, Wednesday, and Friday morning at a regular meeting time. By contrast, *nonperiodic assemblies* include demonstrations, parades, and gatherings at the scene of fires, accidents, and arrests. Such assemblies, for example, the 1989 celebrations at the Berlin Wall after the opening of Germany's borders, often result from word-of-mouth information and are generally less formal than periodic assemblies.

These three approaches to collective behavior give us deeper insight into relatively spontaneous and unstructured situations. Although episodes of collective behavior may seem irrational to outsiders, norms emerge among the participants and organized efforts are made to assemble at a certain time and place.

FORMS OF COLLECTIVE BEHAVIOR

Drawing upon the emergent-norm, value-added, and assembling perspectives—and upon other aspects of sociological examination—sociologists have examined many forms of collective behavior.

Among these are crowds, disaster behavior, fads and fashions, panics and crazes, rumors, public opinion, and social movements.

Crowds

Crowds are temporary groupings of people in close proximity who share a common focus or interest. Spectators at a baseball game, participants at a pep rally, and rioters are all examples of crowds. Sociologists have been interested in what characteristics are common to crowds. Of course, it can be difficult to generalize, since the nature of crowds varies dramatically. For example, in terms of the emotions shared by crowds, hostages on a hijacked airplane experience intense fear, whereas participants in a religious revival feel a deep sense of joy.

Like other forms of collective behavior, crowds are not totally lacking in structure. Even during riots, participants are governed by identifiable social norms and exhibit definite patterns of behavior. Sociologists Richard Berk and Howard Aldrich (1972) examined patterns of vandalism in 15 cities in the United States during the riots of the 1960s. They found that stores of merchants perceived as exploitive were likely to be attacked, while private homes and public agencies with positive reputations were more likely to be spared. Apparently, looters had reached a collective agreement as to what constituted a "proper" or "improper" target for destruction.

If we apply the emergent-norm perspective to urban rioting, we can suggest that a new social norm is accepted (at least temporarily) which basically condones looting. The norms of respect for private property—as well as norms involving obedience to the law—are replaced by a concept of all goods as community property. All desirable items, including those behind locked doors, can be used for the "general welfare." In effect, the emergent norm allows looters to take what they regard as properly theirs (Quarantelli and Dynes, 1970; see also McPhail, 1991).

Disaster Behavior

Newspapers, television reports, and even rumors bring us word of many disasters around the world. The term *disaster* refers to a sudden or disruptive

Doug Miner/Sygma

Illinois residents are shown in August 1993 during efforts to combat the flooding of the Mississippi River. Remarkably, in the wake of many natural and technological disasters, there is increased structure and organization rather than chaos.

event or set of events that overtaxes a community's resources so that outside aid is necessary. Traditionally, disasters have been catastrophes related to nature, such as earthquakes, floods, and fires. Yet, in an industrial age, natural disasters have now been joined by such "technological disasters" as airplane crashes, industrial explosions, nuclear meltdowns, and massive chemical poisonings (Aronoff and Gunter, 1992; J. Thompson and Hawkes, 1962:268).

Sociologists have made enormous strides in disaster research despite the problems inherent in this type of investigation. The work of the Disaster Research Center at the University of Delaware has been especially important. The center has teams of trained researchers prepared to leave for the site of any disaster on four hours' notice. Their field kits include material identifying them as center staff members, recording equipment, and general interview guidelines for use in various types of disasters. En route to the scene, these researchers attempt to obtain news information in order to learn about the conditions they may encounter. Upon arrival, the team establishes a communication post to coordinate fieldwork and maintain contact with the center's headquarters.

Since its founding, the Disaster Research Cen-

ter has conducted more than 520 field studies of natural and technological disasters in the United States, as well as 24 in other nations. Its research has been used to develop effective planning and programming for dealing with disasters in such areas as delivery of emergency health care, establishment and operation of rumor-control centers, coordination of mental health services after disasters, and implementation of disaster-preparedness and emergency-response programs. In addition, the center has provided extensive training and field research for over 100 graduate students. These students maintain a professional commitment to disaster research and often go on to work for such disaster service organizations as the Red Cross and civil defense agencies (D. L. Miller, 1988:55–56; Quarantelli, 1992; see also Cisin and Clark, 1962).

Remarkably, in the wake of many natural and technological disasters, there is increased structure and organization rather than chaos. In the United States, disasters are often followed by the creation of an emergency "operations group" which coordinates public services and even certain services normally carried out by the private sector (such as food distribution). Decision making becomes more centralized than in normal times (Dynes, 1978).

Shown is a "rave" dance club where teenagers meet. Fads (such as "rave" clubs) and fashions are sudden movements involving a particular lifestyle or taste in clothing, music, or recreation.

Fads and Fashions

An almost endless list of objects and behavior patterns seems temporarily to catch the fancy of adults and children. Examples include silly putty, Davy Crockett coonskin caps, hula hoops, *Star Wars* toys, the Rubik cube, break dancing, Cabbage Patch Kids, *The Simpsons* T shirts, and Nintendo games. Fads and fashions are sudden movements toward the acceptance of some lifestyle or particular taste in clothing, music, or recreation (Aguirre et al., 1988; R. Johnson, 1985).

Fads are temporary patterns of behavior involving large numbers of people; they spring up independently of preceding trends and do not give rise to successors. By contrast, *fashions* are pleasurable mass involvements that feature a certain amount of acceptance by society and have a line of historical continuity (Lofland, 1981:442; 1985). Thus, punk haircuts would be considered a fashion, part of the constantly changing standards of hair length and style, whereas adult roller skating would be considered a fad of the early 1980s.

Typically, when people think of *fashions,* they think of clothing, particularly women's clothing. In reality, fads and fashions enter every aspect of life where choices are not dictated by sheer necessity—

vehicles, sports, music, drama, beverages, art, and even selection of pets. Any area of our lives that is subject to continuing change is open to fads and fashions. There is a clear commercial motive behind these forms of collective behavior. For example, in about seven months of 1955, over $100 million of Davy Crockett items was sold (worth about $500 million in 1993 dollars), including coonskin caps, toy rifles, knives, camping gear, cameras, and jigsaw puzzles (Javna, 1986:16; Klapp, 1972:309).

Fads and fashions allow people to identify with something different from the dominant institutions and symbols of a culture. Members of a subculture may break with tradition while remaining "in" with (accepted by) a significant reference group of peers. Fads are generally short-lived and tend to be viewed with amusement or lack of interest by most nonparticipants. Fashions, by contrast, often have wider implications because they can reflect (or falsely give the impression of) wealth and status.

Panics and Crazes

Panics and crazes both represent responses to some generalized belief. A *craze* is an exciting mass involvement which lasts for a relatively long period of time (Lofland, 1981:441; 1985). For example, in late 1973, a press release from a Wisconsin congressman described how the federal bureaucracy had failed to contract for enough toilet paper for government buildings. Then, on December 19, as part of his nightly monologue on the *Tonight Show*, Johnny Carson suggested that it would not be strange if the entire nation experienced a shortage of toilet paper. Millions of people took his humorous comment seriously and immediately began stockpiling this item out of fear that it would soon be unavailable. Shortly thereafter, as a consequence of this craze, a shortage of toilet paper actually resulted. Its effects were felt into 1974 (Malcolm, 1974; *Money*, 1987).

By contrast, a *panic* is a fearful arousal or collective flight based on a generalized belief which may or may not be accurate. In a panic, people commonly perceive that there is insufficient time or inadequate means to avoid injury. Panics often occur on battlefields, in overcrowded burning buildings, or during stock market crashes. The key distinction between panics and crazes is that panics are flights *from* something whereas crazes are movements *to* something.

One of the most famous cases of panic in the United States was touched off by a media event: the 1938 Halloween eve radio dramatization of H. G. Wells's science fiction novel *The War of the Worlds*. This CBS broadcast realistically told of an invasion from Mars, with interplanetary visitors landing in northern New Jersey and taking over New York City 15 minutes later. The announcer indicated at the beginning of the broadcast that the account was fictional, but about 80 percent of the listeners tuned in late.

Clearly, a significant number of listeners became frightened by what they assumed to be a news report. However, some accounts have exaggerated the extent of people's reactions to *The War of the Worlds*. One report concluded that "people all over the United States were praying, crying, fleeing frantically to escape death from the Martians." In contrast, a CBS national survey of listeners found that only 20 percent were genuinely scared by the broadcast. Although perhaps a million people *reacted* to this program, many reacted by switching to other stations to see if the "news" was being carried elsewhere. This "invasion from outer space" set off a limited panic, rather than mass hysteria (R. W.

Brown, 1954:871; Cantril, 1940:102–107; Houseman, 1972).

It is often believed that people engaged in panics or crazes are unaware of their actions, but this is certainly not the case. As the emergent-norm perspective suggests, people take cues from one another as to how to act during such forms of collective behavior. Even in the midst of an escape from a life-threatening situation, such as a fire in a crowded theater, people do not tend to run in a headlong stampede. Rather, they adjust their behavior on the basis of the perceived circumstances and the conduct of others who are assembling in a given location. To outside observers studying the events, people's decisions may seem foolish (pushing against a locked door) or suicidal (jumping from a balcony). Yet, for that individual at that moment, the action may genuinely seem appropriate —or the only desperate choice available (Quarantelli, 1957).

Rumors

"Paul McCartney is dead." According to a popular rumor in 1969, at the height of the Beatles' popularity, the singer died that year at the age of 27. (Or, according to another version of the rumor, he had died in 1966 in an automobile accident after leaving a recording studio tired, sad, and depressed.)

The evidence supporting this rumor seemed clear—at least to some. There was the funeral procession shown on the front of the Beatles' "Abbey Road" album, with McCartney (or perhaps a look-alike?) walking barefoot like a corpse. According to some listeners, if one pays careful attention at the end of the song "Strawberry Fields Forever," one can hear John Lennon say, "I buried Paul!" Moreover, if "Revolution No. 9" is played backwards, one can supposedly hear the terrifying sounds of a traffic accident. As radio stations carried these and other tidbits, Paul McCartney was interviewed by *Life* magazine, thereby establishing that he was indeed alive. But skeptics countered that when a McCartney look-alike contest had been held a few months earlier in Britain, a winner had never been announced. Perhaps *Life* had unwittingly interviewed an imposter standing in for the deceased McCartney? (Kapferer, 1992:54; Neary, 1969; Rosnow, 1991:486).

Rumors about business firms—which can sometimes be damaging—are spread not only by the general public but also by newspapers, radio, and television.

Not all rumors we hear are so astonishing, but none of us is immune from hearing or starting rumors. A *rumor* is a piece of information gathered informally which is used to interpret an ambiguous situation (R. Berk, 1974:78). Viewed from a functionalist perspective, rumors serve a social function by providing a group with a shared belief. As a group strives for consensus, members eliminate those rumors that are least useful or credible.

Although some people may start rumors with a specific intent to spread a falsehood, Jean-Noël Kapferer (1992:53), a professor of communication in France, suggests that rumors are typically "spontaneous social products, devoid of ulterior motives and underlying strategies." Kapferer argues that the existence and spreading of rumors reflect natural processes within groups. In his view, it is misleading to project the responsibility for a rumor outside the group which hears the rumor, finds it meaningful, and mobilizes to pass it on. Kapferer (1992:54) concludes that "in the case of rumors, . . . the public is the main actor."

Rumors about celebrities—whether politicians, movie stars, or members of royal families—have long been a popular pastime around the world. Natural disasters, as well, tend to be a common subject for rumors. For example, after California was shaken (literally and figuratively) in mid-1992 by a

series of powerful earthquakes and aftershocks, rumors abounded that the long-dreaded "big one" was imminent. According to one unfounded account, the California Institute of Technology in Pasadena—the site of the top seismology laboratory in the area—had ordered all its employees to leave town (*New York Times,* 1992d:A8; Rosnow, 1991).

Like celebrities, business firms find that rumors can be damaging. One type of rumor that is particularly worrisome for manufacturers involves ill-founded charges of contamination. In the late 1970s, it was rumored that General Foods' Pop Rocks and Cosmic Candy would explode in children's mouths with tragic results, yet no such explosions took place. Another popular theme of rumors in the marketplace focuses on the charge that a company is using its profits for evil purposes. For example, throughout the 1980s, Procter and Gamble had to counter persistent and unfounded rumors that the company was engaged in satanic activities and that its distinctive corporate trademark was a symbol of Satanism. Businesses can also be hurt by rumors about alleged political activism on controversial issues. In 1992, Snapple Beverage Corporation, the fastest-growing beverage company in the United States, had to counter harmful and unsubstantiated rumors that it was helping to finance Operation Rescue, the militant antiabortion group that attempts to shut down abortion clinics (Koenig, 1985; B. Noble, 1993:D1, D7).

Publics and Public Opinion

The least organized and most individualized form of collective behavior is represented by publics. The term *public* refers to a dispersed group of people, not necessarily in contact with one another, who share interest in an issue. As the term is used in the study of collective behavior, the public does not include everyone. Rather, it is a collective of people who focus on some issue, engage in discussion, agree or disagree, and sometimes dissolve when the issue has been decided (Blumer, 1955:189–191, 1969:195–208; R. Turner and Killian, 1987: 158–185).

The term *public opinion* refers to expressions of attitudes on matters of public policy which are communicated to decision makers. The last part of this definition is particularly important. From the point of view of theorists of collective behavior, there can be no public opinion unless there is both a public and a decision maker. We are not concerned here with the formation of an individual's attitudes on social and political issues; this question was explored in Chapter 15. Instead, in studying public opinion, we focus on the ways in which a public's attitudes are communicated to decision makers and on the ultimate outcome of the public's attempts to influence policymaking (R. Turner and Killian, 1987).

Polls and surveys play a major role in the assessment of public opinion. Using the same techniques that are essential in developing reliable questionnaire and interview schedules (see Chapter 2), survey specialists conduct studies of public opinion for business firms (market analyses), the government, the mass media (ratings of programs), and, of course, politicians. Survey data have become extremely influential not only in preselecting the products we buy but in determining which political candidates are likely to win election and even which possible Supreme Court nominees should be selected (Brower, 1988).

The earliest political polls lacked the scientific rigor that contemporary social scientists require. In a famous example of unscientific and misleading polling, the magazine *Literary Digest* sent 18 million postcard ballots across the United States to assess voters' opinions on the 1936 presidential election. The 2 million replies indicated that Republican candidate Alf Landon would defeat Democratic incumbent Franklin D. Roosevelt. *Literary Digest* predicted a Landon victory, yet Roosevelt was reelected in a landslide.

Today, this method of polling would be regarded as completely unreliable. The magazine took its original sample from automobile registration lists and telephone books. Yet, in 1936, in the midst of the Depression, those people with enough money to own a car or a private telephone were hardly a representative cross section of the nation's voters. Instead, those polled tended to be prosperous citizens who might be likely to support Republican candidates (Squire, 1988).

Current political polls are more precise and representative sampling techniques. As a result, their projections of presidential elections often fall within a few percentage points of the actual vote. The Gallup poll came within 3.7 percent of Ronald Reagan's vote in 1980, within 0.2 percent of Reagan's vote in 1984, and within 0.4 percent of George Bush's vote in 1988. In 1992, the three-way race for president and the high number of undecided voters presented a challenge to pollsters. Although the Gallup poll predicted that Bill Clinton would win 49 percent of the vote, he won only 43 percent, as many undecided voters eventually supported independent candidate Ross Perot (Gallup and Saad, 1992). In Box 20-1, we examine the use of exit polls to sample public opinion in the former Soviet Union.

While political polling has improved dramatically since the *Literary Digest*'s 1936 fiasco, misleading surveys are still with us. Regrettably, telephone companies have marketed call-in "polls" using 1-900 area code numbers. Television viewers or newspaper readers are asked to call one number to register an opinion on an issue, or a second number to register an alternative opinion. There are many problems inherent in this type of "polling." The sample that emerges is hardly representative (see Chapter 2) in that it includes only those people who happened to see the commercial or advertisement for the poll and who feel strongly enough about the issue to spend the typical charge of $1.

BOX 20-1 • AROUND THE WORLD

EXIT POLLING IN THE FORMER SOVIET UNION

Exit polls have been a fact of political life in the United States and other western democracies for more than a decade. In recent years, such polling has been successfully conducted in certain developing countries, notably Mexico. But, in 1993, pollsters addressed the formidable logistics and methodological challenges of surveying a country as vast and politically chaotic as Russia.

As television viewers in the United States have learned, exit polls allow the networks to project the outcome of an election long before all the ballots have been counted. Using sophisticated sampling techniques, interviewers question voters as they leave polling places (hence the term *exit polls*). By studying voting patterns in selected districts, analysts can project the results for an entire city or state.

Exit polling was introduced in Russia in 1993 when a referendum was held to determine the level of support for President Boris Yeltsin and his social and political reforms. Voter Research and Surveys (VRS), a polling firm based in the United States, drew on data from Russia's 1991 presidential elections to develop a representative sample of voters—taking into account such factors as administrative region, type of city or settlement, and political orientation. VRS found that Russian voters were quite willing to speak with interviewers, despite the fact that both democracy and polling are rather new to that country. Indeed, according to Warren Mitofsky, the head of VRS, Russian voters' rate of cooperation with pollsters was much higher than the rate in the United States.

As in the United States, the exit polling in Russia proved to be fairly accurate. Early on the day of the referendum, based on initial analysis of survey data, exit polls began reporting a strong showing of support for Boris Yeltsin. VRS reported that 65 percent of voters had expressed confidence in the president, while a competing polling firm reported a 63 percent approval rating. The final returns of the referendum showed a 59 percent vote of confidence for Yeltsin. A second referendum question asked voters: "Do you approve of the government's social and economic policies conducted by the President and the Government since 1992?" In the exit polls, 56 to 58 percent of those surveyed voiced their approval, as did 53 percent of voters in the referendum.

As in other countries, exit polls in Russia provided information about the preferences of particular types of voters that cannot be obtained from official vote tallies. For example, exit polls showed that support for Boris Yeltsin was stronger among younger voters and those with more years of formal schooling than among older voters and those with less education. Yet, even at best, exit polls reflect the attitudes of *voters,* who are not necessarily a representative sample of all members of a society. The 40 percent of Russian adults who did not participate in the 1993 referendum are likely to be more critical of the government and its policies than the 60 percent who did vote.

On all counts, the initial exit polling in Russia was judged a success. The total cost was $40,000, about half the expense of a similar effort in the United States. Cooperation from voters was high, while interference from police, local politicians, and the traditional communist bureaucracy was minimal. The most serious difficulty faced by VRS was that Russia has a dated telecommunications system. Nevertheless, it is expected that such surveys will become more common in Russia and other parts of the former Soviet Union.

SOURCES: Corning, 1993; Morin, 1993b; Rahr, 1993.

Social Movements

Social movements are the most all-encompassing type of collective behavior, because they may include aspects of other types such as crowds, rumors, publics, and public opinion. Although such factors as physical environment, population, technology, and social inequality serve as sources of change, it is the *collective* effort of individuals organized in social movements that ultimately leads to change. Sociologists use the term **social movements** to refer to organized collective activities to promote or resist change in an existing group or society (Benford, 1992:1880). Herbert Blumer (1955:119), a

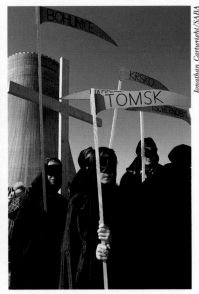

Social movements try to bring about fundamental changes in society. Shown are a 1992 animal rights rally in Washington, D.C.; a demonstration in 1993 against the construction of a nuclear power plant in the Czech Republic; and a protest march by French environmentalists against the dumping of garbage and toxic waste in a river that is home to a population of salmon.

theorist of collective behavior, recognized the special importance of social movements when he defined them as "collective enterprises to establish a new order of life."

Social movements can be contrasted with the forms of collective behavior described earlier in the chapter. Like publics, social movements tend to focus on issues of public policy. Like crowds and fads,

they involve social change—although social movements aim at much more fundamental and long-lasting changes. Social movements persist over longer periods of time than other forms of collective behavior. In part, this is because social movements are more structured; their leadership is frequently well organized and ongoing. Ironically, as Robert Michels (1915) noted (see Chapter 6), political movements fighting for social change eventually take on bureaucratic forms of organization. Leaders dominate the decision-making process without directly consulting their followers.

In many nations, including the United States, social movements have had a dramatic impact on the course of history and the evolution of social structure. It would be naive to ignore the actions of abolitionists, suffragists, civil rights workers, and activists opposed to the war in Vietnam. Members of each social movement stepped outside traditional channels for bringing about social change and yet had a noticeable influence on public policy (J. Wilson, 1973:5).

Although the importance of change and conflict is implicit in the existence of social movements, their activities can also be analyzed from a functionalist perspective. Even when unsuccessful, social movements contribute to the formation of public opinion. Initially, the ideas of Margaret Sanger and other early advocates of birth control were viewed as "radical," yet contraceptives are now widely available in the United States. Moreover, social movements are viewed by functionalists as providing a training ground for leaders of the political establishment. Such heads of state as Cuba's Fidel Castro and Iran's Ayatollah Khomeini came to power after serving as leaders of revolutionary movements. More recently, Poland's Lech Walesa, Russia's Boris Yeltsin, and Czech playwright Vaclav Havel led protest movements against Communist rule and subsequently became leaders of their countries' governments (Heberle, 1968).

How and why do social movements emerge? Obviously, people are often discontented with the way things are. But what causes them to organize at a particular moment in a collective effort to work for change? Sociologists rely on two explanations for why people mobilize: the relative-deprivation and resource-mobilization approaches.

Relative Deprivation   Those members of a society who feel most frustrated and disgruntled by the social and economic conditions of their lives are not necessarily "worst off" in an objective sense. Social scientists have long recognized that what is most significant is how people *perceive* their situation. Karl Marx pointed out that although the misery of the workers was important in reflecting their oppressed state, so was their position relative to the capitalist ruling class (Marx and Engels, 1955:94, original edition 1847).

The term *relative deprivation* is defined as the conscious feeling of a negative discrepancy between legitimate expectations and present actualities (J. Wilson, 1973:69). It may be characterized by scarcity rather than lack of necessities (refer back to the distinction between absolute and relative poverty in Chapter 8). A relatively deprived person is dissatisfied because he or she feels downtrodden relative to some appropriate reference group. Thus, blue-collar workers who live in two-family houses with little lawn space—though hardly at the bottom of the economic ladder—may nevertheless feel deprived in comparison with corporate managers and professionals who live in lavish and exclusive suburbs.

In addition to the feeling of relative deprivation, two other elements must be present before discontent will be channeled into a social movement. People must feel that they have a right to their goals, that they deserve better than what they have. For example, the struggle against European colonialism in Africa (see Chapter 9) intensified when growing numbers of Africans decided that it was legitimate for them to have political and economic independence. At the same time, the disadvantaged group must perceive that it cannot attain its goals through conventional means. This belief may or may not be correct. Yet, whichever is the case, the group will not mobilize into a social movement unless there is a shared perception that its relative deprivation can be ended only through collective action (Morrison, 1971).

Critics of the relative-deprivation approach have noted that an increase in feelings of deprivation is not always necessary before people are moved to act. In addition, this approach fails to explain why certain feelings of deprivation are transformed into social movements, whereas in other situations there is no collective effort to reshape society. Consequently, in recent years sociologists have given increasing attention to the forces needed to bring about the emergence of social movements (Alain, 1985; Finkel and Rule, 1987; Orum, 1978).

Resource Mobilization   Sociologist Anthony Oberschall (1973:199) has argued that in order to sustain social protest or resistance, there must be an "organizational base and continuity of leadership." The term *resource mobilization* is used to refer to the ways in which a social movement utilizes such resources as money, political influence, access to the media, and personnel. The success of a movement for change will depend in good part on how effectively it mobilizes its resources (see also J. Gamson, 1989; Staggenborg, 1989a, 1989b).

As people become part of a social movement, norms develop to guide their behavior. Members of the movement may be expected to attend regular meetings of organizations, pay dues, recruit new adherents, and boycott "enemy" products or speakers. The emergence of new social movement can be evident from the rise of special language or new words for familiar terms. In recent years, social movements have been responsible for such new terms of self-reference as *Blacks* and *African Americans* (used to replace *Negroes*), *senior citizens* (used to replace *old folks*), *gays* (used to replace *homosexuals*), and *people with disabilities* (used to replace *the handicapped*).

Leadership is a central factor in the mobilization of the discontented into social movements. Often a movement will be led by a charismatic figure, such as Dr. Martin Luther King, Jr. As Max Weber described it in 1904, *charisma* is that quality of an individual which sets him or her apart from ordinary people (see Chapter 15). Of course, charisma can fade abruptly; this accounts for the fragility of certain social movements.

Why do certain individuals join a social movement whereas others do not, when all share the same situation of relative deprivation and are subject to the same opportunities for resource mobilization? Karl Marx recognized the importance of recruitment when he called on workers to become aware of their oppressed status and develop a class consciousness (see Chapter 8). Like the contemporary resource-mobilization approach, Marx held that a social movement (specifically, the revolt of the proletariat) would require leaders to sharpen the awareness of the oppressed. They must help workers to overcome feelings of *false consciousness,* or attitudes that do not reflect workers' objective position, in order to organize a revolutionary movement. Similarly, one of the challenges faced by women's liberation activists of the late 1960s and early 1970s was to convince women that they were being deprived of their rights and socially valued resources.

Unlike the relative-deprivation approach, the resource-mobilization perspective focuses on strategic difficulties confronted by social movements (see Box 20-2). Any movement for fundamental change will almost certainly arouse opposition; effective mobilization will depend in part on how the movement deals with resistance to its activities. The reasons people have for resisting social change, and the tactics they employ in resisting, will be discussed later in the chapter. In the following section, we will examine a number of explanations for social change.

THEORIES OF SOCIAL CHANGE

It is clearly a challenge to explain social change in the diverse and complex world of the 1990s. Theorists from several disciplines have sought to analyze social change. In some instances, they have examined historical events in order to arrive at a better understanding of contemporary changes. We will review three theoretical approaches to change: evolutionary theory, functional theory, and conflict theory.

Evolutionary Theory

Nineteenth-century theories of social change reflect the influence of Charles Darwin's (1809–1882) pioneering work in biological evolution. According to his approach, there has been a continuing progression of successive life forms. For example, since human beings came at a later stage of evolution than reptiles, we represent a "higher" form of life. Social theorists sought an analogy to this biological model of development and originated *evolutionary theory,* which views society as moving in a definite direction. Early evolutionary theorists generally agreed that society was inevitably progressing to a higher state. As might be expected, they concluded in an ethnocentric fashion that their own behavior and culture were more advanced than those of earlier civilizations.

Auguste Comte, described in Chapter 1 as a founder of sociology, was an evolutionary theorist

BOX 20-2 • EVERYDAY BEHAVIOR

THE SOCIAL MOVEMENT FOR PROSTITUTES' RIGHTS

In the view of its supporters, prostitution is a service industry, and prostitutes are professional sex workers. However, prostitution is illegal in most of the United States and around the world. Prostitutes are often arrested, though their clients generally are not. Given the common stigma attached to prostitution, it is no easy task to work for the rights of prostitutes.

COYOTE (an acronym for "Call Off Your Old Tired Ethics") was the first and remains the best known of the prostitutes' rights organizations in the United States. Established in 1973, COYOTE has grown into a national organization based in San Francisco, with branches and affiliates in at least 12 major cities in the United States and ties to similar organizations overseas. COYOTE and its allies advocate the repeal of all existing laws against prostitution, the reconstitution of prostitution as a credible service occupation, and the legal protection of prostitutes as legitimate service workers.

Activists in COYOTE view prostitution as a victimless crime (refer back to Chapter 7) and therefore favor full decriminalization of such consensual sexual activity. They flatly oppose legalization of prostitution, whether in the form of registration and licensing, special taxes, compulsory health examinations, or "red light districts." COYOTE believes that any such regulations will inevitably perpetuate the stigma attached to prostitution while unfairly regulating what women do with their bodies.

Sociologist Valerie Jenness (1991, 1992, 1993) suggests that COYOTE has had many successes. Among these are (1) holding conferences and leading demonstrations to raise public awareness concerning the rights of prostitutes, (2) persuading public defenders to assist women charged with prostitution, (3) pressuring government agencies to establish free health clinics for prostitutes, (4) building coalitions in support of prostitutes' rights with certain feminist organizations and other groups, and (5) serving as a crucial link between sex workers and public health agencies as the AIDS crisis has intensified.

By contrast, sociologist Ronald Weitzer (1991) points to the failures of the prostitutes' rights movement. In his view, COYOTE and other activist groups have failed to shift public opinion (which remains hostile to prostitutes' rights), there have been few significant legislative concessions, and movement leaders are rarely consulted by policymakers. Weitzer contends that the movement's resource-mobilization efforts have been largely unsuccessful: the limited resources of activist organizations have not been supplemented by meaningful alliances with other social movements or more established interest groups. Nevertheless, Weitzer acknowledges that the prostitutes' rights movement has enhanced the self-images of activists, while assisting individual prostitutes, attracting media attention, and winning certain legal battles.

It is not easy to assess the success or failure of a social movement; indeed, sociologists do not agree about the criteria that should be utilized. In one study, sociologist William Gamson (1990) traced the activities of a representative sample of 53 social movements that emerged in the United States between 1800 and 1945. Gamson measured the relative success or failure of these movements by examining whether or not they (1) gained new advantages and (2) gained acceptance from their antagonists. He found that 31 of the social movements studied (58 percent) gained either new advantages or acceptance, while another 20 movements (38 percent) gained both. Judged against Gamson's criteria, the prostitutes' rights movement would thus far appear to be a movement (like 4 percent of those studied) which has not genuinely gained either new advantages or acceptance. Nevertheless, despite formal norms against prostitution and negative public opinion, the prostitutes' rights movement has not disappeared and continues to work for what it sees as social justice.

of change. He saw human societies as moving forward in their thinking from mythology to the scientific method. Similarly, Émile Durkheim (1933, original edition 1893) maintained that society progressed from simple to more complex forms of social organization.

The writings of Comte and Durkheim are examples of *unilinear evolutionary theory*. This approach contends that all societies pass through the same successive stages of evolution and inevitably reach the same end. English sociologist Herbert Spencer, also discussed in Chapter 1, used a similar approach: Spencer likened society to a living body with interrelated parts that were moving toward a common destiny. However, contemporary evolutionary theorists such as Gerhard Lenski, Jr., are more likely to picture social change as multilinear than to rely on the more limited unilinear perspective. *Multilinear evolutionary theory* holds that change can occur in several ways and that it does not inevitably lead in the same direction (Haines, 1988; J. Turner, 1985).

Multilinear theorists recognize that human culture has evolved along a number of lines. For example, the theory of demographic transition graphically demonstrates that population change in developing nations has not necessarily followed the model evident in industrialized nations (see Chapter 19). Medical and public health technology was introduced gradually in the developed nations, which gave them time to adjust to falling death rates and resulting rises in population. However, such technology was imported much more rapidly by developing nations, leading to dramatic population growth and severe pressure on social services and natural resources, including food production (R. Appelbaum, 1970:15–64).

Functionalist Theory

As has been stressed throughout this textbook, functionalist sociologists are concerned with the role of cultural elements in preserving the social order as a whole. They focus on what maintains a system, not on what changes it. This might seem to suggest that functionalists can offer little of value to the study of social change. Yet, as the work of sociologist Talcott Parsons demonstrates, functionalists have made a distinctive contribution to this area of sociological investigation.

Parsons, a leading proponent of functionalist theory (refer back to Chapter 1), viewed society as naturally being in a state of equilibrium. By "equilibrium," he meant that society tends toward a state of stability or balance. Parsons would view even prolonged labor strikes or civilian riots as temporary disruptions in the status quo rather than as significant alterations in a society's social structure. Therefore, according to his *equilibrium model*, as changes occur in one part of society, there must be adjustments in other parts. If this does not take place, the society's equilibrium will be threatened and strains will occur.

Reflecting an evolutionary approach, Parsons (1966:21–24) maintained that four processes of social change are inevitable. The first, *differentiation*, refers to the increasing complexity of social organization. A change from "medicine man" to physician, nurse, and pharmacist is an illustration of differentiation in the field of health. This process is accompanied by *adaptive upgrading*, whereby social institutions become more specialized in their purposes. The division of labor among physicians into obstetricians, internists, surgeons, and so forth is an example of adaptive upgrading.

The third process identified by Parsons is the *inclusion* of groups into society which were previously excluded by virtue of such factors as gender, race, and social class background. Medical schools have practiced inclusion by opening their doors to increasing numbers of women and minorities. Finally, Parsons contends that societies experience *value generalization*, the development of new values that tolerate and legitimate a greater range of activities. The acceptance of preventive medicine is an example of value generalization; our society has broadened its view of desirable health care. All four processes identified by Parsons stress consensus—that is, societal agreement on the nature of social organization and values (B. Johnson, 1975; R. Wallace and Wolf, 1980:50–51).

Parsons' approach explicitly incorporates the evolutionary notion of continuing progress. However, as with other functionalist models, the dominant theme in Parsons' model is balance and stability. Society may change, but it remains stable through new forms of integration. In place of the kinship ties that provided social cohesion in the past, there will be laws, judicial processes, and new values and belief systems.

As noted by critics, the functionalist approach virtually disregards the use of coercion by the powerful to maintain the illusion of a stable, well-integrated society. Functionalists assume that social institutions will not persist unless they continue to contribute to the overall society. This leads functionalists to conclude that altering institutions will threaten social equilibrium (Gouldner, 1960).

Conflict Theory

The functionalist perspective minimizes change. It emphasizes the persistence of social life and views gradual change as necessary in order to maintain the equilibrium (or balance) of a society. By contrast, conflict theorists contend that social institutions and practices continue because powerful groups have the ability to maintain the status quo. Change has crucial significance, since it is needed to correct social injustices and inequalities.

Karl Marx accepted the evolutionary argument that societies develop along a particular path. However, unlike Comte and Spencer, he did not view each successive stage as an inevitable improvement over the previous one. History, according to Marx, proceeds through a series of stages, each of which has an exploited class of people. Ancient society exploited slaves; the estate system of feudalism exploited serfs; modern capitalist society exploits the working class. Ultimately, through a socialist revolution led by the proletariat, human society will move toward the final stage of development: a classless communist society, or "community of free individuals" as Marx described it in *Das Kapital* (1955, original edition 1867; Bottomore and Rubel, 1956: 250).

As was noted earlier in this book, Karl Marx had an important influence on the development of sociology. His thinking offered insights into such institutions as the economy, the family, religion, and government. The Marxist view of social change is appealing because it does not restrict people to a passive role in responding to inevitable cycles or changes in material culture. Rather, Marxist theory

Dan Burns/Monkmeyer

An example of the process of inclusion, as described by Talcott Parsons, is the admission of women, African Americans, and Jews into exclusive clubs (including golf clubs) that were previously restricted.

offers a tool for those who wish to seize control of the historical process and gain their freedom from injustice. In contrast to functionalists' emphasis on stability, Marx argues that conflict is a normal and desirable aspect of social change. Indeed, change must be encouraged as a means of eliminating social inequality (Lauer, 1982).

One conflict sociologist, Ralf Dahrendorf (1959), has noted that the contrast between the functionalist emphasis on stability and the conflict perspective's focus on change reflects the contradictory nature of society. Human societies are stable and long-lasting, yet they also experience serious conflict. Indeed, Parsons spoke of new functions that result from social change, and Marx recognized the need for change so that societies could function more equitably. In Dahrendorf's view, the functionalist and conflict approaches are ultimately compatible despite their many areas of disagreement.

RESISTANCE TO SOCIAL CHANGE

As has been stressed through this chapter, efforts to promote social change are likely to be met with resistance. In the midst of rapid scientific and technological innovations, many people are emotionally frightened by the demands of an ever-changing society. However, certain individuals and groups have a stake in maintaining the existing state of affairs.

Social economist Thorstein Veblen (1857–1929) coined the term *vested interests* to refer to those people or groups who will suffer in the event of social change. For example, the American Medical Association (AMA) has taken strong stands against national health insurance and the professionalization of midwifery (refer back to Chapter 17). National health insurance could lead to limits on the income of physicians, and a rise in the status of midwifes could threaten the preeminent position of doctors as the nation's deliverers of babies. In general, those with a disproportionate share of society's wealth, status, and power, such as members of the American Medical Association, have a vested interest in preserving the status quo (Starr, 1982; Veblen, 1919).

Economic factors play an important role in resistance to social change. For example, it can be expensive for manufacturers to meet the highest possible standards for the safety of products and of industrial workers. Conflict theorists argue that, in a capitalist economic system, many firms are not willing to pay the price of meeting strict safety standards. They may resist social change by cutting corners within their plants or by pressuring the government to ease regulations.

As was discussed in Chapter 19, an economic refrain involving "protecting property values" is often heard in communities that claim to be defending their vested interests as they resist social change. The abbreviation "NIMBY" stands for "not in my backyard," a cry often heard when people protest landfills, prisons, nuclear power facilities, and even group homes for those with developmental disabilities. The need for the facility is not necessarily challenged, but the targeted community may simply insist that it be located elsewhere. The "not in my backyard" phenomenon has become so common that it is almost impossible for policymakers to find acceptable locations for such facilities as dump sites for hazardous wastes (Dear, 1992; Piller, 1991).

Like economic factors, cultural factors frequently shape resistance to change. As noted in Chapter 3, William F. Ogburn (1922) distinguished between material and nonmaterial aspects of culture. *Material culture* includes inventions, artifacts, and technology; *nonmaterial culture* encompasses ideas, norms, communication, and social organization. Ogburn pointed out that one cannot devise methods for controlling and utilizing new technology before the introduction of a technique. Thus, nonmaterial culture typically must respond to changes in material culture. Ogburn introduced the term *culture lag* to refer to the period of maladjustment during which the nonmaterial culture is still adapting to new material conditions.

In certain cases, changes in material culture can add strain to the relationships between social institutions. For example, new techniques of birth control have been developed in recent decades. Large families are no longer economically necessary, nor are they commonly endorsed by social norms. But certain religious faiths, among them Roman Catholicism and Mormonism, continue to extol large families and to view methods of limiting family size such as contraception and abortion as undesirable. This represents a lag between aspects of material culture (technology) and nonmaterial culture (religious beliefs). Conflicts may emerge between religion and other social institutions, such as government and the educational system, over the dissemination of birth control and family planning information (Lauer, 1982:152).

Today, social movements often seem to question the traditional basis for a culture. The feminist and gay liberation movements have challenged cultural beliefs long accepted as "natural"—that the male is the dominant member of the species, that heterosexuality is the only healthy form of sexual orientation, and so forth. Not surprisingly, resistance to such movements is often very strong. The re-

Shown are demonstrators opposed to the placement of a new incinerator in a community in Hartford, Connecticut. The phenomenon of "NIMBY" ("not in my backyard") has become so common that it is almost impossible for policymakers to find acceptable locations for incinerators, landfills, and dump sites for hazardous wastes.

source-mobilization approach has focused not only on how social movements mobilize but also on how resistance to change is expressed (R. Roberts and Kloss, 1974:153–157; Zald and McCarthy, 1979). Forms of resistance to social movements include the following:

- *Ridicule.* The women's movement was tagged with the derisive label "women's lib" by its detractors. At the same time, feminists were stereotyped as "bra burners."
- *Cooptation.* One way to pacify members of a social movement is to appear to incorporate, or coopt, its goals or leaders into the political structure. In 1991, while facing strong criticism from Black civil rights groups, President George Bush nominated Judge Clarence Thomas to fill a vacancy on the Supreme Court.
- *Formal social control.* During the 1950s, southern communities passed legislation banning civil rights marches. More recently, certain colleges have denied official recognition of lesbian and gay male student organizations.

- *Violence.* If all other measures used to stop a social movement are unsuccessful, its opponents may resort to violence. When National Guard troops shot and killed four Kent State college students during a 1970 demonstration opposing the United States' invasion of Cambodia, a generation of young protestors learned that participation in a social movement can be extremely risky.

Social movements face a difficult challenge in their struggle for social change. Almost inevitably, powerful individuals and groups in society have a vested interest in opposing change. While members of a social movement attempt to mobilize their resources, the powerful do the same—and the powerful often have more money, more political influence, and greater access to the media. Nevertheless, human history is a history of change; resistance by those in power has often been overcome. In the social policy section which follows, we will see that disability rights activists have overcome resistance to force important changes in society's treatment of people with disabilities.

- How does the medical model of disability compare with the civil rights model?
- In what ways do people with disabilities experience prejudice, discrimination, and other forms of social inequality?
- What difficulties does the disability rights movement face in mobilizing as a political bloc?

Throughout history, people with disabilities have often been subjected to cruel and inhuman treatment. For example, in the early twentieth century the disabled were frequently viewed as subhuman creatures who were a menace to society. As one result, many state legislatures passed compulsory sterilization laws aimed at handicapped people. Drawing on similar prejudices against the disabled, Adolf Hitler's Nazi regime persecuted and put to death perhaps as many as 1 million people with disabilities. In a chilling reminder of this legacy, neo-Nazi groups in Germany launched more than 40 attacks on physically and mentally disabled people during the first two months of 1993 (H. Hahn, 1987:200; M. Rebell, 1986; Waldrop, 1993).

Today, such blatantly hostile treatment of disabled people has generally been replaced by a *medical model* which focuses on the functional impairments of the person. Those with disabilities are therefore viewed as chronic patients. In an adaptation of Talcott Parsons' sick role (refer back to Chapter 17), we can say that society assigns the disabled a "handicapped role." They are viewed as helpless, childlike people who are expected to assume a cheerful and continuing dependence on family members, friends, and health care professionals.

Increasingly, however, people concerned with the rights of the disabled have criticized this medical model. In the view of these activists, it is the unnecessary and discriminatory barriers present in the environment—both physical and attitudinal—that stand in the way of people with disabilities, more than their biological limitations do. Applying a *civil rights model*, activists emphasize that those with disabilities face widespread prejudice, discrimination, and segregation. For example, most voting places are architecturally inaccessible to wheelchair users and fail to offer ballots that can be used by people unable to read print. Many states continue to deny blind and deaf citizens the right to serve on juries. City and state government hearings, school board meetings, and other important public events are typically held in inaccessible locations and without sign language interpreters. Viewed from a conflict perspective, such public policies reflect unequal treatment that helps to keep people with disabilities in a subservient position (A. Asch, 1986:219; H. Hahn, 1987:194).

Labeling theorists, drawing on the earlier work of Erving Goffman (1963a), have suggested that society attaches a stigma to many forms of disability and that this stigma leads to prejudicial treatment. Indeed, people with disabilities frequently observe that the nondisabled see them only as blind, deaf, wheelchair users, and so forth, rather than as complex human beings with individual strengths and weaknesses whose blindness or deafness is merely one aspect of their lives. In this regard, a review of studies of women with disabilities disclosed that most academic research on the disabled does not differentiate by gender—thereby perpetuating the view that when a disability is present, no other personal characteristic can matter. Consequently, as noted in Chapter 5, disability serves as a master status (M. Fine and Asch, 1988; Gove, 1980:237).

The label and master status of "disabled" is commonly viewed as a barrier to any type of accomplishment, as is evident in a story involving John Hockenberry of National Public Radio:

[Hockenberry] had been the network's prolific West Coast correspondent. But Hockenberry's bosses and colleagues had never met him until one day, a few years after he had begun filing his reports, he showed up at NPR's Washington headquarters. His appearance was jolting. Hockenberry is a paraplegic. Only a few in the newsroom knew this. How, his fellow correspondents wondered, had a man in a wheelchair managed to cover political races or the exploding Mount Saint

Disability rights activists have proclaimed July 25 as Disability Independence Day to celebrate the signing of the Americans with Disabilities Act (ADA). The second annual celebration of Disability Independence Day was marked in 1993 with marches and rallies across the nation.

Helens volcano? Then they realized, in a disturbing wave of self-recognition, that had they known of his disability, Hockenberry almost certainly never would have been given such challenging assignments. It would have been assumed that he was not able to cover them (Shapiro, 1993:19).

The mass media have contributed to stereotyping of people with disabilities by treating them with a mixture of pity and fear. Nationwide charity telethons promote negative images of the handicapped by showing them as childlike, incompetent, and nonproductive. By contrast, in literature and film, "evil" characters with disabilities (from Captain Hook to Freddy Krueger) reinforce the view that disability is a punishment for evil and that the handicapped, out of a desire for revenge, would destroy the nondisabled if they could. Even ostensibly more favorable treatments of disabled characters tend to focus on unusually courageous and inspirational individuals who achieve striking personal successes against great odds—rather than on the impact of prejudice and discrimination on "ordinary" disabled people (Longmore, 1985; Shapiro, 1993:31–32; Zola, 1987).

By 1970, a strong social movement for disability rights—drawing on the experiences of the Black civil rights movement, the women's liberation movement, and various self-help movements—had emerged across the United States. This movement now includes organizations of people with a single disability (such as the National Federation of the Blind), organizations of people with different disabilities (such as New York City's Disabled in Action), a legal advocacy organization (the Disability Rights Education and Defense Fund), and an activist publication (the *Disability Rag*). Ironically, the war in Vietnam served as a major factor in advancing the disability rights movement. Because of war-related injuries, a large number of disabled Vietnam veterans joined with other people with disabilities in demanding full civil rights.

Women and men involved in the disability rights movement are working to challenge negative views of disabled people; to gain a greater voice for the disabled in all agency and public policy decisions that affect them; and to reshape laws, institutions, and environments so that people with disabilities can be fully integrated into mainstream society. Disability rights activists argue that there is an important distinction between organizations *for* disabled people and organizations *of* disabled people. The former include service providers, charitable associations, and parental groups. Some activists maintain that since these organizations are not controlled by people with disabilities, they do not give priority to the goals of independence and self-help emphasized by the disability rights movement (Scotch, 1984:33–37, 1989).

Without question, people with disabilities occupy a subordinate position in the United States. According to Mitchell LaPlante, director of the Disability Statistics Program at the University of California at San Francisco, 23 percent of disabled adults in the United States are poor—almost three times the rate for the rest of the population. Many of these low-income people with disabilities survive largely on Social Security payments, Medicaid, and food stamps. Even among the disabled, racial differences are evident. A 1992 study by the federal government's General Accounting Office found that African Americans have more difficulty than others in obtaining benefits from the two largest federal programs for people with severe disabilities: Disability Insurance and Supplementary Security Income (Kilborn, 1992:24; Labaton, 1992).

Architectural barriers and transportation difficulties often add to the problems of disabled people who seek or obtain employment. Simply getting around city streets can be quite difficult; many streets are not properly equipped with curb cuts for wheelchair users. A genuinely barrier-free building needs more than a ramp; it should also include automatic doors, raised letters and braille on signs, and toilets that are accessible to the disabled. But even if a disabled person finds a job, and even if the job is in a barrier-free building, he or she still faces the problem of getting to work in a society where most railroad stations and buses remain inaccessible to wheelchair users and others with disabilities.

With such issues in mind, the disability rights movement won an important victory in 1990 when President George Bush signed the Americans with Disabilities Act (ADA). This civil rights law was passed only after a long legislative struggle, behind-the-scenes lobbying to weaken the bill by business groups, and demonstrations at the Capitol Rotunda by disability rights activists. The ADA affects some 43 million people with a disability (defined as a condition that "substantially limits" a "major life activity," such as walking or sight).

This law, the most sweeping antidiscrimination law to be approved since the 1964 Civil Rights Act, began to go into effect in 1992. It prohibits bias in employment, transportation, public accommodations, and telecommunications against people with disabilities. Businesses with more than 25 employees can no longer refuse to hire a disabled applicant; these companies will be expected to make a "reasonable accommodation" to permit such a worker to do the job. Commercial establishments such as office buildings, hotels, theaters, supermarkets, and dry cleaners have been barred from denying service to people with disabilities. However, as of mid-1993—a year after the ADA had gone into effect—the Justice Department had already received 11,550 complaints of discrimination. About half represented claims from people that they had been unfairly discharged from their jobs because of their disabilities (Kilborn, 1992; Mullins, 1993).

Opponents of various measures mandating accessibility often insist that these measures will be prohibitively expensive. However, disability rights activists argue that these projected costs are often overstated; backers of the ADA add that the law will benefit society by assisting the disabled to find employment and leave the welfare rolls. The federal government spends about $60 billion each year on people with disabilities, but only $3 billion goes for education, training, and rehabilitation, with the rest for benefits. According to one estimate, if even 10,000 disabled people join the work force each year, the government will save $70 million annually in cash benefits and will, in addition, receive millions in taxes from these new workers (Rasky, 1989b; Roth, 1989).

With passage of the ADA, the disability rights movement has begun to emphasize the issue of attendant services. Lack of affordable and reliable home care leaves thousands of severely disabled people powerless to benefit from the ADA—and forces others unnecessarily into nursing homes. Yet state support for home care services varies dramatically. Disability rights activists view attendant services as a civil rights issue. In their view, advances in employment or accessible transportation are meaningless if a disabled person cannot get needed assistance to get up, get ready for work, and get out of the house (Shapiro, 1993:250–257).

In order to win future victories, the disability rights movement will need to become stronger as a political bloc. Yet the social movement for disability rights must overcome certain difficulties related to resource mobilization. Those with disabilities are geographically, socially, and economically dispersed; there is danger of fragmentation because of the diversity evident in the different types and levels of disability. Moreover, many of these individuals—especially those who are successfully employed—may not identify themselves consciously with the movement. Still, activists remain encouraged after passage of the Americans with Disabilities Act. Mary Johnson (1989:446), former editor of the *Disability Rag,* has written: "Discrimination against people with disabilities has now been officially acknowledged. We've got a foot—or a wheel or a cane—in the door" (P. Bradley, 1990; Scotch, 1988).

SUMMARY

Collective behavior is the relatively spontaneous and unstructured behavior of a group that is reacting to an ambiguous situation. *Social change* is significant alteration over time in behavior patterns and culture, including norms and values. This chapter examines sociological theories used to understand collective behavior, forms of collective behavior, theories of social change, and resistance to change.

1 Turner and Killian's *emergent-norm perspective* suggests that new norms of proper behavior may arise in ambiguous situations.

2 Smelser's *value-added model* of collective behavior outlines six important determinants of such behavior: structural conduciveness, structural strain, generalized belief, precipitating factor, mobilization of participants for action, and operation of social control.

3 The *assembling perspective* introduced by McPhail and Miller sought for the first time to examine how and why people move from different points in space to a common location.

4 Unlike certain situations involving collective behavior, *crowds* require people to be in relatively close contact and interaction.

5 The key distinction between a *panic* and a *craze* is that a panic is a flight *from* something whereas a craze is a movement *to* something.

6 A *rumor* serves a social function by providing a group with a shared belief.

7 *Social movements* are more structured than other forms of collective behavior and persist over longer periods of time.

8 Early advocates of *evolutionary theory* of social change believed that society was inevitably progressing to a higher state.

9 Talcott Parsons, a leading advocate of functionalist theory, viewed society as naturally being in a state of equilibrium or balance.

10 Conflict theorists see change as having crucial significance, since it is needed to correct social injustices and inequalities.

11 In general, those with a disproportionate share of society's wealth, status, and power have a *vested interest* in preserving the status quo.

12 By the 1970s, a strong movement for disability rights had emerged across the United States.

CRITICAL THINKING QUESTIONS

1 Are the emergent-norm, value-added, and assembling perspectives aligned with or reminiscent of functionalism, conflict theory, or interactionism? What aspects of each of these theories of collective behavior (if any) seem linked to the broader theoretical perspectives of sociology?

2 Without using any of the examples presented in the textbook, list at least two examples of each of the following types of collective behavior: crowds, disasters, fads, fashions, panics, crazes, rumors, publics, and social movements. Explain why each example belongs in its assigned category. Distinguish between each type of collective behavior based on the type and degree of social structure and interaction that are present.

3 Select one social movement that is currently working for change in the United States. Analyze that movement, drawing on the concepts of relative deprivation, resource mobilization, and false consciousness. Discuss whether the equilibrium model and the conflict theory of social change are useful in analyzing the social movement you have chosen.

Assembling perspective A theory of collective behavior introduced by McPhail and Miller which seeks to examine how and why people move from different points in space to a common location. (page 573)

Collective behavior In the view of sociologist Neil Smelser, the relatively spontaneous and unstructured behavior of a group of people who are reacting to a common influence in an ambiguous situation. (568)

Craze An exciting mass involvement which lasts for a relatively long period of time. (575)

Crowds Temporary gatherings of people in close proximity who share a common focus or interest. (573)

Culture lag Ogburn's term for a period of maladjustment during which the nonmaterial culture is still adapting to new material conditions. (586)

Disaster A sudden or disruptive event or set of events that overtaxes a community's resources so that outside aid is necessary. (573)

Emergent-norm perspective A theory of collective behavior proposed by Turner and Killian which holds that a collective definition of appropriate and inappropriate behavior emerges during episodes of collective behavior. (571)

Equilibrium model Talcott Parsons' functionalist view of society as tending toward a state of stability or balance. (584)

Evolutionary theory A theory of social change which holds that society is moving in a definite direction. (582)

Fads Temporary movements toward the acceptance of some particular taste or lifestyle that involve large numbers of people and are independent of preceding trends. (575)

False consciousness A term used by Karl Marx to describe an attitude held by members of a class that does not accurately reflect its objective position. (582)

Fashions Pleasurable mass involvements in some particular taste or lifestyle that have a line of historical continuity. (575)

Multilinear evolutionary theory A theory of social change which holds that change can occur in several ways and does not inevitably lead in the same direction. (584)

Nonperiodic assemblies Nonrecurring gatherings of people which often result from word-of-mouth information. (573)

Panic A fearful arousal or collective flight based on a generalized belief which may or may not be accurate. (576)

Periodic assemblies Recurring, relatively routine gatherings of people, such as college classes. (573)

Public A dispersed group of people, not necessarily in contact with one another, who share an interest in an issue. (578)

Public opinion Expressions of attitudes on matters of public policy which are communicated to decision makers. (578)

Relative deprivation The conscious feeling of a negative discrepancy between legitimate expectations and present actualities. (581)

Resource mobilization The ways in which a social movement utilizes such resources as money, political influence, access to the media, and personnel. (582)

Rumor A piece of information gathered informally which is used to interpret an ambiguous situation. (577)

Social change Significant alteration over time in behavior patterns and culture, including norms and values. (569)

Social movements Organized collective activities to promote or resist change in an existing group or society. (579)

Unilinear evolutionary theory A theory of social change which holds that all societies pass through the same successive stages of evolution and inevitably reach the same end. (584)

Value-added model A theory of collective behavior proposed by Neil Smelser to explain how broad social conditions are transformed in a definite pattern into some form of collective behavior. (571)

Vested interests Veblen's term for those people or groups who will suffer in the event of social change and who have a stake in maintaining the status quo. (586)

ADDITIONAL READINGS

Brunvand, Jan Harold. *The Baby Train and Other Lusty Urban Legends.* New York: Norton, 1993. The author, an English professor, has collected another series of rumors which have become such an accepted part of our culture that they can perhaps be considered legends or folklore.

Davis, Fred. *Fashions, Culture, and Identity.* Chicago: University of Chicago Press, 1992. A sociologist considers how fashion reflects our sense of identity and is influenced by consumer selection.

Fine, Michelle, and Adrienne Asch (eds.). *Women with Disabilities: Essays in Psychology, Culture, and Politics.* Philadelphia: Temple University Press, 1988. An anthology exploring scholarly and activist concerns on issues ranging from prejudice to employment policy, from friendship to social justice.

Jasper, James M., and Dorothy Nelkin. *The Animal Rights Crusade: The Growth of a Moral Protest.* New York: Free Press, 1992. Two sociologists provide a history and an analysis of a social movement whose members range from associations of kindly pet lovers concerned with "animal welfare" to passionate groups of activists fighting for "animal rights."

Kapferer, Jean-Noël. *Rumors: Uses, Interpretations, and Images.* New Brunswick, N.J.: Transaction, 1990. A comprehensive examination of rumors, gossip, and urban legends drawing upon examples from both Europe and the United States.

Miller, David L. *Introduction to Collective Behavior.* Prospect Heights, Ill.: Waveland, 1988. The author, associated with the assembling perspective, covers all the major theoretical approaches to the field. He examines rumors, riots, social movements, immigration, and other forms of collective behavior.

Shapiro, Joseph P. *No Pity: People with Disabilities Forging a New Civil Rights Movement.* New York: Times Books, 1993. The author, a journalist who writes for *U.S. News and World Report,* draws on hundreds of interviews with disability rights activists to offer a portrait of an emerging social movement.

Turner, Patricia A. *I Heard It through the Grapevine: Rumor in African-American Culture.* Berkeley: University of California Press, 1993. A scholarly examination of folk tales and legends shared among African Americans.

Walton, John. *Western Times and Water Wars: State, Culture, and Rebellion in California.* Berkeley: University of California Press, 1992. A sociological analysis of environmental protests and social movements that developed in the Owens Valley of California.

Zald, Mayer N., and John D. McCarthy (eds.). *Social Movements in an Organizational Society.* Rutgers, N.J.: Transaction, 1986. A detailed analysis of the processes involved when individuals and groups are mobilized for collective action.

Journals

Among those journals which focus on issues of collective behavior are the *International Journal of Mass Emergencies and Disasters* (founded in 1983), the *Journal of Popular Culture* (1967), and *Public Opinion Quarterly* (1937). *The Futurist* (founded in 1967) is a monthly magazine dedicated to exploring possible social and technological changes and their likely impact on society.

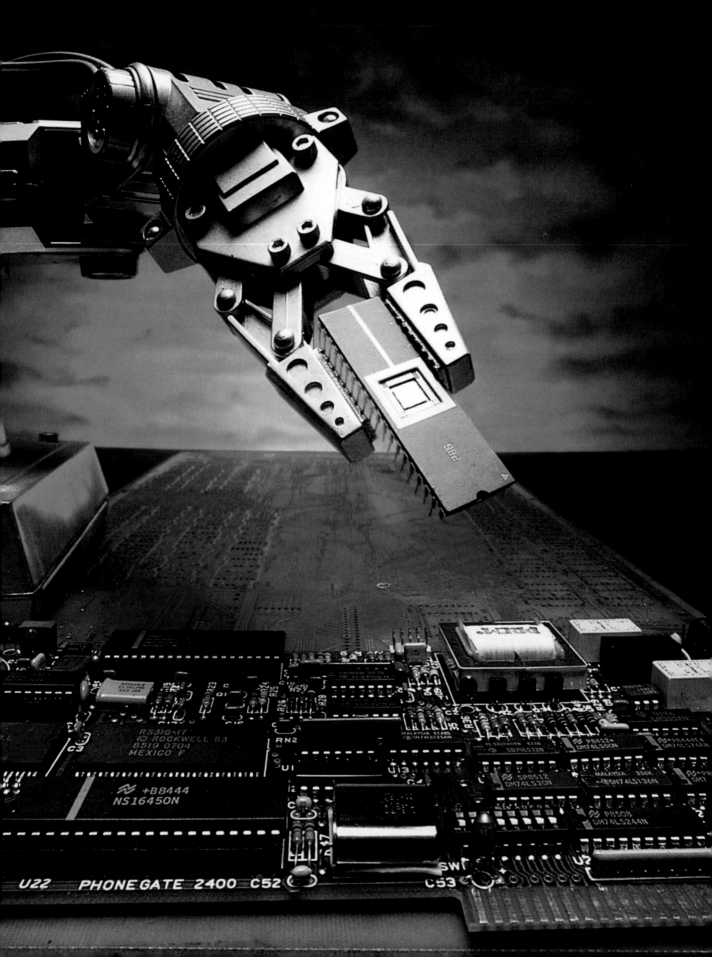

SOCIOLOGY, TECHNOLOGY, AND THE FUTURE

In 1992, sociology in the United States reached a significant milestone. In that year, for the first time, a department of sociology (that of the University of Chicago) marked its centennial anniversary. Clearly, there have been monumental changes since 1892 both in the discipline of sociology and in the society known as the United States. But what is ahead in our discipline, in our country, in our world, as we approach the twenty-first century and beyond?

As noted earlier in this book, *technology* is the application of knowledge to the making of tools and the utilization of natural resources. In this conclusion to our introduction to sociology, we will consider what the sociological imagination tells us about the technology of the present and the decades to come. Technological advances—among them, the airplane, the automobile, the television, the atomic bomb, and more recently, the computer, the FAX machine, and the cellu-

lar phone—have brought dramatic changes in our cultures, our patterns of socialization, our social institutions, and our day-to-day social interactions. Indeed, technological innovations are emerging and being accepted with remarkable speed. It took only eight years for television to make its way into 50 percent of homes in the United States and only 13 years for the VCR to do the same (Maney, 1993).

The technological knowledge we work with today represents only a tiny portion of the knowledge that will be available in the year 2050. We are witnessing an information explosion as well: the number of volumes in major libraries in the United States doubles every 14 years. Consequently, when viewed from a sociological perspective, individuals, institutions, and societies will face unprecedented adaptive challenges in adjusting to the technological advances soon to come (Cetron and Davies, 1991; Wurman, 1989).

In the following sections, we will examine various aspects of our technological future and the strains that will arise owing to technological advances.

Sex Selection 1978 marked the year that the first baby was born as the result of conception outside the womb. Since then, advances in reproductive and screening technology have brought us closer to effective techniques for sex selection. In the United States, the prenatal test of amniocentesis has been used for 20 years to ascertain the presence of certain defects that require medical procedures prior to birth. However, such tests inevitably identify the gender of the fetus.

In many societies, young couples planning to have only one child will want to ensure that this child is a boy because these cultures place a premium on a male heir. Indeed, it has been estimated that if sex selection becomes commonly available in the United States, the nation will experience a 9.5 percent excess of boys over girls. From a functionalist perspective, sex selection can be viewed as an adaptation of the basic family function of regulating reproduction. However, conflict theorists emphasize that sex selection may intensify the male dominance of our society and undermine the advances women have made in entering careers formerly restricted to men (Cornish, 1992; Hawkes, 1993; Nuttall and Watt, 1993; Stacey, 1992:37).

Biotechnology Even more grandiose than sex selection—but not necessarily improbable—is altering human behavior through biotechnology. Fish and plant genes have already been mixed to create frost-resistant potato and tobacco crops; more recently, human genes have been implanted in pigs to provide humanlike kidneys for organ transplants. Criminologist Gene Stephens (1992:42) has written a futuristic scenario of a genetically enhanced police officer scaling a skyscraper to surprise a human "organ rustler" under investigation by the government's Biotech Crime Division.

In 1993, newspapers erroneously reported that a fertility researcher had cloned a human embryo and, in the process, potentially created multiples of the same genetic material that could be implanted into a woman (or several women) who would give birth to genetically identical babies. Actually, the researcher's advances were much more elementary and could not lead to such multiple and identical babies. Nevertheless, the ensuing debate spurred by these reports showed how unprepared we are to deal with such technology. Journalists speculated that if such an embryo grew 7 feet tall and signed a professional basketball contract for $140 million, how much might the still frozen "twin embryos" be worth? In response to those who called for government intervention after initial reports about this supposed advance in genetic engineering, Arthur Caplan, director of the Center for Bioethics at the University of Minnesota, responded critically. "If our politicians can't make up a coherent policy for Haiti . . . ," asked Caplan, "how are we supposed to design our descendants?" (J. Adler, 1993:62; Kolata, 1993).

In examining the issue of biotechnology, we must return to one of the earliest discussions in this textbook: *nature versus nurture* (or heredity versus environment). Today, it is fashionable to proclaim the power of genetics. In February 1993, for example, Phil Donahue aired a show on "How to Tell If Your Child's a Serial Killer!" through genetic analysis. Yet many heralded research findings are already in dispute. The predisposition to crime (or at least violence) for males with an extra Y chromosome—widely reported in the 1960s—has since been found to be mistaken. A 1990 report suggesting that alcoholism may be inherited is currently in dispute. And there are continuing and intense debates concerning the inheritability of intelligence. These controversies serve as a caution in evaluating the more optimistic projections concerning biotechnology (Horgan, 1993).

The prospects of sex selection and other aspects of biotechnology recall observations made in the early 1920s by sociologist William F. Ogburn (1922) in response to then President Herbert Hoover's call for a look at the future. Ogburn and his colleagues believed that our nonmaterial culture of norms, values, and philosophies was not changing fast enough to keep pace with (much less manage) our material culture of technology. Do we have the value system in place to confront the inventions of today, much less biotechnology and other innovations of tomorrow?

Telecommuting As the industrial revolution proceeded, the factory and the office replaced the fam-

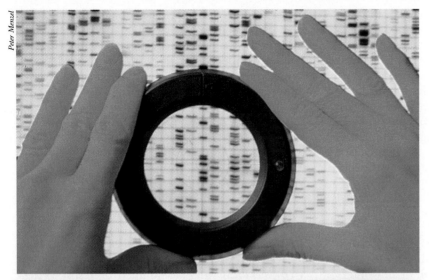

Peter Menzel

Rob Crandall/Stock, Boston

Peter Menzel

In examining technological advances and how they will affect individuals, institutions, and societies, sociologists are interested in such innovations as human genetic engineering, telecommuting, and virtual reality.

ily farm as the typical workplace. However, in 1992, there were about 6.6 million "telecommuters" in the United States, or about 20 percent more than in 1991. *Telecommuters* are employees of business firms or government agencies who work full time or part time at home rather than in an outside office. They are linked to their supervisors and colleagues through computer terminals, phone lines, and FAX machines. Telecommuting can even cross national boundaries, oceans, and continents. For example, noted science-fiction author Arthur C. Clarke, who lives in Sri Lanka (Ceylon), is deeply involved in the publishing world of the United States through electronic networking (Calem, 1993).

There are projections of vast increases in telecommuting in the next decade or two. According to estimates offered by authorities on technology, by the year 2009 as many as half of all workers in the United States will perform their jobs partially at home through use of computer systems (Halal, 1992). How will both work and family life be reshaped if more and more employees are working out of their homes? In what ways will telecommuting expand job possibilities for people with disabilities? Will the emergence of a home-based economy make it impossible for labor unions to organize workers and engage in collective bargaining?

Computers and Privacy While computers offer unquestioned technological advances, they are capable of invading people's privacy. Messages, purchases, financial transactions, and telephone connections can now be monitored in a way that was not previously possible. With such concerns in mind, the Privacy Act of 1974 specifies that the existence of recording systems must be publicly acknowledged, individuals must have access to their own files, they must be able to correct inaccurate or misleading entries, and they must be able to protest improper use of their files. However, all these provisions have restrictions and qualifications, and they do not even apply to all federal government files, much less those maintained by private agencies (Rule, 1993).

Given the absence of strong protective legislation, employees in the United States are subject to increasing and pervasive supervision by computers. It has become easy for even small business firms to gather information on workers' habits, such as casual pauses in entering tedious data or the length of time required to weigh and price a bag of apples at a supermarket checkout station. With "Big Brother" watching in more and more places, computer and video technology have facilitated supervision, control, and even domination by employers or government. How will such supervision affect social interactions in what we have long called a "free society"? Will fears about such intrusions into our lives limit the acceptance of otherwise beneficial technological innovations?

Virtual Reality Imagine putting on a helmet and stepping into a suit complete with gloves and shoes. You are cut off from the real environment around you; through technology, sensations are transmitted to your body so that you feel as if you are swimming in Australia's Great Barrier Reef or initiating a conversation with Mohammed or Jesus. *Virtual reality* is an interactive technology that creates an illusion of being immersed in an artificial world or being present in a remote location in the physical world (Rucker et al., 1992:25).

Currently, virtual reality is utilized primarily as a form of entertainment. However, a 1992 murder trial used computer simulations to "show" the jury how the defendant allegedly committed the murder. Some observers expect that employers will someday use virtual reality to screen job applicants. Counselors, police officers, and teachers, among others, could be placed in virtual reality to test how well they perform in simulated work situations (Bacard, 1993).

We are only at the beginning of the possibilities and ethical dilemmas posed by virtual reality. This technological advance could be used to allow a person to indulge norm-defying or even criminal fantasies. Indeed, by the 1990s, computer software was available that allowed users to engage in activities that ridicule or trivialize women and minority groups.

Technological Accidents Our increasing reliance on technology has led to a growing separation between people and the outcomes of their actions. A carpenter who single-handedly makes a ladder has quite a different investment in the quality of the product than does a technician who develops a small part for a space shuttle.

Sociologist Charles Perrow (1984) introduced

the term *normal accidents* to refer to failures that are inevitable given the manner in which human and technological systems are organized. Whether in a hospital or an aerospace program, catastrophes are often caused not by massive errors but rather by what appear to be (when considered in isolation) almost incidental human misjudgments and minor technical flaws. In studying normal accidents, engineers focus on the system design, the physical environment, and the possibility of mechanical failure; social scientists are hired to evaluate possible operator (or human) error.

Generally, 60 to 80 percent of normal accidents are attributed to human factors. As one example, sociologist Cora Marrett and her colleagues on the President's Commission on the Accident at Three Mile Island studied the 1979 accident at the nuclear power plant near Harrisburg, Pennsylvania. In a controversial finding, the interaction of several operators and supervisors communicating with each other across a shift change was designated as the primary cause of the accident.

System accidents are uncommon, even rare. But, like the death of any individual, which occurs only once, this infrequency is not all that reassuring. Given the possible consequences of a systems failure, we can anticipate that social scientists will work even more closely with engineers to explore how better equipment, training, and organization can reduce the likelihood of normal accidents (Perrow, 1984; see also L. Clarke, 1988).

Technology and Inequality An important continuing theme in sociology is stratification among people. Thus far, there is little evidence to suggest that technology will reduce inequality; indeed, it may only intensify inequality. Technology is costly and it is generally impossible to introduce advances to everyone simultaneously. So who gets this access first? Conflict theorists contend that as we travel further and further along the electronic frontier through advances such as telecommuting and virtual reality, the disenfranchised poor may be isolated from mainstream society in an "information ghetto," just as racial and ethnic minorities have traditionally been subjected to residential segregation (Ouellette, 1993).

In this regard, in 1993 telephone and cable television companies unveiled plans for *interactive* ca-

© D.L. Barstow

"It's for you."

ble television. Home viewers will conceivably be able to access businesses, libraries, and government agencies, as well as sources of entertainment. Will these developments be available to all? Not necessarily, according to the Federal Communications Commission (FCC). FCC commissioner Andrew Barrett has stated:

> Just as we have poor people today, just as we have homeless people today, we will have the information-rich and the information-poor. . . . Our job is to provide access, but I don't want to provide access on the basis of companies having to subsidize all of America (Grady, 1993:1).

The technological advances of the present and future may not be equally beneficial to men and women. Feminist sociologists have brought the issue of women and technology to the forefront by pointing out that technology is not necessarily gender-neutral. For example, many studies have shown that there is differential use of computers by boys and girls. Computer games, which serve as an important means of early socialization to computers, typically involve sports or skills associated with the traditional male gender role. As a result, computer camps and video arcades have become predominantly male settings. Danish scholar Janine Morgall (1993) contends that a feminist approach to technology is essential to ensure that women's needs are served as technological advances reshape our society and our social institutions.

The issue of technology and inequality is especially sensitive when viewed in a cross-cultural perspective. Although industrialization has dramatically improved the standard of living of many workers, it has allowed elites to amass untold wealth. Moreover, as we have seen in this textbook, the activities of multinational corporations have increased the inequality between industrial core nations (such as the United States, Germany, and Japan) and the periphery of developing countries.

A comparison of Great Britain and the African nation of Sierra Leone is illustrative. Sierra Leone gained its independence from Britain in 1961. Although its 4 million residents are not the world's poorest people, their life chances are dramatically different from those of the British population. According to the United Nations Development Programme (1993), life expectancy at birth in Britain is almost 76 years, while in Sierra Leone it is only 42 years. In Sierra Leone, one out of five adults is literate, and the population has had an average of only three months of formal schooling. By contrast, more than 99 percent of adults in Britain are literate, and the population averages 11.5 years of schooling.

Like money, food, and other resources, technology is unevenly distributed within societies and throughout the world. Conflict theorists point out that the world's more developed countries have 10 times as many scientists and engineers per capita as do the developing nations. In addition, the technology gap is widening rather than narrowing. Although nations are exchanging technical data more freely than before, critical technology transfer is often withheld. The technology exported to developing countries may be poorly suited to the conditions of their economies and workplaces (Cetron and Davies, 1991).

These are but a few vignettes of changes viewed from the vantage point of the mid-1990s that raise questions about the future. Sociologists are not fortune-tellers; the focus of the discipline is to examine the society around us, rather than to project decades ahead. But sociologists have no problem in asserting that social change (and technological change) is a given in our world. And so, they remind us, is resistance to change.

One researcher underscored people's mixed feelings about possible changes in a survey of continuing education students in New Zealand. The students were given a list of more than 30 developments that may happen during the next 100 years and were asked to rank each from "very desirable" to "very undesirable." The development ranked most desirable was "Genetic engineering is applied to improve plants and livestock." Not surprisingly, among the least desirable developments were "Governance is by intelligent supercomputer" and "Robots with superior strength and intelligence replace living beings, then proceed to populate the universe" (Mautner, 1992:43).

We cannot know what is ahead. But the sociological imagination—with its probing and theorizing, with its careful empirical studies—can assist us in understanding the past and present and anticipating and adjusting to the future. As we have learned, socialization is a process that continues throughout our lifetimes as we experience personal and societal changes. Anticipatory socialization and resocialization are certainly relevant in dealing with the technological and social developments that we will face in the twenty-first century.

In his acclaimed book *Sociology for Whom?*, Alfred McClung Lee (1986:246), a former president of both the American Sociological Association and the Society for the Study of Social Problems, poignantly observes that social phenomena are seldom what they seem initially. The endless contrasts between what we say and what we do, between the promises of social organizations and their day-to-day performance, remind us of the ever-present need to question and examine. With this in mind, those of us committed to the discipline of sociology, to the beauty and value of the sociological imagination, can only hope that this intellectual enterprise will help us to face the demands and challenges of a technological world far beyond the dreams of Émile Durkheim, Max Weber, and Karl Marx.

GLOSSARY

Note: Numbers following the definitions indicate pages where the terms were identified.
Consult the index for further page references.

Absolute poverty A standard of poverty based on a minimum level of subsistence below which families should not be expected to exist. (226)

Achieved status A social position attained by a person largely through his or her own effort. (124, 212)

Activity theory An interactionist theory of aging which argues that elderly people who remain active will be best-adjusted. (339)

Adoption In a legal sense, a process that allows for the transfer of the legal rights, responsibilities, and privileges of parenthood from legal parents to new legal parents. (371)

Affirmative action Positive efforts to recruit minority group members or women for jobs, promotions, and educational opportunities. (442)

Afrocentricity The use of African cultures, rather than solely the European experience, to better understand human behaviors past and present. (86)

Age grades Cultural categories that identify the stages of biological maturation. (337)

Ageism A term coined by Robert Butler to refer to prejudice and discrimination against the elderly. (344)

Agrarian society The most technologically advanced form of preindustrial society. Members are primarily engaged in the production of food but increase their crop yield through such innovations as the plow. (422)

Alienation The situation of being estranged or disassociated from the surrounding society. (440)

Amalgamation The process by which a majority group and a minority group combine through intermarriage to form a new group. (283)

Anomie Durkheim's term for the loss of direction felt in a society when social control of individual behavior has become ineffective. (12, 182)

Anomie theory of deviance A theory developed by Robert Merton which explains deviance as an adaptation either of socially prescribed goals or of the norms governing their attainment. (182)

Anticipatory socialization Processes of socialization in which a person "rehearses" for future positions, occupations, and social relationships. (104)

Anti-Semitism Anti-Jewish prejudice. (294)

Apartheid The policy of the South African government designed to maintain the separation of Blacks, Coloureds, and Asians from the dominant Whites. (285)

Applied sociology The use of the discipline of sociology with the specific intent of yielding practical applications for human behavior and organizations. (25)

Argot Specialized language used by members of a group or subculture. (78)

Ascribed status A social position "assigned" to a person by society without regard for the person's unique talents or characteristics. (124, 212)

Assembling perspective A theory of collective behavior introduced by McPhail and Miller which seeks to examine how and why people move from different points in space to a common location. (573)

Assimilation The process by which a person forsakes his or her own cultural tradition to become part of a different culture. (284)

Authority Power that has been institutionalized and is recognized by the people over whom it is exercised. (426)

Basic sociology Sociological inquiry conducted with the objective of gaining a more profound knowledge of the fundamental aspects of social phenomena. Also known as *pure sociology*. (25)

Bilateral descent A kinship system in which both sides of a person's family are regarded as equally important. (364)

Bilingualism The use of two or more languages in workplaces or in educational facilities and the treatment of each language as equally legitimate. (69)

Birthrate The number of live births per 1000 population in a given year. Also known as the *crude birthrate*. (544)

Black power A political philosophy promoted by many younger Blacks in the 1960s which supported the creation of Black-controlled political and economic institutions. (286)

Bourgeoisie Karl Marx's term for the capitalist class, comprising the owners of the means of production. (214)

Bureaucracy A component of formal organization in which rules and hierarchical ranking are used to achieve efficiency. (152)

Bureaucratization The process by which a group, organization, or social movement becomes increasingly bureaucratic. (157)

Capitalism An economic system in which the means of production are largely in private hands, and the main incentive for economic activity is the accumulation of profits. (214, 423)

Castes Hereditary systems of rank, usually religiously dictated, that tend to be relatively fixed and immobile. (210)

Causal logic The relationship between a condition or variable and a particular consequence, with one event leading to the other. (36)

Census An enumeration or counting of a population. (543)

Charismatic authority Max Weber's term for power made legitimate by a leader's exceptional personal or emotional appeal to his or her followers. (428)

Class A term used by Max Weber to refer to people who have a similar level of wealth and income. (215)

Class consciousness In Karl Marx's view, a subjective awareness held by members of a class regarding their common vested interests and need for collective political action to bring about social change. (215)

Classical theory An approach to the study of formal organizations which views workers as being motivated almost entirely by economic rewards. (159)

Class system A social ranking based primarily on economic position in which achieved characteristics can influence mobility. (212)

Clinical sociology The use of the discipline of sociology with the specific intent of altering social relationships and facilitating change. (25)

Closed system A social system in which there is little or no possibility of individual mobility. (231)

Coalition A temporary or permanent alliance toward a common goal. (150)

Code of ethics The standards of acceptable behavior developed by and for members of a profession. (46)

Cognitive theory of development Jean Piaget's theory explaining how children's thought progresses through four stages. (102)

Cohabitation The practice of living together as a male-female couple without marrying. (380)

Collective behavior In the view of sociologist Neil Smelser, the relatively spontaneous and unstructured behavior of a group of people who are reacting to a common influence in an ambiguous situation. (568)

Colonialism The maintenance of political, social, economic, and cultural dominance over a people by a foreign power for an extended period of time. (243)

Communism As an ideal type, an economic system under which all property is communally owned and no social distinctions are made on the basis of people's ability to produce. (425)

Community A spatial or territorial unit of social organization in which people have a sense of identity and a feeling of belonging. (510)

Concentric-zone theory A theory of urban growth devised by Ernest Burgess which sees growth in terms of a series of rings radiating from the central business district. (513)

Conflict perspective A sociological approach which assumes that social behavior is best understood in terms of conflict or tension between competing groups. (19)

Conformity Going along with one's peers, individuals of a person's own status, who have no special right to direct that person's behavior. (176)

Contact hypothesis An interactionist perspective which states that interracial contact of people with equal status in noncompetitive circumstances will reduce prejudice. (280)

Content analysis The systematic coding and objective recording of data, guided by some rationale. (45)

Control group Subjects in an experiment who are not introduced to the independent variable by the researcher. (44)

Control variable A factor held constant to test the relative impact of an independent variable. (38)

Correlation A relationship between two variables whereby a change in one coincides with a change in the other. (36)

Correspondence principle A term used by Bowles and Gintis to refer to the tendency of schools to promote the values expected of individuals in each social class and to prepare students for the types of jobs typically held by members of their class. (458)

Cosmology A general theory of the universe advanced by a religion. (402)

Counterculture A subculture that rejects societal norms and values and seeks an alternative lifestyle. (78)

Craze An exciting mass involvement which lasts for a relatively long period of time. (575)

Creationists People who support a literal interpretation of the book of Genesis regarding the origins of the universe and argue that evolution should not be presented as established scientific fact. (402)

Credentialism An increase in the lowest level of education required to enter a field. (456)

Crime A violation of criminal law for which formal penalties are applied by some governmental authority. (190)

Cross-tabulation A table that shows the relationship between two or more variables. (54)

Crowds Temporary gatherings of people in close proximity who share a common focus or interest. (573)

Cult A generally small, secretive religious group that represents either a new religion or a major innovation of an existing faith. (405)

Cultural integration The bringing together of conflicting cultural elements, resulting in a harmonious and cohesive whole. (76)

Cultural relativism The viewing of people's behavior from the perspective of their own culture. (82)

Cultural transmission A school of criminology which argues that criminal behavior is learned through social interactions. (184)

Cultural universals General practices found in every culture. (64, 393)

Culture The totality of learned, socially transmitted behavior. (62)

Culture-bound syndrome A disease or illness that cannot be understood apart from its specific social context. (478)

Culture lag Ogburn's term for a period of maladjustment during which the nonmaterial culture is still adapting to new material conditions. (586)

Culture shock The feeling of surprise and disorientation that is experienced when people witness cultural practices different from their own. (80)

Death rate The number of deaths per 1000 population in a given year. Also known as the *crude death rate*. (544)

Defended neighborhood Suttles's formulation that area residents identify their neighborhood through defined community borders and through a perception that adjacent areas are geographically separate and socially different. (523)

Degradation ceremony An aspect of the socialization process within total institutions, in which people are subjected to humiliating rituals. (105)

Demographic transition A term used to describe the change from high birthrates and death rates to relatively low birthrates and death rates. (545)

Demography The scientific study of population. (541)

Denomination A large, organized religion not officially linked with the state or government. (404)

Dependent variable The variable in a causal relationship which is subject to the influence of another variable. (35)

Deviance Behavior that violates the standards of conduct or expectations of a group or society. (179)

Dialectical process A series of clashes between conflicting ideas and forces. (14)

Differential association A theory of deviance proposed by Edwin Sutherland which holds that violation of rules results from exposure to attitudes favorable to criminal acts. (184)

Diffusion The process by which a cultural item is spread from group to group or society to society. (66)

Disaster A sudden or disruptive event or set of events that overtaxes a community's resources so that outside aid is necessary. (573)

Discovery The process of making known or sharing the existence of an aspect of reality. (64)

Discrimination The process of denying opportunities and equal rights to individuals and groups because of prejudice or for other arbitrary reasons. (282)

Disengagement theory A functionalist theory of aging introduced by Cumming and Henry which contends that society and the aging individual mutually sever many of their relationships. (339)

Domestic partnership Two unrelated adults who have chosen to share one another's lives in a relationship of mutual caring, who reside together, and agree to be jointly responsible for their dependents, basic living expenses, and other common necessities. (381)

Dominant ideology A set of cultural beliefs and practices that help to maintain powerful social, economic, and political interests. (83, 218)

Dramaturgical approach A view of social interaction, popularized by Erving Goffman, under which people are examined as if they were theatrical performers. (23, 100)

Dyad A two-member group. (150)

Dysfunction An element or a process of society that may disrupt a social system or lead to a decrease in stability. (19, 153)

Ecclesia A religious organization that claims to include most of or all the members of a society and is recognized as the national or official religion. (403)

Economic system The social institution through which goods and services are produced, distributed, and consumed. (420)

Education A formal process of learning in which some people consciously teach while others adopt the social role of learner. (450)

Egalitarian family An authority pattern in which the adult members of the family are regarded as equals. (365)

Elite model A view of society as ruled by a small group of individuals who share a common set of political and economic interests. (436)

Emergent-norm perspective A theory of collective behavior proposed by Turner and Killian which holds that a collective definition of appropriate and inappropriate behavior emerges during episodes of collective behavior. (571)

Endogamy The restriction of mate selection to people within the same group. (367)

Equilibrium model Talcott Parsons' functionalist view of society as tending toward a state of stability or balance. (584)

Established sect J. Milton Yinger's term for a religious group that is the outgrowth of a sect, yet remains isolated from society. (405)

Estate system A system of stratification under which peasants were required to work land leased to them by nobles in exchange for military protection and other services. Also known as *feudalism*. (212)

Esteem The reputation that a particular individual has within an occupation. (219)

Ethnic group A group which is set apart from others because of its national origin or distinctive cultural patterns. (273)

Ethnocentrism The tendency to assume that one's culture and way of life are superior to all others. (80, 281)

Euthanasia The act of bringing about the death of a hopelessly ill and suffering person in a relatively quick and painless way for reasons of mercy. (350)

Evangelical faiths Christian faiths which place great emphasis on a personal relationship between the individual and God and believe that each adherent must spread the faith and bear personal witness by openly declaring the religion to nonbelievers. (409)

Evolutionary theory A theory of social change which holds that society is moving in a definite direction. (582)

Exogamy The requirement that people select mates outside certain groups. (367)

Experiment An artificially created situation which allows the researcher to manipulate variables and introduce control variables. (44)

Experimental group Subjects in an experiment who are exposed to an independent variable introduced by a researcher. (44)

Exploitation theory A Marxist theory which views racial subordination in the United States as a manifestation of the class system inherent in capitalism. (280)

Expressiveness A term used by Parsons and Bales to refer to concern for maintenance of harmony and the internal emotional affairs of the family. (311)

Extended family A family in which relatives in addition to parents and children—such as grandparents, aunts, or uncles—live in the same home. (361)

Face-work A term used by Erving Goffman to refer to people's efforts to maintain the proper image and avoid embarrassment in public. (100)

Fads Temporary movements toward the acceptance of some particular taste or lifestyle that involve large numbers of people and are independent of preceding trends. (575)

False consciousness A term used by Karl Marx to describe an attitude held by members of a class that does not accurately reflect its objective position. (215, 582)

Familism Pride in the extended family expressed through the maintenance of close ties and strong obligations to kinfolk. (107)

Family A set of people related by blood, marriage (or some other agreed-upon relationship), or adoption who share the responsibility for reproducing and caring for members of society. (361)

Fashions Pleasurable mass involvements in some particular taste or lifestyle that have a line of historical continuity. (575)

Fertility The amount of reproduction among women of childbearing age. (541)

Folkways Norms governing everyday social behavior whose violation raises comparatively little concern. (72)

Force The actual or threatened use of coercion to impose one's will on others. (426)

Formal norms Norms which have generally been written down and which involve strict rules for punishment of violators. (72)

Formal organization A special-purpose group designed and structured in the interests of maximum efficiency. (151)

Formal social control Social control carried out by authorized agents, such as police officers, judges, school administrators, and employers. (178)

Functionalist perspective A sociological approach which emphasizes the way that parts of a society are structured to maintain its stability. (18)

Fundamentalism Adherence to earlier-accepted religious doctrines, often accompanied by a literal application of historical beliefs and scriptures to today's world. (409)

Gemeinschaft A term used by Ferdinand Tönnies to describe close-knit communities, often found in rural areas, in which strong personal bonds unite members. (135)

Gender identity The self-concept of an individual as being male or female. (307)

Gender roles Expectations regarding the proper behavior, attitudes, and activities of males and females. (106, 307)

Generalized others A term used by George Herbert Mead to refer to the child's awareness of the attitudes, viewpoints, and expectations of society as a whole. (99)

Genocide The deliberate, systematic killing of an entire people or nation. (283)

Gentrification The resettlement of low-income city neighborhoods by prosperous families and business firms. (534)

Gerontocracy Rule by the elderly. (336)

Gerontology The scientific study of the sociological and psychological aspects of aging and the problems of the aged. (338)

Gesellschaft A term used by Ferdinand Tönnies to describe communities, often urban, that are large and impersonal, with little commitment to the group or consensus on values. (135)

Goal displacement Overzealous conformity to official regulations within a bureaucracy. (156)

Goal multiplication The process through which an organization expands its purposes. (164)

Goal succession The process through which an organization identifies an entirely new objective because its traditional goals have been either realized or denied. (165)

Group Any number of people with similar norms, values, and expectations who regularly and consciously interact. (127, 145)

Growth rate The difference between births and deaths, plus the difference between immigrants and emigrants, per 1000 population. (544)

Hawthorne effect The unintended influence that observers or experiments can have on their subjects. (45)

Health As defined by the World Health Organization, a state of complete physical, mental, and social well-being, and not merely the absence of disease and infirmity. (480)

Hidden curriculum Standards of behavior that are deemed proper by society and are taught subtly in schools. (455)

Holistic medicine A means of health maintenance which views the person as an integration of body, mind, and spirit, rather than as a collection of interrelated organ systems. (495)

Homophobia Fear of and prejudice against homosexuality. (139)

Horizontal mobility The movement of an individual from one social position to another of the same rank. (231)

Horticultural societies Preindustrial societies in which people plant seeds and crops rather than subsist merely on available foods. (426)

Human ecology An area of study concerned with the interrelationships among people in their spatial setting and physical environment. (513, 558)

Human relations approach An approach to the study of formal organizations which emphasizes the role of people, communication, and participation within a bureaucracy and tends to focus on the informal structure of the organization. (159)

Human rights Universal moral rights belonging to all people because they are human. (264)

Hunting-and-gathering society A preindustrial society in which people rely on whatever foods and fiber are readily available in order to live. (421)

Hypothesis A speculative statement about the relationship between two or more variables. (35)

Ideal type A construct or model that serves as a measuring rod against which actual cases can be evaluated. (12)

Impression management A term used by Erving Goffman to refer to the altering of the presentation of the self in order to create distinctive appearances and satisfy particular audiences. (100)

Incest taboo The prohibition of sexual relationships between certain culturally specified relatives. (367)

Incidence The number of new cases of a specific disorder occurring within a given population during a stated period of time. (486)

Inclusion An educational experiment under which all children— even those with severe disabilities —are taught in regular public school classrooms. (468)

Income Salaries and wages. (209)

Independent variable The variable in a causal relationship which, when altered, causes or influences a change in a second variable. (35)

Index An indicator of attitudes, behavior, or characteristics of people or organizations. (37)

Index crimes The eight types of crime reported annually by the FBI in the *Uniform Crime Reports*. These are murder, rape, robbery, assault, burglary, theft, motor vehicle theft, and arson. (190)

Industrial city A city characterized by relatively large size, open competition, an open class system, and elaborate specialization in the manufacturing of goods. (512)

Industrial revolution A scientific revolution, largely occurring in England between 1760 and 1830, which focused on the application of nonanimal sources of power to labor tasks. (422, 512)

Industrial society A society which relies chiefly on mechanization for the production of its economic goods and services. (423)

Infant mortality rate The number of deaths of infants under 1 year of age per 1000 live births in a given year. (250, 482, 544)

Influence The exercise of power through a process of persuasion. (426)

Informal economy Transfers of money, goods, or services that are not reported to the government. (251)

Informal norms Norms which are generally understood but which are not precisely recorded. (72)

Informal social control Social control carried out by people casually through such means as laughter, smiles, and ridicule. (178)

In-group Any group or category to which people feel they belong. (147)

Innovation The process of introducing new elements into a culture through either discovery or invention. (64)

Institutional discrimination The denial of opportunities and equal rights to individuals or groups which results from the normal operations of society. (282, 316)

Instrumentality A term used by Parsons and Bales to refer to emphasis on tasks, focus on more distant goals, and a concern for the external relationship between one's family and other social institutions. (311)

Interactionist perspective A sociological approach which generalizes about fundamental or everyday forms of social interaction. (21)

Interest group A voluntary association of citizens who attempt to influence public policy. (434)

Intergenerational mobility Changes in the social position of children relative to their parents. (231)

Interview A face-to-face or telephone questioning of a respondent in order to obtain desired information. (40)

Intragenerational mobility Changes in a person's social position within his or her adult life. (231)

Invention The combination of existing cultural items into a form that did not previously exist. (65)

Iron law of oligarchy A principle of organizational life developed by Robert Michels under which even democratic organizations will become bureaucracies ruled by a few individuals. (158)

Issei The early Japanese immigrants to the United States. (290)

Kinship The state of being related to others. (364)

Labeling theory An approach to deviance popularized by Howard S. Becker which attempts to explain why certain people are *viewed* as deviants while others engaging in the same behavior are not. (187)

Laissez-faire A form of capitalism under which people compete freely, with minimal government intervention in the economy. (423)

Language An abstract system of word meanings and symbols for all aspects of culture. It also includes gestures and other nonverbal communication. (68)

Latent functions Unconscious or unintended functions; hidden purposes. (18)

Law In a political sense, the body of rules made by government for society, interpreted by the courts, and backed by the power of the state. (72, 179)

Legal-rational authority Max Weber's term for power made legitimate by law. (427)

Liberation theology Use of a church, primarily Roman Catholicism, in a political effort to eliminate poverty, discrimination, and other forms of injustice evident in secular society. (399)

Life chances Max Weber's term for people's opportunities to provide themselves with material goods, positive living conditions, and favorable life experiences. (228)

Life expectancy The average number of years a person can be expected to live under current mortality conditions. (544)

Linear-development model A view of community attachment which points to population size as the primary factor influencing patterns of behavior in a community. (519)

Looking-glass self A phrase used by Charles Horton Cooley to emphasize that the self is the product of our social interactions with others. (98)

Machismo A sense of virility, personal worth, and pride in one's maleness. (107)

Macrosociology Sociological investigation which concentrates on large-scale phenomena or entire civilizations. (16)

Mainstreaming The practice, mandated by Public Law 94-142, of integrating handicapped children into "regular" classrooms whenever possible by placing each child in the "least restrictive environment." (468)

Manifest functions Open, stated, and conscious functions. (18)

Marital power A term used by Blood and Wolfe to describe the manner in which decision making is distributed within families. (366, 426)

Master status A status that dominates others and thereby determines a person's general position within society. (125)

Material culture The physical or technological aspects of our daily lives. (67)

Matriarchy A society in which women dominate in family decision making. (365)

Matrilineal descent A kinship system which favors the relatives of the mother. (364)

Matrilocal A pattern of residence in which a married couple lives with the wife's parents. (364)

Mechanical solidarity A term used by Émile Durkheim to describe a society in which people generally all perform the same tasks and in which relationships are close and intimate. (134)

Megalopolis A densely populated area containing two or more cities and their surrounding suburbs. (518)

Microsociology Sociological investigation which stresses study of small groups and often uses laboratory experimental studies. (16)

Midlife crisis A stressful period of self-evaluation, often occurring between the ages of 35 and 50, in which a person realizes that he or she has not achieved certain personal goals and aspirations and that time is running out. (103)

Migration Relatively permanent movement of people with the purpose of changing their place of residence. (553)

Minimum-competency tests (MCTs) Tests which measure a child's knowledge of basic skills, such as reading, writing, and mathematics. (467)

Minority group A subordinate group whose members have significantly less control or power over their own lives than the members of a dominant or majority group have over theirs. (274)

Modernization The far-reaching process by which a society moves from traditional or less developed institutions to those characteristic of more developed societies. (245)

Monogamy A form of marriage in which one woman and one man are married only to each other. (362)

Monopoly Control of a market by a single business firm. (423)

Morbidity rates The incidence of diseases in a given population. (486)

Mores Norms deemed highly necessary to the welfare of a society. (72)

Mortality rate The incidence of death in a given population. (486)

Multiculturalism The effort to revise school and college curricula to give greater emphasis to the contributions and experiences of African Americans, other racial and ethnic minorities, women, and nonwestern peoples. (85)

Multilinear evolutionary theory A theory of social change which holds that change can occur in several ways and does not inevitably lead in the same direction. (584)

Multinational corporations Commercial organizations which, while headquartered in one country, own or control other corporations and subsidiaries throughout the world. (247)

Multiple-nuclei theory A theory of urban growth developed by Harris and Ullman, which views growth as emerging from many centers of development, each of which may reflect a particular urban need or activity. (515)

Natural science The study of the physical features of nature and the ways in which they interact and change. (7)

Negotiated order A social structure that derives its existence from the social interactions through which people define and redefine its character. (123)

Negotiation The attempt to reach agreement with others concerning some objective. (122)

Neocolonialism Continuing dependence of former colonies on foreign countries. (245)

Neolocal A pattern of residence in which a married couple establishes a separate residence. (364)

Nisei Japanese born in the United States who were descendants of the Issei. (292)

Nonmaterial culture Cultural adjustments to material conditions, such as customs, beliefs, patterns of communication, and ways of using material objects. (67)

Nonperiodic assemblies Nonrecurring gatherings of people which often result from word-of-mouth information. (573)

Nonverbal communication The sending of messages through the use of posture, facial expressions, and gestures. (23)

Norms Established standards of behavior maintained by a society. (71)

Nuclear family A married couple and their unmarried children living together. (361)

Obedience Compliance with higher authorities in a hierarchical structure. (176)

Objective method A technique for measuring social class that assigns individuals to classes on the basis of criteria such as occupation, education, income, and place of residence. (219)

Observation A research technique in which an investigator collects information through direct involvement with and observation of a group, tribe, or community. (41)

Oligopoly A market with relatively few sellers. (424)

Open system A social system in which the position of each individual is influenced by his or her achieved status. (231)

Operational definition An explanation of an abstract concept that is specific enough to allow a researcher to measure the concept. (34)

Organic solidarity A term used by Émile Durkheim to describe a society in which members are mutually dependent and in which a complex division of labor exists. (134)

Organized crime The work of a group that regulates relations between various criminal enterprises involved in smuggling and sale of drugs, prostitution, gambling, and other activities. (191)

Out-group A group or category to which people feel they do not belong. (147)

Panic A fearful arousal or collective flight based on a generalized belief which may or may not be accurate. (576)

Patriarchy A society in which men are expected to dominate family decision making. (365)

Patrilineal descent A kinship system which favors the relatives of the father. (364)

Patrilocal A pattern of residence in which a married couple lives with the husband's parents. (364)

Pentecostal faiths Religious groups similar in many respects to evangelical faiths, which in addition believe in the infusion of the Holy Spirit into services and in religious experiences such as faith healing and "speaking in tongues." (409)

Periodic assemblies Recurring, relatively routine gatherings of people, such as college classes. (573)

Personality In everyday speech, a person's typical patterns of attitudes, needs, characteristics, and behavior. (93)

Peter principle A principle of organizational life, originated by Laurence J. Peter, according to which each individual within a hierarchy tends to rise to his or her level of incompetence. (157)

Pluralism Mutual respect between the various groups in a society for one another's cultures, which allows minorities to express their own cultures without experiencing prejudice. (285)

Pluralist model A view of society in which many conflicting groups within a community have access to governmental officials and compete with one another in an attempt to influence policy decisions. (437)

Political action committee (PAC) A political committee established by an interest group—a national bank, corporation, trade association, or cooperative or membership association—to accept voluntary contributions for candidates or political parties. (435)

Political socialization The process by which individuals acquire political attitudes and develop patterns of political behavior. (428)

Political system The social institution which relies on a recognized set of procedures for implementing and achieving the goals of a group. (420)

Politics In Harold D. Lasswell's words, "who gets what, when, how." (426)

Polyandry A form of polygamy in which a woman can have several husbands at the same time. (364)

Polygamy A form of marriage in which an individual can have several husbands or wives simultaneously. (362)

Polygyny A form of polygamy in which a husband can have several wives at the same time. (363)

Population pyramid A special type of bar chart that shows the distribution of the population by gender and age. (549)

Postindustrial society A society whose economic system is engaged in the processing and control of information. (425)

Postmodern society A technologically sophisticated society that is preoccupied with consumer goods and media images. (426)

Power The ability to exercise one's will over others. (215, 426)

Power elite A term used by C. Wright Mills for a small group of military, industrial, and government leaders who control the fate of the United States. (437)

Predestination A Calvinist doctrine which holds that people either will be among the elect, who are rewarded in heaven, or will be condemned to hell and that their futures are not dependent on being righteous or sinful while on earth. (401)

Preindustrial city A city with only a few thousand people living within its borders and characterized by a relatively closed class system and limited mobility. (512)

Prejudice A negative attitude toward an entire category of people, such as racial or ethnic minority. (280)

Pressure groups A term sometimes used to refer to interest groups. (435)

Prestige The respect and admiration with which an occupation is regarded by society. (219)

Prevalence The total number of cases of a specific disorder that exist at a given time. (486)

Primary group A small group characterized by intimate, face-to-face association and cooperation. (146)

Profane The ordinary and commonplace elements of life, as distinguished from the sacred. (395)

Profession An occupation requiring extensive knowledge and governed by a code of ethics. (439)

Professional criminal A person who pursues crime as a day-to-day occupation, developing skilled techniques and enjoying a certain degree of status among other criminals. (190)

Proletariat Karl Marx's term for the working class in a capitalist society. (214)

Protestant ethic Max Weber's term for the disciplined work ethic, this-worldly concerns, and rational orientation to life emphasized by John Calvin and his followers. (400)

Public A dispersed group of people, not necessarily in contact with one another, who share an interest in an issue. (578)

Public opinion Expressions of attitudes on matters of public policy which are communicated to decision makers. (578)

Questionnaire A printed research instrument employed to obtain desired information from a respondent. (40)

Racial group A group which is set apart from others because of obvious physical differences. (273)

Racism The belief that one race is supreme and all others are innately inferior. (281)

Random sample A sample for which every member of the entire population has the same chance of being selected. (36)

Reference group A term used when speaking of any group that individuals use as a standard in evaluating themselves and their own behavior. (147)

Relative deprivation The conscious feeling of a negative discrepancy between legitimate expectations and present actualities. (581)

Relative poverty A floating standard of deprivation by which people at the bottom of a society, whatever their lifestyles, are judged to be disadvantaged in comparison with the nation as a whole. (226)

Reliability The extent to which a measure provides consistent results. (37)

Religion According to Émile Durkheim, a unified system of beliefs and practices relative to sacred things. (395)

Religious beliefs Statements to which members of a particular religion adhere. (401)

Religious experience The feeling or perception of being in direct contact with the ultimate reality, such as a divine being, or of being overcome with religious emotion. (403)

Religious rituals Practices required or expected of members of a faith. (402)

Religious values Shared conceptions of what is good, desirable, and proper that arise out of religious faith. (402)

Representative sample A selection from a larger population that is statistically found to be typical of that population. (36)

Research design A detailed plan or method for obtaining data scientifically. (39)

Resocialization The process of discarding former behavior patterns and accepting new ones as part of a transition in one's life. (104)

Resource mobilization The ways in which a social movement utilizes such resources as money, political influence, access to the media, and personnel. (582)

Reverse socialization The process whereby people normally being socialized are at the same time socializing their socializers. (108)

Rites of passage Rituals marking the symbolic transition from one social position to another. (102)

Role conflict Difficulties that occur when incompatible expectations arise from two or more social positions held by the same person. (125)

Role exit The process of disengagement from a role that is central to one's self-identity, and reestablishment of an identity in a new role. (126)

Role taking The process of mentally assuming the perspective of another, thereby enabling one to respond from that imagined viewpoint. (99)

Rumor A piece of information gathered informally which is used to interpret an ambiguous situation. (577)

Sacred Those elements beyond everyday life which inspire awe, respect, and even fear. (395)

Sanctions Penalties and rewards for conduct concerning a social norm. (73, 176)

Sanctuary movement A movement of loosely connected organizations that offers asylum, often in churches, to those who seek refugee status but are regarded by the Immigration and Naturalization Service as illegal aliens. (399)

Sapir-Whorf hypothesis A hypothesis concerning the role of language in shaping cultures. It holds that language is culturally determined and serves to influence our mode of thought. (68)

Scale An indicator of attitudes, behavior, or characteristics of people or organizations. (37)

Science The body of knowledge obtained by methods based upon systematic observation. (7)

Scientific management approach Another name for the *classical theory* of formal organizations. (159)

Scientific method A systematic, organized series of steps that ensures maximum objectivity and consistency in researching a problem. (38)

Secondary analysis A variety of research techniques that make use of publicly accessible information and data. (45)

Secondary group A formal, impersonal group in which there is little social intimacy or mutual understanding. (146)

Sect A relatively small religious group that has broken away from some other religious organization to renew what it views as the original vision of the faith. (404)

Secularization The process through which religion's influence on other social institutions diminishes. (393)

Segregation The act of physically separating two groups; often imposed on a minority group by a dominant group. (284)

Self According to George Herbert Mead, the sum total of people's conscious perception of their identity as distinct from others. (98)

Self-fulfilling prophecy The tendency of people to respond to and act on the basis of stereotypes, a predisposition which can lead to validation of false definitions. (276)

Self-help group A mutual aid group in which people who face a common concern or condition come together voluntarily for emotional support and practical assistance. (163)

Senilicide The killing of the aged. (335)

Serial monogamy A form of marriage in which a person can have several spouses in her or his lifetime, but can have only one spouse at a time. (362)

Sexism The ideology that one sex is superior to the other. (316)

Sexual harassment Any unwanted and unwelcome sexual advances that interfere with a person's ability to perform a job and enjoy the benefits of a job. (167)

Sick role Societal expectations about the attitudes and behavior of a person viewed as being ill. (480)

Significant others A term used by George Herbert Mead to refer to those individuals who are most important in the development of the self, such as parents, friends, and teachers. (100)

Single-parent families Families in which there is only one parent present to care for children. (382)

Slavery A system of enforced servitude in which people are owned by others and in which enslaved status is transferred from parents to children. (210)

Small group A group small enough for all members to interact simultaneously, that is, to talk with one another or at least be acquainted. (149)

Social change Significant alteration over time in behavior patterns and culture, including norms and values. (569)

Social control The techniques and strategies for regulating human behavior in any society. (176)

Social epidemiology The study of the distribution of disease, impairment, and general health status across a population. (486)

Social inequality A condition in which members of a society have different amounts of wealth, prestige, or power. (208)

Social institutions Organized patterns of beliefs and behavior centered on basic social needs. (130, 357)

Social interaction The ways in which people respond to one another. (120)

Socialism An economic system under which the means of production and distribution are collectively owned. (424)

Socialization The process whereby people learn the attitudes, values, and actions appropriate to individuals as members of a particular culture. (92)

Social mobility Movement of individuals and groups from one position of a society's stratification system to another. (231)

Social movements Organized collective activities to promote or resist change in an existing group or society. (579)

Social network A series of social relationships that link a person directly to others and therefore indirectly to still more people. (127)

Social promotion The practice of passing children from one grade to the next on the basis of age rather than actual education achievement. (467)

Social role A set of expectations of people who occupy a given social position or status. (125)

Social science The study of various aspects of human society. (7)

Social structure The way in which a society is organized into predictable relationships. (120)

Social surplus The production by a group of people of enough goods to cover their own needs, while at the same time sustaining people who are not engaged in agricultural tasks. (422, 511)

Societal-reaction approach Another name for *labeling theory*. (187)

Society A fairly large number of people who live in the same territory, are relatively independent of people outside it, and participate in a common culture. (63)

Sociobiology The systematic study of the biological bases of social behavior. (97)

Sociological imagination An awareness of the relationship between an individual and the wider society. (6)

Sociology The systematic study of social behavior and human groups. (5)

Squatter settlements Areas occupied by the very poor on the fringes of cities, in which housing is often constructed by the settlers themselves from discarded material. (518)

Status A term used by sociologists to refer to any of the full range of socially defined positions within a large group or society. (124)

Status group A term used by Max Weber to refer to people who have the same prestige or lifestyle, independent of their class positions. (215)

Stereotypes Unreliable generalizations about all members of a group that do not recognize individual differences within the group. (276)

Stratification A structured ranking of entire groups of people that perpetuates unequal economic rewards and power in a society. (209)

Stratum mobility Another name for *structural mobility*. (231)

Structural mobility The vertical movement of a specific group, class, or occupation relative to others in the stratification system. (231)

Subculture A segment of society which shares a distinctive pattern of mores, folkways, and values which differs from the pattern of the larger society. (77)

Subsistence technology The tools, processes, and knowledge that a society requires to meet its basic needs for survival. (511)

Suburb According to the Census Bureau, any territory within a metropolitan area that is not included in the central city. (526)

Survey A study, generally in the form of interviews or questionnaires, which provides sociologists and other researchers with information concerning how people think and act. (39)

Symbols The gestures, objects, and language which form the basis of human communication. (98)

Systemic model A model of community attachment proposed by Thomas, Park, and Burgess which emphasizes geographical mobility, rather than population size, as a crucial factor in influencing patterns of behavior. (521)

Teacher-expectancy effect The impact that a teacher's expectations about a student's performance may have on the student's actual achievements. (461)

Techniques of neutralization Justifications for deviant behavior. (186)

Technology The application of knowledge to the making of tools and the utilization of natural resources. (421)

Theory In sociology, a set of statements that seeks to explain problems, actions, or behavior. (9)

Total fertility rate (TFR) The average number of children born alive to a woman, assuming that she conforms to current fertility rates. (544)

Total institutions A term coined by Erving Goffman to refer to institutions which regulate all aspects of a person's life under a single authority, such as prisons, the military, mental hospitals, and convents. (104)

Tracking The practice of placing students in specific curriculum groups on the basis of test scores and other criteria. (458)

Traditional authority Legitimate power conferred by custom and accepted practice. (427)

Trained incapacity The tendency of workers in a bureaucracy to become so specialized that they develop blind spots and cannot notice obvious problems. (153)

Triad A three-member group. (150)

Underclass Long-term poor people who lack training and skills. (225)

Unilinear evolutionary theory A theory of social change which holds that all societies pass through the same successive stages of evolution and inevitably reach the same end. (584)

Urban ecology An area of study which focuses on the interrelationships between people and their environment as they emerge in urban areas. (513)

Urbanism A term used by Wirth to describe distinctive patterns of social behavior evident among city residents. (520)

Validity The degree to which a scale or measure truly reflects the phenomenon under study. (37)

Value-added model A theory of collective behavior proposed by Neil Smelser to explain how broad social conditions are transformed in a definite pattern into some form of collective behavior. (571)

Value neutrality Max Weber's term for objectivity of sociologists in the interpretation of data. (50)

Values Collective conceptions of what is considered good, desirable, and proper—or bad, undesirable, and improper—in a culture. (74)

Variable A measurable trait or characteristic that is subject to change under different conditions. (35)

Verstehen The German word for "understanding" or "insight"; used by Max Weber to stress the need for sociologists to take into account people's emotions, thoughts, beliefs, and attitudes. (12)

Vertical mobility The movement of a person from one social position to another of a different rank. (231)

Vested interests Veblen's term for those people or groups who will suffer in the event of social change and who have a stake in maintaining the status quo. (586)

Veto groups David Riesman's term for interest groups that have the capacity to prevent the exercise of power by others. (437)

Victimization surveys Questionnaires or interviews used to determine whether people have been victims of crime. (197)

Victimless crimes A term used by sociologists to describe the willing exchange among adults of widely desired, but illegal, goods and services. (193)

Vital statistics Records of births, deaths, marriages, and divorces gathered through a registration system maintained by governmental units. (543)

Voluntary associations Organizations established on the basis of common interest whose members volunteer or even pay to participate. (161)

Wealth An inclusive term encompassing all of a person's material assets, including land and other types of property. (209)

White-collar crimes Crimes committed by affluent individuals or corporations in the course of their daily business activities. (192)

World systems theory Immanuel Wallerstein's view of the global economic system as divided between certain industrialized nations who control wealth and developing countries who are controlled and exploited. (245)

Xenocentrism The belief that the products, styles, or ideas of one's society are inferior to those that originate elsewhere. (82)

Zero population growth (ZPG) The state of a population with a growth rate of zero, which is achieved when the number of births plus immigrants is equal to the number of deaths plus emigrants. (551)

Zoning laws Legal provisions stipulating land use and architectural design of housing and often employed as a means of keeping racial minorities and low-income people out of suburban areas. (528)

REFERENCES

Abegglen, James C., and George Stalk, Jr. 1985. *Kaisha: The Japanese Corporation.* New York: Basic Books.

Abelman, Robert, and Kimberly Nevendorf. 1985. "How Religious Is Religious Television Programming," *Journal of Communication, 35*(Winter):98–110.

Abercrombie, Nicholas, Stephen Hill, and Bryan S. Turner. 1980. *The Dominant Ideology Thesis.* London: Allen and Unwin.

——, ——, and —— (eds.). 1990. *Dominant Ideologies.* Cambridge, Mass.: Unwin Hyman.

Aberle, David F., A. K. Cohen, A. K. Davis, M. J. Leng, Jr., and F. N. Sutton. 1950. "The Functional Prerequisites of a Society," *Ethics, 60*(January):100–111.

Abowitz, Deborah A. 1986. "Data Indicate the Feminization of Poverty in Canada, Too," *Sociology and Social Research, 70*(April):209–213.

Abrahams, Ray G. 1968. "Reaching an Agreement over Bridewealth in Labwor, Northern Uganda: A Case Study," in Audrey Richards and Adam Kuer (eds.), Councils in Action. Cambridge, Eng.: Cambridge University Press, pp. 202–215.

Abrahamse, Allan F., Peter A. Morrison, and Linda J. Waite. 1988. *Beyond Stereotypes: Who Becomes a Single Teenage Mother?* Santa Monica, Calif.: Rand Corp.

Abrahamson, Mark. 1978. *Functionalism.* Englewood Cliffs, N.J.: Prentice-Hall.

Adam, Barry D. 1992. "Sociology and People Living with AIDS," in Joan Huber and Beth E. Schneider (eds.), *The Social Context of AIDS.* Newbury Park, Calif.: Sage, pp. 3–18.

Addams, Jane. 1910. *Twenty Years at Hull-House.* New York: Macmillan.

——. 1930. *The Second Twenty Years at Hull-House.* New York: Macmillan.

Adler, Jerry. 1993. "Clone Hype," *Newsweek, 122*(November 8):60–62.

Adler, Patricia A., Peter Adler, and John M. Johnson. 1992. "*Street Corner Society* Revisited," *Journal of Contemporary Ethnography, 21*(April):3–10.

——, Steven J. Kless, and Peter Adler. 1992. "Socialization to Gender Role: Popularity among Elementary School Boys and Girls," *Sociology of Education, 65*(July):169–187.

Aeppel, Timothy. 1987. "'Birth Death' Effects Begin to Show in Some Developed Nations," *Christian Science Monitor* (March 2), p. 6.

Agger, Ben. 1989. "Do Books Write Authors? A Study of Disciplinary Hegemony," *Teaching Sociology,* **17**(July): 365–369.

Aguirre, Benigno E. 1984. "The Conventionalization of Collective Behavior in Cuba," *American Journal of Sociology,* **90**(3):541–566.

———, E. L. Quarantelli, and Jorge L. Mendoza. 1988. "The Collective Behavior of Fads: The Characteristics, Effects, and Career of Streaking," *American Sociological Review,* **53**(August):569–584.

Ahlburg, Dennis, and Carol J. De Vita. 1992. "New Realities of the American Family," *Population Bulletin,* **47**(August).

Aikman, David. 1991. "America's Holy War," *Time,* **138**(December 9):60–66, 68.

Alain, Michel. 1985. "An Empirical Validation of Relative Deprivation," *Human Relations,* **38**(8):739–749.

Alam, Sultana. 1985. "Women and Poverty in Bangladesh," *Women's Studies International Forum,* **8**(4):361–371.

Alba, Richard D. 1990. *Ethnic Identity: The Transformation of White America.* New Haven, Conn.: Yale University Press.

——— and Gwen Moore. 1982. "Ethnicity in the American Elite," *American Sociological Review,* **47**(June):373–383.

Albas, Daniel, and Cheryl Albas. 1988. "Aces and Bombers: The Post-exam Impression Management Strategies of Students," *Symbolic Interaction,* **11**(Fall): 289–302.

Alexander, Ron. 1988. "Aged Homosexuals Celebrate Program," *New York Times* (April 13), p. B3.

Alexander, Vicki, Linda Kahn, Sushaun Robb, and Melanie Tervalon. 1987. "Teenage Mothers: Setting the Record Straight," *AAWO Discussion Paper,* **8**(June):1–8.

Alinsky, Saul. 1946. *Reveille for Radicals.* Chicago: University of Chicago Press.

Allen, Bem P. 1978. *Social Behavior: Fact and Falsehood.* Chicago: Nelson-Hall.

Allen, Katherine R. 1993. "The Relentless Search for Effects of Divorce: Forging New Trails or Tumbling Down the Beaten Path," *Journal of Marriage and the Family,* **55**(February):42–49.

Allport, Gordon W. 1962. "Prejudice: Is It Societal or Personal?" *Journal of Social Issues,* **18**(April):120–134.

———. 1979. *The Nature of Prejudice* (25th anniversary ed.). Reading, Mass.: Addison-Wesley.

Almgren, Gunnar. 1992. "Demographic Transition," in Edgar F. Borgatta and Marie L. Borgatta (eds.), *Encyclopedia of Sociology,* vol. 2. New York: Macmillan, pp. 445–451.

Alonzo, Angelo A. 1989. "Health and Illness and the Definition of the Situation: An Interactionist Perspective." Paper presented at the annual meeting of the Society for the Study of Social Problems, Berkeley, Calif.

Altman, Dennis. 1986. *AIDS in the Mind of America: The Social, Political, and Psychological Impact of a New Epidemic.* Garden City, N.Y.: Anchor/Doubleday.

Altman, Lawrence K. 1992a. "Women Worldwide Nearing Higher Rate of AIDS than Men," *New York Times* (July 21), p. C3.

———. 1992b. "Cost of Treating AIDS Patients Is Soaring," *New York Times* (July 23), p. B8.

——— and Elisabeth Rosenthal. 1990. "Changes in Medicine Bring Pain to Healing Profession," *New York Times* (February 18), pp. 1, 20.

Alvarez, Sonia. 1989. "Contradictions of a 'Women's Space' in a Male-Dominant State: The Political Role of the Commissions on the Status of Women in Pre-authoritarian Brazil," in Kathleen Staudt (ed.), *The Bureaucratic Mire: Women's Programs in Comparative Perspective.* Philadelphia: Temple University Press, pp. 37–78.

Amato, Paul R. 1993. "Family Structure, Family Process, and Family Ideology," *Journal of Marriage and the Family,* **55**(February):50–54.

American Association of University Women. 1992. *How Schools Shortchange Girls.* Washington, D.C.: American Association of University Women.

American Medical Association. 1992. "Physicians and Domestic Violence: Ethical Considerations," *Journal of the American Medical Association,* **267**(June 17):3190–3193.

American Sociological Association. 1977. *Careers in Sociology.* Washington, D.C.: American Sociological Association.

———. 1984. *Code of Ethics.* Washington, D.C.: American Sociological Association.

———. 1989. *Code of Ethics.* Washington, D.C.: American Sociological Association.

Ames, Katrine, et al. [5 authors]. 1991. "Last Rights," *Newsweek,* **118**(August 26): 40–41.

Amnesty International. 1993a. *Amnesty International Report 1993.* New York: Amnesty International.

———. 1993b. "Yugoslavia: Women under the Gun," *Amnesty Action* (Spring), pp. 1, 3.

Anderson, Cheryl, and Linda Rouse. 1988. "Intervention in Cases of Woman Battering: An Application of Symbolic Interactionism and Critical Theory," *Clinical Sociological Review,* **6**:134–137.

Anderson, Elijah. 1990. *Streetwise: Race, Class, and Change in an Urban Community.* Chicago: University of Chicago Press.

Anderson, John Ward, and Molly Moore. 1993. "The Burden of Womanhood," *Washington Post National Weekly Edition,* **10**(March 22–28):6–7.

Anderson, Kevin. 1991. "Health Care Costs More, Serves Fewer," *USA Today* (March 11), pp. B1, B2.

Anderson, Lisa. 1993. "Religious Right Eyes Turf in N.Y. Elections," *Chicago Tribune* (May 23), pp. 19, 21.

Anderson, Roy M., and Robert M. May. 1992. "Understanding the AIDS Pandemic," *Scientific American,* **266**(May): 56–61, 64–66.

Andersson-Brolin, Lillemor. 1988. "Ethnic Residential Segregation: The Case of Sweden," *Scandinavian Journal of Development Alternatives,* **7**(March):33–45.

Angell, Marcia. 1993. "Caring for Women's Health—What Is the Problem?" *New England Journal of Medicine,* **329** (July 22):271–273.

Angier, Natalie. 1993a. "U.S. Opens the Door Just a Crack to Alternative Forms of Medicine," *New York Times* (January 10), pp. 1, 13.

———. 1993b. "Patients Rushing to Alternatives," *New York Times* (January 28), p. A12.

Anti-Defamation League of B'nai B'rith. 1993. *Young Nazi Killers: The Rising Skinhead Danger.* New York: Anti-Defamation League.

———. 1994. *Audit of Anti-Semitic Incidents, 1993.* New York: Anti-Defamation League.

Appelbaum, Richard P. 1970. *Theories of Social Change.* Chicago: Markham.

Arber, Sara. 1990. "Class and the Elderly," *Social Studies Review,* **6**(January).

Archer, Margaret. 1988. *Culture and Agency: The Place of Culture in Social Theory.* Cambridge, Eng.: Cambridge University Press.

Arensberg, Conrad M., and Arthur H. Niehoff. 1964. *Introducing Social Change.* Chicago: Aldine.

Armer, J. Michael, and John Katsillis. 1992. "Modernization Theory," in Edgar F. Borgatta and Marie L. Borgatta (eds.), *Encyclopedia of Sociology,* vol. 4. New York: Macmillan, pp. 1299–1304.

Aronoff, Marilyn, and Valerie Gunter. 1992. "Defining Disaster: Local Constructions for Recovery in the Aftermath of Chemical Contamination," *Social Problems,* **39**(November):345–365.

Aronson, Elliot. 1972. *The Social Animal.* San Francisco: Freeman.

Asante, Molefi Kete. 1992. "Afrocentric Systematics," *Black Issues in Higher Education,* **9**(August 13):16–17, 21–22.

Asch, Adrienne. 1986. "Will Populism Empower Disabled People?" in Harry G. Boyte and Frank Riessman (eds.), *The New Populism: The Politics of Empowerment.* Philadelphia: Temple University Press, pp. 213–228.

———. 1989. "Has the Law Made a Difference? What Some Disabled Students Have to Say," in Dorothy Kerzner Lipsky and Alan Gartner (eds.), *Beyond Separate Education: Quality Education for All.* Baltimore: Brookes, pp. 181–205.

Asch, Solomon. 1952. *Social Psychology.* New York: Prentice-Hall.

Astin, Alexander W., Kenneth C. Green, and William S. Korn. 1987. *The American Freshman: Twenty Year Trends.* Los Angeles: Cooperative Institutional Research Program, University of California at Los Angeles.

———, William S. Korn, and Ellen Riggs. 1993. *The American Freshman: National Norms, Fall 1993.* Los Angeles: Cooperative Institutional Research Program, University of California at Los Angeles.

Astrachan, Anthony. 1986. *How Men Feel: Their Response to Women's Demands for Equality and Power.* New York: Anchor/ Doubleday.

Atchley, Robert C. 1976. *The Sociology of Retirement.* New York: Wiley.

———. 1985. *The Social Forces in Later Life: An Introduction to Social Gerontology* (4th ed.). Belmont, Calif.: Wadsworth.

Auchincloss, Kenneth. 1993. "A Fratricidal Year," *Newsweek,* **121**(January 4):24–26.

Avni, Noga. 1991. "Battered Wives: The Home as a Total Institution," *Violence and Victims,* **6**(Summer):137–149.

Aytac, Isik A. 1987. "Wife's Decision-Making at Work and Contribution to Family Income as Determinate of How Domestic Chores Are Shared." Paper presented at the annual meeting of the Eastern Sociological Society, Boston.

Azumi, Koya, and Jerald Hage. 1972. *Organizational Systems.* Lexington, Mass.: Heath.

Babbie, Earl R. 1980. *Sociology: An Introduction* (2d ed.). Belmont, Calif.: Wadsworth.

Babchuk, Nicholas, and Alan Booth. 1969. "Voluntary Association Membership: A Longitudinal Analysis," *American Sociological Review,* **34**(February):31–45.

Babcock, Charles R. 1993. "Leaders of the PACs: NRA, UPS and Dentists," *Washington Post National Weekly Edition,* **15**(May 16):13.

Bacard, André. 1993. "Technology and Society," *The Humanist,* **53**(March–April): 42–43.

Bachrach, Christine A. 1986. "Adoption Plans, Adopted Children, and Adoptive Mothers," *Journal of Marriage and the Family,* **48**(May):243–253.

Bachrach, Peter, and Morton S. Baratz. 1962. "Two Faces of Power," *American Political Science Review,* **56**(December): 947–952.

Back, Kurt W. 1981. "Small Groups," in Morris Rosenberg and Ralph H. Turner (eds.), *Social Psychology: Sociological Perspectives.* New York: Basic Books, pp. 320–343.

Bacon, John. 1987. "Court Ruling Hasn't Quieted School Prayer," *USA Today* (April 3), p. 34.

Bailey, J. Michael, Richard C. Pillard, Michael C. Neale, and Yvonne Agyei. 1993. "Heritable Factors Influence Sexual Orientation in Women," *Archives of General Psychiatry,* **50**(March):217–223.

Baldassare, Mark. 1992. "Suburban Communities," in Judith Blake and John Ha-

gan (eds.), *Annual Review of Sociology, 1992.* Palo Alto, Calif.: Annual Reviews, pp. 475–494.

Ball, Donald. 1967. "An Abortion Clinic Ethnography," *Social Problems,* **14**(Summer):298–301.

Balswick, Jack, and Charles Peek. 1971. "The Inexpressive Male: A Tragedy of American Society," *Family Coordinator,* **20**(October):363–368.

Baltzell, E. Digby, and Howard G. Schneiderman. 1988. "Social Class in the Oval Office," *Public Opinion,* **25**(September–October):42–49.

Bandura, Albert. 1969. *Principles of Behavior Modification.* New York: Holt.

Banks, Vera J. 1987. *Black Farmers and Their Farms.* Washington, D.C.: U.S. Government Printing Office.

Barak, Gregg (ed.). 1991. *Crimes by the Capitalist State: An Introduction to State Criminality.* Albany: State University of New York Press.

Barkey, Karen. 1991. "The Use of Court Records in the Reconstruction of Village Networks: A Comparative Perspective," *International Journal of Comparative Sociology,* **32**(January–April): 195–216.

Barkun, Michael. 1993. "Reflections after Waco: Millennialists and the State," *Christian Century,* **110**(June 2):596–600.

Barnet, Richard J. 1990. "But What about Africa?" *Harper's,* **280**(May):43–51.

——— and Ronald E. Müller. 1974. *Global Reach: The Power of the Multinational Corporation.* New York: Simon and Schuster.

Baron, James N., and William T. Bielby. 1986. "The Proliferation of Job Titles in Organizations," *Administrative Science Quarterly,* **31**(December):561–586.

Barringer, Felicity. 1993. "School Hallways as Gauntlets of Sexual Taunts," *New York Times* (June 2), p. B7.

Barron, James. 1983. "A Classic Suburb Feels Graying Pains," *New York Times* (July 13), p. E6.

Barron, Milton L. 1953. "Minority Group Characteristics of the Aged in American Society," *Journal of Gerontology,* **8**:477–482.

Bartlett, Kay. 1988. "Sociologist Researches 'Role Exiting' Process," *Galesburg Register-Mail* (August 11), sec. C, p. 1.

Baruch, Grace, Rosalind Barnett, and Caryl Rivers. 1980. "A New Start for

Women at Midlife," *New York Times Magazine* (December 7), pp. 196–201.

———, ———, and ———. 1983. *Lifeprints: New Patterns of Love and Work for Today's Women.* New York: McGraw-Hill.

Basso, Keith H. 1972. "Ice and Travel among the Fort Norman Slave: Folk Taxonomies and Cultural Rules," *Language in Society,* **1**(March):31–49.

Bastian, Lisa D., and Bruce M. Taylor. 1991. *School Crime: A National Crime Victimization Survey Report.* Washington, D.C.: U.S. Government Printing Office.

Battin, Margaret. 1992. "Voluntary Euthanasia and the Risks of Abuse: Can We Learn Anything from the Netherlands?" *Law, Medicine, and Health Care: Current Issues in Biomedical Ethics,* **20**(Spring–Summer):133–143.

Beals, Gregory. 1993. "UN: Third World Life for Blacks, Latinos in U.S.," *New York Daily News* (May 18), p. 2.

Becerra, Rosina M. 1988. "The Mexican American Family," in Charles H. Mindel, Robert W. Habenstein, and Roosevelt Wright, Jr. (eds.), *Ethnic Families in America* (2d ed.). New York: Elsevier, pp. 141–159.

Beck, Melinda. 1993. "The Parent Trap," *Newsweek,* **121**(February 1):34–37.

Becker, Howard S. 1952. "Social Class Variations in the Teacher-Pupil Relationship," *Journal of Educational Sociology,* **25**(April):451–465.

———. 1963. *The Outsiders: Studies in the Sociology of Deviance.* New York: Free Press.

——— (ed.). 1964. *The Other Side: Perspectives on Deviance.* New York: Free Press.

———. 1973. *The Outsiders: Studies in the Sociology of Deviance* (rev. ed.). New York: Free Press.

———, Blanche Greer, Everett C. Hughes, and Anselm Strauss. 1961. *Boys in White: Student Culture in Medical School.* Chicago: University of Chicago Press.

Beeghley, Leonard. 1978. *Social Stratification in America: A Critical Analysis of Theory and Research.* Santa Monica, Calif.: Goodyear.

Belkin, Lisa. 1993. "There's No Simple Suicide," *New York Times Magazine* (November 14), pp. 48–55, 63, 74–75.

Belknap, Penny, and Wilbert Leonard, II. 1991. "A Conceptual Replication and Extension of Erving Goffman's Study of Gender Advertisements," *Sex Roles,* **25**(3,4):103–118.

Bell, Daniel. 1953. "Crime as an American Way of Life," *Antioch Review,* **13**(Summer):131–154.

———. 1973. *The Coming of Postindustrial Society.* New York: Basic Books.

———. 1989. "The Third Technological Revolution," *Dissent,* **36**(Spring):164–176.

Bell, Wendell. 1981a. "Modernization," in *Encyclopedia of Sociology.* Guilford, Conn.: DPG Publishing, pp. 186–187.

———. 1981b. "Neocolonialism," in *Encyclopedia of Sociology.* Guilford, Conn.: DPG Publishing, p. 193.

Bellah, Robert H. 1957. *Tokaguwa Religion. The Values of Pre-industrial Japan.* Glencoe, Ill.: Free Press.

——— and Frederick E. Greenspan (eds.). 1987. *Uncivil Religion: Interreligious Hostility in America.* New York: Crossroads.

———, Richard Madsen, Anne Swidler, William M. Sullivan, and Steven M. Tipton. 1985. *Habits of the Heart: Individualism and Commitment in American Life.* Berkeley: University of California Press.

Bem, Sandra Lipsitz. 1978. "Beyond Androgyny," in Julia A. Sherman and Florence L. Dennsk (eds.), *The Psychology of Women: Future Directions of Research.* New York: Psychological Dimensions, pp. 3–23.

———. 1993. *The Lenses of Gender: Transforming the Debate on Sexual Inequality.* New Haven, Conn.: Yale University Press.

Bendix, B. Reinhard. 1968. "Max Weber," in David L. Sills (ed.), *International Encyclopedia of the Social Sciences.* New York: Macmillan, pp. 493–502.

Benford, Robert D. 1992. "Social Movements," in Edgar F. Borgatta and Marie L. Borgatta (eds.), *Encyclopedia of Sociology,* vol. 4. New York: Macmillan, pp. 1880–1887.

Benner, Richard S., and Susan Tyler Hitchcock. 1986. *Life after Liberal Arts.* Charlottesville: Office of Career Planning and Placement, University of Virginia.

Bennett, Claudette E. 1993. *The Black Population in the United States: March 1992,* ser. P-20, no. 471. Washington, D.C.: U.S. Government Printing Office.

Bensman, David, and Roberta Lynch. 1987. *Rusted Dreams: Hard Times in a Steel Community.* New York: McGraw-Hill.

Berg, Philip L. 1975. "Racism and the Puritan Mind," *Phylon,* **36**(Spring):1–7.

Berger, Peter. 1963. *Invitation to Sociology: A Humanistic Perspective.* New York: Anchor.

———. 1973. "Religious Institutions," in Neil J. Smelser (ed.), *Sociology: An Introduction* (2d ed.). New York: Wiley, pp. 303–346.

——— and Thomas Luckmann. 1966. *The Social Construction of Reality.* New York: Doubleday.

Berk, Marc. 1985. "Medical Manpower and the Labeling of Blindness," *Deviant Behavior,* **6**(3):253–265.

Berk, Richard A. 1974. *Collective Behavior.* Dubuque, Iowa: Brown.

——— and Howard E. Aldrich. 1972. "Patterns of Vandalism during Civil Disorders as an Indicator of Selection of Targets," *American Sociological Review,* **37**(October):533–547.

Berke, Richard L. 1993. "Rising Expectations and Fear of the Bills Create an Opening," *New York Times* (September 26), pp. E1, E6.

Berkeley Wellness Letter. 1990. "The Nest Refilled," **6**(February):1–2.

Berlin, Brent, and Paul Kay. 1991. *Basic Color Terms: Their Universality and Evolution.* Berkeley: University of California Press.

Berman, Paul (ed.). 1992. *Debating P.C.: The Controversy over Political Correctness on College Campuses.* New York: Dell.

Bernard, Jessie. 1972. "The Paradox of the Happy Marriage," in Vivian Gornick and Barbara K. Moran (eds.), *Woman in Sexist Society: Studies in Power and Powerlessness.* New York: Basic Books, pp. 145–162.

Berney, Barbara. 1990. "In Research, Women Don't Matter," *The Progressive,* **54**(October):24–27.

Best, Fred, and Ray Eberhard. 1990. "Education for the 'Era of the Adult,'" *The Futurist,* **21**(May–June):23–28.

Bettelheim, Bruno, and Morris Janowitz. 1964. *Social Change and Prejudice.* New York: Free Press.

Bezilla, Robert E. (ed.). 1993. *Religion in America 1992–1993.* Princeton, N.J.: Princeton Religion Research Center.

Bharadwaj, Lakshmik. 1992. "Human Ecology," in Edgar F. Borgatta and Marie L. Borgatta (eds.), *Encyclopedia of Sociology*, vol. 2. New York: Macmillan, pp. 848–867.

Biggart, Nicole Woolsey. 1989. *Charismatic Capitalism: Direct Selling Organizations in America*. Chicago: University of Chicago Press.

Billson, Janet Mancini, and Bettina J. Huber. 1993. *Embarking upon a Career with an Undergraduate Degree in Sociology* (2d ed.). Washington, D.C.: American Sociological Association.

Binder, David, and Barbara Crossette. 1993. "As Ethnic Wars Multiply, U.S. Strives for a Policy," *New York Times* (February 7), pp. 1, 12.

Binstock, Robert H., and Linda K. George (eds.). 1990. *Handbook of Aging and the Social Sciences* (3d ed.). New York: Van Nostrand Reinhold.

Blakey, G. Robert, Ronald Goldstock, and Charles H. Rogarin. 1978. *Rackets Bureaus: Investigation and Prosecution of Organized Crime*. Report of National Institute of Law Enforcement and Criminal Justice. Washington, D.C.: U.S. Government Printing Office.

Blanc, Ann Klimas. 1984. "Nonmarital Cohabitation and Fertility in the United States and Western Europe," *Population Research and Policy Review*, 3:181–193.

Blanchard, Fletcher A., Teri Lilly, and Leigh Ann Vaughn. 1991. "Reducing the Expression of Racial Prejudice," *Psychological Science*, 2(March):101–105.

Blau, David M. 1993. "The Supply of Child Care Labor," *Journal of Labor Economics*. 11(2):324–347.

Blau, Peter M. 1963. *The Dynamics of Bureaucracy: A Study of Interpersonal Relations in Two Government Agencies* (rev. ed.). Chicago: University of Chicago Press.

———. 1964. *Exchange and Power in Social Life*. New York: Wiley.

——— and Otis Dudley Duncan. 1967. *The American Occupational Structure*. New York: Wiley.

——— and Marshall W. Meyer. 1987. *Bureaucracy in Modern Society* (3d ed.). New York: Random House.

Blauner, Robert. 1972. *Racial Oppression in America*. New York: Harper and Row.

Blee, Kathleen M. 1991. *Women of the Klan: Racism and Gender in the 1920s*. Berkeley: University of California Press.

Blendon, Robert J. 1986. "The Problems of Cost, Access, and Distribution of Medical Care," *Daedalus*, 115(Spring):119–135.

———, Ulrike S. Szalay, and Richard A. Knox. 1992. "Should Physicians Aid Their Patients in Dying?" *Journal of the American Medical Association*, 267(May 20):2658–2662.

——— et al. [4 authors]. 1989. "Access to Medical Care for Black and White Americans," *Journal of the American Medical Association*, 261(January 13):278–281.

Blood, Robert O., Jr., and Donald M. Wolfe. 1960. *Husbands and Wives: The Dynamics of Married Living*. New York: Free Press.

Bloom, Samuel W., and Robert N. Wilson. 1979. "Patient-Practitioner Relationship," in Howard E. Freeman, Sol Levine, and Leo G. Reider (eds.), *Handbook of Medical Sociology* (3d ed.). Englewood Cliffs, N.J.: Prentice-Hall, pp. 275–296.

Bluestone, Barry, and Bennett Harrison. 1982. *The Deindustrialization of America*. New York: Basic Books.

Blumer, Herbert. 1955. "Collective Behavior," in Alfred McClung Lee (ed.), *Principles of Sociology* (2d ed.). New York: Barnes and Noble, pp. 165–198.

———. 1969. *Symbolic Interactionism: Perspective and Method*. Englewood Cliffs, N.J.: Prentice-Hall.

Blumstein, Alfred, Jacqueline Cohen, and Richard Rosenfeld. 1991. "Trend and Deviation in Crime Rates: A Comparison of UCR and NCS Data for Burglary and Robbery," *Criminology*, 29(2):237–264.

Blumstein, Philip, and Pepper Schwartz. 1983. *American Couples: Money, Work, Sex*. New York: Morrow.

Boaz, Rachel Florsheim. 1987. "Early Withdrawal from the Labor Force," *Research on Aging*, 9(December):530–547.

Bogdan, Robert, and Steven J. Taylor. 1989. "Relationship with Severely Disabled People: The Social Construction of Humanness," *Social Problems*, 36(April):135–148.

Bogert, Carroll. 1990. "Chernobyl's Legacy," *Newsweek*, 115(May 7):30–31.

Bohannan, Paul. 1970. "The Six Stations of Divorce," in Paul Bohannan (ed.), *Divorce and After*. New York: Doubleday, pp. 33–62.

Borgatta, Edgar F., and Marie L. Borgatta (eds.). 1992. *Encyclopedia of Sociology*. New York: Macmillan.

Borjas, George. 1990. *Friends or Strangers: The Impact of Immigrants on the U.S. Economy*. New York: Basic Books.

Borman, Kathryn M., and Joel H. Spring. 1984. *Schools in Central Cities: Structure and Process*. New York: Longman.

Bornschier, Volker, and Christopher Chase-Dunn. 1985. *Transnational Corporations and Underdevelopment*. New York: Praeger.

———, ———, and Richard Rubinson. 1978. "Cross-National Evidence of the Effects of Foreign Investment and Aid on Economic Growth and Inequality: A Survey of Findings and a Reanalysis," *American Journal of Sociology*, 84(November):651–683.

Boserup, Ester. 1977. "Preface," in Wellesley Editorial Committee (ed.), *Women and National Development: The Complexities of Change*. Chicago: University of Chicago Press, pp. xi–xiv.

Bosk, Charles L. 1992. *All God's Mistakes: Genetic Counseling in a Pediatric Hospital*. Chicago: University of Chicago Press.

Boston Women's Health Book Collective. 1969. *Our Bodies, Ourselves*. Boston: New England Free Press.

———. 1984. *The New Our Bodies, Ourselves*. New York: Simon and Schuster.

Bottomore, Tom (ed.). 1983. *A Dictionary of Marxist Thought*. Cambridge, Mass.: Harvard University Press.

——— and Maximilien Rubel (eds.). 1956. *Karl Marx: Selected Writings in Sociology and Social Philosophy*. New York: McGraw-Hill.

Bouchard, Thomas J., Jr. 1991. "A Twice-Told Tale: Twins Reared Apart," in W. Grove and D. Ciccehetti (eds.), *Thinking Clearly about Psychology: Essays in Honor of Paul Everett Meehl*, vol. 2: *Personality and Psychopathology*. Minneapolis: University of Minnesota, pp. 188–215.

Bouvier, Leon F. 1980. "America's Baby Boom Generation: The Fateful Bulge," *Population Bulletin*, 35(April).

———. 1984. "Planet Earth 1984–2034: A

Demographic Vision," *Population Bulletin*, **39**(February).

——— and Carol J. De Vita. 1991. "The Baby Boom—Entering Midlife," *Population Bulletin*, **46**(November):1–34.

Bowles, Samuel, and Herbert Gintis. 1976. *Schooling in Capitalist America: Educational Reforms and the Contradictions of Economic Life.* New York: Basic Books.

Bracey, Gerald W. 1993. "No Magic Bullet," *Delta Kappan*, **74**(February):495–496.

Braddock, Jomills Henry, II, and Robert E. Slavin. 1993. "Why Ability Grouping Must End: Achieving Excellence and Equity in American Education," *Journal of Intergroup Relations*, **20**(1):51–64.

Bradley, Martin B., et al. [5 authors]. 1992. *Churches and Church Membership in the United States 1990.* Atlanta, Ga.: Glenmary Research Center.

Bradley, Phil. 1990. "The Growing Clout of Voters with Disabilities," *Illinois Issues*, **16**(April):34.

Bradshaw, York W. 1988. "Reassessing Economic Dependency and Uneven Development: The Kenyan Experience," *American Sociological Review*, **53**(October):693–708.

——— and Jie Huang. 1991. "Intensifying Global Dependency: Foreign Debt, Structural Adjustment, and the Third World Underdevelopment," *Sociological Quarterly*, **32**(3):321–342.

Braithwaite, John. 1989. *Crime, Shame and Reintegration.* Cambridge, Mass.: Cambridge University Press.

Branegan, Jay. 1993. "Is Singapore a Model for the West?" *Time*, **141**(January 18):36–37.

Braun, Denny. 1991. *The Rich Get Richer.* Chicago: Nelson-Hall.

Brazil. 1981. *Ix Recenseamento Geral do Brasil —1980, 1, Pt. 1.* Rio de Janeiro: Secretaria de Planejamento da Presidência da República, Fundação Instituto Brasilerio de Geografia e Estatistica.

Brewer, Rose M. 1989. "Black Women and Feminist Sociology: The Emerging Perspective," *American Sociologist*, **20**(Spring):57–70.

Brinton, Mary C. 1992. *Women and the Economic Miracle: Gender and Work in Postwar Japan.* Berkeley: University of California Press.

Brodeur, Paul. 1985. *Outrageous Misconduct: The Asbestos Industry on Trial.* New York: Pantheon.

———. 1993. "Legacy," *New Yorker*, **69**(June 7):114.

Bromley, David G., and Anson D. Shupe, Jr. 1980. "Financing the New Religions: A Resource Mobilization Approach," *Journal for the Scientific Study of Religion*, **19**(3):227–239.

Brooke, James. 1990a. "Gold's Lure vs. Indian Rights: A Brazilian Conflict Sets the Amazon Aflame," *New York Times* (January 21), p. 3.

———. 1990b. "Brazil's New Chief Gives Radical Plan to Halt Inflation," *New York Times* (March 17), pp. 1, 45.

———. 1990c. "Old Woes Resurge in Brazil," *New York Times* (December 3), pp. D1, D5.

———. 1991a. "'Honor' Killing of Wives Is Outlawed in Brazil," *New York Times* (March 29), p. B16.

———. 1991b. "Brazil Creates Reserve for Imperiled Amazon Tribe," *New York Times* (November 19), p. A3.

———. 1992. "Black Woman in Race to Be Mayor of Rio," *New York Times* (November 14), p. 3.

———. 1993a. "The New Beat of Black Brazil Sets the Pace for Self-Affirmation," *New York Times* (April 11), p. E7.

———. 1993b. "Slavery on Rise in Brazil, as Debt Chains Workers," *New York Times* (May 23), p. 3.

———. 1993c. "Brazil Answers Inflation with Cabinet Shuffle," *New York Times* (May 27), p. A9.

———. 1993d. "In Live-and-Let Live Land, Gay People Are Slain," *New York Times* (August 12), p. A4.

Brooks, Andrée. 1987. "Women in the Clergy: Struggle to Succeed," *New York Times* (February 16), p. 15.

Brower, Brock. 1988. "The Pernicious Power of the Polls," *Money*, **17**(March): 144–163.

Brown, Christopher. 1990. "Discrimination and Immigration Law," *Focus*, **18**(August):3–4, 8.

Brown, Lester R. (ed.). 1993. *State of the World, 1993.* New York: Norton.

Brown, Michael, and Amy Goldin. 1973. *Collective Behavior: A Review and Reinterpretation of the Literature.* Pacific Palisades, Calif.: Goodyear.

Brown, Patricia Leigh. 1987. "Studying Seasons of a Woman's Life," *New York Times* (September 14), p. B17.

———. 1988. "Troubled Millions Heed Call of Self-Help Groups," *New York Times* (July 16), pp. 1, 7.

———. 1993. "The Architecture of Those Called Homeless," *New York Times* (March 28), pp. 1, 32.

Brown, Robert McAfee. 1980. *Gustavo Gutierrez.* Atlanta: John Knox.

Brown, Roger W. 1954. "Mass Phenomena," in Gardner Lindzey (ed.), *Handbook of Social Psychology*, vol. 2. Reading, Mass.: Addison-Wesley, pp. 833–873.

———. 1965. *Social Psychology.* New York: Free Press.

Brown, William J., and Michael J. Cody. 1991. "Effects of a Prosocial Television Soap Opera in Promoting Women's Status," *Human Communication Research*, **18**(September):114–142.

Brozan, Nadine. 1985. "Rate of Pregnancies for U.S. Teenagers Found High in Study," *New York Times* (March 13), pp. A1, C7.

Brunvand, Jan Harold. 1993. *The Baby Train and Other Lusty Urban Legends.* New York: Norton.

Bryant, Bunyan, and Paul Mohai (eds.). 1992. *Race and the Incidence of the Environmental Hazards: A Time for Discourse.* Boulder, Colo.: Westview.

Bryk, Anthony S., Valerie E. Lee, and Peter B. Holland. 1993. *Catholic Schools and the Common Good.* Cambridge, Mass.: Harvard University Press.

Bullard, Robert D. 1990. "Ecological Inequities and the New South: Black Communities under Siege," *Journal of Ethnic Studies*, **17**(Winter):101–115.

Bulle, Wolfgang F. 1987. *Crossing Cultures? Southeast Asian Mainland.* Atlanta: Centers for Disease Control.

Bumpass, Larry L., James A. Sweet, and Teresa Castro Martin. 1990. "Changing Patterns of Remarriage," *Journal of Marriage and the Family*, **52**(August): 747–756.

Bunzel, John H. 1992. *Race Relations on Campus: Stanford Students Speak.* Stanford, Calif.: Portable Stanford.

Burciaga, Cecilia Preciado de Viola Gonzales, and Ruth A. Hepburn. 1977. "The Chicana as Feminist," in Alice G. Sargent (ed.), *Beyond Sex Roles.* St. Paul, Minn.: West, pp. 266–273.

Bureau of the Census. 1975a. *Historical Statistics of the United States, Colonial Times to 1970*. Washington, D.C.: U.S. Government Printing Office.

——. 1975b. *The Social and Economic Status of the Black Population in the United States: 1974*. Washington, D.C.: U.S. Government Printing Office.

——. 1986. "Household Wealth and Asset Ownership: 1984," *Current Population Reports*, ser. P-70, no. 7. Washington, D.C.: U.S. Government Printing Office.

——. 1990a. *Statistical Abstract of the United States: 1990*. Washington, D.C.: U.S. Government Printing Office.

——. 1990b. *Money Income and Poverty Status in the United States, 1989*, ser. P-60, no. 168. Washington, D.C.: U.S. Government Printing Office.

——. 1990c. "Household and Family Characteristics: March 1990 and 1989," *Current Population Reports*, ser. P-20, no. 447. Washington, D.C.: U.S. Government Printing Office.

——. 1990d. *Transitions in Income and Poverty Status: 1985–86*, ser. P-70, no. 18. Washington, D.C.: U.S. Government Printing Office.

——. 1990e. *Residents of Farms and Rural Areas, 1989*, ser. P-20, no. 446. Washington, D.C.: U.S. Government Printing Office.

——. 1991a. *Exports from Manufacturing Establishments*, ser. AR-87, no. 1. Washington, D.C.: U.S. Government Printing Office.

——. 1991b. *Statistical Abstract of the United States, 1991*. Washington, D.C.: U.S. Government Printing Office.

——. 1991c. "Fertility of American Women: June 1990," *Current Population Reports*, ser. P-20, no. 454. Washington, D.C.: U.S. Government Printing Office.

——. 1991d. "Half of the Nation's Population Lives in Large Metropolitan Areas." Press release, February 21.

——. 1991e. "Marital Status and Living Arrangements: March 1990," *Current Population Reports*, ser. P-20, no. 450. Washington, D.C.: U.S. Government Printing Office.

——. 1992. *Statistical Abstract of the United States, 1992*. Washington, D.C.: U.S. Government Printing Office.

——. 1993a. *Poverty in the United States: 1992*, ser. P-60, no. 185. Washington, D.C.: U.S. Government Printing Office.

——. 1993b. *Population Projections of the United States, by Age, Sex, Race, and Hispanic Origin: 1995 to 2050*, ser. P-25, no. 1104. Washington, D.C.: U.S. Government Printing Office.

——. 1993c. "Who's Minding the Kids? Child Care Arrangements: Fall 1988," *Current Population Reports*, ser. P-70, no. 30. Washington, D.C.: U.S. Government Printing Office.

——. 1993d. *Money Income of Households, Families, and Persons in the United States, 1992*, ser. P-60, no. 184. Washington, D.C.: U.S. Government Printing Office.

——. 1993e. *Income, Poverty, and Health Insurance, 1992*. Washington, D.C.: U.S. Government Printing Office.

——. 1994. "Las Vegas Is Fastest Growing Metro Area and Large City." Press release, February 8.

Burek, Deborah (ed.). 1992. *Encyclopedia of Associations, 1993*. Detroit: Gale Research.

Burgess, Ernest W. 1925. "The Growth of the City," in Robert E. Park, Ernest W. Burgess, and Roderick D. McKenzie (eds.), *The City*. Chicago: University of Chicago Press, pp. 47–62.

Burgess, John. 1989. "Exporting Our Office Work," *Washington Post National Weekly Edition*, 6(May 1):22.

Burke, William Kevin. 1993. "The Wise Use Movement: Right Wing Anti-Environmentalism," *The Public Eye* (June), pp. 1–7.

Burrows, William E. 1982. "Cockpit Encounters," *Psychology Today*, 16(November):42–47.

Burstin, Helen R., Stuart R. Lipsitz, and Troyen A. Brennan. 1992. "Socioeconomic Status and Risk for Substandard Medical Care," *Journal of the American Medical Association*, 268(November 4):2383–2387.

Burt, Martha R., and Barbara E. Cohen. 1989. "Differences among Homeless Single Women, Women with Children, and Single Men," *Social Problems*, 36(December):508–524.

Burton, Velmer S., Jr. 1990. "The Consequences of Official Labels: A Research Note on Rights Lost by the Mentally Ill, Mentally Incompetent, and Convicted Felons," *Community Mental Health Journal*, 26(June):267–276.

Bush, Melanie. 1993. "The Doctor Is Out," *Village Voice*, 38(June 22):18.

Butler, Robert N. 1975. *Why Survive? Being Old in America*. New York: Harper and Row.

——. 1990. "A Disease Called Ageism," *Journal of the American Geriatrics Society*, 38(February):178–180.

Byne, William, and Bruce Parsons. 1993. "Human Sexual Orientation: The Biologic Theories Reappraised," *Archives of General Psychiatry*, 30(March):228–239.

Cable, Sherry, and Michael Benson. 1993. "Acting Locally: Environmental Injustice and the Emergence of Grassroots Environmental Organizations," *Social Problems*, 40 (November): 464–477.

Cahill, Spencer E. 1986. "Language Practices and Self Definition: The Case of Gender Identity Acquisition," *Sociological Quarterly*, 27(September):295–312.

Calem, Robert E. 1993. "Working at Home, for Better or Worse," *New York Times* (April 18), sec. 3, pp. 1, 6.

Came, Barry. 1989. "A Growing Menace," *Maclean's*, 102(January 23):43–44.

Camus, Albert. 1948. *The Plague*. New York: Random House.

Cancian, Francesca. 1986. "The Feminization of Love," *Signs*, 11(Summer): 692–708.

Caniglia, Julie. 1993. "Making Body Art," *Utne Reader* (January–February):30–32.

Cannon, James S. 1985. *The Health Costs of Air Pollution*. New York: American Lung Association.

Cantril, Hadley. 1940. *The Invasion from Mars: A Study in the Psychology of Panic*. Princeton, N.J.: Princeton University Press.

Caplan, Arthur L. (ed.). 1978. *The Sociobiology Debate: Readings on Ethical and Scientific Issues*. New York: Harper and Row.

Caplan, Nathan, Marcella H. Gray, and John K. Whitmore. 1992. *Children of the Boat People: A Study of Educational Success*. Ann Arbor: University of Michigan Press.

Caplan, Ronald L. 1989. "The Commodification of American Health Care," *Social Science and Medicine*, 28(11): 1139–1148.

Caplow, Theodore. 1969. *Two against One: Coalitions in Triads*. Englewood Cliffs, N.J.: Prentice-Hall.

Carey, Anne R., and Suzy Parker. 1993. "Women Serving Overseas," *USA Today* (October 28), p. A1.

Cargan, Leonard, and Matthew Melko. 1991. "Being Single on Noah's Ark," in Leonard Cargan and Jeanne H. Ballantine (eds.), *Sociological Footprints* (5th ed.). Belmont, Calif.: Wadsworth, pp. 161–165.

Carmichael, Stokely, and Charles V. Hamilton. 1967. *Black Power: The Politics of Liberation in America*. New York: Random House.

Carmody, Denise Lardner. 1989. *Women and World Religions* (2d ed.). Englewood Cliffs, N.J.: Prentice-Hall.

Carroll, John B. 1953. *The Study of Language*. Cambridge, Mass.: Harvard University Press.

———. 1956. *Language, Thought, and Reality: Selected Writings of Benjamin Lee Whorf*. Cambridge, Mass.: M.I.T. Press.

Carroll, Nicole. 1993. "Salaries Slip for Child-Care Center Workers," *USA Today* (March 25), p. D1.

Carroll, Susan. 1993. "The Gender Gap in the Presidential Race," *CAWP News and Notes*, **9**(Winter):5–6.

Carson, Rachel. 1962. *The Silent Spring*. Boston: Houghton Mifflin.

Carter, Keith. 1989. "Networking Is the Key to Jobs," *USA Today* (August 7), p. B1.

Cassidy, Claire Monod. 1982. "Protein-Energy Malnutrition as a Culture-Bound Syndrome," *Culture, Medicine and Psychiatry*, **6**:325–345.

Cassidy, Frederic G. (ed.). 1985. *Dictionary of American Regional English*. Cambridge, Mass.: Harvard University Press.

Castells, Manuel. 1976. "The Wild City," *Capital and State*, **4,5**(Summer):2–30.

———. 1977. *The Urban Question: A Marxist Approach*. Cambridge, Mass.: M.I.T. Press.

———. 1983. *The City and the Grass Roots*. Berkeley: University of California Press.

———. 1989. *The Informational City*. Oxford, Eng.: Basil Blackwell.

Cauchon, Dennis. 1991. "Study Shows Bias in Sentencing Laws," *USA Today* (August 23), p. 8A.

CBS News. 1979. "I Was Only Following Orders." Transcript of *Sixty Minutes* segment, March 31, pp. 2–8.

Celis, William, III. 1993. "Suburban and Rural Schools Learning that Violence Isn't Confined to the Cities," *New York Times* (April 21), p. B11.

Center for the American Woman and Politics. 1992a. *Women in Elective Office, 1992*. New Brunswick, N.J.: Center for the American Woman and Politics.

———. 1992b. *The Impact of Women in Public Office: Findings at a Glance*. New Brunswick, N.J.: Center for the American Woman and Politics.

Centers for Disease Control. 1992a. "Sexual Behavior among High School Students—United States, 1990," *Morbidity and Mortality Weekly Report*, **40**(January 3):885–889.

———. 1992b. "The Second 100,000 Cases of Acquired Immunodeficiency Syndrome," *Morbidity and Mortality Weekly Report*, **41**(January 17):28–29.

———. 1992c. "Projections of the Number of Persons Diagnosed with AIDS and the Number of Immunosuppressed HIV-Infected Persons—United States, 1992–1994," *Morbidity and Mortality Weekly Report*, **41**(December 25): 1–28.

Cerio, Gregory. 1992. "Playing a Losing Game," *Newsweek*, **119**(May 4):29.

Cetron, Marvin J., and Owen Davies. 1991. "Trends Shaping the World," *Futurist*, **20**(September–October):11–21.

Chafetz, Janet Saltzman. 1988. *Feminist Sociology: An Overview of Contemporary Theories*. Itasca, Ill.: Peacock.

Chalfant, H. Paul, Robert E. Beckley, and C. Eddie Palmer. 1987. *Religion in Contemporary Society* (2d ed.). Palo Alto, Calif.: Mayfield.

——— et al. [6 authors]. 1990. "The Clergy as a Resource for Those Encountering Psychological Distress," *Review of Religious Research*, **31**(March): 305–315.

Chambliss, William. 1972. "Introduction," in Harry King, *Box Man*. New York: Harper and Row, pp. ix–xi.

———. 1973. "The Saints and the Roughnecks," *Society*, **11**(November–December):24–31.

——— and Robert B. Seidman. 1971. *Law, Order, and Power*. Reading, Mass.: Addison-Wesley.

Changing Times. 1981. "When Family Anger Turns to Violence," **35**(March):66–70.

Chapman, Fern Schumer. 1987. "Executive Guilt: Who's Taking Care of the Children," *Fortune*, **115**(February 16):30–37.

Charon, Joel M. 1985. *Symbolic Interactionism: An Introduction, an Interpretation, an Integration* (2d ed.). Englewood Cliffs, N.J.: Prentice-Hall.

Cherlin, Andrew S. 1988. *The Changing American Family and Public Policy*. Washington, D.C.: Urban Institute Press.

——— and Frank Furstenberg. 1986. *The American Grandparent: A Place in the Family, a Life Apart*. New York: Basic Books.

——— et al. [7 authors]. 1991. "Longitudinal Studies of Effects of Divorce on Children in Great Britain and the United States," *Science*, **252**(April–June):1386–1389.

Chernin, Kim. 1981. *The Obsession: Reflections on the Tyranny of Slenderness*. New York: Harper and Row.

Chinoy, Ely. 1954. *Sociological Perspectives: Basic Concepts and Their Applications*. New York: Random House.

Chira, Susan. 1992. "Research Questions Effectiveness of Most School Choice Programs," *New York Times* (October 26), pp. A1, B8.

———. 1993. "When Disabled Students Enter Regular Classrooms," *New York Times* (May 19), pp. A1, A17.

Chow, Effie Poy Yew. 1984. "Traditional Chinese Medicine: A Holistic System," in J. Warren Salmon (ed.), *Alternative Medicines*. New York: Tavistock, pp. 114–137.

Chow, Siu L., Robert Rosenthal, and Hans Werner Beirhoff. 1990. "Teacher's Expectancy and Its Effects: A Tutorial Review," *Zeitschrift-fur-Padagogische-Psychologie*, **4**(September):147–159.

Christensen, Kathleen. 1990. "Bridges over Troubled Water: How Older Workers View the Labor Market," in Peter B. Doeringer (ed.), *Bridges to Retirement*. Ithaca, N.Y.: ILR Press, pp. 175–207.

Chronicle of Higher Education. 1982. "Fact-File: 9-Month Faculty Salaries for 1981–1982," **24**(July 7):10.

Chudacoff, Howard P. 1989. *How Old Are You?* Princeton, N.J.: Princeton University Press.

Cicone, Michael V., and Diane N. Ruble. 1978. "Beliefs about Males," *Journal of Social Issues,* **34**(Winter):5–16.

Cisin, Ira H., and Walter B. Clark. 1962. "The Methodological Challenge of Disaster Research," in George W. Baker and Dwight W. Chapman (eds.), *Man and Society in Disaster.* New York: Basic Books, pp. 23–40.

Cisneros, Henry G. 1993. "A Death on the Nation's Doorstep," *Washington Post National Weekly Edition,* **11** (December 13–19):23.

Clark, Burton R., and Martin Trow. 1966. "The Organizational Context," in Theodore M. Newcomb and Everett K. Wilson (eds.), *The Study of College Peer Groups.* Chicago: Aldine, pp. 17–70.

Clark, Candace. 1983. "Sickness and Social Control," in Howard Robboy and Candace Clark (eds.), *Social Interaction: Readings in Sociology* (2d ed.). New York: St. Martin's, pp. 346–365.

Clarke, Lee. 1988. "Explaining Choices among Technological Risks," *Social Problems,* **35**(February):501–514.

Clausen, John A. 1979. "Mental Disorder," in Howard E. Freeman, Sol Levine, and Leo G. Reeder (eds.), *Handbook of Medical Sociology* (3d ed.). Englewood Cliffs, N.J.: Prentice-Hall, pp. 97–112.

Clements, Mark. 1993. "The Growing Crisis in Health Care," *Parade Magazine* (February 28), pp. 4–5.

Clines, Francis X. 1989. "There's a Crime Wave, or a Perception Wave, in the Soviet Union," *New York Times* (August 17), p. E2.

Cloward, Richard A. 1959. "Illegitimate Means, Anomie, and Deviant Behavior," *American Sociological Review,* **24**(April):164–176.

——— and Frances Fox Piven. 1993. "The Fraud of Workfare," *The Nation* (May 24), pp. 693–696.

Clymer, Adam. 1993. "Congress Passes Measure Providing Emergency Leaves," *New York Times* (February 5), pp. A1, A14.

Cockerham, William C. 1989. *Medical Sociology* (4th ed.). Englewood Cliffs, N.J.: Prentice-Hall.

Cohen, Debra Nussbaum. 1991. "The Right to Be Rabbis Won, Women Face Role's Challenges," *Long Island Jewish World,* **20**(August 23–29):3, 22–23.

Cohn, Bob. 1991. "The Q-Word Charade," *Newsweek,* **117**(June 3):16–18.

Cohn, Steven F., Steven E. Barkan, and William H. Whitaker. 1993. "Activists against Hunger: Membership Characteristics of a National Social Movement Organization," *Sociological Forum,* **8**(March):113–131.

Cohn, Victor. 1992. "How Can We Fix a Broken System?" *Washington Post National Weekly Edition,* **9**(February 3):6–7.

Colasanto, Diane. 1989. "Public Wants Civil Rights Widened for Some Groups, Not for Others," *Gallup Poll Monthly,* **291**(December):13–22.

Colclough, Glenna, and E. M. Beck. 1986. "The American Educational Structure and the Reproduction of Social Class," *Sociological Inquiry,* **56**(Fall):456–476.

Cole, Elizabeth S. 1985. "Adoption: History, Policy, and Program," in Joan Laird and Ann Hartman (eds.), *A Handbook of Child Welfare.* New York: Free Press, pp. 638–666.

Cole, Mike. 1988. *Bowles and Gintis Revisited: Correspondence and Contradiction in Educational Theory.* Philadelphia: Falmer.

Coleman, James S. 1992. "Some Points on Choice in Education," *Sociology of Education,* **65**(October):255–262.

———, Thomas Hoffer, and Sally Kilgore. 1982. *High School Achievement: Public, Catholic, and Other Private Schools Compared.* New York: Basic Books.

Coleman, James William, and Donald R. Cressey. 1980. *Social Problems.* New York: Harper and Row.

Collins, Glenn. 1987. "As Nation Grays, a Mighty Advocate Flexes Its Muscles," *New York Times* (April 2), pp. C1, C8.

Collins, Randall. 1975. *Conflict Sociology: Toward an Explanatory Sociology.* New York: Academic.

———. 1979. *The Credential Society: An Historical Sociology of Education and Stratification.* New York: Academic.

———. 1980. "Weber's Last Theory of Capitalism: A Systematization," *American Sociological Review,* **45**(December):925–942.

———. 1982. *Sociological Insight: An Introduction to Non-obvious Sociology.* New York: Oxford University Press.

——— and Michael Makowsky. 1978. *The Discovery of Society.* New York: Random House.

Collins, Sharon M. 1983. "The Making of the Black Middle Class," *Social Problems,* **30**(April):369–382.

———. 1989. "The Marginalization of Black Executives," *Social Problems,* **36**(October):317–331.

———. 1993. "Blacks on the Bubble: The Vulnerability of Black Executives in White Corporations," *Sociological Quarterly,* **34**(3):429–447.

Commission for Racial Justice. 1987. *Toxic Wastes and Race in the United States.* New York: United Church of Christ.

Commission on Civil Rights. 1976. *A Guide to Federal Laws and Regulations Prohibiting Sex Discrimination.* Washington, D.C.: U.S. Government Printing Office.

———. 1981. *Affirmative Action in the 1980s: Dismantling the Process of Discrimination.* Washington, D.C.: U.S. Government Printing Office.

———. 1992. *Civil Rights Issues Facing Asian Americans in the 1990s.* Washington, D.C.: U.S. Government Printing Office.

———. 1993. "Jackson Speaks to Commission about Discrimination in Professional Sports," *Civil Rights Update* (May–June), p. 4.

Commoner, Barry. 1971. *The Closing Circle.* New York: Knopf.

Conklin, John E. 1981. *Criminology.* New York: Macmillan.

Conley, John J. 1992. "Masks of Autonomy," *Society,* **29**(July–August):11–15.

Conly, Catherine H., and J. Thomas McEwen. 1990. "Computer Crime," *NIJ Reports* (January–February), pp. 2–7.

Conniff, Ruth. 1992. "Cutting the Lifeline: The Real Welfare Fraud," *The Progressive,* **56**(February):25–31.

Conover, Pamela J., and Virginia Gray. 1983. *Feminism and the New Right Conflict over the American Family.* New York: Praeger.

Conrad, Peter. 1975. "The Discovery of Hyperkinesis: Notes on the Medicalization of Deviant Behavior," *Social Problems,* **23**(October):12–21.

——— and Rochelle Kern (eds.). 1986. *The Sociology of Health and Illness: Critical Perspectives* (2d ed.). New York: St. Martin's.

——— and Joseph W. Schneider. 1992. *Deviance and Medicalization: From Baldness to*

Sickness (expanded ed.). Philadelphia: Temple University Press.

Cooley, Charles H. 1902. *Human Nature and the Social Order.* New York: Scribner.

Coontz, Stephanie. 1992. *The Way We Never Were: American Families and the Nostalgia Trap.* New York: Basic Books.

Corea, Gena. 1977. *The Hidden Malpractice.* New York: Morrow.

Corning, Amy. 1993. "The Russian Referendum: An Analysis of Exit Poll Results," *RFE/RL Research Report,* **2**(May 7):6–9.

Cornish, Edward. 1992. "Outlook '93," *Futurist,* **26**(November–December):1–7.

Corral, Thais. 1993. "Brazil's Women-Run Police Stations Fight the Odds," *Ms.,* **4**(November/December):18.

Coser, Lewis A. 1956. *The Functions of Social Conflict.* New York: Free Press.

———. 1977. *Masters of Sociological Thought: Ideas in Historical and Social Context* (2d ed.). New York: Harcourt Brace Jovanovich.

Coser, Rose Laub. 1984. "American Medicine's Ambiguous Progress," *Contemporary Sociology,* **13**(January):9–13.

COSSA (Consortium of Social Science Associations). 1991. "Social Science Triumphs in Congress after Setback on American Teenage Study," *Washington Update,* **15**(August 5):1–4.

Cotton, Paul. 1990. "Is There Still Too Much Extrapolation from Data on Middle-Aged White Men?" *Journal of the American Medical Association,* **263**(February 23):1049–1050.

Couch, Carl. 1990. "Mass Communication and State Structures," *Social Science Journal,* **27**(2):111–128.

Coughlin, Ellen K. 1983. "Alternative Religions or Dangerous Scams: Scholars Assess the Problems of Cults," *Chronicle of Higher Education,* **26**(March 9):5–7.

Council on Ethical and Judicial Affairs, American Medical Association. 1992. "Decisions Near the End of Life," *Journal of the American Medical Association,* **267**(April 22–29):2229–2333.

Council on Scientific Affairs. 1991. "Hispanic Health in the United States," *Journal of the American Medical Association,* **265**(January 9):248–252.

Counts, D. A. 1977. "The Good Death in Kaliai: Preparation for Death in Western New Britain," *Omega,* **7**:367–372.

Courtney, Alice E., and Thomas W. Whipple. 1983. *Sex Stereotyping in Advertising.* Lexington, Mass.: Lexington.

Cowan, Allison Leigh, with James Barron. 1992. "Executives the Economy Left Behind," *New York Times* (November 22), sec. 3, pp. 1, 6.

Cowan, Neil M., and Ruth Schwartz Cowan. 1989. *Our Parents' Lives: The Americanization of Eastern European Jews.* New York: Basic Books.

Cowgill, Donald O. 1986. *Aging around the World.* Belmont, Calif.: Wadsworth.

Cox, Oliver C. 1948. *Caste, Class and Race: A Study in Social Dynamics.* Detroit: Wayne State University Press.

———. 1976. *Race Relations: Elements and Social Dynamics.* Detroit: Wayne State University Press.

Craig, Steve (ed.). 1992. *Men, Masculinity, and the Media.* Newbury Park, Calif.: Sage.

Crawford, Susan. 1993. "A Wink Here, a Leer There: It's Costly," *New York Times* (March 28), p. F17.

Creekmore, C. R. 1985. "Cities Won't Drive You Crazy," *Psychology Today,* **19**(January):46–50, 52–53.

Cressey, Donald R. 1960. "Epidemiology and Individual Contact: A Case from Criminology," *Pacific Sociological Review,* **3**(Fall):47–58.

Crossette, Barbara. 1990. "Campaign to Oust English Is Revived in India," *New York Times* (May 27), p. 4.

———. 1992. "Population Policy in Asia Is Faulted," *New York Times* (September 16), p. A9.

Crouse, James, and Dale Trusheim. 1988. *The Case against the S.A.T.* Chicago: University of Chicago Press.

Crow, Ben, and Alan Thomas. 1983. *Third World Atlas.* Milton Keynes, Eng.: Open University Press.

Cuba, Lee J. 1988. *A Short Guide to Writing about Social Science.* Glenview, Ill.: Scott, Foresman.

Cuff, E. C., and G. C. F. Payne. 1979. *Perspectives on Sociology.* Boston: Allen.

Cullen, Francis T., Jr., and John B. Cullen. 1978. *Toward a Paradigm of Labeling Theory,* ser. 58. Lincoln: University of Nebraska Studies.

Cumming, Elaine, and William E. Henry. 1961. *Growing Old: The Process of Disengagement.* New York: Basic Books.

Cummings, Milton C., Jr., and David Wise. 1993. *Democracy under Pressure: An Introduction to the American Political System* (7th ed.). San Diego: Harcourt Brace Jovanovich.

Cunningham, Kitty. 1993. "Caucus Rebuffs Clinton," *Congressional Quarterly Weekly Report,* **51**(June 12):1452.

Currie, Elliot. 1985. *Confronting Crime: An American Challenge.* New York: Pantheon.

Curry, Timothy Jan. 1993. "A Little Pain Never Hurt Anyone: Athletic Career Socialization and the Normalization of Sports Injury," *Symbolic Interaction,* **26**(Fall):273–290.

Curtis, James E., Edward G. Grabls, and Douglas E. Baer. 1992. "Voluntary Association Membership in Fifteen Countries: A Compositive Analysis," *American Sociological Review,* **57**(April):139–152.

Curtiss, Susan. 1977. *Genie: A Psycholinguistic Study of a Modern Day "Wild Child."* New York: Academic.

———. 1981. "Disassociations between Languages and Cognition: Cases and Implications," *Journal of Autism and Developmental Disabilities,* **11**(March):15–30.

———. 1982. "Developmental Dissociations of Languages and Cognition," in Loraine Obler and Lise Mann (eds.), *Exceptional Language and Linguistics.* New York: Academic, pp. 285–312.

———. 1985. "The Development of Human Cerebral Lateralization," in D. Frank Benson and Eran Zaidel (eds.), *The Dual Brain.* New York: Guilford, pp. 97–116.

Dabrowski, Andrea, Laura López, and Gail Scriven. 1989. "A Chasm of Misery," *Time,* **134**(November 6):64–66.

Dahl, Robert A. 1961. *Who Governs?* New Haven, Conn.: Yale University Press.

Dahrendorf, Ralf. 1958. "Toward a Theory of Social Conflict," *Journal of Conflict Resolution,* **2**(June):170–183.

———. 1959. *Class and Class Conflict in Industrial Sociology.* Stanford, Calif.: Stanford University Press.

———. 1990. *Reflections on the Revolution in Europe.* New York: Random House.

Daniels, Arlene Kaplan. 1987. "Invisible Work," *Social Problems,* **34**(December):403–415.

———. 1988. *Invisible Careers.* Chicago: University of Chicago Press.

Davidman, Lynn. 1991. *Tradition in a Root-*

less World: Women Turn to Orthodox Judaism. Berkeley: University of California Press.

Davies, Christie. 1989. "Goffman's Concept of the Total Institution: Criticisms and Revisions," *Human Studies,* **12**(June): 77–95.

Davis, Fred. 1992. *Fashions, Culture, and Identity.* Chicago: University of Chicago Press.

Davis, James. 1982. "Up and Down Opportunity's Ladder," *Public Opinion,* **5**(June–July):11–15, 48–51.

Davis, Kingsley. 1937. "The Sociology of Prostitution," *American Sociological Review,* **2**(October):744–755.

———. 1940. "Extreme Social Isolation of a Child," *American Journal of Sociology,* **45**(January):554–565.

———. 1947. "Final Note on a Case of Extreme Isolation," *American Journal of Sociology,* **52**(March):432–437.

———. 1949. *Human Society.* New York: Macmillan.

——— and Wilbert E. Moore. 1945. "Some Principles of Stratification," *American Sociological Review,* **10**(April):242–249.

Davis, Mike. 1992. "In L.A., Burning All Illusions," *The Nation,* **254**(June 1):743–746.

Davis, Nancy J., and Robert V. Robinson. 1988. "Class Identification of Men and Women in the 1970s and 1980s," *American Sociological Review,* **53**(February):103–112.

Davis, Nanette J. 1975. *Sociological Constructions of Deviance: Perspectives and Issues in the Field.* Dubuque, Iowa: Brown.

Davis, Phillip. 1992. "Keeping Black Areas Green," *Black Enterprise,* **23**(October):33.

Day, Lincoln H. 1978. "What Will a ZPG Society Be Like?" *Population Bulletin,* **33**(June).

Dear, Michael. 1992. "Understanding and Overcoming the NIMBY Syndrome," *Journal of the American Planning Association,* **50**(Summer):288–300.

de Beauvoir, Simone. 1953. *The Second Sex.* New York: Knopf.

Deegan, Mary Jo. (ed.). 1991. *Women in Sociology: A Bio-Bibliographical Sourcebook.* Westport, Conn.: Greenwood.

——— and Michael Hill (eds.). 1987. *Women and Symbolic Interaction.* Winchester, Mass.: Allen and Unwin.

DeFleur, Melvin L., and Everette E. Dennis. 1981. *Understanding Mass Communication.* Boston: Houghton Mifflin.

Degler, Carl N. 1971. *Neither Black nor White: Slavery and Race Relations in Brazil and the United States.* New York: Macmillan.

Demerath, N. J., II, and Rhys H. Williams. 1992. *A Bridging of Faiths: Religion and Politics in a New England City.* Princeton, N.J.: Princeton University Press.

Denisoff, R. Serge. 1988. *Inside MTV.* Rutgers, N.J.: Transaction.

Dent, David J. 1992. "The New Black Suburbs," *New York Times* (June 14), pp. 18–25.

Dentzer, Susan. 1986. "Back to the Suburbs," *Newsweek,* **107**(April 21):60–62.

Denzin, Norman K. 1987. *The Recovering Alcoholic.* Newbury Park, Calif.: Sage.

———. 1990. "The Sociological Imagination Revisited," *Sociological Quarterly,* **31**(1):1–22.

——— and Yvonna S. Lincoln (eds.). 1994. *Handbook of Qualitative Research.* Thousand Oaks, Calif.: Sage.

DeParle, Jason. 1992a. "Why Marginal Changes Don't Rescue the Welfare System," *New York Times* (March 1), p. E3.

———. 1992b. "'88 Welfare Act Is Falling Short, Researchers Say," *New York Times* (March 30), pp. A1, A11.

———. 1993. "Counter to Trend, a Welfare Program in California Has One Idea: Get a Job!" *New York Times* (May 16), sec. 2, p. 1.

Department of Agriculture. 1992. *Expenditures on a Child by Families, 1992.* Hyattsville, Md.: USDA Family Economics Research Group.

Department of Education. 1992. *Digest of Educational Statistics.* Washington, D.C.: U.S. Government Printing Office.

Department of Justice. 1987. *White Collar Crime.* Washington, D.C.: U.S. Government Printing Office.

———. 1988. *Report of the Nation on Crime and Justice* (2d ed.). Washington, D.C.: U.S. Government Printing Office.

———. 1992. *Criminal Victimization in the United States, 1991.* Washington, D.C.: U.S. Government Printing Office.

———. 1993. *Crime in the U.S.—1992.* Washington, D.C.: U.S. Government Printing Office.

Department of Labor. 1980. *Perspectives on Working Women: A Datebook.* Washington, D.C.: U.S. Government Printing Office.

———. 1993. *Work and Family: Employer-Provided Training among Young Adults.* Washington, D.C.: U.S. Government Printing Office.

Derksen, Linda, and John Gartrell. 1993. "The Social Context of Recycling," *American Sociological Review,* **58**(June): 434–442.

DeSena, Judith N. 1987. "The Defended Neighborhood Revisited." Paper presented at the annual meeting of the Eastern Sociological Society, Boston.

de Sherbinin, Alex. 1990. "Iraq," *Population Today,* **18**(October):12.

Desroches, Frederick J. 1990. "Tearoom Trade: A Research Update," *Qualitative Sociology,* **13**(1):39–61.

DeStefano, Linda, and Diane Colasanto. 1990. "Unlike 1975, Today Most Americans Think Men Have It Better," *Gallup Poll Monthly,* **293**(February):25–36.

DeVault, Marjorie L. 1991. *Feeding the Family: The Social Organization of Caring as Gendered Work.* Chicago: University of Chicago Press.

Devine, Don. 1972. *Political Culture of the United States: The Influence of Member Values on Regime Maintenance.* Boston: Little, Brown.

Dey, Eric L., et al. [3 authors]. 1992. *The American Freshman: National Norms for Fall 1992.* Los Angeles: Higher Education Research Center.

DiMaggio, Paul. 1990. "Review of *Charismatic Capitalism: Direct Selling Organizations in America,*" *Contemporary Sociology,* **19**(March):218–220.

Dingman, P. R. 1974. "The Case for the State Hospital." Mimeograph, Scottsdale, Ariz.: NTIS.

Dittersdorf, Harriet. 1990. "Domestic Partnership: What Used to Define a Traditional Family," *NOW-NYC News,* **14**(July–August):6.

Doblin, Bruce H., Lillian Gelberg, and Howard E. Freeman. 1992. "Patient Care and Professional Staffing Patterns in McKinney Act Clinics Providing Primary Care to the Homeless," *Journal of the American Medical Association,* **267**(February 5):698–701.

Doeringer, Peter B. (ed.). 1990. *Bridges to Retirement: Older Workers in a Changing Labor Market.* Ithaca, N.Y.: ILR Press.

Doerr, Edd. 1993. "Chelsea Goes to School," *Humanist,* **53**(March–April): 38–39.

Doig, Stephen, Reynolds Farley, William Frey, and Dan Gillmor. 1993. *Blacks on the Black—New Patterns of Residential Segregation in a Multi-ethnic Country.* Cambridge, Mass.: Harvard University Press.

Dolbeare, Kenneth M. 1992. *American Public Policy: A Citizen's Guide.* New York: McGraw-Hill.

Dolnick, Edward. 1993. "Deafness as Culture," *Atlantic Monthly,* **272**(September):37–40, 43, 46–48, 50–51.

Domhoff, G. William. 1967. *Who Rules America?* Englewood Cliffs, N.J.: Prentice-Hall.

———. 1970. *The Higher Circles: The Governing Class in America.* New York: Random House.

———. 1978. *Who Really Rules? New Haven and Community Power Reexamined.* New Brunswick, N.J.: Transaction.

———. 1983. *Who Rules America Now? A View for the '80s.* Englewood Cliffs, N.J.: Prentice-Hall.

———. 1993. "Who Rules America?" in *Introduction to Social Problems.* New York: McGraw-Hill, pp. 836–861.

Donnelly, Jack. 1989. *Universal Human Rights in Theory and Practice.* New York: Cornell University Press.

Doob, Christopher Bates. 1993. *Racism: An American Cauldron.* New York: HarperCollins.

Dore, Ronald P. 1976. *The Diploma Disease: Education, Qualification and Development.* Berkeley: University of California Press.

Doress, Irwin, and Jack Nusan Porter. 1977. *Kids in Cults: Why They Join, Why They Stay, Why They Leave.* Brookline, Mass.: Reconciliation Associates.

——— and ———. 1981. "Kids in Cults," in Thomas Robbins and Dick Anthony (eds.), *In Gods We Trust.* New Brunswick, N.J.: Transaction, pp. 297–302.

Dornbusch, Stanford M. 1989. "The Sociology of Adolescence," in W. Richard Scott and Judith Blake (eds.), *Annual Review of Sociology, 1989.* Palo Alto, Calif.: Annual Reviews, pp. 233–259.

Dotson, Floyd. 1991. "Community," in Dushkin Publishing Group, *Encyclopedic Dictionary of Sociology* (4th ed.). Guilford, Conn.: Dushkin, p. 55.

Dougherty, Kevin, and Floyd M. Hammack. 1992. "Education Organization," in Edgar F. Borgatta and Marie L. Borgatta (eds.), *Encyclopedia of Sociology,* vol. 2. New York: Macmillan, pp. 535–541.

Dowd, James J. 1980. *Stratification among the Aged.* Monterey, Calif.: Brooks/Cole.

Downs, Peter. 1987. "Your Money or Your Life," *The Progressive,* **51**(January): 24–28.

Driscoll, Anne. 1988. "For Salem, a Reminder of a Dark Past," *New York Times* (October 30), p. 51.

Duberman, Lucille. 1976. *Social Inequality: Class and Caste in America.* Philadelphia: Lippincott.

Du Bois, W. E. B. 1909. *The Negro American Family.* Atlanta University. Reprinted 1970, Cambridge, Mass.: M.I.T. Press.

Duff, Robert W., and Lawrence K. Hong. 1986. "Impression Management by Competitive Women Bodybuilders." Paper presented at the annual meeting of the Western Social Science Association, Reno, Nev.

——— and ———. 1988. "Management of Deviant Identity among Competitive Women Bodybuilders," in Pelos H. Kelly (ed.), *Deviant Behavior: Readings in the Sociology of Deviance* (3d ed.). New York: St. Martin's.

Dumas, Kitty. 1992. "Vote Likely Buries Anti-crime Bill," *Congressional Quarterly Weekly Report,* **50**(March 21):732.

Duncan, Greg J., and Ken R. Smith. 1989. "The Rising Affluence of the Elderly: How Far, How Fair, and How Frail," in W. Richard Scott and Judith Blake (eds.), *Annual Review of Sociology, 1989,* vol. 15. Palo Alto, Calif.: Annual Reviews, pp. 261–289.

Dundes, Alan. 1962. "Earth-Diver: Creation of the Mythopolic Male," *American Anthropologist,* **54**(October): 1032–1051.

Duneier, Mitchell. 1992. *Slim's Table: Race, Respectability, and Masculinity.* Chicago: University of Chicago Press.

Dunlap, Riley E. 1993. "From Environmental to Ecological Problems," in Craig Calhoun and George Ritzer (eds.), *Introduction to Social Problems.* New York: McGraw-Hill, pp. 707–738.

——— and William R. Catton, Jr. 1983. "What Environmental Sociologists Have in Common," *Sociological Inquiry,* **53**(Spring):113–135.

———, George H. Gallup, Jr., and Alec M. Gallup. 1993. *Health of the Planet.* Princeton, N.J.: George H. Gallup International Institute.

Dunn, William. 1987. "More Blacks Trade Cities for Suburbs," *USA Today* (June 25), p. A1.

———. 1991. "Suburbs See Census 'Action,'" *USA Today* (January 28), p. 1A.

Durkheim, Émile. 1933. *Division of Labor in Society.* Translated by George Simpson. New York: Free Press (originally published in 1893).

———. 1947. *The Elementary Forms of the Religious Life.* Glencoe, Ill.: Free Press (originally published in 1912).

———. 1951. *Suicide.* Translated by John A. Spaulding and George Simpson. New York: Free Press (originally published in 1897).

———. 1964. *The Rules of Sociological Method.* Translated by Sarah A. Solovay and John H. Mueller. New York: Free Press (originally published in 1895).

Durning, Alan B. 1990. "Life on the Brink," *World Watch,* **3**(March–April):22–30.

———. 1993. "Supporting Indigenous Peoples," in Lester R. Brown (ed.), *State of the World, 1993.* New York: Norton, pp. 80–100.

Dushkin Publishing Group. 1991. *Encyclopedic Dictionary of Sociology* (4th ed.). Guilford, Conn.: Dushkin.

Duster, Troy. 1991. "Understanding Self-Segregation on the Campus," *Chronicle of Higher Education,* **38**(September 25):B1, B2.

Dworkin, Anthony Gary. 1987. *Teacher Burnout in the Public Schools: Structural Causes and Consequences for Children.* Albany: State University of New York Press.

Dworkin, Rosalind J. 1982. "A Woman's Report: Numbers Are Not Enough," in Anthony Dworkin and Rosalind Dworkin (eds.), *The Minority Report.* New York: Holt, pp. 375–400.

Dychtwald, Ken, with Joe Flower. 1989. *Age Wave: The Challenges and Opportunities of an Aging America.* Los Angeles: Tarcher.

Dynes, Russell R. 1978. "Interorganizational Relations in Communities under

Stress," in E. L. Quarantelli (ed.), *Disasters: Theory and Research*. Beverly Hills, Calif.: Sage, pp. 50–64.

Dzidzienyo, Anani. 1987. "Brazil," in Jay A. Sigler (ed.), *International Handbook on Race and Race Relations*. New York: Greenwood, pp. 23–42.

Easterbrook, Gregg. 1987. "The Revolution in Medicine," *Newsweek*, **109**(January 26):40–44, 49–54, 56–59, 61–64, 67–68, 70–74.

Ebaugh, Helen Rose Fuchs. 1988. *Becoming an Ex: The Process of Role Exit*. Chicago: University of Chicago Press.

Eckholm, Erik. 1992. "The Riots Bring a Rush to Arm and New Debate," *New York Times* (May 17), p. E18.

——. 1993. "A Little Gun Control, a Lot of Guns," *New York Times* (August 15), sec. 4, p. 1.

The Economist. 1990a. "By Any Other Name," **314**(January 6):42.

——. 1990b. "Thick Skins," **314**(February 24):26.

——. 1991. "The Reincarnation of Caste," **319**(June 8):21–23.

Eden, Dov, and Abraham B. Shani. 1982. "Pygmalion Goes to Boot Camp: Expectancy, Leadership, and Trainee Performance," *Journal of Applied Psychology*, **67**(April):194–199.

Edin, Kathryn. 1991. "Surviving the Welfare System: How AFDC Recipients Make Ends Meet in Chicago," *Social Problems*, **38**(November):462–474.

Edmonston, Barry, and Jeffrey S. Passel. 1993. "U.S. Immigration and Ethnicity in the 21st Century," *Population Today* (October), pp. 6–7.

Edwards, Harry. 1973. *Sociology of Sport*. Homewood, Ill.: Dorsey.

——. 1984. "The Black 'Dumb Jock,'" *College Board Review*, **131**(Spring):8–13.

Egan, Timothy. 1993. "Ballot Measures on Term Limits and Crime Draw Wide Support," *New York Times* (November 4), p. A24.

Ehrenreich, Barbara, and Deidre English. 1973. *Witches, Midwives, and Nurses: A History of Women Healers*. Old Westbury, N.Y.: Feminist Press.

—— and Annette Fuentes. 1981. "Life on the Global Assembly," *Ms.*, **9**(January):53–59, 71.

Ehrlich, Paul R. 1968. *The Population Bomb*. New York: Ballantine.

—— and Anne H. Ehrlich. 1990. *The Population Explosion*. New York: Simon and Schuster.

Eisenberg, David M., et al. [6 authors]. 1993. "Unconventional Medicine in the United States," *New England Journal of Medicine* (January 28), pp. 245–252.

Eitzen, D. Stanley. 1978. *In Conflict and Order: Understanding Society*. Boston: Allyn and Bacon.

——. 1984a. *Sport in Contemporary Society* (2d ed.). New York: St. Martin's.

——. 1984b. *Conflict Theory and the Sociology of American Sport*. Circulated by the Red Feather Institute.

——, with Maxine Baca Zinn. 1988. *In Conflict and Order: Understanding Society* (4th ed.). Boston: Allyn and Bacon.

Ekman, Paul, Wallace V. Friesen, and John Bear. 1984. "The International Language of Gestures," *Psychology Today*, **18**(May):64–69.

Elaide, Mircea. 1978. *A History of Religious Ideas: From the Stone Age to the Eleusinian Mysteries*. Chicago: University of Chicago Press.

Elam, Stanley M. 1990. "The 22nd Annual Gallup Poll of the Public Schools," *Phi Delta Kappan*, **72**(September):41–55.

—— and Alec M. Gallup. 1989. "The 21st Annual Gallup Poll of the Public's Attitudes toward the Public Schools," *Gallup Report*, **288**(August):31–42.

——, Lowell C. Rose, and Alec M. Gallup. 1993. "The 25th Annual Phi Delta Kappa/Gallup Poll of the Public's Attitudes toward the Public Schools," *Phi Delta Kappan*, **75**(October): 137–152.

Elkin, Frederick, and Gerald Handel. 1989. *The Child and Society: The Process of Socialization* (5th ed.). New York: Random House.

Elliott, Marta, and Lauren J. Krivo. 1991. "Structural Determinants of Homelessness in the United States," *Social Problems*, **38**(February):113–131.

Ellis, William N., and Margaret McMahon Ellis. 1989. "Cultures in Transition," *The Futurist*, **23**(March–April):22–26.

Ellison, Ralph. 1952. *Invisible Man*. New York: Random House.

Elsasser, Glen. 1992. "School Prayer Ban Upheld," *Chicago Tribune* (June 25), pp. 1, 10.

Elshtain, Jean. 1981. "A Key to Unlock the Asylum?" *The Nation*, **232**(May 16):585, 602–604.

Elson, John. 1990. "Dumping on the Poor," *Time*, **136**(August 13):46–47.

Ember, Carol R., and Melvin Ember. 1993. *Anthropology* (7th ed.). Englewood Cliffs, N.J.: Prentice-Hall.

Emerson, Ralph Waldo. 1836. *Nature, Addresses, and Lectures*. Boston: Houghton Mifflin.

Emerson, Rupert. 1968. "Colonialism: Political Aspects," in David L. Sills (ed.), *International Encyclopedia of the Social Sciences*, vol. 3. New York: Macmillan, pp. 1–5.

Engels, Friedrich. 1884. "The Origin of the Family, Private Property and the State." Excerpted in Lewis Feuer (ed.), *Marx and Engels: Basic Writings on Politics and Philosophy*. Garden City, N.Y.: Anchor, 1959, pp. 392–394.

England, Paula, and Bahar Norris. 1985. "Comparable Worth: A New Doctrine of Sex Discrimination," *Social Science Quarterly*, **66**(September):629–643.

Enloe, Cynthia. 1990. *Bananas, Beaches, and Bases: Making Feminist Sense of International Politics*. Berkeley: University of California Press.

Epstein, Cynthia Fuchs. 1988. *Deceptive Distinctions: Sex, Gender, and the Social Order*. New Haven, Conn.: Yale University Press.

Erickson, J. David, and Tor Bjerkedal. 1982. "Fetal and Infant Mortality in Norway and the United States," *Journal of the American Medical Association*, **247** (February 19):987–991.

Erikson, Kai. 1966. *Wayward Puritans: A Study in the Sociology of Deviance*. New York: Wiley.

——. 1986. "On Work and Alienation," *American Sociological Review*, **51**(February):1–8.

Esber, George. 1987. "Designing Apache Houses with Apaches," in Robert M. Wulff and Shirley J. Fiske (eds.), *Anthropological Praxis: Translating Knowledge into Action*. Boulder, Colo.: Westview.

Espinosa, Dula. 1992. "Affirmative Action: A Case Study of an Organizational Effort," *Sociological Perspectives*, **35** (1):119–136.

Etzioni, Amitai. 1964. *Modern Organization*. Englewood Cliffs, N.J.: Prentice-Hall.

———. 1985. "Shady Corporate Practices," *New York Times* (November 15), p. A35.

———. 1990. "Going Soft on Corporate Crime," *Washington Post* (April 1), p. C3.

Evans, Peter. 1979. *Dependent Development.* Princeton, N.J.: Princeton University Press.

Evans, Sara. 1980. *Personal Politics: The Roots of Women's Liberation in the Civil Rights Movement and the New Left.* New York: Vintage.

Eve, Raymond A., and Francis B. Harrold. 1991. *The Creationist Movement in Modern America.* Boston: Twayne.

Fager, Marty, Mike Bradley, Lonnie Danchik, and Tom Wodetski. 1971. *Unbecoming Men.* Washington, N.J.: Times Change.

Fallows, Deborah. 1990. "In Japan, Education Isn't a Pastime—It's a Way of Life," *Washington Post National Weekly Edition,* **7**(September 17):25.

Falsey, Barbara, and Barbara Heyns. 1984. "The College Channel: Private and Public Schools Reconsidered," *Sociology of Education,* **57**(April):111–122.

Faludi, Susan. 1991. *Backlash: The Undeclared War against Women.* New York: Crown.

Farnsworth, Clyde H. 1993. "Now Patients Are Paying amid Canadian Cutbacks," *New York Times* (March 7), pp. 1, 18.

Feagin, Joe R. 1983. *The Urban Real Estate Game: Playing Monopoly with Real Money.* Englewood Cliffs, N.J.: Prentice-Hall.

———. 1989. *Minority Group Issues in Higher Education: Learning from Qualitative Research.* Norman: Center for Research on Minority Education, University of Oklahoma.

Featherman, David L., and Robert M. Hauser. 1978. *Opportunity and Change.* New York: Aeodus.

Featherstone, Mike. 1990. *Global Culture: Nationalism, Globalization, and Modernity.* London: Sage.

Feinglass, Joe. 1987. "Next, the McDRG," *The Progressive,* **51**(January):28.

Fenigstein, Alan. 1984. "Self-Consciousness and the Over-perception of Self as a Target," *Journal of Personality and Social Psychology,* **47**(4):860–870.

Ferguson, Kathy E. 1983. "Bureaucracy and Public Life: The Feminization of the Polity," *Administration and Society,* **15**(November):295–322.

———. 1984. *The Feminist Case against Bureaucracy.* Philadelphia: Temple University Press.

Ferguson, Philip M., and Adrienne Asch. 1989. "Lessons from Life: Personal and Parental Perspectives on School, Childhood, and Disability," in Douglas Biklen, Dianne Ferguson, and Alison Ford (eds.), *Schooling and Disability: 88th Yearbook of the National Society for the Study of Education, Part II.* Chicago: National Society for the Study of Education.

Fergusson, D. M., L. J. Horwood, and F. T. Shannon. 1984. "A Proportional Hazards Model of Family Breakdown," *Journal of Marriage and the Family,* **46**(August):539–549.

Ferman, Louis A., Stuart Henry, and Michel Hoyman (eds.). 1987. *The Informal Economy.* Newbury Park, Calif.: Sage. Published as September 1987 issue of *The Annals of the American Academy of Political and Social Science.*

Ferrell, Tom. 1979. "More Choose to Live outside Marriage," *New York Times* (July 1), p. E7.

Feuer, Lewis S. (ed.). 1959. *Karl Marx and Friedrich Engels: Basic Writings on Politics and Philosophy.* Garden City, N.Y.: Doubleday.

Fiala, Robert. 1992. "Postmodernism," in Edgar F. Borgatta and Marie L. Borgatta (eds.), *Encyclopedia of Sociology,* vol. 3. New York: Macmillan, pp. 1512–1522.

Fiechter, Georges-André. 1975. *Brazil since 1964: Modernization under a Military Regime.* New York: Wiley.

Fine, Gary Alan. 1984. "Negotiated Orders and Organizational Cultures," in Ralph Turner (ed.), *Annual Review of Sociology, 1984.* Palo Alto, Calif.: Annual Reviews, pp. 239–262.

———. 1987. *With the Boys: Little League Baseball and Preadolescent Culture.* Chicago: University of Chicago Press.

Fine, Michelle, and Adrienne Asch. 1988. *Women with Disabilities: Essays in Psychology, Culture, and Politics.* Philadelphia: Temple University Press.

Fineberg, Harvey. 1988. "The Social Dimensions of AIDS," *Scientific American,* **259**(October):128–134.

Fingerhut, Lois A. 1993. "Firearm Mortality among Children, Youth, and Young Adults 1–34 Years of Age, Trends and Current Status: United States, 1985–90," *Advance Data,* **231**(March 23):1–20.

——— and Joel C. Kleinman. 1990. "International and Interstate Comparisons of Homicide among Young Males," *Journal of the American Medical Association,* **263**(June 27):3292–3295.

Finkel, Steven E., and James B. Rule. 1987. "Relative Deprivation and Related Psychological Theories of Civil Violence: A Critical Review," *Research in Social Movements,* **9**:47–69.

Fiola, Jan. 1990. "The Informal Economy: Conceptualization, Measurement, Policies." Paper presented at the annual meeting of the Midwest Sociological Society, Chicago.

Firestone, Shulamith. 1970. *The Dialectic of Sex: The Case for Feminist Revolution.* New York: Bantam.

Fischer, Claude S. 1982. *To Dwell among Friends: Personal Networks in Town and City.* Chicago: University of Chicago Press.

Fisher, Arthur. 1992. "Sociobiology: Science or Ideology?" *Society,* **29**(July–August):67–79.

Fisher, B. Aubrey, and Donald G. Ellis. 1990. *Small Group Decision Making: Communication and the Group Process* (3d ed.). New York: McGraw-Hill.

Fisher, Ian. 1993. "Shantytowns, Bulldozers, and Patience: A Dilemma," *New York Times* (September 19), p. E6.

Fiske, Edward B. 1981. "Remarks by Sociologist Stir Debate over Schools," *New York Times* (April 12), p. 11.

———. 1985. "There's a Computer Gap and It's Growing Wider," *New York Times* (August 4), p. E8.

Flacks, Richard. 1971. *Youth and Social Change.* Chicago: Markham.

Flanders, Laura. 1993. "C. MacKinnon in the City of Freud," *The Nation,* **257**(August 9–16):174–177.

Fletcher, Robert S. 1943. *History of Oberlin College to the Civil War.* Oberlin, Ohio: Oberlin College Press.

Flexner, Eleanor. 1972. *Century of Struggle: The Women's Rights Movement in the United States.* New York: Atheneum.

Foner, Nancy. 1984. *Ages in Conflict.* New York: Columbia University Press.

Fong-Torres, Ben. 1986. "The China Syndrome," *Moviegoer*, **5**(July):6–7.

Fontaine, Pierre-Michel (ed.). 1986. *Race, Class, and Power in Brazil*. Los Angeles: UCLA Center for Afro-American Studies.

Ford, Clellan, and Frank Beach. 1951. *Patterns of Sexual Behavior*. New York: Harper and Row.

Ford Foundation. 1989. *Affordable Housing: The Years Ahead*. New York: Ford Foundation.

Forer, Lois G. 1984. *Money and Justice: Who Owns the Courts*. New York: Norton.

Forsythe, David P. 1990. "Human Rights in U.S. Foreign Policy: Retrospect and Prospect," *Political Science Quarterly*, **105**(3):435–454.

Fox, Renée C., and Judith P. Swazey. 1992. *Spare Parts: Organ Replacement in American Society*. New York: Oxford University Press.

Fox, Robert. 1987. *Population Images* (2d ed.). New York: United Nations Fund for Population Activities.

France, David. 1988. "ACT-UP Fires Up," *Village Voice*, **33**(May 3):36.

Frankel, Bruce. 1993. "A New Wave of 'Expendables,'" *USA Today* (June 17), p. 3A.

Franklin, John Hope, and Alfred A. Moss, Jr. 1988. *From Slavery to Freedom* (6th ed.). New York: Knopf.

Freeland, Chrystia. 1992. "Russians 'Doomed for Next 25 Years,'" *Financial Times* (October 8).

Freeman, Howard E., R. R. Dynes, P. H. Rossi, and W. F. Whyte. 1983. *Applied Sociology*. San Francisco: Jossey-Bass.

——— and Peter H. Rossi. 1984. "Furthering the Applied Side of Sociology," *American Sociological Review*, **49**(August): 571–580.

Freeman, Jo. 1973. "The Origins of the Women's Liberation Movement," *American Journal of Sociology*, **78**(January): 792–811.

———. 1975. *The Politics of Women's Liberation*. New York: McKay.

Freeman, Linton C. 1958. "Marriage without Love: Mate Selection in Non-western Societies," in Robert F. Winch (ed.), *Mate Selection*. New York: Harper and Row, pp. 20–30.

Freidson, Eliot. 1970. *Profession of Medicine*. New York: Dodd, Mead.

Freudenheim, Milt. 1990. "Employers Balk at High Cost of High-Tech Medical Care," *New York Times* (April 29), pp. 1, 16.

Frey, William H. 1990. *Metropolitan America: Beyond the Transition*. Washington, D.C.: Population Reference Bureau.

———. 1993. "U.S. Elderly Population Becoming More Concentrated," *Population Today*, **21**(April):6–7, 9.

Friedan, Betty. 1963. *The Feminine Mystique*. New York: Norton.

Friedman, Josh. 1990. "Bulgaria's Deadly Secret," *Newsday* (April 22).

Friedman, Milton. 1962. *Capitalism and Freedom*. Chicago: University of Chicago Press.

Friedman, Norman. 1974. "Cookies and Contest: Notes on Ordinary Deviance and Its Neutralization," *Sociological Symposium*, **11**:1–9.

Friedman, Thomas L. 1993. "Clinton Seeks More Powers to Stem Illegal Immigration," *New York Times* (July 28), p. A13.

Fuller, Bruce, and Xiaoyan Lang. 1993. *The Unfair Search for Child Care*. Cambridge, Mass.: Preschool and Family Choice Project, Harvard University.

Gable, Donna. 1993a. "On TV, Lifestyles of the Slim and Entertaining," *USA Today* (July 27), p. 3D.

———. 1993b. "Series Shortchange Working-Class and Minority Americans," *USA Today* (August 30), p. 3D.

Galbraith, John Kenneth. 1978. *The New Industrial State* (3d ed.). Boston: Houghton Mifflin.

Galinsky, Ellen. 1986. *Investing in Quality Child Care*. Basking Ridge, N.J.: AT&T.

Galloway, Paul. 1992. "Divided We Stand," *Chicago Tribune* (October 28), sec. 2, pp. 1–2.

Gallup, Alec, and Lydia Saad. 1992. "Clinton Holding Lead after Weekend Polls," *Gallup Poll Monthly*, **326**(November):7–10.

Gallup (Opinion Index). 1978. "Religion in America, 1977–78," **145**(January).

———. 1987. "Religion in America, 1987," **259**(April).

Gamson, Josh. 1989. "Silence, Death, and the Invisible Enemy: AIDS Activism and Social Movement 'Newness,'" *Social Problems*, **36**(October):351–367.

Gamson, William A. 1990. *The Strategy of Social Protest* (2d ed.). Belmont, Calif.: Wadsworth.

Gans, Herbert J. 1991. *People, Plans, and Policies: Essays on Poverty, Racism, and Other National Urban Problems*. New York: Columbia University Press and Russell Sage Foundation.

Ganzeboom, Harry B. G., Ruud Luijkx, and Donald J. Treiman. 1989. "Intergenerational Class Mobility in Comparative Perspective," in Arne L. Kalleberg (ed.), *Research in Social Stratification and Mobility*. Greenwich, Conn.: JAI Press, pp. 3–84.

———, Donald J. Truman, and Wout C. Ultee. 1991. "Comparative Intergenerational Stratification Research," in W. Richard Scott (ed.), *Annual Review of Sociology, 1991*. Palo Alto, Calif.: Annual Reviews, pp. 277–302.

Garber, H., and F. R. Herber. 1977. "The Milwaukee Project: Indications of the Effectiveness of Early Intervention in Preventing Mental Retardation," in Peter Mittler (ed.), *Research to Practice in Mental Retardation*, vol. 1. Baltimore: University Park Press, pp. 119–127.

Gardner, Carol Brooks. 1989. "Analyzing Gender in Public Places: Rethinking Goffman's Vision of Everyday Life," *American Sociologist*, **20**(Spring):42–56.

———. 1990. "Safe Conduct: Women, Crime, and Self in Public Places," *Social Problems*, **37**(August):311–328.

Garfinkel, Harold. 1956. "Conditions of Successful Degradation Ceremonies," *American Journal of Sociology*, **61**(March): 420–424.

Gargan, Edward A. 1992a. "Bound to Looms by Poverty and Fear, Boys in India Make a Few Men Rich," *New York Times* (July 9), p. A8.

———. 1992b. "Fundamentalism in South Asia Isn't All Islam," *New York Times* (December 13), sec. 4, pp. 1, 3.

Garreau, Joel. 1991. *Edge City: Life on the New Frontier*. New York: Doubleday.

Gartner, Alan, and Dorothy Kerzner Lipsky. 1987. "Beyond Special Education: Toward a Quality System for All Students," *Harvard Educational Review*, **57**(November):367–395.

Garza, Melita Marie. 1993. "The Cordi-Marian Annual Cotillion," *Chicago Tribune* (May 7), sec. C, pp. 1–5.

Gates, Henry Louis, Jr. 1991. "Delusions of Grandeur," *Sports Illustrated*, **75**(August 19):78.

———. 1992. "Whose Canon Is It, Anyway?" in Paul Berman (ed.), *Debating P.C.: The Controversy over Political Correctness on College Campuses.* New York: Dell, pp. 190–200.

Gaylord, Mark S., and John F. Galliher. 1987. *The Criminology of Edwin Sutherland.* Rutgers, N.J.: Transaction.

Gecas, Viktor. 1981. "Contexts of Socialization," in Morris Rosenberg and Ralph H. Turner (eds.), *Social Psychology: Sociological Perspectives.* New York: Basic Books, pp. 165–199.

———. 1982. "The Self-Concept," in Ralph H. Turner and James F. Short, Jr. (eds.), *Annual Review of Sociology, 1982.* Palo Alto, Calif.: Annual Reviews, pp. 1–33.

———. 1992. "Socialization," in Edgar F. Borgatta and Marie L. Borgatta (eds.), *Encyclopedia of Sociology,* vol. 4. New York: Macmillan, pp. 1863–1872.

Gelles, Richard J. 1993. "Family Violence," in Craig Calhoun and George Ritzer (eds.), *Introduction to Social Problems.* New York: McGraw-Hill, pp. 553–571.

——— and Claire Pedrick Cornell. 1990. *Intimate Violence in Families* (2d ed.). Newbury Park, Calif.: Sage.

———, Murray A. Straus, and John W. Harrop. 1988. "Has Family Violence Decreased? A Response to J. Timothy Stocks," *Journal of Marriage and Family,* **50**(February):286–291.

Gendell, Murray, and Jacob S. Siegel. 1993. "Retirement Quandry," *Population Today,* **21**(March):6–7, 9.

George, Susan. 1988. *A Fate Worse than Debt.* New York: Grove.

Georges, Christopher. 1992. "Old Money," *Washington Monthly,* **24**(June): 16–21.

Gerbner, George, et al. 1984. "Summary: Religion and Television." Philadelphia: Annenberg School of Communications.

Gerstel, Naomi. 1987. "Divorce and Stigma," *Social Problems,* **34**(April): 172–186.

Gerth, H. H., and C. Wright Mills. 1958. *From Max Weber: Essays in Sociology.* New York: Galaxy.

Gesensway, Deborah, and Mindy Roseman. 1987. *Beyond Words: Images from America's Concentration Camps.* Ithaca, N.Y.: Cornell University Press.

Gest, Ted. 1985. "Are White-Collar Crooks Getting Off Too Easy?" *U.S. News and World Report,* **99**(July 1):43.

Giago, Tim, and Sharon Illoway. 1982. "Dying Too Young," *Civil Rights Quarterly Perspective,* **14**(Fall):29, 31, 33.

Gibbs, Nancy. 1993. "Rx for Death," *Time,* **141**(May 31):34–39.

Giddings, Paula. 1984. *When and Where I Enter.* New York: Morrow.

Gilbert, Nigel (ed.). 1993. *Researching Social Life.* Newbury Park, Calif.: Sage.

Gilinsky, Rhoda M. 1983. "Day Care Finds a Home on Campus," *New York Times* (January 9), sec. 12, p. 1.

Gilly, M. C. 1988. "Sex Roles in Advertising: A Comparison of Television Advertisements in Australia, Mexico, and the United States," *Journal of Marketing,* **52**(April):75–85.

Gilmore, David. 1990. "Men and Women in Southern Spain: 'Domestic Power' Revisited," *American Anthropologist,* **92** (December):953–970.

Gimenez, Martha E. 1987. "Black Family: Vanishing or Unattainable," *Humanity and Society,* **11**(November):420–439.

Giordano, Peggy C., Stephen A. Cernkovich, and Alfred DeMaris. 1993. "The Family and Peer Relations of Black Adolescents," *Journal of Marriage and Family,* **55**(May):277–287.

Gittelsohn, John. 1987. "An Asian Norma Rae," *U.S. News and World Report,* **103** (September 14):52.

Glascock, Anthony P. 1990. "By Any Other Name, It Is Still Killing: A Comparison of the Treatment of the Elderly in American and Other Societies," in Jay Sokolovsky (ed.), *The Cultural Context of Aging: Worldwide Perspectives.* New York: Bergen and Garvey, pp. 44–56.

Glaub, Gerald R. 1990. "Gap between State Funding and School Spending Widens," *Illinois School Board Journal,* **58**(July–August):24–26.

Glazer, Nathan, and Mark Lilla (eds.). 1987. *The Public Face of Architecture: Civic Culture and Public Spaces.* New York: Free Press.

Gober, Patricia. 1993. "Americans on the Move," *Population Bulletin,* **48**(November).

———. and Michelle Behr. 1982. "Central Cities and Suburbs as Distinct Place Types: Myth or Fact," *Economic Geography,* **58**(October):371–385.

Godwin, Deborah D., and John Scanzoni. 1989. "Couple Consensus during Marital Joint Decision-Making: A Context, Process, Outcome Model," *Journal of Marriage and the Family,* **31**(November):943–956.

Goffman, Erving. 1959. *The Presentation of Self in Everyday Life.* New York: Doubleday.

———. 1961. *Asylums: Essays on the Social Situation of Mental Patients and Other Inmates.* Garden City, N.Y.: Doubleday.

———. 1963a. *Stigma: Notes on Management of Spoiled Identity.* Englewood Cliffs, N.J.: Prentice-Hall.

———. 1963b. *Behavior in Public Places.* New York: Free Press.

———. 1971. *Relations in Public.* New York: Basic Books.

———. 1977. "The Arrangement between the Sexes," *Theory and Society,* **4**:301–331.

Goldin, Claudia. 1990. *Understanding the Gender Gap: An Economic History of American Women.* New York: Oxford University Press.

Goldman, Ari L. 1992. "Reading, Writing, Arithmetic, and Arabic," *New York Times* (October 3), pp. 25–27.

———. 1993. "Religion Notes," *New York Times* (April 24), p. 11.

Goldscheider, Calvin. 1986. *Jewish Continuity and Change: Emerging Patterns in America.* Bloomington: Indiana University Press.

Goldstein, Melvyn C., and Cynthia M. Beall. 1981. "Modernization and Aging in the Third and Fourth World: Views from the Rural Hinterland in Nepal," *Human Organization,* **40**(Spring):48–55.

Goldstein, Michael S., Dennis T. Joffe, Carol Sutherland, and Josie Wilson. 1987. "Holistic Physicians: Implications for the Study of the Medical Profession," *Journal of Health and Social Behavior,* **28**(June):103–119.

Goleman, Daniel. 1983. "The Electronic Rorschach," *Psychology Today,* **17**(February):36–43.

———. 1990. "Anger over Racism Is Seen as a Cause of Blacks' High Blood Pressure," *New York Times* (April 24), p. C3.

———. 1991. "New Ways to Battle Bias: Fight Acts, Not Feelings," *New York Times* (July 16), pp. C1, C8.

Goodale, Jane C. 1971. *Tiwi Wives: A Study*

of Women of Melville Island, North Australia. Seattle: University of Washington Press.

Goode, William J. 1959. "The Theoretical Importance of Love," *American Sociological Review,* **24**(February):38–47.

———. 1976. "Family Disorganization," in Robert Merton and Robert Nisbet (eds.), *Contemporary Social Problems* (4th ed.). New York: Harcourt Brace Jovanovich, pp. 511–554.

———. 1993. *World Changes in Divorce Patterns.* New Haven, Conn.: Yale University Press.

Goodgame, Dan. 1993. "Welfare for the Well-Off," *Time,* **141**(February 22): 36–38.

Goodman, Ellen. 1977. "Great (Male) Expectations," *Washington Post* (September 3), p. A11.

Gordon, C. Wayne. 1955. "The Role of the Teacher in the School Structure of the High School," *Journal of Educational Sociology,* **29**(September):21–29.

Gordon, Michael R. 1993. "Pentagon Report Tells of Aviators 'Debauchery,'" *New York Times* (April 24), pp. 1, 9.

Gordon, Milton M. 1988. *The Scope of Sociology.* New York: Oxford University Press.

Gordus, Jeanne Prial, and Karen Yamakawa. 1988. "Incomparable Losses: Economic and Labor Market Outcomes for Unemployed Female versus Male Autoworkers," in Patricia Voydanoff and Linda C. Majka (eds.), *Families and Economic Distress.* Newbury Park, Calif.: Sage, pp. 38–54.

Goslin, David A. 1965. *The Schools in Contemporary Society.* Glenview, Ill.: Scott, Foresman.

Gottdiener, Mark. 1985. *The Social Production of Urban Space.* Austin: University of Texas Press.

——— and Joe R. Feagin. 1988. "The Paradigm Shift in Urban Sociology," *Urban Affairs Quarterly,* **24**(December):163–187.

Gough, E. Kathleen. 1974. "Nayar: Central Kerala," in David Schneider and E. Kathleen Gough (eds.), *Matrilineal Kinship.* Berkeley: University of California Press, pp. 298–384.

Gould, Peter, and Joseph Kabel. 1993. "The Geography of AIDS," *Atlantic Monthly,* **271**(January):90–91.

Gouldner, Alvin. 1950. *Studies in Leadership.* New York: Harper and Row.

———. 1960. "The Norm of Reciprocity," *American Sociological Review,* **25**(April): 161–177.

———. 1962. "Anti-Minotaur: The Myth of a Value-Free Sociology," *Social Problems,* **9**(Winter):199–213.

———. 1970. *The Coming Crisis of Western Sociology.* New York: Basic Books.

Gove, Walter R. 1970. "Societal Reaction as an Explanation of Mental Illness: An Evaluation," *American Sociological Review,* **35**(October):873–884.

———. 1975. "The Labelling Theory of Mental Illness: A Reply to Scheff," *American Sociological Review,* **40**(April):242–248.

——— (ed.). 1980. *The Labelling of Deviance* (2d ed.). Beverly Hills, Calif.: Sage.

———. 1987. "Sociobiology Misses the Mark: An Essay on Why Biology but Not Sociobiology Is Very Relevant to Sociology," *American Sociologist,* **18**(Fall): 258–277.

——— and Michael Hughes. 1979. "Possible Causes of the Apparent Sex Differences in Physical Health: An Empirical Investigation," *American Sociological Review,* **44**(February):126–146.

Graber, Laurel. 1992. "Waiting for the Backlash," *New York Times Book Review* (May 17), sec. 7, p. 43.

Grady, William. 1993. "FCC Member: Electronic Highway to Bypass Poor," *Chicago Tribune* (November 6), p. 1.

Graham, Saxon, and Leo G. Reeder. 1979. "Social Epidemiology of Chronic Diseases," in Howard E. Freeman, Sol Levine, and Leo G. Reeder (eds.), *Handbook in Medical Sociology* (3d ed.). Englewood Cliffs, N.J.: Prentice-Hall.

Gramsci, Antonio. 1929. *Selections from the Prison Notebooks,* Quintin Hoare and Geoffrey Nowell Smith (eds.). London: Lawrence and Wishort.

Gray, Jane. 1991. "Tea Room Revisited: A Study of Male Homosexuals in a Public Setting." Paper presented at the annual meeting of the American Criminal Justice Society, Nashville, Tenn.

Greeley, Andrew M. 1972. *The Denominational Society.* Glenview, Ill.: Scott, Foresman.

———. 1989a. "Protestant and Catholic: Is the Analogical Imagination Extinct?" *American Sociological Review,* **54**(August): 485–502.

———. 1989b. *Religious Change in America.* Cambridge, Mass.: Harvard University Press.

Green, Dan S., and Edwin D. Driver. 1978. "Introduction," in Dan S. Green and Edwin D. Driver (eds.), *W.E.B. DuBois on Sociology and the Black Community.* Chicago: University of Chicago Press, pp. 1–60.

Greenfield, Karl Taro. 1993. "Erasing History," *The Nation,* **256**(April 19):508–509.

Greenfield, Sheldon, Dolores M. Blanco, Robert M. Elashoff, and Patricia A. Ganz. 1987. "Patterns of Care Related to Age of Breast Cancer Patients," *Journal of the American Medical Association,* **257**(May 22–29):2766–2770.

Greenhouse, Linda. 1991. "5 Justices Uphold U.S. Rule Curbing Abortion Advice," *New York Times* (May 24), pp. A1, A18.

———. 1992. "High Court, 5-4, Affirms Right to Abortion but Allows Most of Pennsylvania's Limits," *New York Times* (June 30), pp. A1, A15.

———. 1993a. "Court, Citing Religious Freedom, Voids a Ban on Animal Sacrifice," *New York Times* (June 12), pp. 1, 8.

———. 1993b. "High Court Backs Policy of Halting Haitian Refugees," *New York Times* (June 22), pp. 1, 18.

Greil, Arthur L. 1991. *Not Yet Pregnant.* New Brunswick, N.J.: Rutgers University Press.

Grissmer, David, and Sheila Kirby. 1987. *Teacher Attrition: The Uphill Climb to Staff the Nation's Schools.* Santa Monica, Calif.: Rand Corp.

Gross, Edward, and Gregory P. Stone. 1964. "Embarrassment and the Analysis of Role Requirements," *American Journal of Sociology,* **70**(July):1–15.

Gross, Jane. 1987. "An Ever-Widening Epidemic Tears at the City's Life and Spirit," *New York Times* (March 16), p. 17.

———. 1991a. "Surge of Rock Fans, Then Death, Grief, and Anger," *New York Times* (January 25), pp. A1, A16.

———. 1991b. "Female Surgeon's Quitting Touches Nerve at Medical Schools," *New York Times* (July 14), p. 10.

Guemple, D. Lee. 1969. "Human Resource Management: The Dilemma of the Aging Eskimo," *Sociological Symposium,* **2**(Spring):59–74.

Guillemin, Jeanne. 1992. "Planning to Die," *Society,* **29**(July–August):29–33.

Gunset, George. 1992. "Farm a Future for Few," *Chicago Tribune* (November 22), sec. 7, pp. 1, 9.

Guralnik, Jack M., et al. [5 authors]. 1993. "Educational Status and Active Life Expectancy among Older Blacks and Whites," *New England Journal of Medicine,* **329**(July 8):110–116.

Gutiérrez, Gustavo. 1990. "Theology and the Social Sciences," in Paul E. Sigmund, *Liberation Theology at the Crossroads: Democracy or Revolution?* New York: Oxford University Press, pp. 214–225.

Hacker, Andrew. 1964. "Power to Do What?" in Irving Louis Horowitz (ed.), *The New Sociology.* New York: Oxford University Press, pp. 134–146.

———. 1992. *Two Nations: Black and White, Separate, Hostile, Unequal.* New York: Scribner.

Hacker, Helen Mayer. 1951. "Women as a Minority Group," *Social Forces,* **30**(October):60–69.

———. 1973. "Sex Roles in Black Society: Caste versus Caste." Paper presented at the annual meeting of the American Sociological Association, New York City, August 30.

———. 1974. "'Women as a Minority Group,' Twenty Years Later," in Florence Denmark (ed.), *Who Discriminates against Women.* Beverly Hills, Calif.: Sage, pp. 124–134.

Hadjian, Ani, and Lorraine Tritto. 1993. "The World's Largest Industrial Corporations," *Fortune,* **128**(July 26):190–193, 196–197, 200–204, 207–210, 212–215, 218–231.

Hadley, Jack, Earl P. Steinberg, and Judith Feder. 1991. "Comparison of Uninsured and Privately Insured Hospital Patients: Condition on Admission, Resource Use, and Outcome," *Journal of the American Medical Association,* **265** (January 16):374–379.

Hagan, John, and Patricia Parker. 1985. "White-Collar Crime and Punishment: The Class Structure and Legal Sanctioning of Securities Violations," *American Sociological Review,* **50**(June):302–316.

Hahn, Harlan. 1987. "Civil Rights for Disabled Americans: The Foundation of a Political Agenda," in Alan Gartner and Tom Joe (eds.), *Images of the Disabled, Disabling Images.* New York: Praeger, pp. 181–203.

Hahn, Robert A. 1985. "Culture-Bound Syndromes Unbound," *Social Science and Medicine,* **21**(2):165–171.

Haines, Valerie A. 1988. "Is Spencer's Theory an Evolutionary Theory?" *American Journal of Sociology,* **93**(March): 1200–1223.

Halal, William E. 1992. "The Information Technology Revolution," *Futurist,* **26** (July–August):10–15.

Haley, Alex. 1976. *Roots.* New York: Doubleday.

Hall, Edward T., and Mildred Reed Hall. 1990. *Understanding Cultural Differences.* Yarmouth, Maine: Intercultural Press.

Hall, Mimi. 1993a. "Abortion Poll: Militants' Tactics Deemed Improper," *USA Today* (March 16), p. 7A.

———. 1993b. "Painful Path of Homelessness," *USA Today* (December 9), p. 8A.

Hall, Peter. 1977. *The World Cities.* London: Weidenfeld and Nicolson.

Hall, Peter M. 1987. "Interactionism and the Study of Social Organization," *Social Quantity,* **28**(November 1):1–22.

Hall, Richard H. 1963. "The Concept of Bureaucracy: An Empirical Assessment," *American Journal of Sociology,* **69** (July):32–40.

Hall, Robert H. 1982. "The Truth about Brown Lung," *Business and Society Review,* **40**(Winter 1981–1982):15–20.

Haller, Max, Wolfgang König, Peter Krause, and Karin Kurz. 1990. "Patterns of Career Mobility and Structural Positions in Advanced Capitalist Societies: A Comparison of Men in Austria, France, and the United States," *American Sociological Review,* **50**(October): 579–603.

Halliday, M. A. K. 1978. *Language as Social Semiotic.* Baltimore: University Park Press.

Halperin, Jennifer. 1993. "Gender Differences in Lawmakers' Behavior," *Illinois Issues* (February 16), p. 16.

Hamm, Mark S. 1993. *American Skinheads: The Criminology and Control of Hate Crime.* Westport, Conn.: Greenwood.

Hancock, LynNell. 1990. "20 Years of Choice," *Village Voice,* **35**(July 10):11.

Haney, Craig, Curtis Banks, and Philip Zimbardo. 1973. "Interpersonal Dynamics in a Simulated Prison," *International Journal of Criminology and Penology,* **1**(February):69–97.

Harap, Louis. 1982. "Marxism and Religion: Social Functions of Religious Belief," *Jewish Currents,* **36**(January):12–17, 32–35.

Hardgrave, Robert L., Jr. 1969. *The Nadars of Tamilnad. The Political Culture of a Community of Change.* Berkeley: University of California Press.

Harding, Sue (ed.). 1987. *Feminism and Methodology.* Bloomington: Indiana University Press.

Hardy, Melissa. 1992. "Retirement," in Edgar F. Borgatta and Marie L. Borgatta (eds.), *Encyclopedia of Sociology,* vol. 3. New York: Macmillan, pp. 1663–1672.

Hare, A. Paul. 1992. "Group Size," in Edgar F. Borgatta and Marie L. Borgatta (eds.), *Encyclopedia of Sociology,* vol. 2. New York: Macmillan, pp. 788–791.

Harlow, Harry F. 1971. *Learning to Love.* New York: Ballantine.

Harrington, Michael. 1963. *The Other America: Poverty in the United States.* Baltimore: Penguin.

———. 1980. "The New Class and the Left," in B. Bruce-Briggs (ed.), *The New Class.* New Brunswick, N.J.: Transaction, pp. 123–138.

Harris, Chauncy D., and Edward Ullman. 1945. "The Nature of Cities," *Annals of the American Academy of Political and Social Sciences,* **242**(November):7–17.

Harris, Lou. 1987. *Inside America.* New York: Vintage.

Harris, Louis. 1993. *The Commonwealth Fund Survey of Women's Health.* New York: Commonwealth Fund.

Harris, Marlys. 1988. "Where Have All the Babies Gone?" *Money,* **17**(December): 164–176.

Harris, Marvin. 1980. *Culture, People, Nature* (3d ed.). New York: Harper and Row.

Harrison, Bennett, and Barry Bluestone. 1988. *The Great U-Turn.* New York: Basic Books.

Hartjen, Clayton A. 1978. *Crime and Criminalization* (2d ed.). New York: Praeger.

Hartmann, Heidi I. 1981. "The Family as

the Locus of Gender, Class, and Political Struggle: The Example of Housework," *Signs,* **6**(Spring):366–394.

Harvard Law Review. 1993. "Notes," **106** (June):1905–1925.

Hasbrook, Cynthia. 1986. "The Sport Participation–Social Class Relationship: Some Recent Youth Sport Participation Data," *Sociology of Sport Journal,* **3**(June): 154–159.

Hasson, Judi. 1992. "No Simple Cure for Sink System," *USA Today* (October 15), p. 5A.

Haub, Carl. 1988. "The World Population Crisis Was Forgotten, but Not Gone," *Washington Post National Weekly Edition,* **5**(September 5):23.

———— and Machiko Yanagishita. 1993. *World Population Data Sheet, 1993.* Washington, D.C.: Population Reference Bureau.

Haupt, Arthur. 1990. "UN Projections Rise Slightly Higher than 1989," *Population Today,* **18**(November):4.

Hauser, Robert M., and David B. Grusky. 1988. "Cross-National Variation in Occupational Distributions, Relative Mobility Chances, and Intergenerational Shifts in Occupational Distributions," *American Sociological Review,* **53**(October):723–741.

Havemann, Judith. 1988. "Sexual Harassment: The Personnel Problem That Won't Go Away," *Washington Post National Weekly Edition,* **5**(July 11–17): 30–31.

Haviland, William A. 1993. *Cultural Anthropology* (7th ed.). New York: Holt.

Hawkes, Nigel. 1993. "Make Haste When the North Wind Blows . . . ," *London Times* (January 23), p. 3.

Hawley, Amos H. 1950. *Human Ecology: A Theory of Community Structure.* New York: Ronald.

Hayes, Denis. 1990. "Earth Day 1990: Threshold of the Green Decade," *Natural History,* **99**(April):55–58, 67–70.

Hayes, Dianne Williams. 1993. "An Education in Violence: Assaults on Rise in Nation's Schools," *Black Issues in Higher Education,* **10**(July 29):18–20.

Hays, Constance L. 1988. "Study Says Blacks Face More Segregation than Other Groups," *New York Times* (November 23), p. A16.

Hayward, Mark D., William R. Grady, and Steven D. McLaughlin. 1987. "Changes in the Retirement Process," *Demography,* **25**(August):371–386.

Heaven, P. C., and J. M. Niewoudt. 1981. "Authoritarian Attitudes in South Africa," *Journal of Social Psychology,* **115** (December):277–278.

Heberle, Rudolf. 1968. "Social Movements: Types and Functions," in David Sills (ed.), *International Encyclopedia of the Social Sciences,* vol. 14. New York: Macmillan, pp. 438–444.

Hedges, Chris. 1993. "A Sickness in Egypt: Swooning," *New York Times* (April 18), p. 13.

Hedley, R. Alan. 1992. "Industrialization in Less Developed Countries," in Edgar F. Borgatta and Marie L. Borgatta (eds.), *Encyclopedia of Sociology,* vol. 2. New York: Macmillan, pp. 914–920.

Heer, David M. 1975. *Society and Population* (2d ed.). Englewood Cliffs, N.J.: Prentice-Hall.

Heffernan, Orly. 1992. *Los Angeles City Cold Weather Shelter Program Survey Analysis.* Los Angeles: UCLA Graduate School of Architecture and Urban Planning.

Heikes, E. Joel. 1991. "When Men Are the Minority: The Case of Men in Nursing," *Sociological Quarterly,* **32**(3):389–401.

Heisel, Marsel A. 1985. *Aging in the Context of Population Policies in Developing Countries.* New York: United Nations.

Heller, Scott. 1987. "Research on Coerced Behavior Leads Berkeley Sociologist to Key Role as Expert Witness in Controversial Lawsuits," *Chronicle of Higher Education,* **33**(March 8):1, 13.

Hendricks, Jon. 1982. "The Elderly in Society: Beyond Modernization," *Social Science History,* **6**(Summer):321–345.

Hendry, Joy. 1981. *Marriage in Changing Japan.* New York: St. Martin's.

Henley, Nancy, Mykol Hamilton, and Barrie Thorne. 1985. "Womanspeak and Manspeak: Sex Differences and Sexism in Communication, Verbal and Nonverbal," in Alice G. Sargent (ed.), *Beyond Sex Roles* (2d ed.). St. Paul, Minn.: West, pp. 168–185.

Henneberger, Melinda. 1993. "Out of Sight, Out of Mind: Suburbs' Hidden Homeless," *New York Times* (March 4), pp. B1, B6.

Hennon, Charles B., and Ramona Marotz-Baden (eds.). 1987. "Rural Families:

Stability and Change," special issue of *Family Relations,* **36**(October):355–460.

Henry, Mary E. 1989. "The Function of Schooling: Perspectives from Rural Australia," *Discourse,* **9**(April):1–21.

Henry, Tamara. 1993. "Teacher Salaries Up 3.2% Again," *USA Today* (October 14), p. 3D.

Henshaw, Stanley K., and Jennifer Van Vort. 1989. "Teenage Abortion, Birth and Pregnancy Statistics: An Update," *Family Planning Perspective,* **21**(March–April):85–88.

Henslin, James M. (ed.). 1972. *Down to Earth Sociology.* New York: Free Press.

Hentoff, Nat. 1992. "The Silence of Anita Hill," *Village Voice,* **37**(January 21): 20–21.

Herbers, John. 1986. "Suburbs Absorb More Immigrants, Mostly the Affluent and Educated," *New York Times* (December 14), pp. 1, 22.

Herek, Gregory M., and Eric K. Glunt. 1988. "An Epidemic of Stigma," *American Psychologist,* **43**(November):886–891.

Hern, Warren. 1986. "Must Mr. Reagan Tolerate Abortion Clinic Violence?" *New York Times* (June 14), p. 27.

Hershey, Robert D., Jr. 1988. "Underground Economy Is Not Rising to the Bait," *New York Times* (January 24), p. E5.

Herskovits, Melville J. 1930. *The Anthropometry of the American Negro.* New York: Columbia University Press.

————. 1941. *The Myth of the Negro Past.* New York: Harper.

————. 1943. "The Negro in Bahia, Brazil: A Problem in Method," *American Sociological Review,* **8**(August):394–402.

Hertz, Rosanna. 1986. *More Equal than Others: Women and Men in Dual-Career Marriages.* Berkeley: University of California Press.

Hess, Beth B., and Elizabeth W. Markson. 1980. *Aging and Old Age: An Introduction to Social Gerontology.* New York: Macmillan.

———— and ———— (eds.). 1991. *Growing Old in America* (4th ed.). New Brunswick, N.J.: Transaction.

Hess, John L. 1990. "Confessions of a Greedy Geezer," *The Nation,* **250**(April 2):451–455.

Hetherington, E. Mavis. 1979. "Divorce: A

Child's Perspective," *American Psychologist,* **34**(October):851–858.

Hewitt, Paul S., and Neil Howe. 1988. "Future of Generational Politics," *Generations* (Spring), pp. 10–13.

Hiatt, Fred. 1988. "Japanese Kids Are Licking Their Chopsticks," *Washington Post National Weekly Edition,* **5**(March 14–20):19.

Hicks, Jonathan P. 1991. "Women in Waiting," *New York Times* (November 3), sec. 4A, p. 19.

Hill, Robert B. 1972. *The Strengths of Black Families.* New York: Emerson.

———. 1987. "The Future of Black Families," *Colloqui* (Spring), pp. 22–28.

Hillebrand, Barbara. 1992. "Midlife Crisis," *Chicago Tribune* (May 10), sec. 6, pp. 1, 11.

Hilts, Philip J. 1990a. "U.S. Returns to 1820's in Care of Mentally Ill, Study Asserts," *New York Times* (September 12), p. A28.

———. 1990b. "New Study Challenges Estimates of Adopting a Child," *New York Times* (December 10), p. B10.

———. 1991. "Women Still Behind in Medicine," *New York Times* (September 10), p. C7.

———. 1992. "More Teen-agers Being Slain by Guns," *New York Times* (June 10), p. A19.

Hirasawa, Yasumasa. 1992. "The Myth of Homogeneous Japan," *Focus,* **20**(July): 5–6.

Hirschi, Travis, and Michael Gottfredson (eds.). 1994. *The Generality of Deviance.* Rutgers, N.J.: Transaction.

Hively, Robert (ed.). 1990. *The Lurking Evil: Racial and Ethnic Conflict on the College Campus.* Washington, D.C.: American Association of State Colleges and Universities.

Hochschild, Arlie Russell. 1973. "A Review of Sex Role Research," *American Journal of Sociology,* **78**(January):1011–1029.

———. 1990. "The Second Shift: Employed Women and Putting in Another Day of Work at Home," *Utne Reader,* **38**(March–April):66–73.

———, with Anne Machung. 1989. *The Second Shift: Working Parents and the Revolution at Home.* New York: Viking Penguin.

Hodge, Robert W., and Peter H. Rossi.

1964. "Occupational Prestige in the United States, 1925–1963," *American Journal of Sociology,* **70**(November): 286–302.

Hoebel, E. Adamson. 1949. *Man in the Primitive World: An Introduction to Anthropology.* New York: McGraw-Hill.

Hoecker-Drysdale, Susan. 1992. *Harriet Martineau: The First Woman Sociologist.* Oxford, Eng.: Berg.

Hoffman, Lois Waldis. 1977. "Changes in Family Roles, Socialization, and Sex Differences," *American Psychologist,* **32**(August):644–657.

———. 1985. "The Changing Genetics/Socialization Balance," *Journal of Social Issues,* **41**(Spring):127–148.

——— and F. Ivan Nye. 1975. *Working Mothers.* San Francisco: Jossey-Bass.

Hoge, Dean R., and David A. Roozen. 1979. *Understanding Church Growth and Decline, 1950–1979.* New York: Pilgrim.

Holcomb, Betty. 1988. "Nurses Fight Back," *Ms.,* **16**(July):72–78.

Hollingshead, August B. 1975. *Elmtown's Youth and Elmtown Revisited.* New York: Wiley.

Holmes, Steven A. 1990a. "House, 265–145, Votes to Widen Day Care Programs in the Nation," *New York Times* (March 30), pp. A1, A14.

———. 1990b. "Day Care Bill Marks a Turn toward Help for the Poor," *New York Times* (April 8), p. E4.

———. 1990c. "House Passes Measure on Family Leave," *New York Times* (May 11), p. B6.

———. 1993. "Clinton Reverses Policies at U.N. on Rights Issues," *New York Times* (May 9), pp. 1, 15.

Holohan, Ann. 1977. "Diagnosis: The End of Transition," in A. Davis and G. Horobin (eds.), *Medical Encounters: The Experience of Illness and Treatment.* New York: St. Martin's, pp. 87–97.

Homans, George C. 1979. "Nature versus Nurture: A False Dichotomy," *Contemporary Sociology,* **8**(May):345–348.

Hong, Lawrence K., and Robert W. Duff. 1977. "Becoming a Taxi-Dancer: The Significance of Neutralization in a Semi-Deviant Occupation," *Sociology of Work and Occupations,* **4**(August): 327–342.

Hoppe, Robert A., and Herman Bluestone. 1987. "Economic and Social

Conditions Where Black Farmers Live." Paper presented at the annual meeting of the Eastern Sociological Society, Boston.

Horgan, John. 1993. "Eugenics Revisited," *Scientific American,* **268**(June): 122–128, 130–133.

Horn, Jack C., and Jeff Meer. 1987. "The Vintage Years," *Psychology Today,* **21** (May):76–77, 80–84, 88–90.

Hornblower, Margot. 1988. "Gray Power!" *Time,* **131**(January 4):36–37.

Horowitz, Helen Lefkowitz. 1987. *Campus Life.* Chicago: University of Chicago Press.

Horowitz, Irving Louis. 1983. *C. Wright Mills: An American Utopian.* New York: Free Press.

Horwitt, Sanford D. 1989. *Let Them Call Me Rebel: Saul Alinsky—His Life and Legacy.* New York: Knopf.

Hosokawa, William K. 1969. *Nisei: The Quiet Americans.* New York: Morrow.

Houseman, John. 1972. *Run Through.* New York: Simon and Schuster.

Hout, Michael. 1988. "More Universalism, Less Structural Mobility: The American Occupational Structure in the 1980s," *American Journal of Sociology,* **93**(May): 1358–1400.

Howard, Michael C. 1989. *Contemporary Cultural Anthropology* (3d ed.). Glenview, Ill.: Scott, Foresman.

Howe, Neil, and Bill Strauss. 1993. *13th Gen: Abort, Retry, Ignore, Fail?* New York: Vintage.

Howery, Carla B. 1993. "Sociology of Gambling? You Bet!" *Footnotes,* **21** (December):4.

Howlett, Debbie, and Judy Keen. 1991. "Role in Military Splits Minorities," *USA Today* (February 18), p. 2A.

Hoyenga, Katharine Blick, and Kermit T. Hoyenga. 1993. *Gender-Related Differences: Origins and Outcomes.* Boston: Allyn and Bacon.

Huang, Gary. 1988. "Daily Addressing Ritual: A Cross-Cultural Study." Paper presented at the annual meeting of the American Sociological Association, Atlanta.

Huber, Bettina J. 1985. *Employment Patterns in Sociology: Recent Trends and Future Prospects.* Washington, D.C.: American Sociological Association.

———. 1987. "Graduate Education and

the Academic Job Market," *American Sociologist,* **18**(Spring):46–52.

Huber, Joan, and Beth E. Schneider (eds.). 1992. *The Social Context of AIDS.* Newbury Park, Calif.: Sage.

Hubler, Shawn. 1992. "South L.A.'s Poverty Rate Worse than '65," *Los Angeles Times* (May 11), pp. A1, A22–A23.

Hudgins, John L. 1992. "The Strengths of Black Families Revisited," *Urban Review,* **15**(2):9–20.

Huff, Darrell. 1954. *How to Lie with Statistics.* New York: Norton.

Hughes, Everett. 1945. "Dilemmas and Contradictions of Status," *American Journal of Sociology,* **50**(March):353–359.

Hughes, Langston. 1958. *The Langston Hughes Reader.* New York: Braziller.

Hugick, Larry, and Lydia Saad. 1992. "Public Believes Taxes Unfairly Hit Middle Class, Poor," *Gallup Poll Monthly,* **319**(April):32–35.

Hull, Jon D. 1993. "The Knife in the Book Bag," *Time,* **141**(February 8):37.

Humphreys, Laud. 1970a. "Tearoom Trade," *Transaction,* **7**(January):10–25.

———. 1970b. *Tearoom Trade: Impersonal Sex in Public Places.* Chicago: Aldine.

———. 1975. *Tearoom Trade: Impersonal Sex in Public Places* (enlarged ed.). Chicago: Aldine.

Hunt, Geoffrey, et al. [4 authors]. 1993. "Changes in Prison Culture: Prison Gangs and the Case of the 'Pepsi Generation,'" *Social Problems,* **40**(August): 398–401.

Hunter, Herbert M., and Sameer Y. Abraham. 1987. *Race, Class, and the World Systems: The Sociology of Oliver C. Cox.* New York: Monthly Review.

Hunter, James Davison. 1985. "Conservative Protestantism," in Phillip E. Hammond (ed.), *The Sacred in a Secular Age.* Berkeley: University of California Press, pp. 150–166.

———. 1991. *Culture Wars: The Struggle to Define America.* New York: Basic Books.

Hurh, Won Moo, and Kwang Chung Kim. 1986. "The 'Success' Image of Asian Americans: Its Validity, Practical and Theoretical Implications." Paper presented at the annual meeting of the American Sociological Association, New York City.

——— and ———. 1989. "The 'Success' Image of Asian Americans: Its Validity, and Its Practical and Theoretical Implications," *Ethnic and Racial Studies,* **12**(October):512–538.

——— and ———. 1990. "Religious Participation of Korean Immigrants in the United States," *Journal for the Scientific Study of Religion,* **29**(1):19–34.

——— and ———. 1994. *Korean Immigrants in America: A Structural Analysis of Ethnic Confinement and Adhesive Adaptation.* Rutherford, N.J.: Fairleigh Dickinson University Press.

Hurn, Christopher J. 1985. *The Limits and Possibilities of Schooling* (2d ed.). Boston: Allyn and Bacon.

Ibrahim, Youffef M. 1993. "Muslims' Fury Falls on Egypt's Christians," *New York Times* (March 15), pp. A1, A8.

Imhoff, Gary (ed.). 1990. *Learning in Two Languages.* New Brunswick, N.J.: Transaction.

Ingrassia, Michele. 1993. "Daughters of Murphy Brown," *Newsweek,* **122**(August 2):58–59.

Inhaber, Herbert. 1992a. "Yard Sale: Society Should Bid for the Right to Site Its Prisons and Its Dumps," *The Sciences,* **32**(January–February):16–21.

———. 1992b. "Of LULUs, NIMBYs, and NIMTOOs," *Public Interest,* **107**(Spring): 52–64.

Inter-Parliamentary Union. 1993. "Fewer Women in Parliament, New IPU Survey Reveals." Press release. Geneva, Switzerland: Inter-Parliamentary Union.

Isaacson, Walter. 1989. "Should Gays Have Marriage Rights?" *Time,* **134**(November 20):101–102.

Israel, Glenn D., and Steven Stack. 1987. "Another Look at Celebrities and Suicide." Paper presented at the annual meeting of the American Sociological Association, Chicago.

Jackson, Elton F., Charles R. Tittle, and Mary Jean Burke. 1986. "Offense-Specific Models of the Differential Association Process," *Social Problems,* **33** (April):335–356.

Jackson, Kenneth T. 1986. *Crabgrass Frontier: The Suburbanization of the United States.* New York: Oxford University Press.

Jackson, Philip W. 1968. *Life in Classrooms.* New York: Holt.

Jacobs, Jerry A. 1990. *Revolving Doors: Sex Segregation in Women's Careers.* Palo Alto, Calif.: Stanford University Press.

Jacobs, Paul, and Saul Landau (eds.). 1966. *The New Radicals.* New York: Vintage.

Jacobson, Jodi. 1993. "Closing the Gender Gap in Development," in Lester R. Brown (ed.), *State of the World, 1993.* New York: Norton, pp. 61–79.

Jacoby, Henry. 1973. *The Bureaucratization of the World.* Berkeley: University of California Press.

Jaffe, Peter G., David A. Wolfe, and Susan Kaye Wilson. 1990. *Children of Battered Women.* Newbury Park, Calif.: Sage.

Jaimes, M. Annette (ed.). 1992. *The State of Native America.* Boston: South End.

Janis, Irving. 1967. *Victims of Groupthink.* Boston: Houghton Mifflin.

Jarvis, Heather. 1990. "A Nation Wearied by War Emerges from Oblivion," *Times Educational Supplement* (October 12), p. 19.

Jasper, James M., and Dorothy Nelken. 1992. *The Animal Rights Crusade: The Growth of a Moral Protest.* New York: Free Press.

Javna, John. 1986. *Cult TV.* New York: St. Martin's.

Jean, François. 1992. *Populations in Danger: Médecins Sans Frontières.* London: John Libbey.

Jenkins, Richard. 1991. "Disability and Social Stratification," *British Journal of Sociology,* **42**(December):557–580.

Jenness, Valerie. 1991. "Can Coyote Guard the Chicken Coop?: Prostitution and AIDS Activism." Paper presented at the annual meeting of the Society for the Study of Social Problems, Cincinnati.

———. 1992. "In Search of Legitimacy: Prostitutes' Rights Organizations and Contemporary Feminism." Paper presented at the annual meeting of the Pacific Sociological Association, Spokane, Wash.

———. 1993. *Making It Work: The Prostitutes' Rights Movement in Perspective.* New York: Aldine De Gruyter.

Jennings, Jerry T. 1993. "Voting and Registration in the Election of November 1992," *Current Population Reports,* ser. P-20, no. 466. Washington, D.C.: U.S. Government Printing Office.

Jennings, M. Kent, and Richard G. Niemi. 1981. *Generations and Politics.* Princeton, N.J.: Princeton University Press.

Johnson, Benton. 1975. *Functionalism in Modern Sociology: Understanding Talcott Parsons*. Morristown, N.J.: General Learning.

Johnson, Charles S. 1939. "Race Relations and Social Change," in Edgar T. Thompson (ed.), *Race Relations and the Race Problem*. Durham, N.C.: Duke University Press, pp. 217–303.

Johnson, Dirk. 1987. "Fear of AIDS Stirs New Attacks on Homosexuals," *New York Times* (April 24), p. 12.

———. 1990. "Population Decline in Rural America: A Product of Advances in Technology," *New York Times* (September 11), p. A20.

———. 1991. "Census Finds Many Claiming New Identity: Indian," *New York Times* (March 5), pp. A1, A6.

———. 1992. "A Quiet Exodus by the Young Leaves the Future of Family Farms in Doubt," *New York Times* (June 9), p. A22.

———. 1993. "More and More, the Single Parent Is Dad," *New York Times* (August 31), pp. A1, A15.

Johnson, Mary. 1989. "Enabling Act," *The Nation*, **249**(October 23):446.

Johnson, Richard A. 1985. *American Fads*. New York: Beech Tree.

Johnson, William Weber. 1961. *Mexico*. New York: Time-Life.

Johnstone, Ronald L. 1988. *Religion in Society* (3d ed.). Englewood Cliffs, N.J.: Prentice-Hall.

Joint Center for Political Studies. 1992. *National Roster of Black Elected Officials, 1992*. Washington: Joint Center for Political Studies.

Jones, Elise F., et al. [8 authors]. 1985. "Teenage Pregnancy in Developed Countries: Determinants and Policy Implications," *Family Planning Perspectives*, **17**(March–April):53–63.

———. 1986. *Teenage Pregnancy in Industrialized Countries*. New Haven, Conn., and London: Yale University Press.

Jones, James T., IV. 1988. "Harassment Is Too Often Part of the Job," *USA Today* (August 8), p. 5D.

Jones, Landon Y. 1980. *Great Expectations: America and the Baby Boom Generation*. New York: Ballantine.

Jones, Stephen R. G. 1992. "Was There a Hawthorne Effect?" *American Journal of Sociology*, **98**(November):451–568.

Juhasz, Anne McCreary. 1989. "Black Adolescents' Significant Others," *Social Behavior and Personality*, **17**(2):211–214.

Kagay, Michael M. 1991. "Poll Finds AIDS Causes Single People to Alter Behavior," *New York Times* (June 18), p. C3.

Kail, Barbara Lynn, and Eugene Litwak. 1989. "Family, Friends and Neighbors: The Role of Primary Groups in Preventing the Misuse of Drugs," *Journal of Drug Issues*, **19**(2):261–282.

Kalish, Richard A. 1985. *Death, Grief, and Caring Relationships* (2d ed.). Monterey, Calif.: Brooks/Cole.

Kalleberg, Arne L. 1988. "Comparative Perspectives on Work Structures and Inequality," in W. Richard Scott and Judith Blake (eds.), *Annual Review of Sociology, 1988*. Palo Alto, Calif.: Annual Reviews, pp. 203–225.

Kalter, Neil. 1989. "Effects of Divorce on Boys versus Girls," *Medical Aspects of Human Sexuality*, **23**(November):26, 31–34.

Kaminer, Wendy. 1984. *Women Volunteering: The Pleasure, Pain, and Politics of Unpaid Work from 1830 to the Present*. Garden City, N.Y.: Anchor/Doubleday.

———. 1992. *I'm Dysfunctional, You're Dysfunctional: The Recovery Movement and Other Self-Help Fashions*. Reading, Mass.: Addison-Wesley.

Kanter, Rosabeth Moss. 1977a. *Men and Women of the Corporation*. New York: Basic Books.

———. 1977b. "Some Effects of Proportions in Group Life: Skewed Sex Ratios and Responses to Token Women," *American Journal of Sociology*, **82**(5):965–990.

Kantrowitz, Barbara. 1988. "And Thousands More," *Newsweek*, **112**(December 12):58–59.

Kapferer, Jean-Noël. 1990. *Rumors: Uses, Interpretations, and Images*. New Brunswick, N.J.: Transaction.

———. 1992. "How Rumors Are Born," *Society*, **29**(July–August):53–60.

Kaplan, David A. 1991. "The Bank Robbery Boom," *Newsweek*, **119**(December 9):62–63.

Karlins, Marvin, Thomas Coffman, and Gary Walters. 1969. "On the Fading of Social Stereotypes: Studies in Three Generations of College Students," *Journal of Personality and Social Psychology*, **13**(September):1–16.

Kasarda, John D., and Morris Janowitz. 1974. "Community Attachment in Mass Society," *American Sociological Review*, **39**(June):328–339.

Kass, Leon R. 1991. "Suicide Made Easy: The Evil of 'Rational' Humaneness," *Commentary*, **92**(December):19–24.

Kasza, Gregory J. 1987. "Bureaucratic Politics in Radical Military Regimes," *American Political Science Review*, **81**(September):851–872.

Katovich, Michael A. 1987. Correspondence, June 1.

Katz, Michael. 1971. *Class, Bureaucracy, and the Schools: The Illusion of Educational Change in America*. New York: Praeger.

Kaufman, Gladis. 1985. "Power Relations in Middle-Class American Families," *Wisconsin Sociology*, **22**(Winter):13–23.

Kaufman, Michael T. 1993. "21 Reasons to Simply Ask, 'Why?'" *New York Times* (January 9), p. 27.

Kay, Paul, and Willett Kempton. 1984. "What Is the Sapir-Whorf Hypothesis?" *American Anthropologist*, **86**(March): 65–79.

Kearl, Michael C. 1989. *Endings: A Sociology of Death and Dying*. New York and Oxford, Eng.: Oxford University Press.

Keating, Noah, and Brenda Munro. 1988. "Farm Women/Farm Work," *Sex Roles*, **19**(August):155–168.

Keifer, Amy Jo. 1991. "The Death of a Farm," *New York Times* (June 30), p. E15.

Kellerman, Arthur L., et al. [10 authors]. 1993. "Gun Ownership as a Risk Factor for Homicide in the Home," *New England Journal of Medicine*, **329**(October 7):1084–1091.

Kelley, Dean M. 1979. "Is Religion a Dependent Variable," in Dean R. Hoge and David A. Roozen (eds.), *Understanding Church Growth and Decline: 1950–1978*. New York: Pilgrim, pp. 334–343.

Kelly, Dennis. 1990. "Tests, Salaries Are Top Concerns," *USA Today* (November 14), p. 5A.

———. 1993. "More States Join Move to Voucher Plan," *USA Today* (October 20), pp. 1A, 2A.

Kelsoe, John R., et al. [12 authors]. 1989. "Re-evaluation of the Linkage Relationship between Chromosome LTP

Loci and the Gene for Bipolar Affective Disorder in the Old Order Amish," *Nature*, **342**(November 16):238–243.

Kemper, Vicki, and Viveca Novak. 1991. "Health Care Reform: Don't Hold Your Breath," *Washington Post National Weekly Edition*, **8**(October 28):28.

Kennedy, Michael D. 1993. "The End of Soviet-Type Societies and the Future of Postcommunism," in Craig Calhoun and George Ritzer (eds.), *Social Problems*. New York: McGraw-Hill, pp. 643–664.

Kephart, William M., and William M. Zellner. 1994. *Extraordinary Groups: An Examination of Unconventional Life-Styles* (5th ed.). New York: St. Martin's.

Kerbo, Harold R. 1991. *Social Stratification and Inequality*. New York: McGraw-Hill.

Kerr, Clark. 1960. *Industrialization and Industrial Man: The Problems of Labor and Management in Economic Growth*. Cambridge, Mass.: Harvard University Press.

Kerr, Peter. 1986. "The New Homelessness Has Its Roots in Economics," *New York Times* (March 16), p. E5.

———. 1991. "Rural Towns Trying to Lure Retirees to Bolster Economy," *New York Times* (September 22), pp. 1, 30.

Kessler, Ronald C., J. Blake Turner, and James S. House. 1989. "Unemployment, Reemployment, and Emotional Functioning in a Community Sample," *American Sociological Review*, **54**(August): 648–657.

Kiefer, Christie W. 1990. "The Elderly in Modern Japan: Elite, Victims, or Plural Players?" in Jay Sokolovsky (ed.), *The Cultural Context of Aging: Worldwide Perspectives*. New York: Bergin and Garvey, pp. 181–193.

Kilborn, Peter T. 1992. "Big Change Likely as Law Bans Bias toward Disabled," *New York Times* (July 19), pp. 1, 24.

Kim, Illsoo. 1981. *New Urban Immigrants: The Korean Community in New York*. Princeton, N.J.: Princeton University Press.

———. 1988. "A New Theoretical Perspective on Asian Enterprises," *Amerasia*, **14**(Spring):xi–xiii.

Kim, Kwang Chung, and Won Moo Hurh. 1985. "The Wives of Korean Small Businessmen in the U.S.: Business Involvement and Family Roles," in Inn Sook

Lee (ed.), *Korean-American Women: Toward Self-Realization*. Mansfield, Ohio: Association of Korean Christian Scholars in North America, pp. 1–41.

Kimball, Roger. 1992. "The Periphery v. the Center: The MLA in Chicago," in Paul Berman (ed.), *Debating P.C.: The Controversy over Political Correctness on College Campuses*. New York: Dell, pp. 61–84.

Kimmel, Michael S. (ed.). 1987. *Changing Men*. Newbury Park, Calif.: Sage.

King, Martin Luther, Jr. 1968. *Where Do We Go from Here: Chaos or Community?* Boston: Beacon.

King, Stanley H. 1972. "Social-Psychological Factors in Illness," in Howard E. Freeman, Sol Levine, and Leo G. Reeder (eds.), *Handbook of Medical Sociology* (2d ed.). Englewood Cliffs, N.J.: Prentice-Hall, pp. 129–147.

Kinsella, Kevin. 1988. *Aging in the Third World*. International Population Reports, ser. P-95, no. 79. Washington, D.C.: U.S. Government Printing Office.

Kinzer, Stephen. 1993. "German Court Restricts Abortion, Angering Feminists and the East," *New York Times* (May 29), pp. 1, 3.

Kirby, Andrew. 1982. *The Politics of Location: An Introduction*. London: Methuen.

Kirchmeyer, Catherine. 1993. "Multicultural Task Groups: An Account of the Low Contribution Level of Minorities," *Small Group Research*, **24**(February): 127–148.

——— and Aaron Cohen. 1992. "Multicultural Groups: Their Performance and Reactions with Constructive Conflict," *Group and Organization Management*, **17**(June):153–170.

Kitagawa, Evelyn. 1972. "Socioeconomic Differences in the United States and Some Implications for Population Policy," in Charles F. Westoff and Robert Parke, Jr. (eds.), *Demographic and Social Aspects of Population Growth*. Washington, D.C.: U.S. Government Printing Office, pp. 87–110.

Kitchener, Richard F. 1991. "Jean Piaget: The Unknown Sociologist," *British Journal of Sociology*, **42**(September): 421–442.

Klapp, Orvin E. 1972. *Currents of Unrest: An Introduction to Collective Behavior*. New York: Holt.

Klausner, Samuel Z. 1988. "Anti-Semitism in the Executive Suite: Yesterday, Today, and Tomorrow," *Moment*, **13**(September):32–39, 55.

Klein, Abbie Gordan. 1992. *The Debate over Child Care 1969–1990: A Sociohistorical Analysis*. Albany: State University of New York Press.

Kleinman, Dena. 1983. "Less than 40% of Jews in Survey Observe Sabbath," *New York Times* (February 6), pp. 1, 19.

Kling, Rob, Spencer Olin, and Mark Poster (eds.). 1991. *Postsuburban California: The Transformation of Orange County since World War II*. Berkeley: University of California Press.

Koch, Tom. 1990. *Mirrored Lives: Aging Children and Elderly Parents*. New York: Praeger.

Koenig, Frederick W. 1985. *Rumor in the Marketplace*. Dover, Mass.: Auburn House.

Kohn, Alfie. 1988. "Girltalk, Guytalk," *Psychology Today*, **22**(February):65–66.

Kohn, Melvin L. 1970. "The Effects of Social Class on Parental Values and Practices," in David Reiss and H. A. Hoffman (eds.), *The American Family: Dying or Developing*. New York: Plenum, pp. 45–68.

———. 1978. "The Benefits of Bureaucracy," *Human Nature* (August), pp. 60–66.

——— (ed.). 1989. *Cross-National Research in Sociology*. Newbury Park, Calif.: Sage.

Kolata, Gina. 1993. "Cloning Human Embryos: Debate Erupts over Ethics," *New York Times* (October 26), pp. A1, B7.

Kolbert, Elizabeth. 1992. "Maybe the Media DID Treat Bush a Bit Harshly," *New York Times* (November 21), p. E3.

Komarovsky, Mirra. 1991. "Some Reflections on the Feminist Scholarship in Society," in W. Richard Scott and Judith Blake (eds.), *Annual Review of Sociology, 1991*. Palo Alto, Calif.: Annual Reviews, pp. 1–25.

Kornblum, William. 1991. "Who Is the Underclass?" *Dissent*, **38**(Spring): 202–211.

Kornhauser, William. 1961. "'Power Elite' or 'Veto Groups'?" in Seymour Martin Lipset and Leo Lowenthal (eds.), *Culture and Social Character*. New York: Free Press, pp. 252–267.

Kortenhaus, Carole M., and Jack

Demarest. 1993. "Gender Role Stereotyping in Children's Literature: An Update," *Sex Roles,* **28**(3,4):219–232.

Kosmin, Barry A., et al. [6 authors]. 1991. *Highlights of the CJF 1990 National Jewish Population Survey.* New York: Council of Jewish Federations.

—— and Seymour P. Lachman. 1993. *One Nation under God.* New York: Harmony.

Kourvetaris, George A. 1988. "The Greek American Family," in Charles H. Mindel, Robert W. Habenstein, and Roosevelt Wright, Jr. (eds.), *Ethnic Families in America: Patterns and Variations* (3d ed.). New York: Elsevier, pp. 76–108.

Kozol, Jonathan. 1988. *Rachel and Her Children: Homeless Families in America.* New York: Ballantine.

——. 1991. *Savage Inequalities: Children in America's Schools.* New York: Crown.

Kraft, Michael E., and Bruce B. Clary. 1991. "Citizen Participation and the NIMBY Syndrome: Public Response to Radioactive Waste Disposal," *Western Political Quarterly,* **44**(June):299–328.

Kralewski, John E., Laura Pitt, and Deborah Shatin. 1985. "Structural Characteristics of Medical Group Practices," *Administrative Science Quarterly,* **30**(March):34–45.

Kraybill, Donald B. 1989. *The Riddle of Amish Culture.* Baltimore: Johns Hopkins University Press.

Kroeber, Alfred L. 1923. *Anthropology: Culture Patterns and Processes.* New York: Harcourt Brace and World.

Krugman, Paul R. 1992. "The Right, the Rich, and the Facts: Deconstructing the Income Distribution Debate," *American Prospect* (Fall), pp. 19–31.

Kübler-Ross, Elisabeth. 1969. *On Death and Dying.* New York: Macmillan.

Kushnick, Louis. 1993. "Internal Migration," *1993 Encyclopedia Britannica Book of the Year.* Chicago: Encyclopedia Britannica, pp. 252–253.

Kwong, Peter. 1992. "The First Multicultural Riots," *Village Voice,* **37**(June 9): 29–32.

—— and JoAnn Lum. 1988. "Chinese-American Politics: A Silent Minority Tests Its Clout," *The Nation,* **246**(January 16):49–50, 52.

Labaree, David F. 1986. "Curriculum, Credentials, and the Middle Class: A Case Study of a Nineteenth Century High School," *Sociology of Education,* **59**(January):42–57.

Labaton, Stephen. 1992. "Benefits Are Refused More Often to Disabled Blacks, Study Finds," *New York Times* (May 11), p. A1.

Ladner, Joyce. 1981. "Patterns of Age Segregation," *Sociological Focus,* **14**(January):1–13.

——. 1986. "Black Women Face the 21st Century: Major Issues and Problems," *Black Scholar,* **17**(September–October):12–19.

Lamm, Bob. 1977. "Men's Movement Hype," in Jon Snodgrass (ed.), *For Men against Sexism: A Book of Readings.* Albion, Calif.: Times Change, pp. 153–157.

——. 1983. "How Rabbi Faces the Dangers of Deprogramming," *Los Angeles Herald Examiner* (May 7), pp. A2, B8.

Lamont, Michéle, and Marcel Fournier. 1993. *Cultivating Differences: Symbolic Boundaries and the Making of Inequity.* Chicago: University of Chicago Press.

Lancaster, John. 1992. "Does Anyone Allow Gays to Serve in the Military?" *Washington Post National Weekly Edition* (December 7), p. 14.

Landsberger, Henry A., John R. Carlson, and Richard T. Campbell. 1988. "Education Policy in Comparative Perspective: Similarities in the Underlying Issues in Debate among Educational Elites in the U.S., Britain, and the Federal Republic of Germany." Paper presented at the annual meeting of the American Sociological Association, Atlanta.

Landtman, Gunnar. 1968. *The Origin of Inequality of the Social Class.* New York: Greenwood (original edition 1938, Chicago: University of Chicago Press).

Lane, Harlan. 1992. *The Mask of Benevolence: Disabling the Deaf Community.* New York: Knopf.

Lane, Robert E. 1959. *Political Life.* New York: Free Press.

Lang, Eric. 1992. "Hawthorne Effect," in Edgar F. Borgatta and Marie L. Borgatta (eds.), *Encyclopedia of Sociology,* vol. 2. New York: Macmillan, pp. 793–794.

Langan, Patrick A., and Christopher A. Innes. 1985. *The Risk of Violent Crime.* Washington, D.C.: U.S. Government Printing Office.

Lapchick, Richard E., and Jesse L. Jackson. 1993. "Equality in Baseball Is Still Somewhere over Rainbow," *New York Times* (April 4), p. 11.

Lapping, Mark B., Thomas L. Daniels, and John W. Keller. 1989. *Rural Planning and Development.* New York: Guilford.

Larson, Calvin J., and Stan R. Nikkel. 1979. *Urban Problems: Perspectives on Corporations, Governments, and Cities.* Boston: Allyn and Bacon.

Lasswell, Harold D. 1936. *Politics: Who Gets What, When, How.* New York: McGraw-Hill.

Lauer, Robert H. 1982. *Perspectives on Social Change* (3d ed.). Boston: Allyn and Bacon.

Lawton, Millicent. 1992. "Gallup Poll Finds Wide Support for Tuition Vouchers," *Education Week,* **12**(September 23):1, 16.

——. 1993a. "'Anywhere, at Any Time,' Violence in Schools Spreads Past Cities," *Education Week,* **32**(May 5):1, 14.

——. 1993b. "Program Found Curbing Children's Violent Behavior," *Education Week,* **32**(May 5):1, 24.

Lazare, Daniel. 1990. "Planes, Trains, and Automobiles," *Village Voice,* **35**(October 23):39–41.

——. 1991. "Urbancide!" *Village Voice,* **36**(December 10):36–37.

Lazerwitz, Bernard, and Michael Harrison. 1979. "American Jewish Denominations: A Social and Religious Profile," *American Sociological Review,* **44**(August): 656–666.

Leacock, Eleanor Burke. 1969. *Teaching and Learning in City Schools.* New York: Basic Books.

Leavell, Hugh R., and E. Gurney Clark. 1965. *Preventive Medicine for the Doctor in His Community: An Epidemiologic Approach* (3d ed.). New York: McGraw-Hill.

Lee, Alfred McClung. 1978. *Sociology for Whom?* New York: Oxford University Press.

——. 1986. *Sociology for Whom?* Syracuse, N.Y.: Syracuse University Press.

Lee, Barrett A. 1992. "Homelessness," in Edgar F. Borgatta and Marie L. Borgatta (eds.), *Encyclopedia of Sociology,* vol. 2. New York: Macmillan, pp. 843–847.

Lee, D. J., and K. S. Markides. 1990. "Activity and Mortality among Aged People over an Eight-Year Period," *Journal of Gerontology,* **45**(1):39–42.

Lee, Raymond M. 1993. *Doing Research on Sensitive Topics.* Newbury Park, Calif.: Sage.

Leerhsen, Charles. 1990. "Unite and Conquer," *Newsweek,* **115**(February 5): 50–55.

Lemann, Nicholas. 1991. "The Other Underclass," *Atlantic Monthly,* **268**(December):96–102, 104, 107–108, 110.

Lemkow, Louis. 1986. "Socio-Economic Status Differences in Health," *Social Science and Medicine,* **22**(11):1257–1262.

———. 1987. "The Employed Unemployed: The Subterranean Economy in Spain," *Social Science and Medicine,* **25**(2):111–113.

Lenski, Gerhard. 1966. *Power and Privilege: A Theory of Social Stratification.* New York: McGraw-Hill.

———, Jean Lenski, and Patrick Nolan. 1991. *Human Societies: An Introduction to Macrosociology.* New York: McGraw-Hill.

Leo, John. 1987. "Exploring the Traits of Twins," *Time,* **129**(January 12):63.

Leslie, Gerald R., and Sheila K. Korman. 1989. *The Family in Social Context* (7th ed.). New York: Oxford University Press.

Letkemann, Peter. 1973. *Crime as Work.* Englewood Cliffs, N.J.: Prentice-Hall.

Levin, Jack, and William C. Levin. 1980. *Ageism.* Belmont, Calif.: Wadsworth.

Levin, William C. 1988. "Age Stereotyping: College Student Evaluations," *Research on Aging,* **10**(March):134–148.

Levine, Robert. 1987. "Waiting Is a Power Game," *Psychology Today,* **21**(April): 24–26, 28, 30–33.

Levinson, Arlene. 1984. "Laws for Live-In Lovers," *Ms.,* **12**(June):101.

Levinson, Daniel. 1978. *The Seasons of a Man's Life.* New York: Knopf.

Lewandowsky, Stephan, and Ian Spence. 1990. "The Perception of Statistical Graphs," *Sociological Methods and Research,* **18**(February):200–242.

Lewin, Tamar. 1990. "Too Much Retirement Time? A Move Is Afoot to Change It," *New York Times* (April 22), pp. 1, 26.

———. 1991a. "Nude Pictures Are Ruled Sexual Harassment," *New York Times* (January 23), p. A14.

———. 1991b. "Older Women Face Bias in Workplace," *New York Times* (May 11), p. 8.

———. 1992. "Hurdles Increase for Many Women Seeking Abortions," *New York Times* (March 15), pp. 1, 18.

Lewis, Paul. 1993. "Rape Was Weapon of Serbs, U.N. Says," *New York Times* (October 20), pp. A1, A6.

Lewis, Robert. 1973. "A Longitudinal Test of a Developmental Framework for Premarital Dyadic Formation," *Journal of Marriage and the Family,* **35**(February): 16–25.

Lewis, Suzan, Dafna N. Izraeli, and Helen Hootsmans. 1991. *Dual-Earner Families: International Perspectives.* Newbury Park, Calif.: Sage.

Liebman, Charles S. 1973. *The Ambivalent American Jew.* Philadelphia: Jewish Publication Society.

Light, Ivan H., and Edna Bonacich. 1988. *Immigrant Entrepreneurs: Koreans in Los Angeles, 1965–1982.* Berkeley: University of California Press.

Lim, Gerard. 1993. "Homelessness Attracts Attention from Mayors, Civic Organization," *Asian Week* (July 23), p. 5.

Lin, Nan, and Wen Xie. 1988. "Occupational Prestige in Urban China," *American Journal of Sociology,* **93**(January): 793–832.

Linden, Eugene. 1989. "Playing with Fire," *Time,* **136**(September 18):76–80, 82, 85.

Lindsey, Robert. 1987. "Isolated, Strongly Led Sects Growing in U.S.," *New York Times* (June 22), pp. 1, 22.

Lines, Patricia M. 1985. "A Briefing on Tuition Vouchers and Related Plans," *Footnotes,* **22**(Spring):5–7.

Link, Bruce G. 1987. "Understanding Labeling Effects in the Area of Mental Disorders: An Assessment of the Effects of Expectations of Rejection," *American Sociological Review,* **52**(February):96–112.

———, Frances T. Cullen, Elmer Struening, and Patrick E. Shrout. 1989. "A Modified Labeling Theory Approach to Mental Disorders," *American Sociological Review,* **54**(June):400–423.

Linton, Ralph. 1936. *The Study of Man: An Introduction.* New York: Appleton-Century.

Lipset, Seymour Martin. 1990. *Continental Divide: The Values and Institutions of the United States and Canada.* New York: Routledge.

Little, Kenneth. 1988. "The Role of Vol-untary Associations in West African Urbanization," in Johnnetta B. Cole (ed.), *Anthropology for the Nineties: Introductory Readings.* New York: Free Press, pp. 211–230.

Lockheed, Marlaine E., Adriaan M. Verspoor, and associates. 1991. *Improving Primary Education in Developing Countries.* Washington, D.C.: World Bank.

Lofflin, John. 1988. "A Burst of Rural Enterprise," *New York Times* (January 3), sec. 3, pp. 1, 23.

Lofland, John. 1977. *Doomsday Cult* (enlarged ed.). New York: Irvington.

———. 1981. "Collective Behavior: The Elementary Forms," in Morris Rosenberg and Ralph Turner (eds.), *Social Psychology: Sociological Perspectives.* New York: Basic Books, pp. 441–446.

———. 1985. *Protest: Studies of Collective Behavior and Social Movements.* Rutgers, N.J.: Transaction.

London, Kathryn A. 1991. *Cohabitation, Marriage, Marital Dissolution, and Remarriage: United States, 1988.* Washington, D.C.: National Center for Health Statistics.

Longmore, Paul K. 1985. "Screening Stereotypes: Images of Disabled People," *Social Policy,* **16**(Summer):31–37.

———. 1988. "Crippling the Disabled," *New York Times* (November 26), p. 23.

Longworth, R. C. 1993. "UN, Relief Agencies Put Paperwork before People," *Chicago Tribune* (September 14), pp. 1, 9.

Lopreato, Joseph. 1992. "Sociobiology and Human Behavior," in Edgar F. Borgatta and Marie L. Borgatta (eds.), *Encyclopedia of Sociology,* vol. 4. New York: Macmillan, pp. 1995–2000.

Lorch, Donatella. 1993. "Kenya, Calling for Aid, Fights Falling Economy," *New York Times* (June 7), p. A6.

Los Angeles Times. 1992. *Understanding the Riots.* Los Angeles: *Los Angeles Times.*

Lott, Bernice. 1987. *Women's Lives: Themes and Variations in Gender Learning.* Monterey, Calif.: Brooks/Cole.

Louw-Potgieter, J. 1988. "The Authoritarian Personality: An Inadequate Explanation for Intergroup Conflict in South Africa," *Journal of Social Psychology,* **128** (February):75–88.

Lowe, Marcia D. 1992. "Alternatives to Shaping Tomorrow's Cities," *The Futurist,* **26**(July–August):28–34.

Lukacs, Georg. 1923. *History and Class Consciousness*. London: Merlin.

Luker, Kristin. 1984. *Abortion and the Politics of Motherhood*. Berkeley: University of California Press.

Lum, Joann, and Peter Kwong. 1989. "Surviving in America: The Trials of a Chinese Immigrant Woman," *Village Voice,* **34**(October 31):39–41.

Lundberg, George D. 1991. "National Health Care Reform: An Aura of Inevitability Is upon Us," *Journal of the American Medical Association,* **265**(May 15):2565–2566.

Luster, Tom, Kelly Rhoades, and Bruce Haas. 1989. "The Relation between Parental Values and Parenting Behavior: A Test of the Kohn Hypothesis," *Journal of Marriage and the Family,* **51** (February):138–147.

Luxenburg, Joan, and Thomas E. Guild. 1989. "20 Years after the Stonewall: Legal and Political Movement in Gay Rights." Paper presented at the annual meeting of the Society for the Study of Social Problems, Berkeley, Calif.

——— and Lloyd Klein. 1984. "CB Radio Prostitution: Technology and the Displacement of Deviance," *Journal of Offender Counseling, Service, and Rehabilitation,* **9**(Fall–Winter):71–87.

Lyon, Jeff. 1992. "Keeping Score," *Chicago Tribune Magazine* (November 29), pp. 14–16, 28–35.

Lyotard, Jean François. 1993. *The Postmodern Explained: Correspondence 1982–1985*. Minneapolis: University of Minnesota Press.

Mack, Raymond W., and Calvin P. Bradford. 1979. *Transforming America: Patterns of Social Change* (2d ed.). New York: Random House.

Mackenzie, Hilary. 1991. "David vs. Goliath," *Maclean's,* **104**(May 6):24–25.

Mackey, Wade C. 1987. "A Cross-Cultural Perspective on Perceptions of Paternalist Deficiencies in the United States: The Myth of the Derelict Daddy," *Sex Roles,* **12**(March):509–534.

MacKinnon, Catherine A. 1993. "Turning Rape into Pornography: Postmodern Genocide," *Ms.,* **4**(July–August):24–30.

Maddox, G. 1968. "Persistence of Lifestyle among the Elderly," in Bernice L. Neugarten (ed.), *Middle Age and Aging: A Reader in Social Psychology*. Chicago: University of Chicago Press, pp. 181–183.

Maguire, Brendan. 1988. "The Applied Dimension of Radical Criminology: A Survey of Prominent Radical Criminologists," *Sociological Spectrum,* **8**(2):133–151.

Maher, Timothy. 1991. "Race, Class and Trash: Whose Backyard Do We Dump In?" Paper presented at the annual meeting of the North Central Sociological Association, Dearborn, Mich.

Maines, David R. 1977. "Social Organization and Social Structure in Symbolic Interactionist Thought," in Alex Inkleks (ed.), *Annual Review of Sociology, 1977*. Palo Alto, Calif.: Annual Reviews, pp. 235–259.

———. 1982. "In Search of Mesostructure: Studies in the Negotiated Order," *Urban Life,* **11**(July):267–279.

Majors, Richard, and Janet Mancini Bellson. 1992. *Cool Pose: The Dilemmas of Black Manhood in America*. New York: Lexington.

Makepeace, James M. 1986. "Gender Differences in Courtship Violence Victimization," *Family Relations,* **35**(July): 383–388.

———. 1987. "Social Factor and Victim-Offender Differences in Courtship Violence," *Family Relations,* **36**(January): 87–91.

Makihara, Kumiko. 1990. "No Longer Willing to Be Invisible," *Time,* **135**(May 28):36.

Malcolm, Andrew H. 1974. "The 'Shortage' of Bathroom Tissue: A Classic Study in Rumor," *New York Times* (February 3), p. 29.

Malcolm X, with Alex Haley. 1964. *The Autobiography of Malcolm X*. New York: Grove.

Malinowski, Michael J. 1990. "Federal Enclaves and Local Law: Carving Out a Domestic Violence Exception to Exclusive Legislative Jurisdiction," *Yale Law Journal,* **100**:189–208.

Malthus, Thomas, Julian Huxley, and Frederick Osborn. 1960. *Three Essays on Population*. New York: New American Library (originally published in 1824).

Manegold, Catherine S. 1994. "Fewer Men Earn Doctorates, Particularly Among Blacks," *New York Times* (January 18), p. A14.

Maney, Kevin. 1993. "TV Will Take Active Role in the Home," *USA Today* (October 14), pp. A1–A2.

Mangalmurti, Sandeep, and Robert Allan Cooke. 1991. *State Lotteries: Seducing the Less Fortunate*. Chicago: Heartland Institute.

Mann, James. 1983. "One-Parent Family: The Troubles—And the Joys," *U.S. News and World Report,* **95**(November 28):57–58, 62.

Mansnerus, Laura. 1992. "Should Tracking Be Derailed," *New York Times* (November 1), sec. 4A, pp. 14–16.

Manson, Donald A. 1986. *Tracking Offenders: White-Collar Crime*. Bureau of Justice Statistics Special Report. Washington, D.C.: U.S. Government Printing Office.

Marger, Martin. 1981. *Elites and Masses: An Introduction to Political Sociology*. New York: Van Nostrand.

Margolick, David. 1992. "Legal System Is Assailed on AIDS Crisis," *New York Times* (January 19), p. 16.

———. 1993. "Doctor Who Assists Suicides Makes the Macabre Mundane," *New York Times* (February 22), pp. A1, A12.

Marklein, Mary Beth. 1992. "Parents Can Help at Home," *USA Today* (November 18), p. 8A.

Markson, Elizabeth W. 1992. "Moral Dilemmas," *Society,* **29**(July–August):4–6.

Marmor, Theodore R., and John Godfrey. 1992. "Canada's Medical System Is a Model. That's a Fact," *New York Times* (July 23), p. A23.

Marsden, Peter V. 1992. "Social Network Theory," in Edgar F. Borgatta and Marie L. Borgatta (eds.), *Encyclopedia of Sociology,* vol. 4. New York: Macmillan, pp. 1887–1894.

Marshall, Victor W., and Judith A. Levy. 1990. "Aging and Dying," in Robert H. Binstock and Linda K. George (eds.), *Handbook of Aging and the Social Sciences*. San Diego: Academic, pp. 245–260.

Martin, Douglas. 1987. "Indians Seek a New Life in New York," *New York Times* (March 22), p. 17.

Martin, Linda G. 1989. "The Graying of Japan," *Population Bulletin,* **44**(July): 1–43.

Martineau, Harriet. 1896. "Introduction," in the translation of *Positive Philosophy of Auguste Comte*. London: Bell.

———. 1962. *Society in America*. Edited, abridged, with an introductory essay by Seymour Martin Lipset. Garden City,

N.Y.: Doubleday (originally published in 1837).

Martinez, Elizabeth. 1993. "Going Gentle into That Good Night: Is a Rightful Death a Feminist Issue?" *Ms.,* **4**(July–August):65–69.

Marty, Martin E. 1980. "Resurgent Fundamentalism," in *Encyclopedia Britannica Book of the Year, 1980.* Chicago: Encyclopedia Britannica, pp. 606–607.

———. 1987. "Religion in a Troubled Land," in *Encyclopedia Britannica Book of the Year, 1987.* Chicago: Encyclopedia Britannica, pp. 330–331.

Martyna, Wendy. 1983. "Beyond the He/Man Approach: The Case for Nonsexist Language," in Barrie Thorne, Cheris Kramarae, and Nancy Henley (eds.), *Language, Gender and Society.* Rowley, Mass.: Newly House, pp. 25–37.

Marx, Karl, and Friedrich Engels. 1955. *Selected Work in Two Volumes.* Moscow: Foreign Languages Publishing House.

Mascia-Lees, Frances E., and Patricia Sharpe (eds.). 1992. *Tattoo, Torture, Mutilation, and Adornment: The Denaturalization of the Body in Culture and Text.* Albany: State University of New York Press.

Masland, Tim. 1992. "Slavery," *Newsweek,* **119**(May 4):30–32, 37–39.

Masland, Tom, and Ruth Marshall. 1990. 'A Really Nasty Business': False Pharmaceuticals Look like the Real Thing—But They Can Be Lethal," *Newsweek,* **116**(November 5):36, 38, 43.

Mason, Marie K. 1942. "Learning to Speak after Six and One-Half Years of Silence," *Journal of Speech Disorders,* **7**(December):295–304.

Massey, Douglas S., and Nancy A. Denton. 1993. *American Apartheid: Segregation and the Making of the Underclass.* Cambridge, Mass.: Harvard University Press.

Matras, Judah. 1973. *Populations and Societies.* Englewood Cliffs, N.J.: Prentice-Hall.

———. 1977. *Introduction to Population: A Sociological Approach.* Englewood Cliffs, N.J.: Prentice-Hall.

Matyko, Alexander J. 1986. *The Self-Defeating Organization: A Critique of Bureaucracy.* New York: Praeger.

Mauro, Tony. 1993a. "Bigotry vs. Free Speech: Supreme Court's Call," *USA Today* (April 21), p. 7A.

———. 1993b. "Students 'Taking Stand' for Prayer in Schools," *USA Today* (September 15), p. 4A.

Mautner, Michael. 1992. "Human Values and Technical Advances," *Futurist,* **26** (July–August):41–44.

Mayer, Egon. 1983. *Children of Intermarriage.* New York: American Jewish Committee.

———. 1985. *Love and Tradition: Marriage between Jews and Christians.* New York: Plenum.

Mayer, Karl Ulrich, and Urs Schoepflin. 1989. "The State and the Life Course," in W. Richard Scott and Judith Blake (eds.), *Annual Review of Sociology, 1989.* Palo Alto, Calif.: Annual Reviews, pp. 187–209.

McBride, David. 1991. *From TB to AIDS: Epidemics among Urban Blacks since 1900.* Albany: State University of New York.

McBride, Nicholas C. 1987. "Urban Officials Launch Bid for Remodeled US Housing Programs," *Christian Science Monitor* (February 23), p. 6.

McCaghy, Charles H. 1980. *Crime in American Society.* New York: Macmillan.

McCord, William. 1993. "Death with Dignity," *The Humanist,* **53**(January–February):26–29.

McCormick, Kenelm F. 1992. "Attitudes of Primary Case Physicians toward Corporal Punishment," *Journal of the American Medical Association,* **267**(June 17): 3161–3165.

McEnroe, Jennifer. 1991. "Split-Shift Parenting," *American Demographics,* **13**(February):50–52.

McFalls, Joseph A., Jr. 1981. "Where Have All the Children Gone?" *USA Today* (March):30–33.

———. 1991. "Population: A Lively Introduction," *Population Bulletin,* **46**(October).

———, Brian Jones, and Bernard J. Gallegher, III. 1984. "U.S. Population Growth: Prospects and Policy," *USA Today* (January), pp. 30–34.

McGrath, Ellie. 1983. "Schooling for the Common Good," *Time,* **122**(August 1): 66–67.

McGuire, Meredith B. 1981. *Religion: The Social Context.* Belmont, Calif.: Wadsworth.

McGuire, Randall M., and Robert Paynter (eds.). 1991. *The Archaeology of Inequality.* Oxford, Eng.: Basil Blackwell.

McIntosh, Shawn. 1992. "Survey of Those Arrested in the Riots," *USA Today* (May 11), p. 7A.

McKeown, Thomas. 1976. *The Role of Medicine: Dream, Mirage, or Nemesis?* London: Nuffield Provincial Hospitals Trust.

McKinlay, John B., and Sonja M. McKinlay. 1977. "The Questionable Contribution of Medical Measures to the Decline of Mortality in the United States in the Twentieth Century," *Milbank Memorial Fund Quarterly,* **55**(Summer):405–428.

McKinney, Kathleen. 1990. "Sexual Harassment of University Faculty by Colleagues and Students," *Sex Roles,* **23**(October):421–438.

McLean, Elys A. 1992. "Gun Control Lobby Outgunned," *USA Today* (July 31), p. A1.

McNamara, Robert S. 1992. "The Population Explosion," *The Futurist,* **26**(November–December):9–13.

McPhail, Clark. 1991. *The Myth of the Madding Crowd.* New York: De Gruyter.

———. 1994. "The Dark Side of Purpose in Riots: Individual and Collective Violence," *Sociological Quarterly,* **35**(January):i–xx.

——— and David Miller. 1973. "The Assembling Process: A Theoretical and Empirical Examination," *American Sociological Review,* **38**(December):721–735.

McPhail, Thomas L. 1981. *Electronic Colonialism: The Future of International Broadcasting and Communication.* Beverly Hills, Calif.: Sage.

McPherson, J. Miller, and Lynn Smith-Lovin. 1986. "Sex Segregation in Voluntary Associations," *American Sociological Review,* **51**(February):61–79.

McRoberts, Flynn, and Susan Kuczka. 1992. "Morton Grove Gun Ban Failed to Catch U.S. Fancy," *Chicago Tribune* (April 29), pp. 1, 8.

McWilliams, Carey. 1951. *Brothers under the Skin* (rev. ed.). Boston: Little, Brown.

Mead, George H. 1930. "Cooley's Contribution to American Social Thought," *American Journal of Sociology,* **35**(March): 693–706.

———. 1934. In Charles W. Morris (ed.), *Mind, Self and Society.* Chicago: University of Chicago Press.

————. 1964a. In Anselm Strauss (ed.), *On Social Psychology*. Chicago: University of Chicago Press.

————. 1964b. "The Genesis of the Self and Social Control," in Andrew J. Reck (ed.), *Selected Writings: George Herbert Mead*. Indianapolis: Bobbs-Merrill, pp. 267–293.

Mead, Margaret. 1939. "Coming of Age in Samoa," in *From the South Seas: Studies of Adolescence and Sex in Three Primitive Societies*. New York: Morrow.

————. 1963. *Sex and Temperament in Three Primitive Societies*. New York: Morrow (originally published 1935).

————. 1966. "Marriage in Two Steps," *Redbook*, **127**(July):48–49, 84–85.

————. 1970. *Culture and Commitment: A Study of the Generation Gap*. New York: Doubleday.

————. 1973. "Does the World Belong to Men—Or to Women?" *Redbook*, **141** (October):46–52.

Mechanic, David. 1978. *Medical Sociology* (2d ed.). New York: Free Press.

————. 1986. *From Advocacy to Allocation: American Health Care*. New York: Free Press.

Meddis, Sam Vincent. 1993. "Crime Stats Shield Brutal Reality," *USA Today* (October 4), p. 9A.

Meek, Ronald L. (ed.). 1954. *Marx and Engels on Malthus: Selections from the Writings of Marx and Engels Dealing with the Theories of Thomas Robert Malthus*. New York: International Publishers.

Meier, Kenneth J., and Joseph Stewart, Jr. 1991. *The Politics of Hispanic Education*. Albany: State University of New York Press.

Meile, Richard C. 1986. "Pathways to Patienthood: Sick Role and Labeling Perspectives," *Social Science and Medicine*, **22**(1):35–40.

Meisenheimer, Joseph R., II. 1989. "Employer Provisions for Parental Leave," *Monthly Labor Review*, **112**(October):20–24.

Melbin, Murray. 1978. "Night as Frontier," *American Sociological Review*, **43**(February):3–22.

————. 1987. *Night as Frontier: Colonizing the World after Dark*. New York: Free Press.

Melson, Robert. 1986. "Provocation or Nationalism: A Critical Inquiry into the Armenian Genocide of 1915," in Rich-ard G. Hovannisian (ed.), *The Armenian Genocide in Perspective*. New Brunswick, N.J.: Transaction, pp. 61–84.

Memmi, Albert. 1967. *The Colonizer and the Colonized*. Boston: Beacon.

Menard, Scott W., and Elizabeth W. Moen (eds.). 1987. *Perspectives on Population: An Introduction to Concepts and Issues*. New York: Oxford University Press.

Menken, Jane (ed.). 1986. *World Population and U.S. Policy*. New York: Norton.

Merton, Robert K. 1968. *Social Theory and Social Structure*. New York: Free Press.

———— and Alice S. Kitt. 1950. "Contributions to the Theory of Reference Group Behavior," in Robert K. Merton and Paul L. Lazarsfeld (eds.), *Continuities in Social Research: Studies in the Scope and Method of the American Soldier*. New York: Free Press, pp. 40–105.

————, G. C. Reader, and P. L. Kendall. 1957. *The Student Physician*. Cambridge, Mass.: Harvard University Press.

Messner, Michael. 1989. "Masculinities and Athletic Careers," *Gender and Society*, **3**(March):71–88.

Michalowski, Raymond J., and Ronald C. Kramer. 1987. "The Space between Laws: The Problem of Corporate Crime in a Transnational Context," *Social Problems*, **34**(February):34–53.

Michels, Robert. 1915. *Political Parties*. Glencoe, Ill.: Free Press (reprinted 1949).

Middleton, Lorenzo. 1981. "Coleman Study Says Private Schooling Superior to Public; Social Scientists Attack His Findings," *Chronicle of Higher Education*, **22**(April 13):1, 12, 14–15.

Milburn, Norweeta, and Ann D'Ercole. 1991. "Homeless Women: Moving Toward a Comprehensive Model," *American Psychologist*, **46** (November):1161–1169.

Milgram, Stanley. 1963. "Behavioral Study of Obedience," *Journal of Abnormal and Social Psychology*, **67**(October):371–378.

————. 1975. *Obedience to Authority: An Experimental View*. New York: Harper and Row.

Miller, Annetta. 1992. "The World 'S' Ours," *Newsweek*, **114**(March 23):46–47.

Miller, Brent C., and Kristin A. Moore. 1990. "Adolescent Sexual Behavior, Pregnancy, and Parenting: Research through the 1980s," *Journal of Marriage and the Family*, **52**(November):1025–1044.

Miller, David L. 1988. *Introduction to Collective Behavior*. Prospect Heights, Ill.: Waveland.

———— and Richard T. Schaefer. 1993. "Feeding the Hungry: The National Food Bank System as a Non-insurgent Social Movement." Paper presented at the annual meeting of the Midwest Sociological Society, Chicago.

Miller, Delbert C. 1991. *Handbook of Research Design and Social Measurement* (5th ed.). Newbury Park, Calif.: Sage.

Miller, G. Tyler, Jr. 1972. *Replenish the Earth: A Primer in Human Ecology*. Belmont, Calif.: Wadsworth.

Miller, Robert J. 1992. "Hospice Care as an Alternative to Euthanasia," *Law, Medicine, and Health Care; Current Issues in Biomedical Ethics*, **20**(Spring–Summer):127–132.

Millett, Kate. 1969. *Sexual Politics*. New York: Doubleday.

Mills, C. Wright. 1956. *The Power Elite*. New York: Oxford University Press.

————. 1959. *The Sociological Imagination*. London: Oxford University Press.

Mindel, Charles H., Robert W. Habenstein, and Roosevelt Wright, Jr. (eds.). 1988. *Ethnic Families in America: Patterns and Variations* (3d ed.). New York: Elsevier.

Mingle, James R. 1987. *Focus on Minorities*. Denver: Education Commission of the States and the State Higher Education Executive Officers.

Mintz, Steven, and Susan Kellogg. 1988. *Domestic Revolutions: A Social History of American Family Life*. New York: Free Press.

Mishel, Lawrence, and David M. Frankel. 1991. "Hard Times for Working America," *Dissent*, **38**(Spring):282–285.

Mitchell, Richard G., Jr. 1993. *Secrecy and Fieldwork*. Thousand Oaks, Calif.: Sage.

Miyazawa, Setsuo. 1992. *Policing in Japan: A Study on Making Crime*. Albany: State University of New York Press.

Mizrahi, Terry. 1986. *Getting Rid of Patients*. New Brunswick, N.J.: Rutgers University Press.

Moffatt, Michael. 1989. *Coming of Age in New Jersey: College and American Culture*. New Brunswick, N.J.: Rutgers University Press.

Mokhiber, Russell. 1988. *Corporate Crime and Violence.* San Francisco: Sierra Club.

Mollen, Milton. 1992. *"A Failure of Responsibility": Report to Mayor David N. Dinkins on the December 28, 1991, Tragedy at City College of New York.* New York: Office of the Deputy Mayor for Public Safety.

Monaghan, Peter. 1993. "Sociologist Jailed Because He 'Wouldn't Snitch' Ponders the Way Research Ought to Be Done," *Chronicle of Higher Education,* **40**(September 1):A8, A9.

Money. 1987. "A Short History of Shortages," **16**(Fall; special issue):42.

Montgomery, James D. 1992. "Job Search and Network Composition: Implications of the Strength-of-Weak-Ties Hypothesis," *American Sociological Review,* **57**(October):586–596.

Moore, D. R., and S. Davenport. 1988. "High School Choice and Students At-Risk," *Newsletter of the National Center on Effective Secondary Schools,* **3**(2):2–4.

Moore, Joan, and Harry Pachon. 1985. *Hispanics in the United States.* Englewood Cliffs, N.J.: Prentice-Hall.

Moore, Wilbert E. 1967. *Order and Change: Essays in Comparative Sociology.* New York: Wiley.

———. 1968. "Occupational Socialization," in David A. Goslin (ed.), *Handbook of Socialization Theory and Research.* Chicago: Rand McNally, pp. 861–883.

Moran, Theodore. 1978. "Multinational Corporations and Dependency: A Dialogue for Dependentistas and Nondependentistas," *International Organization,* **32**(Winter):79–100.

Morgall, Janine Marie. 1993. "Technology Assessment: A Feminist Approach." Paper presented at the annual meeting of the American Sociological Association, Miami.

Morganthau, Tom. 1988. "The Housing Crunch," *Newsweek,* **111**(January 4):18–20.

Morin, Richard. 1989. "Bringing Up Baby the Company Way," *Washington Post National Weekly Edition,* **6**(September 11–17):37.

———. 1990. "Women Asking Women about Men Asking Women about Men," *Washington Post National Weekly Edition,* **7**(January 21):37.

———. 1993a. "Think Twice Before You Say Another Word," *Washington Post National Weekly Edition,* **10**(January 3):37.

———. 1993b. "Welcome to the World of Exit Surveys," *Washington Post National Weekly Edition,* **10**(May 3):37.

Morris, Michael. 1989. "From the Culture of Poverty to the Underclass: An Analysis of a Shift in Public Language," *American Sociologist,* **20**(Summer):123–133.

Morrison, Denton E. 1971. "Some Notes toward Theory on Relative Deprivation, Social Movements, and Social Change," *American Behavioral Scientist,* **14**(May–June):675–690.

Morrison, Malcolm H. 1988. "Productive Aging and the Future of Retirement," *The World and I* (December), pp. 525–531.

Morse, Arthur D. 1967. *While Six Million Died: A Chronicle of American Apathy.* New York: Ace.

Mortenson, Thomas G. 1992. "College Participation Rates by Family Income," *Postsecondary Education Opportunity* (April), pp. 1–4.

Mortimer, Jeylan E., and Roberta G. Simmons. 1978. "Adult Socialization," in Ralph H. Turner, James Coleman, and Renee C. Fox (eds.), *Annual Review of Sociology, 1978.* Palo Alto, Calif.: Annual Reviews, pp. 421–454.

Moseley, Ray. 1990. "The Night the Wall Fell," *Chicago Tribune* (October 28), pp. 1, 10.

Moskos, Charles C., Jr. 1980. *Greek Americans: Struggle and Success.* Englewood Cliffs, N.J.: Prentice-Hall.

———. 1991. "How Do They Do It?" *New Republic,* **205**(August 5):20.

Ms. 1992. "Family Planning Policies: 1991's Winners and Losers," **2**(March–April):10.

Muedeking, George D. 1992. "Authentic/Inauthentic Identities in the Prison Visiting Room," *Symbolic Interaction,* **15**(2):227–236.

Mullins, Marcy E. 1993. "Reno: Disability Law Will Be Enforced," *USA Today* (July 26), p. 9A.

Murdock, George P. 1945. "The Common Denominator of Cultures," in Ralph Linton (ed.), *The Science of Man in the World Crisis.* New York: Columbia University Press, pp. 123–142.

———. 1949. *Social Structure.* New York: Macmillan.

———. 1957. "World Ethnographic Sample," *American Anthropologist,* **59**(August):664–687.

Murphree, Randall. 1991. "Experts Say TV Has Devastating Effects," *AFA (American Family Association) Journal* (August), p. 5.

Murphy, Caryle. 1993. "Pulling Aside the Veil," *Washington Post National Weekly Edition,* **10**(April 12–18):10–11.

Murray, Douglas L. 1982. "The Abolition of El Cortito, the Short-Handled Hoe: A Case Study in Social Conflict and State Policy in California Agriculture," *Social Problems,* **30**(October), pp. 26–39.

Muskrat, Joe. 1972. "Assimilate or Starve!" *Civil Rights Digest,* **8**(October):27–34.

Mydans, Seth. 1989. "TV Unites, and Divides, Hispanic Groups," *New York Times* (August 2), p. E4.

———. 1992. "A Target of Rioters, Koreatown Is Bitter, Armed, and Determined," *New York Times* (May 3), pp. 1, 16.

———. 1993. "Poll Finds Tide of Immigration Brings Hostility," *New York Times* (June 27), pp. 1, 16.

Myers, James. 1992. "Nonmainstream Body Modification: Genital Piercing, Branding, Burning, and Cutting," *Journal of Contemporary Ethnography,* **21**(October):267–306.

Myers, Steven Lee. 1993. "Captain and Crew Charged in Voyage of Chinese to U.S.," *New York Times* (June 8), pp. A1, B2.

Myrdal, Gunnar, with Richard Steiner and Arnold Rose. 1944. *An American Dilemma: The Negro Problem and Modern Democracy.* New York: Harper.

Nader, Laura. 1986. "The Subordination of Women in Comparative Perspective," *Urban Anthropology,* **15**(Fall–Winter):377–397.

Nader, Ralph. 1965. *Unsafe at Any Speed.* New York: Grossman.

———. 1985. "America's Crime without Criminals," *New York Times* (May 19), p. F3.

———, Mark Green, and Joel Seligman. 1976. *Taming the Giant Corporation.* New York: Norton.

Nakane, Chie. 1970. *Japanese Society.* Berkeley: University of California Press.

Nakao, Keiko, and Judith Treas. 1990a. "Occupational Prestige in the United

States Revisited: Twenty-Five Years of Stability and Change." Paper presented at the annual meeting of the American Sociological Association, Washington, D.C.

——— and ———. 1990b. *Computing 1989 Occupational Prestige Scores.* Chicago: NORC.

NALEO. 1993. "Latino Coverage of the Los Angeles Riots Overwhelming Negative," *Politca,* **3**(May–June):2.

Nasar, Sylvia. 1992. "Even among the Well-Off, the Richest Get Richer," *New York Times* (March 5), pp. A1, D24.

Nash, Manning. 1962. "Race and the Ideology of Race," *Current Anthropology,* **3**(June):285–288.

National Advisory Commission on Criminal Justice. 1976. *Organized Crime.* Washington, D.C.: U.S. Government Printing Office.

National Association of Scholars. 1992. Paid advertisement in *New York Times* (April 5), p. E17.

National Center for Health Statistics. 1974. *Summary Report: Final Divorce Statistics, 1974.* Washington, D.C.: U.S. Government Printing Office.

———. 1990. *Annual Survey of Births, Marriages, Divorces, and Deaths: United States, 1989.* Washington, D.C.: U.S. Government Printing Office.

———. 1992. "Advance Report of Final Mortality Statistics, 1989," *Monthly Vital Statistics Report,* **40**(January 7).

———. 1993a. *Health, United States, 1992.* Washington, D.C.: United States Government Printing Office.

———. 1993b. "Annual Survey of Births, Marriages, Divorces, and Deaths: United States, 1992," *Monthly Vital Statistics Report,* **41**(September 28).

National Center on Women and Family Law. 1991. *Marital Rape Exemption Chart: State-by-State Analysis.* New York: National Center on Women and Family Law.

National Commission on Excellence in Education. 1983. *A Nation at Risk: The Imperative for Educational Reform.* Washington, D.C.: U.S. Government Printing Office.

National Committee for Prevention of Child Abuse. 1993. *NCPCA Fact Sheet No. 9.* Chicago: NCPCA.

National Council of Teachers of English. 1989. *Quarterly Review of Doublespeak,* **15**(January):1–12.

———. 1991. *Quarterly Review of Doublespeak,* **17**(April):1, 6.

———. 1993. *Quarterly Review of Doublespeak,* **19**(April):1.

National Institutes of Health. 1993. "16 Vanguard Centers Selected to Launch Landmark Women's Health Research Studies." News release, March 30, Washington, D.C.: NIH.

Navarro, Mireya. 1993. "Diversity but Conflict under Wider AIDS Umbrella," *New York Times* (May 28), pp. B1, B3.

Navarro, Vicente. 1976. *Medicine under Capitalism: Crisis, Health, and Medicine.* New York: Prodist.

———. 1984. "Medical History as Justification rather than Explanation: A Critique of Starr's 'The Social Transformation of American Medicine,'" *International Journal of Health Services,* **14**(4):511–528.

Neary, John. 1969. "The Magical McCartney Mystery," *Life,* **67**(November 7): 103–106.

Newman, Maria. 1993. "Hunter Gets a Curriculum Covering Many Cultures," *New York Times* (January 28), p. B3.

Newman, William M. 1973. *American Pluralism: A Study of Minority Groups and Social Theory.* New York: Harper and Row.

Newsweek. 1993. "Gunfighting: State by State," **21**(June 21):8.

New York Times. 1990. "Portrait of the Electorate: U.S. House Vote" (November 8), p. B7.

———. 1991a. "Japan Eases Rule on Korean Aliens" (January 11), p. A3.

———. 1991b. "U.S. Reports AIDS Deaths Exceed 100,000" (January 25), p. A18.

———. 1991c. "For 2, an Answer to Years of Doubt on Use of Peyote in Religious Rite" (July 9), p. A14.

———. 1992a. "California Rancher to Pay $1.5 Million in Enslavement Case" (March 25), p. A17.

———. 1992b. "Young Indians Prone to Suicide, Study Finds" (March 25), p. D24.

———. 1992c. "Doctors Are Advised to Screen Women for Abuse" (June 17), p. A26.

———. 1992d. "Californians Confront Wave of Quake Rumors" (July 20), p. A8.

———. 1993a. "Spread of AIDS Is Expected to Slow: 330,000 Deaths Are Seen by '95" (January 15), p. A12.

———. 1993b. "Child Care in Europe: Admirable but Not Perfect, Experts Say" (February 15), p. A13.

———. 1993c. "Dutch May Broaden Euthanasia Guidelines" (February 17), p. A3.

———. 1993d. "New Group Offers to Help the Ill Commit Suicide" (June 13), p. 32.

———. 1993e. "More of Homeless Are Now Families" (December 22), p. A18.

Neysmith, Sheila, and Joey Edwardh. 1984. "Economic Dependency in the 1980s: Its Impact on Third World Elderly," *Ageing and Society,* **4**(1):21–44.

Nikinovich, David G. 1992. "Bureaucracy," in Edgar F. Borgatta and Marie L. Borgatta (eds.), *Encyclopedia of Sociology,* vol. 1. New York: Macmillan, pp. 151–158.

Nixon, Howard L., II. 1979. *The Small Group.* Englewood Cliffs, N.J.: Prentice-Hall.

Noble, Barbara Presley. 1993. "Snapple Escapes the Grip of Rumors," *New York Times* (January 19), pp. D1, D7.

Noble, Kenneth B. 1984. "Plight of Black Family Is Studied Anew," *New York Times* (January 29), p. E20.

Nolan, Patrick D. 1992. "A Standardized Cross-National Comparison of Incomes," *Sociological Quarterly,* **33**(4): 599–609.

NORC (National Opinion Research Center). 1993. *General Social Surveys 1972–1993 Cumulative Code Book.* Chicago: National Opinion Research Center.

Norton, Arthur J., and Louisa F. Miller. 1992. "Marriage, Divorce, and Remarriage in the 1990's," *Current Population Reports,* ser. P-23, no. 180. Washington, D.C.: U.S. Government Printing Office.

Novello, Antonia C., Paul H. Wise, and Dushanka V. Kleinman. 1991. "Hispanic Health: Time for Date, Time for Action," *Journal of the American Medical Association,* **265**(January 9):253–255.

Nuttall, Nick, and Nicholas Watt. 1993. "Sex Selection Clinic Prompts Wave of Protest," *London Times* (January 23), p. 3.

Nyden, Phillip W., and Wim Wiewel. 1991. *Challenging Uneven Development: An Urban Agenda for the 1990s.* New Brunswick, N.J.: Rutgers University Press.

Oakes, Jeannie. 1985. *Keeping Track: How Schools Structure Inequality*. New Haven, Conn.: Yale University Press.

Oberschall, Anthony. 1973. *Social Conflict and Social Movements*. Englewood Cliffs, N.J.: Prentice-Hall.

O'Donnell, Mike. 1992. *A New Introduction to Sociology*. Walton-on-Thames, United Kingdom: Thomas Nelson.

Office of the Federal Register. 1993. *United States Government Manual, 1993–1994*. Washington, D.C.: U.S. Government Printing Office.

Ogbu, John H. 1978. *Minority Education and Caste: The American System in Cross-Cultural Perspective*. New York: Academic.

Ogburn, William F. 1922. *Social Change with Respect to Culture and Original Nature*. New York: Huebsch (reprinted 1966, New York: Dell).

———— and Clark Tibbits. 1934. "The Family and Its Functions," in Research Committee on Social Trends (ed.), *Recent Social Trends in the United States*. New York: McGraw-Hill, pp. 661–708.

O'Hare, Barbara. 1992. "Review of 'Edge City,'" *Population*, **20**(June):11.

O'Hare, William P., and Brenda Curry-White. 1992. "Is There a Rural Underclass?" *Population Today*, **20**(March): 6–8.

Ohnuma, Keiko. 1991. "Study Finds Asians Unhappy at CSU," *Asian Week*, **12**(August 8):5.

Okun, M. A., W. A. Stick, M. J. Haring, and R. A. Witter. 1984. "The Social Activity/Subjective Well-being Relation: A Quantitative Synthesis," *Research on Aging*, **6**:44–65.

Oliner, Pearl M., and Samuel P. Oliner. 1989. *The Roots of Altruism*. New York: American Jewish Committee.

Oliver, Melvin L. 1988. "The Urban Black Community as Network: Toward a Social Network Perspective," *Sociological Quarterly*, **29**(4):623–645.

Olson, Laura Katz. 1982. *The Political Economy of Aging: The State, Private Power, and Social Welfare*. New York: Columbia University Press.

Olson, Philip. 1987. "A Model of Eldercare in the People's Republic of China," *International Journal of Aging and Human Development*, **24**(4):279–300.

————. 1988. "Modernization in the People's Republic of China: The Politicization of the Elderly," *Sociological Quarterly*, **29**(2):241–262.

Omran, Abdel R., and Farzaneh Roudi. 1993. "The Middle East's Population Puzzle," *Population Bulletin*, **48**(July).

O'Reilly, Jane. 1972. "The Housewife's Moment of Truth," *Ms.*, **1**(Spring): 54–55, 57–59.

Ornstein, Norman J., and Mark Schmitt. 1990. "The New World of Interest Politics," *American Enterprise*, **1**(January–February):46–51.

Orum, Anthony M. 1978. *Introduction to Political Sociology: The Social Anatomy of the Body Politic*. Englewood Cliffs, N.J.: Prentice-Hall.

————. 1989. *Introduction to Political Sociology: The Social Anatomy of the Body Politic* (3d ed.). Englewood Cliffs, N.J.: Prentice-Hall.

Orwell, George. 1949. *1984*. New York: Harcourt Brace Jovanovich.

Osborne, Lynn T., Anne H. Rhu, and Ronald W. Smith. 1985. "Labelers in Education: Their Perceptions about Learning Disabilities," *Free Inquiry in Creative Sociology*, **13**:117–122.

Ostling, Richard N. 1989. "Shootouts in the Schools," *Time*, **134**(November 20):116.

————. 1992. "The Second Reformation," *Time*, **140**(November 23):52–58.

Ottaway, David B. 1993. "Ethnic Cleansing's New Diaspora," *Washington Post National Weekly Edition* (August 23): 10–12.

Ouellette, Laurie. 1993. "The Information Lockout," *Utne Reader* (September–October), pp. 25–26.

Oxnam, Robert B. 1986. "Why Asians Succeed Here," *New York Times Magazine* (November 30), pp. 72, 74–75, 88–89, 92.

Page, Charles H. 1946. "Bureaucracy's Other Face," *Social Forces*, **25**(October): 89–94.

Painter, Kim. 1992. "A Better Prognosis for Women's Medical Research," *USA Today* (September 24), p. 6D.

Palen, J. John. 1994. *The Suburbs*. New York: McGraw-Hill.

Palmer, John L., Timothy Smeeding, and Barbara Boyle Torrey (eds.). 1988. *The Vulnerable*. Washington, D.C.: Urban Institute.

Pamperin, Bruce F., Willard F. Bailey, and Richard J. Tyson. 1985. *Students and Community Resources: An Attitudinal Study*. Menominee: University of Wisconsin–Stout.

Paneth, Nigel. 1982. "Editorial: Infant Mortality Reexamined," *Journal of the American Medical Association*, **247**(February 19):1027–1028.

Pappas, Gregory, et al. [4 authors]. 1993. "The Increasing Disparity in Mortality between Socioeconomic Groups in the United States, 1960 and 1986," *New England Journal of Medicine*, **329**(July 8):103–109.

Park, Robert E. 1916. "The City: Suggestions for the Investigation of Human Behavior in the Urban Environment," *American Journal of Sociology*, **20**(March): 577–612.

————. 1936. "Succession, an Ecological Concept," *American Sociological Review*, **1**(April):171–179.

———— and Ernest Burgess. 1921. *Introduction to the Science of Sociology*. Chicago: University of Chicago Press.

———— and ————. 1925. *The City*. Chicago: University of Chicago Press.

Parsons, Talcott. 1951. *The Social System*. New York: Free Press.

————. 1966. *Societies: Evolutionary and Comparative Perspectives*. Englewood Cliffs, N.J.: Prentice-Hall.

————. 1972. "Definitions of Health and Illness in the Light of American Values and Social Structure," in E. Gartley Jaco (ed.), *Patients, Physicians and Illness*. New York: Free Press, pp. 166–187.

————. 1975. "The Sick Role and the Role of the Physician Reconsidered," *Milbank Medical Fund Quarterly, Health and Society*, **53**(Summer):257–278.

———— and Robert Bales. 1955. *Family, Socialization, and Interaction Process*. Glencoe, Ill.: Free Press.

———— and Renee Fox. 1952. "Therapy and the Modern Family," *Journal of Social Issues*, **8**(Fall):31–44.

Patai, Daphne. 1988. *Brazilian Women Speak*. New Brunswick, N.J.: Rutgers University Press.

Paternoster, Raymond. 1991. *Capital Punishment in America*. New York: Lexington.

Patton, Carl V. (ed.). 1988. *Spontaneous Shelter: International Perspectives and Prospects*. Philadelphia: Temple University Press.

Paull, Irene, and Bülbül. 1976. *Everybody's Studying Us: The Ironics of Aging in the Pepsi Generation.* San Francisco: Glide.

Pavalko, Ronald M. 1971. *Sociology of Occupations and Professions.* Itasca, Ill.: Peacock.

——— (ed.). 1972. *Sociological Perspectives on Occupations.* Itasca, Ill.: Peacock.

Payer, Lynn. 1988. *Medicine and Culture: Varieties of Treatment in the United States, England, West Germany, and France.* New York: Holt.

Pear, Robert. 1983. "$1.5 Billion Urged for U.S. Japanese Held in War," *New York Times* (June 17), pp. A1, D16.

Peirce, Kate. 1989. "Sex-Role Stereotyping of Children on Television: A Content Analysis of the Roles and Attributes of Child Characters," *Sociological Spectrum,* 9(3):321–328.

Pelto, Pertti J. 1973. *The Snowmobile Revolution: Technology and Social Change in the Arctic.* Menlo Park, Calif.: Cummings.

People for the American Way. 1993. *Attacks on the Freedom to Learn: 1992–1993 Report.* Washington, D.C.: People for the American Way.

Perez, Miguel. 1986. "The Language of Discrimination," *New York Daily News* (November 13), p. 47.

———. 1989. "'English' Racism Is Now Out in the Open," *New York Daily News* (August 10), p. 42.

Perlez, Jane. 1991. "In Kenya, the Lawyers Lead the Call for Freedom," *New York Times* (March 10), p. E2.

Perrow, Charles. 1984. *Normal Accidents: Living with High Risk Technologies.* New York: Basic Books.

———. 1986. *Complex Organizations* (3d ed.). New York: Random House.

Perrucci, Robert. 1974. *Circle of Madness: On Being Sane and Institutionalized in America.* Englewood Cliffs, N.J.: Prentice-Hall.

Petchesky, Rosalind. 1990. "Giving Women a Real Choice," *The Nation,* 250(May 28): 732–735.

Peter, Laurence J., and Raymond Hull. 1969. *The Peter Principle.* New York: Morrow.

Peters, John F. 1985. "Adolescents as Socialization Agents to Parents," *Adolescence,* 2(Winter):921–933.

Petersen, William. 1975. *Population* (3d ed.). New York: Macmillan.

———. 1979. *Malthus.* Cambridge, Mass.: Harvard University Press.

Peterson, Felix. 1987. "Vietnam 'Battle Deaths': Is There a Race or Class Issue?" *Focus,* 15(July):3–4.

Peterson, Karen. 1992. "Traditions That Put Life in Context," *USA Today* (November 25), pp. D1, D2.

Pettigrew, Thomas. 1981. "Race and Class in the 1980s: An Interactive View," *Daedalus,* 110(Spring):233–255.

Phillips, David P., and Lundie L. Carstensen. 1986. "Clustering of Teenage Suicides after Television News Stories about Suicide," *New England Journal of Medicine,* 315(September 11): 685–689.

Piaget, Jean. 1954. *The Construction of Reality in the Child.* Translated by Margaret Cook. New York: Basic Books.

Pillemer, Karl. 1992. "Disengagement Theory," in Edgar F. Borgatta and Marie L. Borgatta (eds.), *Encyclopedia of Sociology,* vol. 1. New York: Macmillan, pp. 503–505.

Piller, Charles. 1991. *The Fail-Safe Society: Community Defiance and the End of American Technological Optimum.* New York: Basic Books.

Pinderhughes, Dianne. 1987. *Race and Ethnicity in Chicago Politics: A Reexamination of Pluralist Theory.* Urbana: University of Illinois Press.

Pines, Maya. 1981. "The Civilizing of Genie," *Psychology Today,* 15(September):28–29, 31–32, 34.

Piven, Frances Fox, and Richard A. Cloward. 1988. *Why Americans Don't Vote.* New York: Pantheon.

——— and ———. 1993. *Regulating the Poor: The Functions of Public Welfare.* New York: Pantheon.

Platt, Steve. 1993. "Without Walls," *Statesman and Society,* 6(April 2):5–7.

Pleck, Joseph H. 1981. *The Myth of Masculinity.* Cambridge, Mass.: M.I.T. Press.

———. 1985. *Working Wives, Working Husbands.* Beverly Hills, Calif.: Sage.

Plomin, Robert. 1989. "Determinants of Behavior," *American Psychologist,* 44(February):105–111.

Pogash, Carol. 1992. "Risky Business," *Working Woman* (October), pp. 74–77, 101.

Pogrebin, Letty Cottin. 1981. *Growing Up Free: Raising Your Child in the 80's.* New York: McGraw-Hill.

Police Foundation. 1992. *States with Handgun Purchase Laws.* Washington, D.C.: Police Foundation.

Polk, Barbara Bovee. 1974. "Male Power and the Women's Movement," *Journal of Applied Behavioral Sciences,* 10(July): 415–431.

Pollard, Kelvin. 1992. "Income Down, Poverty Up," *Population Today,* 6(November):5, 9.

Population Crisis Committee. 1988. *Country Rankings of the Status of Women: Poor, Powerless and Pregnant.* Washington, D.C.: Population Crisis Committee.

Population Reference Bureau. 1978. "World Population: Growth on the Decline," *Interchange,* 7(May):1–3.

———. 1993. Correspondence.

Population Today. 1986. "Halley's Other Comet," 14(January):3, 10.

Porteous, Skipp. 1993. "The World according to Pat Robertson," *Reform Judaism,* 21(Spring):18, 20–21, 61.

Portes, Alejandro, Manuel Castells, and Lauren Benton. 1989. *The Informal Economy: Studies in Advanced and Less Developed Countries.* Baltimore: Johns Hopkins University Press.

Post, Tom. 1992. "Teaching Sensitivity to Skinheads," *Newsweek,* 119(April 27):34.

Powell, Arthur G., Eleanor Farrar, and David K. Cohen. 1985. *The Shopping Mall High School: Winners and Losers in the Educational Marketplace.* Boston: Houghton Mifflin.

Powers, Mary G., and Joan J. Holmberg. 1978. "Occupational Status Scores: Changes Introduced by the Inclusion of Women," *Demography,* 15(May): 183–204.

Prehn, John W. 1991. "Migration," in Dushkin Publishing Group, *Encyclopedia of Sociology* (4th ed.). Guilford, Conn.: Dushkin, pp. 190–191.

Preston, Julia. 1993. "The Slaves of Necessity," *Washington Post National Weekly Edition,* 10(March 20–April 4):8.

Price, Wayne T. 1993. "Low-tech Prob-lems Hit PC Networks," *USA Today* (August 6), pp. 21, 32.

Prince, Raymond. 1985. "The Concept of Culture-Bound Syndromes: Anorexia Nervosa and Brain-Fog," *Social Science and Medicine,* 21(2):197–203.

Princeton Religion Research Center. 1989. "Prejudice against Fundamentalists

Seen on Rise in Latest Survey," *Emerging Trends,* **11**(March):1–2.

———. 1993a. "Church Attendance Remarkably Constant," *Emerging Trends,* **15**(March):1.

———. 1993b. "Many Teens Say They Are Born-again Christians," *Emerging Trends,* **15**(May):1.

———. 1993c. "Attitudes towards Priests Changing Rapidly," *Emerging Trends,* **15**(October):5.

Pringle, Peter. 1993. "Chinese Gang Uses Immigrants as Slave Labour," *Independent* (London) (June 10), p. 15.

Prud'homme, Alex. 1991. "Chicago's Uphill Battle," *Time,* **137**(June 17):30.

Psychology Today. 1992. "Why Do They Stay?" **25**(May–June):22.

Public Opinion. 1979. "Failing Grades for Local Schools," **2**(August–September): 36–39.

Puente, Maria. 1993a. "Sentiment Sours as Rate of Arrival Rises," *USA Today* (July 14), pp. A1, A2.

———. 1993b. "Study Revises Estimates on Immigrants," *USA Today* (September 3), p. 2A.

Purvis, Andrew. 1990. "Research for Men Only," *Time,* **135**(March 5):59–60.

Pytte, Alyson. 1990. "Congress May Have to Intervene as Garbage Wars Intensify," *Congressional Quarterly Weekly Report,* **48**(January 20):173–177.

Quadagno, Jill (ed.). 1980. *Aging, the Individual and Society: Readings in Social Gerontology.* New York: St. Martin's.

———. 1989. "Generational Conflict and the Politics of Class," *Politics and Society,* **17**(September):353–376.

———. 1991. "Generational Equity and the Politics of the Welfare State," in Beth B. Hess and Elizabeth W. Markson (eds.), *Growing Old in America.* New Brunswick, N.J.: Transaction, pp. 341–351.

———. 1993. "Aging," in Craig Calhoun and George Ritzer (eds.), *Social Problems.* New York: McGraw-Hill, pp. 503–529.

Quarantelli, Enrico L. 1957. "The Behavior of Panic Participants," *Sociology and Social Research,* **41**(January):187–194.

———. 1992. "Disaster Research," in Edgar F. Borgatta and Marie L. Borgatta (eds.), *Encyclopedia of Sociology,* vol. 2. New York: Macmillan, pp. 492–498.

——— and Russell R. Dynes. 1970. "Property Norms and Looting: Their Patterns in Community Crises," *Phylon,* **31**(Summer):168–182.

——— and James R. Hundley, Jr. 1975. "A Test of Some Propositions about Crowd Formation and Behavior," in Robert R. Evans (ed.), *Readings in Collective Behavior.* Chicago: Rand McNally, pp. 538–554.

Quinn, Kathleen, Polly Roskin, and Joyce M. Pruitt. 1984. *Cultural Violence: There Are Many Causes.* Springfield, Ill.: Illinois Coalition Against Sexual Assault and the Illinois Coalition Against Domestic Violence.

Quinney, Richard. 1970. *The Social Reality of Crime.* Boston: Little, Brown.

———. 1974. *Criminal Justice in America.* Boston: Little, Brown.

———. 1979. *Criminology* (2d ed.). Boston: Little, Brown.

———. 1980. *Class, State and Crime* (2d ed.). New York: Longman.

Rabben, Linda. 1990a. "Brazil's Military Stakes Its Claim," *The Nation,* **250**(March 12):341–342.

———. 1990b. "Scorched Earth, Barren Lives," *Discovery Channel Magazine* (April), pp. 24–27.

Radcliffe-Brown, Alfred R. 1964. *The Andaman Islanders.* New York: Free Press.

Radosh, Mary Flannery. 1984. "The Collapse of Midwifery: A Sociological Study of the Decline of a Profession." Unpublished Ph.D. dissertation, Southern Illinois University, Carbondale.

Radosh, Polly F. 1986. "Midwives in the United States: Past and Present," *Population Research and Policy Review,* **5**:129–145.

Rafferty, Kevin. 1993a. "Sexism Charge Brushed Aside," *The Guardian* (London) (May 26), p. 20.

———. 1993b. "Japan's New Imperial Era Ushered in on British Wheels," *The Guardian* (London) (June 10), p. 24.

Rahr, Alexander. 1993. "Yeltsin Receives Support in Referendum," *RFE/RL News Briefs,* **2**(April 30):1.

Randall, Teri. 1990a. "Domestic Violence Intervention Calls for More than Treating Injuries," *Journal of the American Medical Association,* **264**(August 22): 939–940.

———. 1990b. "Domestic Violence Begets Other Problems of Which Physicians Must Be Aware to Be Effective," *Journal of the American Medical Association,* **264**(August 22):940, 943–944.

Randall, Vicky. 1987. *Women in Politics: An International Perspective* (2d ed.). Chicago: University of Chicago Press.

Range, Peter Ross. 1993. "Europe Faces an Immigrant Tide," *National Geographic,* **183**(May):94–124.

Rangel, Jesus. 1984. "Survey Finds Hispanic Groups More Unified," *New York Times* (September 8), p. 22.

Rashid, Salim. 1987. "Malthus's *Essay on Population:* The Facts of 'Super-Growth' and the Rhetoric of Scientific Persuasion," *Journal of the History of the Behavioral Sciences,* **23**(January):22–36.

Rasky, Susan F. 1989a. "Study Finds Sex Bias in News Companies," *New York Times* (April 11), p. C22.

———. 1989b. "Bill Barring Bias against Disabled Holds Wide Impact," *New York Times* (August 14), pp. A1, B6.

Rathje, William L. 1974. "The Garbage Project," *Archaeology,* **27**(October):236–241.

——— and Cullen Murphy. 1992. "Five Major Myths about Garbage, and Why They're Wrong," *Smithsonian,* **23**(July): 113–122.

Ravitch, Diane. 1992. "Multiculturalism: E Pluribus Plures," in Paul Berman (ed.), *Debating P.C.: The Controversy over Political Correctness on College Campuses.* New York: Dell, pp. 271–298.

Raybon, Patricia. 1989. "A Case for 'Severe Bias,'" *Newsweek,* **114**(October 2):11.

Raymond, Chris. 1990. "Scholarship on Homeless Gets Increased Attention from Many Sociologists and Psychologists," *Chronicle of Higher Education,* **37**(September 5):4, 6.

Reardon, Patrick T. 1991. "U.S. Cities Trying to Blend Races without Stirring Up Trouble," *Chicago Tribune* (December 22), sec. 4, pp. 1, 4.

Rebell, Michael A. 1986. "Structural Discrimination and the Rights of the Disabled," *Georgetown Law Journal,* **74**(June): 1435–1489.

Rebell, Susan. 1987. "National Survey:

Americans Call for Child Care," *Ms.*, **15**(March):44.

Rebelsky, Freda, and Cheryl Hanks. 1973. "Fathers' Verbal Interaction with Infants in the First Three Months of Life," in Freda Rebelsky and Lyn Dorman (eds.), *Child Development and Behavior* (2d ed.). New York: Knopf, pp. 145–148.

Reese, William A., II, and Michael A. Katovich. 1989. "Untimely Acts: Extending the Interactionist Conception of Deviance," *Sociological Quarterly*, **30**(2):159–184.

Regier, Darrell, et al. 1988. "One-Month Prevalence of Mental Disorders in the United States," *Archives of General Psychiatry*, **45**(November): 977–986.

Reichard, S., F. Livson, and P. Peterson. 1962. *Aging and Personality: A Study of 87 Older Men.* New York: Wiley.

Reid, J. Norman. 1984. *Availability of Selected Public Facilities in Rural Communities.* Washington, D.C.: U.S. Department of Agriculture.

Reid, T. R. 1990. "Japan Is Making Everything but Babies," *Washington Post National Weekly Edition*, **8**(November 5):18.

Reiman, Jeffrey H. 1984. *The Rich Get Richer and the Poor Get Prison* (2d ed.). New York: Wiley.

Reinharz, Shulamit. 1992. *Feminist Methods in Social Research.* New York: Oxford University Press.

Religion Watch. 1991. "Current Research: New Findings in Religious Attitudes and Behavior," **6**(September):5.

Reskin, Barbara, and Francine Blau. 1990. *Job Queues, Gender Queues: Explaining Women's Inroads into Male Occupations.* Philadelphia: Temple University Press.

Retsinas, Joan. 1988. "A Theoretical Reassessment of the Applicability of Kübler-Ross's Stages of Dying," *Death Studies*, **12**:207–216.

Rexroat, Cynthia, and Constance Shehan. 1987. "The Family Life Cycle and Spouses' Time in Housework," *Journal of Marriage and the Family*, **49**(November):737–750.

Rheingold, Harriet L. 1969. "The Social and Socializing Infant," in David A. Goslin (ed.), *Handbook of Socialization Theory and Research.* Chicago: Rand McNally, pp. 779–790.

Rich, Adrienne. 1979. *On Lies, Secrets, and Silence: Selected Prose 1966–1978.* New York and London: Norton.

Richards, Cara E. 1972. *Man in Perspective: An Introduction to Cultural Anthropology.* New York: Random House.

Richardson, Kenneth, and Robert Caildini. 1981. "Basking and Blasting: Tactics of Indirect Self-Preservation," in James Tedeschi (ed.), *Impression Management: Theory and Research.* New York: Academic, pp. 41–53.

Richardson, Laurel, and Verta Taylor. 1989. *Feminist Frontiers II: Rethinking Sex, Gender, and Society.* New York: Random House.

Richburg, Keith B. 1985. "Learning What Japan Has to Teach," *Washington Post National Weekly Edition*, **3**(November 4):9.

Richlin-Klonsky, Judith, and Ellen Strenski. 1994. *A Guide to Writing Sociology Papers* (3d ed.). New York: St. Martin's.

Richman, Joseph. 1992. "A Rational Approach to Rational Suicide," *Suicide and Life-Threatening Behavior*, **22**(Spring): 130–141.

Riddle, Lyn. 1988. "Shaker Village Buoyed by New Blood," *New York Times* (August 28), p. 43.

Ridgeway, James. 1986. "Que Pasa, U.S. English?" *Village Voice*, **31**(December 2): 32–33.

———. 1988. "Moonrise over Washington," *Village Voice*, **33**(January 19):16–17.

———. 1993. "Worse than the Disease?" *Village Voice*, **37**(September 28):17–18.

Riding, Alan. 1992. "Harassment or Flirting? Europe Tries to Decide," *New York Times* (November 3), p. A8.

———. 1993. "Women Seize Focus at Rights Forum," *New York Times* (June 16), p. A3.

Ries, Lynn M. 1992. "Social Mobility," in Edgar F. Borgatta and Marie L. Borgatta (eds.), *Encyclopedia of Sociology*, vol. 4. New York: Macmillan, pp. 1872–1880.

Riesman, David, with Nathan Glazer and Reuel Denny. 1961. *The Lonely Crowd.* New Haven, Conn.: Yale University Press.

Riessman, Catherine Kohler. 1983. "Women and Medicalization: A New Perspective," *Social Policy*, **14**(Summer): 3–18.

Rigler, David. 1993. "Letters," *New York Times Book Review* (June 13), p. 35.

Riley, John W., Jr. 1992. "Death and Dying," in Edgar F. Borgatta and Marie L. Borgatta (eds.), *Encyclopedia of Sociology*, vol. 1. New York: Macmillan, pp. 413–418.

Ritzer, George. 1977. *Working: Conflict and Change* (2d ed.). Englewood Cliffs, N.J.: Prentice-Hall.

———. 1992a. "Social Problems Theory," in Craig Calhoun and George Ritzer (eds.), *Social Problems.* New York: McGraw-Hill, pp. 33–52.

———. 1992b. *Contemporary Sociological Theory* (3d ed.). New York: McGraw-Hill.

Roberts, D. F. 1975. "The Dynamics of Racial Intermixture in the American Negro—Some Anthropological Considerations," *American Journal of Human Genetics*, **7**(December):361–367.

Roberts, Keith A. 1984. *Religion in Sociological Perspective.* Homewood, Ill.: Dorsey.

Roberts, Ron E. 1991. "Social Control," in Dushkin Publishing Group, *Encyclopedic Dictionary of Sociology* (4th ed.). Guilford, Conn.: Dushkin, p. 274.

———. and Robert March Kloss. 1974. *Social Movements: Between the Balcony and the Barricade.* St. Louis: Mosby.

Robertson, Nan. 1988. "The Changing World of Alcoholics Anonymous," *New York Times Magazine* (February 21), pp. 40, 42–44, 47, 57, 92.

Robertson, Roland. 1988. "The Sociological Significance of Culture: Some General Considerations," *Theory, Culture, and Society*, **5**(February):3–23.

Robinson, James D., and Thomas Skill. 1993. "The Invisible Generation: Portraits of the Elderly on Television." Unpublished paper, University of Dayton.

Robinson, John P. 1988. "Who's Doing the Housework?" *American Demographics*, **10**(December):24–28, 63.

Rochberg-Halton, Eugene. 1991. "From the Walled City to the Malled City." Paper presented at the annual meeting of the American Sociological Association, Cincinnati.

Roddick, Jackie. 1988. *The Dance of the Millions: Latin America and the Debt Crisis.* London: Latin America Bureau, Monthly Review Press.

Rodell, Susanna. 1993. "Memo to Hillary:

Please Have a Look at Australia's System," *New York Times* (July 25), p. E16.

Rodgers, Harrell R., Jr. 1987. *Poor Women, Poor Families.* Armonk, N.Y.: Sharpe.

Roethlisberger, Fritz J., and W. J. Dickson. 1939. *Management and the Worker.* Cambridge, Mass.: Harvard University Press.

Rohlen, Thomas P. 1983. *Japan's High Schools.* Berkeley: University of California Press.

Rohter, Larry. 1991. "Are Women Directors an Endangered Species?" *New York Times* (March 17), pp. H13, H20–H21.

———. 1993. "Rights Groups Fault Decision, as Do Haitians," *New York Times* (June 22), p. 18.

Roof, Wade Clark. 1976. "Traditional Religion in Contemporary Society: A Theory of Local-Cosmopolitan Plausibility," *American Sociological Review,* **41**(April): 195–208.

———. 1978. *Commitment and Community: Religious Plausibility in a Liberal Protestant Church.* New York: Elsevier.

Rooney, James F. 1990. "Organizational Success through Program Failure: Skid Row Rescue Missions," *Social Forces,* **58**(March):904–924.

Rosado, Lourdes. 1991. "Who's Caring for Grandma?" *Newsweek,* **118**(July 29):47.

Rosaldo, Renato. 1985. "Chicano Studies, 1970–1984," in Bernard J. Seigal (ed.), *Annual Review of Anthropology, 1985.* Palo Alto, Calif.: Annual Reviews, pp. 405–427.

Rosario, Ruben, and Tony Marcano. 1989. "A Killer Is Freed," *New York Daily News* (April 1), p. 2.

Rose, Arnold. 1951. *The Roots of Prejudice.* Paris: UNESCO.

Rose, Peter I., Myron Glazer, and Penina Migdal Glazer. 1979. "In Controlled Environments: Four Cases of Intense Resocialization," in Peter I. Rose (ed.), *Socialization and the Life Cycle.* New York: St. Martin's, pp. 320–338.

Rosecrance, John. 1986. "Why Regular Gamblers Don't Quit: A Sociological Perspective," *Sociological Perspective,* **29**(July):357–378.

———. 1987. Correspondence, May 1.

Rosenberg, Douglas H. 1991. "Capitalism," in Dushkin Publishing Group, *Encyclopedic Dictionary of Sociology* (4th ed.). Guilford, Conn.: Dushkin, pp. 33–34.

Rosenberg, Harriet G. 1990. "Complaint Discourse, Aging, and Caregiving among the !Kung San of Botswana," in Jay Sokolovsky (ed.), *The Cultural Context of Aging: Worldwide Perspectives.* New York: Bergin and Garvey, pp. 19–41.

Rosenfeld, Anne, and Elizabeth Stark. 1987. "The Prime of Our Lives," *Psychology Today,* **21**(May):62–64, 66, 68–72.

Rosenthal, R. 1987. "Homelessness in Paradise: A Map of the Terrain." Unpublished doctoral dissertation, University of California, Santa Barbara.

Rosenthal, Robert, and Elisha Y. Babad. 1985. "Pygmalion in the Gymnasium," *Educational Leadership,* **45**(September): 36–39.

——— and Lenore Jacobson. 1968. *Pygmalion in the Classroom.* New York: Holt.

Rosnow, Ralph L. 1991. "Inside Rumor: A Personal Journey," *American Psychologist,* **46**(May):484–496.

Rossi, Alice S. 1968. "Transition to Parenthood," *Journal of Marriage and the Family,* **30**(February):26–39.

———. 1973. *The Feminist Papers: From Adams to de Beauvoir.* New York: Bantam.

———. 1984. "Gender and Parenthood," *American Sociological Review,* **49**(February):1–19.

Rossi, Peter H. 1955. *Why Families Move.* New York: Free Press.

———. 1987. "No Good Applied Social Research Goes Unpunished," *Society,* **25**(November–December):73–79.

———. 1989. *Down and Out in America: The Origins of Homelessness.* Chicago: University of Chicago Press.

———. 1990. "The Politics of Homelessness." Paper presented at the annual meeting of the American Sociological Association, Washington, D.C.

Rossides, Daniel W. 1990. *Social Stratification: The American Class System in Comparative Perspective.* Englewood Cliffs, N.J.: Prentice-Hall.

Roszak, Theodore. 1969. *The Making of a Counterculture.* Garden City, N.Y.: Doubleday.

Roth, Wendy Carol. 1989. "Let Us Work!" *Parade* (September 17), p. 16.

Rothenberg, Paula S. 1992a. "Critics of Attempts to Democratize the Curriculum Are Waging a Campaign to Misrepre-

sent the Work of Responsible Professors," in Paul Berman (ed.), *Debating P.C.: The Controversy over Political Correctness on College Campuses.* New York: Dell, pp. 262–268.

———. 1992b. *Race, Class, and Gender in the United States: An Integrated Study.* New York: St. Martin's.

Rothman, David. 1971. *The Discovery of the Asylum.* Boston: Little, Brown.

Rothmyer, Karen. 1984. "Mapping Out Moon's Media Empire," *Columbia Journalism Review,* **23**(November–December):23–31.

Rothschild-Whitt, Joyce. 1979. "The Collectivist Organization: An Alternative to Rational-Bureaucratic Models," *American Sociological Review,* **44**(August): 509–527.

Rovner, Julie. 1990. "Congress Wraps Up Decision on Child-Care Legislation," *Congressional Quarterly Weekly Report,* **48**(October 27):3605–3606.

Rowen, Hobart. 1993. "The Population Clock Is Ticking," *Washington Post National Weekly Edition,* **10**(March 22):5.

Roybal, Edward R. 1992. "Special Difficulties Face Minority Elderly," *USA Today* (April 6), p. 13A.

Rubin, Charles T. 1994. *The Green Crusade: A History of the Environmental Idea.* New Brunswick, N.J.: Transaction.

Rucker, Rudy, R. V. Sirius, and Queen Ma. 1992. *Mando 2000.* New York: Harper Perennial.

Rudolph, Ellen. 1991. "Women's Talk," *New York Times Magazine* (September 1), p. 8.

Ruggles, Patricia. 1991. "Short- and Long-Term Poverty in the United States: Measuring the American 'Underclass,'" in Lars Osberg (ed.), *Economic Inequity and Poverty: International Perspectives.* Armonk, N.Y.: Sharpe, pp. 157–193.

Rugh, Andrea B. 1984. *Family in Contemporary Egypt.* Syracuse, N.Y.: Syracuse University Press.

Ruhe, J., and J. Eatman. 1977. "Effects of Racial Composition on Small Work Groups," *Small Group Behavior,* **8**:479–486.

Rule, James. 1993. "The Need to Know versus the Right to Privacy," in Craig Calhoun and George Ritzer (eds.), *Introduction to Social Problems.* New York: McGraw-Hill, pp. 729–746.

Rusk, David. 1992. "America's Urban Apartheid," *New York Times* (May 21), p. A29.

Russell, Cheryl. 1984. "The Business of Demographics," *Population Bulletin,* **39** (June).

Ruzek, Sheryl Burt. 1978. *Women's Health Movement: Feminist Alternatives to Medical Control.* New York: Praeger.

Ryan, William. 1976. *Blaming the Victim* (rev. ed.). New York: Random House.

Rymer, Russ. 1992a. "A Silent Childhood—1," *New Yorker,* **68**(April 13): 41–45, 48–51, 54, 64–75, 78–81.

———. 1992b. "A Silent Childhood—2," *New Yorker,* **68**(April 20):43–46, 48–50, 55–58, 60–77.

———. 1993. *Genie: An Abused Child's Flight from Silence.* New York: Harper-Collins.

Saarinen, Thomas F. 1988. "Centering of Mental Maps of the World," *National Geographic Research,* **4**(Winter): 112–127.

Sack, Kevin. 1992. "New, and Volatile, Politics of Welfare," *New York Times* (March 15), p. 24.

———. 1993. "Why Politics as Usual Is Not Helping the Mentally Ill," *New York Times* (July 25), p. E5.

Sadker, Myra, and David Sadker. 1985. "Sexism in the Schoolroom of the '80s," *Psychology Today,* **19**(March):54–57.

——— and ———. 1994. *Failing at Fairness: How America's Schools Cheat Girls.* New York: Scribner's.

Safa, Helen I. 1983. "Women, Production, and Reproduction in Industrial Capitalism: A Comparison of Brazilian and U.S. Factory Workers," in Maria Patricia Fernandez-Kelly (ed.), *Women, Men, and the International Division of Labor.* Albany: State University of New York Press, pp. 95–116.

Sagarin, Edward, and Jose Sanchez. 1988. "Ideology and Deviance: The Case of the Debate over the Biological Factor," *Deviant Behavior,* **9**(1):87–99.

Sale, Kirkpatrick. 1993. "The U.S. Green Movement Today," *The Nation,* **257**(July 19):92–96.

Salem, Richard, and Stanislaus Grabarek. 1986. "Sociology B.A.s in a Corporate Setting: How Can They Get There and of What Value Are They," *Teaching Sociology,* **14**(October):273–275.

Salholz, Eloise. 1990. "Teenagers and Abortion," *Newsweek,* **115**(January 8): 32–33, 36.

———. 1993. "For Better or for Worse," *Newsweek,* **121**(May 24):69.

Saltzman, Amy. 1988. "Hands Off at the Office," *U.S. News and World Report,* **105** (August 1):56–58.

Salvatore, Diane. 1986. "Babies for Sale," *Ladies Home Journal,* **103**(July):54, 56, 60, 64, 136.

Sampson, Anthony. 1973. *The Sovereign State of I.T.T.* New York: Stein and Day.

Sampson, Robert J. 1986. "Effects of Socioeconomic Context on Official Reaction to Juvenile Delinquency," *American Sociological Review,* **51**(December):876–885.

Samuelson, Paul A., and William D. Nordhaus. 1992. *Economics* (14th ed.). New York: McGraw-Hill.

Sanders, Clinton. 1989. *Customizing the Body: The Art and Culture of Tattooing.* Philadelphia: Temple University Press.

Sanger, David. 1992. "Women in Japan Job Market Find the Door Closing Again," *New York Times* (December 1), pp. A1, A10.

Sapir, Edward. 1929. "The Status of Linguistics as a Science," *Language,* **5**(4): 207–214.

Sarti, Cynthia. 1989. "The Panorama of Feminism in Brazil," *New Left Review,* **173**(January–February):75–90.

Sassen, Saskia. 1990. "Economic Restructuring and the American City," in W. Richard Scott (ed.), *Annual Review of Sociology, 1990.* Palo Alto, Calif.: Annual Reviews, pp. 465–490.

Scarce, Rik. 1993. "Confidential Sources," *The Progressive,* **57**(October):38.

Schaefer, Richard T. 1976. *The Extent and Content of Race Prejudice in Great Britain.* San Francisco: R and E Research Association.

———. 1992. "People of Color: The 'Kaleidoscope' May Be a Better Way to Describe America than 'the Melting Pot,'" *Peoria Journal Star* (January 19), p. A7.

———. 1993. *Racial and Ethnic Groups* (5th ed.). New York: HarperCollins.

———. 1995. "Education and Prejudice: Panacea or False Prophet." Paper presented at the annual meeting of the Midwest Sociological Society, Milwaukee.

Scheff, Thomas J. 1975a. *Labeling Madness.* Englewood Cliffs, N.J.: Prentice-Hall.

———. 1975b. "Reply to Chauncey and Gove," *American Sociological Review,* **40** (April):252–257.

———. 1992. *Microsociology: Discourse, Emotion, and Structure.* Chicago: University of Chicago Press.

Schlenker, Barry R. (ed.). 1985. *The Self and Social Life.* New York: McGraw-Hill.

Schmemann, Serge. 1993. "Religion Returns to Russia, with a Vengence," *New York Times* (July 28), pp. A1, A8.

Schmid, Carol. 1980. "Sexual Antagonism: Roots of the Sex-ordered Division of Labor," *Humanity and Society,* **4**(November):243–261.

Schmidt, William E. 1990. "New Vim and Vigor for the Y.M.C.A.," *New York Times* (July 18), pp. C1, C10.

———. 1993. "English Retirement Resort Is a Model for Europe," *New York Times* (July 13), p. A3.

Schmink, Marianne, and Charles Wood (eds.). 1989. *Frontier Expansion in Amazonia.* Gainesville: University of Florida Press.

Schnaiberg, Allan. 1980. *The Environment: From Surplus to Scarcity.* New York: Oxford University Press.

———, Nicholas Watts, and Klaus Zimmerman. 1986. *Distributional Conflicts in Environmental-Resource Policy.* Aldershot, England: Gower.

Schrag, Peter. 1993. "Bailing Out of Public Education," *The Nation,* **257**(October 4):351–354.

Schramm, Wilbur, Lyle M. Nelson, and Mere T. Betham. 1981. *Bold Experiment: The Story of Educational Television in American Samoa.* Stanford, Calif.: Stanford University Press.

Schultz, Terri. 1977. "Though Legal, Abortions Are Not Always Available," *New York Times* (January 1), p. E8.

Schur, Edwin M. 1965. *Crimes without Victims: Deviant Behavior and Public Policy.* Englewood Cliffs, N.J.: Prentice-Hall.

———. 1968. *Law and Society: A Sociological View.* New York: Random House.

———. 1983. *Labeling Women Deviant: Gender, Stigma, and Social Control.* Philadelphia: Temple University Press.

———. 1985. "'Crimes without Victims': A 20 Year Reassessment." Paper presented at the annual meeting of the Society for the Study of Social Problems.

Schwartz, Felice N., with Jean Zimmerman. 1992. *Breaking with Tradition: Women and Work, the New Facts of Life.* New York: Warner.

Schwartz, Howard D. (ed.). 1987. *Dominant Issues in Medical Sociology* (2d ed.). New York: Random House.

Schwartz, Joe. 1990. "Earth Day Today," *American Demographics,* **12**(April):40–41.

———. 1991. "Why Japan's Birthrate Is So Low," *American Demographics,* **13**(April): 20.

Sciolino, Elaine. 1993. "U.S. Rejects Notion that Human Rights Vary with Culture," *New York Times* (June 15), pp. A1, A18.

Scotch, Richard K. 1984. *From Good Will to Civil Rights: Transforming Federal Disability Policy.* Philadelphia: Temple University Press.

———. 1988. "Disability as the Basis for a Social Movement: Advocacy and the Politics of Definition," *Journal of Social Issues,* **44**(1):159–172.

———. 1989. "Politics and Policy in the History of the Disability Rights Movement," *Milbank Quarterly,* **67**(Supplement 2):380–400.

Scott, Ellen Kaye. 1993. "How to Stop the Rapists? A Question of Strategy in Two Rape Crisis Centers," *Social Problems,* **40**(August):343–361.

Scott, Hilda. 1985. *Working Your Way to the Bottom: The Feminization of Poverty.* London: Routledge.

Scott-Samuel, Alex, and Paul Blackburn. 1988. "Crossing the Health Divide—Mortality Attributable to Social Inequality in Great Britain," *Health Promotion,* **2**(3):243–245.

Searle, John. 1992. "The Storm over the University," in Paul Berman (ed.), *Debating P.C.: The Controversy over Political Correctness on College Campuses.* New York: Dell, pp. 85–123.

Seddon, Terri. 1987. "Politics and Curriculum: A Case Study of the Japanese History Textbook Dispute, 1982," *British Journal of Sociology of Education,* **8**(2):213–226.

Selby, David. 1987. *Human Rights.* Cambridge, Eng.: Cambridge University Press.

Select Committee on Aging. 1992. *How Well Do Women Fare under the Nation's Retirement Policies? A Report, September 1992.* Washington, D.C.: U.S. Government Printing Office.

Seligmann, Jean. 1993. "The Art of Flying Solo," *Newsweek,* **121**(March 1):70–73.

Senter, Richard, Terry Miller, Larry T. Reynolds, and Tim Shaffer. 1983. "Bureaucratization and Goal Succession in Alternative Organizations," *Sociological Focus,* **16**(October):239–253.

Shapiro, Joseph P. 1993. *No Pity: People with Disabilities Forging a New Civil Rights Movement.* New York: Times Books.

Sharp, Deborah. 1993. "Teachers Taking a Beating," *USA Today* (October 25), p. 3A.

Sharpe, Rochelle. 1985. "Anti-abortionists Go Activist," *USA Today* (December 2), p. 5A.

Shavit, Yossi. 1993. "From Peasantry to Proletariat: Changes in the Educational Stratification of Arabs in Israel," in Yossi Shavit and Hans-Peter Blossfeld (eds.), *Persistent Inequality: Changing Educational Attainment in Thirteen Countries.* Boulder, Colo.: Westview, pp. 337–349.

Shaw, Marvin E. 1981. *Group Dynamics: The Psychology of Small Group Behavior* (3d ed.). New York: McGraw-Hill.

Shaw, Susan. 1988. "Gender Differences in the Definition and Perception of Household Labor," *Family Relations,* **37**(July):333–337.

Sheehy, Gail. 1976. *Passages: Predictable Crises of Adult Life.* New York: Dutton.

———. 1981. *Pathfinders.* Toronto: Bantam.

Shell, Ellen Rippel. 1988. "Babies in Day Care," *Atlantic,* **262**(August):73–74.

Shelley, Louise I. 1992. "Review of Crime and Justice in Two Societies. Pacific Grove, Calif.: Brooks/Cole.

Shenon, Philip. 1992. "After Years of Denial, Asia Faces Scourge of AIDS," *New York Times* (November 8), pp. 1, 12.

Sherman, Arnold K., and Aliza Kolker. 1987. *The Social Bases of Politics.* Belmont, Calif.: Wadsworth.

Sherwin, Susan. 1992. *No Longer Patient: Feminist Ethics and Health Care.* Philadelphia: Temple University Press.

Shilts, Randy. 1987. *And the Band Played On: Politics, People, and the AIDS Epidemic.* New York: St. Martin's.

———. 1989. "The Era of Bad Feelings," *Mother Jones,* **14**(November):32–36, 58–60.

Shorten, Lynda. 1991. *Without Reserve: Stories from Urban Natives.* Edmonton, Can.: NeWest Press.

Shover, Neal. 1973. "The Social Organization of Burglary," *Social Problems,* **20**(Spring):499–514.

Shupe, Anson D., and David G. Bromley. 1980. "Walking a Tightrope," *Qualitative Sociology,* **2**:8–21.

——— and Jeffrey K. Hadden (eds.). 1988. *The Politics of Religion and Social Change.* New York: Paragon House.

Sidel, Ruth. 1992. *Women and Children Lost: The Plight of Poor Women in Affluent America* (rev. ed.). New York: Penguin.

——— and Victor Sidel. 1984. "Toward the Twenty-First Century," in V. Sidel and R. Sidel (eds.), *Reforming Medicine.* New York: Pantheon, pp. 267–284.

Sidel, Victor, and Ruth Sidel (eds.). 1984. *Reforming Medicine.* New York: Pantheon.

Sigmund, Paul E. 1990. *Liberation Theology at the Crossroads: Democracy or Revolution?* New York: Oxford University Press.

Sills, David L. 1957. *The Volunteers: Means and Ends in a National Organization.* Glencoe, Ill.: Free Press.

———. 1968. "Voluntary Associations: Sociological Aspects," in D. L. Sills (ed.), *International Encyclopedia of the Social Sciences,* vol. 16. New York: Macmillan, pp. 362–379.

——— and Robert K. Merton. 1991. *Social Science Quotations.* New York: Macmillan.

Silva, Nelson De Valle. 1985. "Updating the Cost of Not Being White in Brazil," in Pierre-Michel Fontaine (ed.), *Race, Class, and Power in Brazil.* Los Angeles: Center for Afro-American Studies, University of California at Los Angeles, pp. 42–55.

Silverman, Milton. 1976. *The Drugging of the Americas.* Berkeley: University of California Press.

———, Mia Lydecker, and Philip R. Lee. 1990. "The Drug Swindlers," *International Journal of Health Sciences,* **20**: 561–572.

———, ———, and ———. 1992. *Bad Medicine: The Prescription Drug Industry in the Third World.* Stanford, Calif.: Stanford University Press.

Silverstein, Ken. 1990. "Shock Treatment for the Poor," *The Nation,* **251**(November 12):554–557.

Simmel, Georg. 1950. *Sociology of Georg Simmel.* Translated by K. Wolff. Glencoe, Ill.: Free Press (originally written in 1902–1917).

Simon, John L. 1992. *Population and Development in Poor Countries.* Princeton, N.J.: Princeton University Press.

Simons, Marlise. 1988. "Brazil's Blacks Feel Prejudice 100 Years after Slavery's End," *New York Times* (May 14), pp. 1, 6.

———. 1989. "Abortion Fight Has New Front in Western Europe," *New York Times* (June 28), pp. A1, A9.

———. 1993a. "Out of East Europe, into Sex Slavery," *International Herald Tribune* (June 10), pp. 1, 6.

———. 1993b. "Dutch Move to Enact Law Making Euthanasia Easier," *New York Times* (February 9), pp. A1, A9.

Simpson, Sally. 1993. "Corporate Crime," in Craig Calhoun and George Ritzer (eds.), *Introduction to Social Problems.* New York: McGraw-Hill, pp. 236–256.

Sirott, Larry, and Howard Waitzkin. 1984. "Holism and Self-Care: Can the Individual Succeed Where Society Fails?" in V. Sidel and R. Sidel (eds.), *Reforming Medicine.* New York: Pantheon, pp. 245–264.

Sivy, Michael. 1993. "A Warning Flashes for Stocks," *Money,* **22**(August):55.

Sjoberg, Gideon. 1960. *The Preindustrial City: Past and Present.* Glencoe, Ill.: Free Press.

Skafte, Peter. 1979. "Smoking Out Secrets of the Mysterious 'Snakers' of India," *Smithsonian,* **10**(October):121–126.

Sloan, John Henry, et al. [9 authors]. 1988. "Handgun Regulations, Crime, Assaults, and Homicide: A Tale of Two Cities," *New England Journal of Medicine,* **319**(November 10):1256–1262.

Smart, Barry. 1990. "Modernity, Postmodernity, and the Present," in Bryan S. Turner (ed.), *Theories of Modernity and Postmodernity.* Newbury Park, Calif.: Sage, pp. 14–30.

Smelser, Neil. 1962. *Theory of Collective Behavior.* New York: Free Press.

———. 1963. *The Sociology of Economic Life.* Englewood Cliffs, N.J.: Prentice-Hall.

———. 1981. *Sociology.* Englewood Cliffs, N.J.: Prentice-Hall.

——— (ed.). 1988. *Handbook of Sociology.* Newbury Park, Calif.: Sage.

Smith, Christian. 1991. *The Emergence of Liberation Theology: Radical Religion and Social Movement Theory.* Chicago: University of Chicago Press.

Smith, James P. 1986. *The Distribution of Wealth.* Ann Arbor, Mich.: Survey Research Center.

Smith, Michael Peter. 1988. *City, State, and Market.* New York: Basil Blackwell.

Smith, Ruth Bayard. 1993. "The Rise of the Conservative Student Press," *Change* (January–February), pp. 24–29.

Smolan, Rick, Phillip Moffitt, and Matthew Naythons (eds.). 1990. *The Power to Heal: Ancient Arts and Modern Medicine.* New York: Prentice-Hall.

Smoler, Fredric. 1992. "What Should We Teach Our Children about American History?" *American Heritage,* **43**(February–March):45–50.

Smothers, Ronald. 1992a. "Many State Lotteries Feel the Pinch of Recession, and Perhaps Monotony," *New York Times* (February 2), p. 16.

———. 1992b. "For Black Farmers, Extinction to Be Near," *New York Times* (August 3), p. A10.

Snow, David A., Susan G. Baker, Leon Anderson, and Michael Martin. 1986. "The Myth of Pervasive Mental Illness among the Homeless," *Social Problems,* **33**(June):407–423.

———, Louis A. Zurcher, Jr., and Robert Peters. 1981. "Victory Celebrations as Theater: A Dramaturgical Approach to Crowd Behavior," *Symbolic Interaction,* **4**:21–42.

Sokolovsky, Jay (ed.). 1990. *The Cultural Context of Aging: Worldwide Perspectives.* New York: Bergen and Garvey.

Solórzano, Lucia. 1986. "Teaching in Trouble," *U.S. News and World Report,* **100**(May 26):52–57.

Son, In Soo, Suzanne W. Model, and Gene A. Fisher. 1989. "Polarization and Progress in the Black Community: Earnings and Status Gains for Young Black Males in the Era of Affirmative Action," *Sociological Forum,* **4**(September):309–327.

Sontag, Deborah. 1993a. "Émigrés in New York: Work off the Books," *New York Times* (June 13), pp. 1, 42.

———. 1993b. "Study Sees Illegal Aliens in New Light," *New York Times* (September 2), pp. B1, B8.

Sorokin, Pitirim A. 1959. *Social and Cultural Mobility.* New York: Free Press (original edition 1927, New York: Harper and Brothers).

Sorrentino, Constance. 1990. "The Changing Family in International Perspective," *Monthly Labor Review,* **113**(March):41–56.

Sowell, Thomas. 1993. *Inside American Education: The Decline, the Deception, the Dogmas.* New York: Free Press.

Spain, Daphne. 1992. *Gendered Spaces.* Chapel Hill: University of North Carolina Press.

Spanier, Graham B. 1983. "Married and Unmarried Cohabitation in the United States 1980," *Journal of Marriage and the Family,* **45**(May):277–288.

Spengler, Joseph J. 1978. *Facing Zero Population Growth: Reactions and Interpretations, Past and Present.* Durham, N.C.: Duke University Press.

Spielmann, Peter James. 1992. "11 Population Groups on 'Endangered' List," *Chicago Sun-Times* (November 23), p. 12.

Spradley, James P., and David W. McCurdy. 1980. *Anthropology: The Cultural Perspective* (2d ed.). New York: Wiley.

Squire, Peverill. 1988. "Why the 1936 *Literary Digest* Poll Failed," *Public Opinion Quarterly,* **52**(Spring):125–133.

Stacey, Meg (ed.). 1992. *Changing Human Reproduction: Social Science Perspectives.* London: Sage.

Stack, Steven. 1987. "Celebrities and Suicide: A Taxonomy and Analysis, 1948–1983," *American Sociological Review,* **52**(June):401–412.

Staggenborg, Suzanne. 1988. "Consequences of Professionalization and Formalization," *American Sociological Review,* **53**(August):585–606.

———. 1989a. "Stability and Innovation in the Women's Movement: A Comparison of Two Movement Organizations," *Social Problems,* **36**(February):75–92.

———. 1989b. "Organizational and Environmental Influences on the Development of the Pro-choice Movement," *Social Forces,* **68**(September):204–240.

Stahura, John M. 1986. "Suburban Development, Black Suburbanization and the Civil Rights Movement since World

War II," *American Sociological Review,* **51**(February):131–144.

———. 1987. "Characteristics of Black Suburbs, 1950–1980," *Sociology and Social Research,* **71**(January):135–138.

Stanley, J. P. 1977. "Paradigmatic Woman: The Prostitute," in B. Shores and C. P. Hines (eds.), *Papers in Language Variation.* University: University of Alabama Press, pp. 303–321.

Stark, Rodney, et al. 1973. *Society Today* (2d ed.). Del Mar, Calif.: CRM Books.

——— and William Sims Bainbridge. 1979. "Of Churches, Sects, and Cults: Preliminary Concepts for a Theory of Religious Movements," *Journal for the Scientific Study of Religion,* **18**(June): 117–131.

——— and ———. 1985. *The Future of Religion.* Berkeley: University of California Press.

——— and Laurence R. Iannaccone. 1992. "Sociology of Religion," in Edgar F. Borgatta and Marie L. Borgatta (eds.), *Encyclopedia of Sociology,* vol. 4. New York: Macmillan, pp. 2029–2037.

Starr, Paul. 1982. *The Social Transformation of American Medicine.* New York: Basic Books.

Statham, Ann. 1987. "The Gender Model Revisited: Differences in the Management Styles of Men and Women," *Sex Roles,* **16**(April):409–429.

———, Eleanor M. Miller, and Hans O. Mauksch (eds.). 1988. *The Worth of Women's Work.* Albany: State University of New York Press.

Stearn, J. 1993. "What Crisis?" *Statesmen and Society,* **6**(April 2):7–9.

Steiber, Steven R. 1979. "The World System and World Trade: An Empirical Exploration of Conceptual Conflicts," *Sociological Quarterly,* **20**(Winter):23–36.

Stein, Leonard. 1967. "The Doctor-Nurse Game," *Archives of General Psychiatry,* **16**:699–703.

Stein, Peter J. 1975. "Singlehood: An Alternative to Marriage," *Family Coordinator,* **24**(October):489–503.

——— (ed.). 1981. *Single Life: Unmarried Adults in Social Context.* New York: St. Martin's.

———. 1984. "Men in Families," *Marriage and Family Review,* **7**(Fall–Winter): 143–168.

Stellman, Jeanne Mager, and Joan E.

Bertin. 1990. "Science's Anti-Female Bias," *New York Times* (June 4), p. A23.

Stenning, Derrick J. 1958. "Household Viability among the Pastoral Fulani," in John R. Goody (ed.), *The Developmental Cycle in Domestic Groups.* Cambridge, Eng.: Cambridge University Press, pp. 92–119.

Stephens, Gene. 1992. "Crime and the Biotech Revolution," *Futurist,* **26**(November–December):38–42.

Sterngold, James. 1992. "Japan Ends Fingerprinting of Many Non-Japanese," *New York Times* (May 21), p. A11.

Stets, Jan E., and Maureen A. Pirog-Good. 1987. "Violence in Dating Relationships," *Social Psychology Quarterly,* **50** (September):237–246.

Stevens, William K. 1987a. "Reagan Insurance Plan Appears Helpful to Few," *New York Times* (March 8), p. 24.

———. 1987b. "Despite Defeats, Fundamentalists Vow to Press Efforts to Reshape Schools," *New York Times* (August 29), p. 6.

———. 1987c. "Beyond the Mall: Suburbs Evolving into 'Outer Cities,'" *New York Times* (November 8), p. E5.

Stimpson, Catharine R. 1971. "Thy Neighbor's Wife, Thy Neighbor's Servants; Women's Liberation and Black Civil Rights," in Vivian Gornick and Barbara K. Moran (eds.), *Woman in Sexist Society.* New York: Basic Books, pp. 622–657.

———. 1992. "On Differences: Modern Language Association Presidential Address 1990," in Paul Berman (ed.), *Debating P.C.: The Controversy over Political Correctness on College Campuses.* New York: Dell, pp. 40–60.

Stocks, J. Timothy. 1988. "Has Family Violence Decreased? A Reassessment of the Straus and Gelles Data," *Journal of Marriage and the Family,* **50**(February): 281–285.

Stoeckel, John, and N. L. Sirisena. 1988. "Gender-Specific Socioeconomic Impacts of Development Programs in Sri Lanka," *Journal of Developing Areas,* **23**(October):31–42.

Stone, Andrea. 1991. "Welfare Slash Worst in 10 Years," *USA Today* (December 19), p. A1.

Stone, Gregory P. 1977. "Personal Acts," *Symbolic Interaction,* **1**(Fall):1–21.

Stonich, Susan C. 1989. "The Dynamics of Social Processes and Environmental Destruction: A Central American Case Study," *Population and Development Review,* **15**:269–296.

Straus, Murray A., and Richard J. Gelles (eds.). 1990. *Physical Violence in American Families.* New Brunswick, N.J.: Transaction.

———, ———, and Suzanne K. Steinmetz. 1980. *Behind Closed Doors: Violence in the American Family.* Garden City, N.Y.: Doubleday/Anchor.

Straus, Roger (ed.). 1985. *Using Sociology.* Bayside, N.Y.: General-Hall.

Strauss, Anselm. 1977. *Negotiations: Varieties, Contexts, Processes, and Social Order.* San Francisco: Jossey-Bass.

———. 1985. "Work and the Division of Labor," *Sociological Quarterly,* **26**(Spring):1–19.

Strum, Charles. 1993. "Schools' Tracks and Democracy," *New York Times* (April 1), pp. B1, B7.

Stuart, Reginald. 1982. "Judge Overturns Arkansas Law on Creationism," *New York Times* (January 6), pp. A1, B7, B8.

Sumner, William G. 1906. *Folkways.* New York: Ginn.

Suro, Roberto. 1993. "Pollution-Weary Minorities Try Civil Rights Tack," *New York Times* (January 11), pp. A1, B7.

Sutherland, Edwin H. 1937. *The Professional Thief.* Chicago: University of Chicago Press.

———. 1940. "White-Collar Criminality," *American Sociological Review,* **5**(February):1–11.

———. 1949. *White Collar Crime.* New York: Dryden.

———. 1983. *White Collar Crime: The Uncut Version.* New Haven, Conn.: Yale University Press.

——— and Donald R. Cressey. 1978. *Principles of Criminology* (10th ed.). Philadelphia: Lippincott.

Suttles, Gerald D. 1972. *The Social Construction of Communities.* Chicago: University of Chicago Press.

Swartz, Leslie. 1985. "Anorexia Nervosa as a Culture-Bound Syndrome," *Social Science and Medicine,* **20**(7):725–730.

Swatos, William H., Jr. (ed.). 1993. *Gender and Religion.* New Brunswick, N.J.: Transaction.

Sweet, James A., and Larry L. Bumpass.

1987. *American Families and Households.* New York: Sage.

Swift, Richard N. 1993. "United Nations," in *1993 Britannica Book of the Year.* Chicago: Encyclopedia Britannica, pp. 346–349.

Swinton, David. 1987. "Economic Status of Blacks, 1986," in Janet Dewart (ed.), *The State of Black America.* New York: National Urban League, pp. 49–73.

Swiss, Deborah, and Judith Walker. 1993. *Women and the Work/Family Dilemma: How Today's Professional Women Are Finding Solutions.* New York: Wiley.

Sykes, Gresham, and David Matza. 1957. "Techniques of Neutralization: A Theory of Delinquency," *American Sociological Review,* **22**(December):664–670.

Szasz, Thomas S. 1971. "The Same Slave: An Historical Note on the Use of Medical Diagnosis as Justificatory Rhetoric," *American Journal of Psychotherapy,* **25** (April):228–239.

———. 1974. *The Myth of Mental Illness* (rev. ed.). New York: Harper and Row.

Szulc, Tad. 1988. "How Can We Help Ourselves Age with Dignity?" *Parade* (May 29), pp. 4–7.

Szymanski, Albert. 1983. *Class Structure: A Critical Perspective.* New York: Praeger.

Tachibana, Judy. 1990. "Model Minority Myth Presents Unrepresentative Portrait of Asian Americans, Many Educators Say," *Black Issues in Higher Education,* **6**(March 1):1, 11.

Taeuber, Cynthia M. 1992. "Sixty-five Plus in America," *Current Population Reports,* ser. P-23, no. 178. Washington, D.C.: U.S. Government Printing Office.

Takagi, Dana Y. 1993. *The Retreat from Race: Asian-American Admissions and Racial Politics.* New Brunswick, N.J.: Rutgers University Press.

Takaki, Ronald. 1990. "The Harmful Myth of Asian Superiority," *New York Times* (June 16), p. 21.

———. 1993. *A Different Mirror: A History of Multicultural America.* Boston: Little, Brown.

Tannen, Deborah. 1990. *You Just Don't Understand: Women and Men in Conversation.* New York: Ballantine.

Tashman, Billy. 1992. "Hobson's Choice: Free-Market Education Plan Vouches for Bush's Favorite Class," *Village Voice,* **37**(January 21; educational supplement):9, 14.

Taylor, Paul. 1985. "Uninsured? Find Another Hospital," *Washington Post National Weekly Edition,* **2**(July 22):8–9.

———. 1991. "Baby Steps toward Being Family-Friendly," *Washington Post National Weekly Edition,* **9**(November 25):21.

Taylor, Stuart, Jr. 1987. "High Court Voids Curb on Teaching Evolution Theory," *New York Times* (June 20), pp. 1, 7.

Telsch, Kathleen. 1991. "New Study of Older Workers Finds They Can Become Good Investments," *New York Times* (May 21), p. A16.

Terrell, Ruth Harris. 1992. *A Kid's Guide to How to Stop the Violence.* New York: Avon.

Terry, Don. 1993. "Kevorkian Assists in Death of His 17th Suicide Patient," *New York Times* (August 5), p. A14.

Theberge, Nancy. 1993. "The Construction of Gender in Sport: Women, Coaching, and the Naturalization of Difference," *Social Problems,* **40**(August): 301–313.

Third World Institute. 1993. *Third World Guide 93/94.* Toronto, Can.: Garamond.

Thirlwall, A. P. 1989. *Growth and Development* (4th ed.). London: Macmillan.

Thoits, Peggy A. 1985. "Self-labeling Processes in Mental Illness: The Role of Emotional Deviance," *American Journal of Sociology,* **91**(September):221–249.

Thomas, Gordon, and Max Morgan Witts. 1974. *Voyage of the Damned.* Greenwich, Conn.: Fawcett Crest.

Thomas, Jim. 1984. "Some Aspects of Negotiating Order: Loose Coupling and Mesostructure in Maximum Security Prisons," *Symbolic Interaction,* **7**(Fall): 213–231.

Thomas, Rich. 1993. "Looking like a Leader at Last," *Newsweek,* **122**(July 19): 18–19.

Thomas, William I. 1923. *The Unadjusted Girl.* Boston: Little, Brown.

———. 1927. *The Polish Peasant in Europe and America.* New York: Knopf.

Thompson, James D., and Robert W. Hawkes. 1962. "Disaster, Community Organization, and Administrative Process," in G. W. Baker and D. W. Chapman (eds.), *Man and Society in Disaster.* New York: Basic Books, pp. 268–300.

Thompson, Linda, and Alexis J. Walker. 1989. "Gender in Families: Women and Men in Marriage, Work, and Parenthood," *Journal of Marriage and the Family,* **51**(November):845–871.

Thompson, William E. 1983. "Hanging Tongues: A Sociological Encounter on the Assembly Line," *Qualitative Sociology,* **6**(Fall):215–237.

Thomson, Elizabeth, and Ugo Colella. 1992. "Cohabitation and Marital Stability: Quality or Commitment?" *Journal of Marriage and the Family,* **54**(May):259–267.

Thorne, Barrie. 1987. "Re-visioning Women and Social Change: Where Are the Children?" *Gender and Society,* **1**(March):85–109.

———. 1993. *Gender Play: Girls and Boys in School.* New Brunswick, N.J.: Rutgers University Press.

Thornton, Arland. 1985. "Changing Attitudes toward Separation and Divorce: Causes and Consequences," *American Journal of Sociology,* **90**(January):856–872.

———, Duane F. Alwin, and Donald Camburn. 1983. "Causes and Consequences of Sex-Role Attitudes and Attitude Change," *American Sociological Review,* **48**(April):211–227.

Thornton, Robert Y., and Katsuya Endo. 1990. "Controlling Crime and Delinquency: A Tale of Two Cities," *The Police Chief* (March), pp. 54–58.

Tiano, Susan. 1987. "Gender, Work, and World Capitalism: Third World Women's Role in Development," in Beth B. Hess and Myra Marx Ferree (eds.), *Analyzing Gender: A Handbook of Social Science Research.* Newbury Park, Calif.: Sage, pp. 216–243.

Tiefer, Lenore. 1978. "The Kiss," *Human Nature,* **1**(July):28, 30–37.

Tierney, John. 1990. "Betting the Planet," *New York Times Magazine* (December 2), pp. 52–53, 71, 74, 76, 78, 80–81.

Tierney, Kathleen. 1980. "Emergent Norm Theory as 'Theory': An Analysis and Critique of Turner's Formulation," in Meredith David Pugh (ed.), *Collective Behavior: A Source Book.* St. Paul, Minn.: West, pp. 42–53.

Time. 1971. "Suburbia: The New American Plurality," **97**(March 15):14–20.

———. 1982. "Out Front on Arms Control," **119**(February 1):19.

Tinker, Irene (ed.). 1990. *Persistent Inequalities: Women and World Development.* New York: Oxford University Press.

Tipps, Havens C., and Henry A. Gordon. 1983. "Inequality at Work: Race, Sex, and Underemployment." Paper presented at the annual meeting of the American Sociological Association, Detroit.

Tittle, Charles R. 1989. "Influences on Urbanism: A Test of Predictions from Three Perspectives," *Social Problems,* **36**(June):270–288.

Tobin, Joseph J., David Y. H. Wu, and Dana H. Davidson. 1989. *Preschool in Three Cultures: Japan, China, and the United States.* New Haven, Conn.: Yale University Press.

Tonkinson, Robert. 1978. *The Mardudjara Aborigines.* New York: Holt.

Tönnies, Ferdinand. 1988. *Community and Society.* Rutgers, N.J.: Transaction (originally published in 1887).

Topolnicki, Denise M. 1993. "The World's 5 Best Ideas," *Money,* **22**(June):74–83, 87, 89, 91.

Touraine, Alain. 1974. *The Academic System in American Society.* New York: McGraw-Hill.

Tracy, Martin B., and Roxanne L. Ward. 1986. "Trends in Old-Age Pensions for Women: Benefit Levels in Ten Nations, 1960–1980," *Gerontologist,* **26**(3):286–291.

Treiman, Donald J. 1977. *Occupational Prestige in Comparative Perspective.* New York: Academic.

Treisman, Uri. 1989. *A Study of Mathematics Performance of Black Students at the University of California, Berkeley.* Unpublished manuscript, Dana Center, University of California, Berkeley.

Tsai, Shu-Ling, and Hei-Yuan Chiu. 1993. "Changes in Educational Stratification in Taiwan," in Yossi Shavit and Hans-Peter Blossfeld (eds.), *Persistent Inequality: Changing Educational Attainment in Thirteen Countries,* Boulder, Colo.: Westview, pp. 193–227.

Tsuneyoshi, Ryoko Kato. 1992. "Japanese Corporations and Schools: The Hidden Curricula." Paper presented at the annual meeting of the American Sociological Association, Pittsburgh.

Tuchman, Gaye. 1992. "Feminist Theory," in Edgar F. Borgatta and Marie L. Borgatta (eds.), *Encyclopedia of Sociology,* vol. 2. New York: Macmillan, pp. 695–704.

Tucker, James. 1993. "Everyday Forms of Employee Resistance," *Sociological Forum,* **8**(March):25–45.

Tucker, Jeffrey A. 1993. "Evils of Choice," *National Review,* **45**(March):44–47.

Tumin, Melvin M. 1953. "Some Principles of Stratification: A Critical Analysis," *American Sociological Review,* **18**(August):387–394.

———. 1985. *Social Stratification* (2d ed.). Englewood Cliffs, N.J.: Prentice-Hall.

Turner, Bryan S. 1990. *Theories of Modernity and Postmodernity.* Newbury Park, Calif.: Sage.

Turner, J. H. 1985. *Herbert Spencer: A Renewed Application.* Beverly Hills, Calif.: Sage.

Turner, Margery, Michael Fix, and Raymond J. Struyck. 1991. *Opportunities Denied, Opportunities Diminished: Discrimination in Hiring.* Washington, D.C.: Urban Institute.

Turner, Patricia A. 1993. *I Heard It through the Grapevine: Rumor in African-American Culture.* Berkeley: University of California Press.

Turner, Ralph. 1962. "Role Taking: Process vs. Conformity," in Arnold Rose (ed.), *Human Behavior and Social Processes.* Boston: Houghton Mifflin, pp. 20–40.

——— and Lewis M. Killian. 1987. *Collective Behavior* (3d ed.). Englewood Cliffs, N.J.: Prentice-Hall.

Turque, Bill. 1991. "Reversal of Fortune," *Newsweek,* **118**(September 9):44–45.

Twaddle, Andrew. 1974. "The Concept of Health Status," *Social Science and Medicine,* **8**(January):29–38.

——— and Richard M. Hessler. 1987. *A Sociology of Health* (2d ed.). New York: Macmillan.

Tyler, Charles. 1991. "The World's Manacled Millions," *Geographical Magazine,* **63**(1):30–35.

Tyler, William B. 1985. "The Organizational Structure of the School," in Ralph H. Turner (ed.), *Annual Review of Sociology, 1985.* Palo Alto, Calif.: Annual Reviews, pp. 49–73.

Udy, Stanley H., Jr. 1959. "Bureaucracy and Rationality in Weber's Organizational Theory: An Empirical Study," *American Sociological Review,* **24**(December):791–795.

United Nations. 1993. *World Urbanization Prospects, 1992.* New York: UN Population Division.

United Nations Department of International Economic and Social Affairs. 1991. *The World's Women: Trends and Statistics, 1970–1990.* New York: United Nations.

United Nations Development Programme. 1993. *Human Development Report 1993.* New York: Oxford University Press.

United Nations Environment Programme and World Health Organization. 1988. *Assessment of Urban Air Quality.* Nairobi, Kenya: Global Environmental Monitoring System.

United States National Academy of Sciences and the Royal Society of London. 1992. *Population Growth, Resource Consumption, and a Sustainable World.* London and Washington, D.C.: U.S. National Academy of Sciences and the Royal Society of London.

USA Today. 1991. "Study: Women Hold 2.6% of Top Jobs" (August 27), p. 11A.

Usdansky, Margaret L. 1993a. "Gay Couples, by the Numbers," *USA Today* (April 12), p. 8A.

———. 1993b. "Census: Languages Not Foreign at Home," *USA Today* (April 28), pp. A1, A2.

Vachss, Alice. 1993. *Sex Crimes.* New York: Random House.

van den Berghe, Pierre. 1978. *Race and Racism: A Comparative Perspective* (2d ed.). New York: Wiley.

Vanneman, Reeve, and Lynn Weber Cannon. 1987. *The American Perception of Class.* Philadelphia: Temple University Press.

van Voorst, Bruce. 1992. "The Recycling Bottleneck," *Time,* **140**(September 14):52–54.

van Vucht Tijssen, Lieteke. 1990. "Women between Modernity and Postmodernity," in Bryan S. Turner (ed.), *Theories of Modernity and Postmodernity.* London: Sage, pp. 147–163.

Vasquez, Enriqueta Longauex y. 1970. "The Mexican-American Woman," in Robin Morgan (ed.), *Sisterhood Is Powerful.* New York: Random House, pp. 379–384.

Veblen, Thorstein. 1919. *The Vested Interests and the State of the Industrial Arts.* New York: Huebsch.

Verbrugge, Lois M. 1985. "Gender and Health: An Update on Hypotheses and Evidence," *Journal of Health and Social Behavior,* **26**(September):156–182.

Vernon, Glenn. 1962. *Sociology and Religion.* New York: McGraw-Hill.

Vernon, Jo Etta A., et al. [4 authors]. 1990. "Media Stereotyping: A Comparison of the Way Elderly Women and Men Are Portrayed on Prime-Time Television," *Journal of Women/Aging,* **2** (4):55–68.

Vernon, Raymond. 1977. *Storm over the Multinationals: The Real Issues.* Cambridge, Mass.: Harvard University Press.

Vobejda, Barbara. 1990. "The Overpopulation Scare Has Gotten Lost in the Crowd," *Washington Post National Weekly Edition,* **7**(July 9):31.

———. 1993. "U.S. Ends Survey of Its Dwindling Farm Population," *Chicago Sun-Times* (October 9), p. 6.

Voydanoff, Patricia, and Linda C. Majka (eds.). 1988. *Families and Economic Distress.* Newbury Park, Calif.: Sage.

Wagley, Charles, and Marvin Harris. 1958. *Minorities in the New World: Six Case Studies.* New York: Columbia University Press.

Wagner, David, and Marcia B. Cohen. 1991. "The Power of the People: Homeless Protesters in the Aftermath of Social Movement Participation," *Social Problems,* **38**(November):543–561.

Waitzkin, Howard. 1986. *The Second Sickness: Contradictions of Capitalist Health Care.* Chicago: University of Chicago Press.

Waldrop, Theresa. 1993. "'Slapping Spastis': German Neo-Nazis Turn On the Handicapped," *Newsweek,* **121**(March 1):26.

Walker, Gillian A. 1986. "Burnout: From Metaphor to Ideology," *Canadian Journal of Sociology,* **11**(Spring):35–55.

Wallace, Anthony. 1966. *Religion: An Anthropological View.* New York: Random House.

Wallace, Ruth A., and Alison Wolf. 1980. *Contemporary Sociological Theory.* Englewood Cliffs, N.J.: Prentice-Hall.

Wallace, Stephen. 1984. "Macro and Micro Issues in Intergenerational Relationships within the Latino Family and Community." Paper presented at the annual meeting of the Society for the Study of Social Problems, San Antonio, Tex.

Wallerstein, Immanuel. 1974. *The Modern World System.* New York: Academic Press.

———. 1979. *Capitalist World Economy.* Cambridge, Eng.: Cambridge University Press.

———. 1991. *Geopolitics and Geoculture: Essays on the Changing World System.* Cambridge, Eng.: Cambridge University Press.

Wallerstein, Judith, and Sandra Blakeslee. 1989. *Second Chances: Men, Women, and Children a Decade after Divorce.* New York: Ticknor and Fields.

Wallis, Claudia. 1981. "Southward Ho for Jobs," *Time,* **117**(May 11):23.

———. 1987. "Is Mental Illness Inherited?" *Time,* **129**(March 9):67.

Walton, John. 1992. *Western Times and Water Wars: State, Culture, and Rebellion in California.* Berkeley: University of California Press.

——— and Charles Ragin. 1988. "Global and National Sources of Political Protest: Third World Response to the Debt Crisis." Paper presented at the annual meeting of the American Sociological Association, Atlanta.

——— and ———. 1989. "Austerity and Dissent: Social Basis of Popular Struggle in Latin America," in William L. Canak (ed.), *Lost Promises, Debt, Austerity, and Development in Latin America.* Boulder, Colo.: Westview, pp. 216–232.

Waring, Marilyn. 1988. *If Women Counted: A New Feminist Economics.* San Francisco: Harper and Row.

Warner, Judith. 1993. "The Assassination of Dr. Gunn: Scare Tactics Turn Deadly," *Ms.,* **3**(May–June):86–87.

Warr, Mark, and Mark Stafford. 1991. "The Influence of Delinquent Peers: What They Think or What They Do," *Criminology,* **29**(November):851–866.

Washington Post. 1984. "The Congressional Checkoff," *Washington Post National Weekly Edition,* **1**(October 15): 14–15.

Wasielewski, Patricia. 1985. "The Emotional Basis of Charisma," *Symbolic Interaction,* **8**(2):207–222.

Wasserman, Ira. 1984. "Imitation and Suicide: A Re-examination of the Weorther Effect," *American Sociological Review,* **49**(June):427–436.

Watanabe, Kazuko. 1991. "The New Cold War with Japan: How Are Women Paying for It?" *Ms.,* **2**(November–December):18–22.

Waterfield, Larry W. 1986. *Conflict and Crisis in Rural America.* New York: Praeger.

Waters, Harry F. 1993. "Networks under the Gun," *Newsweek,* **122**(July 12):64–66.

Watkins, Beverly T. 1992. "Foreign Enrollment at U.S. Colleges and Universities Totaled 419,585 in 1991–92, an All-Time High," *Chronicles of Higher Education,* **49**(November 25):A28–A29.

Watson, Kenneth M. 1986. "Birth Families: Living with the Adoption Decision," *Public Welfare,* **44**(Spring):5–10.

Watson, Russell. 1984. "A Hidden Epidemic," *Newsweek,* **103**(May 14):30–36.

Watson, Tracey. 1987. "Women Athletes and Athletic Women: The Dilemmas and Contradictions of Managing Incongruent Identities," *Sociological Inquiry,* **57**(Fall):431–446.

Watts, Jerry G. 1990. "Pluralism Reconsidered," *Urban Affairs Quarterly,* **25** (June):697–704.

Watts, W. David, and Ann Marie Ellis. 1989. "Assessing Sociology Educational Outcomes: Occupational Status and Mobility of Graduates," *Teaching Sociology,* **17**(July):297–306.

Weaver, Warren, Jr. 1982. "Age Discrimination Charges Found in Sharp Rise in U.S.," *New York Times* (February 22), p. A12.

Webb, Eugene J., Donald T. Campbell, Richard D. Schwartz, Lee Sechrest, and Janet Belew Grove. 1981. *Nonreactive Measures in the Social Sciences* (2d ed.). Boston: Houghton Mifflin.

Webb, Marilyn. 1993. "How Old Is Too Old?" *New York,* **26**(March 29):66–73.

Weber, Max. 1947. *The Theory of Social and Economic Organization.* Translated by A. Henderson and T. Parsons. New York: Free Press (originally published during the period 1913–1922).

———. 1949. *Methodology of the Social Sciences.* Translated by Edward A. Shils and Henry A. Finch. Glencoe, Ill.: Free Press (originally published in 1904).

————. 1958a. *The Protestant Ethic and the Spirit of Capitalism.* Translated by Talcott Parsons. New York: Scribner (originally published in 1904).

————. 1958b. *The Religion of India: The Sociology of Hinduism and Buddhism.* New York: Free Press (originally published in 1916).

Weeks, John R. 1988. "The Demography of Islamic Nations," *Population Bulletin,* **43**(December).

————. 1994. *Population: An Introduction to Concepts and Issues* (updated 5th ed.). Belmont, Calif.: Wadsworth.

Weigard, Bruce. 1992. *Off the Books: A Theory and Critique of the Underground Economy.* Dix Hills, N.Y.: General-Hall.

Weinberg, Martin S., and Colin J. Williams. 1980. "Sexual Embourgeoisement? Social Class and Sexual Activity: 1938–1970," *American Sociological Review,* **45**(February):33–48.

Weiner, Tim. 1993. "Pleas for Asylum Inundate System for Immigration," *New York Times* (April 25), pp. 1, 50.

Weinstein, Deena. 1992. *Heavy Metal: A Cultural Sociology.* New York: Lexington.

Weisburd, David, Stanton Wheeler, Elin Warin, and Nancy Bode. 1991. *Crimes of the Middle Classes: White-Collar Offenders in the Federal Courts.* New Haven, Conn.: Yale University Press.

Weisman, Steven R. 1992. "Landmark Harassment Case in Japan," *New York Times* (April 17), p. A3.

Weitz, Shirley. 1977. *Sex Roles: Biological, Psychological, and Social Foundations.* New York: Oxford University Press.

Weitzer, Ronald. 1991. "Prostitutes' Rights in the United States: The Failure of a Movement," *Sociological Quarterly,* **32**(1):23–41.

Weitzman, Lenore J. 1985. *The Divorce Revolution: The Unexpected Social and Economic Consequences for Women and Children in America.* New York: Free Press.

Welch, William M. 1993. "Voters Take Reform Worries, Hopes to Senators," *USA Today* (April 16), p. 5A.

————. 1994. "Welfare Reform Easier Said Than Done," *USA Today* (January 10), p. 3A.

———— and Bill Nicholas. 1993. "Welfare Changes Put on Back Burner," *USA Today* (April 30), p. 6A.

Wells, Ida B. 1970. *Crusade for Justice: The Autobiography of Ida B. Wells.* Chicago: University of Chicago Press.

West, Candace, and Don H. Zimmerman. 1983. "Small Insults: A Study of Interruptions in Cross Sex Conversations between Unacquainted Persons," in Barrie Thorne, Cheris Kramarae, and Nancy Henley (eds.), *Language, Gender, and Society.* Rowley, Mass.: Newbury House, pp. 86–111.

———— and ————. 1987. "Doing Gender," *Gender and Society,* **1**(June):125–151.

West, Cornel. 1993. *Race Matters.* Boston: Beacon Press.

West, Edwin G. 1984. "Are American Schools Working? Disturbing Cost and Quality Trends," *American Education,* **20**(January–February):11–21.

Wheeler, David L. 1993. "Women's Health Study Under Fire," *Chronicle of Higher Education,* **21**(November 10):8.

White, Jack E. 1993. "Growing Up in Black and White," *Time,* **141**(May 17):48–49.

White, Merry. 1987. *The Japanese Educational Challenge: A Commitment to Children.* New York: Free Press.

Whittle, Jeff, Joseph Conigharo, C. B. Good, and Richard P. Lofgren. 1993. "Racial Differences in the Use of Invasive Cardiovascular Procedures in the Department of Veterans Affairs Medical System," *New England Journal of Medicine,* **329**(August 26):621–627.

Whyte, William Foote. 1981. *Street Corner Society: Social Structure of an Italian Slum* (3d ed.). Chicago: University of Chicago Press.

————. 1989. "Advancing Scientific Knowledge through Participatory Action Research," *Sociological Forum,* **4**(September):367–385.

Wickman, Peter M. 1991. "Deviance," in Dushkin Publishing Group, *Encyclopedic Dictionary of Sociology* (4th ed.). Guilford, Conn.: Dushkin, pp. 85–87.

Wilhite, Allen, and John Theilmann. 1986. "Women, Blacks, and PAC Discrimination," *Social Science Quarterly,* **67**(July):283–298.

Wilkerson, Isabel. 1987. "Growth of the Very Poor Is Focus of New Studies," *New York Times* (December 20), p. 15.

————. 1990. "With Rural Towns Vanishing, States Choose Which to Save," *New York Times* (January 3), pp. A1, A16.

————. 1991. "Black-White Marriages Rise, but Social Acceptance Lags," *New York Times* (December 2), pp. A1, B6.

Wilkinson, Doris K. 1980. "A Synopsis: Projections for the Profession in the 1980's," *ASA Footnotes,* **8**(April 1):6–7.

Will, George F. 1992. "Radical English," in Paul Berman (ed.), *Debating P.C.: The Controversy over Political Correctness on College Campuses.* New York: Dell, pp. 258–261.

Will, J. A., P. A. Self, and N. Datan. 1976. "Maternal Behavior and Perceived Sex of Infant," *American Journal of Orthopsychiatry,* **46**:135–139.

Williams, Christine L. 1992. "The Glass Escalator: Hidden Advantages for Men in the 'Female' Professions," *Social Problems,* **39**(3):253–267.

Williams, Ivan. 1991. "Paying the Price for a Low Crime Rate," *Washington Post National Weekly Edition,* **8**(October 21):25.

Williams, J. Allen, Jr., Nicholas Batchuk, and David R. Johnson. 1973. "Voluntary Associations and Minority Status: A Comparative Analysis of Anglo, Black and Mexican Americans," *American Sociological Review,* **38**(October):637–646.

Williams, Robin M., Jr. 1970. *American Society* (3d ed.). New York: Knopf.

————, in collaboration with John P. Dean and Edward A. Suchman. 1964. *Strangers Next Door: Ethnic Relations in American Communities.* Englewood Cliffs, N.J.: Prentice-Hall.

Williams, Simon Johnson. 1986. "Appraising Goffman," *British Journal of Sociology,* **37**(September):348–369.

Willis, Ellen. 1980. (Untitled column), *Village Voice,* **25**(March 3):8.

Willis, John. 1975. "Variations in State Casualty Rates in World War II and the Vietnam War," *Social Problems,* **22**(April):558–568.

Wilson, Edward O. 1975. *Sociobiology: The New Synthesis.* Cambridge, Mass.: Harvard University Press.

————. 1977. "Biology and the Social Sciences," *Daedalus,* **106**(Spring):127–140.

————. 1978. *On Human Nature.* Cambridge, Mass.: Harvard University Press.

Wilson, Franklin D. 1984. "Urban Ecology: Urbanization and Systems of Cities," in Ralph Turner (ed.), *Annual*

Review of Sociology, 1984. Palo Alto, Calif.: Annual Reviews, pp. 283–307.

Wilson, James Q., and Richard J. Hernstein. 1986. *Crime and Human Nature.* New York: Simon and Schuster.

Wilson, John. 1973. *Introduction to Social Movements.* New York: Basic Books.

———. 1978. *Religion in American Society: The Effective Presence.* Englewood Cliffs, N.J.: Prentice-Hall.

Wilson, Warner, Larry Dennis, and Allen P. Wadsworth, Jr. 1976. "Authoritarianism Left and Right," *Bulletin of the Psychonomic Society,* **7**(March):271–274.

Wilson, William Julius. 1980. *The Declining Significance of Race: Blacks and Changing American Institutions* (2d ed.). Chicago: University of Chicago Press.

———. 1987a. *The Truly Disadvantaged: The Inner City, the Underclass and Public Policy.* Chicago: University of Chicago Press.

———. 1987b. "The Ghetto Underclass and the Social Transformation of the Inner City." Paper presented at the annual meeting of the American Association for the Advancement of Science, Chicago.

———. 1988. "The Ghetto Underclass and the Social Transformation of the Inner City," *The Black Scholar,* **19**(May–June):10–17.

——— (ed.). 1989. *The Ghetto Underclass: Social Science Perspectives.* Newbury Park, Calif.: Sage.

———. 1991. "Poverty, Joblessness, and Family Structure in the Inner City: A Comparative Perspective." Paper presented at the Chicago Urban Poverty and Family Life Conference, Chicago.

Wimberley, Dale W. 1990. "Investment Dependence and Alternative Explanations of Third World Mortality: A Cross-National Study," *American Sociological Review,* **55**(February):75–91.

Winter, J. Alan. 1977. *Continuities in the Sociology of Religion.* New York: Harper and Row.

Wirth, Louis. 1928. *The Ghetto.* Chicago: University of Chicago Press.

———. 1931. "Clinical Sociology," *American Journal of Sociology,* **37**(July):49–66.

———. 1938. "Urbanism as a Way of Life," *American Journal of Sociology,* **44**(July):1–24.

Withers, Claudia, and Anne Benaroya.

1989. *Sexual Harassment Update 1989: Selected Issues.* Washington, D.C.: Women's Legal Defense Fund.

Wolf, Eric. 1979. "The Virgin of Guadalupe: A Mexican National Symbol," in William A. Lessa and Evon Z. Vogt (eds.), *Reader in Comparative Religion: An Anthropological Approach* (4th ed.). New York: Harper and Row, pp. 112–115.

Wolfe, Tom. 1980. *The Right Stuff.* New York: Bantam.

Wolinsky, Fredric P. 1980. *The Sociology of Health.* Boston: Little, Brown.

Wolkomir, Richard. 1992. "American Sign Language: 'It's Not Mouth Stuff—It's Brain Stuff,'" *Smithsonian,* **23**(July): 30–41.

Wood, Charles, and José de Carvalho. 1988. *The Demography of Inequality in Brazil.* Cambridge, Eng.: Cambridge University Press.

Work, Clemens P., et al. 1987. "Jam Sessions," *U.S. News and World Report,* **103**(September 7):20–27.

The World Bank. 1987. *World Development Report 1987.* New York: Oxford University Press.

———. 1990. *World Development Report 1990: Poverty.* New York: Oxford University Press.

———. 1992. *World Development Report 1992.* New York: Oxford University Press.

———. 1993. *World Development Report, 1993: Investing in Health.* New York: Oxford University Press.

World Development Forum. 1990. "The Danger of Television," **8**(July 15):4.

Woronoff, John. 1986. *The Japan Syndrome: Symptoms, Ailments and Remedies.* New Brunswick, N.J.: Transaction.

Wright, Erik Olin, David Hachen, Cynthia Costello, and Joy Sprague. 1982. "The American Class Structure," *American Sociological Review,* **47**(December): 709–726.

Wright, Susan. 1993. "Blaming the Victim, Blaming Society, or Blaming the Discipline: Fixing Responsibility for Homelessness," *Sociological Quarterly,* **34**(Spring): 1–16.

Wrong, Dennis H. 1977. *Population and Society* (4th ed.). New York: Random House.

Wurman, Richard Saul. 1989. *Information*

Anxiety. New York: Doubleday.

Wuthnow, Robert, and Marsha Witten. 1988. "New Directions in the Study of Culture," in W. Richard Scott and Judith Blake (eds.), *Annual Review of Sociology, 1988.* Palo Alto, Calif.: Annual Reviews, pp. 49–67.

Yanagishita, Machiko. 1992. "Japan's Declining Fertility: '1.53 Shock,'" *Population Today,* **20**(April):34.

———. 1993. "Slow Growth Will Turn to Decline of the Japanese Population," *Population Today,* **21**(May):4–5.

Yates, Ronald E. 1985. "Japanese Merrily Leave the Christ out of 'Kurisumasu,'" *Chicago Tribune* (December 22), p. 13.

Yinger, J. Milton. 1960. "Countraculture and Subculture," *American Sociological Review,* **25**(October):625–635.

———. 1970. *The Scientific Study of Religion.* New York: Macmillan.

———. 1974. "Religion, Sociology of," in *Encyclopedia Britannica,* vol. 15. Chicago: Encyclopedia Britannica, pp. 604–613.

———. 1982. *Countercultures.* New York: Free Press.

Young, T. R. 1981. "The Typification of Christ at Christmas and Easter: Political and Social Uses of the Jesus Symbol." Paper presented at the annual meeting of the Association of Humanist Sociologists, Cincinnati.

Yzaguirre, Raul. 1993. "Hispanics as an Invisible Minority," *USA Today* (July 15), p. 11A.

Zald, Mayer N. 1970. *Organizational Change: The Political Economy of the YMCA.* Chicago: University of Chicago Press.

——— and John D. McCarthy (eds.). 1979. *The Dynamics of Social Movements.* Cambridge, Mass.: Winthrop.

——— and ———. 1986. *Social Movements in an Organizational Society.* Rutgers, N.J.: Transaction.

Zaslow M. 1988. "Sex Differences in Children's Response to Parental Divorce: 1. Research Methodology and Post-divorce Family Forms," *American Journal of Orthopsychiatry,* **58**(July):355–378.

———. 1989. "Sex Differences in Children's Response to Parental Divorce: 2. Samples, Variables, Ages, and Sources," *American Journal of Orthopsychiatry,* **59**(January):118–141.

Zeitlin, Maurice, Kenneth G. Lutterman,

and James W. Russell. 1973. "Death in Vietnam: Class, Poverty and the Risks of War," *Politics and Society,* **3**(Spring): 313–328.

Zellner, William M. 1978. "Vehicular Suicide: In Search of Incidence." Unpublished M.A. thesis, Western Illinois University, Macomb.

Zelnick, Melvin, and J. Kim Young. 1982. "Sex Education and Its Association with Teenage Sexual Activity, Pregnancy, and Contraceptive Use," *Family Planning Perspectives,* **14**:117–126.

Zia, Helen. 1990. "Midwives: Talking about a Revolution," *Ms.,* **1**(November–December):91.

———. 1993. "Women of Color in Leadership," *Social Policy,* **23**(Summer):51–55.

Zick, Cathleen D., and Jane L. McCullough. 1991. "Trends in Married Couples' Time Use: Evidence from 1977–78 and 1987–88," *Sex Roles,* **24**(April): 459–487.

Zimbardo, Phillip. 1992. *Psychology and Life* (13th ed.). New York: Harper-Collins.

Zimmer, Lynn. 1988. "Tokenism and Women in the Workplace," *Social Problems,* **35**(February):64–77.

Zimmerman, Klaus, Allan Schnaiberg, and Nicholas Watts. 1986. *Distributional Conflicts in Environment: From Surplus to Scarcity.* Aldershot, Eng.: Gower.

Zimmerman, Mary K. 1981. "The Abortion Clinic: Another Look at the Management of Stigma," in Gregory Stone and Harvey Faberman (eds.), *Social Psychology through Symbolic Interaction* (2d ed.). Lexington, Mass.: Ginn, pp. 43–52.

———. 1987. "The Women's Health Movement: A Critique of Medical Enterprise, and the Position of Women," in Beth B. Hess and Myra Marx Ferree (eds.), *Analyzing Gender: A Handbook of Social Science Research.* Newbury Park, Calif.: Sage, pp. 442–472.

Zola, Irving K. 1966. "Culture and Symptoms: An Analysis of Patients Presenting Complaints," *American Sociological Review,* **31**(October):615–630.

———. 1972. "Medicine as an Institution of Social Control," *Sociological Review,* **20**(November):487–504.

———. 1983. *Socio-Medical Inquiries.* Philadelphia: Temple University Press.

———. 1987. "The Portrayal of Disability in the Crime Mystery Genre," *Social Policy,* **17**(Spring):34–39.

Zussman, Robert. 1992. *Intensive Care: Medical Ethics and the Medical Profession.* Chicago: University of Chicago Press.

Zwerdling, Daniel. 1980. *Workplace Democracy.* New York: Harper and Row.

ACKNOWLEDGMENTS

PART-OPENING PHOTOGRAPHS

Part One: Jon Brenneis/Photo 20-20.
Part Two: Brett Froomer/Image Bank.
Part Three: Eric Carle/Stock Boston.
Part Four: Margot Granitsas/Photo Researchers.
Part Five: Daemmrich/Image Works.

CHAPTER 1

Chapter-opening photograph: Will & Deni McIntyre/Photo Researchers.
Table 1-1: Adapted from *Sociological Abstracts,* 1994. Copyright Sociological Abstracts, Inc. All rights reserved.
Box 1-2: Quoted material from Carol Brooks Gardner. 1989. "Analyzing Gender in Public Places: Rethinking Goffman's Vision of Everyday Life," *American Sociologist,* **20**(Spring):45, 49, 56.

Figure for Appendix: W. David Watts and Ann Marie Ellis. 1989. "Assessing Sociology Educational Outcomes: Occupational Status and Mobility of Graduates," *Teaching Sociology,* **17**(July):301. Reprinted by permission of Teaching Sociology and the authors.

CHAPTER 2

Chapter-opening photograph: Gary Crallé/Image Bank.
Figure 2-3: Sharon M. Collins. 1989. "The Marginalization of Black Executives," *Social Problems,* **36**(4; October):317–321. © 1989 by the Society for the Study of Social Problems. Reprinted by permission of Society for the Study of Social Problems and the author.
Box 2-1: Quoted material from Elijah Anderson. 1990. *Streetwise,* pp. 220–221. Copyright © 1990 by The University of Chicago. Reprinted by permission of The University of Chicago Press.
Box 2-2: Quoted material from John Lofland. 1977. *Doomsday Cult* (enlarged ed.), pp. 345–346. Copyright Irvington Publishers, 195 McGregor Street, Manchester, NH 03102. Reprinted by permission of Irvington Publishers, Inc.
Excerpt on page 48: Rik Scarce, 1993. "Confidential Sources," *The Progressive,* **57**(October):38. Reprinted by permission from The Progressive, 409 East Main Street, Madison, WI 53703.
Excerpt on page 51: Peter Rossi, 1987. "No Good Applied Social Research Goes Unpunished," *Society,* **25**(November–December):73–79. Reprinted by permission of Transaction Periodicals Consortium.
Table for Appendix II: Larry Hugick and Lydia Saad. 1992. *Gallup Poll Monthly,* **319**(April):34. Reprinted by permission of Gallup Poll Monthly.

CHAPTER 3

Chapter-opening photograph: Bruce Gordon/Photo Researchers.

Figure 3-2: Thomas F. Saarinen. 1988. "Centering of Mental Maps of the World," *National Geographic Research*, **4**(Winter):124. Reprinted by permission of the author.

Excerpt on page 79: Lynda Shorten. 1991. *Without Reserve: Stories from Urban Natives,* p. 166. Reprinted by permission of NeWest Publishers, Ltd., Edmonton, Alberta, Canada.

Excerpt on page 87: Troy Duster. 1991. "Understanding Self-Segregation on Campus," *Chronicle of Higher Education,* **38**(September 25):B2. Reprinted by permission of the author.

CHAPTER 4

Chapter-opening photograph: Ken Lax/Photo Researchers.

Table 4-1: Adapted in part from Donna Gable. 1993. "On TV, Lifestyles of the Slim and Entertaining," *USA Today,* July 27, p. 3D. Also adapted in part from Donna Gable. 1993. "Series Shortchange Working-Class and Minority Americans," *USA Today,* August 30, p. 3D. Copyright 1993 *USA Today.* Reprinted by permission of *USA Today* and the author.

Excerpt on page 94: Marie K. Mason. 1942. "Learning to Speak after Six and One-Half Years of Silence," *Journal of Speech Disorders,* **7**(December):299. Reprinted by permission of the American Speech-Language-Hearing Association.

CHAPTER 5

Chapter-opening photograph: Scribner/Picture Cube.

Table 5-3: Peter Gould and Joseph Kabel. 1993. "The Geography of AIDS," *Atlantic Monthly,* **271**(January):90–91. Reprinted by permission of *Atlantic Monthly* and Peter Gould, Pennsylvania State University.

Box 5-1: Quoted material from Kay Bartlett. 1988. "Sociologist Researches 'Role Exiting' Process," *Galesburg Regis-ter-Mail* (August 11), p. C1. Reprinted by permission of The Register-Mail, Galesburg, Illinois.

Box 5-2: Quoted material from Jonathan Kozol. 1991. *Savage Inequalities: Children in America's Schools.* Copyright © 1991 by Jonathan Kozol. Reprinted by permission of Crown Publishers, Inc.

Excerpt on page 122: Malcolm X (with Alex Haley). 1964. *The Autobiography of Malcolm X,* p. 37. Reprinted by permission of Grove Press, a division of Random House, Inc.

Excerpt on page 133: William E. Thompson. 1983. "Hanging Tongues: A Sociological Encounter on the Assembly Line," *Qualitative Sociology,* **6**(Fall):215. Reprinted by permission of *Qualitative Sociology,* a division of Plenum Publishing Corp.

CHAPTER 6

Chapter-opening photograph: McLaughlin/Image Works.

Box 6-2: Quoted material from Norman K. Denzin. 1987. *The Recovering Alcoholic,* p. 145. Reprinted by permission of Sage Publications, Inc.

Figure 6-2: National Opinion Research Center. 1991. *General Social Surveys 1972–1991 Cumulative Code Book,* p. 365. Reprinted by permission of the National Opinion Research Center.

Excerpt on page 144: Nicole Woolsey Biggart. 1989. *Charismatic Capitalism: Direct Selling Organizations in America,* pp. 142–143. © 1989 by The University of Chicago. All rights reserved. Reprinted by permission of the University of Chicago Press.

CHAPTER 7

Chapter-opening photograph: Brian W. Robb, Hood River, Oregon.

Table 7-1: William A. Reese, II, and Michael A. Katovich. 1989. "Untimely Acts: Extending the Interactionist Conception of Deviance," *Sociological Quarterly,* **30**(2):159–184. Reprinted by permission of JAI Press, Inc.

Table 7-2: Robert Merton. 1968. *Social Theory and Social Structure,* Revised and Enlarged edition, pp. 194, 480–488. Copyright © 1967, 1968 by Robert K. Merton. Reprinted with the permission of The Free Press, a Division of Macmillan, Inc.

Excerpt on pages 174–175: Clinton Sanders. 1989. *Customizing the Body: The Art and Culture of Tattooing,* pp. 42–55. © 1989 by Temple University. Reprinted by permission of Temple University Press.

Excerpt on pages 177–178: Stanley Milgram. 1975. *Obedience to Authority: An Experimental View,* pp. xi, 5, 19–23, 144–146. Copyright 1975. Reprinted by permission of HarperCollins Publishers.

Excerpt on page 183: William Chambliss. 1972. Introduction to Harry King, *Box Man: A Professional Thief's Journey,* p. x. Published by Harper & Row. Copyright 1972 by William Chambliss. Reprinted by permission.

Excerpt on page 190: Lois Forer. 1984. *Money and Justice: Who Owns the Courts,* p. 9. Reprinted by permission of W.W. Norton and Company, Inc.

CHAPTER 8

Chapter-opening photograph: David Butow/Black Star.

Figure 8-3: Thomas G. Mortenson. 1992. *Postsecondary Education Opportunity* (April), pp. 1–4. Reprinted by permission of the author.

Table 8-2: Adapted in part from Keiko Nakao and Judith Treas. 1990. "Occupational Prestige in the United States Revisited: Twenty-five Years of Stability and Change." Paper presented at the annual ASA meeting, Washington, D.C. Reprinted by permission of the authors. Also adapted in part from the National Opinion Research Center. 1990. *Computing 1989 Occupational Prestige Scores.* Reprinted by permission.

Box 8-2: Quoted material from William Ryan. 1976. "Speaking Out: Blaming the Victim," *Blaming the Victim.* Copyright © 1971, 1976 by William Ryan. Reprinted by permission of Pantheon Books, a division of Random House, Inc.

Excerpt on page 236: Kathryn Edin. 1991. "Surviving the Welfare System: How

AFDC Recipients Make Ends Meet in Chicago," *Social Problems,* **38**(4; November):472. © 1991 by the Society for the Study of Social Problems. Reprinted by permission.

CHAPTER 9

Chapter-opening photograph: Robert Frerck/Woodfin Camp.

Figure 9-1: Adapted in part from Ben Crow and Alan Thomas. 1983. *Third World Atlas,* p. 14. Reprinted by permission of Open University Press. Also adapted in part from Carl Haub and Machiko Yanagishita. 1993. *World Population Data Sheet, 1993.* Washington, D.C.: Population Reference Bureau. Reprinted by permission.

Figure 9-2: The World Bank. 1992. *World Development Report,* pp. 276–277. Reprinted by permission of Oxford University Press.

Table 9-1: Ani Hadjian and Lorraine Tritto. 1993. "The World's Largest Industrial Corporations," *Fortune,* **128** (July 26):191. © 1993 Time Inc. All rights reserved. Reprinted by permission of the publisher.

Table 9-2: Donald J. Treiman. 1977. *Comparative Ranking of Occupational Prestige in Comparative Respect,* pp. 318–405. Reprinted by permission of Academic Press and the author.

Table 9-3: Francois Jean. 1992. *Populations in Danger: Medecins Sans Frontieres.* Reprinted by permission of John Libbey & Company, Ltd. and Medecins Sans Frontieres U.K.

Excerpt on page 242: Julia Preston. 1993. "The Slaves of Necessity," *Washington Post National Weekly Edition,* **10**(March 29–April 4):8. © 1993, The Washington Post. Reprinted with permission.

Excerpt on page 264: Amnesty International. 1993. "Yugoslavia: Women Under the Gun," *Amnesty Action,* Amnesty International Report 1993, p. 70 (AI Index POL 10/01/93), covering January–December 1992.

CHAPTER 10

Chapter-opening photograph: John Running/Black Star.

Figure 10-1: Richard T. Schaefer. 1993. *Racial and Ethnic Groups,* 5th edition. Copyright © 1993 by HarperCollins College Publishers. Reprinted by permission of HarperCollins Publishers, Inc.

Table 10-3: Richard D. Alba and Gwen Moore. 1982. "Ethnicity in the American Elite," *American Sociological Review,* **47**(June):373–383. Reprinted by permission of the American Sociological Review and the authors.

Box 10-1: Quoted material from Raul Yzaguirre. 1993. "Hispanics as an Invisible Minority," *USA Today* (July 15), p. 11A. Reprinted by permission of the National Council of La Raza.

Excerpt on page 272: Countee Cullen. 1925. "Incident." © 1925 by Harper and Brothers. Copyright renewed 1953 by Ida M. Cullen. Reprinted by permission of GRM Associates, Inc., Agents for the Estate of Ida M. Cullen.

CHAPTER 11

Chapter-opening photograph: Bart Bartholomen/Black Star.

Figure 11-2: Linda DeStafano and Diane Colasanto, 1990. "Unlike 1975, Today Most Americans Think Men Have It Better," *Gallup Poll Monthly,* **293**(February):31. Reprinted by permission.

Excerpt on page 309: Mike Bradley, Lonnie Danchik, Marty Fager, and Tom Wodetski. 1971. *Unbecoming Men.* © 1971 by Times Change Press, Box 1380, Ojai, CA 93024. Reprinted by permission.

Excerpt on page 309: Anthony Astrachan. 1986. *How Men Feel: Their Response to Women's Demands for Equality and Power.* Copyright © 1964 by Anthony Astrachan. Reprinted by permission of Georges Borchardt, Inc.

Excerpt on page 310: Margaret Mead. 1963. *Sex and Temperament in Three Primitive Societies,* p. 260 and preface to 1950 edition. Reprinted by permission of William Morrow and Co., Inc.

Excerpt on pages 312, 316: Barbara Bovee Polk. 1974. "Male Power and the Women's Movement," *Journal of Applied Behavioral Science,* **10**(3; July):418, 419.

Copyright 1974. Reprinted with permission from NTL Institute.

Excerpt on page 324: Alice S. Rossi. 1973. *The Feminist Papers: From Adams to de Beauvoir,* edited by Alice S. Rossi. Copyright 1973 by Alice S. Rossi. Reprinted with the permission of Northeastern University Press, Boston.

Excerpt on page 325: Jane O'Reilly, 1972. "The Housewife's Moment of Truth," *Ms.,* **1**(Spring):55. Reprinted by permission of the author.

CHAPTER 12

Chapter-opening photograph: C. Parry/ Image Works.

Box 12-1: Quoted material from Harriet G. Rosenberg. 1990. "Complaint Discourse, Aging, and Caregiving Among the !Kung San of Botswana," *The Cultural Context of Aging: Worldwide Perspectives,* p. 25. Copyright © 1990 by Jay Sokolovsky. Reprinted by permission of Bergin and Garvey, an imprint of Greenwood Publishing Group, Inc., Westport, CT.

Box 12-2: Quoted material from Irene Paull and Bülbül. 1976. *Everybody's Studying Us: The Ironies of Aging in the Pepsi Generation,* pp. 7, 79. © 1976 by Bülbül and Irene Paull. Published by the California Association of Older Americans. For more information, contact Volcano Press, Inc. P.O. Box 270, Volcano, CA 95689 (209) 296-3445.

Excerpt on page 334: "When I'm Sixty-Four." Words and music by John Lennon and Paul McCartney. Copyright © 1967 by Northern Songs. All rights reserved. International copyright secured. Used by permission.

Excerpt on page 348: Robert C. Atchley. 1976. Adapted from *The Sociology of Retirement,* pp. 66, 68–71. Reprinted by permission of Schenkman Publishing Co., Inc.

Excerpt on page 352: William McCord. 1993. "Death with Dignity," *The Humanist,* **53**(January–February), 26–29. Copyright 1993. Reprinted with permission of the American Humanist Association.

CHAPTER 13

Chapter-opening photograph: Daemmrich/Image Works.

Table 13-2: William J. Goode. 1976. *Contemporary Social Problems,* Fourth Edition, pp. 537–538 by Robert K. Merton and Robert A. Nisbet. Copyright © 1976 by Harcourt Brace & Company. Reproduced by permission of the publisher.

Table 13-4: Richard J. Gelles. 1993. "Family Violence," in Craig Calhoun and George Ritzer (eds.), *Introduction to Social Problems,* p. 568. Reproduced with permission of McGraw-Hill, Inc.

Excerpt on page 360: Dennis Ahlburg and Carol J. DeVita. 1992. "New Realities of the American Family," *Population Bulletin,* **47**(August). Reprinted by permission of Population Reference Bureau, Inc.

Excerpt on page 367: Andrea B. Rugh. 1984. *Family Planning in Contemporary Egypt,* p. 137. Reprinted by permission of Syracuse University Press.

Excerpt on page 385: "Why Do They Stay?" 1992. *Psychology Today,* **25**(May/June):22. Reprinted with permission from Psychology Today Magazine. Copyright © 1992 (Sussex Publishers, Inc.).

CHAPTER 14

Chapter-opening photograph: Chuck Fishman/Woodfin Camp.

Figure 14-1: Based on data from 1993 *Britannica Book of the Year,* © 1993, Encyclopaedia Britannica, Inc. Reprinted by permission.

Figure 14-2: B. Martin Bradley, et al. 1992. *Churches and Church Membership in the United States 1990.* Reprinted by permission of Glenmary Research Center, Atlanta, GA.

Figure 14-3: Barry A. Kosmin and Seymour P. Lachman. 1993. *One Nation Under God: Religion in Contemporary American Society,* p. 260. Copyright © 1993 by Barry A. Kosmin and Seymour P. Lachman. Reprinted by permission of Crown Publishers, Inc.

Table 14-1: Glenn Vernon. 1962. *Sociology and Religion.* Reprinted by permission of McGraw-Hill, Inc.

CHAPTER 15

Chapter-opening photograph: Dennis Brack/Black Star.

Figure 15-1: Inter-Parliamentary Union. 1993. *Fewer Women in Parliament New IPU Survey Reveals.* Adapted by permission of the Inter-Parliamentary Union.

Figure 15-2: William Kornhauser. 1961. "'Power Elite' or 'Veto Group'?" in Seymour Lipset and Leo Lowenthal (eds.), *Culture and Social Character.* Copyright © 1961 by The Free Press. Reprinted by permission of The Free Press, a Division of Macmillan, Inc.

Table 15-1: 1993. *General Social Surveys 1972–1993 Cumulative Code Book.* Reprinted with permission of the National Opinion Research Center, Chicago, IL.

Table 15-3: William Kornhauser. 1961. "'Power Elite' or 'Veto Group'?" in Seymour Martin Lipset and Leo Lowenthal (eds.), *Culture and Social Character.* Copyright © 1961 by The Free Press. Reprinted by permission of The Free Press, a Division of Macmillan, Inc.

Box 15-1: Quoted material from Martin Luther King, Jr. 1968. *Where Do We Go From Here: Chaos of Community?* Copyright © 1967 by the Estate of Martin Luther King, Jr. Reprinted by arrangement with the Heirs to the Estate of Martin Luther King, Jr., c/o Joan Daves Agency as agent for the proprietor.

Box 15-2: Quoted material from Douglas L. Murray. 1982. "The Abolition of El Cortito, the Short-Handled Hoe: A Case Study in Social Conflict and State Policy in California Agriculture," *Social Problems,* **30**(October), pp. 28, 29. © 1982 by the Society for the Study of Social Problems. Reprinted by permission.

CHAPTER 16

Chapter-opening photograph: Ellis Herwig/Picture Cube.

Excerpt on page 472: Billy Tashman. 1992. "Hobson's Choice: Free-Market Education Plan Vouches for Bush's Favorite Class," *Village Voice,* **37**(January 21): educational supplement, p. 9. Reprinted by permission of The Village Voice.

CHAPTER 17

Chapter-opening photograph: Michelle Frankfurter/SABA.

Figure 17-1: Carl Haub and Machiko Yanagishita. 1993. *World Population Data Sheet, 1993.* Reprinted by permission of Population Reference Bureau.

Figure 17-3: Judi Hasson. 1992. "No Simple Cure for Sick System," *USA Today* (October 15), p. 5A. Copyright 1992, USA Today. Reprinted with permission.

Excerpt on page 485: Ann Holohan. 1977. "Diagnosis: The End of Transition," in A. Davis and G. Horobin (eds.), *Medical Encounters: The Experience of Illness and Treatment,* p. 88. Copyright © 1977 Alan Davis and Gordon Horobin. All rights reserved. Reprinted by permission of St. Martin's Press.

Excerpt on page 486: Lois M. Verbrugge. 1985. "Gender and Health: An Update on Hypothesis and Evidence," *Journal of Health and Social Behavior,* **26**(September):162–163. Reprinted by permission of the publisher.

CHAPTER 18

Chapter-opening photograph: Karen Kasmauski/Woodfin Camp.

Figure 18-1: Ernest W. Burgess. 1925. "The Growth of the City" in Robert E. Park, Ernest W. Burgess, and Roderick D. McKenzie (eds.), *The City,* p. 55. Copyright © 1925 by The University of Chicago Press. All rights reserved. Reprinted by permission.

Figure 18-2: Joel Garreau. 1991. *Edge City: Life on the New Frontier.* Copyright 1991 by Joel Garreau. Used by permission of Doubleday, a division of Bantam Doubleday Dell Publishing Group, Inc.

Figure 18-3: Robert Fox. 1987. *Population Images* (2d ed.), pp. 10–13. Reprinted by permission of the United Nations Fund for Population Activities.

Table 18-1: Gideon Sjoberg. 1960. *The Preindustrial City: Past and Present,* pp. 323–328. © 1960 by the Free Press; copyright renewed 1988. Adapted by the permission of the Free Press, a Division of Macmillan, Inc.

Excerpt on page 518: Joe R. Feagin. 1983. *The Urban Real Estate Game: Playing Mo-*

nopoly with Real Money, p. 2. © 1983 by Joe R. Feagin. Reprinted by permission of Prentice Hall, a Division of Simon & Schuster, Inc.

CHAPTER 19

Chapter-opening photograph: Claus Meyer/Black Star.

Figure 19-2: John R. Weeks. 1994. *Population: An Introduction to Concepts and Issues,* updated 5th ed., p. 230. Reprinted by permission of Wadsworth, Inc. Copyright 1994.

Figure 19-3. Adapted from Riley E. Dunlap, George H. Gallup, Jr., and Alec M. Gallup. 1993. *Health of the Planet: Results of a 1992 International Environmental Opinion Survey of Citizens in 24 Nations.*

A George H. Gallup Memorial Survey. p. 8. Conducted by The Gallup International Institute. By permission of the George H. Gallup International Institute.

Table 19-1: Population Reference Bureau. "World Population: Number of Years to Add Each Billion," 1993. Reprinted by permission.

Excerpt on page 554: Paul Brodeur. 1993. *Outrageous Misconduct: The Asbestos Industry on Trial,* p. 114. © 1993 Pantheon Books, Random House, Inc. Reprinted by permission.

CHAPTER 20

Chapter-opening photograph: Haviv/ SABA.

Excerpt on pages 588–589: Joseph P. Shapiro. 1993. *No Pity: People with Disabilities Forging a New Civil Rights Movement,* p. 19. Reprinted by permission of Times Books, a division of Pantheon Publishers.

EPILOGUE

Chapter-opening photograph: Don Carroll/Image Bank.

INDEXES

NAME INDEX

Abegglen, James C., 256, 613
Abercrombie, Nicholas, 84, 88, 219, 613
Aberle, David F., 130, 613
Abowitz, Deborah, 224, 613
Abraham, Sameer, 280, 633
Abrahams, Ray G., 123, 613
Abrahamse, Allan F., 384, 613
Abrahamson, Mark, 182, 613
Adam, Barry, 139, 613
Addams, Jane, 15–16, 25, 613
Adler, Jerry, 596, 613
Adler, Patricia, 42, 107, 613
Adler, Peter, 613
Agger, Ben, 19, 613
Aguirre, Benigno E., 430, 575, 613
Ahlburg, Dennis, 360, 371, 614
Aikman, David, 414, 614
Alain, Michael, 581, 614
Alam, Sultana, 259, 614
Alba, Richard D., 296, 302, 614
Albas, Cheryl, 101, 614
Albas, Daniel, 101, 614
Aldrich, Howard E., 573, 616
Alexander, Ron, 347, 614
Alexander, Vicki, 387, 614
Alinsky, Saul, 523, 614

Allen, Bem P., 177–178, 614
Allen, Katherine R., 378, 614
Allport, Gordon W., 278, 280, 282, 614
Almgren, Gunnar, 547, 614
Alonzo, Angelo A., 482, 614
Altman, Dennis, 138, 614
Altman, Lawrence K., 137, 492–493, 614
Alvarez, Sonia, 261, 614
Amato, Paul, 378, 614
Ames, Katrine, 352, 614
Anderson, Cheryl, 386, 614
Anderson, Elijah, 43, 537, 614
Anderson, John Ward, 252, 614
Anderson, Kevin, 491, 614
Anderson, Lisa, 411, 614
Anderson, Roy M., 136, 614
Andersson-Brolin, Lillemor, 285, 614
Angell, Marcia, 488, 614
Angier, Natalie, 496, 614
Appelbaum, Richard P., 584, 615
Arber, Sara, 342, 615
Archer, Margaret, 615
Arensburg, Conrad M., 615
Armer, J. Michael, 246, 615
Aronoff, Marilyn, 574, 615
Aronson, Elliot, 175, 615
Asch, Adrienne, 468, 588, 593, 615, 626
Asch, Solomon, 44, 615

Astin, Alexander W., 75, 465, 615
Astrachan, Anthony, 309, 615
Atchley, Robert C., 341, 347, 615
Auchincloss, Kenneth, 264, 615
Avni, Noga, 385, 615
Aytac, Isik, 366, 615
Azumi, Koya, 152, 615

Babad, Elisha Y., 461, 647
Babbie, Earl R., 336, 618
Babchuk, Nicholas, 164, 615
Babcock, Charles R., 435, 615
Bacard, André, 598, 615
Bachrach, Christine A., 615
Bachrach, Peter, 372, 438, 615
Back, Kurt W., 149, 615
Bacon, John, 414, 615
Baer, Douglas E., 622
Bailey, J. Michael, 97, 615
Bainbridge, William Sims, 406
Baldassare, Mark, 526, 615
Bales, Robert F., 311, 330–331, 606
Ball, Donald, 122, 615
Balswick, Jack, 309, 615
Baltzell, E. Digby, 231, 615
Bandura, Albert, 497, 615
Banks, Curtis, 630

Banks, Vera, 530, 615
Barak, Gregg, 202, 618
Baratz, Morton S., 438, 615
Barkey, Karen, 46, 615
Barkum, Michael, 405, 615
Barnet, Richard J., 246, 250, 615
Barnett, Rosalind, 615
Baron, James N., 154, 615
Barringer, Felicity, 167, 615
Barron, James, 228, 528, 615, 622
Barron, Milton L., 336, 615
Bartlett, Kay, 615
Baruch, Grace, 103–104, 320, 615
Basso, Keith H., 616
Bastian, Lisa D., 464, 616
Battin, Margaret, 351, 616
Beach, Frank, 80, 627
Beall, Cynthia M., 334, 628
Beals, Gregory, 208, 616
Beck, E. M., 458, 621
Becker, Howard S., 22, 112, 187–188, 201, 461, 484, 493, 606, 616
Beeghley, Leonard, 214, 616
Behr, Michelle, 628
Belking, Lisa, 352
Belknap, Penny, 32–33, 616
Bell, Daniel, 191–192, 425, 616
Bell, Wendell, 243, 245, 616
Bellah, Robert, 88, 401, 616
Bem, Sandra Lipsitz, 308, 311, 616
Benaroya, Anne, 167
Bendix, B. Reinhard, 616
Benford, Robert D., 579, 616
Benner, Richard S., 27, 616
Bennett, Clavdette E., 288, 616
Bensman, David, 447, 616
Benson, Michael, 555, 619
Berg, Philip, 616
Berger, Peter L., 5, 29, 133, 398, 616
Berk, Marc, 485–486, 616
Berk, Richard A., 573, 577, 616
Berke, Richard, 489, 616
Berlin, Brent, 919, 616
Berman, Paul, 88, 616
Bernard, Jessie, 315, 616
Berney, Barbara, 488, 616
Best, Fred, 470, 616
Bettelheim, Bruno, 295, 616
Bezilla, Robert E., 393, 407, 616
Bharadwaj, Lakshmik, 557, 559–560, 617
Bielby, William, 114, 615
Biggart, Nicole Woolsey, 144, 171, 617
Billson, Janet Mancini, 27, 617
Binder, David, 264, 617
Binstock, Robert M., 385, 617
Bjerkedal, Tor, 629, 625
Blackburn, Paul, 490, 649
Blakeslee, Sandra, 377, 654
Blakey, G. Robert, 191, 617
Blanc, Ann Klimas, 380, 617
Blanchard, Fletcher, 176, 617
Blau, David M., 114, 617
Blau, Francine, 319, 646
Blau, Peter M., 153, 157, 160, 165, 232, 617
Blauner, Robert, 617
Blee, Katherine M., 171, 617
Blendon, Robert J., 352, 490, 494, 617
Blood, Robert O., Jr., 366, 426, 607, 617
Bloom, Samuel W., 481, 617

Bluestone, Barry, 249, 617, 630
Bluestone, Herman, 530, 632
Blumer, Herbert, 121, 578–579, 617
Blumstein, Philip, 197, 366, 388, 617
Boaz, Rachel Florsheim, 339, 617
Bode, Nancy, 202
Bogdan, Robert, 187, 617
Bogert, Carroll, 557, 617
Bohannan, Paul, 377, 617
Bonacich, Edna, 376, 637
Booth, Alan, 164, 615
Borgatta, Edgar F., 29, 617
Borgutta, Marie L., 29, 617
Borjas, George, 298, 619
Borman, Kathryn M., 463, 617
Bornschier, Volker, 249–250, 253, 267, 617
Boserup, Ester, 259, 617
Bosk, Charles L., 504, 617
Bottomore, Tom B., 84, 585, 617
Bouchard, Thomas, Jr., 97, 617
Bouvier, Leon F., 380, 550–551, 617–618
Bowles, Samuel, 454, 458, 463, 474–475, 603, 618
Bracey, Gerald W., 472–473, 618
Braddock, Jomills Henry, II, 458, 618
Bradford, Calvin, 130, 638
Bradley, Martin G., 408, 618
Bradley, Phil, 591, 618
Bradshaw, York, 247, 250, 252–253, 618
Braithwaite, John, 195, 618
Branegan, Jay, 179, 618
Braun, Denny, 268, 618
Brewer, Rose M., 21, 618
Brinton, Mary, 257, 331, 618
Brodeur, Paul, 192, 554, 618
Bromley, David G., 44, 48, 618, 649
Brooke, James, 259–263, 618
Brooks, Andrée, 410, 618
Brower, Brock, 578, 618
Brown, Christopher, 299, 618
Brown, Lester R., 555–557, 564, 618
Brown, Michael, 572, 618
Brown, Patricia Leigh, 103, 163, 525, 618
Brown, Robert McAfee, 399, 618
Brown, Rodger W., 96, 576, 618
Brown, William, 170, 618
Brozan, Nadine, 383, 618
Brunvand, Jan Harold, 593, 618
Bryant, Bunyan, 562, 564, 618
Bryk, Anthony S., 460, 618
Bülbül, 344, 348, 644
Bullard, Robert D., 562, 618
Bulle, Wolfgang, F., 72, 618
Bumpass, Larry L., 376, 618, 651–652
Bunzel, John H., 281, 302, 618
Burciaga, Cecilia Preciado de, 326, 618
Burek, Deborah, 161, 619
Burgess, Ernest W., 376, 513–514, 521, 523, 611, 619
Burgess, John, 247, 619
Burke, Mary Jean, 633
Burke, William Kevin, 556, 619
Burrows, William E., 149, 619
Burstin, Helen R., 500, 619
Burt, Martha R., 533, 619
Burton, Velmer, S., Jr., 497, 619
Bush, George, 265, 328–329, 373, 433
Butler, Robert N., 344, 355, 611, 619
Byre, William, 97, 619

Cable, Sherry, 555, 619
Cahill, Spencer E., 307, 619
Caildini, Robert, 186, 646
Calem, Robert E., 598, 619
Calvin, John, 400, 401
Came, Barry, 79, 619
Campbell, Donald T., 57, 654
Cancian, Francesa, 369, 619
Caniglia, Julie, 174, 619
Cannon, James S., 557, 619
Cannon, Lynn Weber, 215
Cantril, Hadley, 576, 619
Caplan, Arthur L., 97, 619
Caplan, Nathan, 298, 619
Caplan, Ronald L., 481, 619
Caplow, Theodore, 151, 620
Carey, Anne R., 432, 620
Cargan, Leonard, 381, 411, 620
Carlson, John R., 636
Carmichael, Stokely, 286, 620
Carmody, Denise Lardner, 408, 417, 620
Carroll, John B., 69, 620
Carroll, Nicole, 114, 620
Carroll, Susan, 433, 620
Carson, Rachel, 620
Carstensen, Lundie L., 10
Carter, Jimmy, 231
Carter, Keith, 129, 620
Cassidy, Claire Monod, 478, 620
Cassidy, Frederic G., 78, 620
Castells, Manuel, 518, 525, 537, 620
Cauchon, Dennis, 189, 620
Celis, William, III, 464, 620
Cerio, Gregory, 161, 620
Cetron, Marvin J., 595, 600, 620
Chafetz, Janet Saltzman, 29, 620
Chalfant, H. Paul, 400, 406–407, 415, 620
Chambliss, William J., 179, 183, 186, 191, 620
Chapman, Fern Schumer, 114, 620
Charon, Joel, 122, 620
Chase-Dunn, Christopher, 250, 268, 617
Chavez, Cesar, 441
Cherlin, Andrew, 371, 378, 388, 620
Chernin, Kim, 478, 620
Chinoy, Ely, 157, 620
Chira, Susan, 469, 472–473, 620
Chiv, Hei-Yuan, 489, 653
Chow, Effie, 495, 629
Chow, Siu L., 461, 620
Christensen, Kathleen, 339, 620
Chudacoff, Howard P., 355, 620
Cicone, Michael V., 309, 620
Cisin, Ira H., 574, 621
Cisneros, Henry, 532, 621
Clark, Burton R., 465, 621
Clark, Candace, 484, 621
Clark, E. Gurney, 480, 636
Clark, Walter B., 574, 621
Clarke, Lee, 599, 621
Clary, Michael E., 562, 636
Clausen, John A., 498, 621
Clements, Mark, 500, 621
Clines, Frances X., 194, 621
Clinton, Bill, 236, 265, 329, 373, 430, 433, 548
Clinton, Hillary Rodham, 306
Cloward, Richard A., 184, 226, 235, 239, 431, 621
Clymer, Adam, 374, 621
Cockerham, William C., 486, 497–498, 621
Cody, Michael J., 111, 618

Cohen, Aaron, 148, 635
Cohen, Barbara E., 533, 619
Cohen, David K., 475
Cohen, Debra Nussbaum, 410, 621
Cohen, Marcia B., 534–535, 654
Cohn, Bob, 445, 621
Cohn, Steven F., 5, 621
Cohn, Victor, 501, 621
Colasanto, Diane, 322–323, 443, 621, 623
Colclough, Glenna, 458, 621
Cole, Elizabeth, 371–372, 621
Cole, Mike, 454, 458, 621
Colella, Ugo, 380, 652
Coleman, James S., 459–460, 472, 621
Coleman, James W., 465, 497, 621
Collins, Glenn, 346, 621
Collins, Randall, 14, 29, 217, 219, 313, 401, 456, 621
Collins, Sharon, 34–39, 621
Commission on Civil Rights, 20, 282, 291, 293
Commoner, Barry, 543, 557–558, 621
Comte, Auguste, 11, 15, 582
Conklin, John E., 193, 621
Conley, John J., 353, 621
Conly, Catherine H., 192, 621
Conniff, Ruth, 235, 621
Conover, Pamela J., 327, 621
Conrad, Peter, 481, 487, 497, 504, 621
Cooke, Robert Allan, 230, 638
Cooley, Charles H., 14–15, 22–23, 98, 100–102, 115–116, 146, 611, 622
Coontz, Stephanie, 360, 622
Corea, Gena, 497, 622
Cornell, Claire Pedrick, 385–386, 388, 628
Corning, Amy, 579, 622
Cornish, Edward, 596, 622
Corral, Thais, 262, 622
Coser, Lewis A., 12, 52, 219, 622
Coser, Rose Laub, 492, 622
Cotton, Paul, 488, 622
Couch, Carl, 428, 622
Coughlin, Ellen K., 413, 622
Counts, D. A., 350, 622
Courtney, Alice E., 309, 622
Cowan, Allison, 228, 622
Cowan, Neil M., 302, 622
Cowan, Ruth Schwartz, 302
Cowgill, Donald, 337, 622
Cox, Oliver C., 280, 622
Craig, Steve, 310, 331, 622
Crawford, Susan, 169, 622
Creekmore, C. R., 520, 622
Cressey, Donald R., 185, 465, 497, 622
Crossette, Barbara, 71, 264, 550, 617, 622
Crouse, James, 475, 622
Crow, Ben, 244, 622
Cuba, Lee J., 56, 622
Cuff, E. C., 218, 622
Cullen, Counter, 272
Cullen, Francis T., Jr., 188, 622, 637
Cullen, John B., 186, 622
Cumming, Elaine, 339, 604, 622
Cummings, Milton C., 72, 179, 431, 622
Cunningham, Kitty, 151, 622
Currie, Elliot, 162, 194, 622
Curry, Timothy Jan, 481, 622
Curry-White, Brenda, 225, 643
Curtis, James E., 162, 622
Curtiss, Susan, 94–95, 622

Dabrowski, Andrea, 260, 622
Dahl, Robert A., 437, 622
Dahrendorf, Ralf, 19, 218, 239, 585, 622
Daniels, Arlene Kaplan, 164, 171, 622
Darwin, Charles, 11, 582
Davenport, S., 473, 641
Davidman, Lynn, 417, 622–623
Davies, Christie, 105, 623
Davies, Owen, 595, 600, 611
Davis, Fred, 593, 623
Davis, James, 233, 623
Davis, Kingsley, 18, 94, 217, 512, 540, 623
Davis, Mike, 273, 623
Davis, Nancy, 220, 623
Davis, Nanette J., 182, 188, 623
Davis, Phillip, 562, 623
Day, Lincoln H., 552, 623
Dear, Michael, 561, 586, 623
de Beauvior, Simone, 324, 623
de Carvalho, José, 260–261, 686
Deegan, Mary Jo, 16, 140, 623
DeFleur, Melvin L., 497, 623
Degler, Carl N., 260, 623
Demarest, Jack, 309, 635–636
Demerath, N. J., II, 623
Denisoff, R. Serge, 56, 623
Dennis, Everette E., 497, 623
Dent, David J., 528, 623
Denton, Nancy A., 302, 525, 528–529, 639
Dentzer, Susan, 527, 623
Denzin, Norman, 56, 163, 623
DeParle, Jason, 235–236, 623
Derksen, Linda, 562, 623
DeSena, Judith N., 523, 623
de Sherbinin, Alex, 548, 623
Desroches, Frederick, 49, 623
DeStefano, Linda, 322–323, 623
DeVault, Marjorie L., 447, 623
Devine, Don, 74, 623
DeVita, Carol J., 360, 371, 380, 614, 618
Dey, Eric L., 75, 623
Dickson, W. J., 160, 647
DiMaggio, Paul, 144, 623
Dingman, P. R., 499, 623
Dittersdorf, Harriet, 381, 623
Doblin, Bruce H., 534, 623
Doeringer, Peter B., 339, 355, 623
Doerr, Eda, 471, 624
Doig, Stephen, 285, 624
Dolbeare, Kenneth M., 502, 624
Domhoff, G. William, 437, 447, 624
Donnelly, Jack, 266, 624
Doob, Christopher Bates, 375, 624
Dore, Ronald P., 456, 624
Doress, Irwin, 406, 624
Dornbusch, Stanford M., 109, 624
Dotson, Floyd, 510, 624
Dougherty, Kevin, 462, 624
Dowd, James J., 340–341, 624
Downs, Peter, 495, 624
Driscoll, Anne, 182, 624
Driver, Edwin D., 21, 629
Duberman, Lucille, 216, 624
Du Bois, W. E. B., 15, 21, 23, 286, 624
Duff, Robert W., 186, 624, 632
Duncan, Greg J., 342–343, 624
Duncan, Otis Dudley, 232, 617
Dundes, Alan, 402, 624
Duneier, Mitchell, 140, 624
Dunlap, Riley E., 558–559, 624

Dunn, William, 528, 554, 624
Durkheim, Émile, 10, 12–13, 15, 18, 23, 28, 36, 45, 133–134, 136, 182, 395–396, 440, 584, 601, 607–609, 624
Durning, Alan, 242, 250, 252–253, 266, 559, 624
Duster, Troy, 86–87, 624
Dworkin, Anthony Gary, 475, 624
Dworkin, Rosalind J., 315, 624
Dychtwald, Ken, 355, 624
Dynes, Russell R., 573–574, 624
Dzidzienyo, Anani, 261, 625

Easterbrook, Gregg, 495, 625
Ebaugh, Helen Rose Fuchs, 140, 339, 625
Eberhard, Ray, 470, 616
Eckholm, Erik, 200, 625
Eden, Dov, 451, 625
Edin, Kathryn, 236, 625
Edmonston, Barry, 298, 625
Edward, Joey, 337, 642
Edwards, Harry, 20, 278, 625
Egan, Timothy, 474, 625
Ehrenreich, Barbara, 249, 492, 625
Ehrlich, Anne H., 542, 557, 564, 625
Ehrlich, Paul R., 542, 557, 564, 625
Eisenberg, David M., 495, 625
Eitzen, D. Stanley, 20, 132, 437, 625
Ekman, Paul, 68, 98, 625
Elaide, Mircea, 393, 625
Elam, Stanley M., 454, 465, 467, 625
Elkin, Frederick, 117, 625
Elliott, Marta, 534, 625
Ellis, Donald G., 171, 626
Ellis, Margaret McMahon, 76, 625
Ellis, William N., 76, 625
Ellison, Ralph, 625
Elsasser, Glen, 414, 625
Elshtain, Jean Bethke, 499, 625
Elson, John, 562, 625
Ember, Carol R., 162, 625
Ember, Melvin, 162, 625
Emerson, Rupert, 245, 625
Engels, Friedrich, 13–14, 84, 312, 581, 625, 639
England, Paula, 625
English, Deidre, 492, 625
Enloe, Cynthia, 447, 625
Epstein, Cynthia Fuchs, 331, 625
Erickson, J. David, 229, 625
Erikson, Kai T., 182, 440, 625
Esber, George, Jr., 62, 625
Espinosa, Dula, 444, 625
Etzioni, Amitai, 152, 160, 165–166, 192–193, 625
Evans, Peter, 249, 626
Evans, Sara, 325, 626
Eve, Raymond A., 415, 417, 626

Fager, Marty, 309, 626
Fallows, Deborah, 450, 626
Falsey, Barbara, 460, 626
Faludi, Susan, 331, 626
Farley, Reynolds, 624
Farnsworth, Clyde, 502, 626
Feagin, Joe R., 466, 518–519, 626, 629
Featherman, David L., 232, 626
Featherstone, Mike, 88, 626

Feinglass, Joe, 495, 626
Fenigstein, Alan, 100, 626
Ferguson, Kathy E., 154, 171, 626
Ferguson, Phillip M., 468, 626
Fergusson, D. M., 379, 626
Ferman, Louis A., 251, 268, 626
Ferrell, Tom, 626
Feuer, Lewis S., 313, 626
Fiala, Robert, 426, 626
Fiechter, Georges-André, 626
Fine, Gary A., 20, 122, 626
Fine, Michelle, 588, 593, 626
Fineberg, Harvey, 137, 626
Fingerhut, Lois A., 194, 626
Finkel, Steven E., 581, 626
Fiola, Jan, 251, 261, 626
Firestone, Shulamith, 325, 626
Fischer, Claude, 521, 626
Fisher, Arthur, 98, 626
Fisher, B. Aubrey, 171, 626
Fisher, Gene, 444
Fisher, Ian, 525, 626
Fiske, Edward, 460, 626
Flacks, Richard, 79, 626
Flanders, Laura, 267, 626
Fletcher, Robert S., 260, 469, 626
Flexner, Eleanor, 469, 626
Flower, Joe, 624
Foner, Nancy, 335, 626
Fong-Torres, Ben, 291, 627
Fontaine, Pierre-Michel, 268, 627
Ford, Clellan, 80, 627
Forer, Lois G., 189, 627
Forsythe, David P., 265, 627
Fournier, Marcel, 239, 636
Fox, Renée C., 504, 627
Fox, Robert, 481, 517–518, 627
France, David, 139, 627
Frankel, Bruce, 299, 627
Frankel, David M., 222, 640
Franklin, John Hope, 210, 286, 627
Freeland, Chrystia, 557, 627
Freeman, Howard E., 627
Freeman, Jo, 325, 627
Freeman, Linton C., 368, 627
Freidson, Eliot, 481, 627
Freud, Sigmund, 101
Freudenheim, Milt, 494, 627
Frey, William H., 342, 537, 624, 627
Friedan, Betty, 324, 551, 627
Friedman, James T., 557
Friedman, Milton, 472, 627
Friedman, Norman, 186, 627
Friedman, Thomas L., 300, 627
Fuentes, Annette, 249, 625
Fuller, Bruce, 114, 627
Furstenberg, Frank F., 371

Gable, Donna, 110, 627
Galbraith, John Kenneth, 424, 627
Galinsky, Ellen, 113, 627
Galliher, John F., 202, 628
Galloway, Paul, 397, 627
Gallup, George, 54, 329, 403, 454, 467, 473,
    560, 578, 627
Gamson, Josh, 139, 582, 627
Gamson, William A., 583, 627
Gans, Herbert J., 226, 228, 522–523, 627
Ganzeboom, Harry, 258, 627

Garber, H., 113, 627
Gardner, Carol Brooks, 24, 101, 627
Garfinkel, Harold, 105, 498, 627
Gargan, Edward A., 211, 627
Garreau, Joel, 515–516, 627
Gartner, Alan, 468, 627
Gartrell, John, 562, 623
Garza, Melita Marie, 107, 627
Gates, Henry Louis, Jr., 86, 278, 627
Gaylord, Mark S., 202, 628
Gecas, Viktor, 98, 104–105, 628
Gelles, Richard J., 385–388, 628, 651
Gendell, Murray, 347, 628
George, Linda K., 355, 617
George, Susan, 252, 628
Georges, Christopher, 347, 628
Gerbner, George, 628
Gerstel, Naomi, 377, 379, 628
Gerth, H. H., 13, 216, 228, 457, 628
Gesenway, Deborah, 628
Gest, Ted, 193, 628
Giago, Tim, 289, 628
Gibbs, Nancy, 352–353, 628
Giddings, Paula, 326, 628
Gilbert, Nigel, 56, 628
Gilinsky, Rhoda M., 628
Gilly, M. C., 309, 628
Gilmore, David, 366, 628
Gimenez, Martha, 384, 628
Ginsburg, Ruth, 314
Gintis, Herbert, 108, 454, 458, 463, 474–475,
    603, 618
Giordano, Peggy C., 100, 628
Gittelsohn, John, 249, 628
Glascock, Anthony, 351, 353, 628
Glaub, Gerald R., 457, 628
Glazer, Nathan, 537, 628, 646
Glunt, Erik, 138, 631
Gober, Patricia, 527, 554, 628
Godwin, Deborah D., 366, 628
Goffman, Erving, 15, 23–24, 28, 100–101,
    104–105, 115–117, 127, 313, 385, 498, 588,
    604–606, 611, 628
Goldin, Amy, 572, 618, 628
Goldin, Claudia, 331
Goldman, Ari L., 392, 403, 628
Goldscheider, Calvin, 412, 628
Goldstein, Melvyn C., 334, 628
Goldstein, Michael, 495, 628
Goldstock, Ronald, 617
Goleman, Daniel, 81, 490, 628
Goodale, Jane C., 102, 628–629
Goode, William J., 369, 379, 388, 629
Goodgame, Dan, 234, 629
Gordon, C. Wayne, 463, 629
Gordon, Henry A., 228, 653
Gordon, Michael R., 169, 629
Gordon, Milton, 4, 629
Gordus, Jeanne Prial, 228, 629
Gottdiener, Mark, 518, 629
Gottfredson, Michael, 202, 632
Gough, E. Kathleen, 369, 629
Gould, Peter, 136, 629
Gouldner, Alvin, 51–52, 100, 157, 585, 692
Gove, Walter R., 98, 487, 498, 588, 629
Grabrek, Stanislaus, 27, 648
Graber, Laurel, 163, 629
Grabis, Edward G., 622
Grady, William, 599, 629
Graham, Saxon, 489, 629

Gramsci, Antonio, 84, 629
Gray, Jane, 49, 629
Gray, Virginia, 327, 621
Greeley, Andrew, 396, 401, 417, 629
Green, Dan S., 21, 629
Greenfield, Karl Taro, 452, 629
Greenfield, Sheldon, 344, 629
Greenhouse, Linda, 300, 328–329, 403, 629
Greenspan, Frederick E., 417, 616
Greil, Arthur L., 388, 629
Grissmer, David, 465, 629
Gross, Edward, 72, 629
Gross, Jane, 138, 494, 570, 629
Grove, Janet Belew, 57, 654
Grusky, Oscar, 258
Guemple, D. Lee, 336, 629–630
Guild, Thomas, 638
Guillemin, Jeanne, 353, 630
Gunter, Valerie, 574, 615
Guralnik, Jack M., 229, 487, 630
Gutiérrez, Gustavo, 399, 630

Habenstein, Robert W., 389, 640
Hacker, Andrew, 302, 630
Hacker, Helen Mayer, 315, 326, 630
Hadden, Jeffrey K., 417
Hadjian, Ani, 247–248, 630
Hadley, Jack, 500, 630
Hagan, John, 192, 630
Hage, Jerald, 152
Hahn, Harlan, 588, 630
Hahn, Robert A., 478, 630
Haines, Valerie, 584, 630
Halal, William E., 598, 630
Haley, Alex, 363, 630
Hall, Edward T., 89, 630
Hall, Mildred Hall, 89, 630
Hall, Mimi, 329, 532, 630
Hall, Peter, 630
Hall, Peter M., 122, 527, 630
Hall, Richard H., 157, 489, 630
Hall, Robert H., 630
Haller, Max, 258, 630
Halley, Edward, 541
Halliday, M. A. K., 78, 630
Halperin, Jennifer, 434, 630
Hamilton, Charles V., 286, 620
Hamilton, Mykol, 70
Hamm, Mark S., 79, 630
Hammack, Floyd M., 462, 624
Hancock, LynNell, 123, 630
Handel, Gerald, 117, 625
Haney, Craig, 120, 630
Hanks, Cheryl, 322, 646
Harap, Louis, 398, 630
Hardgrave, Robert L., Jr., 232, 630
Harding, Sue, 56, 349, 630
Hardy, Melissa, 150, 630
Hare, A. Paul, 630
Harlow, Harry F., 95–96, 117, 630
Harrington, Michael, 425, 630
Harris, Chauncy D., 515, 608, 630
Harris, Louis, 443, 487, 528, 630
Harris, Marvin, 97, 274, 372, 630, 654
Harrison, Bennett, 249, 630, 636
Harrold, Francis B., 415, 417, 626
Hartjen, Clayton, 184, 630
Hartmann, Heidi I., 322, 630–631

Hasbrook, Cynthia, 20, 631
Hasson, Judi, 491, 631
Haub, Carl, 243–244, 247, 337, 482, 540, 544–545, 547–548, 550, 631
Haupt, Arthur, 547, 631
Hauser, Robert M., 232, 259, 626, 631
Havemann, Judith, 168, 631
Haviland, William A., 64, 631
Hawkes, Nigel, 574, 652
Hawkes, Robert W., 596, 652
Hawley, Amos H., 542, 631
Hayes, Dianne W., 464, 554, 631
Hays, Constance, 529, 631
Hayward, Mark D., 339, 631
Heaven, P. C., 282, 631
Heberle, Rudolf, 581, 631
Hedges, Chris, 480, 631
Hedley, R. Alan, 246, 631
Heer, David M., 541, 631
Heffernan, Orly, 533, 631
Hegel, Georg, 14
Heikes, E. Joel, 321, 631
Heisel, Marsel, 337, 631
Heller, Scott, 48, 631
Hendricks, Jon, 341, 631
Hendry, Joy, 631
Hendry, Peter, 367
Henley, Nancy, 70, 631
Henneberger, Melinda, 528, 631
Hennon, Charles B., 530, 631
Henry, Mary E., 268
Henry, Tamara, 465, 631
Henry, William E., 339, 604, 622
Henshaw, Stanley, 383, 631
Henslin, James M., 21, 631
Hentoff, Nat, 168, 631
Herber, F. R., 113, 627
Herbers, John 528, 631
Herek, Gregory M., 138, 631
Hernstein, Richard J., 202
Hershey, Robert D., Jr., 251, 631
Hershovits, Melville J., 275, 286, 631
Hertz, Rosanna, 389, 631
Hess, Beth B., 344, 355, 631
Hess, John, 343, 631
Hetherington, E. Mavis, 378, 631–632
Hewitt, Paul S., 346, 632
Heyns, Barbara, 460, 626
Hiatt, Fred, 109, 632
Hicks, Jonathan P., 469, 632
Hill, Anita 167, 169
Hill, Michael, 140, 623
Hill, Robert B., 376, 632
Hill, Stephen, 613
Hillebrand, Barbara, 346, 632
Hilts, Philip J., 198, 320, 372, 494, 499, 632
Hirasawa, Yasumasa, 256, 632
Hirschi, Travis, 202, 632
Hitchcock, Susan Tyler, 27, 616
Hively, Robert, 281, 632
Hochschild, Arlie Russell, 315, 323, 331, 372, 632
Hodge, Robert W., 220, 632
Hoebel, E. Adamson, 279, 632
Hoecker-Drysdale, Susan, 11, 632
Hoffer, Thomas, 621
Hoffman, Lois Wladis, 97, 308, 632
Hoge, Dean R., 409, 632
Holcomb, Betty, 493, 632
Hollingshead, August B., 465, 632
Holmes, John, 115

Holmes, Steven, 113, 265, 373, 632
Holohan, Ann, 485, 632
Homans, George C., 93, 632
Hong, Lawrence K., 186, 624, 632
Hootsman, Helen, 389
Hoppe, Robert A., 530, 632
Horgan, John, 97, 596, 632
Horn, Jack C., 342, 632
Hornblower, Margot, 347, 632
Horowitz, Helen Lefkowitz, 465, 632
Horowitz, Irving Louis, 6, 632
Horwitt, Stanford D., 523, 632
Hosokawa, Bill, 290
House, James S., 635
Houseman, John, 576, 632
Hout, Michael, 233, 632
Howard, Michael C., 98, 632
Howe, Beth B., 346, 355
Howe, Neil, 355, 632
Howery, Carla, 9, 632
Howlett, Debbie, 230, 632
Hoyenga, Katharine, 313, 331, 632
Hoyenga, Kermit, 313, 331, 632
Hoyman, Michele, 268
Huang, Gary, 124, 252–253, 632
Huang, Jai, 618
Huber, Bettina, 26–27, 29, 617, 632–633
Huber, Joan, 140, 632
Hubler, Shawn, 525, 633
Hudgins, John L., 376, 633
Huff, Darrell, 55–56, 633
Hughes, Everett, 125, 633
Hughes, Langston, 633
Hughes, Michael, 487, 629
Hugick, Larry, 54, 633
Hull, Jon D., 157, 464, 633
Humphreys, Laud, 48–50, 633
Hundley, James R., Jr., 572
Hunt, Geoffrey, 19, 633
Hunter, Herbert M., 280, 633
Hunter, James D., 397, 411, 633
Hurh, Won Moo, 291–293, 633, 635
Hurn, Christopher, 455–456, 475, 633

Ibrahim, Youffef M., 411, 633
Illoway, Sharon, 289, 628
Imhoff, Gary, 89, 633
Innes, Christopher, 229, 636
Isaacson, Walter, 381, 633
Israel, Glenn D., 10, 633
Izraeli, Dafna N., 389

Jackson, Elton F., 184–185, 633
Jackson, Jesse L., 20, 636
Jackson, Kenneth, 537, 633
Jackson, Phillip W., 455, 633
Jacobs, Jerry A., 319, 633
Jacobs, Paul, 157, 633
Jacobson, Jodi, 633
Jacobson, Lenore, 318, 461
Jacoby, Henry, 171, 633
Jaffe, Peter, 387, 633
Jaimes, M. Annette, 302, 633
Janis, Irving, 171, 633
Janowitz, Morris, 295, 521, 616, 634
Jarvis, Heather, 450, 633
Jasper, James M., 593, 633
Javna, John, 575, 633

Jean, Francois, 266, 633
Jenkins, Richard, 213, 633
Jenness, Valerie, 583, 633
Jennings, Jerry T., 432, 633
Jennings, M. Kent, 344, 430–431, 633
Johnson, Benton, 584, 634
Johnson, Charles S., 280, 634
Johnson, Dirk, 138, 284, 289, 530, 634
Johnson, John M., 613
Johnson, Mary, 591, 634
Johnson, Richard A., 575, 634
Johnson, William Weber, 397, 634
Johnstone, Ronald L., 406, 634
Jones, Elise, 383, 634
Jones, James T., IV, 634
Jones, Landon Y., 564, 634
Jones, Stephen R., 43, 634
Juhasz, Anne McCleary, 634

Kabel, Joseph, 136, 629
Kagay, Michael R., 138, 634
Kail, Barbara Lynn, 146, 634
Kalish, Richard, 349, 634
Kalleberg, Arne L., 254, 634
Kalter, Neil, 378, 634
Kaminer, Wendy, 163, 171, 634
Kanter, Rosabeth Moss, 133, 321, 634
Kantrowitz, Barbara, 387, 634
Kapferer, Jean-Noël, 576, 593, 634
Kaplan, David A., 276, 634
Karlins, Marvin, 634
Kasarda, John D., 521, 634
Kass, Leon R., 351, 634
Kasza, Gregory, 158–159, 634
Katovich, Michael, 180, 634, 640
Katsillis, John, 246, 615
Katz, Michael, 463, 634
Kaufman, Gladis, 366, 634
Kaufman, Michael T., 533, 634
Kay, Paul, 69, 616, 634
Kearl, Michael C., 350, 352, 634
Keating, Noah, 530, 634
Keen, Judy, 230
Keifer, Amy Jo, 531, 634
Kellermann, Arthur L., 198, 634
Kelley, Dean M., 411, 634
Kellogg, Susan, 389, 640
Kelly, Dennis, 467, 472
Kelsoe, John R., 97, 634–635
Kemper, Vicki, 502, 635
Kempton, Willett, 69, 634
Kendall, P. L., 640
Kennedy, Florynce, 326
Kennedy, John F., 442
Kennedy, Michael D., 425, 635
Kenyatta, Jomo, 246
Kephart, William M., 140, 179, 454, 635
Kerbo, Harold R., 217, 223, 245, 252–253, 256, 635
Kern, Rochelle, 481, 487, 621
Kerr, Clark, 246, 635
Kerr, Peter, 534, 635
Kessler, Ronald, 229, 635
Kiefer, Christie W., 337, 635
Kilborn, Peter T., 590, 635
Kilgore, Sally, 621
Killian, Lewis M., 571, 578, 591–592, 604
Kim, Illsoo, 293, 376, 635
Kim, Kwang Chung, 291–293, 633, 635

Kimball, Roger, 86, 635
Kimmel, Michael, 310, 635
King, Martin Luther, Jr., 398, 429, 635
King, Rodney, 272
King, Stanley, 480, 635
Kinsella, Kevin, 337, 635
Kinzer, Stephen, 329, 635
Kirby, Andrew, 562, 635
Kirby, Sheila, 465, 629
Kirchmeyer, Catherine, 148, 635
Kitagawa, Evelyn, 490, 635
Kitcher, Philip, 102, 635
Kitt, Alice S., 147, 640
Klapp, Orvin, 575, 635
Klausner, Samuel, 635
Klein, Abbie Gorda, 117, 635
Klein, Lloyd, 638
Kleinman, Dena, 411, 635
Kleinman, Dushanka, 642
Kleinman, Joel C., 194, 626
Kling, Rob, 537, 635
Kock, Tom, 635
Koenig, Frederick W., 578, 635
Kohlberg, Lawrence, 102
Kohn, Alfie, 313, 635
Kohn, Melvin, 29, 156, 374, 635
Kolata, Gina, 596, 635
Kolbert, Elizabeth, 46, 635
Kolker, Alice, 434, 438, 649
Komarovsky, Mirra, 21, 635
Korman, Shelia, 360, 637
Kornblum, William, 225, 635
Kornhauser, William, 136, 635
Kortenhaus, Carole M., 309, 635–636
Kosmin, Barry A., 409, 412, 636
Kourvetaris, George A., 376, 636
Kozol, Jonathan, 132, 537, 636
Kraft, Michael E., 562, 636
Kralewski, John E., 154, 636
Kramer, Ronald, 250, 640
Kraybill, Donald B., 89, 636
Krivo, Lauren J., 534, 625
Kroeber, Alfred L., 67, 636
Krugman, Paul R., 222, 636
Kübler-Ross, Elisabeth, 349, 636
Kuczka, Susan, 200, 639
Kushnick, Lovis, 554, 636
Kwong, Peter, 273, 290, 636, 638

Labaree, David F., 457, 636
Labaton, Stephen, 590, 636
Lachman, Seymour P., 409, 636
Ladner, Joyce, 326, 636
Lamm, Robert P., 310, 413, 636
Lamont, Michéle, 239, 636
Lancaster, John, 15, 636
Landau, Saul, 157, 633
Landsberger, Henry, 636
Landtman, Gunnar, 636
Lane, Harlan, 68, 636
Lane, Robert E., 430, 636
Lang, Eric, 45, 636
Langan, Patrick A., 229, 636
Lapchick, Richard E., 20, 636
Lapping, Mark, 532, 636
Larson, Calvin J., 528, 636
Lasswell, Harold D., 426, 609, 636
Lauer, Robert H., 585–586, 636
Lawton, Millicent, 464, 473, 636

Lazare, Daniel, 524, 636
Lazarus, Emma, 297
Lazerwitz, Bernard, 412, 636
Leacock, Eleanor Burke, 455, 636
Leavell, Hugh R., 480, 636
Lee, Alfred McClung, 29, 600, 636
Lee, Barrett, 532, 534, 636
Lee, D. J., 340, 636
Lee, Raymond M., 56, 637
Leehrsen, Charles, 163, 637
Lemann, Nicholas, 294, 637
Lemkow, Louis, 489, 637
Lenski, Gerhard, 219, 421, 423, 511, 584, 637
Leo, John, 97, 637
Leonard, Wilbert, II, 32–33, 616
Leslie, Gerald R., 360, 637
Letkemann, Peter, 191, 637
Levin, Jack, 336, 637
Levin, William C., 336, 637
Levine, Robert, 637
Levinson, Arlene, 380, 637
Levinson, Daniel, 103, 637
Lewandowsky, Stephan, 55, 637
Lewin, Tamar, 167, 327, 340, 345, 637
Lewis, Paul, 264, 637
Lewis, Robert, 367, 637
Lewis, Suzan, 389, 637
Liang, Xiaoyan, 114
Liebman, Charles, 412, 637
Light, Ivan H., 376
Lilla, Mark, 537, 628
Lilly, Teri, 176, 617
Lim, Gerard, 532, 637
Lin, Nan, 220, 255, 637
Lincoln, Yvonna S., 56
Linden, Eugene, 263, 637
Lindsey, Robert, 413, 637
Lines, Patricia M., 473, 637
Link, Bruce G., 187, 497–498
Linton, Ralph, 66, 637
Lipset, Seymour Martin, 74, 637
Lipsky, Dorothy Kerzner, 468, 627
Little, Kenneth, 162, 637
Litwak, Eugene, 146, 634
Lockheed, Marlaine, 459, 637
Lofflin, John, 530, 637
Lofland, John, 47, 575, 637
London, Kathryn, 308, 637
Longmore, Paul K., 589, 637
Longworth, R. C., 153, 637
Lopreato, Joseph, 98, 637
Lorch, Donatella, 247, 637
Lott, Bernice, 117, 637
Louw-Potgieter, J., 281–282, 637
Lowe, Marcia D., 518, 637
Luckmann, Thomas, 133, 616
Luijkx, Ruud, 258
Lukacs, Georg, 83, 638
Luker, Kristin, 329, 638
Lum, JoAnn, 290, 636, 638
Lundberg, George, 500, 638
Luster, Tom, 374, 638
Luxenburg, Joan, 638
Lynch, Roberta, 447, 616
Lyon, Jeff, 52, 638
Lyotard, Jean-Francois, 426, 447, 638

Machung, Anne, 331
Mack, Raymond W., 130, 638

Mackenzie, Hilary, 199
Mackey, Wade, 322, 638
MacKinnon, Catharine A., 264, 638
Maddox, G., 340, 638
Madsen, Richard, 88
Maguire, Brendan, 193, 638
Maher, Timothy, 562, 638
Maines, David R., 123, 638
Majka, Linda C., 239
Majors, Richard, 140, 638
Makepeace, James M., 385, 638
Makihara, Kumiko, 257, 638
Makowsky, Michael, 14, 621
Malcolm, Andrew, 576, 638
Malcolm X, 122, 125
Malinowski, Michael J., 387, 638
Malthus, Thomas Robert, 542, 549, 563, 638
Manegold, Catherine S., 470, 638
Maney, Kevin, 595, 638
Mangalmurti, Sandeys, 230, 638
Mann, James, 383, 638
Mansnerus, Laura, 458, 638
Manson, Donald A., 193, 638
Marcano, Tony, 82
Marger, Martin, 428, 430, 638
Margolick, David, 138, 352, 638
Markides, K. S., 340, 636
Marklein, Mary Beth, 464, 638
Markson, Elizabeth W., 344, 353, 355, 631, 638
Marmor, Theodore R., 502, 638
Marotz-Baden, Ramona, 530, 631
Marsden, Peter V., 127, 638
Marshall, Ruth, 484, 639
Marshall, Victor W., 349–350, 638
Martin, Douglas, 289, 638
Martin, Linda G., 337, 638
Martin, Teresa Castro, 618
Martineau, Harriet, 11, 15, 638
Martinez, Elizabeth, 352, 639
Marty, Martin E., 398, 409, 639
Martyna, Wendy, 69, 639
Marx, Karl, 13–15, 19, 23, 28, 83–84, 214–215, 312, 365, 398, 400, 424–425, 436, 440, 445, 489, 542, 549, 560, 563, 581–582, 585, 592, 602, 604, 605, 609, 639
Mascia-Lees, Francis E., 89, 174, 639
Masland, Tim, 211, 639
Masland, Tom, 484, 639
Mason, Marie K., 94, 639
Massey, Douglas S., 302, 525, 528–529, 639
Matras, Judah, 541, 545, 639
Matyko, Alexander J., 171, 639
Matza, David, 186
Mauksch, Hans O., 447
Mauro, Tony, 281, 414, 639
Mautner, Michael, 600, 639
May, Robert M., 136, 614
Mayer, Egon, 639
Mayer, Karl Ulrich, 112, 639
McBride, Nicholas C., 504, 534, 639
McCaghy, Charles H., 191, 639
McCarthy, John D., 587, 593
McConnell, J. Jeff, 528
McCord, William, 351–352, 639
McCormick, Kenelm F., 387, 639
McCullough, Jane L., 322, 657
McCurdy, David W., 80, 232
McEnroe, Jennifer, 373, 639
McEwen, J. Thomas, 192, 621
McFalls, Joseph A., Jr., 545, 551–552, 639

McGrath, Ellie, 458, 639
McGuire, Meredith, 395, 398, 400, 639
McGuire, Randall M., 239, 639
McIntosh, Shaun, 293, 639
McKeown, Thomas, 545, 639
McKinlay, John B., 481, 639
McKinlay, Sonja M., 481, 639
McKinney, Kathleen, 167, 639
McLean, Elys A., 199, 639
McNamara, Patrick, 552, 556, 558, 639
McPhail, Clark, 571–573, 591–592, 602, 639
McPhail, Thomas, 245, 639
McPherson, J. Miller, 639
McRoberts, Flynn, 200, 639
McWilliams, Carey, 280, 639
Mead, George Herbert, 15, 27, 98, 102, 109, 115, 367, 605, 610, 639
Mead, Margaret, 62, 98–100, 108, 116, 310, 330, 380, 640
Mechanic, David, 480, 492, 640
Meddis, Sam Vincent, 190, 640
Meek, Ronald L., 342, 640
Meer, Jeff, 342, 632
Meier, Kenneth J., 475, 640
Meile, Richard C., 498, 640
Meisenheimer, Joseph R., II, 373, 640
Melbin, Murray, 6, 640
Melko, Matthew, 381, 620
Melson, Robert, 285, 640
Memmi, Albert, 245, 640
Menard, Scott, 564, 640
Mendoza, Jorge L., 614
Menken, Jane, 564, 640
Merton, Robert, 15–16, 18, 23, 29, 147, 156, 182–184, 188, 278, 493, 602, 640
Messner, Michael, 20, 640
Meyer, Marshall W., 157, 617
Michalowski, Raymond J., 250, 640
Michels, Robert, 158, 170, 580, 606, 640
Middleton, Lorenzo, 460, 640
Milburn, Norweeta, 534, 640
Milgram, Stanley, 176–178, 200, 455, 640
Mill, John Stuart, 312
Miller, Annetta, 64, 640
Miller, Brent, 213, 640
Miller, David L, 4–6, 570, 572, 574, 591–593, 639–640
Miller, Delbert C., 56, 640
Miller, Eleanor M., 447
Miller, G. Tyler, Jr., 560, 640
Miller, Louisa F., 376–377, 379, 383, 642
Miller, Robert J., 353, 640
Millett, Kate, 324, 640
Mills, C. Wright, 6, 13, 15, 23, 216, 228, 436–438, 446, 457, 628, 640
Mindel, Charles H., 389, 640
Mingle, James R., 487, 640
Mintz, Steven, 389, 640
Mishel, Lawrence, 222, 640
Mitchell, Richard G., Jr., 47, 640
Mitford, Jessica, 174
Miyazawa, Setsuo, 202, 640
Mizrahi, Terry, 42, 493, 640
Model, Suzanne, 444
Moen, Elizabeth W., 564, 640
Moffatt, Michael, 475, 640
Moffitt, Phillip, 504
Mohai, Paul, 562, 564, 618
Moon, Sun Myung, 47
Moore, D. R., 473, 641

Moore, Gwen, 296, 614
Moore, Joan W., 107, 302, 641
Moore, Kristin, 213, 640
Moore, Molly, 252, 614
Moore, Wilbert E., 111–112, 217, 457, 569, 623, 641
Moran, Theodore, 250, 641
Morganthau, Tom, 534, 641
Morin, Richard, 41, 114, 167, 579, 641
Morris, Michael, 225, 641
Morrison, Denton E., 641
Morrison, Makolm H., 348, 641
Morrison, Peter A., 613
Morse, Arthur D., 297, 641
Mortenson, Thomas, 229, 641
Mortimer, Jeylan E., 112, 641
Moseley, Ray, 568, 641
Moskis, Charles, 129, 376, 641
Moss, Alfred A., Jr., 210, 286, 627
Muedeking, George D., 3, 641
Müller, Ronald E., 250
Mullins, Marcy E., 590, 641
Munro, Brenda, 530, 634
Murdock, George P., 64, 82, 87, 362–364, 511, 535, 641
Murphree, Randall, 110, 641
Murphy, Caryle, 252, 641
Murray, Douglas, 441, 641
Muskrat, Joe, 289, 641
Mydans, Seth, 111, 293, 297–298, 641
Myers, James, 174, 641
Myers, Steven Lee, 211, 641
Myrdal, Gunnar, 300, 315, 641

Nader, Laura, 317, 641
Nader, Ralph, 193, 424, 641
Nakane, Chie, 256, 641
Nakao, Keiko, 220, 641–642
Nasar, Sylvia, 222, 642
Nash, Manning, 279, 283, 642
Navarro, Mirega, 138, 642
Navarro, Vincente, 492, 642
Naythons, Matthew, 504
Neary, John, 576, 642
Newman, Maria, 86, 642
Newman, William, 284–285, 642
Neysmith, Sheila, 337, 642
Niehoff, Arthur H., 615
Niemi, Richard G., 430, 633
Nikinovich, David G., 642
Nikkel, Stan R., 528, 636
Nixon, Howard L., 149, 642
Noble, Barbara Presley, 578, 642
Noble, Kenneth B., 288, 642
Nolan, Patrick D., 254, 642
NORC, 162, 220
Nordhaus, William D., 221, 648
Norris, Bahar, 625
Norton, Arthur J., 376–377, 379, 383, 642
Novak, Viveca, 502, 635
Novello, Antonia, 490, 642
Nuttall, Nick, 596, 642
Nyden, Phillip W., 537, 642
Nye, F. Ivan, 322, 537, 642

Oakes, Jeannie, 458, 475, 643
Oberschall, Anthony, 581, 643

O'Connor, Sandra, 314
O'Donnell, Mike, 156, 221, 246, 380, 643
Ogbu, John H., 489, 643
Ogburn, William F., 67, 112, 586, 596, 603, 643
O'Hare, Barbara, 515, 643
O'Hare, William P., 225, 643
Ohnuma, Keiko, 291, 643
Okun, M. A., 340, 643
Oliner, Pearl M., 127, 643
Oliner, Samuel P., 127, 643
Oliver, Melvin L., 129, 643
Olson, Laura Ketz, 341, 355, 643
Olson, Philip, 335, 643
Omran, Abdel R., 548, 643
O'Reilly, Jane, 325, 643
Ornstein, Norman, 347, 643
Orum, Anthony M., 431, 447, 581, 643
Orwell, George, 208, 643
Osborne, Lynn T., 185, 643
Ostling, Richard, 410, 464, 643
Ovellette, Laurie, 599, 643
Oxnam, Robert B., 291, 643

Pachon, Harry, 107, 302, 641
Page, Charles H., 160, 643
Painter, Kim, 488, 643
Palen, J. John, 528, 643
Palmer, John L., 355, 643
Pamperin, Bruce, 25, 643
Paneth, Nigel, 229, 643
Pappas, Gregory, 229, 487, 643
Park, Robert E., 513, 521, 611, 643
Parker, Patricia, 192, 630
Parker, Suzy, 432, 620
Parsons, Bruce, 97, 619
Parsons, Talcott, 15, 18, 311, 330–331, 480–481, 493, 503, 584, 588, 591, 614–616, 643
Patai, Daphne, 261, 643
Paternoster, Raymond, 202, 643
Patton, Carl, 518, 643
Paull, Irene, 344, 348, 644
Pavalko, Ronald M., 8–9, 440, 644
Payer, Lynn, 504, 644
Payne, G. C. F., 218, 622
Paynter, Robert, 239
Pear, Robert, 292, 644
Peek, Charles, 309, 615
Peirce, Kate, 40, 644
Pelto, Pertti J., 76, 644
Pepper, Claude, 344
Perez, Miguel, 71, 644
Perlez, Jane, 246, 644
Perot, Ross, 433
Perrow, Charles, 59, 598–599, 644
Perrucci, Robert, 498, 644
Petchesky, Rosalind, 327, 644
Peter, Laurence J., 157, 608, 644
Peters, John F., 108, 644
Peters, Robert, 573
Petersen, William, 542, 644
Peterson, Felix, 230, 644
Pettigrew, Thomas, 281, 644
Phillips, David P., 644
Phillips, Leslie, 10
Piaget, Jean, 102, 115, 644
Pillemer, Karl, 339, 644
Piller, Charles, 586, 644

Pinderhughes, Dianne, 438, 644
Pines, Maya, 95, 644
Pirog-Good, Maureen, 386
Pitt, Laura, 636
Piven, Frances Fox, 226, 235, 239, 431, 644, 651
Pleck, Joseph H., 644
Plomin, Robert, 97, 644
Pogash, Carol, 137, 647
Pogrebin, Letty Cottin, 108, 312, 647
Polk, Barbara Bovee, 312, 325, 644
Pollard, Kelvin, 226, 644
Porteous, Skipp, 411, 644
Porter, Jack Nusan, 405–406, 413, 624
Portes, Alejando, 251, 644
Post, Tom, 79, 644
Poster, Mark, 537
Powell, Arthur G., 475, 644
Powers, Mary G., 644
Prehn, John W., 553, 644
Preston, Julia, 242, 644
Price, Wayne T., 167, 644
Prince, Raymond, 478, 480, 644
Pringle, Peter, 211, 645
Prud'homme, Alex, 200, 645
Puente, Maria, 298–299, 645
Purvis, Andrew, 488, 645
Pytte, Alyson, 562, 645

Quadagno, Jill S., 340, 346, 348–349, 658
Quarantelli, Enrico L., 572–574, 576, 614, 645
Quayle, Dan, 375
Quinn, Kathleen, 386, 645
Quinney, Richard, 188–190, 645

Rabben, Linda, 263, 645
Radcliffe-Brown, Alfred R., 336, 645
Radosh, Mary Flanery (Polly), 481, 645
Rafferty, Kevin, 70, 306, 645
Ragin, Charles, 283
Rahr, Alexander, 579, 645
Randall, Teri, 385, 387, 645
Randall, Vicky, 447, 645
Range, Peter Ross, 554, 645
Rangel, Jesus, 645
Rashid, Salim, 542, 645
Rasky, Susan, 319, 590, 645
Rathje, William L., 561, 645
Ravitch, Diane, 86, 645
Raybon, Patricia, 326, 645
Raymond, Chris, 534, 645
Reader, G. C., 640
Reagan, Ronald, 231, 265, 292, 328–329
Reardon, Patrick T., 645
Rebell, Michael A., 645
Rebell, Susan, 114, 588, 645–646
Rebelsky, Freda, 322, 645–646
Reeder, Leo G., 489, 629
Reese, William A., 180, 646
Regier, Darrell, 497, 646
Reichard S., 340, 646
Reid, J. Norman, 530, 646
Reid, T. R., 550, 646
Reiman, Jeffrey H., 192, 646
Reinharz, Shulamit, 57, 646
Reskin, Barbara, 319, 646
Retsinas, Joan, 349, 646
Rexroat, Cynthia, 646

Rheingold, Harriet L., 106, 646
Rich, Adrienne, 315, 646
Richards, Cara E., 82, 646
Richardson, Kenneth, 186, 646
Richardson, Laurel, 646
Richburg, Keith B., 465, 646
Richlin-Klonsky, Judith, 53, 646
Richman, Joseph, 353, 646
Riddle, Lyn, 130, 646
Ridgeway, Cecilia, 146, 413
Ridgeway, James, 502, 646
Riding, Alan, 169, 267, 646
Ries, Lynn M., 259, 646
Riesman, David, 437–438, 447, 612, 646
Riessman, Catherine Kohler, 487, 646
Rigler, David, 95, 646
Riley, John W., Jr., 350, 646
Ritzer, George, 22, 112, 426, 646
Rivers, Caryl, 615
Roberts, D. F., 275, 646
Roberts, Keith, 396, 402, 646
Robertson, Nan, 163, 646
Robertson, Roland, 84, 219, 646
Robinson, J. D., 344, 646
Robinson, John P., 322, 646
Robinson, Robert V., 220, 623
Rochberg-Halton, Eugene, 510, 646
Roddick, Jackie, 252, 646
Rodell, Susanna, 502, 646
Rodgers, Harrell R., Jr., 224, 239, 647
Roethlisberger, Fritz J., 160, 647
Rogarin, Charles H., 617
Rohlen, Thomas P., 458
Rohter, Larry, 300, 319, 647
Roof, Wade Clark, 410, 647
Rooney, James F., 166, 647
Roozen, David A., 409, 632
Rosaldo, Renato, 326, 647
Rosardo, Lourdes, 386, 647
Rosario, Ruben, 82, 647
Rose, Arnold, 279, 647
Rose, Peter I., 105, 647
Rosecrance, John, 8, 647
Roseman, Mindy, 628
Rosenberg, Douglas H., 647
Rosenberg, Harriet G., 338, 647
Rosenfeld, Anne, 104, 647
Rosenthal, Elisabeth, 493, 614
Rosenthal, R., 533, 647
Rosenthal, Robert, 461, 647
Rosnow, Ralph, 576–577, 647
Rossi, Alice S., 369, 647
Rossi, Peter H., 25, 51, 220, 534, 537, 627, 632, 647
Rossides, Daniel W., 212, 647
Roszak, Theodore, 79, 647
Roth, Wendy Carol, 590, 647
Rothenberg, Paula, 86, 331, 647
Rothman, David, 498, 647
Rothmyer, Karen, 413, 624
Rothschild-Whitt, Joyce, 158, 647
Roudi, Farzaneh, 548
Rouse, Linda, 386, 614
Rovner, Julie, 115, 647
Rowen, Hobart, 549, 647
Rubel, Maximilien, 585, 617
Rubin, Charles T., 564, 647
Rubin, Cheryl, 564
Ruble, Diane N., 309, 621
Rucker, Rudy, 598, 647

Rudolph, Ellen, 70, 647
Ruggles, Patricia, 647
Rugh, Andrea B., 367, 647
Ruhe, J., 148, 647
Rule, James B., 581, 598, 626, 647
Rusk, David, 525, 648
Russell, Cheryl, 648
Ruzek, Sheryl Burt, 497, 648
Ryan, William, 227, 648
Rymer, Russ, 95, 648

Saad, Lydia, 54, 578, 633
Saarinen, Thomas F., 648
Sack, Kevin, 234, 499, 648
Sadker, David, 109, 648
Sadker, Myra, 109, 648
Safa, Helen, 261, 648
Sagarin, Edward, 181, 648
Sale, Kirkpatrick, 555–556, 648
Salem, Richard, 27, 648
Salholz, Eloise, 328, 382, 648
Saltzman, Amy, 168, 648
Salvatore, Diane, 372, 648
Sampson, Anthony, 250, 648
Sampson, Robert J., 187, 648
Samuelson, Paul, 221, 254, 648
Sanchez, Jose, 181, 648
Sanders, Clinton, 174, 202, 648
Sanger, David, 257, 648
Sapir, Edward, 69, 648
Sarti, Cynthia, 261, 648
Sassen, Saskia, 525, 648
Scanzoni, John, 366
Scarce, Rik, 48, 648
Schaefer, Richard T., 4–6, 34, 84, 107, 210, 225, 276, 280, 289, 291, 302, 375, 455, 482, 640, 648
Scheff, Thomas J., 141, 498, 648
Schlenker, Barry R., 100, 117, 648
Schmemann, Serge, 393, 648
Schmid, Carol, 313, 648
Schmidt, William E., 165, 337, 648
Schmink, Marianne, 263, 648
Schmitt, Mark, 347, 643
Schnaiberg, Allan, 557, 560, 648
Schneider, Beth E., 140, 633
Schneider, Joseph W., 481, 504, 621–622
Schneiderman, Howard G., 231, 615
Schoepflin, Urs, 112
Schrag, Peter, 474, 648
Schramm, Wilbur, 245, 648
Schultz, Terri, 327, 648
Schur, Edwin, 179, 193, 202, 648–649
Schwartz, Felice N., 331, 649
Schwartz, Howard D., 480, 484, 649
Schwartz, Joe, 545–555, 649
Schwartz, Pepper, 366, 388, 617
Schwartz, Richard D., 57, 654
Sciolino, Elaine, 266, 649
Scotch, Richard K., 590–591, 649
Scott, Ellen Kaye, 158, 649
Scott, Hilda, 224, 649
Scott-Samuel, Alex, 490, 649
Searle, John, 86, 649
Sechrest, Lee, 57, 654
Seddon, Terri, 452, 649
Seidman, Robert B., 179, 191, 620
Selby, David, 264, 649
Seligmann, Jean, 380, 649

Senter, Richard, 158, 649
Shani, Abraham B., 461, 625
Shapiro, Joseph P., 593, 649
Sharpe, Patricia, 89, 174, 639
Shatin, Deborah, 636
Shavit, Yossi, 459, 649
Shaw, Marvin E., 151, 649
Shaw, Susan M., 322, 649
Sheehy, Gail, 649
Shehan, Constano, 646
Shell, Ellen Rippel, 113, 649
Shelley, Louise, 195, 649
Shenon, Philip, 551, 649
Sherman, Arnold K., 438, 649
Sherwin, Susan, 497, 504, 649
Shilts, Randy, 138–139, 649
Shorten, Lynda, 79, 649
Shover, Neal, 123, 649
Shupe, Anson D., Jr., 44, 417, 618, 649
Sidel, Ruth, 239, 497, 649
Sidel, Victor W., 497, 649
Siegel, Jacob S., 347, 628
Sigmund, Paul E., 399, 417, 649
Sills, David L., 29, 162, 164, 166, 649
Silva, Nelson De Valle, 261, 649
Silverman, Milton, 484, 649
Silverstein, Ken, 262, 650
Simmel, Georg, 149–150, 520, 650
Simmons, Roberta G., 112, 641
Simon, John L., 268, 650
Simons, Marlise, 261, 329, 650
Simpson, George Eaton, 192
Sirisena, N. L., 259, 651
Sirott, Larry, 495, 650
Sivy, Michael, 420, 650
Sjoberg, Gideon, 512–513, 535, 650
Skafte, Peter, 104, 650
Slavin, Robert E., 458, 618
Sloan, John Henry, 199, 650
Smart, Barry, 426, 650
Smeeding, Timothy, 355
Smelser, Neil J., 29, 423, 568–569, 571–572,
    602, 612, 650
Smith, Christian, 399, 417, 650
Smith, James P., 223, 650
Smith, Ken R., 342–343, 624
Smith, Michael Peter, 518, 650
Smith, Ruth Bayard, 86, 650
Smith-Lovin, Lynn, 639
Smolan, Rick, 504, 650
Smoler, Fredric, 86, 650
Smothers, Ronald, 230, 530, 650
Snow, David A., 533, 573, 650
Sokolovsky, Jay, 355, 650
Solórzano, Lucia, 465, 650
Son, In Soo, 444, 650
Sontag, Deborah, 251, 297, 650
Sorokin, Pitirim A., 650
Sorrentino, Constance, 363, 650
Sowell, Thomas, 475, 650
Spain, Daphne, 314, 650
Spanier, Graham, 380, 650
Spence, Ian, 55, 637
Spencer, Herbert, 11–12, 15, 584–585
Spengler, Joseph J., 552, 650
Spradley, James P., 80, 232, 650
Spring, Joel H., 463, 617
Squire, Peverill, 650
Stacey, Meg, 596, 650
Stack, Steven, 10, 633, 650

Stafford, Mark, 185
Staggenborg, Suzanne, 158, 582, 650
Stahura, John M., 650
Stalk, Geroge, Jr., 256, 613
Stanley, J. P., 70, 651
Stark, Elizabeth, 104, 647
Stark, Rodney, 152, 393, 406, 651
Starr, Paul, 481, 492, 586, 651
Statham, Anne, 447, 651
Steiber, Steven R., 437, 651
Stein, Leonard, 493, 651
Stein, Peter J., 381, 651
Stellman, Jeanne Mager, 488, 651
Stenning, Derrick J., 335, 651
Stephens, Gene, 596, 651
Sterngold, James, 257, 651
Stets, Jan E., 386, 651
Stevens, William, 411, 492, 527, 651
Stewart, Joseph, Jr., 475, 640
Stimpson, Catharine, 85, 315, 651
Stocks, J. Timothy, 385, 651
Stoeckel, John, 259, 651
Stone, Andrea, 235, 651
Stone, Gregory P., 72, 629, 651
Stonich, Susan, 559, 651
Straus, Murray A., 386–387, 628, 651
Straus, Roger, 25, 29, 651
Strauss, Anselm, 122, 153, 651
Strauss, Bill, 355, 632
Strum, Charles, 458, 651
Stuart, Reginald, 415, 651
Sullivan, William M., 88
Sumner, William Graham, 147, 651
Suro, Roberto, 562, 651
Sutherland, Edwin H., 184–185, 188, 190, 192,
    604, 651
Suttles, Gerald D., 523, 603, 651
Swartz, Leslie, 478, 651
Swatos, William H., Jr., 471, 651
Swazey, Judith P., 504, 627
Sweet, James A., 376, 618, 651–652
Swidler, Anne, 88
Swift, Richard N., 264, 652
Swinton, David, 228, 652
Swiss, Deborah, 324, 652
Sykes, Gresham M., 186, 652
Szasz, Thomas S., 485, 498, 652
Szulc, Tad, 335, 652
Szymanski, Albert, 229, 652

Tachibana, Judy, 291, 652
Taeuber, Cynthia, 341, 343–344, 652
Takaki, Ronald, 291, 302, 652
Tannen, Deborah, 141, 313, 652
Tashman, Billy, 472–473, 652
Taylor, Bruce M., 464, 616
Taylor, Paul, 114, 495, 652
Taylor, Verta, 646
Telsch, Kathleen, 344, 652
Terrell, Ruth Harris, 464, 652
Terry, Don, 350, 652
Theberge, Nancy, 20, 652
Theilmann, John, 435, 655
Thirlwall, A. P., 258, 652
Thoits, Peggy A., 498, 652
Thomas, Alan, 244, 622
Thomas, Gordon, 297, 652
Thomas, Jim, 123, 352
Thomas, Rich, 306, 652

Thomas, William I., 122, 276, 521, 611, 652
Thompson, James D., 574, 652
Thompson, Linda, 369, 380, 652
Thompson, William E., 133, 652
Thorne, Barrie, 70, 108, 331, 652
Thornton, Arland, 195, 379, 652
Tiano, Susan, 259, 652
Tibbits, Clark, 112, 643
Tiefer, Leonore, 80, 652
Tierney, John, 543, 652
Tierney, Kathleen, 572, 652
Tinker, Irene, 268, 652
Tipps, Havens C., 228, 653
Tipton, Steven M., 88
Tittle, Charles R., 521, 633, 653
Tobin, Joseph J., 117, 653
Tocqueville, Alexis de, 144
Tonkinson, Robert, 335, 652
Tönnies, Ferdinand, 134–136, 139, 519–520,
    605, 652
Topolnicki, Denise M., 114, 653
Torrey, Barbara Boyle, 355
Touraine, Alan, 453, 653
Tracy, Martin B., 653
Treas, Judith, 220, 641–642
Treiman, Donald J., 220, 254–255, 258,
    653
Treisman, Urie, 461, 653
Tritto, Lorraine, 247–248, 630
Trow, Martin, 465, 621
Trusheim, Dale, 475, 622
Tsai, Shu-Ling, 459, 653
Tsuneyoshi, Ryoko Kato, 455, 653
Tuchman, Gaye, 21, 313, 653
Tucker, James, 160, 653
Tucker, Jeffrey, 472, 653
Tumin, Melvin, 217, 653
Turner, Bryan S., 426, 613, 653
Turner, J. Blake, 635
Turner, J. H., 504, 653
Turner, Margery, 445, 653
Turner, Patricia A., 593, 653
Turner, Ralph, 99, 571, 578, 591–592, 604,
    653
Turque, Bill, 526, 653
Twaddle, Andrew, 480, 502, 653
Tyler, Charles, 211, 653
Tyler, William B., 463, 653

Udy, Stanley H., Jr., 157, 653
Ullman, Edward, 515, 608, 630
Usdansky, Margaret L., 64, 381, 653

Vachss, Alice, 202, 653
Van den Berghe, Pierre, 653
Vanneman, Reeve, 215, 653
Van Voorst, Bruce, 562, 653
Van Vort, Jennifer, 383
Van Vucht Tijssen, Lieteke, 426, 653
Vasquez, Enriqueta Longauex y, 326, 653
Vaughn, Leigh Ann, 176, 617
Veblen, Thorstein, 586, 612, 654
Verbrugge, Lois M., 486, 654
Vernon, Glenn, 406, 654
Vernon, Jo Etta A., 344, 654
Vernon, Raymond, 250
Vobejda, Barbara, 530, 654
Voydanoff, Patricia, 239, 654

Wagley, Charles, 274, 336, 654
Wagner, David, 534–535, 654
Waite, Linda, 613
Waitzkin, Howard, 490, 495, 504, 650, 654
Waldrop, Theresa, 588, 654
Walker, Alexis J., 652
Walker, Gillian, 442, 654
Wallace, Anthony, 393, 654
Wallace, Ruth, 584, 654
Wallace, Stephen, 654
Wallerstein, Immanuel, 89, 245, 247, 259, 267, 612, 654
Wallerstein, Judith, 249, 377
Wallis, Claudia, 97, 154, 654
Walton, John, 253, 593, 654
Waring, Elin, 202
Waring, Marilyn, 253, 268, 559, 654
Warr, Mark, 185, 654
Wasielewski, Patricia, 428, 654
Wasserman, Ira, 10, 654
Watanaka, Kazuke, 257, 654
Waterfield, Larry W., 537, 654
Waters, Harry F., 654
Watkins, Beverly T., 654
Watson, Kenneth M., 372, 654
Watson, Russell, 394, 654
Watson, Tracey, 127, 654
Watt, Nicholas, 596, 642
Watts, Jerry G., 439, 654
Watts, W. David, 27, 654
Weaver, Warren, Jr., 345, 654
Webb, Eugene J., 57, 654
Weber, Max, 12–13, 15, 18, 28–29, 50–51, 55–56, 153–154, 157, 169–170, 396, 401, 420, 427–428, 446, 462, 582, 602, 607, 609, 611, 612, 654–655
Weeks, John, 540, 543, 545, 548–549, 552, 564, 655
Weigard, Bruce, 251, 268, 655
Weinberg, Martin S., 213, 655
Weiner, Tim, 300, 655
Weinstein, Deena, 89, 655
Weisburd, David, 202, 655
Weisman, Steven R., 169, 257, 655
Weitz, Shirley, 106, 308, 655
Weitzer, Ronald, 583, 655

Weitzman, Lenore, 589, 655
Welch, William M., 235–236, 491, 655
Wells, Ida B., 16, 655
West, Candace, 308, 313, 655
West, Cornel, 655
West, Edwin G., 460, 655
Wheeler, Stanton, 202, 488
Whipple, Thomas, 309, 622
White, Jack E., 106, 622, 655
White, Merry, 458, 475, 655
Whittle, Jeff, 190, 655
Whyte, William Foote, 41–44, 655
Wickman, Peter M., 180, 655
Wiewel, Wim, 537, 642
Wilhite, Allen, 435, 655
Wilkerson, Isabel, 368, 532, 655
Wilkinson, Doris K., 655
Will, George F., 86, 655
Will, J. A., 308, 655
Williams, Christine, 321, 655
Williams, Colin J., 27, 213, 655
Williams, Ivan, 195, 655
Williams, J. Allen, Jr., 162, 655
Williams, Robin M., 74, 455, 655
Williams, Simon Johnson, 101, 655
Willis, Ellen, 327, 655
Willis, John, 230, 655
Wilson, Edward O., 97, 655
Wilson, Franklin D., 511, 655
Wilson, James Q., 202, 656
Wilson, John, 398, 581, 656
Wilson, Robert N., 481, 617
Wilson, Warner, 82, 656
Wilson, William Julius, 225, 239, 656
Wimberly, Dale, 656
Winter, J. Alan, 401, 656
Wirth, Louis, 25, 519–521, 607, 612, 656
Wise, David, 72, 179, 431, 622
Wise, Paul H., 642
Withers, Claudia, 167, 656
Witts, Max Morgan, 297, 652
Wolf, Alison, 584, 654
Wolf, Eric, 397, 656
Wolfe, Donald M., 366, 426, 617
Wolfe, Tom, 78, 656
Wolinsky, Frederic P., 480, 483, 656

Wollstonecraft, Mary, 307, 312
Wood, Charles, 260–261, 263, 648, 656
Work, Clemens P., 524, 656
World Bank, 251, 254, 268
Woronoff, John, 447, 656
Wright, Erik O., 218, 656
Wright, Roosevelt, Jr., 389, 640
Wright, Susan, 225, 656
Wrong, Dennis H., 541, 656
Wurman, Richard Saul, 595, 656
Wuthnow, Robert, 656

Xie, Wen, 220, 255, 637

Yamakawa, Karen, 228
Yanagishita, Machiko, 243–244, 247, 337, 482, 540, 544–545, 547–548, 656
Yates, Ronald E., 67, 656
Yinger, J. Milton, 78, 398, 400, 401, 405, 604, 656
Young, J. Kim, 384, 657
Young, T. R., 402, 656
Yzaguirre, Raul, 277, 656

Zald, Mayer N., 165, 171, 587, 593, 656
Zaslow, M., 378, 656
Zeitlin, Maurice, 230, 656–657
Zellner, William M., 49–50, 140, 179, 454, 635, 657
Zelnick, Melvin, 384, 657
Zia, Helen, 326, 481
Zick, Cathleen D., 322, 657
Zimbardo, Philip G., 120–121, 125, 630, 657
Zimmer, Lynn, 321, 657
Zimmerman, Don H., 122, 497, 655
Zimmerman, Jean, 331
Zimmerman, Klaus, 560, 657
Zimmerman, Mary K., 657
Zinn, Maxine Baca, 625
Zola, Irving K., 480–483, 497, 589, 657
Zurcher, Louis A., 573
Zussman, Robert, 504, 657
Zwerdling, Daniel, 447, 657

SUBJECT INDEX

ABC bill (Act for Better Child Care), 114
Abortion, 41, 122, 327–330
Absolute poverty, 226, 237, 601
Achieved status, 124–125, 139–140, 212, 237, 601
Acquired immune deficiency syndrome (AIDS), 52, 125, 136–139, 352, 485–486, 490–491, 551, 561
Act for Better Child Care (ABC bill), 114
Active euthanasia, 351
Activity theory, 339–340, 353–354, 601
Adolescence, 103, 185
Adoption, 371–372, 388, 601
Adult education, 470, 471
Affirmative action, 38, 442–445, 601
African Americans, 20, 34–39, 43, 100, 122, 129, 137, 168, 189, 210, 212, 228–230, 234, 272, 275–276, 281–282, 286–288, 315–316, 326, 375, 383, 394, 432, 438, 444, 466, 487, 490, 500, 525, 527–528, 562
Afrocentricity, 86–87, 601
Age, stratification by, 333–355
Age grades, 337, 354, 601
Ageism, 344, 354, 601
Aggregate, 145
Agrarian society, 422, 445–446, 601
Aid to Families with Dependent Children (AFDC), 235–237
AIDS (acquired immune deficiency syndrome), 52, 125, 136–139, 352, 485–486, 490–491, 551, 561
Alienation, 440–442, 445–446, 601
Amalgamation, 283–285, 301, 601
American Association of Retired Persons (AARP), 347
American Indians (see Native Americans)
American Sign Language, 68
American Sociological Association (ASA), 46, 48
Americans for Generational Equity, 345–346
Americans with Disabilities Act (ADA), 469, 590–591
Amish, 92–93, 179
Amnesty, 299
Amnesty International, 266
Anomie, 12, 28, 182, 201, 601–602
Anomie theory of deviance, 182–183, 201, 602
Anorexia nervosa, 478
Anticipatory socialization, 104, 112, 115, 348, 602
Anti-Semitism, 294, 301, 602
Apaches, 62
Apartheid, 285, 301, 525, 602
Applied sociology, 25, 28, 44, 602
Arapesh, 310
Argot, 78, 87, 602
Armenia, 283
Ascribed status, 124, 139–140, 212, 237, 602
Asian Americans, 275, 527
Assembling perspective, 284–285, 301, 572–573, 591–592, 602
Assimilation, 284, 301, 602
Authority, 426–428, 445–446, 462, 602
    charismatic, 426, 428, 445–446, 582, 602
    legal-rational, 427–428, 445–446, 607
    traditional, 427, 445, 447, 612

Bakke (Supreme Court case of 1978), 443
Bali, 360
Banaro, 360
Basic sociology, 25, 28, 602
Bell v. Maryland, 295
Bilateral descent, 364, 388, 602
Bilingualism, 69, 71, 87, 294, 453–454, 602
Biotechnology, 592
Birth parents, 371
Birthrate, 544, 551, 563, 602
Black power, 286, 301, 602
Blacks (*see* African Americans)
Blaming the victim, 225–227, 291, 375
Body piercing, 174
"Boomerang generation," 369
Bosnia-Herzegovina, 264–266, 396
Bourgeoisie, 214–215, 237, 602
Brady bill, 200
Brazil, 242, 259–263, 275
Bridge jobs, 339
Brown v. Board of Education, 286
Buraku, 256
Bureau of the Census, 54, 85, 212, 221–224, 226, 234, 248, 253, 275, 286, 288, 294–295, 298, 315, 318–320, 327, 342–343, 362, 369, 372, 374–377, 380, 382–383, 410, 441, 443, 451–452, 461, 469–471, 486–487, 491, 499, 515, 521, 526, 530, 540, 552, 554, 619
Bureaucracy, 152–161, 169–170
Bureaucratization, 157–158, 170
Burnout, 441

Calvinism, 400–401, 417
Canada, 49, 74–75, 79, 322
Capitalism, 214–215, 237, 423–424, 440, 445–446, 459, 542, 586, 602
Career, 26–27, 111
Castes, 210, 237, 265, 602
Category, 145
Causal logic, 36, 55, 602
Census, 543, 563, 602
Charismatic authority, 426, 428, 445–446, 582, 602
Chicanos (*see* Mexican Americans)
Child care, 113–115, 3a77
Childless couples, 382
China, People's Republic of, 255, 335, 550
Chinese Americans, 275, 289–290
Choice programs for schools, 471–474
Civil Liberties Act, 292
Civil rights movement, 286
Class, 212–214, 237, 374, 487, 489, 602
Class consciousness, 215, 237, 325, 602
Class system, 212–214, 237, 602
Classical theory, 159, 170, 602
Clinical sociology, 25, 28, 602
Closed class system, 231, 237, 602
Coalition, 150–151, 170, 602
Code of ethics, 46, 52, 55, 602
Cognitive theory of development, 102, 115, 602
Cohabitation, 380, 388, 602
Collective behavior, 567–582, 588–593, 602
Colonialism, 243, 267, 603
Color gradient, 260

Commitment, 112
Common sense, sociology and, 9
Communism, 14, 425, 446, 603
Communist Manifesto, The, 14
Community, 509–537, 603
Community Mental Health Centers Act (CMHC program), 498–499
Computers, 598
Concentric-zone theory, 513, 536, 603
Concrete operational stage, 102
Conditioning, 112
Conflict perspective, 19–21, 23–24, 28, 34, 69, 81, 84–85, 100, 108–111, 114, 124, 131–133, 137–138, 158–164, 188–189, 192, 194, 199, 212, 215, 217–219, 276, 280, 291, 300, 311–313, 317, 328, 340–341, 343, 372, 386, 397–398, 415, 455–460, 473, 481–482, 487, 489, 495, 502, 518, 523, 549, 556, 559–560, 585–586, 599–600, 603
Conformity, 176–178, 182–183, 200–201, 603
Consciousness:
    false, 215, 237, 325, 398, 582, 592, 605
    class, 215, 237, 325, 602
Contact hypothesis, 280, 301, 603
Content analysis, 45–46, 55, 110, 603
Continuous commitment, 112
Control group, 44, 55, 603
Control variable, 38, 55, 603
"Copycat" behavior, 10
Core nations, 245
Correlation, 36, 55, 603
Correspondence principle, 458, 474, 603
Cosmology, 402, 416, 603
Counterculture, 78–79, 88, 603
Courtship, 367–368
Craze, 575–576, 591–592, 603
Creationists, 402, 413, 416, 603
Credentialism, 456–457, 474, 603
Crime, 190–198, 201, 229–230, 603
    organized, 191–192, 201, 608
    professional, 190–191, 201, 609
    victimless, 188, 193–194, 201, 612
    white-collar, 192–193, 196, 201, 612
Crimes, index, 190–201, 606
Cross-tabulation, 54–55, 603
Crowds, 573, 591–592, 603
Cults, 405–406, 412–413, 416, 603
Cultural integration, 76, 88, 603
Cultural relativism, 82, 87–88, 603
Cultural transmission, 184, 201, 603
Cultural universals, 64, 87–88, 393, 396, 416, 603
Cultural variation, 77–82
Culture, 61–89, 603
Culture-bound syndrome, 478, 503, 603
Culture lag, 586, 592, 603
Culture shock, 79–80, 88, 603

Day care, 113–115, 377
Deaf, 68
Death, 349–353
Death rate, 544, 563, 603
Defended neighborhood, 523, 536, 603
"Definition of the situation," 122, 276
Degradation ceremony, 105, 115, 498, 603

673

Demographic transition, 545–547, 563, 603
Demography, 541, 544, 563, 603
Denomination, 404, 406, 416, 603
Dependent variable, 35–36, 56, 603–604
Descent patterns, 363–364
Deviance, 173–202, 604
 anomie theory of, 182–183, 201, 602
Dialectical process, 14, 28, 604
Differential association, 184, 200–201, 604
Differentiation, 584
Diffusion, 65–66, 88, 604
Direct-selling organizations, 144
Disability, 467–469, 588–591
Disaster Research Center, 574
Disasters, 573–574, 592, 604
Discovery, 64, 88, 604
Discretionary justice, 189
Discrimination, 282–283, 301, 344–345, 383,
 443, 590, 604
 institutional (see Institutional
  discrimination)
Disengagement theory, 339–340, 353–354, 604
Dissertation, 26
Division of labor, 153–154, 462
Divorce, 376–379
Doctor-nurse game, 493
Domestic partnership, 381, 388, 604
Domestic violence, 384–387
Dominant ideology, 83–84, 87–88, 218–219,
 237, 245, 604
Double jeopardy, 320, 325
Doublespeak, 153
Dramaturgical approach, 23, 28, 100, 115, 604
Dual-career families, 372–373
Dyad, 150, 170, 604
Dying, 349–353
Dysfunction, 19, 28, 153, 170, 604

Earth Day, 554
Earth Summit, 555
Ecclesia, 403–404, 406, 416, 604
Economic system, 419–421, 426–439,
 445–447, 604
Economy, informal, 251, 258, 268, 606
Edge cities, 515–516
Education, 131–132, 232–233, 414–416,
 449–475, 604
Egalitarian family, 365, 387–388, 604
Elder abuse, 384–387
Elite model, 436–437, 445–446, 604
Emergent-norm perspective, 569–571, 573,
 591–592, 604
Emigrants, 544
Endogamy, 367, 388, 604
Engel v. Vitale, 414
Environment, 554–564
Equal Employment Opportunity Commission,
 168
Equilibrium model, 584, 592, 604
Established sect, 403–406, 416, 604
Estate system, 210, 212, 237, 604
Esteem, 219, 237, 604
Ethics of research, 46–52
Ethnic cleansing, 264, 283
Ethnic groups, 273–274, 293–299, 301, 522,
 604
Ethnic succession, 191
Ethnocentrism, 80–81, 87–88, 281, 301, 582,
 604

Euthanasia, 350–354, 604
Evangelical faiths, 409, 417, 604
Evolutionary theory, 582, 584, 591–592, 604
Existing sources, 38, 45, 62
Exogamy, 367, 388, 604
Experiment, 38, 44–45, 55–56, 95, 177, 334,
 604
Experimental group, 44, 56, 604
Exploitation theory, 280, 301, 604
Expressiveness, 311, 330, 604–605
Expulsion, 283
Extended family, 361–362, 387–388, 605

Face-work, 100, 115, 605
Fads, 575, 592, 605
False consciousness, 215, 237, 325, 398, 582,
 592, 605
Families, 105–108, 358–389, 605
 dual-career, 372–373
 egalitarian, 365, 387–388, 604
 extended, 361–362, 387–388, 605
 nuclear, 361–362, 387–388, 608
 single-parent, 382–384, 388, 610
Familism, 107, 115–116
Family and Medical Leave Act, 373
Family violence, 384–387
Fashions, 575, 592, 605
Female infanticide, 251, 363
Feminist movement, 325–326
Feminist sociology, 21, 24, 164, 220, 426
Feminization of poverty, 224, 315, 383
Fertility, 541–552, 563, 605
Feudal societies, 212, 237
Filipinos, 275
Folkways, 72, 87–88, 605
Force, 426, 445–446, 605
Formal norms, 72, 87–88, 605
Formal operational stage, 102
Formal organization, 151–161, 440, 462, 605
Formal social control, 178, 201, 605
Free enterprise system, 424
Functional prerequisites, 130–131
Functionalist perspective, 18–21, 28, 34, 69,
 81, 84–85, 102, 109, 130–132, 138, 176, 181,
 190, 217, 219, 279–280, 283, 291, 311, 339,
 365, 371, 396, 452–455, 457, 465, 473,
 480–481, 519, 558, 577, 581, 584–585,
 591–592, 605
Fundamentalism, 409, 411, 415–417, 605

Gambling, 8–9
Game stage, 99
Gemeinschaft, 134–135, 139–140, 162, 519, 521,
 605
Gender and language, 69
Gender gap, 433
Gender identity, 307, 330, 605
Gender roles, 106, 115–116, 127, 154,
 305–331, 605
Gendered spaces, 314
Generalized belief, 571
Generalized others, 99, 116, 605
Genocide, 283, 301, 605
Gentrification, 534, 536, 605
Germany, 553, 568
Gerontocracy, 336, 353–354, 605
Gerontology, 336, 354, 605
Gesellschaft, 134–135, 139–140, 162, 519, 605

Goal displacement, 154, 156, 170, 605
Goal multiplication, 164–165, 170, 605
Goal succession, 165–166, 170, 605
Grandparenting, 369, 371
Gray Panthers, 346–347
Greek Americans, 376
Greenhouse effect, 262, 559
Groups, 127–129, 139–140, 145–151, 170, 605
Growth rate, 545, 563, 605
Gun control, 198–200

Habit training, 106
Hawthorne effect, 45, 56, 605
Hawthorne studies, 45
Health, sociology of, 477–504, 605
Health insurance, 500–502
Heredity versus environment, 93, 96–97, 596
Hidden curriculum, 455, 474, 605
Hierarchy of authority, 154–155
Hispanics, 20, 110–111, 137, 189, 212, 230,
 234, 273, 275, 277, 293–294, 375, 432, 490,
 500, 525, 562
Holistic medicine, 495, 503, 605
Homeless, the, 51, 235, 532–535
Homophobia, 139–146, 605
Homosexuality, 48–49, 137–138, 262, 381–382
Horizontal mobility, 231, 237, 605–606
Horticultural societies, 421, 445–446, 606
Human ecology, 513, 536, 558, 563, 606
Human relations approach, 159, 170, 606
Human rights, 264–267, 606
Hunger, 4
Hunting-and-gathering society, 421, 445–446,
 606
Hyde amendment, 327
Hypothesis, 35, 37–39, 56, 606

Ideal type, 12–13, 29, 606
Immigration, 258, 297–300, 544, 553
Immigration and Naturalization Service, 273,
 297
Immigration Reform and Control Act of 1986,
 299
Impersonality, 154, 157
Impression management, 100–101, 116, 606
Incest taboo, 367, 388, 606
Incidence, 486, 503, 606
Inclusion, 467–469, 474, 606
Income, 209, 221–223, 237, 253–254, 606
Independent variable, 35–36, 56, 606
Index, 37, 56, 606
Index crimes, 190–201, 606
India, 360, 459, 550
Individual marriage, 380
Industrial city, 512–513, 535–536, 606
Industrial revolution, 422, 446, 512, 536, 606
Industrial society, 423, 445–446, 606
Infant mortality rate, 250, 267, 482–483, 503,
 544, 563, 606
Influence, 426, 445–446, 606
Informal economy, 251, 258, 268, 606
Informal norms, 72, 87–88, 606
Informal social control, 178, 201, 606
In-group, 147, 169–170, 274, 277, 606
Innovation, 64, 88, 606
Institutional discrimination, 301, 311,
 330–331, 440, 606
Instrumentality, 311, 331, 606

Interactionist perspective, 21–24, 28–29, 34, 69, 100, 110, 132, 137, 145, 149, 178, 184–185, 278, 313, 415, 460–461, 483, 493, 572, 606
Interest groups, 434–435, 446, 606
Intergenerational mobility, 231–232, 238, 258, 606
Interracial marriage, 367–368
Interview, 40, 56, 62, 606
Intragenerational mobility, 231–232, 238, 258, 606
Invention, 65, 88, 606
Iron law of oligarchy, 158, 170, 606
Issei, 290, 302, 606

Japan, 70, 195, 256–257, 337, 450–451, 458, 545
Japanese Americans, 275, 290, 292
Jews, 126–127, 275, 294–296, 410–412
Juku, 458

Kagemi, 367
Kenya, 246–247
Kinship, 364, 388, 606
Korean Americans, 272–273, 275, 292–293
Koreans, 257, 272–273
Ku Klux Klan, 295
!Kung, 338
Kye, 376

Labeling theory, 186–188, 194, 201, 294, 336, 367, 461, 464, 483–485, 497–498, 588, 606–607
Laissez-faire, 423, 446, 607
Language, 67–71, 87–88, 607
Lapp people, 76
Latent function, 18–19, 29, 130, 607
Latinos (*see* Hispanics)
Law, 88, 179, 200–201, 607
Legal-rational authority, 427–428, 445–446, 607
Lesbians (*see* Homosexuality)
Liberation theology, 399, 417, 607
Life chances and stratification, 228–229, 238, 607
Life expectancy, 545, 563, 607
Linear-development model, 519, 536, 607
Lobbying, 435
Looking-glass self, 98, 116, 439, 607
Los Angeles, 272–273, 375, 380, 572
Lottery, 230
Love, 368–369

Machismo, 107, 116, 607
Macrosociology, 16–17, 23, 28–29, 313, 396, 420, 607
Mainstreaming, 132, 467–469, 474, 607
Manifest function, 18–19, 29, 607
Marital power, 366, 388, 426, 446, 607
Marxism, 13–15, 19, 23, 28, 83–84, 214–215, 312, 365, 398, 400, 424–425, 436, 440, 445, 489, 542, 549, 560, 563, 581–582, 585, 592, 602, 604–605, 609
Mass media, 110–111
Master status, 125, 134–140, 336, 607
Mate selection, 367–368

Material culture, 67, 88, 586, 607
Matriarchy, 365, 388, 607
Matrilineal descent, 364, 388, 607
Matrilocal pattern of residence, 364, 388, 607
MCTs (minimum-competency tests), 467, 475, 607
Mechanical solidarity, 135, 140, 607
Médecins Sans Frontièrer, 266
Medical model, 491, 497–498, 588
Medicalization of society, 481
Medicine, 477–504
  holistic, 495, 503, 605
Megalopolis, 518, 536, 607
Meidung, 179
Melting pot, 284
Men's gender roles, 309–310
Mental health and illness, 497–499, 534
Mexican Americans, 107, 275, 293–294, 326, 376, 441
Mexico, 396–397, 540, 549
Microsociology, 16–17, 23, 28–29, 137, 258, 279, 314, 420, 482, 607
Middle class, 213, 222
Midlife crisis, 103–104, 116, 607
Migration, 342, 553–554, 563, 607
Minimum-competency tests (MCTs), 467, 475, 607
Minority group, 273–274, 277, 301–302, 314–315, 336, 607
Model minority, 240–241
Modernization, 245–246, 267–268, 607
Monogamy, 362, 388, 607
Monopoly, 423–424, 446, 607
Morbidity rates, 486, 503, 607
Mores, 72, 87–88, 607
Mortality rate, 486, 504, 607
  infant (*see* Infant mortality rate)
Multiculturalism, 84–88, 148, 607
Multilinear evolutionary theory, 584, 592, 607–608
Multinational corporations, 247–249, 267–268, 482, 608
Multiple-nuclei theory, 515, 536, 608
Mundugumor, 310
Muslims, 392, 407, 548

Nadars, 232
National Association for the Advancement of Colored People (NAACP), 21, 286
National health insurance, 500–502, 586
National Organization for Women (NOW), 346
Native Americans, 62, 275, 283, 396, 403
Natural science, 7, 29, 608
Nature versus nurture, 93, 596
Negotiated order, 122–123, 140, 608
Negotiation, 122–123, 140, 608
Neocolonialism, 245, 247, 267–268, 608
Neolocal pattern of residence, 364, 388, 608
Neo-Malthusians, 542
Nepal, 334
Netherlands, 351
Networks, 127–128
Neutralization, techniques of, 186, 201, 611
New Zealand, 600
Nigeria, 478
NIMBY, 561, 586
NIMTOO, 561
Nisei, 292, 302, 608

Nonmaterial culture, 67, 88, 586, 608
Nonperiodic assemblies, 573, 592, 608
Nonverbal communication, 23, 28–29, 608
Normal accidents, 599
Norms, 71–74, 87–88, 308, 608
  formal, 72, 87–88, 605
  informal, 72, 87–88, 606
Nuclear family, 361–362, 387–388, 608
Nursing, 321

Obedience, 176–178, 200–201, 608
Objective method, 219, 238, 608
Observation, 38, 41–44, 56, 62, 107, 174, 216, 430, 608
Occupations, 315–319, 463
Older Women's League, 345–347
Oligarchy, 158, 170, 606
  iron law of, 158, 170, 606
Oligopoly, 424, 446, 608
Open class system, 231, 237–238, 608
Operational definition, 34, 55–56, 608
Organic solidarity, 134, 140, 608
Organized crime, 191–192, 201, 608
Out-group, 147, 169–170, 274, 608

PAC (political action committee), 435, 446, 502, 608
Panic, 575–576, 591–592, 608
Papua, New Guinea, 75, 216
Parental marriage, 380
Parenthood, 369, 371
Participant observation, 41, 48
Patriarchy, 365, 387–388, 608
Patrilineal descent, 364, 388, 608
Patrilocal pattern of residence, 364, 388, 608
Peer groups, 109–110
Pentecostal faiths, 409, 417, 608
Periodic assemblies, 573, 592, 608
Periphery nations, 245
Personality, 93, 116, 608
Peter principle, 154, 157, 170, 608
Planned Parenthood v. Casey, 328
Play stage, 99
Pluralism, 285–286, 301–302, 608
Pluralist model, 437–438, 445–446, 608
Political action committee (PAC), 435, 446, 502, 608
Political socialization, 428, 430, 445–446, 608
Political system, 313–315, 419–421, 426–439, 445–447, 608–609
Politics, 426, 446, 609
Pollution (*see* Environment)
Polyandry, 363, 388, 609
Polygamy, 362, 388, 609
Polygyny, 363, 388, 609
Population, 539–544
Population pyramid, 549, 563, 609
Postindustrial society, 425–426, 445–446, 609
Postmodern society, 425, 446, 609
Poverty, 222–224, 226
  absolute, 226, 237, 601
  feminization of, 224, 315, 383
  relative, 226, 238, 609
Poverty line, 226
Power, 215, 238, 426, 445–446, 609
Power elite, 436–437, 446, 609
Precipitating factor, 571
Predestination, 401, 417, 609

Preindustrial city, 512–513, 535–536, 609
Preindustrial societies, 512
Prejudice, 34, 280–281, 302, 344, 609
Pre-operational stage, 102
Preparatory stage, 98
Prescription drugs, 484
Pressure group, 435, 446, 609
Prestige, 219–220, 238, 254–255, 609
Prevalence, 486, 504, 609
Primary group, 146, 169–170, 609
Profane, the, 395, 414, 417, 609
Profession, 439–440, 445–446, 609
Professional criminals, 190–191, 201, 609
Project Head Start, 455
Proletariat, 214–215, 238, 243, 609
Prostitution, 583
Protestant ethic, 400, 417, 609
Public, 578, 592, 609
Public opinion, 578, 592
Public places, 24
Puerto Ricans, 275, 293–294
Pure sociology, 25
Pygmalion study, 461, 475, 611

Questionnaire, 40, 55–56, 609
Quilombo, 260
Quinceañera, 107

Race, 73–76, 86–93
Racial group, 273, 301–302, 609
Racism, 281, 302, 609
Random sample, 36, 56, 609
Reference group, 147–148, 169–170, 609
Relative deprivation, 581, 592, 609
Relative poverty, 226, 238, 609
Reliability, 37, 55–56, 609
Religion, 390–417, 609
Religious beliefs, 401–402, 416–417, 609
Religious experience, 402–403, 416–417, 609
Religious rituals, 402, 416–417, 609
Religious values, 402, 417, 609
Representative sample, 36, 56, 609
Research design, 38–39, 56, 609
Residence, patterns of:
    matrilocal, 364, 388, 607
    neolocal, 364, 388, 608
    patrilocal, 364, 388, 608
Resocialization, 104, 116, 610
Resource mobilization, 581–582, 610
Resurgent fundamentalism, 409–410
Retirement, 347–348
Retreatism, 183
Reverse discrimination, 443
Reverse socialization, 108, 116, 610
Riots, 569–573
Rites of passage, 102, 116, 610
Ritualism, 183
Roe v. Wade, 327–328
Role conflict, 125–126, 140, 610
Role exit, 125–126, 140, 339, 610
Role taking, 99, 116, 610
Roman Catholics, 296, 396, 399, 407, 410
Rules and regulations, 164–165
Rumors, 576–578, 591–592, 610
Rural life, 529–532

Sacred, 395, 414, 417, 610
Sanctions, 73–74, 87–88, 176, 201, 610
Sanctuary movement, 399, 417, 610
Sapir-Whorf hypothesis, 68–69, 87–88, 610
Scale, 37, 56, 610
Science, 7, 29, 610
Scientific management approach, 159, 170, 610
Scientific method, 33–34, 38, 55–56, 610
Second Harvest, 4
Second shift, 323, 373
Secondary analysis, 45, 56, 610
Secondary group, 146, 170, 610
Sects, 404, 406, 412–413, 417, 610
Secularization, 393, 417, 610
Securities and Exchange Commission (SEC), 168
Segregation, 284–285, 301–302, 319, 610
Self, 98–102, 116, 610
Self-fulfilling prophecy, 276, 278, 294, 302, 610
Self-help groups, 162–163, 170, 610
Semiperiphery nations, 245
Senilicide, 335, 354, 610
Senior Action in a Gay Environment (SAGE), 346–347
Serial monogamy, 362, 388, 610
Sex roles (see Gender roles)
Sexism, 316, 331, 469, 488, 599–600, 610
Sexual behavior, 82, 213, 365, 596
Sexual harassment, 167–170, 610
Shakers, 130
Sick role, 480–481, 504, 588, 610
Sierra Leone, 600
Significant others, 100, 116, 367, 610
Singapore, 178–179
Single-parent families, 382–384, 388, 610
Skinheads, 79
Slavery, 210–211, 236, 238, 261, 286, 610
Small group, 148–151, 169, 171, 610
Social change, 569, 582, 583–587, 591–592, 610
Social class (see Class)
Social control, 173–202, 454–455, 571–572, 610
    informal, 178, 201, 606
    formal, 178, 201, 605
Social epidemiology, 486, 504, 610
Social inequality, 205–343, 599–600, 610–611
Social institutions, 130–133, 139–140, 388, 611
Social interaction, 120–141, 611
Social mobility, 230–234, 611
Social movements, 579–583, 587–592, 611
Social network, 127–128, 140, 611
Social norm (see Norms)
Social promotion, 467, 475, 611
Social role, 125, 140, 611
Social science, 7, 28–29, 611
Social structure, 120–141, 611
Social surplus, 422, 446, 511, 535–536, 611
Socialism, 424–425, 440, 446, 611
Socialization, 91–117, 308–309, 325, 365, 611
    anticipatory (see Anticipatory socialization)
Societal-reaction approach, 187, 200–201, 611
Society(ies), 63, 87–88, 611
    agrarian, 422, 445–446, 601
    feudal, 212, 237
    horticultural, 421, 445–446, 606

Society(ies) (Cont.):
    hunting-and-gathering, 421, 445–446, 606
    industrial, 423, 445–446, 606
    medicalization of, 481
    postindustrial, 425–426, 445–446, 609
    postmodern, 425, 446, 609
    preindustrial, 512–513, 535–536, 609
Sociobiology, 97–98, 116, 275, 611
Sociological imagination, 6–7, 28–29, 611
Sociological Practice Association, 25, 46
Sociology, 5, 29, 595, 600, 611
    applied, 25, 28, 44, 602
    basic, 25, 28, 602
    clinical, 25, 28, 602
    and common sense, 9
    feminist, 21, 24, 164, 220, 426
    of health, 477–504, 605
    macro (see Macrosociology)
    micro (see Microsociology)
    pure, 25
Solidarity:
    mechanical, 134, 140, 607
    organic, 134, 140, 608
South Africa, Republic of, 281–282, 284–285
Southern Christian Leadership Conference (SCLC), 286
Sports, 20
Squatter settlements, 518, 536, 611
State, 112
Status, 124–125, 140, 366, 611
    achieved, 124–125, 139–140, 212, 237, 601
    ascribed, 124, 139–140, 212, 237, 602
Status group, 215–216, 238, 611
Stereotypes, 32, 46, 125, 234, 276, 280, 302, 309, 312, 321, 334, 344, 589, 611
Stratification, 207–270, 611
    by age, 333–355
Stratum mobility, 231–232, 238, 611
Structural component of prejudice, 281
Structural mobility, 231, 238, 611
Subculture, 77–78, 87–88, 98, 179, 465–466, 611
Subsistence technology, 511, 536, 611
Suburb, 526–529, 536, 611
Suburbanization, 554
Suicide, 10
Survey, 38–41, 54–56, 228, 329, 368, 403, 443, 454, 467, 473, 487, 528, 560, 579, 611
Sweden, 317
Symbolic interactionist perspective (see Interactionist perspective)
Symbols, 98–99, 116, 611
Systemic model, 521, 536, 611

Tchambuli, 310
Teacher-expectancy effect, 461, 475, 611
Techniques of neutralization, 186, 201, 611
Technology, 421, 446–447, 595–600, 611
Telecommuting, 596, 598
Televangelists, 407
TFR (total fertility rate), 544–545, 548, 563, 611
Theory, 9–10, 28–29, 611
Toda, 360
Total fertility rate (TFR), 544–545, 548, 563, 611
Total institution, 104–105, 116, 611
Tracking, 458, 475, 611–612

Traditional authority, 427, 445, 447, 612
Trained incapacity, 153–154, 171, 612
Triad, 150, 171, 612
Triple jeopardy, 325
Twelve Step program, 163

Unconscious cueing, 126
Underclass, 224–225, 238, 612
Unemployment, 228
Unification church, 47, 413
Uniform Crime Reports, 190
Unilinear evolutionary theory, 584, 592, 612
United Farm Workers, 441
Urban ecology, 513, 536, 612
Urbanism, 520, 536, 612

Validity, 37, 55–56, 612
Value-added model, 571–572, 591–592, 612
Value neutrality, 50, 56, 612
Values, 74–76, 87–88, 612
Variable, 35–36, 38, 56, 612
Verstehen, 12, 28–29, 612
Vertical mobility, 236, 238, 612
Vested interests, 586, 591–592, 612

Veto groups, 437, 447, 612
Victimization surveys, 197, 201, 612
Victimless crimes, 188, 193–194, 201, 612
Vietnamese Americans, 275, 283
Violence:
    family, 384–387
    in schools, 464
Virtual reality, 598
Vital statistics, 543, 563, 612
Voluntary associations, 161–164, 171, 352, 612

War, 429
Wealth, 209, 221–223, 238, 253–254, 612
Welfare, 234–236
Wellness clinics, 495
White-collar crime, 192–193, 196, 201, 612
Wholistic medicine (*see* Holistic medicine)
Women:
    and advertising, 32–33
    and crime, 188
    and developing nations, 248, 251–252, 259,
        261–262
    and education, 469–470
    and gender differences, 24, 102–104,
        154–155, 261–262

Women (*Cont.*):
    and homelessness, 533–534
    in Japan, 257
    and medicine, 486–488, 493
    and politics, 41, 432–434
    and poverty, 314, 533–534
    and public places, 24
    and religion, 410
    and surveys, 41
World systems theory, 245, 247, 259, 268, 612

Xenocentrism, 82, 88, 612

Yanomani Indians, 263
YMCA (Young Men's Christian Association),
    161, 165
Yugoslavia, 397

Zambia, 253
Zero population growth (ZPG), 551–552,
    563–564, 612
Zone in transition, 513
Zoning laws, 528–529, 576, 612